Best American Plays

THIRD SERIES — 1945-1951

Uniform with this volume

BEST PLAYS SERIES

Edited by John Gassner

Containing the complete text of the plays listed, introductory matter, etc.

25 BEST PLAYS OF THE MODERN AMERICAN THEATRE—Early Series
1916-1929

The Hairy Ape
Desire Under the Elms
What Price Glory?
They Knew What They Wanted
Beggar on Horseback
Craig's Wife
Broadway
Paris Bound
The Road to Rome
The Second Man
Saturday's Children
Porgy
The Front Page

Machinal
Gods of the Lightning
Street Scene
Strictly Dishonorable
Berkeley Square
The Clod
Trifles
Ile
Aria da Capo
Poor Aubrey
White Dresses
Minnie Field

20 BEST PLAYS OF THE MODERN AMERICAN THEATRE
1930-1939

Winterset
High Tor
Idiot's Delight
Johnny Johnson
Green Pastures
You Can't Take It with You
End of Summer
The Animal Kingdom
Boy Meets Girl
The Women

Yes, My Darling Daughter
Three Men on a Horse
The Children's Hour
Tobacco Road
Of Mice and Men
Dead End
Bury the Dead
The Fall of the City
Golden Boy
Stage Door

BEST PLAYS OF THE MODERN AMERICAN THEATRE—Second Series
1939-1946

The Glass Menagerie
The Time of Your Life
I Remember Mamma
Life with Father
Born Yesterday
The Voice of the Turtle
The Male Animal
The Man Who Came to Dinner
Dream Girl

The Philadelphia Story
Arsenic and Old Lace
The Hasty Heart
Home of the Brave
Tomorrow the World
Watch on the Rhine
The Patriots
Abe Lincoln in Illinois

Best American
PLAYS

THIRD SERIES — 1945-1951

EDITED WITH AN INTRODUCTION BY
JOHN GASSNER

CROWN PUBLISHERS, INC.

NEW YORK

COPYRIGHT 1952 BY CROWN PUBLISHERS, INC.
LIBRARY OF CONGRESS CATALOG CARD NUMBER: 52-5690
ISBN: 0-517-509504

20   19   18

PRINTED IN THE UNITED STATES OF AMERICA

For JOHN GOLDEN

the American theatre's elder statesman
and most generous friend

PREFACE

This anthology is the latest volume of a series that represents the modern American theatre up to the mid-century mark, the season of 1950-51. Along with three previously published volumes, this book should furnish the reader with a chronicle since 1916 and with representative plays. The reader of this series of "Best Plays" now has available for study or edification no less than seventy-nine plays. Although the "Best" in the title remains questionable, it is a trademark that can no longer be altered; and although more than a few of the plays will not endure strict scrutiny and will certainly not outlast marble, they are part of the record. They should enable us to form an objective estimate of the American drama. These books are not intended to flatter American playwriting but to represent it. If our aim is to know our theatre, it would be a mistake to limit ourselves to masterpieces, even if enough of these could be found to give us an anthology. "A large mind cannot limit itself to what it loves," says Santayana.

The content of the present volume is confined to the period after World War II, which coincides with the second half of the decade of the nineteen-forties. Since the previous volume ended with the Broadway season of 1945-46, some overlapping is caused by the inclusion of *State of the Union,* from that season. *State of the Union,* however, provides a springboard for the present chronicle. It expresses our democratic ideals as affirmed by the war that was concluded in 1945 and jeopardized once more during the peace that followed.

The other plays in this volume illustrate the period's achievements and trends. Arthur Miller and Tennessee Williams, the most important new writers, are represented by their major efforts. These are supplemented with work by the newcomers William Inge and Carson McCullers, whose *Come Back, Little Sheba* and *The Member of the Wedding* supplied the most creative writing after the advent of Miller and Williams. Also new to the Broadway theatre were the authors of *Medea* and *Billy Budd.* And since there is no law forbidding older playwrights from contributing what they can, O'Neill is represented with the one new play that he allowed to be produced on Broadway, Maxwell Anderson with the last of his Elizabethan verse dramas, Sidney Kingsley with his latest realistic moral investigations, Lillian Hellman with another of her dramatic indictments, van Druten with one of his literate comedies, and F. Hugh Herbert with the last and best of his excursions into the field of Broadway entertainment.

My inventory would have been longer if last-minute calculations had not necessitated the elimination of a few other plays, to which reference will be made elsewhere. Nevertheless, the seventeen examples of contemporary playwriting here salvaged should comprise a useful compilation. Our theatre is shown producing new playwrights and drawing upon the resources of their elders, recording the experience of the last war and its aftermath, pondering immediate and general verities, experimenting somewhat with problems of dramatic form and style, working in earnest, and also turning a handspring or two, for which I daresay no apologies are needed.

A more detailed account and some assessment of this activity follow.

JOHN GASSNER

February, 1952.

CONTENTS

Note: Special introductions to plays and playwrights will be found on pages 2-3, 50-51, 96, 174, 206, 252, 282, 318, 366, 396, 416, 456-457, 506, 548, 594, 628, 666-667.

Introduction

THE MID-CENTURY THEATRE, A REPRISE WITH VARIATIONS

By JOHN GASSNER

The American drama during the period immediately following World War II constituted a reprise. Nearly all the motifs to be found in our century's theatre were recapitulated, although some of these were now faint or seemed about to expire. We were still going along our own way in matters dramatic and theatrical; going along haphazardly, as is our wont. No very new experiments in dramatic composition or theatrical style won domination over our playwrights and producers. Our stage remained eclectic. We were still turning out some extraordinarily powerful plays and productions. We were still also multiplying examples of ineptness, mostly entailed by the wayward nature of our undisciplined but lively theatrical enterprise. We seemed bent on proving the truth of the Chestertonian paradox that "if a thing is worth doing it's worth doing badly." And our theatre must surely have had a strong constitution if it could survive so much error and mismanagement. Our work in the drama was still annoying refined and urbane intellects, and we showed little inclination to mend our minds or manners in order to please them. To the dismay of some choice spirits, we were still creating "American" drama, not English or European drama. T. S. Eliot may have captured a number of our graduate schools; he had not yet captured our theatre, although he had successfully invaded it with *The Cocktail Party*. There were also signs of rebellion against humdrum realism and Broadway chaos in the hard-working ranks; and especially in the case of the younger playwrights and producers, this dissatisfaction was keenly felt. But our theatre was indulgent toward their restiveness on Mr. Dooley's principle that it doesn't matter what you teach a boy so long as he doesn't like it, and our stage was the beneficiary of their efforts to write plays according to their own lights. It became evident, too, that the young apples were not falling very far from the old tree, or, to return to my initial metaphor, that the new tunes had been heard before; only the orchestration was somewhat new. Those of us who were familiar with the American stage since the days of the Provincetown Players could assure the youngsters that our way of making theatre had not changed; it had merely become more expensive—and no more so than our making anything else.

It was plain that in playwriting our forte was, as it had been, dramatic or theatrical rather than literary. Genuine literary distinction in *Medea*, a play based on a great Greek poetic drama by one of our best contemporary poets, was the exception. The style of Tennessee Williams was certainly poetic, but it struck admirers as remarkably distinguished only because it was so superior to the commonplace writing to which we were accustomed. Maxwell Anderson's versification did not qualify it for inclusion among specimens of English dramatic poetry. Nor did *Death of a Salesman*, the period's most highly regarded play, commend itself to our attention as a literary masterpiece. A limitation of language long apparent not merely in ordinary plays but in our greatest dramatist O'Neill, and now once more apparent in *The Iceman Cometh*, recurred in the playwriting of the period.

It was also evident that our endowment consisted of strength rather than of subtlety; we displayed sympathy or a certain largeness of heart rather than "judgment" or any observable largeness of intellect. Our theatre had never placed much reliance on the deftness and detachment with which manners and emotions had been treated in England and Western Europe. This deficiency had been present even during our "sophisticated" nineteen-twenties, when it had been merely reduced by the new high-comedic writing of Barry and Behrman. The vogue of strident social drama in the nineteen-thirties naturally had little use for intellectual and esthetic refinements. In the post-war period, there was no marked change. If anything, American playwriting was less intellectual and certainly less detached than it had been a quarter of a century before. It was the large assault upon our emotions that dominated a period whose most impressive original plays were *A Streetcar Named Desire, Death of a Salesman,* and *The Iceman Cometh.*

Finally, our playwriting remained predominantly realistic. Even a verse drama as successful as *Medea* did not engender a breed of poet-playwrights, and the success of some poetic plays in prose, while gratifying, did not alter the face of our theatre. To powder one's face is not the same thing as changing it. Suggestive overtones there had always been in sensitive, high-minded, or simply pretentious writing for our stage. Their continued presence in the mid-century theatre was less than remarkable.

Regardless of any diversity of subject matter and treatment, our drama drew much of its force from the verisimilitude and direct facing up to the realities long present in our theatre. The realism of such plays as *Detective Story, Come Back, Little Sheba, The Autumn Garden, All My Sons,* and *Mister Roberts* remained the norm for playwriting. The fact that stage designers did not always confine the actor to ordinary realistic stage settings makes no difference, for stage art had abandoned facsimiles of environment even before the advent of an art theatre in America after 1918. As for departures from the strictly realistic dramatic technique, their presence was actually less marked than jubilant notices on some sensitive or powerful plays might lead us to believe. The sensitivity of *The Member of the Wedding* confirmed rather than transcended realism of characterization and background. The "symbolism" in *A Streetcar Named Desire* merely added a faint tremolo to the distinctly naturalistic percussion of the drama. If the remembered and hallucinated brother Ben scenes of *Death of a Salesman* had symbolic value, they were nevertheless psychologically justified and they supported a realistic dissection of that deluded materialist Willy Loman. If the authors of such plays as *Death of a Salesman* and *Darkness at Noon* availed themselves of expressionistic intensifications of their story and shuttled back and forth between actual and recollected scenes, they still treated their characterization and general argument realistically. The liberties they took were actually moderate by comparison with those taken by playwrights more than two decades before; by, let us say, O'Neill in *The Emperor Jones, The Hairy Ape* and *The Great God Brown,* by Kaufman and Connelly in *Beggar on Horseback,* and by Elmer Rice in *The Adding Machine.*

The experiments of the forties could be revelations only to playgoers whose experience of playgoing was confined to that period. Certainly, too, it was not the actual writing in our plays that showed conspicuous departure from realism. The creative imagination of the period's playwriting manifested itself chiefly in the manner in which playwrights resorted to flexible and expressive play structure and relied on supplementary theatrical elements, such as music, lighting, and stage design. Our writers continued to write imaginative drama, but they created a *poetry of theatre* rather than dramatic poetry.

Closely considered, then, the period with which this book deals cannot be considered momentous to anyone who requires a totally new dispensation before he can reconcile himself to the American stage. Inevitably, since the times provided no special ferment for the creative life and since the miracle of truly pioneering genius was absent, the period's theatre simply produced the kind of playwriting that our theatre had brought forth hitherto. It would have been quite unreasonable to expect innovation.

Dramatic writing, even more than theatre practice, left, of course, considerable room for discontent on the part of those hardy perennials the idealists who hanker for a type of transfiguring art that the Western world had produced only two or three times since the beginning of its theatre. A valid indictment, moreover, could be drawn up against most of our playwriting even when measured by the standards ordinary playgoers have maintained ever since the exodus of routine farces, melodramas, and tear-jerkers to Hollywood and the broadcasting studios. From this judgment Broadway could appeal only with the reminder that an art should be judged by its best rather than worst examples, which does not, however, invalidate regret at the waste entailed by most of Broadway's efforts. But the problem of drawing a conclusion concerning the best work that the playwrights had to offer during the period involves something else—namely, an appreciation of the characteristically American texture of our more or less broad and vigorous playwriting.

The critical approach of a literary élite would rule out the possibility of merit in virtually anything that prevails on Broadway, and if this attitude is applied to the period under discussion, then it must also be maintained toward the entire modern American drama. In that case, a *nunc dimittis* would have to be read over the dismembered bodies of virtually all American playwrights whose work has been produced on a Broadway stage. In that case, our theatre has labored in vain under increasingly difficult conditions for the greater part of the first half of the century. This view was certainly not held in Europe, which came to rely increasingly on our plays. The new avant-garde criticism, aristocratic and fastidious, that grew up in the nineteen-forties and exerted a strong influence in literary circles, was notable for taste and penetration. But if it had had any effect on Broadway, it would in all probability have eliminated the vitality of American playwriting along with its weaknesses. The operation would have been successful, but the patient would have been dead.

Since the new critical movement has been highly articulate and sometimes quite brilliant, and since it has made a considerable impression on educated young people in recent years, it cannot be ignored. Its estimates of American playwriting are best exemplified by its response to *Death of a Salesman*. The reviews published in *Partisan Review* and the *Hudson Review,* two ably edited organs of advanced criticism, contained some keen observations. But the critic of *Partisan Review* (June, 1949) referred to the play as "a peculiar hodge podge of dated materials and facile new ones" and called it "a very dull business, which departs in no way that is to its credit from the general mediocrity of our commercial theatre." And according to the critic of the *Hudson Review* (summer issue, 1949), the play was "a miserable affair" that proceeded "with unrelieved vulgarity, from cliché to stereotype." It was classified in this learned publication with other Broadway productions "which are completely devoid of merit."

It is hardly necessary to subscribe to extravagant praise of *Death of a Salesman* to conclude that there could be no common ground between the authors of these statements and the men and women who have sustained the American theatre with plays and productions. To please such critics, the playwrights could rehabilitate themselves only by transforming themselves beyond recognition. Perhaps they would all have to become T. S. Eliots in order to be accepted—a consummation that would not have been at all uncongenial at one university where I was assured that the students considered T. S. Eliot the only important American dramatist. Even if Mr. Eliot (who, incidentally, displeased some of his admirers with *The Cocktail Party*) had his British citizenship revoked and were a better playwright than I think he is (or than, as a matter of fact, he considers himself to be), it is plain that there are "new critics" whose standards require a different kind of American theatre than that which has existed for thirty years or that prevailed during the period under consideration. And it is this theatre, with all its manifest limitations as well as with what I consider to be its potencies, that is being represented and reviewed in this volume. Let us look at it, if we may.

The period revealed a declining economy in the professional theatre without any appreciable decline in the quality of its plays except toward the end. Rising costs made the business of stage productions even less feasible than it had become during the war. Fewer and fewer productions managed to make a profit or even pay back the original investment. (At the end of the 1950-51 season, indeed, even long-running plays such as Kingsley's *Darkness at Noon* and Williams' popular piece *The Rose Tattoo* had not yet retrieved their investment.) Consequently, fewer plays were produced, and the season of 1949-50 reached the low ebb of only sixty-two Broadway productions. In our theatre's heyday during the twenties, a season generally had well over two hundred productions.

The curtailment of production was a hardship on playwrights who must have Broadway productions if they are to acquire or retain professional status. Most serious was the situation that required virtually every production to be a smash-hit, since the alternative was usually a crushing failure. There was little room on Broadway for what Brooks Atkinson once called the "in between" play—that is, the play for which only a moderate success can be reasonably expected. If a similar situation had existed in America and Europe twenty-five, fifty, and seventy-five years ago, the modern theatre would have been deprived of most of its authentic masterpieces, including those by Ibsen, Strindberg, Chekhov, Shaw, Synge, and O'Casey. It is even probable that the most important modern playwrights would be unknown today. The economic crisis grew acute, and although its effect on playwriting and theatrical art cannot be accurately assessed, it must have been serious.

Some comfort could be derived from the fact that off-Broadway groups in New York, as well as in the rest of the nation, intensified their activity. Thus the season of 1946-47 had no less than fifty-six "Equity-Library Theatre" productions in New York City—that is, plays economically, though by no means maladroitly, produced in branch libraries before small audiences. This activity, which had its fourth season in 1946-47, was made possible by the generosity and guidance of John Golden, and by the cooperation of George Freedley, Curator of the Theatre Collection of the New York Public Library, and of the Actors' Equity Association under the leadership of Sam Jaffe.

When the libraries withdrew their modest accommodations in the fall of 1947, this low-priced theatrical venture managed to find havens in available little theatres which had better facilities. Budgets were kept down to $100 per production, and further economies were effected when some plays were presented at as low a cost as $25 in the case of so-called Worklight Productions without scenery and costumes. Before long, high school auditoriums were made available to the intrepid venture by New York's Board of Education, and so an "Equity Community Theatre" was born. In its second season, in 1951, the project was responsible for well over five hundred performances and even rolled up a profit of—twenty-one cents. The productions, though hardly of first rank in stage annals, enabled a considerable number of professional actors to use their talents and aspiring stage directors to add some experience, as well as to exhibit their abilities to agents and producers. Along with other off-Broadway groups, the Equity-valiants also compensated somewhat for the lack of state-subsidized repertory companies that supply cosmopolitan playgoers in other lands with opportunities to see their classics year in and year out.

New York needed to be reminded that the theatre is an institution as well as a business. The effort of Eva Le Gallienne, Margaret Webster, and Cheryl Crawford to establish a repertory company, such as Miss Le Gallienne had maintained for years in the nineteen-twenties and early thirties, was short-lived. Their American Repertory

Company, which opened on November 6, 1946, with a production of *Henry VIII,* lasted only one season in spite of unusually strong support from theatre people, and the post-mortems were various and conflicting. A lame attempt to revive this enterprise the next season, in association with the commercial producer Louis J. Singer, expired after rather humdrum productions of *Ghosts* and *Hedda Gabler.* Fortunately, Equity's apprentice labors in the libraries and schools were supplemented by other efforts, although none of these constituted a true repertory system. Notably, the New York City Center, a cavernous playhouse made available by the municipality, provided popular-priced but fully and, indeed, sometimes fulsomely produced revivals, with outstanding performers such as Judith Anderson, Maurice Evans, and José Ferrer contributing their ordinarily expensive services. A number of the revivals given there were return engagements of plays that had previously had long Broadway runs. But Messrs. Evans and Ferrer, who managed some of the seasons at the City Center, brought to that stage new productions of classics or neo-classics, and a successful production at the Center could aspire to a regular run on Broadway. One such production by Evans, *The Devil's Disciple,* which opened on January 25, 1950, was quickly and profitably transferred to the Great White Way.

Other organizations, established for some time or mushrooming as a result of youthful enthusiasm, ventured into full-fledged production of new plays or old that did not have the benefit of previous Broadway success. Young acting groups in Greenwich Village or uptown, such as "On-Stage" and the Abbé Practical Workshop, presented efficient performances of Strindberg's *Creditors* and *The Father,* O'Casey's *The Silver Tassie,* and Synge's *Deirdre of the Sorrows.* At the small midtown President Theatre operated by Erwin Piscator's Dramatic Workshop, from which emerged such able performers as Marlon Brando and Elaine Stritch, New Yorkers could see for the first time such unusual plays as Sartre's *The Flies,* Salacrou's *Nights of Wrath,* and Robert Penn Warren's *All the King's Men.* And an actors' and directors' "Cooperative," calling itself New Stages and establishing itself for several seasons in Greenwich Village, nearly made theatrical history before dissolving as a result of internal dissensions. New Stages won a noteworthy success with a production of Sartre's *The Respectful Prostitute* as staged by the talented Mary Hunter. Although less admired, the group's presentation of another Sartre play, the French underground drama *Morts sans Sépulture* under the title of *The Victors,* was powerful theatre, and Boris Tumarin's staging of *Blood Wedding* brought the genius of the poet-dramatist Lorca closer to the New York public than had ever been the case before—at least as close as that exotic talent can be brought to our public. New Stages, with Boris Tumarin directing, also introduced a generally impressive new play, *Lamp at Midnight,* a drama about Galileo's struggles, by Barrie Stavis. Indeed, a number of the productions might well have been brought to Broadway but for the commercial theatre's unhealthy financial condition.

One unorthodox attempt to overcome this situation suggested itself in 1950 to an enterprising producer David Heilweil, who had played an important part in establishing New Stages. Out-of-town reports, especially from Dallas, Texas, encouraged the belief that costs could be reduced by resorting to central or arena staging—that is, by adopting the long familiar circus type of production which dispenses with scenery and does not have to be presented in Broadway's playhouses, where rentals are high. Reinhardt had achieved notable effects with this style in Germany, Okhlophov had associated it with revolutionary theatricals in Russia, and Professor Glenn Hughes had employed it successfully for about a decade at the Penthouse Theatre of the University of Washington in Seattle. Currently, Margo Jones was making a success of a similar enterprise in her little theatre in Dallas. Her achievement was widely heralded, and Tennessee Williams, by then the enormously successful author of *The Glass Menagerie* and *A Streetcar Named Desire,* proved his admiration of her style by letting her produce his new play *Summer and Smoke* and then sanctioning the transfer of the production to New York.

Heilweil and his associates opened an Arena Theatre in the midtown Edison Hotel, where they presented *The Show-Off, Julius Caesar, The Medium,* and *Arms and the Man* with varying success. It seemed for a while that the enterprise would revolutionize Broadway, but central staging, or "theatre-in-the-round," had a limited appeal to Broadway's clientele. Whatever might be the case in Dallas and other cities, it was apparent in New York that saving money on scenery was not a decisive factor in a theatrical enterprise, that increasing the intimacy between the actors and the audience was not always a desideratum, and that every kind of play was not conspicuously adaptable to the new style of presentation. In 1950, it seemed unlikely that the "fourth-wall" stage convention would be seriously challenged on Broadway and that its playhouses, built along lines that go back to the Renaissance, would be abandoned for the first available hall, ballroom, or nightclub floor; or that anyone would build arena theatres in the heart of Manhattan. It was also debatable whether such reconversion to the original dancing circles of the primitive theatre, even if possible, could guarantee New York better acting performances, productions, and plays. Neither plays nor any genuine esthetic principles specially designed for theatre-in-the-round had been created at the midpoint of the century. The arena stage remained an amateur or semi-amateur development whose real strength was located "out of town." Certainly, besides, it did not bring forth any memorable plays, which is the prime concern of this book. Even *Summer and Smoke* had merely been tested on Margo Jones' Dallas arena stage, rather than written for it. At most it could be expected that increased opportunities of getting new plays produced in the economically run "arenas" would enable more playwrights to learn their craft, in which case the results might be felt in the professional theatre during the next decade.

An additional avenue for talent was opened up by the increasing activity of ANTA, the American National Theatre and Academy. This organization, which had been on paper for a long time with a charter that had been little more than an incorporated hope, was galvanized after the war by the extraordinarily energetic actor-manager Robert Breen. He received much encouragement and support from leaders of the professional theatre such as Helen Hayes and Cheryl Crawford, and, toward the end of the period, ANTA was actually in a position to purchase the Guild Theatre as a permanent home and to embark upon the ambitious program of producing ten plays during the 1950-51 season. The accomplishments of ANTA were a constant source of controversy, and a revised program of play production and training was initiated by Mr. Breen's successor Robert Whitehead, the producer of *Medea* and *The Member of the Wedding.* The new program started very auspiciously in 1952 with an effective revival of O'Neill's *Desire Under the Elms,* staged by Harold Clurman and designed by Mordecai Gorelik, and the production of the pleasing fantasy *Mrs. McThing,* written by Mary Chase.

ANTA's contribution to the refreshment of playgoers' memories of old plays during the 1950-51 season was meager but for an appealing revival of James M. Barrie's elfin, if also somewhat saccharine, fantasy *Mary Rose* and an instructive, though unexhilarating, production of *Getting Married*—Shaw's best example of pure discussion drama. But ANTA, at different times, also promoted the development of new playwrights, and this enterprise enriched the period's harvest of acceptable plays to a greater extent than was realized.

At the Guild Playhouse in 1950, the public could acquaint itself with a playing version of Robinson Jeffers' *Tower Beyond Tragedy,* a rather botched stage play but nonetheless a distinguished poetic drama. In Jan de Hartog's *Skipper Next to God,* a play about a ship captain's heroic efforts to land refugees in Palestine, ANTA, operating an Experimental Theatre, gave New York one of its strongest social dramas.

In the entrancing *Ballet Ballads* by Latouche, with music by Jerome Moross, ANTA introduced the most original theatrical experiment in America since the Federal Theatre's "living newspapers" *Power* and *One-third-of-a-nation* in the late thirties. This series of short plays (*Susanna and the Elders, Willie the Weeper,* and *The Eccentricities of Davy Crockett*) dramatizing American folklore in choreography, dialogue, and song was deservedly given a Broadway run, although it could not survive on a commercial basis. The Experimental Theatre also unfolded, in 1949, *Uniform of Flesh* by Louis O. Coxe and R. H. Chapman that was later staged on Broadway under the simpler title of *Billy Budd.* Out of ANTA's "Six O'Clock Theatre Studio." in 1948, also came the attractive one-acter *Hope Is the Thing with Feathers,* by a new playwright Richard Harrity, of whom much was expected.

All things considered, then, it cannot be maintained that the American stage allowed itself to be immobilized by a nearly paralyzing economic situation hardly of the theatre's own making in an inflationary period. This much must be conceded even without noting Broadway-grown revivals, transatlantic visits by foreign troupes, and productions of foreign plays such as Christopher Fry's *The Lady's Not for Burning,* T. S. Eliot's *The Cocktail Party,* and Jean Giraudoux's *The Madwoman of Chaillot;* and without taking into account numerous productions at universities and at community theatres throughout the country.

It is essential to realize that the stage was busily occupied, that it engaged the energies and talents of a multitude, and that it gathered a varied artistry over the years from both sides of the Atlantic. The question that concerns us here, however, is not how active or even how attractive our theatre was at the mid-century point, but what sort of native playwriting pervaded it. An answer that is neither haughtily negative nor supinely complacent is not easily arrived at. It was generally agreed, for example, that the period gave rise to much achievement in the field of musical entertainment. Was there a comparable richness in musically unaided playwriting? Most observers would agree that the contrary was the case and that in general the quality of our drama began to decline in the late forties. If so, was this decline in dramatic writing purely accidental or is it explainable? Even so, moreover, Broadway offered a number of plays that made a considerable impression. Were we deluded in esteeming them? Perhaps! But surely not by any standards of comparison that do not enforce us to content ourselves only with a small number of the plays written during four or five rather brief periods of human history. And if Broadway's claim must be allowed, where did the creative energy come from when its sources apparently dwindled; and in what direction did that energy flow?

3.

It is apparent that home-grown musical entertainment flourished, and anyone disposed to dismiss Broadway as a desiccated playground would have to ignore our continued progress in the musical comedy and "music drama." The routine musicals inevitably raised their feeble heads, of course, but only, as a rule, to be cut down by wrathful critics and cut dead by an indifferent public. American musical comedy had reached such standards of writing, scoring, and performance (with and without formal ballet) that only very elevated intellects remained unpropitiated. *South Pacific, Finian's Rainbow, Brigadoon,* and *The King and I* were the main peaks of an endeavor which threatened to emerge into the stratosphere of opera, and nearly did with *Allegro, Lost in the Stars,* the semi-operatic *Street Scene* by Kurt Weill, and Gian-Carlo Menotti's musical guignol *The Medium* and refugee-problem melodrama *The Consul.* Diehards of the older and more coarse-grained musical theatre were beginning, in fact, to worry lest Broadway become over-refined. They were comforted when the entrepreneur Mike Todd, the reliable clowns Bert Lahr and Bobby Clark, and the inexhaustible Ethel Merman, triumphant in the Annie Oakley comedy *Annie Get Your Gun,* refused to be refined out of business. Some producers, in fact, played a wide gambit that included such robust literary and unliterary entertainment as *Kiss Me, Kate,* with a nod to Shakespeare, and *Guys and Dolls,* with a bow to Damon Runyon, not to mention a musicalized *Gentlemen Prefer Blondes.* Whatever the change in taste displayed or the degree of success attained, the musical stage triumphed almost as much as in the plush days before the American theatre ever heard of Eugene O'Neill or concerned itself with social and psychological drama, expressionism, and the promises of the Stanislavski method. It was indicative of a change in taste, however, that the "book show" now had to have an acceptable book, that the purely humorous show had to be thoroughly purged of "Blossom Time" and "Heidelberg" oleomargarine, and that the stage productions had to be streamlined rather than lush. These prescriptions were often successfully filled, and it was fortunate that they were when a musical show required a two or three hundred dollar investment.

Prescriptions for successful non-musical plays, however, were less well defined and less easily satisfied. It was characteristic of the period that although its new theatrical groups were many and ardent, they had no end in view other than that of putting on all kinds of interesting plays and giving these a good production in whatever style they found suitable and could manage. This, it will be assumed, should be sufficient. Yet it had not been sufficient hitherto either here or abroad for memorably creative theatre, which was characterized by well-defined developments in playwriting and stage production. Modern theatre had always been the end-product of some fermentation either artistic or social, or both; and the decades of the twenties and thirties virtually seethed with esthetic and social revolt.

During the twenties, our coming-of-age period in the theatre, playwrights and other theatre artists were engaged in a discovery of the modern world, and they assimilated modern philosophies and psychology with the avidity of neophytes. To some extent, the commitment to discovery also led them to strenuous criticism of their world ranging all the way from farcical nose-thumbing to scintillating high-comedy sophistication, and from realistic representations of environment to the spiritual conflicts of O'Neill. Whatever their forte, the playwrights were iconoclasts dedicated either frivolously or soberly to exploding convention, and in the case of strenuous spirits to pursuing a life of inquiry and self-realization or to finding an elusive faith. Whatever the deficiencies and dangers entailed by this attitude, many playwrights found a stimulus and a sense of direction.

America was also a new world for many writers—a world not hitherto observed very honestly. Above all, they felt called upon to create a modern drama for our stage by experimenting with new forms or styles, such as symbolism and expressionism, as well as by assimilating and domesticating naturalism. They found stimulation in modernizing our stage and elevation in creating an "art theatre." Hence the rise of playwrights, a number of whom we still have with us; the development of modern scene design for our stage; and the growth of our "little theatres" throughout the country and of the Provincetown Players and the young Theatre Guild in New York. Obviously, since this first revolution in our theatre was won by the generation of the twenties, it could no longer engage the active interest of the generation of the forties. Merely safeguarding the victory was an obligation, but it was not much of a stimulus. As for the blithe scepticism of the twenties, a good deal of it was apt to seem puerile twenty years later. Nor could it be maintained with so light a heart in a period of rising anxieties and complexities. Also, criticism of our way of life, which had rarely been more than a lovers' quarrel in the secure nineteen-twenties, could constitute disloyalty in a time of crisis, or could be construed as such in a tense and consequently increasingly intolerant period.

Creativity was also no longer sparked by that sense of dismay and shock that gathered force during and immediately after World War I and wrung intense responses of disillusionment and self-examination from writers.

The first World War had been followed by a strong outburst of artistic exertion and probing. So much was this the case, in fact, that we now realize that the "Waste Land" was not really the desert described by the Eliot-Hemingway school, and that the "Lost Generation" was not actually lost. No comparable renascence occurred, however, after the second World War. Few intellectuals could have withdrawn from that struggle or viewed it with scepticism, since the issue had been so clearly drawn by the conduct of Germany and Japan. At the conclusion of hostilities, therefore, writers were not incited to express the kind of anti-war reactions that energized the writing of the post-1918 period of peace or to regard contemporary life with, as it were, newly opened eyes. Only Maxwell Anderson was moved to dramatize disorientation in *Truckline Café,* and this was one of the least successful plays of his long career. If other playwrights gravitated toward disenchantment, they were mostly unknown and unable to gain a foothold in the theatre. The successful war plays after 1945, *Mister Roberts* and *Command Decision,* were different in quality. The first actually dramatized eagerness for combat duty; the second accepted the painful necessity of sacrifice. From neither came those outcries of disillusionment or protest that were heard after 1918. The first World War had stunned the essentially optimistic pre-war company of artists with its unexpectedness, whereas we had been psychologically prepared for the second holocaust ever since 1933 or 1934.

Also, the period before September 1, 1939, had provided no seminal developments in the arts except in French surrealism, which is fundamentally foreign to our pragmatic temperament, and in symbolist poetry and criticism that impressed the literati but made little stir in theatrical circles. The post-war vogue of existentialism was viewed by us from a distance and, largely, with scepticism. The Eliot-inspired British trend toward poetic drama and Anglican theology found admirers in America, but no one writing plays professionally in this country was creatively responsive to that movement. Nothing developed in the European theatre, which had indeed declined in potency after 1930, entranced contemporary American dramatists as a group or even individually, whereas the European theatre from 1880 to 1914 had made a profound impression upon writers of the generation of the twenties.

As suggested earlier, the 1945-50 stage did reprise our 1919-29 theatre in various respects, but with less than the leavening zeal and zest of that decade. John van Druten's comic finesse and Hugh Herbert's vivacity had a familiar quality. George S. Kaufman with a series of ventures such as *Bravo,* Moss Hart with *Light Up the Sky,* Wolcott Gibbs with *Season in the Sun,* Marc Connelly with *A Story for Strangers* had variable success, but even at their best they brought no revelations. They were at most pleasantly sufficient unto the day, and that is virtually all that need be said about their historical position. At the other end of the spectrum, there was *The Iceman Cometh,* actually written by O'Neill in 1939 and close to the mood and style of the semi-naturalistic dramas he had presented in the early nineteen-twenties. Except for O'Neill, the only potent playwright who appeared to be consistently writing for the "art theatre" of our period was Tennessee Williams, who also combined naturalistic action and background with symbolist overtones. *Billy Budd* may also be placed in this category of "art theatre" playwriting by virtue of its symbolism, and *Come Back, Little Sheba* may be included on the strength of its intense naturalism. Their authors, however, made only single contributions to our period.

A sense of direction and purpose had also leavened the theatre of the nineteen-thirties. Some of the purely artistic ardors of the twenties asserted themselves then, too. This was both evident and fruitful in the case of the Group Theatre, whose artistic aims and attainments won high credit. More or less formalistic experiments continued in such plays as *Our Town, Johnny Johnson, The Green Pastures, Hotel Universe, Roll, Sweet Chariot, Waiting for Lefty, Here Come the Clowns, Ten Million Ghosts,* and other pieces good, bad, or indifferent; and this miscellany suggests that the dramatic experiments were made by playwrights regardless of what ideas or social philosophies they entertained. The guardians of the Soviet theatre would surely be annoyed by a number of the left-wing plays of our thirties, considering them as flagrant departures from the orthodox theory of "Socialist Realism."

The earlier intention of treating drama as an exalted art was present during the thirties in O'Neill's continued efforts and in Maxwell Anderson's exertions to produce verse-drama and to attain tragic elevation. Mr. Anderson also offered his poetic aspirations as a gospel for American playwrights in essays collected under the title of *Off Broadway.* Anderson reminded his large public that "the essence of a tragedy, or even of a serious play, is the spiritual awakening, or regeneration, of his hero" (*The Essence of Tragedy*) and said he believed with Goethe "that dramatic poetry is man's greatest achievement on the earth so far, and . . . that theatre is essentially a cathedral of the spirit, devoted to the apostolic succession of inspired high priests which extend further into the past than the Christian line founded by St. Peter" (*Poetry in the Theatre*).

These were ringing proclamations. They were seconded by the critic John Mason Brown in such statements as that "by a convention, born of beauty and our need," the tragic heroes "are fated to leave this earth spiritually cross-ventilated," and that in tragedy "what matters is always the flame and never the lamp; never the body and always the spirit." Some of this idealism glowed, in fact, even in the mundane dramas of the thirties that dealt with the domestic tensions, depression problems, and dreams of a socialist millennium that proliferated during the period. Visions and ardors were present, for example, in the early Odets plays, and their exaltations were different only in immediate point of reference from those invoked by Maxwell Anderson. They were explicit in such adjurations as young Ralph's cry "We don't want life printed on dollar bills" in *Awake and Sing,* Agate's rhetorical call to "put fruit trees where our ashes are" in *Waiting for Lefty* and Leo's peroration in *Paradise Lost*: "Oh, if you could only see the greatness of men. I tremble like a bride to see the time when they'll use it. . . . Heartbreak and terror is not the heritage of mankind! No fruit tree wears a lock and key."

No rhapsodic dispensation, however, whether under the eternal stars or under the banner of social conflict, permeated the theatre of the closing years of the forties. No solace or sop was offered by Tennessee Williams, not even at the foot of the statue of eternity in *Summer and Smoke*. The mood of such plays as *The Iceman Cometh, Billy Budd, Medea, Detective Story,* and *Darkness at Noon* was decidedly grim. Even in *The Member of the Wedding,* the tender treatment of adolescence was crossed by the senseless death of a child and the resigned loneliness of the Negro cook. Resignation to a dire necessity climaxed *Command Decision,* and ruefulness was the temper of *Mister Roberts* despite the standardized capers of its dialogue and its plot. A sense of weariness and defeat dominated the greater part of *The Autumn Garden*. The heroic spirit spoke by rote and royal training in *Anne of the Thousand Days,* although Maxwell Anderson did manage to strike some high notes in his *Joan of Lorraine*. Only Arthur Miller consistently communicated an affirmativeness of sorts, and he was closest in conviction to the writers of social drama in the previous decade.

As for the "social consciousness" that had energized a good deal of the writing of that decade and given rise to many of its new playwrights, only Miller succeeded in expressing it to some degree. And even so, there was considerable difference between the exuberant assertiveness of the Depression plays and the elegiac mood of *Death of a Salesman*. The old left-wing drama, besides, had tended to place responsibility for evil on society, whereas *Death of a Salesman* largely stressed the personal nature of Willy Loman's failure; and personal responsibility was even more distinctly the keynote of Miller's earlier drama, *All My Sons.* Zeal for any drastic transformation of American society was virtually absent from the theatre of a period of economic well-being and of revived disenchantment with Russia after the war-time enthusiasm for an ally. Even mildly liberal protests against racial prejudice and anti-liberal manifestations at home tapered off sharply after *State of the Union* and *Born Yesterday* in the season of 1945-46; only the moderately effective comedy *Goodbye, My Fancy* possessed the same accent among the successful productions as the post-war years rolled on. Lillian Hellman did continue her campaign against the "little foxes" in her sequel *Another Part of the Forest.* But it was a picaresque account of the Hubbards' predatory beginnings in an almost self-contained world of comedy and melodrama. The same author's representation of moral failure and stalemate in *The Autumn Garden,* too, had little discernible basis in contemporary problems.

If anything, the pendulum swung in the opposite direction of a revised estimate of liberalism, in Herman Wouk's intellectual spy melodrama *The Traitor,* and of revolutionary idealism in *Darkness at Noon.* Significantly, the author of this dramatization of Arthur Koestler's novel was Sidney Kingsley, one of the ablest writers of social drama during the thirties. He was not alone in arriving at the conviction that true liberalism would be served best by directing fire against the ruthlessness of communist revolutionary tactics and the suppression of liberties in Russia. Whether the highest ends of art are attainable by this sort of propaganda in reverse is not the question here, even though I believe that Kingsley pitched his play on a distinctly higher level when he drew the "Old Bolshevik" Rubashov than Soviet playwrights were reportedly doing when they presented American characters. The swing of the pendulum was also apparent when Irwin Shaw withdrew his 1936 anti-war drama *Bury the Dead* from the play market to prevent its use as propaganda against our intervention in Korea. And Clifford Odets' first success on Broadway in thirteen years, *The Country Girl,* also happened to be the first produced play he had ever written without relation to social tensions. It was reassuring to realize that Odets' talent for characterization and dramatic conflict was intact, and that his work was not really dependent on the artificial respiration given to some playwrights by ideologies. Still, the nature of this drama about an alcoholic actor's private tribulations was one more indication that the theatre no longer drew any invigoration from the social ferment of the previous decade.

Exuberance, then, was nowhere the shared experience of the period under consideration. Neither the exhilaration of artistic discovery nor the enthusiasm of social conviction was present in the theatre to any marked degree. Nor, for that matter, could any exuberance be found even in comedy, except in musicals. George S. Kaufman enjoyed none of the success that had been his previously. The other members of his school for debunkers no longer made a pleasant din on our stage. Even Moss Hart's expertly contrived *Light Up the Sky* offered little cheer. The latest recruit among the debunking clan, Garson Kanin, failed to come up with anything comparable to *Born Yesterday* in quality or success. Only the indestructible *New Yorker* could be considered a haven for the merrymakers when its drama critic Wolcott Gibbs emerged from its pages to give the stage his amusing *Season in the Sun.* Although George Kelly wrote one of his best comedies in *The Fatal Weakness,* he distilled a decidedly less heady brew in it than in *The Show Off* and *The Torchbearers.* Philip Barry's last comedy *Second Threshold,* completed by Robert Sherwood after Barry's death on December 3, 1949, had many virtues, but a zest for life was not one of them. It was perhaps the most depressed comedy ever produced on our stage with some success. And the scintillating S. N. Behrman's contributions did not rise above the joyless level of *Dunnigan's Daughter* and the routine romantic chronicle *I Know My Love,* tailor-made for the Lunts. Although Behrman wrote a buoyant comedy *Jane* in 1946 or 1947, the New York theatre was not to make its acquaintance until January of 1952. John van Druten alone appeared to have a particularly good time of it during the period, if *Bell, Book and Candle* is any criterion, and the vivacity of this comic fantasy is not altogether sustained.

At the end of the period, indeed, the editor of this book made an accounting for *Theatre Arts* magazine that he morosely entitled *Entropy in the Theatre*. The article ended with a paragraph that expressed a concern which at this writing, in February, 1952, remains justified. "A certain confidence and sure-mindedness, even in negation or rebellious scorn, characterized the theatre of the nineteen-twenties which gave us our first modern dramatists. And this was also true, with added intensification, of the theatre of the nineteen-thirties, which unfolded a second generation of reputable playwrights such as Kingsley, Hellman, Odets, and, by influence, Saroyan, Miller and Williams, who made their mark in the nineteen-forties. That sense of confidence and direction which can lead to both humanistic affirmativeness and artistic integrity will have to be recovered if the present decade is to prove sufficiently fruitful; or some compensation will have to be discovered by playwrights and directors."

4.

Still, when the chronicler of the period is called upon to do something practical, such as compiling this book, his retrospective view takes on an unexpectedly rosy coloration. The chronicler is surprised to discover that the seventeen plays he is allowed to crowd into his volume are too few. Even if he were to throw a few of them out of court on grounds more or less legal in critical circles, he would still be inclined to exceed his allowable space with additions. In any case, the five theatrical seasons from 1946-47 to 1950-51 proved rich enough to make up a book, and it is even arguable whether the present collection of seventeen plays is not actually more impressive than the seventeen in the previous volume of *Best Plays* devoted to the war-period from 1939 to 1945 or the plays in the larger volume of *Best Plays* in which I represented the depression decade of 1929-39.

How this should have been possible in view of my thesis of a diminished stimulus during our period is a large question to which a variety of answers can be made. One explanation would be that creative individuals, who have long been accustomed to making bricks without straw, capitalize on stored-up energy. That is, they are able to do so for a time, if by no means indefinitely unless they have inexhaustible genius; in which case they apparently feed upon inner resources hidden perhaps even from themselves. Writers, besides, are not born as artists at the precise moment when they are writing their best poem or play. Their birth occurred during an indefinite prior period when they accumulated impressions and developed their sensibility and viewpoint.

This much is certain: There was a continuity in our theatre that enriched the period represented in this anthology. Tennessee Williams began to win acceptance on Broadway in 1945 with *The Glass Menagerie*. But anyone who, like the present editor, saw his early work knows that the substance and quality of Williams' later artistry were pre-figured during the depression period. The essence of *A Streetcar Named Desire* and *Summer and Smoke* can be traced in such short early pieces by Williams as *Portrait of a Madonna* and *The Lady of Larkspur Lotion;* only a larger range and a greater degree of transfiguration of the substance still had to come. The hungers of the flesh and spirit, set in a seedy or deteriorating environment, also appeared in several one-acters collectively entitled *American Blues,* and these won a prize in 1938 from that outpost of the "social-consciousness" the Group Theatre. And Williams frankly presented *The Glass Menagerie* as a "memory play" drawn from the prewar depression. Reference may also be made to the distinctly Group Theatre overtones and viewpoint in *All My Sons* and *Death of a Salesman,* whose author received encouragement from the Group Theatre, and whose attitudes and field of observation were already established in early works known to me as long ago as 1938 as one of the Bureau of New Plays judges who gave Arthur Miller a substantial award. O'Neill, who enlarged the theatre with *The Iceman Cometh* in 1946, owed nothing, of course, to the post-war period in which he allowed his 1939 opus to appear. Maxwell Anderson was tilling a field in *Anne of the Thousand Days* that he had opened with *Elizabeth the Queen* nearly twenty years before. The writing and mood in Robinson Jeffers' dramatic poetry in *Medea* were also well seasoned. Jeffers was a fully formed dramatic poet as long ago as 1925 when Boni and Liveright published *The Tower Beyond Tragedy* in the volume *Roan Stallion, Tamar, and Other Poems.*

Enrichment also came from the field of fiction, and this was apparent when Ruth and Arthur Goetz made a moving play out of Henry James's *Washington Square* called *The Heiress,* and when William Archibald made a fascinating dramatization of James's *Turn of the Screw,* ironically entitled *The Innocents.* Louis O. Coxe and Robert Chapman drew upon the substance of Herman Melville's *Billy Budd* in writing a provocative play to express, as they have explained, their own less than cheerful view of the post-war world. Carson McCullers decided to dramatize her short novel *The Member of the Wedding* after dissatisfaction with another writer's attempt to dramatize it in 1947. Kingsley, in 1949, went back to Arthur Koestler's *Darkness at Noon,* published in 1941, and Koestler's novel was inspired by the author's disillusionment with Russian communism some years before the war.

It may also be noted that if the post-war period was not sparked by any outburst of social protest, it did retain a typically American concern with the common man and the realities of his life. Our playwrights brought their customary sympathy and vigor to the common scene. They were no more disposed than previously to keep their nostrils and artistic pretensions elevated. Miller's and Williams' plays, as well as such diverse examples as *Mister Roberts* and *Come Back, Little Sheba,* may be cited to sustain this point. If "high tragedy" did not take wing from most of the theatre's traffic with mortality, if the cosmic wrestlings were few, and if even intellectual drama rarely appeared on our stage, our plays nonetheless drew strength, as previously, from our ample plot of earth. And if memorable poetry was lacking, a considerable rise in sensibility could be noted in our theatre. Sensibility was, indeed, a major virtue in such writing as *The Member of the Wedding, Come Back, Little Sheba, A Streetcar Named Desire, Summer and Smoke,* and even *The Autumn Garden.* There was considerable sensibility, too, in other plays not included in this compilation, in *Second Threshold, The Heiress, The Fatal Weakness, The Rose Tattoo,* and *The Country Girl.* Playwrights and their audiences were inclined to favor responsiveness to refinements of feeling and attention to nuances. One does not have to perform gymnastic feats of textual explication to observe that this was the case and that dramatic writing was improved by it.

5.

Above all, of course, the period managed to acquit itself better than might be expected because it had a number of seasoned playwrights and produced some new talented writers. In previous decades one could point to schools of playwriting, that is, to groups of writers who followed a pattern or expressed a common attitude. In the post-war period, there were no "schools," there were only individual playwrights. Their particular merits, in association with their defects, gave the theatre much of its complexion.

Tennessee Williams, having made an auspicious start in 1945 with *The Glass Menagerie,* became a major figure of the time with *A Streetcar Named Desire.* If his

Summer and Smoke failed on Broadway, it nonetheless possessed considerable sensitivity and depth of characterization. If it lacked the taut dramaturgy and intensity of *Streetcar,* it had a quiet compulsion independent of melodrama except in an ill-considered killing. It was understandable that both Brooks Atkinson and Joseph Wood Krutch, among New York drama critics, should have been inclined to rate it higher than *Streetcar.* And *The Rose Tattoo,* vitiated though it was by a specious symbolism and over-reliance on an overactive libido, had some merit, too, besides indicating that Williams was abandoning the subject of genteel frustration which had become too obviously his stock in trade. He caught some striking folk color in this piece and revealed a humorous tenderness in his treatment of an impetuous suitor and a pair of adolescent lovers.

Of Williams it could be said that he was not only a born theatrician but a dramatist whose heart was singularly attuned to the anguish of passionate souls while his senses were attuned to the nuances of characterization and dialogue. His lapses from good taste, his not always successful use of symbolism, and his occasional straining for motivation imposed limitations upon his artistry. In Williams, however, the American theatre found an artist. In view of the infrequency with which it encountered members of his species, the contemporary stage could not afford to screen him too meticulously.

Close on his heels came Arthur Miller, who had appeared on Broadway briefly in 1944 with a sprawling play, *The Man Who Had All the Luck,* but first gained a foothold there with *All My Sons* in 1947. He brought moral passion and taut playwriting to the theme of human responsibility. If his parable of a man's sacrifice of the welfare of mankind to the egocentric welfare of his family was grounded in a story of war-profiteering, his essential subject was universal rather than topical. If *All My Sons* was not so much "created" as "made," recalling Sardou as well as Hellman, it also had some of Ibsen's largeness of vision and intense character creation. Brooks Atkinson, who declared that there had seldom been on the stage a story "so tightly woven as this one," was also moved to remark on how much "live freight" Miller had "packed into so rigid an area." And when Miller presented *Death of a Salesman* in 1949, only a few obdurate playgoers had any doubt that its author had made a powerful contribution to the contemporary stage.

Time and thought might whittle down the estimate, and reservations could be made even in 1949 as to the dialogue and the logic of Miller's treatment of a little man's calvary. To what degree is Willy Loman's superannuation as a never very successful salesman, which is mere pathos, less decisive in his story than his fiasco as a parent and a responsible person? To what extent can his mistaken values, his materialistic success-worship and large self-delusion, be attributed to social causation, to personal inadequacy, or to Willy's desire to maintain at all costs an ideal image of himself, which Miller considers to be the tragic element in the play? There could be dispute over that question, as well as over the question whether Willy's drama could rise beyond pathos since he failed to rise to the estate of self-recognition that high tragedy affords. Sceptics could ask how this earth-bound matter could be counted among truly estimable works of the theatre. These and other doubts suggested themselves—mostly as afterthoughts by spectators, most of whom were quite shattered by the play's surging emotion and its painful reality in the theatre.

It was plain, however, that Miller held his audience as in a vise, moved it with tidal feelings, and challenged it to arrive at judgment and not a little self-examination. He also engendered a certain sense of fatality not at all remote from true tragedy, and certainly not remote to audiences sensible of insecurity and disappointment in their own lives. Willy, though his shortcomings were exposed by Miller quite objectively, was, besides, lifted above his mental altitude by his intense parental passion and by the desire to realize an ideal of himself through his great expectations for his elder son. He also moved playgoers with his refusal to relinquish his self-esteem, his view of a certain glory in himself and, by projection, in his son, and his tenacious struggle with circumstances. Miller, in short, managed to endow his common hero with an uncommon, if recognizable, heroism, even if Miller could not convince everybody of its presence in the play. (He could not, it is true, convince fastidious spirits in this country or Englishmen, for whom Willy as a "type" was unfamiliar.) Above all, and regardless of the not absolutely relevant question of whether or not the play satisfied standard definitions of high tragedy, Miller compounded a play full of living people, liberally supplied with aspirations, confusions, and feelings. Presenting these imaginatively, in flexible dramatic form composed of realistic scenes, recollected ones, and hallucinated ones, he turned ordinary matter into engrossing theatre.

To the heavy ammunition of the period, too, O'Neill added one of his longest and most saturnine dramas when he allowed the Theatre Guild to produce *The Iceman Cometh,* written in 1939, one of the blackest years in world history and O'Neill's life. Our grimmest playwright was truly heroic here in his anti-heroic reiteration that humanity leads a life so snarled by weaknesses and contradictions that it can subsist only on illusion. He refused to allow a solacing or genial expectation for the race. He was also more loquacious in this "lower depths" drama than is allowable to nay-sayers and to playwrights in general. Still, his intensity and theatrical skill enabled him to hold attention and to reward it on the whole. Finesse of thought had never been O'Neill's strong point in earlier plays; it was not here either. But his huge and tenacious despair gave a certain largeness of spirit to a theatre usually given over to small emotions. The drama tended to grow static as a result of both its dispensable repetitions and its theme of stalemate. Yet *The Iceman Cometh* was tumultuous, too, especially in its various characterizations; for in the case of a number of the characters regrets and anxieties warred with their resignations and rationalized passivity. The power of dramatic art was manifest; by comparison with *The Iceman Cometh,* the existentialist despair of the trimmer, sharper plays of Sartre in France seemed an intellectual exercise, and the sense of original sin in the better-written plays of Eliot in England seemed doctrine rather than felt experience.

The Iceman Cometh, it is true, was hardly a play to captivate the public; even reviewers found it too taxing, and a majority of them favored Miller's *All My Sons* in preference to it when the New York drama critics assembled to make their annual award for the season of 1946-47. But O'Neill's presence in the period's theatre strengthened its claims to some importance. If another of the plays written during his long retirement, *A Moon for the Misbegotten,* had been successfully recast and brought to New York after its Midwestern tryout tour, Broadway would have been further fortified. In time to come, not only the enormous cycle of eleven plays on which he had been working for over a decade, but also a smaller cycle and some individual plays, might become part of our theatrical heritage. Physically afflicted, he might not be able to complete all this work, but probably enough would be available in time to remind us that a giant had labored in our midst. In the meantime, *The Iceman Cometh* was a sufficient reminder.

How even a narrow flame redeems a theatre from what a French critic once called "the vulgar and dramatic"—that is, from the showiness of "show business"—was demonstrated by a new playwright William Inge, who was decidedly not one of the giants before the flood. He gave the period the relentless play *Come Back, Little Sheba,* small in compass but intense in composition. It, too, was a study in stalemate, more familiar than that presented by O'Neill because more proportionate to everyday experience and set in an ordinary middle-class environment. A play about the frustrations of a sensitive alcoholic and a tawdry commonplace wife, *Come Back, Little Sheba* was on the surface an unpromising work. But the drama impacted in this Main Street story had a stirring and perturbing effect as the play rose from a quiet but charged pathos to an uncommonly painful explosion and then simmered down to an unstable equilibrium in the middle-class home, in which every banal detail exuded anxiety and anguish. Whether Inge could attain greater stature remained to be seen in the next decade, and whether the narrowness not merely of subject matter but of dramatic vision in *Come Back, Little Sheba* was altogether redeemed by the play's merits was arguable. But Inge made unpretentious reality yield a true dramatic experience with assistance from the principal actors, Shirley Booth and Sidney Blackmer.

The art of exposure and denudation of people also manifested itself upon a more conspicuous plane in *The Autumn Garden.* That much could be expected of its author Lillian Hellman, whose talent, it often seemed, would have been useful in a district attorney's office. It was the author's contention that allowing oneself to drift in early life made a radical reformation in middle-age impossible, and the life of her characters comprised an entire world of indecisions and self-delusions. This reviewer confesses to having felt some unclarity concerning the common source of all this failure; and perhaps this unclarity was caused by an incomplete commitment to analysis by the author. Still, the perceptive Princeton historian of the drama Alan Downer was correct when he maintained in his *Fifty Years of American Drama* that *The Autumn Garden* "is a broader and deeper view of her society and generation than any Miss Hellman has taken heretofore." In addition to contriving, as Mr. Downer explains, "to bring each of these deluded romantics to a moment of perception, to a moment when his eyes are opened to his precise situation," she allowed each of them an ample measure of life and sensibility. Her departure from tight dramaturgy, which blurred her focus somewhat and deprived her work of some of the dramatic power of several earlier plays, released her characters from subservience to "plot." It also made her indictment a softer impeachment than we had come to expect from her. She humanized her "dark comedy," giving it the quality of mercy without subverting the claims of justice. The shift of focus from one set of characters to another that occurred frequently in the play invited references to *The Autumn Garden* as a "Chekhovian" drama, an inexact description which encouraged invidious comparisons. Miss Hellman was not actually trying to write like Chekhov; she has been too fixed in her own idiom to adopt anyone else's. She was not working atmospheric effects and making poetry out of her characters' frustrations. In fact, she overextended herself in one respect, in striving for a resolution. This occurred in the case of a refugee girl whose grasp of reality, supposed to put the ladies and gentlemen of the play to shame, leads her to blackmail them. In adopting a looser form of drama than she had usually favored, Miss Hellman merely followed the necessities of a drama that contained a variety of people equally subject to scrutiny. She exercised a modern playwright's right to dispense with strict plot-making. *The Autumn Garden* was original rather than imitative, and it grew out of Lillian Hellman's own way of looking at life and thrusting a probing pitchfork into it.

Still, a large perspective was lacking in *The Autumn Garden,* as it was even more conspicuously absent in *Come Back, Little Sheba.* And this limitation could be found in most of the other plays of a period in which no sharp direction was present in the theatre. Although the competent Sidney Kingsley, for example, strove to achieve perspectives in each of his two plays, their power lay in distinct detail and strong foreground drama. In *Detective Story,* Kingsley exposed the fiasco of the overzealous moral will; the catastrophe was caused by the main character's psychologically suspect over-righteousness. Still, it was surface realism, the vivid naturalistic picture of a night court, that stood in the foreground. It was this matter, along with the suspense of progressive discovery by the detective that his own wife was culpable, that gave *Detective Story* its theatrical effectiveness.

Painstaking verisimilitude and technical skill are most apparent in Kingsley's playwriting. And it was technical skill that gave his dramatization *Darkness at Noon* much of its force. He managed to put into effective dramatic form a novel that involves the past and the present, a novel that is therefore difficult to dramatize. The story of efforts to extort a confession in a Soviet prison was masterfully handled— better, indeed, than the complex mentality of the "Old Bolshevik" prisoner Rubashov whose mental processes were Koestler's main concern in the novel. A perspective, largely drawn from Koestler, did appear in the play. It consisted of a demonstration of how ruthless means corrupt ideal ends; how rationalized force can transform moral intentions into crimes for which all humanity pays in the end. The "Old Bolshevik" Rubashov's torment emanates from his realization that in trying to improve civilization he had helped to undermine it. His cold-blooded executioner is his own spiritual heir—his "son." A profound theme was latent in Kingsley's play and raised it above the level of mere melodrama. It concerned the fate of those who not only promise a terrestrial paradise but try to force it on mankind. It dealt with the "priests of politics," as the philosophical Remy de Gourmont called them at the beginning of the century, who "all sell very dearly the tickets of a lottery that will never be drawn." Still, Kingsley's efficacy lay in the immediate drama of interrogation, and the revolutionist's regretful review of his past was limited to the exigencies of this theme. The play expressed the author's outraged feelings as he contemplated the betrayal of a utopian or liberal dream in our time. As is usual in Kingsley's work, the immediate reality, impulse, and conviction were dominant.

By contrast, it was the large or universal theme, rather than any immediately present provocation, that gave *Billy Budd* its main interest. It is always easier to maintain perspective at a distance, and the actual event that served Melville as a basis for a metaphysics of good and evil was fairly remote for Louis Coxe and Robert Chapman when they turned Melville's short novel into a play. Their limitations were the reverse of Kingsley's. The universals in their play were, in the main, better than the specific dramatic realities. The view that absolute good and absolute evil are equally contrary to nature and cannot therefore survive was fascinating. But the facts of the fable that sustained this view—that is, the story of the sailor Billy's sublime innocence, his execution on legalistic grounds, and his blank acceptance of his fate—were rather tenuous. Billy himself was not altogether satisfactory as a character, being partly an individual and partly a symbol. Far sturdier in the play were the drama of one man's (Claggart's) malice in the first two acts of the play and the drama of legalistic rigor, as represented by Captain Vere, in the third act. Still, *Billy Budd* was an uncommonly interesting play. Mind and spirit and a respect for the theatre as a medium for expressive art were present in this work. It was also apparent that the authors discharged personally felt perturbations when they dramatized and in some respects modified and actually amplified Melville's story. If their play proved too elusive or too perturbing for many playgoers, it must nevertheless be enrolled in the period's roster of distinguished dramatic writing.

Not philosophy but a rich sensibility, fully communicated by the noteworthy Harold Clurman stage production, gave distinction to another dramatization, *The Member of the Wedding,* which Carson McCullers, the author of the novel, apparently transformed into a play with almost no effort. But this play, too, departed from standardized drama. It was, in fact, the absence of contriving craftsmanship, replaced by a simple sensitiveness and natural flow, that made this play so fresh and evocative when presented on Broadway.

The Member of the Wedding was a triumph of feeling over plotting and of acute observation over the strenuous dramatics often supposed to be the secret of theatrical success. Although simple enough in construction to accord well with its subject of adolescence, the structure was, nevertheless, subtle; if not theatrically ingenious, it was inwardly or, as one might say, musically compelling. Whether by design or accident, it is difficult to say! One felt as though one were observing the flow of life itself rather than a "made-up" story. The complications depended largely on an adolescent girl's notion that she could go along with her brother and his bride on their honeymoon. Yet the play was anything but the dramatization of a notion. It was the child's restiveness in growth, with all that this involved in irritations and fancies on her part, that compelled motion in the drama. Small ironies and simple truths of life made up the texture of *The Member of the Wedding*. They seemed momentous to the girl, and this constituted her drama. But a larger drama, that of the human condition itself, traced a pattern through the play. It moved to a crescendo of loneliness on the part of the heroine's patient Negro nurse just as the girl's uncertainties and sense of isolation were beginning to vanish, removing the need for the woman's ministrations. The play, then, became not merely a little drama of adolescence, but a poetic realization of the essential loneliness of people. This theme was reinforced by the fact that the youngster's father was a widower and by the death of her delightfully drawn little playmate. In this delicately written play, which had no substantial plot complications, Mrs. McCullers evoked reality by means of revealing inconsequentialities and by means of tone, mood, and suggestion. *The Member of the Wedding* was poetry in the theatre.

The play is another indication of how large a part sensibility had begun to play in a theatre deprived of the stimulus of larger artistic and intellectual challenges. The poetic revival in Britain, sparked by Christopher Fry and T. S. Eliot, was absent here. Jeffers, with his *Medea* and playing version of *The Tower Beyond Tragedy,* and Maxwell Anderson, with *Anne of the Thousand Days,* did not constitute a summer of dramatic nightingales. The success of *Medea,* along with appreciation of the imported plays *The Lady's Not for Burning* and *The Cocktail Party,* simply signified that there was no allergy to contemporary dramatic poetry in our constitution. But we produced our poetry in the theatre in other ways than formal composition, by the exercise of dramatic and theatrical imagination, as in *Death of a Salesman* and *A Streetcar Named Desire,* and by sensitivity to nuances of dialogue, characterization, and play structure. This was apparent not only in the above-mentioned plays but in quite a number of other productions, including failures as well as successes, acceptable plays incorporated in this volume and others excluded, such as *The Heiress, The Innocents,* the Emily Dickinson play *Eastward in Eden* by Dorothy Gardner, and the old-people's-home comedy *The Silver Whistle* by the new playwright Robert McEnroe. We encompassed this poetization of the drama with or without conscious symbolization, and with or without the expressive use of music.

It is questionable whether stage art can be properly sustained over a long period by sensibility alone. But it is a source of artistic achievement at any time and under any circumstances. *The Member of the Wedding,* warmly received on Broadway, may stand for a well-marked attribute of much playwriting. Our stage was secured against devastating banalization in a period of diminishing resources and ferments by our increasingly sensitized playwriting and imaginative use of dramatic art. When energy and passion were also in evidence, as they were in some of the work of Williams, Miller and O'Neill, the American drama was not actually less impressive than it had been before in a theatre of greater abundance and fermentation. The question that agitated some of us was, at first, merely whether enough creativity was making itself felt; and, by 1950, whether creative energy was not running out as we began to navigate around the mid-century point. We certainly could not call it the Cape of Good Hope. But, on the whole and in spite of some foul weather, we had had fair sailing as far as we had gone.

Death of a Salesman

BY ARTHUR MILLER

First presented by Kermit Bloomgarden and Walter Fried at the Morosco Theatre in New York on February 10, 1949, with the following cast:

WILLY LOMAN	Lee J. Cobb	CHARLEY	Howard Smith
LINDA	Mildred Dunnock	UNCLE BEN	Thomas Chalmers
BIFF	Arthur Kennedy	HOWARD WAGNER	Alan Hewitt
HAPPY	Cameron Mitchell	JENNY	Ann Driscoll
BERNARD	Don Keefer	STANLEY	Tom Pedi
THE WOMAN	Winnifred Cushing	MISS FORSYTHE	Constance Ford
	LETTA	Hope Cameron	

The action takes place in Willy Loman's house and yard and in various places he visits in the New York and Boston of today.

AFTER the production of *Death of a Salesman,* Arthur Miller was celebrated throughout the land as the second new dramatist to have assured the survival of significant playwriting in America. (The first had been Tennessee Williams.) The play won both the Pulitzer Prize and the Drama Critics Circle award, as well as sundry other prizes. Although Miller's earlier play, *All My Sons,* had been well received, there had been reason to doubt its author's originality and dramatic range. Once *Death of a Salesman* opened in Manhattan, only his originality could be questioned, since his materials, including his style of dialogue, were familiar. Except in the opinion of a few fastidious observers, however, the vigor of the new play made an academic matter of the question of how new the subject was. The characters and the background were, indeed, fresh precisely because they were so vividly recognizable, and Miller's compassionate scrutiny of little lives communicated itself spontaneously to his public; or so it seemed to audiences, although the author actually kept a firm hand on his sequence of events and revelations. Miller here employed flexible dramaturgy, moving from a present crisis to eruptive scenes of reminiscence. Consequently, he was able to give his story some of the extensiveness and richness of a novel without losing dramatic power. The play displayed life multi-dimensionally or, so to speak, in depth.

For these and other reasons, Miller was acclaimed as the outstanding new dramatist of the forties or, at the least, Tennessee Williams' equal among the decade's discovered playwrights. Although Miller's language was not regarded as equal to Williams' dialogue, his picture of reality was considered more representative and significant. It was in his favor, too, that he demonstrated to those who were familiar with his earlier work that he was capable of artistic growth, having graduated from the "well-made play" grammar school of modern playwriting. As he himself declared, "the conventional play form forces the writer to siphon everything into a single place at a single time, and squeezes the humanity out of a play. Why shouldn't a play have the depth, the completeness, and the diversity of a novel?"

Death of a Salesman climaxed a slow advance on the Broadway scene and a steady development of skills and powers. Born in 1916 in New York, and reared in suburban Brooklyn, Miller had the usual high school education, enlivened by a modest football career not unusual in the case of a tall raw-boned lad. Going on to the University of Michigan, after two and a half years of clerking in an automobile parts warehouse, he found an understanding teacher in Professor Kenneth E. Rowe, the author of *Write That Play.* Miller turned to playwriting with such devotion that he won the university's Avery Hopwood award for two successive years. In 1937 he also received a substantially larger prize from the Bureau of New Plays, established by the Theatre Guild director Theresa Helburn. Upon leaving college in 1938, he first found employment on the playwriting project of the Federal Theatre. Fortunately, since the W.P.A. project expired four months after he joined it, Miller also revealed a talent for radio writing and was able to settle down to a simple, semi-suburban life in Brooklyn with his wife, a former Michigan classmate. During the war, disqualified for military service by an injury he had sustained while playing football, he worked as a steamfitter in the Brooklyn Navy Yard and wrote patriotic radio scripts and one-acters. He also did some work, in 1942, on the notable Ernie Pyle film *The Story of G.I. Joe,* spending six months with the infantry and going on maneuvers while gathering information for the production. Having kept a diary of his research, Miller published it in 1944 under the title of *Situation Normal.* He published a second book in 1945, a successful novel about race hatred entitled *Focus.* By no means neglecting playwriting, Miller also wrote several full-length plays during his apprenticeship, and one of these, *The Man Who Had All the Luck,* a sprawling chronicle, brought him some recognition in 1944.

In 1947 Miller's nine-year-long wrestling with the dramatic medium reaped its first rewards when *All My Sons* (see page 281) had a good run on Broadway, won the Drama Critics Circle award, and was bought by a motion picture producer. Two years later he had Broadway at his feet and met Willy Loman's prescription for success to the letter; he was not only "liked" but "well liked" for *Death of a Salesman.*

Brooks Atkinson, in *The New York Times,* called *Death of a Salesman* "one of the finest dramas in the whole range of the American theatre," and John Mason Brown referred to the production, brilliantly directed by Elia Kazan, as "one of the modern theatre's most overpowering evenings." John Chapman of the *New York Daily News* concurred, describing it as "one of those unforgettable times in which all is right and nothing is wrong." Even the usually more sceptical Wolcott Gibbs, writing in *The New Yorker,* set it down as "a tremendously affecting work . . . told with a mixture of compassion, imagination, and hard technical competence you don't often find in the theatre today." And the hardly less exacting reviewer of *Time,* Louis Kronenberger, described the play as "so simple, central, and terrible that the run of playwrights would neither care nor dare to attempt it." The play also won considerable success abroad, and was received with particular enthusiasm in Vienna. English reviewers and playgoers took a more reserved view of Willy Loman's story. Ivor Brown, writing in *The New York Times* of August 28, 1949, explained that the salesman is not a national type in England, and that the English have too much contempt for "the life of the party" and "smiles into diamonds" philosophy of success to be stirred by Willy's failure. *Death of a Salesman* won greater commendation from the British as "a skillful piece of stagecraft" than as a waterfall of compassion. Yet for the British, too, the play made substantial claims as a "little man's" tragedy. Ivor Brown noted that "now on both sides of the Atlantic we have stool tragedies, not throne tragedies," and that "it is the clerk, not the king, who inspires the tragedian."

ACT ONE

A melody is heard, played upon a flute. It is small and fine, telling of grass and trees and the horizon. The curtain rises.

Before us is the Salesman's house. We are aware of towering, angular shapes behind it, surrounding it on all sides. Only the blue light of the sky falls upon the house and forestage; the surrounding area shows an angry glow of orange. As more light appears, we see a solid vault of apartment houses around the small, fragile-seeming home. An air of the dream clings to the place, a dream rising out of reality. The kitchen at center seems actual enough, for there is a kitchen table with three chairs, and a refrigerator. But no other fixtures are seen. At the back of the kitchen there is a draped entrance, which leads to the living-room. To the right of the kitchen, on a level raised two feet, is a bedroom furnished only with a brass bedstead and a straight chair. On a shelf over the bed a silver athletic trophy stands. A window opens onto the apartment house at the side.

Behind the kitchen, on a level raised six and a half feet, is the boys' bedroom, at present barely visible. Two beds are dimly seen, and at the back of the room a dormer window. (This bedroom is above the unseen living-room.) At the left a stairway curves up to it from the kitchen.

The entire setting is wholly or, in some places, partially transparent. The roof-line of the house is one-dimensional; under and over it we see the apartment buildings. Before the house lies an apron, curving beyond the forestage into the orchestra. This forward area serves as the back yard as well as the locale of all Willy's imaginings and of his city scenes. Whenever the action is in the present the actors observe the imaginary wall-lines, entering the house only through its door at the left. But in the scenes of the past these boundaries are broken, and characters enter or leave a room by stepping "through" a wall onto the forestage.

From the right, Willy Loman, the Salesman, enters, carrying two large sample cases. The flute plays on. He hears but is not aware of it. He is past sixty years of age, dressed quietly. Even as he crosses the stage to the doorway of the house, his exhaustion is apparent. He unlocks the door, comes into the kitchen, and thankfully lets his burden down, feeling the soreness of his palms. A word-sigh escapes his lips—it might be "Oh, boy, oh, boy." He closes the door, then carries his cases out into the living-room, through the draped kitchen doorway.

Linda, his wife, has stirred in her bed at the right. She gets out and puts on a robe, listening. Most often jovial, she has developed an iron repression of her exceptions to Willy's behavior—she more than loves him, she admires him, as though his mercurial nature, his temper, his massive dreams and little cruelties, served her only as sharp reminders of the turbulent longings within him, longings which she shares but lacks the temperament to utter and follow to their end.

———

LINDA (*hearing Willy outside the bedroom, calls with some trepidation*). Willy!

WILLY. It's all right. I came back.

LINDA. Why? What happened? (*Slight pause*) Did something happen, Willy?

WILLY. No, nothing happened.

LINDA. You didn't smash the car, did you?

WILLY (*with casual irritation*). I said nothing happened. Didn't you hear me?

LINDA. Don't you feel well?

WILLY. I'm tired to the death. (*The flute has faded away. He sits on the bed beside her, a little numb*) I couldn't make it. I just couldn't make it, Linda.

LINDA (*very carefully, delicately*). Where were you all day? You look terrible.

WILLY. I got as far as a little above Yonkers. I stopped for a cup of coffee. Maybe it was the coffee.

LINDA. What?

WILLY (*after a pause*). I suddenly couldn't drive any more. The car kept going off onto the shoulder, y'know?

LINDA (*helpfully*). Oh. Maybe it was the steering again. I don't think Angelo knows the Studebaker.

WILLY. No, it's me, it's me. Suddenly I realize I'm goin' sixty miles an hour and I don't remember the last five minutes. I'm —I can't seem to—keep my mind to it.

LINDA. Maybe it's your glasses. You never went for your new glasses.

WILLY. No, I see everything. I came back ten miles an hour. It took me nearly four hours from Yonkers.

LINDA (*resigned*). Well, you'll just have

to take a rest, Willy, you can't continue this way.

WILLY. I just got back from Florida.

LINDA. But you didn't rest your mind. Your mind is overactive, and the mind is what counts, dear.

WILLY. I'll start out in the morning. Maybe I'll feel better in the morning. (*She is taking off his shoes*) These goddam arch supports are killing me.

LINDA. Take an aspirin. Should I get you an aspirin? It'll soothe you.

WILLY (*with wonder*). I was driving along, you understand? And I was fine. I was even observing the scenery. You can imagine, me looking at scenery, on the road every week of my life. But it's so beautiful up there, Linda, the trees are so thick, and the sun is warm. I opened the windshield and just let the warm air bathe over me. And then all of a sudden I'm goin' off the road! I'm tellin' ya, I absolutely forgot I was driving. If I'd've gone the other way over the white line I might've killed somebody. So I went on again—and five minutes later I'm dreamin' again, and I nearly— (*He presses two fingers against his eyes*) I have such thoughts, I have such strange thoughts.

LINDA. Willy, dear. Talk to them again. There's no reason why you can't work in New York.

WILLY. They don't need me in New York. I'm the New England man. I'm vital in New England.

LINDA. But you're sixty years old. They can't expect you to keep traveling every week.

WILLY. I'll have to send a wire to Portland. I'm supposed to see Brown and Morrison tomorrow morning at ten o'clock to show the line. Goddammit, I could sell them! (*He starts putting on his jacket*)

LINDA (*taking the jacket from him*). Why don't you go down to the place tomorrow and tell Howard you've simply got to work in New York? You're too accommodating, dear.

WILLY. If old man Wagner was alive I'd a been in charge of New York now! That man was a prince, he was a masterful man. But that boy of his, that Howard, he don't appreciate. When I went north the first time, the Wagner Company didn't know where New England was!

LINDA. Why don't you tell those things to Howard, dear?

WILLY (*encouraged*). I will, I definitely will. Is there any cheese?

LINDA. I'll make you a sandwich.

WILLY. No, go to sleep. I'll take some milk. I'll be up right away. The boys in?

LINDA. They're sleeping. Happy took Biff on a date tonight.

WILLY (*interested*). That so?

LINDA. It was so nice to see them shaving together, one behind the other, in the bathroom. And going out together. You notice? The whole house smells of shaving lotion.

WILLY. Figure it out. Work a lifetime to pay off a house. You finally own it, and there's nobody to live in it.

LINDA. Well, dear, life is a casting off. It's always that way.

WILLY. No, no, some people—some people accomplish something. Did Biff say anything after I went this morning?

LINDA. You shouldn't have criticized him, Willy, especially after he just got off the train. You mustn't lose your temper with him.

WILLY. When the hell did I lose my temper? I simply asked him if he was making any money. Is that a criticism?

LINDA. But, dear, how could he make any money?

WILLY (*worried and angered*). There's such an undercurrent in him. He became a moody man. Did he apologize when I left this morning?

LINDA. He was crestfallen, Willy. You know how he admires you. I think if he finds himself, then you'll both be happier and not fight any more.

WILLY. How can he find himself on a farm? Is that a life? A farmhand? In the beginning, when he was young, I thought, well, a young man, it's good for him to tramp around, take a lot of different jobs. But it's more than ten years now and he has yet to make thirty-five dollars a week!

LINDA. He's finding himself, Willy.

WILLY. Not finding yourself at the age of thirty-four is a disgrace!

LINDA. Shh!

WILLY. The trouble is he's lazy, goddammit!

LINDA. Willy, please!

WILLY. Biff is a lazy bum!

LINDA. They're sleeping. Get something to eat. Go on down.

WILLY. Why did he come home? I

would like to know what brought him home.

LINDA. I don't know. I think he's still lost, Willy. I think he's very lost.

WILLY. Biff Loman is lost. In the greatest country in the world a young man with such—personal attractiveness, gets lost. And such a hard worker. There's one thing about Biff—he's not lazy.

LINDA. Never.

WILLY (*with pity and resolve*). I'll see him in the morning; I'll have a nice talk with him. I'll get him a job selling. He could be big in no time. My God! Remember how they used to follow him around in high school? When he smiled at one of them their faces lit up. When he walked down the street . . . (*He loses himself in reminiscences*)

LINDA (*trying to bring him out of it*). Willy, dear, I got a new kind of American-type cheese today. It's whipped.

WILLY. Why do you get American when I like Swiss?

LINDA. I just thought you'd like a change—

WILLY. I don't want a change! I want Swiss cheese. Why am I always being contradicted?

LINDA (*with a covering laugh*). I thought it would be a surprise.

WILLY. Why don't you open a window in here, for God's sake?

LINDA (*with infinite patience*). They're all open, dear.

WILLY. The way they boxed us in here. Bricks and windows, windows and bricks.

LINDA. We should've bought the land next door.

WILLY. The street is lined with cars. There's not a breath of fresh air in the neighborhood. The grass don't grow any more, you can't raise a carrot in the back yard. They should've had a law against apartment houses. Remember those two beautiful elm trees out there? When I and Biff hung the swing between them?

LINDA. Yeah, like being a million miles from the city.

WILLY. They should've arrested the builder for cutting those down. They massacred the neighborhood. (*Lost*) More and more I think of those days, Linda. This time of year it was lilac and wisteria. And then the peonies would come out, and the daffodils. What fragrance in this room!

LINDA. Well, after all, people had to move somewhere.

WILLY. No, there's more people now.

LINDA. I don't think there's more people. I think—

WILLY. There's more people! That's what's ruining this country! Population is getting out of control. The competition is maddening! Smell the stink from that apartment house! And another one on the other side . . . How can they whip cheese? (*On Willy's last line, Biff and Happy raise themselves up in their beds, listening.*)

LINDA. Go down, try it. And be quiet.

WILLY (*turning to Linda, guiltily*). You're not worried about me, are you, sweetheart?

BIFF. What's the matter?

HAPPY. Listen!

LINDA. You've got too much on the ball to worry about.

WILLY. You're my foundation and my support, Linda.

LINDA. Just try to relax, dear. You make mountains out of molehills.

WILLY. I won't fight with him any more. If he wants to go back to Texas, let him go.

LINDA. He'll find his way.

WILLY. Sure. Certain men just don't get started till later in life. Like Thomas Edison, I think. Or B. F. Goodrich. One of them was deaf. (*He starts for the bedroom doorway*) I'll put my money on Biff.

LINDA. And, Willy—if it's warm Sunday we'll drive in the country. And we'll open the windshield, and take lunch.

WILLY. No, the windshields don't open on the new cars.

LINDA. But you opened it today.

WILLY. Me? I didn't. (*He stops*) Now isn't that peculiar! Isn't that remarkable— (*He breaks off in amazement and fright as the flute is heard distantly*)

LINDA. What, darling?

WILLY. That is the most remarkable thing.

LINDA. What, dear?

WILLY. I was thinking of the Chevvy (*Slight pause*) Nineteen twenty-eight . . . when I had that red Chevvy—(*Breaks off*) That's funny? I coulda sworn I was driving that Chevvy today.

LINDA. Well, that's nothing. Something must've reminded you.

WILLY. Remarkable. Ts. Remember those days? The way Biff used to simonize that car? The dealer refused to believe there was eighty thousand miles on it. (*He shakes his head*) Heh! (*To Linda*) Close your eyes, I'll be right up. (*He walks out of the bedroom*)

HAPPY (*to Biff*). Jesus, maybe he smashed up the car again!

LINDA (*calling after Willy*). Be careful on the stairs, dear! The cheese is on the middle shelf! (*She turns, goes over to the bed, takes his jacket, and goes out of the bedroom*)

(*Light has risen on the boys' room. Unseen, Willy is heard talking to himself, "Eighty thousand miles," and a little laugh. Biff gets out of bed, comes downstage a bit, and stands attentively. Biff is two years older than his brother Happy, well built, but in these days bears a worn air and seems less self-assured. He has succeeded less, and his dreams are stronger and less acceptable than Happy's. Happy is tall, powerfully made. Sexuality is like a visible color on him, or a scent that many women have discovered. He, like his brother, is lost, but in a different way, for he has never allowed himself to turn his face toward defeat and is thus more confused and hard-skinned, although seemingly more content.*)

HAPPY (*getting out of bed*). He's going to get his license taken away if he keeps that up. I'm getting nervous about him, y'know, Biff?

BIFF. His eyes are going.

HAPPY. No, I've driven with him. He sees all right. He just doesn't keep his mind on it. I drove into the city with him last week. He stops at a green light and then it turns red and he goes. (*He laughs*)

BIFF. Maybe he's color-blind.

HAPPY. Pop? Why he's got the finest eye for color in the business. You know that.

BIFF (*sitting down on his bed*). I'm going to sleep.

HAPPY. You're not still sour on Dad, are you, Biff?

BIFF. He's all right, I guess.

WILLY (*underneath them, in the living-room*). Yes, sir, eighty thousand miles—eighty-two thousand!

BIFF. You smoking?

HAPPY (*holding out a pack of cigarettes*). Want one?

BIFF (*taking a cigarette*). I can never sleep when I smell it.

WILLY. What a simonizing job, heh!

HAPPY (*with deep sentiment*). Funny, Biff, y'know? Us sleeping in here again? The old beds. (*He pats his bed affectionately*) All the talk that went across those two beds, huh? Our whole lives.

BIFF. Yeah. Lotta dreams and plans.

HAPPY (*with a deep and masculine laugh*). About five hundred women would like to know what was said in this room. (*They share a short laugh*)

BIFF. Remember that big Betsy something—what the hell was her name—over on Bushwick Avenue?

HAPPY (*combing his hair*). With the collie dog!

BIFF. That's the one. I got you in there, remember?

HAPPY. Yeah, that was my first time—I think. Boy, there was a pig! (*They laugh, almost crudely*) You taught me everything I know about women. Don't forget that.

BIFF. I bet you forgot how bashful you used to be. Especially with girls.

HAPPY. Oh, I still am, Biff.

BIFF. Oh, go on.

HAPPY. I just control it, that's all. I think I got less bashful and you got more so. What happened, Biff? Where's the old humor, the old confidence? (*He shakes Biff's knee. Biff gets up and moves restlessly about the room*) What's the matter?

BIFF. Why does Dad mock me all the time?

HAPPY. He's not mocking you, he—

BIFF. Everything I say there's a twist of mockery on his face. I can't get near him.

HAPPY. He just wants you to make good, that's all. I wanted to talk to you about Dad for a long time, Biff. Something's—happening to him. He—talks to himself.

BIFF. I noticed that this morning. But he always mumbled.

HAPPY. But not so noticeable. It got so embarrassing I sent him to Florida. And you know something? Most of the time he's talking to you.

BIFF. What's he say about me?

HAPPY. I can't make it out.

BIFF. What's he say about me?

HAPPY. I think the fact that you're not settled, that you're still kind of up in the air . . .

BIFF. There's one or two other things depressing him, Happy.

HAPPY. What do you mean?

BIFF. Never mind. Just don't lay it all to me.

HAPPY. But I think if you just got started —I mean—is there any future for you out there?

BIFF. I tell ya, Hap, I don't know what the future is. I don't know—what I'm supposed to want.

HAPPY. What do you mean?

BIFF. Well, I spent six or seven years after high school trying to work myself up. Shipping clerk, salesman, business of one kind or another. And it's a measly manner of existence. To get on that subway on the hot mornings in summer. To devote your whole life to keeping stock, or making phone calls, or selling or buying. To suffer fifty weeks of the year for the sake of a two-week vacation, when all you really desire is to be outdoors, with your shirt off. And always to have to get ahead of the next fella. And still—that's how you build a future.

HAPPY. Well, you really enjoy it on a farm? Are you content out there?

BIFF (*with rising agitation*). Hap, I've had twenty or thirty different kinds of jobs since I left home before the war, and it always turns out the same. I just realized it lately. In Nebraska where I herded cattle, and the Dakotas, and Arizona, and now in Texas. It's why I came home now, I guess, because I realized it. This farm I work on, it's spring there now, see? And they've got about fifteen new colts. There's nothing more inspiring or—beautiful than the sight of a mare and a new colt. And it's cool there now, see? Texas is cool now, and it's spring. And whenever spring comes to where I am, I suddenly get the feeling, my God, I'm not gettin' anywhere! What the hell am I doing, playing around with horses, twenty-eight dollars a week! I'm thirty-four years old, I oughta be makin' my future. That's when I come running home. And now, I get here, and I don't know what to do with myself. (*After a pause*) I've always made a point of not wasting my life, and everytime I come back here I know that all I've done is to waste my life.

HAPPY. You're a poet, you know that, Biff? You're a—you're an idealist!

BIFF. No, I'm mixed up very bad. Maybe I oughta get married. Maybe I oughta get stuck into something. Maybe that's my trouble. I'm like a boy. I'm not married, I'm not in business, I just—I'm like a boy.

Are you content, Hap? You're a success, aren't you? Are you content?

HAPPY. Hell, no!

BIFF. Why? You're making money, aren't you?

HAPPY (*moving about with energy, expressiveness*). All I can do now is wait for the merchandise manager to die. And suppose I get to be merchandise manager? He's a good friend of mine, and he just built a terrific estate on Long Island. And he lived there about two months and sold it, and now he's building another one. He can't enjoy it once it's finished. And I know that's just what I would do. I don't know what the hell I'm workin' for. Sometimes I sit in my apartment—all alone. And I think of the rent I'm paying. And it's crazy. But then, it's what I always wanted. My own apartment, a car, and plenty of women. And still, goddammit, I'm lonely.

BIFF (*with enthusiasm*). Listen, why don't you come out West with me?

HAPPY. You and I, heh?

BIFF. Sure, maybe we could buy a ranch. Raise cattle, use our muscles. Men built like we are should be working out in the open.

HAPPY (*avidly*). The Loman Brothers, heh?

BIFF (*with vast affection*). Sure, we'd be known all over the counties!

HAPPY (*enthralled*). That's what I dream about, Biff. Sometimes I want to just rip my clothes off in the middle of the store and outbox that goddam merchandise manager. I mean I can outbox, outrun, and outlift anybody in that store, and I have to take orders from those common, petty sons-of-bitches till I can't stand it any more.

BIFF. I'm tellin' you, kid, if you were with me I'd be happy out there.

HAPPY (*enthused*). See, Biff, everybody around me is so false that I'm constantly lowering my ideals . . .

BIFF. Baby, together we'd stand up for one another, we'd have someone to trust.

HAPPY. If I were around you—

BIFF. Hap, the trouble is we weren't brought up to grub for money. I don't know how to do it.

HAPPY. Neither can I!

BIFF. Then let's go!

HAPPY. The only thing is—what can you make out there?

BIFF. But look at your friend. Builds an estate and then hasn't the peace of mind to live in it.

HAPPY. Yeah, but when he walks into the store the waves part in front of him. That's fifty-two thousand dollars a year coming through the revolving door, and I got more in my pinky finger than he's got in his head.

BIFF. Yeah, but you just said—

HAPPY. I gotta show some of those pompous, self-important executives over there that Hap Loman can make the grade. I want to walk into the store the way he walks in. Then I'll go with you, Biff. We'll be together yet, I swear. But take those two we had tonight. Now weren't they gorgeous creatures?

BIFF. Yeah, yeah, most gorgeous I've had in years.

HAPPY. I get that any time I want, Biff. Whenever I feel disgusted. The only trouble is, it gets like bowling or something. I just keep knockin' them over and it doesn't mean anything. You still run around a lot?

BIFF. Naa. I'd like to find a girl—steady, somebody with substance.

HAPPY. That's what I long for.

BIFF. Go on! You'd never come home.

HAPPY. I would! Somebody with character, with resistance! Like Mom, y'know? You're gonna call me a bastard when I tell you this. That girl Charlotte I was with tonight is engaged to be married in five weeks. (*He tries on his new hat*)

BIFF. No kiddin'!

HAPPY. Sure, the guy's in line for the vice-presidency of the store. I don't know what gets into me, maybe I just have an overdeveloped sense of competition or something, but I went and ruined her, and furthermore I can't get rid of her. And he's the third executive I've done that to. Isn't that a crummy characteristic? And to top it all, I go to their weddings! (*Indignantly, but laughing*) Like I'm not supposed to take bribes. Manufacturers offer me a hundred-dollar bill now and then to throw an order their way. You know how honest I am, but it's like this girl, see. I hate myself for it. Because I don't want the girl, and, still, I take it and—I love it!

BIFF. Let's go to sleep.

HAPPY. I guess we didn't settle anything, heh?

BIFF. I just got one idea that I think I'm going to try.

HAPPY. What's that?

BIFF. Remember Bill Oliver?

HAPPY. Sure, Oliver is very big now. You want to work for him again?

BIFF. No, but when I quit he said something to me. He put his arm on my shoulder and he said, "Biff, if you ever need anything, come to me."

HAPPY. I remember that. That sounds good.

BIFF. I think I'll go to see him. If I could get ten thousand or even seven or eight thousand dollars I could buy a beautiful ranch.

HAPPY. I bet he'd back you. 'Cause he thought highly of you, Biff. I mean, they all do. You're well liked, Biff. That's why I say to come back here, and we both have the apartment. And I'm tellin' you, Biff, any babe you want . . .

BIFF. No, with a ranch I could do the work I like and still be something. I just wonder though. I wonder if Oliver still thinks I stole that carton of basketballs.

HAPPY. Oh, he probably forgot that long ago. It's almost ten years. You're too sensitive. Anyway, he didn't really fire you.

BIFF. Well, I think he was going to. I think that's why I quit. I was never sure whether he knew or not. I know he thought the world of me, though. I was the only one he'd let lock up the place.

WILLY (*below*). You gonna wash the engine, Biff?

HAPPY. Shh! (*Biff looks at Happy, who is gazing down, listening. Willy is mumbling in the parlor*)

HAPPY. You hear that? (*They listen. Willy laughs warmly*)

BIFF (*growing angry*). Doesn't he know Mom can hear that?

WILLY. Don't get your sweater dirty, Biff! (*A look of pain crosses Biff's face*)

HAPPY. Isn't that terrible? Don't leave again, will you? You'll find a job here. You gotta stick around. I don't know what to do about him, it's getting embarrassing.

WILLY. What a simonizing job!

BIFF. Mom's hearing that!

WILLY. No kiddin', Biff, you got a date? Wonderful!

HAPPY. Go on to sleep. But talk to him in the morning, will you?

BIFF (*reluctantly getting into bed*). With her in the house. Brother!

HAPPY (*getting into bed*). I wish you'd have a good talk with him.

(*The light on their room begins to fade.*)

BIFF (*to himself, in bed*). That selfish, stupid . . .

HAPPY. Sh . . . Sleep, Biff.

(*Their light is out. Well before they have finished speaking, Willy's form is dimly seen below in the darkened kitchen. He opens the refrigerator, searches in there and takes out a bottle of milk. The apartment houses are fading out, and the entire house and surroundings become covered with leaves. Music insinuates itself as the leaves appear.*)

WILLY. Just wanna be careful with those girls, Biff, that's all. Don't make any promises. No promises of any kind. Because a girl, y'know, they always believe what you tell 'em, and you're very young, Biff, you're too young to be talking seriously to girls.

(*Light rises on the kitchen. Willy, talking, shuts the refrigerator door and comes downstage to the kitchen table. He pours milk into a glass. He is totally immersed in himself, smiling faintly.*)

WILLY. Too young entirely, Biff. You want to watch your schooling first. Then when you're all set, there'll be plenty of girls for a boy like you. (*He smiles broadly at a kitchen chair*) That so? The girls pay for you? (*He laughs*) Boy, you must really be makin' a hit.

(*Willy is gradually addressing—physically —a point offstage, speaking through the wall of the kitchen, and his voice has been rising in volume to that of a normal conversation.*)

WILLY. I been wondering why you polish the car so careful. Ha! Don't leave the hubcaps, boys. Get the chamois to the hubcaps. Happy, use newspapers on the windows, it's the easiest thing. Show him how to do it, Biff! You see, Happy? Pad it up, use it like a pad. That's it, that's it, good work. You're doin' all right, Hap. (*He pauses, then nods in approbation for a few seconds, then looks upward*) Biff, first thing we gotta do when we get time is clip that big branch over the house. Afraid it's gonna fall in a storm and hit the roof. Tell you what. We get a rope and sling her around, and then we climb up there with a couple of saws and take her down. Soon as you finish the car, boys, I wanna see ya. I got a surprise for you, boys.

BIFF (*offstage*). Whatta ya got, Dad?

WILLY. No, you finish first. Never leave a job till you're finished—remember that. (*Looking toward the "big trees"*) Biff, up in Albany I saw a beautiful hammock. I think I'll buy it next trip, and we'll hang it right between those two elms. Wouldn't that be something? Just swingin' there under those branches. Boy, that would be . . .

(*Young Biff and Young Happy appear from the direction Willy was addressing. Happy carries rags and a pail of water. Biff, wearing a sweater with a block "S," carries a football.*)

BIFF (*pointing in the direction of the car offstage*). How's that, Pop, professional?

WILLY. Terrific. Terrific job, boys. Good work, Biff.

HAPPY. Where's the surprise, Pop?

WILLY. In the back seat of the car.

HAPPY. Boy! (*He runs off*)

BIFF. What is it, Dad? Tell me, what'd you buy?

WILLY (*laughing, cuffs him*). Never mind, something I want you to have.

BIFF (*turns and starts off*). What is it, Hap?

HAPPY (*offstage*). It's a punching bag!

BIFF. Oh, Pop!

WILLY. It's got Gene Tunney's signature on it!

(*Happy runs onstage with a punching bag.*)

BIFF. Gee, how'd you know we wanted a punching bag?

WILLY. Well, it's the finest thing for the timing.

HAPPY (*lies down on his back and pedals with his feet*). I'm losing weight, you notice, Pop?

WILLY (*to Happy*). Jumping rope is good too.

BIFF. Did you see the new football I got?

WILLY (*examining the ball*). Where'd you get a new ball?

BIFF. The coach told me to practice my passing.

WILLY. That so? And he gave you the ball, heh?

BIFF. Well, I borrowed it from the locker room. (*He laughs confidentially*)

WILLY (*laughing with him at the theft*). I want you to return that.

HAPPY. I told you he wouldn't like it!

BIFF (*angrily*). Well, I'm bringing it back!

WILLY (*stopping the incipient argument, to Happy*). Sure, he's gotta practice with a regulation ball, doesn't he? (*To Biff*) Coach'll probably congratulate you on your initiative!

BIFF. Oh, he keeps congratulating my initiative all the time, Pop.

WILLY. That's because he likes you. If somebody else took that ball there'd be an uproar. So what's the report, boys, what's the report?

BIFF. Where'd you go this time, Dad? Gee, we were lonesome for you.

WILLY (*pleased, puts an arm around each boy and they come down to the apron*). Lonesome, heh?

BIFF. Missed you every minute.

WILLY. Don't say? Tell you a secret, boys. Don't breathe it to a soul. Someday I'll have my own business, and I'll never have to leave home any more.

HAPPY. Like Uncle Charley, heh?

WILLY. Bigger than Uncle Charley! Because Charley is not liked. He's liked, but he's not—well liked.

BIFF. Where'd you go this time, Dad?

WILLY. Well, I got on the road, and I went north to Providence. Met the Mayor.

BIFF. The Mayor of Providence!

WILLY. He was sitting in the hotel lobby.

BIFF. What'd he say?

WILLY. He said, "Morning!" And I said, "You got a fine city here, Mayor." And then he had coffee with me. And then I went to Waterbury. Waterbury is a fine city. Big clock city, the famous Waterbury clock. Sold a nice bill there. And then Boston—Boston is the cradle of the Revolution. A fine city. And a couple of other towns in Mass., and on to Portland and Bangor and straight home!

BIFF. Gee, I'd love to go with you sometime, Dad.

WILLY. Soon as summer comes.

HAPPY. Promise?

WILLY. You and Hap and I, and I'll show you all the towns. America is full of beautiful towns and fine, upstanding people. And they know me, boys, they know me up and down New England. The finest people. And when I bring you fellas up, there'll be open sesame for all of us, 'cause one thing, boys: I have friends. I can park my car in any street in New England, and the cops protect it like their own. This summer, heh?

BIFF and HAPPY (*together*). Yeah! You bet!

WILLY. We'll take our bathing suits.

HAPPY. We'll carry your bags, Pop!

WILLY. Oh, won't that be somethin'! Me comin' into the Boston stores with you boys carryin' my bags. What a sensation! (*Biff is prancing around, practicing passing the ball.*)

WILLY. You nervous, Biff, about the game?

BIFF. Not if you're gonna be there.

WILLY. What do they say about you in school, now that they made you captain?

HAPPY. There's a crowd of girls behind him everytime the classes change.

BIFF (*taking Willy's hand*). This Saturday, Pop, this Saturday—just for you, I'm going to break through for a touchdown.

HAPPY. You're supposed to pass.

BIFF. I'm takin' one play for Pop. You watch me, Pop, and when I take off my helmet, that means I'm breakin' out. Then you watch me crash through that line!

WILLY (*kisses Biff*). Oh, wait'll I tell this in Boston!

(*Bernard enters in knickers. He is younger than Biff, earnest and loyal, a worried boy.*)

BERNARD. Biff, where are you? You're supposed to study with me today.

WILLY. Hey, looka Bernard. What're you lookin' so anemic about, Bernard?

BERNARD. He's gotta study, Uncle Willy. He's got Regents next week.

HAPPY (*tauntingly, spinning Bernard around*). Let's box, Bernard!

BERNARD. Biff! (*He gets away from Happy*) Listen, Biff, I heard Mr. Birnbaum say that if you don't start studyin' math he's gonna flunk you, and you won't graduate. I heard him!

WILLY. You better study with him, Biff. Go ahead now.

BERNARD. I heard him!

BIFF. Oh, Pop, you didn't see my sneakers! (*He holds up a foot for Willy to look at*)

WILLY. Hey, that's a beautiful job of printing!

BERNARD (*wiping his glasses*). Just because he printed University of Virginia on his sneakers doesn't mean they've got to graduate him, Uncle Willy!

WILLY (*angrily*). What're you talking about? With scholarships to three universities they're gonna flunk him?

BERNARD. But I heard Mr. Birnbaum say—

WILLY. Don't be a pest, Bernard! (*To his boys*) What an anemic!

BERNARD. Okay, I'm waiting for you in my house, Biff.

(*Bernard goes off. The Lomans laugh.*)

WILLY. Bernard is not well liked, is he?

BIFF. He's liked, but he's not well liked.

HAPPY. That's right, Pop.

WILLY. That's just what I mean. Bernard can get the best marks in school, y'understand, but when he gets out in the business world, y'understand, you are going to be five times ahead of him. That's why I thank Almighty God you're both built like Adonises. Because the man who makes an appearance in the business world, the man who creates personal interest, is the man who gets ahead. Be liked and you will never want. You take me, for instance. I never have to wait in line to see a buyer. "Willy Loman is here!" That's all they have to know, and I go right through.

BIFF. Did you knock them dead, Pop?

WILLY. Knocked 'em cold in Providence, slaughtered 'em in Boston.

HAPPY (*on his back, pedaling again*). I'm losing weight, you notice, Pop?

(*Linda enters, as of old, a ribbon in her hair, carrying a basket of washing.*)

LINDA (*with youthful energy*). Hello, dear!

WILLY. Sweetheart!

LINDA. How'd the Chevvy run?

WILLY. Chevrolet, Linda, is the greatest car ever built. (*To the boys*) Since when do you let your mother carry wash up the stairs?

BIFF. Grab hold there, boy!

HAPPY. Where to, Mom?

LINDA. Hang them up on the line. And you better go down to your friends, Biff. The cellar is full of boys. They don't know what to do with themselves.

BIFF. Ah, when Pop comes home they can wait!

WILLY (*laughs appreciatively*). You better go down and tell them what to do, Biff.

BIFF. I think I'll have them sweep out the furnace room.

WILLY. Good work, Biff.

BIFF (*goes through wall-line of kitchen to doorway at back and calls down*). Fellas! Everybody sweep out the furnace room! I'll be right down!

VOICES. All right! Okay, Biff!

BIFF. George and Sam and Frank, come out back! We're hangin' up the wash! Come on, Hap, on the double! (*He and Happy carry out the basket*)

LINDA. The way they obey him!

WILLY. Well, that's training, the training. I'm tellin' you, I was sellin' thousands and thousands, but I had to come home.

LINDA. Oh, the whole block'll be at that game. Did you sell anything?

WILLY. I did five hundred gross in Providence and seven hundred gross in Boston.

LINDA. No! Wait a minute, I've got a pencil. (*She pulls pencil and paper out of her apron pocket*) That makes your commission . . . Two hundred—my God! Two hundred and twelve dollars!

WILLY. Well, I didn't figure it yet, but . . .

LINDA. How much did you do?

WILLY. Well, I—I did—about a hundred and eighty gross in Providence. Well, no —it came to—roughly two hundred gross on the whole trip.

LINDA (*without hesitation*). Two hundred gross. That's . . . (*She figures*)

WILLY. The trouble was that three of the stores were half closed for inventory in Boston. Otherwise I woulda broke records.

LINDA. Well, it makes seventy dollars and some pennies. That's very good.

WILLY. What do we owe?

LINDA. Well, on the first there's sixteen dollars on the refrigerator—

WILLY. Why sixteen?

LINDA. Well, the fan belt broke, so it was a dollar eighty.

WILLY. But it's brand new.

LINDA. Well, the man said that's the way it is. Till they work themselves in, y'know. (*They move through the wall-line into the kitchen.*)

WILLY. I hope we didn't get stuck on that machine.

LINDA. They got the biggest ads of any of them!

WILLY. I know, it's a fine machine. What else?

LINDA. Well, there's nine-sixty for the washing machine. And for the vacuum cleaner there's three and a half due on the fifteenth. Then the roof, you got twenty-one dollars remaining.

WILLY. It don't leak, does it?

LINDA. No, they did a wonderful job. Then you owe Frank for the carburetor.

WILLY. I'm not going to pay that man! That goddam Chevrolet, they ought to prohibit the manufacture of that car!

LINDA. Well, you owe him three and a half. And odds and ends, comes to around a hundred and twenty dollars by the fifteenth.

WILLY. A hundred and twenty dollars! My God, if business don't pick up I don't know what I'm gonna do!

LINDA. Well, next week you'll do better.

WILLY. Oh, I'll knock 'em dead next week. I'll go to Hartford. I'm very well liked in Hartford. You know, the trouble is, Linda, people don't seem to take to me. (*They move onto the forestage.*)

LINDA. Oh, don't be foolish.

WILLY. I know it when I walk in. They seem to laugh at me.

LINDA. Why? Why would they laugh at you? Don't talk that way, Willy.

(*Willy moves to the edge of the stage. Linda goes into the kitchen and starts to darn stockings.*)

WILLY. I don't know the reason for it, but they just pass me by. I'm not noticed.

LINDA. But you're doing wonderful, dear. You're making seventy to a hundred dollars a week.

WILLY. But I gotta be at it ten, twelve hours a day. Other men—I don't know—they do it easier. I don't know why—I can't stop myself—I talk too much. A man oughta come in with a few words. One thing about Charley. He's a man of few words, and they respect him.

LINDA. You don't talk too much, you're just lively.

WILLY (*smiling*). Well, I figure, what the hell, life is short, a couple of jokes. (*To himself*) I joke too much! (*The smile goes*)

LINDA. Why? You're—

WILLY. I'm fat. I'm very—foolish to look at, Linda. I didn't tell you, but Christmas time I happened to be calling on F. H. Stewarts, and a salesman I know, as I was going in to see the buyer I heard him say something about—walrus. And I—I cracked him right across the face. I won't take that. I simply will not take that. But they do laugh at me. I know that.

LINDA. Darling . . .

WILLY. I gotta overcome it. I know I gotta overcome it. I'm not dressing to advantage, maybe.

LINDA. Willy, darling, you're the handsomest man in the world—

WILLY. Oh, no, Linda.

LINDA. To me you are. (*Slight pause*) The handsomest.

(*From the darkness is heard the laughter of a woman. Willy doesn't turn to it, but it continues through Linda's lines.*)

LINDA. And the boys, Willy. Few men are idolized by their children the way you are.

(*Music is heard as behind a scrim, to the left of the house. The Woman, dimly seen, is dressing.*)

WILLY (*with great feeling*). You're the best there is, Linda, you're a pal, you know that? On the road—on the road I want to grab you sometimes and just kiss the life outa you.

(*The laughter is loud now, and he moves into a brightening area at the left, where The Woman has come from behind the scrim and is standing, putting on her hat, looking into a "mirror" and laughing.*)

WILLY. 'Cause I get so lonely—especially when business is bad and there's nobody to talk to. I get the feeling that I'll never sell anything again, that I won't make a living for you, or a business, a business for the boys. (*He talks through The Woman's subsiding laughter; The Woman primps at the "mirror"*) There's so much I want to make for—

THE WOMAN. Me? You didn't make me, Willy. I picked you.

WILLY (*pleased*). You picked me?

THE WOMAN (*who is quite proper-looking, Willy's age*). I did. I've been sitting at that desk watching all the salesmen go by, day in, day out. But you've got such a sense of humor, and we do have such a good time together, don't we?

WILLY. Sure, sure. (*He takes her in his arms*) Why do you have to go now?

THE WOMAN. It's two o'clock . . .

WILLY. No, come on in! (*He pulls her*)

THE WOMAN. . . . . my sisters'll be scandalized. When'll you be back?

WILLY. Oh, two weeks about. Will you come up again?

THE WOMAN. Sure thing. You do make me laugh. It's good for me. (*She squeezes his arm, kisses him*) And I think you're a wonderful man.

WILLY. You picked me, heh?

THE WOMAN. Sure. Because you're so sweet. And such a kidder.

WILLY. Well, I'll see you next time I'm in Boston.

THE WOMAN. I'll put you right through to the buyers.

WILLY (*slapping her bottom*). Right. Well, bottoms up!

THE WOMAN (*slaps him gently and laughs*). You just kill me, Willy. (*He suddenly grabs her and kisses her roughly*) You kill me. And thanks for the stockings. I love a lot of stockings. Well, good night. WILLY. Good night. And keep your pores open!

THE WOMAN. Oh, Willy!

(*The Woman bursts out laughing, and Linda's laughter blends in. The Woman disappears into the dark. Now the area at the kitchen table brightens. Linda is sitting where she was at the kitchen table, but now is mending a pair of her silk stockings.*)

LINDA. You are, Willy. The handsomest man. You've got no reason to feel that—

WILLY (*coming out of The Woman's dimming area and going over to Linda*). I'll make it all up to you. Linda, I'll—

LINDA. There's nothing to make up, dear. You're doing fine, better than—

WILLY (*noticing her mending*). What's that?

LINDA. Just mending my stockings. They're so expensive—

WILLY (*angrily, taking them from her*). I won't have you mending stockings in this house! Now throw them out!

(*Linda puts the stockings in her pocket.*)

BERNARD (*entering on the run*). Where is he? If he doesn't study!

WILLY (*moving to the forestage, with great agitation*). You'll give him the answers!

BERNARD. I do, but I can't on a Regents! That's a state exam! They're liable to arrest me!

WILLY. Where is he? I'll whip him, I'll whip him!

LINDA. And he'd better give back that football, Willy, it's not nice.

WILLY. Biff! Where is he? Why is he taking everything?

LINDA. He's too rough with the girls, Willy. All of the mothers are afraid of him!

WILLY. I'll whip him!

BERNARD. He's driving the car without a license!

(*The Woman's laugh is heard.*)

WILLY. Shut up!

LINDA. All the mothers—

WILLY. Shut up!

BERNARD (*backing quietly away and out*). Mr. Birnbaum says he's stuck up.

WILLY. Get outa here!

BERNARD. If he doesn't buckle down he'll flunk math! (*He goes off*)

LINDA. He's right, Willy, you've gotta—

WILLY (*exploding at her*). There's nothing the matter with him! You want him to be a worm like Bernard? He's got spirit, personality . . .

(*As he speaks, Linda, almost in tears, exits into the living-room. Willy is alone in the kitchen, wilting and staring. The leaves are gone. It is night again, and the apartment houses look down from behind.*)

WILLY. Loaded with it. Loaded! What is he stealing? He's giving it back, isn't he? Why is he stealing? What did I tell him? I never in my life told him anything but decent things.

(*Happy in pajamas has come down the stairs; Willy suddenly becomes aware of Happy's presence.*)

HAPPY. Let's go now, come on.

WILLY (*sitting down at the kitchen table*). Huh! Why did she have to wax the floors herself? Everytime she waxes the floors she keels over. She knows that!

HAPPY. Shh! Take it easy. What brought you back tonight?

WILLY. I got an awful scare. Nearly hit a kid in Yonkers. God! Why didn't I go to Alaska with my brother Ben that time! Ben! That man was a genius, that man was success incarnate! What a mistake! He begged me to go.

HAPPY. Well, there's no use in—

WILLY. You guys! There was a man started with the clothes on his back and ended up with diamond mines!

HAPPY. Boy, some day I'd like to know how he did it.

WILLY. What's the mystery? The man knew what he wanted and went out and got it! Walked into a jungle, and comes out, the age of twenty-one, and he's rich! The world is an oyster, but you don't crack it open on a mattress!

HAPPY. Pop, I told you I'm gonna retire you for life.

WILLY. You'll retire me for life on seventy goddam dollars a week? And your women and your car and your apartment, and you'll retire me for life! Christ's sake, I couldn't get past Yonkers today! Where are you guys, where are you? The woods are burning! I can't drive a car!

(Charley has appeared in the doorway. He is a large man, slow of speech, laconic, immovable. In all he says, despite what he says, there is pity, and, now, trepidation. He has a robe over pajamas, slippers on his feet. He enters the kitchen.)

CHARLEY. Everything all right?

HAPPY. Yeah, Charley, everything's . . .

WILLY. What's the matter?

CHARLEY. I heard some noise. I thought something happened. Can't we do something about the walls? You sneeze in here, and in my house hats blow off.

HAPPY. Let's go to bed, Dad. Come on.
(Charley signals to Happy to go.)

WILLY. You go ahead, I'm not tired at the moment.

HAPPY *(to Willy)*. Take it easy, huh?
(He exits)

WILLY. What're you doin' up?

CHARLEY *(sitting down at the kitchen table opposite Willy)*. Couldn't sleep good. I had a heartburn.

WILLY. Well, you don't know how to eat.

CHARLEY. I eat with my mouth.

WILLY. No, you're ignorant. You gotta know about vitamins and things like that.

CHARLEY. Come on, let's shoot. Tire you out a little.

WILLY *(hesitantly)*. All right. You got cards?

CHARLEY *(taking a deck from his pocket)*. Yeah, I got them. Someplace. What is it with those vitamins?

WILLY *(dealing)*. They build up your bones. Chemistry.

CHARLEY. Yeah, but there's no bones in a heartburn.

WILLY. What are you talkin' about? Do you know the first thing about it?

CHARLEY. Don't get insulted.

WILLY. Don't talk about something you don't know anything about.
(They are playing. Pause.)

CHARLEY. What're you doin' home?

WILLY. A little trouble with the car.

CHARLEY. Oh. *(Pause)* I'd like to take a trip to California.

WILLY. Don't say.

CHARLEY. You want a job?

WILLY. I got a job, I told you that.
(After a slight pause) What the hell are you offering me a job for?

CHARLEY. Don't get insulted.

WILLY. Don't insult me.

CHARLEY. I don't see no sense in it. You don't have to go on this way.

WILLY. I got a good job. *(Slight pause)* What do you keep comin' in here for?

CHARLEY. You want me to go?

WILLY *(after a pause, withering)*. I can't understand it. He's going back to Texas again. What the hell is that?

CHARLEY. Let him go.

WILLY. I got nothin' to give him, Charley, I'm clean, I'm clean.

CHARLEY. He won't starve. None of them starve. Forget about him.

WILLY. Then what have I got to remember?

CHARLEY. You take it too hard. To hell with it. When a deposit bottle is broken you don't get your nickel back.

WILLY. That's easy enough for you to say.

CHARLEY. That ain't easy for me to say.

WILLY. Did you see the ceiling I put up in the living-room?

CHARLEY. Yeah, that's a piece of work. To put up a ceiling is a mystery to me. How do you do it?

WILLY. What's the difference?

CHARLEY. Well, talk about it.

WILLY. You gonna put up a ceiling?

CHARLEY. How could I put up a ceiling?

WILLY. Then what the hell are you bothering me for?

CHARLEY. You're insulted again.

WILLY. A man who can't handle tools is not a man. You're disgusting.

CHARLEY Don't call me disgusting, Willy.

(Uncle Ben, carrying a valise and an umbrella, enters the forestage from around the right corner of the house. He is a stolid man, in his sixties, with a mustache and an authoritative air. He is utterly certain of his destiny, and there is an aura of far places about him. He enters exactly as Willy speaks.)

WILLY. I'm getting awfully tired, Ben.
(Ben's music is heard. Ben looks around at everything.)

CHARLEY. Good, keep playing; you'll sleep better. Did you call me Ben?
(Ben looks at his watch.)

WILLY. That's funny. For a second there you reminded me of my brother Ben.

BEN. I only have a few minutes. *(He strolls, inspecting the place. Willy and Charley continue playing)*

CHARLEY. You never heard from him again, heh? Since that time?

WILLY. Didn't Linda tell you? Couple of weeks ago we got a letter from his wife in Africa. He died.

CHARLEY. That so.

BEN *(chuckling)*. So this is Brooklyn, eh?

CHARLEY. Maybe you're in for some of his money.

WILLY. Naa, he had seven sons. There's just one opportunity I had with that man . . .

BEN. I must make a train, William. There are several properties I'm looking at in Alaska.

WILLY. Sure, sure! If I'd gone with him to Alaska that time, everything would've been totally different.

CHARLEY. Go on, you'd froze to death up there.

WILLY. What're you talking about?

BEN. Opportunity is tremendous in Alaska, William. Surprised you're not up there.

WILLY. Sure, tremendous.

CHARLEY. Heh?

WILLY. There was the only man I ever met who knew the answers.

CHARLEY. Who?

BEN. How are you all?

WILLY *(taking a pot, smiling)*. Fine, fine.

CHARLEY. Pretty sharp tonight.

BEN. Is Mother living with you?

WILLY. No, she died a long time ago.

CHARLEY. Who?

BEN. That's too bad. Fine specimen of a lady, Mother.

WILLY *(to Charley)*. Heh?

BEN. I'd hoped to see the old girl.

CHARLEY. Who died?

BEN. Heard anything from Father, have you?

WILLY *(unnerved)*. What do you mean, who died?

CHARLEY *(taking a pot)*. What're you talkin' about?

BEN *(looking at his watch)*. William, it's half-past eight!

WILLY *(as though to dispel his confusion he angrily stops Charley's hand)*. That's my build!

CHARLEY. I put the ace—

WILLY. If you don't know how to play the game I'm not gonna throw my money away on you!

CHARLEY *(rising)*. It was my ace, for God's sake!

WILLY. I'm through, I'm through!

BEN. When did Mother die?

WILLY. Long ago. Since the beginning you never knew how to play cards.

CHARLEY *(picks up the cards and goes to the door)*. All right! Next time I'll bring a deck with five aces.

WILLY. I don't play that kind of game!

CHARLEY *(turning to him)*. You ought to be ashamed of yourself!

WILLY. Yeah?

CHARLEY. Yeah! *(He goes out)*

WILLY *(slamming the door after him)*. Ignoramus!

BEN *(as Willy comes toward him through the wall-line of the kitchen)*. So you're William.

WILLY *(shaking Ben's hand)*. Ben! I've been waiting for you so long! What's the answer? How did you do it?

BEN. Oh, there's a story in that.

(Linda enters the forestage, as of old, carrying the wash basket.)

LINDA. Is this Ben?

BEN *(gallantly)*. How do you do, my dear.

LINDA. Where've you been all these years? Willy's always wondered why you—

WILLY *(pulling Ben away from her impatiently)*. Where is Dad? Didn't you follow him? How did you get started?

BEN. Well, I don't know how much you remember.

WILLY. Well, I was just a baby, of course, only three or four years old—

BEN. Three years and eleven months.

WILLY. What a memory, Ben!

BEN. I have many enterprises, William, and I have never kept books.

WILLY. I remember I was sitting under the wagon in—was it Nebraska?

BEN. It was South Dakota, and I gave you a bunch of wild flowers.

WILLY. I remember you walking away down some open road.

BEN *(laughing)*. I was going to find Father in Alaska.

WILLY. Where is he?

BEN. At that age I had a very faulty view of geography, William. I discovered after a few days that I was heading due south, so instead of Alaska, I ended up in Africa.

LINDA. Africa!

WILLY. The Gold Coast!

BEN. Principally diamond mines.

LINDA. Diamond mines!

BEN. Yes, my dear. But I've only a few minutes—

WILLY. No! Boys! Boys! (*Young Biff and Happy appear*) Listen to this. This is your Uncle Ben, a great man! Tell my boys, Ben!

BEN. Why, boys, when I was seventeen I walked into the jungle, and when I was twenty-one I walked out. (*He laughs*) And by God I was rich.

WILLY (*to the boys*). You see what I been talking about? The greatest things can happen!

BEN (*glancing at his watch*). I have an appointment in Ketchikan Tuesday week.

WILLY. No, Ben! Please tell about Dad. I want my boys to hear. I want them to know the kind of stock they spring from. All I remember is a man with a big beard, and I was in Mamma's lap, sitting around a fire, and some kind of high music.

BEN. His flute. He played the flute.

WILLY. Sure, the flute, that's right!

(*New music is heard, a high, rollicking tune.*)

BEN. Father was a very great and a very wild-hearted man. We would start in Boston, and he'd toss the whole family into the wagon, and then he'd drive the team right across the country; through Ohio, and Indiana, Michigan, Illinois, and all the Western states. And we'd stop in the towns and sell the flutes that he'd made on the way. Great inventor, Father. With one gadget he made more in a week than a man like you could make in a lifetime.

WILLY. That's just the way I'm bringing them up, Ben—rugged, well liked, all-around.

BEN. Yeah? (*To Biff*) Hit that, boy— hard as you can. (*He pounds his stomach*)

BIFF. Oh, no, sir!

BEN (*taking boxing stance*). Come on, get to me! (*He laughs*)

WILLY. Go to it, Biff! Go ahead, show him!

BIFF. Okay! (*He cocks his fists and starts in*)

LINDA (*to Willy*). Why must he fight, dear?

BEN (*sparring with Biff*). Good boy! Good boy!

WILLY. How's that, Ben, heh?

HAPPY. Give him the left, Biff!

LINDA. Why are you fighting?

BEN. Good boy! (*Suddenly comes in, trips Biff, and stands over him, the point of his umbrella poised over Biff's eye*)

LINDA. Look out, Biff!

BIFF. Gee!

BEN (*patting Biff's knee*). Never fight fair with a stranger, boy. You'll never get out of the jungle that way. (*Taking Linda's hand and bowing*) It was an honor and a pleasure to meet you, Linda.

LINDA (*withdrawing her hand coldly, frightened*). Have a nice—trip.

BEN (*to Willy*). And good luck with your—what do you do?

WILLY. Selling.

BEN. Yes. Well . . . (*He raises his hand in farewell to all*)

WILLY. No, Ben, I don't want you to think . . . (*He takes Ben's arm to show him*) It's Brooklyn, I know, but we hunt too.

BEN. Really, now.

WILLY. Oh, sure, there's snakes and rabbits and—that's why I moved out here. Why, Biff can fell any one of these trees in no time! Boys! Go right over to where they're building the apartment house and get some sand. We're gonna rebuild the entire front stoop right now! Watch this, Ben!

BIFF. Yes, sir! On the double, Hap!

HAPPY (*as he and Biff run off*). I lost weight, Pop, you notice?

(*Charley enters in knickers, even before the boys are gone.*)

CHARLEY. Listen, if they steal any more from that building the watchman'll put the cops on them!

LINDA (*to Willy*). Don't let Biff . . .

(*Ben laughs lustily.*)

WILLY. You shoulda seen the lumber they brought home last week. At least a dozen six-by-tens worth all kinds a money.

CHARLEY. Listen, if that watchman—

WILLY. I gave them hell, understand. But I got a couple of fearless characters there.

CHARLEY. Willy, the jails are full of fearless characters.

BEN (*clapping Willy on the back, with a laugh at Charley*). And the stock exchange, friend!

WILLY (*joining in Ben's laughter*). Where are the rest of your pants?

CHARLEY. My wife bought them.

WILLY. Now all you need is a golf club and you can go upstairs and go to sleep. (*To Ben*) Great athlete! Between him and his son Bernard they can't hammer a nail!

BERNARD (*rushing in*). The watchman's chasing Biff!

WILLY (*angrily*). Shut up! He's not stealing anything!

LINDA (*alarmed, hurrying off left*). Where is he? Biff, dear! (*She exits*)

WILLY (*moving toward the left, away from Ben*). There's nothing wrong. What's the matter with you?

BEN. Nervy boy. Good!

WILLY (*laughing*). Oh, nerves of iron, that Biff!

CHARLEY. Don't know what it is. My New England man comes back and he's bleedin', they murdered him up there.

WILLY. It's contacts, Charley, I got important contacts!

CHARLEY (*sarcastically*). Glad to hear it, Willy. Come in later, we'll shoot a little casino. I'll take some of your Portland money. (*He laughs at Willy and exits*)

WILLY (*turning to Ben*). Business is bad, it's murderous. But not for me, of course.

BEN. I'll stop by on my way back to Africa.

WILLY (*longingly*). Can't you stay a few days? You're just what I need, Ben, because I—I have a fine position here, but I—well, Dad left when I was such a baby and I never had a chance to talk to him and I still feel—kind of temporary about myself.

BEN. I'll be late for my train.

(*They are at opposite ends of the stage.*)

WILLY. Ben, my boys—can't we talk? They'd go into the jaws of hell for me, see, but I—

BEN. William, you're being first-rate with your boys. Outstanding, manly chaps.

WILLY (*hanging on to his words*). Oh, Ben, that's good to hear! Because sometimes I'm afraid that I'm not teaching them the right kind of—Ben, how should I teach them?

BEN (*giving great weight to each word, and with a certain vicious audacity*). William, when I walked into the jungle, I was seventeen. When I walked out I was twenty-one. And, by God, I was rich! (*He goes off into the darkness around the right corner of the house*)

WILLY. . . . was rich! That's just the spirit I want to imbue them with! To walk into a jungle! I was right! I was right! I was right!

(*Ben is gone, but Willy is still speaking to him as Linda, in nightgown and robe, enters the kitchen, glances around for Willy, then goes to the door of the house, looks out and sees him. Comes down to his left. He looks at her.*)

LINDA. Willy, dear? Willy?

WILLY. I was right!

LINDA. Did you have some cheese? (*He can't answer*) It's very late, darling. Come to bed, heh?

WILLY (*looking straight up*). Gotta break your neck to see a star in this yard.

LINDA. You coming in?

WILLY. Whatever happened to that diamond watch fob? Remember? When Ben came from Africa that time? Didn't he give me a watch fob with a diamond in it?

LINDA. You pawned it, dear. Twelve, thirteen years ago. For Biff's radio correspondence course.

WILLY. Gee, that was a beautiful thing. I'll take a walk.

LINDA. But you're in your slippers.

WILLY (*starting to go around the house at the left*). I was right! I was! (*Half to Linda, as he goes, shaking his head*) What a man! There was a man worth talking to. I was right!

LINDA (*calling after Willy*). But in your slippers, Willy!

(*Willy is almost gone when Biff, in his pajamas, comes down the stairs and enters the kitchen.*)

BIFF. What is he doing out there?

LINDA. Sh!

BIFF. God Almighty, Mom, how long has he been doing this?

LINDA. Don't, he'll hear you.

BIFF. What the hell is the matter with him?

LINDA. It'll pass by morning.

BIFF. Shouldn't we do anything?

LINDA. Oh, my dear, you should do a lot of things, but there's nothing to do, so go to sleep.

(*Happy comes down the stairs and sits on the steps.*)

HAPPY. I never heard him so loud, Mom.

LINDA. Well, come around more often; you'll hear him. (*She sits down at the table and mends the lining of Willy's jacket)*

BIFF. Why didn't you ever write me about this, Mom?

LINDA. How would I write to you? For over three months you had no address.

BIFF. I was on the move. But you know I thought of you all the time. You know that, don't you, pal?

LINDA. I know, dear, I know. But he likes to have a letter. Just to know that there's still a possibility for better things.

BIFF. He's not like this all the time, is he?

LINDA. It's when you come home he's always the worst.

BIFF. When I come home?

LINDA. When you write you're coming, he's all smiles, and talks about the future, and—he's just wonderful. And then the closer you seem to come, the more shaky he gets, and then, by the time you get here, he's arguing, and he seems angry at you. I think it's just that maybe he can't bring himself to—open up to you. Why are you so hateful to each other? Why is that?

BIFF *(evasively)*. I'm not hateful, Mom.

LINDA. But you no sooner come in the door than you're fighting!

BIFF. I don't know why, I mean to change. I'm tryin', Mom, you understand?

LINDA. Are you home to stay now?

BIFF. I don't know. I want to look around, see what's doin'.

LINDA. Biff, you can't look around all your life, can you?

BIFF. I just can't take hold, Mom. I can't take hold of some kind of a life.

LINDA. Biff, a man is not a bird, to come and go with the springtime.

BIFF. Your hair . . . *(He touches her hair)* Your hair got so gray.

LINDA. Oh, it's been gray since you were in high school. I just stopped dyeing it, that's all.

BIFF. Dye it again, will ya? I don't want my pal looking old. *(He smiles)*

LINDA. You're such a boy! You think you can go away for a year and . . . You've got to get it into your head now that one day you'll knock on this door and there'll be strange people here—

BIFF. What are you talking about? You're not even sixty, Mom.

LINDA. But what about your father?

BIFF *(lamely)*. Well, I meant him too.

HAPPY. He admires Pop.

LINDA. Biff, dear, if you don't have any feeling for him, then you can't have any feeling for me.

BIFF. Sure I can, Mom.

LINDA. No. You can't just come to see me, because I love him. *(With a threat, but only a threat, of tears)* He's the dearest man in the world to me, and I won't have anyone making him feel unwanted and low and blue. You've got to make up your mind now, darling, there's no leeway any more. Either he's your father and you pay him that respect, or else you're not to come here. I know he's not easy to get along with—nobody knows that better than me—but . . .

WILLY *(from the left, with a laugh)*. Hey, hey, Biffo!

BIFF *(starting to go out after Willy)*. What the hell is the matter with him? *(Happy stops him)*

LINDA. Don't—don't go near him!

BIFF. Stop making excuses for him! He always, always wiped the floor with you! Never had an ounce of respect for you.

HAPPY. He's always had respect for—

BIFF. What the hell do you know about it?

HAPPY *(surlily)*. Just don't call him crazy! *82-125*

BIFF. He's got no character—Charley wouldn't do this. Not in his own house—spewing out that vomit from his mind.

HAPPY. Charley never had to cope with what he's got to.

BIFF. People are worse off than Willy Loman. Believe me, I've seen them!

LINDA. Then make Charley your father, Biff. You can't do that, can you? I don't say he's a great man. Willy Loman never made a lot of money. His name was never in the paper. He's not the finest character that ever lived. But he's a human being, and a terrible thing is happening to him. So attention must be paid. He's not to be allowed to fall into his grave like an old dog. Attention, attention must be finally paid to such a person. You called him crazy—

BIFF. I didn't mean—

LINDA. No, a lot of people think he's lost his—balance. But you don't have to be very smart to know what his trouble is. The man is exhausted.

HAPPY. Sure!

LINDA. A small man can be just as ex-

hausted as a great man. He works for a company thirty-six years this March, opens up unheard-of territories to their trademark, and now in his old age they take his salary away.

HAPPY (*indignantly*). I didn't know that, Mom.

LINDA. You never asked, my dear! Now that you get your spending money someplace else you don't trouble your mind with him.

HAPPY. But I gave you money last—

LINDA. Christmas time, fifty dollars! To fix the hot water it cost ninety-seven fifty! For five weeks he's been on straight commission, like a beginner, an unknown!

BIFF. Those ungrateful bastards!

LINDA. Are they any worse than his sons? When he brought them business, when he was young, they were glad to see him. But now his old friends, the old buyers that loved him so and always found some order to hand him in a pinch—they're all dead, retired. He used to be able to make six, seven calls a day in Boston. Now he takes his valises out of the car and puts them back and takes them out again and he's exhausted. Instead of walking he talks now. He drives seven hundred miles, and when he gets there no one knows him any more, no one welcomes him. And what goes through a man's mind, driving seven hundred miles home without having earned a cent? Why shouldn't he talk to himself? Why? When he has to go to Charley and borrow fifty dollars a week and pretend to me that it's his pay? How long can that go on? How long? You see what I'm sitting here and waiting for? And you tell me he has no character? The man who never worked a day but for your benefit? When does he get the medal for that? Is this his reward—to turn around at the age of sixty-three and find his sons, who he loved better than his life, one a philandering bum—

HAPPY. Mom!

LINDA. That's all you are, my baby! (*To Biff*) And you! What happened to the love you had for him? You were such pals! How you used to talk to him on the phone every night! How lonely he was till he could come home to you!

BIFF. All right, Mom. I'll live here in my room, and I'll get a job. I'll keep away from him, that's all.

LINDA. No, Biff. You can't stay here and fight all the time.

BIFF. He threw me out of this house, remember that.

LINDA. Why did he do that? I never knew why.

BIFF. Because I know he's a fake and he doesn't like anybody around who knows!

LINDA. Why a fake? In what way? What do you mean?

BIFF. Just don't lay it all at my feet. It's between me and him—that's all I have to say. I'll chip in from now on. He'll settle for half my pay check. He'll be all right. I'm going to bed. (*He starts for the stairs*)

LINDA. He won't be all right.

BIFF (*turning on the stairs, furiously*). I hate this city and I'll stay here. Now what do you want?

LINDA. He's dying, Biff.

(*Happy turns quickly to her, shocked.*)

BIFF (*after a pause*). Why is he dying?

LINDA. He's been trying to kill himself.

BIFF (*with great horror*). How?

LINDA. I live from day to day.

BIFF. What're you talking about?

LINDA. Remember I wrote you that he smashed up the car again? In February?

BIFF. Well?

LINDA. The insurance inspector came. He said that they have evidence. That all these accidents in the last year—weren't—weren't—accidents.

HAPPY. How can they tell that? That's a lie.

LINDA. It seems there's a woman . . . (*She takes a breath as*)

BIFF (*sharply but contained*). What woman?

LINDA (*simultaneously*). . . . and this woman . . .

LINDA. What?

BIFF. Nothing. Go ahead.

LINDA. What did you say?

BIFF. Nothing. I just said what woman?

HAPPY. What about her?

LINDA. Well, it seems she was walking down the road and saw his car. She says that he wasn't driving fast at all, and that he didn't skid. She says he came to that little bridge, and then deliberately smashed into the railing, and it was only the shallowness of the water that saved him.

BIFF. Oh, no, he probably just fell asleep again.

LINDA. I don't think he fell asleep.

BIFF. Why not?

LINDA. Last month . . . (*With great difficulty*) Oh, boys, it's so hard to say a thing like this! He's just a big stupid man to you, but I tell you there's more good in him than in many other people. (*She chokes, wipes her eyes*) I was looking for a fuse. The lights blew out, and I went down the cellar. And behind the fuse box —it happened to fall out—was a length of rubber pipe—just short.

HAPPY. No kidding?

LINDA. There's a little attachment on the end of it. I knew right away. And sure enough, on the bottom of the water heater there's a new little nipple on the gas pipe.

HAPPY (*angrily*). That—jerk.

BIFF. Did you have it taken off?

LINDA. I'm—I'm ashamed to. How can I mention it to him? Every day I go down and take away that little rubber pipe. But, when he comes home, I put it back where it was. How can I insult him that way? I don't know what to do. I live from day to day, boys. I tell you, I know every thought in his mind. It sounds so old-fashioned and silly, but I tell you he put his whole life into you and you've turned your backs on him. (*She is bent over in the chair, weeping, her face in her hands*) Biff, I swear to God! Biff, his life is in your hands!

HAPPY (*to Biff*). How do you like that damned fool!

BIFF (*kissing her*). All right, pal, all right. It's all settled now. I've been remiss. I know that, Mom. But now I'll stay, and I swear to you, I'll apply myself. (*Kneeling in front of her, in a fever of self-reproach*) It's just—you see, Mom, I don't fit in business. Not that I won't try. I'll try, and I'll make good.

HAPPY. Sure you will. The trouble with you in business was you never tried to please people.

BIFF. I know, I—

HAPPY. Like when you worked for Harrison's. Bob Harrison said you were tops, and then you go and do some damn fool thing like whistling whole songs in the elevator like a comedian.

BIFF (*against Happy*). So what? I like to whistle sometimes.

HAPPY. You don't raise a guy to a responsible job who whistles in the elevator!

LINDA. Well, don't argue about it now.

HAPPY. Like when you'd go off and

swim in the middle of the day instead of taking the line around.

BIFF (*his resentment rising*). Well, don't you run off? You take off sometimes, don't you? On a nice summer day?

HAPPY. Yeah, but I cover myself!

LINDA. Boys!

HAPPY. If I'm going to take a fade the boss can call any number where I'm supposed to be and they'll swear to him that I just left. I'll tell you something that I hate to say, Biff, but in the business world some of them think you're crazy.

BIFF (*angered*). Screw the business world!

HAPPY. All right, screw it! Great, but cover yourself!

LINDA. Hap, Hap!

BIFF. I don't care what they think! They've laughed at Dad for years, and you know why? Because we don't belong in this nuthouse of a city! We should be mixing cement on some open plain, or— or carpenters. A carpenter is allowed to whistle!

(*Willy walks in from the entrance of the house, at left.*)

WILLY. Even your grandfather was better than a carpenter. (*Pause. They watch him*) You never grew up. Bernard does not whistle in the elevator, I assure you.

BIFF (*as though to laugh Willy out of it*). Yeah, but you do, Pop.

WILLY. I never in my life whistled in an elevator! And who in the business world thinks I'm crazy?

BIFF. I didn't mean it like that, Pop. Now don't make a whole thing out of it, will ya?

WILLY. Go back to the West! Be a carpenter, a cowboy, enjoy yourself!

LINDA. Willy, he was just saying—

WILLY. I heard what he said!

HAPPY (*trying to quiet Willy*). Hey, Pop, come on now . . .

WILLY (*continuing over Happy's line*). They laugh at me, heh? Go to Filene's, go to the Hub, go to Slattery's, Boston. Call out the name Willy Loman and see what happens! Big shot!

BIFF. All right, Pop.

WILLY. Big!

BIFF. All right!

WILLY. Why do you always insult me?

BIFF. I didn't say a word. (*To Linda*) Did I say a word?

LINDA. He didn't say anything, Willy.

WILLY (*going to the doorway of the living-room*). All right, good night, good night.

LINDA. Willy, dear, he just decided . . .

WILLY (*to Biff*). If you get tired hanging around tomorrow, paint the ceiling I put up in the living-room.

BIFF. I'm leaving early tomorrow.

HAPPY. He's going to see Bill Oliver, Pop.

WILLY (*interestedly*). Oliver? For what?

BIFF (*with reserve, but trying, trying*). He always said he'd stake me. I'd like to go into business, so maybe I can take him up on it.

LINDA. Isn't that wonderful?

WILLY. Don't interrupt. What's wonderful about it? There's fifty men in the City of New York who'd stake him. (*To Biff*) Sporting goods?

BIFF. I guess so. I know something about it and—

WILLY. He knows something about it! You know sporting goods better than Spalding, for God's sake! How much is he giving you?

BIFF. I don't know, I didn't even see him yet, but—

WILLY. Then what're you talkin' about?

BIFF (*getting angry*). Well, all I said was I'm gonna see him, that's all!

WILLY (*turning away*). Ah, you're counting your chickens again.

BIFF (*starting left for the stairs*). Oh, Jesus, I'm going to sleep!

WILLY (*calling after him*). Don't curse in this house!

BIFF (*turning*). Since when did you get so clean?

HAPPY (*trying to stop them*). Wait a . . .

WILLY. Don't use that language to me! I won't have it!

HAPPY (*grabbing Biff, shouts*). Wait a minute! I got an idea. I got a feasible idea. Come here, Biff, let's talk this over now, let's talk some sense here. When I was down in Florida last time, I thought of a great idea to sell sporting goods. It just came back to me. You and I, Biff—we have a line, the Loman Line. We train a couple of weeks, and put on a couple of exhibitions, see?

WILLY. That's an idea!

HAPPY. Wait! We form two basketball teams, see? Two water-polo teams. We play each other. It's a million dollars' worth of publicity. Two brothers, see? The Loman Brothers. Displays in the Royal Palms—all the hotels. And banners over the ring and the basketball court: "Loman Brothers." Baby, we could sell sporting goods!

WILLY. That is a one-million-dollar idea!

LINDA. Marvelous!

BIFF. I'm in great shape as far as that's concerned.

HAPPY. And the beauty of it is, Biff, it wouldn't be like a business. We'd be out playin' ball again . . .

BIFF (*enthused*). Yeah, that's . . .

WILLY. Million-dollar . . .

HAPPY. And you wouldn't get fed up with it, Biff. It'd be the family again. There'd be the old honor, and comradeship, and if you wanted to go off for a swim or somethin'—well, you'd do it! Without some smart cooky gettin' up ahead of you!

WILLY. Lick the world! You guys together could absolutely lick the civilized world.

BIFF. I'll see Oliver tomorrow. Hap, if we could work that out . . .

LINDA. Maybe things are beginning to—

WILLY (*wildly enthused, to Linda*). Stop interrupting! (*To Biff*) But don't wear sport jacket and slacks when you see Oliver.

BIFF. No, I'll—

WILLY. A business suit, and talk as little as possible, and don't crack any jokes.

BIFF. He did like me. Always liked me.

LINDA. He loved you!

WILLY (*to Linda*). Will you stop? (*To Biff*) Walk in very serious. You are not applying for a boy's job. Money is to pass. Be quiet, fine, and serious. Everybody likes a kidder, but nobody lends him money.

HAPPY. I'll try to get some myself, Biff. I'm sure I can.

WILLY. I see great things for you kids. I think your troubles are over. But remember, start big and you'll end big. Ask for fifteen. How much you gonna ask for?

BIFF. Gee, I don't know—

WILLY. And don't say "Gee." "Gee" is a boy's word. A man walking in for fifteen thousand dollars does not say "Gee!"

BIFF. Ten, I think, would be top though.

WILLY. Don't be so modest. You always started too low. Walk in with a big laugh. Don't look worried. Start off with a couple of your good stories to lighten things up.

It's not what you say, it's how you say it—because personality always wins the day.

LINDA. Oliver always thought the highest of him—

WILLY. Will you let me talk?

BIFF. Don't yell at her, Pop, will ya?

WILLY (*angrily*). I was talking, wasn't I?

BIFF. I don't like you yelling at her all the time, and I'm tellin' you, that's all.

WILLY. What're you, takin' over this house?

LINDA. Willy—

WILLY (*turning on her*). Don't take his side all the time, goddammit!

BIFF (*furiously*). Stop yelling at her!

WILLY (*suddenly pulling on his cheek, beaten down, guilt ridden*). Give my best to Bill Oliver—he may remember me. (*He exits through the living-room doorway*)

LINDA (*her voice subdued*). What'd you have to start that for? (*Biff turns away*) You see how sweet he was as soon as you talked hopefully? (*She goes over to Biff*) Come up and say good night to him. Don't let him go to bed that way.

HAPPY. Come on, Biff, let's buck him up.

LINDA. Please, dear. Just say good night. It takes so little to make him happy. Come. (*She goes through the living-room doorway, calling upstairs from within the living-room*) Your pajamas are hanging in the bathroom, Willy!

HAPPY (*looking toward where Linda went out*). What a woman! They broke the mold when they made her. You know that, Biff?

BIFF. He's off salary. My God, working on commission!

HAPPY. Well, let's face it: he's no hot-shot selling man. Except that sometimes, you have to admit, he's a sweet personality.

BIFF (*deciding*). Lend me ten bucks, will ya? I want to buy some new ties.

HAPPY. I'll take you to a place I know. Beautiful stuff. Wear one of my striped shirts tomorrow.

BIFF. She got gray. Mom got awful old. Gee, I'm gonna go in to Oliver tomorrow and knock him for a—

HAPPY. Come on up. Tell that to Dad. Let's give him a whirl. Come on.

BIFF (*steamed up*). You know, with ten thousand bucks, boy!

HAPPY (*as they go into the living-room*). That's the talk, Biff, that's the first time I've heard the old confidence out of you!

(*From within the living-room, fading off*) You're gonna live with me, kid, and any babe you want just say the word . . . (*The last lines are hardly heard. They are mounting the stairs to their parents' bedroom*)

LINDA (*entering her bedroom and addressing Willy, who is in the bathroom. She is straightening the bed for him*). Can you do anything about the shower? It drips.

WILLY (*from the bathroom*). All of a sudden everything falls to pieces! Goddam plumbing, oughta be sued, those people. I hardly finished putting it in and the thing . . . (*His words rumble off*)

LINDA. I'm just wondering if Oliver will remember him. You think he might?

WILLY (*coming out of the bathroom in his pajamas*). Remember him? What's the matter with you, you crazy? If he'd've stayed with Oliver he'd be on top by now! Wait'll Oliver gets a look at him. You don't know the average caliber any more. The average young man today—(*He is getting into bed*)—is got a caliber of zero. Greatest thing in the world for him was to bum around.

(*Biff and Happy enter the bedroom. Slight pause.*)

WILLY (*stops short, looking at Biff*). Glad to hear it, boy.

HAPPY. He wanted to say good night to you, sport.

WILLY (*to Biff*). Yeah. Knock him dead, boy. What'd you want to tell me?

BIFF. Just take it easy, Pop. Good night. (*He turns to go*)

WILLY (*unable to resist*). And if anything falls off the desk while you're talking to him—like a package or something—don't you pick it up. They have office boys for that.

LINDA. I'll make a big breakfast—

WILLY. Will you let me finish? (*To Biff*) Tell him you were in the business in the West. Not farm work.

BIFF. All right, Dad.

LINDA. I think everything—

WILLY (*going right through her speech*). And don't undersell yourself. No less than fifteen thousand dollars.

BIFF (*unable to bear him*). Okay. Good night, Mom. (*He starts moving*)

WILLY. Because you got a greatness in you, Biff, remember that. You got all kinds a greatness . . . (*He lies back, exhausted. Biff walks out*)

LINDA (*calling after Biff*). Sleep well, darling!

HAPPY. I'm gonna get married, Mom. I wanted to tell you.

LINDA. Go to sleep, dear.

HAPPY (*going*). I just wanted to tell you.

WILLY. Keep up the good work. (*Happy exits*) God . . . remember that Ebbets Field game? The championship of the city?

LINDA. Just rest. Should I sing to you?

WILLY. Yeah. Sing to me. (*Linda hums a soft lullaby*) When that team came out—he was the tallest, remember?

LINDA. Oh, yes. And in gold.

(*Biff enters the darkened kitchen, takes a cigarette, and leaves the house. He comes downstage into a golden pool of light. He smokes, staring at the night.*)

WILLY. Like a young god. Hercules—something like that. And the sun, the sun all around him. Remember how he waved to me? Right up from the field, with the representatives of three colleges standing by? And the buyers I brought, and the cheers when he came out—Loman, Loman, Loman! God Almighty, he'll be great yet. A star like that, magnificent, can never really fade away!

(*The light on Willy is fading. The gas heater begins to glow through the kitchen wall, near the stairs, a blue flame beneath red coils.*)

LINDA (*timidly*). Willy dear, what has he got against you?

WILLY. I'm so tired. Don't talk any more.

(*Biff slowly returns to the kitchen. He stops, stares toward the heater.*)

LINDA. Will you ask Howard to let you work in New York?

WILLY. First thing in the morning. Everything'll be all right.

(*Biff reaches behind the heater and draws out a length of rubber tubing. He is horrified and turns his head toward Willy's room, still dimly lit, from which the strains of Linda's desperate but monotonous humming rise.*)

WILLY (*staring through the window into the moonlight*). Gee, look at the moon moving between the buildings!

(*Biff wraps the tubing around his hand and quickly goes up the stairs.*)

CURTAIN

ACT TWO

Music is heard, gay and bright. The curtain rises as the music fades away. Willy, in shirt sleeves, is sitting at the kitchen table, sipping coffee, his hat in his lap. Linda is filling his cup when she can.

WILLY. Wonderful coffee. Meal in itself.

LINDA. Can I make you some eggs?

WILLY. No. Take a breath.

LINDA. You look so rested, dear.

WILLY. I slept like a dead one. First time in months. Imagine, sleeping till ten on a Tuesday morning. Boys left nice and early, heh?

LINDA. They were out of here by eight o'clock.

WILLY. Good work!

LINDA. It was so thrilling to see them leaving together. I can't get over the shaving lotion in this house!

WILLY (*smiling*). Mmm—

LINDA. Biff was very changed this morning. His whole attitude seemed to be hopeful. He couldn't wait to get downtown to see Oliver.

WILLY. He's heading for a change. There's no question, there simply are certain men that take longer to get—solidified. How did he dress?

LINDA. His blue suit. He's so handsome in that suit. He could be a—anything in that suit!

(*Willy gets up from the table. Linda holds his jacket for him.*)

WILLY. There's no question, no question at all. Gee, on the way home tonight I'd like to buy some seeds.

LINDA (*laughing*). That'd be wonderful. But not enough sun gets back there. Nothing'll grow any more.

WILLY. You wait, kid, before it's all over we're gonna get a little place out in the country, and I'll raise some vegetables, a couple of chickens . . .

LINDA. You'll do it yet, dear.

(*Willy walks out of his jacket. Linda follows him.*)

WILLY. And they'll get married, and come for a weekend. I'd build a little guest house. 'Cause I got so many fine tools, all I'd need would be a little lumber and some peace of mind.

LINDA (*joyfully*). I sewed the lining . . .

WILLY. I could build two guest houses,

so they'd both come. Did he decide how much he's going to ask Oliver for?

LINDA (*getting him into the jacket*). He didn't mention it, but I imagine ten or fifteen thousand. You going to talk to Howard today?

WILLY. Yeah, I'll put it to him straight and simple. He'll just have to take me off the road.

LINDA. And Willy, don't forget to ask for a little advance, because we've got the insurance premium. It's the grace period now.

WILLY. That's a hundred . . . ?

LINDA. A hundred and eight, sixty-eight. Because we're a little short again.

WILLY. Why are we short?

LINDA. Well, you had the motor job on the car . . .

WILLY. That goddam Studebaker!

LINDA. And you got one more payment on the refrigerator . . .

WILLY. But it just broke again!

LINDA. Well, it's old, dear.

WILLY. I told you we should've bought a well-advertised machine. Charley bought a General Electric and it's twenty years old and it's still good, that son-of-a-bitch.

LINDA. But, Willy—

WILLY. Whoever heard of a Hastings refrigerator. Once in my life I would like to own something outright before it's broken! I'm always in a race with the junkyard! I just finished paying for the car and it's on its last legs. The refrigerator consumes belts like a goddam maniac. They time those things. They time them so when you finally paid for them, they're used up.

LINDA (*buttoning up his jacket as he unbuttons it*). All told, about two hundred dollars would carry us, dear. But that includes the last payment on the mortgage. After this payment, Willy, the house belongs to us.

WILLY. It's twenty-five years!

LINDA. Biff was nine years old when we bought it.

WILLY. Well, that's a great thing. To weather a twenty-five-year mortgage is—

LINDA. It's an accomplishment.

WILLY. All the cement, the lumber, the reconstruction I put in this house! There ain't a crack to be found in it any more.

LINDA. Well, it served its purpose.

WILLY. What purpose? Some stranger'll come along, move in, and that's that. If only Biff would take this house, and raise a family . . . (*He starts to go*) Good-by, I'm late.

LINDA (*suddenly remembering*). Oh, I forgot! You're supposed to meet them for dinner.

WILLY. Me?

LINDA. At Frank's Chop House on Fortyeighth near Sixth Avenue.

WILLY. Is that so! How about you?

LINDA. No, just the three of you. They're gonna blow you to a big meal!

WILLY. Don't say! Who thought of that?

LINDA. Biff came to me this morning, Willy, and he said, "Tell Dad, we want to blow him to a big meal." Be there six o'clock. You and your two boys are going to have dinner.

WILLY. Gee whiz! That's really somethin'. I'm gonna knock Howard for a loop, kid. I'll get an advance, and I'll come home with a New York job. Goddammit, now I'm gonna do it!

LINDA. Oh, that's the spirit, Willy!

WILLY. I will never get behind a wheel the rest of my life!

LINDA. It's changing, Willy, I can feel it changing!

WILLY. Beyond a question. G'by, I'm late. (*He starts to go again*)

LINDA (*calling after him as she runs to the kitchen table for a handkerchief*). You got your glasses?

WILLY (*feels for them, then comes back in*). Yeah, yeah, got my glasses.

LINDA (*giving him the handkerchief*). And a handkerchief.

WILLY. Yeah, handkerchief.

LINDA. And your saccharine?

WILLY. Yeah, my saccharine.

LINDA. Be careful on the subway stairs. (*She kisses him, and a silk stocking is seen hanging from her hand. Willy notices it.*)

WILLY. Will you stop mending stockings? At least while I'm in the house. It gets me nervous. I can't tell you. Please. (*Linda hides the stocking in her hand as she follows Willy across the forestage in front of the house.*)

LINDA. Remember, Frank's Chop House.

WILLY (*passing the apron*). Maybe beets would grow out there.

LINDA (*laughing*). But you tried so many times.

WILLY. Yeah. Well, don't work hard today. (*He disappears around the right corner of the house*)

LINDA. Be careful!

(As Willy vanishes, Linda waves to him. Suddenly the phone rings. She runs across the stage and into the kitchen and lifts it.)

LINDA. Hello? Oh, Biff! I'm so glad you called, I just . . . Yes, sure, I just told him. Yes, he'll be there for dinner at six o'clock, I didn't forget. Listen, I was just dying to tell you. You know that little rubber pipe I told you about? That he connected to the gas heater? I finally decided to go down the cellar this morning and take it away and destroy it. But it's gone! Imagine? He took it away himself, it isn't there! *(She listens)* When? Oh, then you took it. Oh nothing, it's just that I'd hoped he'd taken it away himself. Oh, I'm not worried, darling, because this morning he left in such high spirits, it was like the old days! I'm not afraid any more. Did Mr. Oliver see you? . . . Well, you wait there then. And make a nice impression on him, darling. Just don't perspire too much before you see him. And have a nice time with Dad. He may have big news too! . . . That's right, a New York job. And be sweet to him tonight, dear. Be loving to him. Because he's only a little boat looking for a harbor. *(She is trembling with sorrow and joy)* Oh, that's wonderful, Biff, you'll save his life. Thanks, darling. Just put your arm around him when he comes into the restaurant. Give him a smile. That's the boy . . . Good-by, dear. . . . You got your comb? . . . That's fine. Good-by, Biff dear. *(In the middle of her speech, Howard Wagner, thirty-six, wheels in a small typewriter table on which is a wire-recording machine and proceeds to plug it in. This is on the left forestage. Light slowly fades on Linda as it rises on Howard. Howard is intent on threading the machine and only glances over his shoulder as Willy appears.)*

WILLY. Pst! Pst!

HOWARD. Hello, Willy, come in.

WILLY. Like to have a little talk with you, Howard.

HOWARD. Sorry to keep you waiting. I'll be with you in a minute.

WILLY. What's that, Howard?

HOWARD. Didn't you ever see one of these? Wire recorder.

WILLY. Oh. Can we talk a minute?

HOWARD. Records things. Just got delivery yesterday. Been driving me crazy, the most terrific machine I ever saw in my life. I was up all night with it.

WILLY. What do you do with it?

HOWARD. I bought it for dictation, but you can do anything with it. Listen to this. I had it home last night. Listen to what I picked up. The first one is my daughter. Get this. *(He flicks the switch and "Roll Out the Barrel" is heard being whistled)* Listen to that kid whistle.

WILLY. That is lifelike, isn't it?

HOWARD. Seven years old. Get that tone.

WILLY. Ts, ts. Like to ask a little favor if you . . .

(The whistling breaks off, and the voice of Howard's daughter is heard.)

HIS DAUGHTER. "Now you, Daddy."

HOWARD. She's crazy for me! *(Again the same song is whistled)* That's me! Ha! *(He winks)*

WILLY. You're very good!

(The whistling breaks off again. The machine runs silent for a moment.)

HOWARD. Sh! Get this now, this is my son.

HIS SON. "The capital of Alabama is Montgomery; the capital of Arizona is Phoenix; the capital of Arkansas is Little Rock; the capital of California is Sacramento . . ." *(And on, and on)*

HOWARD *(holding up five fingers)*. Five years old, Willy!

WILLY. He'll make an announcer some day!

HIS SON *(continuing)*. "The capital . . ."

HOWARD. Get that—alphabetical order! *(The machine breaks off suddenly)* Wait a minute. The maid kicked the plug out.

WILLY. It certainly is a—

HOWARD. Sh, for God's sake!

HIS SON. "It's nine o'clock, Bulova watch time. So I have to go to sleep."

WILLY. That really is—

HOWARD. Wait a minute! The next is my wife.

(They wait.)

HOWARD'S VOICE. "Go on, say something." *(Pause)* "Well, you gonna talk?"

HIS WIFE. "I can't think of anything."

HOWARD'S VOICE. "Well, talk—it's turning."

HIS WIFE *(shyly, beaten)*. "Hello." *(Silence)* "Oh, Howard, I can't talk into this . . ."

HOWARD *(snapping the machine off)*. That was my wife.

WILLY. That is a wonderful machine. Can we—

HOWARD. I tell you, Willy, I'm gonna

take my camera, and my bandsaw, and all my hobbies, and out they go. This is the most fascinating relaxation I ever found.

WILLY. I think I'll get one myself.

HOWARD. Sure, they're only a hundred and a half. You can't do without it. Supposing you wanna hear Jack Benny, see? But you can't be at home at that hour. So you tell the maid to turn the radio on when Jack Benny comes on, and this automatically goes on with the radio . . .

WILLY. And when you come home you . . .

HOWARD. You can come home twelve o'clock, one o'clock, any time you like, and you get yourself a Coke and sit yourself down, throw the switch, and there's Jack Benny's program in the middle of the night!

WILLY. I'm definitely going to get one. Because lots of time I'm on the road, and I think to myself, what I must be missing on the radio!

HOWARD. Don't you have a radio in the car?

WILLY. Well, yeah, but who ever thinks of turning it on?

HOWARD. Say, aren't you supposed to be in Boston?

WILLY. That's what I want to talk to you about, Howard. You got a minute? (*He draws a chair in from the wing*)

HOWARD. What happened? What're you doing here?

WILLY. Well . . .

HOWARD. You didn't crack up again, did you?

WILLY. Oh, no. No . . .

HOWARD. Geez, you had me worried there for a minute. What's the trouble?

WILLY. Well, tell you the truth, Howard. I've come to the decision that I'd rather not travel any more.

HOWARD. Not travel! Well, what'll you do?

WILLY. Remember, Christmas time, when you had the party here? You said you'd try to think of some spot for me here in town.

HOWARD. With us?

WILLY. Well, sure.

HOWARD. Oh, yeah, yeah. I remember. Well, I couldn't think of anything for you, Willy.

WILLY. I tell ya, Howard. The kids are all grown up, y'know. I don't need much any more. If I could take home—well,

sixty-five dollars a week, I could swing it.

HOWARD. Yeah, but Willy, see I—

WILLY. I tell ya why, Howard. Speaking frankly and between the two of us, y'know —I'm just a little tired.

HOWARD. Oh, I could understand that, Willy. But you're a road man, Willy, and we do a road business. We've only got a half-dozen salesmen on the floor here.

WILLY. God knows, Howard, I never asked a favor of any man. But I was with the firm when your father used to carry you in here in his arms.

HOWARD. I know that, Willy, but—

WILLY. Your father came to me the day you were born and asked me what I thought of the name of Howard, may he rest in peace.

HOWARD. I appreciate that, Willy, but there just is no spot here for you. If I had a spot I'd slam you right in, but I just don't have a single solitary spot.

(*He looks for his lighter. Willy has picked it up and gives it to him. Pause.*)

WILLY (*with increasing anger*). Howard, all I need to set my table is fifty dollars a week.

HOWARD. But where am I going to put you, kid?

WILLY. Look, it isn't a question of whether I can sell merchandise, is it?

HOWARD. No, but it's a business, kid, and everybody's gotta pull his own weight.

WILLY (*desperately*). Just let me tell you a story, Howard—

HOWARD. 'Cause you gotta admit, business is business.

WILLY (*angrily*). Business is definitely business, but just listen for a minute. You don't understand this. When I was a boy —eighteen, nineteen—I was already on the road. And there was a question in my mind as to whether selling had a future for me. Because in those days I had a yearning to go to Alaska. See, there were three gold strikes in one month in Alaska, and I felt like going out. Just for the ride, you might say.

HOWARD (*barely interested*). Don't say.

WILLY. Oh, yeah, my father lived many years in Alaska. He was an adventurous man. We've got quite a little streak of self-reliance in our family. I thought I'd go out with my older brother and try to locate him, and maybe settle in the North with the old man. And I was almost decided to go, when I met a salesman in the

Parker House. His name was Dave Single-man. And he was eighty-four years old, and he'd drummed merchandise in thirty-one states. And old Dave, he'd go up to his room, y'understand, put on his green velvet slippers—I'll never forget—and pick up his phone and call the buyers, and without ever leaving his room, at the age of eighty-four, he made his living. And when I saw that, I realized that selling was the greatest career a man could want. 'Cause what could be more satisfying than to be able to go, at the age of eighty-four, into twenty or thirty different cities, and pick up a phone, and be remembered and loved and helped by so many different people? Do you know? when he died—and by the way he died the death of a salesman, in his green velvet slippers in the smoker of the New York, New Haven and Hartford, going into Boston—when he died, hundreds of salesmen and buyers were at his funeral. Things were sad on a lotta trains for months after that. (*He stands up. Howard has not looked at him*) In those days there was personality in it, Howard. There was respect, and comradeship, and gratitude in it. Today, it's all cut and dried, and there's no chance for bringing friendship to bear —or personality. You see what I mean? They don't know me any more.

HOWARD (*moving away, to the right*). That's just the thing, Willy.

WILLY. If I had forty dollars a week— that's all I'd need. Forty dollars, Howard.

HOWARD. Kid, I can't take blood from a stone, I—

WILLY (*desperation is on him now*). Howard, the year Al Smith was nominated, your father came to me and—

HOWARD (*starting to go off*). I've got to see some people, kid.

WILLY (*stopping him*). I'm talking about your father! There were promises made across this desk! You mustn't tell me you've got people to see—I put thirty-four years into this firm, Howard, and now I can't pay my insurance! You can't eat the orange and throw the peel away— a man is not a piece of fruit! (*After a pause*) Now pay attention. Your father— in 1928 I had a big year. I averaged a hundred and seventy dollars a week in commissions.

HOWARD (*impatiently*). Now, Willy, you never averaged—

WILLY (*banging his hand on the desk*).

I averaged a hundred and seventy dollars a week in the year of 1928; and your father came to me—or rather, I was in the office here—it was right over this desk— and he put his hand on my shoulder—

HOWARD (*getting up*). You'll have to excuse me, Willy. I gotta see some people. Pull yourself together. (*Going out*) I'll be back in a little while.

(*On Howard's exit, the light on his chair grows very bright and strange.*)

WILLY. Pull myself together! What the hell did I say to him? My God, I was yelling at him! How could I! (*Willy breaks off, staring at the light, which occupies the chair, animating it. He approaches this chair, standing across the desk from it*) Frank, Frank, don't you remember what you told me that time? How you put your hand on my shoulder, and Frank . . . (*He leans on the desk and as he speaks the dead man's name he accidentally switches on the recorder, and instantly*)

HOWARD'S SON. ". . . of New York is Albany. The capital of Ohio is Cincinnati, the capital of Rhode Island is . . ." (*The recitation continues*)

WILLY (*leaping away with fright, shouting*). Ha! Howard! Howard! Howard!

HOWARD (*rushing in*). What happened?

WILLY (*pointing at the machine, which continues nasally, childishly, with the capital cities*). Shut it off! Shut it off!

HOWARD (*pulling the plug out*). Look, Willy . . .

WILLY (*pressing his hands to his eyes*). I gotta get myself some coffee. I'll get some coffee . . .

(*Willy starts to walk out. Howard stops him.*)

HOWARD (*rolling up the cord*). Willy, look . . .

WILLY. I'll go to Boston.

HOWARD. Willy, you can't go to Boston for us.

WILLY. Why can't I go?

HOWARD. I don't want you to represent us. I've been meaning to tell you for a long time now.

WILLY. Howard, are you firing me?

HOWARD. I think you need a good long rest, Willy.

WILLY. Howard—

HOWARD. And when you feel better, come back, and we'll see if we can work something out.

WILLY. But I gotta earn money, Howard. I'm in no position to—

HOWARD. Where are your sons? Why don't your sons give you a hand?

WILLY. They're working on a very big deal.

HOWARD. This is no time for false pride, Willy. You go to your sons and tell them that you're tired. You've got two great boys, haven't you?

WILLY. Oh, no question, no question, but in the meantime . . .

HOWARD. Then that's that, heh?

WILLY. All right, I'll go to Boston tomorrow.

HOWARD. No, no.

WILLY. I can't throw myself on my sons. I'm not a cripple!

HOWARD. Look, kid, I'm busy this morning.

WILLY (*grasping Howard's arm*). Howard, you've got to let me go to Boston!

HOWARD (*hard, keeping himself under control*). I've got a line of people to see this morning. Sit down, take five minutes, and pull yourself together, and then go home, will ya? I need the office, Willy. (*He starts to go, turns, remembering the recorder, starts to push off the table holding the recorder*) Oh, yeah. Whenever you can this week, stop by and drop off the samples. You'll feel better, Willy, and then come back and we'll talk. Pull yourself together, kid, there's people outside.

(*Howard exits, pushing the table off left. Willy stares into space, exhausted. Now the music is heard—Ben's music—first distantly, then closer, closer. As Willy speaks, Ben enters from the right. He carries valise and umbrella.*)

WILLY. Oh, Ben, how did you do it? What is the answer? Did you wind up the Alaska deal already?

BEN. Doesn't take much time if you know what you're doing. Just a short business trip. Boarding ship in an hour. Wanted to say good-by.

WILLY. Ben, I've got to talk to you.

BEN (*glancing at his watch*). Haven't the time, William.

WILLY (*crossing the apron to Ben*). Ben, nothing's working out. I don't know what to do.

BEN. Now, look here, William. I've bought timberland in Alaska and I need a man to look after things for me.

WILLY. God, timberland! Me and my boys in those grand outdoors!

BEN. You've a new continent at your doorstep, William. Get out of these cities, they're full of talk and time payments and courts of law. Screw on your fists and you can fight for a fortune up there.

WILLY. Yes, yes! Linda, Linda!

(*Linda enters, as of old, with the wash.*)

LINDA. Oh, you're back?

BEN. I haven't much time.

WILLY. No, wait! Linda, he's got a proposition for me in Alaska.

LINDA. But you've got— (*To Ben*) He's got a beautiful job here.

WILLY. But in Alaska, kid, I could—

LINDA. You're doing well enough, Willy!

BEN (*to Linda*). Enough for what, dear?

LINDA (*frightened of Ben and angry at him*). Don't say those things to him! Enough to be happy right here, right now. (*To Willy, while Ben laughs*) Why must everybody conquer the world? You're well liked, and the boys love you, and someday— (*To Ben*) —why, old man Wagner told him just the other day that if he keeps it up he'll be a member of the firm, didn't he, Willy?

WILLY. Sure, sure. I am building something with this firm, Ben, and if a man is building something he must be on the right track, mustn't he?

BEN. What are you building? Lay your hand on it. Where is it?

WILLY (*hesitantly*). That's true, Linda, there's nothing.

LINDA. Why? (*To Ben*) There's a man eighty-four years old—

WILLY. That's right, Ben, that's right. When I look at that man I say, what is there to worry about?

BEN. Bah!

WILLY. It's true, Ben. All he has to do is go into any city, pick up the phone, and he's making his living—and you know why?

BEN (*picking up his valise*). I've got to go.

WILLY (*holding Ben back*). Look at this boy!

(*Biff, in his high school sweater, enters carrying suitcase. Happy carries Biff's shoulder guards, gold helmet, and football pants.*)

WILLY. Without a penny to his name, three great universities are begging for him, and from there the sky's the limit, because it's not what you do, Ben. It's who you know and the smile on your face! It's contacts, Ben, contacts! The whole wealth of Alaska passes over the lunch table at the Commodore Hotel, and that's the wonder, the wonder of this country, that a man can end with diamonds here on the basis of being liked! (*He turns to Biff*) And that's why when you get out on that field today it's important. Because thousands of people will be rooting for you and loving you. (*To Ben, who has again begun to leave*) And Ben! when he walks into a business office his name will sound out like a bell and all the doors will open to him! I've seen it, Ben, I've seen it a thousand times! You can't feel it with your hand like timber, but it's there!

BEN. Good-by, William.

WILLY. Ben, am I right? Don't you think I'm right? I value your advice.

BEN. There's a new continent at your doorstep, William. You could walk out rich. Rich! (*He is gone*)

WILLY. We'll do it here, Ben! You hear me? We're gonna do it here!

(*Young Bernard rushes in. The gay music of the Boys is heard.*)

BERNARD. Oh, gee, I was afraid you left already!

WILLY. Why? What time is it?

BERNARD. It's half-past one!

WILLY. Well, come on, everybody! Ebbets Field next stop! Where's the pennants? (*He rushes through the wall-line of the kitchen and out into the living-room*)

LINDA (*to Biff*). Did you pack fresh underwear?

BIFF (*who has been limbering up*). I want to go!

BERNARD. Biff, I'm carrying your helmet, ain't I?

HAPPY. No, I'm carrying the helmet.

BERNARD. Oh, Biff, you promised me.

HAPPY. I'm carrying the helmet.

BERNARD. How am I going to get in the locker room?

LINDA. Let him carry the shoulder guards. (*She puts her coat and hat on in the kitchen*)

BERNARD. Can I, Biff? 'Cause I told everybody I'm going to be in the locker room.

HAPPY. In Ebbets Field it's the clubhouse.

BERNARD. I meant the clubhouse. Biff!

HAPPY. Biff!

BIFF (*grandly, after a slight pause*). Let him carry the shoulder guards.

HAPPY (*as he gives Bernard the shoulder guards*). Stay close to us now.

(*Willy rushes in with the pennants.*)

WILLY (*handing them out*). Everybody wave when Biff comes out on the field. (*Happy and Bernard run off*) You set now, boy?

(*The music has died away.*)

BIFF. Ready to go, Pop. Every muscle is ready.

WILLY (*at the edge of the apron*). You realize what this means?

BIFF. That's right, Pop.

WILLY (*feeling Biff's muscles*). You're comin' home this afternoon captain of the All-Scholastic Championship Team of the City of New York.

BIFF. I got it, Pop. And remember, pal, when I take off my helmet, that touchdown is for you.

WILLY. Let's go! (*He is starting out, with his arm around Biff, when Charley enters, as of old, in knickers*) I got no room for you, Charley.

CHARLEY. Room? For what?

WILLY. In the car.

CHARLEY. You goin' for a ride? I wanted to shoot some casino.

WILLY (*furiously*). Casino! (*Incredulously*) Don't you realize what today is?

LINDA. Oh, he knows, Willy. He's just kidding you.

WILLY. That's nothing to kid about!

CHARLEY. No, Linda, what's goin' on?

LINDA. He's playing in Ebbets Field.

CHARLEY. Baseball in this weather?

WILLY. Don't talk to him. Come on, come on! (*He is pushing them out*)

CHARLEY. Wait a minute, didn't you hear the news?

WILLY. What?

CHARLEY. Don't you listen to the radio? Ebbets Field just blew up.

WILLY. You go to hell! (*Charley laughs. Pushing them out*) Come on, come on! We're late.

CHARLEY (*as they go*). Knock a homer, Biff, knock a homer!

WILLY (*the last to leave, turning to Charley*). I don't think that was funny, Charley. This is the greatest day of his life.

CHARLEY. Willy, when are you going to grow up?

WILLY. Yeah, heh? When this game is

over, Charley, you'll be laughing out of the other side of your face. They'll be calling him another Red Grange. Twenty-five thousand a year.

CHARLEY (*kidding*). Is that so?

WILLY. Yeah, that's so.

CHARLEY. Well, then, I'm sorry, Willy. But tell me something.

WILLY. What?

CHARLEY. Who is Red Grange?

WILLY. Put up your hands. Goddam you, put up your hands!

(*Charley, chuckling, shakes his head and walks away, around the left corner of the stage. Willy follows him. The music rises to a mocking frenzy.*)

WILLY. Who the hell do you think you are, better than everybody else? You don't know everything, you big, ignorant, stupid . . . Put up your hands!

(*Light rises, on the right side of the forestage, on a small table in the reception room of Charley's office. Traffic sounds are heard. Bernard, now mature, sits whistling to himself. A pair of tennis rackets and an overnight bag are on the floor beside him.*)

WILLY (*offstage*). What are you walking away for? Don't walk away! If you're going to say something say it to my face! I know you laugh at me behind my back. You'll laugh out of the other side of your goddam face after this game. Touchdown! Touchdown! Eighty thousand people! Touchdown! Right between the goal posts. (*Bernard is a quiet, earnest, but self-assured young man. Willy's voice is coming from right upstage now. Bernard lowers his feet off the table and listens. Jenny, his father's secretary, enters.*)

JENNY (*distressed*). Say, Bernard, will you go out in the hall?

BERNARD. What is that noise? Who is it?

JENNY. Mr. Loman. He just got off the elevator.

BERNARD (*getting up*). Who's he arguing with?

JENNY. Nobody. There's nobody with him. I can't deal with him any more, and your father gets all upset everytime he comes. I've got a lot of typing to do, and your father's waiting to sign it. Will you see him?

WILLY (*entering*). Touchdown! Touch— (*He sees Jenny*) Jenny, Jenny, good to see you. How're ya? Workin'? Or still honest?

JENNY. Fine. How've you been feeling?

WILLY. Not much any more, Jenny. Ha, ha! (*He is surprised to see the rackets*)

BERNARD. Hello, Uncle Willy.

WILLY (*almost shocked*). Bernard! Well, look who's here! (*He comes quickly, guiltily, to Bernard and warmly shakes his hand*)

BERNARD. How are you? Good to see you.

WILLY. What are you doing here?

BERNARD. Oh, just stopped by to see Pop. Get off my feet till my train leaves. I'm going to Washington in a few minutes.

WILLY. Is he in?

BERNARD. Yes, he's in his office with the accountant. Sit down.

WILLY (*sitting down*). What're you going to do in Washington?

BERNARD. Oh, just a case I've got there, Willy.

WILLY. That so? (*Indicating the rackets*) You going to play tennis there?

BERNARD. I'm staying with a friend who's got a court.

WILLY. Don't say. His own tennis court. Must be fine people, I bet.

BERNARD. They are, very nice. Dad tells me Biff's in town.

WILLY (*with a big smile*). Yeah, Biff's in. Working on a very big deal, Bernard.

BERNARD. What's Biff doing?

WILLY. Well, he's been doing very big things in the West. But he decided to establish himself here. Very big. We're having dinner. Did I hear your wife had a boy?

BERNARD. That's right. Our second.

WILLY. Two boys! What do you know

BERNARD. What kind of a deal has Bi got?

WILLY. Well, Bill Oliver—very big sporting-goods man—he wants Biff very badly. Called him in from the West. Long distance, carte blanche, special deliveries. Your friends have their own private tennis court?

BERNARD. You still with the old firm, Willy?

WILLY (*after a pause*). I'm—I'm overjoyed to see how you made the grade, Bernard, overjoyed. It's an encouraging thing to see a young man really—really— Looks very good for Biff—very—(*He breaks off, then*) Bernard—(*He is so full of emotion, he breaks off again*)

BERNARD. What is it, Willy?

WILLY (*small and alone*). What—what's the secret?

BERNARD. What secret?

WILLY. How—how did you? Why didn't he ever catch on?

BERNARD. I wouldn't know that, Willy.

WILLY (*confidentially, desperately*). You were his friend, his boyhood friend. There's something I don't understand about it. His life ended after that Ebbets Field game. From the age of seventeen nothing good ever happened to him.

BERNARD. He never trained himself for anything.

WILLY. But he did, he did. After high school he took so many correspondence courses. Radio mechanics; television; God knows what, and never made the slightest mark.

BERNARD (*taking off his glasses*). Willy, do you want to talk candidly?

WILLY (*rising, faces Bernard*). I regard you as a very brilliant man, Bernard. I value your advice.

BERNARD. Oh, the hell with the advice, Willy. I couldn't advise you. There's just one thing I've always wanted to ask you. When he was supposed to graduate, and the math teacher flunked him—

WILLY. Oh, that son-of-a-bitch ruined his life.

BERNARD. Yeah, but, Willy, all he had to do was go to summer school and make up that subject.

WILLY. That's right, that's right.

BERNARD. Did you tell him not to go to summer school?

WILLY. Me? I begged him to go. I ordered him to go!

BERNARD. Then why wouldn't he go?

WILLY. Why? Why! Bernard, that question has been trailing me like a ghost for the last fifteen years. He flunked the subject, and laid down and died like a hammer hit him!

BERNARD. Take it easy, kid.

WILLY. Let me talk to you—I got nobody to talk to. Bernard, Bernard, was it my fault? Y'see? It keeps going around in my mind, maybe I did something to him. I got nothing to give him.

BERNARD. Don't take it so hard.

WILLY. Why did he lay down? What is the story there? You were his friend!

BERNARD. Willy, I remember, it was June, and our grades came out. And he'd flunked math.

WILLY. That son-of-a-bitch!

BERNARD. No, it wasn't right then. Biff just got very angry, I remember, and he was ready to enroll in summer school.

WILLY (*surprised*). He was?

BERNARD. He wasn't beaten by it at all. But then, Willy, he disappeared from the block for almost a month. And I got the idea that he'd gone up to New England to see you. Did he have a talk with you then?

(*Willy stares in silence.*)

BERNARD. Willy?

WILLY (*with a strong edge of resentment in his voice*). Yeah, he came to Boston. What about it?

BERNARD. Well, just that when he came back—I'll never forget this, it always mystifies me. Because I'd thought so well of Biff, even though he'd always taken advantage of me. I loved him, Willy, y'know? And he came back after that month and took his sneakers—remember those sneakers with "University of Virginia" printed on them? He was so proud of those, wore them every day. And he took them down in the cellar, and burned them up in the furnace. We had a fist fight. It lasted at least half an hour. Just the two of us, punching each other down the cellar, and crying right through it. I've often thought of how strange it was that I knew he'd given up his life. What happened in Boston, Willy?

(*Willy looks at him as at an intruder.*)

BERNARD. I just bring it up because you asked me.

WILLY (*angrily*). Nothing. What do you mean, "What happened?" What's that got to do with anything?

BERNARD. Well, don't get sore.

WILLY. What are you trying to do, blame it on me? If a boy lays down is that my fault?

BERNARD. Now, Willy, don't get—

WILLY. Well, don't—don't talk to me that way! What does that mean, "What happened?"

(*Charley enters. He is in his vest, and he carries a bottle of bourbon.*)

CHARLEY. Hey, you're going to miss that train. (*He waves the bottle*)

BERNARD. Yeah, I'm going. (*He takes the bottle*) Thanks, Pop. (*He picks up his rackets and bag*) Good-by, Willy, and don't worry about it. You know, "If at first you don't succeed . . ."

WILLY. Yes, I believe in that.

BERNARD. But sometimes, Willy, it's better for a man just to walk away.

WILLY. Walk away?

BERNARD. That's right.

WILLY. But if you can't walk away?

BERNARD (*after a slight pause*). I guess that's when it's tough. (*Extending his hand*) Good-by, Willy.

WILLY (*shaking Bernard's hand*). Good-by, boy.

CHARLEY (*an arm on Bernard's shoulder*). How do you like this kid? Gonna argue a case in front of the Supreme Court.

BERNARD (*protesting*). Pop!

WILLY (*genuinely shocked, pained and happy*). No! The Supreme Court!

BERNARD. I gotta run. 'By, Dad!

CHARLEY. Knock 'em dead, Bernard! (*Bernard goes off.*)

WILLY (*as Charley takes out his wallet*). The Supreme Court! And he didn't even mention it!

CHARLEY (*counting out money on the desk*). He don't have to—he's gonna do it.

WILLY. And you never told him what to do, did you? You never took any interest in him.

CHARLEY. My salvation is that I never took any interest in anything. There's some money—fifty dollars. I got an accountant inside.

WILLY. Charley, look . . . (*With difficulty*) I got my insurance to pay. If you can manage it—I need a hundred and ten dollars.

(*Charley doesn't reply for a moment; merely stops moving.*)

WILLY. I'd draw it from my bank, but Linda would know, and I . . .

CHARLEY. Sit down, Willy.

WILLY (*moving toward the chair*). I'm keeping an account of everything, remember. I'll pay every penny back. (*He sits*)

CHARLEY. Now listen to me, Willy.

WILLY. I want you to know I appreciate . . .

CHARLEY (*sitting down on the table*). Willy, what're you doin'? What the hell is goin' on in your head?

WILLY. Why? I'm simply . . .

CHARLEY. I offered you a job. You can make fifty dollars a week. And I won't send you on the road.

WILLY. I've got a job.

CHARLEY. Without pay? What kind of a job is a job without pay? (*He rises*) Now, look, kid, enough is enough. I'm no genius but I know when I'm being insulted.

WILLY. Insulted!

CHARLEY. Why don't you want to work for me?

WILLY. What's the matter with you? I've got a job.

CHARLEY. Then what're you walkin' in here every week for?

WILLY (*getting up*). Well, if you don't want me to walk in here—

CHARLEY. I am offering you a job.

WILLY. I don't want your goddam job!

CHARLEY. When the hell are you going to grow up?

WILLY (*furiously*). You big ignoramus, if you say that to me again I'll rap you one! I don't care how big you are! (*He's ready to fight*)

(*Pause.*)

CHARLEY (*kindly, going to him*). How much do you need, Willy?

WILLY. Charley, I'm strapped, I'm strapped. I don't know what to do. I was just fired.

CHARLEY. Howard fired you?

WILLY. That snotnose. Imagine that? I named him. I named him Howard.

CHARLEY. Willy, when're you gonna realize that them things don't mean anything? You named him Howard, but you can't sell that. The only thing you got in this world is what you can sell. And the funny thing is that you're a salesman, and you don't know that.

WILLY. I've always tried to think otherwise, I guess. I always felt that if a man was impressive, and well liked, that nothing—

CHARLEY. Why must everybody like you? Who liked J. P. Morgan? Was he impressive? In a Turkish bath he'd look like a butcher. But with his pockets on he was very well liked. Now listen, Willy, I know you don't like me, and nobody can say I'm in love with you, but I'll give you a job because—just for the hell of it, put it that way. Now what do you say?

WILLY. I—I just can't work for you, Charley.

CHARLEY. What're you, jealous of me?

WILLY. I can't work for you, that's all, don't ask me why.

CHARLEY (*angered, takes out more bills*). You been jealous of me all your life, you damned fool! Here, pay your insurance

(*He puts the money in Willy's hand*)

WILLY. I'm keeping strict accounts.

CHARLEY. I've got some work to do. Take care of yourself. And pay your insurance.

WILLY (*moving to the right*). Funny, y'know? After all the highways, and the trains, and the appointments, and the years, you end up worth more dead than alive.

CHARLEY. Willy, nobody's worth nothin' dead. (*After a slight pause*) Did you hear what I said?

(*Willy stands still, dreaming.*)

CHARLEY. Willy!

WILLY. Apologize to Bernard for me when you see him. I didn't mean to argue with him. He's a fine boy. They're all fine boys, and they'll end up big—all of them. Someday they'll all play tennis together. Wish me luck, Charley. He saw Bill Oliver today.

CHARLEY. Good luck.

WILLY (*on the verge of tears*). Charley, you're the only friend I got. Isn't that a remarkable thing? (*He goes out*)

CHARLEY. Jesus!

(*Charley stares after him a moment and follows. All light blacks out. Suddenly raucous music is heard, and a red glow rises behind the screen at right. Stanley, a young waiter, appears, carrying a table, followed by Happy, who is carrying two chairs*)

STANLEY (*putting the table down*). That's all right, Mr. Loman. I can handle it myself. (*He turns and takes the chairs from Happy and places them at the table*)

HAPPY (*glancing around*). Oh, this is better.

STANLEY. Sure, in the front there you're in the middle of all kinds of noise. Whenever you got a party, Mr. Loman, you just tell me and I'll put you back here. Y'know, there's a lotta people they don't like it private, because when they go out they like to see a lotta action around them because they're sick and tired to stay in the house by theirself. But I know you, you ain't from Hackensack. You know what I mean?

HAPPY (*sitting down*). So how's it coming, Stanley?

STANLEY. Ah, it's a dog's life. I only wish during the war they'd a took me in the Army. I coulda been dead by now.

HAPPY. My brother's back, Stanley.

STANLEY. Oh, he come back, heh? From the Far West.

HAPPY. Yeah, big cattle man, my brother, so treat him right. And my father's coming too.

STANLEY. Oh, your father too!

HAPPY. You got a couple of nice lobsters?

STANLEY. Hundred per cent, big.

HAPPY. I want them with the claws.

STANLEY. Don't worry, I don't give you no mice. (*Happy laughs*) How about some wine? It'll put a head on the meal.

HAPPY. No. You remember, Stanley, that recipe I brought you from overseas? With the champagne in it?

STANLEY. Oh, yeah, sure. I still got it tacked up yet in the kitchen. But that'll have to cost a buck apiece anyways.

HAPPY. That's all right.

STANLEY. What'd you, hit a number or somethin'?

HAPPY. No, it's a little celebration. My brother is—I think he pulled off a big deal today. I think we're going into business together.

STANLEY. Great! That's the best for you. Because a family business, you know what I mean?—that's the best.

HAPPY. That's what I think.

STANLEY. 'Cause what's the difference? Somebody steals? It's in the family. Know what I mean? (*Sotto voce*) Like this bartender here. The boss is goin' crazy what kinda leak he's got in the cash register. You put it in but it don't come out.

HAPPY (*raising his head*). Sh!

STANLEY. What?

HAPPY. You notice I wasn't lookin' right or left, was I?

STANLEY. No.

HAPPY. And my eyes are closed.

STANLEY. So what's the—?

HAPPY. Strudel's comin'.

STANLEY (*catching on, looks around*). Ah, no, there's no—

(*He breaks off as a furred, lavishly dressed girl enters and sits at the next table. Both follow her with their eyes.*)

STANLEY. Geez, how'd ya know?

HAPPY. I got radar or something. (*Staring directly at her profile*) Oooooooo . . . Stanley.

STANLEY. I think that's for you, Mr. Loman.

HAPPY. Look at that mouth. Oh, God. And the binoculars.

STANLEY. Geez, you got a life, Mr. Loman.

HAPPY. Wait on her.

STANLEY (*going to the girl's table*). Would you like a menu, ma'am?

GIRL. I'm expecting someone, but I'd like a—

HAPPY. Why don't you bring her—excuse me, miss, do you mind? I sell champagne, and I'd like you to try my brand. Bring her a champagne, Stanley.

GIRL. That's awfully nice of you.

HAPPY. Don't mention it. It's all company money. (*He laughs*)

GIRL. That's a charming product to be selling, isn't it?

HAPPY. Oh, gets to be like everything else. Selling is selling, y'know.

GIRL. I suppose.

HAPPY. You don't happen to sell, do you?

GIRL. No, I don't sell.

HAPPY. Would you object to a compliment from a stranger? You ought to be on a magazine cover.

GIRL (*looking at him a little archly*). I have been.

(*Stanley comes in with a glass of champagne.*)

HAPPY. What'd I say before, Stanley? You see? She's a cover girl.

STANLEY. Oh, I could see, I could see.

HAPPY (*to the Girl*). What magazine?

GIRL. Oh, a lot of them. (*She takes the drink*) Thank you.

HAPPY. You know what they say in France, don't you? "Champagne is the drink of the complexion"—Hya, Biff!

(*Biff has entered and sits with Happy.*)

BIFF. Hello, kid. Sorry I'm late.

HAPPY. I just got here. Uh, Miss—?

GIRL. Forsythe.

HAPPY. Miss Forsythe, this is my brother.

BIFF. Is Dad here?

HAPPY. His name is Biff. You might've heard of him. Great football player.

GIRL. Really? What team?

HAPPY. Are you familiar with football?

GIRL. No, I'm afraid I'm not.

HAPPY. Biff is quarterback with the New York Giants.

GIRL. Well, that is nice, isn't it? (*She drinks*)

HAPPY. Good health.

GIRL. I'm happy to meet you.

HAPPY. That's my name. Hap. It's really Harold, but at West Point they called me Happy.

GIRL (*now really impressed*). Oh, I see. How do you do? (*She turns her profile*)

BIFF. Isn't Dad coming?

HAPPY. You want her?

BIFF. Oh, I could never make that.

HAPPY. I remember the time that idea would never come into your head. Where's the old confidence, Biff?

BIFF. I just saw Oliver—

HAPPY. Wait a minute. I've got to see that old confidence again. Do you want her? She's on call.

BIFF. Oh, no. (*He turns to look at the Girl*)

HAPPY. I'm telling you. Watch this. (*Turning to the Girl*) Honey? (*She turns to him*) Are you busy?

GIRL. Well, I am . . . but I could make a phone call.

HAPPY. Do that, will you, honey? And see if you can get a friend. We'll be here for a while. Biff is one of the greatest football players in the country.

GIRL (*standing up*). Well, I'm certainly happy to meet you.

HAPPY. Come back soon.

GIRL. I'll try.

HAPPY. Don't try, honey, try hard.

(*The Girl exits. Stanley follows, shaking his head in bewildered admiration.*)

HAPPY. Isn't that a shame now? A beautiful girl like that? That's why I can't get married. There's not a good woman in a thousand. New York is loaded with them, kid!

BIFF. Hap, look—

HAPPY. I told you she was on call!

BIFF (*strangely unnerved*). Cut it out, will ya? I want to say something to you.

HAPPY. Did you see Oliver?

BIFF. I saw him all right. Now look, I want to tell Dad a couple of things and I want you to help me.

HAPPY. What? Is he going to back you?

BIFF. Are you crazy? You're out of your goddam head, you know that?

HAPPY. Why? What happened?

BIFF (*breathlessly*). I did a terrible thing today, Hap. It's been the strangest day I ever went through. I'm all numb, I swear.

HAPPY. You mean he wouldn't see you?

BIFF. Well, I waited six hours for him, see? All day. Kept sending my name in.

Even tried to date his secretary so she'd get me to him, but no soap.

HAPPY. Because you're not showin' the old confidence, Biff. He remembered you, didn't he?

BIFF (stopping Happy with a gesture). Finally, about five o'clock, he comes out. Didn't remember who I was or anything. I felt like such an idiot, Hap.

HAPPY. Did you tell him my Florida idea?

BIFF. He walked away. I saw him for one minute. I got so mad I could've torn the walls down! How the hell did I ever get the idea I was a salesman there? I even believed myself that I'd been a salesman for him! And then he gave me one look and—I realized what a ridiculous lie my whole life has been! We've been talking in a dream for fifteen years. I was a shipping clerk.

HAPPY. What'd you do?

BIFF (with great tension and wonder). Well, he left, see. And the secretary went out. I was all alone in the waiting-room. I don't know what came over me, Hap. The next thing I know I'm in his office—paneled walls, everything. I can't explain it. I—Hap, I took his fountain pen.

HAPPY. Geez, did he catch you?

BIFF. I ran out. I ran down all eleven flights. I ran and ran and ran.

HAPPY. That was an awful dumb—what'd you do that for?

BIFF (agonized). I don't know, I just—wanted to take something, I don't know. You gotta help me, Hap, I'm gonna tell Pop.

HAPPY. You crazy? What for?

BIFF. Hap, he's got to understand that . m not the man somebody lends that kind of money to. He thinks I've been spiting him all these years and it's eating him up.

HAPPY. That's just it. You tell him something nice.

BIFF. I can't.

HAPPY. Say you got a lunch date with Oliver tomorrow.

BIFF. So what do I do tomorrow?

HAPPY. You leave the house tomorrow and come back at night and say Oliver is thinking it over. And he thinks it over for a couple of weeks, and gradually it fades away and nobody's the worse.

BIFF. But it'll go on forever!

HAPPY. Dad is never so happy as when he's looking forward to something!

(Willy enters.)

HAPPY. Hello, scout!

WILLY. Gee, I haven't been here in years! (Stanley has followed Willy in and sets a chair for him. Stanley starts off but Happy stops him.)

HAPPY. Stanley!

(Stanley stands by, waiting for an order.)

BIFF (going to Willy with guilt, as to an invalid). Sit down, Pop. You want a drink?

WILLY. Sure, I don't mind.

BIFF. Let's get a load on.

WILLY. You look worried.

BIFF. N-no. (To Stanley) Scotch all around. Make it doubles.

STANLEY. Doubles, right. (He goes)

WILLY. You had a couple already, didn't you?

BIFF. Just a couple, yeah.

WILLY. Well, what happened, boy? (Nodding affirmatively, with a smile) Everything go all right?

BIFF (takes a breath, then reaches out and grasps Willy's hand). Pal . . . (He is smiling bravely, and Willy is smiling too) I had an experience today.

HAPPY. Terrific, Pop.

WILLY. That so? What happened?

BIFF (high, slightly alcoholic, above the earth). I'm going to tell you everything from first to last. It's been a strange day. (Silence. He looks around, composes himself as best he can, but his breath keeps breaking the rhythm of his voice) I had to wait quite a while for him, and—

WILLY. Oliver?

BIFF. Yeah, Oliver. All day, as a matter of cold fact. And a lot of—instances—facts, Pop, facts about my life came back to me. Who was it, Pop? Who ever said I was a salesman with Oliver?

WILLY. Well, you were.

BIFF. No, Dad, I was a shipping clerk.

WILLY. But you were practically—

BIFF (with determination). Dad, I don't know who said it first, but I was never a salesman for Bill Oliver.

WILLY. What're you talking about?

BIFF. Let's hold on to the facts tonight, Pop. We're not going to get anywhere bullin' around. I was a shipping clerk.

WILLY (angrily). All right, now listen to me—

BIFF. Why don't you let me finish?

WILLY. I'm not interested in stories about the past or any crap of that kind because the woods are burning, boys, you understand? There's a big blaze going on all around. I was fired today.

BIFF (*shocked*). How could you be?

WILLY. I was fired, and I'm looking for a little good news to tell your mother, because the woman has waited and the woman has suffered. The gist of it is that I haven't got a story left in my head, Biff. So don't give me a lecture about facts and aspects. I am not interested. Now what've you got to say to me?

(*Stanley enters with three drinks. They wait until he leaves.*)

WILLY. Did you see Oliver?

BIFF. Jesus, Dad!

WILLY. You mean you didn't go up there?

HAPPY. Sure he went up there.

BIFF. I did. I—saw him. How could they fire you?

WILLY (*on the edge of his chair*). What kind of a welcome did he give you?

BIFF. He won't even let you work on commission?

WILLY. I'm out! (*Driving*) So tell me, he gave you a warm welcome?

HAPPY. Sure, Pop, sure!

BIFF (*driven*). Well, it was kind of—

WILLY. I was wondering if he'd remember you. (*To Happy*) Imagine, man doesn't see him for ten, twelve years and gives you that kind of a welcome!

HAPPY. Damn right!

BIFF (*trying to return to the offensive*). Pop, look—

WILLY. You know why he remembered you, don't you? Eecause you impressed him in those days.

BIFF. Let's talk quietly and get this down to the facts, huh?

WILLY (*as though Biff had been interrupting*). Well, what happened? It's great news, Biff. Did he take you into his office or'd you talk in the waiting-room?

BIFF. Well, he came in, see, and—

WILLY (*with a big smile*). What'd he say? Betcha he threw his arm around you.

BIFF. Well, he kinda—

WILLY. He's a fine man. (*To Happy*) Very hard man to see, y'know.

HAPPY (*agreeing*). Oh, I know.

WILLY (*to Biff*). Is that where you had the drinks?

BIFF. Yeah, he gave me a couple of—no, no!

HAPPY (*cutting in*). He told him my Florida idea.

WILLY. Don't interrupt. (*To Biff*) How'd he react to the Florida idea?

BIFF. Dad, will you give me a minute to explain?

WILLY. I've been waiting for you to explain since I sat down here! What happened? He took you into his office and what?

BIFF. Well—I talked. And—and he listened, see.

WILLY. Famous for the way he listens, y'know. What was his answer?

BIFF. His answer was—(*He breaks off, suddenly angry*) Dad, you're not letting me tell you what I want to tell you!

WILLY (*accusing, angered*). You didn't see him, did you?

BIFF. I did see him!

WILLY. What'd you insult him or something? You insulted him, didn't you?

BIFF. Listen, will you let me out of it, will you just let me out of it!

HAPPY. What the hell!

WILLY. Tell me what happened!

BIFF (*to Happy*). I can't talk to him!

(*A single trumpet note jars the ear. The light of green leaves stains the house, which holds the air of night and a dream. Young Bernard enters and knocks on the door of the house.*)

YOUNG BERNARD (*frantically*). Mrs. Loman, Mrs. Loman!

HAPPY. Tell him what happened!

BIFF (*to Happy*). Shut up and leave me alone!

WILLY. No, no! You had to go and flunk math!

BIFF. What math? What're you talking about?

YOUNG BERNARD. Mrs. Loman, Mrs. Loman!

(*Linda appears in the house, as of old.*)

WILLY (*wildly*). Math, math, math!

BIFF. Take it easy, Pop!

YOUNG BERNARD. Mrs. Loman!

WILLY (*furiously*). If you hadn't flunked you'd've been set by now!

BIFF. Now, look, I'm gonna tell you what happened, and you're going to listen to me.

YOUNG BERNARD. Mrs. Loman!

BIFF. I waited six hours—

HAPPY. What the hell are you saying?

BIFF. I kept sending in my name but he wouldn't see me. So finally he . . . (*He continues unheard as light fades low on the restaurant*)

YOUNG BERNARD. Biff flunked math!

LINDA. No!

YOUNG BERNARD. Birnbaum flunked him! They won't graduate him!

LINDA. But they have to. He's gotta go to the university. Where is he? Biff! Biff!

YOUNG BERNARD. No, he left. He went to Grand Central.

LINDA. Grand—You mean he went to Boston!

YOUNG BERNARD. Is Uncle Willy in Boston?

LINDA. Oh, maybe Willy can talk to the teacher. Oh, the poor, poor boy!

(*Light on house area snaps out.*)

BIFF (*at the table, now audible, holding up a gold fountain pen*). . . . so I'm washed up with Oliver, you understand? Are you listening to me?

WILLY (*at a loss*). Yeah, sure. If you hadn't flunked—

BIFF. Flunked what? What're you talking about?

WILLY. Don't blame everything on me! I didn't flunk math—you did! What pen?

HAPPY. That was awful dumb, Biff, a pen like that is worth—

WILLY (*seeing the pen for the first time*). You took Oliver's pen?

BIFF (*weakening*). Dad, I just explained it to you.

WILLY. You stole Bill Oliver's fountain pen!

BIFF. I didn't exactly steal it! That's just what I've been explaining to you!

HAPPY. He had it in his hand and just then Oliver walked in, so he got nervous and stuck it in his pocket!

WILLY. My God, Biff!

BIFF. I never intended to do it, Dad!

OPERATOR'S VOICE. Standish Arms, good evening!

WILLY (*shouting*). I'm not in my room!

BIFF (*frightened*). Dad, what's the matter? (*He and Happy stand up*)

OPERATOR. Ringing Mr. Loman for you!

WILLY. I'm not there, stop it!

BIFF (*horrified, gets down on one knee before Willy*). Dad, I'll make good, I'll make good. (*Willy tries to get to his feet. Biff holds him down*) Sit down now.

WILLY. No, you're no good, you're no good for anything.

BIFF. I am, Dad, I'll find something else, you understand? Now don't worry about anything. (*He holds up Willy's face*) Talk to me, Dad.

OPERATOR. Mr. Loman does not answer. Shall I page him?

WILLY (*attempting to stand, as though to rush and silence the Operator*). No, no, no!

HAPPY. He'll strike something, Pop.

WILLY. No, no . . .

BIFF (*desperately, standing over Willy*). Pop, listen! Listen to me! I'm telling you something good. Oliver talked to his partner about the Florida idea. You listening? He—he talked to his partner, and he came to me . . . I'm going to be all right, you hear? Dad, listen to me, he said it was just a question of the amount!

WILLY. Then you . . . got it?

HAPPY. He's gonna be terrific, Pop!

WILLY (*trying to stand*). Then you got it, haven't you? You got it! You got it!

BIFF (*agonized, holds Willy down*). No, no. Look, Pop, I'm supposed to have lunch with them tomorrow. I'm just telling you this so you'll know that I can still make an impression, Pop. And I'll make good somewhere, but I can't go tomorrow, see?

WILLY. Why not? You simply—

BIFF. But the pen, Pop!

WILLY. You give it to him and tell him it was an oversight!

HAPPY. Sure, have lunch tomorrow!

BIFF. I can't say that—

WILLY. You were doing a crossword puzzle and accidentally used his pen!

BIFF. Listen, kid, I took those balls years ago, now I walk in with his fountain pen? That clinches it, don't you see? I can't face him like that! I'll try elsewhere.

PAGE'S VOICE. Paging Mr. Loman!

WILLY. Don't you want to be anything?

BIFF. Pop, how can I go back?

WILLY. You don't want to be anything, is that what's behind it?

BIFF (*now angry at Willy for not crediting his sympathy*). Don't take it that way! You think it was easy walking into that office after what I'd done to him? A team of horses couldn't have dragged me back to Bill Oliver!

WILLY. Then why'd you go?

BIFF. Why did I go? Why did I go! Look at you! Look at what's become of you!

(*Off left, The Woman laughs.*)

WILLY. Biff, you're going to go to that lunch tomorrow, or—

BIFF. I can't go. I've got no appointment!

HAPPY. Biff, for . . . !

WILLY. Are you spiting me?

BIFF. Don't take it that way! Goddammit!

WILLY (strikes Biff and falters away from the table). You rotten little louse! Are you spiting me?

THE WOMAN. Someone's at the door, Willy!

BIFF. I'm no good, can't you see what I am?

HAPPY (separating them). Hey, you're in a restaurant! Now cut it out, both of you! (The girls enter) Hello, girls, sit down.

(The Woman laughs, off left.)

MISS FORSYTHE. I guess we might as well. This is Letta.

THE WOMAN. Willy, are you going to wake up?

BIFF (ignoring Willy). How're ya, miss, sit down. What do you drink?

MISS FORSYTHE. Letta might not be able to stay long.

LETTA. I gotta get up very early tomorrow. I got jury duty. I'm so excited! Were you fellows ever on a jury?

BIFF. No, but I been in front of them! (The girls laugh) This is my father.

LETTA. Isn't he cute? Sit down with us, Pop.

HAPPY. Sit him down, Biff!

BIFF (going to him). Come on, slugger, drink us under the table. To hell with it! Come on, sit down, pal.

(On Biff's last insistence, Willy is about to sit.)

THE WOMAN (now urgently). Willy, are you going to answer the door!

(The Woman's call pulls Willy back. He starts right, befuddled.)

BIFF. Hey, where are you going?

WILLY. Open the door.

BIFF. The door?

WILLY. The washroom . . . the door . . . where's the door?

BIFF (leading Willy to the left). Just go straight down.

(Willy moves left.)

THE WOMAN. Willy, Willy, are you going to get up, get up, get up, get up?

(Willy exits left.)

LETTA. I think it's sweet you bring your daddy along.

MISS FORSYTHE. Oh, he isn't really your father!

BIFF (at left, turning to her resentfully). Miss Forsythe, you've just seen a prince walk by. A fine, troubled prince. A hardworking, unappreciated prince. A pal, you understand? A good companion. Always for his boys.

LETTA. That's so sweet.

HAPPY. Well, girls, what's the program? We're wasting time. Come on, Biff. Gather round. Where would you like to go?

BIFF. Why don't you do something for him?

HAPPY. Me!

BIFF. Don't you give a damn for him, Hap?

HAPPY. What're you talking about? I'm the one who—

BIFF. I sense it, you don't give a good goddam about him. (He takes the rolled-up hose from his pocket and puts it on the table in front of Happy) Look what I found in the cellar, for Christ's sake. How can you bear to let it go on?

HAPPY. Me? Who goes away? Who runs off and—

BIFF. Yeah, but he doesn't mean anything to you. You could help him—I can't! Don't you understand what I'm talking about? He's going to kill himself, don't you know that?

HAPPY. Don't I know it! Me!

BIFF. Hap, help him! Jesus . . . help him . . . Help me, help me, I can't bear to look at his face! (Ready to weep, he hurries out, up right)

HAPPY (staring after him). Where are you going?

MISS FORSYTHE. What's he so mad about?

HAPPY. Come on, girls, we'll catch up with him.

MISS FORSYTHE (as Happy pushes her out). Say, I don't like that temper of his!

HAPPY. He's just a little overstrung, he'll be all right!

WILLY (off left, as The Woman laughs). Don't answer! Don't answer!

LETTA. Don't you want to tell your father—

HAPPY. No, that's not my father. He's just a guy. Come on, we'll catch Biff, and, honey, we're going to paint this town! Stanley, where's the check! Hey, Stanley! (They exit. Stanley looks toward left.)

STANLEY (calling to Happy indignantly). Mr. Loman! Mr. Loman!

(*Stanley picks up a chair and follows them off. Knocking is heard off left. The Woman enters, laughing. Willy follows her. She is in a black slip; he is buttoning his shirt. Raw, sensuous music accompanies their speech.*)

WILLY. Will you stop laughing? Will you stop?

THE WOMAN. Aren't you going to answer the door? He'll wake the whole hotel.

WILLY. I'm not expecting anybody.

THE WOMAN. Whyn't you have another drink, honey, and stop being so damn self-centered?

WILLY. I'm so lonely.

THE WOMAN. You know you ruined me, Willy? From now on, whenever you come to the office, I'll see that you go right through to the buyers. No waiting at my desk any more, Willy. You ruined me.

WILLY. That's nice of you to say that.

THE WOMAN. Gee, you are self-centered! Why so sad? You are the saddest, self-centeredest soul I ever did see-saw. (*She laughs. He kisses her*) Come on inside, drummer boy. It's silly to be dressing in the middle of the night. (*As knocking is heard*) Aren't you going to answer the door?

WILLY. They're knocking on the wrong door.

THE WOMAN. But I felt the knocking. And he heard us talking in here. Maybe the hotel's on fire!

WILLY (*his terror rising*). It's a mistake.

THE WOMAN. Then tell him to go away!

WILLY. There's nobody there.

THE WOMAN. It's getting on my nerves, Willy. There's somebody standing out there and it's getting on my nerves!

WILLY (*pushing her away from him*). All right, stay in the bathroom here, and don't come out. I think there's a law in Massachusetts about it, so don't come out. It may be that new room clerk. He looked very mean. So don't come out. It's a mistake, there's no fire.

(*The knocking is heard again. He takes a few steps away from her, and she vanishes into the wing. The light follows him, and now he is facing Young Biff, who carries a suitcase. Biff steps toward him. The music is gone.*)

BIFF. Why didn't you answer?

WILLY. Biff! What are you doing in Boston?

BIFF. Why didn't you answer? I've been knocking for five minutes, I called you on the phone—

WILLY. I just heard you. I was in the bathroom and had the door shut. Did anything happen home?

BIFF. Dad—I let you down.

WILLY. What do you mean?

BIFF. Dad . . .

WILLY. Biffo, what's this about? (*Putting his arm around Biff*) Come on, let's go downstairs and get you a malted.

BIFF. Dad, I flunked math.

WILLY. Not for the term?

BIFF. The term. I haven't got enough credits to graduate.

WILLY. You mean to say Bernard wouldn't give you the answers?

BIFF. He did, he tried, but I only got a sixty-one.

WILLY. And they wouldn't give you four points?

BIFF. Birnbaum refused absolutely. I begged him, Pop, but he won't give me those points. You gotta talk to him before they close the school. Because if he saw the kind of man you are, and you just talked to him in your way, I'm sure he'd come through for me. The class came right before practice, see, and I didn't go enough. Would you talk to him? He'd like you, Pop. You know the way you could talk.

WILLY. You're on. We'll drive right back.

BIFF. Oh, Dad, good work! I'm sure he'll change it for you!

WILLY. Go downstairs and tell the clerk I'm checkin' out. Go right down.

BIFF. Yes, sir! See, the reason he hates me, Pop—one day he was late for class so I got up at the blackboard and imitated him. I crossed my eyes and talked with a lithp.

WILLY (*laughing*). You did? The kids like it?

BIFF. They nearly died laughing.

WILLY. Yeah? What'd you do?

BIFF. The thquare root of thixty twee is . . . (*Willy bursts out laughing; Biff joins him*) And in the middle of it he walked in!

(*Willy laughs and The Woman joins in offstage.*)

WILLY (*without hesitation*). Hurry downstairs and—

BIFF. Somebody in there?

WILLY. No, that was next door.

(*The Woman laughs offstage.*)

BIFF. Somebody got in your bathroom!

WILLY. No, it's the next room, there's a party—

THE WOMAN (*enters, laughing. She lisps this*). Can I come in? There's something in the bathtub, Willy, and it's moving! (*Willy looks at Biff, who is staring open-mouthed and horrified at The Woman.*)

WILLY. Ah—you better go back to your room. They must be finished painting by now. They're painting her room so I let her take a shower here. Go back, go back . . . (*He pushes her*)

THE WOMAN (*resisting*). But I've got to get dressed, Willy, I can't—

WILLY. Get out of here! Go back, go back . . . (*Suddenly striving for the ordinary*) This is Miss Francis, Biff, she's a buyer. They're painting her room. Go back, Miss Francis, go back . . .

THE WOMAN. But my clothes, I can't go out naked in the hall!

WILLY (*pushing her offstage*). Get outa here! Go back, go back!

(*Biff slowly sits down on his suitcase as the argument continues offstage.*)

THE WOMAN. Where's my stockings? You promised me stockings, Willy!

WILLY. I have no stockings here!

THE WOMAN. You had two boxes of size nine sheers for me, and I want them!

WILLY. Here, for God's sake, will you get outa here!

THE WOMAN (*enters holding a box of stockings*). I just hope there's nobody in the hall. That's all I hope. (*To Biff*) Are you football or baseball?

BIFF. Football.

THE WOMAN (*angry, humiliated*). That's me too. G'night. (*She snatches her clothes from Willy, and walks out*)

WILLY (*after a pause*). Well, better get going. I want to get to the school first thing in the morning. Get my suits out of the closet. I'll get my valises. (*Biff doesn't move*) What's the matter? (*Biff remains motionless, tears falling*) She's a buyer. Buys for J. H. Simmons. She lives down the hall—they're painting. You don't imagine—(*He breaks off. After a pause*) Now listen, pal, she's just a buyer. She sees merchandise in her room and they have to keep it looking just so . . . (*Pause. Assuming command*) All right, get my suits. (*Biff doesn't move*) Now stop crying and do as I say. I gave you an order. Biff, I gave you an order! Is that what you do when I give you an order? How dare you cry! (*Putting his arm around Biff*) Now look, Biff, when you grow up you'll understand about these things. You mustn't—you mustn't over-emphasize a thing like this. I'll see Birnbaum first thing in the morning.

BIFF. Never mind.

WILLY (*getting down beside Biff*). Never mind! He's going to give you those points. I'll see to it.

BIFF. He wouldn't listen to you.

WILLY. He certainly will listen to me. You need those points for the U. of Virginia.

BIFF. I'm not going there.

WILLY. Heh? If I can't get him to change that mark you'll make it up in summer school. You've got all summer to—

BIFF (*his weeping breaking from him*). Dad . . .

WILLY (*infected by it*). Oh, my boy . . .

BIFF. Dad . . .

WILLY. She's nothing to me, Biff. I was lonely, I was terribly lonely.

BIFF. You—you gave her Mama's stockings! (*His tears break through and he rises to go*)

WILLY (*grabbing for Biff*). I gave you an order!

BIFF. Don't touch me, you—liar!

WILLY. Apologize for that!

BIFF. You fake! You phony little fake! You fake! (*Overcome, he turns quickly and weeping fully goes out with his suitcase. Willy is left on the floor on his knees*)

WILLY. I gave you an order! Biff, come back here or I'll beat you! Come back here! I'll whip you!

(*Stanley comes quickly in from the right and stands in front of Willy.*)

WILLY (*shouts at Stanley*). I gave you an order . . .

STANLEY. Hey, let's pick it up, pick it up, Mr. Loman. (*He helps Willy to his feet*) Your boys left with the chippies. They said they'll see you home.

(*A second waiter watches some distance away.*)

WILLY. But we were supposed to have dinner together.

(*Music is heard, Willy's theme.*)

STANLEY. Can you make it?

WILLY. I'll—sure, I can make it. (*Sud-*

denly concerned about his clothes) Do I—
I look all right?

STANLEY. Sure, you look all right. (*He flicks a speck off Willy's lapel*)

WILLY. Here—here's a dollar.

STANLEY. Oh, your son paid me. It's all right.

WILLY (*putting it in Stanley's hand*). No, take it. You're a good boy.

STANLEY. Oh, no, you don't have to . . .

WILLY. Here—here's some more, I don't need it any more. (*After a slight pause*) Tell me—is there a seed store in the neighborhood?

STANLEY. Seeds? You mean like to plant? (*As Willy turns, Stanley slips the money back into his jacket pocket.*)

WILLY. Yes. Carrots, peas . . .

STANLEY. Well, there's hardware stores on Sixth Avenue, but it may be too late now.

WILLY (*anxiously*). Oh, I'd better hurry. I've got to get some seeds. (*He starts off to the right*) I've got to get some seeds, right away. Nothing's planted. I don't have a thing in the ground.

(*Willy hurries out as the light goes down. Stanley moves over to the right after him, watches him off. The other waiter has been staring at Willy.*)

STANLEY (*to the waiter*). Well, whatta you looking at?

(*The waiter picks up the chairs and moves off right. Stanley takes the table and follows him. The light fades on this area. There is a long pause, the sound of the flute coming over. The light gradually rises on the kitchen, which is empty. Happy appears at the door of the house, followed by Biff. Happy is carrying a large bunch of long-stemmed roses. He enters the kitchen, looks around for Linda. Not seeing her, he turns to Biff, who is just outside the house door, and makes a gesture with his hands, indicating "Not here, I guess." He looks into the living-room and freezes. Inside, Linda, unseen, is seated, Willy's coat on her lap. She rises ominously and quietly and moves toward Happy, who backs up into the kitchen, afraid.*)

HAPPY. Hey, what're you doing up? (*Linda says nothing but moves toward him implacably*) Where's Pop? (*He keeps backing to the right, and now Linda is in full view in the doorway to the living-room*) Is he sleeping?

LINDA. Where were you?

HAPPY (*trying to laugh it off*). We met two girls, Mom, very fine types. Here, we brought you some flowers. (*Offering them to her*) Put them in your room, Ma.

(*She knocks them to the floor at Biff's feet. He has now come inside and closed the door behind him. She stares at Biff, silent.*)

HAPPY. Now what'd you do that for? Mom, I want you to have some flowers—

LINDA (*cutting Happy off, violently to Biff*). Don't you care whether he lives or dies?

HAPPY (*going to the stairs*). Come upstairs, Biff.

BIFF (*with a flare of disgust, to Happy*). Go away from me! (*To Linda*) What do you mean, lives or dies? Nobody's dying around here, pal.

LINDA. Get out of my sight! Get out of here!

BIFF. I wanna see the boss.

LINDA. You're not going near him!

BIFF. Where is he? (*He moves into the living-room and Linda follows*)

LINDA (*shouting after Biff*). You invite him for dinner. He looks forward to it all day—(*Biff appears in his parents' bedroom, looks around, and exits*)—and then you desert him there. There's no stranger you'd do that to!

HAPPY. Why? He had a swell time with us. Listen, when I—(*Linda comes back into the kitchen*)—desert him I hope I don't outlive the day!

LINDA. Get out of here!

HAPPY. Now look, Mom . . .

LINDA. Did you have to go to women tonight? You and your lousy rotten whores! (*Biff re-enters the kitchen.*)

HAPPY. Mom, all we did was follow Biff around trying to cheer him up! (*To Biff*) Boy, what a night you gave me!

LINDA. Get out of here, both of you, and don't come back! I don't want you tormenting him any more. Go on now, get your things together! (*To Biff*) You can sleep in his apartment. (*She starts to pick up the flowers and stops herself*) Pick up this stuff, I'm not your maid any more. Pick it up, you bum, you!

(*Happy turns his back to her in refusal. Biff slowly moves over and gets down on his knees, picking up the flowers.*)

LINDA. You're a pair of animals! Not one, not another living soul would have had the cruelty to walk out on that man in a restaurant!

BIFF (*not looking at her*). Is that what he said?

LINDA. He didn't have to say anything. He was so humiliated he nearly limped when he came in.

HAPPY. But, Mom, he had a great time with us—

BIFF (*cutting him off violently*). Shut up!

(*Without another word, Happy goes upstairs.*)

LINDA. You! You didn't even go in to see if he was all right!

BIFF (*still on the floor in front of Linda, the flowers in his hand; with self-loathing*). No. Didn't. Didn't do a damned thing. How do you like that, heh? Left him babbling in a toilet.

LINDA. You louse. You . . .

BIFF. Now you hit it on the nose! (*He gets up, throws the flowers in the wastebasket*) The scum of the earth, and you're looking at him!

LINDA. Get out of here!

BIFF. I gotta talk to the boss, Mom. Where is he?

LINDA. You're not going near him. Get out of this house!

BIFF (*with absolute assurance, determination*). No. We're gonna have an abrupt conversation, him and me.

LINDA. You're not talking to him!

(*Hammering is heard from outside the house, off right. Biff turns toward the noise.*)

LINDA (*suddenly pleading*). Will you please leave him alone?

BIFF. What's he doing out there?

LINDA. He's planting the garden!

BIFF (*quietly*). Now? Oh, my God!

(*Biff moves outside, Linda following. The light dies down on them and comes up on the center of the apron as Willy walks into it. He is carrying a flashlight, a hoe, and a handful of seed packets. He raps the top of the hoe sharply to fix it firmly, and then moves to the left, measuring off the distance with his foot. He holds the flashlight to look at the seed packets, reading off the instructions. He is in the blue of night.*)

WILLY. Carrots . . . quarter-inch apart. Rows . . . one-foot rows. (*He measures it off*) One foot. (*He puts down a package and measures off*) Beets. (*He puts down another package and measures again*) Let-

tuce. (*He reads the package, puts it down*) One foot—(*He breaks off as Ben appears at the right and moves slowly down to him*) What a proposition, ts, ts. Terrific, terrific. 'Cause she's suffered, Ben, the woman has suffered. You understand me? A man can't go out the way he came in, Ben, a man has got to add up to something. You can't, you can't—(*Ben moves toward him as though to interrupt*) You gotta consider, now. Don't answer so quick. Remember, it's a guaranteed twenty-thousand-dollar proposition. Now look, Ben, I want you to go through the ins and outs of this thing with me. I've got nobody to talk to, Ben, and the woman has suffered, you hear me?

BEN (*standing still, considering*). What's the proposition?

WILLY. It's twenty thousand dollars on the barrelhead. Guaranteed, gilt-edged, you understand?

BEN. You don't want to make a fool of yourself. They might not honor the policy.

WILLY. How can they dare refuse? Didn't I work like a coolie to meet every premium on the nose? And now they don't pay off? Impossible!

BEN. It's called a cowardly thing, William.

WILLY. Why? Does it take more guts to stand here the rest of my life ringing up a zero?

BEN (*yielding*). That's a point, William. (*He moves, thinking, turns*) And twenty thousand—that *is* something one can feel with the hand, it is there.

WILLY (*now assured, with rising power*). Oh, Ben, that's the whole beauty of it! I see it like a diamond, shining in the dark, hard and rough, that I can pick up and touch in my hand. Not like—like an appointment! This would not be another damned-fool appointment, Ben, and it changes all the aspects. Because he thinks I'm nothing, see, and so he spites me. But the funeral—(*Straightening up*) Ben, that funeral will be massive! They'll come from Maine, Massachusetts, Vermont, New Hampshire! All the old-timers with the strange license plates—that boy will be thunder-struck, Ben, because he never realized—I am known! Rhode Island, New York, New Jersey—I am known, Ben, and he'll see it with his eyes once and for all. He'll see what I am, Ben! He's in for a shock, that boy!

BEN (*coming down to the edge of the garden*). He'll call you a coward.

WILLY (*suddenly fearful*). No, that would be terrible.

BEN. Yes. And a damned fool.

WILLY. No, no, he mustn't. I won't have that! (*He is broken and desperate*)

BEN. He'll hate you, William.

(*The gay music of the Boys is heard.*)

WILLY. Oh, Ben, how do we get back to all the great times? Used to be so full of light, and comradeship, the sleigh-riding in winter, and the ruddiness on his cheeks. And always some kind of good news coming up, always something nice coming up ahead. And never even let me carry the valises in the house, and simonizing, simonizing that little red car! Why, why can't I give him something and not have him hate me?

BEN. Let me think about it. (*He glances at his watch*) I still have a little time. Remarkable proposition, but you've got to be sure you're not making a fool of yourself. (*Ben drifts off upstage and goes out of sight. Biff comes down from the left.*)

WILLY (*suddenly conscious of Biff, turns and looks up at him, then begins picking up the packages of seeds in confusion*). Where the hell is that seed? (*Indignantly*) You can't see nothing out here! They boxed in the whole goddam neighborhood!

BIFF. There are, people all around here. Don't you realize that?

WILLY. I'm busy. Don't bother me.

BIFF (*taking the hoe from Willy*). I'm saying good-by to you, Pop. (*Willy looks at him, silent, unable to move*) I'm not coming back any more.

WILLY. You're not going to see Oliver tomorrow?

BIFF. I've got no appointment, Dad.

WILLY. He put his arm around you, and you've got no appointment?

BIFF. Pop, get this now, will you? Every-time I've left it's been a fight that sent me out of here. Today I realized something about myself and I tried to explain it to you and I—I think I'm just not smart enough to make any sense out of it for you. To hell with whose fault it is or anything like that. (*He takes Willy's arm*) Let's just wrap it up, heh? Come on in, we'll tell Mom. (*He gently tries to pull Willy to left*)

WILLY (*frozen, immobile, with guilt in his voice*). No, I didn't want to see her.

BIFF. Come on! (*He pulls again, and Willy tries to pull away*)

WILLY (*highly nervous*). No, no, I don't want to see her.

BIFF (*tries to look into Willy's face, as if to find the answer there*). Why don't you want to see her?

WILLY (*more harshly now*). Don't bother me, will you?

BIFF. What do you mean, you don't want to see her? You don't want them calling you yellow, do you? This isn't your fault; it's me, I'm a bum. Now come inside. (*Willy strains to get away*) Did you hear what I said to you?

(*Willy pulls away and quickly goes by himself into the house. Biff follows.*)

LINDA (*to Willy*). Did you plant, dear?

BIFF (*at the door, to Linda*). All right, we had it out. I'm going and I'm not writing any more.

LINDA (*going to Willy in the kitchen*). I think that's the best way, dear. 'Cause there's no use drawing it out, you'll just never get along.

(*Willy doesn't respond.*)

BIFF. People ask where I am and what I'm doing, you don't know, and you don't care. That way it'll be off your mind and you can start brightening up again. All right? That clears it, doesn't it? (*Willy is silent, and Biff goes to him*) You gonna wish me luck, scout? (*He extends his hand*) What do you say?

LINDA. Shake his hand, Willy.

WILLY (*turning to her, seething with hurt*). There's no necessity to mention the pen at all, y'know.

BIFF (*gently*). I've got no appointment, Dad.

WILLY (*erupting fiercely*). He put his arm around . . . ?

BIFF. Dad, you're never going to see what I am, so what's the use of arguing? If I strike oil I'll send you a check. Meantime, forget I'm alive.

WILLY (*to Linda*). Spite, see?

BIFF. Shake hands, Dad.

WILLY. Not my hand.

BIFF. I was hoping not to go this way.

WILLY. Well, this is the way you're going. Good-by.

(*Biff looks at him a moment, then turns sharply and goes to the stairs.*)

WILLY (*stops him with*). May you rot in hell if you leave this house!

BIFF (*turning*). Exactly what is it that you want from me?

WILLY. I want you to know, on the train, in the mountains, in the valleys, wherever you go, that you cut down your life for spite!

BIFF. No, no.

WILLY. Spite, spite, is the word of your undoing! And when you're down and out, remember what did it. When you're rotting somewhere beside the railroad tracks, remember, and don't you dare blame it on me!

BIFF. I'm not blaming it on you!

WILLY. I won't take the rap for this, you hear?

(*Happy comes down the stairs and stands on the bottom step, watching.*)

BIFF. That's just what I'm telling you!

WILLY (*sinking down into a chair at the table, with full accusation*). You're trying to put a knife in me—don't think I don't know what you're doing!

BIFF. All right, phony! Then let's lay it on the line. (*He whips the rubber tube out of his pocket and puts it on the table*)

HAPPY. You crazy—

LINDA. Biff! (*She moves to grab the hose, but Biff holds it down with his hand*)

BIFF. Leave it there! Don't move it!

WILLY (*not looking at it*). What is that?

BIFF. You know goddam well what that is.

WILLY (*caged, wanting to escape*). I never saw that.

BIFF. You saw it. The mice didn't bring it into the cellar! What is this supposed to do, make a hero out of you? This supposed to make me sorry for you?

WILLY. Never heard of it.

BIFF. There'll be no pity for you, you hear it? No pity!

WILLY (*to Linda*). You hear the spite!

BIFF. No, you're going to hear the truth —what you are and what I am!

LINDA. Stop it!

WILLY. Spite!

HAPPY (*coming down toward Biff*). You cut it now!

BIFF (*to Happy*). The man don't know who we are! The man is gonna know! (*To Willy*) We never told the truth for ten minutes in this house!

HAPPY. We always told the truth!

BIFF (*turning on him*). You big blow, are you the assistant buyer? You're one of the two assistants to the assistant, aren't you?

HAPPY. Well, I'm practically—

BIFF. You're practically full of it! We all are! And I'm through with it! (*To Willy*) Now hear this, Willy, this is me.

WILLY. I know you!

BIFF. You know why I had no address for three months? I stole a suit in Kansas City and I was in jail. (*To Linda, who is sobbing*) Stop crying, I'm through with it. (*Linda turns away from them, her hands covering her face.*)

WILLY. I suppose that's my fault!

BIFF. I stole myself out of every good job since high school!

WILLY. And whose fault is that?

BIFF. And I never got anywhere because you blew me so full of hot air I could never stand taking orders from anybody! That's whose fault it is!

WILLY. I hear that!

LINDA. Don't, Biff!

BIFF. It's goddam time you heard that! I had to be boss big shot in two weeks, and I'm through with it!

WILLY. Then hang yourself! For spite, hang yourself!

BIFF. No! Nobody's hanging himself, Willy! I ran down eleven flights with a pen in my hand today. And suddenly I stopped, you hear me? And in the middle of that office building, do you hear this? I stopped in the middle of that building and I saw—the sky. I saw the things that I love in this world. The work and the food and time to sit and smoke. And I looked at the pen and said to myself, what the hell am I grabbing this for? Why am I trying to become what I don't want to be? What am I doing in an office, making a contemptuous, begging fool of myself, when all I want is out there, waiting for me the minute I say I know who I am! Why can't I say that, Willy? (*He tries to make Willy face him, but Willy pulls away and moves to the left*)

WILLY (*with hatred, threateningly*). The door of your life is wide open!

BIFF. Pop, I'm a dime a dozen, and so are you!

WILLY (*turning on him now in an uncontrolled outburst*). I am not a dime a dozen! I am Willy Loman, and you are Biff Loman!

(*Biff starts for Willy, but is blocked by*

Happy. In his fury, Biff seems on the verge of attacking his father.)

BIFF. I am not a leader of men, Willy, and neither are you. You were never anything but a hard-working drummer who landed in the ash can like all the rest of them! I'm one dollar an hour, Willy! I tried seven states and couldn't raise it. A buck an hour! Do you gather my meaning? I'm not bringing home any prizes any more, and you're going to stop waiting for me to bring them home!

WILLY (*directly to Biff*). You vengeful, spiteful mutt!

(*Biff breaks from Happy. Willy, in fright, starts up the stairs. Biff grabs him.*)

BIFF (*at the peak of his fury*). Pop, I'm nothing! I'm nothing, Pop. Can't you understand that? There's no spite in it any more. I'm just what I am, that's all.

(*Biff's fury has spent itself, and he breaks down, sobbing, holding on to Willy, who dumbly fumbles for Biff's face.*)

WILLY (*astonished*). What're you doing? What're you doing? (*To Linda*) Why is he crying?

BIFF (*crying, broken*). Will you let me go, for Christ's sake? Will you take that phony dream and burn it before something happens? (*Struggling to contain himself, he pulls away and moves to the stairs*) I'll go in the morning. Put him—put him to bed. (*Exhausted, Biff moves up the stairs to his room*)

WILLY (*after a long pause, astonished, elevated*). Isn't that—isn't that remarkable? Biff—he likes me!

LINDA. He loves you, Willy.

HAPPY (*deeply moved*). Always did, Pop.

WILLY. Oh, Biff! (*Staring wildly*) He cried! Cried to me. (*He is choking with his love, and now cries out his promise*) That boy—that boy is going to be magnificent!

(*Ben appears in the light just outside the kitchen.*)

BEN. Yes, outstanding, with twenty thousand behind him.

LINDA (*sensing the racing of his mind, fearfully, carefully*). Now come to bed, Willy. It's all settled now.

WILLY (*finding it difficult not to rush out of the house*). Yes, we'll sleep. Come on. Go to sleep, Hap.

BEN. And it does take a great kind of a man to crack the jungle.

(*In accents of dread, Ben's idyllic music starts up.*)

HAPPY (*his arm around Linda*). I'm getting married, Pop, don't forget it. I'm changing everything. I'm gonna run that department before the year is up. You'll see, Mom. (*He kisses her*)

BEN. The jungle is dark but full of diamonds, Willy.

(*Willy turns, moves, listening to Ben.*)

LINDA. Be good. You're both good boys, just act that way, that's all.

HAPPY. 'Night, Pop. (*He goes upstairs*)

LINDA (*to Willy*). Come, dear.

BEN (*with greater force*). One must go in to fetch a diamond out.

WILLY (*to Linda, as he moves slowly along the edge of the kitchen, toward the door*). I just want to get settled down, Linda. Let me sit alone for a little.

LINDA (*almost uttering her fear*). I want you upstairs.

WILLY (*taking her in his arms*). In a few minutes, Linda. I couldn't sleep right now. Go on, you look awful tired. (*He kisses her*)

BEN. Not like an appointment at all. A diamond is rough and hard to the touch.

WILLY. Go on now. I'll be right up.

LINDA. I think this is the only way, Willy.

WILLY. Sure, it's the best thing.

BEN. Best thing!

WILLY. The only way. Everything is gonna be—go on, kid, get to bed. You look so tired.

LINDA. Come right up.

WILLY. Two minutes.

(*Linda goes into the living-room, then reappears in her bedroom. Willy moves just outside the kitchen door.*)

WILLY. Loves me. (*Wonderingly*) Always loved me. Isn't that a remarkable thing? Ben, he'll worship me for it!

BEN (*with promise*). It's dark there, but full of diamonds.

WILLY. Can you imagine that magnificence with twenty thousand dollars in his pocket?

LINDA (*calling from her room*). Willy! Come up!

WILLY (*calling into the kitchen*). Yes! Yes. Coming! It's very smart, you realize that, don't you, sweetheart? Even Ben sees it. I gotta go, baby. 'By! 'By! (*Going over to Ben, almost dancing*) Imagine? When the mail comes he'll be ahead of Bernard again!

BEN. A perfect proposition all around.

WILLY. Did you see how he cried to me? Oh, if I could kiss him, Ben!

BEN. Time, William, time!

WILLY. Oh, Ben, I always knew one way or another we were gonna make it, Biff and I!

BEN (*looking at his watch*). The boat. We'll be late. (*He moves slowly off into the darkness*)

WILLY (*elegiacally, turning to the house*). Now when you kick off, boy, I want a seventy-yard boot, and get right down the field under the ball, and when you hit, hit low and hit hard, because it's important, boy. (*He swings around and faces the audience*) There's all kinds of important people in the stands, and the first thing you know . . . (*Suddenly realizing he is alone*) Ben, Ben, where do I . . . ? (*He makes a sudden movement of search*) Ben, how do I . . .?

LINDA (*calling*). Willy, you coming up?

WILLY (*uttering a gasp of fear, whirling about as if to quiet her*). Sh! (*He turns around as if to find his way; sounds, faces, voices seem to be swarming in upon him and he flicks at them, crying*) Sh! Sh! (*Suddenly music, faint and high, stops him. It rises in intensity, almost to an unbearable scream. He goes up and down on his toes, and rushes off around the house*) Shhh!

LINDA. Willy?

(*There is no answer. Linda waits. Biff gets up off his bed. He is still in his clothes. Happy sits up. Biff stands listening.*)

LINDA (*with real fear*). Willy, answer me! Willy!

(*There is the sound of a car starting and moving away at full speed.*)

LINDA. No!

BIFF (*rushing down the stairs*). Pop!

(*As the car speeds off, the music crashes down in a frenzy of sound, which becomes the soft pulsation of a single cello string. Biff slowly returns to his bedroom. He and Happy gravely don their jackets. Linda slowly walks out of her room. The music has developed into a death march. The leaves of day are appearing over everything. Charley and Bernard, somberly dressed, appear and knock on the kitchen door. Biff and Happy slowly descend the stairs to the kitchen as Charley and Ber-*

nard enter. All stop a moment when Linda, in clothes of mourning, bearing a little bunch of roses, comes through the draped doorway into the kitchen. She goes to Charley and takes his arm. Now all move toward the audience, through the wall-line of the kitchen. At the limit of the apron, Linda lays down the flowers, kneels, and sits back on her heels. All stare down at the grave.)

REQUIEM

CHARLEY. It's getting dark, Linda.

(*Linda doesn't react. She stares at the grave.*)

BIFF. How about it, Mom? Better get some rest, heh? They'll be closing the gate soon.

(*Linda makes no move. Pause.*)

HAPPY (*deeply angered*). He had no right to do that. There was no necessity for it. We would've helped him.

CHARLEY (*grunting*). Hmmm.

BIFF. Come along, Mom.

LINDA. Why didn't anybody come?

CHARLEY. It was a very nice funeral.

LINDA. But where are all the people he knew? Maybe they blame him.

CHARLEY. Naa. It's a rough world, Linda. They wouldn't blame him.

LINDA. I can't understand it. At this time especially. First time in thirty-five years we were just about free and clear. He only needed a little salary. He was even finished with the dentist.

CHARLEY. No man only needs a little salary.

LINDA. I can't understand it.

BIFF. There were a lot of nice days. When he'd come home from a trip; or on Sundays, making the stoop; finishing the cellar; putting on the new porch; when he built the extra bathroom; and put up the garage. You know something, Charley, there's more of him in that front stoop than in all the sales he ever made.

CHARLEY. Yeah, he was a happy man with a batch of cement.

LINDA. He was so wonderful with his hands.

BIFF. He had the wrong dreams. All, all, wrong.

HAPPY (*almost ready to fight Biff*). Don't say that!

BIFF. He never knew who he was.

CHARLEY (*stopping Happy's movement and reply. To Biff*). Nobody dast blame this man. You don't understand: Willy was a salesman. And for a salesman, there is no rock bottom to the life. He don't put a bolt to a nut, he don't tell you the law or give you medicine. He's the man way out there in the blue riding on a smile and a shoeshine. And when they start not smiling back—that's an earthquake. And then you get yourself a couple of spots on your hat, and you're finished. Nobody dast blame this man. A salesman is got to dream, boy. It comes with the territory.

BIFF. Charley, the man didn't know who he was.

HAPPY (*infuriated*). Don't say that!

BIFF. Why don't you come with me, Happy?

HAPPY. I'm not licked that easily. I'm staying right in this city, and I'm gonna beat this racket! (*He looks at Biff, his chin set*) The Loman Brothers!

BIFF. I know who I am, kid.

HAPPY. All right, boy. I'm gonna show you and everybody else that Willy Loman did not die in vain. He had a good dream. It's the only dream you can have—to come out number-one man. He fought it out here, and this is where I'm gonna win it for him.

BIFF (*with a hopeless glance at Happy, bends toward his mother*). Let's go, Mom.

LINDA. I'll be with you in a minute. Go on, Charley. (*He hesitates*) I want to, just for a minute. I never had a chance to say good-by.

(*Charley moves away, followed by Happy. Biff remains a slight distance up and left of Linda. She sits there, summoning herself. The flute begins, not far away, playing behind her speech.*)

LINDA. Forgive me, dear. I can't cry. I don't know what it is, but I can't cry. I don't understand it. Why did you ever do that? Help me, Willy, I can't cry. It seems to me that you're just on another trip. I keep expecting you. Willy, dear, I can't cry. Why did you do it? I search and search and I search, and I can't understand it, Willy. I made the last payment on the house today. Today, dear. And there'll be nobody home. (*A sob rises in her throat*) We're free and clear. (*Sobbing more fully, released*) We're free. (*Biff comes slowly toward her*) We're free . . . We're free . . . (*Biff lifts her to her feet and moves right with her in his arms. Linda sobs quietly. Bernard and Charley come together and follow them, followed by Happy. Only the music of the flute is left on the darkening stage as over the house the hard towers of the apartment buildings rise into sharp focus, and*)

THE CURTAIN FALLS

A Streetcar Named Desire

BY TENNESSEE WILLIAMS

First presented by Irene Selznick at the Barrymore Theatre in New York on December 3, 1947, with the following cast:

NEGRO WOMAN............................Gee Gee James		MEXICAN WOMAN........................Edna Thomas	
EUNICE HUBBELL.............................Peg Hillias		BLANCHE DUBOIS.........................Jessica Tandy	
STANLEY KOWALSKI.................Marlon Brando		PABLO GONZALES............................Nick Dennis	
STELLA KOWALSKI........................Kim Hunter		A YOUNG COLLECTOR....................Vito Christi	
STEVE HUBBELL..............................Rudy Bond		NURSE ....Ann Dere	
HAROLD MITCHELL (MITCH)......Karl Malden		DOCTOR ....Richard Garrick	

The action of the play takes place in the spring, summer, and early fall in New Orleans. It was performed with intermissions after Scene Four and Scene Six.

WHEN Tennessee Williams' *A Streetcar Named Desire* appeared on the Broadway scene, its critics could barely restrain their admiration for its raw emotional power. Only George Jean Nathan refused to be impressed—perversely, it seemed. John Mason Brown spoke for the strong majority opinion when he called the play "the most probing script to have been written by an American since Clifford Odets wrote *Awake and Sing!*" Brooks Atkinson acclaimed "Mr. Williams' baleful insight into character, his ruthlessness as an observer and his steel-like accuracy as a writer." Other virtues found in the author's artistry were "lyricism" and ability "to evoke mood and transcend realism." John Mason Brown referred to him as a "good Chekhovian." In rebuttal, it could be noted that a considerable portion of the drama was produced by external and not altogether inevitable circumstances. It could also be noted that the play, so tragical in tone and mood, fell short of tragic elevation; that Blanche's story was a singular clinical case rather than a fundamentally representative, "universal" drama. Nevertheless, the play continued to exert a spell over audiences for a long time, and it was appreciated on grounds other than mere sensationalism even when it could not be endorsed as high tragedy.

Atkinson defined *A Streetcar Named Desire* as a play about "an unequal contest between the decadence of a self-conscious civilization and the vitality of animal aimlessness"; and somewhat more accurately, as the drama of a gentlewoman's "panicky flight from the catastrophe of a genteel way of life that can no longer sustain her in an animalized world." This much is certain: There was a substantial, if not absolutely formulable, residuum of meaning in the experience that harrowed the playgoer. The play communicated a sense of crass fatality; of life destroyed by frustration in love, against which pretensions and illusions are a pathetic and futile defense. The epigraph Williams chose from Hart Crane's *The Broken Tower* (Williams belongs to the avant-garde school that favors epigraphs as well as symbols) may speak for his own intentions. It expresses much the same realization of the fragility of love and the same hunger of the soul in a far from clement world that Blanche experiences:

> And so it was I entered the broken world
> To trace the visionary company of love, its voice
> An instant in the wind (I know not whither hurled)
> But not for long to hold each desperate choice.

Not invulnerable to criticism, *A Streetcar Named Desire* nonetheless towered over most of the plays written for the American theatre during the decade of the forties.

Williams was only thirty-three years old when he presented this work after the notable production of *The Glass Menagerie*. Born in 1914 in Columbus, Mississippi, Thomas Lanier ("Tennessee") Williams grew up in the South, for the most part in St. Louis, in a household that introduced him to the struggles of unsheltered gentility. His maternal grandfather, an Episcopalian clergyman, helped to shape his mind and gave him a taste for literature; he also took the impressionable lad on consolatory visits to members of his flock, among whom Williams saw prototypes of the pathetic women of his plays. His sister, to whom he was devoted, had the sort of delicate, vulnerable soul that he was later to represent in these plays, and, like them, suffered mental shipwreck. His father was a none too prosperous shoe salesman who wanted the sensitive lad to earn a living as soon as possible. He went on to the University of Washington, St. Louis, in 1931, but left college after his sophomore year. He worked for two years in the shoe factory that employed his father but after a nervous collapse caused by feverish attempts to write late at night, he returned to college in 1936 and acquired a degree from the University of Iowa. Then came lean years of roving through the South, working at odd jobs, and ushering at a motion picture theatre in New York and performing as a singing waiter in Greenwich Village.

Continuing to write poetry, stories, and plays, Williams, however, found a loyal and energetic play agent, Audrey Wood of the Liebling-Wood office. With Miss Wood's help he won a small cash prize in 1939 from the Group Theatre with four one-act plays on Depression period themes entitled *American Blues,* and in 1940 a scholarship from Theresa Helburn and John Gassner to their seminar for promising playwrights. At the end of the spring semester he submitted his full-length drama of small-town life, *Battle of Angels,* to them. They bought it for the Theatre Guild, and the play went into rehearsal under the direction of Margaret Webster and the supervision of Lawrence Langner, the Guild's co-director.

The "out-of-town" tryout in Boston was disastrous, but fortunately Williams was sustained by American Academy of Arts and Rockefeller Foundation awards and fellowships until the Eddie Dowling production of *The Glass Menagerie* in 1945 gave him material as well as critical success. His collaboration on the dramatization of a D. H. Lawrence short story, *You Touched Me,* was produced less successfully in 1946, but a year later *A Streetcar Named Desire* secured his place in the American theatre. Although his next play, *Summer and Smoke* (see page 665), failed on Broadway, he had another successful production with *The Rose Tattoo* in the season of 1949-50. Williams also published a collection of his one-act plays entitled *27 Wagons Full of Cotton and Other Plays* in 1945, and several of these have been considered well worth staging. The range of his talent was further established by a collection of short stories and a novel. To date, however, it is his plays that ensure him a position in American letters.

SCENE ONE

The exterior of a two-story corner building on a street in New Orleans which is named Elysian Fields and runs between the L & N tracks and the river. The section is poor but, unlike corresponding sections in other American cities, it has a raffish charm. The houses are mostly white frame, weathered gray, with rickety outside stairs and galleries and quaintly ornamented gables. This building contains two flats, upstairs and down. Faded white stairs ascend to the entrances of both.

It is first dark of an evening early in May. The sky that shows around the dim white building is a peculiarly tender blue, almost a turquoise, which invests the scene with a kind of lyricism and gracefully attenuates the atmosphere of decay. You can almost feel the warm breath of the brown river beyond the river warehouses with their faint redolences of bananas and coffee. A corresponding air is evoked by the music of Negro entertainers at a barroom around the corner. In this part of New Orleans you are practically always just around the corner, or a few doors down the street, from a tinny piano being played with the infatuated fluency of brown fingers. This "blue piano" expresses the spirit of the life which goes on here.

Two women, one white and one colored, are taking the air on the steps of the building. The white woman is Eunice, who occupies the upstairs flat; the colored woman a neighbor, for New Orleans is a cosmopolitan city where there is a relatively warm and easy intermingling of races in the old part of town.

Above the music of the "blue piano" the voices of people on the street can be heard overlapping.

———

(Two men come around the corner, Stanley Kowalski and Mitch. They are about twenty-eight or thirty years old, roughly dressed in blue denim work clothes. Stanley carries his bowling jacket and a red-stained package from a butcher's. They stop at the foot of the steps.)

STANLEY *(bellowing)*. Hey, there! Stella, baby!

(Stella comes out on the first floor landing, a gentle young woman, about twenty-five, and of a background obviously quite different from her husband's.)

STELLA *(mildly)*. Don't holler at me like that. Hi, Mitch.

STANLEY. Catch!

STELLA. What?

STANLEY. Meat!

(He heaves the package at her. She cries out in protest but manages to catch it: then she laughs breathlessly. Her husband and his companion have already started back around the corner.)

STELLA *(calling after him)*. Stanley! Where are you going?

STANLEY. Bowling!

STELLA. Can I come watch?

STANLEY. Come on. *(He goes out)*

STELLA. Be over soon. *(To the white woman)* Hello, Eunice. How are you?

EUNICE. I'm all right. Tell Steve to get him a poor boy's sandwich 'cause nothing's left here.

(They all laugh; the colored woman does not stop. Stella goes out.)

NEGRO WOMAN. What was that package he th'ew at 'er? *(She rises from steps, laughing louder)*

EUNICE. You hush, now!

NEGRO WOMAN. Catch *what!*

(She continues to laugh. Blanche comes around the corner, carrying a valise. She looks at a slip of paper, then at the building, then again at the slip and again at the building. Her expression is one of shocked disbelief. Her appearance is incongruous in this setting. She is daintily dressed in a white suit with a fluffy bodice, necklace and earrings of pearl, white gloves and hat, looking as if she were arriving at a summer tea or cocktail party in the garden district. She is about five years older than Stella. Her delicate beauty must avoid a strong light. There is something about her uncertain manner, as well as her white clothes, that suggests a moth.)

EUNICE *(finally)*. What's the matter, honey? Are you lost?

BLANCHE *(with faintly hysterical humor)*. They told me to take a streetcar named Desire, and then transfer to one called Cemeteries and ride six blocks and get off at—Elysian Fields!

EUNICE. That's where you are now.

BLANCHE. At Elysian Fields?

EUNICE. This here is Elysian Fields.

BLANCHE. They mustn't have—understood—what number I wanted . . .

EUNICE. What number you lookin' for?

(Blanche wearily refers to the slip of paper.)

BLANCHE. Six thirty-two.

EUNICE. You don't have to look no further.

BLANCHE *(uncomprehendingly)*. I'm looking for my sister, Stella DuBois. I mean—Mrs. Stanley Kowalski.

EUNICE. That's the party.—You just did miss her, though.

BLANCHE. This—can this be—her home?

EUNICE. She's got the downstairs here and I got the up.

BLANCHE. Oh. She's—out?

EUNICE. You noticed that bowling alley around the corner?

BLANCHE. I'm—not sure I did.

EUNICE. Well, that's where she's at, watchin' her husband bowl. *(There is a pause)* You want to leave your suitcase here an' go find her?

BLANCHE. No.

NEGRO WOMAN. I'll go tell her you come.

BLANCHE. Thanks.

NEGRO WOMAN. You welcome. *(She goes out)*

EUNICE. She wasn't expecting you?

BLANCHE. No. No, not tonight.

EUNICE. Well, why don't you just go in and make yourself at home till they get back.

BLANCHE. How could I—do that?

EUNICE. We own this place so I can let you in.

(She gets up and opens the downstairs door. A light goes on behind the blind, turning it light blue. Blanche slowly follows her into the downstairs flat. The surrounding areas dim out as the interior is lighted.

(Two rooms can be seen, not too clearly defined. The one first entered is primarily a kitchen but contains a folding bed to be used by Blanche. The room beyond this is a bedroom. Off this room is a narrow door to a bathroom.)

EUNICE *(defensively, noticing Blanche's look)*. It's sort of messed up right now but when it's clean it's real sweet.

BLANCHE. Is it?

EUNICE. Uh-huh, I think so. So you're Stella's sister?

BLANCHE. Yes. *(Wanting to get rid of her)* Thanks for letting me in.

EUNICE. *Por nada,* as the Mexicans say, *por nada!* Stella spoke of you.

BLANCHE. Yes?

EUNICE. I think she said you taught school.

BLANCHE. Yes.

EUNICE. And you're from Mississippi, huh?

BLANCHE. Yes.

EUNICE. She showed me a picture of your home-place, the plantation.

BLANCHE. Belle Reve?

EUNICE. A great big place with white columns.

BLANCHE. Yes . . .

EUNICE. A place like that must be awful hard to keep up.

BLANCHE. If you will excuse me, I'm just about to drop.

EUNICE. Sure, honey. Why don't you set down?

BLANCHE. What I meant was I'd like to be left alone.

EUNICE *(offended)*. Aw. I'll make myself scarce, in that case.

BLANCHE. I didn't mean to be rude, but—

EUNICE. I'll drop by the bowling alley an' hustle her up. *(She goes out the door)*

(Blanche sits in a chair very stiffly with her shoulders slightly hunched and her legs pressed close together and her hands tightly clutching her purse as if she were quite cold. After a while the blind look goes out of her eyes and she begins to look slowly around. A cat screeches. She catches her breath with a startled gesture. Suddenly she notices something in a half opened closet. She springs up and crosses to it, and removes a whiskey bottle. She pours a half tumbler of whiskey and tosses it down. She carefully replaces the bottle and washes out the tumbler at the sink. Then she resumes her seat in front of the table.)

BLANCHE *(faintly to herself)*. I've got to keep hold of myself!

(Stella comes quickly around the corner of the building and runs to the door of the downstairs flat.)

STELLA *(calling out joyfully)*. Blanche!

(For a moment they stare at each other. Then Blanche springs up and runs to her with a wild cry.)

BLANCHE. Stella, oh, Stella, Stella! Stella for Star!

(She begins to speak with feverish vivacity as if she feared for either of them to stop and think. They catch each other in a spasmodic embrace.)

BLANCHE. Now, then, let me look at you. But don't you look at me, Stella, no, no, no, not till later, not till I've bathed and rested! And turn that over-light off! Turn that off! I won't be looked at in this merciless glare! *(Stella laughs and complies)* Come back here now! Oh, my baby! Stella! Stella for Star! *(She embraces her again)* I thought you would never come back to this horrible place! What am I saying? I didn't mean to say that. I meant to be nice about it and say—Oh, what a convenient location and such—Ha-a-ha! Precious lamb! You haven't said a *word* to me.

STELLA. You haven't given me a chance to, honey! *(She laughs, but her glance at Blanche is a little anxious)*

BLANCHE. Well, now you talk. Open your pretty mouth and talk while I look around for some liquor! I know you must have some liquor on the place! Where could it be, I wonder? Oh, I spy, I spy! *(She rushes to the closet and removes the bottle; she is shaking all over and panting for breath as she tries to laugh. The bottle nearly slips from her grasp.)*

STELLA *(noticing)*. Blanche, you sit down and let me pour the drinks. I don't know what we've got to mix with. Maybe a coke's in the icebox. Look'n see, honey, while I'm —

BLANCHE. No coke, honey, not with my nerves tonight— Where—where—where is—?

STELLA. Stanley? Bowling! He loves it. They're having a—found some soda!—tournament . . .

BLANCHE. Just water, baby, to chase it! Now don't get worried, your sister hasn't turned into a drunkard, she's just all shaken up and hot and tired and dirty! You sit down, now, and explain this place to me! What are you doing in a place like this?

STELLA. Now, Blanche—

BLANCHE. Oh, I'm not going to be hypocritical, I'm going to be honestly critical about it! Never, never, never in my worst dreams could I picture— Only Poe! Only Mr. Edgar Allan Poe!—could do it justice! Out there I suppose is the ghoul-haunted woodland of Weir! *(She laughs)*

STELLA. No, honey, those are the L & N tracks.

BLANCHE. No, now seriously, putting joking aside. Why didn't you tell me, why didn't you write me, honey, why didn't you let me know?

STELLA *(carefully, pouring herself a drink)*. Tell you what, Blanche?

BLANCHE. Why, that you had to live in these conditions!

STELLA. Aren't you being a little intense about it? It's not that bad at all! New Orleans isn't like other cities.

BLANCHE. This has got nothing to do with New Orleans. You might as well say —forgive me, blessed baby! *(She suddenly stops short)* The subject is closed!

STELLA *(a little drily)*. Thanks.

(During the pause, Blanche stares at her. She smiles at Blanche.)

BLANCHE *(looking down at her glass, which shakes in her hand)*. You're all I've got in the world, and you're not glad to see me!

STELLA *(sincerely)*. Why, Blanche, you know that's not true.

BLANCHE. No?—I'd forgotten how quiet you were.

STELLA. You never did give me a chance to say much, Blanche. So I just got in the habit of being quiet around you.

BLANCHE *(vaguely)*. A good habit to get into . . . *(Then, abruptly)* You haven't asked me how I happened to get away from the school before the spring term ended.

STELLA. Well, I thought you'd volunteer that information—if you wanted to tell me.

BLANCHE. You thought I'd been fired?

STELLA. No, I—thought you might have —resigned . . .

BLANCHE. I was so exhausted by all I'd been through my—nerves broke. *(Nervously tamping cigarette)* I was on the verge of—lunacy, almost! So Mr. Graves— Mr. Graves is the high school superintendent—he suggested I take a leave of absence. I couldn't put all of those details into the wire . . . *(She drinks quickly)* Oh, this buzzes right through me and feels so *good*!

STELLA. Won't you have another?

BLANCHE. No, one's my limit.

STELLA. Sure?

BLANCHE. You haven't said a word about my appearance.

STELLA. You look just fine.

BLANCHE. God love you for a liar! Daylight never exposed so total a ruin! But you—you've put on some weight, yes, you're just as plump as a little partridge! And it's so becoming to you!

STELLA. Now, Blanche—

BLANCHE. Yes, it is, it is or I wouldn't say it! You just have to watch around the hips a little. Stand up.

STELLA. Not now.

BLANCHE. You hear me? I said stand up! *(Stella complies reluctantly)* You messy child, you, you've spilt something on that pretty white lace collar! About your hair— you ought to have it cut in a feather bob with your dainty features. Stella, you have a maid, don't you?

STELLA. No. With only two rooms it's—

BLANCHE. What? *Two* rooms, did you say?

STELLA. This one and—*(She is embarrassed)*

BLANCHE. The other one? *(She laughs sharply. There is an embarrassed silence)* I am going to take just one little tiny nip more, sort of to put the stopper on, so to speak. . . . Then put the bottle away so I won't be tempted. *(She rises)* I want you to look at *my* figure! *(She turns around)* You know I haven't put on one ounce in ten years, Stella? I weigh what I weighed the summer you left Belle Reve. The summer Dad died and you left us . . .

STELLA *(a little wearily)*. It's just incredible, Blanche, how well you're looking.

BLANCHE *(they both laugh uncomfortably)*. But, Stella, there's only two rooms, I don't see where you're going to put me!

STELLA. We're going to put you in here.

BLANCHE. What kind of bed's this—one of those collapsible things? *(She sits on it)*

STELLA. Does it feel all right?

BLANCHE *(dubiously)*. Wonderful, honey. I don't like a bed that gives much. But there's no door between the two rooms, and Stanley—will it be decent?

STELLA. Stanley is Polish, you know.

BLANCHE. Oh, yes. They're something like Irish, aren't they?

STELLA. Well—

BLANCHE. Only not so—highbrow? *(They both laugh again in the same way)* I brought some nice clothes to meet all your lovely friends in.

STELLA. I'm afraid you won't think they are lovely.

BLANCHE. What are they like?

STELLA. They're Stanley's friends.

BLANCHE. Polacks?

STELLA. They're a mixed lot, Blanche.

BLANCHE. Heterogeneous—types?

STELLA. Oh, yes. Yes, types is right!

BLANCHE. Well—anyhow—I brought nice clothes and I'll wear them. I guess you're hoping I'll say I'll put up at a hotel, but I'm not going to put up at a hotel. I want to be *near* you, got to be *with* somebody, I *can't* be *alone!* Because—as you must have noticed—I'm—*not* very *well* . . . *(Her voice drops and her look is frightened)*

STELLA. You seem a little bit nervous or overwrought or something.

BLANCHE. Will Stanley like me, or will I be just a visiting in-law, Stella? I couldn't stand that.

STELLA. You'll get along fine together, if you'll just try not to—well—compare him with men that we went out with at home.

BLANCHE. Is he so—different?

STELLA. Yes. A different species.

BLANCHE. In what way; what's he like?

STELLA. Oh, you can't describe someone you're in love with! Here's a picture of him! *(She hands a photograph to Blanche)*

BLANCHE. An officer?

STELLA. A Master Sergeant in the Engineers' Corps. Those are decorations!

BLANCHE. He had those on when you met him?

STELLA. I assure you I wasn't just blinded by all the brass.

BLANCHE. That's not what I—

STELLA. But of course there were things to adjust myself to later on.

BLANCHE. Such as his civilian background! *(Stella laughs uncertainly)* How did he take it when you said I was coming?

STELLA. Oh, Stanley doesn't know yet.

BLANCHE *(frightened)*. You—haven't told him?

STELLA. He's on the road a good deal.

BLANCHE. Oh. Travels?

STELLA. Yes.

BLANCHE. Good. I mean—isn't it?

STELLA *(half to herself)*. I can hardly stand it when he is away for a night . . .

BLANCHE. Why, Stella!

STELLA. When he's away for a week I nearly go wild!

BLANCHE. Gracious!

STELLA. And when he comes back I cry on his lap like a baby . . . *(She smiles to herself)*

BLANCHE. I guess that is what is meant by being in love . . . (*Stella looks up with a radiant smile*) Stella—

STELLA. What?

BLANCHE (*in an uneasy rush*). I haven't asked you the things you probably thought I was going to ask. And so I'll expect you to be understanding about what *I* have to tell *you*.

STELLA. What, Blanche? (*Her face turns anxious*)

BLANCHE. Well, Stella—you're going to reproach me, I know that you're bound to reproach me—but before you do—take into consideration—you left! I stayed and struggled! You came to New Orleans and looked out for yourself! I stayed at Belle Reve and tried to hold it together! I'm not meaning this in any reproachful way, but *all* the burden descended on *my* shoulders.

STELLA. The best I could do was make my own living, Blanche.

(*Blanche begins to shake again with intensity.*)

BLANCHE. I know, I know. But you are the one that abandoned Belle Reve, not I! I stayed and fought for it, bled for it, almost died for it!

STELLA. Stop this hysterical outburst and tell me what's happened? What do you mean fought and bled? What kind of—

BLANCHE. I knew you would, Stella. I knew you would take this attitude about it!

STELLA. About—what?—please!

BLANCHE (*slowly*). The loss—the loss . . .

STELLA. Belle Reve? Lost, is it? No!

BLANCHE. Yes, Stella.

(*They stare at each other across the yellow-checked linoleum of the table. Blanche slowly nods her head and Stella looks slowly down at her hands folded on the table. The music of the "blue piano" grows louder. Blanche touches her handkerchief to her forehead.*)

STELLA. But how did it go? What happened?

BLANCHE (*springing up*). You're a fine one to ask me how it went!

STELLA. Blanche!

BLANCHE. You're a fine one to sit there *accusing me* of it!

STELLA. *Blanche!*

BLANCHE. I, I, *I* took the blows in my face and my body! All of those deaths! The long parade to the graveyard! Father, mother! Margaret, that dreadful way! So big with it, it couldn't be put in a coffin! But had to be burned like rubbish! You just came home in time for the funerals, Stella. And funerals are pretty compared to deaths. Funerals are quiet, but deaths—not always. Sometimes their breathing is hoarse, and sometimes it rattles, and sometimes they even cry out to you, "Don't let me go!" Even the old, sometimes, say, "Don't let me go." As if you were able to stop them! But funerals are quiet, with pretty flowers. And, oh, what gorgeous boxes they pack them away in! Unless you were there at the bed when they cried out, "Hold me!" you'd never suspect there was the struggle for breath and bleeding. You didn't dream, but I saw! *Saw! Saw!* And now you sit there telling me with your eyes that I let the place go! How in hell do you think all that sickness and dying was paid for? Death is expensive, Miss Stella! And old Cousin Jessie's right after Margaret's, hers! Why, the Grim Reaper had put up his tent on our doorstep! . . . Stella. Belle Reve was his headquarters! Honey—that's how it slipped through my fingers! Which of them left us a fortune? Which of them left a cent of insurance even? Only poor Jessie—one hundred to pay for her coffin. That was all, Stella! And I with my pitiful salary at the school. Yes, accuse me! Sit there and stare at me, thinking I let the place go! *I* let the place go? Where were *you!* In bed with your—Polack!

STELLA (*springing*). Blanche! You be still! That's enough! (*She starts out*)

BLANCHE. Where are you going?

STELLA. I'm going into the bathroom to wash my face.

BLANCHE. Oh, Stella, Stella, you're crying!

STELLA. Does that surprise you?

BLANCHE. Forgive me—I didn't mean to—

(*The sound of men's voices is heard. Stella goes into the bathroom, closing the door behind her. When the men appear, and Blanche realizes it must be Stanley returning, she moves uncertainly from the bathroom door to the dressing table, looking apprehensively towards the front door. Stanley enters, followed by Steve and Mitch. Stanley pauses near his door, Steve by the foot of the spiral stair, and Mitch is slightly above and to the right of them,*) *about to go out. As the men enter, we hear some of the following dialogue.)*

STANLEY. Is that how he got it?

STEVE. Sure that's how he got it. He hit the old weather-bird for 300 bucks on a six-number-ticket.

MITCH. Don't tell him those things; he'll believe it.

(Mitch starts out.)

STANLEY *(restraining Mitch)*. Hey, Mitch—come back here.

(Blanche, at the sound of voices, retires in the bedroom. She picks up Stanley's photo from dressing table, looks at it, puts it down. When Stanley enters the apartment, she darts and hides behind the screen at the head of bed.)

STEVE *(to Stanley and Mitch)*. Hey, are we playin' poker tomorrow?

STANLEY. Sure—at Mitch's.

MITCH *(hearing this, returns quickly to the stair rail)*. No—not at my place. My mother's still sick!

STANLEY. Okay, at my place . . . *(Mitch starts out again)* But you bring the beer! *(Mitch pretends not to hear—calls out "Goodnight all," and goes out, singing. Eunice's voice is heard, above.)*

EUNICE. Break it up down there! I made the spaghetti dish and ate it myself.

STEVE *(going upstairs)*. I told you and phoned you we was playing. *(To the men)* Jax beer!

EUNICE. You never phoned me once.

STEVE. I told you at breakfast—and phoned you at lunch . . .

EUNICE. Well, never mind about that. You just get yourself home here once in a while.

STEVE. You want it in the papers?

(More laughter and shouts of parting come from the men. Stanley throws the screen door of the kitchen open and comes in. He is of medium height, about five feet eight or nine, and strongly, compactly built. Animal joy in his being is implicit in all his movements and attitudes. Since earliest manhood the center of his life has been pleasure with women, the giving and taking of it, not with weak indulgence, dependently, but with the power and pride of a richly feathered male bird among hens. Branching out from this complete and satisfying center are all the auxiliary channels of his life, such as his heartiness with men, his appreciation of rough humor, his love of good drink and food and games, his car, his radio, everything that is his, that bears his emblem of the gaudy seed-bearer. He sizes women up at a glance, with sexual classification, crude images flashing into his mind and determining the way he smiles at them.)

BLANCHE *(drawing involuntarily back from his stare)*. You must be Stanley. I'm Blanche.

STANLEY. Stella's sister?

BLANCHE. Yes.

STANLEY. H'lo. Where's the little woman?

BLANCHE. In the bathroom.

STANLEY. Oh. Didn't know you were coming in town.

BLANCHE. I—uh—

STANLEY. Where you from, Blanche?

BLANCHE. Why, I—live in Laurel.

(He has crossed to the closet and removed the whiskey bottle.)

STANLEY. In Laurel, huh? Oh, yeah. Yeah, in Laurel, that's right. Not in my territory. Liquor goes fast in hot weather. *(He holds the bottle to the light to observe its depletion)* Have a shot?

BLANCHE. No, I—rarely touch it.

STANLEY. Some people rarely touch it, but it touches them often.

BLANCHE *(faintly)*. Ha-ha.

STANLEY. My clothes're stickin' to me. Do you mind if I make myself comfortable? *(He starts to remove his shirt)*

BLANCHE. Please, please do.

STANLEY. Be comfortable is my motto.

BLANCHE. It's mine, too. It's hard to stay looking fresh. I haven't washed or even powdered my face and—here you are!

STANLEY. You know you can catch cold sitting around in damp things, especially when you been exercising hard like bowling is. You're a teacher, aren't you?

BLANCHE. Yes.

STANLEY. What do you teach, Blanche?

BLANCHE. English.

STANLEY. I never was a very good English student. How long you here for, Blanche?

BLANCHE. I—don't know yet.

STANLEY. You going to shack up here?

BLANCHE. I thought I would if it's not inconvenient for you all.

STANLEY. Good.

BLANCHE. Traveling wears me out.

STANLEY. Well, take it easy.

(A cat screeches near the window. Blanche springs up.)

BLANCHE. What's that?

STANLEY. Cats . . . Hey, Stella!

STELLA (*faintly, from the bathroom*). Yes, Stanley.

STANLEY. Haven't fallen in, have you? (*He grins at Blanche. She tries unsuccessfully to smile back. There is a silence*) I'm afraid I'll strike you as being the unrefined type. Stella's spoke of you a good deal. You were married once, weren't you? (*The music of the polka rises up, faint in the distance.*)

BLANCHE. Yes. When I was quite young.

STANLEY. What happened?

BLANCHE. The boy—the boy died. (*She sinks back down*) I'm afraid I'm—going to be sick!

(*Her head falls on her arms.*)

SCENE TWO

It is six o'clock the following evening. Blanche is bathing. Stella is completing her toilette. Blanche's dress, a flowered print, is laid out on Stella's bed.

Stanley enters the kitchen from outside, leaving the door open on the perpetual "blue piano" around the corner.

———

STANLEY. What's all this monkey doings?

STELLA. Oh, Stan! (*She jumps up and kisses him which he accepts with lordly composure*) I'm taking Blanche to Galatoire's for supper and then to a show, because it's your poker night.

STANLEY. How about my supper, huh? I'm not going to no Galatoire's for supper!

STELLA. I put you a cold plate on ice.

STANLEY. Well, isn't that just dandy!

STELLA. I'm going to try to keep Blanche out till the party breaks up because I don't know how she would take it. So we'll go to one of the little places in the Quarter afterwards and you'd better give me some money.

STANLEY. Where is she?

STELLA. She's soaking in a hot tub to quiet her nerves. She's terribly upset.

STANLEY. Over what?

STELLA. She's been through such an ordeal.

STANLEY. Yeah?

STELLA. Stan, we've—lost Belle Reve!

STANLEY. The place in the country?

STELLA. Yes.

STANLEY. How?

STELLA (*vaguely*). Oh, it had to be—sacrificed or something. (*There is a pause while Stanley considers. Stella is changing into her dress*) When she comes in be sure to say something nice about her appearance. And, oh! Don't mention the baby. I haven't said anything yet, I'm waiting until she gets in a quieter condition.

STANLEY (*ominously*). So?

STELLA. And try to understand her and be nice to her, Stan.

BLANCHE (*singing in the bathroom*). "From the land of the sky blue water, They brought a captive maid!"

STELLA. She wasn't expecting to find us in such a small place. You see I'd tried to gloss things over a little in my letters.

STANLEY. So?

STELLA. And admire her dress and tell her she's looking wonderful. That's important with Blanche. Her little weakness!

STANLEY. Yeah. I get the idea. Now let's skip back a little to where you said the country place was disposed of.

STELLA. Oh!—yes . . .

STANLEY. How about that? Let's have a few more details on that subjeck.

STELLA. It's best not to talk much about it until she's calmed down.

STANLEY. So that's the deal, huh? Sister Blanche cannot be annoyed with business details right now!

STELLA. You saw how she was last night.

STANLEY. Uh-hum, I saw how she was. Now let's have a gander at the bill of sale.

STELLA. I haven't seen any.

STANLEY. She didn't show you no papers, no deed of sale or nothing like that, huh?

STELLA. It seems like it wasn't sold.

STANLEY. Well, what in hell was it then, give away? To charity?

STELLA. Shhh! She'll hear you.

STANLEY. I don't care if she hears me. Let's see the papers!

STELLA. There weren't any papers, she didn't show any papers, I don't care about papers.

STANLEY. Have you ever heard of the Napoleonic code?

STELLA. No, Stanley, I haven't heard of the Napoleonic code and if I have, I don't see what it—

STANLEY. Let me enlighten you on a point or two, baby.

STELLA. Yes?

STANLEY. In the state of Louisiana we have the Napoleonic code according to which what belongs to the wife belongs to the husband and vice versa. For instance if I had a piece of property, or you had a piece of property—

STELLA. My head is swimming!

STANLEY. All right. I'll wait till she gets through soaking in a hot tub and then I'll inquire if *she* is acquainted with the Napoleonic code. It looks to me like you have been swindled, baby, and when you're swindled under the Napoleonic code I'm swindled *too*. And I don't like to be *swindled*.

STELLA. There's plenty of time to ask her questions later but if you do now she'll go to pieces again. I don't understand what happened to Belle Reve but you don't know how ridiculous you are being when you suggest that my sister or I or anyone of our family could have perpetrated a swindle on anyone else.

STANLEY. Then where's the money if the place was sold?

STELLA. Not sold—*lost, lost!* (*He stalks into bedroom, and she follows him*) Stanley!

(*He pulls open the wardrobe trunk standing in middle of room and jerks out an armful of dresses.*)

STANLEY. Open your eyes to this stuff! You think she got them out of a teacher's pay?

STELLA. Hush!

STANLEY. Look at these feathers and furs that she come here to preen herself in! What's this here? A solid-gold dress, I believe! And this one! What is these here? Fox-pieces! (*He blows on them*) Genuine fox fur-pieces, a half a mile long! Where are your fox-pieces, Stella? Bushy snow-white ones, no less! Where are your white fox-pieces?

STELLA. Those are inexpensive summer furs that Blanche has had a long time.

STANLEY. I got an acquaintance who deals in this sort of merchandise. I'll have him in here to appraise it. I'm willing to bet you there's thousands of dollars invested in this stuff here!

STELLA. Don't be such an idiot, Stanley! (*He hurls the furs to the daybed. Then he jerks open small drawer in the trunk and pulls up a fist-full of costume jewelry.*)

STANLEY. And what have we here? The treasure chest of a pirate!

STELLA. Oh, Stanley!

STANLEY. Pearls! Ropes of them! What is this sister of yours, a deep-sea diver? Bracelets of solid gold, too! Where are your pearls and gold bracelets?

STELLA. Shhh! Be still, Stanley!

STANLEY. And diamonds! A crown for an empress!

STELLA. A rhinestone tiara she wore to a costume ball.

STANLEY. What's rhinestone?

STELLA. Next door to glass.

STANLEY. Are you kidding? I have an acquaintance that works in a jewelry store. I'll have him in here to make an appraisal of this. Here's your plantation, or what was left of it, here!

STELLA. You have no idea how stupid and horrid you're being! Now close that trunk before she comes out of the bathroom!

(*He kicks the trunk partly closed and sits on the kitchen table.*)

STANLEY. The Kowalskis and the DuBois have different notions.

STELLA (*angrily*). Indeed they have, thank heavens—*I'm* going outside. (*She snatches up her white hat and gloves and crosses to the outside door*) You come out with me while Blanche is getting dressed.

STANLEY. Since when do you give me orders?

STELLA. Are you going to stay here and insult her?

STANLEY. You're damn tootin' I'm going to stay here.

(*Stella goes out to the porch. Blanche comes out of the bathroom in a red satin robe.*)

BLANCHE (*airily*). Hello, Stanley! Here I am, all freshly bathed and scented, and feeling like a brand new human being!

(*He lights a cigarette.*)

STANLEY. That's good.

BLANCHE (*drawing the curtains at the window*). Excuse me while I slip on my pretty new dress!

STANLEY. Go right ahead, Blanche.

(*She closes the drapes between the rooms.*)

BLANCHE. I understand there's to be a little card party to which we ladies are cordially *not* invited!

STANLEY (*ominously*). Yeah?

(*Blanche throws off her robe and slips into a flowered print dress.*)

BLANCHE. Where's Stella?

STANLEY. Out on the porch.

BLANCHE. I'm going to ask a favor of you in a moment.

STANLEY. What could that be, I wonder?

BLANCHE. Some buttons in back! You may enter! *(He crosses through drapes with a smoldering look)* How do I look?

STANLEY. You look all right.

BLANCHE. Many thanks! Now the buttons!

STANLEY. I can't do nothing with them.

BLANCHE. You men with your big clumsy fingers. May I have a drag on your cig?

STANLEY. Have one for yourself.

BLANCHE. Why, thanks! . . . It looks like my trunk has exploded.

STANLEY. Me an' Stella were helping you unpack.

BLANCHE. Well, you certainly did a fast and thorough job of it!

STANLEY. It looks like you raided some stylish shops in Paris.

BLANCHE. Ha-ha! Yes—clothes are my passion!

STANLEY. What does it cost for a string of fur-pieces like that?

BLANCHE. Why, those were a tribute from an admirer of mine!

STANLEY. He must have had a lot of—admiration!

BLANCHE. Oh, in my youth I excited some admiration. But look at me now! *(She smiles at him radiantly)* Would you think it possible that I was once considered to be—attractive?

STANLEY. Your looks are okay.

BLANCHE. I was fishing for a compliment, Stanley.

STANLEY. I don't go in for that stuff.

BLANCHE. What—stuff?

STANLEY. Compliments to women about their looks. I never met a woman that didn't know if she was good-looking or not without being told, and some of them give themselves credit for more than they've got. I once went out with a doll who said to me, "I am the glamorous type, I am the glamorous type!" I said, "So what?"

BLANCHE. And what did she say then?

STANLEY. She didn't say nothing. That shut her up like a clam.

BLANCHE. Did it end the romance?

STANLEY. It ended the conversation—that was all. Some men are took in by this Hollywood glamor stuff and some men are not.

BLANCHE. I'm sure you belong in the second category.

STANLEY. That's right.

BLANCHE. I cannot imagine any witch of a woman casting a spell over you.

STANLEY. That's—right.

BLANCHE. You're simple, straightforward and honest, a little bit on the primitive side I should think. To interest you a woman would have to—*(She pauses with an indefinite gesture)*

STANLEY *(slowly)*. Lay . . . her cards on the table.

BLANCHE *(smiling)*. Well, I never cared for wishy-washy people. That was why, when you walked in here last night, I said to myself—"My sister has married a man!" —Of course that was all that I could tell about you.

STANLEY *(booming)*. Now let's cut the re-bop!

BLANCHE *(pressing hands to her ears* Ouuuuu!

STELLA *(calling from the steps)*. Stanley! You come out here and let Blanche finish dressing!

BLANCHE. I'm through dressing, honey.

STELLA. Well, you come out, then.

STANLEY. Your sister and I are having a little talk.

BLANCHE *(lightly)*. Honey, do me a favor. Run to the drugstore and get me a lemon-coke with plenty of chipped ice in it!—Will you do that for me, Sweetie?

STELLA *(uncertainly)*. Yes. *(She goes around the corner of the building)*

BLANCHE. The poor little thing was out there listening to us, and I have an idea she doesn't understand you as well as I do. . . . All right; now, Mr. Kowalski, let us proceed without any more double-talk. I'm ready to answer all questions. I've nothing to hide. What is it?

STANLEY. There is such a thing in this state of Louisiana as the Napoleonic code, according to which whatever belongs to my wife is also mine—and vice versa.

BLANCHE. My, but you have an impressive judicial air!

(She sprays herself with her atomizer; then playfully sprays him with it. He seizes the atomizer and slams it down on the dresser. She throws back her head and laughs.)

STANLEY. If I didn't know that you was my wife's sister I'd get ideas about you!

BLANCHE. Such as what!

STANLEY. Don't play so dumb. You know!

BLANCHE (*she puts the atomizer on the table*). All right. Cards on the table. That suits me. (*She turns to Stanley*) I know I fib a good deal. After all, a woman's charm is fifty per cent illusion, but when a thing is important I tell the truth, and this is the truth: I haven't cheated my sister or you or anyone else as long as I have lived.

STANLEY. Where's the papers? In the trunk?

BLANCHE. Everything that I own is in that trunk.

(*Stanley crosses to the trunk, shoves it roughly open and begins to open compartments.*)

BLANCHE. What in the name of heaven are you thinking of! What's in the back of that little boy's mind of yours? That I am absconding with something, attempting some kind of treachery on my sister? —Let me do that! It will be faster and simpler . . . (*She crosses to the trunk and takes out a box*) I keep my papers mostly in this tin box. (*She opens it*)

STANLEY. What's them underneath? (*He indicates another sheaf of paper*)

BLANCHE. These are love-letters, yellowing with antiquity, all from one boy. (*He snatches them up. She speaks fiercely*) Give those back to me!

STANLEY. I'll have a look at them first!

BLANCHE. The touch of your hands insults them!

STANLEY. Don't pull that stuff!

(*He rips off the ribbon and starts to examine them. Blanche snatches them from him, and they cascade to the floor.*)

BLANCHE. Now that you've touched them I'll burn them!

STANLEY (*staring, baffled*). What in hell are they?

BLANCHE (*on the floor, gathering them up*). Poems a dead boy wrote. I hurt him the way that you would like to hurt me, but you can't! I'm not young and vulnerable any more. But my young husband was and I—never mind about that! Just give them back to me!

STANLEY. What do you mean by saying you'll have to burn them?

BLANCHE. I'm sorry, I must have lost my head for a moment. Everyone has something he won't let others touch because of their—intimate nature . . . (*She now seems faint with exhaustion and she sits down with the strong box and puts on a pair of glasses and goes methodically through a large stack of papers*) Ambler & Ambler. Hmmmmm. . . . Crabtree. . . . More Ambler & Ambler.

STANLEY. What is Ambler & Ambler?

BLANCHE. A firm that made loans on the place.

STANLEY. Then it *was* lost on a mortgage?

BLANCHE (*touching her forehead*). That must've been what happened.

STANLEY. I don't want no ifs, ands or buts! What's all the rest of them papers? (*She hands him the entire box. He carries it to the table and starts to examine the papers.*)

BLANCHE (*picking up a large envelope containing more papers*). There are thousands of papers, stretching back over hundreds of years, affecting Belle Reve as, piece by piece, our improvident grandfathers and father and uncles and brothers exchanged the land for their epic fornications—to put it plainly! (*She removes her glasses with an exhausted laugh*) The four-letter word deprived us of our plantation, till finally all that was left—and Stella can verify that!—was the house itself and about twenty acres of ground, including a graveyard, to which now all but Stella and I have retreated. (*She pours the contents of the envelope on the table*) Here all of them are, all papers! I hereby endow you with them! Take them, peruse them— commit them to memory, even! I think it's wonderfully fitting that Belle Reve should finally be this bunch of old papers in your big, capable hands! . . . I wonder if Stella's come back with my lemon-coke . . . (*She leans back and closes her eyes*)

STANLEY. I have a lawyer acquaintance who will study these out.

BLANCHE. Present them to him with a box of aspirin tablets.

STANLEY (*becoming somewhat sheepish*). You see, under the Napoleonic code—a man has to take an interest in his wife's affairs—especially now that she's going to have a baby.

(*Blanche opens her eyes. The "blue piano" sounds louder.*)

BLANCHE. Stella? Stella going to have a

baby? *(Dreamily)* I didn't know she was
going to have a baby!
*(She gets up and crosses to the outside
door. Stella appears around the corner
with a carton from the drugstore.*
*(Stanley goes into the bedroom with the
envelope and the box.*
*(The inner rooms fade to darkness and
the outside wall of the house is visible.
Blanche meets Stella at the foot of the
steps to the sidewalk.)*
  BLANCHE. Stella, Stella for star! How
lovely to have a baby! It's all right. Everything's all right.
  STELLA. I'm sorry he did that to you.
  BLANCHE. Oh, I guess he's just not the
type that goes for jasmine perfume, but
maybe he's what we need to mix with our
blood now that we've lost Belle Reve. We
thrashed it out. I feel a bit shaky, but I
think I handled it all nicely, I laughed and
treated it all as a joke. *(Steve and Pablo
appear, carrying a case of beer)* I called
him a little boy and laughed and flirted.
Yes, I was flirting with your husband! *(As
the men approach)* The guests are gathering for the poker party. *(The two men
pass between them, and enter the house)*
Which way do we go now, Stella—this
way?
  STELLA. No, this way. *(She leads Blanche
away)*
  BLANCHE *(laughing)*. The blind are
leading the blind!
(A tamale vendor is heard calling.)
  VENDOR'S VOICE. Red-hot!

SCENE THREE

THE POKER NIGHT

  *There is a picture of Van Gogh's of a
billiard-parlor at night. The kitchen now
suggests that sort of lurid nocturnal brilliance, the raw colors of childhood's spectrum. Over the yellow linoleum of the
kitchen table hangs an electric bulb with
a vivid green glass shade. The poker players—Stanley, Steve, Mitch and Pablo—
wear colored shirts, solid blues, a purple, a
red-and-white check, a light green, and
they are men at the peak of their physical
manhood, as coarse and direct and powerful as the primary colors. There are vivid
slices of watermelon on the table, whiskey
bottles and glasses. The bedroom is relatively dim with only the light that spills*

*between the portieres and through the
wide window on the street.*
  *For a moment, there is absorbed silence
as a hand is dealt.*

———

  STEVE. Anything wild this deal?
  PABLO. One-eyed jacks are wild.
  STEVE. Give me two cards.
  PABLO. You, Mitch?
  MITCH. I'm out.
  PABLO. One.
  MITCH. Anyone want a shot?
  STANLEY. Yeah, me.
  PABLO. Why don't somebody go to the
Chinaman's and bring back a load of chop
suey?
  STANLEY. When I'm losing you want to
eat! Ante up! Openers? Openers! Get y'r
ass off the table, Mitch. Nothing belongs
on a poker table but cards, chips and
whiskey. *(He lurches up and tosses some
watermelon rinds to the floor)*
  MITCH. Kind of on your high horse, ain't
you?
  STANLEY. How many?
  STEVE. Give me three.
  STANLEY. One.
  MITCH. I'm out again. I oughta go home
pretty soon.
  STANLEY. Shut up.
  MITCH. I gotta sick mother. She don't go
to sleep until I come in at night.
  STANLEY. Then why don't you stay home
with her?
  MITCH. She says to go out, so I go, but
I don't enjoy it. All the while I keep won-
dering how she is.
  STANLEY. Aw, for the sake of Jesus, go
home, then!
  PABLO. What've you got?
  STEVE. Spade flush.
  MITCH. You all are married. But I'll be
alone when she goes.—I'm going to the
bathroom.
  STANLEY. Hurry back and we'll fix you a
sugar-tit.
  MITCH. Aw, go rut. *(He crosses through
the bedroom into the bathroom)*
  STEVE *(dealing a hand)*. Seven card stud.
(Telling his joke as he deals) This ole
farmer is out in back of his house sittin'
down th'owing corn to the chickens when
all at once he hears a loud cackle and this
young hen comes lickety split around the
side of the house with the rooster right behind her and gaining on her fast.

STANLEY *(impatient with the story)*. Deal!

STEVE. But when the rooster catches sight of the farmer th'owing the corn he puts on the brakes and lets the hen get away and starts pecking corn. And the old farmer says, "Lord God, I hopes I never gits *that* hongry!"

(Steve and Pablo laugh. The sisters appear around the corner of the building.)

STELLA. The game is still going on.

BLANCHE. How do I look?

STELLA. Lovely, Blanche.

BLANCHE. I feel so hot and frazzled. Wait till I powder before you open the door. Do I look done in?

STELLA. Why no. You are as fresh as a daisy.

BLANCHE. One that's been picked a few days.

(Stella opens the door and they enter.)

STELLA. Well, well, well. I see you boys are still at it!

STANLEY. Where you been?

STELLA. Blanche and I took in a show. Blanche, this is Mr. Gonzales and Mr. Hubbell.

BLANCHE. Please don't get up.

STANLEY. Nobody's going to get up, so don't be worried.

STELLA. How much longer is this game going to continue?

STANLEY. Till we get ready to quit.

BLANCHE. Poker is so fascinating. Could I kibitz?

STANLEY. You could not. Why don't you women go up and sit with Eunice?

STELLA. Because it is nearly two-thirty. *(Blanche crosses into the bedroom and partially closes the portieres)* Couldn't you call it quits after one more hand?

(A chair scrapes. Stanley gives a loud whack of his hand on her thigh.)

STELLA *(sharply)*. That's not fun, Stanley.

(The men laugh. Stella goes into the bedroom.)

STELLA. It makes me so mad when he does that in front of people.

BLANCHE. I think I will bathe.

STELLA. Again?

BLANCHE. My nerves are in knots. Is the bathroom occupied?

STELLA. I don't know.

(Blanche knocks. Mitch opens the door and comes out, still wiping his hands on a towel.)

BLANCHE. Oh!—good evening.

MITCH. Hello. *(He stares at her)*

STELLA. Blanche, this is Harold Mitchell. My sister, Blanche DuBois.

MITCH *(with awkward courtesy)*. How do you do, Miss DuBois.

STELLA. How is your mother now, Mitch?

MITCH. About the same, thanks. She appreciated your sending over that custard. —Excuse me, please.

(He crosses slowly back into the kitchen, glancing back at Blanche and coughing a little shyly. He realizes he still has the towel in his hands and with an embarrassed laugh hands it to Stella. Blanche looks after him with a certain interest.)

BLANCHE. That one seems—superior to the others.

STELLA. Yes, he is.

BLANCHE. I thought he had a sort of sensitive look.

STELLA. His mother is sick.

BLANCHE. Is he married?

STELLA. No.

BLANCHE. Is he a wolf?

STELLA. Why, Blanche! *(Blanche laughs)* I don't think he would be.

BLANCHE. What does—what does he do? *(She is unbuttoning her blouse)*

STELLA. He's on the precision bench in the spare parts department. At the plant Stanley travels for.

BLANCHE. Is that something much?

STELLA. No. Stanley's the only one of his crowd that's likely to get anywhere.

BLANCHE. What makes you think Stanley will?

STELLA. Look at him.

BLANCHE. I've looked at him.

STELLA. Then you should know.

BLANCHE. I'm sorry, but I haven't noticed the stamp of genius even on Stanley's forehead.

(She takes off the blouse and stands in her pink silk brassiere and white skirt in the light through the portieres. The game has continued in undertones.)

STELLA. It isn't on his forehead and it isn't genius.

BLANCHE. Oh. Well, what is it, and where? I would like to know.

STELLA. It's a drive that he has. You're standing in the light, Blanche!

BLANCHE. Oh, am I!

(She moves out of the yellow streak of

light. Stella has removed her dress and put on a light blue satin kimono.)

STELLA *(with girlish laughter)*. You ought to see their wives.

BLANCHE *(laughingly)*. I can imagine. Big, beefy things, I suppose.

STELLA. You know that one upstairs? *(More laughter)* One time *(laughing)* the plaster—*(laughing)* cracked—

STANLEY. You hens cut out that conversation in there!

STELLA. You can't hear us.

STANLEY. Well, you can hear me and I said to hush up!

STELLA. This is my house and I'll talk as much as I want to!

BLANCHE. Stella, don't start a row.

STELLA. He's half drunk!—I'll be out in a minute.

(She goes into the bathroom. Blanche rises and crosses leisurely to a small white radio and turns it on.)

STANLEY. Awright, Mitch, you in?

MITCH. What? Oh!—No, I'm out!

(Blanche moves back into the streak of light. She raises her arms and stretches, as she moves indolently back to the chair.

(Rhumba music comes over the radio. Mitch rises at the table.)

STANLEY. Who turned that on in there?

BLANCHE. I did. Do you mind?

STANLEY. Turn it off!

STEVE. Aw, let the girls have their music.

PABLO. Sure, that's good, leave it on!

STEVE. Sounds like Xavier Cugat!

(Stanley jumps up and, crossing to the radio, turns it off. He stops short at the sight of Blanche in the chair. She returns his look without flinching. Then he sits again at the poker table.

(Two of the men have started arguing hotly.)

STEVE. I didn't hear you name it.

PABLO. Didn't I name it, Mitch?

MITCH. I wasn't listenin'.

PABLO. What were you doing, then?

STANLEY. He was looking through them drapes. *(He jumps up and jerks roughly at curtains to close them)* Now deal the hand over again and let's play cards or quit. Some people get ants when they win. *(Mitch rises as Stanley returns to his seat.)*

STANLEY *(yelling)*. Sit down!

MITCH. I'm going to the "head. Deal me out.

PABLO. Sure he's got ants now. Seven

five-dollar bills in his pants pocket folded up tight as spitballs.

STEVE. Tomorrow you'll see him at the cashier's window getting them changed into quarters.

STANLEY. And when he goes home he'll deposit them one by one in a piggy bank his mother give him for Christmas. *(Dealing)* This game is Spit in the Ocean.

(Mitch laughs uncomfortably and continues through the portieres. He stops just inside.)

BLANCHE *(softly)*. Hello! The Little Boys' Room is busy right now.

MITCH. We've—been drinking beer.

BLANCHE. I hate beer.

MITCH. It's—a hot weather drink.

BLANCHE. Oh, I don't think so; it always makes me warmer. Have you got any cigs? *(She has slipped on the dark red satin wrapper)*

MITCH. Sure.

BLANCHE. What kind are they?

MITCH. Luckies.

BLANCHE. Oh, good. What a pretty case. Silver?

MITCH. Yes. Yes; read the inscription.

BLANCHE. Oh, is there an inscription? I can't make it out. *(He strikes a match and moves closer)* Oh! *(Reading with feigned difficulty)* "And if God choose, I shall but love thee better—after—death!" Why, that's from my favorite sonnet by Mrs. Browning!

MITCH. You know it?

BLANCHE. Certainly I do!

MITCH. There's a story connected with that inscription.

BLANCHE. It sounds like a romance.

MITCH. A pretty sad one.

BLANCHE. Oh?

MITCH. The girl's dead now.

BLANCHE *(in a tone of deep sympathy)*. Oh!

MITCH. She knew she was dying when she give me this. A very strange girl, very sweet—very!

BLANCHE. She must have been fond of you. Sick people have such deep, sincere attachments.

MITCH. That's right, they certainly do.

BLANCHE. Sorrow makes for sincerity, I think.

MITCH. It sure brings it out in people.

BLANCHE. The little there is belongs to people who have experienced some sorrow.

MITCH. I believe you are right about that.

BLANCHE. I'm positive that I am. Show me a person who hasn't known any sorrow and I'll show you a shuperficial— Listen to me! My tongue is a little—thick! You boys are responsible for it. The show let out at eleven and we couldn't come home on account of the poker game so we had to go somewhere and drink. I'm not accustomed to having more than one drink. Two is the limit—and *three! (She laughs)* Tonight I had three.

STANLEY. Mitch!

MITCH. Deal me out. I'm talking to Miss—

BLANCHE. DuBois.

MITCH. Miss DuBois?

BLANCHE. It's a French name. It means woods and Blanche means white, so the two together mean white woods. Like an orchard in spring! You can remember it by that.

MITCH. You're French?

BLANCHE. We are French by extraction. Our first American ancestors were French Huguenots.

MITCH. You are Stella's sister, are you not?

BLANCHE. Yes, Stella is my precious little sister. I call her little in spite of the fact she's somewhat older than I. Just slightly. Less than a year. Will you do something for me?

MITCH. Sure. What?

BLANCHE. I bought this adorable little colored paper lantern at a Chinese shop on Bourbon. Put it over the light bulb! Will you, please?

MITCH. Be glad to.

BLANCHE. I can't stand a naked light bulb, any more than I can a rude remark or a vulgar action.

MITCH *(adjusting the lantern)*. I guess we strike you as being a pretty rough bunch.

BLANCHE. I'm very adaptable—to circumstances.

MITCH. Well, that's a good thing to be. You are visiting Stanley and Stella?

BLANCHE. Stella hasn't been so well lately, and I came down to help her for a while. She's very rundown.

MITCH. You're not—?

BLANCHE. Married? No, no. I'm an old maid schoolteacher!

MITCH. You may teach school but you're certainly not an old maid.

BLANCHE. Thank you, sir! I appreciate your gallantry!

MITCH. So you are in the teaching profession?

BLANCHE. Yes. Ah, yes . . .

MITCH. Grade school or high school or—

STANLEY *(bellowing)*. *Mitch!*

MITCH. *Coming!*

BLANCHE. Gracious, what lung-power! . . . I teach high school. In Laurel.

MITCH. What do you teach? What subject?

BLANCHE. Guess!

MITCH. I bet you teach art or music? *(Blanche laughs delicately)* Of course I could be wrong. You might teach arithmetic.

BLANCHE. Never arithmetic, sir; never arithmetic! *(With a laugh)* I don't even know my multiplication tables! No, I have the misfortune of being an English instructor. I attempt to instill a bunch of bobby-soxers and drugstore Romeos with reverence for Hawthorne and Whitman and Poe!

MITCH. I guess that some of them are more interested in other things.

BLANCHE. How very right you are! Their literary heritage is not what most of them treasure above all else! But they're sweet things! And in the spring, it's touching to notice them making their first discovery of love! As if nobody had ever known it before! *(The bathroom door opens and Stella comes out. Blanche continues talking to Mitch)* Oh! Have you finished? Wait—I'll turn on the radio.

(She turns the knobs on the radio and it begins to play "Wien, Wien, nur du allein." Blanche waltzes to the music with romantic gestures. Mitch is delighted and moves in awkward imitation like a dancing bear.

(Stanley stalks fiercely through the portieres into the bedroom. He crosses to the small white radio and snatches it off the table. With a shouted oath, he tosses the instrument out the window.)

STELLA. *Drunk—drunk—animal thing, you! (She rushes through to the poker table)* All of you—please go home! If any of you have one spark of decency in you—

BLANCHE *(wildly)*. Stella, watch out, he's—

(Stanley charges after Stella.)

MEN *(feebly)*. Take it easy, Stanley. **Easy,** fellow.—Let's all—

STELLA. You lay your hands on me and I'll—

(*She backs out of sight. He advances and disappears. There is the sound of a blow. Stella cries out. Blanche screams and runs into the kitchen. The men rush forward and there is grappling and cursing. Something is overturned with a crash.*)

BLANCHE (*shrilly*). My sister is going to have a baby!

MITCH. This is terrible.

BLANCHE. Lunacy, absolute lunacy!

MITCH. Get him in here, men.

(*Stanley is forced, pinioned by the two men, into the bedroom. He nearly throws them off. Then all at once he subsides and is limp in their grasp.*

(*They speak quietly and lovingly to him and he leans his face on one of their shoulders.*)

STELLA (*in a high, unnatural voice, out of sight*). I want to go away, I want to go away!

MITCH. Poker shouldn't be played in a house with women.

(*Blanche rushes into the bedroom.*)

BLANCHE. I want my sister's clothes! We'll go to that woman's upstairs!

MITCH. Where is the clothes?

BLANCHE (*opening the closet*). I've got them! (*She rushes through to Stella*) Stella, Stella, precious! Dear, dear little sister, don't be afraid!

(*With her arms around Stella, Blanche guides her to the outside door and upstairs.*)

STANLEY (*dully*). What's the matter; what's happened?

MITCH. You just blew your top, Stan.

PABLO. He's okay, now.

STEVE. Sure, my boy's okay!

MITCH. Put him on the bed and get a wet towel.

PABLO. I think coffee would do him a world of good, now.

STANLEY (*thickly*). I want water.

MITCH. Put him under the shower!

(*The men talk quietly as they lead him to the bathroom.*)

STANLEY. Let the rut go of me, you sons of bitches!

(*Sounds of blows are heard. The water goes on full tilt.*)

STEVE. Let's get quick out of here!

(*They rush to the poker table and sweep up their winnings on their way out.*)

MITCH (*sadly but firmly*). Poker should not be played in a house with women.

(*The door closes on them and the place is still. The Negro entertainers in the bar around the corner play "Paper Doll" slow and blue. After a moment Stanley comes out of the bathroom dripping water and still in his clinging wet polka dot drawers.*)

STANLEY. Stella! (*There is a pause*) My baby doll's left me! (*He breaks into sobs. Then he goes to the phone and dials, still shuddering with sobs*) Eunice? I want my baby! (*He waits a moment; then he hangs up and dials again*) Eunice! I'll keep on ringin' until I talk with my baby!

(*An indistinguishable shrill voice is heard. He hurls phone to floor. Dissonant brass and piano sounds as the rooms dim out to darkness and the outer walls appear in the night light. The "blue piano" plays for a brief interval.*

(*Finally, Stanley stumbles half-dressed out to the porch and down the wooden steps to the pavement before the building. There he throws back his head like a baying hound and bellows his wife's name: "Stella! Stella, sweetheart! Stella!"*)

STANLEY. Stell-*lahhhhh!*

EUNICE (*calling down from the door of her upper apartment*). Quit that howling out there an' go back to bed!

STANLEY. I want my baby down here. Stella, Stella!

EUNICE. She ain't comin' down so you quit! Or you'll git th' law on you!

STANLEY. Stella!

EUNICE. You can't beat on a woman an' then call 'er back! She won't come! And her goin' t' have a baby! . . . You stinker! You whelp of a Polack, you! I hope they do haul you in and turn the fire hose on you, same as the last time!

STANLEY (*humbly*). Eunice, I want my girl to come down with me!

EUNICE. Hah! (*She slams her door*)

STANLEY (*with heaven-splitting violence*). STELL-LAHHHHH!

(*The low-tone clarinet moans. The door upstairs opens again. Stella slips down the rickety stairs in her robe. Her eyes are glistening with tears and her hair loose about her throat and shoulders. They stare at each other. Then they come together with low animal moans. He falls to his knees on the steps and presses his face to her belly, curving a little with maternity. Her eyes go blind with tenderness as she*

catches his head and raises him level with her. He snatches the screen door open and lifts her off her feet and bears her into the dark flat.
(Blanche comes out on the upper landing in her robe and slips fearfully down the steps.)

BLANCHE. Where is my little sister? Stella? Stella?
(She stops before the dark entrance of her sister's flat. Then catches her breath as if struck. She rushes down to the walk before the house. She looks right and left as if for a sanctuary.
(The music fades away. Mitch appears from around the corner.)

MITCH. Miss DuBois?

BLANCHE. Oh!

MITCH. All quiet on the Potomac now?

BLANCHE. She ran downstairs and went back in there with him.

MITCH. Sure she did.

BLANCHE. I'm terrified!

MITCH. Ho-ho! There's nothing to be scared of. They're crazy about each other.

BLANCHE. I'm not used to such—

MITCH. Naw, it's a shame this had to happen when you just got here. But don't take it serious.

BLANCHE. Violence! Is so—

MITCH. Set down on the steps and have a cigarette with me.

BLANCHE. I'm not properly dressed.

MITCH. That don't make no difference in the Quarter.

BLANCHE. Such a pretty silver case.

MITCH. I showed you the inscription, didn't I?

BLANCHE. Yes. *(During the pause she looks up at the sky)* There's so much—so much confusion in the world . . . *(He coughs diffidently)* Thank you for being so kind! I need kindness now.

SCENE FOUR

It is early the following morning. There is a confusion of street cries like a choral chant.
Stella is lying down in the bedroom. Her face is serene in the early morning sunlight. One hand rests on her belly, rounding slightly with new maternity. From the other dangles a book of colored comics. Her eyes and lips have that almost narcotized tranquility that is in the faces of Eastern idols.
The table is sloppy with remains of breakfast and the debris of the preceding night, and Stanley's gaudy pyjamas lie across the threshold of the bathroom. The outside door is slightly ajar on a sky of summer brilliance.
Blanche appears at this door. She has spent a sleepless night and her appearance entirely contrasts with Stella's. She presses her knuckles nervously to her lips as she looks through the door, before entering.

———

BLANCHE. Stella?

STELLA *(stirring lazily).* Hmmh?
(Blanche utters a moaning cry and runs into the bedroom, throwing herself down beside Stella in a rush of hysterical tenderness.)

BLANCHE. Baby, my baby sister!

STELLA *(drawing away from her).* Blanche, what is the matter with you?
(Blanche straightens up slowly and stands beside the bed looking down at her sister with knuckles pressed to her lips.)

BLANCHE. He's left?

STELLA. Stan? Yes.

BLANCHE. Will he be back?

STELLA. He's gone to get the car greased. Why?

BLANCHE. Why! I've been half crazy, Stella! When I found out you'd been insane enough to come back in here after what happened—I started to rush in after you!

STELLA. I'm glad you didn't.

BLANCHE. What were you thinking of?
(Stella makes an indefinite gesture) Answer me! What? What?

STELLA. Please, Blanche! Sit down and stop yelling.

BLANCHE. All right, Stella. I will repeat the question quietly now. How could you come back in this place last night? Why, you must have slept with him!
(Stella gets up in a calm and leisurely way.)

STELLA. Blanche, I'd forgotten how excitable you are. You're making much too much fuss about this.

BLANCHE. Am I?

STELLA. Yes, you are, Blanche. I know how it must have seemed to you and I'm awful sorry it had to happen, but it wasn't anything as serious as you seem to take it. In the first place, when men are drinking and playing poker anything can happen. It's always a powder-keg. He didn't know what he was doing. . . . He was as good as a lamb when I came back and he's really very, very ashamed of himself.

BLANCHE. And that—that makes it all right?

STELLA. No, it isn't all right for anybody to make such a terrible row, but—people do sometimes. Stanley's always smashed things. Why, on our wedding night—soon as we came in here—he snatched off one of my slippers and rushed about the place smashing the light-bulbs with it.

BLANCHE. He did—*what?*

STELLA. He smashed all the light-bulbs with the heel of my slipper! *(She laughs)*

BLANCHE. And you—you *let* him? Didn't *run,* didn't *scream?*

STELLA. I was—sort of—thrilled by it. *(She waits for a moment)* Eunice and you had breakfast?

BLANCHE. Do you suppose I wanted any breakfast?

STELLA. There's some coffee left on the stove.

BLANCHE. You're so—matter of fact about it, Stella.

STELLA. What other can I be? He's taken the radio to get it fixed. It didn't land on the pavement so only one tube was smashed.

BLANCHE. And you are standing there smiling!

STELLA. What do you want me to do?

BLANCHE. Pull yourself together and face the facts.

STELLA. What are they, in your opinion?

BLANCHE. In my opinion? You're married to a madman!

STELLA. No!

BLANCHE. Yes, you are, your fix is worse than mine is! Only you're not being sensible about it. I'm going to *do* something. Get hold of myself and make myself a new life!

STELLA. Yes?

BLANCHE. But you've given in. And that isn't right, you're not old! You can get out.

STELLA *(slowly and emphatically)*. I'm not in anything I want to get out of.

BLANCHE *(incredulously)*. What—Stella?

STELLA. I said I am not in anything that I have a desire to get out of. Look at the mess in this room! And those empty bottles! They went through two cases last night! He promised this morning that he

was going to quit having these poker parties, but you know how long such a promise is going to keep. Oh, well, it's his pleasure, like mine is movies and bridge. People have got to tolerate each other's habits, I guess.

BLANCHE. I don't understand you. *(Stella turns toward her)* I don't understand your indifference. Is this a Chinese philosophy you've—cultivated?

STELLA. Is what—what?

BLANCHE. This shuffling about and mumbling—"One tube smashed—beer-bottles—mess in the kitchen!"—as if nothing out of the ordinary has happened! *(Stella laughs uncertainly, and picking up the broom, twirls it in her hands)*

BLANCHE. Are you deliberately shaking that thing in my face?

STELLA. No.

BLANCHE. Stop it. Let go of that broom. I won't have you cleaning up for him!

STELLA. Then who's going to do it? Are you?

BLANCHE. I? I!

STELLA. No, I didn't think so.

BLANCHE. Oh, let me think, if only my mind would function! We've got to get hold of some money, that's the way out!

STELLA. I guess that money is always nice to get hold of.

BLANCHE. Listen to me. I have an idea of some kind. *(Shakily she twists a cigarette into her holder)* Do you remember Shep Huntleigh? *(Stella shakes her head)* Of course you remember Shep Huntleigh. I went out with him at college and wore his pin for a while. Well—

STELLA. Well?

BLANCHE. I ran into him last winter. You know I went to Miami during the Christmas holidays?

STELLA. No.

BLANCHE. Well, I did. I took the trip as an investment, thinking I'd meet someone with a million dollars.

STELLA. Did you?

BLANCHE. Yes. I ran into Shep Huntleigh—I ran into him on Biscayne Boulevard, on Christmas Eve, about dusk . . . getting into his car—Cadillac convertible; must have been a block long!

STELLA. I should think it would have been—inconvenient in traffic!

BLANCHE. You've heard of oil-wells?

STELLA. Yes—remotely.

BLANCHE. He has them, all over Texas.

Texas is literally spouting gold in his pockets.

STELLA. My, my.

BLANCHE. Y'know how indifferent I am to money. I think of money in terms of what it does for you. But he could do it, he could certainly do it!

STELLA. Do what, Blanche?

BLANCHE. Why—set us up in a—shop!

STELLA. What kind of a shop?

BLANCHE. Oh, a—shop of some kind! He could do it with half what his wife throws away at the races.

STELLA. He's married?

BLANCHE. Honey, would I be here if the man weren't married? *(Stella laughs a little. Blanche suddenly springs up and crosses to phone. She speaks shrilly)* How do I get Western Union?—Operator! Western Union!

STELLA. That's a dial phone, honey.

BLANCHE. I can't dial, I'm too—

STELLA. Just dial O.

BLANCHE. O?

STELLA. Yes, "O" for Operator! *(Blanche considers a moment; then she puts the phone down)*

BLANCHE. Give me a pencil. Where is a slip of paper? I've got to write it down first—the message, I mean ... *(She goes to the dressing table, and grabs up a sheet of Kleenex and an eyebrow pencil for writing equipment)* Let me see now ... *(She bites the pencil)* "Darling Shep. Sister and I are in desperate situation."

STELLA. I beg your pardon!

BLANCHE. "Sister and I in desperate situation. Will explain details later. Would you be interested in—?" *(She bites the pencil again)* "Would you be—interested—in . . ." *(She smashes the pencil on the table and springs up)* You never get anywhere with direct appeals!

STELLA *(with a laugh)*. Don't be so ridiculous, darling!

BLANCHE. But I'll think of something, I've *got* to think of—*something*! Don't, don't laugh at me, Stella! Please, please don't—I—I want you to look at the contents of my purse! Here's what's in it! *(She snatches her purse open)* Sixty-five measly cents in coin of the realm!

STELLA *(crossing to bureau)*. Stanley doesn't give me a regular allowance, he likes to pay bills himself, but—this morning he gave me ten dollars to smooth things over. You take five of .t, Blanche, and I'll keep the rest.

BLANCHE. Oh, no. No, Stella.

STELLA *(insisting)*. I know how it helps your morale just having a little pocket-money on you.

BLANCHE. No, thank you—I'll take to the streets!

STELLA. Talk sense! How did you happen to get so low on funds?

BLANCHE. Money just goes—it goes places. *(She rubs her forehead)* Sometime today I've got to get hold of a bromo!

STELLA. I'll fix you one now.

BLANCHE. Not yet—I've got to keep thinking!

STELLA. I wish you'd just let things go, at least for a—while . . .

BLANCHE. Stella, I can't live with him! You can, he's your husband. But how could I stay here with him, after last night, with just those curtains between us?

STELLA. Blanche, you saw him at his worst last night.

BLANCHE. On the contrary, I saw him at his best! What such a man has to offer is animal force and he gave a wonderful exhibition of that! But the only way to live with such a man is to—go to bed with him! And that's your job—not mine!

STELLA. After you've rested a little, you'll see it's going to work out. You don't have to worry about anything while you're here. I mean—expenses . . .

BLANCHE. I have to plan for us both, to get us both—out!

STELLA. You take it for granted that I am in something that I want to get out of.

BLANCHE. I take it for granted that you still have sufficient memory of Belle Reve to find this place and these poker players impossible to live with.

STELLA. Well, you're taking entirely too much for granted.

BLANCHE. I can't believe you're in earnest.

STELLA. No?

BLANCHE. I understand how it happened—a little. You saw him in uniform, an officer, not here but—

STELLA. I'm not sure it would have made any difference where I saw him.

BLANCHE. Now don't say it was one o. those mysterious electric things between people! If you do I'll laugh in your face.

STELLA. I am not going to say anything more at all about it

BLANCHE. All right, then, don't!

STELLA. But there are things that happen between a man and a woman in the dark —that sort of make everything else seem —unimportant. *(Pause)*

BLANCHE. What you are talking about is brutal desire—just—Desire!—the name of that rattle-trap streetcar that bangs through the Quarter, up one old narrow street and down another . . .

STELLA. Haven't you ever ridden on that streetcar?

BLANCHE. It brought me here.—Where I'm not wanted and where I'm ashamed to be . . .

STELLA. Then don't you think your superior attitude is a bit out of place?

BLANCHE. I am not being or feeling at all superior, Stella. Believe me I'm not! It's just this. This is how I look at it. A man like that is someone to go out with—once —twice—three times when the devil is in you. But live with? Have a child by?

STELLA. I have told you I love him.

BLANCHE. Then I tremble for you! I just —*tremble* for you. . . .

STELLA. I can't help your trembling if you insist on trembling!

(There is a pause.)

BLANCHE. May I—speak—*plainly?*

STELLA. Yes, do. Go ahead. As plainly as you want to.

(Outside, a train approaches. They are silent till the noise subsides. They are both in the bedroom.

(Under cover of the train's noise Stanley enters from outside. He stands unseen by the women, holding some packages in his arms, and overhears their following conversation. He wears an undershirt and grease-stained seersucker pants.)

BLANCHE. Well—if you'll forgive me— he's *common!*

STELLA. Why, yes, I suppose he is.

BLANCHE. Suppose! You can't have forgotten that much of our bringing up, Stella, that you just *suppose* that any part of a gentleman's in his nature! *Not one particle, no!* Oh, if he was just—*ordinary!* Just *plain*—but good and wholesome, but —*no.* There's something downright—*bestial*—about him! You're hating me saying this, aren't you?

STELLA *(coldly)*. Go on and say it all, Blanche.

BLANCHE. He acts like an animal, has an animal's habits! Eats like one, moves like one, talks like one! There's even something —sub-human—something not quite to the stage of humanity yet! Yes, something— ape-like about him, like one of those pictures I've seen in—anthropological studies! Thousands and thousands of years have passed him right by, and there he is— Stanley Kowalski—survivor of the stone age! Bearing the raw meat home from the kill in the jungle! And you—*you* here— *waiting* for him! Maybe he'll strike you or maybe grunt and kiss you! That is, if kisses have been discovered yet! Night falls and the other apes gather! There in the front of the cave, all grunting like him, and swilling and gnawing and hulking! His poker night!—you call it—this party of apes! Somebody growls—some creature snatches at something—the fight is on! *God!* Maybe we are a long way from being made in God's image, but Stella—my sister—there has been *some* progress since then! Such things as art—as poetry and music—such kinds of new light have come into the world since then! In some kinds of people some tenderer feelings have had some little beginning! That we have got to make *grow!* And *cling* to, and hold as our flag! In this dark march toward whatever it is we're approaching. . . . *Don't—don't hang back with the brutes!*

(Another train passes outside. Stanley hesitates, licking his lips. Then suddenly he turns stealthily about and withdraws through front door. The women are still unaware of his presence. When the train has passed he calls through the closed front door.)

STANLEY. Hey! Hey, Stella!

STELLA *(who has listened gravely to Blanche)*. Stanley!

BLANCHE. Stell, I—

(But Stella has gone to the front door. Stanley enters casually with his packages.)

STANLEY. Hiyuh, Stella. Blanche back?

STELLA. Yes, she's back.

STANLEY. Hiyuh, Blanche. *(He grins at her)*

STELLA. You must've got under the car.

STANLEY. Them darn mechanics at Fritz's don't know their ass fr'm— *Hey!* *(Stella has embraced him with both arms, fiercely, and full in the view of Blanche. He laughs and clasps her head to him. Over her head he grins through the curtains at Blanche.*

(As the lights fade away, with a lingering

brightness on their embrace, the music of the "blue piano" and trumpet and drums is heard.)

SCENE FIVE

Blanche is seated in the bedroom fanning herself with a palm leaf as she reads over a just completed letter. Suddenly she bursts into a peal of laughter. Stella is dressing in the bedroom.

———

STELLA. What are you laughing at, honey?

BLANCHE. Myself, myself, for being such a liar! I'm writing a letter to Shep. *(She picks up the letter)* "Darling Shep. I am spending the summer on the wing, making flying visits here and there. And who knows, perhaps I shall take a sudden notion to *swoop* down on *Dallas!* How would you feel about that? Ha-ha!" *(She laughs nervously and brightly, touching her throat as if actually talking to Shep)* "Forewarned is forearmed, as they say!"— How does that sound?

STELLA. Uh-huh . . .

BLANCHE *(going on nervously)*. "Most of my sister's friends go north in the summer but some have homes on the Gulf and there has been a continued round of entertainments, teas, cocktails, and luncheons—"

(A disturbance is heard upstairs at the Hubbells' apartment.)

STELLA. Eunice seems to be having some trouble with Steve.

(Eunice's voice shouts in terrible wrath.)

EUNICE. I heard about you and that blonde!

STEVE. That's a damn lie!

EUNICE. You ain't pulling the wool over my eyes! I wouldn't mind if you'd stay down at the Four Deuces, but you always going up.

STEVE. Who ever seen me up?

EUNICE. I seen you chasing her 'round the balcony—I'm gonna call the vice squad!

STEVE. Don't you throw that at me!

EUNICE *(shrieking)*. You hit me! I'm gonna call the police!

(A clatter of aluminum striking a wall is heard, followed by a man's angry roar, shouts and overturned furniture. There is a crash; then a relative hush.)

BLANCHE *(brightly)*. Did he *kill* her?

(Eunice appears on the steps in daemonic disorder.)

STELLA. No! She's coming downstairs.

EUNICE. Call the police, I'm going to call the police! *(She rushes around the corner)*

(They laugh lightly. Stanley comes around the corner in his green and scarlet silk bowling shirt. He trots up the steps and bangs into the kitchen. Blanche registers his entrance with nervous gestures.)

STANLEY. What's a matter with Eun-uss?

STELLA. She and Steve had a row. Has she got the police?

STANLEY. Naw. She's gettin' a drink.

STELLA. That's much more practical!

(Steve comes down nursing a bruise on his forehead and looks in the door.)

STEVE. *She here?*

STANLEY. Naw, naw. At the Four Deuces.

STEVE. That rutting hunk! *(He looks around the corner a bit timidly, then turns with affected boldness and runs after her)*

BLANCHE. I must jot that down in my notebook. Ha-ha! I'm compiling a notebook of quaint little words and phrases I've picked up here.

STANLEY. You won't pick up nothing here you ain't heard before.

BLANCHE. Can I count on that?

STANLEY. You can count on it up to five hundred.

BLANCHE. That's a mighty high number. *(He jerks open the bureau drawer, slams it shut and throws shoes in a corner. At each noise Blanche winces slightly. Finally she speaks)* What sign were you born under?

STANLEY *(while he is dressing)*. Sign?

BLANCHE. Astrological sign. I bet you were born under Aries. Aries people are forceful and dynamic. They dote on noise! They love to bang things around! You must have had lots of banging around in the army and now that you're out, you make up for it by treating inanimate objects with such a fury!

(Stella has been going in and out of closet during this scene. Now she pops her head out of the closet.)

STELLA. Stanley was born just five minutes after Christmas.

BLANCHE. Capricorn—the Goat!

STANLEY. What sign were *you* born under?

BLANCHE. Oh, my birthday's next month,

the fifteenth of September; that's under Virgo.

STANLEY. What's Virgo?

BLANCHE. Virgo is the Virgin.

STANLEY (*contemptuously*). Hah! (*He advances a little as he knots his tie*) Say, do you happen to know somebody named Shaw?

(*Her face expresses a faint shock. She reaches for the cologne bottle and dampens her handkerchief as she answers carefully.*)

BLANCHE. Why, everybody knows somebody named Shaw!

STANLEY. Well, this somebody named Shaw is under the impression he met you in Laurel, but I figure he must have got you mixed up with some other party because this other party is someone he met at a hotel called the Flamingo.

(*Blanche laughs breathlessly as she touches the cologne-dampened handkerchief to her temples.*)

BLANCHE. I'm afraid he does have me mixed up with this "other party." The Hotel Flamingo is not the sort of establishment I would dare to be seen in!

STANLEY. You know of it?

BLANCHE. Yes, I've seen it and smelled it.

STANLEY. You must've got pretty close if you could smell it.

BLANCHE. The odor of cheap perfume is penetrating.

STANLEY. That stuff you use is expensive?

BLANCHE. Twenty-five dollars an ounce! I'm nearly out. That's just a hint if you want to remember my birthday! (*She speaks lightly but her voice has a note of fear*)

STANLEY. Shaw must've got you mixed up. He goes in and out of Laurel all the time so he can check on it and clear up any mistake.

(*He turns away and crosses to the portieres. Blanche closes her eyes as if to faint. Her hand trembles as she lifts the handkerchief again to her forehead.*)

(*Steve and Eunice come around the corner. Steve's arm is around Eunice's shoulder and she is sobbing luxuriously and he is cooing love-words. There is a murmur of thunder as they go slowly upstairs in a tight embrace.*)

STANLEY (*to Stella*). I'll wait for you at the Four Deuces!

STELLA. Hey! Don't I rate one kiss?

STANLEY. Not in front of your sister.

(*He goes out. Blanche rises from her chair. She seems faint; looks about her with an expression of almost panic.*)

BLANCHE. Stella! What have you heard about me?

STELLA. Huh?

BLANCHE. What have people been telling you about me?

STELLA. Telling?

BLANCHE. You haven't heard any—unkind—gossip about me?

STELLA. Why, no, Blanche, of course not!

BLANCHE. Honey, there was—a good deal of talk in Laurel.

STELLA. About *you*, Blanche?

BLANCHE. I wasn't so good the last two years or so, after Belle Reve had started to slip through my fingers.

STELLA. All of us do things we—

BLANCHE. I never was hard or self-sufficient enough. When people are soft—soft people have got to shimmer and glow—they've got to put on soft colors, the colors of butterfly wings, and put a—paper lantern over the light. . . . It isn't enough to be soft. You've got to be soft *and attractive*. And I—I'm fading now! I don't know how much longer I can turn the trick.

(*The afternoon has faded to dusk. Stella goes into the bedroom and turns on the light under the paper lantern. She holds a bottled soft drink in her hand.*)

BLANCHE. Have you been listening to me?

STELLA. I don't listen to you when you are being morbid! (*She advances with the bottled coke*)

BLANCHE (*with abrupt change to gaiety*). Is that coke for me?

STELLA. Not for anyone else!

BLANCHE. Why, you precious thing, you! Is it just coke?

STELLA (*turning*). You mean you want a shot in it!

BLANCHE. Well, honey, a shot never does a coke any harm! Let me! You mustn't wait on me!

STELLA. I like to wait on you, Blanche. It makes it seem more like home. (*She goes into the kitchen, finds a glass and pours a shot of whiskey into it*)

BLANCHE. I have to admit I love to be waited on . . . (*She rushes into the bedroom. Stella goes to her with the glass. Blanche suddenly clutches Stella's free hand with a moaning sound and presses the hand to her lips. Stella is embarrassed by her show of emotion. Blanche speaks in a choked voice)* You're—you're so *good* to me! And I—

STELLA. Blanche.

BLANCHE. I know, I won't! You hate me to talk sentimental! But honey, *believe* I feel things more than I *tell* you! I *won't* stay long! I won't, I *promise* I—

STELLA. Blanche!

BLANCHE *(hysterically)*. I won't, I promise, *I'll* go! Go *soon!* I will really! I *won't* hang around until he—throws me out . . .

STELLA. Now will you stop talking foolish?

BLANCHE. Yes, honey. Watch how you pour—that fizzy stuff foams over!

(Blanche laughs shrilly and grabs the glass, but her hand shakes so it almost slips from her grasp. Stella pours the coke into the glass. It foams over and spills. Blanche gives a piercing cry.)

STELLA *(shocked by the cry)*. Heavens!

BLANCHE. Right on my pretty white skirt!

STELLA. Oh . . . Use my hanky. Blot gently.

BLANCHE *(slowly recovering)*. I know—gently—gently . . .

STELLA. Did it stain?

BLANCHE. Not a bit. Ha-ha! Isn't that lucky? *(She sits down shakily, taking a grateful drink. She holds the glass in both hands and continues to laugh a little)*

STELLA. Why did you scream like that?

BLANCHE. I don't know why I screamed! *(Continuing nervously)* Mitch—Mitch is coming at seven. I guess I am just feeling nervous about our relations. *(She begins to talk rapidly and breathlessly)* He hasn't gotten a thing but a goodnight kiss, that's all I have given him, Stella. I want his respect. And men don't want anything they get too easy. But on the other hand men lose interest quickly. Especially when the girl is over—thirty. They think a girl over thirty ought to—the vulgar term is—"put out." . . . And I—I'm not "putting out." Of course he—he doesn't know—I mean I haven't informed him—of my real age!

STELLA. Why are you sensitive about your age?

BLANCHE. Because of hard knocks my vanity's been given. What I mean is—he thinks I'm sort of—prim and proper, you know! *(She laughs out sharply)* I want to

deceive him enough to make him—want me . . .

STELLA. Blanche, do you want *him?*

BLANCHE. I want to *rest!* I want to breathe quietly again! Yes—I *want* Mitch . . . *very badly!* Just think! If it happens! I can leave here and not be anyone's problem . . .

(Stanley comes around the corner with a drink under his belt.)

STANLEY *(bawling)*. Hey, Steve! Hey, Eunice! Hey, Stella!

(There are joyous calls from above. Trumpet and drums are heard from around the corner.)

STELLA *(kissing Blanche impulsively)*. It *will* happen!

BLANCHE *(doubtfully)*. It will?

STELLA. It *will!* *(She goes across into the kitchen, looking back at Blanche)* It will, honey, it *will*. . . . But don't take another drink! *(Her voice catches as she goes out the door to meet her husband)*

(Blanche sinks faintly back in her chair with her drink. Eunice shrieks with laughter and runs down the steps. Steve bounds after her with goat-like screeches and chases her around corner. Stanley and Stella twine arms as they follow, laughing. Dusk settles deeper. The music from the Four Deuces is slow and blue.)

BLANCHE. Ah, me, ah, me, ah, me . . .

(Her eyes fall shut and the palm leaf fan drops from her fingers. She slaps her hand on the chair arm a couple of times. There is a little glimmer of lightning about the building.

(A Young Man comes along the street and rings the bell.)

BLANCHE. Come in.

(The Young Man appears through the portieres. She regards him with interest.)

BLANCHE. Well, well! What can I do for *you?*

YOUNG MAN. I'm collecting for *The Evening Star.*

BLANCHE. I didn't know that stars took up collections.

YOUNG MAN. It's the paper.

BLANCHE. I know, I was joking—feebly! Will you—have a drink?

YOUNG MAN. No, ma'am. No, thank you, I can't drink on the job.

BLANCHE. Oh, well, now, let's see. . . . No, I don't have a dime! I'm not the lady of the house. I'm her sister from Mississippi. I'm one of those poor relations you've heard about.

YOUNG MAN. That's all right. I'll drop by later. (*He starts to go out. She approaches a little*)

BLANCHE. Hey! (*He turns back shyly. She puts a cigarette in a long holder*) Could you give me a light? (*She crosses toward him. They meet at the door between the two rooms*)

YOUNG MAN. Sure. (*He takes out a lighter*) This doesn't always work.

BLANCHE. It's temperamental? (*It flares*) Ah!—thank you. (*He starts away again*) Hey! (*He turns again, still more uncertainly. She goes close to him*) Uh—what time is it?

YOUNG MAN. Fifteen of seven, ma'am.

BLANCHE. So late? Don't you just love these long rainy afternoons in New Orleans when an hour isn't just an hour—but a little piece of eternity dropped into your hands—and who knows what to do with it? (*She touches his shoulders*) You—uh—didn't get wet in the rain?

YOUNG MAN. No, ma'am. I stepped inside.

BLANCHE. In a drugstore? And had a soda?

YOUNG MAN. Uh-huh.

BLANCHE. Chocolate?

YOUNG MAN. No, ma'am. Cherry.

BLANCHE (*laughing*). Cherry!

YOUNG MAN. A cherry soda.

BLANCHE. You make my mouth water. (*She touches his cheek lightly, and smiles. Then she goes to the trunk*)

YOUNG MAN. Well, I'd better be going—

BLANCHE. (*stopping him*). Young man! (*He turns. She takes a large, gossamer scarf from the trunk and drapes it about her shoulders.*

(*In the ensuing pause, the "blue piano" is heard. It continues through the rest of this scene and the opening of the next. The young man clears his throat and looks yearningly at the door.*)

Young man! Young, young, young man! Has anyone ever told you that you look like a young Prince out of the Arabian Nights?

(*The Young Man laughs uncomfortably and stands like a bashful kid. Blanche speaks softly to him.*)

Well, you do, honey lamb! Come here. I want to kiss you, just once, softly and sweetly on your mouth!

(*Without waiting for him to accept, she crosses quickly to him and presses her lips to his.*)

Now run along, now, quickly! It would be nice to keep you, but I've got to be good—and keep my hands off children.

(*He stares at her a moment. She opens the door for him and blows a kiss at him as he goes down the steps with a dazed look. She stands there a little dreamily after he has disappeared. Then Mitch appears around the corner with a bunch of roses.*)

BLANCHE (*gaily*). Look who's coming! My Rosenkavalier! Bow to me first . . . now present them! Ahhhh—Merciiii!

(*She looks at him over them, coquettishly pressing them to her lips. He beams at her self-consciously.*)

SCENE SIX

It is about two A.M. on the same evening. The outer wall of the building is visible. Blanche and Mitch come in. The utter exhaustion which only a neurasthenic personality can know is evident in Blanche's voice and manner. Mitch is stolid but depressed. They have probably been out to the amusement park on Lake Pontchartrain, for Mitch is bearing, upside down, a plaster statuette of Mae West, the sort of prize won at shooting-galleries and carnival games of chance.

BLANCHE (*stopping lifelessly at the steps*). Well—(*Mitch laughs uneasily*) Well . . .

MITCH. I guess it must be pretty late—and you're tired.

BLANCHE. Even the hot tamale man has deserted the street, and he hangs on till the end. (*Mitch laughs uneasily again*) How will you get home?

MITCH. I'll walk over to Bourbon and catch an owl-car.

BLANCHE (*laughing grimly*). Is that streetcar named Desire still grinding along the tracks at this hour?

MITCH (*heavily*). I'm afraid you haven't gotten much fun out of this evening, Blanche.

BLANCHE. I spoiled it for *you*.

MITCH. No, you didn't, but I felt all the time that I wasn't giving you much—entertainment.

BLANCHE. I simply couldn't rise to the occasion. That was all. I don't think I've ever tried so hard to be gay and made such a dismal mess of it. I get ten points for trying!—I *did* try.

MITCH. Why did you try if you didn't feel like it, Blanche?

BLANCHE. I was just obeying the law of nature.

MITCH. Which law is that?

BLANCHE. The one that says the lady must entertain the gentleman—or no dice! See if you can locate my door-key in this purse. When I'm so tired my fingers are all thumbs!

MITCH *(rooting in her purse)*. This it?

BLANCHE. No, honey, that's the key to my trunk which I must soon be packing.

MITCH. You mean you are leaving here soon?

BLANCHE. I've outstayed my welcome.

MITCH. This it?

(The music fades away.)

BLANCHE. Eureka! Honey, you open the door while I take a last look at the sky. *(She leans on the porch rail. He opens the door and stands awkwardly behind her)* I'm looking for the Pleiades, the Seven Sisters, but these girls are not out tonight. Oh, yes they are, there they are! God bless them! All in a bunch going home from their little bridge party. . . . Y' get the door open? Good boy! I guess you—want to go now . . .

(He shuffles and coughs a little.)

MITCH. Can I—uh—kiss you—good-night?

BLANCHE. Why do you always ask me if you may?

MITCH. I don't know whether you want me to or not.

BLANCHE. Why should you be so doubtful?

MITCH. That night when we parked by the lake and I kissed you, you—

BLANCHE. Honey, it wasn't the kiss I objected to. I liked the kiss very much. It was the other little—familiarity—that I—felt obliged to—discourage. . . . I didn't resent it! Not a bit in the world! In fact, I was somewhat flattered that you—desired me! But, honey, you know as well as I do that a single girl, a girl alone in the world, has got to keep a firm hold on her emotions or she'll be lost!

MITCH *(solemnly)*. Lost?

BLANCHE. I guess you are used to girls that like to be lost. The kind that get lost immediately, on the first date!

MITCH. I like you to be exactly the way that you are, because in all my—experience—I have never known anyone like you.

(Blanche looks at him gravely; then she bursts into laughter and then claps a hand to her mouth.)

MITCH. Are you laughing at me?

BLANCHE. No, honey. The lord and lady of the house have not yet returned, so come in. We'll have a night-cap. Let's leave the lights off. Shall we?

MITCH. You just—do what you want to.

(Blanche precedes him into the kitchen. The outer wall of the building disappears and the interiors of the two rooms can be dimly seen.)

BLANCHE *(remaining in the first room)*. The other room's more comfortable—go on in. This crashing around in the dark is my search for some liquor.

MITCH. You want a drink?

BLANCHE. I want *you* to have a drink! You have been so anxious and solemn all evening, and so have I; we have both been anxious and solemn and now for these few last remaining moments of our lives together—I want to create—*joie de vivre!* I'm lighting a candle.

MITCH. That's good.

BLANCHE. We are going to be very Bohemian. We are going to pretend that we are sitting in a little artists' cafe on the Left Bank in Paris! *(She lights a candle stub and puts it in a bottle)* Je suis la Dame aux Camellias! Vous êtes—Armand! Understand French?

MITCH *(heavily)*. Naw. Naw, I—

BLANCHE. *Voulez-vous couchez avec moi ce soir? Vous ne comprenez pas? Ah, quelle dommage!*—I mean it's a damned good thing. . . . I've found some liquor! Just enough for two shots without any dividends, honey . . .

MITCH *(heavily)*. That's—good.

(She enters the bedroom with the drinks and the candle.)

BLANCHE. Sit down! Why don't you take off your coat and loosen your collar?

MITCH. I better leave it on.

BLANCHE. No. I want you to be comfortable.

MITCH. I am ashamed of the way I perspire. My shirt is sticking to me.

BLANCHE. Perspiration is healthy. If people didn't perspire they would die in five minutes. *(She takes his coat from him)* This is a nice coat. What kind of material is it?

MITCH. They call that stuff alpaca.

BLANCHE. Oh. Alpaca.

MITCH. It's very lightweight alpaca.

BLANCHE. Oh. Lightweight alpaca.

MITCH. I don't like to wear a wash-coat even in summer because I sweat through it.

BLANCHE. Oh.

MITCH. And it don't look neat on me. A man with a heavy build has got to be careful of what he puts on him so he don't look too clumsy.

BLANCHE. You are not too heavy.

MITCH. You don't think I am?

BLANCHE. You are not the delicate type. You have a massive bone-structure and a very imposing physique.

MITCH. Thank you. Last Christmas I was given a membership to the New Orleans Athletic Club.

BLANCHE. Oh, good.

MITCH. It was the finest present I ever was given. I work out there with the weights and I swim and I keep myself fit. When I started there, I was getting soft in the belly but now my belly is hard. It is so hard now that a man can punch me in the belly and it don't hurt me. Punch me! Go on! See? *(She pokes lightly at him)*

BLANCHE. Gracious. *(Her hand touches her chest)*

MITCH. Guess how much I weigh, Blanche?

BLANCHE. Oh, I'd say in the vicinity of— one hundred and eighty?

MITCH. Guess again.

BLANCHE. Not that much?

MITCH. No. More.

BLANCHE. Well, you're a tall man and you can carry a good deal of weight without looking awkward.

MITCH. I weigh two hundred and seven pounds and I'm six feet one and one half inches tall in my bare feet—without shoes on. And that is what I weigh stripped.

BLANCHE. Oh, my goodness, me! It's awe-inspiring.

MITCH *(embarrassed)*. My weight is not a very interesting subject to talk about. *(He hesitates for a moment)* What's yours?

BLANCHE. My weight?

MITCH. Yes.

BLANCHE. Guess!

MITCH. Let me lift you.

BLANCHE. Samson! Go on, lift me. *(He comes behind her and puts his hands on her waist and raises her lightly off the ground)* Well?

MITCH. You are light as a feather.

BLANCHE. Ha-ha! *(He lowers her but keeps his hands on her waist. Blanche speaks with an affectation of demureness)* You may release me now.

MITCH. Huh?

BLANCHE *(gaily)*. I said unhand me, sir. *(He fumblingly embraces her. Her voice sounds gently reproving)* Now, Mitch. Just because Stanley and Stella aren't at home is no reason why you shouldn't behave like a gentleman.

MITCH. Just give me a slap whenever I step out of bounds.

BLANCHE. That won't be necessary. You're a natural gentleman, one of the very few that are left in the world. I don't want you to think that I am severe and old maid schoolteacherish or anything like that. It's just—well—

MITCH. Huh?

BLANCHE. I guess it is just that I have— old-fashioned ideals! *(She rolls her eyes, knowing he cannot see her face. Mitch goes to the front door. There is a considerable silence between them. Blanche sighs and Mitch coughs self-consciously)*

MITCH *(finally)*. Where's Stanley and Stella tonight?

BLANCHE. They have gone out. With Mr. and Mrs. Hubbell upstairs.

MITCH. Where did they go?

BLANCHE. I think they were planning to go to a midnight prevue at Loew's State.

MITCH. We should all go out together some night.

BLANCHE. No. That wouldn't be a good plan.

MITCH. Why not?

BLANCHE. You are an old friend of Stanley's?

MITCH. We was together in the Two-forty-first.

BLANCHE. I guess he talks to you frankly?

MITCH. Sure.

BLANCHE. Has he talked to you about me?

MITCH. Oh—not very much.

BLANCHE. The way you say that, I suspect that he has.

MITCH. No, he hasn't said much.

BLANCHE. But what he *has* said. What would you say his attitude toward me was?

MITCH. Why do you want to ask that?

BLANCHE. Well—

MITCH. Don't you get along with him?

BLANCHE. What do you think?

MITCH. I don't think he understands you.

BLANCHE. That is putting it mildly. If it weren't for Stella about to have a baby, I wouldn't be able to endure things here.

MITCH. He isn't—nice to you?

BLANCHE. He is insufferably rude. Goes out of his way to offend me.

MITCH. In what way, Blanche?

BLANCHE. Why, in every conceivable way.

MITCH. I'm surprised to hear that.

BLANCHE. Are you?

MITCH. Well, I—don't see how anybody could be rude to you.

BLANCHE. It's really a pretty frightful situation. You see, there's no privacy here. There's just these portieres between the two rooms at night. He stalks through the rooms in his underwear at night. And I have to ask him to close the bathroom door. That sort of commonness isn't necessary. You probably wonder why I don't move out. Well, I'll tell you frankly. A teacher's salary is barely sufficient for her living-expenses. I didn't save a penny last year and so I had to come here for the summer. That's why I have to put up with my sister's husband. And he has to put up with me, apparently so much against his wishes. . . . Surely he must have told you how much he hates me!

MITCH. I don't think he hates you.

BLANCHE. He hates me. Or why would he insult me? The first time I laid eyes on him I thought to myself, that man is my executioner! That man will destroy me, unless—

MITCH. Blanche—

BLANCHE. Yes, honey?

MITCH. Can I ask you a question?

BLANCHE. Yes. What?

MITCH. How old are you?

(She makes a nervous gesture.)

BLANCHE. Why do you want to know?

MITCH. I talked to my mother about you and she said, "How old is Blanche?" And I wasn't able to tell her. *(There is another pause)*

BLANCHE. You talked to your mother about me?

MITCH. Yes.

BLANCHE. Why?

MITCH. I told my mother how nice you were, and I liked you.

BLANCHE. Were you sincere about that?

MITCH. You know I was.

BLANCHE. Why did your mother want to know my age?

MITCH. Mother is sick.

BLANCHE. I'm sorry to hear it. Badly?

MITCH. She won't live long. Maybe just a few months.

BLANCHE. Oh.

MITCH. She worries because I'm not settled.

BLANCHE. Oh.

MITCH. She wants me to be settled down before she—*(His voice is hoarse and he clears his throat twice, shuffling nervously around with his hands in and out of his pockets)*

BLANCHE. You love her very much, don't you?

MITCH. Yes.

BLANCHE. I think you have a great capacity for devotion. You will be lonely when she passes on, won't you? *(Mitch clears his throat and nods)* I understand what that is.

MITCH. To be lonely?

BLANCHE. I loved someone, too, and the person I loved I lost.

MITCH. Dead? *(She crosses to the window and sits on the sill, looking out. She pours herself another drink)* A man?

BLANCHE. He was a boy, just a boy, when I was a very young girl. When I was sixteen, I made the discovery—love. All at once and much, much too completely. It was like you suddenly turned a blinding light on something that had always been half in shadow, that's how it struck the world for me. But I was unlucky. Deluded. There was something different about the boy, a nervousness, a softness and tenderness which wasn't like a man's, although he wasn't the least bit effeminate looking—still—that thing was there. . . . He came to me for help. I didn't know that. I didn't find out anything till after our marriage when we'd run away and come back and all I knew was I'd failed him in some mysterious

way and wasn't able to give the help he
needed but couldn't speak of! He was in
the quicksands and clutching at me—but
I wasn't holding him out, I was slipping
in with him! I didn't know that. I didn't
know anything except I loved him un-
endurably but without being able to help
him or help myself. Then I found out. In
the worst of all possible ways. By coming
suddenly into a room that I thought was
empty—which wasn't empty, but had two
people in it . . . the boy I had married
and an older man who had been his friend
for years . . .
*(A locomotive is heard approaching out-
side. She claps her hands to her ears and
crouches over. The headlight of the locomotive glares into the room as it thunders
past. As the noise recedes she straightens
slowly and continues speaking.)*
Afterwards we pretended that nothing had
been discovered. Yes, the three of us drove
out to Moon Lake Casino, very drunk and
laughing all the way.
*(Polka music sounds, in a minor key
faint with distance.)*
We danced the Varsouviana! Suddenly in
the middle of the dance the boy I had
married broke away from me and ran out
of the casino. A few moments later—a
shot!
(The Polka stops abruptly.
*(Blanche rises stiffly. Then, the Polka re-
sumes in a major key.)*
I ran out—all did!—all ran and gathered
about the terrible thing at the edge of the
lake! I couldn't get near for the crowding.
Then somebody caught my arm. "Don't
go any closer! Come back! You don't want
to see!" See? See what! Then I heard
voices say—Allan! Allan! The Grey boy!
He'd stuck the revolver into his mouth,
and fired—so that the back of his head had
been—blown away!
(She sways and covers her face.)
It was because—on the dance-floor—unable to stop myself—I'd suddenly said—"I
saw! I know! You disgust me . . ." And
then the searchlight which had been
turned on the world was turned off again
and never for one moment since has there
been any light that's stronger than this—
kitchen—candle . . .
*(Mitch gets up awkwardly and moves
toward her a little. The Polka music in-
creases. Mitch stands beside her.)*
MITCH *(drawing her slowly into his
arms).* You need somebody. And I need
somebody, too. Could it be—you and me,
Blanche?
*(She stares at him vacantly for a moment.
Then with a soft cry huddles in his embrace. She makes a sobbing effort to speak
but the words won't come. He kisses her
forehead and her eyes and finally her lips.
The Polka tune fades out. Her breath is
drawn and released in long, grateful sobs.)*
BLANCHE. Sometimes—there's God—so
quickly!

SCENE SEVEN

It is late afternoon in mid-September.
*The portieres are open and a table is set
for a birthday supper, with cake and
flowers.*
*Stella is completing the decorations as
Stanley comes in.*

STANLEY. What's all this stuff for?
STELLA. Honey, it's Blanche's birthday.
STANLEY. She here?
STELLA. In the bathroom.
STANLEY *(mimicking).* "Washing out
some things"?
STELLA. I reckon so.
STANLEY. How long she been in there?
STELLA. All afternoon.
STANLEY *(mimicking).* "Soaking in a
hot tub"?
STELLA. Yes.
STANLEY. Temperature 100 on the nose,
and she soaks herself in a hot tub.
STELLA. She says it cools her off for the
evening.
STANLEY. And you run out an' get her
cokes, I suppose? And serve 'em to Her
Majesty in the tub? *(Stella shrugs)* Set
down here a minute.
STELLA. Stanley, I've got things to do.
STANLEY. Set down! I've got th' dope
on your big sister, Stella.
STELLA. Stanley, stop picking on
Blanche.
STANLEY. That girl calls *me* common!
STELLA. Lately you been doing all you
can think of to rub her the wrong way,
Stanley, and Blanche is sensitive and
you've got to realize that Blanche and I
grew up under very different circum-
stances than you did.
STANLEY. So I been told. And told and

told and told! You know she's been feeding us a pack of lies here?

STELLA. No, I don't, and—

STANLEY. Well, she has, however. But now the cat's out of the bag! I found out some things!

STELLA. What—things?

STANLEY. Things I already suspected. But now I got proof from the most reliable sources—which I have checked on! *(Blanche is singing in the bathroom a saccharine popular ballad which is used contrapuntally with Stanley's speech.)*

STELLA *(to Stanley)*. Lower your voice!

STANLEY. Some canary-bird, huh!

STELLA. Now please tell me quietly what you think you've found out about my sister.

STANLEY. Lie Number One: All this squeamishness she puts on! You should just know the line·she's been feeding to Mitch. He thought she had never been more than kissed by a fellow! But Sister Blanche is no lily! Ha-ha! Some lily she is!

STELLA. What have you heard and who from?

STANLEY. Our supply-man down at the plant has been going through Laurel for years and he knows all about her and everybody else in the town of Laurel knows all about her. She is as famous in Laurel as if she was the President of the United States, only she is not respected by any party! This supply-man stops at a hotel called the Flamingo.

BLANCHE *(singing blithely)*. "Say, it's only a paper moon, Sailing over a cardboard sea—But it wouldn't be make-believe If you believed in me!"

STELLA. What about the—Flamingo?

STANLEY. She stayed there, too.

STELLA. My sister lived at Belle Reve.

STANLEY. This is after the home-place had slipped through her lily-white fingers! She moved to the Flamingo! A second-class hotel which has the advantage of not interfering in the private social life of the personalities there! The Flamingo is used to all kinds of goings-on. But even the management of the Flamingo was impressed by Dame Blanche! In fact they was so impressed by Dame Blanche that they requested her to turn in her room-key—for permanently! This happened a couple of weeks before she showed here.

BLANCHE *(singing)*. "It's a Barnum and

Bailey world, Just as phony as it can be—

But it wouldn't be make-believe If you believed in me!"

STELLA. What—contemptible—lies!

STANLEY. Sure, I can see how you would be upset by this. She pulled the wool over your eyes as much as Mitch's!

STELLA. It's pure invention! There's not a word of truth in it and if I were a man and this creature had dared to invent such things in my presence—

BLANCHE *(singing)*. "Without your love, It's a honky-tonk parade!
Without your love,
It's a melody played In a penny arcade . . ."

STANLEY. Honey, I told you I thoroughly checked on these stories! Now wait till I'm finished. The trouble with Dame Blanche was that she couldn't put on her act any more in Laurel! They got wised up after two or three dates with her and then they quit, and she goes on to another, the same old line, same old act, same old hooey! But the town was too small for this to go on forever! And as time went by she became a town character. Regarded as not just different but downright loco—nuts. *(Stella draws back)* And for the last year or two she has been washed up like poison. That's why she's here this summer, visiting royalty, putting on all this act—because she's practically told by the mayor to get out of town! Yes, did you know there was an army camp near Laurel and your sister's was one of the places called "Out-of-Bounds"?

BLANCHE. "It's only a paper moon, Just as phony as it can be—

But it wouldn't be make-believe If you believed in me!"

STANLEY. Well, so much for her being such a refined and particular type of girl. Which brings us to Lie Number Two.

STELLA. I don't want to hear any more!

STANLEY. She's not going back to teach school! In fact I am willing to bet you that she never had no idea of returning to Laurel! She didn't resign temporarily from the high school because of her nerves! No, siree, Bob! She didn't. They kicked her out of that high school before the spring term ended—and I hate to tell you the reason that step was taken! A seventeen-year-old boy—she'd gotten mixed up with!

BLANCHE. "It's a Barnum and Bailey

world, Just as phony as it can be—"
(In the bathroom the water goes on loud; little breathless cries and peals of laughter are heard as if a child were frolicking in the tub.)

STELLA. This is making me—sick!

STANLEY. The boy's dad learned about it and got in touch with the high school superintendent. Boy, oh, boy, I'd like to have been in that office when Dame Blanche was called on the carpet! I'd like to have seen her trying to squirm out of that one! But they had her on the hook good and proper that time and she knew that the jig was all up! They told her she better move on to some fresh territory. Yep, it was practickly a town ordinance passed against her!

(The bathroom door is opened and Blanche thrusts her head out, holding a towel about her hair.)

BLANCHE. Stella!

STELLA *(faintly)*. Yes, Blanche?

BLANCHE. Give me another bath-towel to dry my hair with. I've just washed it.

STELLA. Yes, Blanche. *(She crosses in a dazed way from the kitchen to the bathroom door with a towel)*

BLANCHE. What's the matter, honey?

STELLA. Matter? Why?

BLANCHE. You have such a strange expression on your face!

STELLA. Oh—*(She tries to laugh)* I guess I'm a little tired!

BLANCHE. Why don't you bathe, too, soon as I get out?

STANLEY *(calling from the kitchen)*. How soon is that going to be?

BLANCHE. Not so terribly long! Possess your soul in patience!

STANLEY. It's not my soul, it's my kidneys I'm worried about!

(Blanche slams the door. Stanley laughs harshly. Stella comes slowly back into the kitchen.)

STANLEY. Well, what do you think of it?

STELLA. I don't believe all of those stories and I think your supply-man was mean and rotten to tell them. It's possible that some of the things he said are partly true. There are things about my sister I don't approve of—things that caused sorrow at home. She was always—flighty!

STANLEY. Flighty!

STELLA. But when she was young, very young, she married a boy who wrote poetry. . . . He was extremely good-looking.

I think Blanche didn't just love him but worshipped the ground he walked on! Adored him and thought him almost too fine to be human! But then she found out—

STANLEY. What?

STELLA. This beautiful and talented young man was a degenerate. Didn't your supply-man give you that information?

STANLEY. All we discussed was recent history. That must have been a pretty long time ago.

STELLA. Yes, it was—a pretty long time ago . . .

(Stanley comes up and takes her by the shoulders rather gently. She gently withdraws from him. Automatically she starts sticking little pink candles in the birthday cake.)

STANLEY. How many candles you putting in that cake?

STELLA. I'll stop at twenty-five.

STANLEY. Is company expected?

STELLA. We asked Mitch to come over for cake and ice-cream.

(Stanley looks a little uncomfortable. He lights a cigarette from the one he has just finished.)

STANLEY. I wouldn't be expecting Mitch over tonight.

(Stella pauses in her occupation with candles and looks slowly around at Stanley.)

STELLA. *Why?*

STANLEY. Mitch is a buddy of mine. We were in the same outfit together—Two-forty-first Engineers. We work in the same plant and now on the same bowling team. You think I could face him if—

STELLA. Stanley Kowalski, did you—did you repeat what that—?

STANLEY. You're goddam right I told him! I'd have that on my conscience the rest of my life if I knew all that stuff and let my best friend get caught!

STELLA. Is Mitch through with her?

STANLEY. Wouldn't you be if—?

STELLA. I said, *Is Mitch through with her?*

(Blanche's voice is lifted again, serenely as a bell. She sings "But it wouldn't be make believe if you believed in me.")

STANLEY. No, I don't think he's necessarily through with her—just wised up!

STELLA. Stanley, she thought Mitch was —going to—going to marry her. I was hoping so, too.

STANLEY. Well, he's not going to marry her. Maybe he *was,* but he's not going to jump in a tank with a school of sharks—now! *(He rises)* Blanche! Oh, Blanche! Can I please get in my bathroom? *(There is a pause)*

BLANCHE. Yes, indeed, sir! Can you wait one second while I dry?

STANLEY. Having waited one hour I guess one second ought to pass in a hurry.

STELLA. And she hasn't got her job? Well, what will she do!

STANLEY. She's not stayin' here after Tuesday. You know that, don't you? Just to make sure I bought her ticket myself. A bus-ticket!

STELLA. In the first place, Blanche wouldn't go on a bus.

STANLEY. She'll go on a bus and like it.

STELLA. No, she won't, no, she won't, Stanley!

STANLEY. *She'll go!* Period. P.S. She'll go *Tuesday!*

STELLA *(slowly).* What'll — she — do! What on earth will she—*do!*

STANLEY. Her future is mapped out for her.

STELLA. What do you mean?

(Blanche sings.)

STANLEY. Hey, canary bird! Toots! Get *OUT* of the *BATHROOM!*

(The bathroom door flies open and Blanche emerges with a gay peal of laughter, but as Stanley crosses past her, a frightened look appears in her face, almost a look of panic. He doesn't look at her but slams the bathroom door shut as he goes in.)

BLANCHE *(snatching up a hair-brush).* Oh, I feel so good after my long, hot bath, I feel so good and cool and—rested!

STELLA *(sadly and doubtfully from the kitchen).* Do you, Blanche?

BLANCHE *(brushing her hair vigorously).* Yes, I do, so refreshed! *(She tinkles her highball glass)* A hot bath and a long, cold drink always give me a brand new outlook on life! *(She looks through the portieres at Stella, standing between them, and slowly stops brushing)* Something has happened!—What is it?

STELLA *(turning away quickly).* Why, nothing has happened, Blanche.

BLANCHE. You're lying! Something has! *(She stares fearfully at Stella, who pretends to be busy at the table. The distant piano goes into a hectic breakdown.)*

SCENE EIGHT

Three-quarters of an hour later.

The view through the big windows is fading gradually into a still-golden dusk. A torch of sunlight blazes on the side of a big water-tank or oil-drum across the empty lot toward the business district which is now pierced by pinpoints of lighted windows or windows reflecting the sunset.

The three people are completing a dismal birthday supper. Stanley looks sullen. Stella is embarrassed and sad.

Blanche has a tight, artificial smile on her drawn face. There is a fourth place at the table which is left vacant.

—

BLANCHE *(suddenly).* Stanley, tell us a joke, tell us a funny story to make us all laugh. I don't know what's the matter, we're all so solemn. Is it because I've been stood up by my beau? *(Stella laughs feebly)* It's the first time in my entire experience with men, and I've had a good deal of all sorts, that I've actually been stood up by anybody! Ha-ha! I don't know how to take it. . . . Tell us a funny little story, Stanley! Something to help us out.

STANLEY. I didn't think you liked my stories, Blanche.

BLANCHE. I like them when they're amusing but not indecent.

STANLEY. I don't know any refined enough for your taste.

BLANCHE. Then let me tell one.

STELLA. Yes, you tell one, Blanche. You used to know lots of good stories.

(The music fades.)

BLANCHE. Let me see, now. . . . I must run through my repertoire! Oh, yes—I love parrot stories! Do you all like parrot stories? Well, this one's about the old maid and the parrot. This old maid, she had a parrot that cursed a blue streak and knew more vulgar expressions than Mr. Kowalski!

STANLEY. Huh.

BLANCHE. And the only way to hush the parrot up was to put the cover back on its cage so it would think it was night and go back to sleep. Well, one morning the old maid had just uncovered the parrot for the day—when who should she see coming up the front walk but the preacher! Well, she rushed back to the parrot and slipped the cover back on the cage and then she let in the preacher. And the parrot was perfectly still, just as quiet as a mouse, but just as she was asking the preacher how much sugar he wanted in his coffee—the parrot broke the silence with a loud—*(She whistles)*—and said—"God *damn,* but that was a short day!"

(She throws back her head and laughs. Stella also makes an ineffectual effort to seem amused. Stanley pays no attention to the story but reaches way over the table to spear his fork into the remaining chop which he eats with his fingers.)

BLANCHE. Apparently Mr. Kowalski was not amused.

STELLA. Mr. Kowalski is too busy making a pig of himself to think of anything else!

STANLEY. That's right, baby.

STELLA. Your face and your fingers are disgustingly greasy. Go and wash up and then help me clear the table.

(He hurls a plate to the floor.)

STANLEY. That's how I'll clear the table! *(He seizes her arm)* Don't ever talk that way to me! "Pig—Polack—disgusting—vulgar—greasy!"—them kind of words have been on your tongue and your sister's too much around here! What do you two think you are? A pair of queens? Remember what Huey Long said—"Every Man Is a King!" And I am the king around here, so don't forget it! *(He hurls a cup and saucer to the floor)* My place is cleared! You want me to clear your places? *(Stella begins to cry weakly. Stanley stalks out on the porch and lights a cigarette. (The Negro entertainers around the corner are heard.)*

BLANCHE. What happened while I was bathing? What did he tell you, Stella?

STELLA. Nothing, nothing, nothing!

BLANCHE. I think he told you something about Mitch and me! You know why Mitch didn't come but you won't tell me! *(Stella shakes her head helplessly)* I'm going to call him!

STELLA. I wouldn't call him, Blanche.

BLANCHE. I am, I'm going to call him on the phone.

STELLA *(miserably).* I wish you wouldn't.

BLANCHE. I intend to be given some explanation from someone!

(She rushes to the phone in the bedroom. Stella goes out on the porch and stares reproachfully at her husband. He grunts and turns away from her.)

STELLA. I hope you're pleased with your doings. I never had so much trouble swallowing food in my life, looking at that girl's face and the empty chair! *(She cries quietly)*

BLANCHE *(at the phone).* Hello. Mr. Mitchell, please. . . . Oh. . . . I would like to leave a number if I may. Magnolia 9047. And say it's important to call. . . . Yes, very important. . . . Thank you. *(She remains by the phone with a lost, frightened look)*

(Stanley turns slowly back toward his wife and takes her clumsily in his arms.)

STANLEY. Stell, it's gonna be all right after she goes and after you've had the baby. It's gonna be all right again between you and me the way that it was. You remember that way that it was? Them nights we had together? God, honey, it's gonna be sweet when we can make noise in the night the way that we used to and get the colored lights going with nobody's sister behind the curtains to hear us! *(Their upstairs neighbors are heard in bellowing laughter at something. Stanley chuckles)* Steve an' Eunice. . . .

STELLA. Come on back in. *(She returns to the kitchen and starts lighting the candles on the white cake)* Blanche?

BLANCHE. Yes. *(She returns from the bedroom to the table in the kitchen)* Oh, those pretty, pretty little candles! Oh, don't burn them, Stella.

STELLA. I certainly will.

(Stanley comes back in.)

BLANCHE. You ought to save them for baby's birthdays. Oh, I hope candles are going to glow in his life and I hope that his eyes are going to be like candles, like two blue candles lighted in a white cake!

STANLEY *(sitting down).* What poetry!

BLANCHE *(she pauses reflectively for a moment).* I shouldn't have called him.

STELLA. There's lots of things could have happened.

BLANCHE. There's no excuse for it, Stella. I don't have to put up with insults. I won't be taken for granted.

STANLEY. Goddamn, it's hot in here with the steam from the bathroom.

BLANCHE. I've said I was sorry three times. *(The piano fades out)* I take hot baths for my nerves. Hydro-therapy, they call it. You healthy Polack, without a nerve in your body, of course you don't know what anxiety feels like!

STANLEY. I am not a Polack. People from Poland are Poles, not Polacks. But what I am is a one hundred percent American, born and raised in the greatest country on earth and proud as hell of it, so don't ever call me a Polack.

(The phone rings. Blanche rises expectantly.)

BLANCHE. Oh, that's for me, I'm sure.

STANLEY. *I'm* not sure. Keep your seat. *(He crosses leisurely to phone)* H'lo. Aw, yeh, hello, Mac.

(He leans against wall, staring insultingly in at Blanche. She sinks back in her chair with a frightened look. Stella leans over and touches her shoulder.)

BLANCHE. Oh, keep your hands off me, Stella. What is the matter with you? Why do you look at me with that pitying look?

STANLEY *(bawling)*. Q U I E T I N THERE!—We've got a noisy woman on the place.—Go on, Mac. At Riley's? No, I don't wanta bowl at Riley's. I had a little trouble with Riley last week. I'm the team-captain, ain't I? All right, then, we're not gonna bowl at Riley's, we're gonna bowl at the West Side or the Gala! All right, Mac. See you! *(He hangs up and returns to the table. Blanche fiercely controls herself, drinking quickly from her tumbler of water. He doesn't look at her but reaches in a pocket. Then he speaks slowly and with false amiability)* Sister Blanche, I've got a little birthday remembrance for you.

BLANCHE. Oh, have you, Stanley? I wasn't expecting any, I—I don't know why Stella wants to observe my birthday! I'd much rather forget it—when you—reach twenty-seven! Well—age is a subject that you'd prefer to—ignore!

STANLEY. Twenty-seven?

BLANCHE *(quickly)*. What is it? Is it for *me*?

(He is holding a little envelope toward her.)

STANLEY. Yes, I hope you like it!

BLANCHE. Why, why—Why, it's a—

STANLEY. Ticket! Back to Laurel! On the Greyhound! Tuesday! *(The Varsouviana music steals in softly and continues playing. Stella rises abruptly and turns her back. Blanches tries to smile. Then she tries to laugh. Then she gives both up and springs from the table and runs into the next room. She clutches her throat and*

then runs into the bathroom. Coughing, gagging sounds are heard) Well!

STELLA. You didn't need to do that.

STANLEY. Don't forget all that I took off her.

STELLA. You needn't have been so cruel to someone alone as she is.

STANLEY. Delicate piece she is.

STELLA. She is. She was. You didn't know Blanche as a girl. Nobody, nobody, was tender and trusting as she was. But people like you abused her, and forced her to change. *(He crosses into the bedroom, ripping off his shirt, and changes into a brilliant silk bowling shirt. She follows him)* Do you think you're going bowling now?

STANLEY. Sure.

STELLA. You're not going bowling. *(She catches hold of his shirt)* Why did you do this to her?

STANLEY. I done nothing to no one. Let go of my shirt. You've torn it.

STELLA. I want to know why. Tell me why.

STANLEY. When we first met, me and you, you thought I was common. How right you was, baby. I was common as dirt. You showed me the snapshot of the place with the columns. I pulled you down off them columns and how you loved it, having them colored lights going! And wasn't we happy together, wasn't it all okay till she showed here? *(Stella makes a slight movement. Her look goes suddenly inward as if some interior voice had called her name. She begins a slow, shuffling progress from the bedroom to the kitchen, leaning and resting on the back of the chair and then on the edge of a table with a blind look and listening expression. Stanley, finishing with his shirt, is unaware of her reaction)* And wasn't we happy together? Wasn't it all okay? Till she showed here. Hoity-toity, describing me as an ape. *(He suddenly notices the change in Stella)* Hey, what is it, Stel? *(He crosses to her)*

STELLA *(quietly)*. Take me to the hospital.

(He is with her now, supporting her with his arm, murmuring indistinguishably as they go outside.)

SCENE NINE

A while later that evening. Blanche is

seated in a tense hunched position in a bedroom chair that she has re-covered with diagonal green and white stripes. She has on her scarlet satin robe. On the table beside chair is a bottle of liquor and a glass. The rapid, feverish polka tune, the "Varsouviana," is heard. The music is in her mind; she is drinking to escape it and the sense of disaster closing in on her, and she seems to whisper the words of the song. An electric fan is turning back and forth across her.

Mitch comes around the corner in work clothes: blue denim shirt and pants. He is unshaven. He climbs the steps to the door and rings. Blanche is startled.

BLANCHE. Who is it, please?

MITCH *(hoarsely).* Me. Mitch.

(The polka tune stops.)

BLANCHE. Mitch!—Just a minute. *(She rushes about frantically, hiding the bottle in a closet, crouching at the mirror and dabbing her face with cologne and powder. She is so excited that her breath is audible as she dashes about. At last she rushes to the door in the kitchen and lets him in)* Mitch!—Y'know, I really shouldn't let you in after the treatment I have received from you this evening! So utterly uncavalier! But hello, beautiful! *(She offers him her lips. He ignores it and pushes past her into the flat. She looks fearfully after him as he stalks into the bedroom)* My, my, what a cold shoulder! And such uncouth apparel! Why, you haven't even shaved! The unforgivable insult to a lady! But I forgive you. I forgive you because it's such a relief to see you. You've stopped that polka tune that I had caught in my head. Have you ever had anything caught in your head? No, of course you haven't, you dumb angel-puss, you'd never get anything awful caught in your head!

(He stares at her while she follows him while she talks. It is obvious that he has had a few drinks on the way over.)

MITCH. Do we have to have that fan on?

BLANCHE. No!

MITCH. I don't like fans.

BLANCHE. Then let's turn it off, honey. I'm not partial to them! *(She presses the switch and the fan nods slowly off. She clears her throat uneasily as Mitch plumps himself down on the bed in the bedroom and lights a cigarette)* I don't know what

there is to drink. I—haven't investigated.

MITCH. I don't want Stan's liquor.

BLANCHE. It isn't Stan's. Everything here isn't Stan's. Some things on the premises are actually mine! How is your mother? Isn't your mother well?

MITCH. Why?

BLANCHE. Something's the matter tonight, but never mind. I won't cross-examine the witness. I'll just— *(She touches her forehead vaguely. The polka tune starts up again)*—pretend I don't notice anything different about you! That—music again . . .

MITCH. What music?

BLANCHE. The "Varsouviana"! The polka tune they were playing when Allan— Wait! *(A distant revolver shot is heard. Blanche seems relieved)* There now, the shot! It always stops after that. *(The polka music dies out again)* Yes, now it's stopped.

MITCH. Are you boxed out of your mind?

BLANCHE. I'll go and see what I can find in the way of— *(She crosses into the closet, pretending to search for the bottle)* Oh, by the way, excuse me for not being dressed. But I'd practically given you up! Had you forgotten your invitation to supper?

MITCH. I wasn't going to see you any more.

BLANCHE. Wait a minute. I can't hear what you're saying and you talk so little that when you do say something, I don't want to miss a single syllable of it. . . . What am I looking around here for? Oh, yes—liquor! We've had so much excitement around here this evening that I *am* boxed out of my mind! *(She pretends suddenly to find the bottle. He draws his foot up on the bed and stares at her contemptuously)* Here's something. Southern Comfort! What is that, I wonder?

MITCH. If you don't know, it must belong to Stan.

BLANCHE. Take your foot off the bed. It has a light cover on it. Of course you boys don't notice things like that. I've done so much with this place since I've been here.

MITCH. I bet you have.

BLANCHE. You saw it before I came. Well, look at it now! This room is almost —dainty! I want to keep it that way. I wonder if this stuff ought to be mixed with something? Ummm, it's sweet, so sweet! It's terribly, terribly sweet! Why, it's a *liqueur,* I believe! Yes, that's what it *is,* a liqueur! *(Mitch grunts)* I'm afraid you won't like it, but try it, and maybe you will.

MITCH. I told you already I don't want none of his liquor and I mean it. You ought to lay off his liquor. He says you been lapping it up all summer like a wildcat!

BLANCHE. What a fantastic statement! Fantastic of him to say it, fantastic of you to repeat it! I won't descend to the level of such cheap accusations to answer them, even!

MITCH. Huh.

BLANCHE. What's in your mind? I see something in your eyes!

MITCH *(getting up).* It's dark in here.

BLANCHE. I like it dark. The dark is comforting to me.

MITCH. I don't think I ever seen you in the light. *(Blanche laughs breathlessly)* That's a fact!

BLANCHE. Is it?

MITCH. I've never seen you in the afternoon.

BLANCHE. Whose fault is that?

MITCH. You never want to go out in the afternoon.

BLANCHE. Why, Mitch, you're at the plant in the afternoon!

MITCH. Not Sunday afternoon. I've asked you to go out with me sometimes on Sundays but you always make an excuse. You never want to go out till after six and then it's always some place that's not lighted much.

BLANCHE. There is some obscure meaning in this but I fail to catch it.

MITCH. What it means is I've never had a real good look at you, Blanche. Let's turn the light on here.

BLANCHE *(fearfully).* Light? Which light? What for?

MITCH. This one with the paper thing on it. *(He tears the paper lantern off the light bulb. She utters a frightened gasp)*

BLANCHE. What did you do that for?

MITCH. So I can take a look at you good and plain!

BLANCHE. Of course you don't really mean to be insulting!

MITCH. No, just realistic.

BLANCHE. I don't want realism. I want magic! *(Mitch laughs)* Yes, yes, magic! I try to give that to people. I misrepresent things to them. I don't tell truth, I tell what *ought* to be truth. And if that is sinful, then let me be damned for it!—*Don't turn the light on!*

(Mitch crosses to the switch. He turns the light on and stares at her. She cries out and covers her face. He turns the light off again.)

MITCH *(slowly and bitterly).* I don't mind you being older than what I thought. But all the rest of it—Christ! That pitch about your ideals being so old-fashioned and all the malarkey that you've dished out all summer. Oh, I knew you weren't sixteen any more. But I was a fool enough to believe you was straight.

BLANCHE. Who told you I wasn't—"straight"? My loving brother-in-law. And you believed him.

MITCH. I called him a liar at first. And then I checked on the story. First I asked our supply-man who travels through Laurel. And then I talked directly over long-distance to this merchant.

BLANCHE. Who is this merchant?

MITCH. Kiefaber.

BLANCHE. The merchant Kiefaber of Laurel! I know the man. He whistled at me. I put him in his place. So now for revenge he makes up stories about me.

MITCH. Three people, Kiefaber, Stanley and Shaw, swore to them!

BLANCHE. Rub-a-dub-dub, three men in a tub! And such a filthy tub!

MITCH. Didn't you stay at a hotel called The Flamingo?

BLANCHE. Flamingo? No! Tarantula was the name of it! I stayed at a hotel called The Tarantula Arms!

MITCH *(stupidly).* Tarantula?

BLANCHE. Yes, a big spider! That's where I brought my victims. *(She pours herself another drink)* Yes, I had many intimacies with strangers. After the death of Allan—intimacies with strangers was all I seemed able to fill my empty heart with. . . . I think it was panic, just panic, that drove me from one to another, hunting for some protection—here and there, in the most—unlikely places—even, at last, in a seventeen-year-old boy but—somebody wrote the superintendent about it—"This woman is morally unfit for her position!" *(She throws back her head with convulsive, sobbing laughter. Then she repeats the statement, gasps, and drinks)* True? Yes, I suppose—unfit somehow—anyway. . . . So I came here. There was nowhere else I could go. I was played out. You know what played out is? My youth was suddenly gone up the water-spout, and—I met you. You said you needed somebody. Well, I needed somebody, too. I thanked God for you, because you seemed to be gentle—a cleft in the rock of the world that I could hide in! But I guess I was asking, hoping—too much! Kiefaber, Stanley and Shaw have tied an old tin can to the tail of the kite.

(There is a pause. Mitch stares at her dumbly.)

MITCH. You lied to me, Blanche.

BLANCHE. Don't say I lied to you.

MITCH. Lies, lies, inside and out, all lies.

BLANCHE. Never inside, I didn't lie in my heart . . .

(A vendor comes around the corner. She is a blind Mexican woman in a dark shawl, carrying bunches of those gaudy tin flowers that lower class Mexicans display at funerals and other festive occasions. She is calling barely audibly. Her figure is only faintly visible outside the building.)

MEXICAN WOMAN. Flores. Flores. Flores para los muertos. Flores. Flores.

BLANCHE. What? Oh! Somebody outside . . . *(She goes to the door, opens it and stares at the Mexican Woman)*

MEXICAN WOMAN *(she is at the door and offers Blanche some of her flowers)*. Flores? Flores para los muertos?

BLANCHE *(frightened)*. No, no! Not now! Not now! *(She darts back into the apartment, slamming the door)*

MEXICAN WOMAN *(she turns away and starts to move down the street)*. Flores para los muertos.

(The polka tune fades in.)

BLANCHE *(as if to herself)*. Crumble and fade and—regrets—recriminations . . . "If you'd done this, it wouldn't've cost me that!"

MEXICAN WOMAN. Corones para los muertos. Corones . . .

BLANCHE. Legacies! Huh . . . And other things such as bloodstained pillow-slips—"Her linen needs changing"—"Yes, Mother. But couldn't we get a colored girl to do it?" No, we couldn't of course. Everything gone but the—

MEXICAN WOMAN. Flores.

BLANCHE. Death—I used to sit here and she used to sit over there and death was as close as you are. . . . We didn't dare even admit we had ever heard of it!

MEXICAN WOMAN. Flores para los muertos, flores—flores . . .

BLANCHE. The opposite is desire. So do you wonder? How could you possibly wonder! Not far from Belle Reve, before we had lost Belle Reve, was a camp where they trained young soldiers. On Saturday nights they would go in town to get drunk—

MEXICAN WOMAN *(softly)*. Corones . . .

BLANCHE. —and on the way back they would stagger onto my lawn and call—"Blanche! Blanche!"—The deaf old lady remaining suspected nothing. But sometimes I slipped outside to answer their calls. . . . Later the paddy-wagon would gather them up like daisies . . . the long way home . . .

(The Mexican Woman turns slowly and drifts back off with her soft mournful cries. Blanche goes to the dresser and leans forward on it. After a moment, Mitch rises and follows her purposefully. The polka music fades away. He places his hands on her waist and tries to turn her about.)

BLANCHE. What do you want?

MITCH *(fumbling to embrace her)*. What I been missing all summer.

BLANCHE. Then marry me, Mitch!

MITCH. I don't think I want to marry you any more.

BLANCHE. No?

MITCH *(dropping his hands from her waist)*. You're not clean enough to bring in the house with my mother.

BLANCHE. Go away, then. *(He stares at her)* Get out of here quick before I start screaming fire! *(Her throat is tightening with hysteria)* Get out of here quick before I start screaming fire. *(He still remains staring. She suddenly rushes to the big window with its pale blue square of the soft summer light and cries wildly)* Fire! Fire! Fire!

(With a startled gasp, Mitch turns and goes out the outer door, clatters awkwardly down the steps and around the corner of the building. Blanche staggers back from the window and falls to her knees. The distant piano is slow and blue.)

SCENE TEN

It is a few hours later that night.
Blanche has been drinking fairly steadily since Mitch left. She has dragged her

wardrobe trunk into the center of the bed-room. It hangs open with flowery dresses thrown across it. As the drinking and packing went on, a mood of hysterical ex-hilaration came into her and she has decked herself out in a somewhat soiled and crumpled white satin evening gown and a pair of scuffed silver slippers with brilliants set in their heels.

Now she is placing the rhinestone tiara on her head before the mirror of the dressing-table and murmuring excitedly as if to a group of spectral admirers.

BLANCHE. How about taking a swim, a moonlight swim at the old rock-quarry? If anyone's sober enough to drive a car! Ha-ha! Best way in the world to stop your head buzzing! Only you've got to be care-ful to dive where the deep pool is—if you hit a rock you don't come up till tomor-row . . .
(Tremblingly she lifts the hand mirror for a closer inspection. She catches her breath and slams the mirror face down with such violence that the glass cracks. She moans a little and attempts to rise.
(Stanley appears around the corner of the building. He still has on the vivid green silk bowling shirt. As he rounds the cor-ner the honky-tonk music is heard. It con-tinues softly throughout the scene.
(He enters the kitchen, slamming the door. As he peers in at Blanche, he gives a low whistle. He has had a few drinks on the way and has brought some quart beer bottles home with him.)
BLANCHE. How is my sister?
STANLEY. She is doing okay.
BLANCHE. And how is the baby?
STANLEY *(grinning amiably)*. The baby won't come before morning so they told me to go home and get a little shut-eye.
BLANCHE. Does that mean we are to be alone in here?
STANLEY. Yep. Just me and you, Blanche. Unless you got somebody hid under the bed. What've you got on those fine feath-ers for?
BLANCHE. Oh, that's right. You left be-fore my wire came.
STANLEY. You got a wire?
BLANCHE. I received a telegram from an old admirer of mine.
STANLEY. Anything good?
BLANCHE. I think so. An invitation.
STANLEY. What to? A fireman's ball?

BLANCHE *(throwing back her head)*. A cruise of the Caribbean on a yacht!
STANLEY. Well, well. What do you know?
BLANCHE. I have never been so surprised in my life.
STANLEY. I guess not.
BLANCHE. It came like a bolt from the blue!
STANLEY. Who did you say it was from?
BLANCHE. An old beau of mine.
STANLEY. The one that give you the white fox-pieces?
BLANCHE. Mr. Shep Huntleigh. I wore his ATO pin my last year at college. I hadn't seen him again until last Christmas. I ran in to him on Biscayne Boulevard. Then—just now—this wire—inviting me on a cruise of the Caribbean! The problem is clothes. I tore into my trunk to see what I have that's suitable for the tropics!
STANLEY. And come up with that—gor-geous—diamond—tiara?
BLANCHE. This old relic? Ha-ha! It's only rhinestones.
STANLEY. Gosh. I thought it was Tiffany diamonds. *(He unbuttons his shirt)*
BLANCHE. Well, anyhow, I shall be enter-tained in style.
STANLEY. Uh-huh. It goes to show, you never know what is coming.
BLANCHE. Just when I thought my luck had begun to fail me—
STANLEY. Into the picture pops this Mi-ami millionaire.
BLANCHE. This man is not from Miami. This man is from Dallas.
STANLEY. This man is from Dallas?
BLANCHE. Yes, this man is from Dallas where gold spouts out of the ground!
STANLEY. Well, just so he's from some-where! *(He starts removing his shirt)*
BLANCHE. Close the curtains before you undress any further.
STANLEY *(amiably)*. This is all I'm going to undress right now. *(He rips the sack off a quart beer-bottle)* Seen a bottle-opener? *(She moves slowly toward the dresser, where she stands with her hands knotted together)* I used to have a cousin who could open a beer-bottle with his teeth. *(Pounding the bottle cap on the cor-ner of table)* That was his only accom-plishment, all he could do—he was just a human bottle-opener. And then one time, at a wedding party, he broke his front teeth off! After that he was so ashamed of

elf he used t' sneak out of the house
n company came . . . *(The bottle cap
s off and a geyser of foam shoots up.
Stanley laughs happily, holding up the
bottle over his head)* Ha-ha! Rain from
heaven! *(He extends the bottle toward
her)* Shall we bury the hatchet and make
it a loving-cup? Huh?

BLANCHE. No, thank you.

STANLEY. Well, it's a red letter night for
us both. You having an oil-millionaire and
me having a baby.

*(He goes to the bureau in the bedroom
and crouches to remove something from
the bottom drawer.)*

BLANCHE *(drawing back)*. What are you
doing in here?

STANLEY. Here's something I always
break out on special occasions like this.
The silk pyjamas I wore on my wedding
night!

BLANCHE. Oh.

STANLEY. When the telephone rings and
they say, "You've got a son!" I'll tear this
off and wave it like a flag! *(He shakes out
a brilliant pyjama coat)* I guess we are
both entitled to put on the dog. *(He goes
back to the kitchen with the coat over his
arm)*

BLANCHE. When I think of how divine
it is going to be to have such a thing as
privacy once more—I could weep with joy!

STANLEY. This millionaire from Dallas is
not going to interfere with your privacy
any?

BLANCHE. It won't be the sort of thing
you have in mind. This man is a gentleman and he respects me. *(Improvising fe-
verishly)* What he wants is my companionship. Having great wealth sometimes
makes people lonely! A cultivated woman,
a woman of intelligence and breeding, can
enrich a man's life—immeasurably! I have
those things to offer, and this doesn't take
them away. Physical beauty is passing. A
transitory possession. But beauty of the
mind and richness of the spirit and tenderness of the heart—and I have all of those
things—aren't taken away, but grow! Increase with the years! How strange that I
should be called a destitute woman! When
I have all of these treasures locked in my
heart. *(A choked sob comes from her)* I
think of myself as a very, very rich
woman! But I have been foolish—casting
my pearls before swine!

STANLEY. Swine, huh?

BLANCHE. Yes, swine! Swine! And I'm
thinking not only of you but of your
friend, Mr. Mitchell. He came to see me
tonight. He dared to come here in his
work-clothes! And to repeat slander to me,
vicious stories that he had gotten from
you! I gave him his walking papers . . .

STANLEY. You did, huh?

BLANCHE. But then he came back. He
returned with a box of roses to beg my
forgiveness! He implored my forgiveness.
But some things are not forgivable. Deliberate cruelty is not forgivable. It is the one
unforgivable thing in my opinion and it is
the one thing of which I have never, never
been guilty. And so I told him, I said to
him, "Thank you," but it was foolish of
me to think that we could ever adapt ourselves to each other. Our ways of life are
too different. Our attitudes and our backgrounds are incompatible. We have to be
realistic about such things. So farewell, my
friend! And let there be no hard feelings . . .

STANLEY. Was this before or after the
telegram came from the Texas oil millionaire?

BLANCHE. What telegram? No! No,
after! As a matter of fact, the wire came
just as—

STANLEY. As a matter of fact there wasn't
no wire at all!

BLANCHE. Oh, oh!

STANLEY. There isn't no millionaire! And
Mitch didn't come back with roses 'cause
I know where he is—

BLANCHE. Oh!

STANLEY. There isn't a goddam thing but
imagination!

BLANCHE. Oh!

STANLEY. And lies and conceit and
tricks!

BLANCHE. Oh!

STANLEY. And look at yourself! Take a
look at yourself in that worn-out Mardi
Gras outfit, rented for fifty cents from
some rag-picker! And with the crazy
crown on! What queen do you think you
are?

BLANCHE. Oh—God . . .

STANLEY. I've been on to you from the
start! Not once did you pull any wool over
this boy's eyes! You come in here and
sprinkle the place with powder and spray
perfume and cover the light-bulb with a
paper lantern, and lo and behold the place
has turned into Egypt and you are the

Queen of the Nile! Sitting on your throne and swilling down my liquor! I say—*Ha! —Ha!* Do you hear me? *Ha—ha—ha! (He walks into the bedroom)*

BLANCHE. Don't come in here! *(Lurid reflections appear on the walls around Blanche. The shadows are of a grotesque and menacing form. She catches her breath, crosses to the phone and jiggles the hook. Stanley goes into the bathroom and closes the door)* Operator, operator! Give me long-distance, please. . . . I want to get in touch with Mr. Shep Huntleigh of Dallas. He's so well-known he doesn't require any address. Just ask anybody who—Wait! —No, I couldn't find it right now. . . . Please understand. I—No! No, wait! . . . One moment! Someone is—Nothing! Hold on, please!

(She sets the phone down and crosses warily into the kitchen. The night is filled with inhuman voices like cries in a jungle. (The shadows and lurid reflections move sinuously as flames along the wall spaces. (Through the back wall of the rooms, which have become transparent, can be seen the sidewalk. A prostitute has rolled a drunkard. He pursues her along the walk, overtakes her and there is a struggle. A policeman's whistle breaks it up. The figures disappear.

(Some moments later the Negro Woman appears around the corner with a sequined bag which the prostitute had dropped on the walk. She is rooting excitedly through it.

(Blanche presses her knuckles to her lips and returns slowly to the phone. She speaks in a hoarse whisper.)

BLANCHE. Operator! Operator! Never mind long-distance. Get Western Union. There isn't time to be—Western—Western Union! *(She waits anxiously)* Western Union? Yes! I—want to— Take down this message! "In desperate, desperate circumstances! Help me! Caught in a trap. Caught in—" *Oh!*

(The bathroom door is thrown open and Stanley comes out in the brilliant silk pyjamas. He grins at her as he knots the tasseled sash about his waist. She gasps and backs away from the phone. He stares at her for a count of ten. Then a clicking becomes audible from the telephone, steady and rasping.)

STANLEY. You left th' phone off th' hook.

(He crosses to it deliberately and sets it back on the hook. After he has replaced it, he stares at her again, his mouth slowly curving into a grin, as he weaves between Blanche and the outer door.

(The barely audible "blue piano" begins to drum up louder. The sound of it turns into the roar of an approaching locomotive. Blanche crouches, pressing her fists to her ears until it has gone by.)

BLANCHE *(finally straightening)*. Let me —let me get by you!

STANLEY. Get by me? Sure. Go ahead. *(He moves back a pace in the doorway)*

BLANCHE. You—you stand over there! *(She indicates a further position)*

STANLEY *(grinning)*. You got plenty of room to walk by me now.

BLANCHE. Not with you there! But I've got to get out somehow!

STANLEY. You think I'll interfere with you? Ha-ha!

(The "blue piano" goes softly. She turns confusedly and makes a faint gesture. The inhuman jungle voices rise up. He takes a step toward her, biting his tongue which protrudes between his lips.)

STANLEY *(softly)*. Come to think of it— maybe you wouldn't be bad to—interfere with . . .

(Blanche moves backward through the door into the bedroom.)

BLANCHE. Stay back! Don't you come toward me another step or I'll—

STANLEY. What?

BLANCHE. Some awful thing will happen! It will!

STANLEY. What are you putting on now? *(They are now both inside the bedroom.)*

BLANCHE. I warn you, don't, I'm in danger!

(He takes another step. She smashes a bottle on the table and faces him, clutching the broken top.)

STANLEY. What did you do that for?

BLANCHE. So I could twist the broken end in your face!

STANLEY. I bet you would do that!

BLANCHE. I would! I will if you—

STANLEY. Oh! So you want some roughhouse! All right, let's have some roughhouse! *(He springs toward her, overturning the table. She cries out and strikes at him with the bottle top but he catches her wrist)* Tiger—tiger! Drop the bottle-top! Drop it! We've had this date with each other from the beginning!

(She moans. The bottle-top falls. She sinks

to her knees. He picks up her inert figure and carries her to the bed. The hot trumpet and drums from the Four Deuces sound loudly.)

SCENE ELEVEN

It is some weeks later. Stella is packing Blanche's things. Sound of water can be heard running in the bathroom.

The portieres are partly open on the poker players—Stanley, Steve, Mitch and Pablo—who sit around the table in the kitchen. The atmosphere of the kitchen is now the same raw, lurid one of the disastrous poker night.

The building is framed by the sky of turquoise. Stella has been crying as she arranges the flowery dresses in the open trunk.

Eunice comes down the steps from her flat above and enters the kitchen. There is an outburst from the poker table.

STANLEY. Drew to an inside straight and made it, by God.

PABLO. *Maldita sea tu suerto!*

STANLEY. Put it in English, greaseball.

PABLO. I am cursing your rutting luck.

STANLEY *(prodigiously elated)*. You know what luck is? Luck is believing you're lucky. Take at Salerno. I believed I was lucky. I figured that four out of five would not come through but I would . . . and I did. I put that down as a rule. To hold front position in this rat-race you've got to believe you are lucky.

MITCH. You . . . you . . . you. . . . Brag . . . brag . . . bull . . . bull.

(Stella goes into the bedroom and starts folding a dress.)

STANLEY. What's the matter with him?

EUNICE *(walking past the table)*. I always did say that men are callous things with no feelings, but this does beat anything. Making pigs of yourselves. *(She comes through the portieres into the bedroom)*

STANLEY. What's the matter with her?

STELLA. How is my baby?

EUNICE. Sleeping like a little angel. Brought you some grapes. *(She puts them on a stool and lowers her voice)* Blanche?

STELLA. Bathing.

EUNICE. How is she?

STELLA. She wouldn't eat anything but asked for a drink.

EUNICE. What did you tell her?

STELLA. I—just told her that—we'd made arrangements for her to rest in the country. She's got it mixed in her mind with Shep Huntleigh.

(Blanche opens the bathroom door slightly.)

BLANCHE. Stella.

STELLA. Yes, Blanche?

BLANCHE. If anyone calls while I'm bathing take the number and tell them I'll call right back.

STELLA. Yes.

BLANCHE. That cool yellow silk—the bouclé. See if it's crushed. If it's not too crushed I'll wear it and on the lapel that silver and turquoise pin in the shape of a seahorse. You will find them in the heart-shaped box I keep my accessories in. And Stella . . . Try and locate a bunch of artificial violets in that box, too, to pin with the seahorse on the lapel of the jacket.

(She closes the door. Stella turns to Eunice.)

STELLA. I don't know if I did the right thing.

EUNICE. What else could you do?

STELLA. I couldn't believe her story and go on living with Stanley.

EUNICE. Don't ever believe it. Life has got to go on. No matter what happens, you've got to keep on going.

(The bathroom door opens a little.)

BLANCHE *(looking out)*. Is the coast clear?

STELLA. Yes, Blanche. *(To Eunice)* Tell her how well she's looking.

BLANCHE. Please close the curtains before I come out.

STELLA. They're closed.

STANLEY. —How many for you?

PABLO. —Two.

STEVE. —Three.

(Blanche appears in the amber light of the door. She has a tragic radiance in her red satin robe following the sculptural lines of her body. The "Varsouviana" rises audibly as Blanche enters the bedroom.)

BLANCHE *(with faintly hysterical vivacity)*. I have just washed my hair.

STELLA. Did you?

BLANCHE. I'm not sure I got the soap out.

EUNICE. Such fine hair!

BLANCHE *(accepting the compliment)*. It's a problem. Didn't I get a call?

STELLA. Who from, Blanche?

BLANCHE. Shep Huntleigh . . .

STELLA. Why, not yet, honey!

BLANCHE. How strange! I—

(At the sound of Blanche's voice, Mitch's arm supporting his cards has sagged and his gaze is dissolved into space. Stanley slaps him on the shoulder.)

STANLEY. Hey, Mitch, come to!

(The sound of this new voice shocks Blanche. She makes a shocked gesture, forming his name with her lips. Stella nods and looks quickly away. Blanche stands quite still for some moments—the silverbacked mirror in her hand and a look of sorrowful perplexity as though all human experience shows on her face. Blanche finally speaks but with sudden hysteria.)

BLANCHE. What's going on here?

(She turns from Stella to Eunice and back to Stella. Her rising voice penetrates the concentration of the game. Mitch ducks his head lower but Stanley shoves back his chair as if about to rise. Steve places a restraining hand on his arm.)

BLANCHE *(continuing)*. What's happened here? I want an explanation of what's happened here.

STELLA *(agonizingly)*. Hush! Hush!

EUNICE. Hush! Hush! Honey.

STELLA. Please, Blanche.

BLANCHE. Why are you looking at me like that? Is something wrong with me?

EUNICE. You look wonderful, Blanche. Don't she look wonderful?

STELLA. Yes.

EUNICE. I understand you are going on a trip.

STELLA. Yes, Blanche *is*. She's going on a vacation.

EUNICE. I'm green with envy.

BLANCHE. Help me, help me get dressed!

STELLA *(handing her dress)*. Is this what you—

BLANCHE. Yes, it will do! I'm anxious to get out of here—this place is a trap!

EUNICE. What a pretty blue jacket.

STELLA. It's lilac colored.

BLANCHE. You're both mistaken. It's Della Robbia blue. The blue of the robe in the old Madonna pictures. Are these grapes washed?

(She fingers the bunch of grapes which Eunice had brought in.)

EUNICE. Huh?

BLANCHE. Washed, I said. Are they washed?

EUNICE. They're from the French Market.

BLANCHE. That doesn't mean they've been washed. *(The cathedral bells chime)* Those cathedral bells—they're the only clean thing in the Quarter. Well, I'm going now. I'm ready to go.

EUNICE *(whispering)*. She's going to walk out before they get here.

STELLA. Wait, Blanche.

BLANCHE. I don't want to pass in front of those men.

EUNICE. Then wait'll the game breaks up.

STELLA. Sit down and . . .

(Blanche turns weakly, hesitantly about. She lets them push her into a chair.)

BLANCHE. I can smell the sea air. The rest of my time I'm going to spend on the sea. And when I die, I'm going to die on the sea. You know what I shall die of? *(She plucks a grape)* I shall die of eating an unwashed grape one day out on the ocean. I will die—with my hand in the hand of some nice-looking ship's doctor, a very young one with a small blond mustache and a big silver watch. "Poor lady," they'll say, "the quinine did her no good. That unwashed grape has transported her soul to heaven." *(The cathedral chimes are heard)* And I'll be buried at sea sewn up in a clean white sack and dropped overboard—at noon—in the blaze of summer—and into an ocean as blue as *(Chimes again)* my first lover's eyes!

(A Doctor and a Matron have appeared around the corner of the building and climbed the steps to the porch. The gravity of their profession is exaggerated—the unmistakable aura of the state institution with its cynical detachment. The Doctor rings the doorbell. The murmur of the game is interrupted.)

EUNICE *(whispering to Stella)*. That must be them.

(Stella presses her fists to her lips.)

BLANCHE *(rising slowly)*. What is it?

EUNICE *(affectedly casual)*. Excuse me while I see who's at the door.

STELLA. Yes.

(Eunice goes into the kitchen.)

BLANCHE *(tensely)*. I wonder if it's for me.

(A whispered colloquy takes place at the door.)

EUNICE *(returning, brightly)*. Someone is calling for Blanche.

BLANCHE. It *is* for me, then! (*She looks fearfully from one to the other and then to the portieres. The "Varsouviana" faintly plays*) Is it the gentleman I was expecting from Dallas?

EUNICE. I think it is, Blanche.

BLANCHE. I'm not quite ready.

STELLA. Ask him to wait outside.

BLANCHE. I . . .

(*Eunice goes back to the portieres. Drums sound very softly.*)

STELLA. Everything packed?

BLANCHE. My silver toilet articles are still out.

STELLA. Ah!

EUNICE (*returning*). They're waiting in front of the house.

BLANCHE. They! Who's "they"?

EUNICE. There's a lady with him.

BLANCHE. I cannot imagine who this "lady" could be! How is she dressed?

EUNICE. Just—just a sort of a—plain-tailored outfit.

BLANCHE. Possibly she's—(*Her voice dies out nervously*)

STELLA. Shall we go, Blanche?

BLANCHE. Must we go through that room?

STELLA. I will go with you.

BLANCHE. How do I look?

STELLA. Lovely.

EUNICE (*echoing*). Lovely.

(*Blanche moves fearfully to the portieres. Eunice draws them open for her. Blanche goes into the kitchen.*)

BLANCHE (*to the men*). Please don't get up. I'm only passing through.

(*She crosses quickly to outside door. Stella and Eunice follow. The poker players stand awkwardly at the table—all except Mitch, who remains seated, looking down at the table. Blanche steps out on a small porch at the side of the door. She stops short and catches her breath.*)

DOCTOR. How do you do?

BLANCHE. You are not the gentleman I was expecting. (*She suddenly gasps and starts back up the steps. She stops by Stella, who stands just outside the door, and speaks in a frightening whisper*) That man isn't Shep Huntleigh.

(*The "Varsouviana" is playing distantly.*) (*Stella stares back at Blanche. Eunice is holding Stella's arm. There is a moment of silence—no sound but that of Stanley steadily shuffling the cards.*)

(*Blanche catches her breath again and slips back into the flat. She enters the flat with a peculiar smile, her eyes wide and brilliant. As soon as her sister goes past her, Stella closes her eyes and clenches her hands. Eunice throws her arms comfortingly about her. Then she starts up to her flat. Blanche stops just inside the door. Mitch keeps staring down at his hands on the table, but the other men look at her curiously. At last she starts around the table toward the bedroom. As she does, Stanley suddenly pushes back his chair and rises as if to block her way. The Matron follows her into the flat.*)

STANLEY. Did you forget something?

BLANCHE (*shrilly*). Yes! Yes, I forgot something!

(*She rushes past him into the bedroom. Lurid reflections appear on the walls in odd, sinuous shapes. The "Varsouviana" is filtered into a weird distortion, accompanied by the cries and noises of the jungle. Blanche seizes the back of a chair as if to defend herself.*)

STANLEY (*sotto voce*). Doc, you better go in.

DOCTOR (*sotto voce, motioning to the Matron*). Nurse, bring her out.

(*The Matron advances on one side, Stanley on the other. Divested of all the softer properties of womanhood, the Matron is a peculiarly sinister figure in her severe dress. Her voice is bold and toneless as a firebell.*)

MATRON. Hello, Blanche.

(*The greeting is echoed and re-echoed by other mysterious voices behind the walls, as if reverberated through a canyon of rock.*)

STANLEY. She says that she forgot something.

(*The echo sounds in threatening whispers.*)

MATRON. That's all right.

STANLEY. What did you forget, Blanche?

BLANCHE. I—I—

MATRON. It don't matter. We can pick it up later.

STANLEY. Sure. We can send it along with the trunk.

BLANCHE (*retreating in panic*). I don't know you—I don't know you. I want to be—left alone—please!

MATRON. Now, Blanche!

ECHOES (*rising and falling*). Now, Blanche—now, Blanche—now, Blanche!

STANLEY. You left nothing here but spilt

talcum and old empty perfume bottles—unless it's the paper lantern you want to take with you. You want the lantern?

(He crosses to dressing table and seizes the paper lantern, tearing it off the light bulb, and extends it toward her. She cries out as if the lantern was herself. The Matron steps boldly toward her. She screams and tries to break past the Matron. All the men spring to their feet. Stella runs out to the porch, with Eunice following to comfort her, simultaneously with the confused voices of the men in the kitchen. Stella rushes into Eunice's embrace on the porch.)

STELLA. Oh, my God, Eunice, help me! Don't let them do that to her, don't let them hurt her! Oh, God, oh, please God, don't hurt her. What are they doing to her? What are they doing? *(She tries to break from Eunice's arms)*

EUNICE. No, honey, no, no, honey. Stay here. Don't go back in there. Stay with me and don't look.

STELLA. What have I done to my sister? Oh, God, what have I done to my sister?

EUNICE. You done the right thing, the only thing you could do. She couldn't stay here; there wasn't no other place for her to go.

(While Stella and Eunice are speaking on the porch the voices of the men in the kitchen overlap them. Mitch has started toward the bedroom. Stanley crosses to block him. Stanley pushes him aside. Mitch lunges and strikes at Stanley. Stanley pushes Mitch back. Mitch collapses at the table, sobbing.

(During the preceding scenes, the Matron catches hold of Blanche's arm and prevents her flight. Blanche turns wildly and scratches at the Matron. The heavy woman pinions her arms. Blanche cries out hoarsely and slips to her knees.)

MATRON. These fingernails have to be trimmed. *(The Doctor comes into the room and she looks at him)* Jacket, Doctor?

DOCTOR. Not unless necessary.

(He takes off his hat and now he becomes personalized. The inhuman quality goes. His voice is gentle and reassuring as he crosses to Blanche and crouches in front of her. As he speaks her name, her terror subsides a little. The lurid reflections fade from the walls, the inhuman cries and noises die out and her own hoarse crying is calmed.)

DOCTOR. Miss DuBois. *(She turns her face to him and stares at him with desperate pleading. He smiles; then he speaks to the Matron)* It won't be necessary.

BLANCHE *(faintly)*. Ask her to let go of me.

DOCTOR *(to the Matron)*. Let go.

(The Matron releases her. Blanche extends her hands toward the Doctor. He draws her up gently and supports her with his arm and leads her through the portieres.)

BLANCHE *(holding tight to his arm)*. Whoever you are—I have always depended on the kindness of strangers.

(The poker players stand back as Blanche and the Doctor cross the kitchen to the front door. She allows him to lead her as if she were blind. As they go out on the porch, Stella cries out her sister's name from where she is crouched a few steps up on the stairs.)

STELLA. Blanche! Blanche, Blanche!

(Blanche walks on without turning, followed by the Doctor and the Matron. They go around the corner of the building.

(Eunice descends to Stella and places the child in her arms. It is wrapped in a pale blue blanket. Stella accepts the child, sobbingly. Eunice continues downstairs and enters the kitchen where the men, except for Stanley, are returning silently to their places about the table. Stanley has gone out on the porch and stands at the foot of the steps looking at Stella.)

STANLEY *(a bit uncertainly)*. Stella?

(She sobs with inhuman abandon. There is something luxurious in her complete surrender to crying now that her sister is gone.)

STANLEY *(voluptuously, soothingly)*. Now, honey. Now, love. Now, now, love. *(He kneels beside her and his fingers find the opening of her blouse)* Now, now, love. Now, love. . . .

(The luxurious sobbing, the sensual murmur fade away under the swelling music of the "blue piano" and the muted trumpet.)

STEVE. This game is seven-card stud.

CURTAIN

The Iceman Cometh

BY EUGENE O'NEILL

First presented by The Theatre Guild at the Martin Beck Theatre on October 9, 1946, with the following cast:

HARRY HOPE..................................Dudley Digges	LARRY SLADE..........................Carl Benton Reid
ED MOSHER.............................Morton L. Stevens	ROCKY PIOGGI.....................................Tom Pedi
PAT McGLOIN...............................Al McGranary	DON PARRITT................................Paul Crabtree
WILLIE OBAN.............................E. G. Marshall	PEARL ....Ruth Gilbert
JOE MOTT...John Marriott	MARGIE ....Jeanne Cagney
PIET WETJOEN ("THE GENERAL")	CORA ....Marcella Markham
Frank Tweddell	CHUCK MORELLO................................Joe Marr
CECIL LEWIS ("THE CAPTAIN")..Nicholas Joy	THEODORE HICKMAN (HICKEY)
JAMES CAMERON ("JIMMY TOMORROW")	James Barton
Russell Collins	MORAN ....Michael Wyler
HUGO KALMAR................................Leo Chalzel	LIEB ....Charles Hart

---

ACT ONE

Back room and a section of the bar at Harry Hope's—early morning in summer, 1912.

ACT TWO

Back room, around midnight of the same day.

ACT THREE

Bar and a section of the back room—morning of the following day.

ACT FOUR

Same as *Act One*. Back room and a section of the bar—around 1:30 A.M. of the next day.

The action takes place in the Back Room and the Bar at Harry Hope's lower West Side New York City waterfront saloon in the summer of 1912.

ACCORDING to George Jean Nathan, the New York Drama Critics Circle's elder statesman and mathematician, *The Iceman Cometh* was presented on Broadway exactly
twelve years and nine months after the last premiere of an O'Neill play—*Days Without
End,* in the spring of 1935. It took that long for O'Neill to return from his Babylonian
exile. Although *The Iceman Cometh* had been written in the critical year of 1939,
O'Neill had resisted all temptations to allow a production during the war years. Ill and
depressed, and residing far from New York, O'Neill had waited until he could be
present at the rehearsals. He had also waited for the mood of anxiety and depression to
leave the nation before contributing his own decidedly substantial load of pessimism to
the theatre.

Contrary to a widely held notion, O'Neill is capable of humor, as *Ah, Wilderness*
alone would prove. In fact, his sense of comedy is actually more robust than that of
most writers for the stage who pass for humorists. Nevertheless, he had discharged a
grim view of man's destiny ever since his novitiate in 1913-14, when he wrote the one-
acters *Thirst* and *Bound East for Cardiff.* The sea-pieces *In the Zone, Ile, the Long
Voyage Home* and *Moon of the Caribees,* all composed in 1917, were anything but con-
ducive to cheerfulness. His picture was essentially one of human frustration and loneliness, of obsessive passion and spiritual bankruptcy, and of futile writhings in the grip
of fate. The full-length plays that followed the one-acters year after year offered scant
relief, whether they were chiefly (though never wholly) realistic dramas, such as *Beyond
the Horizon, Anna Christie,* and *Desire Under the Elms,* or expressionistic or otherwise
stylized pieces, such as *Emperor Jones, The Hairy Ape,* or *The Great God Brown.*

When O'Neill finally wrote *The Iceman Cometh* he seems to have rolled up all his
melancholy view of humanity, testimonially, into four and a half hours of strenuous
theatre. He made the play a summary of all-encompassing human failure, of which his
characters' stalemate and the shattering of their illusions of freedom were merely the
consummation. The play is more dynamic than either the theme of stalemate or the
unfortunate overwriting of a number of the scenes allows us to realize.

That there is more to the play than a bleak naturalistic picture is evident even if one
refrains from the now popular game of symbol-hunting, which O'Neill himself invites
with his death-symbol of "the Iceman." *The Iceman Cometh* is rich in psychological
meaning, especially in the case of Hickey, and there are implications in the drama concerning love and hate, failure and salvation that are deeply perturbing. They are likely
to sound banal only when formulated; the felt experience is, as usual in an O'Neill
drama, far more impressive than O'Neill's intellectual formulations. Fortunately, the
drama of character in *The Iceman Cometh* is substantial and is not easily lost in a metaphysical mist. Most of O'Neill's critics were not at all happy with his various excursions
into expressionism and mask-drama in *All God's Chillun Got Wings, The Great
God Brown, Dynamo, Lazarus Laughed,* and *Days Without End.* More realistically
grounded, *The Iceman Cometh* recalls the lives and idiom with which O'Neill first won
our attention. In some respects, in fact, it is a reminiscence of O'Neill's early days "on
the beach" at the waterfront saloon of "Jimmy the Priest." In a sense, *The Iceman
Cometh* was a reprise in America's most notable playwriting career.

ACT ONE

SCENE: *The back room and a section of the bar of Harry Hope's saloon on an early morning in summer, 1912. The right wall of the back room is a dirty black curtain which separates it from the bar. At rear, this curtain is drawn back from the wall so the bartender can get in and out. The back room is crammed with round tables and chairs placed so close together that it is a difficult squeeze to pass between them. In the middle of the rear wall is a door opening on a hallway. In the left corner, built out into the room, is the toilet with a sign "This is it" on the door. Against the middle of the left wall is a nickel-in-the-slot phonograph. Two windows, so glazed with grime one cannot see through them, are in the left wall, looking out on a backyard. The walls and ceiling once were white, but it was a long time ago, and they are now so splotched, peeled, stained and dusty that their color can best be described as dirty. The floor, with iron spittoons placed here and there, is covered with sawdust. Lighting comes from single wall brackets, two at left and two at rear.*

There are three rows of tables, from front to back. Three are in the front line. The one at left-front has four chairs; the one at center-front, four; the one at right-front, five. At rear of, and half between, front tables one and two is a table of the second row with five chairs. A table, similarly placed at rear of front tables two and three, also has five chairs. The third row of tables, four chairs to one and six to the other, is against the rear wall on either side of the door.

At right of this dividing curtain is a section of the barroom, with the end of the bar seen at rear, a door to the hall at left of it. At front is a table with four chairs. Light comes from the street windows off right, the gray subdued light of early morning in a narrow street. In the back room, Larry Slade and Hugo Kalmar are at the table at left-front, Hugo in a chair facing right, Larry at rear of table facing front, with an empty chair between them. A fourth chair is at right of table, facing left. Hugo is a small man in his late fifties. He has a head much too big for his body, a high forehead, crinkly long black hair streaked with gray, a square face with a pug nose, a walrus mustache, black eyes which peer near-sightedly from behind thick-lensed spectacles, tiny hands and feet. He is dressed in threadbare black clothes and his white shirt is frayed at collar and cuffs, but everything about him is fastidiously clean. Even his flowing Windsor tie is neatly tied. There is a foreign atmosphere about him, the stamp of an alien radical, a strong resemblance to the type Anarchist as portrayed, bomb in hand, in newspaper cartoons. He is asleep now, bent forward in his chair, his arms folded on the table, his head resting sideways on his arms.

Larry Slade is sixty. He is tall, rawboned, with coarse straight white hair, worn long and raggedly cut. He has a gaunt Irish face with a big nose, high cheekbones, a lantern jaw with a week's stubble of beard, a mystic's meditative pale-blue eyes with a gleam of sharp sardonic humor in them. As slovenly as Hugo is neat, his clothes are dirty and much slept in. His gray flannel shirt, open at the neck, has the appearance of having never been washed. From the way he methodically scratches himself with his long-fingered, hairy hands, he is lousy and reconciled to being so. He is the only occupant of the room who is not asleep. He stares in front of him, an expression of tired tolerance giving his face the quality of a pitying but weary old priest's.

All four chairs at the middle table, front, are occupied. Joe Mott sits at left-front of the table, facing front. Behind him, facing right-front, is Piet Wetjoen ("The General"). At center of the table, rear, James Cameron ("Jimmy Tomorrow") sits facing front. At right of table, opposite Joe, is Cecil Lewis ("The Captain").

Joe Mott is a Negro, about fifty years old, brown-skinned, stocky, wearing a light suit that had once been flashily sporty but is now about to fall apart. His pointed tan buttoned shoes, faded pink shirt and bright tie belong to the same vintage. Still, he manages to preserve an atmosphere of nattiness and there is nothing dirty about his appearance. His face is only mildly negroid in type. The nose is thin and his lips are not noticeably thick. His hair is crinkly and he is beginning to get bald. A scar from a knife slash runs from his left cheekbone to jaw. His face would be hard and tough if it were not for its good nature and lazy humor. He is asleep, his nodding head supported by his left hand.

Piet Wetjoen, the Boer, is in his fifties, a huge man with a bald head and a long grizzled beard. He is slovenly dressed in a dirty shapeless patched suit, spotted by food. A Dutch farmer type, his once great muscular strength has been debauched into flaccid tallow. But despite his blubbery mouth and sodden bloodshot blue eyes, there is still a suggestion of old authority lurking in him like a memory of the drowned. He is hunched forward, both elbows on the table, his hand on each side of his head for support.

James Cameron ("Jimmy Tomorrow") is about the same size and age as Hugo, a small man. Like Hugo, he wears threadbare black, and everything about him is clean. But the resemblance ceases there. Jimmy has a face like an old well-bred, gentle bloodhound's, with folds of flesh hanging from each side of his mouth, and big brown friendly guileless eyes, more bloodshot than any bloodhound's ever were. He has mouse-colored thinning hair, a little bulbous nose, buck teeth in a small rabbit mouth. But his forehead is fine, his eyes are intelligent and there once was a competent ability in him. His speech is educated, with the ghost of a Scotch rhythm in it. His manners are those of a gentleman. There is a quality about him of a prim, Victorian old maid, and at the same time of a likable, affectionate boy who has never grown up. He sleeps, chin on chest, hands folded in his lap.

Cecil Lewis ("The Captain") is as obviously English as Yorkshire pudding and just as obviously the former army officer. He is going on sixty. His hair and military mustache are white, his eyes bright blue, his complexion that of a turkey. His lean figure is still erect and square-shouldered. He is stripped to the waist, his coat, shirt, undershirt, collar and tie crushed up into a pillow on the table in front of him, his head sideways on this pillow, facing front, his arms dangling toward the floor. On his lower left shoulder is the big ragged scar of an old wound.

At the table at right, front, Harry Hope, the proprietor, sits in the middle, facing front, with Pat McGloin on his right and

Ed Mosher on his left, the other two chairs being unoccupied.

Both McGloin and Mosher are big paunchy men. McGloin has his old occupation of policeman stamped all over him. He is in his fifties, sandy-haired, bullet-headed, jowly, with protruding ears and little round eyes. His face must once have been brutal and greedy, but time and whiskey have melted it down into a good-humored, parasite's characterlessness. He wears old clothes and is slovenly. He is slumped sideways on his chair, his head drooping jerkily toward one shoulder.

Ed Mosher is going on sixty. He has a round kewpie's face—a kewpie who is an unshaven habitual drunkard. He looks like an enlarged, elderly, bald edition of the village fat boy—a sly fat boy, congenitally indolent, a practical joker, a born grafter and con merchant. But amusing and essentially harmless, even in his most enterprising days, because always too lazy to carry crookedness beyond petty swindling. The influence of his old circus career is apparent in his get-up. His worn clothes are flashy; he wears phony rings and a heavy brass watch-chain (not connected to a watch). Like McGloin, he is slovenly. His head is thrown back, his big mouth open.

Harry Hope is sixty, white-haired, so thin the description "bag of bones" was made for him. He has the face of an old family horse, prone to tantrums, with balkiness always smoldering in its wall eyes, waiting for any excuse to shy and pretend to take the bit in its teeth. Hope is one of those men whom everyone likes on sight, a softhearted slob, without malice, feeling superior to no one, a sinner among sinners, a born easy mark for every appeal. He attempts to hide his defenselessness behind a testy truculent manner, but this has never fooled anyone. He is a little deaf, but not half as deaf as he sometimes pretends. His sight is failing but is not as bad as he complains it is. He wears five-and-ten-cent-store spectacles which are so out of alignment that one eye at times peers half over one glass while the other eye looks half under the other. He has badly fitting store teeth, which click like castanets when he begins to fume. He is dressed in an old coat from one suit and pants from another.

In a chair facing right at the table in

the second line, between the first two tables, front, sits Willie Oban, his head on his left arm outstretched along the table edge. He is in his late thirties, of average height, thin. His haggard, dissipated face has a small nose, a pointed chin, blue eyes with colorless lashes and brows. His blond hair, badly in need of a cut, clings in a limp part to his skull. His eyelids flutter continually as if any light were too strong for his eyes. The clothes he wears belong on a scarecrow. They seem constructed of an inferior grade of dirty blotting paper. His shoes are even more disreputable, wrecks of imitation leather, one laced with twine, the other with a bit of wire. He has no socks, and his bare feet show through holes in the soles, with his big toes sticking out of the uppers. He keeps muttering and twitching in his sleep.

As the curtain rises, Rocky, the night bartender, comes from the bar through the curtain and stands looking over the back room. He is a Neapolitan-American in his late twenties, squat and muscular, with a flat, swarthy face and beady eyes. The sleeves of his collarless shirt are rolled up on his thick, powerful arms and he wears a soiled apron. A tough guy but sentimental, in his way, and good-natured. He signals to Larry with a cautious "Sstt" and motions him to see if Hope is asleep. Larry rises from his chair to look at Hope and nods to Rocky. Rocky goes back in the bar but immediately returns with a bottle of bar whiskey and a glass. He squeezes between the tables to Larry.

————

ROCKY *(in a low voice out of the side of his mouth).* Make it fast. *(Larry pours a drink and gulps it down. Rocky takes the bottle and puts it on the table where Willie Oban is)* Don't want de Boss to get wise when he's got one of his tightwad buns on. *(He chuckles with an amused glance at Hope)* Jees, ain't de old bastard a riot when he starts dat bull about turnin' over a new leaf? "Not a damned drink on de house," he tells me, "and all dese bums got to pay up deir room rent. Beginnin' tomorrow," he says. Jees, yuh'd tink he meant it! *(He sits down in the chair at Larry's left)*

LARRY *(grinning).* I'll be glad to pay up—tomorrow. And I know my fellow inmates will promise the same. They've

all a touching credulity concerning tomorrows. *(A half-drunken mockery in his eyes)* It'll be a great day for them, tomorrow—the Feast of All Fools, with brass bands playing! Their ships will come in, loaded to the gunwales with cancelled regrets and promises fulfilled and clean slates and new leases!

ROCKY *(cynically).* Yeah, and a ton of hop!

LARRY *(leans toward him, a comical intensity in his low voice).* Don't mock the faith! Have you no respect for religion, you unregenerate Wop? What's it matter if the truth is that their favoring breeze has the stink of nickel whiskey on its breath, and their sea is a growler of lager and ale, and their ships are long since looted and scuttled and sunk on the bottom? To hell with the truth! As the history of the world proves, the truth has no bearing on anything. It's irrelevant and immaterial, as the lawyers say. The lie of a pipe dream is what gives life to the whole misbegotten mad lot of us, drunk or sober. And that's enough philosophic wisdom to give you for one drink of rot-gut.

ROCKY *(grins kiddingly).* De old Foolosopher, like Hickey calls yuh, ain't yuh? I s'pose you don't fall for no pipe dream?

LARRY *(a bit stiffly).* I don't, no. Mine are all dead and buried behind me. What's before me is the comforting fact that death is a fine long sleep, and I'm damned tired, and it can't come too soon for me.

ROCKY. Yeah, just hangin' around hopin' you'll croak, ain't yuh? Well, I'm bettin' you'll have a good long wait. Jees, somebody'll have to take an axe to croak you!

LARRY *(grins).* Yes, it's my bad luck to be cursed with an iron constitution that even Harry's booze can't corrode.

ROCKY. De old anarchist wise guy dat knows all de answers! Dat's you, huh?

LARRY *(frowns).* Forget the anarchist part of it. I'm through with the Movement long since. I saw men didn't want to be saved from themselves, for that would mean they'd have to give up greed, and they'll never pay that price for liberty. So I said to the world, God bless all here, and may the best man win and die of gluttony! And I took a seat in the grandstand of philosophical detachment to fall asleep observing the cannibals do their death dance. *(He chuckles at his own fancy—reaches over and shakes Hugo's shoulder)* Ain't I telling him the truth, Comrade Hugo?

ROCKY. Aw, fer Chris' sake, don't get dat bughouse bum started!

HUGO *(raises his head and peers at Rocky blearily through his thick spectacles —in a guttural declamatory tone).* Capitalist swine! Bourgeois stool pigeons! Have the slaves no right to sleep even? *(Then he grins at Rocky and his manner changes to a giggling, wheedling playfulness, as though he were talking to a child)* Hello, leedle Rocky! Leedle monkey-face! Vere is your leedle slave girls? *(With an abrupt change to a bullying tone)* Don't be a fool! Loan me a dollar! Damned bourgeois Wop! The great Malatesta is my good friend! Buy me a trink! *(He seems to run down, and is overcome by drowsiness. His head sinks to the table again and he is at once fast asleep)*

ROCKY. He's out again. *(More exasperated than angry)* He's lucky no one don't take his cracks serious or he'd wake up every mornin' in a hospital.

LARRY *(regarding Hugo with pity).* No. No one takes him seriously. That's his epitaph. Not even the comrades any more. If I've been through with the Movement long since, it's been through with him, and, thanks to whiskey, he's the only one doesn't know it.

ROCKY. I've let him get by wid too much. He's goin' to pull dat slave-girl stuff on me once too often. *(His manner changes to defensive argument)* Hell, yuh'd tink I wuz a pimp or somethin'. Everybody knows me knows I ain't. A pimp don't hold no job. I'm a bartender. Dem tarts, Margie and Poil, dey're just a side line to pick up some extra dough. Strictly business, like dey was fighters and I was deir manager, see? I fix the cops fer dem so's dey can hustle widout gettin' pinched. Hell, dey'd be on de Island most of de time if it wasn't fer me. And I don't beat dem up like a pimp would. I treat dem fine. Dey like me. We're pals, see? What if I do take deir dough? Dey'd on'y trow it away. Tarts can't hang on to dough. But I'm a bartender and I work hard for my livin' in dis dump. You know dat, Larry.

LARRY *(with inner sardonic amusement —flatteringly).* A shrewd business man, who doesn't miss any opportunity to get on in the world. That's what I'd call you.

ROCKY *(pleased).* Sure ting. Dat's me. Grab another ball, Larry. *(Larry pours a drink from the bottle on Willie's table and gulps it down. Rocky glances around the room)* Yuh'd never tink all dese bums had a good bed upstairs to go to. Scared if dey hit the hay dey wouldn't be here when Hickey showed up, and dey'd miss a coupla drinks. Dat's what kept you up too, ain't it?

LARRY. It is. But not so much the hope of booze, if you can believe that. I've got the blues and Hickey's a great one to make a joke of everything and cheer you up.

ROCKY. Yeah, some kidder! Remember how he woiks up dat gag about his wife, when he's cockeyed, cryin' over her picture and den springin' it on yuh all of a sudden dat he left her in de hay wid de iceman? *(He laughs)* I wonder what's happened to him. Yuh could set your watch by his periodicals before dis. Always got here a coupla days before Harry's birthday party, and now he's on'y got till tonight to make it. I hope he shows soon. Dis dump is like de morgue wid all dese bums passed out. *(Willie Oban jerks and twitches in his sleep and begins to mumble. They watch him)*

WILLIE *(blurts from his dream).* It's a lie! *(Miserably)* Papa! Papa!

LARRY. Poor devil *(Then angry with himself)* But to hell with pity! It does no good. I'm through with it!

ROCKY. Dreamin' about his old man. From what de old-timers say, de old gent sure made a pile of dough in de bucket-shop game before de cops got him. *(He considers Willie frowningly)* Jees, I've seen him bad before but never dis bad. Look at dat get-up. Been playin' de old reliever game. Sold his suit and shoes at Solly's two days ago. Solly give him two bucks and a bum outfit. Yesterday he sells de bum one back to Solly for four bits and gets dese rags to put on. Now he's through. Dat's Solly's final edition he wouldn't take back for nuttin'. Willie sure is on de bottom. I ain't never seen no one so bad, except Hickey on de end of a coupla his bats.

LARRY *(sardonically).* It's a great game, the pursuit of happiness.

ROCKY. Harry don't know what to do

about him. He called up his old lady's lawyer like he always does when Willie gets licked. Yuh remember dey used to send down a private dick to give him the rush to a cure, but de lawyer tells Harry nix, de old lady's off of Willie for keeps dis time and he can go to hell.

LARRY (*watches Willie, who is shaking in his sleep like an old dog*). There's the consolation that he hasn't far to go! (*As if replying to this, Willie comes to a crisis of jerks and moans. Larry adds in a comically intense, crazy whisper*) Be God, he's knocking on the door right now!

WILLIE (*suddenly yells in his nightmare*). It's a God-damned lie! (*He begins to sob*) Oh, Papa! Jesus! (*All the occupants of the room stir on their chairs but none of them wakes up except Hope*)

ROCKY (*grabs his shoulder and shakes him*). Hey, you! Nix! Cut out de noise! (*Willie opens his eyes to stare around him with a bewildered horror.*)

HOPE (*opens one eye to peer over his spectacles—drowsily*). Who's that yelling?

ROCKY. Willie, Boss. De Brooklyn boys is after him.

HOPE (*querulously*). Well, why don't you give the poor feller a drink and keep him quiet? Bejees, can't I get a wink of sleep in my own back room?

ROCKY (*indignantly to Larry*). Listen to that blind-eyed, deef old bastard, will yuh? He give me strict orders not to let Willie hang up no more drinks, no matter—

HOPE (*mechanically puts a hand to his ear in the gesture of deafness*). What's that? I can't hear you. (*Then drowsily irascible*) You're a cockeyed liar. Never refused a drink to anyone needed it bad in my life! Told you to use your judgment. Ought to know better. You're too busy thinking up ways to cheat me. Oh, I ain't as blind as you think. I can still see a cash register, bejees!

ROCKY (*grins at him affectionately now —flatteringly*). Sure, Boss. Swell chance of foolin' you!

HOPE. I'm wise to you and your sidekick, Chuck. Bejees, you're burglars, not barkeeps! Blind-eyed, deef old bastard, am I? Oh, I heard you! Heard you often when you didn't think. You and Chuck laughing behind my back, telling people you throw the money up in the air and

whatever sticks to the ceiling is my share! A fine couple of crooks! You'd steal the pennies off your dead mother's eyes!

ROCKY (*winks at Larry*). Aw, Harry, me and Chuck was on'y kiddin'.

HOPE (*more drowsily*). I'll fire both of you. Bejees, if you think you can play me for an easy mark, you've come to the wrong house. No one ever played Harry Hope for a sucker!

ROCKY (*to Larry*). No one but everybody.

HOPE (*his eyes shut again—mutters*). Least you could do—keep things quiet— (*He falls asleep*)

WILLIE (*pleadingly*). Give me a drink, Rocky. Harry said it was all right. God, I need a drink.

ROCKY. Den grab it. It's right under your nose.

WILLIE (*avidly*). Thanks. (*He takes the bottle with both twitching hands and tilts it to his lips and gulps down the whiskey in big swallows*)

ROCKY (*sharply*). When! When! (*He grabs the bottle*) I didn't say, take a bath! (*Showing the bottle to Larry—indignantly*) Jees, look! He's killed a half pint or more! (*He turns on Willie angrily, but Willie has closed his eyes and is sitting quietly, shuddering, waiting for the effect*)

LARRY (*with a pitying glance*). Leave him be, the poor devil. A half pint of that dynamite in one swig will fix him for a while—if it doesn't kill him.

ROCKY (*shrugs his shoulders and sits down again*). Aw right by me. It ain't my booze. (*Behind him, in the chair at left of the middle table, Joe Mott, the Negro, has been waking up*)

JOE (*his eyes blinking sleepily*). Whose booze? Gimme some. I don't care whose. Where's Hickey? Ain't he come yet? What time's it, Rocky?

ROCKY. Gettin' near time to open up. Time you begun to sweep up in de bar.

JOE (*lazily*). Never mind de time. If Hickey ain't come, it's time Joe goes to sleep again. I was dreamin' Hickey come in de door, crackin' one of dem drummer's jokes, wavin' a big bankroll and we was all goin' be drunk for two weeks. Wake up and no luck. (*Suddenly his eyes open wide*) Wait a minute, dough. I got idea. Say, Larry, how 'bout dat young guy, Parritt, came to look you up last night and rented a room? Where's he at?

LARRY. Up in his room, asleep. No hope in him, anyway, Joe. He's broke.

JOE. Dat what he told you? Me and Rocky knows different. Had a roll when he paid you his room rent, didn't he, Rocky? I seen it.

ROCKY. Yeah. He flashed it like he forgot and den tried to hide it quick.

LARRY (surprised and resentful). He did, did he?

ROCKY. Yeah, I figgered he don't belong, but he said he was a friend of yours.

LARRY. He's a liar. I wouldn't know him if he hadn't told me who he was. His mother and I were friends years ago on the Coast. (He hesitates—then lowering his voice) You've read in the papers about that bombing on the Coast when several people got killed? Well, the one woman they pinched, Rosa Parritt, is his mother. They'll be coming up for trial soon, and there's no chance for them. She'll get life, I think. I'm telling you this so you'll know why if Don acts a bit queer, and not jump on him. He must be hard hit. He's her only kid.

ROCKY (nods—then thoughtfully). Why ain't he out dere stickin' by her?

LARRY (frowns). Don't ask questions. Maybe there's a good reason.

ROCKY (stares at him—understandingly). Sure. I get it. (Then wonderingly) But den what kind of a sap is he to hang on to his right name?

LARRY (irritably). I'm telling you I don't know anything and I don't want to know. To hell with the Movement and all connected with it! I'm out of it, and everything else, and damned glad to be.

ROCKY (shrugs his shoulders—indifferently). Well, don't tink I'm interested in dis Parritt guy. He's nuttin' to me.

JOE. Me neider. If dere's one ting more'n anudder I cares nuttin' about, it's de sucker game you and Hugo call de Movement. (He chuckles—reminiscently) Reminds me of damn fool argument me and Mose Porter has de udder night. He's drunk and I'm drunker. He says, "Socialist and Anarchist, we ought to shoot dem dead. Dey's all no-good sons of bitches." I says, "Hold on, you talk's if Anarchists and Socialists was de same." "Dey is," he says. "Dey's both no-good bastards." "No, dey ain't," I says. "I'll explain the difference. De Anarchist he never works. He drinks but he never buys, and if he do ever get a nickel, he blows it in on bombs, and he wouldn't give you nothin'. So go ahead and shoot him. But de Socialist, sometimes, he's got a job, and if he gets ten bucks, he's bound by his religion to split fifty-fifty wid you. You say—how about my cut, Comrade? And you gets de five. So you don't shoot no Socialists while I'm around. Dat is, not if dey got anything. Of course, if dey's broke, den dey's no-good bastards, too." (He laughs, immensely tickled)

LARRY (grins with sardonic appreciation). Be God, Joe, you've got all the beauty of human nature and the practical wisdom of the world in that little parable.

ROCKY (winks at Joe). Sure, Larry ain't de on'y wise guy in dis dump, hey Joe? (At a sound from the hall he turns as Don Parritt appears in the doorway. Rocky speaks to Larry out of the side of his mouth) Here's your guy.

(Parritt comes forward. He is eighteen, tall and broad-shouldered but thin, gangling and awkward. His face is good-looking, with blond curly hair and large regular features, but his personality is unpleasant. There is a shifting defiance and ingratiation in his light-blue eyes and an irritating aggressiveness in his manner. His clothes and shoes are new, comparatively expensive, sporty in style. He looks as though he belonged in a pool room patronized by would-be sports. He glances around defensively, sees Larry and comes forward.)

PARRITT. Hello, Larry. (He nods to Rocky and Joe) Hello. (They nod and size him up with expressionless eyes)

LARRY (without cordiality). What's up? I thought you'd be asleep.

PARRITT. Couldn't make it. I got sick of lying awake. Thought I might as well see if you were around.

LARRY (indicates the chair on the right of table). Sit down and join the bums then. (Parritt sits down. Larry adds meaningfully) The rules of the house are that drinks may be served at all hours.

PARRITT (forcing a smile). I get you. But, hell, I'm just about broke. (He catches Rocky's and Joe's contemptuous glances—quickly) Oh, I know you guys saw— You think I've got a roll. Well, you're all wrong. I'll show you. (He takes a small wad of dollar bills from his *pocket)* It's all ones. And I've got to live on it till I get a job. *(Then with defensive truculence)* You think I fixed up a phony, don't you? Why the hell would I? Where would I get a real roll? You don't get rich doing what I've been doing. Ask Larry. You're lucky in the Movement if you have enough to eat. *(Larry regards him puzzledly)*

ROCKY *(coldly).* What's de song and dance about? We ain't said nuttin'.

PARRITT *(lamely—placating them now).* Why, I was just putting you right. But I don't want you to think I'm a tightwad. I'll buy a drink if you want one.

JOE *(cheering up).* If? Man, when I don't want a drink, you call de morgue, tell dem come take Joe's body away, cause he's sure enuf dead. Gimme de bottle quick, Rocky, before he changes his mind!

Rocky passes him the bottle and glass. He pours a brimful drink and tosses it down his throat, and hands the bottle and glass to Larry.)

ROCKY. I'll take a cigar when I go in de bar. What're you havin'?

PARRITT. Nothing. I'm on the wagon. What's the damage? *(He holds out a dollar bill)*

ROCKY. Fifteen cents. *(He makes change from his pocket)*

PARRITT. Must be some booze!

LARRY. It's cyanide cut with carbolic acid to give it a mellow flavor. Here's luck! *(He drinks)*

ROCKY. Guess I'll get back in de bar and catch a coupla winks before opening-up time. *(He squeezes through the tables and disappears, right-rear, behind the curtain. In the section of bar at right, he comes forward and sits at the table and slumps back, closing his eyes and yawning)*

JOE *(stares calculatingly at Parritt and then looks away—aloud to himself, philosophically).* One-drink guy. Dat well done run dry. No hope till Harry's birthday party. 'Less Hickey shows up. *(He turns to Larry)* If Hickey comes, Larry, you wake me up if you has to bat me wid a chair. *(He settles himself and immediately falls asleep)*

PARRITT. Who's Hickey?

LARRY. A hardware drummer. An old friend of Harry Hope's and all the gang. He's a grand guy. He comes here twice a year regularly on a periodical drunk and blows in all his money.

PARRITT *(with a disparaging glance around).* Must be hard up for a place to hang out.

LARRY. It has its points for him. He never runs into anyone he knows in his business here.

PARRITT *(lowering his voice).* Yes, that's what I want, too. I've got to stay under cover, Larry, like I told you last night.

LARRY. You did a lot of hinting. You didn't tell me anything.

PARRITT. You can guess, can't you? *(He changes the subject abruptly)* I've been in some dumps on the Coast, but this is the limit. What kind of joint is it, anyway?

LARRY *(with a sardonic grin).* What is it? It's the No Chance Saloon. It's Bedrock Bar, The End of the Line Café, The Bottom of the Sea Rathskeller! Don't you notice the beautiful calm in the atmosphere? That's because it's the last harbor. No one here has to worry about where they're going next, because there is no farther they can go. It's a great comfort to them. Although even here they keep up the appearances of life with a few harmless pipe dreams about their yesterdays and tomorrows, as you'll see for yourself if you're here long.

PARRITT *(stares at him curiously).* What's your pipe dream, Larry?

LARRY *(hiding resentment).* Oh, I'm the exception. I haven't any left, thank God. *(Shortly)* Don't complain about this place. You couldn't find a better for lying low.

PARRITT. I'm glad of that, Larry. I don't feel any too damned good. I was knocked off my base by that business on the Coast, and since then it's been no fun dodging around the country, thinking every guy you see might be a dick.

LARRY *(sympathetically now).* No, it wouldn't be. But you're safe here. The cops ignore this dump. They think it's as harmless as a graveyard. *(He grins sardonically)* And, be God, they're right.

PARRITT. It's been lonely as hell. *(Impulsively)* Christ, Larry, I was glad to find you. I kept saying to myself, "If I can only find Larry. He's the one guy in the world who can understand—" *(He hesitates, staring at Larry with a strange appeal)*

LARRY (*watching him puzzledly*). Understand what?

PARRITT (*hastily*). Why, all I've been through. (*Looking away*) Oh, I know you're thinking, This guy has a hell of a nerve. I haven't seen him since he was a kid. I'd forgotten he was alive. But I've never forgotten you, Larry. You were the only friend of Mother's who ever paid attention to me, or knew I was alive. All the others were too busy with the Movement. Even Mother. And I had no Old Man. You used to take me on your knee and tell me stories and crack jokes and make me laugh. You'd ask me questions and take what I said seriously. I guess I got to feel in the years you lived with us that you'd taken the place of my Old Man. (*Embarrassedly*) But, hell, that sounds like a lot of mush. I suppose you don't remember a damned thing about it.

LARRY (*moved in spite of himself*). I remember well. You were a serious lonely little shaver. (*Then resenting being moved, changes the subject*) How is it they didn't pick you up when they got your mother and the rest?

PARRITT (*in a lowered voice but eagerly, as if he wanted this chance to tell about it*). I wasn't around, and as soon as I heard the news I went under cover. You've noticed my glad rags. I was staked to them—as a disguise, sort of. I hung around pool rooms and gambling joints and hooker shops, where they'd never look for a Wobblie, pretending I was a sport. Anyway, they'd grabbed everyone important, so I suppose they didn't think of me until afterward.

LARRY. The papers say the cops got them all dead to rights, that the Burns dicks knew every move before it was made, and someone inside the Movement must have sold out and tipped them off.

PARRITT (*turns to look Larry in the eyes—slowly*). Yes, I guess that must be true, Larry. It hasn't come out who it was. It may never come out. I suppose whoever it was made a bargain with the Burns men to keep him out of it. They won't need his evidence.

LARRY (*tensely*). By God, I hate to believe it of any of the crowd, if I am through long since with any connection with them. I know they're damned fools, most of them, as stupidly greedy for power as the worst capitalist they attack, but I'd swear there couldn't be a yellow stool pigeon among them.

PARRITT. Sure. I'd have sworn that, too, Larry.

LARRY. I hope his soul rots in hell, whoever it is!

PARRITT. Yes, so do I.

LARRY (*after a pause—shortly*). How did you locate me? I hoped I'd found a place of retirement here where no one in the Movement would ever come to disturb my peace.

PARRITT. I found out through Mother.

LARRY. I asked her not to tell anyone.

PARRITT. She didn't tell me, but she'd kept all your letters and I found where she'd hidden them in the flat. I sneaked up there one night after she was arrested.

LARRY. I'd never have thought she was a woman who'd keep letters.

PARRITT. No, I wouldn't, either. There's nothing soft or sentimental about Mother.

LARRY. I never answered her last letters. I haven't written her in a couple of years—or anyone else. I've gotten beyond the desire to communicate with the world—or, what's more to the point, let it bother me any more with its greedy madness.

PARRITT. It's funny Mother kept in touch with you so long. When she's finished with anyone, she's finished. She's always been proud of that. And you know how she feels about the Movement. Like a revivalist preacher about religion. Anyone who loses faith in it is more than dead to her; he's a Judas who ought to be boiled in oil. Yet she seemed to forgive you.

LARRY (*sardonically*). She didn't, don't worry. She wrote to denounce me and try to bring the sinner to repentance and a belief in the One True Faith again.

PARRITT. What made you leave the Movement, Larry? Was it on account of Mother?

LARRY (*starts*). Don't be a damned fool! What the hell put that in your head?

PARRITT. Why, nothing—except I remember what a fight you had with her before you left.

LARRY (*resentfully*). Well, if you do, I don't. That was eleven years ago. You were only seven. If we did quarrel, it was because I told her I'd become convinced the Movement was only a beautiful pipe dream.

PARRITT (*with a strange smile*). I don't remember it that way.

LARRY. Then you can blame your imagination—and forget it. (*He changes the subject abruptly*) You asked me why I quit the Movement. I had a lot of good reasons. One was myself, and another was my comrades, and the last was the breed of swine called men in general. For myself, I was forced to admit, at the end of thirty years' devotion to the Cause, that I was never made for it. I was born condemned to be one of those who has to see all sides of a question. When you're damned like that, the questions multiply for you until in the end it's all question and no answer. As history proves, to be a worldly success at anything, especially revolution, you have to wear blinkers like a horse and see only straight in front of you. You have to see, too, that this is all black, and that is all white. As for my comrades in the Great Cause, I felt as Horace Walpole did about England, that he could love it if it weren't for the people in it. The material the ideal free society must be constructed from is men themselves and you can't build a marble temple out of a mixture of mud and manure. When man's soul isn't a sow's ear, it will be time enough to dream of silk purses. (*He chuckles sardonically—then irritably as if suddenly provoked at himself for talking so much*) Well, that's why I quit the Movement, if it leaves you any wiser. At any rate, you see it had nothing to do with your mother.

PARRITT (*smiles almost mockingly*). Oh, sure, I see. But I'll bet Mother has always thought it was on her account. You know her, Larry. To hear her go on sometimes, you'd think she was the Movement.

LARRY (*stares at him, puzzled and repelled—sharply*). That's a hell of a way for you to talk, after what happened to her!

PARRITT (*at once confused and guilty*). Don't get me wrong. I wasn't sneering, Larry. Only kidding. I've said the same thing to her lots of times to kid her. But you're right. I know I shouldn't now. I keep forgetting she's in jail. It doesn't seem real. I can't believe it about her. She's always been so free. I— But I don't want to think of it. (*Larry is moved to a puzzled pity in spite of himself. Parritt changes the subject*) What have you been doing all the years since you left—the Coast, Larry?

LARRY (*sardonically*). Nothing I could help doing. If I don't believe in the Movement, I don't believe in anything else either, especially not the State. I've refused to become a useful member of its society. I've been a philosophical drunken bum, and proud of it. (*Abruptly his tone sharpens with resentful warning*) Listen to me. I hope you've deduced that I've my own reason for answering the impertinent questions of a stranger, for that's all you are to me. I have a strong hunch you've come here expecting something of me. I'm warning you, at the start, so there'll be no misunderstanding, that I've nothing left to give, and I want to be left alone, and I'll thank you to keep your life to yourself. I feel you're looking for some answer to something. I have no answer to give anyone, not even myself. Unless you can call what Heine wrote in his poem to morphine an answer. (*He quotes a translation of the closing couplet sardonically*)

"Lo, sleep is good; better is death; in sooth,
The best of all were never to be born."

PARRITT (*shrinks a bit frightenedly*). That's the hell of an answer. (*Then with a forced grin of bravado*) Still, you never know when it might come in handy. (*He looks away, Larry stares at him puzzledly, interested in spite of himself and at the same time vaguely uneasy*)

LARRY (*forcing a casual tone*). I don't suppose you've had much chance to hear news of your mother since she's been in jail?

PARRITT. No. No chance. (*He hesitates —then blurts out*) Anyway, I don't think she wants to hear from me. We had a fight just before that business happened. She bawled me out because I was going around with tarts. That got my goat, coming from her. I told her, "You've always acted the free woman, you've never let anything stop you from—" (*He checks himself—goes on hurriedly*) That made her sore. She said she wouldn't give a damn what I did except she'd begun to suspect I was too interested in outside things and losing interest in the Movement.

LARRY (*stares at him*). And were you?

PARRITT (*hesitates—then with inten-*

sity). Sure I was! I'm no damned fool! I couldn't go on believing forever that gang was going to change the world by shooting off their loud traps on soapboxes and sneaking around blowing up a lousy building or a bridge! I got wise it was all a crazy pipe dream! *(Appealingly)* The same as you did, Larry. That's why I came to you. I knew you'd understand. What finished me was this last business of someone selling out. How can you believe anything after a thing like that happens? It knocks you cold! You don't know what the hell is what! You're through! *(Appealingly)* You know how I feel, don't you, Larry? *(Larry stares at him, moved by sympathy and pity in spite of himself, disturbed, and resentful at being disturbed, and puzzled by something he feels about Parritt that isn't right. But before he can reply, Hugo suddenly raises his head from his arms in a half-awake alcoholic daze and speaks)*

HUGO *(quotes aloud to himself in a guttural declamatory style).* "The days grow hot, O Babylon! 'Tis cool beneath thy villow trees!" *(Parritt turns startledly as Hugo peers muzzily without recognition at him. Hugo exclaims automatically in his tone of denunciation)* Gottammed stool pigeon!

PARRITT *(shrinks away—stammers).* What? Who do you mean? *(Then furiously)* You lousy bum, you can't call me that! *(He draws back his fist)*

HUGO *(ignores this—recognizing him now, bursts into his childish teasing giggle).* Hello, leedle Don! Leedle monkey-face. I did not recognize you. You have grown big boy. How is your mother? Where you come from? *(He breaks into his wheedling, bullying tone)* Don't be a fool! Loan me a dollar! Buy me a trink! *(As if this exhausted him, he abruptly forgets it and plumps his head down on his arms again and is asleep)*

PARRITT *(with eager relief).* Sure, I'll buy you a drink, Hugo. I'm broke, but I can afford one for you. I'm sorry I got sore. I ought to have remembered when you're soused you call everyone a stool pigeon. But it's no damned joke right at this time. *(He turns to Larry, who is regarding him now fixedly with an uneasy expression as if he suddenly were afraid of his own thoughts—forcing a smile)* Gee, he's passed out again. *(He stiffens*

defensively) What are you giving me the hard look for? Oh, I know. You thought I was going to hit him? What do you think I am? I've always had a lot of respect for Hugo. I've always stood up for him when people in the Movement panned him for an old drunken has-been. He had the guts to serve ten years in the can in his own country and get his eyes ruined in solitary. I'd like to see some of them here stick that. Well, they'll get a chance now to show— *(Hastily)* I don't mean— But let's forget that. Tell me some more about this dump. Who are all these tanks? Who's that guy trying to catch pneumonia? *(He indicates Lewis)*

LARRY *(stares at him almost frightenedly—then looks away and grasps eagerly this chance to change the subject. He begins to describe the sleepers with sardonic relish but at the same time showing his affection for them).* That's Captain Lewis, a one-time hero of the British Army. He strips to display that scar on his back he got from a native spear whenever he's completely plastered. The bewhiskered bloke opposite him is General Wetjoen, who led a commando in the War. The two of them met when they came to work in the Boer War spectacle at the St. Louis Fair and they've been bosom pals ever since. They dream the hours away in happy dispute over the brave days in South Africa when they tried to murder each other. The little guy between them was in it, too, as correspondent for some English paper. His nickname here is Jimmy Tomorrow. He's the leader of our Tomorrow Movement.

PARRITT. What do they do for a living?

LARRY. As little as possible. Once in a while one of them makes a successful touch somewhere, and some of them get a few dollars a month from connections at home who pay it on condition they never come back. For the rest, they live on free lunch and their old friend, Harry Hope, who doesn't give a damn what anyone does or doesn't do, as long as he likes you.

PARRITT. It must be a tough life.

LARRY. It's not. Don't waste your pity. They wouldn't thank you for it. They manage to get drunk, by hook or crook, and keep their pipe dreams, and that's all they ask of life. I've never known more contented men. It isn't often that men attain the true goal of their heart's desire. The same applies to Harry himself and his two cronies at the far table. He's so satisfied with life he's never set foot out of this place since his wife died twenty years ago. He has no need of the outside world at all. This place has a fine trade from the Market people across the street and the waterfront workers, so in spite of Harry's thirst and his generous heart, he comes out even. He never worries in hard times because there's always old friends from the days when he was a jitney Tammany politician, and a friendly brewery to tide him over. Don't ask me what his two pals work at because they don't. Except at being his life-time guests. The one facing this way is his brother-in-law, Ed Mosher, who once worked for a circus in the ticket wagon. Pat McGloin, the other one, was a police lieutenant back in the flush times of graft when everything went. But he got too greedy and when the usual reform investigation came he was caught red-handed and thrown off the Force. *(He nods at Joe)* Joe here has a yesterday in the same flush period. He ran a colored gambling house then and was a hell of a sport, so they say. Well, that's our whole family circle of inmates, except the two barkeeps and their girls, three ladies of the pavement that room on the third floor.

PARRITT *(bitterly)*. To hell with them! I never want to see a whore again! *(As Larry flashes him a puzzled glance, he adds confusedly)* I mean, they always get you in dutch. *(While he is speaking Willie Oban has opened his eyes. He leans toward them, drunk now from the effect of the huge drink he took, and speaks with a mocking suavity)*

WILLIE. Why omit me from your Who's Who in Dypsomania, Larry? An unpardonable slight, especially as I am the only inmate of royal blood. *(To Parritt—ramblingly)* Educated at Harvard, too. You must have noticed the atmosphere of culture here. My humble contribution. Yes, Generous Stranger—I trust you're generous—I was born in the purple, the son, but unfortunately not the heir, of the late world-famous Bill Oban, King of the Bucket Shops. A revolution deposed him, conducted by the District Attorney. He was sent into exile. In fact, not to

mince matters, they locked him in the can and threw away the key. Alas, his was an adventurous spirit that pined in confinement. And so he died. Forgive these reminiscences. Undoubtedly all this is well known to you. Everyone in the world knows.

PARRITT *(uncomfortably)*. Tough luck. No, I never heard of him.

WILLIE *(blinks at him incredulously)*. Never heard? I thought everyone in the world— Why, even at Harvard I discovered my father was well known by reputation, although that was some time before the District Attorney gave him so much unwelcome publicity. Yes, even as a freshman I was notorious. I was accepted socially with all the warm cordiality that Henry Wadsworth Longfellow would have shown a drunken Negress dancing the can can at high noon on Brattle Street. Harvard was my father's idea. He was an ambitious man. Dictatorial, too. Always knowing what was best for me. But I did make myself a brilliant student. A dirty trick on my classmates, inspired by revenge, I fear. *(He quotes)* "Dear college days, with pleasure rife! The grandest gladdest days of life!" But, of course, that is a Yale hymn, and they're given to rah-rah exaggeration at New Haven. I was a brilliant student at Law School, too. My father wanted a lawyer in the family. He was a calculating man. A thorough knowledge of the law close at hand in the house to help him find fresh ways to evade it. But I discovered the loophole of whiskey and escaped his jurisdiction. *(Abruptly to Parritt)* Speaking of whiskey, sir, reminds me—and, I hope, reminds you—that when meeting a Prince the customary salutation is "What'll you have?"

PARRITT *(with defensive resentment)*. Nix! All you guys seem to think I'm made of dough. Where would I get the coin to blow everyone?

WILLIE *(sceptically)*. Broke? You haven't the thirsty look of the impecunious. I'd judge you to be a plutocrat, your pockets stuffed with ill-gotten gains. Two or three dollars, at least. And don't think we will question how you got it. As Vespasian remarked, the smell of all whiskey is sweet.

PARRITT. What do you mean, how I got it? *(To Larry, forcing a laugh)* It's a laugh, calling me a plutocrat, isn't it, Larry, when I've been in the Movement all my life. *(Larry gives him an uneasy suspicious glance, then looks away, as if avoiding something he does not wish to see)*

WILLIE *(disgustedly)*. Ah, one of those, eh? I believe you now, all right! Go away and blow yourself up, that's a good lad. Hugo is the only licensed preacher of that gospel here. A dangerous terrorist, Hugo! He would as soon blow the collar off a schooner of beer as look at you! *(To Larry)* Let us ignore this useless youth, Larry. Let us join in prayer that Hickey, the Great Salesman, will soon arrive bringing the blessed bourgeois long green! Would that Hickey or Death would come! Meanwhile, I will sing a song. A beautiful old New England folk ballad which I picked up at Harvard amid the debris of education. *(He sings in a boisterous baritone, rapping on the table with his knuckles at the indicated spots in the song)*

"Jack, oh, Jack, was a sailor lad
And he came to a tavern for gin.
He rapped and he rapped with a *(Rap, rap, rap)*
But never a soul seemed in."

(The drunks at the tables stir. Rocky gets up from his chair in the bar and starts back for the entrance to the back room. Hope cocks one irritable eye over his specs. Joe Mott opens both of his and grins. Willie interposes some drunken whimsical exposition to Larry.)

The origin of this beautiful ditty is veiled in mystery, Larry. There was a legend bruited about in Cambridge lavatories that Waldo Emerson composed it during his uninformative period as a minister, while he was trying to write a sermon. But my own opinion is, it goes back much further, and Jonathan Edwards was the author of both words and music. *(He sings)*

"He rapped and rapped, and tapped and tapped
Enough to wake the dead
Till he heard a damsel *(Rap, rap, rap)*
On a window right over his head."

(The drunks are blinking their eyes now, grumbling and cursing. Rocky appears from the bar at rear, right, yawning.)

HOPE *(with yawning irritation)*. Rocky! Bejees, can't you keep that crazy bastard quiet? *(Rocky starts for Willie)*

WILLIE. And now the influence of a good woman enters our mariner's life. Well, perhaps "good" isn't the word. But very, very kind. *(He sings)*

"Oh, come up," she cried, "my sailor lad,
And you and I'll agree,
And I'll show you the prettiest *(Rap, rap, rap)*
That ever you did see."

(He speaks) You see, Larry? The lewd Puritan touch, obviously, and it grows more marked as we go on. *(He sings)*

"Oh, he put his arm around her waist,
He gazed in her bright blue eyes
And then he—"

(But here Rocky shakes him roughly by the shoulder.)

ROCKY. Piano! What d'yuh tink dis dump is, a dump?

HOPE. Give him the bum's rush upstairs! Lock him in his room!

ROCKY *(yanks Willie by the arm)*. Come on, Bum.

WILLIE *(dissolves into pitiable terror)*. No! Please, Rocky! I'll go crazy up in that room alone! It's haunted! I— *(He calls to Hope)* Please, Harry! Let me stay here! I'll be quiet!

HOPE *(immediately relents—indignantly)*. What the hell you doing to him, Rocky? I didn't tell you to beat up the poor guy. Leave him alone, long as he's quiet. *(Rocky lets go of Willie disgustedly and goes back to his chair in the bar)*

WILLIE *(huskily)*. Thanks, Harry. You're a good scout. *(He closes his eyes and sinks back in his chair exhaustedly, twitching and quivering again)*

HOPE *(addressing McGloin and Mosher, who are sleepily awake—accusingly)*. Always the way. Can't trust nobody. Leave it to that Dago to keep order and it's like bedlam in a cathouse, singing and everything. And you two big barflies are a hell of a help to me, ain't you? Eat and sleep and get drunk! All you're good for, bejees! Well, you can take that "I'll-have-the-same" look off your maps! There ain't going to be no more drinks on the house till hell freezes over! *(Neither of the two is impressed either by his insults or his threats. They grin hangover grins of tolerant affection at him and wink at each other. Harry fumes)* Yeah, grin! Wink, bejees! Fine pair of sons of bitches to have glued on me for life! (*But he can't get a rise out of them and he subsides into a fuming mumble. Meanwhile, at the middle table, Captain Lewis and General Wetjoen are as wide awake as heavy hangovers permit. Jimmy Tomorrow nods, his eyes blinking. Lewis is gazing across the table at Joe Mott, who is still chuckling to himself over Willie's song. The expression on Lewis's face is that of one who can't believe his eyes*)

LEWIS (*aloud to himself, with a muzzy wonder*). Good God! Have I been drinking at the same table with a bloody Kaffir?

JOE (*grinning*). Hello, Captain. You comin' up for air? Kaffir? Who's he?

WETJOEN (*blurrily*). Kaffir, dot's a nigger, Joe. (*Joe stiffens and his eyes narrow. Wetjoen goes on with heavy jocosity*) Dot's joke on him, Joe. He don't know you. He's still plind drunk, the ploody Limey chentleman! A great mistake I missed him at the pattle of Modder River. Vit mine rifle I shoot damn fool Limey officers py the dozen, but him I miss. De pity of it! (*He chuckles and slaps Lewis on his bare shoulder*) Hey, wake up, Cecil, you ploody fool! Don't you know your old friend, Joe? He's no damned Kaffir! He's white, Joe is!

LEWIS (*light dawning—contritely*). My profound apologies, Joseph, old chum. Eyesight a trifle blurry, I'm afraid. Whitest colored man I ever knew. Proud to call you my friend. No hard feelings, what? (*He holds out his hand*)

JOE (*at once grins good-naturedly and shakes his hand*). No, Captain, I know it's mistake. Youse regular, if you is a Limey. (*Then his face hardening*) But I don't stand for "nigger" from nobody. Never did. In de old days, people calls me "nigger" wakes up in de hospital. I was de leader ob de Dirty Half-Dozen Gang. All six of us colored boys, we was tough and I was de toughest.

WETJOEN (*inspired to boastful reminiscence*). Me, in old days in Transvaal, I vas so tough and strong I grab axle of ox wagon mit full load and lift like feather.

LEWIS (*smiling amiably*). As for you, my balmy Boer that walks like a man, I say again it was a grave error in our foreign policy ever to set you free, once we nabbed you and your commando with Cronje. We should have taken you to the London zoo and incarcerated you in the baboons' cage. With a sign: "Spectators may distinguish the true baboon by his blue behind."

WETJOEN (*grins*). Gott! To dink, ten better Limey officers, at least, I shoot clean in the mittle of forehead at Spion Kopje, and you I miss! I neffer forgive myself! (*Jimmy Tomorrow blinks benignantly from one to the other with a gentle drunken smile*)

JIMMY (*sentimentally*). Now, come, Cecil, Piet! We must forget the War. Boer and Briton, each fought fairly and played the game till the better man won and then we shook hands. We are all brothers within the Empire united beneath the flag on which the sun never sets. (*Tears come to his eyes. He quotes with great sentiment, if with slight application*) "Ship me somewhere east of Suez—"

LARRY (*breaks in sardonically*). Be God, you're there already, Jimmy. Worst is best here, and East is West, and tomorrow is yesterday. What more do you want?

JIMMY (*with bleary benevolence, shaking his head in mild rebuke*). No, Larry, old friend, you can't deceive me. You pretend a bitter, cynic philosophy, but in your heart you are the kindest man among us.

LARRY (*disconcerted—irritably*). The hell you say!

PARRITT (*leans toward him—confidentially*). What a bunch of cuckoos!

JIMMY (*as if reminded of something—with a pathetic attempt at a brisk, no-more-nonsense air*). Tomorrow, yes. It's high time I straightened out and got down to business again. (*He brushes his sleeve fastidiously*) I must have this suit cleaned and pressed. I can't look like a tramp when I—

JOE (*who has been brooding—interrupts*). Yes, suh, white folks always said I was white. In de days when I was flush, Joe Mott's de only colored man dey allows in de white gamblin' houses. "You're all right, Joe, you're white," dey says. (*He chuckles*) Wouldn't let me play craps, dough. Dey know I could make dem dice behave. "Any odder game and any limit you like, Joe," dey says. Man, de money I lost! (*He chuckles—then with an underlying defensiveness*) Look at de Big Chief in dem days. He knew I was white. I'd saved my dough so I could start my own gamblin' house. Folks in de know tells me, see de man at de top, den you never has trouble. You git Harry Hope give you a letter to de Chief. And Harry does. Don't you, Harry?

HOPE (*preoccupied with his own thoughts*). Eh? Sure. Big Bill was a good friend of mine. I had plenty of friends high up in those days. Still could have if I wanted to go out and see them. Sure, I gave you a letter. I said you was white. What the hell of it?

JOE (*to Captain Lewis who has relapsed into a sleepy daze and is listening to him with an absurd strained attention without comprehending a word*). Dere. You see, Captain. I went to see de Chief, shakin' in my boots, and dere he is sittin' behind a big desk, lookin' as big as a freight train. He don't look up. He keeps me waitin' and waitin', and after 'bout an hour, seems like to me, he says slow and quiet like dere wasn't no harm in him, "You want to open a gamblin' joint, does you, Joe?" But he don't give me no time to answer. He jumps up, lookin' as big as two freight trains, and he pounds his fist like a ham on de desk, and he shouts, "You black son of a bitch, Harry says you're white and you better be white or dere's a little iron room up de river waitin' for you!" Den he sits down and says quiet again, "All right. You can open. Git de hell outa here!" So I opens, and he finds out I'se white, sure 'nuff, 'cause I run wide open for years and pays my sugar on de dot, and de cops and I is friends. (*He chuckles with pride*) Dem old days! Many's de night I come in here. Dis was a first-class hangout for sports in dem days. Good whiskey, fifteen cents, two for two bits. I t'rows down a fifty-dollar bill like it was trash paper and says, "Drink it up, boys, I don't want no change." Ain't dat right, Harry?

HOPE (*caustically*). Yes, and bejees, if I ever seen you throw fifty cents on the bar now, I'd know I had delirium tremens! You've told that story ten million times and if I have to hear it again, that'll give me D.T.s anyway!

JOE (*chuckling*). Gittin' drunk every day for twenty years ain't give you de Brooklyn boys. You needn't be scared of me!

LEWIS (*suddenly turns and beams on Hope*). Thank you, Harry, old chum. I will have a drink, now you mention it,

seeing it's so near your birthday. (*The others laugh*)

HOPE (*puts his hand to his ear—angrily*). What's that? I can't hear you.

LEWIS (*sadly*). No, I fancied you wouldn't.

HOPE. I don't have to, bejees! Booze is the only thing you ever talk about!

LEWIS (*sadly*). True. Yet there was a time when my conversation was more comprehensive. But as I became burdened with years, it seemed rather pointless to discuss my other subject.

HOPE. You can't joke with me! How much room rent do you owe me, tell me that?

LEWIS. Sorry. Adding has always baffled me. Subtraction is my forte.

HOPE (*snarling*). Arrh! Think you're funny! Captain, bejees! Showing off your wounds! Put on your clothes, for Christ's sake! This ain't no Turkish bath! Lousy Limey army! Took 'em years to lick a gang of Dutch hayseeds!

WETJOEN. Dot's right, Harry. Gif him hell!

HOPE. No lip out of you, neither, you Dutch spinach! General, hell! Salvation Army, that's what you'd ought t'been General in! Bragging what a shot you were, and, bejees, you missed him! And he missed you, that's just as bad! And now the two of you bum on me! (*Threateningly*) But you've broke the camel's back this time, bejees! You pay up tomorrow or out you go!

LEWIS (*earnestly*). My dear fellow, I give you my word of honor as an officer and a gentleman, you shall be paid tomorrow.

WETJOEN. Ve swear it, Harry! Tomorrow vidout fail!

MCGLOIN (*a twinkle in his eye*). There you are, Harry. Sure, what could be fairer?

MOSHER (*with a wink at McGloin*). Yes, you can't ask more than that, Harry. A promise is a promise—as I've often discovered.

HOPE (*turns on them*). I mean the both of you, too! An old grafting flatfoot and a circus bunco steerer! Fine company for me, bejees! Couple of con men living in my flat since Christ knows when! Getting fat as hogs, too! And you ain't even got the decency to get me upstairs where I got a good bed! Let me sleep on a chair like a bum! Kept me down here waitin' for Hickey to show up, hoping I'd blow you to more drinks!

MCGLOIN. Ed and I did our damnedest to get you up, didn't we, Ed?

MOSHER. We did. But you said you couldn't bear the flat because it was one of those nights when memory brought poor old Bessie back to you.

HOPE *(his face instantly becoming long and sad and sentimental—mournfully).* Yes, that's right, boys. I remember now. I could almost see her in every room just as she used to be—and it's twenty years since she— *(His throat and eyes fill up. A suitable sentimental hush falls on the room)*

LARRY *(in a sardonic whisper to Parritt).* Isn't a pipe dream of yesterday a touching thing? By all accounts, Bessie nagged the hell out of him.

JIMMY *(who has been dreaming, a look of prim resolution on his face, speaks aloud to himself).* No more of this sitting around and loafing. Time I took hold of myself. I must have my shoes soled and heeled and shined first thing tomorrow morning. A general spruce-up. I want to have a well-groomed appearance when I— *(His voice fades out as he stares in front of him. No one pays any attention to him except Larry and Parritt)*

LARRY *(as before, in a sardonic aside to Parritt).* The tomorrow movement is a sad and beautiful thing, too!

MCGLOIN *(with a huge sentimental sigh —and a calculating look at Hope).* Poor old Bessie! You don't find her like in these days. A sweeter woman never drew breath.

MOSHER *(in a similar calculating mood).* Good old Bess. A man couldn't want a better sister than she was to me.

HOPE *(mournfully).* Twenty years, and I've never set foot out of this house since the day I buried her. Didn't have the heart. Once she'd gone, I didn't give a damn for anything. I lost all my ambition. Without her, nothing seemed worth the trouble. You remember, Ed, you, too, Mac —the boys was going to nominate me for Alderman. It was all fixed. Bessie wanted it and she was so proud. But when she was taken, I told them, "No, boys, I can't do it. I simply haven't the heart. I'm through." I would have won the election easy, too. *(He says this a bit defiantly)* Oh, I know there was jealous wise guys said the boys was giving me the nomination because they knew they couldn't win that year in this ward. But that's a damned lie! I knew every man, woman and child in the ward, almost. Bessie made me make friends with everyone, helped me remember all their names. I'd have been elected easy.

MCGLOIN. You would, Harry. It was a sure thing.

MOSHER. A dead cinch, Harry. Everyone knows that.

HOPE. Sure they do. But after Bessie died, I didn't have the heart. Still, I know while she'd appreciate my grief, she wouldn't want it to keep me cooped up in here all my life. So I've made up my mind I'll go out soon. Take a walk around the ward, see all the friends I used to know, get together with the boys and maybe tell 'em I'll let 'em deal me a hand in their game again. Yes, bejees, I'll do it. My birthday, tomorrow, that'd be the right time to turn over a new leaf. Sixty. That ain't too old.

MCGLOIN *(flatteringly).* It's the prime of life, Harry.

MOSHER. Wonderful thing about you, Harry, you keep young as you ever was.

JIMMY *(dreaming aloud again).* Get my things from the laundry. They must still have them. Clean collar and shirt. If I wash the ones I've got on any more, they'll fall apart. Socks, too. I want to make a good appearance. I met Dick Trumbull on the street a year or two ago. He said, "Jimmy, the publicity department's never been the same since you got—resigned. It's dead as hell." I said, "I know. I've heard rumors the management were at their wits' end and would be only too glad to have me run it for them again. I think all I'd have to do would be go and see them and they'd offer me the position. Don't you think so, Dick?" He said, "Sure, they would, Jimmy. Only take my advice and wait a while until business conditions are better. Then you can strike them for a bigger salary than you got before, do you see?" I said, "Yes, I do see, Dick, and many thanks for the tip." Well, conditions must be better by this time. All I have to do is get fixed up with a decent front tomorrow, and it's as good as done.

HOPE *(glances at Jimmy with a condescending affectionate pity—in a hushed voice).* Poor Jimmy's off on his pipe dream again. Bejees, he takes the cake! *(This is too much for Larry. He cannot restrain a sardonic guffaw. But no one pays any attention to him)*

LEWIS *(opens his eyes, which are drowsing again—dreamily to Wetjoen).* I'm sorry we had to postpone our trip again this April, Piet. I hoped the blasted old estate would be settled up by then. The damned lawyers can't hold up the settlement much longer. We'll make it next year, even if we have to work and earn our passage money, eh? You'll stay with me at the old place as long as you like, then you can take the *Union Castle* from Southampton to Cape Town. *(Sentimentally, with real yearning)* England in April. I want you to see that, Piet. The old veldt has its points, I'll admit, but it isn't home—especially home in April.

WETJOEN *(blinks drowsily at him—dreamily).* Ja, Cecil, I know how beautiful it must be, from all you tell me many times. I vill enjoy it. But I shall enjoy more ven I am home, too. The veldt, ja! You could put England on it, and it would look like a farmer's small garden. Py Gott, there is space to be free, the air like vine is, you don't need booze to be drunk! My relations vill so surprised be. They vill not know me, it is so many years. Dey vill be so glad I haf come home at last.

JOE *(dreamily).* I'll make my stake and get my new gamblin' house open before you boys leave. You got to come to de openin'. I'll treat you white. If you're broke, I'll stake you to buck any game you chooses. If you wins, dat's velvet for you. If you loses, it don't count. Can't treat you no whiter dan dat, can I?

HOPE *(again with condescending pity).* Bejees, Jimmy's started them off smoking the same hop. *(But the three are finished, their eyes closed again in sleep or a drowse)*

LARRY *(aloud to himself—in his comically tense, crazy whisper).* Be God, this bughouse will drive me stark, raving loony yet!

HOPE *(turns on him with fuming suspicion).* What? What d'you say?

LARRY *(placatingly).* Nothing, Harry. I had a crazy thought in my head.

HOPE *(irascibly).* Crazy is right! Yah! The old wise guy! Wise, hell! A damned old fool Anarchist I-Won't-Worker! I'm sick of you and Hugo, too. Bejees, you'll pay up tomorrow, or I'll start a Harry Hope Revolution! I'll tie a dispossess bomb to your tails that'll blow you out in the street! Bejees, I'll make your Movement move! *(The witticism delights him and he bursts into a shrill cackle. At once McGloin and Mosher guffaw enthusiastically)*

MOSHER *(flatteringly).* Harry, you sure say the funniest things! *(He reaches on the table as if he expected a glass to be there—then starts with well-acted surprise)* Hell, where's my drink? That Rocky is too damned fast cleaning tables. Why, I'd only taken one sip of it.

HOPE *(his smiling face congealing).* No, you don't! *(Acidly)* Any time you only take one sip of a drink, you'll have lockjaw and paralysis! Think you can kid me with those old circus con games?—me, that's known you since you was knee-high, and, bejees, you was a crook even then!

MCGLOIN *(grinning).* It's not like you to be so hard-hearted, Harry. Sure, it's hot, parching work laughing at your jokes so early in the morning on an empty stomach!

HOPE. Yah! You, Mac! Another crook! Who asked you to laugh? We was talking about poor old Bessie, and you and her no-good brother start to laugh! A hell of a thing! Talking mush about her, too! "Good old Bess." Bejees, she'd never forgive me if she knew I had you two bums living in her flat, throwing ashes and cigar butts on her carpet. You know her opinion of you, Mac. "That Pat McGloin is the biggest drunken grafter that ever disgraced the police force," she used to say to me. "I hope they send him to Sing Sing for life."

MCGLOIN *(unperturbed).* She didn't mean it. She was angry at me because you used to get me drunk. But Bess had a heart of gold underneath her sharpness. She knew I was innocent of all the charges.

WILLIE *(jumps to his feet drunkenly and points a finger at McGloin—imitating the manner of a cross-examiner—coldly).* One moment, please. Lieutenant McGloin! Are you aware you are under oath? Do you realize what the penalty for perjury is? *(Purringly)* Come now, Lieutenant, isn't it a fact that you're as guilty as hell? No, don't say, "How about your old man?" I am asking the questions. The fact that he was a crooked old bucket-shop bastard has no bearing on your case. *(With a change to maudlin joviality)* Gentlemen of the Jury, court will now recess while the D.A. sings out a little ditty he learned at Harvard. It was composed in a wanton moment by the Dean of the Divinity School on a moonlight night in July, 1776, while sobering up in a Turkish bath. *(He sings)*

"Oh, come up," she cried, "my sailor lad,
And you and I'll agree.
And I'll show you the prettiest *(Rap, rap, rap on table)*
That ever you did see."

(Suddenly he catches Hope's eyes fixed on him condemningly, and sees Rocky appearing from the bar. He collapses back on his chair, pleading miserably) Please, Harry! I'll be quiet! Don't make Rocky bounce me upstairs! I'll go crazy alone! *(To McGloin)* I apologize, Mac. Don't get sore. I was only kidding you. *(Rocky, at a relenting glance from Hope, returns to the bar)*

MCGLOIN *(good-naturedly)*. Sure, kid all you like, Willie. I'm hardened to it. *(He pauses—seriously)* But I'm telling you some day before long I'm going to make them reopen my case. Everyone knows there was no real evidence against me, and I took the fall for the ones higher up. I'll be found innocent this time and reinstated. *(Wistfully)* I'd like to have my old job on the Force back. The boys tell me there's fine pickings these days, and I'm not getting rich here, sitting with a parched throat waiting for Harry Hope to buy a drink. *(He glances reproachfully at Hope)*

WILLIE. Of course, you'll be reinstated, Mac. All you need is a brilliant young attorney to handle your case. I'll be straightened out and on the wagon in a day or two. I've never practiced but I was one of the most brilliant students in Law School, and your case is just the opportunity I need to start. *(Darkly)* Don't worry about my not forcing the D.A. to reopen your case. I went through my father's papers before the cops destroyed them, and I remember a lot of people, even if I can't prove— *(Coaxingly)* You will let me take your case, won't you, Mac?

MCGLOIN *(soothingly)*. Sure I will and it'll make your reputation, Willie. *(Mosher winks at Hope, shaking his head, and*

Hope answers with identical pantomime, as though to say, "Poor dopes, they're off again!")*

LARRY *(aloud to himself more than to Parritt—with irritable wonder)*. Ah, be damned! Haven't I heard their visions a thousand times? Why should they get under my skin now? I've got the blues, I guess. I wish to hell Hickey'd turn up.

MOSHER *(calculatingly solicitous—whispering to Hope)*. Poor Willie needs a drink bad, Harry—and I think if we all joined him it'd make him feel he was among friends and cheer him up.

HOPE. More circus con tricks! *(Scathingly)* You talking of your dear sister! Bessie had you sized up. She used to tell me, "I don't know what you can see in that worthless, drunken, petty-larceny brother of mine. If I had my way," she'd say, "he'd get booted out in the gutter on his fat behind." Sometimes she didn't say behind, either.

MOSHER *(grins genially)*. Yes, dear old Bess had a quick temper, but there was no real harm in her. *(He chuckles reminiscently)* Remember the time she sent me down to the bar to change a ten-dollar bill for her?

HOPE *(has to grin himself)*. Bejees, do I! She coulda bit a piece out of a stove lid, after she found it out. *(He cackles appreciatively)*

MOSHER. I was sure surprised when she gave me the ten spot. Bess usually had better sense, but she was in a hurry to go out to church. I didn't really mean to do it, but you know how habit gets you. Besides, I still worked then, and the circus season was going to begin soon, and I needed a little practice to keep my hand in. Or, you never can tell, the first rube that came to my wagon for a ticket might have left with the right change and I'd be disgraced. *(He chuckles)* I said, "I'm sorry, Bess, but I had to take it all in dimes. Here, hold out your hands and I'll count it out for you, so you won't kick afterwards I short-changed you." *(He begins a count which grows more rapid as he goes on)* Ten, twenty, thirty, forty, fifty, sixty, seventy, eighty, ninety, a dollar. Ten, twenty, thirty, forty, fifty, sixty— You're counting with me, Bess, aren't you?— eighty, ninety, two dollars. Ten, twenty— Those are pretty shoes you got on, Bess— forty, fifty, seventy, eighty, ninety, three dollars. Ten, twenty, thirty— What's on at the church tonight, Bess?—fifty, sixty, seventy, ninety, four dollars. Ten, twenty, thirty, fifty, seventy, eighty, ninety—That's a swell new hat, Bess, looks very becoming—six dollars. *(He chuckles)* And so on. I'm bum at it now for lack of practice, but in those days I could have short-changed the Keeper of the Mint.

HOPE *(grinning)*. Stung her for two dollars and a half, wasn't it, Ed?

MOSHER. Yes. A fine percentage, if I do say so, when you're dealing to someone who's sober and can count. I'm sorry to say she discovered my mistakes in arithmetic just after I beat it around the corner. She counted it over herself. Bess somehow never had the confidence in me a sister should. *(He sighs tenderly)* Dear old Bess.

HOPE *(indignant now)*. You're a fine guy bragging how you short-changed your own sister! Bejees, if there was a war and you was in it, they'd have to padlock the pockets of the dead!

MOSHER *(a bit hurt at this)*. That's going pretty strong, Harry. I always gave a sucker some chance. There wouldn't be no fun robbing the dead. *(He becomes reminiscently melancholy)* Gosh, thinking of the old ticket wagon brings those days back. The greatest life on earth with the greatest show on earth! The grandest crowd of regular guys ever gathered under one tent! I'd sure like to shake their hands again!

HOPE *(acidly)*. They'd have guns in theirs. They'd shoot you on sight. You've touched every damned one of them. Bejees, you've even borrowed fish from the trained seals and peanuts from every elephant that remembered you! *(This fancy tickles him and he gives a cackling laugh)*

MOSHER *(overlooking this—dreamily)*. You know, Harry, I've made up my mind I'll see the boss in a couple of days and ask for my old job. I can get back my magic touch with change easy, and I can throw him a line of bull that'll kid him I won't be so unreasonable about sharing the profits next time. *(With insinuating complaint)* There's no percentage in hanging around this dive, taking care of you and shooing away your snakes, when I don't even get an eye-opener for my trouble.

HOPE *(implacably)*. No! *(Mosher sighs*

and gives up and closes his eyes. The others, except Larry and Parritt, are all dozing again now. Hope goes on grumbling)* Go to hell or the circus, for all I care. Good riddance, bejees! I'm sick of you! *(Then worriedly)* Say, Ed, what the hell you think's happened to Hickey? I hope he'll turn up. Always got a million funny stories. You and the other bums have begun to give me the graveyard fantods. I'd like a good laugh with old Hickey. *(He chuckles at a memory)* Remember that gag he always pulls about his wife and the iceman? He'd make a cat laugh! *(Rocky appears from the bar. He comes front, behind Mosher's chair, and begins pushing the black curtain along the rod to the rear wall)*

ROCKY. Openin' time, Boss. *(He presses a button which switches off the lights. The back room becomes drabber and dingier than ever in the gray daylight that comes from the street windows, off right, and what light can penetrate the grime of the two backyard windows at left. Rocky turns back to Hope—grumpily)* Why don't you go up to bed, Boss? Hickey'd never turn up dis time of de mornin'!

HOPE *(starts and listens)*. Someone's coming now.

ROCKY *(listens)*. Aw, dat's on'y my two pigs. It's about time dey showed. *(He goes back toward the door at left of the bar)*

HOPE *(sourly disappointed)*. You keep them dumb broads quiet. I don't want to go to bed. I'm going to catch a couple more winks here and I don't want no damn-fool laughing and screeching. *(He settles himself in his chair, grumbling)* Never thought I'd see the day when Harry Hope's would have tarts rooming in it. What'd Bessie think? But I don't let 'em use my rooms for business. And they're good kids. Good as anyone else. They got to make a living. Pay their rent, too, which is more than I can say for— *(He cocks an eye over his specs at Mosher and grins with satisfaction)* Bejees, Ed, I'll bet Bessie is doing somersaults in her grave! *(He chuckles. But Mosher's eyes are closed, his head nodding, and he doesn't reply, so Hope closes his eyes. Rocky has opened the barroom door at rear and is standing in the hall beyond it, facing right. A girl's laugh is heard)*

ROCKY *(warningly)*. Nix! Piano!

(He comes in, beckoning them to follow. He goes behind the bar and gets a whiskey bottle and glasses and chairs. Margie and Pearl follow him, casting a glance around. Everyone except Larry and Parritt is asleep or dozing. Even Parritt has his eyes closed. The two girls, neither much over twenty, are typical dollar street walkers, dressed in the usual tawdry get-up. Pearl is obviously Italian with black hair and eyes. Margie has brown hair and hazel eyes, a slum New Yorker of mixed blood. Both are plump and have a certain prettiness that shows even through their blobby make-up. Each retains a vestige of youthful freshness, although the game is beginning to get them and give them hard, worn expressions. Both are sentimental, feather-brained, giggly, lazy, good-natured and reasonably contented with life. Their attitude toward Rocky is much that of two maternal, affectionate sisters toward a bullying brother whom they like to tease and spoil. His attitude toward them is that of the owner of two performing pets he has trained to do a profitable act under his management. He feels a proud proprietor's affection for them, and is tolerantly lax in his discipline.)

MARGIE *(glancing around)*. Jees, Poil, it's de Morgue wid all dè stiffs on deck. *(She catches Larry's eye and smiles affectionately)* Hello, Old Wise Guy, ain't you died yet?

LARRY *(grinning)*. Not yet, Margie. But I'm waiting impatiently for the end. *(Parritt opens his eyes to look at the two girls, but as soon as they glance at him he closes them again and turns his head away)*

MARGIE *(as she and Pearl come to the table at right, front, followed by Rocky)*. Who's de new guy? Friend of yours, Larry? *(Automatically she smiles seductively at Parritt and addresses him in a professional chant)* Wanta have a good time, kid?

PEARL. Aw, he's passed out. Hell wid him!

HOPE *(cocks an eye over his specs at them—with drowsy irritation)*. You dumb broads cut the loud talk. *(He shuts his eye again)*

ROCKY *(admonishing them good-naturedly)*. Sit down before I knock yuh down. *(Margie and Pearl sit at left, and rear, of table, Rocky at right of it. The girls pour drinks. Rocky begins in a brisk, business-like manner but in a lowered voice with an eye on Hope)* Well, how'd you tramps do?

MARGIE. Pretty good. Didn't we, Poil?

PEARL. Sure. We nailed a coupla all-night guys.

MARGIE. On Sixth Avenoo. Boobs from de sticks.

PEARL. Stinko, de bot' of 'em.

MARGIE. We thought we was in luck. We steered dem to a real hotel. We figgered dey was too stinko to bother us much and we could cop a good sleep in beds that ain't got cobble stones in de mattress like de ones in dis dump.

PEARL. But we was outa luck. Dey didn't bother us much dat way, but dey wouldn't go to sleep either, see? Jees, I never hoid such gabby guys.

MARGIE. Dey got onta politics, drinkin' outa de bottle. Dey forgot we was around. "De Bull Moosers is de on'y reg'lar guys," one guy says. And de other guy says, "You're a God-damned liar! And I'm a Republican!" Den dey'd laugh.

PEARL. Den dey'd get mad and make a bluff dey was goin' to scrap, and den dey'd make up and cry and sing "School Days." Jees, imagine tryin' to sleep wid dat on de phonograph!

MARGIE. Maybe you tink we wasn't glad when de house dick come up and told us all to git dressed and take de air!

PEARL. We told de guys we'd wait for dem 'round de corner.

MARGIE. So here we are.

ROCKY *(sententiously)*. Yeah. I see you. But I don't see no dough yet.

PEARL *(with a wink at Margie—teasingly)*. Right on de job, ain't he, Margie?

MARGIE. Yeah, our little business man! Dat's him!

ROCKY. Come on! Dig! *(They both pull up their skirts to get the money from their stockings. Rocky watches this move carefully)*

PEARL *(amused)*. Pipe him keepin' cases, Margie.

MARGIE *(amused)*. Scared we're holdin' out on him.

PEARL. Way he gabs, yuh'd tink it was him done de woik. *(She holds out a little roll of bills to Rocky)* Here y'are, Grafter!

MARGIE *(holding hers out)*. We hope it chokes yuh. *(Rocky counts the money quickly and shoves it in his pocket)*

ROCKY (*genially*). You dumb baby dolls gimme a pain. What would you do wid money if I wasn't around? Give it all to some pimp.

PEARL (*teasingly*). Jees, what's the difference—? (*Hastily*) Aw, I don't mean dat, Rocky.

ROCKY (*his eyes growing hard—slowly*). A lotta difference, get me?

PEARL. Don't get sore. Jees, can't yuh take a little kiddin'?

MARGIE. Sure, Rocky, Poil was on'y kiddin'. (*Soothingly*) We know yuh got a reg'lar job. Dat's why we like yuh, see? Yuh don't live offa us. Yuh're a bartender.

ROCKY (*genially again*). Sure, I'm a bartender. Everyone knows me knows dat. And I treat you goils right, don't I? Jees, I'm wise yuh hold out on me, but I know it ain't much, so what the hell, I let yuh get away wid it. I tink yuh're a coupla good kids. Yuh're aces wid me, see?

PEARL. You're aces wid us, too. Ain't he, Margie?

MARGIE. Sure, he's aces. (*Rocky beams complacently and takes the glasses back to the bar. Margie whispers*) Yuh sap, don't yuh know enough not to kid him on dat? Serve yuh right if he beat yuh up!

PEARL (*admiringly*). Jees, I'll bet he'd give yuh an awful beatin', too, once he started. Ginnies got awful tempers.

MARGIE. Anyway, we wouldn't keep no pimp, like we was reg'lar old whores. We ain't dat bad.

PEARL. No. We're tarts, but dat's all.

ROCKY (*rinsing glasses behind the bar*). Cora got back around three o'clock. She woke up Chuck and dragged him outa de hay to go to a chop suey joint. (*Disgustedly*) Imagine him standin' for dat stuff!

MARGIE (*disgustedly*). I'll bet dey been sittin' around kiddin' demselves wid dat old pipe dream about gettin' married and settlin' down on a farm. Jees, when Chuck's on de wagon, dey never lay off dat dope! Dey give yuh an earful every time yuh talk to 'em!

PEARL. Yeah. Chuck wid a silly grin on his ugly map, de big boob, and Cora gigglin' like she was in grammar school and some tough guy'd just told her babies wasn't brung down de chimney by a boid!

MARGIE. And her on de turf long before me and you was! And bot' of 'em arguin' all de time, Cora sayin' she's scared to marry him because he'll go on drunks again. Just as dough any drunk could scare Cora!

PEARL. And him swearin', de big liar, he'll never go on no more periodicals! An' den her pretendin'— But it gives me a pain to talk about it. We ought to phone de booby hatch to send round de wagon for 'em.

ROCKY (*comes back to the table—disgustedly*). Yeah, of all de pipe dreams in dis dump, dey got de nuttiest! And nuttin' stops dem. Dey been dreamin' it for years, every time Chuck goes on de wagon. I never could figger it. What would gettin' married get dem? But de farm stuff is de sappiest part. When bot' of 'em was dragged up in dis ward and ain't never been nearer a farm dan Coney Island! Jees, dey'd tink dey'd gone deef if dey didn't hear de El rattle! Dey'd get D.T.s if dey ever hoid a cricket choip! I hoid crickets once on my cousin's place in Joisey. I couldn't sleep a wink. Dey give me de heebie-jeebies. (*With deeper disgust*) Jees, can yuh picture a good barkeep like Chuck diggin' spuds? And imagine a whore hustlin' de cows home! For Christ sake! Ain't dat a sweet picture!

MARGIE (*rebukingly*). Yuh oughtn't to call Cora dat, Rocky. She's a good kid. She may be a tart, but—

ROCKY (*considerately*). Sure, dat's all I meant, a tart.

PEARL (*giggling*). But he's right about de damned cows, Margie. Jees, I bet Cora don't know which end of de cow has de horns! I'm goin' to ask her. (*There is the noise of a door opening in the hall and the sound of a man's and woman's arguing voices*)

ROCKY. Here's your chance. Dat's dem two nuts now.

(*Cora and Chuck look in from the hallway and then come in. Cora is a thin peroxide blonde, a few years older than Pearl and Margie, dressed in similar style, her round face showing more of the wear and tear of her trade than theirs, but still with traces of a doll-like prettiness. Chuck is a tough, thick-necked, barrel-chested Italian-American, with a fat, amiable, swarthy face. He has on a straw hat with a vivid band, a loud suit, tie and shirt, and yellow shoes. His eyes are clear and he looks healthy and strong as an ox.*)

CORA (*gaily*). Hello, bums. (*She looks*

around) Jees, de Morgue on a rainy Sunday night! (*She waves to Larry—affectionately*) Hello, Old Wise Guy! Ain't you croaked yet?

LARRY (*grins*). Not yet, Cora. It's damned tiring, this waiting for the end.

CORA. Aw, gwan, you'll never die! Yuh'll have to hire someone to croak yuh wid an axe.

HOPE (*cocks one sleepy eye at her—irritably*). You dumb hookers, cut the loud noise! This ain't a cat-house!

CORA (*teasingly*). My, Harry! Such language!

HOPE (*closes his eyes—to himself with a gratified chuckle*). Bejees, I'll bet Bessie's turning over in her grave!

(*Cora sits down between Margie and Pearl. Chuck takes an empty chair from Hope's table and puts it by hers and sits down. At Larry's table, Parritt is glaring resentfully toward the girls.*)

PARRITT. If I'd known this dump was a hooker hangout, I'd never have come here.

LARRY (*watching him*). You seem down on the ladies.

PARRITT (*vindictively*). I hate every bitch that ever lived! They're all alike! (*Catching himself guiltily*) You can understand how I feel, can't you, when it was getting mixed up with a tart that made me have that fight with Mother? (*Then with a resentful sneer*) But what the hell does it matter to you? You're in the grandstand. You're through with life.

LARRY (*sharply*). I'm glad you remember it. I don't want to know a damned thing about your business. (*He closes his eyes and settles on his chair as if preparing for sleep. Parritt stares at him sneeringly. Then he looks away and his expression becomes furtive and frightened*)

CORA. Who's de guy wid Larry?

ROCKY. A tightwad. To hell wid him.

PEARL. Say, Cora, wise me up. Which end of a cow is de horns on?

CORA (*embarrassed*). Aw, don't bring dat up. I'm sick of hearin' about dat farm.

ROCKY. You got nuttin' on us!

CORA (*ignoring this*). Me and dis overgrown tramp has been scrappin' about it. He says Joisey's de best place, and I says Long Island because we'll be near Coney. And I tells him, How do I know yuh're off of periodicals for life? I don't give a damn how drunk yuh get, the way we are, but I don't wanta be married to no soak.

CHUCK. And I tells her I'm off de stuff for life. Den she beefs we won't be married a month before I'll trow it in her face she was a tart. "Jees, Baby," I tells her. "Why should I? What de hell yuh tink I tink I'm marryin', a voigin? Why should I kick as long as yuh lay off it and don't do no cheatin' wid de iceman or nobody? (*He gives her a rough hug*) Dat's on de level, Baby. (*He kisses her*)

CORA (*kissing him*). Aw, yuh big tramp!

ROCKY (*shakes his head with profound disgust*). Can yuh tie it? I'll buy a drink. I'll do anything. (*He gets up*)

CORA. No, dis round's on me. I run into luck. Dat's why I dragged Chuck outa bed to celebrate. It was a sailor. I rolled him. (*She giggles*) Listen, it was a scream. I've run into some nutty souses, but dis guy was de nuttiest. De booze dey dish out around de Brooklyn Navy Yard must be as turrible bug-juice as Harry's. My dogs was givin' out when I seen dis guy holdin' up a lamppost, so I hurried to get him before a cop did. I says, "Hello, Handsome, wanta have a good time?" Jees, he was paralyzed! One of dem polite jags. He tries to bow to me, imagine, and I had to prop him up or he'd fell on his nose. And what d'yuh tink he said? "Lady," he says, "can yuh kindly tell me de nearest way to de Museum of Natural History?" (*They all laugh*) Can yuh imagine! At two A.M. As if I'd know where de dump was anyway. But I says, "Sure ting, Honey Boy, I'll be only too glad." So I steered him into a side street where it was dark and propped him against a wall and give him a frisk. (*She giggles*) And what d'yuh tink he does? Jees, I ain't lyin', he begins to laugh, de big sap! He says, "Quit ticklin' me." While I was friskin' him for his roll! I near died! Den I toined him 'round and give him a push to start him. "Just keep goin'," I told him. "It's a big white building on your right. You can't miss it." He must be swimmin' in de North River yet! (*They all laugh*)

CHUCK. Ain't Uncle Sam de sap to trust guys like dat wid dough!

CORA (*with a business-like air*). I picked twelve bucks offa him. Come on, Rocky,

Set 'em up. (*Rocky goes back to the bar. Cora looks around the room*) Say, Chuck's kiddin' about de iceman a minute ago reminds me. Where de hell's Hickey?

ROCKY. Dat's what we're all wonderin'.

CORA. He oughta be here. Me and Chuck seen him.

ROCKY (*excited, comes back from the bar, forgetting the drinks*). You seen Hickey? (*He nudges Hope*) Hey, Boss, come to! Cora's seen Hickey.

(*Hope is instantly wide awake and everyone in the place, except Hugo and Parritt, begins to rouse up hopefully, as if a mysterious wireless message had gone round.*)

HOPE. Where'd you see him, Cora?

CORA. Right on de next corner. He was standin' dere. We said, "Welcome to our city. De gang is expectin' yuh wid deir tongues hangin' out a yard long." And I kidded him, "How's de iceman, Hickey? How's he doin' at your house?" He laughs and says, "Fine." And he says, "Tell de gang I'll be along in a minute. I'm just finishin' figurin' out de best way to save dem and bring dem peace."

HOPE (*chuckles*). Bejees, he's thought up a new gag! It's a wonder he didn't borry a Salvation Army uniform and show up in that! Go out and get him, Rocky. Tell him we're waitin' to be saved! (*Rocky goes out, grinning*)

CORA. Yeah, Harry, he was only kiddin'. But he was funny, too, somehow. He was different, or somethin'.

CHUCK. Sure, he was sober, Baby. Dat's what made him different. We ain't never seen him when he wasn't on a drunk, or had de willies gettin' over it.

CORA. Sure! Gee, ain't I dumb?

HOPE (*with conviction*). The dumbest broad I ever seen! (*Then puzzledly*) Sober? That's funny. He's always lapped up a good starter on his way here. Well, bejees, he won't be sober long! He'll be good and ripe for my birthday party tonight at twelve. (*He chuckles with excited anticipation—addressing all of them*) Listen! He's fixed some new gag to pull on us. We'll pretend to let him kid us, see? And we'll kid the pants off him.

(*They all say laughingly, "Sure, Harry," "Righto," "That's the stuff," "We'll fix him," etc., etc., their faces excited with the same eager anticipation. Rocky appears in the doorway at the end of the bar with Hickey, his arm around Hickey's shoulders.*)

ROCKY (*with an affectionate grin*). Here's the old son of a bitch!

(*They all stand up and greet him with affectionate acclaim, "Hello, Hickey!" etc. Even Hugo comes out of his coma to raise his head and blink through his thick spectacles with a welcoming giggle.*)

HICKEY (*jovially*). Hello, Gang! (*He stands a moment, beaming around at all of them affectionately. He is about fifty, a little under medium height, with a stout, roly-poly figure. His face is round and smooth and big-boyish with bright blue eyes, a button nose, a small, pursed mouth. His head is bald except for a fringe of hair around his temples and the back of his head. His expression is fixed in a salesman's winning smile of self-confident affability and hearty good fellowship. His eyes have the twinkle of a humor which delights in kidding others but can also enjoy equally a joke on himself. He exudes a friendly, generous personality that makes everyone like him on sight. You get the impression, too, that he must have real ability in his line. There is an efficient, business-like approach in his manner, and his eyes can take you in shrewdly at a glance. He has the salesman's mannerisms of speech, an easy flow of glib, persuasive convincingness. His clothes are those of a successful drummer whose territory consists of minor cities and small towns—not flashy but conspicuously spic and span. He immediately puts on an entrance act, places a hand affectedly on his chest, throws back his head, and sings in a falsetto tenor*) "It's always fair weather, when good fellows get together!" (*Changing to a comic bass and another tune*) "And another little drink won't do us any harm!" (*They all roar with laughter at this burlesque which his personality makes really funny. He waves his hand in a lordly manner to Rocky*) Do your duty, Brother Rocky. Bring on the rat poison! (*Rocky grins and goes behind the bar to get drinks amid an approving cheer from the crowd. Hickey comes forward to shake hands with Hope—with affectionate heartiness*) How goes it, Governor?

HOPE (*enthusiastically*). Bejees, Hickey, you old bastard, it's good to see you! (*Hickey shakes hands with Mosher and*)

McGloin; leans right to shake hands with Margie and Pearl; moves to the middle table to shake hands with Lewis, Joe Mott, Wetjoen and Jimmy; waves to Willie, Larry and Hugo. He greets each by name with the same affectionate heartiness and there is an interchange of "How's the kid?" "How's the old scout?" "How's the boy?" "How's everything?" etc., etc. Rocky begins setting out drinks, whiskey glasses with chasers, and a bottle for each table, starting with Larry's table. Hope says:) Sit down, Hickey. Sit down. *(Hickey takes the chair, facing front, at the front of the table in the second row which is half between Hope's table and the one where Jimmy Tomorrow is. Hope goes on with excited pleasure)* Bejees, Hickey, it seems natural to see your ugly, grinning map. *(With a scornful nod to Cora)* This dumb broad was tryin' to tell us you'd changed, but you ain't a damned bit. Tell us about yourself. How've you been doin'? Bejees, you look like a million dollars.

ROCKY *(coming to Hickey's table, puts a bottle of whiskey, a glass and a chaser on it—then hands Hickey a key)*. Here's your key, Hickey. Same old room.

HICKEY *(shoves the key in his pocket)*. Thanks, Rocky. I'm going up in a little while and grab a snooze. Haven't been able to sleep lately and I'm tired as hell. A couple of hours good kip will fix me.

HOPE *(as Rocky puts drinks on his table)*. First time I ever heard you worry about sleep. Bejees, you never would go to bed. *(He raises his glass, and all the others except Parritt do likewise)* Get a few slugs under your belt and you'll forget sleeping. Here's mud in your eye, Hickey. *(They all join in with the usual humorous toasts)*

HICKEY *(heartily)*. Drink hearty, boys and girls! *(They all drink, but Hickey drinks only his chaser)*

HOPE. Bejees, is that a new stunt, drinking your chaser first?

HICKEY. No, I forgot to tell Rocky— You'll have to excuse me, boys and girls, but I'm off the stuff. For keeps. *(They stare at him in amazed incredulity)*

HOPE. What the hell— *(Then with a wink at the others, kiddingly)* Sure! Joined the Salvation Army, ain't you? Been elected President of the W.C.T.U.? Take that bottle away from him, Rocky.

We don't want to tempt him into sin. *(He chuckles and the others laugh)*

HICKEY *(earnestly)*. No, honest, Harry. I know it's hard to believe but— *(He pauses—then adds simply)* Cora was right, Harry. I have changed. I mean, about booze. I don't need it any more. *(They all stare, hoping it's a gag, but impressed and disappointed and made vaguely uneasy by the change they now sense in him)*

HOPE *(his kidding a bit forced)*. Yeah, go ahead, kid the pants off us! Bejees, Cora said you was coming to save us! Well, go on. Get this joke off your chest! Start the service! Sing a God-damned hymn if you like. We'll all join in the chorus. "No drunkard can enter this beautiful home." That's a good one. *(He forces a cackle)*

HICKEY *(grinning)*. Oh, hell, Governor! You don't think I'd come around here peddling some brand of temperance bunk, do you? You know me better than that! Just because I'm through with the stuff don't mean I'm going Prohibition. Hell, I'm not that ungrateful! It's given me too many good times. I feel exactly the same as I always did. If anyone wants to get drunk, if that's the only way they can be happy, and feel at peace with themselves, why the hell shouldn't they? They have my full and entire sympathy. I know all about that game from soup to nuts. I'm the guy that wrote the book. The only reason I've quit is— Well, I finally had the guts to face myself and throw overboard the damned lying pipe dream that'd been making me miserable, and do what I had to do for the happiness of all concerned—and then all at once I found I was at peace with myself and I didn't need booze any more. That's all there was to it. *(He pauses. They are staring at him, uneasy and beginning to feel defensive. Hickey looks round and grins affectionately—apologetically)* But what the hell! Don't let me be a wet blanket, making fool speeches about myself. Set 'em up again, Rocky. Here. *(He pulls a big roll from his pocket and peels off a ten-dollar bill. The faces of all brighten)* Keep the balls coming until this is killed. Then ask for more.

ROCKY. Jees, a roll dat'd choke a hippopotamus! Fill up, youse guys. *(They all pour out drinks)*

HOPE. That sounds more like you, Hickey. That water-wagon bull— Cut out the act and have a drink, for Christ's sake.

HICKEY. It's no act, Governor. But don't get me wrong. That don't mean I'm a teetotal grouch and can't be in the party. Hell, why d'you suppose I'm here except to have a party, same as I've always done, and help celebrate your birthday tonight? You've all been good pals to me, the best friends I've ever had. I've been thinking about you ever since I left the house—all the time I was walking over here—

HOPE. Walking? Bejees, do you mean to say you walked?

HICKEY. I sure did. All the way from the wilds of darkest Astoria. Didn't mind it a bit, either. I seemed to get here before I knew it. I'm a bit tired and sleepy but otherwise I feel great. *(Kiddingly)* That ought to encourage you, Governor— show you a little walk around the ward is nothing to be so scared about. *(He winks at the others. Hope stiffens resentfully for a second. Hickey goes on)* I didn't make such bad time either for a fat guy, considering it's a hell of a ways, and I sat in the park a while thinking. It was going on twelve when I went in the bedroom to tell Evelyn I was leaving. Six hours, say. No, less than that. I'd been standing on the corner some time before Cora and Chuck came along, thinking about all of you. Of course, I was only kidding Cora with that stuff about saving you. *(Then seriously)* No, I wasn't either. But I didn't mean booze. I meant save you from pipe dreams. I know now, from my experience, they're the things that really poison and ruin a guy's life and keep him from finding any peace. If you knew how free and contented I feel now. I'm like a new man. And the cure for them is so damned simple, once you have the nerve. Just the old dope of honesty is the best policy—honesty with yourself, I mean. Just stop lying about yourself and kidding yourself about tomorrows. *(He is staring ahead of him now as if he were talking aloud to himself as much as to them. Their eyes are fixed on him with uneasy resentment. His manner becomes apologetic again)* Hell, this begins to sound like a damned sermon on the way to lead the good life. Forget that

part of it. It's in my blood, I guess. My old man used to whale salvation into my heinie with a birch rod. He was a preacher in the sticks of Indiana, like I've told you. I got my knack of sales gab from him, too. He was the boy who could sell those Hoosier hayseeds building lots along the Golden Street! *(Taking on a salesman's persuasiveness)* Now listen, boys and girls, don't look at me as if I was trying to sell you a goldbrick. Nothing up my sleeve, honest. Let's take an example. Any one of you. Take you, Governor. That walk around the ward you never take—

HOPE *(defensively sharp)*. What about it?

HICKEY *(grinning affectionately)*. Why, you know as well as I do, Harry. Everything about it.

HOPE *(defiantly)*. Bejees, I'm going to take it!

HICKEY. Sure, you're going to—this time. Because I'm going to help you. I know it's the thing you've got to do before you'll ever know what real peace means. *(He looks at Jimmy Tomorrow)* Same thing with you, Jimmy. You've got to try and get your old job back. And no tomorrow about it! *(As Jimmy stiffens with a pathetic attempt at dignity— placatingly)* No, don't tell me, Jimmy. I know all about tomorrow. I'm the guy that wrote the book.

JIMMY. I don't understand you. I admit I've foolishly delayed, but as it happens, I'd just made up my mind that as soon as I could get straightened out—

HICKEY. Fine! That's the spirit! And I'm going to help you. You've been damned kind to me, Jimmy, and I want to prove how grateful I am. When it's all over and you don't have to nag at yourself any more, you'll be grateful to me, too! *(He looks around at the others)* And all the rest of you, ladies included, are in the same boat, one way or another.

LARRY *(who has been listening with sardonic appreciation—in his comically intense, crazy whisper)*. Be God, you've hit the nail on the head, Hickey! This dump is the Palace of Pipe Dreams!

HICKEY *(grins at him with affectionate kidding)*. Well, well! The Old Grandstand Foolosopher speaks! You think you're the big exception, eh! Life doesn't mean a damn to you any more, does it?

You're retired from the circus. You're just waiting impatiently for the end—the good old Long Sleep! (*He chuckles*) Well, I think a lot of you, Larry, you old bastard. I'll try and make an honest man of you, too!

LARRY (*stung*). What the devil are you hinting at, anyway?

HICKEY. You don't have to ask me, do you, a wise old guy like you? Just ask yourself. I'll bet you know.

PARRITT (*is watching Larry's face with a curious sneering satisfaction*). He's got your number all right, Larry! (*He turns to Hickey*) That's the stuff, Hickey. Show the old faker up! He's got no right to sneak out of everything.

HICKEY (*regards him with surprise at first, then with a puzzled interest*). Hello. A stranger in our midst. I didn't notice you before, Brother.

PARRITT (*embarrassed, his eyes shifting away*). My name's Parritt. I'm an old friend of Larry's. (*His eyes come back to Hickey to find him still sizing him up— defensively*) Well? What are you staring at?

HICKEY (*continuing to stare—puzzledly*). No offense, Brother. I was trying to figure— Haven't we met before some place?

PARRITT (*reassured*). No. First time I've ever been East.

HICKEY. No, you're right. I know that's not it. In my game, to be a shark at it, you teach yourself never to forget a name or a face. But still I know damned well I recognized something about you. We're members of the same lodge—in some way.

PARRITT (*uneasy again*). What are you talking about? You're nuts.

HICKEY (*dryly*). Don't try to kid me, Little Boy. I'm a good salesman—so damned good the firm was glad to take me back after every drunk—and what made me good was I could size up anyone. (*Frowningly puzzled again*) But I don't see— (*Suddenly breezily good-natured*) Never mind. I can tell you're having trouble with yourself and I'll be glad to do anything I can to help a friend of Larry's.

LARRY. Mind your own business, Hickey. He's nothing to you—or to me, either. (*Hickey gives him a keen inquisitive glance. Larry looks away and goes on sarcastically*) You're keeping us all in sus-pense. Tell us more about how you're going to save us.

HICKEY (*good-naturedly but seeming a little hurt*). Hell, don't get sore, Larry. Not at me. We've always been good pals, haven't we? I know I've always liked you a lot.

LARRY (*a bit shamefaced*). Well, so have I liked you. Forget it, Hickey.

HICKEY (*beaming*). Fine! That's the spirit! (*Looking around at the others, who have forgotten their drinks*) What's the matter, everybody? What is this, a funeral? Come on and drink up! A little action! (*They all drink*) Have another. Hell, this is a celebration! Forget it, if anything I've said sounds too serious. I don't want to be a pain in the neck. Any time you think I'm talking out of turn, just tell me to go chase myself! (*He yawns with growing drowsiness and his voice grows a bit muffled*) No, boys and girls, I'm not trying to put anything over on you. It's just that I know now from experience what a lying pipe dream can do to you—and how damned relieved and contented with yourself you feel when you're rid of it. (*He yawns again*) God, I'm sleepy all of a sudden. That long walk is beginning to get me. I better go upstairs. Hell of a trick to go dead on you like this. (*He starts to get up but relaxes again. His eyes blink as he tries to keep them open*) No, boys and girls, I've never known what real peace was until now. It's a grand feeling, like when you're sick and suffering like hell and the Doc gives you a shot in the arm, and the pain goes, and you drift off. (*His eyes close*) You can let go of yourself at last. Let yourself sink down to the bottom of the sea. Rest in peace. There's no farther you have to go. Not a single damned hope or dream left to nag you. You'll all know what I mean after you— (*He pauses—mumbles*) Excuse—all in—got to grab forty winks— Drink up, everybody—on me— (*The sleep of complete exhaustion overpowers him. His chin sags to his chest. They stare at him with puzzled uneasy fascination*)

HOPE (*forcing a tone of irritation*). Bejees, that's a fine stunt, to go to sleep on us! (*Then fumingly to the crowd*) Well, what the hell's the matter with you bums? Why don't you drink up? You're always crying for booze, and now you've got it under your nose, you sit like dummies! *(They start and gulp down their whiskies and pour another. Hope stares at Hickey)* Bejees, I can't figure Hickey. I still say he's kidding us. Kid his own grandmother, Hickey would. What d'you think, Jimmy?

JIMMY *(unconvincingly).* It must be another of his jokes, Harry, although— Well, he does appear changed. But he'll probably be his natural self again tomorrow— *(Hastily)* I mean, when he wakes up.

LARRY *(staring at Hickey frowningly— more aloud to himself than to them).* You'll make a mistake if you think he's only kidding.

PARRITT *(in a low confidential voice).* I don't like that guy, Larry. He's too damned nosy. I'm going to steer clear of him. *(Larry gives him a suspicious glance, then looks hastily away)*

JIMMY *(with an attempt at open-minded reasonableness).* Still, Harry, I have to admit there was some sense in his nonsense. It is time I got my job back— although I hardly need him to remind me.

HOPE *(with an air of frankness).* Yes, and I ought to take a walk around the ward. But I don't need no Hickey to tell me, seeing I got it all set for my birthday tomorrow.

LARRY *(sardonically).* Ha! *(Then in his comically intense, crazy whisper)* Be God, it looks like he's going to make two sales of his peace at least! But you'd better make sure first it's the real McCoy and not poison.

HOPE *(disturbed—angrily).* You bughouse I-Won't-Work harp, who asked you to shove in an oar? What the hell d'you mean, poison? Just because he has your number—*(He immediately feels ashamed of this taunt and adds apologetically)* Bejees, Larry, you're always croaking about something to do with death. It gets my nanny. Come on, fellers, let's drink up. *(They drink. Hope's eyes are fixed on Hickey again)* Stone cold sober and dead to the world! Spilling that business about pipe dreams! Bejees, I don't get it. *(He bursts out again in angry complaint)* He ain't like the old Hickey! He'll be a fine wet blanket to have around at my birthday party! I wish to hell he'd never turned up!

MOSHER *(who has been the least impressed by Hickey's talk and is the first to recover and feel the effect of the drinks on top of his hangover—genially).* Give him time, Harry, and he'll come out of it. I've watched many cases of almost fatal teetotalism, but they all came out of it completely cured and as drunk as ever. My opinion is the poor sap is temporarily bughouse from overwork. *(Musingly)* You can't be too careful about work. It's the deadliest habit known to science, a great physician once told me. He practiced on street corners under a torchlight. He was positively the only doctor in the world who claimed that rattlesnake oil, rubbed on the prat, would cure heart failure in three days. I remember well his saying to me, "You are naturally delicate, Ed, but if you drink a pint of bad whiskey before breakfast every evening, and never work if you can help it, you may live to a ripe old age. It's staying sober and working that cuts men off in their prime." *(While he is talking, they turn to him with eager grins. They are longing to laugh, and as he finishes they roar. Even Parritt laughs. Hickey sleeps on like a dead man, but Hugo, who had passed into his customary coma again, head on table, looks up through his thick spectacles and giggles foolishly)*

HUGO *(blinking around at them. As the laughter dies he speaks in his giggling, wheedling manner, as if he were playfully teasing children).* Laugh, leedle bourgeois monkey-faces! Laugh like fools, leedle stupid peoples! *(His tone suddenly changes to one of guttural soapbox denunciation and he pounds on the table with a small fist)* I vill laugh, too! But I vill laugh last! I vill laugh at you! *(He declaims his favorite quotation)* "The days grow hot, O Babylon! 'Tis cool beneath thy villow trees!" *(They all hoot him down in a chorus of amused jeering. Hugo is not offended. This is evidently their customary reaction. He giggles good-naturedly. Hickey sleeps on. They have all forgotten their uneasiness about him now and ignore him)*

LEWIS *(tipsily).* Well, now that our little Robespierre has got the daily bit of guillotining off his chest, tell me more about your doctor friend, Ed. He strikes me as the only bloody sensible medico I ever heard of. I think we should appoint him house physician here without a moment's delay. *(They all laughingly assent)*

MOSHER *(warming to his subject, shakes his head sadly).* Too late! The old Doc has passed on to his Maker. A victim of overwork, too. He didn't follow his own advice. Kept his nose to the grindstone and sold one bottle of snake oil too many. Only eighty years old when he was taken. The saddest part was that he knew he was doomed. The last time we got paralyzed together he told me: "This game will get me yet, Ed. You see before you a broken man, a martyr to medical science. If I had any nerves I'd have a nervous breakdown. You won't believe me, but this last year there was actually one night I had so many patients, I didn't even have time to get drunk. The shock to my system brought on a stroke which, as a doctor, I recognized was the beginning of the end." Poor old Doc! When he said this he started crying. "I hate to go before my task is completed, Ed," he sobbed. "I'd hoped I'd live to see the day when, thanks to my miraculous cure, there wouldn't be a single vacant cemetery lot left in this glorious country." *(There is a roar of laughter. He waits for it to die and then goes on sadly)* I miss Doc. He was a gentleman of the old school. I'll bet he's standing on a street corner in hell right now, making suckers of the damned, telling them there's nothing like snake oil for a bad burn. *(There is another roar of laughter. This time it penetrates Hickey's exhausted slumber. He stirs on his chair, trying to wake up, managing to raise his head a little and force his eyes half open. He speaks with a drowsy, affectionately encouraging smile. At once the laughter stops abruptly and they turn to him startledly)*

HICKEY. That's the spirit—don't let me be a wet blanket—all I want is to see you happy— *(He slips back into heavy sleep again. They all stare at him, their faces again puzzled, resentful and uneasy)*

CURTAIN

ACT TWO

SCENE: *The back room only. The black curtain dividing it from the bar is the right wall of the scene. It is getting on toward midnight of the same day.*

The back room has been prepared for a festivity. At center, front, four of the circular tables are pushed together to form one long table with an uneven line of chairs behind it, and chairs at each end. This improvised banquet table is covered with old table cloths, borrowed from a neighboring beanery, and is laid with glasses, plates and cutlery before each of the seventeen chairs. Bottles of bar whiskey are placed at intervals within reach of any sitter. An old upright piano and stool have been moved in and stand against the wall at left, front. At right, front, is a table without chairs. The other tables and chairs that had been in the room have been moved out, leaving a clear floor space at rear for dancing. The floor has been swept clean of sawdust and scrubbed. Even the walls show evidence of having been washed, although the result is only to heighten their splotchy leprous look. The electric light brackets are adorned with festoons of red ribbon. In the middle of the separate table at right, front, is a birthday cake with six candles. Several packages, tied with ribbon, are also on the table. There are two necktie boxes, two cigar boxes, a fifth containing a half dozen handkerchiefs, the sixth is a square jeweler's watch box.

As the curtain rises, Cora, Chuck, Hugo, Larry, Margie, Pearl and Rocky are discovered. Chuck, Rocky and the three girls have dressed up for the occasion. Cora is arranging a bouquet of flowers in a vase, the vase being a big schooner glass from the bar, on top of the piano. Chuck sits in a chair at the foot (left) of the banquet table. He has turned it so he can watch her. Near the middle of the row of chairs behind the table, Larry sits, facing front, a drink of whiskey before him. He is staring before him in frowning, disturbed meditation. Next to him, on his left, Hugo is in his habitual position, passed out, arms on table, head on arms, a full whiskey glass by his head. By the separate table at right, front, Margie and Pearl are arranging the cake and presents, and Rocky stands by them. All of them, with the exception of Chuck and Rocky, have had plenty to drink and show it, but no one, except Hugo, seems to be drunk. They are trying to act up in the spirit of the occasion but there is something forced about their manner, an undercurrent of nervous irritation and preoccupation.

CORA *(standing back from the piano to regard the flower effect).* How's dat, Kid?

CHUCK *(grumpily).* What de hell do I know about flowers?

CORA. Yuh can see dey're pretty, can't yuh, yuh big dummy?

CHUCK *(mollifyingly).* Yeah, Baby, sure. If yuh like 'em, dey're aw right wid me. *(Cora goes back to give the schooner of flowers a few more touches)*

MARGIE *(admiring the cake).* Some cake, huh, Poil? Lookit! Six candles. Each for ten years.

PEARL. When do we light de candles, Rocky?

ROCKY *(grumpily).* Ask dat bughouse Hickey. He's elected himself boss of dis boithday racket. Just before Harry comes down, he says. Den Harry blows dem out wid one breath, for luck. Hickey was goin' to have sixty candles, but I says, Jees, if de old guy took dat big a breath, he'd croak himself.

MARGIE *(challengingly).* Well, anyways, it's some cake, ain't it?

ROCKY *(without enthusiasm).* Sure, it's aw right by me. But what de hell is Harry goin' to do wid a cake? If he ever et a hunk, it'd croak him.

PEARL. Jees, yuh're a dope! Ain't he, Margie?

MARGIE. A dope is right!

ROCKY *(stung).* You broads better watch your step or—

PEARL *(defiantly).* Or what?

MARGIE. Yeah! Or what? *(They glare at him truculently)*

ROCKY. Say, what de hell's got into youse? It'll be twelve o'clock and Harry's boithday before long. I ain't lookin' for no trouble.

PEARL *(ashamed).* Aw, we ain't neider, Rocky. *(For the moment this argument subsides)*

CORA *(over her shoulder to Chuck—acidly).* A guy what can't see flowers is pretty must be some dumbbell.

CHUCK. Yeah? Well, if I was as dumb as you— *(Then mollifyingly)* Jees, yuh got your scrappin' pants on, ain't yuh? *(Grins good-naturedly)* Hell, Baby, what's eatin' yuh? All I'm tinkin' is, flowers is dat louse Hickey's stunt. We never had

no flowers for Harry's boithday before. What de hell can Harry do wid flowers? He don't know a cauliflower from a geranium.

ROCKY. Yeah, Chuck, it's like I'm tellin' dese broads about de cake. Dat's Hickey's wrinkle, too. *(Bitterly)* Jees, ever since he woke up, yuh can't hold him. He's taken on de party like it was his boithday.

MARGIE. Well, he's payin' for everything, ain't he?

ROCKY. Aw, I don't mind de boithday stuff so much. What gets my goat is de way he's tryin' to run de whole dump and everyone in it. He's buttin' in all over de place, tellin' everybody where dey get off. On'y he don't really tell yuh. He just keeps hintin' around.

PEARL. Yeah. He was hintin' to me and Margie.

MARGIE. Yeah, de lousy drummer.

ROCKY. He just gives yuh an earful of dat line of bull about yuh got to be honest wid yourself and not kid yourself, and have de guts to be what yuh are. I got sore. I told him dat's aw right for de bums in dis dump. I hope he makes dem wake up. I'm sick of listenin' to dem hop demselves up. But it don't go wid me, see? I don't kid myself wid no pipe dream. *(Pearl and Margie exchange a derisive look. He catches it and his eyes narrow)* What are yuh grinnin' at?

PEARL *(her face hard—scornfully).* Nuttin'.

MARGIE. Nuttin'.

ROCKY. It better be nuttin'! Don't let Hickey put no ideas in your nuts if you wanta stay healthy! *(Then angrily)* I wish de louse never showed up! I hope he don't come back from de delicatessen. He's gettin' everyone nuts. He's ridin' someone every minute. He's got Harry and Jimmy Tomorrow run ragged, and de rest is hidin' in deir rooms so dey won't have to listen to him. Dey're all actin' cagey wid de booze, too, like dey was scared if dey get too drunk, dey might spill deir guts, or somethin'. And everybody's gettin' a prize grouch on.

CORA. Yeah, he's been hintin' round to me and Chuck, too. Yuh'd tink he suspected me and Chuck hadn't no real intention of gettin' married. Yuh'd tink he suspected Chuck wasn't goin' to lay off periodicals—or maybe even didn't want to.

CHUCK. He didn't say it right out or I'da socked him one. I told him, "I'm on de wagon for keeps and Cora knows it."

CORA. I told him, "Sure, I know it. And Chuck ain't never goin' to trow it in my face dat I was a tart, neider. And if yuh tink we're just kiddin' ourselves, we'll show yuh!"

CHUCK. We're goin' to show him!

CORA. We got it all fixed. We've decided Joisey is where we want de farm, and we'll get married dere, too, because yuh don't need no license. We're goin' to get married tomorrow. Ain't we, Honey?

CHUCK. You bet, Baby.

ROCKY (disgusted). Christ, Chuck, are yuh lettin' dat bughouse louse Hickey kid yuh into—

CORA (turns on him angrily). Nobody's kiddin' him into it, nor me neider! And Hickey's right. If dis big tramp's goin' to marry me, he ought to do it, and not just shoot off his old bazoo about it.

ROCKY (ignoring her). Yuh can't be dat dumb, Chuck.

CORA. You keep outa dis! And don't start beefin' about crickets on de farm drivin' us nuts. You and your crickets! Yuh'd tink dey was elephants!

MARGIE (coming to Rocky's defense—sneeringly). Don't notice dat broad, Rocky. Yuh heard her say "tomorrow," didn't yuh? It's de same old crap.

CORA (glares at her). Is dat so?

PEARL (lines up with Margie—sneeringly). Imagine Cora a bride! Dat's a hot one! Jees, Cora, if all de guys you've stayed wid was side by side, yuh could walk on 'em from here to Texas!

CORA (starts moving toward her threateningly). Yuh can't talk like dat to me, yuh fat Dago hooker! I may be a tart, but I ain't a cheap old whore like you!

PEARL (furiously). I'll show yuh who's a whore! (They start to fly at each other, but Chuck and Rocky grab them from behind)

CHUCK (forcing Cora onto a chair). Sit down and cool off, Baby.

ROCKY (doing the same to Pearl). Nix on de rough stuff, Poil.

MARGIE (glaring at Cora). Why don't you leave Poil alone, Rocky? She'll fix dat blonde's clock! Or if she don't, I will!

ROCKY. Shut up, you! (Disgustedly) Jees, what dames! D'yuh wanta gum Harry's party?

PEARL (a bit shamefaced—sulkily). Who wants to? But nobody can't call me a —

ROCKY (exasperatedly). Aw, bury it! What are you, a voigin?

(Pearl stares at him, her face growing hard and bitter. So does Margie.)

PEARL. Yuh mean yuh tink I'm a whore, too, huh?

MARGIE. Yeah, and me?

ROCKY. Now don't start nuttin'!

PEARL. I suppose it'd tickle you if me and Margie did what dat louse, Hickey, was hintin' and come right out and admitted we was whores.

ROCKY. Aw right! What of it? It's de truth, ain't it?

CORA (lining up with Pearl and Margie —indignantly). Jees, Rocky, dat's a fine hell of a ting to say to two goils dat's been as good to yuh as Poil and Margie! (To Pearl) I didn't mean to call yuh dat, Poil. I was on'y mad.

PEARL (accepts the apology gratefully). Sure, I was mad, too, Cora. No hard feelin's.

ROCKY (relieved). Dere. Dat fixes everyting, don't it?

PEARL (turns on him—hard and bitter). Aw right, Rocky. We're whores. You know what dat makes you, don't you?

ROCKY (angrily). Look out, now!

MARGIE. A lousy little pimp, dat's what!

ROCKY. I'll loin yuh! (He gives her a slap on the side of the face)

PEARL. A dirty little Ginny pimp, dat's what!

ROCKY (gives her a slap, too). And dat'll loin you! (But they only stare at him with hard sneering eyes)

MARGIE. He's provin' it to us, Poil.

PEARL. Yeah! Hickey's convoited him. He's give up his pipe dream!

ROCKY (furious and at the same time bewildered by their defiance). Lay off me or I'll beat de hell—

CHUCK (growls). Aw, lay off dem. Harry's party ain't no time to beat up your stable.

ROCKY (turns to him). Whose stable? Who d'yuh tink yuh're talkin' to? I ain't never beat dem up! What d'yuh tink I am? I just give dem a slap, like any guy would his wife, if she got too gabby. Why don't you tell dem to lay off me? I don't want no trouble on Harry's boithday party.

MARGIE (a victorious gleam in her eye—

tauntingly). Aw right, den, yuh poor little Ginny. I'll lay off yuh till de party's over if Poil will.

PEARL *(tauntingly).* Sure, I will. For Harry's sake, not yours, yuh little Wop!

ROCKY *(stung).* Say, listen, youse! Don't get no wrong idea— *(But an interruption comes from Larry who bursts into a sardonic laugh. They all jump startledly and look at him with unanimous hostility. Rocky transfers his anger to him)* Who de hell yuh laughin' at, yuh half-dead old stew bum?

CORA *(sneeringly).* At himself, he ought to be! Jees, Hickey's sure got his number!

LARRY *(ignoring them, turns to Hugo and shakes him by the shoulder—in his comically intense, crazy whisper).* Wake up, Comrade! Here's the Revolution starting on all sides of you and you're sleeping through it! Be God, it's not to Bakunin's ghost you ought to pray in your dreams, but to the great Nihilist, Hickey! He's started a movement that'll blow up the world!

HUGO *(blinks at him through his thick spectacles—with guttural denunciation).* You, Larry! Renegade! Traitor! I vill have you shot! *(He giggles)* Don't be a fool! Buy me a trink! *(He sees the drink in front of him, and gulps it down. He begins to sing the Carmagnole in a guttural basso, pounding on the table with his glass)* "Dansons la Carmagnole! Vive le son! Vive le son! Dansons la Carmagnole! Vive le son des canons!"

ROCKY. Can dat noise!

HUGO *(ignores this—to Larry, in a low tone of hatred).* That bourgeois svine, Hickey! He laughs like good fellow, he makes jokes, he dares make hints to me so I see what he dares to think. He thinks I am finish, it is too late, and so I do not vish the Day come because it vill not be my Day. Oh, I see what he thinks! He thinks lies even vorse, dat I— *(He stops abruptly with a guilty look, as if afraid he was letting something slip—then revengefully)* I vill have him hanged the first one of all on de first lamppost! *(He changes his mood abruptly and peers around at Rocky and the others—giggling again)* Vhy you so serious, leedle monkey-faces? It's all great joke, no? So ve get drunk, and ve laugh like hell, and den ve die, and de pipe dream vanish! *(A bitter mocking contempt creeps into his tone)* But be

of good cheer, leedle stupid peoples! "The days grow hot, O Babylon!" Soon, leedle proletarians, ve vill have free picnic in the cool shade, ve vill eat hot dogs and trink free beer beneath the villow trees! Like hogs, yes! Like beautiful leedle hogs! *(He stops startledly, as if confused and amazed at what he has heard himself say. He mutters with hatred)* Dot Gottamned liar, Hickey. It is he who makes me sneer. I want to sleep. *(He lets his head fall forward on his folded arms again and closes his eyes. Larry gives him a pitying look, then quickly drinks his drink)*

CORA *(uneasily).* Hickey ain't overlookin' no bets, is he? He's even give Hugo de woiks.

LARRY. I warned you this morning he wasn't kidding.

MARGIE *(sneering).* De old wise guy!

PEARL. Yeah, still pretendin' he's de one exception, like Hickey told him. He don't do no pipe dreamin'! Oh, no!

LARRY *(sharply resentful).* I—! *(Then abruptly he is drunkenly good-natured, and you feel this drunken manner is an evasive exaggeration)* All right, take it out on me, if it makes you more content. Sure, I love every hair of your heads, my great big beautiful baby dolls, and there's nothing I wouldn't do for you!

PEARL *(stiffly).* De old Irish bunk, huh? We ain't big. And we ain't your baby dolls! *(Suddenly she is mollified and smiles)* But we admit we're beautiful. Huh, Margie?

MARGIE *(smiling).* Sure ting! But what would he do wid beautiful dolls, even if he had de price, de old goat? *(She laughs teasingly—then pats Larry on the shoulder affectionately)* Aw, yuh're aw right at dat, Larry, if yuh are full of bull!

PEARL. Sure. Yuh're aces wid us. We're noivous, dat's all. Dat lousy drummer— why can't he be like he's always been. I never seen a guy change so. You pretend to be such a fox, Larry. What d'yuh tink's happened to him?

LARRY. I don't know. With all his gab I notice he's kept that to himself so far. Maybe he's saving the great revelation for Hugo's party. *(Then irritably)* To hell with him! I don't want to know. Let him mind his own business and I'll mind mine.

CHUCK. Yeah, dat's what I say.

CORA. Say, Larry, where's dat young friend of yours disappeared to?

LARRY. I don't care where he is, except I wish it was a thousand miles away! (*Then, as he sees they are surprised at his vehemence, he adds hastily*) He's a pest.

ROCKY (*breaks in with his own preoccupation*). I don't give a damn what happened to Hickey, but I know what's gonna happen if he don't watch his step. I told him, "I'll take a lot from you, Hickey, like everyone else in dis dump, because yuh've always been a grand guy. But dere's tings I don't take from you nor nobody, see? Remember dat, or you'll wake up in a hospital—or maybe worse, wid your wife and de iceman walkin' slow behind yuh."

CORA. Aw, yuh shouldn't make dat iceman crack, Rocky. It's aw right for him to kid about it but—I notice Hickey ain't pulled dat old iceman gag dis time. (*Excitedly*) D'yuh suppose dat he did catch his wife cheatin'? I don't mean wid no iceman, but wid some guy.

ROCKY. Aw, dat's de bunk. He ain't pulled dat gag or showed her photo around because he ain't drunk. And if he'd caught her cheatin' he'd be drunk, wouldn't he? He'd have beat her up and den gone on de woist drunk he'd ever staged. Like any other guy'd do. (*The girls nod, convinced by this reasoning*)

CHUCK. Sure! Rocky's got de right dope, Baby. He'd be paralyzed.

(*While he is speaking, the Negro, Joe, comes in from the hallway. There is a noticeable change in him. He walks with a tough, truculent swagger and his good-natured face is set in sullen suspicion.*)

JOE (*to Rocky—defiantly*). I's stood tellin' people dis dump is closed for de night all I's goin' to. Let Harry hire a doorman, pay him wages, if he wants one.

ROCKY (*scowling*). Yeah? Harry's pretty damned good to you.

JOE (*shamefaced*). Sure he is. I don't mean dat. Anyways, it's all right. I told Schwartz, de cop, we's closed for de party. He'll keep folks away. (*Aggressively again*) I want a big drink, dat's what!

CHUCK. Who's stoppin' yuh? Yuh can have all yuh want on Hickey.

JOE (*has taken a glass from the table and has his hand on a bottle when Hickey's name is mentioned. He draws his hand back as if he were going to refuse—then grabs it defiantly and pours a big drink*). All right, I's earned all de drinks

on him I could drink in a year for listenin' to his crazy bull. And here's hopin' he gets de lockjaw! (*He drinks and pours out another*) I drinks on him but I don't drink wid him. No, suh, never no more!

ROCKY. Aw, bull! Hickey's aw right. What's he done to you?

JOE (*sullenly*). Dat's my business. I ain't buttin' in yours, is I? (*Bitterly*) Sure, you think he's all right. He's a white man, ain't he? (*His tone becomes aggressive*) Listen to me, you white boys! Don't you get it in your heads I's pretendin' to be what I ain't, or dat I ain't proud to be what I is, get me? Or you and me's goin' to have trouble! (*He picks up his drink and walks left as far away from them as he can get and slumps down on the piano stool*)

MARGIE (*in a low angry tone*). What a noive! Just because we act nice to him, he gets a swelled nut! If dat ain't a coon all over!

CHUCK. Talkin' fight talk, huh? I'll moider de nigger! (*He takes a threatening step toward Joe, who is staring before him guiltily now*)

JOE (*speaks up shamefacedly*). Listen, boys, I's sorry. I didn't mean dat. You been good friends to me. I's nuts, I guess. Dat Hickey, he gets my head all mixed up wit' craziness. (*Their faces at once clear of resentment against him*)

CORA. Aw, dat's aw right, Joe. De boys wasn't takin' yuh serious. (*Then to the others, forcing a laugh*) Jees, what'd I say, Hickey ain't overlookin' no bets. Even Joe. (*She pauses—then adds puzzledly*) De funny ting is, yuh can't stay sore at de bum when he's around. When he forgets de bughouse preachin', and quits tellin' yuh where yuh get off, he's de same old Hickey. Yuh can't help likin' de louse. And yuh got to admit he's got de right dope— (*She adds hastily*) I mean, on some of de bums here.

MARGIE (*with a sneering look at Rocky*). Yeah, he's coitinly got one guy I know sized up right! Huh, Poil?

PEARL. He coitinly has!

ROCKY. Cut it out, I told yuh!

LARRY (*is staring before him broodingly. He speaks more aloud to himself than to them*). It's nothing to me what happened to him. But I have a feeling he's dying to tell us, inside of him, and yet he's afraid. He's like that damned kid. It's strange the queer way he seemed to recognize him. If he's afraid, it explains why he's off booze. Like that damned kid again. Afraid if he got drunk, he'd tell— *(While he is speaking, Hickey comes in the doorway at rear. He looks the same as in the previous act, except that now his face beams with the excited expectation of a boy going to a party. His arms are piled with packages)*

HICKEY *(booms in imitation of a familiar Polo Grounds bleacherite cry—with rising volume).* Well! Well!! Well!!! *(They all jump startledly. He comes forward, grinning)* Here I am in the nick of time. Give me a hand with these bundles, somebody. *(Margie and Pearl start taking them from his arms and putting them on the table. Now that he is present, all their attitudes show the reaction Cora has expressed. They can't help liking him and forgiving him)*

MARGIE. Jees, Hickey, yuh scared me outa a year's growth, sneakin' in like dat.

HICKEY. Sneaking? Why, me and the taxi man made enough noise getting my big surprise in the hall to wake the dead. You were all so busy drinking in words of wisdom from the Old Wise Guy here, you couldn't hear anything else. *(He grins at Larry)* From what I heard, Larry, you're not so good when you start playing Sherlock Holmes. You've got me all wrong. I'm not afraid of anything now— not even myself. You better stick to the part of Old Cemetery, the Barker for the Big Sleep—that is, if you can still let yourself get away with it! *(He chuckles and gives Larry a friendly slap on the back. Larry gives him a bitter angry look)*

CORA *(giggles).* Old Cemetery! That's him, Hickey. We'll have to call him dat.

HICKEY *(watching Larry quizzically).* Beginning to do a lot of puzzling about me, aren't you, Larry? But that won't help you. You've got to think of yourself. I couldn't give you my peace. You've got to find your own. All I can do is help you, and the rest of the gang, by showing you the way to find it. *(He has said this with a simple persuasive earnestness. He pauses, and for a second they stare at him with fascinated resentful uneasiness)*

ROCKY *(breaks the spell).* Aw, hire a church!

HICKEY *(placatingly).* All right! All right! Don't get sore, boys and girls. I guess that did sound too much like a lousy preacher. Let's forget it and get busy on the party. *(They look relieved)*

CHUCK. Is dose bundles grub, Hickey? You bought enough already to feed an army.

HICKEY *(with boyish excitement again).* Can't be too much! I want this to be the biggest birthday Harry's ever had. You and Rocky go in the hall and get the big surprise. My arms are busted lugging it. *(They catch his excitement. Chuck and Rocky go out, grinning expectantly. The three girls gather around Hickey, full of thrilled curiosity)*

PEARL. Jees, yuh got us all het up! What is it, Hickey?

HICKEY. Wait and see. I got it as a treat for the three of you more than anyone. I thought to myself, I'll bet this is what will please those whores more than anything. *(They wince as if he had slapped them, but before they have a chance to be angry, he goes on affectionately)* I said to myself, I don't care how much it costs, they're worth it. They're the best little scouts in the world, and they've been damned kind to me when I was down and out! Nothing is too good for them. *(Earnestly)* I mean every word of that, too—and then some! *(Then, as if he noticed the expression on their faces for the first time)* What's the matter? You look sore. What—? *(Then he chuckles)* Oh, I see. But you know how I feel about that. You know I didn't say it to offend you. So don't be silly now.

MARGIE *(lets out a tense breath).* Aw right, Hickey. Let it slide.

HICKEY *(jubilantly, as Chuck and Rocky enter carrying a big wicker basket).* Look! There it comes! Unveil it, boys. *(They pull off a covering burlap bag. The basket is piled with quarts of champagne)*

PEARL *(with childish excitement).* It's champagne! Jees, Hickey, if you ain't a sport! *(She gives him a hug, forgetting all animosity, as do the other girls)*

MARGIE. I never been soused on champagne. Let's get stinko, Poil.

PEARL. You betcha my life! De bot' of us! *(A holiday spirit of gay festivity has seized them all. Even Joe Mott is standing up to look at the wine with an admiring grin, and Hugo raises his head to blink at it)*

JOE. You sure is hittin' de high spots, Hickey. *(Boastfully)* Man, when I runs my gamblin' house, I drinks dat old bubbly water in steins! *(He stops guiltily and gives Hickey a look of defiance)* I's goin' to drink it dat way again, too, soon's I make my stake! And dat ain't no pipe dream, neider! *(He sits down where he was, his back turned to them)*

ROCKY. What'll we drink it outa, Hickey? Dere ain't no wine glasses.

HICKEY *(enthusiastically)*. Joe has the right idea! Schooners! That's the spirit for Íarry's birthday! *(Rocky and Chuck carry the basket of wine into the bar. The three girls go back and stand around the entrance to the bar, chatting excitedly among themselves and to Chuck and Rocky in the bar)*

HUGO *(with his silly giggle)*. Ve vill trink vine beneath the villow trees!

HICKEY *(grins at him)*. That's the spirit, Brother—and let the lousy slaves drink vinegar! *(Hugo blinks at him startledly, then looks away)*

HUGO *(mutters)*. Gottamned liar! *(He puts his head back on his arms and closes his eyes, but this time his habitual passout has a quality of hiding)*

LARRY *(gives Hugo a pitying glance— in a low tone of anger)*. Leave Hugo be! He rotted ten years in prison for his faith! He's earned his dream! Have you no decency or pity?

HICKEY *(quizzically)*. Hello, what's this? I thought you were in the grandstand. *(Then with a simple earnestness, taking a chair by Larry, and putting a hand on his shoulder)* Listen, Larry, you're getting me all wrong. Hell, you ought to know me better. I've always been the best-natured slob in the world. Of course, I have pity. But now I've seen the light, it isn't my old kind of pity—the kind yours is. It isn't the kind that lets itself off easy by encouraging some poor guy to go on kidding himself with a lie—the kind that leaves the poor slob worse off because it makes him feel guiltier than ever—the kind that makes his lying hopes nag at him and reproach him until he's a rotten skunk in his own eyes. I know all about that kind of pity. I've had a bellyful of it in my time, and it's all wrong! *(With a salesman's persuasiveness)* No, sir. The kind of pity I feel now is after final results that will really save the poor guy, and make him contented with what he is, and quit battling himself, and find peace for the rest of his life. Oh, I know how you resent the way I have to show you up to yourself. I don't blame you. I know from my own experience it's bitter medicine, facing yourself in the mirror with the old false whiskers off. But you forget that, once you're cured. You'll be grateful to me when all at once you find you're able to admit, without feeling ashamed, that all the grandstand foolosopher bunk and the waiting for the Big Sleep stuff is a pipe dream. You'll say to yourself, I'm just an old man who is scared of life, but even more scared of dying. So I'm keeping drunk and hanging on to life at any price, and what of it? Then you'll know what real peace means, Larry, because you won't be scared of either life or death any more. You simply won't give a damn! Any more than I do!

LARRY *(has been staring into his eyes with a fascinated wondering dread)*. Be God, if I'm not beginning to think you've gone mad! *(With a rush of anger)* You're a liar!

HICKEY *(injuredly)*. Now, listen, that's no way to talk to an old pal who's trying to help you. Hell, if you really wanted to die, you'd just take a hop off your fire escape, wouldn't you? And if you really were in the grandstand, you wouldn't be pitying everyone. Oh, I know the truth is tough at first. It was for me. All I ask is for you to suspend judgment and give it a chance. I'll absolutely guarantee— Hell, Larry, I'm no fool. Do you suppose I'd deliberately set out to get under everyone's skin and put myself in dutch with all my old pals, if I wasn't certain, from my own experience, that it means contentment in the end for all of you? *(Larry again is staring at him fascinatedly. Hickey grins)* As for my being bughouse, you can't crawl out of it that way. Hell, I'm too damned sane. I can size up guys, and turn 'em inside out, better than I ever could. Even where they're strangers like that Parritt kid. He's licked, Larry. I think there is only one possible way out you can help him to take. That is, if you have the right kind of pity for him.

LARRY *(uneasily)*. What do you mean? *(Attempting indifference)* I'm not advising him, except to leave me out of his troubles. He's nothing to me.

HICKEY *(shakes his head)*. You'll find he won't agree to that. He'll keep after you until he makes you help him. Because he has to be punished, so he can forgive himself. He's lost all his guts. He can't manage it alone, and you're the only one he can turn to.

LARRY. For the love of God, mind your own business! *(With forced scorn)* A lot you know about him! He's hardly spoken to you!

HICKEY. No, that's right. But I do know a lot about him just the same. I've had hell inside me. I can spot it in others. *(Frowning)* Maybe that's what gives me the feeling there's something familiar about him, something between us. *(He shakes his head)* No, it's more than that. I can't figure it. Tell me about him. For instance, I don't imagine he's married, is he?

LARRY. No.

HICKEY. Hasn't he been mixed up with some woman? I don't mean trollops. I mean the old real love stuff that crucifies you.

LARRY *(with a calculating relieved look at him—encouraging him along this line).* Maybe you're right. I wouldn't be surprised.

HICKEY *(grins at him quizzically).* I see. You think I'm on the wrong track and you're glad I am. Because then I won't suspect whatever he did about the Great Cause. That's another lie you tell yourself, Larry, that the good old Cause means nothing to you any more. *(Larry is about to burst out in denial but Hickey goes on)* But you're all wrong about Parritt. That isn't what's got him stopped. It's what's behind that. And it's a woman. I recognize the symptoms.

LARRY *(sneeringly).* And you're the boy who's never wrong! Don't be a damned fool. His trouble is he was brought up a devout believer in the Movement and now he's lost his faith. It's a shock, but he's young and he'll soon find another dream just as good. *(He adds sardonically)* Or as bad.

HICKEY. All right. I'll let it go at that, Larry. He's nothing to me except I'm glad he's here because he'll help me make you wake up to yourself. I don't even like the guy, or the feeling there's anything between us. But you'll find I'm right just the same, when you get to the final showdown with him.

LARRY. There'll be no showdown! I don't give a tinker's damn—

HICKEY. Sticking to the old grandstand, eh? Well, I knew you'd be the toughest to convince of all the gang, Larry. And, along with Harry and Jimmy Tomorrow, you're the one I want most to help. *(He puts an arm around Larry's shoulder and gives him an affectionate hug)* I've always liked you a lot, you old bastard! *(He gets up and his manner changes to his bustling party excitement—glancing at his watch)* Well, well, not much time before twelve. Let's get busy, boys and girls. *(He looks over the table where the cake is)* Cake all set. Good. And my presents, and yours, girls, and Chuck's, and Rocky's. Fine. Harry'll certainly be touched by your thought of him. *(He goes back to the girls)* You go in the bar, Pearl and Margie, and get the grub ready so it can be brought right in. There'll be some drinking and toasts first, of course. My idea is to use the wine for that, so get it all set. I'll go upstairs now and root everyone out. Harry the last. I'll come back with him. Somebody light the candles on the cake when you hear us coming, and you start playing Harry's favorite tune, Cora. Hustle now, everybody. We want this to come off in style. *(He bustles into the hall. Margie and Pearl disappear in the bar. Cora goes to the piano. Joe gets off the stool sullenly to let her sit down)*

CORA. I got to practice. I ain't laid my mits on a box in Gawd knows when. *(With the soft pedal down, she begins gropingly to pick out "The Sunshine of Paradise Alley")* Is dat right, Joe? I've forgotten dat has-been tune. *(She picks out a few more notes)* Come on, Joe, hum de tune so I can follow. *(Joe begins to hum and sing in a low voice and correct her. He forgets his sullenness and becomes his old self again)*

LARRY *(suddenly gives a laugh—in his comically intense, crazy tone).* Be God, it's a second feast of Belshazzar, with Hickey to do the writing on the wall!

CORA. Aw, shut up, Old Cemetery! Always beefin'! *(Willie comes in from the hall. He is in a pitiable state, his face pasty, haggard with sleeplessness and nerves, his eyes sick and haunted. He is sober. Cora greets him over her shoulder kiddingly)* If it ain't Prince Willie! *(Then kindly)* Gee, kid, yuh look sick. Git a coupla shots in yuh.

WILLIE *(tensely).* No, thanks. Not now.

I'm tapering off. (*He sits down weakly on Larry's right*)

CORA (*astonished*). What d'yuh know? He means it!

WILLIE (*leaning toward Larry confidentially—in a low shaken voice*). It's been hell up in that damned room, Larry! The things I've imagined! (*He shudders*) I thought I'd go crazy. (*With pathetic boastful pride*) But I've got it beat now. By tomorrow morning I'll be on the wagon. I'll get back my clothes the first thing. Hickey's loaning me the money. I'm going to do what I've always said—go to the D.A.'s office. He was a good friend of my Old Man's. He was only assistant, then. He was in on the graft, but my Old Man never squealed on him. So he certainly owes it to me to give me a chance. And he knows that I really was a brilliant law student. (*Self-reassuringly*) Oh, I know I can make good, now I'm getting off the booze forever. (*Moved*) I owe a lot to Hickey. He's made me wake up to myself—see what a fool— It wasn't nice to face but— (*With bitter resentment*) It isn't what he says. It's what you feel behind—what he hints— Christ, you'd think all I really wanted to do with my life was sit here and stay drunk. (*With hatred*) I'll show him!

LARRY (*masking pity behind a sardonic tone*). If you want my advice, you'll put the nearest bottle to your mouth until you don't give a damn for Hickey!

WILLIE (*stares at a bottle greedily, tempted for a moment—then bitterly*). That's fine advice! I thought you were my friend! (*He gets up with a hurt glance at Larry, and moves away to take a chair in back of the left end of the table, where he sits in dejected, shaking misery, his chin on his chest*)

JOE (*to Cora*). No, like dis. (*He beats time with his finger and sings in a low voice*) "She is the sunshine of Paradise Alley." (*She plays*) Dat's more like it. Try it again. (*She begins to play through the chorus again. Don Parritt enters from the hall. There is a frightened look on his face. He slinks in furtively, as if he were escaping from someone. He looks relieved when he sees Larry and comes and slips into the chair on his right. Larry pretends not to notice his coming, but he instinctively shrinks with repulsion. Parritt leans* toward him and speaks ingratiatingly in a low secretive tone*)

PARRITT. Gee, I'm glad you're here, Larry. That damned fool, Hickey, knocked on my door. I opened up because I thought it must be you, and he came busting in and made me come downstairs. I don't know what for. I don't belong in this birthday celebration. I don't know this gang and I don't want to be mixed up with them. All I came here for was to find you.

LARRY (*tensely*). I've warned you—

PARRITT (*goes on as if he hadn't heard*). Can't you make Hickey mind his own business? I don't like that guy, Larry. The way he acts, you'd think he had something on me. Why, just now he pats me on the shoulder, like he was sympathizing with me, and says, "I know how it is, Son, but you can't hide from yourself, not even here on the bottom of the sea. You've got to face the truth and then do what must be done for your own peace and the happiness of all concerned." What did he mean by that, Larry?

LARRY. How the hell would I know?

PARRITT. Then he grins and says, "Never mind, Larry's getting wise to himself. I think you can rely on his help in the end. He'll have to choose between living and dying, and he'll never choose to die while there is a breath left in the old bastard!" And then he laughs like it was a joke on you. (*He pauses. Larry is rigid on his chair, staring before him. Parritt asks him with a sudden taunt in his voice*) Well, what do you say to that, Larry?

LARRY. I've nothing to say. Except you're a bigger fool than he is to listen to him.

PARRITT (*with a sneer*). Is that so? He's no fool where you're concerned. He's got your number, all right! (*Larry's face tightens but he keeps silent. Parritt changes to a contrite, appealing air*) I don't mean that. But you keep acting as if you were sore at me, and that gets my goat. You know what I want most is to be friends with you, Larry. I haven't a single friend left in the world. I hoped you— (*Bitterly*) And you could be, too, without it hurting you. You ought to, for Mother's sake. She really loved you. You loved her, too, didn't you?

LARRY (*tensely*). Leave what's dead in its grave.

PARRITT. I suppose, because I was only a

kid, you didn't think I was wise about you and her. Well, I was. I've been wise, ever since I can remember, to all the guys she's had, although she'd tried to kid me along it wasn't so. That was a silly stunt for a free Anarchist woman, wasn't it, being ashamed of being free?

LARRY. Shut your damned trap!

PARRITT (*guiltily but with a strange undertone of satisfaction*). Yes, I know I shouldn't say that now. I keep forgetting she isn't free any more. (*He pauses*) Do you know, Larry, you're the one of them all she cared most about? Anyone else who left the Movement would have been dead to her, but she couldn't forget you. She'd always make excuses for you. I used to try and get her goat about you. I'd say, "Larry's got brains and yet he thinks the Movement is just a crazy pipe dream." She'd blame it on booze getting you. She'd kid herself that you'd give up booze and come back to the Movement—tomorrow! She'd say, "Larry can't kill in himself a faith he's given his life to, not without killing himself." (*He grins sneeringly*) How about it, Larry? Was she right? (*Larry remains silent. He goes on insistently*) I suppose what she really meant was, come back to her. She was always getting the Movement mixed up with herself. But I'm sure she really must have loved you, Larry. As much as she could love anyone besides herself. But she wasn't faithful to you, even at that, was she? That's why you finally walked out on her, isn't it? I remember that last fight you had with her. I was on your side, even if she was my mother, because I liked you so much; you'd been so good to me—like a father. I remember her putting on her high-and-mighty free-woman stuff, saying you were still a slave to bourgeois morality and jealousy and you thought a woman you loved was a piece of private property you owned. I remember that you got mad and you told her, "I don't like living with a whore, if that's what you mean!"

LARRY (*bursts out*). You lie! I never called her that!

PARRITT (*goes on as if Larry hadn't spoken*). I think that's why she still respects you, because it was you who left her. You were the only one to beat her to it. She got sick of the others before they did of her. I don't think she ever cared much about them, anyway. She just had

to keep on having lovers to prove to herself how free she was. (*He pauses—then with a bitter repulsion*) It made home a lousy place. I felt like you did about it. I'd get feeling it was like living in a whorehouse—only worse, because she didn't have to make her living—

LARRY. You bastard! She's your mother! Have you no shame?

PARRITT (*bitterly*). No! She brought me up to believe that family-respect stuff is all bourgeois, property-owning crap. Why should I be ashamed?

LARRY (*making a move to get up*). I've had enough!

PARRITT (*catches his arm—pleadingly*). No! Don't leave me! Please! I promise I won't mention her again! (*Larry sinks back in his chair*) I only did it to make you understand better. I know this isn't the place to— Why didn't you come up to my room, like I asked you? I kept waiting. We could talk everything over there.

LARRY. There's nothing to talk over!

PARRITT. But I've got to talk to you. Or I'll talk to Hickey. He won't let me alone! I feel he knows, anyway! And I know he'd understand, all right—in his way. But I hate his guts! I don't want anything to do with him! I'm scared of him, honest. There's something not human behind his damned grinning and kidding.

LARRY (*starts*). Ah! You feel that, too?

PARRITT (*pleadingly*). But I can't go on like this. I've got to decide what I've got to do. I've got to tell you, Larry!

LARRY (*again starts up*). I won't listen!

PARRITT (*again holds him by the arm*). All right! I won't. Don't go! (*Larry lets himself be pulled down on his chair. Parritt examines his face and becomes insultingly scornful*) Who do you think you're kidding? I know damned well you've guessed—

LARRY. I've guessed nothing!

PARRITT. But I want you to guess now! I'm glad you have! I know now, since Hickey's been after me, that I meant you to guess right from the start. That's why I came to you. (*Hurrying on with an attempt at a plausible frank air that makes what he says seem doubly false*) I want you to understand the reason. You see, I began studying American history. I got admiring Washington and Jefferson and Jackson and Lincoln. I began to feel patriotic and love this country. I saw it was the best government in the world, where everybody was equal and had a chance. I saw that all the ideas behind the Movement came from a lot of Russians like Bakunin and Kropotkin and were meant for Europe, but we didn't need them here in a democracy where we were free already. I didn't want this country to be destroyed for a damned foreign pipe dream. After all, I'm from old American pioneer stock. I began to feel I was a traitor for helping a lot of cranks and bums and free women plot to overthrow our government. And then I saw it was my duty to my country—

LARRY (*nauseated—turns on him*). You stinking rotten liar! Do you think you can fool me with such hypocrite's cant! (*Then turning away*) I don't give a damn what you did! It's on your head—whatever it was! I don't want to know—and I won't know!

PARRITT (*as if Larry had never spoken —falteringly*). But I never thought Mother would be caught. Please btlieve that, Larry. You know I never would have—

LARRY (*his face haggard, drawing a deep breath and closing his eyes—as if he were trying to hammer something into his own brain*). All I know is I'm sick of life! I'm through! I've forgotten myself! I'm drowned and contented on the bottom of a bottle. Honor or dishonor, faith or treachery are nothing to me but the opposites of the same stupidity which is ruler and king of life, and in the end they rot into dust in the same grave. All things are the same meaningless joke to me, for they grin at me from the one skull of death. So go away. You're wasting breath. I've forgotten your mother.

PARRITT (*jeers angrily*). The old foolosopher, eh? (*He spits out contemptuously*) You lousy old faker!

LARRY (*so distracted he pleads weakly*). For the love of God, leave me in peace the little time that's left to me!

PARRITT. Aw, don't pull that pitiful old-man junk on me! You old bastard, you'll never die as long as there's a free drink of whiskey left!

LARRY (*stung—furiously*). Look out how you try to taunt me back into life, I warn you! I might remember the thing they call justice there, and the punishment for— (*He checks himself with an effort— then with a real indifference that comes*

from exhaustion) I'm old and tired. To hell with you! You're as mad as Hickey, and as big a liar. I'd never let myself believe a word you told me.

PARRITT (*threateningly*). The hell you won't! Wait till Hickey gets through with you! (*Pearl and Margie come in from the bar. At the sight of them, Parritt instantly subsides and becomes self-conscious and defensive, scowling at them and then quickly looking away*)

MARGIE (*eyes him jeeringly*). Why, hello, Tightwad Kid. Come to join de party? Gee, don't he act bashful, Poil?

PEARL. Yeah. Especially wid his dough. (*Parritt slinks to a chair at the left end of the table, pretending he hasn't heard them. Suddenly there is a noise of angry, cursing voices and a scuffle from the hall. Pearl yells*) Hey, Rocky! Fight in de hall! (*Rocky and Chuck run from behind the bar curtain and rush into the hall. Rocky's voice is heard in irritated astonishment, "What de hell?" and then the scuffle stops and Rocky appears holding Captain Lewis by the arm, followed by Chuck with a similar hold on General Wetjoen. Although these two have been drinking they are both sober, for them. Their faces are sullenly angry, their clothes disarranged from the tussle*)

ROCKY (*leading Lewis forward—astonished, amused and irritated*). Can yuh beat it? I've heard youse two call each odder every name yuh could think of but I never seen you— (*Indignantly*) A swell time to stage your first bout, on Harry's boithday party! What started de scrap?

LEWIS (*forcing a casual tone*). Nothing, old chap. Our business, you know. That bloody ass, Hickey, made some insinuation about me, and the boorish Boer had the impertinence to agree with him.

WETJOEN. Dot's a lie! Hickey made joke about me, and this Limey said yes, it was true!

ROCKY. Well, sit down, de bot' of yuh, and cut out de rough stuff. (*He and Chuck dump them down in adjoining chairs toward the left end of the table, where, like two sulky boys, they turn their backs on each other as far as possible in chairs which both face front.*)

MARGIE (*laughs*). Jees, lookit de two bums! Like a coupla kids! Kiss and make up, for Gawd's sakes!

ROCKY. Yeah. Harry's party begins in a

minute and we don't want no soreheads around.

LEWIS *(stiffly)*. Very well. In deference to the occasion, I apologize, General Wetjoen—provided that you do also.

WETJOEN *(sulkily)*. I apologize, Captain Lewis—because Harry is my goot friend.

ROCKY. Aw, hell! If yuh can't do better'n dat—!

(Mosher and McGloin enter together from the hall. Both have been drinking but are not drunk)

PEARL. Here's de star boarders.

(They advance, their heads together, so interested in a discussion they are oblivious to everyone)

MCGLOIN. I'm telling you, Ed, it's serious this time. That bastard, Hickey, has got Harry on the hip. *(As he talks, Margie, Pearl, Rocky and Chuck prick up their ears and gather round. Cora, at the piano, keeps running through the tune, with soft pedal, and singing the chorus half under her breath, with Joe still correcting her mistakes. At the table, Larry, Parritt, Willie, Wetjoen and Lewis sit motionless, staring in front of them. Hugo seems asleep in his habitual position)* And you know it isn't going to do us no good if he gets him to take that walk tomorrow.

MOSHER. You're damned right. Harry'll mosey around the ward, dropping in on everyone who knew him when. *(Indignantly)* And they'll all give him a phony glad hand and a ton of good advice about what a sucker he is to stand for us.

MCGLOIN. He's sure to call on Bessie's relations to do a little cryin' over dear Bessie. And you know what that bitch and all her family thought of me.

MOSHER *(with a flash of his usual humor—rebukingly)*. Remember, Lieutenant, you are speaking of my sister! Dear Bessie wasn't a bitch. She was a Goddamned bitch! But if you think my loving relatives will have time to discuss you, you don't know them. They'll be too busy telling Harry what a drunken crook I am and saying he ought to have me put in Sing Sing!

MCGLOIN *(dejectedly)*. Yes, once Bessie's relations get their hooks in him, it'll be as tough for us as if she wasn't gone.

MOSHER *(dejectedly)*. Yes, Harry has always been weak and easily influenced, and now he's getting old he'll be an easy mark

for those grafters. *(Then with forced re assurance)* Oh, hell, Mac, we're saps to worry. We've heard Harry pull that bluf about taking a walk every birthday he's had for twenty years.

MCGLOIN *(doubtfully)*. But Hickey wasn't sicking him on those times. Jus the opposite. He was asking Harry wha he wanted to go out for when there wa plenty of whiskey here.

MOSHER *(with a change to forced care lessness)*. Well, after all, I don't care whether he goes out or not. I'm clearing out tomorrow morning anyway. I'm jus sorry for you, Mac.

MCGLOIN *(resentfully)*. You needn't be then. Ain't I going myself. I was onl feeling sorry for you.

MOSHER. Yes, my mind is made up Hickey may be a lousy, interfering pest now he's gone teetotal on us, but there's a lot of truth in some of his bull. Hanging around here getting plastered with you Mac, is pleasant, I won't deny, but the old booze gets you in the end, if you keep lapping it up. It's time I quit for a while *(With forced enthusiasm)* Besides, I fee the call of the old carefree circus life is my blood again. I'll see the boss tomor row. It's late in the season but he'll b glad to take me on. And won't all the old gang be tickled to death when I show up on the lot!

MCGLOIN. Maybe—if they've got a rop handy!

MOSHER *(turns on him—angrily)*. Lis ten! I'm damned sick of that kidding!

MCGLOIN. You are, are you? Well, I'n sicker of your kidding me about getting reinstated on the Force. And whateve you'd like, I can't spend my life sitting here with you, ruining my stomach with rotgut. I'm tapering off, and in the morn ing I'll be fresh as a daisy. I'll go and hav a private chin with the Commissioner *(With forced enthusiasm)* Man alive from what the boys tell me, there's suga galore these days, and I'll soon be ridin around in a big red automobile—

MOSHER *(derisively—beckoning an im aginary Chinese)*. Here, One Lung Hop Put fresh peanut oil in the lamp and coo the Lieutenant another dozen pills! It's hi gowed-up night!

MCGLOIN *(stung—pulls back a fis threateningly)*. One more crack like tha and I'll—!

MOSHER *(putting up his fists).* Yes? Just start—!

(Chuck and Rocky jump between them.)

ROCKY. Hey! Are you guys nuts? Jees, it's Harry's boithday party! *(They both look guilty)* Sit down and behave.

MOSHER *(grumpily).* All right. Only tell him to lay off me. *(He lets Rocky push him in a chair, at the right end of the table, rear)*

MCGLOIN *(grumpily).* Tell him to lay off me. *(He lets Chuck push him into the chair on Mosher's left. At this moment Hickey bursts in from the hall, bustling and excited)*

HICKEY. Everything all set? Fine *(He glances at his watch)* Half a minute to go. Harry's starting down with Jimmy. I had a hard time getting them to move! They'd rather stay hiding up there, kidding each other along. *(He chuckles)* Harry don't even want to remember it's his birthday now! *(He hears a noise from the stairs)* Here they come! *(Urgently)* Light the candles! Get ready to play, Cora! Stand up, everybody! Get that wine ready, Chuck and Rocky! *(Margie and Pearl light the candles on the cake. Cora gets her hands set over the piano key, watching over her shoulder. Rocky and Chuck go in the bar. Everybody at the table stands up mechanically. Hugo is the last, suddenly coming to and scrambling to his feet. Harry Hope and Jimmy Tomorrow appear in the hall outside the door. Hickey looks up from his watch)* On the dot! It's twelve! *(Like a cheer leader)* Come on now, everybody, with a Happy Birthday, Harry!

(With his voice leading they all shout "Happy Birthday, Harry!" in a spiritless chorus. Hickey signals to Cora, who starts playing and singing in a whiskey soprano "She's the Sunshine of Paradise Alley." Hope and Jimmy stand in the doorway. Both have been drinking heavily. In Hope the effect is apparent only in a bristling, touchy, pugnacious attitude. It is entirely different from the usual irascible beefing he delights in which no one takes seriously. Now he really has a chip on his shoulder. Jimmy, on the other hand, is plainly drunk, but it has not had the desired effect, for beneath a pathetic assumption of gentlemanly poise, he is obviously frightened and shrinking back within himself. Hickey grabs Hope's hand and pumps it up and down. For a moment Hope appears unconscious of this handshake. Then he jerks his hand away angrily.)

HOPE. Cut out the glad hand, Hickey. D'you think I'm a sucker? I know you, bejees, you sneaking, lying drummer! *(With rising anger, to the others)* And all you bums! What the hell you trying to do, yelling and raising the roof? Want the cops to close the joint and get my license taken away? *(He yells at Cora who has stopped singing but continues to play mechanically with many mistakes)* Hey, you dumb tart, quit banging that box! Bejees, the least you could do is learn the tune!

CORA *(stops—deeply hurt).* Aw, Harry, Jees, ain't I— *(Her eyes begin to fill)*

HOPE *(glaring at the other girls).* And you two hookers, screaming at the top of your lungs! What d'you think this is, a dollar cathouse? Bejees, that's where you belong!

PEARL *(miserably).* Aw, Harry— *(She begins to cry)*

MARGIE. Jees, Harry, I never thought you'd say that—like yuh meant it. *(She puts her arm around Pearl—on the verge of tears herself)* Aw, don't bawl, Poil. He don't mean it.

HICKEY *(reproachfully).* Now, Harry! Don't take it out on the gang because you're upset about yourself. Anyway, I've promised you you'll come through all right, haven't I? So quit worrying. *(He slaps Hope on the back encouragingly. Hope flashes him a glance of hate)* Be yourself, Governor. You don't want to bawl out the old gang just when they're congratulating you on your birthday, do you? Hell, that's no way!

HOPE *(looking guilty and shamefaced now—forcing an unconvincing attempt at his natural tone).* Bejees, they ain't as dumb as you. They know I was only kidding them. They know I appreciate their congratulations. Don't you, fellers? *(There is a listless chorus of "Sure, Harry," "Yes," "Of course we do," etc. He comes forward to the two girls,· with Jimmy and Hickey following him, and pats them clumsily)* Bejees, I like you broads. You know I was only kidding. *(Instantly they forgive him and smile affectionately)*

MARGIE. Sure we know, Harry.

PEARL. Sure.

HICKEY (*grinning*). Sure. Harry's the greatest kidder in this dump and that's saying something! Look how he's kidded himself for twenty years! (*As Hope gives him a bitter, angry glance, he digs him in the ribs with his elbow playfully*) Unless I'm wrong, Governor, and I'm betting I'm not. We'll soon know, eh? Tomorrow morning. No, by God, it's *this* morning now!

JIMMY (*with a dazed dread*). This morning?

HICKEY. Yes, it's today at last, Jimmy. (*He pats him on the back*) Don't be so scared! I've promised I'll help you.

JIMMY (*trying to hide his dread behind an offended, drunken dignity*). I don't understand you. Kindly remember I'm fully capable of settling my own affairs!

HICKEY (*earnestly*). Well, isn't that exactly what I want you to do, settle with yourself once and for all? (*He speaks in his ear in confidential warning*) Only watch out on the booze, Jimmy. You know, not too much from now on. You've had a lot already, and you don't want to let yourself duck out of it by being too drunk to move—not this time! (*Jimmy gives him a guilty, stricken look and turns away and slumps into the chair on Mosher's right*)

HOPE (*to Margie—still guiltily*). Bejees, Margie, you know I didn't mean it. It's that lousy drummer riding me that's got my goat.

MARGIE. I know. (*She puts a protecting arm around Hope and turns him to face the table with the cake and presents*) Come on. You ain't noticed your cake yet. Ain't it grand?

HOPE (*trying to brighten up*). Say, that's pretty. Ain't ever had a cake since Bessie — Six candles. Each for ten years, eh? Bejees, that's thoughtful of you.

PEARL. It was Hickey got it.

HOPE (*his tone forced*). Well, it was thoughtful of him. He means well, I guess. (*His eyes, fixed on the cake, harden angrily*) To hell with his cake. (*He starts to turn away. Pearl grabs his arm*)

PEARL. Wait, Harry. Yuh ain't seen de presents from Margie and me and Cora and Chuck and Rocky. And dere's a watch all engraved wid your name and de date from Hickey.

HOPE. To hell with it! Bejees, he can keep it! (*This time he does turn away*)

PEARL. Jees, he ain't even goin' to look at our presents.

MARGIE (*bitterly*). Dis is all wrong. We gotta put some life in dis party or I'll go nuts! Hey, Cora, what's de matter wid dat box? Can't yuh play for Harry? Yuh don't have to stop just because he kidded yuh!

HOPE (*rouses himself—with forced heartiness*). Yes, come on, Cora. You was playing it fine. (*Cora begins to play half-heartedly. Hope suddenly becomes almost tearfully sentimental*) It was Bessie's favorite tune. She was always singing it. It brings her back. I wish—(*He chokes up*)

HICKEY (*grins at him—amusedly*). Yes, we've all heard you tell us you thought the world of her, Governor.

HOPE (*looks at him with frightened suspicion*). Well, so I did, bejees! Everyone knows I did! (*Threateningly*) Bejees, if you say I didn't—

HICKEY (*soothingly*). Now, Governor. I didn't say anything. You're the only one knows the truth about that.

(*Hopes stares at him confusedly. Cora continues to play. For a moment there is a pause, broken by Jimmy Tomorrow who speaks with muzzy, self-pitying melancholy out of a sentimental dream.*)

JIMMY. Marjorie's favorite song was "Loch Lomond." She was beautiful and she played the piano beautifully and she had a beautiful voice. (*With gentle sorrow*) You were lucky, Harry. Bessie died. But there are more bitter sorrows than losing the woman one loves by the hand of death—

HICKEY (*with an amused wink at Hope*). Now, listen, Jimmy, you needn't go on. We've all heard that story about how you came back to Cape Town and found her in the hay with a staff officer. We know you like to believe that was what started you on the booze and ruined your life.

JIMMY (*stammers*). I—I'm talking to Harry. Will you kindly keep out of— (*With a pitiful defiance*) My life is not ruined!

HICKEY (*ignoring this—with a kidding grin*). But I'll bet when you admit the truth to yourself, you'll confess you were pretty sick of her hating you for getting drunk. I'll bet you were really damned relieved when she gave you such a good excuse. *(Jimmy stares at him strickenly. Hickey pats him on the back again—with sincere sympathy)* I know how it is, Jimmy. I —*(He stops abruptly and for a second he seems to lose his self-assurance and become confused)*

LARRY *(seizing on this with vindictive relish)*. Ha! So that's what happened to you, is it? Your iceman joke finally came home to roost, did it? *(He grins tauntingly)* You should have remembered there's truth in the old superstition that you'd better look out what you call because in the end it comes to you!

HICKEY *(himself again—grins to Larry kiddingly)*. Is that a fact, Larry? Well, well! Then you'd better watch out how you keep calling for that old Big Sleep! *(Larry starts and for a second looks superstitiously frightened. Abruptly Hickey changes to his jovial, bustling, master-of-ceremonies manner)* But what are we waiting for, boys and girls? Let's start the party rolling! *(He shouts to the bar)* Hey, Chuck and Rocky! Bring on the big surprise! Governor, you sit at the head of the table here. *(He makes Harry sit down on the chair at the end of the table, right. To Margie and Pearl)* Come on, girls, sit down. *(They sit side by side on Jimmy's right. Hickey bustles down to the left end of table)* I'll sit here at the foot. *(He sits, with Cora on his left and Joe on her left. Rocky and Chuck appear from the bar, each bearing a big tray laden with schooners of champagne which they start shoving in front of each member of the party.)*

ROCKY *(with forced cheeriness)*. Real champagne, bums! Cheer up! What is dis, a funeral? Jees, mixin' champagne wid Harry's redeye will knock yuh paralyzed! Ain't yuh never satisfied? *(He and Chuck finish serving out the schooners, grab the last two themselves and sit down in the two vacant chairs remaining near the middle of the table. As they do so, Hickey rises, a schooner in his hand.)*

HICKEY *(rapping on the table for order when there is nothing but a dead silence)*. Order! Order, Ladies and Gents! *(He catches Larry's eyes on the glass in his hand)* Yes, Larry, I'm going to drink with you this time. To prove I'm not teetotal because I'm afraid booze would make me spill my secrets, as you think.

(Larry looks sheepish. Hickey chuckles and goes on) No, I gave you the simple truth about that. I don't need booze or anything else any more. But I want to be sociable and propose a toast in honor of our old friend, Harry, and drink it with you. *(His eyes fix on Hugo, who is out again, his head on his plate— To Chuck, who is on Hugo's left)* Wake up our demon bomb-tosser, Chuck. We don't want corpses at this feast.

CHUCK *(gives Hugo a shake)*. Hey, Hugo, come up for air! Don't yuh see de champagne? *(Hugo blinks around and giggles foolishly)*

HUGO. Ve vill eat birthday cake and trink champagne beneath the villow tree! *(He grabs his schooner and takes a greedy gulp—then sets it back on the table with a grimace of distaste—in a strange, arrogantly disdainful tone, as if he were rebuking a butler)* Dis vine is unfit to trink. It has not properly been iced.

HICKEY *(amusedly)*. Always a high-toned swell at heart, eh, Hugo? God help us poor bums if you'd ever get to telling us where to get off! You'd have been drinking our blood beneath those willow trees! *(He chuckles. Hugo shrinks back in his chair, blinking at him, but Hickey is now looking up the table at Hope. He starts his toast, and as he goes on he becomes more moved and obviously sincere)* Here's the toast, Ladies and Gents! Here's to Harry Hope, who's been a friend in need to every one of us! Here's to the old Governor, the best sport and the kindest, biggest-hearted guy in the world! Here's wishing you all the luck there is, Harry, and long life and happiness! Come on, everybody! To Harry! Bottoms up! *(They have all caught his sincerity with eager relief. They raise their schooners with an enthusiastic chorus of "Here's how, Harry!" "Here's luck, Harry!" etc., and gulp half the wine down, Hickey leading them in this.)*

HOPE *(deeply moved—his voice husky)*. Bejees, thanks, all of you. Bejees, Hickey, you old son of a bitch, that's white of you! Bejees, I know you meant it, too.

HICKEY *(moved)*. Of course I meant it, Harry, old friend! And I mean it when I say I hope today will be the biggest day in your life, and in the lives of everyone here, the beginning of a new life of peace and contentment where no pipe dreams can ever nag at you again. Here's to that, Harry! *(He drains the remainder of his drink, but this time he drinks alone. In an instant the attitude of everyone has reverted to uneasy, suspicious defensiveness)*

ROCKY *(growls)*. Aw, forget dat bughouse line of bull for a minute, can't yuh?

HICKEY *(sitting down—good-naturedly)*. You're right, Rocky, I'm talking too much. It's Harry we want to hear from. Come on, Harry! *(He pounds his schooner on the table)* Speech! Speech!

(They try to recapture their momentary enthusiasm, rap their schooners on the table, call "Speech," but there is a hollow ring in it. Hope gets to his feet reluctantly, with a forced smile, a smoldering resentment beginning to show in his manner.)

HOPE *(lamely)*. Bejees, I'm no good at speeches. All I can say is thanks to everybody again for remembering me on my birthday. *(Bitterness coming out)* Only don't think because I'm sixty I'll be a bigger damned fool easy mark than ever! No, bejees! Like Hickey says, it's going to be a new day! This dump has got to be run like other dumps, so I can make some money and not just split even. People has got to pay what they owe me! I'm not running a damned orphan asylum for bums and crooks! Not a God-damned hooker shanty, either! Nor an Old Men's Home for lousy Anarchist tramps that ought to be in jail! I'm sick of being played for a sucker! *(They stare at him with stunned, bewildered hurt. He goes on in a sort of furious desperation, as if he hated himself for every word he said, and yet couldn't stop)* And don't think you're kidding me right now, either! I know damned well you're giving me the laugh behind my back, thinking to yourselves, The old, lying, pipe-dreaming faker, we've heard his bull about taking a walk around the ward for years, he'll never make it! He's yellow, he ain't got the guts, he's scared he'll find out— *(He glares around at them almost with hatred)* But I'll show you, bejees! *(He glares at Hickey)* I'll show you, too, you son of a bitch of a frying-pan-peddling bastard!

HICKEY *(heartily encouraging)*. That's the stuff, Harry! Of course you'll try to show me! That's what I want you to do!

(Harry glances at him with helpless dread —then drops his eyes and looks furtively around the table. All at once he becomes miserably contrite)

HOPE *(his voice catching)*. Listen, all of you! Bejees, forgive me. I lost my temper! I ain't feeling well! I got a hell of a grouch on! Bejees, you know you're all as welcome here as the flowers in May! *(They look at him with eager forgiveness. Rocky is the first one who can voice it)*

ROCKY. Aw, sure, Boss, you're always aces wid us, see?

HICKEY *(rises to his feet again. He addresses them now with the simple, convincing sincerity of one making a confession of which he is genuinely ashamed)*. Listen, everybody! I know you are sick of my gabbing, but I think this is the spot where I owe it to you to do a little explaining and apologize for some of the rough stuff I've had to pull on you. I know how it must look to you. As if I was a damned busybody who was not only interfering in your private business, but even sicking some of you on to nag at each other. Well, I have to admit that's true, and I'm damned sorry about it. But it simply had to be done! You must believe that! You know old Hickey. I was never one to start trouble. But this time I had to—for your own good! I had to make you help me with each other. I saw I couldn't do what I was after alone. Not in the time at my disposal. I knew when I came here I wouldn't be able to stay with you long. I'm slated to leave on a trip. I saw I'd have to hustle and use every means I could. *(With a joking boastfulness)* Why, if I had enough time, I'd get a lot of sport out of selling my line of salvation to each of you all by my lonesome. Like it was fun in the old days, when I traveled house to house, to convince some dame, who was sicking the dog on me, her house wouldn't be properly furnished unless she bought another wash boiler. And I could do it with you, all right. I know every one of you, inside and out, by heart. I may have been drunk when I've been here before, but old Hickey could never be so drunk he didn't have to see through people. I mean, everyone except himself. And, finally, he had to see through himself, too. *(He pauses. They stare at him, bitter, uneasy and fascinated. His manner changes to deep earnestness)* But here's the point to get. I swear I'd never act like I have if I wasn't absolutely sure it will be worth it to you in the end, after you're rid of the damned guilt that makes you lie to yourselves you're something you're not, and the remorse that nags at you and makes you hide behind lousy pipe dreams about tomorrow. You'll be in a today where there is no yesterday or tomorrow to worry you. You won't give a damn what you are any more. I wouldn't say this unless I knew, Brothers and Sisters. This peace is real! It's a fact! I know! Because I've got it! Here! Now! Right in front of you! You see the difference in me! You remember how I used to be! Even when I had two quarts of rotgut under my belt and joked and sang "Sweet Adeline," I still felt like a guilty skunk. But you can all see that I don't give a damn about anything now. And I promise you, by the time this day is over, I'll have every one of you feeling the same way! *(He pauses. They stare at him fascinatedly. He adds with a grin)* I guess that'll be about all from me, boys and girls—for the present. So let's get on with the party. *(He starts to sit down)*

LARRY *(sharply)*. Wait! *(Insistently—with a sneer)* I think it would help us poor pipe-dreaming sinners along the sawdust trail to salvation if you told us now what it was happened to you that converted you to this great peace you've found. *(More and more with a deliberate, provocative taunting)* I notice you didn't deny it when I asked you about the iceman. Did this great revelation of the evil habit of dreaming about tomorrow come to you after you found your wife was sick of you? *(While he is speaking the faces of the gang have lighted up vindictively, as if all at once they saw a chance to revenge themselves. As he finishes, a chorus of sneering taunts begins, punctuated by nasty, jeering laughter)*

HOPE. Bejees, you've hit it, Larry! I've noticed he hasn't shown her picture around this time!

MOSHER. He hasn't got it! The iceman took it away from him!

MARGIE. Jees, look at him! Who could blame her?

PEARL. She must be hard up to fall for an iceman!

CORA. Imagine a sap like him advisin' me and Chuck to git married!

CHUCK. Yeah! He done so good wid it!

JIMMY. At least I can say Marjorie chose an officer and a gentleman.

LEWIS. Come to look at you, Hickey, old chap, you've sprouted horns like a bloody antelope!

WETJOEN. Pigger, py Gott! Like a water buffalo's!

WILLIE *(sings to his Sailor Lad tune)*.
"Come up," she cried, "my iceman lad,
And you and I'll agree—"
(They all join in a jeering chorus, rapping with knuckles or glasses on the table at the indicated spot in the lyric.)
"And I'll show you the prettiest *(Rap, rap, rap)*
That ever you did see!"
(A roar of derisive, dirty laughter. But Hickey has remained unmoved by all this taunting. He grins good-naturedly, as if he enjoyed the joke at his expense, and joins in the laughter.)

HICKEY. Well, boys and girls, I'm glad to see you getting in good spirits for Harry's party, even if the joke is on me. I admit I asked for it by always pulling that iceman gag in the old days. So laugh all you like. *(He pauses. They do not laugh now. They are again staring at him with baffled uneasiness. He goes on thoughtfully)* Well, this forces my hand, I guess, your bringing up the subject of Evelyn. I didn't want to tell you yet. It's hardly an appropriate time, I meant to wait until the party was over. But you're getting the wrong idea about poor Evelyn, and I've got to stop that. *(He pauses again. There is a tense stillness in the room. He bows his head a little and says quietly)* I'm sorry to tell you my dearly beloved wife is dead. *(A gasp comes from the stunned company. They look away from him, shocked and miserably ashamed of themselves, except Larry who continues to stare at him)*

LARRY *(aloud to himself with a superstitious shrinking)*. Be God, I felt he'd brought the touch of death on him! *(Then suddenly he is even more ashamed of himself than the others and stammers)* Forgive me, Hickey! I'd like to cut my dirty tongue out! *(This releases a chorus of shame-faced mumbles from the crowd. "Sorry, Hickey." "I'm sorry, Hickey." "We're sorry, Hickey")*

HICKEY (*looking around at them—in a kindly, reassuring tone*). Now look here, everybody. You mustn't let this be a wet blanket on Harry's party. You're still getting me all wrong. There's no reason— You see, I don't feel any grief. (*They gaze at him startledly. He goes on with convincing sincerity*) I've got to feel glad, for her sake. Because she's at peace. She's rid of me at last. Hell, I don't have to tell you—you all know what I was like. You can imagine what she went through, married to a no-good cheater and drunk like I was. And there was no way out of it for her. Because she loved me. But now she is at peace like she always longed to be. So why should I feel sad? She wouldn't want me to feel sad. Why, all that Evelyn ever wanted out of life was to make me happy. (*He stops, looking around at them with a simple, gentle frankness. They stare at him in bewildered, incredulous confusion*)

CURTAIN

ACT THREE

SCENE: *Barroom of Harry Hope's, including a part of what had been the back room in Acts One and Two. In the right wall are two big windows, with the swinging doors to the street between them. The bar itself is at rear. Behind it is a mirror, covered with white mosquito netting to keep off the flies, and a shelf on which are barrels of cheap whiskey with spiggots and a small show case of bottled goods. At left of the bar is the doorway to the hall. There is a table at left, front, of barroom proper, with four chairs. At right, front, is a small free-lunch counter, facing left, with a space between it and the window for the dealer to stand when he dishes out soup at the noon hour. Over the mirror behind the bar are framed photographs of Richard Croker and Big Tim Sullivan, flanked by framed lithographs of John L. Sullivan and Gentleman Jim Corbett in ring costume.*

At left, in what had been the back room, with the dividing curtain drawn, the banquet table of Act Two has been broken up, and the tables are again in the crowded arrangement of Act One. Of these, we see one in the front row with five chairs at left of the barroom table, another with five chairs at left-rear of it, a third back by the rear wall with five chairs, and finally, at extreme left-front, one with four chairs, partly on and partly off stage, left.

It is around the middle of the morning of Hope's birthday, a hot summer day. There is sunlight in the street outside, but it does not hit the windows and the light in the back-room section is dim.

Jot Mott is moving around, a box of sawdust under his arm, strewing it over the floor. His manner is sullen, his face set in gloom. He ignores everyone. As the scene progresses, he finishes his sawdusting job, goes behind the lunch counter and cuts loaves of bread. Rocky is behind the bar, wiping it, washing glasses, etc. He wears his working clothes, sleeves rolled up. He looks sleepy, irritable and worried. At the barroom table, front, Larry sits in a chair, facing right-front. He has no drink in front of him. He stares ahead, deep in harried thought. On his right, in a chair facing right, Hugo sits sprawled forward, arms and head on the table as usual, a whiskey glass beside his limp hand. At rear of the front table at left of them, in a chair facing left, Parritt is sitting. He is staring in front of him in a tense, strained immobility.

As the curtain rises, Rocky finishes his work behind the bar. He comes forward and drops wearily in the chair at right of Larry's table, facing left.

ROCKY. Nuttin' now till de noon rush from de Market. I'm goin' to rest my fanny. (*Irritably*) If I ain't a sap to let Chuck kid me into workin' his time so's he can take de mornin' off. But I got sick of arguin' wid 'im. I says, "Aw right, git married! What's it to me?" Hickey's got de bot' of dem bums. (*Bitterly*) Some party last night, huh? Jees, what a funeral! It was jinxed from de start, but his tellin' about his wife croakin' put de K.O on it.

LARRY. Yes, it turned out it wasn't a birthday feast but a wake!

ROCKY. Him promisin' he'd cut out de bughouse bull about peace—and den he went on talkin' and talkin' like he couldn't stop! And all de gang sneakin' upstairs, leavin' free booze and eats like dey was poison! It didn't do dem no good if dey thought dey'd shake him. He's been hoppin' from room to room all night. Yuh can't stop him. He's got his Reform Wave goin' strong dis mornin'! Did yuh notice him drag Jimmy out de foist ting to get his laundry and his clothes pressed so he wouldn't have no excuse? And he give Willie de dough to buy his stuff back from Solly's. And all de rest been brushin' and shavin' demselves wid de shakes—

LARRY (*defiantly*). He didn't come to my room! He's afraid I might ask him a few questions.

ROCK. (*scornfully*). Yeah? It don't look to me he's scared of yuh. I'd say you was scared of him.

LARRY (*stung*). You'd lie, then!

PARRITT (*jerks round to look at Larry —sneeringly*). Don't let him kid you, Rocky. He had his door locked. I couldn't get in, either.

ROCKY. Yeah, who d'yuh tink yuh're kiddin', Larry? He's showed you up, aw right. Like he says, if yuh was so anxious to croak, why wouldn't yuh hop off your fire escape long ago?

LARRY (*defiantly*). Because it'd be a coward's quitting, that's why!

PARRITT. He's all quitter, Rocky. He's a yellow old faker!

LARRY (*turns on him*). You lying punk! Remember what I warned you—!

ROCKY (*scowls at Parritt*). Yeah, keep outta dis, you! Where d'yuh get a license to butt in? Shall I gave him de bum's rush, Larry? If you don't want him around, nobody else don't.

LARRY (*forcing an indifferent tone*). No. Let him stay. I don't mind him. He's nothing to me. (*Rocky shrugs his shoulders and yawns sleepily*)

PARRITT. You're right, I have nowhere to go. You're the only one in the world I can turn to.

ROCKY (*drowsily*). Yuh're a soft old sap, Larry. He's a no-good louse like Hickey. He don't belong. (*He yawns*) I'm all in. Not a wink of sleep. Can't keep my peepers open. (*His eyes close and his head nods. Parritt gives him a glance and then gets up and slinks over to slide into the chair on Larry's left, between him and Rocky. Larry shrinks away, but determinedly ignores him*)

PARRITT (*bending toward him—in a low, ingratiating, apologetic voice*). I'm sorry for riding you, Larry. But you get my goat when you act as if you didn't care a damn what happened to me, and keep your door locked so I can't talk to you. (*Then hopefully*) But that was to keep Hickey out, wasn't it? I don't blame you. I'm getting to hate him. I'm getting more and more scared of him. Especially since he told us his wife was dead. It's that queer feeling he gives me that I'm mixed up with him some way. I don't know why, but it started me thinking about Mother—as if she was dead. (*With a strange undercurrent of something like satisfaction in his pitying tone*) I suppose she might as well be. Inside herself, I mean. It must kill her when she thinks of me—I know she doesn't want to, but she can't help it. After all, I'm her only kid. She used to spoil me and made a pet of me. Once in a great while, I mean. When she remembered me. As if she wanted to make up for something. As if she felt guilty. So she must have loved me a little, even if she never let it interfere with her freedom. (*With a strange pathetic wistfulness*) Do you know, Larry, I once had a sneaking suspicion that maybe, if the truth was known, you were my father.

LARRY (*violently*). You damned fool! Who put that insane idea in your head? You know it's a lie! Anyone in the Coast crowd could tell you I never laid eyes on your mother till after you were born.

PARRITT. Well, I'd hardly ask them, would I? I know you're right, though, because I asked her. She brought me up to be frank and ask her anything, and she'd always tell me the truth. (*Abruptly*) But I was talking about how she must feel now about me. My getting through with the Movement. She'll never forgive that. The Movement is her life. And it must be the final knockout for her if she knows I was the one who sold—

LARRY. Shut up, damn you!

PARRITT. It'll kill her. And I'm sure she knows it must have been me. (*Suddenly with desperate urgency*) But I never thought the cops would get her! You've got to believe that! You've got to see what my only reason was! I'll admit what I told you last night was a lie—that bunk about getting patriotic and my duty to my country. But here's the true reason, Larry— the only reason! It was just for money! I got stuck on a whore and wanted dough to blow in on her and have a good time!

That's all I did it for! Just money! Honest! *(He has the terrible grotesque air, in confessing his sordid baseness, of one who gives an excuse which exonerates him from any real guilt)*

LARRY *(grabs him by the shoulder and shakes him).* God damn you, shut up! What the hell is it to me? *(Rocky starts awake)*

ROCKY. What's comin' off here?

LARRY *(controlling himself).* Nothing. This gabby young punk was talking my ear off, that's all. He's a worse pest than Hickey.

ROCKY *(drowsily).* Yeah, Hickey— Say, listen, what d'yuh mean about him bein' scared you'd ask him questions? What questions?

LARRY. Well, I feel he's hiding something. You notice he didn't say what his wife died of.

ROCKY *(rebukingly).* Aw, lay off dat. De poor guy— What are yuh gettin' at, anyway? Yuh don't tink it's just a gag of his?

LARRY. I don't. I'm damned sure he's brought death here with him. I feel the cold touch of it on him.

ROCKY. Aw, bunk! You got croakin' on de brain, Old Cemetery. *(Suddenly Rocky's eyes widen)* Say! D'yuh mean yuh tink she committed suicide, 'count of his cheatin' or someting?

LARRY *(grimly).* It wouldn't surprise me. I'd be the last to blame her.

ROCKY *(scornfully).* But dat's crazy! Jees, if she'd done dat, he wouldn't tell us he was glad about it, would he? He ain't dat big a bastard.

PARRITT *(speaks up from his own preoccupation—strangely).* You know better than that, Larry. You know she'd never commit suicide. She's like you. She'll hang on to life even when there's nothing left but—

LARRY *(stung—turns on him viciously).* And how about you? Be God, if you had any guts or decency—! *(He stops guiltily)*

PARRITT *(sneeringly).* I'd take that hop off your fire escape you're too yellow to take, I suppose?

LARRY *(as if to himself).* No! Who am I to judge? I'm done with judging.

PARRITT *(tauntingly).* Yes, I suppose you'd like that, wouldn't you?

ROCKY *(irritably mystified).* What de hell's all dis about? *(To Parritt)* What d'you know about Hickey's wife? How d'yuh know she didn't—?

LARRY *(with forced belittling casualness).* He doesn't. Hickey's addled the little brains he's got. Shove him back to his own table, Rocky. I'm sick of him.

ROCKY *(to Parritt, threateningly).* Yuh heard Larry? I'd like an excuse to give yuh a good punch in de snoot. So move quick!

PARRITT *(gets up—to Larry).* If you think moving to another table will get rid of me! *(He moves away—then adds with bitter reproach)* Gee, Larry, that's a hell of a way to treat me, when I've trusted you, and I need your help. *(He sits down in his old place and sinks into a wounded, self-pitying brooding)*

ROCKY *(going back to his train of thought).* Jees, if she committed suicide, yuh got to feel sorry for Hickey, huh? Yuh can understand how he'd go bughouse and not be responsible for all de crazy stunts he's stagin' here. *(Then puzzledly)* But how can yuh be sorry for him when he says he's glad she croaked, and yuh can tell he means it? *(With weary exasperation)* Aw, nuts! I don't get nowhere tryin' to figger his game. *(His face hardening)* But I know dis. He better lay off me and my stable! *(He pauses—then sighs)* Jees, Larry, what a night dem two pigs give me! When de party went dead, dey pinched a coupla bottles and brung dem up deir room and got stinko. I don't get a wink of sleep, see? Just as I'd drop off on a chair here, dey'd come down lookin' for trouble. Or else dey'd raise hell upstairs, laughin' and. singin', so I'd get scared dey'd get de joint pinched and go up to tell dem to can de noise. And every time dey'd crawl my frame wid de same old argument. Dey'd say, "So yuh agreed wid Hickey, do yuh, yuh dirty little Ginny? We're whores, are we? Well, we agree wid Hickey about you, see! Yuh're nuttin' but a lousy pimp!" Den I'd slap dem. Not beat 'em up, like a pimp would. Just slap dem. But it don't do no good. Dey'd keep at it over and over. Jees, I get de earache just thinkin' of it! "Listen," dey'd say, "if we're whores we gotta right to have a reg'lar pimp and not stand for no punk imitation! We're sick of wearin' out our dogs poundin' sidewalks for a double-crossin' bartender, when all de thanks we get is he looks down on us.

We'll find a guy who really needs us to take care of him and ain't ashamed of it. Don't expect us to work tonight, 'cause we won't, see? Not if de streets was blocked wid sailors! We're goin' on strike and yuh can like it or lump it!" (*He shakes his head*) Whores goin' on strike! Can yuh tie that? (*Going on with his story*) Dey says, "We're takin' a holiday. We're goin' to beat it down to Coney Island and shoot the chutes and maybe we'll come back and maybe we won't. And you can go to hell!" So dey put on deir lids and beat it, de bot' of dem stinko. (*He sighs dejectedly. He seems grotesquely like a harried family man, henpecked and browbeaten by a nagging wife. Larry is deep in his own bitter preoccupation and hasn't listened to him. Chuck enters from the hall at rear. He has his straw hat with the gaudy band in his hand and wears a Sunday-best blue suit with a high stiff collar. He looks sleepy, hot, uncomfortable and grouchy*)

CHUCK (*glumly*). Hey, Rocky. Cora wants a sherry flip. For her noives.

ROCKY (*turns indignantly*). Sherry flip! Christ, she don't need nuttin' for her noive! What's she tink dis is, de Waldorf?

CHUCK. Yeah, I told her, what would we use for sherry, and dere wasn't no egg unless she laid one. She says, "Is dere a law yuh can't go out and buy de makings, yuh big tramp?" (*Resentfully puts his straw hat on his head at a defiant tilt*) To hell wid her! She'll drink booze or nuttin'! (*He goes behind the bar to draw a glass of whiskey from a barrel*)

ROCKY (*sarcastically*). Jees, a guy oughta give his bride anything she wants on de weddin' day, I should tink! (*As Chuck comes from behind the bar, Rocky surveys him derisively*) Pipe de bridegroom, Larry! All dolled up for de killin'! (*Larry pays no attention*)

CHUCK. Aw, shut up!

ROCKY. One week on dat farm in Joisey, dat's what I give yuh! Yuh'll come runnin' in here some night yellin' for a shot of booze 'cause de crickets is after yuh! (*Disgustedly*) Jees, Chuck, dat louse Hickey's coitinly made a prize coupla suckers outa youse.

CHUCK (*unguardedly*). Yeah. I'd like to give him one sock in de puss—just one! (*Then angrily*) Aw, can dat! What's he got to do wid it? Ain't we always said we

was goin' to? So we're goin' to, see? And don't give me no argument! (*He stares at Rocky truculently. But Rocky only shrugs his shoulders with weary disgust and Chuck subsides into complaining gloom*) If on'y Cora'd cut out de beefin'. She don't gimme a minute's rest all night. De same old stuff over and over! Do I really want to marry her? I says, "Sure, Baby, why not?" She says, "Yeah, but after a week yuh'll be tinkin' what a sap you was. Yuh'll make dat an excuse to go off on a periodical, and den I'll be tied for life to a no-good soak, and de foist ting I know yuh'll have me out hustlin' again, your own wife!" Den she'd bust out cryin', and I'd get sore. "Yuh're a liar," I'd say. "I ain't never taken your dough 'cept when I was drunk and not workin'!" "Yeah," she'd say, "and how long will yuh stay sober now? Don't tink yuh can kid me wid dat water-wagon bull! I've heard it too often." Dat'd make me sore and I'd say, "Don't call me a liar. But I wish I was drunk right now, because if I was, yuh wouldn't be keepin' me awake all night beefin'. If yuh opened your yap, I'd knock de stuffin' outa yuh!" Den she'd yell, "Dat's a sweet way to talk to de goil yuh're goin' to marry." (*He sighs explosively*) Jees, she's got me hangin' on de ropes! (*He glances with vengeful yearning at the drink of whiskey in his hand*) Jees, would I like to get a quart of dis redeye under my belt!

ROCKY. Well, why de hell don't yuh?

CHUCK (*instantly suspicious and angry*). Sure! You'd like dat, wouldn't yuh? I'm wise to you! Yuh don't wanta see me get married and settle down like a reg'lar guy! Yuh'd like me to stay paralyzed all de time, so's I'd be like you, a lousy pimp!

ROCKY (*springs to his feet, his face hardened viciously*). Listen! I don't take dat even from you, see!

CHUCK (*puts his drink on the bar and clenches his fists*). Yeah? Wanta make somethin' of it? (*Jeeringly*) Don't make me laugh! I can lick ten of youse wid one mit!

ROCKY (*reaching for his hip pocket*). Not wid lead in your belly, yuh won't!

JOE (*has stopped cutting when the quarrel started—expostulating*). Hey, you, Rocky and Chuck! Cut it out! You's ole friends! Don't let dat Hickey make you crazy!

CHUCK *(turns on him)*. Keep outa our business, yuh black bastard!

ROCKY *(like Chuck, turns on Joe, as if their own quarrel was forgotten and they became natural allies against an alien)*. Stay where yuh belong, yuh doity nigger!

JOE *(snarling with rage, springs from behind the lunch counter with the bread knife in his hand)*. You white sons of bitches! I'll rip your guts out! *(Chuck snatches a whiskey bottle from the bar and raises it above his head to hurl at Joe. Rocky jerks a short-barreled, nickel-plated revolver from his hip pocket. At this moment Larry pounds on the table with his fist and bursts into a sardonic laugh)*

LARRY. That's it! Murder each other, you damned loons, with Hickey's blessing! Didn't I tell you he'd brought death with him? *(His interruption startles them. They pause to stare at him, their fighting fury suddenly dies out and they appear deflated and sheepish)*

ROCKY *(to Joe)*. Aw right, you. Leggo dat shiv and I'll put dis gat away.

(Joe sullenly goes back behind the counter and slaps the knife on top of it. Rocky slips the revolver back in his pocket. Chuck lowers the bottle to the bar. Hugo, who has awakened and raised his head when Larry pounded on the table, now giggles foolishly.)

HUGO. Hello, leedle peoples! Neffer mind! Soon you vill eat hot dogs beneath the villow trees and trink free vine— *(Abruptly in a haughty fastidious tone)* The champagne vas not properly iced. *(With guttural anger)* Gottamned liar, Hickey! Does that prove I vant to be aristocrat? I love only the proletariat! I vill lead them! I vill be like a Gott to them! They vill be my slaves! *(He stops in bewildered self-amazement—to Larry appealingly)* I am very trunk, no, Larry? I talk foolishness. I am so trunk, Larry, old friend, am I not, I don't know vhat I say?

LARRY *(pityingly)*. You're raving drunk, Hugo. I've never seen you so paralyzed. Lay your head down now and sleep it off.

HUGO *(gratefully)*. Yes. I should sleep. I am too crazy trunk. *(He puts his head on his arms and closes his eyes)*

JOE *(behind the lunch counter—brooding superstitiously)*. You's right, Larry. Bad luck come in de door when Hickey come. I's an ole gamblin' man and I knows bad luck when I feels it! *(Then defiantly)* But it's white man's bad luck. He can't jinx me! *(He comes from behind the counter and goes to the bar—addressing Rocky stiffly)* De bread's cut and I's finished my job. Do I get de drink I's earned? *(Rocky gives him a hostile look but shoves a bottle and glass at him. Joe pours a brimful drink—sullenly)* I's finished wid dis dump for keeps. *(He takes a key from his pocket and slaps it on the bar)* Here's de key to my room. I ain't comin' back. I's goin' to my own folks where I belong. I don't stay where I's not wanted. I's sick and tired of messin' round wid white men. *(He gulps down his drink —then looking around defiantly he deliberately throws his whiskey glass on the floor and smashes it)*

ROCKY. Hey! What de hell—!

JOE *(with a sneering dignity)*. I's on'y savin' you de trouble, White Boy. Now you don't have to break it, soon's my back's turned, so's no white man kick about drinkin' from de same glass. *(He walks stiffly to the street door—then turns for a parting shot—boastfully)* I's tired of loafin' 'round wid a lot of bums. I's a gamblin' man. I's gonna get in a big crap game and win me a big bankroll. Den I'll get de okay to open up my old gamblin' house for colored men. Den maybe I comes back here sometime to see de bums. Maybe I throw a twenty-dollar bill on de bar and say, "Drink it up," and listen when dey all pat me on de back and say, "Joe, you sure is white." But I'll say, "No, I'm black and my dough is black man's dough, and you's proud to drink wid me or you don't get no drink!" Or maybe I just says, "You can all go to hell. I don't lower myself drinkin' wid no white trash!" *(He opens the door to go out—then turns again)* And dat ain't no pipe dream! I'll git de money for my stake today, somehow, somewheres! If I has to borrow a gun and stick up some white man, I gets it! You wait and see! *(He swaggers out through the swinging doors)*

CHUCK *(angrily)*. Can yuh beat de noive of dat dinge! Jees, if I wasn't dressed up, I'd go out and mop up de street wid him!

ROCKY. Aw, let him go, de poor old dope! Him and his gamblin' house! He'll be back tonight askin' Harry for his room and bummin' me for a ball. *(Vengefully)* Den I'll be de one to smash de glass! I'll loin him his place!

(The swinging doors are pushed open and Willie Oban enters from the street. He is shaved and wears an expensive, well-cut suit, good shoes and clean linen. He is absolutely sober, but his face is sick, and his nerves in a shocking state of shakes.)

CHUCK. Another guy all dolled up! Got your clothes from Solly's, huh, Willie? *(Derisively)* Now yuh can sell dem back to him again tomorrow.

WILLIE *(stiffly)*. No, I—I'm through with that stuff. Never again. *(He comes to the bar)*

ROCKY *(sympathetically)*. Yuh look sick, Willie. Take a ball to pick yuh up. *(He pushes a bottle toward him)*

WILLIE *(eyes the bottle yearningly but shakes his head—determinedly)*. No, thanks. The only way to stop is to stop. I'd have no chance if I went to the D.A.'s office smelling of booze.

CHUCK. Yuh're really goin' dere?

WILLIE *(stiffly)*. I said I was, didn't I? I just came back here to rest a few minutes, not because I needed any booze. I'll show that cheap drummer I don't have to have any Dutch courage— *(Guiltily)* But he's been very kind and generous staking me. He can't help his insulting manner, I suppose. *(He turns away from the bar)* My legs are a bit shaky yet. I better sit down a while. *(He goes back and sits at the left of the second table, facing Parritt, who gives him a scowling, suspicious glance and then ignores him. Rocky looks at Chuck and taps his head disgustedly. Captain Lewis appears in the doorway from the hall)*

CHUCK *(mutters)*. Here's anudder one. *(Lewis looks spruce and clean-shaven. His ancient tweed suit has been brushed and his frayed linen is clean. His manner is full of a forced, jaunty self-assurance. But he is sick and beset by katzenjammer.)*

LEWIS. Good morning, gentlemen. *(He passes along the front of bar to look out in the street)* A jolly fine morning, too. *(He turns back to the bar)* An eye-opener? I think not. Not required, Rocky, old chum. Feel extremely fit, as a matter of fact. Though can't say I slept much, thanks to that interfering ass, Hickey, and that stupid bounder of a Boer. *(His face hardens)* I've had about all I can take from that fellow. It's my own fault, of course, for allowing a brute of a Dutch farmer to become familiar. Well, it's come

to a parting of the ways now, and good riddance. Which reminds me, here's my key. *(He puts it on the bar)* I shan't be coming back. Sorry to be leaving good old Harry and the rest of you, of course, but I can't continue to live under the same roof with that fellow. *(He stops, stiffening into hostility as Wetjoen enters from the hall, and pointedly turns his back on him. Wetjoen glares at him sneeringly. He, too, has made an effort to spruce up his appearance, and his bearing has a forced swagger of conscious physical strength. Behind this, he is sick and feebly holding his booze-sodden body together)*

ROCKY *(to Lewis—disgustedly putting the key on the shelf in back of the bar)*. So Hickey's kidded the pants offa you, too? Yuh tink yuh're leavin' here, huh?

WETJOEN *(jeeringly)*. Ja! Dot's vhat he kids himself.

LEWIS *(ignores him—airily)*. Yes, I'm leaving. But that ass, Hickey, has nothing to do with it. Been thinking things over. Time I turned over a new leaf, and all that.

WETJOEN. He's going to get a job! Dot's what he says!

ROCKY. What at, for Chris' sake?

LEWIS *(keeping his airy manner)*. Oh, anything. I mean, not manual labor, naturally, but anything that calls for a bit of brains and education. However humble. Beggars can't be choosers. I'll see a pal of mine at the Consulate. He promised any time I felt an energetic fit he'd get me a post with the Cunard—clark in the office or something of the kind.

WETJOEN. Ja! At Limey Consulate they promise anything to get rid of him vhen he comes there tronk! They're scared to call the police and have him pinched because it vould scandal in the papers make about a Limey officer and chentleman!

LEWIS. As a matter of fact, Rocky, I only wish a post temporarily. Means to an end, you know. Save up enough for a first-class passage home, that's the bright idea.

WETJOEN. He's sailing back to home, sveet home! Dot's biggest pipe dream of all. What leetle brain the poor Limey has left, dot isn't in whiskey pickled, Hickey has made crazy! *(Lewis' fists clench, but he manages to ignore this)*

CHUCK *(feels sorry for Lewis and turns on Wetjoen—sarcastically)*. Hickey ain't made no sucker outa you, huh? You're too foxy, huh? But I'll bet you tink yuh're goin' out and land a job, too.

WETJOEN (*bristles*). I am, ja. For me, it is easy. Because I put on no airs of chentleman. I am not ashamed to vork vith my hands. I vas a farmer before the war ven ploody Limey thieves steal my country. (*Boastfully*) Anyone I ask for job can see vith one look I have the great strength to do work of ten ordinary mens.

LEWIS (*sneeringly*). Yes, Chuck, you remember he gave a demonstration of his extraordinary muscles last night when he helped to move the piano.

CHUCK. Yuh couldn't even hold up your corner. It was your fault de damned box almost fell down de stairs.

WETJOEN. My hands vas sweaty! Could I help dot my hands slip? I could de whole veight of it lift! In old days in Transvaal, I lift loaded oxcart by the axle! So vhy shouldn't I get job? Dot longshoreman boss, Dan, he tell me any time I like, he take me on. And Benny he from de Market he promise me same.

LEWIS. You remember, Rocky, it was one of those rare occasions when the Boer that walks like a man—spelled with a double o, by the way—was buying drinks and Dan and Benny were stony. They'd bloody well have promised him the moon.

ROCKY. Yeah, yuh big boob, dem boids was on'y kiddin' yuh.

WETJOEN (*angrily*). Dot's lie! You vill see dis morning I get job! I'll show dot bloody Limey chentleman, and dot liar, Hickey! And I need vork only leetle vhile to save money for my passage home. I need not much money because I am not ashamed to travel steerage. I don't put on first-cabin airs! (*Tauntingly*) Und *I* can go home to my country! Vhen I get there, they vill let *me* come in!

LEWIS (*grows rigid—his voice trembling with repressed anger*). There was a rumor in South Africa, Rocky, that a certain Boer officer—if you call the leaders of a rabble of farmers officers—kept advising Cronje to retreat and not stand and fight—

WETJOEN. And I vas right! I vas right! He got surrounded at Poardeberg! He had to surrender!

LEWIS (*ignoring him*). Good strategy, no doubt, but a suspicion grew afterwards into a conviction among the Boers that the officer's caution was prompted by a desire to make his personal escape. His country-

men felt extremely savage about it, and his family disowned him. So I imagine there would be no welcoming committee waiting on the dock, nor delighted relatives making the veldt ring with their happy cries—

WETJOEN (*with guilty rage*). All lies! You Gottamned Limey— (*Trying to control himself and copy Lewis' manner*) I also haf heard rumors of a Limey officer who, after the war, lost all his money gambling vhen he was tronk. But they found out it vas regiment money, too, he lost—

LEWIS (*loses his control and starts for him*). You bloody Dutch scum!

ROCKY (*leans over the bar and stops Lewis with a straight-arm swipe on the chest*). Cut it out! (*At the same moment Chuck grabs Wetjoen and yanks him back*)

WETJOEN (*struggling*). Let him come! I saw them come before—at Modder River, Magersfontein, Spion Kopje—waving their silly swords, so afraid they couldn't show off how brave they vas!—and I kill them vith my rifle so easy! (*Vindictively*) Listen to me, you Cecil! Often when I am tronk and kidding you I say I am sorry I missed you, but now, py Gott, I am sober, and I don't joke, and I say it!

LARRY (*gives a sardonic guffaw—with his comically crazy, intense whisper*). Be God, you can't say Hickey hasn't the miraculous touch to raise the dead, when he can start the Boer War raging again! (*This interruption acts like a cold douche on Lewis and Wetjoen. They subside, and Rocky and Chuck let go of them. Lewis turns his back on the Boer*)

LEWIS (*attempting a return of his jaunty manner, as if nothing had happened*). Well, time I was on my merry way to see my chap at the Consulate. The early bird catches the job, what? Good-bye and good luck, Rocky, and everyone. (*He starts for the street door*)

WETJOEN. Py Gott, if dot Limey can go, I can go! (*He hurries after Lewis. But Lewis, his hand about to push the swinging doors open, hesitates, as though struck by a sudden paralysis of the will, and Wetjoen has to jerk back to avoid bumping into him. For a second they stand there, one behind the other, staring over the swinging doors into the street*)

ROCKY. Well, why don't yuh beat it?

LEWIS (*guiltily casual*). Eh? Oh, just

happened to think. Hardly the decent thing to pop off without saying good-bye to old Harry. One of the best, Harry. And good old Jimmy, too. They ought to be down any moment. *(He pretends to notice Wetjoen for the first time and steps away from the door—apologizing as to a stranger)* Sorry. I seem to be blocking your way out.

WETJOEN *(stiffly)*. No. I vait to say good-bye to Harry and Jimmy, too. *(He goes to right of door behind the lunch counter and looks through the window, his back to the room. Lewis takes up a similar stand at the window on the left of door)*

CHUCK. Jees, can yuh beat dem simps! *(He picks up Cora's drink at the end of the bar)* Hell, I'd forgot Cora. She'll be trowin' a fit. *(He goes into the hall with the drink)*

ROCKY *(looks after him disgustedly)*. Dat's right, wait on her and spoil her, yuh poor sap! *(He shakes his head and begins to wipe the bar mechanically)*

WILLIE *(is regarding Parritt across the table from him with an eager, calculating eye. He leans over and speaks in a low confidential tone)*. Look here, Parritt. I'd like to have a talk with you.

PARRITT *(starts—scowling defensively)*. What about?

WILLIE *(his manner becoming his idea of a crafty criminal lawyer's)*. About the trouble you're in. Oh, I know. You don't admit it. You're quite right. That's my advice. Deny everything. Keep your mouth shut. Make no statements whatever without first consulting your attorney.

PARRITT. Say! What the hell—?

WILLIE. But you can trust me. I'm a lawyer, and it's just occurred to me you and I ought to co-operate. Of course I'm going to see the D.A. this morning about a job on his staff. But that may take time. There may not be an immediate opening. Meanwhile it would be a good idea for me to take a case or two, on my own, and prove my brilliant record in law school was no flash in the pan. So why not retain me as your attorney?

PARRITT. You're crazy! What do I want with a lawyer?

WILLIE. That's right. Don't admit anything. But you can trust me, so let's not beat about the bush. You got in trouble out on the Coast, eh? And now you're

hiding out. Any fool can spot that. *(Lowering his voice still more)* You feel safe here, and maybe you are, for a while. But remember, they get you in the end. I know from my father's experience. No one could have felt safer than he did. When anyone mentioned the law to him, he nearly died laughing. But—

PARRITT. You crazy mutt! *(Turning to Larry with a strained laugh)* Did you get that, Larry? This damned fool thinks the cops are after me!

LARRY *(bursts out with his true reaction before he thinks to ignore him)*. I wish to God they were! And so should you, if you had the honor of a louse! *(Parritt stares into his eyes guiltily for a second. Then he smiles sneeringly)*

PARRITT. And you're the guy who kids himself he's through with the Movement! You old lying faker, you're still in love with it! *(Larry ignores him again now)*

WILLIE *(disappointedly)*. Then you're not in trouble, Parritt? I was hoping— But never mind. No offense meant. Forget it.

PARRITT *(condescendingly—his eyes on Larry)*. Sure. That's all right, Willie. I'm not sore at you. It's that damned old faker that gets my goat. *(He slips out of his chair and goes quietly over to sit in the chair beside Larry he had occupied before —in a low, insinuating, intimate tone)* I think I understand, Larry. It's really Mother you still love—isn't it?—in spite of the dirty deal she gave you. But hell, what did you expect? She was never true to anyone but herself and the Movement. But I understand how you can't help still feeling—because I still love her, too. *(Pleading in a strained, desperate tone)* You know I do, don't you? You must! So you see I couldn't have expected they'd catch her! You've got to believe me that I sold them out just to get a few lousy dollars to blow in on a whore. No other reason, honest! There couldn't possibly be any other reason! *(Again he has a strange air of exonerating himself from guilt by this shameless confession)*

LARRY *(trying not to listen, has listened with increasing tension)*. For the love of Christ will you leave me in peace! I've told you you can't make me judge you! But if you don't keep still, you'll be saying something soon that will make you vomit your own soul like a drink of nickel rot-

gut that won't stay down! *(He pushes
back his chair and springs to his feet)* To
hell with you! *(He goes to the bar)*

PARRITT *(jumps up and starts to follow him—desperately).* Don't go, Larry!
You've got to help me! *(But Larry is at
the bar, back turned, and Rocky is scowling at him. He stops, shrinking back into
himself helplessly, and turns away. He
goes to the table where he had been before, and this time he takes the chair at
rear facing directly front. He puts his elbows on the table, holding his head in his
hands as if he had a splitting headache)*

LARRY. Set 'em up, Rocky. I swore I'd
have no more drinks on Hickey, if I died
of drought, but I've changed my mind!
Be God, he owes it to me, and I'd get
blind to the world now if it was the Iceman of Death himself treating! *(He stops,
startledly, a superstitious awe coming into
his face)* What made me say that, I wonder. *(With a sardonic laugh)* Well, be
God, it fits, for Death was the Iceman
Hickey called to his home!

ROCKY. Aw, forget dat iceman gag! De
poor dame is dead. *(Pushing a bottle and
glass at Larry)* Gwan and get paralyzed!
I'll be glad to see one bum in dis dump
act natural. *(Larry downs a drink and
pours another)*

*(Ed Mosher appears in the doorway from
the hall. The same change which is apparent in the manner and appearance of the
others shows in him. He is sick, his nerves
are shattered, his eyes are aprehensive, but
he, too, puts on an exaggeratedly self-
confident bearing. He saunters to the bar
between Larry and the street entrance.)*

MOSHER. Morning, Rocky. Hello, Larry.
Glad to see Brother Hickey hasn't cor-
rupted you to temperance. I wouldn't
mind a shot myself. *(As Rocky shoves a
bottle toward him he shakes his head)* But
I remember the only breath-killer in this
dump is coffee beans. The boss would
never fall for that. No man can run a circus successfully who believes guys chew
coffee beans because they like them. *(He
pushes the bottle away)* No, much as I
need one after the hell of a night I've
had— *(He scowls)* That drummer son of
a drummer! I had to lock him out. But I
could hear him through the wall doing
his spiel to someone all night long. Still at
it with Jimmy and Harry when I came
down just now. But the hardest to take

was that flannel-mouth, flat-foot Mick trying to tell me where I got off! I had to
lock him out, too. *(As he says this, Mc-
Gloin comes in the doorway from the hall.
The change in his appearance and manner
is identical with that of Mosher and the
others)*

MCGLOIN. He's a liar, Rocky! It was me
locked him out! *(Mosher starts to flare up
—then ignores him. They turn their backs
on each other. McGloin starts into the
back-room section)*

WILLIE. Come and sit here, Mac. You're
just the man I want to see. If I'm to take
your case, we ought to have a talk before
we leave.

MCGLOIN *(contemptuously).* We'll have
no talk. You damned fool, do you think
I'd have your father's son for my lawyer?
They'd take one look at you and bounce
us both out on our necks! *(Willie winces
and shrinks down in his chair. McGloin
goes to the first table beyond him and sits
with his back to the bar)* I don't need a
lawyer, anyway. To hell with the law! All
I've got to do is see the right ones and get
them to pass the word. They will, too.
They know I was framed. And once
they've passed the word, it's as good as
done, law or no law.

MOSHER. God, I'm glad I'm leaving this
madhouse! *(He pulls his key from his
pocket and slaps it on the bar)* Here's my
key, Rocky.

MCGLOIN *(pulls his from his pocket).*
And here's mine. *(He tosses it to Rocky)*
I'd rather sleep in the gutter than pass another night under the same roof with that
loon, Hickey, and a lying circus grifter!
(He adds darkly) And if that hat fits anyone here, let him put it on! *(Mosher turns
toward him furiously but Rocky leans
over the bar and grabs his arm)*

ROCKY. Nix! Take it easy! *(Mosher subsides. Rocky tosses the key on the shelf—
disgustedly)* You boids gimme a pain. It'd
soive you right if I wouldn't give de keys
back to yuh tonight.

*(They both turn on him resentfully, but
there is an interruption as Cora appears
in the doorway from the hall with Chuck
behind her. She is drunk, dressed in her
gaudy best, her face plastered with rouge
and mascara, her hair a bit disheveled, her
hat on anyhow.)*

CORA *(comes a few steps inside the bar
—with a strained bright giggle).* Hello,

everybody! Here we go! Hickey just told us, ain't it time we beat it, if we're really goin'. So we're showin' de bastard, ain't we, Honey? He's comin' right down wid Harry and Jimmy. Jees, dem two look like dey was goin' to de electric chair! *(With frightened anger)* If I had to listen to any more of Hickey's bunk, I'd brain him. *(She puts her hand on Chuck's arm)* Come on, Honey. Let's get started before he comes down.

CHUCK *(sullenly)*. Sure, anyting yuh say, Baby.

CORA *(turns on him truculently)*. Yeah? Well, I say we stop at de foist reg'lar dump and yuh gotta blow me to a sherry flip—or four or five, if I want 'em!—or all bets is off!

CHUCK. Aw, yuh got a fine bun on now!

CORA. Cheap skate! I know what's eatin' you, Tightwad! Well, use my dough, den, if yuh're so stingy. Yuh'll grab it all, anyway, right after de ceremony. I know you! *(She hikes her skirt up and reaches inside the top of her stocking)* Here, yuh big tramp!

CHUCK *(knocks her hand away—angrily)*. Keep your lousy dough! And don't show off your legs to dese bums when yuh're goin' to be married, if yuh don't want a sock in de puss!

CORA *(pleased—meekly)*. Aw right, Honey. *(Looking around with a foolish laugh)* Say, why don't all you barflies come to de weddin'? *(But they are all sunk in their own apprehensions and ignore her. She hesitates, miserably uncertain)* Well, we're goin', guys. *(There is no comment. Her eyes fasten on Rocky—desperately)* Say, Rocky, yuh gone deaf? I said me and Chuck was goin' now.

ROCKY *(wiping the bar—with elaborate indifference)*. Well, good-bye. Give my love to Joisey.

CORA *(tearfully indignant)*. Ain't yuh goin' to wish us happiness, yuh doity little Ginny?

ROCKY. Sure. Here's hopin' yuh don't moider each odder before next week.

CHUCK *(angrily)*. Aw, Baby, what d'we care for dat pimp? *(Rocky turns on him threateningly, but Chuck hears someone upstairs in the hall and grabs Cora's arm)* Here's Hickey comin'! Let's get outa here! *(They hurry into the hall. The street door is heard slamming behind them)*

ROCKY *(gloomily pronounces an obitu-ary)*. One regular guy and one all-right tart gone to hell! *(Fiercely)* Dat louse Hickey oughta be croaked!

(There is a muttered growl of assent from most of the gathering. Then Harry Hope enters from the hall, followed by Jimmy Tomorrow, with Hickey on his heels. Hope and Jimmy are both putting up a front of self-assurance, but Cora's description of them was apt. There is a desperate bluff in their manner as they walk in, which suggests the last march of the condemned. Hope is dressed in an old black Sunday suit, black tie, shoes, socks, which gives him the appearance of being in mourning. Jimmy's clothes are pressed, his shoes shined, his white linen immaculate. He has a hangover and his gently appealing dog's eyes have a boiled look. Hickey's face is a bit drawn from lack of sleep and his voice is hoarse from continual talking, but his bustling energy appears nervously intensified, and his beaming expression is one of triumphant accomplishment.)

HICKEY Well, here we are! We've got this far, at least! *(He pats Jimmy on the back)* Good work, Jimmy. I told you you weren't half as sick as you pretended. No excuse whatever for postponing—

JIMMY. I'll thank you to keep your hands off me! I merely mentioned I would feel more fit tomorrow. But it might as well be today, I suppose.

HICKEY. Finish it now, so it'll be dead forever, and you can be free! *(He passes him to clap Hope encouragingly on the shoulder)* Cheer up, Harry. You found your rheumatism didn't bother you coming downstairs, didn't you? I told you it wouldn't. *(He winks around at the others. With the exception of Hugo and Parritt, all their eyes are fixed on him with bitter animosity. He gives Hope a playful nudge in the ribs)* You're the damnedest one for alibis, Governor! As bad as Jimmy!

HOPE *(putting on his deaf manner)*. Eh? I can't hear— *(Defiantly)* You're a liar! I've had rheumatism on and off for twenty years. Ever since Bessie died. Everybody knows that.

HICKEY. Yes, we know it's the kind of rheumatism you turn on and off! We're on to you, you old faker! *(He claps him on the shoulder again, chuckling)*

HOPE *(looks humiliated and guilty—by way of escape he glares around at the others)*. Bejees, what are all you bums hanging round staring at me for? Think you was watching a circus! Why don't you get the hell out of here and 'tend to your own business, like Hickey's told you? *(They look at him reproachfully, their eyes hurt. They fidget as if trying to move)*

HICKEY. Yes, Harry, I certainly thought they'd have had the guts to be gone by this time. *(He grins)* Or maybe I did have my doubts. *(Abruptly he becomes sincerely sympathetic and earnest)* Because I know exactly what you're up against, boys. I know how damned yellow a man can be when it comes to making himself face the truth. I've been through the mill, and I had to face a worse bastard in myself than any of you will have to in yourselves. I know you become such a coward you'll grab at any lousy excuse to get out of killing your pipe dreams. And yet, as I've told you over and over, it's exactly those damned tomorrow dreams which keep you from making peace with yourself. So you've got to kill them like I did mine. *(He pauses. They glare at him with fear and hatred. They seem about to curse him, to spring at him. But they remain silent and motionless. His manner changes and he becomes kindly bullying)* Come on, boys! Get moving! Who'll start the ball rolling? You, Captain, and you, General. You're nearest the door. And besides, you're old war heroes! You ought to lead the forlorn hope! Come on, now, show us a little of that good old battle of Modder River spirit we've heard so much about! You can't hang around all day looking as if you were scared the street outside would bite you!

LEWIS *(turns with humiliated rage—with an attempt at jaunty casualness)*. Right you are, Mister Bloody Nosey Parker! Time I pushed off. Was only waiting to say good-bye to you, Harry, old chum.

HOPE *(dejectedly)*. Good-bye, Captain. Hope you have luck.

LEWIS. Oh, I'm bound to, Old Chap, and the same to you. *(He pushes the swinging doors open and makes a brave exit, turning to his right and marching off outside the window at right of door)*

WETJOEN. Py Gott, if dot Limey can, I can! *(He pushes the door open and lumbers through it like a bull charging an obstacle. He turns left and disappears off rear, outside the farthest window)*

HICKEY *(exhortingly)*. Next? Come on, Ed. It's a fine summer's day and the call of the circus lot must be in your blood! *(Mosher glares at him, then goes to the door. McGloin jumps up from his chair and starts moving toward the door. Hickey claps him on the back as he passes)* That's the stuff, Mac.

MOSHER. Good-bye, Harry. *(He goes out, turning right outside)*

MCGLOIN *(glowering after him)*. If that crooked grifter has the guts— *(He goes out, turning left outside. Hickey glances at Willie who, before he can speak, jumps from his chair)*

WILLIE. Good-bye, Harry, and thanks for all your kindness.

HICKEY *(claps him on the back)*. That's the way, Willie! The D.A.'s a busy man. He can't wait all day for you, you know. *(Willie hurries to the door)*

HOPE *(dully)*. Good luck, Willie. *(Willie goes out and turns right outside. While he is doing so, Jimmy, in a sick panic, sneaks to the bar and furtively reaches for Larry's glass of whiskey)*

HICKEY. And now it's your turn, Jimmy, old pal. *(He sees what Jimmy is at and grabs his arm just as he is about to down the whiskey)* Now, now, Jimmy! You can't do that to yourself. One drink on top of your hangover and an empty stomach and you'll be oreyeyed. Then you'll tell yourself you wouldn't stand a chance if you went up soused to get your old job back.

JIMMY *(pleads abjectly)*. Tomorrow! I will tomorrow! I'll be in good shape tomorrow! *(Abruptly getting control of himself—with shaken firmness)* All right. I'm going. Take your hands off me.

HICKEY. That's the ticket! You'll thank me when it's all over.

JIMMY *(in a burst of futile fury)*. You dirty swine! *(He tries to throw the drink in Hickey's face, but his aim is poor and it lands on Hickey's coat. Jimmy turns and dashes through the door, disappearing outside the window at right of door)*

HICKEY *(brushing the whiskey off his coat—humorously)*. All set for an alcohol rub! But no hard feelings. I know how he feels. I wrote the book. I've seen the day when if anyone forced me to face the truth about my pipe dreams, I'd have shot them dead. *(He turns to Hope—encouragingly)* Well, Governor, Jimmy made the grade. It's up to you. If he's got the guts to go through with the test, then certainly you—

LARRY (*bursts out*). Leave Harry alone, damn you!

HICKEY (*grins at him*). I'd make up my mind about myself if I was you, Larry, and not bother over Harry. He'll come through all right. I've promised him that. He doesn't need anyone's bum pity. Do you, Governor?

HOPE (*with a pathetic attempt at his old fuming assertiveness*). No, bejees! Keep your nose out of this, Larry. What's Hickey got to do with it? I've always been going to take this walk, ain't I? Bejees, you bums want to keep me locked up here 's if I was in jail! I've stood it long enough! I'm free, white and twenty-one, and I'll do as I damned please, bejees! You keep your nose out, too, Hickey! You'd think you was boss of this dump, not me. Sure, I'm all right! Why shouldn't I be? What the hell's to be scared of, just taking a stroll around my own ward? (*As he talks he has been moving toward the door. Now he reaches it*) What's the weather like outside, Rocky?

ROCKY. Fine day, Boss.

HOPE. What's that? Can't hear you. Don't look fine to me. Looks 's if it'd pour down cats and dogs any minute. My rheumatism— (*He catches himself*) No, must be my eyes. Half blind, bejees. Makes things look black. I see now it's a fine day. Too damned hot for a walk, though, if you ask me. Well, do me good to sweat the booze out of me. But I'll have to watch out for the damned automobiles. Wasn't none of them around the last time, twenty years ago. From what I've seen of 'em through the window, they'd run over you as soon as look at you. Not that I'm scared of 'em. I can take care of myself. (*He puts a reluctant hand on the swinging door*) Well, so long— (*He stops and looks back—with frightened irascibility*) Bejees, where are you, Hickey? It's time we got started.

HICKEY (*grins and shakes his head*). No, Harry. Can't be done. You've got to keep a date with yourself alone.

HOPE (*with forced fuming*). Hell of a guy, you are! Thought you'd be willing to help me across the street, knowing I'm half blind. Half deaf, too. Can't bear those damned automobiles! Hell with you! Bejees, I've never needed no one's help and I don't now! (*Egging himself on*) I'll take a good long walk now I've started. See all my old friends. Bejees, they must have given me up for dead. Twenty years is a long time. But they know it was grief over Bessie's death that made me— (*He puts his hand on the door*) Well, the sooner I get started— (*Then he drops his hand—with sentimental melancholy*) You know, Hickey, that's what gets me. Can't help thinking the last time I went out was to Bessie's funeral. After she'd gone, I didn't feel life was worth living. Swore I'd never go out again. (*Pathetically*) Somehow, I can't feel it's right for me to go, Hickey, even now. It's like I was doing wrong to her memory.

HICKEY. Now, Governor, you can't let yourself get away with that one any more!

HOPE (*cupping his hand to his ear*). What's that? Can't hear you. (*Sentimentally again but with desperation*) I remember now clear as day the last time before she— It was a fine Sunday morning. We went out to church together. (*His voice breaks on a sob*)

HICKEY (*amused*). It's a great act, Governor. But I know better, and so do you. You never did want to go to church with her or any place else with her. She was always on your neck, making you have ambition and go out and do things, when all you wanted was to get drunk in peace.

HOPE (*falteringly*). Can't hear a word you're saying. You're a God-damned liar, anyway! (*Then in a sudden fury, his voice trembling with hatred*) Bejees, you son of a bitch, if there was a mad dog outside I'd go and shake hands with it rather than stay here with you! (*The momentum of his fit of rage does it. He pushes the door open and strides blindly out into the street and as blindly past the window behind the free-lunch counter*)

ROCKY (*in amazement*). Jees, he made it! I'd a give yuh fifty to one he'd never— (*He goes to the end of the bar to look through the window—disgustedly*) Aw, he's stopped. I'll bet yuh he's comin' back.

HICKEY. Of course, he's coming back. So are all the others. By tonight they'll all be here again. You dumbbell, that's the whole point.

ROCKY (*excitedly*). No, he ain't neider! He's gone to de coib. He's lookin' up and down. Scared stiff of automobiles. Jees, dey ain't more'n two an hour comes down dis street, de old boob! (*He watches excitedly, as if it were a race he had a bet on, oblivious to what happens in the bar*)

LARRY (*turns on Hickey with bitter defiance*). And now it's my turn, I suppose? What is it I'm to do to achieve this blessed peace of yours?

HICKEY (*grins at him*). Why, we've discussed all that, Larry. Just stop lying to yourself—

LARRY. You think when I say I'm finished with life, and tired of watching the stupid greed of the human circus, and I'll welcome closing my eyes in the long sleep of death—you think that's a coward's lie?

HICKEY (*chuckling*). Well, what do you think, Larry?

LARRY (*with increasing bitter intensity, more as if he were fighting with himself than with Hickey*). I'm afraid to live, am I?—and even more afraid to die! So I sit here, with my pride drowned on the bottom of a bottle, keeping drunk so I won't see myself shaking in my britches with fright, or hear myself whining and praying: Beloved Christ, let me live a little longer at any price! If it's only for a few days more, or a few hours even, have mercy, Almighty God, and let me still clutch greedily to my yellow heart this sweet treasure, this jewel beyond price, the dirty, stinking bit of withered old flesh which is my beautiful little life! (*He laughs with a sneering, vindictive self-loathing, staring inward at himself with contempt and hatred. Then abruptly he makes Hickey again the antagonist*) You think you'll make me admit that to myself?

HICKEY (*chuckling*). But you just did admit it, didn't you?

PARRITT (*lifts his head from his hands to glare at Larry—jeeringly*). That's the stuff, Hickey! Show the old yellow faker up! He can't play dead on me like this! He's got to help me!

HICKEY. Yes, Larry, you've got to settle with him. I'm leaving you entirely in his hands. He'll do as good a job as I could at making you give up that old grandstand bluff.

LARRY (*angrily*). I'll see the two of you in hell first!

ROCKY (*calls excitedly from the end of the bar*). Jees, Harry's startin' across de street! He's goin' to fool yuh, Hickey, yuh bastard! (*He pauses, watching—then worriedly*) What de hell's he stoppin' for? Right in de middle of de street! Yuh'd tink he was paralyzed or somethin'! (*Disgustedly*) Aw, he's quittin'! He's turned back! Jees, look at de old bastard travel! Here he comes!

(*Hope passes the window outside the free-lunch counter in a shambling, panic-stricken run. He comes lurching blindly through the swinging doors and stumbles to the bar at Larry's right.*)

HOPE. Bejees, give me a drink quick! Scared me out of a year's growth! Bejees, that guy ought to be pinched! Bejees, it ain't safe to walk in the streets! Bejees, that ends me! Never again! Give me that bottle! (*He slops a glass full and drains it and pours another— To Rocky, who is regarding him with scorn—appealingly*) You seen it, didn't you, Rocky?

ROCKY. Seen what?

HOPE. That automobile, you dumb Wop! Feller driving it must be drunk or crazy. He'd run right over me if I hadn't jumped. (*Ingratiatingly*) Come on, Larry, have a drink. Everybody have a drink. Have a cigar, Rocky. I know you hardly ever touch it.

ROCKY (*resentfully*). Well, dis is de time I do touch it! (*Pouring a drink*) I'm goin' to get stinko, see! And if yuh don't like it, yuh know what yuh can do! I gotta good mind to chuck my job, anyways. (*Disgustedly*) Jees, Harry, I thought yuh had some guts! I was bettin' yuh'd make it and show dat four-flusher up. (*He nods at Hickey—then snorts*) Automobile, hell! Who d'yuh tink yuh're kiddin'? Dey wasn' no automobile! Yuh just quit cold!

HOPE (*feebly*). Guess I ought to know! Bejees, it almost killed me!

HICKEY (*comes to the bar between him and Larry, and puts a hand on his shoulder—kindly*). Now, now, Governor. Don't be foolish. You've faced the test and come through. You're rid of all that nagging dream stuff now. You know you can't believe it any more.

HOPE (*appeals pleadingly to Larry*). Larry, you saw it, didn't you? Drink up! Have another! Have all you want! Bejees, we'll go on a grand old souse together! You saw that automobile, didn't you?

LARRY (*compassionately, avoiding his eyes*). Sure, I saw it, Harry. You had a narrow escape. Be God, I thought you were a goner!

HICKEY (*turns on him with a flash of sincere indignation*). What the hell's the matter with you, Larry? You know what I told you about the wrong kind of pity. Leave Harry alone! You'd think I was trying to harm him, the fool way you act! My oldest friend! What kind of a louse do you think I am? There isn't anything I wouldn't do for Harry, and he knows it! All I've wanted to do is fix it so he'll be finally at peace with himself for the rest of his days! And if you'll only wait until the final returns are in, you'll find that's exactly what I've accomplished! (*He turns to Hope and pats his shoulder —coaxingly*) Come now, Governor. What's the use of being stubborn, now when it's all over and dead? Give up that ghost automobile.

HOPE (*beginning to collapse within himself—dully*). Yes, what's the use—now? All a lie! No automobile. But, bejees, something ran over me! Must have been myself, I guess. (*He forces a feeble smile —then wearily*) Guess I'll sit down. Feel all in. Like a corpse, bejees. (*He picks a bottle and glass from the bar and walks to the first table and slumps down in the chair, facing left-front. His shaking hand misjudges the distance and he sets the bottle on the table with a jar that rouses Hugo, who lifts his head from his arms and blinks at him through his thick spectacles. Hope speaks to him in a flat, dead voice*) Hello, Hugo. Coming up for air? Stay passed out, that's the right dope. There ain't any cool willow trees—except you grow your own in a bottle. (*He pours a drink and gulps it down*)

HUGO (*with his silly giggle*). Hello, Harry, stupid proletarian monkey-face! I vill trink champagne beneath the villow— (*With a change to aristocratic fastidiousness*) But the slaves must ice it properly! (*With guttural rage*) Gottamned Hickey! Peddler pimp for nouveau-riche capitalism! Vhen I lead the jackass mob to the sack of Babylon, I vill make them hang him to a lamppost the first one!

HOPE (*spiritlessly*). Good work. I'll help pull on the rope. Have a drink, Hugo.

HUGO (*frightenedly*). No, thank you. I am too trunk now. I hear myself say crazy things. Do not listen, please. Larry vill tell you I haf never been so crazy trunk. I must sleep it off. (*He starts to put his head on his arms but stops and stares at Hope with growing uneasiness*) Vhat's matter, Harry? You look funny. You look dead. Vhat's happened? I don't know you. Listen, I feel I am dying, too. Because I am so crazy trunk! It is very necessary I sleep. But I can't sleep here vith you. You look dead. (*He scrambles to his feet in a confused panic, turns his back on Hope and settles into the chair at the next table which faces left. He thrusts his head down on his arms like an ostrich hiding its head in the sand. He does not notice Parritt, nor Parritt him*)

LARRY (*to Hickey with bitter condemnation*). Another one who's begun to enjoy your peace!

HICKEY. Oh, I know it's tough on him right now, the same as it is on Harry. But that's only the first shock. I promise you they'll both come through all right.

LARRY. And you believe that! I see you do! You mad fool!

HICKEY. Of course, I believe it! I tell you I know from my own experience!

HOPE (*spiritlessly*). Close that big clam of yours, Hickey. Bejees, you're a worse gabber than that nagging bitch, Bessie, was. (*He drinks his drink mechanically and pours another*)

ROCKY (*in amazement*). Jees, did yuh hear dat?

HOPE (*dully*). What's wrong with this booze? There's no kick in it.

ROCKY (*worriedly*). Jees, Larry, Hugo had it right. He does look like he'd croaked.

HICKEY (*annoyed*). Don't be a damned fool! Give him time. He's coming along all right. (*He calls to Hope with a first trace of underlying uneasiness*) You're all right, aren't you, Harry?

HOPE (*dully*). I want to pass out like Hugo.

LARRY (*turns to Hickey—with bitter anger*). It's the peace of death you've brought him.

HICKEY (*for the first time loses his temper*). That's a lie! (*But he controls this instantly and grins*) Well, well, you did manage to get a rise out of me that time. I think such a hell of a lot of Harry— (*Impatiently*) You know that's damned foolishness. Look at me. I've been through it. Do I look dead? Just leave Harry alone and wait until the shock wears off and you'll see. He'll be a new man. Like I am. (*He calls to Hope coaxingly*) How's it coming, Governor? Beginning to feel free, aren't you? Relieved and not guilty any more?

HOPE (*grumbles spiritlessly*). Bejees, you must have been monkeying with the booze, too, you interfering bastard! There's no life in it now. I want to get drunk and pass out. Let's all pass out. Who the hell cares?

HICKEY (*lowering his voice—worriedly to Larry*). I admit I didn't think he'd be hit so hard. He's always been a happy-go-lucky slob. Like I was. Of course, it hit me hard, too. But only for a minute. Then I felt as if a ton of guilt had been lifted off my mind. I saw what had happened was the only possible way for the peace of all concerned.

LARRY (*sharply*). What was it happened? Tell us that! And don't try to get out of it! I want a straight answer! (*Vindictively*) I think it was something you drove someone else to do!

HICKEY (*puzzled*). Someone else?

LARRY (*accusingly*). What did your wife die of? You've kept that a deep secret, I notice—for some reason!

HICKEY (*reproachfully*). You're not very considerate, Larry. But, if you insist on knowing now, there's no reason you shouldn't. It was a bullet through the head that killed Evelyn. (*There is a second's tense silence*)

HOPE (*dully*). Who the hell cares? To hell with her and that nagging old hag, Bessie.

ROCKY. Christ. You had de right dope, Larry.

LARRY (*revengefully*). You drove your poor wife to suicide? I knew it! Be God, I don't blame her! I'd almost do as much myself to be rid of you! It's what you'd like to drive us all to— (*Abruptly he is ashamed of himself and pitying*) I'm sorry, Hickey. I'm a rotten louse to throw that in your face.

HICKEY (*quietly*). Oh, that's all right, Larry. But don't jump at conclusions. I didn't say poor Evelyn committed suicide. It's the last thing she'd ever have done, as long as I was alive for her to take care of and forgive. If you'd known her at all, you'd never get such a crazy suspicion. (*He pauses—then slowly*) No, I'm sorry to have to tell you my poor wife was killed. (*Larry stares at him with growing horror and shrinks back along the bar*

away from him. Parritt jerks his head up from his hands and looks around frightenedly, not at Hickey, but at Larry. Rocky's round eyes are popping. Hope stares dully at the table top. Hugo, his head hidden in his arms, gives no sign of life)

LARRY (*shakenly*). Then she—was murdered.

PARRITT (*springs to his feet—stammers defensively*). You're a liar, Larry! You must be crazy to say that to me! You know she's still alive! (*But no one pays any attention to him*)

ROCKY (*blurts out*). Moidered? Who done it?

LARRY (*his eyes fixed with fascinated horror on Hickey—frightenedly*). Don't ask questions, you dumb Wop! It's none of our damned business! Leave Hickey alone!

HICKEY (*smiles at him with affectionate amusement*). Still the old grandstand bluff, Larry? Or is it some more bum pity? (*He turns to Rocky—matter-of-factly*) The police don't know who killed her yet, Rocky. But I expect they will before very long. (*As if that finished the subject, he comes forward to Hope and sits beside him, with an arm around his shoulder—affectionately coaxing*) Coming along fine now, aren't you, Governor? Getting over the first shock? Beginning to feel free from guilt and lying hopes and at peace with yourself?

HOPE (*with a dull callousness*). Somebody croaked your Evelyn, eh? Bejees, my bets are on the iceman! But who the hell cares? Let's get drunk and pass out. (*He tosses down his drink with a lifeless, automatic movement—complaining*) Bejees, what did you do to the booze, Hickey? There's no damned life left in it.

PARRITT (*stammers, his eyes on Larry, whose eyes in turn remain fixed on Hickey*). Don't look like that, Larry! You've got to believe what I told you! It had nothing to do with her! It was just to get a few lousy dollars!

HUGO (*suddenly raises his head from his arms and, looking straight in front of him, pounds on the table frightenedly with his small fists*). Don't be a fool! Buy me a trink! But no more vine! It is not properly iced! (*With guttural rage*) Gottamned stupid proletarian slaves! Buy me a trink or I vill have you shot! (*He col-*

lapses into abject begging) Please, for Gott's sake! I am not trunk enough! I cannot sleep! Life is a crazy monkey-face! Always there is blood beneath the villow trees! I hate it and I am afraid! *(He hides his face on his arms, sobbing muffledly)* Please, I am crazy trunk! I say crazy things! For Gott's sake, do not listen to me! *(But no one pays any attention to him. Larry stands shrunk back against the bar. Rocky is leaning over it. They stare at Hickey. Parritt stands looking pleadingly at Larry)*

HICKEY *(gazes with worried kindliness at Hope)*. You're beginning to worry me, Governor. Something's holding you up somewhere. I don't see why— You've faced the truth about yourself. You've done what you had to do to kill your nagging pipe dreams. Oh, I know it knocks you cold. But only for a minute. Then you see it was the only possible way to peace. And you feel happy. Like I did. That's what worries me about you, Governor. It's time you began to feel happy—

CURTAIN

ACT FOUR

SCENE: *Same as Act One—the back room with the curtain separating it from the section of the barroom with its single table at right of curtain, front. It is around half past one in the morning of the following day.*

The tables in the back room have a new arrangement. The one at left, front, before the window to the yard, is in the same position. So is the one at the right, rear, of it in the second row. But this table now has only one chair. This chair is at right of it, facing directly front. The two tables on either side of the door at rear are unchanged. But the table which was at center, front, has been pushed toward right so that it and the table at right, rear, of it in the second row, and the last table at right in the front row, are now jammed so closely together that they form one group.

Larry, Hugo and Parritt are at the table at left, front. Larry is at left of it, beside the window, facing front. Hugo sits at

rear, facing front, his head on his arms in his habitual position, but he is not asleep. On Hugo's left is Parritt, his chair facing left, front. At right of table, an empty chair, facing left. Larry's chin is on his chest, his eyes fixed on the floor. He will not look at Parritt, who keeps staring at him with a sneering, pleading challenge.

Two bottles of whiskey are on each table, whiskey and chaser glasses, a pitcher of water.

The one chair by the table at right, rear, of them is vacant.

At the first table at right of center, Cora sits at left, front, of it, facing front. Around the rear of this table are four empty chairs. Opposite Cora, in a sixth chair, is Captain Lewis, also facing front. On his left, McGloin is facing front in a chair before the middle table of his group. At right, rear, of him, also at this table, General Wetjoen sits facing front. In back of this table are three empty chairs.

At right, rear, of Wetjoen, but beside the last table of the group, sits Willie. On Willie's left, at rear of table, is Hope. On Hope's left, at right, rear, of table, is Mosher. Finally, at right of table is Jimmy Tomorrow. All of the four sit facing front.

There is an atmosphere of oppressive stagnation in the room, and a quality of insensibility about all the people in this group at right. They are like wax figures, set stiffly on their chairs, carrying out mechanically the motions of getting drunk but sunk in a numb stupor which is impervious to stimulation.

In the bar section, Joe is sprawled in the chair at right of table, facing left. His head rolls forward in a sodden slumber. Rocky is standing behind his chair, regarding him with dull hostility. Rocky's face is set in an expression of tired, callous toughness. He looks now like a minor Wop gangster.

ROCKY *(shakes Joe by the shoulder)*. Come on, yuh damned nigger! Beat it in de back room! It's after hours. *(But Joe remains inert. Rocky gives up)* Aw, to hell wid it. Let de dump get pinched. I'm through wid dis lousy job, anyway! *(He hears someone at rear and calls)* Who's dat? *(Chuck appears from rear. He has been drinking heavily, but there is no lift to his jag; his manner is grouchy and sullen. He has evidently been brawl-*

ing. His knuckles are raw and there is a mouse under one eye. He has lost his straw hat, his tie is awry, and his blue suit is dirty. Rocky eyes him indifferently) Been scrappin', huh? Started off on your periodical, ain't yuh? *(For a second there is a gleam of satisfaction in his eyes)*

CHUCK. Yeah, ain't yuh glad? *(Truculently)* What's it to yuh?

ROCKY. Not a damn ting. But dis is someting to me. I'm out on my feet holdin' down your job. Yuh said if I'd take your day, yuh'd relieve me at six, and here it's half past one A.M. Well, yuh're takin' over now, get me, no matter how plastered yuh are!

CHUCK. Plastered, hell! I wisht I was. I've lapped up a gallon, but it don't hit me right. And to hell wid de job. I'm goin' to tell Harry I'm quittin'.

ROCKY. Yeah? Well, I'm quittin', too.

CHUCK. I've played sucker for dat crummy blonde long enough, lettin' her kid me into woikin'. From now on I take it easy.

ROCKY. I'm glad yuh're gettin' some sense.

CHUCK. And I hope yuh're gettin' some. What a prize sap you been, tendin' bar when yuh got two good hustlers in your stable!

ROCKY. Yeah, but I ain't no sap now. I'll loin dem, when dey get back from Coney. *(Sneeringly)* Jees, dat Cora sure played you for a dope, feedin' yuh dat marriage-on-de-farm hop!

CHUCK *(dully)*. Yeah. Hickey got it right. A lousy pipe dream. It was her pulling sherry flips on me woke me up. All de way walkin' to de ferry, every gin-mill we come to she'd drag me in to blow her. I got tinkin', Christ, what won't she want when she gets de ring on her finger and I'm hooked? So I tells her at de ferry, "Kiddo, yuh can go to Joisey, or to hell, but count me out."

ROCKY. She says it was her told you to go to hell, because yuh'd started hittin' de booze.

CHUCK *(ignoring this)*. I got tinkin', too, Jees, won't I look sweet wid a wife dat if yuh put all de guys she's stayed wid side by side, dey'd reach to Chicago. *(He sighs gloomily)* Dat kind of dame, yuh can't trust 'em. De minute your back is toined, dey're cheatin' wid de iceman or someone. Hickey done me a favor, makin'

me wake up. *(He pauses—then adds pathetically)* On'y it was fun, kinda, me and Cora kiddin' ourselves— *(Suddenly his face hardens with hatred)* Where is dat son of a bitch, Hickey? I want one good sock at dat guy—just one!—and next buttin' in he'll do will be in de morgue! I'll take a chance on goin' to de Chair—!

ROCKY *(starts—in a low warning voice)*. Piano! Keep away from him, Chuck! He ain't here now, anyway. He went out to phone, he said. He wouldn't call from here. I got a hunch he's beat it. But if he does come back, yuh don't know him, if anyone asks yuh, get me? *(As Chuck looks at him with dull surprise he lowers his voice to a whisper)* De Chair, maybe dat's where he's goin'. I don't know nuttin', see, but it looks like he croaked his wife.

CHUCK *(with a flash of interest)*. Yuh mean she really was cheatin' on him? Den I don't blame de guy—

ROCKY. Who's blamin' him? When a dame asks for it— But I don't know nuttin' about it, see?

CHUCK. Is any of de gang wise?

ROCKY. Larry is. And de boss ought to be. I tried to wise de rest of dem up to stay clear of him, but dey're all so licked, I don't know if dey got it. *(He pauses—vindictively)* I don't give a damn what he done to his wife, but if he gets de Hot Seat I won't go into no mournin'!

CHUCK. Me, neider!

ROCKY. Not after his trowin' it in my face I'm a pimp. What if I am? Why de hell not? And what he's done to Harry. Jees, de poor old slob is so licked he can't even get drunk. And all de gang. Dey're all licked. I couldn't help feelin' sorry for de poor bums when dey showed up tonight, one by one, lookin' like pooches wid deir tails between deir legs, dat everyone'd been kickin' till dey was too punch-drunk to feel it no more. Jimmy Tomorrow was de last. Schwartz, de copper, brung him in. Seen him sittin' on de dock on West Street, lookin' at de water and cryin'! Schwartz thought he was drunk and I let him tink it. But he was cold sober. He was tryin' to jump in and didn't have de noive, I figgered it. Noive! Jees, dere ain't enough guts left in de whole gang to battle a mosquito!

CHUCK. Aw, to hell wid 'em! Who

cares? Gimme a drink. *(Rocky pushes the bottle toward him apathetically)* I see you been hittin' de redeye, too.

ROCKY. Yeah. But it don't do no good. I can't get drunk right. *(Chuck drinks. Joe mumbles in his sleep. Chuck regards him resentfully)* Dis doity dinge was able to get his snootful and pass out. Jees, even Hickey can't faze a nigger! Yuh'd tink he was fazed if yuh'd seen him come in. Stinko, and he pulled a gat and said he'd plug Hickey for insultin' him. Den he dropped it and begun to cry and said he wasn't a gamblin' man or a tough guy no more; he was yellow. He'd borrowed de gat to stick up someone, and den didn't have de guts. He got drunk panhandlin' drinks in nigger joints, I s'pose. I guess dey felt sorry for him.

CHUCK. He ain't got no business in de bar after hours. Why don't yuh chuck him out?

ROCKY *(apathetically)*. Aw, to hell wid it. Who cares?

CHUCK *(lapsing into the same mood)*. Yeah. I don't.

JOE *(suddenly lunges to his feet dazedly—mumbles in humbled apology)*. Scuse me, White Boys. Scuse me for livin'. I don't want to be where I's not wanted. *(He makes his way swayingly to the opening in the curtain at rear and tacks down to the middle table of the three at right, front. He feels his way around it to the table at its left and gets to the chair in back of Captain Lewis)*

CHUCK *(gets up—in a callous, brutal tone)*. My pig's in de back room, ain't she? I wanna collect de dough I wouldn't take dis mornin', like a sucker, before she blows it. *(He goes rear)*

ROCKY *(getting up)*. I'm comin', too. I'm trough woikin'. I ain't no lousy bartender. *(Chuck comes through the curtain and looks for Cora as Joe flops down in the chair in back of Captain Lewis)*

JOE *(taps Lewis on the shoulder—servilely apologetic)*. If you objects to my sittin' here, Captain, just tell me and I pulls my freight.

LEWIS. No apology required, old chap. Anybody could tell you I should feel honored a bloody Kaffir would lower himself to sit beside me.

(Joe stares at him with sodden perplexity—then closes his eyes. Chuck comes forward to take the chair behind Cora's, as Rocky enters the back room and starts over toward Larry's table.)

CHUCK *(his voice hard)*. I'm waitin', Baby. Dig!

CORA *(with apathetic obedience)*. Sure. I been expectin' yuh. I got it all ready. Here. *(She passes a small roll of bills she has in her hand over her shoulder, without looking at him. He takes it, glances at it suspiciously, then shoves it in his pocket without a word of acknowledgment. Cora speaks with a tired wonder at herself rather than resentment toward him)* Jees, imagine me kiddin' myself I wanted to marry a drunken pimp.

CHUCK. Dat's nuttin', Baby. Imagine de sap I'da been, when I can get your dough just as easy widout it!

ROCKY *(takes the chair on Parritt's left, facing Larry—dully)*. Hello, Old Cemetery. *(Larry doesn't seem to hear. To Parritt)* Hello, Tightwad. You still around?

PARRITT *(keeps his eyes on Larry—in a jeeringly challenging tone)*. Ask Larry! He knows I'm here, all right, although he's pretending not to! He'd like to forget I'm alive! He's trying to kid himself with that grandstand philosopher stuff! But he knows he can't get away with it now! He kept himself locked in his room until a while ago, alone with a bottle of booze, but he couldn't make it work! He couldn't even get drunk! He had to come out! There must have been something there he was even more scared to face than he is Hickey and me! I guess he got looking at the fire escape and thinking how handy it was, if he was really sick of life and only had the nerve to die! *(He pauses sneeringly. Larry's face has tautened, but he pretends he doesn't hear. Rocky pays no attention. His head has sunk forward, and he stares at the table top, sunk in the same stupor as the other occupants of the room. Parritt goes on, his tone becoming more insistent)* He's been thinking of me, too, Rocky. Trying to figure a way to get out of helping me! He doesn't want to be bothered understanding. But he does understand all right! He used to love her, too. So he thinks I ought to take a hop off the fire escape! *(He pauses. Larry's hands on the table have clinched into fists, as his nails dig into his palms, but he remains silent. Parritt breaks and starts pleading)* For God's sake, Larry, can't you say something? Hickey's got me all balled up. Thinking of what he must have done has got me so I don't know any more what I did or why. I can't go on like this! I've got to know what I ought to do—

LARRY (*in a stifled tone*). God damn you! Are you trying to make me your executioner?

PARRITT (*starts frightenedly*). Execution? Then you do think—?

LARRY. I don't think anything!

PARRITT (*with forced jeering*). I suppose you think I ought to die because I sold out a lot of loud-mouthed fakers, who were cheating suckers with a phony pipe dream, and put them where they ought to be, in jail? (*He forces a laugh*) Don't make me laugh! I ought to get a medal! What a damned old sap you are! You must still believe in the Movement! (*He nudges Rocky with his elbow*) Hickey's right about him, isn't he, Rocky? An old no-good drunken tramp, as dumb as he is, ought to take a hop off the fire escape!

ROCKY (*dully*). Sure. Why don't he? Or you? Or me? What de hell's de difference? Who cares? (*There is a faint stir from all the crowd, as if this sentiment struck a responsive chord in their numbed minds. They mumble almost in chorus as one voice, like sleepers talking out of a dully irritating dream, "The hell with it!" "Who cares?" Then the sodden silence descends again on the room. Rocky looks from Parritt to Larry puzzledly. He mutters*) What am I doin' here wid youse two? I remember I had someting on my mind to tell yuh. What—? Oh, I got it now. (*He looks from one to the other of their oblivious faces with a strange, sly, calculating look—ingratiatingly*) I was tinking how you was bot' reg'lar guys. I tinks, ain't two guys like dem saps to be hangin' round like a coupla stew bums and wastin' demselves. Not dat I blame yuh for not woikin'. On'y suckers woik. But dere's no percentage in bein' broke when yuh can grab good jack for yourself and make someone else woik for yuh, is dere? I mean, like I do. So I tinks, Dey're my pals and I ought to wise up two good guys like dem to play my system, and not be lousy barflies, no good to demselves or nobody else. (*He addresses Parritt now—persuasively*) What yuh

tink, Parritt? Ain't I right? Sure, I am. So don't be a sucker, see? Yuh ain't a bad-lookin' guy. Yuh could easy make some gal who's a good hustler, an' start a stable. I'd help yuh and wise yuh up to de inside dope on de game. (*He pauses inquiringly. Parritt gives no sign of having heard him. Rocky asks impatiently*) Well, what about it? What if dey do call yuh a pimp? What de hell do you care—any more'n I do.

PARRITT (*without looking at him—vindictively*). I'm through with whores. I wish they were all in jail—or dead!

ROCKY (*ignores this—disappointedly*). So yuh won't touch it, huh? Aw right, stay a bum! (*He turns to Larry*) Jees, Larry, he's sure one dumb boob, ain't he? Dead from de neck up! He don't know a good ting when he sees it. (*Oily, even persuasive again*) But how about you, Larry? You ain't dumb. So why not, huh? Sure, yuh're old, but dat don't matter. All de hustlers tink yuh're aces. Dey fall for yuh like yuh was deir uncle or old man or someting. Dey'd like takin' care of yuh. And de cops 'round here, dey like yuh, too. It'd be a pipe for yuh, 'specially wid me to help yuh and wise yuh up. Yuh wouldn't have to worry where de next drink's comin' from, or wear doity clothes. (*Hopefully*) Well, don't it look good to yuh?

LARRY (*glances at him—for a moment he is stirred to sardonic pity*). No, it doesn't look good, Rocky. I mean, the peace Hickey's brought you. It isn't contented enough, if you have to make everyone else a pimp, too.

ROCKY (*stares at him stupidly—then pushes his chair back and gets up, grumbling*). I'm a sap to waste time on yuh. A stew bum is a stew bum and yuh can't change him. (*He turns away—then turns back for an afterthought*) Like I was sayin' to Chuck, yuh better keep away from Hickey. If anyone asks yuh, yuh don't know nuttin', get me? Yuh never even hoid he had a wife. (*His face hardens*) Jees, we all ought to git drunk and stage a celebration when dat bastard goes to de Chair.

LARRY (*vindictively*). Be God, I'll celebrate with you and drink long life to him in hell! (*Then guiltily and pityingly*) No! The poor mad devil— (*Then with angry self-contempt*) Ah, pity again!

The wrong kind! He'll welcome the Chair!

PARRITT *(contemptuously).* Yes, what are you so damned scared of death for? I don't want your lousy pity.

ROCKY. Christ, I hope he don't come back, Larry, We don't know nuttin' now. We're on'y guessin', see? But if de bastard keeps on talkin'—

LARRY *(grimly).* He'll come back. He'll keep on talking. He's got to. He's lost his confidence that the peace he's sold us is the real McCoy, and it's made him uneasy about his own. He'll have to prove to us— *(As he is speaking Hickey appears silently in the doorway at rear. He has lost his beaming salesman's grin. His manner is no longer self-assured. His expression is uneasy, baffled and resentful. It has the stubborn set of an obsessed determination. His eyes are on Larry as he comes in. As he speaks, there is a start from all the crowd, a shrinking away from him)*

HICKEY *(angrily).* That's a damned lie, Larry! I haven't lost confidence a damned bit! Why should I? *(Boastfully)* By God, whenever I made up my mind to sell someone something I knew they ought to want, I've sold 'em! *(He suddenly looks confused—haltingly)* I mean— It isn't kind of you, Larry, to make that kind of crack when I've been doing my best to help—

ROCKY *(moving away from him toward right—sharply).* Keep away from me! I don't know nuttin' about yuh, see?

(His tone is threatening but his manner as he turns his back and ducks quickly across to the bar entrance is that of one in flight. In the bar he comes forward and slumps in a chair at the table, facing front.)

HICKEY *(comes to the table at right, rear, of Larry's table and sits in the one chair there, facing front. He looks over the crowd at right, hopefully and then disappointedly. He speaks with a strained attempt at his old affectionate jollying manner).* Well, well! How are you coming along, everybody? Sorry I had to leave you for a while, but there was something I had to get finally settled. It's all fixed now.

HOPE *(in the voice of one reiterating mechanically a hopeless complaint).* When are you going to do something about this booze, Hickey? Bejees, we all know you did something to take the life out of it. It's like drinking dishwater! We can't pass out! And you promised us peace. *(His group all join in in a dull, complaining chorus, "We can't pass out! You promised us peace!")*

HICKEY *(bursts into resentful exasperation).* For God's sake, Harry, are you still harping on that damned nonsense! You've kept it up all afternoon and night! And you've got everybody else singing the same crazy tune! I've had about all I can stand— That's why I phoned— *(He controls himself)* Excuse me, boys and girls. I don't mean that. I'm just worried about you, when you play dead on me like this. I was hoping by the time I got back you'd be like you ought to be! I thought you were deliberately holding back, while I was around, because you didn't want to give me the satisfaction of showing me I'd had the right dope. And I did have! I know from my own experience. *(Exasperatedly)* But I've explained that a million times! And you've all done what you needed to do! By rights you should be contented now, without a single damned hope or lying dream left to torment you! But here you are, acting like a lot of stiffs cheating the undertaker! *(He looks around accusingly)* I can't figure it— unless it's just your damned pigheaded stubbornness! *(He breaks—miserably)* Hell, you oughn't to act this way with me! You're my old pals, the only friends I've got. You know the one thing I want is to see you all happy before I go— *(Rousing himself to his old brisk, master-of-ceremonies manner)* And there's damned little time left now. I've made a date for two o'clock. We've got to get busy right away and find out what's wrong. *(There is a sodden silence. He goes on exasperatedly)* Can't you appreciate what you've got, for God's sake? Don't you know you're free now to be yourselves, without having to feel remorse or guilt, or lie to yourselves about reforming tomorrow? Can't you see there is no tomorrow now? You're rid of it forever! You've killed it! You don't have to care a damn about anything any more! You've finally got the game of life licked, don't you see that? *(Angrily exhorting)* Then why the hell don't you get pie-eyed and celebrate? Why don't you laugh and sing "Sweet Adeline"? *(With bitterly hurt accusation)* The only reason I can think of is, you're putting on this rotten half-dead act just to get back at me! Because you hate my guts! *(He breaks again)* God, don't do that, gang! It makes me feel like hell to think you hate me. It makes me feel you suspect I must have hated you. But that's a lie! Oh, I know I used to hate everyone in the world who wasn't as rotten a bastard as I was! But that was when I was still living in hell—before I faced the truth and saw the one possible way to free poor Evelyn and give her the peace she'd always dreamed about. *(He pauses. Everyone in the group stirs with awakening dread and they all begin to grow tense on their chairs)*

CHUCK *(without looking at Hickey—with dull, resentful viciousness)*. Aw, put a bag over it! To hell wid Evelyn! What if she was cheatin'? And who cares what yuh did to her? Dat's your funeral. We don't give a damn, see? *(There is a dull, resentful chorus of assent, "We don't give a damn." Chuck adds dully)* All we want outa you is keep de hell away from us and give us a rest. *(A muttered chorus of assent)*

HICKEY *(as if he hadn't heard this—an obsessed look on his face)*. The one possible way to make up to her for all I'd made her go through, and get her rid of me so I couldn't make her suffer any more, and she wouldn't have to forgive me again! I saw I couldn't do it by killing myself, like I wanted to for a long time. That would have been the last straw for her. She'd have died of a broken heart to think I could do that to her. She'd have blamed herself for it, too. Or I couldn't just run away from her. She'd have died of grief and humiliation if I'd done that to her. She'd have thought I'd stopped loving her. *(He adds with a strange impressive simplicity)* You see, Evelyn loved me. And I loved her. That was the trouble. It would have been easy to find a way out if she hadn't loved me so much. Or if I hadn't loved her. But as it was, there was only one possible way. *(He pauses—then adds simply)* I had to kill her. *(There is a second's dead silence as he finishes—then a tense indrawn breath like a gasp from the crowd, and a general shrinking movement)*

LARRY *(bursts out)*. You mad fool, can't you keep your mouth shut! We may hate you for what you've done here this time, but we remember the old times, too, when you brought kindness and laughter with you instead of death! We don't want to know things that will make us help send you to the Chair!

PARRITT *(with angry scorn)*. Ah, shut up, you yellow faker! Can't you face anything? Wouldn't I deserve the Chair, too, if I'd—It's worse if you kill someone and they have to go on living. I'd be glad of the Chair! It'd wipe it out! It'd square me with myself!

HICKEY *(disturbed—with a movement of repulsion)*. I wish you'd get rid of that bastard, Larry. I can't have him pretending there's something in common between him and me. It's what's in your heart that counts. There was love in my heart, not hate.

PARRITT *(glares at him in angry terror)*. You're a liar! I don't hate her! I couldn't! And it had nothing to do with her, anyway! You ask Larry!

LARRY *(grabs his shoulder and shakes him furiously)*. God damn you, stop shoving your rotten soul in my lap! *(Parritt subsides, hiding his face in his hands and shuddering)*

HICKEY *(goes on quietly now)*. Don't worry about the Chair, Larry. I know it's still hard for you not to be terrified by death, but when you've made peace with yourself, like I have, you won't give a damn. *(He addresses the group at right again—earnestly)* Listen, everybody. I've made up my mind the only way I can clear things up for you, so you'll realize how contented and carefree you ought to feel, now I've made you get rid of your pipe dreams, is to show you what a pipe dream did to me and Evelyn. I'm certain if I tell you about it from the beginning, you'll appreciate what I've done for you and why I did it, and how damned grateful you ought to be—instead of hating me. *(He begins eagerly in a strange running narrative manner)* You see, even when we were kids, Evelyn and me—

HOPE *(bursts out, pounding with his glass on the table)*. No! Who the hell cares? We don't want to hear it. All we want is to pass out and get drunk and a little peace! *(They are all, except Larry and Parritt, seized by the same fit and pound with their glasses, even Hugo, and Rocky in the bar, and shout in chorus, "Who the hell cares? We want to pass out!")*

HICKEY *(with an expression of wounded hurt).* All right, if that's the way you feel. I don't want to cram it down your throats. I don't need to tell anyone. I don't feel guilty. I'm only worried about you.

HOPE. What did you do to this booze? That's what we'd like to hear. Bejees, you done something. There's no life or kick in it now. *(He appeals mechanically to Jimmy Tomorrow)* Ain't that right, Jimmy?

JIMMY *(more than any of them, his face has a wax-figure blankness that makes it look embalmed. He answers in a precise, completely lifeless voice, but his reply is not to Harry's question, and he does not look at him or anyone else).* Yes. Quite right. It was all a stupid lie—my nonsense about tomorrow. Naturally, they would never give me my position back. I would never dream of asking them. It would be hopeless. I didn't resign. I was fired for drunkenness. And that was years ago. I'm much worse now. And it was absurd of me to excuse my drunkenness by pretending it was my wife's adultery that ruined my life. As Hickey guessed, I was a drunkard before that. Long before. I discovered early in life that living frightened me when I was sober. I have forgotten why I married Marjorie. I can't even remember now if she was pretty. She was a blonde, I think, but I couldn't swear to it. I had some idea of wanting a home, perhaps. But, of course, I much preferred the nearest pub. Why Marjorie married me, God knows. It's impossible to believe she loved me. She soon found I much preferred drinking all night with my pals to being in bed with her. So, naturally, she was unfaithful. I didn't blame her. I really didn't care. I was glad to be free—even grateful to her, I think, for giving me such a good tragic excuse to drink as much as I damned well pleased. *(He stops like a mechanical doll that has run down. No one gives any sign of having heard him. There is a heavy silence. Then Rocky, at the table in the bar, turns grouchily as he hears a noise behind him. Two men come quietly forward. One, Moran, is middle-aged. The other, Lieb, is in his twenties. They look ordinary in every way, without anything distinctive to indicate what they do for a living)*

ROCKY *(grumpily).* In de back room if yuh wanta drink.

(Moran makes a peremptory sign to be quiet. All of a sudden Rocky senses they are detectives and springs up to face them, his expression freezing into a wary blankness. Moran pulls back his coat to show his badge.)

MORAN *(in a low voice).* Guy named Hickman in the back room?

ROCKY. Tink I know de names of all de guys—?

MORAN. Listen, you! This is murder. And don't be a sap. It was Hickman himself phoned in and said we'd find him here around two.

ROCKY *(dully).* So dat's who he phoned to. *(He shrugs his shoulders)* Aw right, if he asked for it. He's de fat guy sittin' alone. *(He slumps down in his chair again)* And if yuh want a confession all yuh got to do is listen. He'll be tellin' all about it soon. Yuh can't stop de bastard talkin'.

(Moran gives him a curious look, then whispers to Lieb, who disappears rear and a moment later appears in the hall doorway of the back room. He spots Hickey and slides into a chair at the left of the doorway, cutting off escape by the hall. Moran goes back and stands in the opening in the curtain leading to the back room. He sees Hickey and stands watching him and listening.)

HICKEY *(suddenly bursts out).* I've got to tell you! Your being the way you are now gets my goat! It's all wrong! It puts things in my mind—about myself. It makes me think, if I got balled up about you, how do I know I wasn't balled up about myself? And that's plain damned foolishness. When you know the story of me and Evelyn, you'll see there wasn't any other possible way out of it, for her sake. Only I've got to start way back at the beginning or you won't understand. *(He starts his story, his tone again becoming musingly reminiscent)* You see, even as a kid I was always restless. I had to keep on the go. You've heard the old saying, "Ministers' sons are sons of guns." Well, that was me, and then some. Home was like a jail. I didn't fall for the religious bunk. Listening to my old man whooping up hell fire and scaring those Hoosier suckers into shelling out their dough only handed me a laugh, although I had to hand it to him, the way he sold them nothing for something. I guess I take after him, and that's what made me a good salesman. Well, anyway, as I said, home was like jail, and so was school, and so was that damned hick town. The only place I liked was the pool rooms, where I could smoke Sweet Caporals, and mop up a couple of beers, thinking I was a hell-on-wheels sport. We had one hooker shop in town, and, of course, I liked that, too. Not that I hardly ever had entrance money. My old man was a tight old bastard. But I liked to sit around in the parlor and joke with the girls, and they liked me because I could kid 'em along and make 'em laugh. Well, you know what a small town is. Everyone got wise to me. They all said I was a no-good tramp. I didn't give a damn what they said. I hated everybody in the place. That is, except Evelyn. I loved Evelyn. Even as a kid. And Evelyn loved me. *(He pauses. No one moves or gives any sign except by the dread in their eyes that they have heard him. Except Parritt, who takes his hands from his face to look at Larry pleadingly)*

PARRITT. I loved Mother, Larry! No matter what she did! I still do! Even though I know she wishes now I was dead! You believe that, don't you? Christ, why can't you say something?

HICKEY *(too absorbed in his story now to notice this—goes on in a tone of fond, sentimental reminiscence)*. Yes, sir, as far back as I can remember, Evelyn and I loved each other. She always stuck up for me. She wouldn't believe the gossip—or she'd pretend she didn't. No one could convince her I was no good. Evelyn was stubborn as all hell once she'd made up her mind. Even when I'd admit things and ask her forgiveness, she'd make excuses for me and defend me against myself. She'd kiss me and say she knew I didn't mean it and I wouldn't do it again. So I'd promise I wouldn't. I'd have to promise, she was so sweet and good, though I knew darned well— *(A touch of strange bitterness comes into his voice for a moment)* No, sir, you couldn't stop Evelyn. Nothing on earth could shake her faith in me. Even I couldn't. She was a sucker for a pipe dream. *(Then quickly)* Well, naturally, her family forbid her seeing me. They were one of the town's best, rich for that hick burg, owned the trolley line and lumber company. Strict Methodists, too. They hated my guts. But they couldn't stop Evelyn. She'd sneak notes to me and meet me on the sly. I was getting more restless. The town was getting more like a jail. I made up my mind to beat it. I knew exactly what I wanted to be by that time. I'd met a lot of drummers around the hotel and liked 'em. They were always telling jokes. They were sports. They kept moving. I liked their life. And I knew I could kid people and sell things. The hitch was how to get the railroad fare to the Big Town. I told Mollie Arlington my trouble. She was the madame of the cathouse. She liked me. She laughed and said, "Hell, I'll stake you, Kid! I'll bet on you. With that grin of yours and that line of bull, you ought to be able to sell skunks for good ratters!" *(He chuckles)* Mollie was all right. She gave me confidence in myself. I paid her back, the first money I earned. Wrote her a kidding letter, I remember, saying I was peddling baby carriages and she and the girls had better take advantage of our bargain offer. *(He chuckles)* But that's ahead of my story. The night before I left town, I had a date with Evelyn. I got all worked up, she was so pretty and sweet and good. I told her straight, "You better forget me, Evelyn, for your own sake. I'm no good and never will be. I'm not worthy to wipe your shoes." I broke down and cried. She just said, looking white and scared, "Why, Teddy? Don't you still love me?" I said, "Love you? God, Evelyn, I love you more than anything in the world. And I always will!" She said, "Then nothing else matters, Teddy, because nothing but death could stop my loving you. So I'll wait, and when you're ready you send for me and we'll be married. I know I can make you happy, Teddy, and once you're happy you won't want to do any of the bad things you've done any more." And I said, "Of course, I won't, Evelyn!" I meant it, too. I believed it. I loved her so much she could make me believe anything. *(He sighs. There is a suspended, waiting silence. Even the two detectives are drawn into it. Then Hope breaks into dully exasperated, brutally callous protest)*

HOPE. Get it over, you long-winded bastard! You married her, and you caught her cheating with the iceman, and you croaked her, and who the hell cares? What's she to us? All we want is to pass out in peace, bejees! *(A chorus of dull, resentful protest from all the group. They mumble, like sleepers who curse a person who keeps awakening them, "What's it to us? We want to pass out in peace!" Hope drinks and they mechanically follow his example. He pours another and they do the same. He complains with a stupid, nagging insistence)* No life in the booze! No kick! Dishwater. Bejees, I'll never pass out!

HICKEY *(goes on as if there had been no interruption)*. So I beat it to the Big Town. I got a job easy, and it was a cinch for me to make good. I had the knack. It was like a game, sizing people up quick, spotting what their pet pipe dreams were, and then kidding 'em along that line, pretending you believed what they wanted to believe about themselves. Then they liked you, they trusted you, they wanted to buy something to show their gratitude. It was fun. But still, all the while I felt guilty, as if I had no right to be having such a good time away from Evelyn. In each letter I'd tell her how I missed her, but I'd keep warning her, too. I'd tell her all my faults, how I liked my booze every once in a while, and so on. But there was no shaking Evelyn's belief in me, or her dreams about the future. After each letter of hers, I'd be as full of faith as she was. So as soon as I got enough saved to start us off, I sent for her and we got married. Christ, wasn't I happy for a while! And wasn't she happy! I don't care what anyone says, I'll bet there never was two people who loved each other more than me and Evelyn. Not only then but always after, in spite of everything I did— *(He pauses— then sadly)* Well, it's all there, at the start, everything that happened afterwards. I never could learn to handle temptation. I'd want to reform and mean it. I'd promise Evelyn, and I'd promise myself, and I'd believe it. I'd tell her, it's the last time. And she'd say, "I know it's the last time, Teddy. You'll never do it again." That's what made it so hard. That's what made me feel such a rotten skunk—her always

forgiving me. My playing around with women, for instance. It was only a harmless good time to me. Didn't mean anything. But I'd know what it meant to Evelyn. So I'd say to myself, never again. But you know how it is, traveling around. The damned hotel rooms. I'd get seeing things in the wall paper. I'd get bored as hell. Lonely and homesick. But at the same time sick of home. I'd feel free and I'd want to celebrate a little. I never drank on the job, so it had to be dames. Any tart. What I'd want was some tramp I could be myself with without being ashamed— someone I could tell a dirty joke to and she'd laugh.

CORA *(with a dull, weary bitterness)*. Jees, all de lousy jokes I've had to listen to and pretend was funny!

HICKEY *(goes on obliviously)*. Sometimes I'd try some joke I thought was a corker on Evelyn. She'd always make herself laugh. But I could tell she thought it was dirty, not funny. And Evelyn always knew about the tarts I'd been with when I came home from a trip. She'd kiss me and look in my eyes, and she'd know. I'd see in her eyes how she was trying not to know, and then telling herself even if it was true, he couldn't help it, they tempt him, and he's lonely, he hasn't got me, it's only his body, anyway, he doesn't love them, I'm the only one he loves. She was right, too. I never loved anyone else. Couldn't if I wanted to. *(He pauses)* She forgave me even when it all had to come out in the open. You know how it is when you keep taking chances. You may be lucky for a long time, but you get nicked in the end. I picked up a nail from some tart in Altoona.

CORA *(dully, without resentment)*. Yeah. And she picked it up from some guy. It's all in de game. What de hell of it?

HICKEY. I had to do a lot of lying and stalling when I got home. It didn't do any good. The quack I went to got all my dough and then told me I was cured and I took his word. But I wasn't, and poor Evelyn— But she did her best to make me believe she fell for my lie about how traveling men get things from drinking cups on trains. Anyway, she forgave me. The same way she forgave me every time I'd turn up after a periodical drunk. You all know what I'd be like at the end of one.

You've seen me. Like something lying in the gutter that no alley cat would lower itself to drag in—something they threw out of the D.T. ward in Bellevue along with the garbage, something that ought to be dead and isn't! *(His face is convulsed with self-loathing)* Evelyn wouldn't have heard from me in a month or more. She'd have been waiting there alone, with the neighbors shaking their heads and feeling sorry for her out loud. That was before she got me to move to the outskirts, where there weren't any next-door neighbors. And then the door would open and in I'd stumble—looking like what I've said—into her home, where she kept everything so spotless and clean. And I'd sworn it would never happen again, and now I'd have to start swearing again this was the last time. I could see disgust having a battle in her eyes with love. Love always won. She'd make herself kiss me, as if nothing had happened, as if I'd just come home from a business trip. She'd never complain or bawl me out. *(He bursts out in a tone of anguish that has anger and hatred beneath it)* Christ, can you imagine what a guilty skunk she made me feel! If she'd only admitted once she didn't believe any more in her pipe dream that some day I'd behave! But she never would. Evelyn was stubborn as hell. Once she'd set her heart on anything, you couldn't shake her faith that it had to come true—tomorrow! It was the same old story, over and over, for years and years. It kept piling up, inside her and inside me. God, can you picture all I made her suffer, and all the guilt she made me feel, and how I hated myself! If she only hadn't been so damned good—if she'd been the same kind of wife I was a husband. God, I used to pray sometimes she'd—I'd even say to her, "Go on, why don't you, Evelyn? It'd serve me right. I wouldn't mind. I'd forgive you." Of course, I'd pretend I was kidding—the same way I used to joke here about her being in the hay with the iceman. She'd have been so hurt if I'd said it seriously. She'd have thought I'd stopped loving her. *(He pauses—then looking around at them)* I suppose you think I'm a liar, that no woman could have stood all she stood and still loved me so much—that it isn't human for any woman to be so pitying and forgiving. Well, I'm not lying, and if you'd ever seen her, you're realize I wasn't. It was written all over her face, sweetness and love and pity and forgiveness. *(He reaches mechanically for the inside pocket of his coat)* Wait! I'll show you. I always carry her picture. *(Suddenly he looks startled. He stares before him, his hand falling back—quietly)* No, I'm forgetting I tore it up—afterwards. I didn't need it any more. *(He pauses. The silence is like that in the room of a dying man where people hold their breath, waiting for him to die)*

CORA *(with a muffled sob)*. Jees, Hickey! Jees! *(She shivers and puts her hands over her face)*

PARRITT *(to Larry in a low insistent tone)*. I burnt up Mother's picture, Larry. Her eyes followed me all the time. They seemed to be wishing I was dead!

HICKEY. It kept piling up, like I've said. I got so I thought of it all the time. I hated myself more and more, thinking of all the wrong I'd done to the sweetest woman in the world who loved me so much. I got so I'd curse myself for a lousy bastard every time I saw myself in the mirror. I felt such pity for her it drove me crazy. You wouldn't believe a guy like me, that's knocked around so much, could feel such pity. It got so every night I'd wind up hiding my face in her lap, bawling and begging her forgiveness. And, of course, she'd always comfort me and say, "Never mind, Teddy, I know you won't ever again." Christ, I loved her so, but I began to hate that pipe dream! I began to be afraid I was going bughouse, because sometimes I couldn't forgive her for forgiving me. I even caught myself hating her for making me hate myself so much. There's a limit to the guilt you can feel and the forgiveness and the pity you can take! You have to begin blaming someone else, too. I got so sometimes when she'd kiss me it was like she did it on purpose to humiliate me, as if she'd spit in my face! But all the time I saw how crazy and rotten of me that was, and it made me hate myself all the more. You'd never believe I could hate so much, a good-natured, happy-go-lucky slob like me. And as the time got nearer to when I was due to come here for my drunk around Harry's birthday, I got nearly crazy. I kept swearing to her every night that this time I really wouldn't, until I'd made it a real final test to myself—and to her. And she kept encouraging me and saying, "I can see you really mean it now, Teddy. I know you'll conquer it this time, and we'll be so happy, dear." When she'd say that and kiss me, I'd believe it, too. Then she'd go to bed, and I'd stay up alone because I couldn't sleep and I didn't want to disturb her, tossing and rolling around. I'd get so damned lonely. I'd get thinking how peaceful it was here, sitting around with the old gang, getting drunk and forgetting love, joking and laughing and singing and swapping lies. And finally I knew I'd have to come. And I knew if I came this time, it was the finish. I'd never have the guts to go back and be forgiven again, and that would break Evelyn's heart because to her it would mean I didn't love her any more. (*He pauses*) That last night I'd driven myself crazy trying to figure some way out for her. I went in the bedroom. I was going to tell her it was the end. But I couldn't do that to her. She was sound asleep. I thought, God, if she'd only never wake up, she'd never know! And then it came to me—the only possible way out, for her sake. I remembered I'd given her a gun for protection while I was away and it was in the bureau drawer. She'd never feel any pain, never wake up from her dream. So I—

HOPE (*tries to ward this off by pounding with his glass on the table—with brutal, callous exasperation*). Give us a rest, for the love of Christ! Who the hell cares? We want to pass out in peace!

(*They all, except Parritt and Larry, pound with their glasses and grumble in chorus: "Who the hell cares? We want to pass out in peace!" Moran, the detective, moves quietly from the entrance in the curtain across the back of the room to the table where his companion, Lieb, is sitting. Rocky notices his leaving and gets up from the table in the rear and goes back to stand and watch in the entrance. Moran exchanges a glance with Lieb, motioning him to get up. The latter does so. No one notices them. The clamor of banging glasses dies out as abruptly as it started. Hickey hasn't appeared to hear it.*)

HICKEY (*simply*). So I killed her. (*There is a moment of dead silence. Even the detectives are caught in it and stand motionless*)

PARRITT (*suddenly gives up and relaxes limply in his chair—in a low voice in which there is a strange exhausted relief*). I may as well confess, Larry. There's no use lying any more. You know, anyway. I didn't give a damn about the money. It was because I hated her.

HICKEY (*obliviously*). And then I saw I'd always known that was the only possible way to give her peace and free her from the misery of loving me. I saw it meant peace for me, too, knowing she was at peace. I felt as though a ton of guilt was lifted off my mind. I remember I stood by the bed and suddenly I had to laugh. I couldn't help it, and I knew Evelyn would forgive me. I remember I heard myself speaking to her, as if it was something I'd always wanted to say: "Well, you know what you can do with your pipe dream now, you damned bitch!" (*He stops with a horrified start, as if shocked out of a nightmare, as if he couldn't believe he heard what he had just said. He stammers*) No! I never—!

PARRITT (*to Larry—sneeringly*). Yes, that's it! Her and the damned old Movement pipe dream! Eh, Larry?

HICKEY (*bursts into frantic denial*). No! That's a lie! I never said—! Good God, I couldn't have said that! If I did, I'd gone insane! Why, I loved Evelyn better than anything in life! (*He appeals brokenly to the crowd*) Boys, you're all my old pals! You've known old Hickey for years! You know I'd never— (*His eyes fix on Hope*) You've known me longer than anyone, Harry. You know I must have been insane, don't you, Governor?

HOPE (*at first with the same defensive callousness—without looking at him*). Who the hell cares? (*Then suddenly he looks at Hickey and there is an extraordinary change in his expression. His face lights up, as if he were grasping at some dawning hope in his mind. He speaks with a groping eagerness*) Insane? You mean—you really went insane? (*At the tone of his voice, all the group at the tables by him start and stare at him as if they caught his thought. Then they all look at Hickey eagerly, too*)

HICKEY. Yes! Or I couldn't have laughed! I couldn't have said that to her! (*Moran walks up behind him on one side, while the second detective, Lieb, closes in on him from the other*)

MORAN (*taps Hickey on the shoulder*). That's enough, Hickman. You know who we are. You're under arrest. (*He nods to Lieb, who slips a pair of handcuffs on Hickey's wrists. Hickey stares at them with stupid incomprehension. Moran takes his arm*) Come along and spill your guts where we can get it on paper.

HICKEY. No, wait, Officer! You owe me a break! I phoned and made it easy for you, didn't I? Just a few minutes! (*To Hope—pleadingly*) You know I couldn't say that to Evelyn, don't you, Harry—unless—

HOPE (*eagerly*). And you've been crazy ever since? Everything you've said and done here—

HICKEY (*for a moment forgets his own obsession and his face takes on its familiar expression of affectionate amusement and he chuckles*). Now, Governor! Up to your old tricks, eh? I see what you're driving at, but I can't let you get away with— (*Then, as Hope's expression turns to resentful callousness again and he looks away, he adds hastily with pleading desperation*) Yes, Harry, of course, I've been out of my mind ever since! All the time I've been here! You saw I was insane, didn't you?

MORAN (*with cynical disgust*). Can it! I've had enough of your act. Save it for the jury. (*Addressing the crowd, sharply*) Listen, you guys. Don't fall for his lies. He's starting to get foxy now and thinks he'll plead insanity. But he can't get away with it. (*The crowd at the grouped tables are grasping at hope now. They glare at him resentfully*)

HOPE (*begins to bristle in his old-time manner*). Bejees, you dumb dick, you've got a crust trying to tell us about Hickey! We've known him for years, and every one of us noticed he was nutty the minute he showed up here! Bejees, if you'd heard all the crazy bull he was pulling about bringing us peace—like a bughouse preacher escaped from an asylum! If you'd seen all the damnedfool things he made us do! We only did them because— (*He hesitates—then defiantly*) Because we hoped he'd come out of it if we kidded him along and humored him. (*He looks around at the others*) Ain't that right, fellers? (*They burst into a chorus of eager assent: "Yes, Harry!" "That's it, Harry!"*

"That's why!" "We knew he was crazy!" "Just to humor him!"*)

MORAN. A fine bunch of rats! Covering up for a dirty, cold-blooded murderer.

HOPE (*stung into recovering all his old fuming truculence*). Is that so? Bejees, you know the old story, when Saint Patrick drove the snakes out of Ireland they swam to New York and joined the police force! Ha! (*He cackles insultingly*) Bejees, we can believe it now when we look at you, can't we, fellers? (*They all growl assent, glowering defiantly at Moran. Moran glares at them, looking as if he'd like to forget his prisoner and start cleaning out the place. Hope goes on pugnaciously*) You stand up for your rights, bejees, Hickey! Don't let this smartaleck dick get funny with you. If he pulls any rubber-hose tricks, you let me know! I've still got friends at the Hall! Bejees, I'll have him back in uniform pounding a beat where the only graft he'll get will be stealing tin cans from the goats!

MORAN (*furiously*). Listen, you cock-eyed old bum, for a plugged nickel I'd— (*Controlling himself, he turns to Hickey, who is oblivious to all this, and yanks his arm*) Come on, you!

HICKEY (*with a strange mad earnestness*). Oh, I want to go, Officer. I can hardly wait now. I should have phoned you from the house right afterwards. It was a waste of time coming here. I've got to explain to Evelyn. But I know she's forgiven me. She knows I was insane. You've got me all wrong, Officer. I want to go to the Chair.

MORAN. Crap!

HICKEY (*exasperatedly*). God, you're a dumb dick! Do you suppose I give a damn about life now? Why, you bonehead, I haven't got a single damned lying hope or pipe dream left!

MORAN (*jerks him around to face the door to the hall*). Get a move on!

HICKEY (*as they start walking toward rear—insistently*). All I want you to see is I was out of my mind afterwards, when I laughed at her! I was a raving rotten lunatic or I couldn't have said— Why, Evelyn was the only thing on God's earth I ever loved! I'd have killed myself before I'd ever have hurt her! (*They disappear in the hall. Hickey's voice keeps on protesting*)

HOPE *(calls after him)*. Don't worry, Hickey! They can't give you the Chair! We'll testify you was crazy! Won't we, fellers? *(They all assent. Two or three echo Hope's "Don't worry, Hickey." Then from the hall comes the slam of the street door. Hope's face falls—with genuine sorrow)* He's gone. Poor crazy son of a bitch! *(All the group around him are sad and sympathetic, too. Hope reaches for his drink)* Bejees, I need a drink. *(They grab their glasses. Hope says hopefully)* Bejees, maybe it'll have the old kick, now he's gone. *(He drinks and they follow suit)*

ROCKY *(comes forward from where he has stood in the bar entrance—hopefully)*. Yeah, Boss, maybe we can get drunk now. *(He sits in the chair by Chuck and pours a drink and tosses it down. Then they all sit still, waiting for the effect, as if this drink were a crucial test, so absorbed in hopeful expectancy that they remain oblivious to what happens at Larry's table)*

LARRY *(his eyes full of pain and pity—in a whisper, aloud to himself)*. May the Chair bring him peace at last, the poor tortured bastard!

PARRITT *(leans toward him—in a strange low insistent voice)*. Yes, but he isn't the only one who needs peace, Larry. I can't feel sorry for him. He's lucky. He's through, now. It's all decided for him. I wish it was decided for me. I've never been any good at deciding things. Even about selling out, it was the tart the detective agency got after me who put it in my mind. You remember what Mother's like, Larry. She makes all the decisions. She's always decided what I must do. She doesn't like anyone to be free but herself. *(He pauses, as if waiting for comment, but Larry ignores him)* I suppose you think I ought to have made those dicks take me away with Hickey. But how could I prove it, Larry? They'd think I was nutty. Because she's still alive. You're the only one who can understand how guilty I am. Because you know her and what I've done to her. You know I'm really much guiltier than he is. You know what I did is a much worse murder. Because she is dead and yet she has to live. For a while. But she can't live long in jail. She loves freedom too much. And I can't kid myself like Hickey, that she's at peace. As long as she lives, she'll never be able to forget what I've done to her even in her sleep. She'll

never have a second's peace. *(He pauses—then bursts out)* Jesus, Larry, can't you say something? *(Larry is at the breaking point. Parritt goes on)* And I'm not putting up any bluff, either, that I was crazy afterwards when I laughed to myself and thought, "You know what you can do with your freedom pipe dream now, don't you, you damned old bitch!"

LARRY *(snaps and turns on him, his face convulsed with detestation. His quivering voice has a condemning command in it)*. Go! Get the hell out of life, God damn you, before I choke it out of you! Go up—!

PARRITT *(his manner is at once transformed. He seems suddenly at peace with himself. He speaks simply and gratefully)*. Thanks, Larry. I just wanted to be sure. I can see now it's the only possible way I can ever get free from her. I guess I've really known that all my life. *(He pauses—then with a derisive smile)* It ought to comfort Mother a little, too. It'll give her the chance to play the great incorruptible Mother of the Revolution, whose only child is the Proletariat. She'll be able to say: "I am glad he's dead! Long live the Revolution!" *(He adds with a final implacable jeer)* You know her, Larry! Always a ham!

LARRY *(pleads distractedly)*. Go, for the love of Christ, you mad tortured bastard, for your own sake! *(Hugo is roused by this. He lifts his head and peers uncomprehendingly at Larry. Neither Larry nor Parritt notices him)*

PARRITT *(stares at Larry. His face begins to crumble as if he were going to break down and sob. He turns his head away, but reaches out fumblingly and pats Larry's arm and stammers)*. Jesus, Larry, thanks. That's kind. I knew you were the only one who could understand my side of it. *(He gets to his feet and turns toward the door)*

HUGO *(looks at Parritt and bursts into his silly giggle)*. Hello, leedle Don, leedle monkey-face! Don't be a fool! Buy me a trink!

PARRITT *(puts on an act of dramatic bravado—forcing a grin)*. Sure, I will, Hugo! Tomorrow! Beneath the willow trees! *(He walks to the door with a careless swagger and disappears in the hall. From now on, Larry waits, listening for the sound he knows is coming from the backyard out-side the window, but trying not to listen, in an agony of horror and cracking nerve)*

HUGO *(stares after Parritt stupidly).* Stupid fool! Hickey make you crazy, too. *(He turns to the oblivious Larry—with a timid eagerness)* I'm glad, Larry, they take that crazy Hickey avay to asylum. He makes me have bad dreams. He makes me tell lies about myself. He makes me want to spit on all I have ever dreamed. Yes, I am glad they take him to asylum. I don't feel I am dying now. He vas selling death to me, that crazy salesman. I think I have a trink now, Larry. *(He pours a drink and gulps it down)*

HOPE *(jubilantly).* Bejees, fellers, I'm feeling the old kick, or I'm a liar! It's putting life back in me! Bejees, if all I've lapped up begins to hit me, I'll be paralyzed before I know it! It was Hickey kept it from— Bejees, I know that sounds crazy, but he was crazy, and he'd got all of us as bughouse as he was. Bejees, it does queer things to you, having to listen day and night to a lunatic's pipe dreams—pretending you believe them, to kid him along and doing any crazy thing he wants to humor him. It's dangerous, too. Look at me pretending to start for a walk just to keep him quiet. I knew damned well it wasn't the right day for it. The sun was broiling and the streets full of automobiles. Bejees, I could feel myself getting sunstroke, and an automobile damn near ran over me. *(He appeals to Rocky, afraid of the result, but daring it)* Ask Rocky. He was watching. Didn't it, Rocky?

ROCKY *(a bit tipsily).* What's dat, Boss? Jees, all de booze I've mopped up is beginning to get to me. *(Earnestly)* De automobile, Boss? Sure, I seen it! Just missed yuh! I thought yuh was a goner. *(He pauses—then looks around at the others, and assumes the old kidding tone of the inmates, but hesitantly, as if still a little afraid)* On de woid of a honest bartender! *(He tries a wink at the others. They all respond with smiles that are still a little forced and uneasy)*

HOPE *(flashes him a suspicious glance. Then he understands—with his natural testy manner).* You're a bartender, all right. No one can say different. *(Rocky looks grateful)* But, bejees, don't pull that honest junk! You and Chuck ought to have cards in the Burglars' Union! *(This*

time there is an eager laugh from the group. Hope is delighted) Bejees, it's good to hear someone laugh again! All the time that bas—poor old Hickey was here, I didn't have the heart— Bejees, I'm getting drunk and glad of it! *(He cackles and reaches for the bottle)* Come on, fellers. It's on the house. *(They pour drinks. They begin rapidly to get drunk now. Hope becomes sentimental)* Poor old Hickey! We mustn't hold him responsible for anything he's done. We'll forget that and only remember him the way we've always known him before—the kindest, biggest-hearted guy ever wore shoe leather. *(They all chorus hearty sentimental assent: "That's right, Harry!" "That's all!" "Finest fellow!" "Best scout!" etc. Hope goes on)* Good luck to him in Matteawan! Come on, bottoms up! *(They all drink. At the table by the window Larry's hands grip the edge of the table. Unconsciously his head is inclined toward the window as he listens)*

LARRY *(cannot hold back an anguished exclamation).* Christ! Why don't he—!

HUGO *(beginning to be drunk again—peers at him).* Vhy don't he what? Don't be a fool! Hickey's gone. He vas crazy. Have a trink. *(Then as he receives no reply—with vague uneasiness)* What's matter vith you, Larry? You look funny. What you listen to out in backyard, Larry? *(Cora begins to talk in the group at right)*

CORA *(tipsily).* Well, I thank Gawd now me and Chuck did all we could to humor de poor nut. Jees, imagine us goin' off like we really meant to git married, when we ain't even picked out a farm yet!

CHUCK *(eagerly).* Sure ting, Baby. We kidded him we was serious.

JIMMY *(confidently—with a gentle, drunken unction).* I may as well say I detected his condition almost at once. All that talk of his about tomorrow, for example. He had the fixed idea of the insane. It only makes them worse to cross them.

WILLIE *(eagerly).* Same with me, Jimmy. Only I spent the day in the park. I wasn't such a damned fool as to—

LEWIS *(getting jauntily drunk).* Picture my predicament if I *had* gone to the Consulate. The pal of mine there is a humorous blighter. He would have got me a job out of pure spite. So I strolled about and finally came to roost in the park. (*He grins with affectionate kidding at Wetjoen*) And lo and behold, who was on the neighboring bench but my old battlefield companion, the Boer that walks like a man —who, if the British Government had taken my advice, would have been removed from his fetid kraal on the veldt straight to the baboon's cage at the London Zoo, and little children would now be asking their nurses: "Tell me, Nana, is that the Boer General, the one with the blue behind?" (*They all laugh uproariously. Lewis leans over and slaps Wetjoen affectionately on the knee*) No offense meant, Piet, old chap.

WETJOEN (*beaming at him*). No offense taken, you tamned Limey! (*Wetjoen goes on—grinningly*) About a job, I felt the same as you, Cecil.

(*At the table by the window Hugo speaks to Larry again.*)

HUGO (*with uneasy insistence*). What's matter, Larry? You look scared. What you listen for out there? (*But Larry doesn't hear, and Joe begins talking in the group at right*)

JOE (*with drunken self-assurance*). No, suh, I wasn't fool enough to git in no crap game. Not while Hickey's around. Crazy people puts a jinx on you.

(*McGloin is now heard. He is leaning across in front of Wetjoen to talk to Ed Mosher on Hope's left.*)

MCGLOIN (*with drunken earnestness*). I know you saw how it was, Ed. There was no good trying to explain to a crazy guy, but it ain't the right time. You know how getting reinstated is.

MOSHER (*decidedly*). Sure, Mac. The same way with the circus. The boys tell me the rubes are wasting all their money buying food and times never was so hard. And I never was one to cheat for chicken feed.

HOPE (*looks around him in an ecstasy of bleary sentimental content*). Bejees, I'm cockeyed! Bejees, you're all cockeyed! Bejees, we're all right! Let's have another! (*They pour out drinks. At the table by the window Larry has unconsciously shut his eyes as he listens. Hugo is peering at him frightenedly now*)

HUGO (*reiterates stupidly*). What's matter, Larry? Why you keep eyes shut? You look dead. What you listen for in back-

yard? (*Then, as Larry doesn't open his eyes or answer, he gets up hastily and moves away from the table, mumbling with frightened anger*) Crazy fool! You vas crazy like Hickey! You give me bad dreams, too. (*He shrinks quickly past the table where Hickey had sat to the rear of the group at right*)

ROCKY (*greets him with boisterous affection*). Hello, dere, Hugo! Welcome to de party!

HOPE. Yes, bejees, Hugo! Sit down! Have a drink! Have ten drinks, bejees!

HUGO (*forgetting Larry and bad dreams, gives his familiar giggle*). Hello, leedle Harry! Hello, nice, leedle, funny monkeyfaces! (*Warming up, changes abruptly to his usual declamatory denunciation*) Gottamned stupid bourgeois! Soon comes the Day of Judgment! (*They make derisive noises and tell him to sit down. He changes again, giggling good-naturedly, and sits at rear of the middle table*) Give me ten trinks, Harry. Don't be a fool. (*They laugh. Rocky shoves a glass and bottle at him. The sound of Margie's and Pearl's voices is heard from the hall, drunkenly shrill. All of the group turn toward the door as the two appear. They are drunk and look blowsy and disheveled. Their manner as they enter hardens into a brazen defensive truculence*)

MARGIE (*stridently*). Gangway for two good whores!

PEARL. Yeah! And we want a drink quick!

MARGIE (*glaring at Rocky*). Shake de lead outa your pants, Pimp! A little soivice!

ROCKY (*his black bullet eyes sentimental, his round Wop face grinning welcome*). Well, look who's here! (*He goes to them unsteadily, opening his arms*) Hello, dere, Sweethearts! Jees, I was beginnin' to worry about yuh, honest! (*He tries to embrace them. They push his arms away, regarding him with amazed suspicion*)

PEARL. What kind of a gag is dis?

HOPE (*calls to them effusively*). Come on and join the party, you broads! Bejees, I'm glad to see you! (*The girls exchange a bewildered glance, taking in the party and the changed atmosphere*)

MARGIE. Jees, what's come off here?

PEARL. Where's dat louse, Hickey?

ROCKY. De cops got him. He'd gone crazy and croaked his wife. *(The girls exclaim, "Jees!" But there is more relief than horror in it. Rocky goes on)* He'll get Matteawan. He ain't responsible. What he's pulled don't mean nuttin'. So forget dat whore stuff. I'll knock de block off anyone calls you whores! I'll fill de bastard full of lead! Yuh're tarts, and what de hell of it? Yuh're as good as anyone. So forget it, see? *(They let him get his arms around them now. He gives them a hug. All the truculence leaves their faces. They smile and exchange maternally amused glances)*

MARGIE *(with a wink)*. Our little bartender, ain't he, Poil?

PEARL. Yeah, and a cute little Ginny at dat! *(They laugh)*

MARGIE. And is he stinko!

PEARL. Stinko is right. But he ain't got nuttin' on us. Jees, Rocky, did we have a big time at Coney!

HOPE. Bejees, sit down, you dumb broads! Welcome home! Have a drink! Have ten drinks, bejees! *(They take the empty chairs on Chuck's left, warmly welcomed by all. Rocky stands in back of them, a hand on each of their shoulders, grinning with proud proprietorship. Hope beams over and under his crooked spectacles with the air of a host whose party is a huge success, and rambles on happily)* Bejees, this is all right! We'll make this my birthday party, and forget the other. We'll get paralyzed! But who's missing? Where's the Old Wise Guy? Where's Larry?

ROCKY. Over by de window, Boss. Jees, he's got his eyes shut. De old bastard's asleep. *(They turn to look. Rocky dismisses him)* Aw, to hell wid him. Let's have a drink. *(They turn away and forget him)*

LARRY *(torturedly arguing to himself in a shaken whisper)*. It's the only way out for him! For the peace of all concerned, as Hickey said! *(Snapping)* God damn his yellow soul, if he doesn't soon, I'll go up and throw him off!—like a dog with its guts ripped out you'd put out of misery! *(He half rises from his chair just as from outside the window comes the sound of something hurtling down, followed by a muffled, crunching thud. Larry gasps and drops back on his chair, shuddering, hiding his face in his hands. The group at right hear it but are too preoccupied with drinks to pay much attention.)*

HOPE *(wonderingly)*. What the hell was that?

ROCKY. Aw, nuttin'. Someting fell off de fire escape. A mattress, I'll bet. Some of dese bums been sleepin' on de fire escapes.

HOPE *(his interest diverted by this excuse to beef—testily)*. They've got to cut it out! Bejees, this ain't a fresh-air cure. Mattresses cost money.

MOSHER. Now don't start crabbing at the party, Harry. Let's drink up. *(Hope forgets it and grabs his glass, and they all drink)*

LARRY *(in a whisper of horrified pity)*. Poor devil! *(A long-forgotten faith returns to him for a moment and he mumbles)* God rest his soul in peace. *(He opens his eyes—with a bitter self-derision)* Ah, the damned pity—the wrong kind, as Hickey said! Be God, there's no hope! I'll never be a success in the grandstand—or anywhere else! Life is too much for me! I'll be a weak fool looking with pity at the two sides of everything till the day I die! *(With an intense bitter sincerity)* May that day come soon! *(He pauses startledly, surprised at himself—then with a sardonic grin)* Be God, I'm the only real convert to death Hickey made here. From the bottom of my coward's heart I mean that now!

HOPE *(calls effusively)*. Hey there, Larry! Come over and get paralyzed! What the hell you doing, sitting there? *(Then as Larry doesn't reply he immediately forgets him and turns to the party. They are all very drunk now, just a few drinks ahead of the passing-out stage, and hilariously happy about it)* Bejees, let's sing! Let's celebrate! It's my birthday party! Bejees, I'm oreyeyed! I want to sing! *(He starts the chorus of "She's the Sunshine of Paradise Alley," and instantly they all burst into song. But not the same song. Each starts the chorus of his or her choice. Jimmy Tomorrow's is "A Wee Dock and Doris"; Ed Mosher's, "Break the News to Mother"; Willie Oban's, the Sailor Lad ditty he sang in Act One; General Wetjoen's, "Waiting at the Church"; McGloin's, "Tammany"; Captain Lewis's, "The Old Kent Road"; Joe's, "All I Got Was Sympathy"; Pearl's and Margie's, "Everybody's Doing It"; Rocky's, "You*

Great Big Beautiful Doll"; Chuck's, "The Curse of an Aching Heart"; Cora's, "The Oceana Roll"; while Hugo jumps to his feet and, pounding on the table with his fist, bellows in his guttural basso the French Revolutionary "Carmagnole." A weird cacophony results from this mixture and they stop singing to roar with laughter. All but Hugo, who keeps on with drunken fervor.)

HUGO. "Dansons la Carmagnole!

Vive le son! Vive le son!

Dansons la Carmagnole!

Vive le son des canons!"

(They all turn on him and howl him down with amused derision. He stops singing to denounce them in his most fiery style) Capitalist svine! Stupid bourgeois monkeys! *(He declaims)* "The days grow hot, O Babylon!" *(They all take it up and shout in enthusiastic jeering chorus)* " 'Tis cool beneath thy willow trees!" *(They pound their glasses on the table, roaring with laughter, and Hugo giggles with them. In his chair by the window, Larry stares in front of him, oblivious to their racket)*

CURTAIN

The Member of the Wedding

BY CARSON McCULLERS

First presented by Robert Whitehead, Oliver Rea and Stanley Martineau at the Empire Theatre in New York on January 5, 1950, with the following cast:

BERENICE SADIE BROWN	Ethel Waters	MRS. WEST	Margaret Barker
FRANKIE ADDAMS	Julie Harris	HELEN FLETCHER	Mitzie Blake
JOHN HENRY WEST	Brandon de Wilde	DORIS	Joan Shepard
JARVIS	James Holden	SIS LAURA	Phyllis Walker
JANICE	Janet de Gore	T. T. WILLIAMS	Harry Bolden
MR. ADDAMS	William Hansen	HONEY CAMDEN BROWN	Henry Scott
	BARNEY MacKEAN	Jimmy Dutton	

ACT ONE

A late afternoon in August.

ACT TWO

Afternoon of the next day.

ACT THREE

Scene One: The wedding day—afternoon of the next day following Act Two.
Scene Two: 4 A.M. the following morning.
Scene Three: Late afternoon, in the following November.

Time: August, 1945
Place: A small Southern town

ALTHOUGH Carson McCullers, who was born in Columbus, Georgia, in 1917, has been writing since the age of sixteen, her first interest was music and the pursuit of a career as a concert pianist. In fact, she came to New York at the age of seventeen in order to study at Columbia University's Juilliard School of Music. This laudable intention died virtually aborning when she lost her tuition money in the subway during her second day in the city. Since she had no other resources, she took on a variety of jobs she was fortunately (in retrospect) unable to retain while settling for an inexpensive writing course at New York University. And fate apparently had her definitely marked for a literary and theatrical career by then, since she found herself living in the same house in Brooklyn as the poet W. H. Auden and the now prominent British opera composer Benjamin Britten.

A year later, Mrs. Carson McCullers (she was married in 1937 to a Southerner, Reeves McCullers) sold two short stories to *Story Magazine* and began a novel, *The Heart Is a Lonely Hunter,* published in 1940, which won her high critical acclaim. In 1941 she published a second book, the short novel *Reflections in a Golden Eye,* which *Time Magazine* compared favorably to *The Turn of the Screw.* Her third and longer novel *The Member of the Wedding,* published in 1946, indicated the addition of a humorous tenderness to her intense talent. In 1951 the last two novels, along with a new novella and six of her stories, were collected in another volume, *The Ballad of the Sad Café.* For these contributions she was awarded two Guggenheim Fellowships and was made a member of the American Academy of Art.

A young Southerner having made a dramatization of *The Member of the Wedding* that did not please her, although it was optioned by the Theatre Guild, Mrs. McCullers decided to dramatize the book herself. In venturing upon this enterprise, she worked without preparation in the field of playwriting, having, in fact, seen only two Broadway productions and a few plays while still at school. All the assistance she had was encouragement from Tennessee Williams, who urged her to make the dramatization. All her novels had stressed the fact of loneliness and human isolation. Her dramatization simply translated this reality into dialogue and dramatic representation. Mrs. McCullers was acutely aware of her intentions and, as she later explained, she was not writing a "conventional" or "literal kind of play." It was, she declared, "an inward play," in which the conflict was inward and the antagonist was not a person, but "a human condition." To give proper realization to her theme, she concerned herself, she declared, with "the weight of time, the hazard of human existence, bolts of chance." As a result the play was inevitably "fragmentary." It could be argued quite reasonably, however, that the "fragmentariness" of the play is an essential expression of the transitory experience Mrs. McCullers was intent upon evoking. A "well-made play," a methodical elaboration of meshing plot elements, would have violated the integrity of the novel's substance.

ACT ONE

A part of a Southern back yard and kitchen. At stage left there is a scuppernong arbor. A sheet, used as a stage curtain, hangs raggedly at one side of the arbor. There is an elm tree in the yard. The kitchen has in the center a table with chairs. The walls are drawn with child drawings. There is a stove to the right and a small coal heating stove with coal scuttle in rear center of kitchen. The kitchen opens on the left into the yard. At the interior right a door leads to a small inner room. A door at the left leads into the front hall. The lights go on dimly, with a dreamlike effect, gradually revealing the family in the yard and Berenice Sadie Brown in the kitchen. Berenice, the cook, is a stout, motherly Negro woman with an air of great capability and devoted protection. She is about forty-five years old. She has a quiet, flat face and one of her eyes is made of blue glass. Sometimes, when her socket bothers her, she dispenses with the false eye and wears a black patch. When we first see her she is wearing the patch and is dressed in a simple print work dress and apron.

Frankie, a gangling girl of twelve with blonde hair cut like a boy's, is wearing shorts and a sombrero and is standing in the arbor gazing adoringly at her brother Jarvis and his fiancée Janice. She is a dreamy, restless girl, and periods of energetic activity alternate with a rapt attention to her inward world of fantasy. She is thin and awkward and very much aware of being too tall. Jarvis, a good-looking boy of twenty-one, wearing an army uniform, stands by Janice. He is awkward when he first appears because this is his betrothal visit. Janice, a young, pretty, fresh-looking girl of eighteen or nineteen, is charming but rather ordinary, with brown hair done up in a small knot. She is dressed in her best clothes and is anxious to be liked by her new family. Mr. Addams, Frankie's father, is a deliberate and absent-minded man of about forty-five. A widower of many years, he has become set in his habits. He is dressed conservatively, and there is about him an old-fashioned look and manner. John Henry, Frankie's small cousin, aged seven, picks and eats any scuppernongs he can reach. He is a delicate, active boy and wears gold-rimmed spectacles which give him an oddly judicious look. He is blond and sun-burned and when we first see him he is wearing a sun-suit and is barefooted.

(Berenice Sadie Brown is busy in the kitchen.)

JARVIS. Seems to me like this old arbor has shrunk. I remember when I was a child it used to seem absolutely enormous. When I was Frankie's age, I had a vine swing here. Remember, Papa?

FRANKIE. It don't seem so absolutely enormous to me, because I am so tall.

JARVIS. I never saw a human grow so fast in all my life. I think maybe we ought to tie a brick to your head.

FRANKIE *(hunching down in obvious distress)*. Oh, Jarvis! Don't.

JANICE. Don't tease your little sister. I don't think Frankie is too tall. She probably won't grow much more. I had the biggest portion of my growth by the time I was thirteen.

FRANKIE. But I'm just twelve. When I think of all the growing years ahead of me, I get scared.

(Janice goes to Frankie and puts her arms around her comfortingly. Frankie stands rigid, embarrassed and blissful.)

JANICE. I wouldn't worry.

(Berenice comes from the kitchen with a tray of drinks. Frankie rushes eagerly to help her serve them.)

FRANKIE. Let me help.

BERENICE. Them two drinks is lemonade for you and John Henry. The others got liquor in them.

FRANKIE. Janice, come sit down on the arbor seat. Jarvis, you sit down too.

(Jarvis and Janice sit close together on the wicker bench in the arbor. Frankie hands the drinks around, then perches on the ground before Janice and Jarvis and stares adoringly at them.)

FRANKIE. It was such a surprise when Jarvis wrote home you are going to be married.

JANICE. I hope it wasn't a bad surprise.

FRANKIE. Oh, Heavens no! *(With great feeling)* As a matter of fact . . . *(She strokes Janice's shoes tenderly and Jarvis' army boot)* If only you knew how I feel.

MR. ADDAMS. Frankie's been bending my ears ever since your letter came, Jarvis. Going on about weddings, brides, grooms, etc.

JANICE. It's lovely that we can be married at Jarvis' home.

MR. ADDAMS. That's the way to feel, Janice. Marriage is a sacred institution.

FRANKIE. Oh, it will be beautiful.

JARVIS. Pretty soon we'd better be shoving off for Winter Hill. I have to be back in barracks tonight.

FRANKIE. Winter Hill is such a lovely, cold name. It reminds me of ice and snow.

JANICE. You know it's just a hundred miles away, darling.

JARVIS. Ice and snow indeed! Yesterday the temperature on the parade ground reached 102.

(Frankie takes a palmetto fan from the table and fans first Janice, then Jarvis.)

JANICE. That feels so good, darling. Thanks.

FRANKIE. I wrote you so many letters, Jarvis, and you never, never would answer me. When you were stationed in Alaska, I wanted so much to hear about Alaska. I sent you so many boxes of home-made candy, but you never answered me.

JARVIS. Oh, Frankie. You know how it is . . .

FRANKIE *(sipping her drink)*. You know this lemonade tastes funny. Kind of sharp and hot. I believe I got the drinks mixed up.

JARVIS. I was thinking my drink tasted mighty sissy. Just plain lemonade—no liquor at all.

(Frankie and Jarvis exchange their drinks. Jarvis sips his.)

JARVIS. This is better.

FRANKIE. I drank a lot. I wonder if I'm drunk. It makes me feel like I had four legs instead of two. I think I'm drunk. *(She gets up and begins to stagger around in imitation of drunkenness)* See! I'm drunk! Look, Papa, how drunk I am! *(Suddenly she turns a handspring; then there is a blare of music from the club house gramophone off to the right)*

JANICE. Where does the music come from? It sounds so close.

FRANKIE. It is. Right over there. They have club meetings and parties with boys on Friday nights. I watch them here from the yard.

JANICE. It must be nice having your club house so near.

FRANKIE. I'm not a member now. But they are holding an election this afternoon, and maybe I'll be elected.

JOHN HENRY. Here comes Mama.

(Mrs. West, John Henry's mother, crosses the yard from the right. She is a vivacious, blonde woman of about thirty-three. She is dressed in sleazy, rather dowdy summer clothes.)

MR. ADDAMS. Hello, Pet. Just in time to meet our new family member.

MRS. WEST. I saw you out here from the window.

JARVIS *(rising, with Janice)*. Hi, Aunt Pet. How is Uncle Eustace?

MRS. WEST. He's at the office.

JANICE *(offering her hand with the engagement ring on it)*. Look, Aunt Pet. May I call you Aunt Pet?

MRS. WEST *(hugging her)*. Of course, Janice. What a gorgeous ring!

JANICE. Jarvis just gave it to me this morning. He wanted to consult his father and get it from his store, naturally.

MRS. WEST. How lovely.

MR. ADDAMS. A quarter carat—not too flashy but a good stone.

MRS. WEST *(to Berenice, who is gathering up the empty glasses)*. Berenice, what have you and Frankie been doing to my John Henry? He sticks over here in your kitchen morning, noon and night.

BERENICE. We enjoys him and Candy seems to like it over here.

MRS. WEST. What on earth do you do to him?

BERENICE. We just talks and passes the time of day. Occasionally plays cards.

MRS. WEST. Well, if he gets in your way just shoo him home.

BERENICE. Candy don't bother nobody.

JOHN HENRY *(walking around bare-footed in the arbor)*. These grapes are so squelchy when I step on them.

MRS. WEST. Run home, darling, and wash your feet and put on your sandals.

JOHN HENRY. I like to squelch on the grapes.

(Berenice goes back to the kitchen.)

JANICE. That looks like a stage curtain. Jarvis told me how you used to write plays and act in them out here in the arbor. What kind of shows do you have?

FRANKIE. Oh, crook shows and cowboy shows. This summer I've had some cold shows—about Esquimos and explorers—on account of the hot weather.

JANICE. Do you ever have romances?

FRANKIE. Naw . . . *(With bravado)* I had crook shows for the most part. You see I never believed in love until now. *(Her look lingers on Janice and Jarvis. She hugs Janice and Jarvis, bending over them from back of the bench)*

MRS. WEST. Frankie and this little friend of hers gave a performance of "The Vagabond King" out here last spring.

(John Henry spreads out his arms and imitates the heroine of the play from memory, singing in his high childish voice.

JOHN HENRY. Never hope to bind me. Never hope to know. *(Speaking)* Frankie was the king-boy. I sold the tickets.

MRS. WEST. Yes, I have always said that Frankie has talent.

FRANKIE. Aw, I'm afraid I don't have much talent.

JOHN HENRY. Frankie can laugh and kill people good. She can die, too.

FRANKIE *(with some pride)*. Yeah, I guess I die all right.

MR. ADDAMS. Frankie rounds up John Henry and those smaller children, but by the time she dresses them in the costumes, they're worn out and won't act in the show.

JARVIS *(looking at his watch)*. Well, it's time we shove off for Winter Hill— Frankie's land of icebergs and snow— where the temperature goes up to 102.

(Jarvis takes Janice's hand. He gets up and gazes fondly around the yard and the arbor. He pulls her up and stands with his arm around her, gazing around him at the arbor and yard.)

JARVIS. It carries me back—this smell of mashed grapes and dust. I remember all the endless summer afternoons of my childhood. It does carry me back.

FRANKIE. Me too. It carries me back, too.

MR. ADDAMS *(putting one arm around Janice and shaking Jarvis' hand)*. Merciful Heavens! It seems I have two Methuselahs in my family! Does it carry you back to your childhood too, John Henry?

JOHN HENRY. Yes, Uncle Royal.

MR. ADDAMS. Son, this visit was a real pleasure. Janice, I'm mighty pleased to see my boy has such lucky judgment in choosing a wife.

FRANKIE. I hate to think you have to go. I'm just now realizing you're here.

JARVIS. We'll be back in two days. The wedding is Sunday.

(The family move around the house toward the street. John Henry enters the kitchen through the back door. There are

the sounds of "good-byes" from the front yard.)

JOHN HENRY. Frankie was drunk. She drank a liquor drink.

BERENICE. She just made out like she was drunk—pretended.

JOHN HENRY. She said, "Look, Papa, how drunk I am," and she couldn't walk.

FRANKIE'S VOICE. Good-bye, Jarvis. Good-bye, Janice.

JARVIS' VOICE. See you Sunday.

MR. ADDAMS' VOICE. Drive carefully, son. Good-bye, Janice.

JANICE'S VOICE. Good-bye and thanks, Mr. Addams. Good-bye, Frankie darling.

ALL THE VOICES. Good-bye! Good-bye!

JOHN HENRY. They are going now to Winter Hill.

(There is the sound of the front door opening, then of steps in the hall. Frankie enters through the hall.)

FRANKIE. Oh, I can't understand it! The way it all just suddenly happened.

BERENICE. Happened? Happened?

FRANKIE. I have never been so puzzled.

BERENICE. Puzzled about what?

FRANKIE. The whole thing. They are so beautiful.

BERENICE *(after a pause)*. I believe the sun done fried your brains.

JOHN HENRY *(whispering)* Me too.

BERENICE. Look here at me. You jealous.

FRANKIE. Jealous?

BERENICE. Jealous because your brother's going to be married.

FRANKIE *(slowly)*. No. I just never saw any two people like them. When they walked in the house today it was so queer.

BERENICE. You jealous. Go and behold yourself in the mirror. I can see from the color of your eyes.

(Frankie goes to the mirror and stares. She draws up her left shoulder, shakes her head, and turns away.)

FRANKIE *(with feeling)*. Oh! They were the two prettiest people I ever saw. I just can't understand how it happened.

BERENICE. Whatever ails you?—actin' so queer.

FRANKIE. I don't know. I bet they have a good time every minute of the day.

JOHN HENRY. Less us have a good time.

FRANKIE. Us have a good time? Us?

(She rises and walks around the table)

BERENICE. Come on. Less have a game of three-handed bridge.

(They sit down at the table, shuffle the cards, deal, and play a game.)

FRANKIE. Oregon, Alaska, Winter Hill, the wedding. It's all so queer.

BERENICE. I can't bid, never have a hand these days.

FRANKIE. A spade.

JOHN HENRY. I want to bid spades. That's what I was going to bid.

FRANKIE. Well, that's your tough luck. I bid them first.

JOHN HENRY. Oh, you fool jackass! It's not fair!

BERENICE. Hush quarreling, you two. *(She looks at both their hands)* To tell the truth, I don't think either of you got such a grand hand to fight over the bid about. Where is the cards? I haven't had no kind of a hand all week.

FRANKIE. I don't give a durn about it. It is immaterial with me. *(There is a long pause. She sits with her head propped on her hand, her legs wound around each other)* Let's talk about them—and the wedding.

BERENICE. What you want to talk about?

FRANKIE. My heart feels them going away—going farther and farther away—while I am stuck here by myself.

BERENICE. You ain't here by yourself. By the way, where's your Pa?

FRANKIE. He went to the store. I think about them, but I remembered them more as a feeling than as a picture.

BERENICE. A feeling?

FRANKIE. They were the two prettiest people I ever saw. Yet it was like I couldn't see all of them I wanted to see. My brains couldn't gather together quick enough to take it all in. And then they were gone.

BERENICE. Well, stop commenting about it. You don't have your mind on the game.

FRANKIE *(playing her cards, followed by John Henry)*. Spades are trumps and you got a spade. I have some of my mind on the game.

(John Henry puts his donkey necklace in his mouth and looks away.)

FRANKIE. Go on, cheater.

BERENICE. Make haste.

JOHN HENRY. I can't. It's a king. The only spade I got is a king, and I don't want to play my king under Frankie's ace. And I'm not going to do it either.

FRANKIE *(throwing her cards down on the table)*. See, Berenice, he cheats!

BERENICE. Play your king, John Henry. You have to follow the rules of the game.

JOHN HENRY. My king. It isn't fair.

FRANKIE. Even with this trick, I can't win.

BERENICE. Where is the cards? For three days I haven't had a decent hand. I'm beginning to suspicion something. Come on less us count these old cards.

FRANKIE. We've worn these old cards out. If you would eat these old cards, they would taste like a combination of all the dinners of this summer together with a sweaty-handed, nasty taste. Why, the jacks and the queens are missing.

BERENICE. John Henry, how come you do a thing like that? So that's why you asked for the scissors and stole off quiet behind the arbor. Now, Candy, how come you took our playing cards and cut out the pictures?

JOHN HENRY. Because I wanted them. They're cute.

FRANKIE. See? He's nothing but a child. It's hopeless. Hopeless!

BERENICE. Maybe so.

FRANKIE. We'll just have to put him out of the game. He's entirely too young.

(John Henry whimpers.)

BERENICE. Well, we can't put Candy out of the game. We gotta have a third to play. Besides, by the last count he owes me close to three million dollars.

FRANKIE. Oh, I am sick unto death. *(She sweeps the cards from the table, then gets up and begins walking around the kitchen. John Henry leaves the table and picks up a large blonde doll on the chair in the corner)* I wish they'd taken me with them to Winter Hill this afternoon. I wish tomorrow was Sunday instead of Saturday.

BERENICE. Sunday will come.

FRANKIE. I doubt it. I wish I was going somewhere for good. I wish I had a hundred dollars and could just light out and never see this town again.

BERENICE. It seems like you wish for a lot of things.

FRANKIE. I wish I was somebody else except me.

JOHN HENRY *(holding the doll)*. You serious when you gave me the doll a while ago?

FRANKIE. It gives me a pain just to think about them.

BERENICE. It is a known truth that gray-eyed people are jealous.

(There are sounds of children playing in the neighboring yard.)

JOHN HENRY. Let's go out and play with the children.

FRANKIE. I don't want to.

JOHN HENRY. There's a big crowd, and they sound like they having a mighty good time. Less go.

FRANKIE. You got ears. You heard me.

JOHN HENRY. I think maybe I better go home.

FRANKIE. Why, you said you were going to spend the night. You just can't eat dinner and then go off in the afternoon like that.

JOHN HENRY. I know it.

BERENICE. Candy, Lamb, you can go home if you want to.

JOHN HENRY. But less go out, Frankie. They sound like they having a lot of fun.

FRANKIE. No, they're not. Just a crowd of ugly, silly children. Running and hollering and running and hollering. Nothing to it.

JOHN HENRY. Less go!

FRANKIE. Well, then I'll entertain you. What do you want to do? Would you like for me to read to you out of The Book of Knowledge, or would you rather do something else?

JOHN HENRY. I rather do something else. *(He goes to the back door, and looks into the yard. Several young girls of thirteen or fourteen, dressed in clean print frocks, file slowly across the back yard)* Look. Those big girls.

FRANKIE *(running out into the yard)*. Hey, there. I'm mighty glad to see you. Come on in.

HELEN. We can't. We were just passing through to notify our new member.

FRANKIE *(overjoyed)*. Am I the new member?

DORIS. No, you're not the one the club elected.

FRANKIE. Not elected?

HELEN. Every ballot was unanimous for Mary Littlejohn.

FRANKIE. Mary Littlejohn! You mean that girl who just moved in next door? That pasty fat girl with those tacky pigtails? The one who plays the piano all day long?

DORIS. Yes. The club unanimously elected Mary.

FRANKIE. Why, she's not even cute.

HELEN. She is too; and, furthermore, she's talented.

FRANKIE. I think it's sissy to sit around the house all day playing classical music.

DORIS. Why, Mary is training for a concert career.

FRANKIE. Well, I wish to Jesus she would train somewhere else.

DORIS. You don't have enough sense to appreciate a talented girl like Mary.

FRANKIE. What are you doing in my yard? You're never to set foot on my Papa's property again. *(Frankie shakes Helen)* Son-of-a-bitches. I could shoot you with my Papa's pistol.

JOHN HENRY *(shaking his fists)*. Son-of-a-bitches.

FRANKIE. Why didn't you elect me? *(She goes back into the house)* Why can't I be a member?

JOHN HENRY. Maybe they'll change their mind and invite you.

BERENICE. I wouldn't pay them no mind. All my life I've been wantin' things that I ain't been gettin'. Anyhow those club girls is fully two years older than you.

FRANKIE. I think they have been spreading it all over town that I smell bad. When I had those boils and had to use that black bitter-smelling ointment, old Helen Fletcher asked me what was that funny smell I had. Oh, I could shoot every one of them with a pistol.

(Frankie sits with her head on the table. John Henry approaches and pats the back of Frankie's neck.)

JOHN HENRY. I don't think you smell so bad. You smell sweet, like a hundred flowers.

FRANKIE. The son-of-a-bitches. And there was something else. They were telling nasty lies about married people. When I think of Aunt Pet and Uncle Eustace! And my own father! The nasty lies! I don't know what kind of fool they take me for.

BERENICE. That's what I tell you. They too old for you.

(John Henry raises his head, expands his nostrils and sniffs at himself. Then Frankie goes into the interior bedroom and returns with a bottle of perfume.)

FRANKIE. Boy! I bet I use more perfume than anybody else in town. Want some on you, John Henry? You want some, Berenice? *(She sprinkles perfume)*

JOHN HENRY. Like a thousand flowers.

BERENICE. Frankie, the whole idea of a club is that there are members who are included and the non-members who are not included. Now what you ought to do is to round you up a club of your own. And you could be the president yourself. *(There is a pause)*

FRANKIE. Who would I get?

BERENICE. Why, those little children you hear playing in the neighborhood.

FRANKIE. I don't want to be the president of all those little young left-over people.

BERENICE. Well, then enjoy your misery. That perfume smells so strong it kind of makes me sick.

(John Henry plays with the doll at the kitchen table and Frankie watches.)

FRANKIE. Look here at me, John Henry. Take off those glasses. *(John Henry takes off his glasses)* I bet you don't need those glasses. *(She points to the coal scuttle)* What is this?

JOHN HENRY. The coal scuttle.

FRANKIE *(taking a shell from the kitchen shelf)*. And this?

JOHN HENRY. The shell we got at Saint Peter's Bay last summer.

FRANKIE. What is that little thing crawling around on the floor?

JOHN HENRY. Where?

FRANKIE. That little thing crawling around near your feet.

JOHN HENRY. Oh. *(He squats down)* Why, it's an ant. How did that get in here?

FRANKIE. If I were you I'd just throw those glasses away. You can see good as anybody.

BERENICE. Now quit picking with John Henry.

FRANKIE. They don't look becoming. *(John Henry wipes his glasses and puts them back on)* He can suit himself. I was only telling him for his own good. *(She walks restlessly around the kitchen)* I bet Janice and Jarvis are members of a lot of clubs. In fact, the army is kind of like a club.

(John Henry searches through Berenice's pocketbook.)

BERENICE. Don't root through my pocketbook like that, Candy. Ain't a wise policy to search folks' pocketbooks. They might think you trying to steal their money.

JOHN HENRY. I'm looking for your new glass eye. Here it is. *(He hands Berenice the glass eye)* You got two nickels and a dime.

(Berenice takes off her patch, turns away and inserts the glass eye.)

BERENICE. I ain't used to it yet. The socket bothers me. Maybe it don't fit properly.

JOHN HENRY. The blue glass eye looks very cute.

FRANKIE. I don't see why you had to get that eye. It has a wrong expression—let alone being blue.

BERENICE. Ain't anybody ask your judgment, wise-mouth.

JOHN HENRY. Which one of your eyes do you see out of the best?

BERENICE. The left eye, of course. The glass eye don't do me no seeing good at all.

JOHN HENRY. I like the glass eye better. It is so bright and shiny—a real pretty eye. Frankie, you serious when you gave me this doll a while ago?

FRANKIE. Janice and Jarvis. It gives me this pain just to think about them.

BERENICE. It is a known truth that gray-eyed people are jealous.

FRANKIE. I told you I wasn't jealous. I couldn't be jealous of one of them without being jealous of them both. I 'sociate the two of them together. Somehow they're just so different from us.

BERENICE. Well, I were jealous when my foster-brother, Honey, married Clorina. I sent a warning I could tear the ears off her head. But you see I didn't. Clorina's got ears just like anybody else. And now I love her.

FRANKIE *(stopping her walking suddenly)*. J.A.—Janice and Jarvis. Isn't that the strangest thing?

BERENICE. What?

FRANKIE. J.A.—Both their names begin with "J.A."

BERENICE. And? What about it?

FRANKIE *(walking around the kitchen table)*. If only my name was Jane. Jane or Jasmine.

BERENICE. I don't follow your frame of mind.

FRANKIE. Jarvis and Janice and Jasmine. See?

BERENICE. No. I don't see.

FRANKIE. I wonder if it's against the law to change your name. Or add to it.

BERENICE. Naturally. It's against the law.

FRANKIE (*impetuously*). Well, I don't care. F. Jasmine Addams.

JOHN HENRY (*approaching with the doll*). You serious when you give me this? (*He pulls up the doll's dress and pats her*) I will name her Belle.

FRANKIE. I don't know what went on in Jarvis' mind when he brought me that doll. Imagine bringing me a doll! I had counted on Jarvis bringing me something from Alaska.

BERENICE. Your face when you unwrapped that package was a study.

FRANKIE. John Henry, quit pickin' at the doll's eyes. It makes me so nervous. You hear me! (*He sits the doll up*) In fact, take the doll somewhere out of my sight.

JOHN HENRY. Her name is Lily Belle. (*John Henry goes out and props the doll up on the back steps. There is the sound of an unseen Negro singing from the neighboring yard.*)

FRANKIE (*going to the mirror*). The big mistake I made was to get this close crew cut. For the wedding, I ought to have long brunette hair. Don't you think so?

BERENICE. I don't see how come brunette hair is necessary. But I warned you about getting your head shaved off like that before you did it. But nothing would do but you shave it like that.

FRANKIE (*stepping back from the mirror and slumping her shoulders*). Oh, I am so worried about being so tall. I'm twelve and five-sixth years old and already five feet five and three-fourths inches tall. If I keep on growing like this until I'm twenty-one, I figure I will be nearly ten feet tall.

JOHN HENRY (*re-entering the kitchen*). Lily Belle is taking a nap on the back steps. Don't talk so loud, Frankie.

FRANKIE (*after a pause*). I doubt if they ever get married or go to a wedding. Those freaks.

BERENICE. Freaks. What freaks you talking about?

FRANKIE. At the fair. The ones we saw there last October.

JOHN HENRY. Oh, the freaks at the fair! (*He holds out an imaginary skirt and begins to skip around the room with one finger resting on the top of his head*) Oh, she was the cutest little girl I ever saw. I never saw anything so cute in my whole life. Did you, Frankie?

FRANKIE. No. I don't think she was cute.

BERENICE. Who is that he's talking about?

FRANKIE. That little old pin-head at the fair. A head no bigger than an orange. With the hair shaved off and a big pink bow at the top. Bow was bigger than the head.

JOHN HENRY. Shoo! She was too cute.

BERENICE. That little old squeezed-looking midget in them little trick evening clothes. And that giant with the hang-jaw face and them huge loose hands. And that morphidite! Half man—half woman. With that tiger skin on one side and that spangled skirt on the other.

JOHN HENRY. But that little-headed girl was cute.

FRANKIE. And that wild colored man they said came from a savage island and ate those real live rats. Do you think they make a very big salary?

BERENICE. How would I know? In fact, all them freak folks down at the fair every October just gives me the creeps.

FRANKIE (*after a pause, and slowly*). Do I give you the creeps?

BERENICE. You?

FRANKIE. Do you think I will grow into a freak?

BERENICE. You? Why certainly not, I trust Jesus!

FRANKIE (*going over to the mirror, and looking at herself*). Well, do you think I will be pretty?

BERENICE. Maybe. If you file down them horns a inch or two.

FRANKIE (*turning to face Berenice, and shuffling one bare foot on the floor*). Seriously.

BERENICE. Seriously, I think when you fill out you will do very well. If you behave.

FRANKIE. But by Sunday, I want to do something to improve myself before the wedding.

BERENICE. Get clean for a change. Scrub your elbows and fix yourself nice. You will do very well.

JOHN HENRY. You will be all right if you file down them horns.

FRANKIE (*raising her right shoulder and turning from the mirror*). I don't know what to do. I just wish I would die.

BERENICE. Well, die then!

JOHN HENRY. Die.

FRANKIE (suddenly exasperated). Go home! (There is a pause) You heard me! (She makes a face at him and threatens him with the fly swatter. They run twice around the table) Go home! I'm sick and tired of you, you little midget.

(John Henry goes out, taking the doll with him.)

BERENICE. Now what makes you act like that? You are too mean to live.

FRANKIE. I know it. (She takes a carving knife from the table drawer) Something about John Henry just gets on my nerves these days. (She puts her left ankle over her right knee and begins to pick with the knife at a splinter in her foot) I've got a splinter in my foot.

BERENICE. That knife ain't the proper thing for a splinter.

FRANKIE. It seems to me that before this summer I used always to have such a good time. Remember this spring when Evelyn Owen and me used to dress up in costumes and go down town and shop at the five-and-dime? And how every Friday night we'd spend the night with each other either at her house or here? And then Evelyn Owen had to go and move away to Florida. And now she won't even write to me.

BERENICE. Honey, you are not crying, is you? Don't that hurt you none?

FRANKIE. It would hurt anybody else except me. And how the wisteria in town was so blue and pretty in April but somehow it was so pretty it made me sad. And how Evelyn and me put on that show the Glee Club did at the High School Auditorium? (She raises her head and beats time with the knife and her fist on the table, singing loudly with sudden energy) Sons of toil and danger! Will you serve a stranger! And bow down to Burgundy! (Berenice joins in on "Burgundy." Frankie pauses, then begins to pick her foot again, humming the tune sadly)

BERENICE. That was a nice show you children copied in the arbor. You will meet another girl friend you like as well as Evelyn Owen. Or maybe Mr. Owen will move back into town. (There is a pause) Frankie, what you need is a needle.

FRANKIE. I don't care anything about my feet. (She stomps her foot on the floor and lays down the knife on the table) It was just so queer the way it happened this afternoon. The minute I laid eyes on the pair of them I had this funny feeling. (She goes over and picks up a saucer of milk near the cat-hole in back of the door and pours the milk in the sink) How old were you, Berenice, when you married your first husband?

BERENICE. I were thirteen years old.

FRANKIE. What made you get married so young for?

BERENICE. Because I wanted to.

FRANKIE. You never loved any of your four husbands but Ludie.

BERENICE. Ludie Maxwell Freeman was my only true husband. The other ones were just scraps.

FRANKIE. Did you marry with a veil every time?

BERENICE. Three times with a veil.

FRANKIE (pouring milk into the saucer and returning the saucer to the cat-hole). If only I just knew where he is gone. Ps, ps, ps . . . Charles, Charles.

BERENICE. Quit worrying yourself about that old alley cat. He's gone off to hunt a friend.

FRANKIE. To hunt a friend?

BERENICE. Why certainly. He roamed off to find himself a lady friend.

FRANKIE. Well, why don't he bring his friend home with him? He ought to know I would be only too glad to have a whole family of cats.

BERENICE. You done seen the last of that old alley cat.

FRANKIE (crossing the room). I ought to notify the police force. They will find Charles.

BERENICE. I wouldn't do that.

FRANKIE (at the telephone). I want the police force, please . . . Police force? . . . I am notifying you about my car . . . Cat! He's lost. He is almost pure Persian.

BERENICE. As Persian as I is.

FRANKIE. But with short hair. A lovely color of gray with a little white spot on his throat. He answers to the name of Charles, but if he don't answer to that, he might come if you call "Charlina." . . . My name is Miss F. Jasmine Addams and the address is 124 Grove Street.

BERENICE (giggling as Frankie re-enters). Gal, they going to send around here and tie you up and drag you off to Milledgeville. Just picture them fat blue police chasing tomcats around alleys and hollering, "Oh Charles! Oh come here, Charlina!" Merciful Heavens.

FRANKIE. Aw, shut up!

(*Outside a voice is heard calling in a drawn-out chant, the words almost indistinguishable: "Lot of okra, peas, fresh butter beans . . .")*

BERENICE. The trouble with you is that you don't have no sense of humor no more.

FRANKIE (*disconsolately*). Maybe I'd be better off in jail.

(*The chanting voice continues and an ancient Negro woman, dressed in a clean print dress with several petticoats, the ruffle of one of which shows, crosses the yard. She stops and leans on a gnarled stick.*)

FRANKIE. Here comes the old vegetable lady.

BERENICE. Sis Laura is getting mighty feeble to peddle this hot weather.

FRANKIE. She is about ninety. Other old folks lose their faculties, but she found some faculty. She reads futures, too.

BERENICE. Hi, Sis Laura. How is your folks getting on?

SIS LAURA. We ain't much, and I feels my age these days. Want any peas today? (*She shuffles across the yard*)

BERENICE. I'm sorry, I still have some left over from yesterday. Good-bye, Sis Laura.

SIS LAURA. Good-bye. (*She goes off behind the house to the right, continuing her chant*)

(*When the old woman is gone Frankie begins walking around the kitchen.*)

FRANKIE. I expect Janice and Jarvis are almost to Winter Hill by now.

BERENICE. Sit down. You make me nervous.

FRANKIE. Jarvis talked about Granny. He remembers her very good. But when I try to remember Granny, it is like her face is changing—like a face seen under water. Jarvis remembers Mother too, and I don't remember her at all.

BERENICE. Naturally! Your mother died the day that you were born.

FRANKIE (*standing with one foot on the seat of the chair, leaning over the chair back and laughing*). Did you hear what Jarvis said?

BERENICE. What?

FRANKIE (*after laughing more*). They were talking about whether to vote for C. P. MacDonald. And Jarvis said, "Why I wouldn't vote for that scoundrel if he was running to be dogcatcher." I never heard anything so witty in my life. (*There is a silence during which Berenice watches Frankie, but does not smile*) And you know what Janice remarked? When Jarvis mentioned about how much I've grown, she said she didn't think I looked so terribly big. She said she got the major portion of her growth before she was thirteen. She said I was the right height and had acting talent and ought to go to Hollywood. She did, Berenice.

BERENICE. O.K. All right! She did!

FRANKIE. She said she thought I was a lovely size and would probably not grow any taller. She said all fashion models and movie stars . . .

BERENICE. She did not. I heard her from the window. She only remarked that you probably had already got your growth. But she didn't go on and on like that or mention Hollywood.

FRANKIE. She said to me . . .

BERENICE. She said to you! This is a serious fault with you, Frankie. Somebody just makes a loose remark and then you cozen it in your mind until nobody would recognize it. Your Aunt Pet happened to mention to Clorina that you had sweet manners and Clorina passed it on to you. For what it was worth. Then next thing I know you are going all around and bragging how Mrs. West thought you had the finest manners in town and ought to go to Hollywood, and I don't know whatall you didn't say. And that is a serious fault.

FRANKIE. Aw, quit preaching at me.

BERENICE. I ain't preaching. It's the solemn truth and you know it.

FRANKIE. I admit it a little. (*She sits down at the table and puts her forehead on the palms of her hands. There is a pause, and then she speaks softly*) What I need to know is this. Do you think I made a good impression?

BERENICE. Impression?

FRANKIE. Yes.

BERENICE. Well, how would I know?

FRANKIE. I mean, how did I act? What did I do?

BERENICE. Why, you didn't do anything to speak of.

FRANKIE. Nothing?

BERENICE. No. You just watched the pair of them like they was ghosts. Then, when they talked about the wedding, them ears of yours stiffened out the size of cabbage leaves . . .

FRANKIE *(raising her hand to her ears).* They didn't!

BERENICE. They did.

FRANKIE. Some day you going to look down and find that big fat tongue of yours pulled out by the roots and laying there before you on the table.

BERENICE. Quit talking so rude.

FRANKIE *(after a pause).* I'm so scared I didn't make a good impression.

BERENICE. What of it? I got a date with T. T. and he's supposed to pick me up here. I wish him and Honey would come on. You make me nervous. *(Frankie sits miserably, her shoulders hunched. Then with a sudden gesture she bangs her forehead on the table. Her fists are clenched and she is sobbing.)*

BERENICE. Come on. Don't act like that.

FRANKIE *(her voice muffled).* They were so pretty. They must have such a good time. And they went away and left me.

BERENICE. Sit up. Behave yourself.

FRANKIE. They came and went away, and left me with this feeling.

BERENICE. Hosee! I bet I know something. *(She begins tapping with her heel: one, two, three—bang! After a pause, in which the rhythm is established, she begins singing)* Frankie's got a crush! Frankie's got a crush! Frankie's got a crush on the *wedding!*

FRANKIE. Quit!

BERENICE. Frankie's got a crush! Frankie's got a crush!

FRANKIE. You better quit! *(She rises suddenly and snatches up the carving knife)*

BERENICE. You lay down that knife.

FRANKIE. Make me. *(She bends the blade slowly)*

BERENICE. Lay it down, *Devil.* *(There is a silence)* Just throw it! You just!

(After a pause Frankie aims the knife carefully at the closed door leading to the bedroom and throws it. The knife does not stick in the wall.)

FRANKIE. I used to be the best knife thrower in this town.

BERENICE. Frances Addams, you goin' to try that stunt once too often.

FRANKIE. I warned you to quit pickin' with me.

BERENICE. You are not fit to live in a house.

FRANKIE. I won't be living in this one much longer; I'm going to run away from home.

BERENICE. And a good riddance to big old bag of rubbage.

FRANKIE. You wait and see. I'm leavin town.

BERENICE. And where do you think you are going?

FRANKIE *(gazing around the walls).* I don't know.

BERENICE. You're going crazy. That's where you going.

FRANKIE. No. *(Solemnly)* This coming Sunday after the wedding, I'm leaving town. And I swear to Jesus by my two eyes I'm never coming back here any more.

BERENICE *(going to Frankie and pushing her damp bangs back from her forehead).* Sugar? You serious?

FRANKIE *(exasperated).* Of course! Do you think I would stand here and say that swear and tell a story? Sometimes, Berenice, I think it takes you longer to realize a fact than it does anybody who ever lived.

BERENICE. But you say you don't know where you going. You going, but you don't know where. That don't make no sense to me.

FRANKIE *(after a long pause in which she again gazes around the walls of the room).* I feel just exactly like somebody has peeled all the skin off me. I wish I had some good cold peach ice cream. *(Berenice takes her by the shoulders)* *(During the last speech, T. T. Williams and Honey Camden Brown have been approaching through the back yard. T. T. is a large and pompous-looking Negro man of about fifty. He is dressed like a church deacon, in a black suit with a red emblem in the lapel. His manner is timid and over-polite. Honey is a slender, limber Negro boy of about twenty. He is quite light in color and he wears loud-colored, snappy clothes. He is brusque and there is about him an odd mixture of hostility and playfulness. He is very high-strung and volatile. They are trailed by John Henry. John Henry is dressed for afternoon in a clean white linen suit, white shoes and socks. Honey carries a horn. They cross the back yard and knock at the back door. Honey holds his hand to his head.)*

FRANKIE. But every word I told you was the solemn truth. I'm leaving here after the wedding.

BERENICE *(taking her hands from Frankie's shoulders and answering the door).* Hello, Honey and T. T. I didn't hear you coming.

T. T. You and Frankie too busy discussing something. Well, your foster-brother, Honey, got into a ruckus standing on the sidewalk in front of the Blue Moon Café. Police cracked him on the haid.

BERENICE *(turning on the kitchen light).* What! *(She examines Honey's head)* Why, it's a welt the size of a small egg.

HONEY. Times like this I feel like I got to bust loose or die.

BERENICE. What were you doing?

HONEY. Nothing. I was just passing along the street minding my own business when this drunk soldier came out of the Blue Moon Café and ran into me. I looked at him and he gave me a push. I pushed him back and he raised a ruckus. This white M.P. came up and slammed me with his stick.

T. T. It was one of those accidents can happen to any colored person.

JOHN HENRY *(reaching for the horn).* Toot some on your horn, Honey.

FRANKIE. Please blow.

HONEY *(to John Henry, who has taken the horn).* Now, don't bother my horn, Butch.

JOHN HENRY. I want to toot it some. *(John Henry takes the horn, tries to blow it, but only succeeds in slobbering in it. He holds the horn away from his mouth and sings: "Too-ty-toot, too-ty-toot." Honey snatches the horn away from him and puts it on the sewing table.)*

HONEY. I told you not to touch my horn. You got it full of slobber inside and out. It's ruined! *(He loses his temper, grabs John Henry by the shoulders and shakes him hard)*

BERENICE *(slapping Honey).* Satan! Don't you dare touch that little boy! I'm going to stomp out your brains!

HONEY. You ain't mad because John Henry is a little boy. It's because he's a white boy. John Henry knows he needs a good shake. Don't you, Butch?

BERENICE. Ornery—no good!

(Honey lifts John Henry and swings him, then reaches in his pocket and brings out some coins.)

HONEY. John Henry, which would you rather have—the nigger money or the white money?

JOHN HENRY. I rather have the dime. *(He takes it)* Much obliged. *(He goes out and crosses the yard to his house)*

BERENICE. You troubled and beat down and try to take it out on a little boy. You and Frankie just alike. The club girls don't elect her and she turns on John Henry too. When folks are lonesome and left out, they turn so mean. T. T., do you wish a small little quickie before we start?

T. T. *(looking at Frankie and pointing toward her).* Frankie ain't no tattle-tale. Is you? *(Berenice pours a drink for T. T.)*

FRANKIE *(disdaining his question).* That sure is a cute suit you got on, Honey. Today I heard somebody speak of you as Lightfoot Brown. I think that's such a grand nickname. It's on account of your travelling—to Harlem, and all the different places where you have run away, and your dancing. Lightfoot! I wish somebody would call me Lightfoot Addams.

BERENICE. It would suit me better if Honey Camden had brick feets. As it is, he keeps me so anxious-worried. C'mon, Honey and T. T. Let's go! *(Honey and T. T. go out)*

FRANKIE. I'll go out into the yard. *(Frankie, feeling excluded, goes out into the yard. Throughout the act the light in the yard has been darkening steadily. Now the light in the kitchen is throwing a yellow rectangle in the yard.)*

BERENICE. Now Frankie, you forget all that foolishness we were discussing. And if Mr. Addams don't come home by good dark, you go over to the Wests'. Go play with John Henry.

HONEY AND T. T. *(from outside).* So long!

FRANKIE. So long, you all. Since when have I been scared of the dark? I'll invite John Henry to spend the night with me.

BERENICE. I thought you were sick and tired of him.

FRANKIE. I am.

BERENICE (*kissing Frankie*). Good night, Sugar!

FRANKIE. Seems like everybody goes off and leaves me. (*She walks toward the Wests' yard, calling, with cupped hands*) John Henry. John Henry.

JOHN HENRY'S VOICE. What do you want, Frankie?

FRANKIE. Come over and spend the night with me.

JOHN HENRY'S VOICE. I can't.

FRANKIE. Why?

JOHN HENRY. Just because.

FRANKIE. Because why? (*John Henry does not answer*) I thought maybe me and you could put up my Indian tepee and sleep out here in the yard. And have a good time. (*There is still no answer*) Sure enough. Why don't you stay and spend the night?

JOHN HENRY (*quite loudly*). Because, Frankie. I don't want to.

FRANKIE (*angrily*). Fool Jackass! Suit yourself! I only asked you because you looked so ugly and so lonesome.

JOHN HENRY (*skipping toward the arbor*). Why, I'm not a bit lonesome.

FRANKIE (*looking at the house*). I wonder when that Papa of mine is coming home. He always comes home by dark. I don't want to go into that empty, ugly house all by myself.

JOHN HENRY. Me neither.

FRANKIE (*standing with outstretched arms, and looking around her*). I think something is wrong. It is too quiet. I have a peculiar warning in my bones. I bet you a hundred dollars it's going to storm.

JOHN HENRY. I don't want to spend the night with you.

FRANKIE. A terrible, terrible dog-day storm. Or maybe even a cyclone.

JOHN HENRY. Huh.

FRANKIE. I bet Jarvis and Janice are now at Winter Hill. I see them just plain as I see you. Plainer. Something is wrong. It is too quiet.

(*A clear horn begins to play a blues tune in the distance.*)

JOHN HENRY. Frankie?

FRANKIE. Hush! It sounds like Honey. '*The horn music becomes jazzy and pangling, then the first blues tune is re-peated. Suddenly, while still unfinished, the music stops. Frankie waits tensely.*)

FRANKIE. He has stopped to bang the spit out of his horn. In a second he will

finish. (*After a wait*) Please, Honey, go on finish!

JOHN HENRY (*softly*). He done quit now.

FRANKIE (*moving restlessly*). I told Berenice that I was leavin' town for good and she did not believe me. Sometimes I honestly think she is the biggest fool that ever drew breath. You try to impress something on a big fool like that, and it's just like talking to a block of cement. I kept on telling and telling and telling her. I told her I had to leave this town for good because it is inevitable. Inevitable. (*Mr. Addams enters the kitchen from the house, calling: "Frankie, Frankie."*)

MR. ADDAMS (*calling from the kitchen door*). Frankie, Frankie.

FRANKIE. Yes, Papa.

MR. ADDAMS (*opening the back door*). You had supper?

FRANKIE. I'm not hungry.

MR. ADDAMS. Was a little later than I intended, fixing a timepiece for a railroad man. (*He goes back through the kitchen and into the hall, calling: "Don't leave the yard!"*)

JOHN HENRY. You want me to get the weekend bag?

FRANKIE. Don't bother me, John Henry. I'm thinking.

JOHN HENRY. What you thinking about?

FRANKIE. About the wedding. About my brother and the bride. Everything's been so sudden today. I never believed before about the fact that the earth turns at the rate of about a thousand miles a day. I didn't understand why it was that if you jumped up in the air you wouldn't land in Selma or Fairview or somewhere else instead of the same back yard. But now it seems to me I feel the world going around very fast. (*Frankie begins turning around in circles with arms outstretched. John Henry copies her. They both turn*) I feel it turning and it makes me dizzy.

JOHN HENRY. I'll stay and spend the night with you.

FRANKIE (*suddenly stopping her turning*). No. I just now thought of something.

JOHN HENRY. You just a little while ago was begging me.

FRANKIE. I know where I'm going. (*There are sounds of children playing in the distance.*)

JOHN HENRY. Let's go play with the children, Frankie.

FRANKIE. I tell you I know where I'm going. It's like I've known it all my life. Tomorrow I will tell everybody.

JOHN HENRY. Where?

FRANKIE (dreamily). After the wedding I'm going with them to Winter Hill. I'm going off with them after the wedding.

JOHN HENRY. You serious?

FRANKIE. Shush, just now I realized something. The trouble with me is that for a long time I have been just an "I" person. All other people can say "we." When Berenice says "we" she means her lodge and church and colored people. Soldiers can say "we" and mean the army. All people belong to a "we" except me.

JOHN HENRY. What are we going to do?

FRANKIE. Not to belong to a "we" makes you too lonesome. Until this afternoon I didn't have a "we," but now after seeing Janice and Jarvis I suddenly realize something.

JOHN HENRY. What?

FRANKIE. I know that the bride and my brother are the "we" of me. So I'm going with them, and joining with the wedding. This coming Sunday when my brother and the bride leave this town, I'm going with the two of them to Winter Hill. And after that to whatever place that they will ever go. (There is a pause) I love the two of them so much and we belong to be together. I love the two of them so much because they are the *we* of me.

THE CURTAIN FALLS.

ACT TWO

The scene is the same: the kitchen of the Addams home. Berenice is cooking. John Henry sits on the stool, blowing soap bubbles with a spool. It is the afternoon of the next day.

———

(*The front door slams and Frankie enters from the hall.*)

BERENICE. I been phoning all over town trying to locate you. Where on earth have you been?

FRANKIE. Everywhere. All over town.

BERENICE. I been so worried I got a good mind to be seriously mad with you. Your Papa came home to dinner today. He was mad when you didn't show up. He's taking a nap now in his room.

FRANKIE. I walked up and down Main Street and stopped in almost every store. Bought my wedding dress and silver shoes. Went around by the mills. Went all over the complete town and talked to nearly everybody in it.

BERENICE. What for, pray tell me?

FRANKIE. I was telling everybody about the wedding and my plans. (*She takes off her dress and remains barefooted in her slip*)

BERENICE. You mean just people on the street? (*She is creaming butter and sugar for cookies*)

FRANKIE. Everybody. Storekeepers. The monkey and monkey-man. A soldier. Everybody. And you know the soldier wanted to join with me and asked me for a date this evening. I wonder what you do on dates.

BERENICE. Frankie, I honestly believe you have turned crazy on us. Walking all over town and telling total strangers this big tale. You know in your soul this mania of yours is pure foolishness.

FRANKIE. Please call me F. Jasmine. I don't wish to have to remind you any more. Everything good of mine has got to be washed and ironed so I can pack them in the suitcase. (*She brings in a suitcase and opens it*) Everybody in town believes that I'm going. All except Papa. He's stubborn as an old mule. No use arguing with people like that.

BERENICE. Me and Mr. Addams has some sense.

FRANKIE. Papa was bent over working on a watch when I went by the store. I asked him could I buy the wedding clothes and he said charge them at MacDougals. But he wouldn't listen to any of my plans. Just sat there with his nose to the grindstone and answered with—kind of grunts. He never listens to what I say. (*There is a pause*) Sometimes I wonder if Papa loves me or not.

BERENICE. Course he loves you. He is just a busy widowman—set in his ways.

FRANKIE. Now I wonder if I can find some tissue paper to line this suitcase.

BERENICE. Truly, Frankie, what makes you think they want you taggin' along with them? Two is company and three is a crowd. And that's the main thing about a wedding. Two is company and three is a crowd.

FRANKIE. You wait and see.

BERENICE. Remember back to the time of the flood. Remember Noah and the Ark.

FRANKIE. And what has that got to do with it?

BERENICE. Remember the way he admitted them creatures.

FRANKIE. Oh, shut up your big old mouth!

BERENICE. Two by two. He admitted them creatures two by two.

FRANKIE (after a pause). That's all right. But you wait and see. They will take me.

BERENICE. And if they don't?

FRANKIE (turning suddenly from washing her hands at the sink). If they don't, I will kill myself.

BERENICE. Kill yourself, how?

FRANKIE. I will shoot myself in the side of the head with the pistol that Papa keeps under his handkerchiefs with Mother's picture in the bureau drawer.

BERENICE. You heard what Mr. Addams said about playing with that pistol. I'll just put this cookie dough in the icebox. Set the table and your dinner is ready. Set John Henry a plate and one for me. (Berenice puts the dough in the icebox. Frankie hurriedly sets the table. Berenice takes dishes from the stove and ties a napkin around John Henry's neck) I have heard of many a peculiar thing. I have knew men to fall in love with girls so ugly that you wonder if their eyes is straight.

JOHN HENRY. Who?

BERENICE. I have knew women to love veritable satans and thank Jesus when they put their split hooves over the threshold. I have knew boys to take it into their heads to fall in love with other boys. You know Lily Mae Jenkins?

FRANKIE. I'm not sure. I know a lot of people.

BERENICE. Well, you either know him or you don't know him. He prisses around in a girl's blouse with one arm akimbo. Now this Lily Mae Jenkins fell in love with a man name Juney Jones. A man, mind you. And Lily Mae turned into a girl. He changed his nature and his sex and turned into a girl.

FRANKIE. What?

BERENICE. He did. To all intents and purposes. (Berenice is sitting in the center chair at the table. She says grace) Lord, make us thankful for what we are about to receive to nourish our bodies. Amen.

FRANKIE. It's funny I can't think who you are talking about. I used to think I knew so many people.

BERENICE. Well, you don't need to know Lily Mae Jenkins. You can live without knowing him.

FRANKIE. Anyway, I don't believe you.

BERENICE. I ain't arguing with you. What was we speaking about?

FRANKIE. About peculiar things.

BERENICE. Oh, yes. As I was just now telling you I have seen many a peculiar thing in my day. But one thing I never knew and never heard tell about. No, siree. I never in all my days heard of anybody falling in love with a wedding. (There is a pause) And thinking it all over I have come to a conclusion.

JOHN HENRY. How? How did that boy change into a girl? Did he kiss his elbow? (He tries to kiss his elbow)

BERENICE. It was just one of them things, Candy Lamb. Yep, I have come to the conclusion that what you ought to be thinking about is a beau. A nice little white boy beau.

FRANKIE. I don't want any beau. What would I do with one? Do you mean something like a soldier who would maybe take me to the Idle Hour?

BERENICE. Who's talking about soldiers? I'm talking about a nice little white boy beau your own age. How 'bout that little old Barney next door?

FRANKIE. Barney MacKean! That nasty Barney!

BERENICE. Certainly! You could make out with him until somebody better comes along. He would do.

FRANKIE. You are the biggest crazy in this town.

BERENICE. The crazy calls the sane the crazy.

(Barney MacKean, a boy of twelve, shirtless and wearing shorts, and Helen Fletcher, a girl of twelve or fourteen, cross the yard from the left, go through the arbor and out on the right. Frankie and John Henry watch them from the window.)

FRANKIE. Yonder's Barney now with Helen Fletcher. They are going to the alley behind the Wests' garage. They do something bad back there. I don't know what it is.

BERENICE. If you don't know what it is, how come you know it is bad?

FRANKIE. I just know it. I think maybe they look at each other and peepee or something. They don't let anybody watch them.

JOHN HENRY. I watched them once.

FRANKIE. What do they do?

JOHN HENRY. I saw. They don't peepee.

FRANKIE. Then what do they do?

JOHN HENRY. I don't know what it was. But I watched them. How many of them did you catch, Berenice? Them beaus?

BERENICE. How many? Candy Lamb, how many hairs is in this plait? You're talking to Miss Berenice Sadie Brown.

FRANKIE. I think you ought to quit worrying about beaus and be content with T. T. I bet you are forty years old.

BERENICE. Wise-mouth. How do you know so much? I got as much right as anybody else to continue to have a good time as long as I can. And as far as that goes, I'm not so old as some peoples would try and make me. I ain't changed life yet.

JOHN HENRY. Did they all treat you to the picture show, them beaus?

BERENICE. To the show, or one thing or another. Wipe off your mouth.

(There is the sound of piano tuning.)

JOHN HENRY. The piano tuning man.

BERENICE. Ye Gods, I seriously believe this will be the last straw.

JOHN HENRY. Me too.

FRANKIE. It makes me sad. And jittery too. *(She walks around the room)* They tell me that when they want to punish the crazy people in Milledgeville, they tie them up and make them listen to piano tuning. *(She puts the empty coal scuttle on her head and walks around the table)*

BERENICE. We could turn on the radio and drown him out.

FRANKIE. I don't want the radio on. *(She goes into the interior room and takes off her dress, speaking from inside)* But I advise you to keep the radio on after I leave. Some day you will very likely hear us speak over the radio.

BERENICE. Speak about what, pray tell me?

FRANKIE. I don't know exactly what about. But probably some eye witness account about something. We will be asked to speak.

BERENICE. I don't follow you. What are we going to eye witness? And who will ask you to speak?

JOHN HENRY *(excitedly)*. What, Frankie? Who is speaking on the radio?

FRANKIE. When I said *we,* you thought I meant you and me and John Henry West. To speak over the world radio. I have never heard of anything so funny since I was born.

JOHN HENRY *(climbing up to kneel on the seat of the chair)*. Who? What?

FRANKIE. Ha! Ha! Ho! Ho! Ho! Ho! *(Frankie goes around punching things with her fist, and shadow boxing. Berenice raises her right hand for peace. Then suddenly they all stop. Frankie goes to the window, and John Henry hurries there also and stands on tiptoe with his hands on the sill. Berenice turns her head to see what has happened. The piano is still. Three young girls in clean dresses are passing before the arbor. Frankie watches them silently at the window.)*

JOHN HENRY *(softly)*. The club of girls.

FRANKIE. What do you son-of-a-bitches mean crossing my yard? How many times must I tell you not to set foot on my Papa's property?

BERENICE. Just ignore them and make like you don't see them pass.

FRANKIE. Don't mention those crooks to me.

(T. T. and Honey approach by way of the back yard. Honey is whistling a blues tune.)

BERENICE. Why don't you show me the new dress? I'm anxious to see what you selected. *(Frankie goes into the interior room. T. T. knocks on the door. He and Honey enter)* Why T. T., what you doing around here this time of day?

T. T. Good afternoon, Miss Berenice. I'm here on a sad mission.

BERENICE *(startled)*. What's wrong?

T. T. It's about Sis Laura Thompson. She suddenly had a stroke and died.

BERENICE. What! Why she was by here just yesterday. We just ate her peas. They in my stomach right now, and her lyin' dead on the cooling board this minute. The Lord works in strange ways.

T. T. Passed away at dawn this morning.

FRANKIE *(putting her head in the doorway)*. Who is it that's dead?

BERENICE. Sis Laura, Sugar. That old vegetable lady.

FRANKIE *(unseen, from the interior room)*. Just to think—she passed by yesterday.

T. T. Miss Berenice, I'm going around to take up a donation for the funeral. The policy people say Sis Laura's claim has lapsed.

BERENICE. Well, here's fifty cents. The poor old soul.

T. T. She was brisk as a chipmunk to the last. The Lord had appointed the time for her. I hope I go that way.

FRANKIE *(from the interior room)*. I've got something to show you all. Shut your eyes and don't open them until I tell you. *(She enters the room dressed in an orange satin evening dress with silver shoes and stockings)* These are the wedding clothes. *(Berenice, T. T. and John Henry stare)*

JOHN HENRY. Oh, how pretty!

FRANKIE. Now tell me your honest opinion. *(There is a pause)* What's the matter? Don't you like it, Berenice?

BERENICE. No. It don't do.

FRANKIE. What do you mean? It don't do.

BERENICE. Exactly that. It just don't do. *(She shakes her head while Frankie looks at the dress)*

FRANKIE. But I don't see what you mean. What is wrong?

BERENICE. Well, if you don't see it I can't explain it to you. Look there at your head, to begin with. *(Frankie goes to the mirror)* You had all your hair shaved off like a convict and now you tie this ribbon around this head without any hair. Just looks peculiar.

FRANKIE. But I'm going to wash and try to stretch my hair tonight.

BERENICE. Stretch your hair! How you going to stretch your hair? And look at them elbows. Here you got on a grown woman's evening dress. And that brown crust on your elbows. The two things just don't mix. *(Frankie, embarrassed, covers her elbows with her hands. Berenice is still shaking her head)* Take it back down to the store.

T. T. The dress is too growny looking.

FRANKIE. But I can't take it back. It's bargain basement.

BERENICE. Very well then. Come here. Let me see what I can do.

FRANKIE *(going to Berenice, who works with the dress)*. I think you're just not accustomed to seeing anybody dressed up.

BERENICE. I'm not accustomed to seein' a human Christmas tree in August.

JOHN HENRY. Frankie's dress looks like a Christmas tree.

FRANKIE. Two-faced Judas! You just now said it was pretty. Old double-faced Judas! *(The sounds of piano tuning are heard again)* Oh, that piano tuner!

BERENICE. Step back a little now.

FRANKIE *(looking in the mirror)*. Don't you honestly think it's pretty? Give me your candy opinion.

BERENICE. I never knew anybody so unreasonable! You ask me my candy opinion, I give you my candy opinion. You ask me again, and I give it to you again. But what you want is not my honest opinion, but my good opinion of something I know is wrong.

FRANKIE. I only want to look pretty.

BERENICE. Pretty is as pretty does. Ain't that right, T. T.? You will look well enough for anybody's wedding. Excepting your own.

(Mr. Addams enters through the hall door.)

MR. ADDAMS. Hello, everybody. *(To Frankie)* I don't want you roaming around the streets all morning and not coming home at dinner time. Looks like I'll have to tie you up in the back yard.

FRANKIE. I had business to tend to. Papa, look!

MR. ADDAMS. What is it, Miss Picklepriss?

FRANKIE. Sometimes I think you have turned stone blind. You never even noticed my new dress.

MR. ADDAMS. I thought it was a show costume.

FRANKIE. Show costume! Papa, why is it you don't ever notice what I have on or pay any serious mind to me? You just walk around like a mule with blinders on, not seeing or caring.

MR. ADDAMS. Never mind that now. *(To T. T. and Honey)* I need some help down at my store. My porter failed me again. I wonder if you or Honey could help me next week.

T. T. I will if I can, sir, Mr. Addams.

What days would be convenient for you, sir?

MR. ADDAMS. Say Wednesday afternoon.

T. T. Now, Mr. Addams, that's one afternoon I promised to work for Mr. Finny, sir. I can't promise anything, Mr. Addams. But if Mr. Finny changes his mind about needing me, I'll work for you, sir.

MR. ADDAMS. How about you, Honey?

HONEY (shortly). I ain't got the time.

MR. ADDAMS. I'll be so glad when the war is over and you biggety, worthless niggers get back to work. And, furthermore, you sir me! Hear me!

HONEY (reluctantly). Yes—sir.

MR. ADDAMS. I getter go back to the store now and get my nose down to the grindstone. You stay home, Frankie. (He goes out through the hall door)

JOHN HENRY. Uncle Royal called Honey a nigger. Is Honey a nigger?

BERENICE. Be quiet now, John Henry. (To Honey) Honey, I got a good mind to shake you till you spit. Not saying sir to Mr. Addams, and acting so impudent.

HONEY. T. T. said sir enough for a whole crowd of niggers. But for folks that calls me nigger, I got a real good nigger razor. (He takes a razor from his pocket. Frankie and John Henry crowd close to look. When John Henry touches the razor, Honey says) Don't touch it, Butch, it's sharp. Liable to hurt yourself.

BERENICE. Put up that razor, Satan! I worry myself sick over you. You going to die before your appointed span.

JOHN HENRY. Why is Honey a nigger?

BERENICE. Jesus knows.

HONEY. I'm so tensed up. My nerves been scraped with a razor. Berenice, loan me a dollar.

BERENICE. I ain't handing you no dollar, worthless, to get high on them reefer cigarettes.

HONEY. Gimme, Berenice, I'm so tensed up and miserable. The nigger hole. I'm sick of smothering in the nigger hole. I can't stand it no more.

(Relenting, Berenice gets her pocketbook from the shelf, opens it, and takes out some change.)

BERENICE. Here's thirty cents. You can buy two beers.

HONEY. Well, thankful for tiny, infinitesimal favors. I better be dancing off now.

T. T. Same here. I still have to make a good deal of donation visits this afternoon. (Honey and T. T. go to the door)

BERENICE. So long, T. T. I'm counting on you for tomorrow and you too, Honey.

FRANKIE and JOHN HENRY. So long.

T. T. Good-bye, you all. Good-bye. (He goes out, crossing the yard)

BERENICE. Poor ole Sis Laura. I certainly hope that when my time comes I will have kept up my policy. I dread to think the church would ever have to bury me. When I die.

JOHN HENRY. Are you going to die, Berenice?

BERENICE. Why, Candy, everybody has to die.

JOHN HENRY. Everybody? Are you going to die, Frankie?

FRANKIE. I doubt it. I honestly don't think I'll ever die.

JOHN HENRY. What is "die"?

FRANKIE. It must be terrible to be nothing but black, black, black.

BERENICE. Yes, baby.

FRANKIE. How many dead people do you know? I know six dead people in all. I'm not counting my mother. There's William Boyd who was killed in Italy. I knew him by sight and name. An' that man who climbed poles for the telephone company. An' Lou Baker. The porter at Finny's place who was murdered in the alley back of Papa's store. Somebody drew a razor on him and the alley people said that his cut throat shivered like a mouth and spoke ghost words to the sun.

JOHN HENRY. Ludie Maxwell Freeman is dead.

FRANKIE. I didn't count Ludie; it wouldn't be fair. Because he died just before I was born. (To Berenice) Do you think very frequently about Ludie?

BERENICE. You know I do. I think about the five years when me and Ludie was together, and about all the bad times I seen since. Sometimes I almost wish I had never knew Ludie at all. It leaves you too lonesome afterward. When you walk home in the evening on the way from work, it makes a little lonesome quinch come in you. And you take up with too many sorry men to try to get over the feeling.

FRANKIE. But T. T. is not sorry.

BERENICE. I wasn't referring to T. T. He is a fine upstanding colored gentleman, who has walked in a state of grace all his life.

FRANKIE. When are you going to marry with him?

BERENICE. I ain't going to marry with him.

FRANKIE. But you were just now saying . . .

BERENICE. I was saying how sincerely I respect T. T. and sincerely regard T. T. *(There is a pause)* But he don't make me shiver none.

FRANKIE. Listen, Berenice, I have something queer to tell you. It's something that happened when I was walking around town today. Now I don't exactly know how to explain what I mean.

BERENICE. What is it?

FRANKIE *(now and then pulling her bangs or lower lip)*. I was walking along and I passed two stores with a alley in between. The sun was frying hot. And just as I passed this alley, I caught a *glimpse* of something in the corner of my left eye. A dark double shape. And this glimpse brought to my mind—so sudden and clear—my brother and the bride that I just stood there and couldn't hardly bear to look and see what it was. It was like they were there in that alley, although I knew that they are in Winter Hill almost a hundred miles away. *(There is a pause)* Then I turn slowly and look. And you know what was there? *(There is a pause)* It was just two colored boys. That was all. But it gave me such a queer feeling.

(Berenice has been listening attentively. She stares at Frankie, then draws a package of cigarettes from her bosom and lights one.)

BERENICE. Listen at me! Can you see through these bones in my forehead? *(She points to her forehead)* Have you, Frankie Addams, been reading my mind? *(There is a pause)* That's the most remarkable thing I ever heard of.

FRANKIE. What I mean is that . . .

BERENICE. I know what you mean. You mean right here in the corner of your eye. *(She points to her eye)* You suddenly catch something there. And this cold shiver run all the way down you. And you whirl around. And you stand there facing Jesus knows what. But not Ludie, not who you want. And for a minute you feel like you been dropped down a well.

FRANKIE. Yes. That is it. *(Frankie reaches for a cigarette and lights it, coughing a bit)*

BERENICE. Well, that is mighty remarkable. This is a thing been happening to me all my life. Yet just now is the first time I ever heard it put into words. *(There is a pause)* Yes, that is the way it is when you are in love. A thing known and not spoken.

FRANKIE *(patting her foot)*. Yet I always maintained I never believed in love. I didn't admit it and never put any of it in my shows.

JOHN HENRY. I never believed in love.

BERENICE. Now I will tell you something. And it is to be a warning to you. You hear me, John Henry. You hear me, Frankie.

JOHN HENRY. Yes. *(He points his forefinger)* Frankie is smoking.

BERENICE *(squaring her shoulders)*. Now I am here to tell you I was happy. There was no human woman in all the world more happy than I was in them days. And that includes everybody. You listening to me, John Henry? It includes all queens and millionaires and first ladies of the land. And I mean it includes people of all color. You hear me, Frankie? No human woman in all the world was happier than Berenice Sadie Brown.

FRANKIE. The five years you were married to Ludie.

BERENICE. From that autumn morning when I first meet him on the road in front of Campbell's Filling Station until the very night he died, November, the year 1933.

FRANKIE. The very year and the very month I was born.

BERENICE. The coldest November I ever seen. Every morning there was frost and puddles were crusted with ice. The sunshine was pale yellow like it is in winter time. Sounds carried far away, and I remember a hound dog that used to howl toward sundown. And everything I seen come to me as a kind of sign.

FRANKIE. I think it is a kind of sign I was born the same year and the same month he died.

BERENICE. And it was a Thursday towards six o'clock. About this time of day. Only November. I remember I went to the passage and opened the front door. Dark was coming on; the old hound was howling far away. And I go back in the room and lay down on Ludie's bed. I lay myself down over Ludie with my arms spread out and my face on his face. And I pray that the Lord would contage my strength to him. And I ask the Lord to let it be anybody, but not let it be Ludie. And I lay there and pray for a long time. Until night.

JOHN HENRY. How? *(In a higher, wailing voice)* How, Berenice?

BERENICE. That night he died. I tell you he died. Ludie! Ludie Freeman! Ludie Maxwell Freeman died! *(She hums)*

FRANKIE *(after a pause)*. It seems to me I feel sadder about Ludie than any other dead person. Although I never knew him. I know I ought to cry sometimes about my mother, or anyhow Granny. But it looks like I can't. But Ludie—maybe it was because I was born so soon after Ludie died. But you were starting out to tell some kind of a warning.

BERENICE *(looking puzzled for a moment)*. Warning? Oh, yes! I was going to tell you how this thing we was talking about applies to me. *(As Berenice begins to talk Frankie goes to a shelf above the refrigerator and brings back a fig bar to the table)* It was the April of the following year that I went one Sunday to the church where the congregation was strange to me. I had my forehead down on the top of the pew in front of me, and my eyes were open—not peeping around in secret, mind you, but just open. When suddenly this shiver ran all the way through me. I had caught sight of something from the corner of my eye. And I looked slowly to the left. There on the pew, just six inches from my eyes, was this *thumb*.

FRANKIE. What thumb?

BERENICE. Now I have to tell you. There was only one small portion of Ludie Freeman which was not pretty. Every other part about him was handsome and pretty as anyone would wish. All except this right thumb. This one thumb had a mashed, chewed appearance that was not pretty. You understand?

FRANKIE. You mean you suddenly saw Ludie's thumb when you were praying?

BERENICE. I mean I seen *this* thumb. And as I knelt there just staring at this thumb, I begun to pray in earnest. I prayed out loud! Lord, manifest! Lord, manifest!

FRANKIE. And did He—manifest?

BERENICE. Manifest, my foot! *(Spitting)* You know who that thumb belonged to?

FRANKIE. Who?

BERENICE. Why, Jamie Beale. That big old no-good Jamie Beale. It was the first time I ever laid eyes on him.

FRANKIE. Is that why you married him? Because he had a mashed thumb like Ludie's?

BERENICE. Lord only knows. I don't. I guess I felt drawn to him on account of that thumb. And then one thing led to another. First thing I know I had married him.

FRANKIE. Well, I think that was silly. To marry him just because of that thumb.

BERENICE. I'm not trying to dispute with you. I'm just telling you what actually happened. And the very same thing occurred in the case of Henry Johnson.

FRANKIE. You mean to sit there and tell me Henry Johnson had one of those mashed thumbs too?

BERENICE. No. It was not the thumb this time. It was the coat. *(Frankie and John Henry look at each other in amazement. After a pause Berenice continues)* Now when Ludie died, them policy people cheated me out of fifty dollars so I pawned everything I could lay hands on, and I sold my coat and Ludie's coat. Because I couldn't let Ludie be put away cheap.

FRANKIE. Oh! Then you mean Henry Johnson bought Ludie's coat and you married him because of it?

BERENICE. Not exactly. I was walking down the street one evening when I suddenly seen this shape appear before me. Now the shape of this boy ahead of me was so similar to Ludie through the shoulders and the back of the head that I almost dropped dead there on the sidewalk. I followed and run behind him. It was Henry Johnson. Since he lived in the country and didn't come into town, he had chanced to buy Ludie's coat and from the back view it looked like he was Ludie's ghost or Ludie's twin. But how I married him I don't exactly know, for, to begin with, it was clear that he did not have his share of sense. But you let a boy hang around you and you get fond of him. Anyway, that's how I married Henry Johnson.

FRANKIE. He was the one went crazy on you. Had eatin' dreams and swallowed the corner of the sheet. *(There is a pause)* But I don't understand the point of what you was telling. I don't see how that about

Jamie Beale and Henry Johnson applies to me.

BERENICE. Why, it applies to everybody and it is a warning.

FRANKIE. But how?

BERENICE. Why, Frankie, don't you see what I was doing? I loved Ludie and he was the first man I loved. Therefore I had to go and copy myself forever afterward. What I did was to marry off little pieces of Ludie whenever I come across them. It was just my misfortune they all turned out to be the wrong pieces. My intention was to repeat me and Ludie. Now don't you see?

FRANKIE. I see what you're driving at. But I don't see how it is a warning applied to me.

BERENICE. You don't! Then I'll tell you. *(Frankie does not nod or answer. The piano tuner plays an arpeggio)* You and that wedding tomorrow. That is what I am warning about. I can see right through them two gray eyes of yours like they was glass. And what I see is the saddest piece of foolishness I ever knew.

JOHN HENRY *(in a low voice)*. Gray eyes is glass.

(Frankie tenses her brows and looks steadily at Berenice.)

BERENICE. I see what you have in mind. Don't think I don't. You see something unheard of tomorrow, and you right in the center. You think you going to march to the preacher right in between your brother and the bride. You think you going to break into that wedding, and then Jesus knows what else.

FRANKIE. No. I don't see myself walking to the preacher with them.

BERENICE. I see through them eyes. Don't argue with me.

JOHN HENRY *(repeating softly)*. Gray eyes is glass.

BERENICE. But what I'm warning is this. If you start out falling in love with some unheard-of thing like that, what is going to happen to you? If you take a mania like this, it won't be the last time and of that you can be sure. So what will become of you? Will you be trying to break into weddings the rest of your days?

FRANKIE. It makes me sick to listen to people who don't have any sense. *(She sticks her fingers in her ears and hums)*

BERENICE. You just settin' yourself this fancy trap to catch yourself in trouble. And you know it.

FRANKIE. They will take me. You wait and see.

BERENICE. Well, I been trying to reason seriously. But I see it is no use.

FRANKIE. You are just jealous. You are just trying to deprive me of all the pleasure of leaving town.

BERENICE. I am just trying to head this off. But I still see it is no use.

JOHN HENRY. Gray eyes is glass.

(The piano is played to the seventh note of the scale and this is repeated.)

FRANKIE *(singing)*. Do, ray, mee, fa, sol, la, tee, do. Tee. Tee. It could drive you wild. *(She crosses to the screen door and slams it)* You didn't say anything about Willis Rhodes. Did he have a mashed thumb or a coat or something? *(She returns to the table and sits down)*

BERENICE. Lord, now that really was something.

FRANKIE. I only know he stole your furniture and was so terrible you had to call the Law on him.

BERENICE. Well, imagine this! Imagine a cold bitter January night. And me laying all by myself in the big parlor bed. Alone in the house because everybody else had gone for the Saturday night. Me, mind you, who hates to sleep in a big empty bed all by myself at any time. Past twelve o'clock on this cold, bitter January night. Can you remember winter time, John Henry? *(John Henry nods)* Imagine! Suddenly there comes a sloughing sound and a tap, tap, tap. So Miss Me ... *(She laughs uproariously and stops suddenly, putting her hand over her mouth)*

FRANKIE. What? *(Leaning closer across the table and looking intently at Berenice)* What happened?

(Berenice looks from one to the other, shaking her head slowly. Then she speaks in a changed voice.)

BERENICE. Why, I wish you would look yonder. I wish you would look. *(Frankie glances quickly behind her, then turns back to Berenice)*

FRANKIE. What? What happened?

BERENICE. Look at them two little pitchers and them four big ears. *(Berenice gets up suddenly from the table)* Come on, chillin, less us roll out the dough for the cookies tomorrow. *(Berenice clears the table and begins washing dishes at the sink)*

FRANKIE. If it's anything I mortally despise, it's a person who starts out to tell something and works up people's interest, and then stops.

BERENICE *(still laughing)*. I admit it. And I am sorry. But it was just one of them things I suddenly realized I couldn't tell you and John Henry.

(John Henry skips up to the sink.)

JOHN HENRY *(singing)*. Cookies! Cookies! Cookies!

FRANKIE. You could have sent him out of the room and told me. But don't think I care a particle about what happened. I just wish Willis Rhodes had come in about that time and slit your throat. *(She goes out into the hall)*

BERENICE *(still chuckling)*. That is a ugly way to talk. You ought to be ashamed. Here, John Henry, I'll give you a scrap of dough to make a cookie man. *(Berenice gives John Henry some dough. He climbs up on a chair and begins to work with it. Frankie enters with the evening newspaper. She stands in the doorway, then puts the newspaper on the table.)*

FRANKIE. I see in the paper where we dropped a new bomb—the biggest one dropped yet. They call it a atom bomb. I intend to take two baths tonight. One long soaking bath and scrub with a brush. I'm going to try to scrape this crust off my elbows. Then let out the dirty water and take a second bath.

BERENICE. Hooray, that's a good idea. I will be glad to see you clean.

JOHN HENRY. I will take two baths.

(Berenice has picked up the paper and is sitting in a chair against the pale white light of the window. She holds the newspaper open before her and her head is twisted down to one side as she strains to see what is printed there.)

FRANKIE. Why is it against the law to change your name?

BERENICE. What is that on your neck? I thought it was a head you carried on that neck. Just think. Suppose I would suddenly up and call myself Mrs. Eleanor Roosevelt. And you would begin naming yourself Joe Louis. And John Henry here tried to pawn himself off as Henry Ford.

FRANKIE. Don't talk childish; that is not the kind of changing I mean. I mean from

a name that doesn't suit you to a name you prefer. Like I changed from Frankie to F. Jasmine.

BERENICE. But it would be a confusion. Suppose we all suddenly change to entirely different names. Nobody would ever know who anybody was talking about. The whole world would go crazy.

FRANKIE. I don't see what that has to do with it.

BERENICE. Because things accumulate around your name. You have a name and one thing after another happens to you and things have accumulated around the name.

FRANKIE. But what has accumulated around my old name? *(Berenice does not reply)* Nothing! See! My name just didn't mean anything. Nothing ever happened to me.

BERENICE. But it will. Things will happen.

FRANKIE. What?

BERENICE. You pin me down like that and I can't tell you truthfully. If I could, I wouldn't be sitting here in this kitchen right now, but making a fine living on Wall Street as a wizard. All I can say is that things will happen. Just what, I don't know.

FRANKIE. Until yesterday, nothing ever happened to me.

(John Henry crosses to the door and puts on Berenice's hat and shoes, takes her pocketbook and walks around the table twice.)

BERENICE. John Henry, take off my hat and my shoes and put up my pocketbook. Thank you very much. *(John Henry does so)*

FRANKIE. Listen, Berenice. Doesn't it strike you as strange that I am I and you are you? Like when you are walking down a street and you meet somebody. And you are you. And he is him. Yet when you look at each other, the eyes make a connection. Then you go off one way. And he goes off another way. You go off into different parts of town, and maybe you never see each other again. Not in your whole life. Do you see what I mean?

BERENICE. Not exactly.

FRANKIE. That's not what I meant to say anyway. There are all these people here in town I don't even know by sight or name. And we pass alongside each other and don't have any connection. And they don't know me and I don't know them. And now I'm leaving town and there are all these people I will never know.

BERENICE. But who do you want to know?

FRANKIE. Everybody. Everybody in the world.

BERENICE. Why, I wish you would listen to that. How about people like Willis Rhodes? How about them Germans? How about them Japanese?

(Frankie knocks her head against the door jamb and looks up at the ceiling.)

FRANKIE. That's not what I mean. That's not what I'm talking about.

BERENICE. Well, what *is* you talking about?

(A child's voice is heard outside, calling: "Batter up! Batter up!")

JOHN HENRY *(in a low voice)*. Less play out, Frankie.

FRANKIE. No. You go. *(After a pause)* This is what I mean.

(Berenice waits, and when Frankie does not speak again, says:)

BERENICE. What on earth is wrong with you?

FRANKIE *(after a long pause, then suddenly, with hysteria)*. Boyoman! Manoboy! When we leave Winter Hill we're going to more places than you ever thought about or even knew existed. Just where we will go first I don't know, and it don't matter. Because after we go to that place we're going on to another. Alaska, China, Iceland, South America. Traveling on trains. Letting her rip on motorcycles. Flying around all over the world in airplanes. Here today and gone tomorrow. All over the world. It's the damn truth. Boyoman! *(She runs around the table)*

BERENICE. Frankie!

FRANKIE. And talking of things happening. Things will happen so fast we won't hardly have time to realize them. Captain Jarvis Addams wins highest medals and is decorated by the President. Miss F. Jasmine Addams breaks all records. Mrs. Janice Addams elected Miss United Nations in beauty contest. One thing after another happening so fast we don't hardly notice them.

BERENICE. Hold still, fool.

FRANKIE *(her excitement growing more and more intense)*. And we will meet them. Everybody. We will just walk up to people and know them right away. We will be walking down a dark road and see a lighted house and knock on the door and strangers will rush to meet us and say: "Come in! Come in!" We will know decorated aviators and New York people and movie stars. We will have thousands and thousands of friends. And we will belong to so many clubs that we can't even keep track of all of them. We will be members of the whole world. Boyoman! Manoboy!

(Frankie has been running round and round the table in wild excitement and when she passes the next time Berenice catches her slip so quickly that she is caught up with a jerk.)

BERENICE. *Is* you gone raving wild? *(She pulls Frankie closer and puts her arm around her waist)* Sit here in my lap and rest a minute. *(Frankie sits in Berenice's lap. John Henry comes close and jealously pinches Frankie)* Leave Frankie alone. She ain't bothered you.

JOHN HENRY. I'm sick.

BERENICE. Now no, you ain't. Be quiet and don't grudge your cousin a little bit love.

JOHN HENRY *(hitting Frankie)*. Old mean bossy Frankie.

BERENICE. What she doing so mean right now? She just laying here wore out. *(They continue sitting. Frankie is relaxed now)*

FRANKIE. Today I went to the Blue Moon—this place that all the soldiers are so fond of and I met a soldier—a red-headed boy.

BERENICE. What is all this talk about the Blue Moon and soldiers?

FRANKIE. Berenice, you treat me like a child. When I see all these soldiers milling around town I always wonder where they came from and where they are going.

BERENICE. They were born and they going to die.

FRANKIE. There are so many things about the world I do not understand.

BERENICE. If you did understand you would be God. Didn't you know that?

FRANKIE. Maybe so. *(She stares and stretches herself on Berenice's lap, her long legs sprawled out beneath the kitchen table)* Anyway, after the wedding I won't have to worry about things any more.

BERENICE. You don't have to now. Nobody requires you to solve the riddles of the world.

FRANKIE (*looking at newspaper*). The paper says this new atom bomb is worth twenty thousand tons of T.N.T.

BERENICE. Twenty thousand tons? And there ain't but two tons of coal in the coal house—all that coal.

FRANKIE. The paper says the bomb is a very important science discovery.

BERENICE. The figures these days have got too high for me. Read in the paper about ten million peoples killed. I can't crowd that many people in my mind's eye.

JOHN HENRY. Berenice, is the glass eye your mind's eye?

(*John Henry has climbed up on the back rungs of Berenice's chair and has been hugging her head. He is now holding her ears.*)

BERENICE. Don't yank my head back like that, Candy. Me and Frankie ain't going to float up through the ceiling and leave you.

FRANKIE. I wonder if you have ever thought about this? Here we are—right now. This very minute. Now. But while we're talking right now, this minute is passing. And it will never come again. Never in all the world. When it is gone, it is gone. No power on earth could bring it back again.

JOHN HENRY (*beginning to sing*).
I sing because I'm happy,
I sing because I'm free,
For His eye is on the sparrow,
And I know He watches me.

BERENICE (*singing*).
Why should I feel discouraged?
Why should the shadows come?
Why should my heart be lonely,
Away from heaven and home?
For Jesus is my portion,
My constant friend is He,
For His eye is on the sparrow,
And I know He watches me.
So, I sing because I'm happy.

(*John Henry and Frankie join on the last three lines.*)

I sing because I'm happy,
I sing because I'm free,
For His eye is on the sparrow,
And I know He watches . . .

BERENICE. Frankie, you got the sharpest set of human bones I ever felt.

THE CURTAIN FALLS

ACT THREE

SCENE ONE

The scene is the same: the kitchen. It is the day of the wedding. When the curtain rises Berenice, in her apron, and T. T. Williams in a white coat have just finished preparations for the wedding refreshments. Berenice has been watching the ceremony through the half-open door leading into the hall. There are sounds of congratulations offstage, the wedding ceremony having just finished.

———

BERENICE (*to T. T. Williams*). Can't see much from this door. But I can see Frankie. And her face is a study. And John Henry's chewing away at the bubble gum that Jarvis bought him. Well, sounds like it's all over. They crowding in now to kiss the bride. We better take this cloth off the sandwiches. Frankie said she would help you serve.

T. T. From the way she's been acting, I don't think we can count much on her.

BERENICE. I wish Honey was here. I'm so worried about him since what you told me. It's going to storm. It's a mercy they didn't decide to have the wedding in the back yard like they first planned.

T.T. I thought I'd better not minch the matter. Honey was in a bad way when I saw him this morning.

BERENICE. Honey Camden don't have too large a share of judgment as it is, but when he gets high on them reefers, he's got on more judgment than a four-year-old child. Remember that time he swung at the police and nearly got his eyes beat out?

T. T. Not to mention six months on the road.

BERENICE. I haven't been so anxious in all my life. I've got two people scouring Sugarville to find him. (*In a fervent voice*) God, you took Ludie but please watch over my Honey Camden. He's all the family I got.

T. T. And Frankie behaving this way about the wedding. Poor little critter.

BERENICE. And the sorry part is that she's perfectly serious about all this foolishness. (*Frankie enters the kitchen through the hall door*) Is it all over? (*T. T. crosses to the icebox with sandwiches*)

FRANKIE. Yes. And it was such a pretty wedding I wanted to cry.

BERENICE. You told them yet?

FRANKIE. About my plans—no, I haven't yet told them.

(John Henry comes in and goes out.)

BERENICE. Well, you better hurry up and do it, for they going to leave the house right after the refreshments.

FRANKIE. Oh, I know it. But something just seems to happen to my throat; every time I tried to tell them, different words came out.

BERENICE. What words?

FRANKIE. I asked Janice how come she didn't marry with a veil. *(With feeling)* Oh, I'm so embarrassed. Here I am all dressed up in this tacky evening dress. Oh, why didn't I listen to you! I'm so ashamed. *(T. T. goes out with a platter of sandwiches.)*

BERENICE. Don't take everything so strenuous like.

FRANKIE. I'm going in there and tell them now! *(She goes)*

JOHN HENRY *(coming out of the interior bedroom, carrying several costumes)*. Frankie sure gave me a lot of presents when she was packing the suitcase. Berenice, she gave me all the beautiful show costumes.

BERENICE. Don't set so much store by all those presents. Come tomorrow morning and she'll be demanding them back again.

JOHN HENRY. And she even gave me the shell from the Bay. *(He puts the shell to his ear and listens)*

BERENICE. I wonder what's going on up there. *(She goes to the door and opens it and looks through)*

T. T. *(returning to the kitchen)*. They all complimenting the wedding cake. And drinking the wine punch.

BERENICE. What's Frankie doing? When she left the kitchen a minute ago she was going to tell them. I wonder how they'll take this total surprise. I have a feeling like you get just before a big thunder storm.

(Frankie enters, holding a punch cup.)

BERENICE. You told them yet?

FRANKIE. There are all the family around and I can't seem to tell them. I wish I had written it down on the typewriter beforehand. I try to tell them and the words just—die.

BERENICE. The words just die because the very idea is so silly.

FRANKIE. I love the two of them so much. Janice put her arms around me and said she had always wanted a little sister. And she kissed me. She asked me again what grade I was in school. That's the third time she's asked me. In fact, that's the main question I've been asked at the wedding.

(John Henry comes in, wearing a fairy costume, and goes out. Berenice notices Frankie's punch and takes it from her.)

FRANKIE. And Jarvis was out in the street seeing about this car he borrowed for the wedding. And I followed him out and tried to tell him. But while I was trying to reach the point, he suddenly grabbed me by the elbows and lifted me up and sort of swung me. He said: "Frankie, the lankie, the alaga fankie, the tee-legged, toe-legged, bow-legged Frankie." And he gave me a dollar bill.

BERENICE. That's nice.

FRANKIE. I just don't know what to do. I have to tell them and yet I don't know how to.

BERENICE. Maybe when they're settled, they will invite you to come and visit with them.

FRANKIE. Oh no! I'm going *with* them. *(Frankie goes back into the house. There are louder sounds of voices from the interior. John Henry comes in again.)*

JOHN HENRY. The bride and the groom are leaving. Uncle Royal is taking their suitcases out to the car.

(Frankie runs to the interior room and returns with her suitcase. She kisses Berenice.)

FRANKIE. Good-bye, Berenice. Good-bye, John Henry. *(She stands a moment and looks around the kitchen)* Farewell, old ugly kitchen. *(She runs out)*

(There are sounds of good-byes as the wedding party and the family guests move out of the house to the sidewalk. The voices get fainter in the distance. Then, from the front sidewalk there is the sound of disturbance. Frankie's voice is heard, diminished by distance, although she is speaking loudly.)

FRANKIE'S VOICE. That's what I am telling you. *(Indistinct protesting voices are heard)*

MR. ADDAMS' VOICE *(indistinctly)*. Now be reasonable, Frankie.

FRANKIE'S VOICE *(screaming)*. I have to go. Take me! Take me!

JOHN HENRY (entering excitedly). Frankie is in the wedding car and they can't get her out. (He runs out but soon returns) Uncle Royal and my Daddy are having to haul and drag old Frankie. She's holding onto the steering wheel.

MR. ADDAMS' VOICE. You march right along here. What in the world has come into you? (He comes into the kitchen with Frankie who is sobbing) I never heard of such an exhibition in my life. Berenice, you take charge of her.

(Frankie flings herself on the kitchen chair and sobs with her head in her arms on the kitchen table.)

JOHN HENRY. They put old Frankie out of the wedding. They hauled her out of the wedding car.

MR. ADDAMS (clearing his throat). That's sufficient, John Henry. Leave Frankie alone. (He puts a caressing hand on Frankie's head) What makes you want to leave your old papa like this? You've got Janice and Jarvis all upset on their wedding day.

FRANKIE. I love them so!

BERENICE (looking down the hall). Here they come. Now please be reasonable, Sugar.

(The bride and groom come in. Frankie keeps her face buried in her arms and does not look up. The bride wears a blue suit with a white flower corsage pinned at the shoulder.)

JARVIS. Frankie, we came to tell you good-bye. I'm sorry you're taking it like this.

JANICE. Darling, when we are settled we want you to come for a nice visit with us. But we don't yet have any place to live. (She goes to Frankie and caresses her head. Frankie jerks) Won't you tell us good-bye now?

FRANKIE (with passion). We! When you say we, you only mean you and Jarvis. And I am not included. (She buries her head in her arms again and sobs)

JANICE. Please, darling, don't make us unhappy on our wedding day. You know we love you.

FRANKIE. See! We—when you say we, I am not included. It's not fair.

JANICE. When you come visit us you must write beautiful plays, and we'll all act in them. Come, Frankie, don't hide your sweet face from us. Sit up. (Frankie raises her head slowly and stares with a look of wonder and misery) Good-bye, Frankie, darling.

JARVIS. So long, now, kiddo.

(They go out and Frankie still stares at them as they go down the hall. She rises, crosses towards the door and falls on her knees.)

FRANKIE. Take me! Take me!

(Berenice puts Frankie back on her chair.)

JOHN HENRY. They put Frankie out of the wedding. They hauled her out of the wedding car.

BERENICE. Don't tease your cousin, John Henry.

FRANKIE. It was a frame-up all around.

BERENICE. Well, don't bother no more about it. It's over now. Now cheer up.

FRANKIE. I wish the whole world would die.

BERENICE. School will begin now in only three more weeks and you'll find another bosom friend like Evelyn Owens you so wild about.

JOHN HENRY (seated below the sewing machine). I'm sick, Berenice. My head hurts.

BERENICE. No you're not. Be quiet, I don't have the patience to fool with you.

FRANKIE (hugging her hunched shoulders). Oh, my heart feels so cheap!

BERENICE. Soon as you get started in school and have a chance to make these here friends, I think it would be a good idea to have a party.

FRANKIE. These baby promises rasp on my nerves.

BERENICE. You could call up the society editor of the Evening Journal and have the party written up in the paper. And that would make the fourth time your name has been published in the paper.

FRANKIE (with a trace of interest). When my bike ran into that automobile, the paper called me Fankie Addams, F-A-N-K-I-E. (She puts her head down again)

JOHN HENRY. Frankie, don't cry. This evening we can put up the tepee and have a good time.

FRANKIE. Oh, hush up your mouth.

BERENICE. Listen to me. Tell me what you would like and I will try to do it if it is in my power.

FRANKIE. All I wish in the world, is for no human being ever to speak to me as long as I live.

BERENICE. Bawl, then, misery.

(Mr. Addams enters the kitchen, carrying Frankie's suitcase, which he sets in the middle of the kitchen floor. He cracks his finger joints. Frankie stares at him resentfully, then fastens her gaze on the suitcase.)

MR. ADDAMS. Well, it looks like the show is over and the monkey's dead.

FRANKIE. You think it's over, but it's not.

MR. ADDAMS. You want to come down and help me at the store tomorrow? Or polish some silver with the shammy rag? You can even play with those old watch springs.

FRANKIE *(still looking at her suitcase)*. That's my suitcase I packed. If you think it's all over, that only shows how little you know. *(T. T. comes in)* If I can't go with the bride and my brother as I was meant to leave this town, I'm going anyway. Somehow, anyhow, I'm leaving town. *(Frankie raises up in her chair)* I can't stand this existence—this kitchen—this town—any longer! I will hop a train and go to New York. Or hitch rides to Hollywood, and get a job there. If worse comes to worse, I can act in comedies. *(She rises)* Or I could dress up like a boy and join the Merchant Marines and run away to sea. Somehow, anyhow, I'm running away.

BERENICE. Now, quiet down—

FRANKIE *(grabbing the suitcase and running into the hall)*. Please, Papa, don't try to capture me.

(Outside the wind starts to blow.)

JOHN HENRY *(from the doorway)*. Uncle Royal, Frankie's got your pistol in her suitcase.

(There is the sound of running footsteps and of the screen door slamming.)

BERENICE. Run, catch her.

(T. T. and Mr. Addams rush into the hall, followed by John Henry.)

MR. ADDAMS' VOICE. Frankie! Frankie! Frankie!

(Berenice is left alone in the kitchen. Outside the wind is higher and the hall door is blown shut. There is a rumble of thunder, then a loud clap. Thunder and flashes of lightning continue. Berenice is seated in her chair, when John Henry comes in.)

JOHN HENRY. Uncle Royal is going with my Daddy, and they are chasing her in our car. *(There is a thunder clap)* The thunder scares me, Berenice.

BERENICE *(taking him in her lap)*. Ain't nothing going to hurt you.

JOHN HENRY. You think they're going to catch her?

BERENICE *(putting her hand to her head)*. Certainly. They'll be bringing her home directly. I've got such a headache. Maybe my eye socket and all these troubles.

JOHN HENRY *(with his arms around Berenice)*. I've got a headache, too. I'm sick, Berenice.

BERENICE. No, you ain't. Run along, Candy. I ain't got the patience to fool with you now.

(Suddenly the lights go out in the kitchen, plunging it in gloom. The sound of wind and storm continues and the yard is a dark storm-green.)

JOHN HENRY. Berenice!

BERENICE. Ain't nothing. Just the lights went out.

JOHN HENRY. I'm scared.

BERENICE. Stand still, I'll just light a candle. *(Muttering)* I always keep one around, for such like emergencies. *(She opens a drawer)*

JOHN HENRY. What makes the lights go out so scarey like this?

BERENICE. Just one of them things, Candy.

JOHN HENRY. I'm scared. Where's Honey?

BERENICE. Jesus knows. I'm scared, too. With Honey snow-crazy and loose like this—and Frankie run off with a suitcase and her Papa's pistol. I feel like every nerve had been picked out of me.

JOHN HENRY *(holding out his seashell and stroking Berenice)*. You want to listen to the ocean?

THE CURTAIN FALLS

SCENE TWO

The scene is the same. There are still signs in the kitchen of the wedding: punch glasses and the punch bowl on the drainboard. It is four o'clock in the morning. As the curtain rises, Berenice and Mr Addams are alone in the kitchen. There is a crepuscular glow in the yard.

———

MR. ADDAMS. I never was a believer in corporal punishment. Never spanked

Frankie in my life, but when I lay my hands on her . . .

BERENICE. She'll show up soon—but I know how you feel. What with worrying about Honey Camden, John Henry's sickness and Frankie, I've never lived through such a anxious night. (*She looks through the window. It is dawning now*)

MR. ADDAMS. I'd better go and find out the last news of John Henry, poor baby. (*He goes through the hall door*)
(*Frankie comes into the yard and crosses to the arbor. She looks exhausted and almost beaten. Berenice has seen her from the window, rushes into the yard and grabs her by the shoulders and shakes her.*)

BERENICE. Frankie Addams, you ought to be skinned alive. I been worried.

FRANKIE. I've been so worried too.

BERENICE. Where have you been this night? Tell me everything.

FRANKIE. I will, but quit shaking me.

BERENICE. Now tell me the A and the Z of this.

FRANKIE. When I was running around the dark scarey streets, I begun to realize that my plans for Hollywood and the Merchant Marines were child plans that would not work. I hid in the alley behind Papa's store, and it was dark and I was scared. I opened the suitcase and took out Papa's pistol. (*She sits down on her suitcase*) I vowed I was going to shoot myself. I said I was going to count three and on three pull the trigger. I counted one—two—but I didn't count three—because at the last minute, I changed my mind.

BERENICE. You march right along with me. You going to bed.

FRANKIE. Oh, Honey Camden!
(*Honey Camden Brown, who has been hiding behind the arbor, has suddenly appeared.*)

BERENICE. Oh, Honey, Honey. (*They embrace*)

HONEY. Shush, don't make any noise; the law is after me.

BERENICE (*in a whisper*). Tell me.

HONEY. Mr. Wilson wouldn't serve me so I drew a razor on him.

BERENICE. You kill him?

HONEY. Didn't have no time to find out. I been runnin' all night.

FRANKIE. Lightfoot, if you drew a razor on a white man, you'd better not let them catch you.

BERENICE. Here's six dolla's. If you can get to Fork Falls and then to Atlanta. But be careful slippin' through the white folks' section. They'll be combing the county looking for you.

HONEY (*with passion*). Don't cry, Berenice.

BERENICE. Already I feel that rope.

HONEY. Don't you dare cry. I know now all my days have been leading up to this minute. No more "boy this—boy that"— no bowing, no scraping. For the first time, I'm free and it makes me happy. (*He begins to laugh hysterically*)

BERENICE. When they catch you, they'll string you up.

HONEY (*beside himself, brutally*). Let them hang me—I don't care. I tell you I'm glad. I tell you I'm happy. (*He goes out behind the arbor*)

FRANKIE (*calling after him*). Honey, remember you are Lightfoot. Nothing can stop you if you want to run away.
(*Mrs. West, John Henry's mother, comes into the yard.*)

MRS. WEST. What was all that racket? John Henry is critically ill. He's got to have perfect quiet.

FRANKIE. John Henry's sick, Aunt Pet?

MRS. WEST. The doctors say he has meningitis. He must have perfect quiet.

BERENICE. I haven't had time to tell you yet. John Henry took sick sudden last night. Yesterday afternoon when I complained of my head, he said he had a headache too and thinking he copies me I said, "Run along, I don't have the patience to fool with you." Looks like a judgment on me. There won't be no more noise, Mrs. West.

MRS. WEST. Make sure of that. (*She goes away*)

FRANKIE (*putting her arm around Berenice*). Oh, Berenice, what can we do?

BERENICE (*stroking Frankie's head*). Ain't nothing we can do but wait.

FRANKIE. The wedding—Honey—John Henry—so much has happened that my brain can't hardly gather it in. Now for the first time I realize that the world is certainly—a sudden place.

BERENICE. Sometimes sudden, but when you are waiting, like this, it seems so slow.

THE CURTAIN FALLS

SCENE THREE

The scene is the same: the kitchen and arbor. It is months later, a November day, about sunset.

The arbor is brittle and withered. The elm tree is bare except for a few ragged leaves. The yard is tidy and the lemonade stand and sheet stage curtain are now missing. The kitchen is neat and bare and the furniture has been removed. Berenice, wearing a fox fur, is sitting in a chair with an old suitcase and doll at her feet. Frankie enters.

——

FRANKIE. Oh, I am just mad about these Old Masters.

BERENICE. Humph!

FRANKIE. The house seems so hollow. Now that the furniture is packed. It gives me a creepy feeling in the front. That's why I came back here.

BERENICE. Is that the only reason why you came back here?

FRANKIE. Oh, Berenice, you know. I wish you hadn't given quit notice just because Papa and I are moving into a new house with Uncle Eustace and Aunt Pet out in Limewood.

BERENICE. I respect and admire Mrs. West but I'd never get used to working for her.

FRANKIE. Mary is just beginning this Rachmaninoff Concerto. She may play it for her debut when she is eighteen years old. Mary playing the piano and the whole orchestra playing at one and the same time, mind you. Awfully hard.

BERENICE. Ma-ry Littlejohn.

FRANKIE. I don't know why you always have to speak her name in a tinged voice like that.

BERENICE. Have I ever said anything against her? All I said was that she is too lumpy and marshmallow white and it makes me nervous to see her just setting there sucking them pigtails.

FRANKIE. Braids. Furthermore, it is no use our discussing a certain party. You could never possibly understand it. It's just not in you.

(Berenice looks at her sadly, with faded stillness, then pats and strokes the fox fur.)

BERENICE. Be that as it may. Less us not fuss and quarrel this last afternoon.

FRANKIE. I don't want to fuss either.

Anyway, this is not our last afternoon. I will come and see you often.

BERENICE. No, you won't, baby. You'll have other things to do. Your road is already strange to me.

(Frankie goes to Berenice, pats her on the shoulder, then takes her fox fur and examines it.)

FRANKIE. You still have the fox fur that Ludie gave you. Somehow this little fur looks so sad—so thin and with a sad little fox-wise face.

BERENICE *(taking the fur back and continuing to stroke it).* Got every reason to be sad. With what has happened in these two last months. I just don't know what I have done to deserve it. *(She sits, the fur in her lap, bent over with her forearms on her knees and her hands limply dangling)* Honey gone and John Henry, my little boy gone.

FRANKIE. You did all you could. You got poor Honey's body and gave him a Christian funeral and nursed John Henry.

BERENICE. It's the way Honey died and the fact that John Henry had to suffer so. Little soul!

FRANKIE. It's peculiar—the way it all happened so fast. First Honey caught and hanging himself in the jail. Then later in that same week, John Henry died and then I met Mary. As the irony of fate would have it, we first got to know each other in front of the lipstick and cosmetics counter at Woolworth's. And it was the week of the fair.

BERENICE. The most beautiful September I ever seen. Countless white and yellow butterflies flying around them autumn flowers—Honey dead and John Henry suffering like he did and daisies, golden weather, butterflies—such strange death weather.

FRANKIE. I never believed John Henry would die. *(There is a long pause. She looks out the window)* Don't it seem quiet to you in here? *(There is another, longer pause)* When I was a little child I believed that out under the arbor at night there would come three ghosts and one of the ghosts wore a silver ring. *(Whispering)* Occasionally when it gets so quiet like this I have a strange feeling. It's like John Henry is hovering somewhere in this kitchen—solemn looking and ghost-grey.

A BOY'S VOICE *(from the neighboring yard).* Frankie, Frankie.

FRANKIE (*calling to the boy*). Yes, Barney. (*To Berenice*) Clock stopped. (*She shakes the clock*)

THE BOY'S VOICE. Is Mary there?

FRANKIE (*to Berenice*). It's Barney MacKean. (*To the boy, in a sweet voice*) Not yet. I'm meeting her at five. Come on in, Barney, won't you?

BARNEY. Just a minute.

FRANKIE (*to Berenice*). Barney puts me in mind of a Greek god.

BERENICE. What? Barney puts you in mind of a what?

FRANKIE. Of a Greek god. Mary remarked that Barney reminded her of a Greek god.

BERENICE. It looks like I can't understand a thing you say no more.

FRANKIE. You know, those old-timey Greeks worship those Greek gods.

BERENICE. But what has that got to do with Barney MacKean?

FRANKIE. On account of the figure. (*Barney MacKean, a boy of thirteen, wearing a football suit, bright sweater and cleated shoes, runs up the back steps into the kitchen.*)

BERENICE. Hi, Greek god Barney. This afternoon I saw your initials chalked down on the front sidewalk. M.L. loves B.M.

BARNEY. If I could find out who wrote it, I would rub it out with their faces. Did you do it, Frankie?

FRANKIE (*drawing herself up with sudden dignity*). I wouldn't do a kid thing like that. I even resent you asking me. (*She repeats the phrase to herself in a pleased undertone*) Resent you asking me.

BARNEY. Mary can't stand me anyhow.

FRANKIE. Yes she can stand you. I am her most intimate friend. I ought to know. As a matter of fact she's told me several lovely compliments about you. Mary and I are riding on the moving van to our new house. Would you like to go?

BARNEY. Sure.

FRANKIE. O.K. You will have to ride back with the furniture 'cause Mary and I are riding on the front seat with the driver. We had a letter from Jarvis and Janice this afternoon. Jarvis is with the Occupation Forces in Germany and they took a vacation trip to Luxembourg. (*She repeats in a pleased voice*) Luxembourg. Berenice, don't you think that's a lovely name?

BERENICE. It's kind of a pretty name, but it reminds me of soapy water.

FRANKIE. Mary and I will most likely pass through Luxembourg when we—are going around the world together.

(*Frankie goes out followed by Barney and Berenice sits in the kitchen alone and motionless. She picks up the doll, looks at it and hums the first two lines of "I Sing Because I'm Happy." In the next house the piano is heard again, as the curtain falls.*)

The Autumn Garden

BY LILLIAN HELLMAN

First presented by Kermit Bloomgarden at the Coronet Theater in New York on March 7, 1951, with the following cast:

ROSE GRIGGS...........................Florence Eldridge
MRS. MARY ELLIS...........................Ethel Griffies
GENERAL BENJAMIN GRIGGS
                  Colin Keith-Johnston
EDWARD CROSSMAN......................Kent Smith
FREDERICK ELLIS.......................James Lipton

CARRIE ELLIS............................Margaret Barker
SOPHIE TUCKERMAN.....................Joan Lorring
LEON ....Maxwell Glanville
CONSTANCE TUCKERMAN.......Carol Goodner
NICHOLAS DENERY.....................Fredric March
NINA DENERY...................................Jane Wyatt

HILDA ....Lois Holmes

ACT ONE
Monday night after dinner.

ACT TWO

Scene One: The following Sunday morning.
Scene Two: That night.

ACT THREE
Early the next morning.

The time is September, 1949. The place is the Tuckerman house in a summer resort on the Gulf of Mexico, about one hundred miles from New Orleans.

Miss Hellman won her success mainly with the tight dramaturgy of three "well-made plays," *The Children's Hour* (1934), *The Little Foxes* (1939), and *Watch on the Rhine* (1941). Each of these surged forward to a sharp dramatic resolution by means of distinct plot complications. Yet we must note that each assault upon the emotions was also a challenge to the spectator's intellect; each play was surely something more than a piece of theatrical contrivance from the Scribe-Sardou play factory. Miss Hellman's characters, in fact, frequently had independent reality even while functioning in a tightly knit plot. In two other plays, *Days to Come* and *The Searching Wind*, Miss Hellman also exhibited an interest in looser plot construction. In *The Autumn Garden*, however, Miss Hellman virtually left plot alone and allowed the characters to demonstrate themselves with nearly complete freedom from anything but the necessities of their own personalities.

The above-mentioned plays, along with her "little Foxes" sequel *Another Part of the Forest* (1946) and an adaptation of an "existentialist" French play *Montserrat*, comprise Miss Hellman's total dramatic output. The foundation for this work, which gave this New-Orleans-born playwright an international reputation, was laid down after study at Columbia University and graduation in 1924 at the age of nineteen. Miss Hellman did publicity for a stock company in Rochester, worked as a book reviewer and a Broadway playreader, and published articles and stories. A flair for theatre seems to have come naturally to Miss Hellman. She collaborated on a play with Louis Kronenberger early in her career. Most of her plays have been singularly successful, and she was also profitably employed, for some time, in Hollywood.

Miss Hellman has been a meticulous, hard-working playwright who leaves no doubt that she knows her own mind and, what is at least equally important, that she knows her characters. Having scant patience for bumbling, she often chivvies her characters, but, as a rule, only after she has made them live. In fact, they are frequently so alive in the theatre that the indictments she incorporates in her plays seem indictments of human nature itself, giving rise to the complaint that she does not like people. In *The Autumn Garden* she liked them well enough to include a considerable amount of tenderness in her writing, although here, too, she refused to overlook moral bankruptcy or to romanticize evasions of reality.

ACT ONE

SCENE: *The living room of the Tucker-man house in a town on the Gulf of Mex-ico, a hundred miles from New Orleans. A September evening, 1949, after dinner. To the right of the living room is a side porch, separated from the room by a glass door. Upstage left is a door leading into the entrance hall of the house: through this door we can see the hall and stair-case. On the porch are chairs and tables. The furniture of the living room is hand-some but a little shabby. It is all inherited from another day. (Right and left are the audience's right and left.)*

ON THE STAGE AT RISE OF CURTAIN: *Gen-eral Griggs, a good-looking man of fifty-three, is seated at one side of the room reading a newspaper. His wife—Rose Griggs, ex-pretty, soft-looking and about forty-three, is seated at a table wearing an evening dress that is much too young for her. She is chatting across the room with—Carrie Ellis, a distinguished-look-ing woman of about forty-five, who is sit-ting on a side chair, near her son, Fred-erick, and her mother-in-law—Mrs. Mary Ellis, in her seventies, sprightly in man-ner and movement when she wishes to be, broken and senile when she wishes to be broken and senile. She has piled cushions on her chair so she can read a manuscript over the shoulder of her grandson—Frederick Ellis, a pleasant-looking young man of around twenty-five. Occasionally he makes a correction in the manuscript, looks up amused and annoyed at his grandmother. On the right porch—Edward Crossman, about forty-six, tired and worn-looking as if he is not in good health, is sitting alone, his back to those in the room. There is a second of silence after the curtain goes up.*

———

ROSE *(gets up from her chair. She finds silence uncomfortable and breaks into song "We Stroll the Lane Together").* Now where is it? Everything's been so topsy-turvy all evening. If I can't have it immediately after dinner than I just about don't want it. At home you can bet it's right waiting for us when we leave the dining room, isn't it, Ben? Too bad it's Thursday. I'd almost rather go and see him than go to the party. *(To Mrs. Ellis)* I think it's what keeps you awake, Mrs.

Ellis. I mean a little is good for your heart, the doctor told me always to have a little, but my goodness the amount you have every night.

MRS. ELLIS *(pleasantly).* Would you mind telling me what you're talking about, Mrs. Griggs? You said if it wasn't for the party you'd go and see *him,* but you thought *I* drank too much on a Thursday?

ROSE *(giggles).* Coffee. I mean you drink too much coffee.

MRS. ELLIS. Then it is coffee you wish to go and see?

ROSE. Now, now. You're teasing. You know very well I mean Robert Taylor in that thing.

MRS. ELLIS. Believe me, I did *not* know you meant Robert Taylor in that thing. You know, General Griggs, after seven summers I have come to the conclusion that your wife considers it vulgar to men-tion anything by name. There's nothing particularly genteel about pronouns, my dear. Coffee is coffee and not it, Robert Taylor is Robert Taylor and not him, I suppose, and a fool is a fool and not her.

ROSE *(pleasantly).* I know. It's a naughty habit. Ben has been telling me for years. *(She is close to Ben)* Do you like my dress, Ben?

GRIGGS. It's nice.

ROSE. Have I too much rouge? *(To others)* Know what she used to say? *(Quickly)* Ben's mother, I mean. She used to say it before she died. *(To Cross-man)* Come and join us. *(To others)* She used to say that Southern women painted a triangle of rouge on their faces as if they were going out to square the hypote-nuse. Ben came from Boston, and his mother was sometimes a little sharp about Southerners.

MRS. ELLIS. Who could have blamed her?

ROSE *(calling out to Crossman).* Know what she told me last winter when I met her at the Club?

CROSSMAN *(turns, smiles).* Ben's mother?

ROSE. No. Your sister, of course. She said we see more of you here on your summer vacation than she sees all year round in New Orleans. She says you're getting to be a regular old hermit. You have to watch that as you get older. You might get to like being alone—and that's dangerous.

MRS. ELLIS. I used to like being alone. When you get old, of course, then you don't any more. But somewhere in the middle years, it's fine to be alone. A room of one's own isn't nearly enough. A house, or, best, an island of one's own. Don't you agree, General Griggs? (*Very quickly*) Happiest year of my life was when my husband died. Every month was springtime and every day I seemed to be tipsy, as if my blood had turned a lovely *vin rosé*.

CARRIE. You're lyrical, Mother.

MRS. ELLIS (*to Frederick*). Do you know I almost divorced your grandfather, Frederick? During the racing season in 1901.

FREDERICK (*looks up, laughs*). You don't feel it's a little late to talk about it? (*The phone rings.*)

MRS. ELLIS. Thought you might like to write my biography—when you're finished with regional poetry.

(*As the phone rings again, Sophie comes into the hall to answer it.*)

SOPHIE (*into the phone*). No, sir. We do not take transient guests. No, never, sir. Only permanent guests. You might telephone to Mrs. Prescott in the village. Thank you, sir.

ROSE (*calls into hall*). Dear Sophie, where is coffee?

(*Sophie comes to the hall door. She is a plain-looking, shy girl of about seventeen. She has a hesitant, overpolite manner and speaks with a slight accent. She has on a party dress, covered by a kitchen apron.*)

SOPHIE. Aunt Constance is most sorry for the delay. We bring it immediately. (*She disappears.*)

ROSE. Frederick, do you know I've been giving Sophie dancing lessons, or trying to? She's a charming child, your intended, but she's never going to be a dancer.

FREDERICK (*pleasantly*). Terrible expression, Mrs. Griggs: my intended. Sounds like my indentured. Did you tell Mrs. Griggs, Mother? I thought we agreed that since there were no definite plans as yet—

CARRIE (*a little uncomfortable*). It's natural that I should speak about my son's marriage, isn't it?

ROSE. Why, goodness, yes indeed it is. I'd have felt hurt—

GRIGGS. Don't you know that women have no honor, Frederick, when it comes to keeping secrets about marriage or cancer?

FREDERICK (*looks at his mother*). No, sir. I didn't know. I'm too young for my age.

MRS. ELLIS (*who has been busy reading the manuscript*). I know I'm too young to be reading Payson's book. Full of the most confused sex. I can't tell who is what. And all out of doors. Is that new, so much sex out of doors? Is it, General?

GRIGGS. I don't think it's a question of "new." I think it's a question of climate.

MRS. ELLIS (*points to book*). But aren't sexual relations the way they used to be: between *men* and *women*? It's so twitched about in Mr. Payson's book. You know, I think the whole country is changing.

GRIGGS (*as if he wished to help Frederick*). Has Payson written a good book, Fred?

FREDERICK. It's a wonderful book. I think he's going to be the most important young writer—

CARRIE. You said the first two books were wonderful, Frederick. And they didn't sell very well.

MRS. ELLIS. I don't know why they didn't—I always thought houses of prostitution had a big lending-library trade. (*Frederick gets up, as if he were angry.*)

CARRIE. Will this new book sell, Frederick?

FREDERICK. I don't know, Mother.

CARRIE. I hope it sells. Any man is better off supporting himself.

FREDERICK (*smiles*). Mother, sometimes I think no people are quite so moral about money as those who clip coupons for a living.

MRS. ELLIS. And why not? Particularly your mother who is given the coupons already clipped by me who has the hardship of clipping them. That leaves her more time to grow moral. And then, of course, you who don't even have that much trouble are left at leisure to be moral about those who have to go to the trouble of living on unearned money.

CARRIE (*to General Griggs*). You mustn't look uncomfortable, General. You should know by this time that my mother-in-law enjoys discussing family matters in public. And the more uncomfortable you look, the longer she will continue.

GRIGGS. Do I look uncomfortable? I was thinking how hard it is to be young.

ROSE (*to Ben*). Won't you come to the party? (*To others*) Ben has never gone to the Carter party. I am sure they're just as insulted every year—

GRIGGS. I don't think so.

ROSE. But what will you do with yourself? Why don't you go to see Robert Taylor? It's that war picture where he does so well and you'll want to see if it's accurate.

GRIGGS. No. I don't want to see if it's accurate.

ROSE. Do you like my dress?

GRIGGS. It's nice.

MRS. ELLIS. You are a patient man. (*To Rose*) Do you know you've asked him that five times since rising from dinner?

ROSE. Well, I feel young and gay, and I'm going to a party. I wish the Denerys would come before we leave. I like meeting new people and they sound so interesting. I thought they were supposed to arrive in time for dinner. (*To Carrie*) Is he absolutely fascinating?

CARRIE. I don't know, Mrs. Griggs. I haven't seen him in twenty years or more.

ROSE (*calling to Crossman*). Is he fascinating, Mr. Crossman?

CROSSMAN (*pleasantly*). You're making it a little harder than usual. Is who fascinating?

ROSE. Nicholas Denery, of course.

CROSSMAN. Of course. I don't know.

ROSE. But, goodness. Didn't you all grow up together? I mean you and Constance and Mrs. Ellis and—

CROSSMAN. I don't remember any of us as fascinating. Do you, Carrie?

(*Carrie shakes her head, laughs.*)

(*Sophie, carrying a tray with brandy and brandy glasses, comes into the room. She is followed by Leon, a young, colored butler, carrying coffee and coffee cups. Frederick rises and takes the tray from Sophie. She looks at him and smiles.*)

ROSE. Let's see your dress, Sophie. (*Sophie smiles shyly, begins to take off her apron as Leon pours coffee*) Oh. It's right nice. But you should wear tighter things, dear. (*Comes in back of her, begins to fool with her hair*) I'd like to try your hair again. (*Sophie moves to help Leon but is cornered by Rose*) Now you just sit down. How's this?

(*Crossman comes into the room.*)

CROSSMAN. Makes her look like everybody else. That's desirable, isn't it?

ROSE. What does Frederick think? We're out to please Frederick, after all, aren't we, dear?

FREDERICK (*turns to look*). I like Sophie her own way.

SOPHIE (*smiles*). I have no "way."

ROSE. But most European girls have such chic—(*General Griggs gets up, as if he were annoyed*) They have, Ben. You said it yourself when you came back from the Pacific, and I was jealous.

MRS. ELLIS. Pacific? I thought you fought in Europe.

GRIGGS. I did. Robert Taylor fought in the Pacific.

(*He rises, wanders off to the porch.*)

ROSE (*holding Sophie's hair another way*). Or is *this* better?

FREDERICK (*smiles to Sophie*). Don't you mind being pulled about?

SOPHIE. No. Well. (*Gently pulls away*) I am grateful for the trouble that Mrs. Griggs—Thank you.

CROSSMAN. Sophie doesn't mind anything. All she has said all summer is thank you.

(*Through his speech the phone rings. Frederick starts for the phone. At the same time, Constance Tuckerman comes through the hall. She is a handsome woman of forty-three or forty-four. She is carrying two flower vases. She puts down one of the vases in order to answer the phone.*)

CONSTANCE. Yes. Just a minute. Frederick. Mr. Payson would like to speak to you. (*She picks up the other vase, comes into the door, as if she were in a hurry. Frederick immediately moves to the phone*) Sorry coffee was late. You all want more just ring. And do, Carrie, explain to the Carters why I can't come to their party this year—

ROSE. Any news from them, Constance?

CONSTANCE (*carefully*). News from whom?

ROSE (*laughs*). Oh, come now. Stop pretending. When do the Denerys arrive?

CONSTANCE. Don't wait up for them, Rose. You'll see them at breakfast.

(*She turns, goes out and goes up the stairs.*)

ROSE. My, Constance is nervous. Well, I suppose I should be if I were seeing an old beau for the first time in— But I don't believe in old beaux. Beaux should be brand-new, or just friends, don't you think? *(Crossman starts out to porch, carrying his coffee and the brandy bottle. Rose points outside, meaning General Griggs and Crossman)* Now are you boys just going to sit here and share the bottle—

CROSSMAN. General Griggs is only being kind when he says he shares the bottle with me.
(He goes off. Frederick comes in, starts to speak, changes his mind.)

CARRIE *(carefully)*. Was that Mr. Payson on the phone? Is he coming to the party?

FREDERICK. How many generations do you have to summer in this joint before you're invited to the Carters'?

MRS. ELLIS. Oh, that's not true. They're very liberal lately. *(Points to Rose)* After all, the last few years they've always included Mrs. Griggs. *(To Rose)* And nobody can be more *nouveau riche* than your family, can they? I mean your brother during the war and all that.

ROSE *(giggles)*. My. Everybody is so jealous of Henry.

MRS. ELLIS. Well, of course we are. I wish we were *nouveau riche* again.

FREDERICK *(sharply)*. All right, Grandma.

ROSE. Oh, I don't mind. I enjoy your grandmother.

FREDERICK *(to his mother)*. I'm sorry I'm not going to be able to take you to the party. I hope you'll excuse me, Sophie. Mother. Grandma.

CARRIE *(carefully)*. What has happened, Frederick?

FREDERICK. Payson had a wire from his publishers. They want the manuscript in the mail tomorrow morning. *(He goes to take the manuscript from the table)* So I'll have to proofread it with him tonight. It's a nasty job alone, almost impossible—

CARRIE *(slowly)*. I don't understand.

ROSE *(hurriedly)*. I must fix my face. As you get older your face needs arranging more often.
(She goes off.)

CARRIE. We're ready to leave, Frederick.

FREDERICK. Mother, I'm not going to the party. I wasn't making a joke.

CARRIE. Oh. I hoped you were. You have no obligation to us, or Sophie? An appointment broken, because Payson summons you?

FREDERICK. I am sorry, Sophie, Maybe I can pick you up later. *(Haltingly)* I am sorry.

SOPHIE. I do not mind, really. It is better this way.

CARRIE. Don't you? Why not? *(No answer)* Why don't you mind, Sophie?

SOPHIE *(smiles)*. I do not like parties. I did not want to go. Now Frederick has some important business and must leave quickly—

CARRIE. Perhaps you are going to make *too* good a wife.

FREDERICK. Suppose you let me decide that, Mother. Good night. Have a good time. See you in the morning—

CARRIE. I want to talk to you, Frederick.

FREDERICK *(stops, smiles)*. When you use that tone of voice you need two hours. Let's make it in the morning. Mother.
(Sophie has turned away, gone upstage, as if she wanted to be as far away as possible.)

CARRIE. I ask you to break your appointment with Payson. As a favor to me.

FREDERICK. There's nothing important about my being at the party and it is important to him. He wants to consult me—

CARRIE *(sharply)*. He is always consulting you. You talk like a public accountant or a landscape gardener. Why should he want to consult *you* about his work?

FREDERICK *(hurt)*. Maybe because I try to write and maybe because he thinks I know a little. I realize that's hard for you to believe—

CARRIE. I didn't mean that.

FREDERICK. I think you did. Good night.

CARRIE. You have no sense of obligation to me. *(Looks around for Sophie who is trying at this minute to leave the room)* And none to Sophie. Who evidently won't speak for herself. Do stay here, Sophie, it's your business as well as mine— *(Sophie stands still)* I am getting tired of Mr. Payson, Frederick, and with good reason. When he came to stay with us in town last winter, I fully understood that he was a brilliant and gifted man and I was glad for you to have such a friend. But when he followed you down here this summer—

FREDERICK *(slowly, angrily)*. He did not follow me down here and I wouldn't like you to put it that way again. He came here for the summer and is that your business, Mother?

CARRIE. There is just too much of Mr.

Payson. Every day or every evening—
How often do you take Sophie with you?
(Sharply) How often have you seen Mr.
Payson this summer, Sophie? *(There is
no answer)* Please answer me.

FREDERICK. And please stop using that
tone to Sophie. Say what you have to say
to me.

CARRIE *(turning to Mrs. Ellis, who has
been watching them)*. Mother—

MRS. ELLIS. I've been dozing. How many
hours have passed?

CARRIE *(slowly)*. You are always dozing
when there is something unpleasant to
face out with Frederick.

MRS. ELLIS. What better time? You all
want to know something's been worrying
me all day? Nobody in the South has
tapeworm any more. In my day that was
all you ever heard. Tapeworm, tapeworm,
tapeworm. *(Gets up)* Now kiss your
mother good night, boy. Otherwise she'll
be most unhappy. And say you forgive
her.

FREDERICK. I have nothing to forgive her
for, Grandma.

MRS. ELLIS. Of course not. But even
when your mother starts out being right
she talks and talks until she gets around
to being wrong.
(She exits. There is silence.)

CARRIE *(softly)*. I'm sorry if I spoke
unfairly, or at the wrong time—

FREDERICK *(comes to her, smiling)*. You
didn't, you didn't. Now don't feel bad.
Nothing's happened. And don't let Grandma tease you.

CARRIE. I know. *(She turns to go)* You
go ahead, dear. Try to join us later.
*(He kisses her. She smiles, pleased, and
goes out. Frederick turns to Sophie.)*

FREDERICK. Sophie, Mother didn't mean
to be sharp with you. But when she is,
you mustn't let her. She's a little bossy
from time to time, but no harm in it. You
look so worried.

SOPHIE *(very puzzled)*. Your mother is
not angry now?

FREDERICK. Of course not. You mustn't
take these things too seriously. Mother is
like that.

SOPHIE *(smiles)*. You know it is most
difficult in another language. Everything
in English sounds so important. I get a
headache from the strain of listening.

FREDERICK *(laughs)*. Don't. It's not
worth it. *(Looks at her, then slowly)*

Mother is right: I have been rude and
neglectful. But I haven't meant to be,
Sophie.

SOPHIE. No, no. You have not been.

FREDERICK. And in two weeks Mother
and I will be going off to Europe. I hope
you don't mind about the European trip.
It was all arranged long before you and
I— *(Stares at her, smiles)* got engaged.
*(Sophie smiles at him as if she were em-
barrassed, then she coughs and clears her
throat)* We're an awkward pair. I like
you, Sophie.

SOPHIE *(warmly)*. I like you, Frederick.

FREDERICK. Sophie, I think we'll have to
sit down soon and talk about ourselves. I
don't think we even know how we got
engaged. We haven't said much of anything—

SOPHIE. Sometimes it is better not to say
things. There is time and things will
come as they come.

FREDERICK. The day we got engaged,
we tried to speak as honestly as we both
knew how but we didn't say very much—

SOPHIE. And I think we should not try
so hard to talk. Sometimes it is wise to
let things grow more roots before one
blows them away with many words—
(Shyly touches his hand) It will come
better if we give it time.

FREDERICK. We will give it time. And
you'll make no decisions and set no dates
until you are sure about what you think
and feel.

SOPHIE. Oh, I have made the decision
for myself. And I am pleased.

FREDERICK *(pleased)*. And you are quite
sure of your decision?

SOPHIE. You know, sometimes I have
thought that with rich people—*(Very
quickly)* with educated people, I mean,
decisions are made only in order to speak
about changing them. It happens often
with Aunt Constance and with your
mother, also, I think. And the others.

FREDERICK. Yes. *(Takes her hand)* We'll
get along fine. I want you to know that I
feel very lucky—

SOPHIE. Lucky? You will have to be
patient with me. I am not a good success
here.

FREDERICK. Now, you stop that. I don't
want you a good success. And you're to
stop thinking it. You're to stop a lot of
things: letting Mother boss you about,

letting Mrs. Griggs tell you what to wear, or pull your hair—

SOPHIE. Oh, I do not mind. Because I look so bad makes Mrs. Griggs think she looks so good.

FREDERICK (*smiles*). Good night, my dear.

SOPHIE (*smiles*). Good night.

(*He exits. Sophie begins to pick up the coffee cups, brandy glasses, etc. After a minute Rose Griggs comes down the steps carrying a light summer wrap. She comes in the room.*)

ROSE. Where are the Ellises?

SOPHIE. They went to the party, Mrs. Griggs.

ROSE. No! Without me? I *must* say that's very rude. They can't have done that, Sophie—(*She hurries to the hall, looks out. Then she comes back in, goes to the porch*) Ben. (*He looks up*) The Ellises left without me, Ben!

GRIGGS. Yes?

ROSE. You'll have to walk me over. I just won't go in, alone.

GRIGGS. It's across the street, Rose. Not a very dangerous journey.

ROSE (*gently*). Ben. (*He rises, comes in*) You know, I think it's shocking. In front of other people. God knows what they know or guess this summer. (*Suddenly notices Sophie who is collecting cups*) Sophie. Don't wait here listening. (*Sophie turns, surprised, but before she can speak . . .*)

GRIGGS (*sharply*). Rose!

ROSE (*who is always charming at this point. To Sophie*). I am sorry, my dear. Please most earnestly I ask your pardon—

SOPHIE. Yes, ma'am.

ROSE (*tries to catch her at door*). I'm just a nervous old silly these days. Now say you forgive me—

(*Sophie disappears.*)

GRIGGS (*smiles, as if he has seen this before*). All right, Rose. You're charming.

ROSE. You won't even walk over with me, just to the door?

GRIGGS. Certainly I will.

ROSE (*smiles*). No, you don't have to. I just wanted to see if you would. Will you call for me, at twelve, say?

GRIGGS. No.

ROSE. Then will you meet me at twelve, at the tavern?

GRIGGS. No. What mischief is this, Rose?

ROSE. Is it mischief to want to talk with you?

GRIGGS. Again? Tonight? And every night and every day? The same things over and over? We're worn out, Rose, both of us. (*Kindly*) There is no more to say.

ROSE (*softly*). No more to say. Do people get divorces, after twenty-five years, by just saying they want them and that's all and walking off?

GRIGGS. I suppose some men do. But I haven't walked off and I have said all I know how to say.

ROSE. But you haven't really explained anything to me. You tell me that you want a divorce— And I ask why, why, why. We've been happy together.

GRIGGS (*looks at her*). You don't believe that.

ROSE. When people get our age, well, the worst is over—and what else can one do? (*Exasperated*) I never really heard of such a thing. I'm just not taking you seriously and I do wish you'd stop talking about it. (*After a pause*) You've never given me a good reason. I ask you ten times a day if there's another woman. I could understand that. Of course you say no, naturally—

GRIGGS. There is no other woman.

ROSE (*giggles*). You know what I think? I think it's that little blonde at the drugstore, and the minute my back is turned—

GRIGGS. Please, Rose. Please stop that.

ROSE. Never at any time, during this divorce talk, have you mentioned them. You'd think we didn't have sons, and the awful effect on them. Did you write them today?

GRIGGS. I did not write them because you begged me not to.

ROSE. Oh, yes, I forgot. It will break their hearts.

GRIGGS. Their hearts won't be broken. They won't even bother to finish the letter.

ROSE (*softly, shocked*). You can't love them, to speak that way.

GRIGGS. I don't love them. I did love them but I don't now. They're hard men to love.

ROSE. Oh, I don't believe a word you say. You've always enjoyed shocking me. You've been a wonderful father and you're just as devoted to them as they are to you.

GRIGGS. They aren't the least devoted to me—when they think about me it is to find my name useful and when it isn't useful they disapprove of me.

ROSE (moving to door). Look, Ben. I just can't stay and talk all night. I'm late now. There's no use our saying the same things over and over again— (He laughs) If you won't come to the party what are you going to do?

GRIGGS. I am going down by the water, sit on a bench and study from a Chinese grammar.

ROSE. You'll be lonely.

GRIGGS. Yes, but not for parties.

ROSE. It's very hard to take seriously a man who spends the evening with a Chinese grammar. I'll never forget that winter with the Hebrew phonograph records. (Pats his arm) Now, good night, darling. And don't worry about me: I am going to try to have a good time. We'll talk about all this another day.
(She starts out.)

GRIGGS (sharply). No. No, we're not going to do that. You're turning it into a pleasure, Rose, something to chatter about on a dull winter night in the years to come. I've told you it isn't going to be that way. (She is in the hall) It isn't going to be that way. When you go back to town next week I'm not going with you. (He turns to see that she has gone.)

ROSE's VOICE (from the hall). Good night, darling.

GRIGGS (he stands still for a minute. Then he turns, see his book on the porch table. Goes out to the porch, realizes the doors have been open. To Crossman). I guess we thought the doors were closed. I am sorry.

CROSSMAN. Don't be.

GRIGGS. There are so many things I want to do that I don't know which to do first. Have you ever thought about starting a new life?

CROSSMAN (smiles). I've often thought that if I started all over again, I'd go right back to where I started and start from there. Otherwise, it wouldn't prove anything.

GRIGGS (laughs). Where'd you start from?

CROSSMAN (laughs). Nowhere. That's the trouble.

GRIGGS. I started with mathematics. Seems strange now, but that's why I went to West Point—wonderful mathematics department. So I got myself two wars instead. I want to go somewhere now and study for a few years, or—(Smiles) Anyway, sit down by myself and think.

CROSSMAN. Europe?

GRIGGS. I don't think so. Europe seemed like a tourist joint the last time. With all the aimless, dead bitterness of—tourist joints. I don't want sentimental journeys to old battlefields. I'll start tame enough: I've written my sister that I'd like to stay with her for a month or two.

CROSSMAN. Isn't that a sentimental journey?

GRIGGS. I suppose it is. I really want to see her because she looks like my mother. The last six months I've thought a lot about my mother. If I could just go back to her for a day. Crazy at my age—

CROSSMAN. I know. We all do at times. Age has nothing to do with it. It's when we're in trouble.

GRIGGS. I don't know why I want to say this but, well, don't think too badly of my wife.

CROSSMAN. Why should I think badly of anybody?

GRIGGS (as he turns to go). All professional soldiers marry Rose. It's in the Army Manual. She is as she always was. It is my fault, not hers.

CROSSMAN. Haven't you lived in the South long enough to know that nothing is ever anybody's fault?
(General Griggs laughs, starts out as Constance comes down stairs. Constance has on a different dress and is buttoning the belt as she comes into the room. General Griggs crosses the room and exits by the stage left windows. Constance looks around, finds the room is neat, goes out to the porch, talking as she goes.)

CONSTANCE. I think everything is ready. I've put Nick in Sophie's room—Sophie says she doesn't mind sleeping down here. Anyway it happens every summer. And I've given Mrs. Denery the yellow room. They wanted two rooms, Nick said on the phone.

CROSSMAN. Fashionable people don't sleep together, don't you know that? It's not sanitary.

CONSTANCE (sits down). I'm tired, Ned.

CROSSMAN. Have a brandy.

CONSTANCE. No. It would make me nervous.

CROSSMAN. Remarkable the things that make people nervous: coffee, brandy, relatives, running water, too much sun, too little sun. Never anything in themselves, eh, Constance?

CONSTANCE. They have a maid and a chauffeur. I'll have to put them in the boathouse. It's all so much work at the end of the season. Sophie's been cleaning all day, and I've been cooking—Why did I say they could come?

CROSSMAN (smiles). I wonder why.

CONSTANCE. Well, of course, I want to see Nick again. But I am nervous about meeting her. (Points to his glass) Do you think perhaps a sip?

CROSSMAN. Only drunkards borrow other people's drinks. Have one of your own. (Through her next speech he pours her a drink and hands it to her. When she finishes it, he will take back the glass and pour himself a drink.)

CONSTANCE. I got out Mama's good, old linen sheets. I don't care how rich the Denerys are, or where they've been, they never could have had finer linen. And I've stuffed some crabs and there's white wine—Remember how Nick loved stuffed crabs?

CROSSMAN (smiles). No. I don't remember.

CONSTANCE. It was twenty-three years ago, the eighteenth of next month. I mean the night he decided to go to Paris to study. Not so many young men from New Orleans went to Paris in those days.

CROSSMAN. Just as many young men met rich young ladies on boats.

CONSTANCE (sharply). He fell in love. People can't be blamed for changing their hearts—it just happens. They've had a fine marriage, and that's given me happiness all these years.

CROSSMAN. How do you know they've had a "fine" marriage?

CONSTANCE (smiles). I know.

CROSSMAN. The rest of us don't know anything about any marriage—but you know all about one you've never seen. You're very wise, Constance. It must come from not thinking.

CONSTANCE. Is this dress all right?

CROSSMAN. You've changed your dress three times since dinner.

CONSTANCE. My dresses are all so sort of —She'll think they're cheap. (Smiles) Well, and so they are. (There is silence. Then) Have we changed much, Ned?

CROSSMAN. Yes, my dear. You've changed, I've changed. But you're still handsome, if that's what you mean.

CONSTANCE. Ned, you don't look so well this summer. (He is pouring himself another brandy. She points to bottle) I wanted to tell you—Don't you think—

CROSSMAN (very pleasantly). Don't I think you should mind your business? Yes, I do.

(Sophie comes into living room carrying sheets, a quilt, a pillow, puts them down and moves to porch.)

CONSTANCE. Isn't what happens to you my business?

SOPHIE. You look pretty, Aunt Constance.

CONSTANCE (to Crossman). Sophie made this dress for me. Last winter. What could the girls at school have thought? Sophie sitting sewing for an old country aunt when she could have been out dancing—

SOPHIE. I sew better than I dance.

CONSTANCE (to Crossman). Sophie's mother taught her to sew. You know that Ann-Marie is a modiste?

SOPHIE (laughs). Oh, she is not. She is what you call here a home-seamstress, or sometimes a factory worker.

CONSTANCE. But she designs. She wrote me and you told me—

SOPHIE (laughs). Oh no. You did not understand. She does—

(Outside the house there is the noise of a car coming to a stop. Constance turns towards the room, then steps back, moves around the table and suddenly runs into the house. Crossman turns to stare at her.)

SOPHIE (timidly, pointing out towards living room). Should I—Should I stay, Mr. Ned?

CROSSMAN. I don't know the etiquette of such meetings.

SOPHIE. Why is Aunt Constance so nervous about the visit of this lady and gentleman?

CROSSMAN. Because she was once in love with Nicholas Denery, this gentleman.

SOPHIE. Oh. Such a long, long time to stay nervous. (Sententious) Great love in tender natures. And things of such kind. (As he turns to stare at her) It always happens that way with ladies. For them it is once and not again: it is their good breeding that makes it so.

CROSSMAN. What is the matter with you?

SOPHIE (laughs). I try very hard to sound nice. I try too hard, perhaps? (She begins to move out into the room; then, as she hears voices, she runs out of the room, exits off porch.)

NICK'S VOICE (offstage). Constance! (Nick appears in the hall and comes into the room. He is about forty-five, handsome, a little soft-looking and in a few years will be too heavy. He is followed by Nina Denery, who is a woman of about forty, good-looking, chic, tired and delicate. She stops and stands in the doorway.)

NICK (calling). Constance! (Nick and Nina are followed by a maid, Hilda, who stands waiting in the hall. She is carrying a jewelry case, an overnight bag, two coats. Crossman starts to come forward, changes his mind, draws back.)

HILDA (in German). Shall I take the bags upstairs, madame?

NINA (in German). We don't know where upstairs is.

NICK. Oh, I know where upstairs is. I know every foot of this house. (Examining the room) It was the great summer mansion and as kids we were here more than we were at home—(Softly) The great summer mansion! Did the house change, or me? (Sees Nina in doorway) Come on in.

NINA. Perhaps it would be pleasanter for you to see old friends without me. In any case, I am very tired—

NICK. Oh, now don't get tired. We've just come. What have you got to be tired about? Do you realize how often these days you're tired?

NINA. I realize it very well. And I know it bores you.

NICK. It worries me. (By this time, Nick, wandering around the room, has reached the porch. Crossman turns and, realizing that he has been seen, now comes forward) Could you tell me where we could find Miss Tuckerman?

CROSSMAN. Hello, Nick. Good to see you.

NICK (after a second). My God, Willy. How many years, how many years? (He puts his arm around Crossman, embraces him) Nina, this may be my oldest and best friend in the world. Nina, tell Willy how often I've talked about him and what I said.

CROSSMAN (who is shaking hands with Nina, amused). Then I hope he told you that my name is Edward, not Willy.

NINA (amused). I hope so—but I am not sure.

NICK. Your mother always called you Willy. Don't you remember?

CROSSMAN (goes out into the hall). No, I thought it was my brother's name. (Calls out, loudly) Constance, Nick is here.

NICK (coming to Crossman). Tell me before I see her. What has happened here? I don't know anything.

CROSSMAN. There's very little to know. Old man Tuckerman surprised everybody by dying broke. Constance sold the New Orleans house and managed to hang on to this by turning it into what is called a summer guest house. That's about all, Nick.

NICK. Where is Mrs. Tuckerman? I was crazy about her, Nina: she had style.

CROSSMAN. I don't know where she is, although I've asked myself often enough. She died shortly after Mr. Tuckerman— just to show him anybody could do it.

NICK (laughs, pats Crossman). Good to see you, boy. You know, if anybody had asked me, I would have said this room was as large as an eighteenth-century ballroom and as elegant. I think it shrank. All the fine things were sold?

CROSSMAN. The size hasn't changed. And nothing was sold.

NICK. Could I have been so wrong all these years? Seems so shabby now and—

NINA (quickly). I think it is a pleasant room.

NICK. Does Sam live here?

CROSSMAN. Sam died during the war. He went to Europe, oh, in the thirties, married there and never came back. You'll meet his daughter. Constance imported her five years ago.

NICK. Well, Sam was always the devoted brother until it came to being devoted. And Constance sacrificed her life for him.

CROSSMAN (to Nina). Nick is still a Southerner. With us every well-born lady sacrifices her life for something: a man, a house, sometimes a gardenia bush. Is it the same where you come from?

NINA *(smiles)*. New York is too cold for gardenias.

(Through Crossman's speech, Constance appears in the hall. As she moves into the room, she trips, recovers herself, smiles nervously and waits for Nick to come to her. He takes her face in his hands and kisses her. Then he stands back to look at her.)

NICK. This is a good hour of my life, Constance.

CONSTANCE *(softly)*. And of mine.

NICK *(holds her face)*. You've changed and you've changed well. Do you still have the portrait, Constance?

CONSTANCE *(smiles)*. *Still* have the portrait! It's the only important thing I have got— *(Then she remembers Nina, becomes confused, moves away from him and comes to Nina)* Forgive me, Mrs. Denery.

NINA *(puts out her hand, warmly)*. Hello.

CONSTANCE *(flossy)*. I should have been here to make you as welcome as you truly are. I was reading when you arrived, reading a book, and I didn't hear the car. *(She sees Crossman is staring at her and she looks nervously away from him)*

NICK. I had expected you standing in the driveway with the sun in your face, in the kind of lovely pink thing you used to wear—

NINA. The sun is not usually out at night—even for you.

NICK *(to Constance)*. Instead, you are reading. As if you were waiting for the groceries to come.

CONSTANCE *(quickly)*. I wasn't reading. It was a silly lie. I was just pretending— *(Embarrassed)* Well, I'm even forgetting my manners. You must be hungry, Mrs. Denery, and I've got—

NICK *(laughs, takes her hands, pulls her to the couch)*. No, no. Stop your manners, girl. There's a great deal I want to know. *(They sit down)* Now. Is the portrait as good as I remember it? I want Nina to see it. Nina knows a great deal about painting. Sometimes I think she knows more than I.

CONSTANCE *(smiles to Nina, nods. Then to Nick)*. You know, Nick, I subscribe to the New York Sunday *Times*. Because of the art section. I wanted to follow your career.

NICK *(carefully)*. You haven't often

found me in the *Times*. I've only exhibited in Europe.

CONSTANCE *(relieved)*. Oh. That explains it. *(There is a slight, awkward pause)* I like painting. I like Renoir best. The summer ladies in the gardens, so very, very pretty.

NICK *(bored)*. Yes, very pretty. This is the same wonderful place— My God, we had happy summers here, all of us. We loved each other so very much. Remember, Ned?

CROSSMAN. I don't remember that much love.

NINA *(laughs)*. I like you, Mr. Crossman.

NICK. Of course you like him. These are my oldest friends. I think as one grows older it is more and more necessary to reach out your hand for the sturdy old vines you knew when you were young and let them lead you back to the roots of things that matter. *(Nina coughs. Crossman moves away, smiling. Even Constance is a little overwhelmed)* Isn't that true, Ned? Now what have you been up to all these years?

CROSSMAN. I still work in the bank and come here for my vacation. That's about all.

NICK. I bumped into Louis Prescott in Paris a couple of years ago and he told me you and Constance had never married— *(Pats Constance's hand; Constance looks embarrassed)* Couldn't understand it. No wonder you drink too much, Ned.

CROSSMAN. Louis Prescott go all the way to Paris to tell you that?

NICK *(anxious, gets up)*. Oh, look, old boy. I didn't mean anything—I drink too much myself. I only want to know about you and have you know about me. I hope you didn't mind, Ned.

CROSSMAN. Not a bit. I want to know about you, too. Ever had syphilis, Nick? Kind of thing one has to know right off, if you understand me.

CONSTANCE *(gets up, very disturbed)*. Ned, how can you speak that way?

NICK *(smiles)*. You've grown edgy. I didn't remember you that way.

CROSSMAN *(pleasantly)*. Oh, I don't think I've changed. See you in the morning.

NICK. Hope you'll take me around, show me all the old places—

CROSSMAN. Of course I will. Good night, Mrs. Denery.

(He exits up staircase.)

NICK *(to Constance, meaning Crossman)*. I'm sorry if I said anything—

CONSTANCE. You know, for years I've been meeting you and Mrs. Denery—in my mind, I mean—and I've played all kinds of roles. Sometimes I was the dignified old friend, and sometimes I was a very, very old lady welcoming you to a gracious table. It was so important to me —our first meeting— *(Sadly)* And now when it happens—

NICK *(heartily)*. Nonsense. My homecoming is just as it should be. It's as if I had gone away yesterday. We took right up where we left off: even Ned and I. Let us be as we were, my dear, with no years between us, and no pretending.

CONSTANCE *(delighted with him, warmly)*. Thank you. *(Goes to Nina)* All these years I wanted to write you. I did write but I never sent the letters. It seemed so intrusive of me. I could see you getting the letter and just not knowing who I was.

NICK. I told Nina about you the first night I met her and through the years she has done quite a little teasing— You are too modest, Constance. *(Suddenly)* Now are you going to let me do another portrait of you?

CONSTANCE *(laughs)*. Another portrait? No, no, indeed. I want to remember myself as I was in the picture upstairs.

NICK. Go and get it for me. I want to look at it with you. *(She smiles, exits. There is silence)* You haven't been too warm or gracious, Nina.

NINA. What can I do when I don't even know the plot?

NICK. What are you talking about?

NINA. You told me about Constance Tuckerman the first night we met? And about dear Willy or Ned, and I've done quite a little teasing about her all these years?

NICK. I did tell you about her immediately—

NINA. You mentioned her very casually, last week, years after the night you met me and you said that you could hardly remember anything more about her than a rather silly—

NICK *(quickly)*. Are you going to be bad-tempered for our whole visit here? For years I've looked forward to coming back—

(Nina laughs.)

NINA. So you came to do her portrait?

NICK. No, I didn't "come to do her portrait." I thought about it driving down here. If the one I did is as good as I remember, it would be wonderful for the show. The young girl, the woman at forty-five. She's aged. Have we changed that much? I don't think you've changed, darling.

NINA. I've changed a great deal. And I wouldn't want it pointed out to me in a portrait to be hung side by side with a picture of what I used to be. *(He doesn't answer her)* That isn't a nice reason for being here and if I had known it—

NICK. We have no "reason" for being here. I just wanted to come back. Nothing mysterious about it—

NINA. You're simply looking for a new area in which to exercise yourself. It has happened many, many times before. But it *always* happens when we return from Europe and spend a month in New York. It's been too important to you, for many years, that you cannot manage to charm my family. And so, when our visit is finished there, you inevitably look around for— Well, you know. You know what's been and the trouble.

NICK *(cheerfully)*. I don't know what the hell you're talking about.

NINA. I'm tired of such troubles, Nick—

NICK. Do you know that these sharp moods of yours grow more sharp with time? Now I would like to have a happy visit here. But if something is disturbing you and you'd prefer not to stay, I'll arrange immediately—

NINA *(as if she were a little frightened)*. I'd only prefer to go to bed. Sorry if I've been churly about your—home-coming. *(She starts out, meets Constance who comes in carrying portrait)* Will you excuse me, Constance? The long drive gave me a headache.

CONSTANCE. I am sorry. Will I bring you a tray upstairs?

NINA. No, thank you.

(Constance moves as if to show her the way.)

NICK. Come, I want to see the picture. Nina will find her way.

(He takes the picture from Constance.)

CONSTANCE. The yellow room on the left. Your maid is unpacking. I peeked in.

What lovely clothes. Can I come and see them tomorrow?

NINA (*going up the stairs*). Yes, of course. Thank you and good night.

(*Constance watches her and then comes into room.*)

NICK (*who is looking at the picture*). I was nervous about seeing it. Damn good work for a boy eighteen.

CONSTANCE. You were twenty-two, Nick.

NICK. No, I wasn't. I—

CONSTANCE. You finished it the morning of your birthday. (*She points to windows*) And when you put down your brushes you said damn good work for a boy of twenty-two, and then you asked me to marry you. Don't you remember— (*She stops, embarrassed*) Why should you remember? And I don't want to talk that way.

NICK (*who is preoccupied with the picture*). Oh, nonsense. Talk any way you like. We were in love, very much in love, and why shouldn't we speak of it?

CONSTANCE (*hastily, very embarrassed*). After I die, the picture will go to the Delgado Museum.

NICK (*laughs*). I want to borrow it first. I'm having a retrospective show this winter, in London. I've done a lot of fancy people in Europe, you know that, but I'll be more proud of this— And I want to do another portrait of you as you are now. (*Moves toward window, excited*) You standing there. As before. Wonderful idea; young girl, woman at— Be a sensation. Constance, it's fascinating how faces change, mold firm or loose, have lines that start in youth and—

CONSTANCE (*amazed*). Oh, Nick. I don't want to see myself now. I don't want to see all the changes. And I don't want other people to stand and talk about them. I don't want people to laugh at me or pity me. (*Hurt*) Oh, Nick.

NICK. I see. (*Turns*) Well, it would have meant a lot to me. But that's that. I'll be off to bed now—

CONSTANCE (*coming after him*). But we haven't had a minute. And I have supper all ready for you—

NICK. Good night, my dear.

CONSTANCE (*slowly*). You think I'm being selfish and vain? I mean, am I the only woman who wouldn't like—

NICK. No, I think most women would feel the same way.

(*He starts out.*)

CONSTANCE. Do you prefer breakfast in bed? And what shall I make for your dinner? Pompano—

(*He is at the door as Carrie and Rose come into the hall. Carrie is holding Rose's arm.*)

CARRIE. Hello, Nick.

NICK (*takes her hands*). My God, Carrie. I didn't know you were here. How come? It's wonderful—

CARRIE. We come every summer.

NICK. You're handsome, Carrie. But you always were.

CARRIE (*smiles*). And you always remembered to say so. (*Rose coughs delicately*) This is Mrs. Griggs. (*To Constance*) Mrs. Griggs didn't feel well, so I brought her home. She became a little dizzy, dancing.

ROSE (*to Nick, who is shaking hands with her*). You're a famous gentleman in this town, sir, and I've been looking forward so to seeing you. We lead dull lives here, you know—

NICK (*laughs*). You don't look as if you do.

ROSE. Oh, thank you. But I don't look well tonight. I became suddenly a little ill—

CARRIE (*tartly*). Yes. Well, come along. If you still feel ill.

NICK. Can I help you, Mrs. Griggs?

ROSE (*delightedly*). Oh, thank you. That would be nice. I haven't been well this summer—

(*Nick starts into hall.*)

CONSTANCE. Nick—

(*He pays no attention. Carrie moves quickly ahead of him, takes Rose's arm.*)

CARRIE. Come. Good night, Nick. I look forward to seeing you in the morning. Hope you're staying for a while.

NICK. I think we'll have to leave tomorrow.

ROSE. Oh, don't do that. (*Then*) Constance, if Ben comes in would you tell him I was taken ill?

(*Carrie impatiently pushes her ahead and up the steps.*)

NICK (*meaning Rose*). Pretty woman, or was. (*Looks at Constance*) What is it Con?

CONSTANCE. How can you talk of leaving tomorrow? (*He doesn't answer*) Don't be mad with me, Nick.

NICK. I don't get mad, darling.

CONSTANCE *(catches him as he is almost out the door).* Please, Nick, let me change my mind. You are welcome to take this picture and I am flattered you wish to do another. But I'll have to pose early, before they're all down for breakfast—

NICK *(turns casually).* Good. We'll start in the morning. Do you make a living out of this place, darling?

CONSTANCE *(gaily).* Not much of one. The last few years have been a little hard. I brought Sam's daughter from Europe— she and her mother went through the occupation and were very poor—and I've tried to send her to the best school and then she was to make her debut only now she wants to get married, I think, and—

NICK. The girl expected all that from you?

CONSTANCE. Oh, no. Her mother didn't want to come and Sophie didn't want to leave her mother. I finally had really to *demand* that Sam's daughter was not to grow up— Well, I just can't describe it. At thirteen she was working in a fish store or whatever you call it over there. I just *made* her come over—

NICK. Why didn't you ever marry Ned?

CONSTANCE. I can't answer such questions, Nick. Even for you.

NICK. Why not? I'd tell you about myself or Nina.

CONSTANCE. Oh, it's one thing to talk about lives that have been good and full and happy and quite another— Well, I don't know. We just never did marry.

NICK *(bored).* Well, then, tomorrow morning. I'll do a good portrait of you because it's the face of a good woman—

(He stops as Sophie comes in. She sees Nick and Constance and draws back a little.)

CONSTANCE. Sophie. *(Sophie comes into the room)* This is Sam's daughter.

NICK *(very warmly to Sophie).* I've been looking forward to meeting you for many years.

(Constance turns, puzzled.)

SOPHIE. How do you do, sir?

NICK. You follow in the great tradition of Tuckerman good looks.

SOPHIE. Er. Er.

CONSTANCE *(smiles).* Don't er, dear. Say thank you. *(Griggs enters from left porch)* Do come in. *(Griggs comes in)* This is General Griggs. My very old friend, Nicholas Denery.

NICK. Are you General Benjamin Griggs? I've read about you in Raymond's book and Powell's.

GRIGGS *(as they shake hands).* I hear they disagree about me.

NICK. We almost met before this. When your boys marched into Paris. I was in France during the German occupation. *(Sophie turns sharply.)*

GRIGGS. That must have been unpleasant for you.

NICK. Yes, it was. But in the end, one has to be just; the Germans were damn smart about the French. They acted like gentlemen.

GRIGGS *(pleasantly).* That's a side of them I didn't see. *(Looks over at Sophie)* You didn't either, Sophie?

(During his speech Hilda, the maid, appears in the doorway.)

HILDA *(in German).* Excuse me, Mr. Denery. Mrs. Denery would like you to come for a minute before you retire. She has a little surprise gift she bought for you in New Orleans.

NICK *(in German).* No. Tell Mrs. Denery I will see her in the morning. Tell her to take a sleeping pill.

HILDA *(in German).* Thank you, sir.

CONSTANCE *(who hasn't understood the German but who is puzzled because Sophie is frowning and Griggs has turned away).* Can I— Does Nina want something?

NICK. No, no. She's fine. *(Sophie begins to make up the couch. Nick turns to her)* That means one of us must have put you out of your room. I'm sorry and I thank you.

SOPHIE. Not at all, sir. It is nothing.

NICK *(comes to her).* You're a sweet child and I look forward to knowing you. Good night. *(To Griggs)* Good night, sir. A great pleasure. *(Griggs bows. Nick kisses Constance)* Wonderful to be here, darling.

(He goes out. Constance moves to help Sophie make up the couch. There is silence for a minute while they arrange the bedclothes. Griggs watches them.)

CONSTANCE. I suppose I shouldn't ask but what did the German maid want? Something from the kitchen or— *(No answer)* Sophie. *(No answer)* Sophie.

SOPHIE *(slowly).* Mrs. Denery wanted to say good night to Mr. Denery.

GRIGGS. Mrs. Denery had bought a little

gift for him in New Orleans and wanted to give it to him.

CONSTANCE. After all these years. To have a little gift for him. Isn't that nice? *(She looks at Griggs and Sophie. Neither answers her. She becomes conscious of something strained)* What did Nick say?

SOPHIE. He said she should take a sleeping pill and go to sleep.

CONSTANCE. Just like that?

SOPHIE. Down at the beach there is the frankfurter concession. I think I will get the sleeping-pill concession and grow very rich.

CONSTANCE. Why, Sophie. Are you disturbed about something, dear? *(Looks at her dress)* You didn't go to the party! I've been so busy, I didn't realize— Why, where's Fred and—

SOPHIE. I did not wish to go to the party, Aunt Constance. And Frederick had a most important appointment.

CONSTANCE. More important than being with you? Young people get engaged and act toward each other with such—I don't know. *(To Griggs)* In our day we made marriage more romantic and I must say I think we had more fun. If you can't have fine dreams now, then when can you have them? *(Pats Sophie)* Never mind. I guess the new way is more sensible. But I liked our way better. *(To Griggs)* Didn't you? Oh, what's the matter with me? I forgot. Rose came back from the party. She said she was ill. I mean, I think she just didn't feel well—Carrie is upstairs with her. *(He doesn't move)* I think Carrie probably wants to go back to the party and is waiting for you to come.

GRIGGS. Yes. Of course. Thank you. Good night.

(He exits.)

CONSTANCE *(she kisses Sophie)*. You'll be comfortable? See you in the morning, dear.

(She exits through the hall. Sophie finishes with the couch, goes out. After a second, Crossman comes down the stairs. He sticks his head in the door, sees nobody, crosses the room, goes out to the porch, takes the bottle of brandy and a glass, moves back into the room and crosses it as Sophie returns carrying pajamas and a robe.)

CROSSMAN *(his voice and manner are slightly different now)*. I needed another book and another bottle. Royalty gone to bed? Does anybody improve with age? Just tell me that, Sophie, and I'll have something to lie awake and think about.

SOPHIE. I do not know, Mr. Ned.

CROSSMAN. For God's sake, Sophie, have an opinion about *something*. Try it, and see what comes out.

SOPHIE *(laughs)*. Some people improve with age, some do not.

CROSSMAN *(nods, amused)*. Wonderful, Sophie, wonderful. Some improve with age, some do not. Medical statistics show that 61 per cent of those who improve have bought our book on Dianetics and smoke Iflewitz cigarettes. You're beginning to talk like an advertisement, which is the very highest form of American talk. *(Sharply)* It's not *your* language, nor your native land. You don't have to care about it. You shouldn't even understand it.

SOPHIE. Sometimes I understand.

CROSSMAN. That's dangerous to admit, Sophie. You've been so busy cultivating a pseudo-stupidity. Not that you'd ever be a brilliant girl, but at least you used to be normal. Another five years and you won't be *pseudo*-stupid.

SOPHIE *(smiles)*. I will not mind. It will be easier. *(Carefully)* You notice me too much, Mr. Ned. Please do not feel sorry or notice me so much.

CROSSMAN. You came here a nice little girl who had seen a lot of war and trouble. You had spirit, in a quiet way, and you were gay, in a quiet way, which is the only way women should be gay since they are never really gay at all. Only serious people are ever gay and women are very seldom serious people. They are earnest instead. But earnestness has nothing to do with seriousness. So. *(Suddenly)* What the hell is this marriage business between you and Fred Ellis?

SOPHIE *(softly)*. It is the marriage business between me and Fred Ellis.

CROSSMAN. But what's the matter with you? Haven't you got sense enough to know—

SOPHIE *(quickly)*. I do the best I can. I do the best I can. And I thank you for worrying about me, but you are an educated man with ideas in English that I am not qualified to understand.

CROSSMAN. Listen to me, Sophie. Sometimes when I've had enough to drink— just exactly enough—I feel as if I were given to understand that which I may not understand again. And sometimes then— but rarely—I have an urge to speak out. Fewer drinks, more drinks, and I'm less certain that I see the truth, or I get bored, and none of my opinions and none of the people and issues involved seem worth the trouble. Right now, I've had just enough: so listen to me, Sophie. I say turn yourself around and go home. Beat it quick.

SOPHIE. You take many words to say simple things. All of you. And you make the simple things—like going to sleep—so hard, and the hard things—like staying awake—so easy. Go home, shall I? Just like that, you say it. Aunt Constance has used up all her money on me, wasted it, and for why and what? How can I go home?

CROSSMAN. If that's all it is I'll find you the money to go home.

SOPHIE (wearily). Oh, Mr. Ned. We owe money in our village, my mother and I. In my kind of Europe you can't live where you owe money. Go home. Did I ever want to come? I have no place here and I am lost and homesick. I like my mother, I— Every night I plan to go. But it is five years now and there is no plan and no chance to find one. Therefore I will do the best I can. (Very sharply) And I will not cry about it and I will not speak of it again.

CROSSMAN (softly, as if he were moved). The best you can?

SOPHIE. I think so. (Sweetly) Maybe you've never tried to do that, Mr. Ned. Maybe none of you have tried.

CROSSMAN. Sophie, lonely people talking to each other can make each other lonelier. They should be careful because maybe lonely people are the only people who can't afford to cry. I'm sorry.

(He exits through the hall, goes up the stairs as the curtain falls.)

CURTAIN

ACT TWO

SCENE ONE

SCENE: The same as Act One. A week later, eight-thirty Sunday morning.

AT RISE: Constance is standing against the outside edge of the porch, leaning on the railing. Nick is standing in front of an easel. Constance has on a most unbecoming house dress and her hair is drawn back tight. She looks ten years older. In the living room, Sophie has finished folding her bedclothes and is hurrying around the room with a carpet sweeper. After a second, Leon appears from the direction of the dining room with a tray and dishes and moves out to the porch. He puts down the tray, moves the table, begins to place the dishes. Constance tries desperately to ask him if everything is all right in the kitchen. She does this by moving her lips and trying not to move her head. Leon sees her motions but doesn't understand what she is trying to say. The noise of the rattling dishes, and the carpet sweeper, becomes sharp.

———

NICK. Constance, please ask them to stop that noise. (Waves his hand to Leon and Sophie) Go away, both of you.

CONSTANCE. They can't, Nick. I explain it to you every morning! We simply have to get ready for breakfast. (Quietly) Sophie, is everything all right in the kitchen?

SOPHIE. Yes, ma'am. Everything is fine.

NICK (to Constance, sharply). Please keep the pose. Just a few minutes more.

CONSTANCE (to Leon). Tell Sadie not to cook the liver until everybody is downstairs, like she always does. Did she remember about the grits this Sunday? (To Nick, sees his face) All right. I'm sorry. But really, I can't run a boardinghouse and pose for—

(She sighs, settles back. Sophie picks up her bedclothes and exits through the hall. Leon finishes with the porch table and comes back into the living room as Mrs. Ellis comes down the steps.)

MRS. ELLIS (to Leon). My breakfast ready?

LEON. No, ma'am. We'll ring the bell.

MRS. ELLIS. What's the matter with my breakfast?

LEON. Nothing the matter with it. It will be like always.

MRS. ELLIS. It gets later and later every day.

LEON. No, ma'am. That's just you. Want it in the dining room or on the porch?

MRS. ELLIS. Too damp on the porch. Whole house is damp. I haven't slept all summer, Leon.

LEON. Just as well not to sleep in summer.

MRS. ELLIS (as Leon exits). You're going

to have to explain that to me sometime. *(She turns, goes toward porch, comes around in front of Constance)* Constance, he's made you look right mean and ten years older. Why have you done that, Nicholas?

(Sophie comes back into living room with a large urn of coffee and small cups. She puts the tray on a table.)

NICK *(to Mrs. Ellis)*. Shoo, shoo. This is forbidden ground.

MRS. ELLIS *(calls)*. Sophie, give me a cup. I have to stay awake for church. *(To Constance)* Ten years older. When you pay an artist to paint your portrait he makes you ten years younger. I had my portrait done when I was twenty-one, holding my first baby. And the baby looked older than I did. Was rather a scandal or like those people in Tennessee.

NICK. You know if you wouldn't interrupt me every morning, I think I'd fall in love with you.

MRS. ELLIS *(she goes toward Sophie to get her coffee. During her speech, Sophie puts three spoons of sugar in the small cup)*. I wouldn't like that. Even if I was the right age I wouldn't like it. Although I realize it would make me dangerously different from every other woman in the world. You would never have been my dish of tea, and isn't that a silly way of saying it? *(To Sophie: she is now in the living room)* You're the only one who ever remembers about my sugar. Sophie, will you come up to town *(Crossman comes down the steps and into the room)* and stay with me for a few weeks while Carrie and Frederick are in Europe?

SOPHIE. I would like that.

MRS. ELLIS. Ned, what shall I give Sophie for her wedding present? My pearls or my mother's diamonds?

CROSSMAN *(to Sophie)*. The rich always give something old and precious to their new brides. Something that doesn't cost them new money. Same thing true in your country?

SOPHIE *(smiles)*. I do not know the rich in my country.

MRS. ELLIS. He's quite right, Sophie. Not only something old but something so old that we're sick of it.

CROSSMAN. Why don't you give her a nice new check?

MRS. ELLIS. Only if I have to.

CONSTANCE *(on porch)*. Nick, my neck is breaking—

NICK. All right. All finished for this morning.

(Turns the picture around so that Constance cannot see it. Sophie brings two cups of coffee to the porch.)

CONSTANCE *(collapsing in a chair)*. Whew. *(Takes the coffee from Sophie, pats her arm. Sophie takes the other cup to Nick.)*

NICK. You're the girl I want to paint. Change your mind and we'll start today. Why not, Sophie?

(He is holding her hand.)

SOPHIE. I am not pretty, Mr. Nicholas.

NICK. You are better than pretty.

(Crossman comes out to the porch. Sophie disengages her hand, moves off.)

CROSSMAN *(staring at Constance)*. My God, you look awful, Constance. What did you get done up like that for? You're poor enough not to have to pretend you are poor.

NICK *(laughing)*. Go way, Ned. You've got a hangover. I know I have.

(Nina comes down the steps, comes into the room, says good morning to Mrs. Ellis who says good morning to her. She pours herself a cup of coffee. She is close enough to the porch to hear what is said.)

CONSTANCE. You know, I waited up until twelve o'clock for you both—

NICK. We were late. We had a good get-together last night. Like old times, wasn't it, Ned? *(To Constance)* If you have the normal vanity you'd be pleased at the amount of time we spent on you. Ned loosened up and talked—

CROSSMAN. I did? I thought that was you.

NICK *(laughs)*. I knew you wouldn't remember what you'd said— Don't regret it: did you good to speak your heart out —for once.

CROSSMAN. My heart, eh?

NICK. In a juke-box song called Constance.

CONSTANCE. What? I don't understand.

CROSSMAN *(who has turned sharply, then decided to laugh)*. Neither do I. The stage of not remembering, or speaking out of my heart, will come in time, I am sorry to say. But I hope it hasn't come yet.

(As he turns to go out, Leon appears in the hall with a bell and begins to ring the bell.)

NINA (*a little timidly*). Good morning, Mr. Crossman.

CROSSMAN. Good morning, Mrs. Denery. I'm sorry you didn't join us last night—to hear me pour my heart out.

NINA. I'm never invited to the pouring of a heart.

CROSSMAN. I looked for you, but Nick said you had a headache.

NINA. Nick always says I have a headache when he doesn't want me to come along, or sees to it that I do have one.

MRS. ELLIS (*gets up quickly*). All right, Leon. I'm ready. I haven't eaten since four this morning. (*Goes out. As she passes stairs, she shouts up*) Carrie! Frederick! I simply won't wait breakfast any longer.

(*Crossman follows her out.*)

CONSTANCE (*gets up*). Well, they seemed to have managed in the kitchen without me. I reckon I better change now. Where'd you get this dress, Nick?

NICK. Place on Dreyenen Street.

CONSTANCE. In a Negro store! You bought this dress in a Negro store! (*He looks at her and laughs*) I don't mean that. I mean Ned's right. You must have wanted to make me look just about as awful as— For some reason I don't understand. Nick, what *are* you doing? And why won't you let me see the portrait?

NICK. Haven't you yet figured out that Ned is jealous?

CONSTANCE. Jealous of what?

NICK. He's in love with you, girl. As much as he was when we were kids. You're all he talked about last night. How lonely he's been, how much he's wanted you, how often he asked you to marry him—

CONSTANCE. I just don't believe you. Ned never talks about himself. I just don't believe he said such things—

NICK. You know damn well he loves you and you know he's rotting away for you. He said last night—

CONSTANCE (*prissy*). Nick, if he did talk, and it's most out of character, I don't think I should hear what he said in confidence just to you.

NICK. Oh, run along, honey. You're pleased as punch. When you're not pretending to be genteel.

CONSTANCE (*laughs*). Genteel? How awful of me. Mama used to say gentility was the opposite of breeding and— (*She has*

started to move out of the room) Did Ned say—er—

(*Nick laughs, she laughs, and exits. Nick begins to put away portrait and to fold easel as Nina puts down her coffee and comes out to the porch.*)

NICK (*kisses her*). Morning, darling. (*Nina sits down, watches him*) What's the matter?

(*Leon appears with breakfast dishes. He serves Nick and Nina during the next few speeches.*)

NINA. Why have you done that? To Constance?

NICK. Done what? Tell her the truth?

NINA. How could you know it to be the truth? I don't believe Crossman talked to you—

NICK. Look, it makes her happy—and if I can get a little sense into her head it will make him happy. I don't have to have an affidavit to know what's going on in the human heart.

(*He leans over, kisses her, sits down to eat his breakfast.*)

NINA (*laughs*). Oh, you are enjoying yourself so much here. I've seldom seen it this hog-wild. (*Leon exits*) You're on a rampage of good will. Makes me nervous for even the trees outside. But there's something impertinent about warning an oak tree. How should I do it?

NICK (*laughs*). First tell me how to understand what you're talking about.

(*They eat in silence for a minute.*)

NINA. Are we staying much longer, Nick?

NICK. A few more days. The house officially closes this week, Constance says. The Ellises go tomorrow and the Griggses on Tuesday, I think. Just till I finish.

NINA. Finish what?

NICK (*carefully*). The portrait, Nina.

(*Rose Griggs comes down the stairs, carrying a small overnight case. She is done up in a pretty, too fussy, hat and a pretty, too fussy, dress. She looks in the room, puts the case down, comes hurrying out to the porch.*)

ROSE. Oh, good morning. Sorry to interrupt. You look so handsome together. (*Makes a gesture to Nick meaning "Could you come here"?*) Nick—

NICK (*hospitable*). Come on out.

ROSE. I'd rather. Could you—

NICK. Come and join us.

ROSE (*hesitantly*). Well, I wanted to tell

you but I don't want to worry Nina. You see—

NINA. I'd go away, Mrs. Griggs, but I've been dismissed from so many meals lately that I'm getting hungry.

ROSE *(smiles to Nina. Speaks to Nick)*. I called him last night. Just like you advised. And I'm driving right over now. He's the executor of my trust fund, you know. He's very wise: I've got gilt-edged securities.

NICK. Who is this?

ROSE. My brother, of course. Henry, like I told you. *(To Nina)* It sounds so mysterious, but it isn't. He's much older. You know he builds ships, I mean during our wars. I'll tell him the whole story, Nick, and he'll know what to do.

NICK *(amused)*. Of course he will.

ROSE. I'm going to drive over to my doctor's. He's going to wait for me on a hot Sunday. It'll be expensive— *(To Nina)* I had a heart murmur. They had to take me out of school for a year.

NINA. Recently?

ROSE *(giggles)*. That's charming—"recently." *(To Nick)* There's so much I wanted to consult you about. I waited up for you last night, but—well. Should I do *just* as you told me yesterday?

NICK *(who doesn't remember what he told her)*. Sure.

ROSE. Everything?

NICK. Well—

NINA. I think, Mrs. Griggs, you'll have to remind Nick what he told you. Yesterday is a long time ago when you have so many ladies to attend to—

ROSE *(as Nick laughs)*. I shouldn't have brought it up like this. Oh, Mrs. Denery, you might as well know: it's about a divorce, and Nick has been most kind.

NINA. I am sure of it.

ROSE. Just one more thing. What should I do about our boys? Should I telephone them or let Henry? One of our sons works on the atom bomb, you know. He's the religious one and it will be traumatic for him. What do you think, Nick?

NINA *(gets up quickly, trying not to laugh, moves away)*. Goodness.

NICK. I think you should go and have your breakfast. It's my firm belief that women only look well in hats after they've eaten.

ROSE *(to Nick, softly, secretly)*. And I'm going to just *make* Henry commission the

portrait—and for the very good price that he can afford to pay. You remember though that I told you she can't take the braces off her teeth for another six months.

NICK *(laughs)*. Go along now, my dear.

ROSE *(pleased)*. Thank you for all you've done. And forgive me, Nina. I'll be back tonight, Nick, before you go to bed because you'll want to know how everything turns out.

(She exits through room. Nina stands without speaking.)

NICK *(looks up at her)*. There was a day when we would have laughed together about this. Don't you have fun any more?

NINA. I don't think so.

NICK. She's quite nice, really. And very funny.

NINA. I suppose it's all right to flirt with, or to charm, women and men and children and animals but nowadays it seems to me you include books-in-vellum and sirloin steaks, red squirrels and lamp shades.

NICK *(smiles)*. Are you crazy? Flirt with that silly woman? Come and eat your breakfast, Nina. I've had enough seriousness where none is due.

(Through this speech, Carrie has come down the steps. She meets Sophie who is going through the hall to the dining room. Sophie is carrying a tray.)

CARRIE. Good morning, dear. Is Frederick in the dining room?

SOPHIE. No. He has not come down as yet.

(She goes on past. Carrie comes into the room, continues on to the porch.)

CARRIE *(to Nick and Nina)*. Good morning. Your maid said you wanted to see me, Nick.

NICK *(hesitantly)*. Carrie, I hesitated all day yesterday. I told myself perhaps you knew, but maybe, just maybe, you didn't.

NINA *(laughs)*. Oh, it sounds so serious.

CARRIE *(smiles)*. It does indeed.

NICK *(carefully)*. Don't you know that man's reputation, Carrie? You can't travel around Europe with him.

CARRIE. Travel around Europe with him? I'm going to Europe with Frederick. *(Then sharply, as she sees his face)* What do you mean, Nick?

NICK. I—

(Sophie comes into room, goes out to porch. During next few speeches, she pours coffee.)

CARRIE. Please tell me.

NICK. I saw Frederick in the travel agency yesterday with a man I once met in Europe. Not the sort of man you'd expect to see Frederick with.

CARRIE. Are you talking about Mr. Payson?

NICK. Yes, I am. Well, I waited until they left the travel place and then I went in.

NINA. Why did you go in?

NICK. Luther hadn't seen me since we were kids and we got to talking. He said he had booked your passage on the *Elizabeth* and now he had another for Mr. Payson and Fred had just paid for it— (*Carrie gets up, turns sharply, does not speak*) I didn't know whether you knew, Carrie, or if I should tell you—

CARRIE. I didn't know. I thank you for telling me. (*After a second, she turns*) What did you mean, Nick, when you asked me if I know Payson's reputation? I don't like to press you for gossip, but—

NINA. He didn't mean anything, Mrs. Ellis—

NICK. Oh, look here, Nina, you know he's part of Count Denna's set, and on the nasty fringe of that.

(*Sophie, very quietly, leaves the porch.*)

CARRIE. What does that mean: Count Denna's set and the nasty fringe of that?

NINA (*quickly*). It means very little. The Count is a foolish old man who gives large parties—

NICK (*to Nina*). Would you want your young son with such people at such parties?

NINA (*angrily*). I have no son. And I don't know: perhaps I would have wanted only to leave him alone—

CARRIE (*gently*). All people who have no children think that, Mrs. Denery. But it just isn't true. (*To Nick*) I don't know much about Mr. Payson but I've been worried for a long time that he's taken Frederick in. Frederick admires his writing, and— Yet I know so little about him. He stayed with us a few weeks in town last winter. He'd just come back from Europe then—

NICK. He'd just come back from a filthy little scandal in Rome. It was all over the papers.

NINA. You don't know it was true.

CARRIE. What kind of scandal? (*No answer. Softly*) Please help me. I don't understand.

NICK (*gets up*). Look, Carrie, there's nothing to understand. The guy is just no good. That's all you need to know. He's nobody to travel around Europe with.

CARRIE. How could Fred have— (*She hesitates for a minute*) It was kind and friendly of you to tell me that. I am grateful to you both.

(*She goes slowly across the room and into the hall toward the dining room. There is a long pause: Nick takes a sip of coffee, looks around at Nina.*)

NICK. What would you have done?

NINA (*idly*). I don't know. Have you ever tried leaving things alone?

NICK. I like Carrie. She doesn't know what the hell it's all about—and the chances are the boy doesn't either. I'm sorry for them. Aren't you? (*When she doesn't answer*) What's the matter, Nina?

NINA. I can smell it: it's all around us. The flowerlike odor right before it becomes troublesome and heavy. It travels ahead of you, Nick, whenever you get most helpful, most loving and most lovable. Down through the years it runs ahead of us—I smell it—and I want to leave.

NICK (*pleasantly*). I think maybe you're one of the few neurotics in the world who didn't marry a neurotic. I wonder how that happened?

NINA. *I want to leave.*

NICK (*sharply*). Then leave.

NINA (*after a second*). You won't come?

NICK. I told you: we'll go Friday. If you want to go before, then go. But stop talking about it, Nina. Or we'll be in for one of your long farewells—and long returns. I don't think I can stand another. Spare yourself, darling. You pay so heavy, inside. (*Comes to her, puts his arms around her*) Friday, then. And in the meantime, gentle down to the pretty lady you truly are.

(*He kisses her. Exits. Nina stands quietly for a minute. Sophie comes onto the porch, begins to gather the dishes.*)

SOPHIE (*gently*). Would you like something, Mrs. Denery?

NINA (*softly*). No, thank you.

(*She moves off, through the room and toward the staircase. As she starts up the stairs, Frederick comes down.*)

FREDERICK. Good morning.

NINA. Good morning, Mr. Ellis. (*Stops

as if she wanted to tell him something)
I—er. Good morning.
(She goes up as Sophie, who has heard their voices, leaves the dishes and comes quickly into the room.)

SOPHIE *(calling into the hall)*. Fred. Fred. *(He comes in. Shyly)* Would you like to have your breakfast on the kitchen porch?

FREDERICK. Sure. Why?

SOPHIE. Your mother is—er— *(Points toward dining room)* She has found out that— Come.

FREDERICK. Denery told her he saw me in the travel agency. I was sure he would. There's nothing to worry about. I intended to tell her this morning.

SOPHIE. But perhaps it would be more wise—

FREDERICK *(smiles to her)*. We'll be leaving here tomorrow and for Europe on the sixteenth. You and I won't see each other for six months. Sophie, you're sure you feel all right about my going?

SOPHIE *(quickly)*. Oh, I do.

FREDERICK. We will visit your mother. And—

SOPHIE *(very quickly)*. No, no, please do not do that. I have not written to her about us—

FREDERICK. Oh.

SOPHIE. You see, we have as yet no date of time, or—

FREDERICK *(smiles)*. I don't think you want a date of time, Sophie. And you don't have to be ashamed of wishing you could find another way. But if there isn't any other way for you, then I'll be just as good to you as I know how. And I know you will be to me.

SOPHIE. You are a kind man. And I will also be kind, I hope.

FREDERICK. It isn't any deal for you. You are a girl who should love, and will one day, of course.

SOPHIE *(puts her hand up to her mouth)*. Shssh. Such things should not be said. *(Cheerfully)* It will be nice in your house with you, and I will be grateful for it.

FREDERICK. I have no house, Sophie. People like me never have their own house, so-to-speak.

SOPHIE. Never mind. Whatever house. It will be nice. We will make it so.
(He smiles, pats her arm.)

FREDERICK. Everybody in the dining room? *(She nods. He starts for hall)* Might as well face it out.

SOPHIE. I would not. No, I would not. All of you face out too much. Every act of life should not be of such importance—

FREDERICK *(calling into dining room)*. Mother. *(Sophie shrugs, smiles, shakes her head, and exits. Frederick comes back into room, pours himself a cup of coffee. After a minute, Carrie appears. She comes into the room obviously very disturbed. But she does not speak)* There's nothing to be so upset about.

CARRIE *(after a pause)*. You think that, really?
(Mrs. Ellis appears in the hall.)

FREDERICK. We're going to have a companion. That's all. We know nothing of traveling and Payson knows all of Europe.

MRS. ELLIS. Of course. You're lucky to get Mr. Payson to come along.
(Both of them turn to look at her.)

FREDERICK *(after a second, to Carrie)*. What is it, Mother?

CARRIE. I can't say it. It's shocking of you to take along a guest without consulting me. You and I have planned this trip for three years and—

FREDERICK. I didn't consult you because the idea came up quickly and Payson had to get his ticket before the travel office closed for the week end—

CARRIE. *Payson* had to get *his* ticket?

FREDERICK. I thought you'd given up going through my checkbooks.

CARRIE. *Please don't speak that way to me. (Pause, quietly, delicately)* We are not going to Europe.

FREDERICK *(after a second, quietly)*. I am.

CARRIE. We are not going, Fred. We are not going.

MRS. ELLIS. Your mother's feelings are hurt. She had looked forward to being alone with you. Of course.

FREDERICK *(uncomfortably)*. We'll still be together.

CARRIE *(to Mrs. Ellis)*. I don't wish to be interpreted, Mother. *(To Frederick)* There's no sense talking about it; we'll go another time.

FREDERICK *(laughs, unpleasantly)*. Will you stop acting as if you're taking me back to school? I will be disappointed if you don't wish to come with me but I am sailing on the sixteenth. *(Then, quietly)* I've never had much fun. Never seen the things I wished to see, never met the people I wanted to meet or been the places where I could. There are wonderful things to see and to learn about and to try to understand. We're lucky to have somebody who knows about them and who is willing to have *us* tag along. *I'm* not much to drag around— *(Softly)* I'll come back, and you can take up my life again. Six months isn't much to ask.

MRS. ELLIS. Six months? Sad to ask so little.

CARRIE *(as if she recognized a tone of voice)*. Mother, please. I—

MRS. ELLIS. Perhaps you won't want to come back at all? I wouldn't blame you.

CARRIE *(nervously)*. Fred, don't make a decision now. Promise me you'll think about it until tomorrow and then we'll talk quietly and—

MRS. ELLIS *(to Frederick)*. Don't make bargains with your mother. Everything always ends that way between you. I advise you to go now, or stay.

FREDERICK. I am going. There is nothing to think about. I'm going.

(He turns and exits, going up staircase. There is a pause.)

CARRIE *(angry)*. You always do that, Mother. You always arrange to come out his friend and make me his enemy. You've been amusing yourself that way all his life.

MRS. ELLIS. There's no time for all that, Carrie. I warned you to say and do nothing. I told you to make the best of it and go along with them.

CARRIE *(softly)*. How could I do that? That man is a scoundrel and Fred doesn't know it, and won't believe it. What am I to do now?

MRS. ELLIS. You're to go upstairs and say that you are reconciled to his leaving without you but that Frederick is to make clear to his guest that his ten thousand a year ends today and will not begin again. Tell him you've decided young people have a happier time in Europe without American money—

CARRIE *(sharply)*. I couldn't do that. He'd hate me for it. Maybe we'd better let him go, and perhaps I can join him later. Time will— *(Sees Mrs. Ellis's face)* I will not cut off his allowance.

MRS. ELLIS. I didn't know it was you who wrote the check.

CARRIE *(with dignity)*. Are you quite sure you wish to speak this way?

MRS. ELLIS. Relatively sure.

CARRIE. Then I will say as sharply that the money is his father's money, and not yours to threaten him, or deprive him, in any proper sense.

MRS. ELLIS. In any *proper* sense. There is no morality to money, Carrie, and very immoral of you to think so.

CARRIE. If you stop his allowance, Mother, I will simply send him mine.

MRS. ELLIS. Then I won't give you yours. *(Carrie turns sharply, as if she were deeply shocked. Mrs. Ellis now speaks, gently)* Yes, old people are often harsh, Carrie, when they control the purse. You'll see, when your day comes. And then, too, one comes to be bored with those who fool themselves. I say to myself—one should have power, or give it over. But if one keeps it, it might as well be used, with as little mealymouthness as possible. Go up now, and press him hard, and do it straight. *(Carrie turns slowly to exit)* Tell yourself you're doing it for his own good.

CARRIE *(softly)*. I wouldn't be doing it otherwise.

MRS. ELLIS. Perhaps. Perhaps not. Doesn't really matter. *(Laughs, amused)* I'm off to church now. You can skip church today, Carrie.

CARRIE. Thank you for the dispensation. *(She begins to move off toward hall and toward stairs as Rose comes from the direction of the dining room and into the room.)*

MRS. ELLIS *(to Carrie, as Carrie moves off)*. Quite all right. You have God's work to do. *(She turns to watch Rose who is elaborately settling herself in a chair as if she were arranging for a scene—which is what she is doing)* What are you doing, Mrs. Griggs? *(Rose nervously points to left window. Mrs. Ellis looks toward it, watches Rose fix her face)* Is it Robert Taylor you're expecting or Vice-President Barkley? *(Griggs comes in from the left windows. He has on riding pants and an old shirt)* Oh.

GRIGGS *(to them both)*. Good morning.

MRS. ELLIS. Your wife's getting ready to flirt. You'd be safer in church with me. *(She exits as Griggs laughs. He goes to coffee urn.)*

ROSE *(meaning Mrs. Ellis)*. Nasty old thing. *(Then)* I'm driving over to see him. I'm sorry I had to make such a decision, but I felt it was necessary now.

GRIGGS. Are you talking about your brother?

ROSE. Yes, of course. Now, I know it will be bad for you, Ben, but since *you're* being so stubborn, I didn't know what else to do.

GRIGGS. I think you should see Henry.

ROSE. But he's going to be very, very angry, Ben. And you know how much influence he has in Washington.

GRIGGS *(turns, carefully)*. Tell him to use his influence. And tell him to go to hell.

ROSE *(giggles)*. On a Sunday?

GRIGGS *(gently)*. Rose, no years will make you serious.

ROSE. You used to like me that way.

GRIGGS. So you always wanted to believe.

ROSE. How can I just walk into Henry's happy house and say Ben wants a divorce, and I don't even know the reason. I *ask* him and I *ask* him but he says there is no reason—

GRIGGS. I never said there was no reason. But it isn't the reason that you like, or will accept. If I were in love with another woman you'd rather enjoy that. And certainly Henry would.

ROSE. It would at least be human. And I am not convinced it isn't so. I've done a good deal of thinking about it, and I've just about decided it's why you stayed in Europe so long.

GRIGGS. I didn't arrange World War II and don't listen to the rumors that I did.

ROSE. He said it at the time. He said he had known a good many professional soldiers but nobody had managed to make so much fuss about the war as you did, or to stay away so long. Henry said that.

GRIGGS. I guessed it was Henry who said that.

ROSE *(laughs)*. But you didn't guess that it was Henry who got you the last promotion.

GRIGGS. Rose, stop that. You're lying. You always do it about now. *(Turns to her)* Give Henry this reason: tell him my wife's too young for me. For Henry's simple mind, a simple reason.

ROSE. I've wanted to stay young, I've—

GRIGGS. You've done more than stay young: you've stayed a child.

ROSE. What about your mother, Ben, have you thought of her? It would kill her—

GRIGGS. She's been dead sixteen years. Do you think this will kill her?

ROSE. You know what I mean. She loved me and she was happy for our marriage.

GRIGGS. No, she didn't. She warned me not to marry— *(With feeling)* I began my life with a serious woman. I doubt if any man gets over that, or ever really wants any other kind of woman.

ROSE. *Your mother loved me.* You have no right to malign the dead. I say she loved me, I know she did.

GRIGGS *(wearily)*. What differences does it make?

ROSE. You never think anybody loves me. Quite a few men have found me attractive—

GRIGGS *(quickly)*. And many more will, my dear.

ROSE. I always knew in the end I would have to tell you although I haven't seen him since you came home. That I promise you. I told him you were a war hero with a glorious record and he said he wouldn't either any longer—

GRIGGS *(who is at the left window)*. Henry's chauffeur is outside, Rose.

ROSE. He was very, very, very, very much in love with me while he was at the Pentagon.

GRIGGS. Good place to be in love. The car is outside, Rose.

ROSE. Even after we both knew it, he kept on saying that you didn't make love to a friend, more than a friend's, wife.

GRIGGS *(gently)*. Rose, don't let's talk this way.

ROSE. Does it hurt you? Well, you've hurt me enough. The third time you went to Europe was when it really began, maybe the second. Because I, too, wanted affection.

GRIGGS *(gently)*. I can understand that.

ROSE. Ask me who it was. Ask me, Ben, and I will tell you. *(No answer)* Just ask me.

GRIGGS. No, I won't do that, Rose.

ROSE. Remember when the roses came from Teheran, I mean wired from Teheran, last birthday? That's who sent them. You didn't even like Teheran. You said it was filthy and the people downtrodden. But he sent roses.

GRIGGS. He sounds like the right man. Go to him, Rose, the flying time is nothing now.

ROSE *(angrily)*. You just stop being nasty. *(Then)* And now I am going to tell you who it is.

GRIGGS *(begins to move toward door, as if he were backing away from her)*. Please, Rose. We have had so many years of this— Please. *(As she is closer to him)* Do I have to tell you that I don't care who it is?

ROSE *(she begins to move on him)*. I'd like to whisper it. I knew if I ever told you I'd have to whisper it. *(He begins now really to back away)* Ben, you come right here. Ben stand still. *(He starts to laugh)* Stop that laughing. *(Very loudly, very close to him)* It was your cousin, Ralph Sommers. There. *(She turns away)* There. You won't ever speak with him about it?

GRIGGS. You can be sure of that.

ROSE *(outside an automobile horn is sounded)*. Oh, I'm late. I can't talk any more now, Ben. *(She starts for door, stops)* What am I going to tell Henry? Anyway, you know Henry is going to allow me to give you a divorce. You know that, Ben. *(Carefully)* And therefore I won't be able to do what you want, and the whole day is just wasted. Please tell me not to go, Ben.

GRIGGS *(as if he has held on to himself long enough)*. Tell Henry that I want a divorce. But in any case I am going away. I am leaving. That is all that matters to me or need matter to you or him. I would prefer a divorce. But I am going, whatever you and Henry decide. Understand that, Rose, the time has come to understand it.

ROSE *(gently, smiling)*. I am going to try, dear. Really I am. It's evidently important to you.

(She exits through hall. Griggs sits down as if he were very tired. A minute later, Crossman comes from the direction of the dining room, carrying the Sunday papers. He looks at Ben, goes to him, hands him the front page. Ben takes it, nods, sits holding it. Crossman crosses to a chair, sits down, begins to read the comic section. A second later, Nina comes down the stairs, comes into the room, starts to speak to Ben and Crossman, changes her mind and sits down. Then Constance, in an old-fashioned flowered hat and carrying a large palmetto fan, comes through the hall and into the room.)

CONSTANCE. I'm off to church. Anybody want anything just ring for Leon or Sophie. *(Bravely)* Want to come to church with me, Ned? *(He peers over his paper, amazed)* All right. I just thought— Well, Nick told us that you told him last night—

CROSSMAN *(laughs)*. I think perhaps I shall never again go out at night.

CONSTANCE. Oh, it's good for all of us to confide in somebody— *(She becomes conscious of Nina and Griggs, smiles awkwardly and then with great determination leans over and kisses Crossman)* Good-by, darling.

(Surprised, he gets up, stands watching her leave the room. Then he sits down, staring ahead.)

NINA *(after a minute, hesitantly)*. I've got a car and a full picnic basket and a cold bottle of wine. Would you— *(Turning to Crossman and then to Griggs)* like to come along? I don't know where to go, but—

CROSSMAN. Got enough in your picnic basket for lunch *and* dinner?

NINA *(smiles)*. I think so.

CROSSMAN. Got a mandolin?

NINA *(smiles)*. No. Does that rule me out?

CROSSMAN. Almost. But we'll make do. The General whistles very well.

GRIGGS *(smiles, gets up)*. Is one bottle of wine enough on a Sunday?

NINA *(laughs as she goes toward hall)*. Not for the pure in heart. I'll get five or six more.

(Griggs follows her out through hall. Crossman gets up, folds the comic section, puts it under his arm, exits through hall. As he exits, Sophie comes on the porch. She begins to pile the breakfast dishes on a tray. She sees a half-used roll and a piece of bacon, fixes it for herself, goes out carrying the tray and chewing on the roll as the curtain falls.)

CURTAIN

SCENE TWO

SCENE: *The same. Nine-thirty that evening.*

AT RISE: *Nick is lying on the couch. Next to him, on the floor, is an empty champagne glass. On the table, in a sil-*

ver cooler, is a bottle of champagne. Constance is sitting at the table playing solitaire and humming to the record on the phonograph. On the porch, Sophie is reading to Mrs. Mary Ellis.

————

NICK *(looks up from couch to Constance, irritably)*. Please don't hum.

CONSTANCE. Sorry. I always like that so much, I—

NICK. And please don't talk. Mozart doesn't need it.

CONSTANCE. Haydn.

NICK. Mozart.

CONSTANCE *(tartly)*. I'm sorry but it's Haydn.

NICK. You know damn well I know what I'm talking about.

CONSTANCE. You don't know what you're talking about. Go look.

NICK *(gets up, picks up his glass, goes to phonograph, shuts it off, looks down, turns away annoyed, picks up a champagne bottle, pours himself a drink, then brings the bottle to Constance)*. Ready for another?

CONSTANCE. I haven't finished this.

(Nick carries the bottle out to the porch.)

MRS. ELLIS *(looks up at him)*. For the fourth time, we don't want any. Please go away. We're having a nice time. We're in the part I like best.

NICK. A nice time? Will I think such a time is a nice time when I am your age? I suppose so.

MRS. ELLIS. No, Mr. Denery. If you haven't learned to read at your age, you won't learn at mine.

NICK *(laughs, pats her shoulder)*. Never mind, I like you.

MRS. ELLIS. You must be damn hard up. People seldom like those who don't like them.

NICK *(pleased)*. You haven't forgotten how to flirt. Come on inside and talk to me. My wife disappears, everybody disappears— *(Stretches)* I'm bored, I'm bored.

MRS. ELLIS. And that's a state of sin, isn't it?

NICK. Unfortunately, it isn't. I've always said I can stand any pain, any trouble—but not boredom.

MRS. ELLIS. My advice is to try something intellectual for a change. Sit down with your champagne—on which you've been chewing since early afternoon—and try to make a paper hat out of the news-paper or get yourself a nice long piece of string.

NICK *(goes to Sophie)*. Sophie, come in and dance with me.

MRS. ELLIS *(calls in)*. Constance, whistle for Mr. Denery, please.

NICK *(to Sophie)*. You don't want to sit here and read to Mrs. Ellis.

SOPHIE. Yes, sir, I do. I enjoy the adventures of Odysseus. And the dollar an hour Mrs. Ellis pays me for reading to her.

NICK *(laughs, as Mrs. Ellis laughs)*. Give you two dollars an hour to dance with me.

MRS. ELLIS. It's not nearly enough, Sophie.

NICK *(pats Mrs. Ellis)*. You're a corrupter of youth—you steal the best hours.

MRS. ELLIS *(shakes his hand off her shoulder)*. And you're a toucher: you constantly touch people or lean on them. Little moments of sensuality. One should have sensuality whole or not at all. Don't you find pecking at it ungratifying? There are many of you: the touchers and the leaners. All since the depression, is my theory.

NICK *(laughs, pats her again)*. You must have been quite a girl in your day.

MRS. ELLIS. I wasn't. I wasn't at all. *(Nick wanders into the room. Mrs. Ellis speaks to Sophie)* I was too good for those who wanted me and not good enough for those I wanted. Like Frederick, Sophie. Life can be hard for such people and they seldom understand why and end bitter and confused.

SOPHIE. I know.

MRS. ELLIS. Do you? Frederick is a nice boy, Sophie—and that is all. But that's more than most, and precious in a small way.

SOPHIE. Yes, I think so.

(Mrs. Ellis smiles, pats her hand; Sophie begins again to read.)

NICK *(near the phonograph, to Constance)*. Dance with me?

CONSTANCE. I don't know how any more.

NICK *(turns away from the phonograph)*. Has it been wise, Constance, to lose all the graces in the service of this house?

CONSTANCE. Do you think I wanted it that way?

NICK. I'm not sure you didn't. You

could have married Ned, instead of dangling him around, the way you've done.

CONSTANCE. Ned has come here each summer because, well, because I guess this is about the only home he has. I loved Ned and honored him, but—I just wasn't in love with him when we were young. You know that, and you'd have been the first to tell me that you can't marry unless you're in love—*(He begins to laugh)* What are you laughing at?

NICK. "Can't marry unless you're in love." What do you think the rest of us did? I was in love with you. I've never been in love again.

CONSTANCE *(very sharply).* I don't want you to talk to me that way. And I don't believe you. You fell in love with Nina and that's why you didn't come back—*(Desperately)* You're *very* much in love with Nina. Then and now. Then—

NICK. Have it your way. What are you so angry about? Want to know something: I've never been angry in my life. *(Turns to her, smiles)* In the end, we wouldn't have worked out. You're a good woman and I am not a good man.

CONSTANCE. Well, whatever the reason, things turned out for the best. *(Carefully)* About Ned. What did he say last night? I mean did he really talk about me?

NICK *(expansively).* He said he loved you and wanted you and had wasted his life loving you and wanting you. And that he wasn't coming here any more. This is his last summer in this house.

CONSTANCE *(she turns, pained, startled).* His last summer? He said that? He really said it was his last summer—*(Carrie comes quickly into the room.)*

CARRIE. Has Fred come back?

NICK *(to her).* Well, where have *you* been? Come and have a drink and talk to me.

(He moves to pour her a drink as she crosses to the porch.)

CARRIE *(softly, to Mrs. Ellis).* I've been everywhere. Everywhere possible. I even forced myself to call on Mr. Payson.

MRS. ELLIS. And what did he say?

CARRIE. That Fred came in to see him after he left here this morning, stayed a few minutes, no more, and he hasn't seen him since.

MRS. ELLIS. Ah, that's good.

CARRIE. What's good about it? It means we don't know where he's been since ten this morning. *(Softly, as she sits down)* I don't know what else to do or where else to look. What should I do? Shall I call the police, what else is there to do?

MRS. ELLIS. Nothing.

CARRIE. How can I do nothing? You shouldn't have made me threaten him. We were wrong. It wasn't important that he wanted to go to Europe with a man his own age. What harm was there in it?

MRS. ELLIS. All his life you've been plucking him this way and plucking him that. Do what you like. Call the police.

NICK *(who has come to the door carrying a glass for Carrie. He hears the last few speeches; gently).* Can I do anything, Carrie?

CARRIE. I don't know, Nick. I only found one person who had seen him, down by the water—

NICK. Is he—would he have—is that what you're thinking, Carrie?

CARRIE. I'm afraid, I'm afraid.

NICK *(quickly, the kind of efficiency that comes with liquor and boredom).* Then come on, Carrie. You must go to the police right away. I'll get a boat. Tell the police to follow along. Right away. *(Carrie gets up. Starts toward Nick. Sophie gets up.)*

SOPHIE *(angrily, in French, to Nick).* Do not enjoy the excitement so much. Stop being a fool.

NICK *(amazed).* What?

SOPHIE *(in German).* I said don't enjoy yourself so much. Mind your business.

CARRIE. What? What is it, Sophie?

SOPHIE *(to Carrie).* Frederick is in the cove down by the dock. He has been there all day.

NICK *(to Sophie).* You said I was a fool. I don't like such words, Sophie. I don't.

CARRIE *(carefully, to Sophie).* You've let me go running about all day, frantic with terror—

SOPHIE. He wanted to be alone, Mrs. Ellis. That is not so terrible a thing to want.

CARRIE. How dare you take this on yourself? How dare you—

MRS. ELLIS. I hope this is not a sample of you as a mother-in-law.

SOPHIE *(gently, to Carrie).* He will return, Mrs. Ellis. Leave him alone.

NICK *(softly).* Sophie, I think you owe me an apology. You are by way of being a rather sharp little girl underneath all that shyness, aren't you? I'm waiting. *(No answer)* I'm waiting.

MRS. ELLIS. Well, wait outside, will you?

(He stares at her, turns, goes in the room.)

NICK *(very hurt, to Constance)*. I don't think I like it around here, Constance. No, I don't like it.

(He goes out left windows as Constance stares at him.)

CARRIE. Since Frederick has confided in you, Sophie, perhaps you should go to him.

SOPHIE. He has not confided in me. Sometimes his troubles are his own.

(She gets up, walks through room, sits down near Constance, who looks at her curiously. On the porch, Mrs. Ellis leans over and whispers to Carrie.)

CARRIE. Not tonight.

MRS. ELLIS. Why not tonight? We'll be leaving in the morning.

CARRIE. Because I've changed my mind. I think it best now that we let him go to Europe.

MRS. ELLIS *(gets up)*. He will not want to go to Europe. Haven't you understood that much?

CARRIE *(hesitantly)*. How do you know what he wants or feels—

MRS. ELLIS. I know. *(She comes into room, sits near Constance and Sophie. After a second Carrie follows her in, stands near them)* Sophie, I think a decision had best be made now. There should be no further postponement.

CARRIE *(very nervous)*. This isn't the time. Fred will be angry—

MRS. ELLIS *(to Sophie)*. I don't want to push you, child, but nothing will change, nothing. I know you've wanted to wait, and so did Frederick, both of you hoping that maybe— But it will all be the same a year from now. Miracles don't happen. I'm telling you the truth, Sophie.

SOPHIE. Yes, Mrs. Ellis, and I agree with you. Nothing will change. If Frederick is willing for an early marriage then I am also willing.

CONSTANCE. Is this the way it's been? *Willing* to marry, *willing to marry*—

SOPHIE *(looks at her)*. I do not use the correct word?

CONSTANCE *(to Mrs. Ellis and Carrie)*. If that's the way it is, then I am not willing. I thought it was two young people

who—who—who loved each other. I didn't ever understand it, and I didn't ask questions, but— Willing to get married. What have you been thinking of, why— *(Sharply, hurt)* What kind of unpleasant thing has this been?

CARRIE. I—I know. I can't—

MRS. ELLIS *(to Constance and Carrie)*. Why don't you take each other by the hand and go outside and gather in the dew?

SOPHIE. I think Aunt Constance is sad that we do not speak of it in the romantic words of love.

CONSTANCE. Yes, I am. And shocked. When Carrie first talked to me about the marriage, I asked you immediately and you told me you were in love—

SOPHIE. I never told you that, Aunt Constance.

CONSTANCE. I don't remember your exact words but of course I understood— You mean you and Frederick have never been in love? Why? Then why have you—

SOPHIE. Aunt Constance. I do not wish to go on with my life as it has been. I have not been happy, and I cannot continue here. I cannot be what you have wished me to be, and I do not want the world you want for me. It is too late—

CONSTANCE *(softly)*. Too late? You were thirteen years old when you came here. I've tried to give you everything—

SOPHIE. I came from another world and in that world thirteen is not young. I know what you have tried to give me, and I am grateful. But it has been a foolish waste for us both.

CONSTANCE *(softly)*. Were you happy at home, Sophie?

SOPHIE. I did not think in such words.

CONSTANCE. Please tell me.

SOPHIE. I was comfortable with myself, if that is what you mean, and I am no longer.

CONSTANCE *(gently, takes her hand)*. I have been so wrong. And so careless in not seeing it. Do you want to go home now?

SOPHIE. No. My mother cannot— Well, it is not that easy. I do not— *(As if it were painful)* I do not wish to go home now.

CONSTANCE *(puzzled)*. It's perfectly simple for you to go home. Why, why isn't it?

SOPHIE. I do not want to say, Aunt Constance. I do not want to. *(With feeling)* Please do not talk of it any more. Please allow me to do what I wish to do, and know is best for me. *(Smiles)* And don't look such a way. Frederick and I will have a nice life, we will make it so. *(Goes out)*

CARRIE *(sharply)*. Don't be too disturbed, Constance. I have decided that Frederick should go to Europe and this time I am not going to allow any interference of any kind.

(Frederick appears in the hall, comes into the room.)

FREDERICK. I'm not going to Europe, Mother.

CARRIE *(turns to him)*. I have had a bad day. And I have thought of many things. I was mistaken and you were right. You must go wherever you want—however you want to go.

FREDERICK. I am not going, Mother. Payson made that very clear to me this morning.

MRS. ELLIS. Don't, Frederick. It's not necessary. I know.

FREDERICK. But evidently Mother doesn't. . . . Payson made it clear to me that I was not wanted and never had been unless I supplied the money.

(Constance gets up, moves off to the porch.)

CARRIE *(after a second)*. I—Er—I don't believe he meant that. You just tell him that it's all been a mistake and there will certainly be money for the trip. Just go right back and say that, Frederick—

FREDERICK *(very sharply)*. Mother! I don't want to see him again! Ever.

CARRIE. You often imagine people don't like you for yourself. *I'll* go and tell Mr. Payson that it's all fixed now—

MRS. ELLIS. Carrie, you're an ass. *(To Frederick)* But I hope you haven't wasted today feeling bitter about Mr. Payson. You have no right to bitterness. No right at all. Why shouldn't Mr. Payson have wanted your money, though I must say he seems to have been rather boorish about not getting it. People like us should pay for the interest of people like him. Why should they want us otherwise? I don't believe he ever pretended to feel anything else about you.

FREDERICK *(softly)*. No, he never pretended.

MRS. ELLIS. Then understand that you've been the fool, and not he the villain. Take next week to be sad: a week's long enough to be sad in, if it's true sadness. Plenty long enough.

FREDERICK *(smiles)*. All right, Grandma. I'll take a week.

(Sophie appears at the hall door.)

SOPHIE *(to Frederick)*. You have had no dinner? *(Puts out her hand)* Then come. I have made a tray for you.

(He turns, goes to her, takes her hand, goes out.)

MRS. ELLIS *(gets up, looks at Carrie)*. Are you going to interfere this time, Carrie? *(No answer. Gently)* I hope not.

(She goes out. Carrie stands for a minute near the porch. Then she goes out to Constance.)

CARRIE. I don't like it either.

CONSTANCE *(wearily)*. Whole thing sounds like the sale of a short-front property. I don't know. Seems to me I've been so mixed up about so much. Well, maybe you all know what you're doing.

CARRIE. I don't know what I'm doing.

CONSTANCE. Why did you want the marriage, Carrie? I mean a month ago when you spoke to me—

CARRIE. I don't even know that.

CONSTANCE. You always seem so clear about everything. And so strong. Even when we were girls. I envied you that, Carrie, and wanted to be like you.

CARRIE *(laughs)*. Clear and strong. I wish I could tell you what I've missed and what I've wanted. Don't envy me, Con.

(She exits toward hall and staircase. As she does, Nick comes in. He is now a little more drunk than when he went out.)

NICK. Come on out, Carrie. It's wonderful night. Take you for a sail.

CARRIE *(laughs)*. Good night, Nick.

NICK *(as she goes up steps)*. I'm lonely, Carrie. I wouldn't leave you if you were lonely. *(When she doesn't answer, he goes into room, looks around, sees Constance sitting on the porch, goes over, stands in the door looking out. After a second)* I wish I wanted to go to bed with you, Con. I just can't want to. I don't know why. I just don't want it.

CONSTANCE *(very sharply)*. Stop talking that way. You've had too much to drink.

(She gets up, comes into room. He grabs her arm.)

NICK. Now you're angry again. *(Puts his arms around her)* I'll sing you a lullaby. Will you like that?

CONSTANCE. Look, Nick, you've been rather a trial tonight. Do go to bed.

NICK. I'm not going to bed. I'm lonely. I'm—

(The phone rings. Constance goes to it. Nick pours himself a glass of champagne.)

CONSTANCE. Yes? General Griggs isn't in, Rose. Oh. Yes. Just a minute. *(To Nick)* Rose Griggs wants to talk to *you*.

NICK. What's the matter, she got some new trouble?

CONSTANCE *(annoyed)*. Do you want the call or don't you?

NICK. Tell her I'm busy.

CONSTANCE *(in phone)*. He's busy drinking, Rose. Shall I leave a message for General Griggs— Oh. *(She puts the phone down, annoyed)* She says it's absolutely and positively urgent that she speak with *you*. Not her husband. Absolutely and positively.

(She exits through hall. Nick rises and goes to phone.)

NICK. Look here, my dear, don't be telling people you want to speak to me and not to your husband. Sounds awful. *(Laughs)* Oh. A most agreeable doctor. Must get to know him. Look, you don't have to convince me. Save it for your husband. Oh, come on. You're getting like those people who believe their own press agents. Anyway, I once knew a woman with heart trouble and it gave her a nice color. You didn't go to the doctor to believe him—*(Sighs, listens)* All right, of course I'm sorry. It sounds jolly nice and serious and I apologize. *(Listens)* Oh. Well, that is kind of you. Yes, tell your brother I'd like to stay with him. Oh, by Friday, certainly. How old is your niece? Is she the one with the braces on her teeth? *(Nina appears from the hall entrance. She is followed by Griggs who is carrying the picnic basket)* No, I won't paint anything out. That big a hack I'm not. Yes, we'll have plenty of time together. You're a good friend. *(To Nina and Griggs)* Had a nice day? *(Into phone)* No, I'm talking to your husband. Oh. Good-by. Take care of yourself. *(He hangs up. To Griggs)* That was Rose.

(Gaily, to Nina) I've had a dull day, darling. *(Crossman comes in)* Where'd you skip to?

NINA. We drove over to Pass Christian.

NICK. Did you put the car in the garage?

CROSSMAN *(gives Nina the keys)*. Yes, all safe.

NICK. Did you drive, Ned? That heavy Isotta? *(To Nina)* Nobody who drinks as much as Ned should be driving that car. Or any car belonging to me.

NINA. And nobody as tight as you are should talk that way.

NICK *(laughs)*. Have a drink, Ned.

(He brings Crossman a glass.)

CROSSMAN. Thank you, no.

(Nick turns, hands glass to Griggs.)

GRIGGS. No, thank you.

NICK. What the hell is this? Refusing to have a drink with me— *(To Crossman)* I'm trying to apologize to you. Now take the drink—

NINA. Nick, please—

NICK. Stay out of it, Nina. Women don't know anything about the etiquette of drinking.

CROSSMAN *(laughs)*. Has it got etiquette now? *(As Nick again hands him glass. Shakes his head)* Thank you.

NICK *(drunk, hurt)*. Look here, old boy, I say in the light of what's happened, you've just got to take this. It's my way of apologizing and I shouldn't have to explain that to a gentleman.

(He grabs Crossman's arm, playfully presses the glass to Crossman's lips.)

CROSSMAN *(quietly)*. Don't do that.

NICK. Come on, old boy. If I have to pour it down you—

CROSSMAN. Don't do that.

(Nick, laughing, presses the glass hard against Crossman's mouth. Crossman pushes the glass and it falls to the floor.)

NINA *(sits down)*. Well, we got rid of that glass. But there are plenty more, Nick.

NICK *(sad, but firm to Crossman)*. Now you've put *yourself* on the defensive, my friend. That's always tactically unwise, isn't it, General Griggs?

GRIGGS. I know nothing of tactics, Mr. Denery. Certainly not of yours.

NICK. Then what the hell are you doing as a general?

GRIGGS. Masquerading. They had a costume left over and they lent it to me.

NICK *(to Crossman)*. I'm waiting, Ned. Pour yourself a drink, and make *your* apologies.

CROSSMAN. You are just exactly the way I remember you. And that I wouldn't have believed of any man. *(He turns, goes out.)*

NICK *(like a hurt child)*. What the hell does that mean? *(Calling)* Hey, Ned. Come on back and have it your way. *(Gets no answer, turns, hearty again)* Come on, General. Have a bottle with me.

NINA. Are we going to start again?

NICK. General, got something to tell you: your wife telephoned but she didn't want to speak to you.

GRIGGS. That's most understandable. Good night, Mrs. Denery, and thank you for a pleasant day.

NICK. But she'll want to speak to you in the morning. Better stick around in the morning.

GRIGGS *(stares at him)*. Thank you. Good night.

NICK *(following him)*. I think you're doing the wrong thing, wanting to leave Rose. You're going to be lonely at your age without—

GRIGGS. If my wife wishes to consult you, Mr. Denery, that's her business. But I don't wish to consult you. *(He exits.)*

NICK. Sorry. Forget it. *(Nick turns, takes his drink to the couch, lies down.)*

NINA *(after a pause)*. You know, it's a nasty business hating yourself.

NICK. Who's silly enough to do that?

NINA. Me.

NICK *(warmly)*. Come on over here, darling, and tell me about yourself. I've missed you.

NINA. To hate yourself, all the time.

NICK. I love you, Nina.

NINA *(gets up)*. Here we go with that routine. Now you'll bait me until I tell you that you've never loved any woman, or any man, nor ever will. *(Wearily)* I'll be glad to get out of this house before Constance finds you out. She can go back to sleeping with her dreams. *(After a second)* You still think you can wind up everybody's affairs by Friday?

NICK. Oh, sure. Friday. Then we're going up to spend a month with Rose's brother, Henry something or other. In New Orleans.

NINA *(carefully)*. What are you talking about?

NICK. Rose fixed it for me. I'm going to do a portrait of her niece, the heiress to the fortune. The girl is balding and has braces. *(Looks at her)* Five thousand dollars.

NINA. Are you crazy?

NICK. Not a bit.

NINA. It's all right to kid around here—

NICK *(gets up)*. I *don't* know what you mean.

NINA *(violently)*. Please don't let's talk this way. Just tell Mrs. Griggs that you've changed your mind—

NICK. I demand that you tell me what you mean.

NINA *(angrily)*. How many years have we avoided saying it? Why must you walk into it now? *(Pauses, looks at him)* All right. Maybe it's time: you haven't finished a portrait in twelve years. And money isn't your reason for wanting to do this portrait. You're setting up a silly flirtation with Mrs. Griggs. I'm not going to New Orleans, Nick. I am not going to watch it all again. I can't go on this way with myself— *(Then softly)* Don't go. Call it off. You know how it will end. Please let's don't this time—We're not young any more, Nick. Somewhere we must have learned something.

NICK *(softly, carefully)*. If I haven't finished every picture I started it's because I'm good enough to know they weren't good enough. All these years you never understood that? I think I will never forgive you for talking that way.

NINA. Your trouble is that you're an amateur, a gifted amateur. And like all amateurs you have very handsome reasons for what you do not finish—between trains and boats.

NICK. You have thought that about me, all these years?

NINA. Yes.

NICK. Then it was good of you and loyal to pretend you believed in me.

NINA. Good? Loyal? What do they mean? I loved you.

NICK. Yes, good and loyal. But I, too, have a little vanity—*(She laughs; he comes to her)* And no man can bear to live with a woman who feels that way about his work. I think you ought to leave tomorrow, Nina. For good and forever.

NINA (softly). Yes. (She turns) Yes, of course.

(She starts to exit. He follows behind her, talking.)

NICK. But it must be different this time. Remember I said years ago—"Ten times of threatening is out, Nina," I said—the tenth time you stay gone.

NINA. All right. Ten times is out. (Quietly, desperately) I promise for good and forever.

NICK (she is climbing the staircase). This time, spare yourself the return. And the begging and the self-humiliation and the self-hate. And the disgusting self-contempt. This time they won't do any good. (He is following her but we cannot see him) Let's write it down, darling. And have a drink to seal it.

(On the words "disgusting self-contempt," Constance comes into the hall. She hears the words, recognizes Nick's voice and stands, frowning, and thoughtful. Then she turns out the lights on the porch, puts on all lights except one lamp, comes back into the living room and begins to empty the ashtrays, etc. Sophie comes into the room carrying pillow, sheets, quilts, a glass of milk, and crosses to couch. Without speaking, Constance moves to help her and together they begin to make the couch for the night.)

SOPHIE (after a minute, smiles). Do not worry for me, Aunt Constance.

CONSTANCE. I can't help it.

SOPHIE. I think perhaps you worry sometimes in order that you should not think.

CONSTANCE (smiles). Yes, maybe. I won't say any more. I'll be lonely without you, Sophie. I don't like being alone, any more. It's not a good way to live. And with you married, I'll be alone forever, unless—Well, Ned's loved me and it's been such a waste, such a waste. I know it now but—well—I don't know. (Shyly, as a young girl would say it) I wanted you to understand. You understand, Sophie? (Sophie stares at her, frowning. Then Constance speaks happily) Sleep well, dear.

(She comes to Sophie, kisses her, exits, closing door. Sophie finishes with the bed, brings her milk to the bed table, takes off her robe, puts it around her shoulders, gets into bed, and lies quietly, thinking. Then she turns as she hears footsteps in the hall and she is staring at the door as Nick opens it. He trips over a chair, recovers himself, turns on a lamp.)

NICK (sharply). Constance! What is this —a boys' school with lights out at eleven! (He sees Sophie) Where's your aunt? I want to talk to her. What are you doing?

SOPHIE. I think I am asleep, Mr. Denery.

NICK. You're cute. Maybe too cute. (He pours himself a drink) I'm going down to the tavern and see if I can get up a beach party. Tell your aunt. Just tell her that. (Going toward door) Want to come? You couldn't be more welcome. (She shakes her head) Oh, come on. Throw on a coat. I'm not mad at you any more. (He comes back toward her, looks down at her) I couldn't paint you, Sophie. You're too thin. Damn shame you're so thin. (Suddenly sits down on bed) I'm sick of trouble. Aren't you? Like to drive away with me for a few days? (Smiles at her) Nobody would care. And we could be happy. I hate people not being happy. (He lies down. His head is now on her knees) Move your knees, baby, they're bony. And get me a drink.

SOPHIE. Take the bottle upstairs, Mr. Denery.

NICK. Get me a drink. And make it poison. (Slowly, wearily, she gets up, takes his glass, goes to bottle, pours drink. He begins to sing. She brings glass back to him. He reaches up to take the glass, decides to pull her toward him, and spills the liquid on the bed) Clumsy, honey, clumsy. But I'll forgive you.

(He is holding her, and laughing.)

SOPHIE (calmly). Please go somewhere else, Mr. Denery.

NICK (springs up, drunk-angry). People aren't usually rude to me, Sophie. Poor little girls always turn rude when they're about to marry rich little boys. What a life you're going to have. That boy doesn't even know what's the matter with him—

SOPHIE (very sharply). Please, Mr. Denery, go away.

NICK (laughs). Oh, you know what's the matter with him? No European would be as innocent of the world as you pretend. (Delighted) I tricked you into telling me. Know that?

SOPHIE. You are drunk and I am tired.

Please go away.

NICK (*sits down across the room*). Go to sleep, child. I'm not disturbing you. (*She stares at him, decides she can't move him, gets into bed, picks up a book, begins to read*) I won't say a word. Ssh. Sophie's reading. Do you like to read? Know the best way to read? With someone you love. Out loud. Ever try it that way, honey? (*He gets up, comes to bed, stands near her, speaking over her shoulder*) I used to know a lot of poetry. Brought up on Millay. My candle and all that. "I had to be a liar. My mother was a leprechaun, my father was a friar." Crazy for the girl. (*Leans over and kisses her hair. She pulls her head away*) Ever wash your hair in champagne, darling? I knew a woman once. (*Tips the glass over her head*) Let's try it.

SOPHIE (*sharply*). Let us not try it again.

NICK (*sits down beside her*). Now for God's sake don't get angry. (*Takes her shoulders and shakes her*) I'm sick of angry women. All men are sick of angry women, if angry women know the truth. Sophie, we can always go away and starve. I'll manage to fall in love with you.

SOPHIE (*he is holding her*). Mr. Denery, I am sick of you.

NICK (*softly*). Tell me you don't like me and I will go away and not come back.

SOPHIE. No, sir. I do not like you.

NICK. People have hated me. But nobody's ever not liked me. If I thought you weren't flirting, I'd be hurt. Is there any aspirin downstairs? If you kiss me, Sophie, be kind to me for just a minute, I'll go away. I may come back another day, but I'll go all by myself—(*Desperately*) Please, Sophie, please.

SOPHIE (*sighs, holds up her side face to him*). All right. Then you will go, remember. (*He takes her in his arms, pulls her down on the bed. She struggles to get away from him. She speaks angrily*) Do not make yourself such a clown. (*When she cannot get away from him*) I will call your wife, Mr. Denery.

NICK (*delighted*). That would be fun, go ahead. We're getting a divorce. Sophie, let's make this night our night. God, Julie, if you only knew what I've been through—

SOPHIE (*violently*). Oh shut up.

(*She pulls away from him with great effort. He catches her robe and rolls over on it.*)

NICK (*giggles as he settles down comfortably*). Come on back. It's nice and warm here and I love you very much. But we've got to get some sleep, darling. Really we have to.

(*Then he turns over and lies still. She stands looking at him.*)

SOPHIE (*after a minute*). Get up, Mr. Denery. I will help you upstairs. (*No answer*) Please, please get up.

NICK (*gently, half passed-out*). It's raining out. Just tell the concierge I'm your brother. She'll understa—(*The words fade off. Sophie waits a second and then leans over and with great strength begins to shake him*) Stop that. (*He passes out, begins to breathe heavily. She turns, goes to hall, stands at the foot of the steps. Then she changes her mind and comes back into the room. She goes to the couch, stands, looking at him, decides to pull him by the legs*) (*Softly*) I'll go away in a few minutes. Don't be so young. Have a little pity. I am old and sick.

(*Sophie draws back, moves slowly to the other side of the room as the curtain falls.*)

CURTAIN

ACT THREE

SCENE: *Seven o'clock the next morning. Nick is asleep on the couch. Sophie is sitting in a chair, drinking a cup of coffee. A minute after the rise of the curtain, Mrs. Ellis comes down the steps, comes into the room.*

———

MRS. ELLIS. I heard you bumping around in the kitchen, Sophie. The older you get the less you sleep, and the more you look forward to meals. Particularly breakfast, because you've been alone all night, and the nights are the hardest—(*She sees Nick, stares, moves over to look at him*) What is this?

SOPHIE. It is Mr. Denery.

MRS. ELLIS (*turns to stare at her*). What's he doing down here?

SOPHIE. He became drunk and went to sleep.

MRS. ELLIS. He has been here all night?

(Sophie nods) What's the matter with you? Get him out of here immediately.

SOPHIE. I cannot move him. I tried. Shall I get you some coffee?

MRS. ELLIS *(staring at her)*. Are you being silly, Sophie? Sometimes it is very hard to tell with you. Why didn't you call Constance or Mrs. Denery?

SOPHIE. I did not know what to do. Mr. and Mrs. Denery had some trouble between them, or so he said, and I thought it might be worse for her if—*(Smiles)* Is it so much? He was just a little foolish and sleepy. *(Goes toward door)* I will get Leon and Sadie and we will take him upstairs.

MRS. ELLIS *(crosses to door)*. You will not get Leon and Sadie. Rose Griggs may be President of the gossip club for summer Anglo-Saxons, but Leon is certainly President of the Negro chapter. You will get this, er, out of here before anybody else sees him. *(She crosses back to bed, pulls blanket off Nick)* At least he's dressed. Bring me that cup of coffee. *(Sophie brings cup)* Mr. Denery! Sit up! *(Nick moves his head slightly. To Sophie)* Hold his head up.
(Sophie holds Nick's head; Mrs. Ellis tries to make him drink.)

NICK. *(very softly)*. Please leave me alone.

MRS. ELLIS *(shouting in his ear)*. Mr. Denery, listen to me. *You are to get up and get out of here immediately.*

NICK *(giving a bewildered look around the room; then he closes his eyes)*. Julie.

SOPHIE. He has been speaking of Julie most of the night.

MRS. ELLIS *(very sharply)*. Shall I wake your wife and see if she can locate Julie for you, or would you rather be cremated here? Get up, Mr. Denery. *(He opens his eyes, shuts them again)*

SOPHIE. You see how it is? *(She tries to pull her robe from under him)* Would you get off my robe, Mr. Denery?

MRS. ELLIS *(stares at her)*. Sophie, you're a damned little ninny. *(Very loudly, to Nick)* Now get up. You have no right to be here. You must get up immediately. I say *you*, you get up. *(Shouting)* Get to your room. Get out of here.

NICK *(turns, opens his eyes, half sits up, speaks gently)*. Don't scream at me, Mrs. Ellis. *(Sees Sophie, begins to realize where he is, groans deeply)* I passed out?

SOPHIE. Yes, sir. Most deeply.

MRS. ELLIS. I'm sure after this he won't mind if you don't call him "sir."

NICK. Champagne's always been a lousy drink for me. How did I get down here? *(He turns over)* I'm sorry, child. What happened?

SOPHIE. You fell asleep.

NICK *(hesitantly)*. Did I—God, I'm a fool. What did I—Did I do anything or say anything? Tell me, Sophie.

MRS. ELLIS. Please get up and get out of here.

NICK. I'm thirsty. I want a quart of water. Or a bottle of beer. Get me a bottle of cold beer, Sophie, will you? *(Looks around the bed)* Where'd you sleep? Get me the beer, will you?

MRS. ELLIS *(carefully)*. Mr. Denery, you are in Sophie's bed, in the living room of a house in a small Southern town where for a hundred and fifty years it has been impossible to take a daily bath without everybody in town advising you not to dry out your skin. You know that as well as I do. Now get up and go out by the side lawn to the boathouse. Put your head under water, or however you usually treat these matters, and come back through the front door for breakfast.

NICK *(laughs)*. I couldn't eat breakfast.

MRS. ELLIS. I don't find you cute. I find only that you can harm a young girl. Do please understand that.

NICK. Yes, I do. And I'm sorry. *(He sits up, untangling himself from the robe)* What's this? Oh, Sophie, child, I must have been a nuisance. I am *so* sorry.

MRS. ELLIS *(very loudly)*. Get up and get the hell out of here.
(The door opens and Rose, carrying her overnight handbag, sticks her head in.)

ROSE *(to Mrs. Ellis, who is directly on a line with the door)*. You frightened me. I could hear you outside on the lawn, so early. Oh, Nick. How nice you're downstairs. I never expected it— *(Her voice trails off as she sees Sophie and realizes Nick is on the bed)* Oh. *(Giggles, hesitantly)* You look like you just woke up, Nick. I mean, just woke up where you are.

MRS. ELLIS *(to Nick)*. Well, that's that. Perhaps you wanted it this way, Mr. Denery.
(She starts out as Leon appears carrying

the coffee urn. Rose stands staring at Nick.)

LEON *(very curious, but very hesitant in doorway)*. Should I put it here this morning, like every day, or—

MRS. ELLIS. Who told you, Leon?

LEON. Told me what, Mrs. Ellis? Sadie says take on in the urn—

MRS. ELLIS. I'm not talking about the urn. Who told you about Mr. Denery being here?

LEON. Told me? Why Miss Sophie came in for coffee for them.

MRS. ELLIS *(after a second, shrugs, points to coffee urn)*. Take it into the dining room.

LEON. You want me to come back and straighten up, Miss Sophie?

MRS. ELLIS *(waves him out)*. Mrs. Griggs will be glad to straighten up. *(She exits.)*

ROSE *(softly to Nick)*. You were here all night? I come back needing your help and advice as I've never before needed anything. And I find you—

NICK. Rose, please stop moving about. You're making me seasick. And would you go outside? I'd like to speak to Sophie.

ROSE. I am waiting for you to explain, Nick. I don't understand.

NICK. There is no need for you to understand.

ROSE. I'm not judging you. I know that there's probably a good explanation— But please tell me, Nick, what happened and then I won't be angry.

NICK. What the hell are you talking about? What's it your business? Now go upstairs, Rose.

ROSE *(softly, indignant)*. "Go upstairs, Rose." "What's it your business?" After I work my head off getting the commission of the portrait for you and after I go to the doctor's on your advice, although I never would have gone if I had known, and I come back here and find you this way. *(Sits down)* You've hurt me and you picked a mighty bad day to do it.

(The door opens and Constance comes in. She goes to Nick, stands looking at him.)

CONSTANCE. Nick, I want you to go to that window and look across the street. *(He stares at her. Then he gets up slowly and slowly moves to the window)* The Carters have three extra guests on their breakfast porch, the Gable sisters are unexpectedly entertaining— *(With feeling)* This house was not built to be stared at.

NICK *(gently)*. It can't be that bad, Constance.

CONSTANCE. It is just that bad.

NICK. I'm sorry. I was silly and drunk but there's no sense making more out of it than that.

CONSTANCE. I am not making anything out of it. But I know what is being made out of it. In your elegant way of life, I daresay this is an ordinary occurrence. But not in our village. *(The telephone rings. Constance picks up phone, says "Hello," pauses, "Hello, Mrs. Sims." Then her face becomes angry and she hangs up. She stands looking at the phone, and then takes it off the hook. Turns to Nick)* Please explain to me what happened. *(Points to telephone and then across the street)* I only know what they know.

SOPHIE. Mr. Denery came down looking for someone to talk to. He saw me, recited a little poetry, spoke to me of his troubles, tried to embrace me in a most mild fashion. He was uncertain of my name and continued throughout the night to call me Julie although twice he called for Cecile. And fell into so deep a sleep that I could not move him. Alcohol. It is the same in my country, every country.

CONSTANCE *(softly, as if it pained her)*. You are taking a very light tone about it, Sophie.

SOPHIE *(turns away, goes toward couch, and through the next speeches will strip the bed and pile the clothes)*. I will speak whichever way you think most fits the drama, Aunt Constance.

CONSTANCE. Will you tell me why you stayed in the room? Why didn't you come and call me, or—

NICK. Oh, look here. It's obvious. The kid didn't want to make any fuss and thought I'd wake up and go any minute. Damn nice of you, Sophie, and I'm grateful.

CONSTANCE. It was the most dangerous "niceness" I've ever heard of. *(Sophie looks up, stares at Constance.)*

NICK. I know it's hard for you, Constance, but it's not all that much.

CONSTANCE. Isn't it? You've looked out of the window. Now go down to the drugstore and listen to them and I think you'll change your mind.

NICK. Look. A foolish guy drinks, passes out—

ROSE *(amazed as she turns to look at Sophie)*. Why look at Sophie. Just as calm as can be. Making the bed. Like it happened to her every night.

CONSTANCE *(turns, realizes Rose is in the room)*. What are you doing here, Rose?

ROSE. Sitting here thinking that no man sleeps in a girl's bed unless she gives him to understand— *(Constance stares at her)* You can blame Nick all you like. But you know very well that a nice girl would have screamed.

CONSTANCE. How dare you talk this way? Whatever gave you the right— I hope it will be convenient for you to leave today. I will apologize to the General.

ROSE *(softly)*. That's all right, Constance. I must leave today, in any case. You see, I have to— *(Sighs, sincerely)* You won't be mad at me for long when you know the story. Oh, I'm very tired now. Could I have my breakfast in bed? Doctor's orders. *(She goes out, passes Crossman who is coming in. In sepulchral tones)* Good morning, dear Ned. *(Then in a sudden burst)* Have you heard—?

CROSSMAN *(cheerful)*. Good morning. Yes, I've heard. I'm not the one deaf man in town.

(Passes her. She stares at his back, reluctantly exits.)

CONSTANCE *(turns)*. Ned, what should we do?

CROSSMAN. Is there always something that can be done, remedied, patched, pulled apart and put together again? There is nothing to "do," Con. *(Smiles to Sophie, amused)* How are you, Sophie?

SOPHIE. I am all right, Mr. Ned.

NICK. Ned, is it as bad as *(Gestures toward window and Constance)* Constance thinks?

CONSTANCE. What's the difference to you? You're just sitting there telling yourself what provincial people we are and how you wish you were in the Ritz bar with people who would find it amusing with their lunch. *(Very angrily)* You came here as my friend and in our small life—in our terms—you have dishonored my house. It has taken me too many years to find out that you—

CROSSMAN. All right, Con, maybe that's the truth; but what's the good of discussing Nick's character and habits now?

NICK *(sincerely, to Constance)*. Whatever you think of me, I didn't want this.

I know what it will mean to Sophie and I'll stay here and face anything that will help you. Anything I can say or do—

SOPHIE *(she finishes folding the clothes)*. What will it "mean" to me, Mr. Ned?

CONSTANCE *(softly)*. You're old enough to know. And I believe you do know.

SOPHIE. I want to know from Mr. Ned what he thinks.

CROSSMAN *(to Sophie)*. I know what you want to know: the Ellis name is a powerful name. They won't be gossiped about out loud. They won't gossip about you and they won't listen to gossip about you. In their own way they'll take care of things. *(Carefully)* You can be quite sure of that. Quite sure.

SOPHIE *(after a second)*. And that is all?

CROSSMAN. That is all.

SOPHIE *(softly, carefully)*. Thank you, Mr. Ned.

CONSTANCE. Take care of things? She hasn't done anything. Except be stupid. The Tuckerman name is as good as the Ellis name—

CROSSMAN. Yes, yes. Sure enough.

(Sophie looks at Crossman, exits. She passes Leon in the hall. He is carrying his hat.)

LEON. Mrs. Ellis is cutting up about her breakfast. And Sadie's waiting for orders. We're messed this morning, for good.

CONSTANCE. Not at all. Tell Sadie I'm coming. *(She goes toward door)* What's your hat for, Leon?

LEON. Well, kind of a hot sun today.

CONSTANCE. Not in here. Rest your hat: you'll have plenty of time to gossip when the sun goes down.

(She goes out.)

NICK *(miserably)*. Ned. Ned, you understand I never thought it would make all this— Is Constance being—I mean, is she being old-maid fussy or is it really unpleasant—

CROSSMAN. It is unpleasant. She loves the girl, and she's worried for her.

NICK *(groans)*. If I could do something—

CROSSMAN. You did; but don't make too much of it.

NICK *(the first kind word he's heard)*. Thank you, boy.

CROSSMAN. Or too little. *(Nick groans)* Nobody will blame you too much. The girl's a foreigner and they don't understand her and therefore don't like her.

You're a home-town boy and as such you didn't do anything they wouldn't do. Boys will be boys and in the South there's no age limit on boyishness. Therefore, she led you on, or whatever is this morning's phrase. You'll come off all right. But then I imagine you always do.

NICK. You think this is coming off all right?

CROSSMAN. No, I don't.

NICK. I didn't even want her. Never thought of her that way.

CROSSMAN (too sympathetic). That is too bad. Better luck next time. You're young —in spirit.

(He exits into hall toward dining room as Hilda, carrying a jewel case, and hat box, comes down the steps. She has on her hat and gloves.)

NICK (who is sitting on a line with the door and sees her, speaks in German). Where you going?

HILDA (in German). Good morning, sir. I am taking madame's luggage to the nine-thirty train.

(She moves off as Nina appears. Nina has on a hat and gloves. On her heels is Rose in a fluffy negligee. Rose is talking as she follows Nina down the steps.)

ROSE. I'm not trying to excuse him. Of course it was indiscreet but you're a woman of the world, Nina, and you know what young girls are with a tipsy man. Nina, do believe that I saw them this morning and he didn't have the slightest interest in her. Nina—

NINA (turns to her, very pleasantly). I know it's eccentric of me, Mrs. Griggs, but I dislike being called by my first name before midnight.

ROSE (hurt, softly). You shouldn't allow yourself such a nasty snub. I'm only trying to help Nick. I know him well enough to know that he didn't do a thing— (Nina laughs) He's been my good friend. I'm trying to be a friend to him.

NINA. You will have every opportunity.

NICK (very angry). Will you please not stand there in the hall discussing me?

ROSE. Oh! (Looks at Nick, then at Nina, steps back into hall, calls toward kitchen) Leon! Could I have my tray upstairs? (As she goes past room and upstairs) Anybody seen my husband this morning? (Exits.)

NICK. Nina. (She comes in) I just want to say before you go that they're making an awful row about nothing—

NINA. You don't owe me an explanation, Nick.

NICK. Nothing happened, Nina, I swear. Nothing happened.

NINA. Try out phrases like "nothing happened" on women like Mrs. Griggs.

NICK (smiles). I'm sorry as all hell but they sure are cutting up—

NINA. Well, it is a tasty little story. Particularly for a girl who is going to be married.

NICK. My God, I'd forgotten about the boy. I must say he's an easy boy to forget about. Now I'll have to take him out and explain—

NINA. Don't do that, Nick. He isn't a fool.

NICK (looks around, thinking of anything to keep her in the room). Shall I get you a cup of coffee, darling?

NINA. No. Darling will have it on the train.

(She turns.)

NICK. Nina, I swear I didn't sleep with her.

NINA. I believe you. The girl doesn't like you.

NICK. Doesn't she? She's been very kind to me. She could have raised hell. That doesn't sound as if she doesn't like me. (Nina laughs) Don't laugh at me this morning. (After a second) What can I do for her, Nina.

NINA. You used to send wicker hampers of white roses. With a card saying "White for purity and sad parting."

NICK. Stop being nasty to me. (Then he smiles and comes toward her) Or maybe it's a good sign.

NINA. It isn't. I just say these things by rote. (Turns) I don't know how long I'll be in New York, but you can call Horace and he'll take care of the legal stuff for us.

NICK (close to her). I told you last night that I would agree to the separation because I knew with what justice you wanted to leave me.

NINA (coldly). That's not at all what you said.

NICK. I was tight. It was what I meant to say—

NINA (very angry). You're lying. You said just what you meant to say: I was to leave. And not make you sick with my usual begging to come back—

NICK. Stop, Nina. Take any kind of revenge you want, but—please—some other day. *(Leans down, puts his face against her face)* Don't ever leave me. Don't ever leave me. We've had good times, wild times. They made up for what was bad and they always will. Most people don't get that much. We've only had one trouble; you hate yourself for loving me. Because you have contempt for me.

NINA. For myself. I have no right—

NICK. No, nobody has. No right at all.

NINA. I wouldn't have married you, Nick, if I had known—

NICK. You would have married me. Or somebody like me. You've needed to look down on me, darling. You've needed to make fun of me. And to be ashamed of yourself for doing it.

NINA *(softly)*. Am I that sick?

NICK. I don't know about such words. You found the man you deserved. That's all. I am no better and no worse than what you really wanted. You like to—to demean yourself. And so you chose me. You must say I haven't minded much. Because I've always loved you and known we'd last it out. Come back to me, Nina, without shame in wanting to. *(He leans down, kisses her neck)* Put up with me a little longer, kid. I'm getting older and I'll soon wear down.

NINA *(she smiles, touched)*. I've never heard you speak of getting old.

NICK *(quickly)*. Yes. *(Then)* The Ile sails next week. Let's get on. We'll have fun. Tell me we're together again and you're happy. Say it, Nina, quick.

NINA. I'm happy.

(He takes her in his arms, kisses her. Then he stands away, looks at her, and smiles shyly.)

NICK. There'll be no more of what you call my "home-comings." Old friends and all that. They are damn bores, with empty lives.

NINA. Is that so different from us?

NICK. If we could only do something for the kid. Take her with us, get her out of here until they get tired of the gossip—

NINA *(laughs)*. I don't think we will take her with us.

NICK *(laughs)*. Now, now. You know what I mean.

NINA. I know what you mean—and we're not taking her with us.

NICK. I suppose there isn't anything to do. *(Softly, his hand to his head)* I feel sick, Nina.

NINA. You've got a hangover.

NICK. It's more than that. I've got a sore throat and my back aches. Come on, darling, let's get on the train.

NINA. You go. I'll stay and see if there's anything I can do. That's what you really want. Go on, Nicky. Maybe it's best.

NICK. I couldn't do that.

NINA. Don't waste time, darling. You'll miss the train. I'll bring your clothes with me.

NICK *(laughs, ruefully)*. If you didn't see through me so fast, you wouldn't dislike yourself so much. *(Comes to her)* You're a wonderful girl. It's wonderful of you to take all this on—

NINA. I've had practice.—

NICK *(hurt)*. That's not true. You know this never happened before.

NINA *(smiles)*. Nicky, it always confuses you that the fifth time something happens it varies slightly from the second and fourth. No, it never happened in this house before. Cora had a husband and Sylvia wanted one. And this isn't a hotel in Antibes, and Sophie is not a rich Egyptian. And this time you didn't break your arm on a boat deck and it isn't 1928—

NICK. This is your day, Nina. But pass up the chance to play it too hard, will you? Take me or leave me now but don't—

NINA. You're right. Please go, darling. Your staying won't do any good. Neither will mine, but maybe—

NICK. When will you come? I'll tell you what: you take the car and drive to Mobile. I'll get off there and wait at the Battle House. Then we can drive the rest of the way together. Must be somewhere in Mobile I can waste time for a few hours—

NINA *(gaily)*. I'm sure. But let's have a week's rest. Now go on.

NICK *(takes her in his arms)*. I love you, Nina. And we'll have the best time of our lives. Good luck, darling. And thank you. *(He kisses her)* They won't rag you, nobody ever does. We'll get the bridal suite on the Ile and have all our meals in bed. *(He moves away)* If you possibly can, bring the new portrait with you. I can finish it now. And try to get me the old portrait, darling. Maybe Constance will sell it to you— *(Nina laughs)* All right. Think what you want and I'll be what I

am. I love you and you love me and that's
that and always will be.
(He exits. She stands quietly.)

NINA. You love me and I love you and
that's that and always will be. *(Then she
turns, goes to bell cord, pulls it. After a
second, Constance appears in the hall.
Nina does not turn)* Leon, could I have
breakfast on the porch?

CONSTANCE *(in the doorway. She is carrying a tray)*. Yes, of course. I'll tell Leon
to bring it.
(Nina turns, stares at her.)

NINA. I am very sorry, Constance.

CONSTANCE. I am sorry, too, my dear.

NINA. I don't know what else to say. I
wish—

CONSTANCE. There's nothing for us to
say. *(There is an awkward pause)* Well.
I'll tell Leon. Old lady Ellis is having her
second breakfast. She always does on her
last day. I don't know why. *(She starts
out as Carrie, followed by Frederick,
comes down the steps. Carrie has on her
hat, etc., as if she were ready for traveling.
Frederick is carrying two valises)* Shall I
send breakfast up to Nick?

NINA *(very quickly)*. No, no. I'll just
have mine and—

FREDERICK *(calling to Constance)*.
Where's Sophie?

CONSTANCE. I'll send her in.

FREDERICK *(smiles)*. Don't sound so solemn, Miss Constance.

CONSTANCE *(sharply)*. I didn't mean to.
*(She disappears in the direction of the din-
ing room. Frederick and Carrie come into
the room.)*

NINA. Mr. Ellis, I should be carrying a
sign that says my husband is deeply sorry
and so am I.
*(He smiles at her. She turns, goes out on
the porch, closes the door behind her.)*

CARRIE *(hesitantly)*. She's a nice woman,
I think. Must be a hard life for her.

FREDERICK *(laughs)*. I don't think so.
(Turns as he hears Sophie in the hall)
Now remember, Mother. *(Sophie appears
in the door. Frederick goes to her, takes
her chin in his hand, kisses her)* I want to
tell you something fast. I don't know how
to explain it but I'm kind of glad this
foolishness happened. It makes you seem
closer to me, some silly way. You must believe that, although I can't make it clear.
Now there are two things to do right
away. Your choice.

SOPHIE. I have made bad gossip for you,
Frederick. We must speak about that.
Right away.

FREDERICK. There's no need to speak
about it again. It's a comic story and
that's all. And you must begin to laugh
about it.

SOPHIE *(smiles)*. I did laugh but nobody
would laugh with me. And nobody will
laugh in New Orleans, either. Is that not
so, Mrs. Ellis?

CARRIE. I think you should travel up
with us, Sophie. Right now. Whatever is
to be faced, we will do much better if we
face it all together and do it quickly.

FREDERICK *(looks at her, as if they had
had previous talk)*. You're putting it much
too importantly. There's nothing to be
faced.

CARRIE. I didn't mean to make it too
important. Of course, it isn't—

SOPHIE *(puts her hand on his arm)*. It
is important to you. And you must not be
kind and pretend that—

FREDERICK *(firmly)*. I'm not being kind.
I told you the truth. I've been in trouble,
now you've been in a little. That's all, now
or ever. *(Shyly)* As far as I'm concerned,
it makes us seem less like strangers. I'd
hoped you'd feel the same way—

CARRIE *(quickly)*. Run and pack a bag,
Sophie. It's a lovely day for driving and
we'll be in town for lunch. I think you
and I will have it at the club— Now let's
not talk about it any more—

SOPHIE. No. It would be most mistaken
of me to come now. My leaving here
would seem as if I must be ashamed and
you shamed for me. I must not come with
you today. I must stay here. *(Smiles)* It
must be faced.

FREDERICK. All right. That makes sense.
Mother and Grandma will drive up and
I'll stay here—

SOPHIE *(very quickly)*. No, no. You
must not stay here. *(Points to window,
meaning town)* They knew you had made
plans to leave today as usual. And so you
must leave. We must act as if nothing had
happened, and if we do that, and are not
worried, it will all end more quickly.
(Goes to Frederick) Believe me, Frederick. You know what I say is true. All
must seem to be as it has been. *(To Mrs.
Ellis)* You tell him that, please, Mrs. Ellis.

CARRIE. I don't know. You belong with
us now, Sophie. We don't want to leave

you, or Constance. I think she should come along and—

SOPHIE. Oh, she would not do that. You know she would not. *(Smiles, very cheerful)* Now. You are both very kind. But you know what I say is best for us all, and of no importance whether I come one week or the next. *(Takes Frederick's arm)* You have said I must laugh about it. I do laugh, and so it will be nothing for me to stay.

(Mrs. Ellis comes to the door from the direction of the dining room.)

CARRIE. Good-by, Sophie. We will be waiting for you.

(She exits, passing Mrs. Ellis without speaking.)

FREDERICK *(unhappily)*. You all seem to know what's right, what's best, so much faster than I do. I—

SOPHIE *(smiles, puts her hand over his mouth)*. This is best. Please.

FREDERICK. Then let us come back this week end. Can I do that?

SOPHIE *(she touches his face)*. I think so. You are a nice man, Frederick.

FREDERICK *(kisses her)*. And you're a nice girl to think so. See you in a few days. *(Turns to go out, passes Mrs. Ellis)* I feel happy, Grandma.

(Mrs. Ellis nods, waits for him to exit. Sophie sits down).

MRS. ELLIS *(after a second)*. Sophie.

SOPHIE *(smiles as if she knew what was coming)*. Yes.

MRS. ELLIS. Did *Carrie* ask you to leave with us? *(Sophie nods)* Ah. That's not good. When Carrie gets smart she gets very smart. Sophie, Frederick meant what he said to you. But I know them both and I would guess that in a week, or two or three, he will agree to go to Europe with his mother and he will tell you that it is only a postponement. And he will believe what he says. Time and decisions melt and merge for him and ten years from now he will be convinced that you refused to marry him. And he will always be a little sad about what could have been.

SOPHIE. Yes. Of course.

MRS. ELLIS. Carrie never will want him to marry. And she will never know it. Well, she, too, got cheated a long time ago. There is very little I can do—perhaps very little I want to do any more. Don't judge him too harshly, child.

SOPHIE *(smiles)*. No, I will not judge. I will write a letter to him.

MRS. ELLIS. That's my girl. Don't take from us what you don't have to take, or waste yourself on defeat. *(She gets up)* Oh, Sophie, feel sorry for Frederick. He is nice and he is nothing. And his father before him and my other sons. And myself. Another way. Well. If there is ever a chance, come and see me.

(She moves out. Sophie remains seated. After a second Constance comes in from the hall. She looks at Sophie.)

CONSTANCE *(hesitantly)*. Carrie tells me you'll be going up to town in a few weeks to stay with them. I'm glad. *(No answer)* Er. Why don't you go up to my room, dear, and lie down for a while? *(Points to porch)* She's on the porch. I'm going to ask the Denerys to leave today. I am sure they will want to, anyway. And the Griggses will be going and then just you and I—

SOPHIE. I will not be going to New Orleans, Aunt Constance, and there will be no marriage between Frederick and me.

CONSTANCE *(stares at her)*. But Carrie told me—

SOPHIE. Now she believes that she wants me. But it will not be so.

CONSTANCE *(after a second)*. I wish I could say I was surprised or angry. But I'm not sorry. No marriage without love—

SOPHIE *(pleasantly)*. Yes. Yes.

CONSTANCE *(gently)*. You're not to feel bad or hurt.

SOPHIE. I do not.

CONSTANCE. I'm—I'm glad. Mighty glad. Everything will work out for the best. You'll see. After everybody goes, we'll get the house and the accounts cleaned up and straightened out as usual. *(Gaily)* And then I think you and I will take a little trip. I haven't seen Memphis in years and maybe in a few months— *(Gently)* You know what? We can even sell, rent, the place, if we want to. We can pick up and go anywhere we want. You'll see, dear. We'll have a nice time.

SOPHIE *(almost as if she were speaking to a child)*. Yes, Aunt Constance. *(Constance goes out. Sophie turns to watch Leon who, during Constance's speech, has come out on the porch and is serving breakfast to Nina. Sophie rises and goes out to the porch. She takes the coffee pot from Leon—he has finished placing the other dishes—nods to him, and pours*

Nina's coffee. Leon exits. Nina turns, sees Sophie, turns back) You are a pretty woman, Mrs. Denery, when your face is happy.

NINA. And you think my face is happy *this* morning?

SOPHIE. Oh, yes. You and Mr. Denery have had a nice reconciliation.

NINA *(stares at her)*. Er. Yes, I suppose so.

SOPHIE. I am glad for you. That is as it has been and will always be. *(She sits down)* Now could I speak with you and Mr. Denery?

NINA *(uncomfortably)*. Sophie, if there was anything I can do— Er. Nick isn't here. I thought it best for us all—

SOPHIE *(softly)*. Ah. Ah, my aunt will be most sad.

NINA. Sophie, there's no good my telling you how sorry, how— What can I do?

SOPHIE. You can give me five thousand dollars, Mrs. Denery. American dollars, of course. *(Demurely; her accent from now on grows more pronounced)* I have been subjected to the most degrading experience from which no young girl easily recovers. *(In French)* A most degrading experience from which no young girl easily recovers—

NINA *(stares at her)*. It sounds exactly the same in French.

SOPHIE. Somehow sex and money are simpler in French. Well. In English, then, I have lost or will lose my most beloved fiancé; I cannot return to school and the comrades with whom my life has been so happy; my aunt is uncomfortable and unhappy in the only life she knows and is now burdened with me for many years to come. I am utterly, utterly miserable, Mrs. Denery. I am ruined. *(Nina bursts out laughing. Sophie smiles)* Please do not laugh at me.

NINA. I suppose I should be grateful to you for making a joke of it.

SOPHIE. You make a mistake. I am most serious.

NINA *(stops laughing)*. Are you? Sophie, it is an unpleasant and foolish incident and I don't wish to minimize it. But don't you feel you're adding considerable drama to it?

SOPHIE. No, ma'am. I did not say that is the way I thought of it. But that is the way it will be considered in this place, in this life. Little is made into very much here.

NINA. It's just the same in your country.

SOPHIE. No, Mrs. Denery. You mean it is the same in Brussels or Strasbourg or Paris, with those whom you would meet. In my class, in my town, it is not so. In a poor house if a man falls asleep drunk— and certainly it happens with us each Saturday night—he is not alone with an innocent young girl because the young girl, at my age, is not so innocent and because her family is in the same room, not having any other place to go. It arranges itself differently; you have more rooms and therefore more troubles.

NINA. Yes. I understand the lecture. *(Pauses)* Why do you want five thousand dollars, Sophie?

SOPHIE. I wish to go home.

NINA *(gently)*. Then I will be happy to give it to you. Happier than you know to think we can do something.

SOPHIE. Yes. I am sure. But I will not accept it as largesse—to make you happy. We will call it a loan, come by through blackmail. One does not have to be grateful for blackmail money, nor think of oneself as a charity girl.

NINA *(after a second)*. Blackmail money?

SOPHIE. Yes, ma'am. You will give me five thousand dollars because if you do not I will say that Mr. Denery seduced me last night. *(Nina stares at her, laughs)* You are gay this morning, madame.

NINA *(shocked)*. Sophie, Sophie. What a child you are. It's not necessary to talk this way.

SOPHIE. I wish to prevent you from giving favors to me.

NINA. I intended no favors. And I don't like this kind of talk. Nick did not seduce you and I want no more jokes about it. *(Pleasantly)* Suppose we try to be friends—

SOPHIE. I am not joking, Mrs. Denery. And I do not wish us to be friends.

NINA *(gets up)*. I would like to give you the money. And I will give it to you for that reason and no other.

SOPHIE. It does not matter to me what you would like. You will give it to me for my reason—or I will not take it.

(Angrily, Nina goes toward door, goes into the room, then turns and smiles at Sophie.)

NINA. You are serious? Just for a word.

a way of calling something, you would hurt my husband and me?

SOPHIE. For me it is more than a way of calling something.

NINA. You're a tough little girl.

SOPHIE. Don't you think people often say other people are tough when they do not know how to cheat them?

NINA (angrily). I was not trying to cheat you of anything—

SOPHIE. Yes, you were. You wish to be the kind lady who most honorably stays to discharge—within reason—her obligations. And who goes off, as she has gone off many other times, to make the reconciliation with her husband. How would you and Mr. Denery go on living without such incidents as me? I have been able to give you a second, or a twentieth, honeymoon

NINA (angrily). Is that speech made before you raise your price?

SOPHIE (smiles). No. A blackmail bargain is still a bargain.

(Crossman appears in the hall, Sophie sees him.)

NINA. How would— How shall we make the arrangements?

SOPHIE (calling). Mr. Ned. (Pleasantly, to Nina) Mr. Ned will know what to do.

NINA (after a second to Crossman). I'd like to get a check cashed. It's rather a large check. Could you vouch for me at the bank?

CROSSMAN. Sure. That's easy enough. The bank's just around the corner.

SOPHIE. Would you like me to come with you, Mrs. Denery?

NINA (smiles). You know, I think perhaps it's wisest for you to stay right here. You and I in a bank, cashing a check, this morning, could well be interpreted as a pay-off, or blackmail.

(She goes out.)

SOPHIE. I will be going home, Mr. Ned.

CROSSMAN (smiles). Good. (Looks at her, turns to stare at Nina, as she passes him and goes into hall) At least I hope it's good.

SOPHIE. I think it is more good than it is not good.

(He goes out. Rose comes down the steps. Her manner is hurried, nervous. She goes immediately to windows. She looks out as if she saw somebody coming. Then she turns and sees Sophie.)

ROSE (very nervous). Oh. Good morning, Sophie.

SOPHIE. We have seen each other earlier this morning, Mrs. Griggs.

ROSE. Oh. It's like a nightmare to me, as if a year had gone by. I've asked for my breakfast tray twice and nobody pays any attention. And the doctor says that's the way it must be.

SOPHIE (exiting). I will get it for you.

ROSE (back at the window, speaks to Sophie who has left the room). Not you, Sophie. You have your own troubles, God knows. I don't know how any of us can eat anything today. (Griggs, in riding pants and old shirt, comes in through the windows. Because she is upstage of the windows, he does not see her until she speaks) I've been looking everywhere for you, Ben.

GRIGGS (turns). Rose. You knew where I was.

ROSE. That was all we needed here today: a telephone call to the stables. Oh, Ben, it was I who found them. But you don't know about it—

GRIGGS. I've heard all about it.

ROSE. Terrible, isn't it?

GRIGGS. Not very.

ROSE. He's been a disappointment to me. I've been lying on the bed thinking about it. Nick Denery, I mean.

GRIGGS. I'm sorry.

ROSE. You know, Ben, I've just about come to the conclusion that I'm often wrong about people, mostly men.

GRIGGS. And what did you and Henry— ah—put together, Rose?

ROSE. It was so hot in town. Henry's got that wonderful air conditioning, of course, but it's never like your own air. I think Sunday's the hottest day of the year, anyway. Athalia's braces cost twenty-five hundred dollars at that Greek dentist's and believe me they don't make anybody look prettier—

GRIGGS. What point did you come to about my decision?

ROSE. Decision? Your decision—

GRIGGS (tensely). Please stop playing the fool. I'm afraid of you when you start playing that game.

ROSE. You afraid of me?

GRIGGS. Yes, me afraid of you. This very minute. Be kind, Rose, and tell me what has been decided for me.

ROSE (softly. very nervous). It wasn't

like that. Before I saw Henry I went to see Dr. Wills. You know he won't ever see patients on Sunday.

GRIGGS. Not unless the fee is over a hundred.

ROSE. I've always been sorry you didn't like Howard Wills. He's known as the best man in the South, Ben. He gave up a beach picnic with that woman, you know. Only that famous a man could buck having an open mistress—

GRIGGS. I don't want to hear about Wills. Come to the point. What did you and Henry—

ROSE (*grows sober, recognizing the tone*). I've been uneasy. I've sometimes been in pain, all summer. But I guess I knew because I guess I've known since that army doctor in 1934— I didn't want to talk about it— (*Moves toward him, frightened*) I have bad heart trouble, Ben.

GRIGGS (*after a second, as if he were sick*). Don't play that trick, Rose. It's just too ugly.

ROSE. I am not playing a trick. Wills wrote you a letter about it.

(*She reaches in the pocket of her robe, hands him a folded paper. He takes it from her, reads it.*)

GRIGGS (*violently*). How much did Henry pay Wills for this?

ROSE (*gently, seriously*). It wasn't bought. Even Henry couldn't buy it.

(*She turns, goes toward door, as if she were a dignified woman.*)

GRIGGS (*softly*). Tell me about it.

ROSE. There isn't much to tell. I've known some of it for years, and so have you. I just didn't know it was this bad, or didn't want to. Wills says I must lead a —well, a very different life. I'll have to go to the country somewhere and rest most of the day—not climb steps or go to parties or even see people much. I like people, I— Well, I just don't understand what I can do, except sit in the sun, and I hate sun— Oh, I don't know. He said worse than I am saying— I can't say it—

GRIGGS. Yes. (*After a second*) I'm sorry.

ROSE. I know you are. You've been my good friend. I'm frightened, Ben. I play the fool, but I'm not so big a fool that I don't know I haven't got anybody to help me. I pretend about the boys and what they're like but I know just as well as you do that they're not very kind men and won't want me and won't come to help

me. (*With feeling*) And of course I know about Henry—I always have. I've got nobody and I'm not young and I'm scared. Awful scared.

GRIGGS. You don't have to be.

ROSE (*who is crying, very quietly*). Wills says that if I take good care I might be, probably will be, in fine shape at the end of a year. Please stay with me this year, just this year. I will swear a solemn oath —believe me I'm telling you the truth now—I will give you a divorce at the end of the year without another word. I'll go and do it without any fuss, any talk. But please help me now. I'm so scared. Help me, please. One year's a lot to ask, I know, but—

(*Griggs comes to her, presses her arm.*)

GRIGGS. Of course. Of course. Now don't let's speak of it again and we'll do what has to be done.

(*She turns, goes out. He stands where he is. A minute later, Crossman comes in, stares at Griggs as if he knew something was wrong. Then he speaks casually.*)

CROSSMAN. Seen Sophie?

GRIGGS (*as if it were an effort, idly*). In the kitchen, I guess. Tough break for the kid, isn't it?

CROSSMAN. Perhaps it isn't. I don't know. (*He watches as Griggs takes out a cigarette and lights it. Griggs' hands are shaking and as he puts out the match, he stares at them.*)

GRIGGS (*smiles*). My hands are shaking.

CROSSMAN. What's the matter?

GRIGGS. Worst disease of all. I'm all gone. I've just looked and there's no Benjamin Griggs.

CROSSMAN (*after a second*). Oh, that. And you've just found that out?

GRIGGS. Just today. Just now.

CROSSMAN. My God, you're young.

GRIGGS (*laughs*). I guess I was. (*Slowly, carefully*) So at any given moment you're only the sum of your life up to then. There are no big moments you can reach unless you've a pile of smaller moments to stand on. That big hour of decision, the turning point in your life, the someday you've counted on when you'd suddenly wipe out your past mistakes, do the work you'd never done, think the way you'd never thought, have what you'd never had —it just doesn't come suddenly. You've trained yourself for it while you waited— or you've let it all run past you and frittered yourself away. *(Shakes his head)* I've frittered myself away, Crossman.

CROSSMAN. Most people like us.

GRIGGS. That's no good to me. Most people like us haven't done anything to themselves; they've let it be done to them. I had no right to let it be done to me, but I let it be done. What consolation can I find in not having made myself any more useless than an Ellis, a Denery, a Tuckerman, a—

CROSSMAN. Say it. I won't mind. Or a Crossman.

GRIGGS. The difference is you've meant to fritter yourself away.

CROSSMAN. And does that make it better?

GRIGGS. Better? Worse? All I know is it makes it different. Rose is a sick woman. But you know I'm not talking only about Rose and me, don't you?

CROSSMAN. I know.

GRIGGS *(very slowly)*. I am not any too sure I didn't partly welcome the medical opinion that made it easier for me to give up. *(Then in a low voice as if to himself)* And I don't like Rose. And I'll live to like her less.

(He starts toward door. Constance appears in the hall carrying a tray. She is followed by Sophie who is carrying a carpet sweeper and a basket filled with cleaning rags, etc. Constance comes to the door. She speaks wearily.)

CONSTANCE *(to Griggs)*. Sorry about Rose's breakfast. I forgot it. Sophie is going to help Rose to get packed. I don't mean to sound inhospitable but since you were going tomorrow, anyway— *(Gently)* I'm just tired and it would be easier for us. Please forgive me but you're an old friend and you will understand.

GRIGGS *(smiles, pats her arm)*. I'll take the tray.

(He takes it from her, goes up the steps. Constance comes in the room, sighs, sits down.)

CROSSMAN. Sophie. *(Sophie comes to him)* I was asked to give you this.

(He hands her an envelope.)

SOPHIE. Thank you, Mr. Ned.

CONSTANCE *(idly, without much interest)*. Secrets?

CROSSMAN. That's right. Secrets. Old love letters or something.

(Sophie laughs, goes out.)

CONSTANCE *(after a silence)*. I hate this house today.

CROSSMAN. Well, they'll all be gone soon.

CONSTANCE. You won't go? Please.

CROSSMAN. I'll stay for a few days if you'd like me to.

CONSTANCE. Oh, yes. I need you to stay.

CROSSMAN *(points out of window)*. Don't worry about what the town thinks. Just act as if nothing had happened and they'll soon stop talking.

CONSTANCE. Oh, I'm not worrying about that. *(Pauses)* I feel so lost, Ned. As if I distrusted myself, didn't have anything to stand on. I mean, right now, if you asked me, I just wouldn't know what I thought or believed, or ever had, or— *(Shyly)* Well, what *have* I built my life on? Do you know what I mean?

CROSSMAN. Sure. I know.

CONSTANCE *(as if she had trouble with the words)*. It's—it's so painful. *(Then as if she wished to change the subject quickly)* Sophie will be going back to Europe. She just told me. She *wants* to go. Did you know that?

CROSSMAN. Is that so?

CONSTANCE. I was so sure I was doing the right thing, bringing her here. You see? That's part of what I mean by not knowing the things I thought I knew. Well. She wants me to come with her and live with them, but I told her I'd be no happier in a new life than she was. *(Pauses as if she were coming to something that frightens her)* Nick said you wouldn't be coming here next summer. Did you say anything like that, or was it one of Nick's lies? *(He does not answer her. She stares at him)* Why, Ned?

CROSSMAN. Hasn't anything to do with you, Con. Just think I'd be better off. You know, it's kind of foolish—two weeks a year—coming back here and living a life that isn't me any more. *(Laughs)* It's too respectable for me, Con. I ain't up to it any more.

CONSTANCE. Oh. It's what I look forward to every summer. What will I— *(Very quickly)* Where is Nick? I haven't seen him. I wish they'd leave—

CROSSMAN. They've gone.

CONSTANCE *(stares at him)*. Without a word to me? Exactly the way he left years ago. I didn't ever tell you that, did I? We had a date for dinner. He didn't come. He just got on the boat. I didn't ever tell anybody before. *(Violently)* What a fool. All these years of making a shabby man into the kind of hero who would come back some day all happy and shining—

CROSSMAN. Oh, don't do that. He never asked you to make him what he wasn't. Or to wait twenty years to find him out.

CONSTANCE. No, he didn't. That's true. *(She rises, goes to the portrait and stands staring at it)* Do I look like this?

CROSSMAN. You look nice.

CONSTANCE. Come and look at it.

CROSSMAN. No. I don't want to.

CONSTANCE. Much older than I thought or— And I don't look very bright. *(Puts the picture away from her)* Well, I haven't been very bright. I want to say something to you. I can't wait any longer. Would you forgive me?

CROSSMAN. Forgive you? For what?

CONSTANCE. For wasting all these years. For not knowing what I felt about you, or not wanting to. Ned, would you have me now?

CROSSMAN *(after a second)*. What did you say?

CONSTANCE. Would you marry me? *(There is a pause. Then Sophie comes from the direction of the dining room carrying a carpet sweeper and a cleaning basket. As she goes up the steps she is singing a cheerful French song. Constance smiles)* She's happy. That's good. I think she'll come out all right, always.

CROSSMAN *(stares at Constance, then slowly, carefully)*. I live in a room and I go to work and I play a game called getting through the day while you wait for me. The night's for me—just me—and I can do anything with it I want. There used to be a lot of things to do with it, good things, but now there's a bar and another bar and the same people in each bar. When I've had enough I go back to my room—or somebody else's room—and that never means much one way or the other. A few years ago I'd have weeks of reading—night after night—just me. But I don't do that much any more. Just read, all night long. You can feel good that way.

CONSTANCE. I never did that. I'm not a reader.

CROSSMAN *(as if he hadn't heard her)*. And a few years ago I'd go on the wagon twice a year. Now I don't do that any more. And I don't care. *(Smiles)* And all these years I told myself that if you'd loved me everything would have been different. I'd have had a good life, been worth something to myself. I wanted to tell myself that. I wanted to believe it. Griggs was right. I not only wasted myself, but I wanted it that way. All my life, I guess, I wanted it that way.

CONSTANCE. And you're not in love with me, Ned?

CROSSMAN. No, Con. Not now.

CONSTANCE *(gets up, goes to him)*. Let's have a nice dinner together, just you and me, and go to the movies. Could we do that?

CROSSMAN. I've kept myself busy looking into other people's hearts so I wouldn't have to look into my own. *(Softly)* If I made you think I was still in love, I'm sorry. Sorry I fooled you and sorry I fooled myself. And I've never liked liars—least of all those who lie to themselves.

CONSTANCE. Never mind. Most of us lie to ourselves, darling, most of us.

CURTAIN

Come Back, Little Sheba

BY WILLIAM INGE

First presented by The Theatre Guild at the Booth Theatre in New York on February 15, 1950, with the following cast:

DOC	Sidney Blackmer	MRS. COFFMAN	Olga Fabian
MARIE	Joan Lorring	MILKMAN	John Randolph
LOLA	Shirley Booth	MESSENGER	Arnold Schulman
TURK	Lonny Chapman	BRUCE	Robert Cunningham
POSTMAN	Daniel Reed	ED ANDERSON	Wilson Brooks
	ELMO HUSTON	Paul Krauss	

ACT ONE

Scene One: Morning in late spring.
Scene Two: The same evening, after supper.

ACT TWO

Scene One: The following morning.
Scene Two: Late afternoon the same day.
Scene Three: 5:30 the next morning.
Scene Four: Morning, a week later.

The action takes place in a rundown neighborhood of a Midwestern city.

BORN in Independence, Kansas, in 1913, and the holder of a B.A. from the University of Kansas and an M.A. from Peabody College of Nashville, Tennessee, William Inge is a genuine Midwesterner. His claims to that distinction—and it is a distinction in his case since the tone and quality of *Come Back, Little Sheba* cannot conceivably have been drawn from any other region!—were strengthened by his professional work. He taught at Stephens College in Columbia, Missouri, where the celebrated Maude Adams headed the theatre department during the last years of her life; and he gave an extension course in playwriting at Washington University in St. Louis, where he also filled the post of drama, film and music critic on the *St. Louis Star-Times*.

While occupying this position, Mr. Inge went to see the pre-Broadway production of Tennessee Williams' *The Glass Menagerie* in Chicago. Profoundly impressed by what he later called "the first real experience I had felt in the theatre for years," he proceeded to write his first play, *Farther Off From Heaven.* Margo Jones produced it in her Dallas arena theatre in 1947. *Come Back, Little Sheba* was his second play, and it introduced an authentic new talent to Broadway in 1950. Although that talent is as remote from the Great White Way as any that has won acclaim there for many years, it was instantly welcomed by the Theatre Guild and loyally supported by the Guild's able play editor Phyllis Anderson, whose faith in the author proved justified. At this writing, Mr. Inge has a new play, *Picnic,* scheduled for the season of 1952-1953 and resides within commuting distance of New York in Old Greenwich, Connecticut.

Both *Farther Off From Heaven* and *Come Back, Little Sheba* have in common with *The Glass Menagerie* a concern with small lives and a sparing expenditure of plot. But, unlike Tennessee Williams, Mr. Inge resolutely allowed the facts of a constricted, essentially small-town life to speak for themselves, without the accessory machinery of narrations, flashbacks, and symbolism. In this respect, too, his work, remote from literary sophistication, remained inviolately Midwestern. To *Come Back, Little Sheba,* however, the author gave a universality which he once defined by referring us to Thoreau's statement in *Walden* that "the mass of men lead lives of quiet desperation." Thoreau added, "What is called resignation is confirmed desperation," and it would be difficult to find an apter description of the first and third acts of Inge's play. *Come Back, Little Sheba* brings a large if quietly dispensed compassion to bear upon ordinary lives.

Inge's artistry may be described as Naturalism with a heart. It does not pitch the drama on the heights, but neither does it artificially inflate the human condition. It does not scintillate, but neither does it purvey the factitious glitter of verbal gymnasts. The play belongs to Main Street and Gopher Prairie, and if this is a limitation in the work, it is also evidence of its authenticity. There are too many examples of disingenuous artistry by contemporaries who think they are on Parnassus when they are merely in literary society. Inge gave the impression of being a lonely writer who was disinclined to run with any literary pack, and his play is a genuine middle-class drama that pretends to be nothing else. It does not varnish a St. Louis background with a British accent. Is it, for that reason, any the less universal?

ACT ONE

SCENE ONE

The stage is empty.

It is the downstairs of an old house in one of those semi-respectable neighborhoods in a Midwestern city. The stage is divided into two rooms, the living room at right and the kitchen at left, with a stairway and a door between. At the foot of the stairway is a small table with a telephone on it. The time is about 8:00 A.M., a morning in the late spring.

At rise of curtain the sun hasn't come out in full force and outside the atmosphere is a little gray. The house is extremely cluttered and even dirty. The living room somehow manages to convey the atmosphere of the twenties, decorated with cheap pretense at niceness and respectability. The general effect is one of fussy awkwardness. The furniture is all heavy and rounded-looking, the chairs and davenport being covered with a shiny mohair. The davenport is littered and there are lace antimacassars on all the chairs. In such areas, houses are so close together they hide each other from the sunlight. What sun could come through the window, at right, is dimmed by the smoky glass curtains. In the kitchen there is a table, center. On it are piled dirty dishes from supper the night before. Woodwork in the kitchen is dark and grimy. No industry whatsoever has been spent in making it one of those white, cheerful rooms that we commonly think kitchens should be. There is no action on stage for several seconds.

Doc comes downstairs to kitchen. His coat is on back of chair, center. He straightens chair, takes roll from bag on drainboard, folds bag and tucks it behind sink. He lights stove and goes to table, fills dishpan there and takes it to sink. Turns on water, tucks towel in vest for apron. He goes to chair and says prayer. Then he crosses to stove, takes frying pan to sink and turns on water.

Marie, a young girl of eighteen or nineteen who rooms in the house, comes out of her bedroom (next to the living room), skipping airily into the kitchen. Her hair is piled in curls on top of her head and she wears a sheer dainty negligee and smart, feathery mules on her feet. She has the cheerfulness only youth can feel in the morning.

MARIE *(goes to chair, opens pocketbook there)*. Hi!

DOC. Well, well, how is our star boarder this morning?

MARIE. Fine.

DOC. Want your breakfast now?

MARIE. Just my fruit juice. I'll drink it while I dress and have my breakfast later.

DOC *(places two glasses on table)*. Up a little early, aren't you?

MARIE. I have to get to the library and check out some books before anyone else gets them.

DOC. Yes, you want to study hard, Marie, learn to be a fine artist some day. Paint lots of beautiful pictures. I remember a picture my mother had over the mantelpiece at home, a picture of a cathedral in a sunset, one of those big cathedrals in Europe somewhere. Made you feel religious just to look at it.

MARIE. These books aren't for art, they're for biology. I have an exam.

DOC. Biology? Why do they make you take biology?

MARIE *(laughs)*. It's required. Didn't you have to take biology when you were in college?

DOC. Well . . . yes, but I was preparing to study medicine, so of course I *had* to take biology and things like that. You see —I was going to be a real doctor then— only I left college my third year.

MARIE. What's the matter? Didn't you like the pre-med course?

DOC. Yes, of course . . . I had to give it up.

MARIE. Why?

DOC *(goes to stove with roll on plate— evasive)*. I'll put your sweet roll in now, Marie, so it will be nice and warm for you when you want it.

MARIE. Dr. Delaney, you're so nice to your wife, and you're so nice to me, as a matter of fact, you're so nice to everyone. I hope my husband is as nice as you are. Most husbands would never think of getting their own breakfast.

DOC *(very pleased with this)*. . . . uh . . . you might as well sit down now and . . . yes, sit here and I'll serve you your breakfast now, Marie, and we can eat it together, the two of us.

MARIE *(a light little laugh as she starts*

dancing away from him). No, I like to bathe first and feel that I'm all fresh and clean to start the day. I'm going to hop into the tub now. See you later. *(She goes upstairs)*

DOC *(the words appeal to him).* Yes, fresh and clean— *(Doc shows disappointment but goes on in businesslike way setting his breakfast on the table)*

MARIE *(offstage).* Mrs. Delaney.

LOLA *(offstage).* 'Mornin', honey. *(Then Lola comes downstairs. She is a contrast to Doc's neat cleanliness, and Marie's Over a nightdress she wears a lumpy kimono. Her eyes are dim with a morning expression of disillusionment, as though she had had a beautiful dream during the night and found on waking none of it was true. On her feet are worn dirty comfies)*

LOLA *(with some self-pity).* I can't sleep late like I used to. It used to be I could sleep till noon if I wanted to, but I can't any more. I don't know why.

DOC. Habits change. Here's your fruit juice.

LOLA *(taking it).* I oughta be gettin' your breakfast, Doc, instead of you gettin' mine.

DOC. I have to get up anyway, Baby.

LOLA *(sadly).* I had another dream last night.

DOC *(pours coffee).* About Little Sheba?

LOLA *(with sudden animation).* It was just as real. I dreamt I put her on a leash and we walked downtown—to do some shopping. All the people on the street turned around to admire her, and I felt so proud. Then we started to walk, and the blocks started going by so fast that Little Sheba couldn't keep up with me. Suddenly, I looked around and Little Sheba was gone. Isn't that funny? I looked everywhere for her but I couldn't find her. And I stood there feeling sort of afraid. *(Pause)* Do you suppose that means anything?

DOC. Dreams are funny.

LOLA. Do you suppose it means Little Sheba is going to come back?

DOC. I don't know, Baby.

LOLA *(petulant).* I miss her so, Doc. She was such a cute little puppy. Wasn't she cute?

DOC *(smiles with the reminiscence).* Yes, she was cute.

LOLA. Remember how white and fluffy she used to be after I gave her a bath?

And how her little hind-end wagged from side to side when she walked?

DOC *(an appealing memory).* I remember.

LOLA. She was such a cute little puppy. I hated to see her grow old, didn't you, Doc?

DOC. Yah. Little Sheba should have stayed young forever. Some things should never grow old. That's what it amounts to, I guess.

LOLA. She's been gone for such a long time. What do you suppose ever happened to her?

DOC. You can't ever tell.

LOLA *(with anxiety).* Do you suppose she got run over by a car? Or do you think that old Mrs. Coffman next door poisoned her? I wouldn't be a bit surprised.

DOC. No, Baby. She just disappeared. That's all we know.

LOLA *(redundantly).* Just vanished one day . . . vanished into thin air. *(As though in a dream)*

DOC. I told you I'd find another one, Baby.

LOLA *(pessimistically).* You couldn't ever find another puppy as cute as Little Sheba.

DOC *(back to reality).* Want an egg?

LOLA. No, just this coffee. *(He pours coffee and sits down to breakfast, Lola, suddenly)* Have you said your prayer, Doc?

DOC. Yes, Baby.

LOLA. And did you ask God to be with you—all through the day, and keep you strong?

DOC. Yes, Baby.

LOLA. Then God will be with you, Docky. He's been with you almost a year now and I'm so proud of you.

DOC *(preening himself a little).* Sometimes I feel sorta proud of myself.

LOLA. Say your prayer, Doc. I like to hear it.

DOC *(matter-of-factly).* God grant me the serenity to accept the things I cannot change, courage to change the things I can, and wisdom always to tell the difference.

LOLA. That's nice. That's so pretty. When I think of the way you used to drink, always getting into fights, we had so much trouble. I was so scared! I never knew what was going to happen.

DOC. That was a long time ago, Baby.

LOLA. I know it, Daddy. I know how you're going to be when you come home now. *(She kisses him lightly)*

DOC. *I* don't know what I would have done without you.

LOLA. And now you've been sober almost a year.

DOC. Yep. A year next month. *(He rises and goes to the sink with coffee cup and two glasses, rinsing them)*

LOLA. Do you have to go to the meeting tonight?

DOC. No. I can skip the meetings now for a while.

LOLA. Oh, good! Then you can take me to a movie.

DOC. Sorry, Baby. I'm going out on some Twelfth Step work with Ed Anderson.

LOLA. What's that?

DOC *(drying the glasses)*. I showed you that list of twelve steps the Alcoholics Anonymous have to follow. This is the final one. After you learn to stay dry yourself, then you go out and help other guys that need it.

LOLA. Oh!

DOC *(goes to sink)*. When we help others, we help ourselves.

LOLA. I know what you mean. Whenever I help Marie in some way, it makes me feel good.

DOC. Yah. *(Lola takes her cup to Doc and he washes it)* Yes, but this is a lot different, Baby. When I go out to help some poor drunk, I have to give him courage—to stay sober like I've stayed sober. Most alcoholics are disappointed men . . . They need courage . . .

LOLA. You weren't ever disappointed, were you, Daddy?

DOC *(after another evasive pause)*. The important thing is to forget the past and live for the present. And stay sober doing it.

LOLA. Who do you have to help tonight?

DOC. Some guy they picked up on Skid Row last night. *(Gets his coat from back of chair)* They got him at the City Hospital. I kinda dread it.

LOLA. I thought you said it helped you.

DOC *(puts on coat)*. It does, if you can stand it. I did some Twelfth Step work down there once before. They put alcoholics right in with the crazy people. It's horrible—these men all twisted and shaking—eyes all foggy and full of pain. Some

guy there with his fists clamped together, so he couldn't kill anyone. There was a young man, just a *young* man, had scratched his eyes out.

LOLA *(cringing)*. Don't, Daddy. Seems a shame to take a man there just 'cause he got drunk.

DOC. Well, they'll sober a man up. That's the important thing. Let's not talk about it any more.

LOLA *(with relief)*. Rita Hayworth's on tonight, out at the Plaza. Don't you want to see it?

DOC. Maybe Marie will go with you.

LOLA. Oh, no. She's probably going out with Turk tonight.

DOC. She's too nice a girl to be going out with a guy like Turk.

LOLA. I don't know why, Daddy. Turk's nice. *(Cuts coffee cake)*

DOC. A guy like that doesn't have any respect for *nice* young girls. You can tell that by looking at him.

LOLA. I never saw Marie object to any of the lovemaking.

DOC. A big, brawny bozo like Turk, he probably forces her to kiss him.

LOLA. Daddy, that's not so at all. I came in the back way once when they were in the living room, and she was kissing him like he was Rudolph Valentino.

DOC *(an angry denial)*. Marie is a nice girl.

LOLA. I know she's nice. I just said she and Turk were doing some tall spooning. It wouldn't surprise me any if . . .

DOC. Honey, I don't want to hear any more about it.

LOLA. You try to make out like every young girl is Jennifer Jones in the *Song of Bernadette*.

DOC. I do not. I just like to believe that young people like her are clean and decent . . . *(Marie comes downstairs)*

MARIE. Hi! *(Gets cup and saucer from drainboard)*

LOLA *(at stove)*. There's an extra sweet roll for you this morning, honey. I didn't want mine.

MARIE. One's plenty, thank you.

DOC. How soon do you leave this morning? *(Lola brings coffee)*

MARIE *(eating)* As soon as I finish my breakfast.

DOC. Well, I'll wait and we can walk to the corner together.

MARIE. Oh, I'm sorry, Doc. Turk's coming by. He has to go to the library, too.

DOC. Oh, well, I'm not going to be competition with a football player. (*To Lola*) It's a nice spring morning. Wanta walk to the office with me?

LOLA. I look too terrible, Daddy. I ain't even dressed.

DOC. Kiss Daddy good-bye.

LOLA (*gets up and kisses him softly*). Bye, bye, Daddy. If you get hungry, come home and I'll have something for you.

MARIE (*joking*). Aren't you going to kiss *me*, Dr. Delaney? (*Lola eggs Doc to go ahead*)

DOC (*startled, hesitates, forces himself to realize she is only joking and manages to answer*). Can't spend my time kissing all the girls.

(*Marie laughs. Doc goes into living room while Lola and Marie continue talking. Marie's scarf is tossed over his hat on chair, so he picks it up, then looks at it fondly, holding it in the air inspecting its delicate gracefulness. He drops it back on chair and goes out.*)

MARIE. I think Dr. Delaney is so nice.

LOLA (*she is by the closet now, where she keeps a few personal articles. She is getting into a more becoming smock*). When did you say Turk was coming by?

MARIE. Said he'd be here about 9:30. (*Doc exits, hearing the line about Turk*) That's a pretty smock.

LOLA (*goes to table, sits in chair and changes shoes*). It'll be better to work around the house in.

MARIE (*not sounding exactly cheerful*). Mrs. Delaney, I'm expecting a telegram this morning. Would you leave it on my dresser for me when it comes?

LOLA. Sure, honey. No bad news, I hope.

MARIE. Oh, no! It's from Bruce.

LOLA (*Marie's boy friends are one of her liveliest interests*). Oh, your boy friend in Cincinnati. Is he coming to see you?

MARIE. I guess so.

LOLA. I'm just dying to meet him.

MARIE (*changing the subject*). Really, Mrs. Delaney, you and Doc have been so nice to me. I just want you to know I appreciate it.

LOLA. Thanks, honey.

MARIE. You've been like a father and mother to me. I appreciate it.

LOLA. Thanks, honey.

MARIE. Turk was saying just the other night what good sports you both are.

LOLA (*brushing hair*). That so?

MARIE. Honest. He said it was just as much fun being with you as with kids our own age.

LOLA (*couldn't be more flattered*). Oh, I like that Turk. He reminds me of a boy I used to know in high school, Dutch Mc-Coy. Where did you ever meet him?

MARIE. In art class.

LOLA. Turk take art?

MARIE (*laughs*). No. It was in a life class. He was modeling. Lots of the athletes do that. It pays them a dollar an hour.

LOLA. That's nice.

MARIE. Mrs. Delaney? I've got some corrections to make in some of my drawings. Is it all right if I bring Turk home this morning to pose for me? It'll just take a few minutes.

LOLA. Sure, honey.

MARIE. There's a contest on now. They're giving a prize for the best drawing to use for advertising the Spring Relays.

LOLA. And you're going to do a picture of Turk? That's nice. (*A sudden thought*) Doc's gonna be gone tonight. You and Turk can have the living room if you want to. (*A little secretively*)

MARIE (*this is a temptation*). O.K. Thanks. (*Exits to bedroom*)

LOLA. Tell me more about Bruce. (*Follows her to bedroom door*)

MARIE (*offstage in bedroom. Remembering her affinity*). Well, he comes from one of the best families in Cincinnati. And they have a great big house. And they have a maid, too. And he's got a wonderful personality. He makes $300 a month.

LOLA. That so?

MARIE. And he stays at the best hotels. His company insists on it. (*Enters*)

LOLA. Do you like him as well as Turk? (*Buttoning up back of Marie's blouse*)

MARIE (*evasive*). Bruce is so dependable, and . . . he's a gentleman, too.

LOLA. Are you goin' to marry him, honey?

MARIE. Maybe, after I graduate from college and he feels he can support a wife and children. I'm going to have lots and lots of children.

LOLA. I wanted children, too. When I

lost my baby and found out I couldn't have any more, I didn't know what to do with myself. I wanted to get a job, but Doc wouldn't hear of it.

MARIE. Bruce is going to come into a lot of money some day. His uncle made a fortune in men's garters. (*Exits into her room*)

LOLA (*leaning on door frame*). Doc was a rich boy when I married him. His mother left him $25,000 when she died. (*Disillusioned*) It took him a lot to get his office started and everything . . . then, he got sick. (*She makes a futile gesture; then on the bright side*) But Doc's always good to me . . . now.

MARIE (*re-enters*). Oh, Doc's a peach.

LOLA. I used to be pretty, something like you. (*She gets her picture from table*) I was Beauty Queen of the senior class in high school. My dad was awful strict, though. Once he caught me holding hands with that good-looking Dutch McCoy. Dad sent Dutch home, and wouldn't let me go out after supper for a whole month. Daddy would never let me go out with boys much. Just because I was pretty. He was afraid all the boys would get the wrong idea—*you* know. I never had any fun at all until I met Doc.

MARIE. Sometimes I'm glad I didn't know my father. Mom always let me do pretty much as I please.

LOLA. Doc was the first boy Dad ever let me go out with. We got married that spring. (*Replaces picture. Marie sits on couch, puts on shoes and socks*)

MARIE. What did your father think of that?

LOLA. We came right to the city then. And, well, Doc gave up his pre-med course and went to Chiropractor School instead.

MARIE. You must have been married awful young.

LOLA. Oh, yes. Eighteen.

MARIE. That must have made your father really mad.

LOLA. Yes, it did. I never went home after that, but my mother comes down here from Green Valley to visit me sometimes.

TURK (*bursts into the front room from outside. He is a young, big, husky, good-looking boy, nineteen or twenty. He has the openness, the generosity, vigor and health of youth. He's had a little time in* the service, but he is not what one would call disciplined. He wears faded dungarees and a T-shirt. He always enters unannounced. He hollers for Marie). Hey, Marie! Ready?

MARIE (*calling. Runs and exits into bedroom, closing door*). Just a minute, Turk.

LOLA (*confidentially*). I'll entertain him until you're ready. (*She is by nature coy and kittenish with any attractive man. Picks up papers—stuffs them under table*) The house is such a mess, Turk! I bet you think I'm an awful housekeeper. Some day I'll surprise you. But you're like one of the family now. (*Pause*) My, you're an early caller.

TURK. Gotta get to the library. Haven't cracked a book for a biology exam and Marie's gotta help me.

LOLA (*unconsciously admiring his stature and physique and looking him over*). My, I'd think you'd be chilly running around in just that thin little shirt.

TURK. Me? I go like this in the middle of winter.

LOLA. Well, you're a big husky man.

TURK (*laughs*). Oh, I'm a brute, *I* am.

LOLA. You should be out in Hollywood making those Tarzan movies.

TURK. I had enough of that place when I was in the Navy.

LOLA. That so?

TURK (*calling*). Hey, Marie, hurry up.

MARIE. Oh, be patient, Turk.

TURK (*to Lola*). She doesn't realize how busy I am. I'll only have a half hour to study at most. I gotta report to the coach at 10:30.

LOLA. What are you in training for now?

TURK. Spring track. They got me throwing the javelin.

LOLA. The javelin? What's that?

TURK (*laughs at her ignorance*). It's a big, long lance. (*Assumes the magnificent position*) You hold it like this, erect— then you let go and it goes singing through the air, and lands yards away, if you're any good at it, and sticks in the ground, quivering like an arrow. I won the State championship last year.

LOLA (*she has watched as though fascinated*). My!

TURK (*very generous*). Get Marie to take you to the track field some afternoon, and you can watch me.

LOLA. That would be thrilling.

MARIE (comes dancing in). Hi, Turk.

TURK. Hi, juicy.

LOLA (as the young couple moves to the doorway). Remember, Marie, you and Turk can have the front room tonight. All to yourselves. You can play the radio and dance and make a plate of fudge, or anything you want.

MARIE (to Turk). O.K.?

TURK (with eagerness). Sure.

MARIE. Let's go. (Exits)

LOLA. 'Bye, kids.

TURK. 'Bye, Mrs. Delaney. (Gives her a chuck under the chin) You're a swell skirt.

(Lola couldn't be more flattered. For a moment she is breathless. They speed out the door and Lola stands, sadly watching them depart. Then a sad, vacant look comes over her face. Her arms drop in a gesture of futility. Slowly she walks out on the front porch and calls.)

LOLA. Little Sheba! Come, Little She-ba. Come back . . . come back, Little Sheba! (She waits for a few moments, then comes wearily back into the house, closing the door behind her. Now the morning has caught up with her. She goes to the kitchen, kicks off her pumps and gets back into comfies. The sight of the dishes on the drainboard depresses her. Clearly she is bored to death. Then the telephone rings with the promise of relieving her. She answers it) Hello—Oh, no, you've got the wrong number—Oh, that's all right. (Again it looks hopeless. She hears the postman. Now her spirits are lifted. She runs to the door, opens it and awaits him. When he's within distance, she lets loose a barrage of welcome) 'Morning, Mr. Postman.

POSTMAN. 'Morning, ma'am.

LOLA. You better have something for me today. Sometimes I think you don't even know I live here. You haven't left me anything for two whole weeks. If you can't do better than that, I'll just have to get a new postman.

POSTMAN (on the porch). You'll have to get someone to write you some letters, lady. Nope, nothing for you.

LOLA. Well, I was only joking. You knew I was joking, didn't you? I bet you're thirsty. You come right in here and I'll bring you a glass of cold water. Come in and sit down for a few minutes and rest your feet awhile.

POSTMAN. I'll take you up on that, lady. I've worked up quite a thirst. (Coming in)

LOLA. You sit down. I'll be back in just a minute. (Goes to kitchen, gets pitcher out of refrigerator and brings it back)

POSTMAN. Spring is turnin' into summer awful soon.

LOLA. You feel free to stop here and ask me for a drink of water any time you want to. (Pouring drink) That's what we're all here for, isn't it? To make each other comfortable?

POSTMAN. Thank you, ma'am.

LOLA (clinging, not wanting to be left alone so soon; she hurries her conversation to hold him). You haven't been our postman very long, have you?

POSTMAN (she pours him a glass of water, stands holding pitcher as he drinks). No.

LOLA. You postmen have things pretty nice, don't you? I hear you get nice pensions after you been working for the government twenty years. I think that's dandy. It's a good job, too. (Pours him a second glass) You may get tired but I think it's good for a man to be outside and get a lot of exercise. Keeps him strong and healthy. My husband, he's a doctor, a chiropractor; he has to stay inside his office all day long. The only exercise he gets is rubbin' peoples' backbones. (They laugh. Lola goes to table, leaves pitcher) It makes his hands strong. He's got the strongest hands you ever did see. But he's got a poor digestion. I keep tellin' him he oughta get some fresh air once in a while and some exercise. (Postman rises as if to go, and this hurries her into a more absorbing monologue) You know what? My husband is an Alcoholics Anonymous. He doesn't care if I tell you that 'cause he's proud of it. He hasn't touched a drop in almost a year. All that time we've had a quart of whiskey in the pantry for company and he hasn't even gone near it. Doesn't even want to. You know, alcoholics can't drink like ordinary people; they're allergic to it. It affects them different. They get started drinking and can't stop. Liquor transforms them. Sometimes they get mean and violent and wanna fight, but if they let liquor alone, they're perfectly all right, just like you and me. (Postman tries to leave) You should have seen Doc before he gave it up. He lost all his patients, wouldn't even go to the office; just wanted to stay drunk all day long and he'd come home at night and . . . You just wouldn't believe it if you saw him now. He's got his patients all back, and he's just doing fine.

POSTMAN. Sure, I know Dr. Delaney. I deliver his office mail. He's a fine man.

LOLA. Oh, thanks. You don't ever drink, do you?

POSTMAN. Oh, a few beers once in a while. *(He is ready to go)*

LOLA. Well, I guess that stuff doesn't do any of us any good.

POSTMAN. No. *(Crosses down for mail on floor center)* Well, good day, ma'am.

LOLA. Say, you got any kids?

POSTMAN. Three grandchildren.

LOLA *(getting it from console table)*. We don't have any kids, and we got this toy in a box of breakfast food. Why don't you take it home to them?

POSTMAN. Why, that's very kind of you, ma'am. *(He takes it, and goes)*

LOLA. Good-bye, Mr. Postman.

POSTMAN *(on porch)*. I'll see that you get a letter, if I have to write it myself.

LOLA. Thanks. Good-bye. *(Left alone, she turns on radio. Then she goes to kitchen to start dishes, showing her boredom in the half-hearted way she washes them. Takes water back to icebox. Then she spies Mrs. Coffman hanging baby clothes on lines just outside kitchen door. Goes to door)* My, you're a busy woman this morning, Mrs. Coffman.

MRS. COFFMAN *(German accent. She is outside, but sticks her head in for some of the following)*. Being busy is being happy.

LOLA. I guess so.

MRS. COFFMAN. I don't have it as easy as you. When you got seven kids to look after, you got no time to sit around the house, Mrs. Delaney.

LOLA. I s'pose not.

MRS. COFFMAN. But you don't hear me complain.

LOLA. Oh, no. You never complain. *(Pause)* I guess my little doggie's gone for good, Mrs. Coffman. I sure miss her.

MRS. COFFMAN. The only way to keep from missing one dog is to get another.

LOLA *(goes to sink, turns off water)*. Oh, I never could find another doggie as cute as Little Sheba.

MRS. COFFMAN. Did you put an ad in the paper?

LOLA. For two whole weeks. No one answered it. It's just like she vanished—into thin air. *(She likes this metaphor)* Every day, though, I go out on the porch and call her. You can't tell; she might be around. Don't you think?

MRS. COFFMAN. You should get busy and forget her. You should get busy, Mrs. Delaney.

LOLA. Yes, I'm going to. I'm going to start my spring house-cleaning one of these days real soon. Why don't you come in and have a cup of coffee with me, Mrs. Coffman, and we can chat awhile?

MRS. COFFMAN. I got work to do, Mrs. Delaney. I got work. *(Exit) (Lola turns from the window, annoyed at her rejection. Is about to start in on the dishes when the milkman arrives. She opens the back door and detains him)*

MILKMAN. 'Morning, Mrs. Coffman.

MRS. COFFMAN. 'Morning.

LOLA. Hello there, Mr. Milkman. How are you today?

MILKMAN. 'Morning, Lady.

LOLA. I think I'm going to want a few specials today. Can you come in a minute? *(Goes to icebox)*

MILKMAN *(coming in)*. What'll it be? *(He probably is used to her. He is not a handsome man but is husky and attractive in his uniform)*

LOLA *(at refrigerator)*. Well, now, let's see. You got any cottage cheese?

MILKMAN. We always got cottage cheese, Lady. *(Showing her card)* All you gotta do is check the items on the card and we leave 'em. Now I gotta go back to the truck.

LOLA. Now, don't scold me. I always mean to do that but you're always here before I think of it. Now, I guess I'll need some coffee cream, too—half a pint.

MILKMAN. Coffee cream. OK.

LOLA. Now let me see . . . Oh, yes, I want a quart of buttermilk. My husband has liked buttermilk ever since he stopped drinking. My husband's an alcoholic. Had to give it up. Did I ever tell you? *(Starts out. Stops at sink)*

MILKMAN. Yes, Lady. *(Starts to go. She follows)*

LOLA. Now he can't get enough to eat. Eats six times a day. He comes home in the middle of the morning, and I fix him a snack. In the middle of the afternoon he has a malted milk with an egg in it. And then another snack before he goes to bed.

MILKMAN. What'd ya know?

LOLA. Keeps his energy up.

MILKMAN. I'll bet. Anything else, Lady?

LOLA. No, I guess not.

MILKMAN (*going out*). Be back in a jiffy. (*Gives her slip*)

LOLA. I'm just so sorry I put you to so much extra work. (*He goes. Returns shortly with dairy products*) After this I'm going to do my best to remember to check the card. I don't think it's right to put people to extra work. (*Goes to icebox, puts things away*)

MILKMAN (*smiles, is willing to forget*). That's all right, Lady.

LOLA. Maybe you'd like a piece of cake or a sandwich. Got some awfully good cold cuts in the icebox.

MILKMAN. No, thanks, Lady.

LOLA. Or maybe you'd like a cup of coffee.

MILKMAN. No. thanks. (*He's checking the items, putting them on the bill*)

LOLA. You're just a young man. You oughta be going to college. I think everyone should have an education. Do you like your job?

MILKMAN. It's O.K. (*Looks at Lola*)

LOLA. You're a husky young man. You oughta be out in Hollywood making those Tarzan movies.

MILKMAN (*steps back. Feels a little flattered*). When I first began on this job I didn't get enough exercise, so I started working out on the bar-bell.

LOLA. Bar-bells?

MILKMAN. Keeps you in trim.

LOLA (*fascinated*). Yes, I imagine.

MILKMAN. I sent my picture in to *Strength and Health* last month. (*Proudly*) It's a physique study! If they print it, I'll bring you a copy.

LOLA. Oh, will you? I think we should all take better care of ourselves, don't you?

MILKMAN. If you ask me, Lady, that's what's wrong with the world today. We're not taking care of ourselves.

LOLA. I wouldn't be surprised.

MILKMAN. Every morning, I do forty push-ups before I eat my breakfast.

LOLA. Push-ups?

MILKMAN. Like this. (*He spreads himself on the floor and demonstrates, doing three rapid push-ups. Lola couldn't be more fascinated. Then he springs to his feet*) That's good for shoulder development. Wanta feel my shoulders?

LOLA. Why . . . why, yes. (*He makes one arm tense and puts her hand on his shoulder*) Why, it's just like a rock.

MILKMAN. I can do seventy-nine without stopping.

LOLA. Seventy-nine!

MILKMAN. Now feel my arm.

LOLA (*does so*). Goodness!

MILKMAN. You wouldn't believe what a puny kid I was. Sickly, no appetite.

LOLA. Is that a fact? And, my! Look at you now.

MILKMAN (*very proud*). Shucks, any man could do the same . . . if he just takes care of himself.

LOLA. Oh, sure, sure. (*A horn is heard offstage*)

MILKMAN. There's my buddy. I gotta beat it. (*Picks up his things, shakes hands, leaves hurriedly*) See you tomorrow, Lady.

LOLA. 'Bye.

(*She watches him from kitchen window until he gets out of sight. There is a look of some wonder on her face, an emptiness, as though she were unable to understand anything that ever happened to her. She looks at clock, runs into living room, turns on radio. A pulsating tom-tom is heard as a theme introduction. Then the announcer.*)

ANNOUNCER (*in dramatic voice*). TA-BOOoooo! (*Now in a very soft, highly personalized voice. Lola sits on couch, eats candy*) It's Ta-boo, radio listeners, your fifteen minutes of temptation. (*An alluring voice*) Won't you join me? (*Lola swings feet up*) Won't you leave behind your routine, the dull cares that make up your day-to-day existence, the little worries, the uncertainties, the confusions of the work-a-day world and follow me where pagan spirits hold sway, where lithe natives dance on a moon-enchanted isle, where palm trees sway with the restless ocean tide, restless surging on the white shore? Won't you come along? (*More tom-tom*) (*Now in an oily voice*) But remember, it's TA-BOOOOOoooo-OOO! (*Now the tom-tom again, going into a sensual, primitive rhythm melody. Lola has been transfixed from the beginning of the program. She lies down on the davenport, listening, then slowly, growing more and more comfortable.)*

WESTERN UNION BOY *(at door).* Telegram for Miss Marie Buckholder.

LOLA. She's not here.

WESTERN UNION BOY. Sign here.

(Lola does, then she closes the door and brings the envelope into the house, looking at it wonderingly. This is a major temptation for her. She puts the envelope on the table but can't resist looking at it. Finally she gives in and takes it to the kitchen to steam it open. Then Marie and Turk burst into the room. Lola, confused, wonders what to do with the telegram, then decides, just in the nick of time, to jam it in her apron pocket.)

MARIE. Mrs. Delaney! *(Turns off radio. At the sound of Marie's voice, Lola embarrassedly slips the message into her pocket and runs in to greet them)* Mind if we turn your parlor into an art studio?

LOLA. Sure, go right ahead. Hi, Turk. *(Turk gives a wave of his arm)*

MARIE *(to Turk, indicating her bedroom).* You can change in there, Turk. *(Exit to bedroom)*

LOLA *(puzzled).* Change?

MARIE. He's gotta take off his clothes.

LOLA. Huh? *(Closes door)*

MARIE. These drawings are for my life class.

LOLA *(consoled but still mystified).* Oh.

MARIE *(sits on couch).* Turk's the best male model we've had all year. Lotsa athletes pose for us 'cause they've all got muscles. They're easier to draw.

LOLA. You mean . . . he's gonna pose *naked?*

MARIE *(laughs).* No. The women do, but the men are always more proper. Turk's going to pose in his track suit.

LOLA. Oh. *(Almost to herself)* The women pose naked but the men don't. *(This strikes her as a startling inconsistency)* If it's all right for a woman, it oughta be for a man.

MARIE *(businesslike).* The man always keeps covered. *(Calling to Turk)* Hurry up, Turk.

TURK *(with all his muscles in place, he comes out. He is not at all self-conscious about his semi-nudity. His body is something he takes very much for granted. Lola is* ⋯ *'e dazed by the spectacle of*

flesh). How do you want this lovely body? Same pose I took in Art Class?

MARIE. Yah. Over there where I can get more light on you.

TURK *(opens door. Starts pose).* Anything in the house I can use for a javelin?

MARIE. Is there, Mrs. Delaney?

LOLA. How about the broom?

TURK. O.K. *(Lola runs out to get it. Turk goes to her in kitchen, takes it, returns to living room and resumes pose)*

MARIE *(from her sofa, studying Turk in relation to her sketch-pad, moves his leg).* Your left foot a little more this way. *(Studying it)* O.K., hold it. *(Starts sketching rapidly and industriously. Lola looks on, lingeringly)*

LOLA *(starts unwillingly into kitchen, changes her mind and returns to the scene of action. Marie and Turk are too busy to comment. Lola looks at sketch, inspecting it).* Well . . . that's real pretty, Marie. *(Marie is intent. Lola moves closer to look at the drawing)* It . . . it's real artistic. *(Pause)* I wish *I* was artistic.

TURK. Baby, I can't hold this pose very long at a time.

MARIE. Rest whenever you feel like it.

TURK. O.K.

MARIE *(to Lola).* If I make a good drawing, they'll use it for the posters for the Spring Relays.

LOLA. Ya. You told me.

MARIE *(to Turk).* After I'm finished with these sketches I won't have to bother you any more.

TURK. No bother. *(Rubs his shoulder—he poses)* Hard pose, though. Gets me in the shoulder. *(Marie pays no attention. Lola peers at him so closely he becomes a little self-conscious and breaks pose. This also breaks Lola's concentration)*

LOLA. I'll heat you up some coffee. *(Goes to kitchen)*

TURK *(softly to Marie).* Hey, can't you keep her out of here? She makes me feel naked.

MARIE *(laughs).* I can't keep her out of her own house, can I?

TURK. Didn't she ever see a man before?

MARIE. Not a big, beautiful man like you, Turky. *(Turk smiles, is flattered by any recognition of his physical worth, takes it as an immediate invitation to lovemaking. Pulling her up, he kisses her as Doc comes up on porch. Marie pushes*

Turk away) Turk, get back in your corner. *(Doc comes in from outside)*

DOC *(cheerily).* Hi, everyone.

MARIE. Hi.

TURK. Hi, Doc. *(Doc then sees Turk, feels immediate resentment. Goes into kitchen to Lola)* What's goin' on here?

LOLA *(getting cups).* Oh, hello, Daddy. Marie's doin' a drawin'.

DOC *(trying to size up the situation. Marie and Turk are too busy to speak).* Oh.

LOLA. I've just heated up the coffee, want some?

DOC. Yeah. What happened to Turk's clothes?

LOLA. Marie's doing some drawings for her *life* class, Doc.

DOC. Can't she draw him with his clothes on?

LOLA *(with coffee. Very professional now).* No, Doc, it's not the same. See, it's a *life* class. They draw bodies. They all do it, right in the classroom.

DOC. Why, Marie's just a young girl; she shouldn't be drawing things like that. I don't care if they do teach it at college. It's not right.

LOLA *(disclaiming responsibility).* I don't know, Doc.

TURK *(turns).* I'm tired.

MARIE *(squats at his feet).* Just let me finish the foot.

DOC. Why doesn't she draw something else, a bowl of flowers or a cathedral . . . or a sunset?

LOLA. All she told me, Doc, was if she made a good drawing of Turk, they'd use it for the posters for the Spring Relay. *(Pause)* So I guess they don't want sunsets.

DOC. What if someone walked into the house now? What would they think?

LOLA. Daddy, Marie just asked me if it was all right if Turk came in and posed for her. Now that's all she said, and I said O.K. But if you think it's wrong I won't let them do it again.

DOC. I just don't like it.

MARIE. Hold it a minute more.

TURK. O.K.

LOLA. Well, then you speak to Marie about it if . . .

DOC *(he'd never mention anything disapprovingly to Marie).* No, Baby. I couldn't do that.

LOLA. Well, then . . .

DOC. Besides, it's not her fault. If those college people make her do drawings like that, I suppose she has to do them. I just don't think it's right she should have to, that's all.

LOLA. Well, if you think it's wrong . . .

DOC *(ready to dismiss it).* Never mind.

LOLA. I don't see any harm in it, Daddy.

DOC. Forget it.

LOLA *(goes to icebox).* Would you like some buttermilk?

DOC. Thanks. *(Marie finishes sketch)*

MARIE. O.K. That's all I can do for today.

TURK. Is there anything I can do for *you?*

MARIE. Yes—get your clothes on.

TURK. O.K., coach. *(Turk exits)*

LOLA. You know what Marie said, Doc? She said that the women pose naked, but the men don't.

DOC. Why, of course, honey.

LOLA. Why is that?

DOC *(stumped).* Well . . .

LOLA. If it's all right for a woman it oughta be for a man. But the man always keeps covered. That's what she said.

DOC. Well, that's the way it should be, honey. A man, after all, is a man, and he . . . well, he has to protect himself.

LOLA. And a woman doesn't?

DOC. It's different, honey.

LOLA. Is it? I've got a secret, Doc. Bruce is comin'.

DOC. Is that so?

LOLA *(after a glum silence).* You know Marie's boy friend from Cincinnati. I promised Marie a long time ago, when her fiancé came to town, dinner was on me. So I'm getting out the best china and cooking the best meal you ever sat down to.

DOC. When did she get the news?

LOLA. The telegram came this morning.

DOC. That's fine. That Bruce sounds to me like just the fellow for her. I think I'll go in and congratulate her.

LOLA *(nervous).* Not now, Doc.

DOC. Why not?

LOLA. Well, Turk's there. It might make him feel embarrassed.

DOC. Well, why doesn't Turk clear out now that Bruce is coming? What's he hanging around for? She's engaged to marry Bruce, isn't she? *(Turk enters from bedroom and goes to Marie, starting to make advances)*

LOLA. Marie's just doing a picture of him, Doc.

DOC. You always stick up for him. You encourage him.

LOLA. Shhh, Daddy. Don't get upset.

DOC *(very angrily)*. All right, but if anything happens to the girl I'll never forgive you. *(Doc goes upstairs. Turk then grabs Marie, kisses her passionately)*

CURTAIN

SCENE TWO

The same evening, after supper. Outside it is dark. There has been an almost miraculous transformation of the entire house. Lola, apparently, has been working hard and fast all day. The rooms are spotlessly clean and there are such additions as new lampshades, fresh curtains, etc. In the kitchen all the enamel surfaces glisten, and piles of junk that have lain around for months have been disposed of. Lola and Doc are in the kitchen, he washing up the dishes and she puttering around putting the finishing touches on her housecleaning.

LOLA *(at stove)*. There's still some beans left. Do you want them, Doc?

DOC. I had enough.

LOLA. I hope you got enough to eat tonight, Daddy. I been so busy cleaning I didn't have time to fix you much.

DOC. I wasn't very hungry.

LOLA *(at table, cleaning up)*. You know what? Mrs. Coffman said I could come over and pick all the lilacs I wanted for my centerpiece tomorrow. Isn't that nice? I don't think she poisoned Little Sheba, do you?

DOC. I never did think so, Baby. Where'd you get the new curtains?

LOLA. I went out and bought them this afternoon. Aren't they pretty? Be careful of the woodwork, it's been varnished.

DOC. How come, honey?

LOLA *(gets broom and dustpan from closet)*. Bruce is comin'. I figured I had to do my spring housecleaning some time.

DOC. You got all this done in one day? The house hasn't looked like this in years.

LOLA. I can be a good housekeeper when I want to be, can't I, Doc?

DOC *(holding dustpan for Lola)*. I never

had any complaints. Where's Marie now?

LOLA. I don't know, Doc. I haven't seen her since she left here this morning with Turk.

DOC *(with a look of disapproval)*. Marie's too nice to be wasting her time with him.

LOLA. Daddy, Marie can take care of herself. Don't worry. *(Returns broom to closet)*

DOC *(goes into living room)*. 'Bout time for Fibber McGee and Molly.

LOLA *(untying apron. Goes to closet and then back door)*. Daddy, I'm gonna run over to Mrs. Coffman's and see if she's got any silver polish. I'll be right back. *(Doc goes to radio. Lola exits) (At the radio Doc starts twisting the dial. He rejects one noisy program after another, then very unexpectedly he comes across a rendition of Shubert's famous "Ave Maria," sung in a high soprano voice. Probably he has encountered the piece before somewhere, but it is now making its first impression on him. Gradually he is transported into a world of ethereal beauty which he never knew existed. He listens intently. The music has expressed some ideal of beauty he never fully realized and he is even a little mystified. Then Lola comes in the back door, letting it slam, breaking the spell, and announcing in a loud, energetic voice:)* Isn't it funny? I'm not a bit tired tonight. You'd think after working so hard all day I'd be pooped.

DOC *(in the living room; he cringes)*. Baby, don't use that word.

LOLA *(to Doc on couch. Sets silver polish down and joins Doc)*. I'm sorry, Doc. I hear Marie and Turk say it all the time, and I thought it was kinda cute.

DOC. It . . . it sounds vulgar.

LOLA *(kisses Doc)*. I won't say it again, Daddy. Where's Fibber McGee?

DOC. Not quite time yet.

LOLA. Let's get some peppy music.

DOC *(tuning in a sentimental dance band)*. That what you want?

LOLA. That's O.K. *(Doc takes a pack of cards off radio and starts shuffling them, very deftly)* I love to watch you shuffle cards, Daddy. You use your hands so gracefully. *(She watches closely)* Do me one of your card tricks.

DOC. Baby, you've seen them all.

LOLA. But I never get tired of them.

DOC. O.K. Take a card. *(Lola does)* Keep it now. Don't tell me what it is.

LOLA. I won't.

DOC *(shuffling cards again)*. Now put it back in the deck. I won't look. *(He closes his eyes)*

LOLA *(with childish delight)*. All right.

DOC. Put it back.

LOLA. Uh-huh.

DOC. O.K. *(Shuffles cards again, cutting them, taking top half off, exposing Lola's card, to her astonishment)* That your card?

LOLA *(unbelievingly)*. Daddy, how did you do it?

DOC. Baby, I've pulled that trick on you dozens of times.

LOLA. But I never understand how you do it.

DOC. Very simple.

LOLA. Docky, show me how you do that.

DOC *(you can forgive him a harmless feeling of superiority)*. Try it for yourself.

LOLA. Doc, you're clever. I never could do it.

DOC. Nothing to it.

LOLA. There is *too*. Show me how you do it, Doc.

DOC. And give away all my secrets? It's a gift, honey. A magic gift.

LOLA. Can't you give it to me?

DOC *(picks up newspaper)*. A man has to keep some things to himself.

LOLA. It's not a gift at all, it's just some trick you *learned*.

DOC. O.K., Baby, any way you want to look at it.

LOLA. Let's have some music. How soon do you have to meet Ed Anderson? *(Doc turns on radio)*

DOC. I still got a little time. *(Pleased)*

LOLA. Marie's going to be awfully happy when she sees the house all fixed up. She can entertain Bruce here when he comes, and maybe we could have a little party here and you can do your card tricks.

DOC. O.K.

LOLA. I think a young girl should be able to bring her friends home.

DOC. Sure.

LOLA. We never liked to sit around the house 'cause the folks always stayed there with us. *(Rises—starts dancing alone)* Remember the dances we used to go to, Daddy?

DOC. Sure.

LOLA. We had awful good times—for a while, didn't we?

DOC. Yes, Baby.

LOLA. Remember the homecoming dance, when Charlie Kettlekamp and I won the Charleston contest?

DOC. Please, honey, I'm trying to read.

LOLA. And you got mad at him 'cause he thought he should take me home afterwards.

DOC. I did not.

LOLA. Yes, you did—Charlie was all right, Doc, really he was. You were just jealous.

DOC. I *wasn't* jealous.

LOLA *(she has become very coy and flirtatious now, an old dog playing old tricks)*. You got jealous every time we went out any place and I even looked at another boy. There was never anything between Charlie and me; there never was.

DOC. That was a long time ago . . .

LOLA. Lots of other boys called me up for dates . . . Sammy Knight . . . Hand Biderman . . . Dutch McCoy.

DOC. Sure, Baby. You were the "it" girl.

LOLA *(pleading for his attention now)*. But I saved all my dates for *you*, didn't I, Doc?

DOC *(trying to joke)*. As far as *I* know, Baby.

LOLA *(hurt)*. Daddy, I did. You *got* to believe that. I never took a date with any other boy but you.

DOC *(a little weary and impatient)*. That's all forgotten now. *(Turns off radio)*

LOLA. How can you talk that way, Doc? That was the happiest time of our lives. I'll never forget it.

DOC *(disapprovingly)*. Honey!

LOLA *(at the window)*. That was a nice spring. The trees were so heavy and green and the air smelled so sweet. Remember the walks we used to take, down to the old chapel, where it was so quiet and still? *(Sits on couch)*

DOC. In the spring a young man's fancy turns . . . pretty fancy.

LOLA *(in the same tone of reverie)*. I was pretty then, wasn't I, Doc? Remember the first time you kissed me? You were scared as a young girl, I believe, Doc; you trembled so. *(She is being very soft and delicate. Caught in the reverie, he chokes a little and cannot answer)* We'd been going together all year and you were always so shy. Then for the first time you grabbed me and kissed me. Tears came to your eyes, Doc, and you said you'd love me forever and ever, Remember? You said . . . if I didn't marry you, you wanted to die . . . I remember 'cause it scared me for anyone to say a thing like that.

DOC (*in a repressed tone*). Yes, Baby.

LOLA. And when the evening came on, we stretched out on the cool grass and you kissed me all night long.

DOC (*opens doors*). Baby, you've got to forget those things. That was twenty years ago.

LOLA. I'll soon be forty. Those years have just vanished—vanished into thin air.

DOC. Yes.

LOLA. Just disappeared—like Little Sheba. (*Pause*) Maybe you're sorry you married me now. You didn't know I was going to get old and fat and sloppy . . .

DOC. Oh, Baby!

LOLA. It's the truth. That's what I am. But I didn't know it, either. Are you sorry you married me, Doc?

DOC. Of course not.

LOLA. I mean, are you sorry you *had* to marry me?

DOC (*goes to porch*). We were never going to talk about that, Baby.

LOLA (*following Doc out*). You *were* the first one, Daddy, the *only* one. I'd just die if you didn't believe that.

DOC (*tenderly*). I know, Baby.

LOLA. You were so nice and so proper, Doc; I thought nothing we could do together could ever be wrong—or make us unhappy. Do you think we did wrong, Doc?

DOC (*consoling*). No, Baby, of course I don't.

LOLA. I don't think anyone knows about it except my folks, do you?

DOC. Of course not, Baby.

LOLA (*follows him in*). I wish the baby had lived, Doc. I don't think that woman knew her business, do you, Doc?

DOC. I guess not.

LOLA. If we'd gone to a doctor, she would have lived, don't you think?

DOC. Perhaps.

LOLA. A doctor wouldn't have known we'd just got married, would he? Why were we so afraid?

DOC (*sits on couch*). We were just kids. Kids don't know how to look after things.

LOLA (*sits on couch*). If we'd had the baby she'd be a young girl now; then maybe you'd have *saved* your money, Doc, and she could be going to college—like Marie.

DOC. Baby, what's done is done.

LOLA. It must make you feel bad at times to think you had to give up being a doctor and to think you don't have any money like you used to.

DOC. No . . . no, Baby. We should never feel bad about what's past. What's in the past can't be helped. You . . . you've got to forget it and live for the present. If you can't forget the past, you stay in it and never get out. I might be a big M.D. today, instead of a chiropractor; we might have had a family to raise and be with us now; I might still have a lot of money if I'd used my head and invested it carefully, instead of gettin' drunk every night. We might have a nice house, and comforts, and friends. But we don't have any of those things. So what! We gotta keep on living, don't we? I can't stop just 'cause I made a few mistakes. I gotta keep goin' . . . somehow.

LOLA. Sure, Daddy.

DOC (*sighs and wipes brow*). I . . . I wish you wouldn't ask me questions like that, Baby. Let's not talk about it any more. I gotta keep goin', and not let things upset me, or . . . or . . . *I* saw enough at the City Hospital to keep me sober for a long time.

LOLA. I'm sorry, Doc. I didn't mean to upset you.

DOC. I'm not upset.

LOLA. What time'll you be home tonight?

DOC. 'Bout eleven o'clock.

LOLA. I wish you didn't have to go tonight. I feel kinda lonesome.

DOC. Yah, so am I, Baby, but some time soon, we'll go *out* together. I kinda hate to go to those night clubs and places since I stopped drinking, but some night I'll take you out to dinner.

LOLA. Oh, will you, Daddy?

DOC. We'll get dressed up and go to the Windermere and have a fine dinner and dance between courses.

LOLA (*eagerly*). Let's do it, Daddy. I got a little money saved up. I got about forty dollars out in the kitchen. We can take that if you need it.

DOC. I'll have plenty of money the first of the month.

LOLA (*she has made a quick response to the change of mood, seeing a future evening of carefree fun*). What are we sitting around here so serious for? (*Turns to radio*) Let's have some music. (*Lola gets a lively foxtrot on the radio, dances with Doc. They begin dancing vigorously as though to dispense with the sadness of the preceding dialogue, but slowly it winds them and leaves Lola panting*) We oughta go dancing . . . all the time, Docky . . . It'd be good for us. Maybe if I danced more often, I'd lose . . . some of . . . this fat. I remember . . . I used to be able to dance like this . . . all night . . . and not even notice . . . it. (*Lola breaks into a Charleston routine as of yore*) Remember the Charleston, Daddy? (*Doc is clapping his hands in rhythm. Then Marie bursts in through the front door, the personification of the youth that Lola is trying to recapture*)

DOC. Hi, Marie.

MARIE. What are you trying to do, a jig, Mrs. Delaney? (*Marie doesn't intend her remark to be cruel, but it wounds Lola. Lola stops abruptly in her dancing, losing all the fun she has been able to create for herself. She feels she might cry; so to hide her feelings she hurries quietly out to kitchen, but Doc and Marie do not notice. Marie notices the change in atmosphere*) Hey, what's been happening around here?

DOC. Lola got to feeling industrious. You oughta see the kitchen.

MARIE (*running to kitchen, where she is too observant of the changes to notice Lola weeping in corner. Lola, of course, straightens up as soon as Marie enters*). What got into you, Mrs. Delaney? You've done wonders with the house. It looks marvelous.

LOLA (*quietly*). Thanks, Marie.

MARIE (*darting back into living room*). I can hardly believe I'm in the same place.

DOC. Think your boy friend'll like it? (*Meaning Bruce*)

MARIE (*thinking of Turk*). You know how men are. Turk never notices things like that. (*Starts into her room blowing*

a kiss to Doc on her way. Lola comes back in, dabbing at her eyes*)

DOC. Turk? (*Marie is gone; he turns to Lola*) What's the matter, honey?

LOLA. I don't know.

DOC. Feel bad about something.

LOLA. I didn't want her to see me dancing that way. Makes me feel sorta silly.

DOC. Why, you're a fine dancer.

LOLA. I feel kinda silly.

MARIE (*jumps back into the room with her telegram*). My telegram's here. When did it come?

LOLA. It came about an hour ago, honey. (*Lola looks nervously at Doc. Doc looks puzzled and a little sore*)

MARIE. Bruce is coming! "Arriving tomorrow 5:00 P.M. CST, Flight 22, Love, Bruce." When did the telegram come?

DOC (*looking hopelessly at Lola*). So it came an hour ago.

LOLA (*nervously*). Isn't it nice I got the house all cleaned? Marie, you bring Bruce to dinner with us tomorrow night. It'll be a sort of wedding present.

MARIE. That would be wonderful, Mrs. Delaney, but I don't want you to go to any trouble.

LOLA. No trouble at all. Now I insist. (*Front doorbell rings*) That must be Turk.

MARIE (*whisper*). Don't tell *him*. (*Goes to door. Lola scampers to kitchen*) Hi, Turk. Come on in.

TURK (*entering. Stalks her*). Hi. (*Looks around to see if anyone is present, then takes her in his arms and starts to kiss her*)

LOLA. I'm sorry, Doc. I'm sorry about the telegram.

DOC. Baby, people don't do things like that. Don't you understand? *Nice* people don't.

MARIE. Stop it!

TURK. What's the matter?

MARIE. They're in the kitchen. (*Turk sits with book*)

DOC. Why didn't you give it to her when it came?

LOLA. Turk was posing for Marie this morning and I couldn't give it to her while he was here. (*Turk listens at door*)

DOC. Well, it just isn't nice to open other people's mail. (*Turk goes to Marie's door*)

LOLA. I guess I'm not nice then. That what you mean?

MARIE. Turk, will you get away from that door?

DOC. No, Baby, but . . .

LOLA. I don't see any harm in it, Doc. I steamed it open and sealed it back. *(Turk at switch in living room)* She'll never know the difference. I don't see any harm in that, Doc.

DOC *(gives up)*. O.K., Baby, if you don't see any harm in it, I guess I can't explain. *(Starts getting ready to go)*

LOLA. I'm sorry, Doc. Honest, I'll never do it again. Will you forgive me?

DOC *(giving her a peck of a kiss)*. I forgive you.

MARIE *(comes back with book)*. Let's look like we're studying.

LOLA. What time'll you be home tonight?

TURK. Biology? Hot dog!

LOLA *(after Marie leaves her room)*. Now I feel better. Do you have to go now? *(Turk sits by Marie on the couch)*

DOC. Yah.

LOLA. Before you go, why don't you show your tricks to Marie?

DOC *(reluctantly)*. Not now.

LOLA. Oh, please do. They'd be crazy about them.

DOC *(with pride)*. O.K. *(Preens himself a little)* If you think they'd enjoy them . . . *(Lola, starting to living room, stops suddenly upon seeing Marie and Turk spooning behind a book. A broad, pleased smile breaks on her face and she stands silently watching. Doc is at sink)* Well . . . what's the matter, Baby?

LOLA *(in a soft voice)*. Oh . . . nothing . . . nothing . . . Doc.

DOC. Well, do you want me to show 'em my tricks or don't you?

LOLA *(coming back to center kitchen; in a secretive voice with a little giggle)*. I guess they wouldn't be interested now.

DOC *(with injured pride. A little sore)*. Oh, very well.

LOLA. Come and look, Daddy.

DOC *(shocked and angry)*. No!

LOLA. Just one little look. They're just kids, Daddy. It's sweet. *(Drags him by arm)*

DOC *(jerking loose)*. Stop it, Baby. I won't do it. It's not decent to snoop around spying on people like that. It's cheap and mischievous and mean.

LOLA *(this had never occurred to her)*. Is it?

DOC. Of course it is.

LOLA. I don't spy on Marie and Turk to be mischievous and mean.

DOC. Then why *do* you do it?

LOLA. You watch young people make love in the movies, don't you, Doc? There's nothing wrong with that. And I *know* Marie and I like her, and Turk's nice, too. They're both so young and pretty. Why shouldn't I watch them?

DOC. I give up.

LOLA. Well, why shouldn't I?

DOC. I don't know, Baby, but it's not nice. *(Turk kisses Marie's ear)*

LOLA *(plaintive)*. I think it's one of the nicest things I know.

MARIE. Let's go out on the porch. *(They steal out)*

DOC. It's not right for Marie to do that, particularly since Bruce is coming. We shouldn't allow it.

LOLA. Oh, they don't do any harm, Doc. I think it's all right. *(Turk and Marie go to porch)*

DOC. It's not all right. I don't know why you encourage that sort of thing.

LOLA. I don't encourage it.

DOC. You do, too. You like that fellow Turk. You said so. And I say he's no good. Marie's sweet and innocent; she doesn't understand guys like him. I think I oughta run him outa the house.

LOLA. Daddy, you wouldn't do that.

DOC *(very heated)*. Then you talk to her and tell her how we feel.

LOLA. Hush, Daddy. They'll hear you.

DOC. I don't care if they do hear me.

LOLA *(to Doc at stove)*. Don't get upset, Daddy. Bruce is coming and Turk won't be around any longer. I promise you.

DOC. All right. I better go.

LOLA. I'll go with you, Doc. Just let me run up and get a sweater. Now wait for me.

DOC. Hurry, Baby.

(Lola goes upstairs. Doc is at platform when he hears Turk laugh on the porch. Doc sees whiskey bottle. Reaches for it and hears Marie giggle. Turns away as Turk laughs again. Turns back to the bottle and hears Lola's voice from upstairs.)

LOLA. I'll be there in a minute, Doc. *(Enters downstairs)* I'm all ready. *(Doc turns out kitchen lights and they go into living room)* I'm walking Doc down to the bus. *(Doc sees Turk with Lola's picture. Takes it out of his hand, puts it on shelf as Lola leads him out. Doc is off-stage)* Then I'll go for a long walk in the moonlight. Have a good time. *(She exits)*

MARIE. 'Bye, Mrs. Delaney. *(Exits)*

TURK. He hates my guts. *(Goes to front door)*

MARIE. Oh, he does not. *(Follows Turk, blocks his exit in door)*

TURK. Yes, he does. If you ask me, he's jealous.

MARIE. Jealous?

TURK. I've always thought he had a crush on you.

MARIE. Now, Turk, don't be silly. Doc is nice to me. It's just in a few little things he does, like fixing my breakfast, but he's nice to everyone.

TURK. He ever make a pass?

MARIE. No. He'd never get fresh.

TURK. He'd better not.

MARIE. Turk, don't be ridiculous. Doc's such a nice, quiet man; if he gets any fun out of being nice to me, why not?

TURK. He's got a wife of his own, hasn't he? Why doesn't he make a few passes at her?

MARIE. Things like that are none of our business.

TURK. O.K. How about a snuggle, lovely?

MARIE *(a little prim and businesslike)*. No more for tonight, Turk.

TURK. Why's tonight different from any other night?

MARIE. I think we should make it a rule, every once in a while, just to sit and talk. *(Starts to sit on couch, but goes to chair)*

TURK *(restless, sits on couch)*. O.K. What'll we talk about?

MARIE. Well . . . there's lotsa things.

TURK. O.K. Start in.

MARIE. A person doesn't start a conversation that way.

TURK. Start it any way you want to.

MARIE. Two people should have something to talk about, like politics or psychology or religion.

TURK. How 'bout sex?

MARIE. Turk!

TURK *(chases her around couch)*. Have you read the Kinsey Report, Miss Buckholder?

MARIE. I should say not.

TURK. How old were you when you had your first affair, Miss Buckholder? And did you ever have relations with your grandfather?

MARIE. Turk, stop it.

TURK. You wanted to talk about something; I was only trying to please. Let's have a kiss.

MARIE. Not tonight.

TURK. Who you savin' it up for?

MARIE. Don't talk that way.

TURK *(gets up, yawns)*. Well, thanks, Miss Buckholder, for a nice evening. It's been a most enjoyable talk.

MARIE *(anxious)*. Turk, where are you going?

TURK. I guess I'm a man of action, Baby.

MARIE. Turk, don't go.

TURK. Why not? I'm not doing any good here.

MARIE. Don't go.

TURK *(returns and she touches him. They sit on couch)*. Now why didn't you think of this before? C'mon, let's get to work.

MARIE. Oh, Turk, this is all we ever do.

TURK. Are you complaining?

MARIE *(weakly)*. No.

TURK. Then what do you want to put on such a front for?

MARIE. It's not a front.

TURK. What else is it? *(Mimicking)* Oh, no, Turk. Not tonight, Turk. I want to talk about philosophy, Turk. *(Himself again)* When all the time you know that if I went outa here without givin' you a good lovin' up you'd be sore as hell . . . Wouldn't you?

MARIE *(she has to admit to herself it's true; she chuckles)*. Oh . . . Turk . . .

TURK. It's true, isn't it?

MARIE. Maybe.

TURK. How about tonight, lovely; going to be lonesome?

MARIE. Turk, you're in training.

TURK. What of it? I can throw the old javelin any old time, *any* old time. C'mon, Baby, we've got by with it before, haven't we?

MARIE. I'm not so sure.

TURK. What do you mean?

MARIE. Sometimes I think Mrs. Delaney knows.

TURK. Well, bring her along. I'll take care of her, too, if it'll keep her quiet.

MARIE *(a pretense of being shocked)*. Turk!

TURK. What makes you think so?

MARIE. Women just sense those things. She asks so many questions.

TURK. She ever *say* anything?

MARIE. No.

TURK. Now *you're* imagining things.

MARIE. Maybe.

TURK. Well, stop it.

MARIE. O.K.

TURK *(follows Marie)*. Honey, I know I talk awful rough around you at times; I never was a very gentlemanly bastard, but you really don't mind it . . . do you? *(She only smiles mischievously)* Anyway, you know I'm nuts about you.

MARIE *(smug)*. Are you?

(Now they engage in a little rough-house, he cuffing her like an affectionate bear, she responding with "Stop it," "Turk, that hurt," etc. And she slaps him playfully. Then they laugh together at their own pretense. Now Lola enters the back way very quietly, tiptoeing through the dark kitchen, standing by the doorway where she can peek at them. There is a quiet, satisfied smile on her face. She watches every move they make, alertly.)

TURK. Now, Miss Buckholder, what is your opinion of the psychodynamic pressure of living in the atomic age?

MARIE *(playfully)*. Turk, don't make fun of me.

TURK. Tonight?

MARIE *(her eyes dance as she puts him off just a little longer)*. Well.

TURK. Tonight will never come again. *(This is true. She smiles)* O.K.?

MARIE. Tonight will never come again. . . . *(They embrace and start to dance)* Let's go out somewhere first and have a few beers. We can't come back till they're asleep.

TURK. O.K.

(They dance slowly out the door. Then Lola moves quietly into the living room and out onto the porch. There she can be heard calling plaintively in a lost voice.)

LOLA. Little Sheba . . . Come back . . . Come back, Little Sheba. Come back.

CURTAIN

ACT TWO

SCENE ONE

The next morning. Lola and Doc are at breakfast again. Lola is rambling on while Doc sits meditatively, his head down, his face in his hands.

———

LOLA *(in a light, humorous way, as though the faults of youth were as blameless as the uncontrollable actions of a puppy. Chuckles)*. Then they danced for a while and went out together, arm in arm. . . .

DOC *(sitting at table, very nervous and tense)*. I don't wanna hear any more about it, Baby.

LOLA. What's the matter, Docky?

DOC. Nothing.

LOLA. You look like you didn't feel very good.

DOC. I didn't sleep well last night.

LOLA. You didn't take any of those sleeping pills, did you?

DOC. No.

LOLA. Well, don't. The doctors say they're terrible for you.

DOC. I'll feel better after a while.

LOLA. Of course you will.

DOC. What time did Marie come in last night?

LOLA. I don't know, Doc. I went to bed early and went right to sleep. Why?

DOC. Oh . . . nothing.

LOLA. You musta slept if you didn't hear her.

DOC. I heard her; it was after .midnight.

LOLA. Then what did you ask me for?

DOC. I wasn't sure it was her.

LOLA. What do you mean?

DOC. I thought I heard a man's voice.

LOLA. Turk probably brought her inside the door.

DOC *(troubled)*. I thought I heard someone laughing. A man's laugh . . . I guess I was just hearing things.

LOLA. Say your prayer?

DOC *(gets up)*. Yes.

LOLA. Kiss me 'bye. *(He leans over and kisses her, then puts on his coat and starts to leave)* Do you think you could get home a little early? I want you to help me entertain Bruce. Marie said he'd be here about 5:30. I'm going to have a lovely dinner: stuffed pork chops, twice-baked potatoes, and asparagus, and for dessert a big chocolate cake and maybe ice cream . . .

DOC. Sounds fine.

LOLA. So you get home and help me.

DOC. O.K.

(Doc leaves kitchen and goes into living room. Again on the chair is Marie's scarf. He picks it up as before and fondles it. Then there is the sound of Turk's laughter, soft and barely audible. It sounds like

the laugh of a sated Bacchus. Doc's body stiffens. It is a sickening fact he must face and it has been revealed to him in its ugliest light. The lyrical grace, the spiritual ideal of Ave Maria is shattered. He has been fighting the truth, maybe suspecting all along that he was deceiving himself. Now he looks as though he might vomit. All his blind confusion is inside him. With an immobile expression of blankness on his face, he stumbles into the table above the sofa.)

LOLA *(still in kitchen).* Haven't you gone yet, Docky?

DOC *(dazed).* No . . . no, Baby.

LOLA *(in doorway).* Anything the matter?

DOC. No . . . no, I'm all right now. *(Drops scarf, takes hat, exits. He has managed to sound perfectly natural. He braces himself and goes out. Lola stands a moment, looking after him with a little curiosity. Then Mrs. Coffman enters, sticks her head in back door.)*

MRS. COFFMAN. Anybody home?

LOLA *(on platform).* 'Morning, Mrs. Coffman.

MRS. COFFMAN *(inspecting the kitchen's new look).* So this is what you've been up to, Mrs. Delaney.

LOLA *(proud).* Yes, I been busy.

(Marie's door opens and closes. Marie sticks her head out of her bedroom to see if the coast is clear, then sticks her head back in again to whisper to Turk that he can leave without being observed.)

MRS. COFFMAN. Busy? Good Lord, I never seen such activity. What got into you, Lady?

LOLA. Company tonight. I thought I'd fix things up a little.

MRS. COFFMAN. You mean you done all this in one day?

LOLA *(with simple pride).* I said I been busy.

MRS. COFFMAN. Dear God, you done your spring housecleaning all in one day. *(Turk appears in living room)*

LOLA *(appreciating this).* I fixed up the living room a little, too.

MRS. COFFMAN. I must see it. *(Goes into living room. Turk overhears her and ducks back into Marie's room, shutting the door behind himself and Marie)* I declare! Overnight you turn the place into something really swanky.

LOLA. Yes, and I bought a few things, too.

MRS. COFFMAN. Neat as a pin, and so warm and cozy. I take my hat off to you, Mrs. Delaney. I didn't know you had it in you. All these years, now, I've been sayin' to myself, "That Mrs. Delaney is a good for nothing, sits around the house all day, and never so much as shakes a dust mop." I guess it just shows, we never really know what people are like.

LOLA. I still got some coffee.

MRS. COFFMAN. Not now, Mrs. Delaney. Seeing your house so clean makes me feel ashamed. I gotta get home and get to work. *(Goes to kitchen)*

LOLA *(follows).* I hafta get busy, too. I got to get out all the silver and china. I like to set the table early, so I can spend the rest of the day looking at it. *(Both laugh)*

MRS. COFFMAN. Good day, Mrs. Delaney. *(Exits)*

(Hearing the screen door slam, Marie guards the kitchen door and Turk slips out the front. But neither has counted on Doc's reappearance. After seeing that Turk is safe, Marie blows a good-bye kiss to him and joins Lola in the kitchen. But Doc is coming in the front door just as Turk starts to go out. There is a moment of blind embarrassment, during which Doc only looks stupefied and Turk, after mumbling an unintelligible apology, runs out. First Doc is mystified, trying to figure it all out. His face looks more and more troubled. Meanwhile, Marie and Lola are talking in the kitchen.)

MARIE. Boo! *(Sneaking up behind Lola at back porch)*

LOLA *(jumping around).* Heavens! You scared me, Marie. You up already?

MARIE. Yah.

LOLA. This is Saturday. You could sleep as late as you wanted.

MARIE *(pouring a cup of coffee).* I thought I'd get up early and help you.

LOLA. Honey, I'd sure appreciate it. You can put up the table in the living room, after you've had your breakfast. That's where we'll eat. Then you can help me set it. *(Doc closes door)*

MARIE. O.K.

LOLA. Want a sweet roll?

MARIE. I don't think so. Turk and I had so much beer last night. He got kinda tight.

LOLA. He shouldn't do that, Marie.

MARIE *(starts for living room)* Just keep the coffee hot for me. I'll want another cup in a minute. *(Stops on seeing Doc)* Why, Dr. Delaney! I thought you'd gone.

DOC *(trying to sustain his usual manner)*. Good morning, Marie. *(But not looking at her)*

MARIE *(she immediately wonders)*. Why . . . why . . . how long have you been here, Doc?

DOC. Just got here, just this minute.

LOLA *(comes in)*. That you, Daddy?

DOC. It's me.

LOLA. What are you doing back?

DOC. I . . . I just thought maybe I'd feel better . . . if I took a glass of soda water . . .

LOLA. I'm afraid you're not well, Daddy.

DOC. I'm all right. *(Starts for kitchen)*

LOLA *(helping Marie with table)*. The soda's on the drainboard. *(Doc goes to kitchen, fixes some soda, and stands a moment, just thinking. Then he sits sipping the soda, as though he were trying to make up his mind about something)* Marie, would you help me move the table? It'd be nice now if we had a dining room, wouldn't it? But if we had a dining room, I guess we wouldn't have you, Marie. It was my idea to turn the dining room into a bedroom and rent it. I thought of lots of things to do for extra money . . . a few years ago . . . when Doc was so . . . so sick. *(They set up table—Lola gets cloth from cabinet)*

MARIE. This is a lovely tablecloth.

LOLA. Irish linen. Doc's mother gave it to us when we got married. She gave us all our silver and china, too. The china's Havelin. I'm so proud of it. It's the most valuable possession we own. I just washed it. . . . Will you help me bring it in? *(Getting china from kitchen)* Doc was sorta Mama's boy. He was an only child and his mother thought the sun rose and set in him. Didn't she, Docky? She brought Doc up like a real gentleman.

MARIE. Where are the napkins?

LOLA. Oh, I forgot them. They're so nice I keep them in my bureau drawer with my handkerchiefs. Come upstairs and we'll get them.

(Lola and Marie go upstairs. Then Doc listens to be sure Lola and Marie are upstairs, looks cautiously at the whiskey bottle on pantry shelf but manages to resist several times. Finally he gives in to temptation, grabs bottle off shelf, then starts wondering how to get past Lola with it. Finally, it occurs to him to wrap it inside his trench coat which he gets from pantry and carries over his arm. Lola and Marie are heard upstairs. They return to the living room and continue setting table as Doc enters from kitchen on his way out.)

LOLA *(coming downstairs)*. Did you ever notice how nice he keeps his fingernails? Not many men think of things like that. And he used to take his mother to church every Sunday.

MARIE *(at table)*. Oh, Doc's a real gentleman.

LOLA. Treats women like they were all beautiful angels. We went together a whole year before he even kissed me. *(Doc comes through the living room with coat and bottle, going to front door)* On your way back to the office now, Docky?

DOC *(his back to them)*. Yes.

LOLA. Aren't you going to kiss me goodbye before you go, Daddy? *(She goes to him and kisses him. Marie catches Doc's eye and smiles. Then she exits to her room, leaving door open)* Get home early as you can. I'll need you. We gotta give Bruce a royal welcome.

DOC. Yes, Baby.

LOLA. Feeling all right?

DOC. Yes.

LOLA *(in doorway, Doc is on porch)*. Take care of yourself.

DOC *(in a toneless voice)*. Good-bye. *(He goes)*

LOLA *(coming back to table with pleased expression, which changes to a puzzled look, calls to Marie)*. Now that's funny. Why did Doc take his raincoat? It's a beautiful day. There isn't a cloud in sight.

CURTAIN

SCENE TWO

It is now 5:30. The scene is the same as the preceding except that more finishing touches have been added and the two women, still primping the table, lighting the tapers, are dressed in their best. Lola is arranging the centerpiece.

LOLA *(above table, fixing flowers)*. I just love lilacs, don't you, Marie? *(Takes one and studies it)* Mrs. Coffman was nice;

she let me have all I wanted. *(Looks at it very closely)* Aren't they pretty? And they smell so sweet. I think they're the nicest flower there is.

MARIE. They don't last long.

LOLA *(respectfully)*. No. Just a few days. Mrs. Coffman's started blooming just day before yesterday.

MARIE. By the first of the week they'll all be gone.

LOLA. Vanish . . . they'll vanish into thin air. *(Gayer now)* Here, honey, we have them to spare *now*. Put this in your hair. There. *(Marie does)* Mrs. Coffman's been so nice lately. I didn't use to like her. Now where could Doc be? He promised he'd get here early. He didn't even come home for lunch.

MARIE *(gets two chairs from bedroom)*. Mrs. Delaney, you're a peach to go to all this trouble.

LOLA *(gets salt and pepper)*. Shoot, I'm gettin' more fun out of it than you are. Do you think Bruce is going to like us?

MARIE. If he doesn't, I'll never speak to him again.

LOLA *(eagerly)*. I'm just dying to meet him. But I feel sorta bad I never got to do anything nice for Turk.

MARIE *(carefully prying)*. Did . . . Doc ever say anything to you about Turk . . . and me?

LOLA. About Turk and you? No, honey. Why?

MARIE. I just wondered.

LOLA. What if Bruce finds out that you've been going with someone else?

MARIE. Bruce and I had a very business-like understanding before I left for school that we weren't going to sit around lonely just because we were separated.

LOLA. Aren't you being kind of mean to Turk?

MARIE. I don't think so.

LOLA. How's he going to feel when Bruce comes?

MARIE. He may be sore for a little while, but he'll get over it.

LOLA. Won't he feel bad?

MARIE. He's had his eye on a pretty little Spanish girl in his history class for a long time. I like Turk, but he's not the marrying kind.

LOLA. No! Really? *(Lola, with a look of sad wonder on her face, sits on arm of couch. It's been a serious disillusionment)*

MARIE. What's the matter?

LOLA. I . . . I just felt kinda tired. *(Sharp buzzing of doorbell. Marie runs to answer it)*

MARIE. That must be Bruce. *(She skips to the mirror again, then to door)* Bruce!

BRUCE. How are you, sweetheart?

MARIE. Wonderful.

BRUCE. Did you get my wire?

MARIE. Sure.

BRUCE. You're looking swell.

MARIE. Thanks. What took you so long to get here?

BRUCE. Well, honey, I had to go to my hotel and take a bath.

MARIE. Bruce, this is Mrs. Delaney.

BRUCE *(now he gets the cozy quality out of his voice)*. How do you do, ma'am?

LOLA. How d'ya do?

BRUCE. Marie has said some very nice things about you in her letters.

MARIE. Mrs. Delaney has fixed the grandest dinner for us.

BRUCE. Now that was to be my treat. I have a big expense account now, honey. I thought we could all go down to the hotel and have dinner there, and celebrate first with a few cocktails.

LOLA. Oh, we can have cocktails, too. Excuse me, just a minute. *(She hurries to the kitchen and starts looking for the whiskey. Bruce kisses Marie)*

MARIE *(whispers)*. Now, Bruce, she's been working on this dinner all day. She even cleaned the house for you.

BRUCE *(with a surveying look)*. Did she?

MARIE. And Doc's joining us. You'll like Doc.

BRUCE. Honey, are we going to have to stay here the whole evening?

MARIE. We can't just eat and run. We'll get away as soon as we can.

BRUCE. I hope so. I got the raise, sweetheart. They're giving me new territory. *(Lola is frantic in the kitchen, having found the bottle missing. She hurries back into the living room)*

LOLA. You kids are going to have to entertain yourselves awhile 'cause I'm going to be busy in the kitchen. Why don't you turn on the radio, Marie? Get some dance music. I'll shut the door so . . . so I won't disturb you. *(Lola does so, then goes to the telephone)*

MARIE. Come and see my room, Bruce. I've fixed it up just darling. And I've got your picture in the prettiest frame right on my dresser. *(They exit and their voices are heard from the bedroom while Lola is phoning)*

LOLA *(at the phone)*. This is Mrs. Delaney. Is . . . Doc there? Well, then, is Ed Anderson there? Well, would you give me Ed Anderson's telephone number? You see, he sponsored Doc into the club and helped him . . . you know . . . and . . . and I was a little worried tonight. . . . Oh, thanks. Yes, I've got it. *(She writes down number)* Could you have Ed Anderson call me if he comes in? Thank you. *(She hangs up. On her face is a dismal expression of fear, anxiety and doubt. She searches flour bin, icebox, closet. Then she goes into the living room, calling to Marie and Bruce as she comes)* I . . . I guess we'll go ahead without Doc, Marie.

MARIE *(enters from her room)*. What's the matter with Doc, Mrs. Delaney?

LOLA. Well . . . he got held up at the office . . . just one of those things, you know. It's too bad. It would have to happen when I needed him most.

MARIE. Sure you don't need any help?

LOLA. Huh? Oh, no. I'll make out. Everything's ready. I tell you what I'm going to do. There's a crowd, so I'm going to be the butler and serve the dinner to you two young lovebirds *(The telephone rings)* Pardon me . . . pardon me for just a minute. *(She rushes to phone, closing the door behind her)* Hello? Ed? Have you seen Doc? He went out this morning and hasn't come back. We're having company for dinner and he was supposed to be home early. . . . That's not all. This time we've had a quart of whiskey in the kitchen and Doc's never gone near it. I went to get it tonight. I was going to serve some cocktails. It was *gone.* Yes, I saw it there yesterday. No, I don't think so. . . . He said this morning he had an upset stomach but . . . Oh, would you? . . . Thank you, Mr. Anderson. Thank you a million times. And you let me know when you find out anything. Yes, I'll be here . . . yes. *(Hangs up and crosses back to living room)* Well, I guess we're all ready.

BRUCE. Aren't you going to look at your present?

MARIE. Oh, sure, let's get some scissors. *(Their voices continue in bedroom)*

MARIE *(enters with Bruce)*. Mrs. Delaney, we think you should eat with us.

LOLA. Oh, no, honey, I'm not very hun-gry. Besides, this is the first time you've been together in months and I think you should be alone. Marie, why don't you light the candles? Then we'll have just the right atmosphere. *(She goes into kitchen, gets tomato-juice glasses from icebox while Bruce lights the candles)*

BRUCE. Do we have to eat by candle-light? I won't be able to see. *(Lola returns)*

LOLA. Now, Bruce, you sit here. *(He and Marie sit)* Isn't that going to be cozy? Dinner for two. Sorry we won't have time for cocktails. Let's have a little music. *(She turns on the radio and a Viennese waltz swells up as the curtain falls with Lola looking at the young people eating.)*

CURTAIN

SCENE THREE

Funereal atmosphere. It is about 5:30 the next morning. The sky is just beginning to get light outside, while inside the room the shadows still cling heavily to the corners. The remains of last night's dinner clutter the table in the living room. The candles have guttered down to stubs amid the dirty dinner plates, and the lilacs in the centerpiece have wilted. Lola is sprawled on the davenport, sleeping. Slowly she awakens and regards the morning light. She gets up and looks about strangely, beginning to show despair for the situation she is in. She wears the same spiffy dress she had on the night before but it is wrinkled now, and her marcelled coiffure is awry. One silk stocking has twisted loose and falls around her ankle. When she is sufficiently awake to realize her situation, she rushes to the telephone and dials a number.

———

LOLA *(at telephone. She sounds frantic)*. Mr. Anderson? Mr. Anderson, this is Mrs. Delaney again. I'm sorry to call you so early, but I just *had* to. . . . Did you find Doc? . . . No, he's not home yet. I don't suppose he'll come home till he's drunk all he can hold and wants to sleep. . . . I don't know what else to think, Mr. Anderson. I'm scared, Mr. Anderson. I'm awful scared. Will you come right over? . . . Thanks, Mr. Anderson. *(She hangs up and goes to kitchen to make coffee. She finds some left from the night before, so turns on the fire to warm it up. She wanders around vaguely, trying to get her thoughts in order, jumping at every sound. Pours herself a cup of coffee, then takes it to living room, sits and sips it. Very quietly Doc enters through the back way into the kitchen. He carries a big bottle of whiskey which he carefully places back in the pantry, not making a sound, hangs up overcoat, then puts suitcoat on back of chair. Starts to go upstairs. But Lola speaks)* Doc? That you, Doc? *(Then Doc quietly walks in from kitchen. He is staggering drunk, but he is managing for a few minutes to appear as though he were perfectly sober and nothing had happened. His steps, however, are not too sure and his eyes are like blurred ink spots. Lola is too frightened to talk. Her mouth is gaping and she is breathless with fear)*

DOC. Good morning, honey.

LOLA. Doc! You all right?

DOC. The morning paper here? I wanta see the morning paper.

LOLA. Doc, we don't get a morning paper. *You* know that.

DOC. Oh, then I suppose I'm drunk or something. That what you're trying to say?

LOLA. No, Doc . . .

DOC. Then give me the morning paper.

LOLA *(scampering to get last night's paper from console table)*. Sure, Doc. Here it is. Now you just sit there and be quiet.

DOC *(resistance rising)*. Why shouldn't I be quiet?

LOLA. Nothin', Doc . . .

DOC *(has trouble unfolding paper. He places it before his face in order not to be seen. But he is too blind even to see)*. Nothing, Doc. *(Mockingly)*

LOLA *(cautiously, after a few minutes' silence)*. Doc, are you all right?

DOC. Of course, I'm all right. Why shouldn't I be all right?

LOLA. Where you been?

DOC. What's it your business where I been? I been to London to see the Queen. What do you think of that? *(Apparently she doesn't know what to think of it)* Just let me alone. That's all I ask. I'm all right.

LOLA *(whimpering)*. Doc, what made you do it? You said you'd be home last night . . . 'cause we were having company. Bruce was here and I had a big dinner

fixed . . . and you never came. What was the matter, Doc?

DOC *(mockingly)*. We had a big dinner for *Bruce.*

LOLA. Doc, it was for you, too.

DOC. Well . . . I don't want it.

LOLA. Don't get mad, Doc.

DOC *(threateningly)*. Where's Marie?

LOLA. I don't know, Doc. She didn't come in last night. She was out with Bruce.

DOC *(back to audience)*. I suppose you tucked them in bed together and peeked through the keyhole and applauded.

LOLA *(sickened)*. Doc, don't talk that way. Bruce is a nice boy. They're gonna get married.

DOC. He probably *has* to marry her, the poor bastard. Just 'cause she's pretty and he got amorous one day . . . Just like I had to marry *you.*

LOLA. Oh, Doc!

DOC. You and Marie are both a couple of sluts.

LOLA. Doc, please don't talk like that.

DOC. What are you good for? You can't even get up in the morning and cook my breakfast.

LOLA *(mumbling)*. I will, Doc. I will after this.

DOC. You won't even sweep the floors, till some bozo comes along to make love to Marie, and then you fix things up like Buckingham Palace or a Chinese whorehouse with perfume on the lampbulbs, and flowers, and the gold-trimmed china *my mother* gave us. We're not going to use these any more. My mother didn't buy those dishes for whores to eat off of. *(He jerks the cloth off the table, sending the dishes rattling to the floor)*

LOLA. Doc! Look what you done.

DOC. Look what I *did,* not done. I'm going to get me a drink. *(Goes to kitchen)*

LOLA *(follows to platform)*. Oh, no, Doc! You know what it does to you!

DOC. You're damn right I know what it does to me. It makes me willing to come home here and look at you, you two-ton old heifer! *(Takes a long swallow)* There! And pretty soon I'm going to have another, then another.

LOLA *(with dread)*. Oh, Doc! *(Lola takes phone. Doc sees this, rushes for the butcher-knife from kitchen-cabinet drawer. Not finding it, he gets a hatchet from the back porch)* Mr. Anderson? Come quick,

Mr. Anderson. He's back. He's *back!* He's got a hatchet!

DOC. God damn you! Get away from that telephone. (*He chases her into living room where she gets the couch between them*) That's right, phone! Tell the world I'm drunk. Tell the whole damn world. Scream your head off, you fat slut. Holler till all the neighbors think I'm beatin' hell outuv you. Where's Bruce now—under Marie's bed? You got all fresh and pretty for him, didn't you? Combed your hair for once—you even washed the back of your neck and put on a girdle. You were willing to harness all that fat into one bundle.

LOLA (*about to faint under the weight of the crushing accusations*). Doc, don't say any more . . . I'd rather you hit me with an axe, Doc. . . Honest I would. But I can't stand to hear you talk like that.

DOC. I oughta hack off all that fat, and then wait for Marie and chop off those pretty ankles she's always dancing around on . . . then start lookin' for Turk and fix him too.

LOLA. Daddy, you're talking crazy!

DOC. I'm making sense for the first time in my life. You didn't know I knew about it, did you? But I saw him coming outa there, I saw him. You knew about it all the time and thought you were hidin' something . . .

LOLA. Daddy, I didn't know anything about it at all. Honest, Daddy.

DOC. Then *you're* the one that's crazy, if you think I didn't know. You were running a regular house, weren't you? It's probably been going on for years, ever since we were married. (*He lunges for her. She breaks for kitchen. They struggle in front of sink*)

LOLA. Doc, it's not so; it's not so. You gotta believe me, Doc.

DOC. You're lyin'. But none a that's gonna happen any more. I'm gonna fix you now, once and for all. . . .

LOLA. Doc . . . don't do that to me. (*Lola, in a frenzy of fear, clutches him around the neck holding arm with axe by his side*) Remember, Doc. It's *me*, Lola! You said I was the prettiest girl you ever saw. Remember, Doc! It's me! Lola!

DOC (*the memory has overpowered him. He collapses, slowly mumbling*). Lola . . . my pretty Lola. (*He passes out on the floor. Lola stands now, as though in a*

trance. *Quietly Mrs. Coffman comes creeping in through the back way*)

MRS. COFFMAN (*calling softly*). Mrs. Delaney! (*Lola doesn't even hear. Mrs. Coffman comes in*) Mrs. Delaney! Here you are, Lady. I heard screaming and I was frightened for you.

LOLA. I . . . I'll be all right . . . some men are comin' pretty soon; everything'll be all right.

MRS. COFFMAN. I'll stay until they get here.

LOLA (*feeling a sudden need*). Would you . . . would you *please*, Mrs. Coffman? (*Breaks into sobs*)

MRS. COFFMAN. Of course, Lady. (*Regarding Doc*) The doctor got "sick" again?

LOLA (*mumbling*). Some men . . . 'll be here pretty soon . . .

MRS. COFFMAN. I'll try to straighten things up before they get here. . . .
(*She rights chair, hangs up telephone and picks up the axe, which she is holding when Ed Anderson and Elmo Huston enter unannounced. They are experienced AA's. Neatly dressed businessmen approaching middle-age.*)

ED. Pardon us for walking right in, Mrs. Delaney, but I didn't want to waste a second. (*Kneels by Doc*)

LOLA (*weakly*). It's all right. . . .
(*Both men observe Doc on the floor, and their expressions hold understanding mixed with a feeling of irony. There is even a slight smile of irony on Ed's face. They have developed the surgeon's objectivity.*)

ED. Where is the hatchet? (*To Elmo as though appraising Doc's condition*) What do you think, Elmo?

ELMO. We can't leave him here if he's gonna play around with hatchets.

ED. Give me a hand, Elmo. We'll get him to sit up and then try to talk some sense into him. (*They struggle with the lumpy body, Doc grunting his resistance*) Come on, Doc, old boy. It's Ed and Elmo. We're going to take care of you. (*They seat him at table*)

DOC (*through a thick fog*). Lemme alone.

ED. Wake up. We're taking you away from here.

DOC. Lemme 'lone, God damn it. (*Falls forward, head on table*)

ELMO *(to Mrs. Coffman)*. Is there any coffee?

MRS. COFFMAN. I think so, I'll see. *(Goes to stove with cup from drainboard. Lights fire under coffee and waits for it to get heated)*

ED. He's way beyond coffee.

ELMO. It'll help some. Get something hot into his stomach.

ED. If we could get him to eat. How 'bout some hot food, Doc? *(Doc gestures and they don't push the matter)*

ELMO. City Hospital, Ed?

ED. I guess that's what it will have to be.

LOLA. Where you going to take him? *(Elmo goes to phone; speaks quietly to City Hospital)*

ED. Don't know; wanta talk to him first.

MRS. COFFMAN *(coming in with the coffee)*. Here's the coffee.

ED *(taking cup)*. Hold him, Elmo, while I make him swallow this.

ELMO. Come on, Doc, drink your coffee. *(Doc only blubbers)*

DOC *(after the coffee is down)*. Uh . . . what . . . what's goin' on here?

ED. It's me, Doc. Your old friend Ed. I got Elmo with me.

DOC *(twisting his face painfully)*. Get out, both of you. Lemme 'lone.

ED *(with certainty)*. We're takin' you with us, Doc.

DOC. Hell you are. I'm all right. I just had a little slip. We all have slips. . . .

ED. Sometimes, Doc, but we gotta get over 'em.

DOC. I'll be O.K. Just gimme a day to sober up. I'll be as good as new.

ED. Remember the last time, Doc? You said you'd be all right in the morning and we found you with a broken collar bone. Come on.

DOC. Boys, I'll be all right. Now lemme alone.

ED. How much has he had, Mrs. Delaney?

LOLA. I don't know. He had a quart when he left here yesterday and he didn't get home till now.

ED. He's probably been through a *couple* of quarts. He's been dry for a long time. It's going to hit him pretty hard. Yah, he'll be a pretty sick man for a few days. *(Louder to Doc, as though he were talking to a deaf man)* Wanta go to the City Hospital, Doc?

DOC *(this has a sobering effect on him.*

He looks about him furtively for possible escape). No . . . no, boys. Don't take me there. That's a torture chamber. No, Ed. You wouldn't do that to me.

ED. They'll sober you up.

DOC. Ed, I been there; I've seen the place. That's where they take the crazy people. You can't do that to me, Ed.

ED. Well, *you're* crazy, aren't you? Goin' after your wife with a hatchet.

(They lift Doc to his feet. Doc looks with dismal pleading in his eyes at Lola, who has her face in her hands.)

DOC *(so plaintive, a sob in his voice)*. Honey! Honey! *(Lola can't look at him. Now Doc tries to make a getaway, bolting blindly into the living room before the two men catch him and hold him in front of living room table)* Honey, don't let 'em take me there. They'll believe *you*. Tell 'em you won't *let* me take a drink.

LOLA. Isn't there any place else you could take him?

ED. Private sanitariums cost a lotta dough.

LOLA. I got forty dollars in the kitchen.

ED. That won't be near enough.

DOC. I'll be at the meeting tomorrow night sober as you are now.

ED *(to Lola)*. All the king's horses couldn't keep him from takin' another drink now, Mrs. Delaney. He got himself into this; he's gotta sweat it out.

DOC. I won't go to the City Hospital. That's where they take the crazy people. *(Stumbles into chair)*

ED *(using all his patience now)*. Look, Doc. Elmo and I are your friends. You know that. Now if you don't come along peacefully, we're going to call the cops and you'll have to wear off this jag in the cooler. How'd you like that? *(Doc is as though stunned)* The important thing is for you to get sober.

DOC. I don't wanta go.

ED. The City Hospital or the City Jail. Take your choice. We're not going to leave you here. Come on, Elmo. *(They grab hold of him)*

DOC *(has collected himself and now given in)*. O.K., boys. Gimme another drink and I'll go.

LOLA. Oh, no, Doc.

ED. Might as well humor him, ma'am. Another few drinks couldn't make much difference now. *(Mrs. Coffman runs for bottle and glass in pantry and comes right*

back with them. She hands them to Lola)
O.K., Doc, we're goin' to give you a
drink. Take a good one; it's gonna be
your last for a long, long time to come.
*(Ed takes the bottle, removes the cork
and gives Doc a glass of whiskey. Doc
takes his fill, straight, coming up once or
twice for air. Then Ed takes the bottle
from him and hands it to Lola. To Lola)*
That'll keep him three or four days, Mrs.
Delaney; then he'll be home again, good
as new. *(Modestly)* I . . . I don't want to
pry into personal affairs, ma'am . . . but
he'll need you then, pretty bad . . . Come
on, Doc. Let's go.
*(Ed has a hold of Doc's coat sleeve trying
to maneuver him. A faraway look is in
Doc's eyes, a dazed look containing panic
and fear. He gets to his feet.)*
DOC *(struggling to sound reasonable).*
Just a minute, boys . . .
ED. What's the matter?
DOC. I . . . I wanta glass of water.
ED. You'll get a glass of water later.
Come on.
DOC *(beginning to twist a little in Ed's
grasp).* . . . a glass of water . . . that's all
. . . *(One furious, quick twist of his body
and he eludes Ed)*
ED. Quick, Elmo.
*(Elmo acts fast and they get Doc before
he gets away. Then Doc struggles with all
his might, kicking and screaming like a
pampered child. Ed and Elmo holding him
tightly to usher him out.)*
DOC *(as he is led out).* Don't let 'em
take me there. Don't take me there. Stop
them, somebody. Stop them. That's where
they take the crazy people. Oh, God, stop
them, somebody. Stop them.
*(Lola looks on blankly while Ed and Elmo
depart with Doc. Now there are several
moments of deep silence.)*
MRS. COFFMAN *(clears up. Very softly).*
Is there anything more I can do for you
now, Mrs. Delaney?
LOLA. I guess not.
MRS. COFFMAN *(puts a hand on Lola's
shoulder).* Get busy, Lady. Get busy and
forget it.
LOLA. Yes . . . I'll get busy right away.
Thanks, Mrs. Coffman.
MRS. COFFMAN. I better go. I've got to
make breakfast for the children. If you
want me for anything, let me know.
LOLA. Yes . . . yes . . . good-bye, Mrs.
Coffman. *(Mrs. Coffman exits. Lola is too
exhausted to move from the big chair. At
first she can't even cry; then the tears
come slowly, softly. In a few moments
Bruce and Marie enter, bright and merry.
Lola turns her head slightly to regard
them as creatures from another planet)*
MARIE *(springing into room. Bruce fol-
lows).* Congratulate me, Mrs. Delaney.
LOLA. Huh?
MARIE. We're going to be married.
LOLA. Married? *(It barely registers)*
MARIE *(showing ring).* Here it is. My
engagement ring. *(Marie and Bruce are
too engrossed in their own happiness to
notice Lola's stupor)*
LOLA. That's lovely . . . lovely.
MARIE. We've had the most wonderful
time. We danced all night and then drove
out to the lake and saw the sun rise.
LOLA. That's nice.
MARIE. We've made all our plans. I'm
quitting school and flying back to Cincinnati with Bruce this afternoon. His mother
has invited me to visit them before I go
home. Isn't that wonderful?
LOLA. Yes . . . yes, indeed.
MARIE. Going to miss me?
LOLA. Yes, of course, Marie. We'll miss
you very much . . . uh . . . congratulations.
MARIE. Thanks, Mrs. Delaney. *(Goes to
bedroom door)* Come on, Bruce, help me
get my stuff. *(To Lola)* Mrs. Delaney,
would you throw everything into a big
box and send it to me at home? We
haven't had breakfast yet. We're going
down to the hotel and celebrate.
BRUCE. I'm sorry we're in such a hurry,
but we've got a taxi waiting. *(They go
into room)*
LOLA *(goes to telephone, dials).* Long-
distance? I want to talk to Green Valley
223. Yes. This is Delmar 1887. *(She hangs
up. Marie comes from bedroom, followed
by Bruce, who carries suitcase)*
MARIE. Mrs. Delaney, I sure hate to say
good-bye to you. You've been so wonderful to me. But Bruce says I can come and
visit you once in a while, didn't you,
Bruce?
BRUCE. Sure thing.
LOLA. You're going?
MARIE. We're going downtown and have
our breakfast, then do a little shopping
and catch our plane. And thanks for everything, Mrs. Delaney.

BRUCE. It was very nice of you to have us to dinner.

LOLA. Dinner? Oh, don't mention it.

MARIE *(to Lola)*. There isn't much time for good-bye now, but I just want you to know Bruce and I wish you the best of everything. You and Doc both. Tell Doc good-bye for me, will you, and remember I think you're both a coupla peaches.

BRUCE. Hurry, honey.

MARIE. 'Bye, Mrs. Delaney! *(She goes out)*

BRUCE. 'Bye, Mrs. Delaney. Thanks for being nice to my girl. *(He goes out and off porch with Marie)*

LOLA *(waves. The phone rings. She goes to it quickly)*. Hello. Hello, Mom. It's Lola, Mom. How are you? Mom, Doc's sick again. Do you think Dad would let me come home for a while? I'm awfully unhappy, Mom. Do you think . . . just till I made up my mind? . . . All right. No, I guess it wouldn't do any good for you to come here . . . I . . . I'll let you know what I decide to do. That's all, Mom. Thanks. Tell Daddy hello. *(She hangs up)*

CURTAIN

SCENE FOUR

It is morning, a week later. The house is neat again. Lola is dusting in the living room as Mrs. Coffman enters.

————

MRS. COFFMAN. Mrs. Delaney! Good morning, Mrs. Delaney.

LOLA. Come in, Mrs. Coffman.

MRS. COFFMAN *(coming in)*. It's a fine day for the games. I've got a box lunch ready, and I'm taking all the kids to the Stadium. My boy's got a ticket for you, too. You better get dressed and come with us.

LOLA. Thanks, Mrs. Coffman, but I've got work to do.

MRS. COFFMAN. But it's a big day. The Spring Relays . . . All the athletes from the colleges are supposed to be there.

LOLA. Oh, yes. You know that boy, Turk, who used to come here to see Marie —he's one of the big stars.

MRS. COFFMAN. Is that so? Come on . . . do. We've got a ticket for you. . . .

LOLA. Oh, no, I have to stay here and clean up the house. Doc may be coming home today. I talked to him on the phone. He wasn't sure what time they'd let him out, but I wanta have the place all nice for him.

MRS. COFFMAN. Well, I'll tell you all about it when I come home. Everybody and his brother will be there.

LOLA. Have a good time.

MRS. COFFMAN. 'Bye, Mrs. Delaney.

LOLA. 'Bye.

(Mrs. Coffman leaves, and Lola goes into kitchen. The mailman comes onto porch and leaves a letter, but Lola doesn't even know he's there. Then the milkman knocks on the kitchen door.)

LOLA. Come in.

MILKMAN *(entering with armful of bottles, etc.)*. I see you checked the list, lady. You've got a lot of extras.

LOLA. Yah—I think my husband's coming home.

MILKMAN *(he puts the supplies on table, then pulls out magazine)*. Remember, I told you my picture was going to appear in *Strength and Health*. *(Showing her magazine)* Well, see that pile of muscles? That's me.

LOLA. My goodness. You got your picture in a magazine.

MILKMAN. Yes, ma'am. See what it says about my chest development? For the greatest self-improvement in a three months' period.

LOLA. Goodness sakes. You'll be famous, won't you?

MILKMAN. If I keep busy on these barbells. I'm working now for "muscular separation."

LOLA. That's nice.

MILKMAN *(cheerily)*. Well, good day, ma'am.

LOLA. You forgot your magazine.

MILKMAN. That's for you. *(Exits. Lola puts away the supplies in the icebox. Then Doc comes in the front door, carrying the little suitcase she previously packed for him. His quiet manner and his serious demeanor are the same as before. Lola is shocked by his sudden appearance. She jumps and can't help showing her fright)*

LOLA. Docky! *(Without thinking she assumes an attitude of fear. Doc observes this and it obviously pains him)*

DOC. Good morning, honey. *(Pause)*

LOLA *(on platform)*. Are . . . are you all right, Doc?

DOC. Yes, I'm all right. *(An awkward*

pause. Then Doc tries to reassure her)
Honest, I'm all right, honey. Please don't
stand there like that . . . like I was gonna
. . . gonna . . .

LOLA *(tries to relax)*. I'm sorry, Doc.

DOC. How you been?

LOLA. Oh, I been all right, Doc. Fine.

DOC. Any news?

LOLA. I told you about Marie—over the
phone.

DOC. Yah.

LOLA. He was a very nice boy, Doc.
Very nice.

DOC. That's good. I hope they'll be
happy.

LOLA *(trying to sound bright)*. She said
. . . maybe she'd come back and visit us
some time. That's what she *said*.

DOC *(pause)*. It . . . it's good to be home.

LOLA. Is it, Daddy?

DOC. Yah. *(Beginning to choke up, just
a little)*

LOLA. Did everything go all right . . . I
mean . . . did they treat you well and . . .

DOC *(now loses control of his feelings.
Tears in his eyes, he all but lunges at her,
gripping her arms, drilling his head into
her bosom)*. Honey, don't ever leave me.
Please don't ever leave me. If you do,
they'd have to keep me down at that place
all the time. I don't know what I said to
you or what I did, I can't remember hardly anything. But please forgive me . . .
please . . . please . . . And I'll try to make
everything up.

LOLA *(there is surprise on her face and
new contentment. She becomes almost
angelic in demeanor. Tenderly she places
a soft hand on his head)*. Daddy! Why, of
course I'll never leave you. *(A smile of
satisfaction)* You're all I've got. You're all
I ever had. *(Very tenderly he kisses her)*

DOC *(collecting himself now. Lola sits
beside Doc)*. I . . . I feel better . . . already.

LOLA *(almost gay)*. So do I. Have you
had your breakfast?

DOC. No. The food there was terrible.
When they told me I could go this morning, I decided to wait and fix myself
breakfast here.

LOLA *(happily)*. Come on out in the
kitchen and I'll get you a nice, big breakfast. I'll scramble some eggs and . . .
You see I've got the place all cleaned up
just the way you like it. *(Doc goes to
kitchen)* Now you sit down here and I'll

get your fruit juice. *(He sits and she gets
fruit juice from refrigerator)* I've got
bacon this morning, too. My, it's expensive now. And I'll light the oven and
make you some toast, and here's some
orange marmalade, and . . .

DOC *(with a new feeling of control)*.
Fruit juice. I'll need lots of fruit juice for
a while. The doctor said it would restore
the vitamins. You see, that damn whiskey
kills all the vitamins in your system, eats
up all the sugar in your kidneys. They
came around every morning and shot
vitamins in my arm. Oh, it didn't hurt.
And the doctor told me to drink a quart
of fruit juice every day. And you better
get some candy bars for me at the grocery
this morning. Doctor said to eat lots of
candy, try to replace the sugar.

LOLA. I'll do that, Doc. Here's another
glass of this pineapple juice now. I'll get
some candy bars first thing.

DOC. The doctor said I should have a
hobby. Said I should go out more. That's
all that's wrong with me. I thought maybe I'd go hunting once in a while.

LOLA. Yes, Doc. And bring home lots of
good things to eat.

DOC. I'll get a big bird dog, too. Would
you like a sad-looking old bird dog
around the house?

LOLA. Of course, I would. *(All her life
and energy have been restored)* You know
what, Doc? I had another dream last
night.

DOC. About Little Sheba?

LOLA. Oh, it was about everyone and
everything. *(In a raptured tone. She gets
bacon from icebox and starts to cook it)*
Marie and I were going to the Olympics
back in our old high school stadium.
There were thousands of people there.
There was Turk out in the center of the
field throwing the javelin. Every time he
threw it, the crowd would roar . . . and
you know who the man in charge was?
It was my father. Isn't that funny? . . .
But Turk kept changing into someone
else all the time. And then my father disqualified him. So he had to sit on the
sidelines . . . and guess who took his
place, Daddy? You! You came trotting
out there on the field just as big as you
please . . .

DOC *(smilingly)*. How did I do, Baby?

LOLA. Fine. You picked the javelin up
real careful, like it was awful heavy. But

you threw it, Daddy, clear, *clear* up into the sky. And it never came down again. *(Doc looks very pleased with himself. Lola goes on)* Then it started to rain. And I couldn't find Little Sheba. I almost went crazy looking for her and there were so many people, I didn't even know where to look. And you were waiting to take me home. And we walked and walked through the slush and mud, and people were hurrying all around us and . . . and . . . *(Leaves stove and sits. Sentimental tears come to her eyes)* But this part is sad, Daddy. All of a sudden I saw Little Sheba . . . she was lying in the middle of the field . . . dead. . . . It made me cry, Doc. No one paid any attention . . . I cried and cried. It made me feel so bad, Daddy. That sweet little puppy . . . her curly white fur was smeared with mud, and no one to stop and take care of her . . .

DOC. Why couldn't *you?*

LOLA. I wanted to, but you wouldn't let me. You kept saying, "We can't stay here, honey; we must go on. We gotta go on." *(Pause)* Now, isn't that strange?

DOC. Dreams are funny.

LOLA. I don't think Little Sheba's ever coming back, Doc. I'm not going to call her any more.

DOC. Not much point in it, Baby. I guess she's gone for good.

LOLA. I'll fix your eggs.

(She gets up, embraces Doc, and goes to stove. Doc remains at table sipping his fruit juice. The curtain comes slowly down.)

All My Sons

BY ARTHUR MILLER

First presented by Elia Kazan, Harold Clurman, and Walter Fried (in association with Herbert Harris) at the Coronet Theatre in New York on January 29, 1947, with the following cast:

JOE KELLER................................Ed Begley		DR. JIM BAYLISS..................John McGovern	
KATE KELLER............................Beth Merrill		SUE BAYLISS......................Peggy Meredith	
CHRIS KELLER......................Arthur Kennedy		FRANK LUBEY.......................Dudley Sadler	
ANN DEEVER............................Lois Wheeler		LYDIA LUBEY......................Hope Cameron	
GEORGE DEEVER.......................Karl Malden		BERT ....Eugene Steiner	

ACT ONE

The back yard of the Keller home in the outskirts of an American town. August of our era.

ACT TWO

Scene, as before. The same evening, as twilight falls.

ACT THREE

Scene, as before. Two o'clock the following morning.

ARTHUR MILLER's first successful play, *All My Sons,* grew out of the war only in so far as the subject of Joe Keller's sale of defective machine parts to the air force had the war as a frame of reference or "objective correlate." *All My Sons* was rooted in Miller's conviction that social responsibility transcends self-interest. Miller did not intend to present war profiteering in *All My Sons.* His concern was with ethics in the context of common reality; he pursued, as one critic noted, a "moral jurisprudence." In this respect, and in the construction of the play, as well as in the symbolism of the failing apple tree, Miller could be described as one of Ibsen's numerous descendants in the modern theatre.

Thematically, too, the play raised the old Ibsen battlecry against "Gyntism" or self-indulgence, the conviction that the evasion of individual human responsibility is unforgivable despite the presence of extenuating circumstances, such as a sense of economic insecurity and a strong devotion to family. Perhaps unintentionally, Harold Clurman, the co-producer of the play, made plain a considerable divergence between Miller's views and the overemphasis of social determinism in the theatre of the thirties in declaring that "the man who blames society for his betrayal of it is a weakling and a coward." Nevertheless, the villain of *All My Sons* is not Joe Keller, who is merely "smart" and has tried to be "tough," as much as the notion of practicality that is shared by Keller's well-intentioned wife. The conflict is between all-encompassing humanity as expressed in the title and the narrow practicality that the Kellers' soldier-son denounces when he protests: "The cats in the alley are practical. The bums who ran away when we were fighting were practical. Only the dead ones weren't practical."

A severe critic could also trace Miller's ancestry back to Sardou, the master of the "well-made play" formula for stage craftsmen, and in retrospect Miller was inclined to concede the reproof. "I felt," he wrote, "I had to perfect conventional technique first and *All My Sons* was an exercise." Still it was no small feat to compose so taut and driving a problem play and at the same time to create a living background and to present a flow of real human relationships that recalled the early work of Odets. The observation and passion in the play, moreover, were singularly Miller's own expression of personality. As John Mason Brown noted, "Mr. Miller's own voice could be heard in *All My Sons,* rising strong and clear. . . . It spoke with heat, fervor, and compassion."

ACT ONE

The back yard of the Keller home in the outskirts of an American town. August of our era.

The stage is hedged on R. and L. by tall, closely planted poplars which lend the yard a secluded atmosphere. Upstage is filled with the back of the house and its open, unroofed porch which extends into the yard some six feet. The house is two stories high and has seven rooms. It would have cost perhaps fifteen thousand in the early twenties when it was built. Now it is nicely painted, looks tight and comfortable, and the yard is green with sod, here and there plants whose season is gone. At the R., beside the house, the entrance of the driveway can be seen, but the poplars cut off view of its continuation downstage. In the L. corner, downstage, stands the four-foot high stump of a slender apple tree whose upper trunk and branches lie toppled beside it, fruit still clinging to its branches.

Downstage R. is a small, trellised arbor, shaped like a sea-shell, with a decorative bulb hanging from its forward-curving roof. Garden chairs and a table are scattered about. A garbage pail on the ground next to the porch steps, a wire leaf-burner near it.

On the rise: It is early Sunday morning. Joe Keller is sitting in the sun reading the want ads of the Sunday paper, the other sections of which lie neatly on the ground beside him. Behind his back, inside the arbor, Doctor Jim Bayliss is reading part of the paper at the table.

Keller is nearing sixty. A heavy man of stolid mind and build, a business man these many years, but with the imprint of the machine-shop worker and boss still upon him. When he reads, when he speaks, when he listens, it is with the terrible concentration of the uneducated man for whom there is still wonder in many commonly known things, a man whose judgments must be dredged out of experience and a peasant-like common sense. A man among men.

Doctor Bayliss is nearly forty. A wry self-controlled man, an easy talker, but with a wisp of sadness that clings even to his self-effacing humor.

At curtain, Jim is standing at L., staring at the broken tree. He taps a pipe on it,

blows through the pipe, feels in his pockets for tobacco, then speaks.

———

JIM. Where's your tobacco?

KELLER. I think I left it on the table. (Jim goes slowly to table on the arbor, finds a pouch, and sits there on the bench, filling his pipe) Gonna rain tonight.

JIM. Paper says so?

KELLER. Yeah, right here.

JIM. Then it can't rain.

(Frank Lubey enters, through a small space between the poplars. Frank is thirty-two but balding. A pleasant, opinionated man, uncertain of himself, with a tendency toward peevishness when crossed, but always wanting it pleasant and neighborly. He rather saunters in, leisurely, nothing to do. He does not notice Jim in the arbor. On his greeting, Jim does not bother looking up.)

FRANK. Hya.

KELLER. Hello, Frank. What's doin'?

FRANK. Nothin'. Walking off my breakfast. (Looks up at the sky) That beautiful? Not a cloud.

KELLER (looks up) Yeah, nice.

FRANK. Every Sunday ought to be like this.

KELLER (indicating the sections beside him). Want the paper?

FRANK. What's the difference, it's all bad news. What's today's calamity?

KELLER. I don't know, I don't read the news part any more. It's more interesting in the want ads.

FRANK. Why, you trying to buy something?

KELLER. No, I'm just interested. To see what people want, y'know? For instance, here's a guy is lookin' for two Newfoundland dogs. Now what's he want with two Newfoundland dogs?

FRANK. That is funny.

KELLER. Here's another one. Wanted— Old Dictionaries. High prices paid. Now what's a man going to do with an old dictionary?

FRANK. Why not? Probably a book collector.

KELLER. You mean he'll make a living out of that?

FRANK. Sure, there's a lot of them.

KELLER (shakes his head). All the kind of business goin' on. In my day, either you were a lawyer, or a doctor, or you worked in a shop. Now . . .

FRANK. Well, I was going to be a forester once.

KELLER. Well, that shows you; in my day, there was no such thing. *(Scanning the page, sweeping it with his hand)* You look at a page like this you realize how ignorant you are. *(Softly, with wonder, as he scans page)* Psss!

FRANK *(noticing tree)*. Hey, what happened to your tree?

KELLER. Ain't that awful? The wind must've got it last night. You heard the wind, didn't you?

FRANK. Yeah, I got a mess in my yard, too. *(Goes to tree)* What a pity. *(Turns to Keller)* What'd Kate say?

KELLER. They're all asleep yet. I'm just waiting for her to see it.

FRANK *(struck)*. You know?—it's funny.

KELLER. What?

FRANK. Larry was born in August. He'd been twenty-seven this month. And his tree blows down.

KELLER *(touched)*. I'm surprised you remember his birthday, Frank. That's nice.

FRANK. Well, I'm working on his horoscope.

KELLER. How can you make him a horoscope? That's for the future, ain't it?

FRANK. Well, what I'm doing is this, see. Larry was reported missing on November 25th, right?

KELLER. Yeah?

FRANK. Well, then, we assume that if he was killed it was on November 25th. Now, what Kate wants . . .

KELLER. Oh, Kate asked you to make a horoscope?

FRANK. Yeah, what she wants to find out is whether November 25th was a favorable day for Larry.

KELLER. What is that, favorable day?

FRANK. Well, a favorable day for a person is a fortunate day, according to his stars. In other words it would be practically impossible for him to have died on his favorable day.

KELLER. Well, was that his favorable day?—November 25th?

FRANK. That's what I'm working on to find out. It takes time! See, the point is, if November 25th was his favorable day, then it's completely possible he's alive somewhere, because . . . I mean it's possible. *(He notices Jim now. Jim is looking at him as though at an idiot. To Jim—*

with an uncertain laugh) I didn't even see you.

KELLER *(to Jim)*. Is he talkin' sense?

JIM. Him? He's all right. He's just completely out of his mind, that's all.

FRANK *(peeved)*. The trouble with you is, you don't *believe* in anything.

JIM. And your trouble is that you believe in *anything*. *You* didn't see my kid this morning, did you?

FRANK. No.

KELLER. Imagine? He walked off with his thermometer. Right out of his bag.

JIM *(gets up)*. What a problem. One look at a girl and he takes her temperature. *(Goes to driveway, looks upstage toward street)*

FRANK. That boy's going to be a real doctor; he's smart.

JIM. Over my dead body he'll be a doctor. A good beginning, too.

FRANK. Why? It's an honorable profession.

JIM *(looks at him tiredly)*. Frank, will you stop talking like a civics book? *(Keller laughs)*

FRANK. Why, I saw a movie a couple of weeks ago, reminded me of you. There was a doctor in that picture . . .

KELLER. Don Ameche!

FRANK. I think it was, yeah. And he worked in his basement discovering things. That's what you ought to do; you could help humanity, instead of . . .

JIM. I would love to help humanity on a Warner Brothers salary.

KELLER *(points at him, laughing)*. That's very good, Jim.

JIM *(looks toward house)*. Well, where's the beautiful girl was supposed to be here?

FRANK *(excited)*. Annie came?

KELLER. Sure, sleepin' upstairs. We picked her up on the one o'clock train last night. Wonderful thing. Girl leaves here, a scrawny kid. Couple of years go by, she's a regular woman. Hardly recognized her, and she was running in and out of this yard all her life. That was a very happy family used to live in your house, Jim.

JIM. Like to meet her. The block can use a pretty girl. In the whole neighborhood there's not a damned thing to look at. *(Enter Sue, Jim's wife. She is rounding forty, an overweight woman who fears it. On seeing her Jim wryly adds:)* . . . Except my wife, of course.

SUE *(in same spirit)*. Mrs. Adams is on the phone, you dog.

JIM *(to Keller)*. Such is the condition which prevails—*(Going to his wife)* my love, my light. . . .

SUE. Don't sniff around me. *(Points to their house)* And give her a nasty answer. I can smell her perfume over the phone.

JIM. What's the matter with her now?

SUE. I don't know, dear. She sounds like she's in terrible pain—unless her mouth is full of candy.

JIM. Why don't you just tell her to lay down?

SUE. She enjoys it more when you tell her to lay down. And when are you going to see Mr. Hubbard?

JIM. My dear; Mr. Hubbard is not sick, and I have better things to do than to sit there and hold his hand.

SUE. It seems to me that for ten dollars you could hold his hand.

JIM *(to Keller)*. If your son wants to play golf tell him I'm ready. Or if he'd like to take a trip around the world for about thirty years. *(He exits)*

KELLER. Why do you needle him? He's a doctor, women are supposed to call him up.

SUE. All I said was Mrs. Adams is on the phone. Can I have some of your parsley?

KELLER. Yeah, sure. *(She goes to parsley box and pulls some parsley)* You were a nurse too long, Susie. You're too . . . too . . . realistic.

SUE *(laughing, points at him)*. Now you said it! *(Enter Lydia Lubey. She is a robust, laughing girl of twenty-seven.)*

LYDIA. Frank, the toaster . . . *(Sees the others)* Hya.

KELLER. Hello!

LYDIA *(to Frank)*. The toaster is off again.

FRANK. Well, plug it in, I just fixed it.

LYDIA *(kindly, but insistently)*. Please, dear, fix it back like it was before.

FRANK. I don't know why you can't learn to turn on a simple thing like a toaster! *(Frank exits.)*

SUE *(laughs)*. Thomas Edison.

LYDIA *(apologetically)*. He's really very handy. *(She sees broken tree)* Oh, did the wind get your tree?

KELLER. Yeah, last night.

LYDIA. Oh, what a pity. Annie get in?

KELLER. She'll be down soon. Wait'll you meet her, Sue, she's a knockout.

SUE. I should've been a man. People are always introducing me to beautiful women. *(To Joe)* Tell her to come over later; I imagine she'd like to see what we did with her house. And thanks. *(Sue exits.)*

LYDIA. Is she still unhappy, Joe?

KELLER. Annie? I don't suppose she goes around dancing on her toes, but she seems to be over it.

LYDIA. She going to get married? Is there anybody . . . ?

KELLER. I suppose . . . say, it's a couple years already. She can't mourn a boy forever.

LYDIA. It's so strange . . . Annie's here and not even married. And I've got three babies. I always thought it'd be the other way around.

KELLER. Well, that's what a war does. I had two sons, now I got one. It changed all the tallies. In my day when you had sons it was an honor. Today a doctor could make a million dollars if he could figure out a way to bring a boy into the world without a trigger finger.

LYDIA. You know, I was just reading . . . *(Enter Chris Keller from house, stands in doorway)*

LYDIA. Hya, Chris . . . *(Frank shouts from offstage)*

FRANK. Lydia, come in here! If you want the toaster to work don't plug in the malted mixer.

LYDIA *(embarrassed, laughs)*. Did I . . . ?

FRANK. And the next time I fix something don't tell me I'm crazy! Now come in here!

LYDIA *(to Keller)*. I'll never hear the end of this one.

KELLER *(calling to Frank)*. So what's the difference? Instead of toast have a malted!

LYDIA. Sh! sh! *(She exits, laughing)* *(Chris watches her off. He is thirty-two; like his father, solidly built, a listener. A man capable of immense affection and loyalty. He has a cup of coffee in one hand, part of a doughnut in other.)*

KELLER. You want the paper?

CHRIS. That's all right, just the book section. *(He bends down and pulls out part of paper on porch floor)*

KELLER. You're always reading the book section and you never buy a book.

CHRIS (*coming down to settee*). I like to keep abreast of my ignorance. (*He sits on settee*)

KELLER. What is that, every week a new book comes out?

CHRIS. Lot of new books.

KELLER. All different.

CHRIS. All different.

KELLER (*shakes his head, puts knife down on bench, takes oilstone up to the cabinet*). Psss! Annie up yet?

CHRIS. Mother's giving her breakfast in the dining-room.

KELLER (*looking at broken tree*). See what happened to the tree?

CHRIS (*without looking up*). Yeah.

KELLER. What's Mother going to say? (*Bert runs on from driveway. He is about eight. He jumps on stool, then on Keller's back*)

BERT. You're finally up.

KELLER (*swinging him around and putting him down*). Ha! Bert's here! Where's Tommy? He's got his father's thermometer again.

BERT. He's taking a reading.

CHRIS. What!

BERT. But it's only oral.

KELLER. Oh, well, there's no harm in oral. So what's new this morning, Bert?

BERT. Nothin'. (*He goes to broken tree, walks around it*)

KELLER. Then you couldn't've made a complete inspection of the block. In the beginning, when I first made you a policeman you used to come in every morning with something new. Now, nothin's ever new.

BERT. Except some kids from Thirtieth Street. They started kicking a can down the block, and I made them go away because you were sleeping.

KELLER. Now you're talkin', Bert. Now you're on the ball. First thing you know I'm liable to make you a detective.

BERT (*pulls him down by the lapel and whispers in his ear*). Can I see the jail now?

KELLER. Seein' the jail ain't allowed, Bert. You know that.

BERT. Aw, I betcha there isn't even a jail. I don't see any bars on the cellar windows.

KELLER. Bert, on my word of honor there's a jail in the basement. I showed you my gun, didn't I?

BERT. But that's a hunting gun.

KELLER. That's an arresting gun!

BERT. Then why don't you ever arrest anybody? Tommy said another dirty word to Doris yesterday, and you didn't even demote him.

KELLER (*he chuckles and winks at Chris, who is enjoying all this*). Yeah, that's a dangerous character, that Tommy. (*Beckons him closer*) What word does he say?

BERT (*backing away quickly in great embarrassment*). Oh, I can't say that.

KELLER (*grabs him by the shirt and pulls him back*). Well, gimme an idea.

BERT. I can't. It's not a nice word.

KELLER. Just whisper it in my ear. I'll close my eyes. Maybe I won't even hear it.

BERT (*on tiptoe, puts his lips to Keller's ear, then in unbearable embarrassment steps back*). I can't, Mr. Keller.

CHRIS (*laughing*). Don't make him do that.

KELLER. Okay, Bert. I take your word. Now go out, and keep both eyes peeled.

BERT (*interested*). For what?

KELLER. For what! Bert, the whole neighborhood is depending on you. A policeman don't ask questions. Now peel them eyes!

BERT (*mystified, but willing*). Okay. (*He runs off stage back of arbor*)

KELLER (*calling after him*). And mum's the word, Bert.

BERT (*stops and sticks his head through the arbor*). About what?

KELLER. Just in general. Be v-e-r-y careful.

BERT (*nods in bewilderment*). Okay. (*Bert exits.*)

KELLER (*laughs*). I got all the kids crazy!

CHRIS. One of these days, they'll all come in here and beat your brains out.

KELLER. What's she going to say? Maybe we ought to tell her before she sees it.

CHRIS. She saw it.

KELLER. How could she see it? I was the first one up. She was still in bed.

CHRIS. She was out here when it broke.

KELLER. When?

CHRIS. About four this morning. (*Indicating window above them*) I heard it cracking and I woke up and looked out.

She was standing right here when it cracked.

KELLER. What was she doing out here four in the morning?

CHRIS. I don't know. When it cracked she ran back into the house and cried in the kitchen.

KELLER. Did you talk to her?

CHRIS. No, I . . . I figured the best thing was to leave her alone. *(Pause)*

KELLER *(deeply touched)*. She cried hard?

CHRIS. I could hear her right through the floor of my room.

KELLER *(slight pause)*. What was she doing out here at that hour? *(Chris silent. An undertone of anger showing)* She's dreaming about him again. She's walking around at night.

CHRIS. I guess she is.

KELLER. She's getting just like after he died. *(Slight pause)* What's the meaning of that?

CHRIS. I don't know the meaning of it. *(Slight pause)* But I know one thing, Dad. We've made a terrible mistake with Mother.

KELLER. What?

CHRIS. Being dishonest with her. That kind of thing always pays off, and now it's paying off.

KELLER. What do you mean, dishonest?

CHRIS. You know Larry's not coming back and I know it. Why do we allow her to go on thinking that we believe with her?

KELLER. What do you want to do, argue with her?

CHRIS. I don't want to argue with her, but it's time she realized that nobody believes Larry is alive any more. *(Keller simply moves away, thinking, looking at the ground)* Why shouldn't she dream of him, walk the nights waiting for him? Do we contradict her? Do we say straight out that we have no hope any more? That we haven't had any hope for years now?

KELLER *(frightened at the thought)*. You can't say that to her.

CHRIS. We've got to say it to her.

KELLER. How're you going to prove it? Can you prove it?

CHRIS. For God's sake, three years! Nobody comes back after three years. It's insane.

KELLER. To you it is, and to me. But not to her. You can talk yourself blue in the face, but there's no body and there's no grave, so where are you?

CHRIS. Sit down, Dad. I want to talk to you.

KELLER *(looks at him searchingly a moment, and sitting . . .)*. The trouble is the Goddam newspapers. Every month some boy turns up from nowhere, so the next one is going to be Larry, so . . .

CHRIS. All right, all right, listen to me. *(Slight pause. Keller sits on settee)* You know why I asked Annie here, don't you?

KELLER *(he knows, but . . .)*. Why?

CHRIS. You know.

KELLER. Well, I got an idea, but . . . What's the story?

CHRIS. I'm going to ask her to marry me. *(Slight pause)*

KELLER *(nods)*. Well, that's only your business, Chris.

CHRIS. You know it's not only my business.

KELLER. What do you want me to do? You're old enough to know your own mind.

CHRIS *(asking, annoyed)*. Then it's all right, I'll go ahead with it?

KELLER. Well, you want to be sure Mother isn't going to . . .

CHRIS. Then it isn't just my business.

KELLER. I'm just sayin'. . . .

CHRIS. Sometimes you infuriate me, you know that? Isn't it your business, too, if I tell this to Mother and she throws a fit about it? You have such a talent for ignoring things.

KELLER. I ignore what I gotta ignore. The girl is Larry's girl . . .

CHRIS. She's not Larry's girl.

KELLER. From Mother's point of view he is not dead and you have no right to take his girl. *(Slight pause)* Now you can go on from there if you know where to go, but I'm tellin' you I don't know where to go. See? I don't know. Now what can I do for you?

CHRIS. I don't know why it is, but every time I reach out for something I want, I have to pull back because other people will suffer. My whole bloody life, time after time after time.

KELLER. You're a considerate fella, there's nothing wrong in that.

CHRIS. To hell with that.

KELLER. Did you ask Annie yet?

CHRIS. I wanted to get this settled first.

KELLER. How do you know she'll marry you? Maybe she feels the same way Mother does?

CHRIS. Well, if she does, then that's the end of it. From her letters I think she's forgotten him. I'll find out. And then we'll thrash it out with Mother? Right? Dad, don't avoid me.

KELLER. The trouble is, you don't see enough women. You never did.

CHRIS. So what? I'm not fast with women.

KELLER. I don't see why it has to be Annie. . . .

CHRIS. Because it is.

KELLER. That's a good answer, but it don't answer anything. You haven't seen her since you went to war. It's five years.

CHRIS. I can't help it. I know her best. I was brought up next door to her. These years when I think of someone for my wife, I think of Annie. What do you want, a diagram?

KELLER. I don't want a diagram . . . I . . . I'm . . . She thinks he's coming back, Chris. You marry that girl and you're pronouncing him dead. Now what's going to happen to Mother? Do you know? I don't! *(Pause)*

CHRIS. All right, then, Dad.

KELLER *(thinking Chris has retreated)*. Give it some more thought.

CHRIS. I've given it three years of thought. I'd hoped that if I waited, Mother would forget Larry and then we'd have a regular wedding and everything happy. But if that can't happen here, then I'll have to get out.

KELLER. What the hell is *this?*

CHRIS. I'll get out. I'll get married and live some place else. Maybe in New York.

KELLER. Are you crazy?

CHRIS. I've been a good son too long, a good sucker. I'm through with it.

KELLER. You've got a business here, what the hell is this?

CHRIS. The business! The business doesn't inspire me.

KELLER. Must you be inspired?

CHRIS. Yes. I like it an hour a day. If I have to grub for money all day long at least at evening I want it beautiful. I want a family, I want some kids, I want to build something I can give myself to. Annie is in the middle of that. Now . . . where do I find it?

KELLER. You mean . . . *(Goes to him)* Tell me something, you mean you'd leave the business?

CHRIS. Yes. On this I would.

KELLER *(pause)*. Well . . . you don't want to think like that.

CHRIS. Then help me stay here.

KELLER. All right, but . . . but don't think like that. Because what the hell did I work for? That's only for you, Chris, the whole shootin' match is for you!

CHRIS. I know that, Dad. Just you help me stay here.

KELLER *(puts a fist up to Chris' jaw)*. But don't think that way, you hear me?

CHRIS. I am thinking that way.

KELLER *(lowering his hand)*. I don't understand you, do I?

CHRIS. No, you don't. I'm a pretty tough guy.

KELLER. Yeah. I can see that. *(Mother appears on porch. She is in her early fifties, a woman of uncontrolled inspirations, and an overwhelming capacity for love)*

MOTHER. Joe?

CHRIS *(going toward porch)*. Hello, Mom.

MOTHER *(indicating house behind her. To Keller)*. Did you take a bag from under the sink?

KELLER. Yeah, I put it in the pail.

MOTHER. Well, get it out of the pail. That's my potatoes. *(Chris bursts out laughing—goes up into alley)*

KELLER *(laughing)*. I thought it was garbage.

MOTHER. Will you do me a favor, Joe? Don't be helpful.

KELLER. I can afford another bag of potatoes.

MOTHER. Minnie scoured that pail in boiling water last night. It's cleaner than your teeth.

KELLER. And I don't understand why, after I worked forty years and I got a maid, why I have to take out the garbage.

MOTHER. If you would make up your mind that every bag in the kitchen isn't full of garbage you wouldn't be throwing out my vegetables. Last time it was the onions. *(Chris comes on, hands her bag)*

KELLER. I don't like garbage in the house.

MOTHER. Then don't eat. *(She goes into the kitchen with bag)*

CHRIS. That settles you for today.

KELLER. Yeah, I'm in last place again. I don't know, once upon a time I used to think that when I got money again I would have a maid and my wife would take it easy. Now I got money, and I got a maid, and my wife is workin' for the maid. *(He sits in one of the chairs. Mother comes out on last line. She carries a pot of stringbeans)*

MOTHER. It's her day off, what are you crabbing about?

CHRIS *(to Mother)*. Isn't Annie finished eating?

MOTHER *(looking around preoccupiedly at yard)*. She'll be right out. *(Moves)* That wind did some job on this place. *(Of the tree)* So much for that, thank God.

KELLER *(indicating chair beside him)*. Sit down, take it easy.

MOTHER *(she presses her hand to top of her head)*. I've got such a funny pain on the top of my head.

CHRIS. Can I get you an aspirin?

MOTHER *(picks a few petals off ground, stand there smelling them in her hand, then sprinkles them over plants)*. No more roses. It's so funny . . . everything decides to happen at the same time. This month is his birthday; his tree blows down, Annie comes. Everything that happened seems to be coming back. I was just down the cellar, and what do I stumble over? His baseball glove. I haven't seen it in a century.

CHRIS. Don't you think Annie looks well?

MOTHER. Fine. There's no question about it. She's a beauty . . . I still don't know what brought her here. Not that I'm not glad to see her, but . . .

CHRIS. I just thought we'd all like to see each other again. *(Mother just looks at him, nodding ever so slightly—almost as though admitting something)* And I wanted to see her myself.

MOTHER *(her nods halt. To Keller)*. The only thing is I think her nose got longer. But I'll always love that girl. She's one that didn't jump into bed with somebody else as soon as it happened with her fella.

KELLER *(as though that were impossible for Annie)*. Oh, what're you . . .?

MOTHER. Never mind. Most of them didn't wait till the telegrams were opened. I'm just glad she came, so you can see I'm not *completely* out of my mind. *(Sits, and rapidly breaks stringbeans in the pot)*

CHRIS. Just because she isn't married doesn't mean she's been mourning Larry.

MOTHER *(with an undercurrent of observation)*. Why then isn't she?

CHRIS *(a little flustered)*. Well . . . it could've been any number of things.

MOTHER *(directly at him)*. Like what, for instance?

CHRIS *(embarrassed, but standing his ground)*. I don't know. Whatever it is. Can I get you an aspirin? *(Mother puts her hand to her head)*

MOTHER *(she gets up and goes aimlessly toward the trees on rising)*. It's not like a headache.

KELLER. You don't sleep, that's why. She's wearing out more bedroom slippers than shoes.

MOTHER. I had a terrible night. *(She stops moving)* I never had a night like that.

CHRIS *(looks at Keller)*. What was it, Mom? Did you dream?

MOTHER. More, more than a dream.

CHRIS *(hesitantly)*. About Larry?

MOTHER. I was fast asleep, and . . . *(Raising her arm over the audience)* Remember the way he used to fly low past the house when he was in training? When we used to see his face in the cockpit going by? That's the way I saw him. Only high up. Way, way up, where the clouds are. He was so real I could reach out and touch him. And suddenly he started to fall. And crying, crying to me . . . Mom, Mom! I could hear him like he was in the room. Mom! . . . it was his voice! If I could touch him I knew I could stop him, if I could only . . . *(Breaks off, allowing her outstretched hand to fall)* I woke up and it was so funny . . . The wind . . . it was like the roaring of his engine. I came out here . . . I must've still been half asleep. I could hear that roaring like he was going by. The tree snapped right in front of me . . . and I like . . . came awake. *(She is looking at tree. She suddenly realizes something, turns with a reprimanding finger shaking slightly at Keller)* See? We should never have planted that tree. I said so in the first place; it was too soon to plant a tree for him.

CHRIS *(alarmed)*. Too soon!

MOTHER *(angering)*. We rushed into it. Everybody was in such a hurry to bury him. I *said* not to plant it yet *(To Keller)* I *told* you to . . .!

CHRIS. Mother, Mother! *(She looks into his face)* The wind blew it down. What significance has that got? What are you talking about? Mother, please . . . Don't go through it all again, will you? It's no good, it doesn't accomplish anything. I've been thinking, y'know?—maybe we ought to put our minds to forgetting him?

MOTHER. That's the third time you've said that this week.

CHRIS. Because it's not right; we never took up our lives again. We're like at a railroad station waiting for a train that never comes in.

MOTHER *(presses top of her head)*. Get me an aspirin, heh?

CHRIS. Sure, and let's break out of this, heh, Mom? I thought the four of us might go out to dinner a couple of nights, maybe go dancing out at the shore.

MOTHER. Fine. *(To Keller)* We can do it tonight.

KELLER. Swell with me!

CHRIS. Sure, let's have some fun. *(To Mother)* You'll start with this aspirin. *(He goes up and into house with new spirit. Her smile vanishes)*

MOTHER *(with an accusing undertone)*. Why did he invite her here?

KELLER. Why does that bother you?

MOTHER. She's been in New York three and a half years, why all of a sudden . . .?

KELLER. Well, maybe . . . maybe he just wanted to see her . . .

MOTHER. Nobody comes seven hundred miles "just to see."

KELLER. What do you mean? He lived next door to the girl all his life, why shouldn't he want to see her again? *(Mother looks at him critically)* Don't look at me like that, he didn't tell me any more than he told you.

MOTHER *(a warning and a question)*. He's not going to marry her.

KELLER. How do you know he's even thinking of it?

MOTHER. It's got that about it.

KELLER *(sharply watching her reaction)*. Well? So what?

MOTHER *(alarmed)*. What's going on here, Joe?

KELLER. Now listen, kid . . .

MOTHER *(avoiding contact with him)*. She's not his girl, Joe; she knows she's not.

KELLER. You can't read her mind.

MOTHER. Then why is she still single? New York is full of men, why isn't she married? *(Pause)* Probably a hundred people told her she's foolish, but she's waited.

KELLER. How do you know why she waited?

MOTHER. She knows what I know, that's why. She's faithful as a rock. In my worst moments, I think of her waiting, and I know again that I'm right.

KELLER. Look, it's a nice day. What are we arguing for?

MOTHER *(warningly)*. Nobody in this house dast take her faith away, Joe. Strangers might. But not his father, not his brother.

KELLER *(exasperated)*. What do you want me to do? What do you want?

MOTHER. I want you to act like he's coming back. Both of you. Don't think I haven't noticed you since Chris invited her. I won't stand for any nonsense.

KELLER. But, Kate . . .

MOTHER. Because if he's not coming back, then I'll kill myself! Laugh. Laugh at me. *(She points to tree)* But why did that happen the very night she came back? Laugh, but there are meanings in such things. She goes to sleep in his room and his memorial breaks in pieces. Look at it; look. *(She sits on bench.)* Joe . . .

KELLER. Calm yourself.

MOTHER. Believe with me, Joe. I can't stand all alone.

KELLER. Calm yourself.

MOTHER. Only last week a man turned up in Detroit, missing longer than Larry. You read it yourself.

KELLER. All right, all right, calm yourself.

MOTHER. You above all have got to believe, you . . .

KELLER *(rises)*. Why me above all?

MOTHER. . . . Just don't stop believing . . .

KELLER. What does that mean, me above all? *(Bert comes rushing on)*

BERT. Mr. Keller! Say, Mr. Keller . . . *(Pointing up driveway)* Tommy just said it again!

KELLER *(not remembering any of it)*. Said what? . . . Who? . . .

BERT. The dirty word.

KELLER. Oh. Well . . .

BERT. Gee, aren't you going to arrest him? I warned him.

MOTHER *(with suddenness).* Stop that, Bert. Go home. *(Bert backs up, as she advances)* There's no jail here.

KELLER *(as though to say, "Oh-what-the-hell-let-him-believe-there-is").* Kate . . .

MOTHER *(turning on Keller furiously).* There's no jail here! I want you to stop that jail business! *(He turns, shamed, but peeved)*

BERT *(past her to Keller).* He's right across the street . . .

MOTHER. Go home, Bert. *(Bert turns around and goes up driveway. She is shaken. Her speech is bitten off, extremely urgent)* I want you to stop that, Joe. That whole jail business!

KELLER *(alarmed, therefore angered).* Look at you, look at you shaking.

MOTHER *(trying to control herself, moving about clasping her hands).* I can't help it.

KELLER. What have I got to hide? What the hell is the matter with you, Kate?

MOTHER. I didn't say you had anything to hide, I'm just telling you to stop it! Now stop it! *(As Ann and Chris appear on porch. Ann is twenty-six, gentle but despite herself capable of holding fast to what she knows. Chris opens door for her)*

ANN. Hya, Joe! *(She leads off a general laugh that is not self-conscious because they know one another too well)*

CHRIS *(bringing Ann down, with an outstretched, chivalric arm).* Take a breath of that air, kid. You never get air like that in New York.

MOTHER *(genuinely overcome with it).* Annie, where did you get that dress!

ANN. I couldn't resist. I'm taking it right off before I ruin it. *(Swings around)* How's that for three weeks' salary?

MOTHER *(to Keller).* Isn't she the most . . . ? *(To Ann)* It's gorgeous, simply gor . . .

CHRIS *(to Mother).* No kidding, now, isn't she the prettiest gal you ever saw?

MOTHER *(caught short by his obvious admiration, she finds herself reaching out for a glass of water and aspirin in his hand, and . . .).* You gained a little weight, didn't you, darling? *(She gulps pill and drinks)*

ANN. It comes and goes.

KELLER. Look how nice her legs turned out!

ANN *(she runs to fence).* Boy, the poplars got thick, didn't they?

KELLER *(moves to settee and sits).* Well, it's three years, Annie. We're gettin' old, kid.

MOTHER. How does Mom like New York? *(Ann keeps looking through trees)*

ANN *(a little hurt).* Why'd they take our hammock away?

KELLER. Oh, no, it broke. Couple of years ago.

MOTHER. What broke? He had one of his light lunches and flopped into it.

ANN *(she laughs and turns back toward Jim's yard . . .).* Oh, excuse me! *(Jim has come to fence and is looking over it. He is smoking a cigar. As she cries out, he comes on around on stage)*

JIM. How do you do. *(To Chris)* She looks very intelligent!

CHRIS. Ann, this is Jim . . . Doctor Bayliss.

ANN *(shaking Jim's hand).* Oh, sure, he writes a lot about you.

JIM. Don't you believe it. He likes everybody. In the Battalion he was known as Mother McKeller.

ANN. I can believe it . . . You know—? *(To Mother)* It's so strange seeing him come out of that yard. *(To Chris)* I guess I never grew up. It almost seems that Mom and Pop are in there now. And you and my brother doing Algebra, and Larry trying to copy my home-work. Gosh, those dear dead days beyond recall.

JIM. Well, I hope that doesn't mean you want me to move out?

SUE *(calling from offstage).* Jim, come in here! Mr. Hubbard is on the phone!

JIM. I told you I don't want . . .

SUE *(commandingly sweet).* Please, dear! Please!

JIM *(resigned).* All right, Susie. *(Trailing off)* All right, all right . . . *(To Ann)* I've only met you, Ann, but if I may offer you a piece of advice— When you marry, never—even in your mind—never count your husband's money.

SUE *(from offstage).* Jim?!

JIM. At once! *(Turns and goes off)* At once. *(He exits)*

MOTHER *(Ann is looking at her. She speaks meaningfully).* I told her to take up the guitar. It'd be a common interest for them. *(They laugh)* Well, he loves the guitar!

ANN *(as though to overcome Mother,*

she becomes suddenly lively, crosses to Keller on settee, sits on his lap). Let's eat at the shore tonight! Raise some hell around here, like we used to before Larry went!

MOTHER *(emotionally).* You think of him! You see? *(Triumphantly)* She thinks of him!

ANN *(with an uncomprehending smile).* What do you mean, Kate?

MOTHER. Nothing. Just that you . . . remember him, he's in your thoughts.

ANN. That's a funny thing to say; how could I help remembering him?

MOTHER *(it is drawing to a head the wrong way for her; she starts anew. She rises and comes to Ann).* Did you hang up your things?

ANN. Yeah . . . *(To Chris)* Say, you've sure gone in for clothes. I could hardly find room in the closet.

MOTHER. No, don't you remember? That's Larry's room.

ANN. You mean . . . they're Larry's?

MOTHER. Didn't you recognize them?

ANN *(slowly rising, a little embarrassed).* Well, it never occurred to me that you'd . . . I mean the shoes are all shined.

MOTHER. Yes, dear. *(Slight pause. Ann can't stop staring at her. Mother breaks it by speaking with the relish of gossip, putting her arm around Ann and walking with her)* For so long I've been aching for a nice conversation with you, Annie. Tell me something.

ANN. What?

MOTHER. I don't know. Something nice.

CHRIS *(wryly).* She means do you go out much?

MOTHER. Oh, shut up.

KELLER. And are any of them serious?

MOTHER *(laughing, sits in her chair).* Why don't you both choke?

KELLER. Annie, you can't go into a restaurant with that woman any more. In five minutes thirty-nine strange people are sitting at the table telling her their life story.

MOTHER. If I can't ask Annie a personal question . . .

KELLER. Askin' is all right, but don't beat her over the head. You're beatin' her, you're beatin' her. *(They are laughing)*

ANN *(to Mother. Takes pan of beans off stool, puts them on floor under chair and sits).* Don't let them bulldoze you. Ask me anything you like. What do you want

to know, Kate? Come on, let's gossip.

MOTHER *(to Chris and Keller).* She's the only one is got any sense. *(To Ann)* Your mother . . . she's not getting a divorce, heh?

ANN. No, she's calmed down about it now. I think when he gets out they'll probably live together. In New York, of course.

MOTHER. That's fine. Because your father is still . . . I mean he's a decent man after all is said and done.

ANN. I don't care. She can take him back if she likes.

MOTHER. And you? You . . . *(Shakes her head negatively)* . . . go out much? *(Slight pause)*

ANN *(delicately).* You mean am I still waiting for him?

MOTHER. Well, no, I don't expect you to wait for him but . . .

ANN *(kindly).* But that's what you mean, isn't it?

MOTHER. . . . Well . . . yes.

ANN. Well, I'm not, Kate.

MOTHER *(faintly).* You're not?

ANN. Isn't it ridiculous? You don't really imagine he's . . . ?

MOTHER. I know, dear, but don't say it's ridiculous, because the papers were full of it; I don't know about New York, but there was half a page about a man missing even longer than Larry, and he turned up from Burma.

CHRIS *(coming to Ann).* He couldn't have wanted to come home very badly, Mom.

MOTHER. Don't be so smart.

CHRIS. You can have a helluva time in Burma.

ANN *(rises and swings around in back of Chris).* So I've heard.

CHRIS. Mother, I'll bet you money that you're the only woman in the country who after three years is still . . .

MOTHER. You're sure?

CHRIS. Yes, I am.

MOTHER. Well, if you're sure then you're sure. *(She turns her head away an instant)* They don't say it on the radio but I'm sure that in the dark at night they're still waiting for their sons.

CHRIS. Mother, you're absolutely—

MOTHER *(waving him off).* Don't be so damned smart! Now stop it! *(Slight pause)* There are just a few things you *don't* know. All of you. And I'll tell you one of them, Annie. Deep, deep in your heart you've always been waiting for him.

ANN (*resolutely*). No, Kate.

MOTHER (*with increasing demand*). But deep in your heart, Annie!

CHRIS. She ought to know, shouldn't she?

MOTHER. Don't let them tell you what to think. Listen to your heart. Only your heart.

ANN. Why does your heart tell you he's alive?

MOTHER. Because he has to be.

ANN. But why, Kate?

MOTHER (*going to her*). Because certain things have to be, and certain things can never be. Like the sun has to rise, it has to be. That's why there's God. Otherwise anything could happen. But there's God, so certain things can never happen. I would know, Annie—just like I knew the day he (*Indicates Chris*) went into that terrible battle. Did he write me? Was it in the papers? No, but that morning I couldn't raise my head off the pillow. Ask Joe. Suddenly, I knew. I knew! And he was nearly killed that day. Ann, you *know* I'm right!

ANN (*she stands there in silence, then turns trembling, going upstage*). No, Kate.

MOTHER. I have to have some tea. (*Frank appears, carrying ladder*)

FRANK. Annie! (*Coming down*) How are you, gee whiz!

ANN (*taking his hand*). Why, Frank, you're losing your hair.

KELLER. He's got responsibility.

FRANK. Gee whiz!

KELLER. Without Frank the stars wouldn't know when to come out.

FRANK (*laughs. To Ann*). You look more womanly. You've matured. You . . .

KELLER. Take it easy, Frank, you're a married man.

ANN (*as they laugh*). You still haberdashering?

FRANK. Why not? Maybe I too can get to be president. How's your brother? Got his degree, I hear.

ANN. Oh, George has his own office now!

FRANK. Don't say! (*Funereally*) And your dad? Is he . . . ?

ANN (*abruptly*). Fine. I'll be in to see Lydia.

FRANK (*sympathetically*). How about it, does Dad expect a parole soon?

ANN (*with growing ill-ease*). I really don't know, I' . . .

FRANK (*staunchly defending her father for her sake*). I mean because I feel, y' know, that if an intelligent man like your father is put in prison, there ought to be a law that says either you execute him, or let him go after a year.

CHRIS (*interrupting*). Want a hand with that ladder, Frank?

FRANK (*taking cue*). That's all right, I'll . . . (*Picks up ladder*) I'll finish the horoscope tonight, Kate. (*Embarrassed*) See you later, Ann, you look wonderful. (*He exits. They look at Ann*)

ANN (*to Chris, sits slowly on stool*). Haven't they stopped talking about Dad?

CHRIS (*comes down and sits on arm of chair*). Nobody talks about him any more.

KELLER (*rises and comes to her*). Gone and forgotten, kid.

ANN. Tell me. Because I don't want to meet anybody on the block if they're going to . . .

CHRIS. I don't want you to worry about it.

ANN (*to Keller*). Do they still remember the case, Joe? Do they talk about you?

KELLER. The only one still talks about it is my wife.

MOTHER. That's because you keep on playing policeman with the kids. All their parents hear out of you is jail, jail, jail.

KELLER. Actually what happened was that when I got home from the penitentiary the kids got very interested in me. You know kids. I was (*Laughs*) like the expert on the jail situation. And as time passed they got it confused and . . . I ended up a detective. (*Laughs*)

MOTHER. Except that *they* didn't get it confused. (*To Ann*) He hands out police badges from the Post Toasties boxes. (*They laugh*)

ANN (*wondrously at them, happily. She rises and comes to Keller, putting her arm around his shoulder*). Gosh, it's wonderful to hear you laughing about it.

CHRIS. Why, what'd you expect?

ANN. The last thing I remember on this block was one word—"Murderers!" Remember that, Kate? . . . Mrs. Hammond standing in front of our house and yelling that word . . . She's still around, I suppose?

MOTHER. They're all still around.

KELLER. Don't listen to her. Every Sat

urday night the whole gang is playin' poker in this arbor. All the ones who yelled murderer takin' my money now.

MOTHER. Don't, Joe; she's a sensitive girl, don't fool her. (*To Ann*) They still remember about Dad. It's different with him— (*Indicates Joe*) —he was exonerated, your father's still there. That's why I wasn't so enthusiastic about your coming. Honestly, I know how sensitive you are, and I told Chris, I said . . .

KELLER. Listen, you do like I did and you'll be all right. The day I come home, I got out of my car;—but not in front of the house . . . on the corner. You should've been here, Annie, and you too, Chris; you'd-a seen something. Everybody knew I was getting out that day; the porches were loaded. Picture it now; none of them believed I was innocent. The story was, I pulled a fast one getting myself exonerated. So I get out of my car, and I walk down the street. But very slow. And with a smile. The beast! I was the beast; the guy who sold cracked cylinder heads to the Army Air Force; the guy who made twenty-one P-40's crash in Australia. Kid, walkin' down the street that day I was guilty as hell. Except I wasn't, and there was a court paper in my pocket to prove I wasn't, and I walked . . . past . . . the porches. Result? Fourteen months later I had one of the best shops in the state again, a respected man again; bigger than ever.

CHRIS (*with admiration*). Joe McGuts.

KELLER (*now with great force*). That's the only way you lick 'em is guts! (*To Ann*) The worst thing you did was to move away from here. You made it tough for your father when he gets out. That's why I tell you, I like to see him move back right on this block.

MOTHER (*pained*). How could they move back?

KELLER. It ain't gonna end *till* they move back! (*To Ann*) Till people play cards with him again, and talk with him, and smile with him—you play cards with a man you know he can't be a murderer. And the next time you write him I like you to tell him just what I said. (*Ann simply stares at him*) You hear me?

ANN (*surprised*). Don't you hold anything against him?

KELLER. Annie, I never believed in crucifying people.

ANN (*mystified*). But he was your partner, he dragged you through the mud . . .

KELLER. Well, he ain't my sweetheart, but you gotta forgive, don't you?

ANN. You, either, Kate? Don't you feel any . . . ?

KELLER (*to Ann*). The next time you write Dad . . .

ANN. I don't write him.

KELLER (*struck*). Well, every now and then you . . .

ANN (*a little shamed, but determined*). No, I've *never* written to him. Neither has my brother. (*To Chris*) Say, do you feel this way, too?

CHRIS. He murdered twenty-one pilots.

KELLER. What the hell kinda talk is that?

MOTHER. That's not a thing to say about a man.

ANN. What else can you say? When they took him away I followed him, went to him every visiting day. I was crying all the time. Until the news came about Larry. Then I realized. It's wrong to pity a man like that. Father or no father, there's only one way to look at him. He knowingly shipped out parts that would crash an airplane. And how do you know Larry wasn't one of them?

MOTHER. I was waiting for that. (*Going to her*) As long as you're here, Annie, I want to ask you never to say that again.

ANN. You surprise me. I thought you'd be mad at him.

MOTHER. What your father did had nothing to do with Larry. Nothing.

ANN. But we can't know that.

MOTHER (*striving for control*). As long as you're here!

ANN (*perplexed*). But, Kate . . .

MOTHER. Put that out of your head!

KELLER. Because . . .

MOTHER (*quickly to Keller*). That's all, that's enough. (*Places her hand on her head*) Come inside now, and have some tea with me. (*She turns and goes up steps*)

KELLER (*to Ann*). The one thing you . . .

MOTHER (*sharply*). He's not dead, so there's no argument! Now come!

KELLER (*angrily*). In a minute! (*Mother turns and goes into house*) Now look, Annie . . .

CHRIS. All right, Dad, forget it.

KELLER. No, she dasn't feel that way. Annie . . .

CHRIS. I'm sick of the whole subject, now cut it out.

KELLER. You want her to go on like this? *(To Ann)* Those cylinder heads went into P-40's only. What's the matter with you? You know Larry never flew a P-40.

CHRIS. So who flew those P-40's, pigs?

KELLER. The man was a fool, but don't make a murderer out of him. You got no sense? Look what it does to her! *(To Ann)* Listen, you gotta appreciate what was doin' in that shop in the war. The both of you! It was a madhouse. Every half hour the Major callin' for cylinder heads, they were whippin' us with the telephone. The trucks were hauling them away hot, damn near. I mean just try to see it human, see it human. All of a sudden a batch comes out with a crack. That happens, that's the business. A fine, hairline crack. All right, so . . . so he's a little man, your father, always scared of loud voices. What'll the Major say?—Half a day's production shot. . . . What'll I say? You know what I mean? Human. *(He pauses)* So he takes out his tools and he . . . covers over the cracks. All right . . . that's bad, it's wrong, but that's what a little man does. If I could have gone in that day I'd a told him—junk 'em, Herb, we can afford it. But alone he was afraid. But I know he meant no harm. He believed they'd hold up a hundred percent. That's a mistake, but it ain't murder. You mustn't feel that way about him. You understand me? It ain't right.

ANN *(she regards him a moment)*. Joe, let's forget it.

KELLER. Annie, the day the news came about Larry he was in the next cell to mine . . . Dad. And he cried, Annie . . . he cried half the night.

ANN *(touched)*. He shoulda cried all night. *(Slight pause)*

KELLER *(almost angered)*. Annie, I do not understand why you . . . !

CHRIS *(breaking in—with nervous urgency)*. Are you going to stop it?!

ANN. Don't yell at him. He just wants everybody happy.

KELLER *(clasps her around waist, smiling)*. That's my sentiments. Can you stand steak?

CHRIS. And champagne!

KELLER. Now you're operatin'! I'll call Swanson's for a table! Big time tonight, Annie!

ANN. Can't scare me.

KELLER *(to Chris, pointing at Ann)*. I like that girl. Wrap her up. *(They laugh. Goes up porch)* You got nice legs, Annie! . . . I want to see everybody drunk tonight. *(Pointing to Chris)* Look at him, he's blushin'! *(He exits, laughing, into house)*

CHRIS *(calling after him)*. Drink your tea, Casanova. *(He turns to Ann)* Isn't he a great guy?

ANN. You're the only one I know who loves his parents.

CHRIS. I know. It went out of style didn't it?

ANN *(with a sudden touch of sadness)* It's all right. It's a good thing. *(She looks about)* You know? It's lovely here. The air is sweet.

CHRIS *(hopefully)*. You're not sorry you came?

ANN. Not sorry, no. But I'm . . . not going to stay . . .

CHRIS. Why?

ANN. In the first place, your mother as much as told me to go.

CHRIS. Well . . .

ANN. You saw that . . . and then you . . . you've been kind of . . .

CHRIS. What?

ANN. Well . . . kind of embarrassed ever since I got here.

CHRIS. The trouble is I planned on kind of sneaking up on you over a period of a week or so. But they take it for granted that we're all set.

ANN. I knew they would. Your mother anyway.

CHRIS. How did you know?

ANN. From *her* point of view, why else would I come?

CHRIS. Well . . . would you want to? *(Ann still studies him)* I guess you know this is why I asked you to come.

ANN. I guess this is why I came.

CHRIS. Ann, I love you. I love you a great deal. *(Finally)* I love you. *(Pause. She waits)* I have no imagination . . . that's all I know to tell you. *(Ann, waiting, ready)* I'm embarrassing you. I didn't want to tell it to you here. I wanted some place we'd never been; a place where we'd be brand new to each other. . . . You feel it's wrong here, don't you? This yard, this chair? I want you to be ready for me. I don't want to win you away from anything.

ANN *(putting her arms around him)*. Oh, Chris, I've been ready a long, long time!

CHRIS. Then he's gone forever. You're sure.

ANN. I almost got married two years ago.

CHRIS. . . . why didn't you?

ANN. You started to write to me . . . *(Slight pause)*

CHRIS. You felt something that far back?

ANN. Every day since!

CHRIS. Ann, why didn't you let me know?

ANN. I was waiting for you, Chris. Till then you never wrote. And when you did, what did you say? You sure can be ambiguous, you know.

CHRIS *(he looks toward house, then at her, trembling)*. Give me a kiss, Ann. Give me a . . . *(They kiss)* God, I kissed you, Annie, I kissed Annie. How long, how long I've been waiting to kiss you!

ANN. I'll never forgive you. Why did you wait all these years? All I've done is sit and wonder if I was crazy for thinking of you.

CHRIS. Annie, we're going to live now! I'm going to make you so happy. *(He kisses her, but without their bodies touching)*

ANN *(a little embarrassed)*. Not like that you're not.

CHRIS. I kissed you . . .

ANN. Like Larry's brother. Do it like you, Chris. *(He breaks away from her abruptly)* What is it, Chris?

CHRIS. Let's drive some place . . . I want to be alone with you.

ANN. No . . . what is it, Chris, your mother?

CHRIS. No . . . nothing like that . . .

ANN. Then what's wrong? . . . Even in your letters, there was something ashamed.

CHRIS. Yes. I suppose I have been. But it's going from me.

ANN. You've got to tell me—

CHRIS. I don't know how to start. *(He takes her hand. He speaks quietly, factually at first)*

ANN. It wouldn't work this way. *(Slight pause)*

CHRIS. It's all mixed up with so many other things. . . . You remember, overseas, I was in command of a company?

ANN. Yeah, sure.

CHRIS. Well, I lost them.

ANN. How many?

CHRIS. Just about all.

ANN. Oh, gee!

CHRIS. It takes a little time to toss that off. Because they weren't just men. For instance, one time it'd been raining several days and this kid came to me, and gave me his last pair of dry socks. Put them in my pocket. That's only a little thing . . . but . . . that's the kind of guys I had. They didn't die; they killed themselves for each other. I mean that exactly; a little more selfish and they'd 've been here today. And I got an idea—watching them go down. Everything was being destroyed, see, but it seemed to me that one new thing was made. A kind of . . . responsibility. Man for man. You understand me? —To show that, to bring that on to the earth again like some kind of a monument and everyone would feel it standing there, behind him, and it would make a difference to him. *(Pause)* And then I came home and it was incredible. I . . . there was no meaning in it here; the whole thing to them was a kind of a— bus accident. I went to work with Dad, and that rat-race again. I felt . . . what you said . . . ashamed somehow. Because nobody was changed at all. It seemed to make suckers out of a lot of guys. I felt wrong to be alive, to open the bank-book, to drive the new car, to see the new refrigerator. I mean you can take those things out of a war, but when you drive that car you've got to know that it came out of the love a man can have for a man, you've got to be a little better because of that. Otherwise what you have is really loot, and there's blood on it. I didn't want to take any of it. And I guess that included you.

ANN. And you still feel that way?

CHRIS. I want you now, Annie.

ANN. Because you mustn't feel that way any more. Because you have a right to whatever you have. Everything, Chris, understand that? To me, too . . . And the money, there's nothing wrong in your money. Your father put hundreds of planes in the air, you should be proud. A man should be paid for that . . .

CHRIS. Oh Annie, Annie . . . I'm going to make a fortune for you!

KELLER *(offstage)*. Hello . . . Yes. Sure.

ANN *(laughing softly)*. What'll I do with

a fortune . . . ? *(They kiss. Keller enters from house)*

KELLER *(thumbing toward house)*. Hey, Ann, your brother . . . *(They step apart shyly. Keller comes down, and wryly . . .)* What is this, Labor Day?

CHRIS *(waving him away, knowing the kidding will be endless)*. All right, all right . . .

ANN. You shouldn't burst out like that.

KELLER. Well, nobody told me it was Labor Day. *(Looks around)* Where's the hot dogs?

CHRIS *(loving it)*. All right. You said it once.

KELLER. Well, as long as I know it's Labor Day from now on, I'll wear a bell around my neck.

ANN *(affectionately)*. He's so subtle!

CHRIS. George Bernard Shaw as an elephant.

KELLER. George!—hey, you kissed it out of my head—your brother's on the phone.

ANN *(surprised)*. My brother?

KELLER. Yeah, George. Long distance.

ANN. What's the matter, is anything wrong?

KELLER. I don't know, Kate's talking to him. Hurry up, she'll cost him five dollars.

ANN *(she takes a step upstage, then comes down toward Chris)*. I wonder if we ought to tell your mother yet? I mean I'm not very good in an argument.

CHRIS. We'll wait till tonight. After dinner. Now don't get tense, just leave it to me.

KELLER. What're you telling her?

CHRIS. Go ahead, Ann. *(With misgivings, Ann goes up and into house)* We're getting married, Dad. *(Keller nods indecisively)* Well, don't you say anything?

KELLER *(distracted)*. I'm glad, Chris, I'm just . . . George is calling from Columbus.

CHRIS. Columbus!

KELLER. Did Annie tell you he was going to see his father today?

CHRIS. No, I don't think she knew anything about it.

KELLER *(asking uncomfortably)*. Chris! You . . . you think you know her pretty good?

CHRIS *(hurt and apprehensive)* What kind of a question . . . ?

KELLER. I'm just wondering. All these years George don't go to see his father. Suddenly he goes . . . and she comes here.

CHRIS. Well, what about it?

KELLER. It's crazy, but it comes to my mind. She don't hold nothin' against me, does she?

CHRIS *(angry)*. I don't know what you're talking about.

KELLER *(a little more combatively)*. I'm just talkin'. To his last day in court the man blamed it all on me; and this is his daughter. I mean if she was sent here to find out something?

CHRIS *(angered)*. Why? What is there to find out?

ANN *(on phone, offstage)*. Why are you so excited, George? What happened there?

KELLER. I mean if they want to open up the case again, for the nuisance value, to hurt us?

CHRIS. Dad . . . how could you think that of her?

ANN *(still on phone)*. But what did he say to you, for God's sake?

(Together)

KELLER. It couldn't be, heh. You know.

CHRIS. Dad, you amaze me . . .

KELLER *(breaking in)*. All right, forget it, forget it. *(With great force, moving about)* I want a clean start for you, Chris. I want a new sign over the plant—Christopher Keller, Incorporated.

CHRIS *(a little uneasily)*. J. O. Keller is good enough.

KELLER. We'll talk about it. I'm going to build you a house, stone, with a driveway from the road. I want you to spread out, Chris, I want you to use what I made for you . . . *(He is close to him now)* . . . I mean, with joy, Chris, without shame . . . with joy.

CHRIS *(touched)*. I will, Dad.

KELLER *(with deep emotion)*. . . . . Say it to me.

CHRIS. Why?

KELLER. Because sometimes I think you're . . . ashamed of the money.

CHRIS. No, don't feel that.

KELLER. Because it's good money, there's nothing wrong with that money.

CHRIS *(a little frightened)*. Dad, you don't have to tell me this.

KELLER *(with overriding affection and self-confidence now. He grips Chris by the back of the neck, and with laughter between his determined jaws)*. Look, Chris, I'll go to work on Mother for you. We'll get her so drunk tonight we'll all get married! *(Steps away, with a wide gesture of his arm)* There's gonna be a wedding, kid, like there never was seen! Champagne, tuxedoes . . . !

(He breaks off as Ann's voice comes out loud from the house where she is still talking on phone.)

ANN. Simply because when you get excited you don't control yourself. . . . *(Mother comes out of house)* Well, what did he tell you for God's sake? *(Pause)* All right, come then. *(Pause)* Yes, they'll all be here. Nobody's running away from you. And try to get hold of yourself, will you? *(Pause)* All right, all right. Goodbye. *(There is a brief pause as Ann hangs up receiver, then comes out of kitchen)*

CHRIS. Something happen?

KELLER. He's coming here?

ANN. On the seven o'clock. He's in Columbus. *(To Mother)* I told him it would be all right.

KELLER. Sure, fine! Your father took sick?

ANN *(mystified).* No, George didn't say he was sick. I . . . *(Shaking it off)* I don't know, I suppose it's something stupid, you know my brother . . . *(She comes to Chris)* Let's go for a drive, or something . . .

CHRIS. Sure. Give me the keys, Dad.

MOTHER. Drive through the park. It's beautiful now.

CHRIS. Come on, Ann. *(To them)* Be back right away.

ANN *(as she and Chris exit up driveway).* See you. *(Mother comes down toward Keller, her eyes fixed on him)*

KELLER. Take your time. *(To Mother)* What does George want?

MOTHER. He's been in Columbus since this morning with Steve. He's gotta see Annie right away, he says.

KELLER. What for?

MOTHER. I don't know. *(She speaks with warning)* He's a lawyer now, Joe. George is a lawyer. All these years he never even sent a postcard to Steve. Since he got back from the war, not a postcard.

KELLER. So what?

MOTHER *(her tension breaking out).* Suddenly he takes an airplane from New York to see him. An airplane!

KELLER. Well? So?

MOTHER *(trembling).* Why?

KELLER. I don't read minds. Do you?

MOTHER. Why, Joe? What has Steve suddenly got to tell him that he takes an airplane to see him?

KELLER. What do I care what Steve's got to tell him?

MOTHER. You're sure, Joe?

KELLER *(frightened, but angry).* Yes, I'm sure.

MOTHER *(she sits stiffly in a chair).* Be smart now, Joe. The boy is coming. Be smart.

KELLER *(desperately).* Once and for all, did you hear what I said? I said I'm sure!

MOTHER *(she nods weakly).* All right, Joe. *(He straightens up)* Just . . . be smart. *(Keller, in hopeless fury, looks at her, turns around, goes up to porch and into house, slamming screen door violently behind him. Mother sits in chair downstage, stiffly, staring, seeing.)*

CURTAIN

ACT TWO

As twilight falls, that evening.

On the rise, Chris is discovered sawing the broken-off tree, leaving stump standing alone. He is dressed in good pants, white shoes, but without a shirt. He disappears with tree up the alley when Mother appears on porch. She comes down and stands watching him. She has on a dressing-gown, carries a tray of grape-juice drink in a pitcher, and glasses with sprigs of mint in them.

MOTHER *(calling up alley).* Did you have to put on good pants to do that? *(She comes downstage and puts tray on table in the arbor. Then looks around uneasily, then feels pitcher for coolness. Chris enters from alley brushing off his hands)* You notice there's more light with that thing gone?

CHRIS. Why aren't you dressing?

MOTHER. It's suffocating upstairs. I made a grape drink for Georgie. He always liked grape. Come and have some.

CHRIS *(impatiently).* Well, come on, get dressed. And what's Dad sleeping so much for? *(He goes to table and pours a glass of juice)*

MOTHER. He's worried. When he's worried he sleeps. *(Pauses. Looks into his eyes)* We're dumb, Chris. Dad and I are stupid people. We don't know anything. You've got to protect us.

CHRIS. You're silly; what's there to be afraid of?

MOTHER. To his last day in court Steve never gave up the idea that Dad made him do it. If they're going to open the case again I won't live through it.

CHRIS. George is just a damn fool, Mother. How can you take him seriously?

MOTHER. That family hates us. Maybe even Annie. . . .

CHRIS. Oh, now, Mother . . .

MOTHER. You think just because you like everybody, they like you!

CHRIS. All right, stop working yourself up. Just leave everything to me.

MOTHER. When George goes home tell her to go with him.

CHRIS (noncommittally). Don't worry about Annie.

MOTHER. Steve is her father, too.

CHRIS. Are you going to cut it out? Now, come.

MOTHER (going upstage with him). You don't realize how people can hate, Chris, they can hate so much they'll tear the world to pieces. . . . (Ann, dressed up, appears on porch)

CHRIS. Look! She's dressed already. (As he and Mother mount porch) I've just got to put on a shirt.

ANN (in a preoccupied way). Are you feeling well, Kate?

MOTHER. What's the difference, dear. There are certain people, y'know, the sicker they get the longer they live. (She goes into house)

CHRIS. You look nice.

ANN. We're going to tell her tonight.

CHRIS. Absolutely, don't worry about it.

ANN. I wish we could tell her now. I can't stand scheming. My stomach gets hard.

CHRIS. It's not scheming, we'll just get her in a better mood.

MOTHER (offstage, in the house). Joe, are you going to sleep all day!

ANN (laughing). The only one who's relaxed is your father. He's fast asleep.

CHRIS. I'm relaxed.

ANN. Are you?

CHRIS. Look. (He holds out his hand and makes it shake) Let me know when George gets here. (He goes into the house. She moves aimlessly, and then is drawn toward tree stump. She goes to it, hesitantly touches broken top in the hush of her thoughts. Offstage Lydia calls, "Johnny! Come get your supper!" Sue enters, and halts, seeing Ann)

SUE. Is my husband . . . ?

ANN (turns, startled). Oh!

SUE. I'm terribly sorry.

ANN. It's all right, I . . . I'm a little silly about the dark.

SUE (looks about). It is getting dark.

ANN. Are you looking for your husband?

SUE. As usual. (Laughs tiredly) He spends so much time here, they'll be charging him rent.

ANN. Nobody was dressed so he drove over to the depot to pick up my brother.

SUE. Oh, your brother's in?

ANN. Yeah, they ought to be here any minute now. Will you have a cold drink?

SUE. I will, thanks. (Ann goes to table and pours) My husband. Too hot to drive me to beach.—Men are like little boys; for the neighbors they'll always cut the grass.

ANN. People like to do things for the Kellers. Been that way since I can remember.

SUE. It's amazing. I guess your brother's coming to give you away, heh?

ANN (giving her drink). I don't know. I suppose.

SUE. You must be all nerved up.

ANN. It's always a problem getting yourself married, isn't it?

SUE. That depends on your shape, of course. I don't see why you should have had a problem.

ANN. I've had chances—

SUE. I'll bet. It's romantic . . . it's very unusual to me, marrying the brother of your sweetheart.

ANN. I don't know. I think it's mostly that whenever I need somebody to tell me the truth I've always thought of Chris. When he tells you something you know it's so. He relaxes me.

SUE. And he's got money. That's important, you know.

ANN. It wouldn't matter to me.

SUE. You'd be surprised. It makes all the difference. I married an interne. On my salary. And that was bad, because as soon as a woman supports a man he owes her something. You can never owe somebody without resenting them. (Ann laughs) That's true, you know.

ANN. Underneath, I think the doctor is very devoted.

SUE. Oh, certainly. But it's bad when a

man always sees the bars in front of him. Jim thinks he's in jail all the time.

ANN. Oh . . .

SUE. That's why I've been intending to ask you a small favor, Ann . . . it's something very important to me.

ANN. Certainly, if I can do it.

SUE. You can. When you take up housekeeping, try to find a place away from here.

ANN. Are you fooling?

SUE. I'm very serious. My husband is unhappy with Chris around.

ANN. How is that?

SUE. Jim's a successful doctor. But he's got an idea he'd like to do medical research. Discover things. You see?

ANN. Well, isn't that good?

SUE. Research pays twenty-five dollars a week minus laundering the hair shirt. You've got to give up your life to go into it.

ANN. How does Chris?

SUE *(with growing feeling)*. Chris makes people want to be better than it's possible to be. He does that to people.

ANN. Is that bad?

SUE. My husband has a family, dear. Every time he has a session with Chris he feels as though he's compromising by not giving up everything for research. As though Chris or anybody else isn't compromising. It happens with Jim every couple of years. He meets a man and makes a statue out of him.

ANN. Maybe he's right. I don't mean that Chris is a statue, but . . .

SUE. Now darling, you know he's not right.

ANN. I don't agree with you. Chris . . .

SUE. Let's face it, dear. Chris is working with his father, isn't he? He's taking money out of that business every week in the year.

ANN. What of it?

SUE. You ask me what of it?

ANN. I certainly do. *(She seems about to burst out)* You oughtn't cast aspersions like that, I'm surprised at you.

SUE. You're surprised at me!

ANN. He'd never take five cents out of that plant if there was anything wrong with it.

SUE. You know that.

ANN. I know it. I resent everything you've said.

SUE *(moving toward her)*. You know what I resent, dear?

ANN. Please, I don't want to argue.

SUE. I resent living next door to the Holy Family. It makes me look like a bum, you understand?

ANN. I can't do anything about that.

SUE. Who is he to ruin a man's life? Everybody knows Joe pulled a fast one to get out of jail.

ANN. That's not true!

SUE. Then why don't you go out and talk to people? Go on, talk to them. There's not a person on the block who doesn't know the truth.

ANN. That's a lie. People come here all the time for cards and . . .

SUE. So what? They give him credit for being smart. I do, too, I've got nothing against Joe. But if Chris wants people to put on the hair shirt let him take off his broadcloth. He's driving my husband crazy with that phony idealism of his, and I'm at the end of my rope on it! *(Chris enters on porch, wearing shirt and tie now. She turns quickly, hearing. With a smile)* Hello, darling. How's Mother?

CHRIS. I thought George came.

SUE. No, it was just us.

CHRIS *(coming down to them)*. Susie, do me a favor, heh? Go up to Mother and see if you can calm her. She's all worked up.

SUE. She still doesn't know about you two?

CHRIS *(laughs a little)*. Well, she senses it, I guess. You know my mother.

SUE *(going up to porch)*. Oh, yeah, she's psychic.

CHRIS. Maybe there's something in the medicine chest.

SUE. I'll give her one of everything. *(On porch)* Don't worry about Kate; couple of drinks, dance her around a little . . . she'll love Ann. *(To Ann)* Because you're the female version of him. *(Chris laughs)* Don't be alarmed, I said version. *(She goes into house)*

CHRIS. Interesting woman, isn't she?

ANN. Yeah, she's very interesting.

CHRIS. She's a great nurse, you know, she . . .

ANN *(in tension, but trying to control it)*. Are you still doing that?

CHRIS *(sensing something wrong, but still smiling)*. Doing what?

ANN. As soon as you get to know somebody you find a distinction for them. How do you know she's a great nurse?

CHRIS. What's the matter, Ann?

ANN. The woman hates you. She despises you!

CHRIS. Hey . . . what's hit you?

ANN. Gee, Chris . . .

CHRIS. What happened here?

ANN. You never . . . Why didn't you tell me?

CHRIS. Tell you what?

ANN. She says they think Joe is guilty.

CHRIS. What difference does it make what they think?

ANN. I don't care what they think, I just don't understand why you took the trouble to deny it. You said it was all forgotten.

CHRIS. I didn't want you to feel there was anything wrong in you coming here, that's all. I know a lot of people think my father was guilty, and I assumed there might be some question in your mind.

ANN. But I never once said I suspected him.

CHRIS. Nobody says it.

ANN. Chris, I know how much you love him, but it could never . . .

CHRIS. Do you think I could forgive him if he'd done that thing?

ANN. I'm not here out of a blue sky, Chris. I turned my back on my father, if there's anything wrong here now . . .

CHRIS. I know that, Ann.

ANN. George is coming from Dad, and I don't think it's with a blessing.

CHRIS. He's welcome here. You've got nothing to fear from George.

ANN. Tell me that . . . just tell me that.

CHRIS. The man is innocent, Ann. Remember he was falsely accused once and it put him through hell. How would you behave if you were faced with the same thing again? Annie, believe me, there's nothing wrong for you here, believe me, kid.

ANN. All right, Chris, all right. *(They embrace as Keller appears quietly on porch. Ann simply studies him)*

KELLER. Every time I come out here it looks like Playland! *(They break and laugh in embarrassment)*

CHRIS. I thought you were going to shave?

KELLER *(sitting on bench)*. In a minute. I just woke up, I can't see nothin'.

ANN. You look shaved.

KELLER. Oh, no. *(Massages his jaw)* Gotta be extra special tonight. Big night, Annie. So how's it feel to be a married woman?

ANN *(laughs)*. I don't know, yet.

KELLER *(to Chris)*. What's the matter, you slippin'? *(He takes a little box of apples from under the bench as they talk)*

CHRIS. The great roué!

KELLER. What is that, roué?

CHRIS. It's French.

KELLER. Don't talk dirty. *(They laugh)*

CHRIS *(to Ann)*. You ever meet a bigger ignoramus?

KELLER. Well, somebody's got to make a living.

ANN *(as they laugh)*. That's telling him.

KELLER. I don't know, everybody's gettin' so Goddam educated in this country there'll be nobody to take away the garbage. *(They laugh)* It's gettin' so the only dumb ones left are the bosses.

ANN. You're not so dumb, Joe.

KELLER. I know, but you go into our plant, for instance. I got so many lieutenants, majors and colonels that I'm ashamed to ask somebody to sweep the floor. I gotta be careful I'll insult somebody. No kiddin'. It's a tragedy: you stand on the street today and spit, you're gonna hit a college man.

CHRIS. Well, don't spit.

KELLER *(breaks apple in half, passing it to Ann and Chris)*. I mean to say, it's comin' to a pass. *(He takes a breath)* I been thinkin', Annie . . . your brother, George. I been thinkin' about your brother George. When he comes I like you to *brooch* something to him.

CHRIS. Broach.

KELLER. What's the matter with brooch?

CHRIS *(smiling)*. It's not English.

KELLER. When I went to night school it was brooch.

ANN *(laughing)*. Well, in day school it's broach.

KELLER. Don't surround me, will you? Seriously, Ann . . . You say he's not well. George, I been thinkin', why should he knock himself out in New York with that cut-throat competition, when I got so many friends here; I'm very friendly with some big lawyers in town. I could set George up here.

ANN. That's awfully nice of you, Joe.

KELLER. No, kid, it ain't nice of me. I want you to understand me. I'm thinking of Chris. *(Slight pause)* See . . . this is what I mean. You get older, you want to feel that you . . . accomplished something. My only accomplishment is my son. I ain't brainy. That's all I accomplished. Now, a year, eighteen months, your father'll be a free man. Who is he going to come to, Annie? His baby. You. He'll come, old, mad, into your house.

ANN. That can't matter any more, Joe.

KELLER. I don't want that to come between us. *(Gestures between Chris and himself)*

ANN. I can only tell you that that could never happen.

KELLER. You're in love now, Annie, but believe me, I'm older than you and I know —a daughter is a daughter, and a father is a father. And it could happen. *(He pauses)* I like you and George to go to him in prison and tell him . . . "Dad, Joe wants to bring you into the business when you get out."

ANN *(surprised, even shocked)*. You'd have him as a partner?

KELLER. No, no partner. A good job. *(Pause. He sees she is shocked, a little mystified. He gets up, speaks more nervously)* I want him to know, Annie . . . while he's sitting there I want him to know that when he gets out he's got a place waitin' for him. It'll take his bitterness away. To know you got a place . . . it sweetens you.

ANN. Joe, you owe him nothing.

KELLER. I owe him a good kick in the teeth, but he's your father. . . .

CHRIS. Then kick him in the teeth! I don't want him in the plant, so that's that! You understand? And besides, don't talk about him like that. People misunderstand you!

KELLER. And I don't understand why she has to crucify the man.

CHRIS. Well, it's her father, if she feels . . .

KELLER. No, no . . .

CHRIS *(almost angrily)*. What's it to you? Why . . . ?

KELLER *(a commanding outburst in high nervousness)*. A father is a father! *(As though the outburst had revealed him, he looks about, wanting to retract it. His hand goes to his cheek)* I better . . . I better shave. *(He turns and a smile is on his face. To Ann)* I didn't mean to yell at you, Annie.

ANN. Let's forget the whole thing, Joe.

KELLER. Right. *(To Chris)* She's likeable.

CHRIS *(a little peeved at the man's stupidity)*. Shave, will you?

KELLER. Right again.

(As he turns to porch Lydia comes hurrying from her house.)

LYDIA. I forgot all about it . . . *(Seeing Chris and Ann)* Hya. *(To Joe)* I promised to fix Kate's hair for tonight. Did she comb it yet?

KELLER. Always a smile, hey, Lydia?

LYDIA. Sure, why not?

KELLER *(going up on porch)*. Come on up and comb my Katie's hair. *(Lydia goes up on porch)* She's got a big night, make her beautiful.

LYDIA. I will.

KELLER *(he holds door open for her and she goes into kitchen. To Chris and Ann)*. Hey, that could be a song. *(He sings softly)*

"Come on up and comb my Katie's hair . . .

Oh, come on up, 'cause she's my lady fair—"

(To Ann) How's that for one year of night school? *(He continues singing as he goes into kitchen)*

"Oh, come on up, come on up, and comb my lady's hair—"

(Jim Bayliss rounds corner of driveway, walking rapidly. Jim crosses to Chris, motions him and pulls him down excitedly. Keller stands just inside kitchen door, watching them.)

CHRIS. What's the matter? Where is he?

JIM. Where's your mother?

CHRIS. Upstairs, dressing.

ANN *(crossing to them rapidly)*. What happened to George?

JIM. I asked him to wait in the car. Listen to me now. Can you take some advice? *(They wait)* Don't bring him in here.

ANN. Why?

JIM. Kate is in bad shape, you can't explode this in front of her.

ANN. Explode what?

JIM. You know why he's here, don't try to kid it away. There's blood in his eye; drive him somewhere and talk to him alone.

(Ann turns to go up drive, takes a couple of steps, sees Keller and stops. He goes quietly on into house.)

CHRIS *(shaken, and therefore angered)*. Don't be an old lady.

JIM. He's come to take her home. What does that mean? *(To Ann)* You know what that means. Fight it out with him some place else.

ANN *(she comes back down toward Chris)*. I'll drive . . . him somewhere.

CHRIS *(goes to her)*. No.

JIM. Will you stop being an idiot?

CHRIS. Nobody's afraid of him here. Cut that out! *(He starts for driveway, but is brought up short by George, who enters there. George is Chris' age, but a paler man, now on the edge of his self-restraint. He speaks quietly, as though afraid to find himself screaming. An instant's hesitation and Chris steps up to him, hand extended, smiling)* Helluva way to do; what're you sitting out there for?

GEORGE. Doctor said your mother isn't well, I . . .

CHRIS. So what? She'd want to see you, wouldn't she? We've been waiting for you all afternoon. *(He puts his hand on George's arm, but George pulls away, coming across toward Ann)*

ANN *(touching his collar)*. This is filthy, didn't you bring another shirt? *(George breaks away from her, and moves down, examining the yard. Door opens, and he turns rapidly, thinking it is Kate, but it's Sue. She looks at him, he turns away and moves to fence. He looks over it at his former home. Sue comes down stage)*

SUE *(annoyed)*. How about the beach, Jim?

JIM. Oh, it's too hot to drive.

SUE. How'd you get to the station—Zeppelin?

CHRIS. This is Mrs. Bayliss, George. *(Calling, as George pays no attention, staring at house)* George! *(George turns)* Mrs. Bayliss.

SUE. How do you do.

GEORGE *(removing his hat)*. You're the people who bought our house, aren't you?

SUE. That's right. Come and see what we did with it before you leave.

GEORGE *(he walks down and away from her)*. I liked it the way it was.

SUE *(after a brief pause)*. He's frank, isn't he?

JIM *(pulling her off)*. See you later. . . . Take it easy, fella. *(They exit)*

CHRIS *(calling after them)*. Thanks for driving him! *(Turning to George)* How about some grape juice? Mother made it especially for you.

GEORGE *(with forced appreciation)*. Good old Kate, remembered my grape juice.

CHRIS. You drank enough of it in this house. How've you been, George?—Sit down.

GEORGE *(he keeps moving)*. It takes me a minute. *(Looking around)* It seems impossible.

CHRIS. What?

GEORGE. I'm back here.

CHRIS. Say, you've gotten a little nervous, haven't you?

GEORGE. Yeah, toward the end of the day. What're you, big executive now?

CHRIS. Just kind of medium. How's the law?

GEORGE. I don't know. When I was studying in the hospital it seemed sensible, but outside there doesn't seem to be much of a law. The trees got thick, didn't they? *(Points to stump)* What's that?

CHRIS. Blew down last night. We had it there for Larry. You know.

GEORGE. Why, afraid you'll forget him?

CHRIS *(starts for George)*. Kind of a remark is that?

ANN *(breaking in, putting a restraining hand on Chris)*. When did you start wearing a hat?

GEORGE *(discovers hat in his hand)*. Today. From now on I decided to look like a lawyer, anyway. *(He holds it up to her)* Don't you recognize it?

ANN. Why? Where . . . ?

GEORGE. Your father's . . . he asked me to wear it.

ANN. . . . How is he?

GEORGE. He got smaller.

ANN. Smaller?

GEORGE. Yeah, little. *(Holds out his hand to measure)* He's a little man. That's what happens to suckers, you know. It's good I went to him in time—another year there'd be nothing left but his smell.

CHRIS. What's the matter, George, what's the trouble?

GEORGE. The trouble? The trouble is when you make suckers out of people once, you shouldn't try to do it twice.

CHRIS. What does that mean?

GEORGE *(to Ann)*. You're not married yet, are you?

ANN. George, will you sit down and stop—?

GEORGE. Are you married yet?

ANN. No, I'm not married yet.

GEORGE. You're not going to marry him.

ANN. Why am I not going to marry him?

GEORGE. Because his father destroyed your family.

CHRIS. Now look, George . . .

GEORGE. Cut it short, Chris. Tell her to come home with me. Let's not argue, you know what I've got to say.

CHRIS. George, you don't want to be the voice of God, do you?

GEORGE. I'm . . .

CHRIS. That's been your trouble all your life, George, you dive into things. What kind of a statement is that to make? You're a big boy now.

GEORGE. I'm a big boy now.

CHRIS. Don't come bulling in here. If you've got something to say, be civilized about it.

GEORGE. Don't civilize me!

ANN. Shhh!

CHRIS (ready to hit him). Are you going to talk like a grown man or aren't you?

ANN (quickly, to forestall an outburst). Sit down, dear. Don't be angry, what's the matter? (He allows her to seat him, looking at her) Now what happened? You kissed me when I left, now you . . .

GEORGE (breathlessly). My life turned upside down since then. I couldn't go back to work when you left. I wanted to go to Dad and tell him you were going to be married. It seemed impossible not to tell him. He loved you so much . . . (He pauses) Annie . . . we did a terrible thing. We can never be forgiven. Not even to send him a card at Christmas. I didn't see him once since I got home from the war! Annie, you don't know what was done to that man. You don't know what happened.

ANN (afraid). Of course I know.

GEORGE. You can't know, you wouldn't be here. Dad came to work that day. The night foreman came to him and showed him the cylinder heads . . . they were coming out of the process with defects. There was something wrong with the process. So Dad went directly to the phone and called here and told Joe to come down right away. But the morning passed. No sign of Joe. So Dad called again. By this time he had over a hundred defectives. The Army was screaming for stuff and

Dad didn't have anything to ship. So Joe told him . . . on the phone he told him to weld, cover up the cracks in any way he could, and ship them out.

CHRIS. Are you through now?

GEORGE (surging up at him). I'm not through now! (Back to Ann) Dad was afraid. He wanted Joe there if he was going to do it. But Joe can't come down . . . he's sick. Sick! He suddenly gets the flu! Suddenly! But he promised to take responsibility. Do you understand what I'm saying? On the telephone you can't have responsibility! In a court you can always deny a phone call and that's exactly what he did. They knew he was a liar the first time, but in the appeal they believed that rotten lie and now Joe is a big shot and your father is the patsy. (He gets up) Now what're you going to do? Eat his food, sleep in his bed? Answer me; what're you going to do?

CHRIS. What're you going to do, George?

GEORGE. He's too smart for me, I can't prove a phone call.

CHRIS. Then how dare you come in here with that rot?

ANN. George, the court . . .

GEORGE. The court didn't know your father! But you know him. You know in your heart Joe did it.

CHRIS (whirling him around). Lower your voice or I'll throw you out of here!

GEORGE. She knows. She knows.

CHRIS (to Ann). Get him out of here, Ann. Get him out of here.

ANN. George, I know everything you've said. Dad told that whole thing in court, and they . . .

GEORGE (almost a scream). The court did not know him, Annie!

ANN. Shhh!—But he'll say anything, George. You know how quick he can lie.

GEORGE (turning to Chris, with deliberation). I'll ask you something, and look me in the eye when you answer me.

CHRIS. I'll look you in the eye.

GEORGE. You know your father . . .

CHRIS. I know him well.

GEORGE. And he's the kind of boss to let a hundred and twenty-one cylinder heads be repaired and shipped out of his shop without even knowing about it?

CHRIS. He's that kind of boss.

GEORGE. And that's the same Joe Keller who never left his shop without first go ing around to see that all the lights were out.

CHRIS (*with growing anger*). The same Joe Keller.

GEORGE. The same man who knows how many minutes a day his workers spend in the toilet.

CHRIS. The same man.

GEORGE. And my father, that frightened mouse who'd never buy a shirt without somebody along—that man would dare do such a thing on his own?

CHRIS. On his own. And because he's a frightened mouse this is another thing he'd do;—throw the blame on somebody else because he's not man enough to take it himself. He tried it in court but it didn't work, but with a fool like you it works!

GEORGE. Oh, Chris, you're a liar to yourself!

ANN (*deeply shaken*). Don't talk like that!

CHRIS (*sits facing George*). Tell me, George. What happened? The court record was good enough for you all these years, why isn't it good now? Why did you believe it all these years?

GEORGE (*after a slight pause*). Because you believed it. . . . That's the truth, Chris. I believed everything, because I thought you did. But today I heard it from his mouth. From his mouth it's altogether different than the record. Anyone who knows him, and knows your father, will believe it from his mouth. Your Dad took everything we have. I can't beat that. But she's one item he's not going to grab. (*He turns to Ann*) Get your things. Everything they have is covered with blood. You're not the kind of a girl who can live with that. Get your things.

CHRIS. Ann . . . you're not going to believe that, are you?

ANN (*she goes to him*). You know it's not true, don't you?

GEORGE. How can he tell you? It's his father. (*To Chris*) None of these things ever even cross your mind?

CHRIS. Yes, they crossed my mind. Anything can cross your mind!

GEORGE. *He knows*, Annie. He knows!

CHRIS. The Voice of God!

GEORGE. Then why isn't your name on the business? Explain that to her!

CHRIS. What the hell has that got to do with . . .?

GEORGE. Annie, why isn't his name on it?

CHRIS. Even when I don't own it!

GEORGE. Who're you kidding? Who gets it when he dies? (*To Ann*) Open your eyes, you know the both of them, isn't that the first thing they'd do, the way they love each other?—J. O. Keller & Son? (*Pause. Ann looks from him to Chris*) I'll settle it. Do you want to settle it, or are you afraid to?

CHRIS. . . . What do you mean?

GEORGE. Let me go up and talk to your father. In ten minutes you'll have the answer. Or are you afraid of the answer?

CHRIS. I'm not afraid of the answer. I know the answer. But my mother isn't well and I don't want a fight here now.

GEORGE. Let me go to him.

CHRIS. You're not going to start a fight here now.

GEORGE (*to Ann*). What more do you want!!! (*There is a sound of footsteps in the house*)

ANN (*turns her head suddenly toward house*). Someone's coming.

CHRIS (*to George, quietly*). You won't say anything now.

ANN. You'll go soon. I'll call a cab.

GEORGE. You're coming with me.

ANN. And don't mention marriage, because we haven't told her yet.

GEORGE. You're coming with me.

ANN. You understand? Don't . . . George, you're not going to start anything now! (*She hears footsteps*) Shsh!

(*Mother enters on porch. She is dressed almost formally, her hair is fixed. They are all turned toward her. On seeing George she raises both hands, comes down toward him.*)

MOTHER. Georgie, Georgie.

GEORGE (*he has always liked her*). Hello, Kate.

MOTHER (*she cups his face in her hands*). They made an old man out of you. (*Touches his hair*) Look, you're gray.

GEORGE (*her pity, open and unabashed, reaches into him, and he smiles sadly*). I know, I . . .

MOTHER. I told you when you went away, don't try for medals.

GEORGE (*he laughs, tiredly*). I didn't try, Kate. They made it very easy for me.

MOTHER (*actually angry*). Go on. You're all alike. (*To Ann*) Look at him, why did you say he's fine? He looks like a ghost.

GEORGE (*relishing her solicitude*). I feel all right.

MOTHER. I'm sick to look at you. What's the matter with your mother, why don't she feed you?

ANN. He just hasn't any appetite.

MOTHER. If he ate in my house he'd have an appetite. (*To Ann*) I pity your husband! (*To George*) Sit down. I'll make you a sandwich.

GEORGE (*sits with an embarrassed laugh*). I'm really not hungry.

MOTHER. Honest to God, it breaks my heart to see what happened to all the children. How we worked and planned for you, and you end up no better than us.

GEORGE (*with deep feeling for her*). You ... you haven't changed at all, you know that, Kate?

MOTHER. None of us changed, Georgie. We all love you. Joe was just talking about the day you were born and the water got shut off. People were carrying basins from a block away—a stranger would have thought the whole neighborhood was on fire? (*They laugh. She sees the juice. To Ann*) Why didn't you give him some juice!

ANN (*defensively*). I offered it to him.

MOTHER (*scoffingly*). You offered it to him! (*Thrusting glass into George's hand*) Give it to him! (*To George, who is laughing*) And now you're going to sit here and drink some juice ... and look like something!

GEORGE (*sitting*). Kate, I feel hungry already.

CHRIS (*proudly*). She could turn Mahatma Ghandi into a heavyweight!

MOTHER (*to Chris, with great energy*). Listen, to hell with the restaurant! I got a ham in the icebox, and frozen strawberries, and avocados, and ...

ANN. Swell, I'll help you!

GEORGE. The train leaves at eight-thirty, Ann.

MOTHER (*to Ann*). You're leaving?

CHRIS. No, Mother, she's not ...

ANN (*breaking through it, going to George*). You hardly got here; give yourself a chance to get acquainted again.

CHRIS. Sure, you don't even know us any more.

MOTHER. Well, Chris, if they can't stay, don't ...

CHRIS. No, it's just a question of George, Mother, he planned on ...

GEORGE (*he gets up politely, nicely, for Kate's sake*). Now wait a minute, Chris ...

CHRIS (*smiling and full of command, cutting him off*). If you want to go, I'll drive you to the station now, but if you're staying, no arguments while you're here.

MOTHER (*at last confessing the tension*). Why should he argue? (*She goes to him, and with desperation and compassion, stroking his hair*) Georgie and us have no argument. How could we have an argument, Georgie? We all got hit by the same lightning, how can you ...? Did you see what happened to Larry's tree, Georgie? (*She has taken his arm, and unwillingly he moves across stage with her*) Imagine? While I was dreaming of him in the middle of the night, the wind came along and ... (*Lydia enters on porch. As soon as she sees him*)

LYDIA. Hey, Georgie! Georgie! Georgie! Georgie! Georgie! (*She comes down to him eagerly. She has a flowered hat in her hand, which Kate takes from her as she goes to George*)

GEORGE (*they shake hands eagerly, warmly*). Hello, Laughy. What'd you do, grow?

LYDIA. I'm a big girl now.

MOTHER (*taking hat from her*). Look what she can do to a hat!

ANN (*to Lydia, admiring the hat*). Did you make that?

MOTHER. In ten minutes! (*She puts it on*)

LYDIA (*fixing it on her head*). I only rearranged it.

GEORGE. You still make your own clothes?

CHRIS (*of Mother*). Ain't she classy! All she needs now is a Russian wolfhound.

MOTHER (*moving her head*). It feels like somebody is sitting on my head.

ANN. No, it's beautiful, Kate.

MOTHER (*kisses Lydia—to George*). She's a genius! You should've married her. (*They laugh*) This one can feed you!

LYDIA (*strangely embarrassed*). Oh, stop that, Kate.

GEORGE (*to Lydia*). Didn't I hear you had a baby?

MOTHER. You don't hear so good. She's got three babies.

GEORGE (*a little hurt by it—to Lydia*) No kidding, three?

LYDIA. Yeah, it was one, two, three—You've been away a long time, Georgie—

GEORGE. I'm beginning to realize.

MOTHER (*to Chris and George*). The trouble with you kids is you *think* too much.

LYDIA. Well, we think, too.

MOTHER. Yes, but not all the time.

GEORGE (*with almost obvious envy*). They never took Frank, heh?

LYDIA (*a little apologetically*). No, he was always one year ahead of the draft.

MOTHER. It's amazing. When they were calling boys twenty-seven Frank was just twenty-eight, when they made it twenty-eight he was just twenty-nine. That's why he took up astrology. It's all in when you were born, it just goes to show.

CHRIS. What does it go to show?

MOTHER (*to Chris*). Don't be so intelligent. Some superstitions are very nice! (*To Lydia*) Did he finish Larry's horoscope?

LYDIA. I'll ask him now, I'm going in. (*To George, a little sadly, almost embarrassed*) Would you like to see my babies? Come on.

GEORGE. I don't think so, Lydia.

LYDIA (*understanding*). All right. Good luck to you, George.

GEORGE. Thanks. And to you . . . And Frank. (*She smiles at him, turns and goes off to her house. George stands staring after her*)

LYDIA (*as she runs off*). Oh, Frank!

MOTHER (*reading his thoughts*). She got pretty, heh?

GEORGE (*sadly*). Very pretty.

MOTHER (*as a reprimand*). She's beautiful, you damned fool!

GEORGE (*looks around longingly; and softly, with a catch in his throat*). She makes it seem so nice around here.

MOTHER (*shaking her finger at him*). Look what happened to you because you wouldn't listen to me! I told you to marry that girl and stay out of the war!

GEORGE (*laughs at himself*). She used to laugh too much.

MOTHER. And you didn't laugh enough. While you were getting mad about Fascism Frank was getting into her bed.

GEORGE (*to Chris*). He won the war, Frank.

CHRIS. All the battles.

MOTHER (*in pursuit of this mood*). The day they started the draft, Georgie, I told you you loved that girl.

CHRIS (*laughs*). And truer love hath no man!

MOTHER. I'm smarter than any of you.

GEORGIE (*laughing*). She's wonderful!

MOTHER. And now you're going to listen to me, George. You had big principles, Eagle Scouts the three of you; so now I got a tree, and this one (*Indicating Chris*) when the weather gets bad he can't stand on his feet; and that big dope (*Pointing to Lydia's house*) next door who never reads anything but Andy Gump has three children and his house paid off. Stop being a philosopher, and look after yourself. Like Joe was just saying—you move back here, he'll help you get set, and I'll find you a girl and put a smile on your face.

GEORGE. Joe? Joe wants me here?

ANN (*eagerly*). He asked me to tell you, and I think it's a good idea.

MOTHER. Certainly. Why must you make believe you hate us? Is that another principle?—that you have to hate us? You don't hate us, George, I know you, you can't fool me, I diapered you. (*Suddenly, to Ann*) You remember Mr. Marcy's daughter?

ANN (*laughing, to George*). She's got you hooked already! (*George laughs, is excited*)

MOTHER. You look her over, George; you'll see she's the most beautiful . . .

CHRIS. She's got warts, George.

MOTHER (*to Chris*). She hasn't got warts! (*To George*) So the girl has a little beauty mark on her chin . . .

CHRIS. And two on her nose.

MOTHER. You remember. Her father's the retired police inspector.

CHRIS. Sergeant, George.

MOTHER. He's a very kind man!

CHRIS. He looks like a gorilla.

MOTHER (*to George*). He never shot anybody.

(*They all burst out laughing, as Keller appears in doorway. George rises abruptly, stares at Keller, who comes rapidly down to him.*)

KELLER (*the laughter stops. With strained joviality*). Well! Look who's here! (*Extending his hand*) Georgie, good to see ya.

GEORGE (*shakes hands—somberly*). How're you, Joe?

KELLER. So-so. Gettin' old. You comin' out to dinner with us?

GEORGE. No, got to be back in New York.

ANN. I'll call a cab for you. *(She goes up into the house)*

KELLER. Too bad you can't stay, George. Sit down. *(To Mother)* He looks fine.

MOTHER. He looks terrible.

KELLER. That's what I said, you look terrible, George. *(They laugh)* I wear the pants and she beats me with the belt.

GEORGE. I saw your factory on the way from the station. It looks like General Motors.

KELLER. I wish it was General Motors, but it ain't. Sit down, George. Sit down. *(Takes cigar out of his pocket)* So you finally went to see your father, I hear?

GEORGE. Yes, this morning. What kind of stuff do you make now?

KELLER. Oh, little of everything. Pressure cookers, an assembly for washing machines. Got a nice, flexible plant now. So how'd you find Dad? Feel all right?

GEORGE *(searching Keller, he speaks indecisively)*. No, he's not well, Joe.

KELLER *(lighting his cigar)*. Not his heart again, is it?

GEORGE. It's everything, Joe. It's his soul.

KELLER *(blowing out smoke)*. Uh huh—

CHRIS. How about seeing what they did with your house?

KELLER. Leave him be.

GEORGE *(to Chris, indicating Keller)*. I'd like to talk to him.

KELLER. Sure, he just got here. That's the way they do, George. A little man makes a mistake and they hang him by the thumbs; the big ones becomes ambassadors. I wish you'd-a told me you were going to see Dad.

GEORGE *(studying him)*. I didn't know you were interested.

KELLER. In a way, I am. I would like him to know, George, that as far as I'm concerned, any time he wants, he's got a place with me. I would like him to know :hat.

GEORGE. He hates your guts, Joe. Don't you know that?

KELLER. I imagined it. But that can change, too.

MOTHER. Steve was never like that.

GEORGE. He's like that now. He'd like to take every man who made money in the war and put him up against a wall.

CHRIS. He'll need a lot of bullets.

GEORGE. And he'd better not get any.

KELLER. That's a sad thing to hear.

GEORGE *(with bitterness dominant)*. Why? What'd you expect him to think of you?

KELLER *(the force of his nature rising, but under control)*. I'm sad to see he hasn't changed. As long as I know him, twenty-five years, the man never learned how to take the blame. You know that, George.

GEORGE *(he does)*. Well, I . . .

KELLER. But you do know it. Because the way you come in here you don't look like you remember it. I mean like in 1937 when we had the shop on Flood Street. And he damn near blew us all up with that heater he left burning for two days without water. He wouldn't admit that was his fault, either. I had to fire a mechanic to save his face. You remember that.

GEORGE. Yes, but . . .

KELLER. I'm just mentioning it, George. Because this is just another one of a lot of things. Like when he gave Frank that money to invest in oil stock.

GEORGE *(distressed)*. I know that, I . . .

KELLER *(driving in, but restrained)*. But it's good to remember those things, kid. The way he cursed Frank because the stock went down. Was that Frank's fault? To listen to him Frank was a swindler. And all the man did was give him a bad tip.

GEORGE *(gets up, moves away)*. I know those things . . .

KELLER. Then remember them, remember them. *(Ann comes out of house)* There are certain men in the world who rather see everybody hung before they'll take blame. You understand me, George? *(They stand facing each other, George trying to judge him)*

ANN *(coming downstage)*. The cab's on its way. Would you like to wash?

MOTHER *(with the thrust of hope)*. Why must he go? Make the midnight, George.

KELLER. Sure, you'll have dinner with us!

ANN. How about it? Why not? We're eating at the lake, we could have a swell time.

GEORGE *(long pause, as he looks at Ann. Chris, Keller, then back to her)*. All right.

MOTHER. Now you're talking.

CHRIS. I've got a shirt that'll go right with that suit.

MOTHER. Size fifteen and a half, right, George?

GEORGE. Is Lydia . . .? I mean—Frank and Lydia coming?

MOTHER. I'll get you a date that'll make her look like a . . . *(She starts upstage)*

GEORGE *(laughs).* No, I don't want a date.

CHRIS. I know somebody just for you! Charlotte Tanner! *(He starts for the house)*

KELLER. Call Charlotte, that's right.

MOTHER. Sure, call her up. *(Chris goes into house)*

ANN. You go up and pick out a shirt and tie.

GEORGE *(he stops, looks around at them and the place).* I never felt at home anywhere but here. I feel so . . . *(He nearly laughs, and turns away from them)* Kate, you look so young, you know? You didn't change at all. It . . . rings an old bell. *(Turns to Keller)* You too, Joe, you're amazingly the same. The whole atmosphere is.

KELLER. Say, I ain't got time to get sick.

MOTHER. He hasn't been laid up in fifteen years. . . .

KELLER. Except my flu during the war.

MOTHER. Huhh?

KELLER. My flu, when I was sick during . . . the war.

MOTHER. Well, sure . . . *(To George)* I mean except for that flu. *(George stands perfectly still)* Well, it slipped my mind, don't look at me that way. He wanted to go to the shop but he couldn't lift himself off the bed. I thought he had pneumonia.

GEORGE. Why did you say he's never . . .?

KELLER. I know how you feel, kid, I'll never forgive myself. If I could've gone in that day I'd never allow Dad to touch those heads.

GEORGE. She said you've never been sick.

MOTHER. I said he was sick, George.

GEORGE *(going to Ann).* Ann, didn't you hear her say . . .?

MOTHER. Do you remember every time you were sick?

GEORGE. I'd remember pneumonia. Especially if I got it just the day my partner was going to patch up cylinder heads . . . What happened that day, Joe?

FRANK *(enters briskly from driveway, holding Larry's horoscope in his hand. He comes to Kate).* Kate! Kate!

MOTHER. Frank, did you see George?

FRANK *(extending his hand).* Lydia told me, I'm glad to . . . you'll have to pardon me. *(Pulling Mother over)* I've got something amazing for you, Kate, I finished Larry's horoscope.

MOTHER. You'd be interested in this, George. It's wonderful the way he can understand the . . .

CHRIS *(entering from house).* George, the girl's on the phone . . .

MOTHER *(desperately).* He finished Larry's horoscope!

CHRIS. Frank, can't you pick a better time than this?

FRANK. The greatest men who ever lived believed in the stars!

CHRIS. Stop filling her head with that junk!

FRANK. Is it junk to feel that there's a greater power than ourselves? I've studied the stars of his life! I won't argue with you, I'm telling you. Somewhere in this world your brother is alive!

MOTHER *(instantly to Chris).* Why isn't it possible?

CHRIS. Because it's insane.

FRANK. Just a minute now. I'll tell you something and you can do as you please. Just let me say it. He was supposed to have died on November twenty-fifth. But November twenty-fifth was his favorable day.

CHRIS. Mother!

MOTHER. Listen to him!

FRANK. It was a day when everything good was shining on him, the kind of day he should've married on. You can laugh at a lot of it, I can understand you laughing. But the odds are a million to one that a man won't die on his favorable day. That's known, that's known, Chris!

MOTHER. Why isn't it possible, why isn't it possible, Chris!

GEORGE *(to Ann).* Don't you understand what she's saying? She just told you to go. What are you waiting for now?

CHRIS. Nobody can tell her to go. *(A car horn is heard)*

MOTHER *(to Frank).* Thank you, darling, for your trouble. Will you tell him to wait, Frank?

FRANK *(as he goes).* Sure thing.

MOTHER *(calling out)*. They'll be right out, driver!

CHRIS. She's not leaving, Mother.

GEORGE. You heard her say it, he's never been sick!

MOTHER. He misunderstood me, Chris! *(Chris looks at her, struck)*

GEORGE *(to Ann)*. He simply told your father to kill pilots, and covered himself in bed!

CHRIS. You'd better answer him, Annie. Answer him.

MOTHER. I packed your bag, darling . . .

CHRIS. What?

MOTHER. I packed your bag. All you've got to do is close it.

ANN. I'm not closing anything. He asked me here and I'm staying till he tells me to go. *(To George)* Till Chris tells me!

CHRIS. That's all! Now get out of here, George!

MOTHER *(to Chris)*. But if that's how he feels . . .

CHRIS. That's all, nothing more till Christ comes, about the case or Larry as long as I'm here! *(To Ann)* Now get out of here, George!

GEORGE *(to Ann)*. You tell me. I want to hear you tell me.

ANN. Go, George!

(They disappear up the driveway, Ann saying "Don't take it that way, Georgie! Please don't take it that way.")

CHRIS *(turns to his mother)*. What do you mean, you packed her bag? How dare you pack her bag?

MOTHER. Chris . . .

CHRIS. How dare you pack her bag?

MOTHER. She doesn't belong here.

CHRIS. Then I don't belong here.

MOTHER. She's Larry's girl.

CHRIS. And I'm his brother and he's dead, and I'm marrying his girl.

MOTHER. Never, never in this world!

KELLER. You lost your mind?

MOTHER. You have nothing to say!

KELLER *(cruelly)*. I got plenty to say. Three and a half years you been talking like a maniac—

MOTHER *(she smashes him across the face)*. Nothing. You have nothing to say. Now I say. He's coming back, and everybody has got to wait.

CHRIS. Mother, Mother . . .

MOTHER. Wait, wait . . .

CHRIS. How long? How long?

MOTHER *(rolling out of her)*. Till he comes; forever and ever till he comes!

CHRIS *(as an ultimatum)*. Mother, I'm going ahead with it.

MOTHER. Chris, I've never said no to you in my life, now I say no!

CHRIS. You'll never let him go till I do it.

MOTHER. I'll never let him go and you'll never let him go . . .!

CHRIS. I've let him go. I've let him go a long . . .

MOTHER *(with no less force, but turning from him)*. Then let your father go. *(Pause. Chris stands transfixed)*

KELLER. She's out of her mind.

MOTHER. Altogether! *(To Chris, but not facing them)* Your brother's alive, darling, because if he's dead, your father killed him. Do you understand me now? As long as you live, that boy is alive. God does not let a son be killed by his father. Now you see, don't you? Now you see. *(Beyond control, she hurries up and into house)*

KELLER *(Chris has not moved. He speaks insinuatingly, questioningly)*. She's out of her mind.

CHRIS *(a broken whisper)*. Then . . . you did it?

KELLER *(the beginning of plea in his voice)*. He never flew a P-40—

CHRIS *(struck. Deadly)*. But the others.

KELLER *(insistently)*. She's out of her mind. *(He takes a step toward Chris, pleadingly)*

CHRIS *(unyielding)*. Dad . . . you did it?

KELLER. He never flew a P-40, what's the matter with you?

CHRIS *(still asking, and saying)*. Then you did it. To the others.

(Both hold their voices down.)

KELLER *(afraid of him, his deadly insistence)*. What's the matter with you? What the hell is the matter with you?

CHRIS *(quietly, incredibly)*. How could you do that? How?

KELLER. What's the matter with you!

CHRIS. Dad . . . Dad, you killed twenty-one men!

KELLER. What, killed?

CHRIS. You killed them, you murdered them.

KELLER *(as though throwing his whole nature open before Chris)*. How could I kill anybody?

CHRIS. Dad! Dad!

KELLER (*trying to hush him*). I didn't kill anybody!

CHRIS. Then explain it to me. What did you do? Explain it to me or I'll tear you to pieces!

KELLER (*horrified at his overwhelming fury*). Don't, Chris, don't . . .

CHRIS. I want to know what you did, now what did you do? You had a hundred and twenty cracked engine-heads, now what did you do?

KELLER. If you're going to hang me then I . . .

CHRIS. I'm listening. God Almighty, I'm listening!

KELLER (*their movements now are those of subtle pursuit and escape. Keller keeps a step out of Chris' range as he talks*). You're a boy, what could I do! I'm in business, a man is in business; a hundred and twenty cracked, you're out of business; you got a process, the process don't work you're out of business; you don't know how to operate, your stuff is no good; they close you up, they tear up your contracts, what the hell's it to them? You lay forty years into a business and they knock you out in five minutes, what could I do, let them take forty years, let them take my life away? (*His voice cracking*) I never thought they'd install them. I swear to God. I thought they'd stop 'em before anybody took off.

CHRIS. Then why'd you ship them out?

KELLER. By the time they could spot them I thought I'd have the process going again, and I could show them they needed me and they'd let it go by. But weeks passed and I got no kick-back, so I was going to tell them.

CHRIS. Then why didn't you tell them?

KELLER. It was too late. The paper, it was all over the front page, twenty-one went down, it was too late. They came with handcuffs into the shop, what could I do? (*He sits on bench*) Chris . . . Chris, I did it for you, it was a chance and I took it for you. I'm sixty-one years old, when would I have another chance to make something for you? Sixty-one years old you don't get another chance, do ya?

CHRIS. You even knew they wouldn't hold up in the air.

KELLER. I didn't say that . . .

CHRIS. But you were going to warn them not to use them . . .

KELLER. But that don't mean . . .

CHRIS. It means you knew they'd crash.

KELLER. It don't mean that.

CHRIS. Then you *thought* they'd crash.

KELLER. I was afraid maybe . . .

CHRIS. You were afraid maybe! God in heaven, what kind of a man are you? Kids were hanging in the air by those heads. You knew that!

KELLER. For you, a business for you!

CHRIS (*with burning fury*). For me! Where do you live, where have you come from? For me!—I was dying every day and you were killing my boys and you did it for me? What the hell do you think I was thinking of, the Goddam business? Is that as far as your mind can see, the business? What is that, the world—the business? What the hell do you mean, you did it for me? Don't you have a country? Don't you live in the world? What the hell are you? You're not even an animal, no animal kills his own, what are you? What must I do to you? I ought to tear the tongue out of your mouth, what must I do? (*With his fist he pounds down upon his father's shoulder. He stumbles away, covering his face as he weeps*) What must I do, Jesus God, what must I do?

KELLER. Chris . . . My Chris . . .

CURTAIN

ACT THREE

Two o'clock the following morning, Mother is discovered on the rise, rocking ceaselessly in a chair, staring at her thoughts. It is an intense, slight, sort of rocking. A light shows from upstairs bedroom, lower floor windows being dark. The moon is strong and casts its bluish light.

Presently Jim, dressed in jacket and hat, appears, and seeing her, goes up beside her.

———

JIM. Any news?

MOTHER. No news.

JIM (*gently*). You can't sit up all night, dear, why don't you go to bed?

MOTHER. I'm waiting for Chris. Don't worry about me, Jim, I'm perfectly all right.

JIM. But it's almost two o'clock.

MOTHER. I can't sleep. (*Slight pause*) You had an emergency?

JIM (*tiredly*). Somebody had a head-ache and thought he was dying. (*Slight pause*) Half of my patients are quite mad. Nobody realizes how many people are walking around loose, and they're cracked as coconuts. Money. Money-money-money-money. You say it long enough it doesn't mean anything. (*She smiles, makes a silent laugh*) Oh, how I'd love to be around when that happens!

MOTHER (*shakes her head*). You're so childish, Jim! Sometimes you are.

JIM (*looks at her a moment*). Kate. (*Pause*) What happened?

KATE. I told you. He had an argument with Joe. Then he got in the car and drove away.

JIM. What kind of an argument?

MOTHER. An argument, Joe . . . he was crying like a child, before.

JIM. They argued about Ann?

MOTHER (*slight hesitation*). No, not Ann. Imagine? (*Indicates lighted window above*) She hasn't come out of that room since he left. All night in that room.

JIM (*looks at window, then at her*). What'd Joe do, tell him?

MOTHER (*she stops rocking*). Tell him what?

JIM. Don't be afraid, Kate, I know. I've always known.

MOTHER. How?

JIM. It occurred to me a long time ago.

MOTHER. I always had the feeling that in the back of his head, Chris . . . almost knew. I didn't think it would be such a shock.

JIM (*gets up*). Chris would never know how to live with a thing like that. It takes a certain talent . . . for lying. You have it, and I do. But not him.

MOTHER. What do you mean . . . he's not coming back?

JIM. Oh, no, he'll come back. We all come back, Kate. These private little revolutions always die. The compromise is always made. In a peculiar way. Frank is right—every man does have a star. The star of one's honesty. And you spend your life groping for it, but once it's out it never lights again. I don't think he went very far. He probably just wanted to be alone to watch his star go out.

MOTHER. Just as long as he comes back.

JIM. I wish he wouldn't, Kate. One year I simply took off, went to New Orleans; for two months I lived on bananas and milk, and studied a certain disease. It was beautiful. And then she came, and she cried. And I went back home with her. And now I live in the usual darkness; I can't find myself; it's even hard some times to remember the kind of man I wanted to be. I'm a good husband; Chris is a good son—he'll come back.

(*Keller comes out on porch in dressing-gown and slippers. He goes upstage—to alley. Jim goes to him.*)

JIM. I have a feeling he's in the park. I'll look around for him. Put her to bed, Joe; this is no good for what she's got. (*Jim exits up driveway*)

KELLER (*coming down*). What does he want here?

MOTHER. His friend is not home.

KELLER (*his voice is husky. Comes down to her*). I don't like him mixing in so much.

MOTHER. It's too late, Joe. He knows.

KELLER (*apprehensively*). How does he know?

MOTHER. He guessed a long time ago.

KELLER. I don't like that.

MOTHER (*laughs dangerously, quietly into the line*). What you don't like . . .

KELLER. Yeah, what I don't like.

MOTHER. You can't bull yourself through this one, Joe, you better be smart now. This thing—this thing is not over yet.

KELLER (*indicating lighted window above*). And what is she doing up there? She don't come out of the room.

MOTHER. I don't know, what is she doing? Sit down, stop being mad. You want to live? You better figure out your life.

KELLER. She don't know, does she?

MOTHER. She saw Chris storming out of here. It's one and one—she knows how to add.

KELLER. Maybe I ought to talk to her.

MOTHER. Don't ask me, Joe.

KELLER (*almost an outburst*). Then who do I ask? But I don't think she'll do anything about it.

MOTHER. You're asking me again.

KELLER. I'm askin' you. What am I, a stranger? I thought I had a family here. What happened to my family?

MOTHER. You've got a family. I'm simply telling you that I have no strength to think anymore.

KELLER. You have no strength. The minute there's trouble you have no strength.

MOTHER. Joe, you're doing the same thing again; all your life whenever there's trouble you yell at me and you think that settles it.

KELLER. Then what do I do? Tell me, talk to me, what do I do?

MOTHER. Joe . . . I've been thinking this way. If he comes back . . .

KELLER. What do you mean "if"? . . . he's comin' back!

MOTHER. I think if you sit him down and you . . . explain yourself. I mean you ought to make it clear to him that you know you did a terrible thing. *(Not looking into his eyes)* I mean if he saw that you realize what you did. You see?

KELLER. What ice does that cut?

MOTHER *(a little fearfully)*. I mean if you told him that you want to pay for what you did.

KELLER *(sensing . . . quietly)*. How can I pay?

MOTHER. Tell him . . . you're willing to go to prison. *(Pause)*

KELLER *(struck, amazed)*. I'm willing to . . . ?

MOTHER *(quickly)*. You wouldn't go, he wouldn't ask you to go. But if you told him you wanted to, if he could feel that you wanted to pay, maybe he would forgive you.

KELLER. He would forgive me! For what?

MOTHER. Joe, you know what I mean.

KELLER. I don't know what you mean! You wanted money, so I made money. What must I be forgiven? You wanted money, didn't you?

MOTHER. I didn't want it that way.

KELLER. I didn't want it that way, either! What difference is it what you want? I spoiled the both of you. I should've put him out when he was ten like I was put out, and make him earn his keep. Then he'd know how a buck is made in this world. Forgiven! I could live on a quarter a day myself, but I got a family so I . . .

MOTHER. Joe, Joe . . . it don't excuse it that you did it for the family.

KELLER. It's got to excuse it!

MOTHER. There's something bigger than the family to him.

KELLER. Nothin' is bigger!

MOTHER. There is to him.

KELLER. There's nothin' he could do that I wouldn't forgive. Because he's my son. Because I'm his father and he's my son.

MOTHER. Joe, I tell you . . .

KELLER. Nothin's bigger than that. And you're goin' to tell him, you understand? I'm his father and he's my son, and if there's something bigger than that I'll put a bullet in my head!

MOTHER. You stop that!

KELLER. You heard me. Now you know what to tell him. *(Pause. He moves from her—halts)* But he wouldn't put me away though . . . He wouldn't do that . . . Would he?

MOTHER. He loved you, Joe, you broke his heart.

KELLER. But to put me away . . .

MOTHER. I don't know. I'm beginning to think we don't really know him. They say in the war he was such a killer. Here he was always afraid of mice. I don't know him. I don't know what he'll do.

KELLER. Goddam, if Larry was alive he wouldn't act like this. He understood the way the world is made. He listened to me. To him the world had a forty-foot front, it ended at the building line. This one, everything bothers him. You make a deal, overcharge two cents, and his hair falls out. He don't understand money. Too easy, it came too easy. Yes, sir. Larry. That was a boy we lost. Larry. Larry. *(He slumps on chair in front of her)* What am I gonna do, Kate . . .

MOTHER. Joe, Joe, please . . . you'll be all right, nothing is going to happen . . .

KELLER *(desperately, lost)*. For you, Kate, for both of you, that's all I ever lived for . . .

MOTHER. I know, darling, I know . . . *(Ann enters from house. They say nothing, waiting for her to speak.)*

ANN. Why do you stay up? I'll tell you when he comes.

KELLER *(rises, goes to her)*. You didn't eat supper, did you? *(To Mother)* Why don't you make her something?

MOTHER. Sure, I'll . . .

ANN. Never mind, Kate, I'm all right. *(They are unable to speak to each other)* There's something I want to tell you. *(She starts, then halts)* I'm not going to do anything about it. . . .

MOTHER. She's a good girl! *(To Keller)* You see? She's a . . .

ANN. I'll do nothing about Joe, but you're going to do something for me.

(Directly to Mother) You made Chris feel guilty with me. Whether you wanted to or not, you've crippled him in front of me. I'd like you to tell him that Larry is dead and that you know it. You understand me? I'm not going out of here alone. There's no life for me that way. I want you to set him free. And then I promise you, everything will end, and we'll go away, and that's all.

KELLER. You'll do that. You'll tell him.

ANN. I know what I'm asking, Kate. You had two sons. But you've only got one now.

KELLER. You'll tell him . . .

ANN. And you've got to say it to him so he knows you mean it.

MOTHER. My dear, if the boy was dead, it wouldn't depend on my words to make Chris know it. . . . The night he gets into your bed, his heart will dry up. Because he knows and you know. To his dying day he'll wait for his brother! No, my dear, no such thing. You're going in the morning, and you're going alone. That's your life, that's your lonely life. *(She goes to porch, and starts in)*

ANN. Larry is dead, Kate.

MOTHER *(she stops)*. Don't speak to me.

ANN. I said he's dead. I know! He crashed off the coast of China November twenty-fifth! His engine didn't fail him. But he died. I know . . .

MOTHER. How did he die? You're lying to me. If you know, how did he die?

ANN. I loved him. You know I loved him. Would I have looked at anyone else if I wasn't sure? That's enough for you.

MOTHER *(moving on her)*. What's enough for me? What're you talking about? *(She grasps Ann's wrists)*

ANN. You're hurting my wrists.

MOTHER. What are you talking about! *(Pause. She stares at Ann a moment, then turns and goes to Keller)*

ANN. Joe, go in the house . . .

KELLER. Why should I . . .

ANN. Please go.

KELLER. Lemme know when he comes. *(Keller goes into house)*

MOTHER *(sees Ann take a letter from her pocket)*. What's that?

ANN. Sit down . . . *(Mother moves left to chair, but does not sit)* First you've got to understand. When I came, I didn't have any idea that Joe . . . I had nothing against him or you. I came to get married. I hoped . . . So I didn't bring this to hurt you. I thought I'd show it to you only if there was no other way to settle Larry in your mind.

MOTHER. Larry? *(Snatches letter from Ann's hand)*

ANN. He wrote it to me just before he— *(Mother opens and begins to read letter)* I'm not trying to hurt you, Kate. You're making me do this, now remember you're —Remember. I've been so lonely, Kate . . . I can't leave here alone again. *(A long, low moan comes from Mother's throat as she reads)* You made me show it to you. You wouldn't believe me. I told you a hundred times, why wouldn't you believe me!

MOTHER. Oh, my God . . .

ANN *(with pity and fear)*. Kate, please, please . . .

MOTHER. My God, my God . . .

ANN. Kate, dear, I'm so sorry . . . I'm so sorry.

(Chris enters from driveway. He seems exhausted.)

CHRIS. What's the matter . . . ?

ANN. Where were you? . . . you're all perspired. *(Mother doesn't move)* Where were you?

CHRIS. Just drove around a little. I thought you'd be gone.

ANN. Where do I go? I have nowhere to go.

CHRIS *(to Mother)*. Where's Dad?

ANN. Inside lying down.

CHRIS. Sit down, both of you. I'll say what there is to say.

MOTHER. I didn't hear the car . . .

CHRIS. I left it in the garage.

MOTHER. Jim is out looking for you.

CHRIS. Mother . . . I'm going away. There are a couple of firms in Cleveland, I think I can get a place. I mean, I'm going away for good. *(To Ann alone)* I know what you're thinking, Annie. It's true. I'm yellow. I was made yellow in this house because I suspected my father and I did nothing about it, but if I knew that night when I came home what I know now, he'd be in the district attorney's office by this time, and I'd have brought him there. Now if I look at him, all I'm able to do is cry.

MOTHER. What are you talking about? What else can you do?

CHRIS. I could jail him! I could jail him, if I were human any more. But I'm like everybody else now. I'm practical now. You made me practical.

MOTHER. But you have to be.

CHRIS. The cats in that alley are practical, the bums who ran away when we were fighting were practical. Only the dead ones weren't practical. But now I'm practical, and I spit on myself. I'm going away. I'm going now.

ANN (goes up to him). I'm coming with you. . . .

CHRIS. No, Ann.

ANN. Chris, I don't ask you to do anything about Joe.

CHRIS. You do, you do . . .

ANN. I swear I never will.

CHRIS. In your heart you always will.

ANN. Then do what you have to do!

CHRIS. Do what? What is there to do? I've looked all night for a reason to make him suffer.

ANN. There's reason, there's reason!

CHRIS. What? Do I raise the dead when I put him behind bars? Then what'll I do it for? We used to shoot a man who acted like a dog, but honor was real there, you were protecting something. But here? This is the land of the great big dogs, you don't love a man here, you eat him! That's the principle; the only one we live by—it just happened to kill a few people this time, that's all. The world's that way, how can I take it out on him? What sense does that make? This is a zoo, a zoo!

ANN (to Mother). You know what he's got to do! Tell him!

MOTHER. Let him go.

ANN. I won't let him go. You'll tell him what he's got to do . . .

MOTHER. Annie!

ANN. Then I will!

(Keller enters from house. Chris sees him, goes down near arbor.)

KELLER. What's the matter with you? I want to talk to you.

CHRIS. I've got nothing to say to you.

KELLER (taking his arm). I want to talk to you!

CHRIS (pulling violently away from him). Don't do that, Dad. I'm going to hurt you if you do that. There's nothing to say, so say it quick.

KELLER. Exactly what's the matter? What's the matter? You got too much money? Is that what bothers you?

CHRIS (with an edge of sarcasm). It bothers me.

KELLER. If you can't get used to it, then throw it away. You hear me? Take every cent and give it to charity, throw it in the sewer. Does that settle it? In the sewer, that's all. You think I'm kidding? I'm tellin' you what to do, if it's dirty then burn it. It's your money, that's not my money. I'm a dead man, I'm an old dead man, nothing's mine. Well, talk to me!— what do you want to do!

CHRIS. It's not what I want to do. It's what you want to do.

KELLER. What should I want to do? (Chris is silent) Jail? You want me to go to jail? If you want me to go, say so! Is that where I belong?—then tell me so! (Slight pause) What's the matter, why can't you tell me? (Furiously) You say everything else to me, say that! (Slight pause) I'll tell you why you can't say it. Because you know I don't belong there. Because you know! (With growing emphasis and passion, and a persistent tone of desperation) Who worked for nothin' in that war? When they work for nothin', I'll work for nothin'. Did they ship a gun or a truck outa Detroit before they got their price? Is that clean? It's dollars and cents, nickels and dimes; war and peace, it's nickels and dimes, what's clean? Half the Goddam country is gotta go if I go! That's why you can't tell me.

CHRIS. That's exactly why.

KELLER. Then . . . why am *I* bad?

CHRIS. *I* know you're no worse than most men but I thought you were better. I never saw you as a man. I saw you as my father. (Almost breaking) I can't look at you this way, I can't look at myself!

(He turns away unable to face Keller. Ann goes quickly to Mother, takes letter from her and starts for Chris. Mother instantly rushes to intercept her.)

MOTHER. Give me that!

ANN. He's going to read it! (She thrusts letter into Chris' hand) Larry. He wrote it to me the day he died. . . .

KELLER. Larry!?

MOTHER. Chris, it's not for you. (He starts to read) Joe . . . go away . . .

KELLER (mystified, frightened). Why'd she say, Larry, what . . . ?

MOTHER (she desperately pushes him toward alley, glancing at Chris). Go to the street, Joe, go to the street! (She comes down beside Keller) Don't, Chris . . .

(Pleading from her whole soul) Don't tell him . . .

CHRIS *(quietly)*. Three and one half years . . . talking, talking. Now you tell me what you must do. . . . This is how he died, now tell me where you belong.

KELLER *(pleading)*. Chris, a man can't be a Jesus in this world!

CHRIS. I know all about the world. I know the whole crap story. Now listen to this, and tell me what a man's got to be! *(Reads)* "My dear Ann: . . ." You listening? He wrote this the day he died. Listen, don't cry . . . listen! "My dear Ann: It is impossible to put down the things I feel. But I've got to tell you something. Yesterday they flew in a load of papers from the States and I read about Dad and your father being convicted. I can't express myself. I can't tell you how I feel— I can't bear to live any more. Last night I circled the base for twenty minutes before I could bring myself in. How could he have done that? Every day three or four men never come back and he sits back there doing business. . . . I don't know how to tell you what I feel . . . I can't face anybody . . . I'm going out on a mission in a few minutes. They'll probably report me missing. If they do, I want you to know that you mustn't wait for me. I tell you, Ann, if I had him here now I could kill him—" *(Keller grabs letter from Chris' hand and reads it. After a long pause)* Now blame the world. Do you understand that letter?

KELLER *(he speaks almost inaudibly)*. I think I do. Get the car. I'll put on my jacket. *(He turns and starts slowly for the house. Mother rushes to intercept him)*

MOTHER. Why are you going? You'll sleep, why are you going?

KELLER. I can't sleep here. I'll feel better if I go.

MOTHER. You're so foolish. Larry was your son too, wasn't he? You know he'd never tell you to do this.

KELLER *(looking at letter in his hand)*.

Then what is this if it isn't telling me? Sure, he was my son. But I think to him they were all my sons. And I guess they were, I guess they were. I'll be right down. *(Exits into house)*

MOTHER *(to Chris, with determination)*. You're not going to take him!

CHRIS. I'm taking him.

MOTHER. It's up to you, if you tell him to stay he'll stay. Go and tell him!

CHRIS. Nobody could stop him now.

MOTHER. You'll stop him! How long will he live in prison?—are you trying to kill him?

CHRIS *(holding out letter)*. I thought you read this!

MOTHER *(of Larry, the letter)*. The war is over! Didn't you hear?—it's over!

CHRIS. Then what was Larry to you? A stone that fell into the water? It's not enough for him to be sorry. Larry didn't kill himself to make you and Dad sorry.

MOTHER. What more can we be!

CHRIS. You can be better! Once and for all you can know there's a universe of people outside and you're responsible to it, and unless you know that, you threw away your son because that's why he died.

(A shot is heard in the house. They stand frozen for a brief second. Chris starts for porch, pauses at step, turns to Ann.)

CHRIS. Find Jim! *(He goes on into the house and Ann runs up driveway. Mother stands alone, transfixed)*

MOTHER *(softly, almost moaning)*. Joe . . . Joe . . . Joe . . . Joe . . . *(Chris comes out of house, down to Mother's arms)*

CHRIS *(almost crying)*. Mother, I didn't mean to . . .

MOTHER. Don't dear. Don't take it on yourself. Forget now. Live. *(Chris stirs as if to answer)* Shhh . . . *(She puts his arms down gently and moves toward porch)* Shhh . . . *(As she reaches porch steps she begins sobbing, as*

THE CURTAIN FALLS

Detective Story

BY SIDNEY KINGSLEY

First presented by Howard Lindsay and Russel Crouse at the Hudson Theatre in New York on March 23, 1949, with the following cast:

DETECTIVE DAKIS	Robert Strauss	SUSAN CARMICHAEL	Joan Copeland
SHOPLIFTER	Lee Grant	PATROLMAN KEOGH	Byron C. Halstead
DETECTIVE GALLAGHER	Edward Binns	PATROLMAN BAKER	Joe Roberts
MRS. FARRAGUT	Jean Adair	WILLY	Carl Griscom
JOE FEINSON	Lou Gilbert	MISS HATCH	Maureen Stapleton
DETECTIVE CALLAHAN	Patrick McVey	MRS. FEENEY	Sarah Grable
DETECTIVE O'BRIEN	John Boyd	MR. FEENEY	Jim Flynn
DETECTIVE BRODY	James Westerfield	CRUMB-BUM	Archie Benson
MR. SIMS	Les Tremayne	MR. GALLANTZ	Garney Wilson
DETECTIVE McLEOD	Ralph Bellamy	MR. PRITCHETT	James Maloney
ARTHUR KINDRED	Warren Stevens	MARY McLEOD	Meg Mundy
PATROLMAN BARNES	Earl Sydnor	TAMI GIACOPPETTI	Alexander Scourby
1st BURGLAR (CHARLEY)	Joseph Wiseman	PHOTOGRAPHER	Michael Lewin
2nd BURGLAR (LEWIS)	Michael Strong	LADY	Ruth Storm
MRS. BAGATELLE	Michelette Burani	GENTLEMAN	John Alberts
DR. SCHNEIDER	Harry Worth	MR. BAGATELLE	Joseph Ancona
LT. MONOGHAN	Horace McMahon	INDIGNANT CITIZEN	Jacqueline Paige

ACT ONE

A day in August. 5:30 P.M.

ACT TWO

7:30 P.M.

ACT THREE

8:30 P.M.

Time—the present. The entire action of the play takes place in the detective squad-room of a New York precinct police station.

SIDNEY KINGSLEY, who was born in 1906 and educated at Cornell University, has had a considerable reputation as a playwright ever since the 1933 Group Theatre production of his hospital drama, *Men in White,* staged by Lee Strasberg. As is usual when Kingsley writes a play, it had more than its meticulously established surface realism or verisimilitude to recommend it. It revolved around a young physician's need to make a difficult decision between practicing his profession for pecuniary gain and dedicating himself to the advancement of medical knowledge. Under the influence of a farsighted and humane senior physician, the young man dedicated himself to science. The author, who had not yet attained his thirty-first year when the play opened, won the Pulitzer Prize and embarked on a highly successful Broadway and Hollywood career, started at Cornell, where he acted, won two prizes for debating, and received the Drummond award for playwriting.

Kingsley's second success on Broadway came with the production of his drama about the crime-breeding slums of the Depression period, *Dead End,* in 1935. And again the realism of the writing and staging sustained a thesis. The play even had some practical effect; no less an authority than the late Senator Robert Wagner attributed Congressional action on slum clearance to the stimulus provided by this extremely successful drama, from which Hollywood soon made a powerful motion picture. In 1939 Kingsley also made an impressive, if decidedly less successful, dramatization *The World We Make,* an account of a neurotic girl's redemption when she learns to face a world of hard labor and poverty. From 1940 to 1944, Mr. Kingsley was in the army as an enlisted man and then as a first lieutenant in the Signal Corps. But he found time to write another honorable play, *The Patriots.* It dramatized the sharp political conflicts of Jefferson and Hamilton and culminated in the latter's support of Jefferson for the presidency for patriotic reasons when the country was in danger of subversion by Aaron Burr. This work also won a number of prizes after its production in 1943. In the last seasons of the nineteen-forties the author showed no signs of flagging energy or talent, giving the Broadway stage two successful pieces, *Detective Story* and *Darkness at Noon* (see page 505).

Detective Story is a typical piece of Kingsley realism, in which an environment is recreated with striking fidelity and translated into vivid theatre while the well-paced and tense action carries a significant theme—namely, the dangers of extreme righteousness in a world of fallible human beings. It may be described as Kingsley's *Measure for Measure,* although the wealth of realistic detail overshadows the theme, so that the play prevails largely as a dramatic representation of a detective's experiences and of life in a typical night court. For all its accent on melodrama, *Detective Story* is also a "slice of life" drama written by a thoughtful playwright.

ACT ONE

SCENE: *The 21st Detective Squad, second floor of the 21st Precinct Police Station, New York City. The major area of the stage is occupied by the squad-room; to the right separated by a door and an invisible wall we glimpse a fragment of the Lieutenant's office. Severe, nakedly institutional, ghost-ridden, these rooms are shabby, three-quarters of a century old, with an effluvium of their own compounded of seventy-five years of the tears and blood of human anguish, despair, passion, rage, terror and violent death. The walls are olive green to the waist and light green above. In the wall upstage, two ceiling-high windows guarded by iron-grill work. The entrance, stage left, is surrounded by an iron railing with a swinging gate. Tacked to the wall, a height chart; next to it a folding fingerprint shelf; above that a green-shaded light. Adjoining, a bulletin board upon which are tacked several notices and photographs of criminals, etc. In the center of the room is the phone desk, on which are two phones. Downstage left is another desk, on it a typewriter. High on the main wall a large electric clock, beneath it a duty board with replaceable celluloid letters, reading "On Duty—Det. Gallagher, Det. Dakis, Lt. Monoghan." In the segment of the Lieutenant's office, a desk, a swivel chair, several small chairs, some files, a water-cooler, a coat-rack, etc. A small window in the Lieutenant's office looks out upon an air shaft. Through it we catch a glimpse of the window of the wash-room, the door to which is upstage right.*

The light is fading. It is late afternoon, five-twenty by the clock on the wall. Through the main windows a magnificent view of the city and its towering sky-scrapers; dominating the panorama are a General Motors sign, a church spire and a cross.

At the curtain's rise, Nicholas Dakis is seated at the typewriter desk making out a form and interrogating a young woman who has been picked up for shoplifting. At the phone desk his partner, Gallagher, is writing up some "squeals," and sipping Coca-Cola from the bottle. A traffic policeman in uniform pauses momentarily in the doorway to murmur a greeting to another uniformed policeman; then they vanish. Detective Gallagher is a young man, third-grade, a novice about 27 years of age, and good-looking in spite of a broken nose. The heat has him a little down: he is sweating profusely and every once in a while he plucks at his moist shirt which clings to his body. He and his partner, Detective Dakis, are in their shirt sleeves, their collars open.

Dakis is a bull of a man as wide as he is high. He has a voice like the roll of a kettle-drum. He is a middle-aged Greek American. He tackles his job efficiently and unemotionally, in an apparently off-hand, casual manner—as indeed do most of the detectives.

The shoplifter is a shapeless, moronic little creature with a Bronx accent. Her voice is the blat of a moose-calf, and, in spite of her avowed guilt, she has all the innocence of ignorance.

———

DAKIS. Hair? *(Squints at her frazzled hair)*

SHOPLIFTER. Brown.

DAKIS *(typing, hunt and peck system)*. Brown. *(He squints at her eyes)* Eyes?

SHOPLIFTER. Blue.

DAKIS *(types)*. Blue.

(The phone rings. Gallagher picks up the receiver.)

GALLAGHER. 21st Squad Detectives, Gallagher. Yes, Madame, what is your name, please? *(He reaches for a pencil and pad, glances at the clock, writes)* Address? Phone number? Plaza 9-1855 . . .

DAKIS. Weight?

GALLAGHER *(as the other desk phone rings)*. One second, please. *(He picks up the other receiver, balancing the first on his shoulder)* 21st Squad Detectives, Gallagher.

SHOPLIFTER. 109, I think.

DAKIS *(types)*. 109 will do. . . . *(He squints at her potato sack of a figure)* Height?

SHOPLIFTER. I don't know. About . . .

DAKIS. Stand up against the wall! *(He waves her to the height chart)* Over there.

GALLAGHER *(on phone)*. Hello, Loot. No, nothing. A shoplifter. Best's. A pocketbook. *(He calls to Dakis)* Hey, Nick, what was the price on that purse she lifted?

SHOPLIFTER *(mournfully)*. Six dollars.

DAKIS *(to the shoplifter)*. Five foot one.

All right, come back. (*The shoplifter returns to the desk*)

GALLAGHER (*on the phone*). Six bucks.

DAKIS. Age?

SHOPLIFTER. Twenty-seven. (*Corrects herself, quickly*) Twenty-two.

DAKIS (*squints at her, types*). Twenty—seven.

GALLAGHER (*on the phone*). Right, Loot. It come in too late. Night court. Right, chief. (*He hangs up, applies the other receiver*) Sorry, Mrs. . . . (*Glances at his pad*) Andrews. Yes. Have you a list of just what's missing? It would help. Any cash? You do? One of the servants? All right. I'll be there. Yes, Madame. (*Hangs up, makes some notes on the scratch pad, sips at the Coca-Cola bottle*)

SHOPLIFTER. My God, the times I spent twice as much for a pocketbook.

DAKIS (*matter of fact, no animus*). Well, you took it.

SHOPLIFTER. I don't know why. It was crazy.

DAKIS (*shrugs it off*). It's your first offense. You'll get off on probation.

SHOPLIFTER. I didn't need it. I didn't even like it. Crazy!

(*A burst of song offstage: an overmellow baritone pouring out Canio's heartbreak from I Pagliacci, making up in vigar all that it lacks in sweetness: "Ma il vizio alberga sol ne l' alma tua negletta." The shoplifter, puzzled, glances about, hunches her shoulders at Dakis inquisitively, but he is absorbed in his work and he does not even glance up. The singing comes closer. More heartbreak! "Tu viscere non hai . . . sol legge." Enter Gus Keogh, a uniformed policeman with a normally smiling, smooth, white Irish face, twisted for the moment with the agony of the tragic song he is pouring forth.*)

KEOGH. "è 'l senso a te . . ." (*Breaks off, beaming*) Got any 61's?

GALLAGHER. A couple. You're off key today, Gus. (*Hands him several slips. Keogh studies them; his face contorts again with the emotion of the song as he goes off*)

KEOGH. "vo' ne lo sprezzo mio schiacciarti . . . (*And fades off down the hall with a sob*) sotto piè."

DAKIS (*rises, crosses to fingerprint board, rolls ink on pad, beckons to the shoplifter*). Come here! (*The shoplifter crosses to Dakis. He takes her hand. She stiffens. He reassures her gently—in the interests*

of efficiency*) Take it easy, girlie. Let me do the work. You just supply the finger.

SHOPLIFTER. Ooh!!

DAKIS. This finger. Relax, now, I'm not going to hurt you. Just r-r-r-roll it. . . . (*He presses her finger down on the sheet*)

GALLAGHER (*glances up, toward door into hallway at someone approaching*). Uh, uh! Here comes trouble. (*To Dakis*) Look at the calendar!

DAKIS (*glances at the calendar on the wall*). A full moon tonight.

GALLAGHER (*groans*). It never fails. (*Enter an elderly, aristocratic-looking woman, dressed in the style of a by-gone era. Gallagher rises gallantly*) Come in, Mrs. Farragut! Are those people still bothering you?

MRS. FARRAGUT. Worse than ever, Officer. If I hadn't awakened last night and smelled that gas coming through the walls, I'd be gone—we'd all be gone.

GALLAGHER (*solicitously*). Have a chair.

MRS. FARRAGUT. Why haven't you given me protection? I demand protection.

GALLAGHER (*"conning" her*). I got twelve men on duty guarding you.

MRS. FARRAGUT. But whose side are they really on? Are you sure you can trust them?

GALLAGHER (*wounded*). Mrs. Farragut! One of them is my own *brother*.

MRS. FARRAGUT. Oh, I'm sorry! I didn't mean to offend you. (*She sits, leans toward him, confidentially*) Only it's so important. You see, they know I know all about it— Atom bombs! (*Gallagher nods sagely*) They're making them—these foreigners next door and they blow this atomic vapor through the wall at me. And they have a man watching me from the top of the Empire State Building . . . with radar . . .

GALLAGHER. That man we got covered.

MRS. FARRAGUT. You have?

GALLAGHER. Day and night.

MRS. FARRAGUT. Does the President know about this?

GALLAGHER. I talked to him only an hour ago.

MRS. FARRAGUT. That's important, very important. These foreigners know I have electronic vision. I can see everything around us vibrating with electricity. . . . Billions of atoms like stars in a universe, turning, vibrating, vibrating. Out there in the streets ten million living dynamos—

coming and going . . . They create cross-currents; and those great tall skyscrapers draw all this human electricity to the top of the Empire State Building, where that man sits, and he turns it back and shoots it down on us. It's a terrifying situation . . . terrifying!! Do something!—Or it's the end of the world!! *(She rises, having worked herself into a frenzy of terror)* *(Joe Feinson, police-reporter, enters, leans his head on the rail watching; a tiny man, few inches more than five feet, exaggerated nose, crooked features, Joe's superficially wise-cracking police-reporter attitude is only the persona with which he cloaks a genuine philosophic, humanistic outlook. Nothing escapes his humorous, beady, bird-like eyes.)*

GALLAGHER *(rises, crosses around to her, takes her arm reassuringly)*. Now, Mrs. Farragut, I'm watching it, every second; and I got it all under control. Tell you what—I'm going to *double* the men I got guarding you. Twenty-five picked men day and night. How's that?

MRS. FARRAGUT *(calms down)*. Oh, that's better. Much better. Thank you. *(Exit Mrs. Farragut)*

GALLAGHER *(plucking at his damp shirt)*. Get out the butterfly net.

JOE. You give the customers a good massage.

GALLAGHER. Hell, this job is ninety percent salesmanship!

DAKIS *(finishes the fingerprints)*. O.K., girlie, wash your hands. In there! *(He points to the wash-room door. The shoplifter crosses to the wash-room, dangling her lamp-blacked fingers before her so as not to soil her dress)*

JOE. What's new?

GALLAGHER. It's quiet. *(Knocks wood)*

JOE. The town's dead as Kelcey's. *(He saunters over to Gallagher's desk)*

SHOPLIFTER *(opens the door, frowning, calls out)*. There isn't any lock on the door.

DAKIS. Just wash your hands, girlie.

SHOPLIFTER *(indignantly)*. A fine how-doyoudo! *(She slams the door)*

JOE. Story for me?

GALLAGHER. No. Shoplifter.

JOE. She anybody?

GALLAGHER. Nobody at all.

JOE. Any angles?

GALLAGHER. Nah! Just a slob.

(Two detectives enter. One of them, Cal-lahan, is very exuberant and high-spirited, Tenth Avenue in his speech, dressed in a yellow polo shirt and baggy trousers, which do not match his wrinkled jacket. The other, Detective O'Brien, is an older man, spectacled, neatly dressed, soft-spoken.)

CALLAHAN *(tears off his jacket, revealing the full splendor of his polo shirt—Hawaiian in motif, with brilliant foliage woven into the pattern)*. Hi, Tom, Nick, Joe! Phew, it's hot out! Sweat your ko-lonjas off!

JOE. What the hell are you dressed up for? Must be Halloween?

CALLAHAN. I wonder what he means?

O'BRIEN. Saks-Fifth Avenue pays Mike to advertise their clothes.

CALLAHAN. Gese, were we given a run around! We tailed a guy for two hours, from Fifty-thoid to Ninety-foist and back. I thought for sure, "This one belongs to us."

O'BRIEN. Looked like a good man.

CALLAHAN. Then the jerko took a bus. *(Glances at the schedule hanging on the wall)* Moider! Sunday again! What the hell am I?—A Sunday detective? My kids'll grow up, they won't even know me. *(To Joe)* Say, Joe, there's a big story on Third Avenue. You get it? The brewery truck?

JOE. No, what about it?

CALLAHAN. A brewery truck backed up into the sidewalk and a barrel of beer fell right out inna baby carriage.

JOE *(rising)*. Was the baby in it?

CALLAHAN. Yeah.

JOE. Was it killed?

CALLAHAN. No, it was light beer! Boy-eeng! *(He doubles over, holding his sides with laughter)* Ha, ha, ha!

JOE *(groans and sinks back into his chair)*. You're a cute kid. What's your name, Berle?

(The shoplifter returns from the wash-room. As she crosses Callahan studies her face, squinting his eyes professionally.)

O'BRIEN. Busy day?

GALLAGHER. Quiet.

O'BRIEN. Good. *(He knocks wood)*

GALLAGHER. Too quiet.

O'BRIEN. We're due. We're ripe for a homicide.

GALLAGHER. Ssh. Wait till I get out of here. *(The desk phone rings, Gallagher groans)* Can't you keep your big mouth shut? *(He picks up the receiver)* 21st Squad Detectives, Gallagher. Yes, Madame. That's right. Where? Now what is it you lost?

JOE. Her virginity.

GALLAGHER. In a taxicab?

JOE. Hell of a place!

GALLAGHER. Did you get his number? Can you describe it?

JOE. This is going to be educational.

GALLAGHER. What's your name? Address? Yes, Madame. I'll check that for you. Not at all.

JOE *(simultaneously with Gallagher's last speech)*. I got a squeal for you. I lost something. My manhood.

CALLAHAN. We don't take cases *that* old, Joe.

GALLAGHER *(hanging up)*. Outlawed by the statute of limitations.

(Detective Lou Brody enters with several containers of coffee, Coca-Colas, and a bag of sandwiches. Brody is a huge man, deceptively obese and clumsy in appearance; bald-head, ugly, carbuncled face, lit up, however, by sad, soft, gentle eyes. He hands one bag to Dakis.)

BRODY. Here you are, Nick!

DAKIS. I appreciate that.

BRODY. My pleasure. Here you are, Miss.

SHOPLIFTER. With Russian Dressing? *(Standing up, searching in her purse)*

BRODY. They ran out. *(He crosses, places the remaining sandwiches and coffee on the long table, then goes into the Lieutenant's office, hangs his hat and packet on the coat-tree)*

SHOPLIFTER. How much do I owe you?

DAKIS. It's on the house.

SHOPLIFTER. You're all awful decent, really, awful decent.

DAKIS. Well, you didn't kill anyone.

(A man carrying a briefcase enters, stands at the gate a moment, taps on it impatiently. He is about thirty-five, erect in bearing, sharply chiseled features, self-possessed, apparently immune to the heat; he is crisp and cool even to the starched collar. When he speaks his voice is equally crisp and starched, and carries considerable authority.)

GALLAGHER. Yes, sir?

(The man fishes a card out of his wallet and presents it.)

MAN. My name is Sims, Endicott Sims. I'm an attorney.

GALLAGHER. What can we do for you, Counselor?

SIMS. I represent Mr. Kurt Schneider. Your office has a warrant out for him?

DAKIS. Hey, Lou! This is Jim's squeal, ain't it? Kurt Schneider?

BRODY. Yeah, I'll take it. *(Crosses to Sims)* This is my partner's case. What about Schneider, Counselor? Where is he?

SIMS. He's ready to surrender himself into your custody.

BRODY. Fine, bring him in.

SIMS. First, however, I have here some photographs. . . . *(He takes some pictures from his briefcase, and hands them to Brody)* He had these taken half an hour ago.

BRODY *(examines them)*. Nudes? Ugly, ain't he?

SIMS *(smiles wryly)*. He's no Mr. America.

BRODY. No, that he ain't.

SIMS. The purpose is not aesthetic. I don't want any rubber hoses used on him.

BRODY. Counselor, how long have you been practicing law? We don't assault our prisoners.

SIMS. Who's handling this case here?

BRODY. My partner.

SIMS. A man named James McLeod?

BRODY. Yeah.

SIMS. I've heard a good deal about him. A law unto himself. You will please tell him for me . . .

BRODY. Wait a minute. Tell him for yourself. Here he is.

(James McLeod enters, his big hand gripping the arm of a stunned, sensitive-looking young man whom he guides into the room. James McLeod is tall, lean, handsome, has powerful shoulders, uncompromising mouth, a studied, immobile, mask-like face betrayed by the deep-set, impatient, mocking eyes which reveal the quick flickers of mood, the deep passions of the man possessed by his own demon.)

BRODY. Oh, Jim, this is your squeal. *(To Sims)* This is Detective McLeod, Mr. Sims.

MCLEOD. How do you do, sir? *(Takes out a handkerchief, mops his brow, wipes the sweat-band of his hat)*

SIMS. How do you do?

BRODY. Mr. Sims is an attorney.

MCLEOD. And very clever. I've seen him in court.

SIMS. Thank you.

BRODY. He's here for Kurt Schneider.

MCLEOD (*the quick flicker of mockery in his eyes*). Oh, yes. (*To Sims*) I had the pleasure of arresting your client a year ago.

SIMS. So I am informed.

MCLEOD. He's changed his lawyer since, if not his business.

SIMS. Kurt Schneider is a successful truck farmer from New Jersey.

MCLEOD. With a little abortion mill in New York for a sideline. Nothing fancy, just a quick ice-tong job. I've a considerable yen for your client.

SIMS. I'm aware of that. (*To Brody*) Show him those pictures! (*Brody hands the photographs to McLeod*)

MCLEOD (*looks at the pictures, grimaces*). There's no doubt the process of evolution is beginning to reverse itself.

SIMS. You understand, Officer, that my client has certain rights. I am here to see that those rights are respected.

MCLEOD (*urbanely*). One second, Counselor. I'll be right with you. Have a chair. (*He guides the young man into the squad room*)

GALLAGHER. Jim, call your wife!

MCLEOD. Thanks, Tom. (*He searches the young man for weapons; the quick "frisk," ankles, legs, thighs, front and rear*) All right, Buster. Sit down over there. (*To Gallagher*) When'd she phone?

GALLAGHER. Twenty minutes ago. (*The phone rings*) 21st Squad Detectives, Gallagher. Yes, sir. (*He hands the phone to McLeod*) The Lieutenant.

MCLEOD (*takes the phone and it is evident from his grimace at the phone that he has no great love for his lieutenant. He sits on the desk*). Yes, Lieutenant? I just got back.

JOE (*crosses down, drapes himself on the chair next to McLeod*). Hiya, Seamus!

MCLEOD (*smothers the mouthpiece of the phone, murmurs quickly*). Oh, Yussel, Yussel! You're supposed to be an intelligent reporter.

JOE. What's the matter, Seamus?

MCLEOD. That Langdon story!

JOE. Didn't I spell your name right?

MCLEOD. It's the only thing you did get right. (*On the phone*) Yes, Lieutenant. I just brought him in. (*To Arthur*) Arthur, were you arrested before?

ARTHUR. I told you.

MCLEOD. Tell me again.

ARTHUR. No.

MCLEOD (*back to phone*). Says no. We'll check his prints. Yes, sir. Yes, sir. (*He covers the mouthpiece*) You're degenerating into a real sob-sister, Yussel. Grrrim grray prrrison walls! Wish you'd have seen Langdon in the bull-pen. "Hiya, Jack! Hiya, Charley!" Smiling. He was happy! He was home again! (*On phone*) Yes, Lieutenant. Yes, sir.

JOE. The mortal God—McLeod! Captain Ahab pursuing the great gray Leviathan! A fox with rabies bit him in the ass when he was two years old, and neither of them recovered. Don't throw water on him. He goes rabid!

MCLEOD (*hangs up, pulls Joe's bow-tie*). You apple-headed member of the fourth estate, to look natural you should have a knife and fork sticking out of the top of your head. City College is going to be proud of you yet! (*Rises, talks Yiddish*) Mir daft ihr dihagginun!

JOE (*laughs, ties his tie*). Is this story worth a picture?

MCLEOD. Mm . . . Possibly. (*To Arthur*) Don't try running for it, Buster. You'd just about reach that door and suddenly you'd put on weight. Bullets are supersonic.

ARTHUR. Don't worry.

MCLEOD. I won't. Either way. (*Brody, at the sound of the young man's voice, stops and turns quickly. He comes over, scrutinizes the young man's face.*)

MCLEOD. Know him?

BRODY. No . . . No . . . I . . . (*Shakes his head*)

MCLEOD (*calls across the room to Mr. Sims*). One second, Counselor. (*He crosses to the Lieutenant's office, comes face to face with Callahan. He pauses to survey Callahan's sartorial splendor. Shakes his head*) Strictly Pier 6!

CALLAHAN. I ain't no friggin barber-college detective with pleats in my pants.

MCLEOD (*sardonically*). No, you ain't. . . . (*Goes into Lieutenant's office, closes the door, dials a number*)

CALLAHAN (*miffed*). Remind me to get that college graduate a bicycle pump for Christmas to blow up that big head of his. (*O'Brien and Gallagher laugh.*)

O'BRIEN. He needling you again?

CALLAHAN. Mm! Big needle-man from sew-and-sew.

MCLEOD (on the phone). Hello, darling. (His voice at once takes on warmth and tenderness; his eyes, his smile, his whole being seem to undergo a metamorphosis) What did the doctor say? . . . Thank God! Nothing organic? Sure, now, Mary? . . . How does he explain those palpitations? . . . Psychosomatic? Mm! And how does he explain that? . . . What tensions? (Laughs) What'd he prescribe, short of a new world? Phenobarbital and Vitamin B-one? The history of our time. (He laughs) Oh, Mary! You're wonderful! I love you! Of course, I was worried sick. Mm. Yes . . . Thank you, my angel. I'll call you later. Good-bye.

(In the squad-room, Arthur's face turns gray, he clutches his stomach and bites his lip. Brody, who has been studying him, crosses to him.)

BRODY. What's the matter, sonny?

ARTHUR. Nothing.

(Brody points to the wash-room. Arthur crosses to it, quickly. Once inside, alone, his bravado falls away. He is a sick and desperate boy. He dry-retches over the sink for a moment. Breathing heavily, he looks about in sudden panic.)

BRODY (glances toward the wash-room, goes to his files, takes out a bottle, goes to the wash-room, props open the door, stands there, watching. Arthur controls himself, turns on the water in the sink, buries his face in it. Brody takes a paper cup, pours out a drink, offers it to him). Have a bomb?

ARTHUR. No, thanks. (Dries his face) (Brody tosses off the drink, himself. They return to the squad-room. The desk phone rings. Gallagher reaches for it.)

BRODY (glances at the clock). O.K., Tom. I'll take over now. Go on home. (Picks up the phone)

GALLAGHER. Home? I got a squeal. (Goes off into the next room)

BRODY (on the phone). 21st Squad, Detective Brody. Yeah? Get his license number? . . . (He glances at the clock, scribbles data on a pad)

MCLEOD (enters the squad-room, crosses to Mr. Sims). Now, Counselor?

SIMS (presents him with the photographs again). You will observe there are no scars or lacerations of any kind! (Points to photos) This is the way I'm delivering my client to you, and this is the way I want him back.

MCLEOD (studies them gravely). I should think that any change whatsoever would be an improvement, Counselor.

SIMS. I want you to know I'm not going to allow you to violate his Constitutional rights. You're not to abuse him physically or degrade his dignity as a human being, do you understand?

MCLEOD (bites this off sharply). Counselor, I never met a criminal yet who didn't wrap himself in the Constitution from head to toe, or a hoodlum who wasn't filled to the nostrils with habeas corpus and the rights of human dignity. Did you ever see the girl your client operated on last year—in the morgue—on a marble slab? Wasn't much human left of her, Counselor—and very little dignity!

SIMS. My client was innocent of that charge. The court acquitted him.

MCLEOD. He was guilty.

SIMS. Are you setting yourself above the courts of the land?

MCLEOD. There's a higher court, Counselor.

SIMS. I'm sure there is, Officer. Are you qualified to speak for it? I'm not. God doesn't come down and whisper in my ear. But when it comes to the man-made law on terra firma, I know it, I obey it, and I respect it.

MCLEOD. What do you want to do?— Try the case here? This isn't a court. Save it for the Judge. Now, Counselor, I'm busy. Your client will be treated with as much delicacy as he is entitled to. So bring him in—or get off the pot.

SIMS. I've heard about you. You're quite an anomaly, McLeod, quite an anomaly. It's going to be a real pleasure to examine you on the witness stand.

MCLEOD. Anything to give you a thrill, Counselor.

SIMS. We may have a thrill or two in store for you.

MCLEOD. Meaning?

SIMS. For over a year you personally have been making my client's life a living hell. Why?

MCLEOD. I beg your pardon?

SIMS. Why?

MCLEOD (sardonically). Because I'm annoyed by criminals that get away with murder. They upset me.

SIMS. You're easily upset.

MCLEOD. Oh, I'm very sensitive. (Dismissing him) To me your client is just another criminal. *(Turns away)* O.K., Arthur! In there! *(He indicates the Lieutenant's office. Arthur rises, enters the office)*

SIMS. That's your story. At considerable expense we have investigated and discovered *otherwise*.

(McLeod turns to stare at him. Sims smiles knowingly and goes.)

BRODY. What the hell's he driving at?

MCLEOD. A fishing expedition. That's a shrewd mouthpiece. I've seen him operate. *(He enters the Lieutenant's office. To Arthur)* Empty your pockets! Take everything out. Put it on the desk! *(Arthur empties the contents of his pockets on the desk)* That all?

ARTHUR. Yes.

MCLEOD. Turn your pockets inside out. *(Arthur obeys)* Sit down! Over there! What'd you do with the money?

ARTHUR. I spent it.

MCLEOD *(examines the articles one by one, very carefully)*. All of it?

ARTHUR. Yes.

MCLEOD *(picks up a book of matches)*. When were you at the Stork Club?

ARTHUR. Wednesday night.

MCLEOD. Been doing the hot spots?

ARTHUR. Some.

MCLEOD. Any of the money left?

ARTHUR. How far can you go with four hundred dollars?

MCLEOD. Four hundred and eighty.

ARTHUR. Was it four eighty?

MCLEOD. So your employer claims.

ARTHUR. He ought to know.

MCLEOD. Arthur, why'd you take the money?

ARTHUR. What's the difference? I took it, I admit it, I took it!

MCLEOD. Where'd you spend last night?

ARTHUR. In my room.

MCLEOD. I was there. Where were you? Under the bed?

ARTHUR. I sat in the Park.

MCLEOD. All night?

ARTHUR. Yes.

MCLEOD. It rained.

ARTHUR. Drizzled.

MCLEOD. You sat in the drizzle?

ARTHUR. Yes.

MCLEOD. What were you doing?

ARTHUR. Just dreaming.

MCLEOD. In the park at night?—Dreaming?

ARTHUR. Night is the time for dreams.

MCLEOD. And *thieves!* *(He examines the articles in Arthur's pockets. . . . The phone in the squad-room rings. Brody answers)*

BRODY. 21st Squad, Detective Brody . . . Callahan, for you!

CALLAHAN *(crosses to phone, throwing a parking ticket on the desk)*. A kiss from Judge Bromfield. *(Into phone)* Callahan, 21st.

JOE *(examines the ticket)*. You got a parking ticket?

DAKIS *(morosely)*. I got one, too. In front of the Criminal Court Building. You're such a big shot, Joe, why don't you throw a little weight around?

JOE. Mind if I use the phone?

BRODY *(nods.)* The outside one.

(Joe dials a number.)

O'BRIEN. Some of these judges haven't the brains God gave them. They refrigerate them in law-school.

DAKIS. It ain't enough we use our own cars to take prisoners to court, and our own gas—we can't even deduct it from our income tax. Where's your justice?

JOE *(into phone)*. Hello, Jerry—this is Joe Feinson. *(Suddenly yelling at the top of his lungs)* Who the hell does that Judge Bromfield think he is? . . . He's persecutin' cops, that's what! Parkin' tickets on duty. I'm going to stir up the goddamnedest hornet's nest! . . . All right! All right! . . . *(Calmly)* Yeah. Fine. Sure. I got one here. Yeah. *(He hangs up, takes the ticket)* O.K. Forget it. It's fixed. *(Crosses to get Dakis' ticket)*

O'BRIEN. You frighten him?

JOE. I frightened myself. *(Holds up his trembling hand)* Look at my hand! Shaking!

(Dakis laughs—a bellow that makes the room vibrate.)

CALLAHAN. A cop's got to get a reporter to fix a ticket for him. I seen everything now.

JOE. That's the way it should be. A free press is the tocsin of a free people. The law keeps you in line, we keep the law in line, the people keep us in line, you keep the people in line. Everybody kicks everybody else in the ass! That way nobody gets too big for his britches. That's democracy! *(Crosses to the gate)*

DAKIS. You have the gall to call that yellow, monopolistic sheet—a free press? Ha! Ha! *(Bellows again)* You kill me!

(Exit Joe, waving the ticket triumphantly.)

SHOPLIFTER. So.

DAKIS. So what?

SHOPLIFTER. So what happens to me now?

DAKIS. We wait here till night court opens. Nine o'clock. Then the magistrate will probably set bail for you.

O'BRIEN. Have you got a lawyer? You might save the bail bond.

SHOPLIFTER. My brother-in-law's a lawyer.

DAKIS (belches). Excuse me. Call him up . . .

SHOPLIFTER. Gee, I hate to. He's kind of a new brother-in-law. If my sister finds out, oh, God! she'll die! And she's in the fourth month, too.

O'BRIEN. It's up to you.

DAKIS. Suit yourself. The court'll appoint you one.

SHOPLIFTER. Gee, I don't know what to do!

MCLEOD (completes his examination of the articles in Arthur's pockets). Ever been arrested before, Arthur?

ARTHUR. I told you no.

MCLEOD. You sure?

ARTHUR. Yes.

MCLEOD. It would help your case if you returned the money.

ARTHUR. I know. But I can't. I told you it's gone.

(Brody enters the Lieutenant's office and listens to the interrogation.)

MCLEOD. What's this pawn ticket for?

ARTHUR. Textbooks.

MCLEOD. Where did you get them?

ARTHUR. College.

MCLEOD. Graduate?

ARTHUR. No.

MCLEOD. What stopped you?

ARTHUR. World War Two, the first time.

MCLEOD. And the second time?

ARTHUR. World War Three.

MCLEOD. Foolish question, foolish answer. (Examining contents of Arthur's pockets) Have you any identifying marks on you, Arthur? Any scars? . . . Roll up your sleeves. . . . (Arthur obeys. On his left wrist is a tattoo mark) A tattoo mark. A heart. And what's the name? J—O—Y! Who's Joy?

ARTHUR. A girl.

MCLEOD. Your girl?

ARTHUR. No.

MCLEOD. Whose girl?

ARTHUR. What's the difference?

MCLEOD. What branch of the service were you in?

ARTHUR. Navy.

MCLEOD. How long?

ARTHUR. Five years.

MCLEOD. What rank?

ARTHUR. Chief Petty Officer.

MCLEOD. You married?

ARTHUR. No.

MCLEOD. How old are you?

ARTHUR. Twenty-seven.

MCLEOD. How long you been in New York?

ARTHUR. A year.

MCLEOD. Where you from?

ARTHUR. Ann Arbor, Michigan.

MCLEOD. What's your father's business?

ARTHUR. My father's dead.

MCLEOD. What was his business?

ARTHUR. He was a teacher. Music. History of music.

MCLEOD. History of music? He must've been proud of you. Where's your mother?

ARTHUR. She's dead.

MCLEOD (looking through Arthur's address book). Ah! Here's Joy again—Joy Carmichael. Maybe I better give her a ring.

ARTHUR. What for? Why drag her into this? She doesn't know anything about it.

MCLEOD (mockingly). You wouldn't lie to me, would you, Arthur?

ARTHUR. Why should I lie?

MCLEOD. I don't know. Why should you steal? Maybe it's because you're just no damn good, hm, Arthur? The judge asks me and I'm going to throw the book at you.—Tattoo that on your arm! (McLeod rises)

BRODY. Admission?

MCLEOD. Yes.

BRODY. Get the money?

MCLEOD. No. He doesn't milk easily. A superman. I've got an angle. (Crosses into the squad-room, dials phone)

BRODY (to Arthur). Sonny, you look like a nice boy. How'd you get into this mess?

ARTHUR (rises). What is this? Are you going to give me a sermon?

BRODY. Don't get funny with me, son. I'll knock you right through the floor! Sit down! (Arthur sits) How'd you get into this mess, son?

ARTHUR. I don't know. You get trapped.

BRODY. Where's the money?

ARTHUR (*shakes his head*). Gone! It's gone.

BRODY. What did you do with it?

ARTHUR. Spent it.

BRODY (*pauses, takes out a cigarette, offers Arthur one, lights them*). You went to college? What did you study?

ARTHUR. Majored in History.

BRODY. History? What for?

ARTHUR. To teach. I wanted to be a teacher.

BRODY. Much of a career in that?

ARTHUR. I used to think so.

BRODY. You're a long way from home?

ARTHUR. Yes.

BRODY. Why didn't you finish?

ARTHUR. No time. The war washed that up. There's no time. You can't start from scratch at 25.

(*Brody studies him, shakes his head. The sudden babble of voices is heard, off.*)

MCLEOD (*looks up from phone*). Uh-uh! Here comes trouble! A couple of customers.

(*A uniformed policeman, Negro, enters herding in front of him two burglars handcuffed to each other. They are followed by other policemen, a hysterical woman, and at the tail of the parade, Willy, the janitor, with broom, pail and inquisitive look. (The Negro policeman is a big man of erect carriage, with a fine, intelligent face. The two burglars are a study in contrasting personalities. The first is nervous, thin, short, wiry, with long expressive hands that are never still, forever weaving in and out. He has jet-black hair which keeps falling over his forehead in bangs, tiny black eyes, an olive complexion and a slight Italian accent. He is protesting his innocence with percussive indignation. He is wearing an expensive suit and a pink shirt with no tie. The second burglar is a chunky, sandy-haired young fellow, slow-moving, slower-thinking, who is inclined to take this arrest as a minor nuisance at worst. He is wearing a "zoot suit" with extremely narrow cuffs on the trousers. He moves slouching slowly, swaying from side to side. There is something "off-beat," something disturbing about both these men. Willy, the janitor, is a thin, sour, grizzled man with a pockmarked face and a moth-eaten tooth-brush moustache. He wears a worn black shirt and old, torn trousers. The hysterical woman is a short, dumpy, elderly Frenchwoman whose hair*

is in disarray and whose slip is showing. She is wringing her hands, crying and gabbling half in French, half in English. As they enter, they are all talking at once. The first burglar's percussive cries and the Frenchwoman's wails dominate the hubbub.)

(*Brody, hearing the noise, crosses back into squad-room.*)

MCLEOD. What have you got there?

BARNES (NEGRO PATROLMAN). Burglars. Caught 'em red-handed. Forcible entry.

WOMAN (*in a French accent*). I come up to my apartment. The door was open. The lock was burst wide open. The jamb was broken down. They were inside. I started to run. This one grabbed me and choked me.

FIRST BURGLAR. It's a lie! It's a pack of lies! I don't know what she's talking about. . . .

BARNES. I was right across the street when I heard her scream. They come running down the stairs. I collared them. . . . This one put up a struggle.

FIRST BURGLAR (*screaming*). I was walkin' down the stairs mindin' my own business—the cop jumps on me and starts beatin' the crap outa me. . . .

MCLEOD (*roars*). All right! (*The first burglar stops screaming, pantomimes his innocence*) We'll come to you. (*He takes his revolver out of his holster, puts it in his pocket. Brody takes out his revolver, places it in the desk drawer. Dakis does likewise. This is official routine which Callahan alone neglects to observe*)

FIRST BURGLAR (*softly*). Think I'm crazy to do a thing like this?

BRODY. Sh! You'll get your turn to talk. Sit down.

BARNES. On this one I found this jimmy, and this . . . (*Takes out a jimmy and a revolver, hands them to McLeod*)

BRODY. Twenty-two?

MCLEOD (*nods*). Loaded. (*He unloads the cylinder, places the cartridges on the desk*)

BRODY (*to the first burglar*). What's your name? Stand up! (*Searches him more thoroughly*)

FIRST BURGLAR. Gennini. Charles Gennini. And I don't know nothin'. I don't even know this guy. Ask him! (*To the other burglar*) Do I know you? (*To Brody*) No!

BRODY. Take it easy, **Charley**. Sit down!

(To the other burglar) What's your name?

SECOND BURGLAR. Lewis Abbott.

BRODY *(brandishes revolver and jimmy).* Were you carrying these, Lewis?

LEWIS *(thinks for a moment, nods, unemotionally).* Ya.

WOMAN *(begins to cry).* By the throat he grabbed me! How can this happen in New York?

MCLEOD *(gently).* Take it easy, Madame. You're all right, now. Sit down, Madame. I'll get you a glass of water.

WOMAN. Oh, please, please!

(McLeod crosses to the water-cooler.)

BRODY *(searches Lewis).* You're a bad boy, Lewis, and what's more, you're a bad thief. Don't you know a good thief never carries a loaded pistol? It means five years added to your sentence, Lewis.

LEWIS. I'd never use it.

BRODY. That's what you think, Lewis. But it'd happen. You're lucky you were picked up. Probably saved you from a murder rap. Just once you'd walk in, a woman, she'd scream, resist, you'd get scared . . .

CALLAHAN. Boom! Boom! *(Sings a funeral dirge)* Ta da de da da de da de da de dum . . .

BRODY. You like the smell a burning flesh? Your own?

LEWIS *(thinks, shakes his head).* Na.

(McLeod returns with the glass of water, hands it to the hysterical woman.)

BRODY. Getting dropped today was the luckiest thing ever happened to you, Lewis. *(Turns to Charley)* Now, *you!*

(Charley rises. Brody searches him more carefully.)

CHARLEY *(his hands weaving).* I got nothing to do with this, I swear. You think I got rocks in my head?

BRODY *(producing a large wad of bills from Charley's pockets).* Look at this!

MCLEOD. Quite a bundle! How much is here, Charley?

CHARLEY. Fourteen hundred bucks.

MCLEOD *(digs into his own pocket, takes out a slim roll of bills).* Eleven! Why is it every time one of you bums comes in, you've got fourteen hundred dollars in your kick and I've got eleven in mine?

BRODY. You don't live right.

MCLEOD. No, evidently not. *(To Charley)* Where'd you get this?

CHARLEY. I saved it. I worked.

MCLEOD. Where?

CHARLEY. I was a bricklayer.

MCLEOD *(hands the money to the patrolman).* Count it! This goes to the custodian. We don't want Charley suing us. *(To Charley)* Let's see your hands! *(He feels them)* The only thing you ever "laid," Charley, was a two-dollar floozy.

CALLAHAN. Do you always carry so much money around?

CHARLEY. Yeah.

MCLEOD. What's the matter, Charley, don't you trust the banks?

BRODY. When were you in stir last Charley?

CHARLEY. Me? In jail? Never! I swear to God on a stack of Bibles!

MCLEOD. What's your B number?

CHARLEY. I ain't got none.

MCLEOD. You sure?

CHARLEY. On my mother's grave, I ain't got no B card.

CALLAHAN. You're stupid.

MCLEOD *(looks at the others, shakes his head and laughs softly).* You just gave yourself away, Charley. How do you know what a B card is if you never had one?

CHARLEY. I . . . heard. I been around.

MCLEOD. I'll bet you have. You've been working this precinct since October.

CHARLEY. No. I swear . . .

MCLEOD *(laughs in his face).* Who the hell do you think you're kidding? *(Charley glares at him)* I know that face. This is a good man. He's been in jail before.

CHARLEY. Never, so help me God! What are you tryin' to do, hang me? I wanta call my lawyer.

MCLEOD. Shut up! Print him. You'll find he's got a sheet as long as your arm.

CHARLEY. I don't know what you're talkin' about. I swear to God! I get down on my knees . . . *(He falls to his knees, crying)* What do you want me to . . .

MCLEOD. Get up! Get up! I can smell you. He's a cat burglar. A real murderer!

CALLAHAN. How many women you raped? *(Callahan stands near by, his back to the prisoner, his revolver sticking out of the holster. Charley looks at it, licks his lips)*

MCLEOD *(to Callahan).* Watch the roscoe! What's the matter with you? *(Callahan takes his revolver out of his holster, puts it in his pocket. To Charley)* Sit down! Over there.

WOMAN. Isn't anybody going to take care of me?

MCLEOD. Look, Madame! You're very upset. We don't need you here. Why don't you go home and rest up?

WOMAN. No, no, no! I am afraid to go back there now. I'm afraid even to go out in the street.

MCLEOD (laughs). Now, come on! You've got nothing to be afraid of.

WOMAN. No, no! I am! I am afraid!

MCLEOD. Suppose I send a policeman with you? . . . What time do you expect your husband back?

WOMAN. Seven o'clock.

MCLEOD. I'll send a policeman home with you to keep you company. A nice handsome Irish cop. How's that?

WOMAN (thinks it over, giggles at him, nods). That would be fine. Thank you, very much.

MCLEOD (turns her over to Keogh). Gus, see that this lady gets home safely. (Gus, grinning, takes her in tow. Exit Gus and the woman, giggling.)

SHOPLIFTER. I think I better call my brother-in-law.

DAKIS. What's the number?

SHOPLIFTER. Jerome 7-2577.

(Dakis crosses to phone, dials the number.)

BRODY (moves a chair center, turns to Lewis). Now, Lewis, sit down! (Lewis sits) You're in trouble.

MCLEOD (steps close to Lewis). You help us, we'll help you. We'll ask the D.A. to give you a break.

BRODY. Tell us the truth. How many burglaries you committed here? (Lewis is silent. Brody hands him a cigarette)

CALLAHAN (comes in from behind, lights his cigarette). Be a man. You got dropped! Face it!

O'BRIEN (closes the circle around Lewis). Why not get the agony over with?

CALLAHAN. If you don't, we're gonna get the D.A. to throw away the key.

DAKIS (to shoplifter, holding out the phone). Here you are, girlie! Come and get it.

SHOPLIFTER (crossing rapidly). Oh, God, what'll I tell her? What should I say? (She takes the phone and assumes her most casual sing-song) Hello, Milly! . . . Yeah! . . . Nothin'! I just didn't have any change. How are you? Yeah? Fine! How was the party? You went to Brooklyn? In your delicate condition? Milly! (She laughs feebly) Say, Milly, is Jack there by

any chance? Could I talk to him? Oh, nothin'! Some friend of mine wants some advice on somethin'. I don't know what. (She puts phone down) He's there. What should I tell him? I don't know what to tell him.

DAKIS. Tell him to meet you at night court, 100 Center Street.

SHOPLIFTER. Shall I tell him to bring hard cash?

DAKIS. He'll know better than we.

SHOPLIFTER (whispers hoarsely into phone). Hello, Jack? Listen—can Milly hear me? I don't want her to know, but I'm in a jam. I need your help. So don't let on. Make out like it's nothing. I can't give you all the details. I'm at the police station. Yeah. I took a bag. Best's. (Blatting) I had to admit it, Jack, it was on my arm. Thanks, Jack! 100 Center Street. If Milly asks, tell her . . . Gee, Jack, you're a . . . (She hangs up slowly, sighs with relief to Detective Dakis) Boy! Am I relieved!

(Endicott Sims appears with Kurt Schneider, and they stand within the gate, talking softly. Schneider is gaunt, neatly attired, dark, sullen, narrow, ferret-like face, bulging eyes, well-trimmed, waxed moustache.)

MCLEOD (coming out of the Lieutenant's office, crosses to them). Hello, Kurt! Come on in.

SIMS (to McLeod). I have advised my client of his legal rights. He will answer no questions other than his name and address. Remember, Kurt! Name and address, that's all. Is that understood?

MCLEOD. As you say, Counselor.

SIMS. When are you going to book him?

MCLEOD. In a couple of hours, when we get around to it.

SIMS. I want to arrange his bail bond.

MCLEOD. You'll have to get Judge Crater to stand bail for him.

SIMS. Suppose you tend to your business and I'll tend to mine.

MCLEOD. I'll be glad to, if you'll get the hell out of here and let me.

SIMS. Remember, Kurt! Name and address, that's all. (Exit)

MCLEOD. Sit down, Kurt. Over here! How've you been?

KURT. So, so.

MCLEOD. You look fit. That farm life agrees with you. Some coffee, Kurt?

KURT. You got enough?

MCLEOD. There's plenty. *(Pours some)* Here you are! Sandwich?

KURT. I just ate.

MCLEOD. Cruller?

KURT. I'm full—

MCLEOD. Be right with you. *(Hands him a newspaper, crosses to the phone, looks up a number in his notebook, dials it)*

BRODY *(to Patrolman Barnes, pointing at Charley and indicating the wash-room)*. Steve!

PATROLMAN BARNES *(nods)*. Come on, Charley, in here! *(Takes Charley off into the wash-room)*

BRODY *(to Lewis)*. Charley let *you* carry the gun and the jimmy. . . . You're the one that's going to burn. Don't you see how he's crossed you?

CALLAHAN. You ever hear of the guy who sold his buddy up the river for thirty pieces of silver?

LEWIS. Ya. *(The ring of men closes around Lewis)*

O'BRIEN. Well? Think!

BRODY. When were you in jail last? *(Silence)*

MCLEOD. Look, Lewis, we're gonna finger-print you. In half an hour we'll know your whole record, anyway.

BRODY. Make it easy for yourself. How many burglaries you committed in New York, Lewis?

LEWIS. What'll I get?

CALLAHAN. Were you in jail before?

LEWIS. Ya. Elmira. I got out in March.

BRODY. How long were you in?

LEWIS. Three and a half years.

BRODY. What for?

LEWIS. Burglary.

BRODY. Well, I'd say, seven and a half, to ten; maybe less, if you co-operate, if not—fifteen to twenty!

LEWIS. What do you want to know?

BRODY. How many burglaries you committed in New York?

LEWIS. Nine or ten.

CALLAHAN. That's better.

BRODY. What'd you do with the stuff?

LEWIS. Gave it to Charley.

CALLAHAN. He was in on it then?

LEWIS. Ya.

BRODY. You sell it?

LEWIS. Ya.

BRODY. Where?

LEWIS. In Boston . . . I think.

BRODY. You *think?* Didn't he tell you?

LEWIS. Na.

CALLAHAN. You're a bit of a shmuck, ain't you, Lewis?

BRODY. No, Lewis is regular. He's co-operating. *(To Lewis)* How much did he give you altogether?

LEWIS. Half. Four hundred dollars.

CALLAHAN. Wha . . . a . . . t?

BRODY. This stuff was worth thirty to forty thousand dollars.

LEWIS. Charley said it was mostly fake.

BRODY. Look! Here's the list! See for yourself!

(Lewis looks at it, his face drops.)

MCLEOD. Lewis, you've been robbed!

LEWIS. Ya.

BRODY. Where does Charley live?

LEWIS. 129th Street, West. I know the house. I don't know the number. I can show it to you.

BRODY. Fine.

(Dakis crosses to the toilet, opens the door, nods to Patrolman Barnes who brings Charley back into the room.)

CALLAHAN. That's using your . . . *(Taps Lewis' head)* . . . tokas, Lewis.

(Lieutenant Monoghan enters. He is an old-time police officer, ruddy, moon-faced, a cigar always thrust in the jaw, gray hair, muscle gone a bit to fat, his speech, crude New Yorkese interlarded with the vivid thieves' vernacular, crackles with authority.)

O'BRIEN. Hello, Chief!

BRODY. Hi, Lieutenant!

LIEUTENANT *(looking around)*. Busy house!

O'BRIEN. Yes, sir, we're bouncin', all of a sudden.

CALLAHAN. John! Got your car here? *(O'Brien nods)* Run us over? We're gonna hit this bum's flat, Chief.

LIEUTENANT *(squints at Lewis)*. What's your name?

LEWIS. Lewis. Abbott.

CALLAHAN *(shows Lieutenant the jimmy)*. Look at this . . . *(Shows him the gun)* . . . and this.

LIEUTENANT. Loaded?

CALLAHAN. Yeah.

BRODY *(indicating Charley)*. The other burglar.

LIEUTENANT. What's your name?

CHARLEY. Gennini. I don't know nothing about this, Lieutenant. I was . . .

LIEUTENANT (*snorts, turns his back on Charley*). Print him!

CALLAHAN. Yes, sir.

LIEUTENANT. Who made the collar?

BRODY. Uniform arrest. Patrolman Barnes.

LIEUTENANT (*to Barnes*). Nice goin'!

MCLEOD (*indicating Kurt to Lieutenant*). Kurt Schneider. Turned himself in.

LIEUTENANT. That mouthpiece of his got hold of me downstairs, chewed my ear off. I wanna have a talk with you. (*Beckons him inside*)

DAKIS. Charley, on your feet! Let's go. (*Leads Charley over to the finger-print board and "prints" him*)

MCLEOD (*in the Lieutenant's office, indicates Arthur*). Kindred. The Pritchett complaint.

LIEUTENANT. Admission?

MCLEOD. Yes.

LIEUTENANT. Step inside, lad.—In there. (*He indicates an ante-room off right. Arthur exits off right. To McLeod*) Shut the door. (*McLeod shuts door to the squad-room. The Lieutenant takes off his hat and jacket, tosses them onto the coat-rack*) On Schneider—what's your poisonal angle?

MCLEOD (*subtly mimics the Lieutenant's speech*). Poisonal angle! None. Why?

LIEUTENANT (*looks up sharply*). His mouthpiece hinted at something or other.

MCLEOD. Fishing expedition.

LIEUTENANT. You sure?

MCLEOD. Sure, I'm sure. What did Mr. Sims imply?

LIEUTENANT (*takes off his shoulder holstel, hangs it on the rack, transferring the revolver to his hip-pocket*). Just vague hints.

MCLEOD. You can write those on the air!

LIEUTENANT. What've you got? (*Takes off his shirt, hangs it up*)

MCLEOD. Girl—Miss Marris in the hospital. Critical. I called the D.A.'s office. I'm taking Schneider over to the hospital for a positive identification. I've got a corroborating witness. I phoned her. She's on her way over here. And I want to get a signed statement from Schneider.

LIEUTENANT. How?

MCLEOD. "Persuasion."

(*Joe saunters into the outer office.*)

LIEUTENANT. Keep your big mitts off. That's an order.

MCLEOD. Were you ever in those railroad flats of his? Did you ever see that kitchen table covered by a filthy, blood-stained oilcloth on which Kurt Schneider performs his delicate operations?

LIEUTENANT (*crosses to desk, opens drawer, takes out shaving articles and towel*). This is an impoisonal business! Your moral indignation is beginning to give me a quick pain in the butt. You got a Messianic complex. You want to be the judge and the jury, too. Well, you can't do it. It says so in the book. I don't like lawyers coming in here with photos. It marks my squad lousy. I don't like it— and I won't have it. You understand?

MCLEOD. Yes, sir.

LIEUTENANT. Can't you say, "yes, sir," without making it sound like an insult? (*Pause*)

MCLEOD (*the sting still in his voice*). Yes, sir.

LIEUTENANT (*furious*). You're too damn superior, that's your trouble. For the record, I don't like you any more'n you like me; but you got a value here and I need you on my squad. That's the only reason you're not wearing a white badge again.

MCLEOD (*reaches in his pocket for his shield*). You wouldn't want it back now, would you?

LIEUTENANT. When I do, I'll ask for it.

MCLEOD. Because you can have it—with instructions.

LIEUTENANT (*controls himself*). Get what you can out of Schneider, but no roughhouse! You know the policy of this administration.

MCLEOD. I don't hold with it.

LIEUTENANT. What the hell ice does that cut?

MCLEOD. I don't believe in coddling criminals.

LIEUTENANT. Who tells you to?

MCLEOD. You do. The whole damn system does.

LIEUTENANT. Sometimes, McLeod, you talk like a maniac.

MCLEOD (*starts to speak*). May I . . .

LIEUTENANT. No! You got your orders. That's all.

MCLEOD. May I have the keys to the files, *sir*?

LIEUTENANT. You got to have the last word, don't you? (*Tosses the keys on the desk, stalks off right*)

DAKIS (*finishes finger-printing Charley,*

waves him to the wash-room). Charley, wash up! In there!

JOE *(to Brody).* How many burglaries?

BRODY. Nine or ten.

(A tall, slender girl enters and stands at the gate. Her face is handsome with a bony, freckled, intelligent, scrubbed handsomeness; wide, soft, generous lips, huge clear eyes, at the moment very troubled, indeed.)

JOE. Any important names? Any good addresses?

BRODY *(moans).* We don't know yet. You'll get it. Don't rush us, will you, Joey?

YOUNG GIRL. Is Detective McLeod here?

CALLAHAN *(crosses up to gate).* Yes, Miss?

YOUNG GIRL. May I see Detective McLeod?

CALLAHAN. He's busy. Anything I can do for you? *(He scrutinizes her, grins, a little "on the make")* I seen your face before?

YOUNG GIRL. No.

CALLAHAN. I never forget a face.

(Joe looks at her, then wanders into the Lieutenant's office.)

YOUNG GIRL. You probably saw my sister.

CALLAHAN. Who's your sister?

YOUNG GIRL. Please tell him Miss Susan Carmichael is here.

CALLAHAN. Yes, Miss. Just a minute. *(Replaces the cards in the files)*

MCLEOD *(in the Lieutenant's office, examining burglary sheets, still fuming at his Lieutenant).* Ignorant, gross wardheeler! Why don't you print the truth for once, Yussel?

JOE. Which truth?—Yours, his, theirs, mine?

MCLEOD. *The* truth.

JOE. Oh, that one? Who would know it? If it came up and blew in your ear, who would know it?

CALLAHAN *(pokes his head into the doorway, addresses McLeod).* Kid outside for you! *(Returns to his files)*

JOE. A nice, tall, long-stemmed kid. *(He sits down, picks his teeth, rambles on, almost to himself. McLeod, who is going through the files and grinding his teeth in anger, pays no heed to Joe's reflections)* I love these tall kids today. I got a nephew, 17, six-foot-three, blond hair, blue eyes. *(Sucks his teeth)* Science

tells us at the turn of the century the average man and woman's going to be seven-foot tall. Seven foot! That's for me. We know the next fifty years are gonna be lousy: war, atom-bombs, whole friggin' civilization's caving in. But I don't wake up at four A.M. to bury myself, any more. I got the whole thing licked—I'm skipping the next fifty years. I'm concentrating on the twenty-first century and all those seven-foot beauties. . . .

MCLEOD *(impatiently).* I've no time for a philosophic discussion today, Yussel. *(Starts for outer office)*

JOE *(following, murmurs).* Don't throw water on McLeod. He goes rabid.

BARNES *(to Charley as he comes out of wash-room).* O.K., Charley. Come with me. *(They exit through gate)*

MCLEOD *(calls to O'Brien who is about to exit with Lewis in tow).* Hey, John, I need eight or ten fellows up here for a line-up. Ask a couple of the men downstairs to get into civvies!

O'BRIEN. Line-up? Sure. *(Exit)*

MCLEOD *(coming down to the desk, addresses the young lady at the gate).* Miss Carmichael?

SUSAN. Yes. I'm Susan Carmichael.

MCLEOD. Come in, please!

SUSAN *(enters through the gate, crosses down to the desk facing McLeod).* Are you the officer who phoned?

MCLEOD. Yes. I'm Detective McLeod.

SUSAN. Where's Arthur? What happened to him? What's this about?

MCLEOD. Did you contact your sister?

SUSAN *(hesitating).* N . . . no!

MCLEOD. Why not?

SUSAN. I couldn't reach her.

MCLEOD. Where is she?

SUSAN. Visiting some friends in Connecticut. I don't know the address. Where's Arthur? Is he all right?

MCLEOD. Yes. He's inside. How well do you know Arthur Kindred?

SUSAN. Very. All my life. We lived next door to each other in Ann Arbor.

MCLEOD. Kind of a wild boy, wasn't he?

SUSAN. Arthur?? Not at all. He was always very serious. Why?

MCLEOD. Did he give your sister any money?

SUSAN. My sister earns $25 an hour. She's a very successful model. She averages $300 to $400 a week for herself. Will you please tell me what this is about?

MCLEOD. Let me ask the questions? Do you mind?

SUSAN. Sorry!

MCLEOD. Arthur was in the Navy?

SUSAN. Five years.

MCLEOD. He got a dishonorable discharge.

SUSAN. What are you talking about?

(Brody becomes interested, edges over, listening.)

MCLEOD. That's a question.

SUSAN. You didn't punctuate it.

MCLEOD. Correction. *(He smiles)* Did he?

SUSAN. Arthur was cited four times. He got the silver star. He carried a sailor up three decks of a burning ship. He had two ships sunk under him. He floated around once in the Pacific Ocean for seventeen hours with sharks all around him. When they picked him up, he was out of his head, trying to climb onto a concrete platform that wasn't there. He was in the hospital for ten weeks after that. Any more questions?

MCLEOD. What is his relationship to your sister?

SUSAN. I told you, we all grew up together.

MCLEOD. Is he in love with her?

SUSAN. My sister is one of the most beautiful girls in New York. A lot of men are in love with her. May I talk to Arthur, now, please?

MCLEOD. He didn't give her any money, then?

SUSAN *(impatiently)*. No.

MCLEOD. Did he give it to you?

SUSAN. Are you kidding?

MCLEOD. I'm afraid not. Your sister's boy-friend is in trouble.

SUSAN. What trouble?

MCLEOD. He's a thief.

SUSAN. Who says so?

MCLEOD. He does.

SUSAN. I don't believe you.

MCLEOD. Sit down. *(He calls through door of the Lieutenant's office, off right)* Arthur! In here!

(Arthur enters, sees Susan, stops in his tracks.)

SUSAN. Jiggs! What happened?

ARTHUR. Suzy! *(He glares indignantly at MCLEOD)* Did you have to drag children into this?

MCLEOD *(ironically)*. Now, Jiggs!

ARTHUR. Susan, you shouldn't have come here.

SUSAN. What happened?

ARTHUR. I took some money.

SUSAN. Who from?

ARTHUR. The man I worked for.

SUSAN. But why, Jiggs, why?

ARTHUR. None of your business.

BRODY *(scanning a list)*. Say, Jim!

MCLEOD. Yes?

(Brody beckons to him. McLeod turns up, talks to Brody sotto voce. Arthur whispers to Susan, urgently.)

ARTHUR. Suzy, go home—quick—go home—get out of here.

SUSAN *(whispers)*. Jiggs, what happened? Have you got a lawyer?

ARTHUR. No!

SUSAN. I'll phone Joy and tell her.

ARTHUR. Do you want to get her involved? There are newspapermen here. You want to ruin her career?

SUSAN *(whispering)*. But, Jiggs—

ARTHUR *(whispering)*. Get out of here, will you?

(McLeod returns.)

MCLEOD. Well, young lady—satisfied?

SUSAN. How much did he take?

MCLEOD. $480.

ARTHUR. What's the difference? Will you please tell her to go home, Officer? She's only a kid.

SUSAN *(indignantly)*. I'm not. I wish you'd . . .

ARTHUR. She shouldn't be here. She's got nothing to do with this.

MCLEOD. All right, young lady. I'm sorry to have bothered you. Have your sister get in touch with me as soon as you hear from her.

ARTHUR. What for? Don't you do it, Suzy—you don't have to. *(To McLeod)* You're not going to get her involved in this.

MCLEOD. You shut up! *(To Susan)* O.K. *(Motions Susan to go. She bites her lip to keep from crying, and goes)*

BRODY *(comes down to Arthur)*. Is it true that you carried a wounded sailor on your shoulders up three decks of a burning ship?

ARTHUR. Yes.

BRODY. Pretty good.

ARTHUR. Could I have that drink now? Please!

BRODY. Sure. *(Crosses up to his files, takes out a bottle of whiskey, cleans a*

*glass, pours a drink. McLeod ambles
down to Kurt, sipping coffee from a container)*

MCLEOD. You're looking pretty well,
Kurt.

KURT. Could be better.

MCLEOD *(sits at typewriter, inserts a
sheet of paper).* How's the farm?

KURT. All right!

MCLEOD. Wasn't there a drought in Jersey this year? *(Starts to type statement)*

KURT. I irrigate my crops. I've got
plenty of water.

MCLEOD. What do you raise?

KURT. Cabbage . . . Lettuce . . . Kale!
Truck stuff!

MCLEOD *(typing).* That's the life. Pic-
turesque country, North Jersey. Nice hills,
unexpected!

KURT. Yes. How're things with you?

MCLEOD. This is one business never has
a depression. *(Drinks—surveys his container)* They make a pretty good cup of
coffee across the street.

KURT. Mm. So, so.

BRODY *(comes down, hands drink to
Arthur).* Here you are, son! *(Crosses up
again to replace bottle in his file. Arthur
tosses down the drink)*

MCLEOD *(types).* When I retire I'm going to buy myself a little farm like yours,
settle down. Does it really pay for itself?

KURT. If you work it.

MCLEOD. How much can a man average
a year? *(Types)*

KURT. Varies. Two thousand a good
year.

MCLEOD. Clear? That's pretty good.
(Types)

KURT. Sometimes you lose a crop.

MCLEOD *(types).* How long you had
that farm?

KURT. Eleven years.

MCLEOD. And you average two thousand
a year? *(Stops typing, fixes him with a
sharp, searching glance)*

KURT. What's . . . ?

MCLEOD. Then how'd you manage to
accumulate $56,000 in the bank, Kurt?
Hm? *(Silence)* Hm, Kurt? How?

KURT. Who says I have?

MCLEOD. I do. I checked. $56,000. That's
a lot of kale. *(Takes out a note-book
from his pocket)* You got it in four
banks. Passaic—Oakdale—two in Newark. Here are the figures. How'd you get
that money, Kurt?

KURT. I got it honestly.

MCLEOD. How? How?

KURT. I don't have to tell you that.

MCLEOD. Oh, come on, Kurt. How?
(Kurt shakes his head) Make it easy for
yourself. You're still running that abortion mill, aren't you?

KURT. My name is Kurt Schneider—I
live in Oakdale, New Jersey. That's all I
have to answer.

MCLEOD. You operated on Miss Harris,
didn't you?

KURT. No, I did not!

MCLEOD. She identified your picture.
*(He rips the sheet of paper out of the
typewriter and sets it down before Kurt)*
Sign that, Kurt!

KURT. What is it?

MCLEOD. An admission.

KURT. You think I'm crazy.

MCLEOD. We've got you dead to rights.
Make it easy for yourself.

KURT. I'm not saying anything more on
advice of counsel!

MCLEOD. I'm getting impatient! You better talk, Kurt.

KURT. I'm standing on my Constitutional rights!

MCLEOD *(rising nervously, moving
above the desk and down to Kurt).* Hold
your hats, boys, here we go again. *(Looking down on Kurt from behind him,
murmurs softly)* You're lucky, Kurt. You
got away with it once. But the postman
rings twice. And this time we've got you,
Kurt. Why don't you cop a plea? Miss
Harris is waiting for you. We're going to
visit her in the hospital. She's anxious to
see you. And what you don't know is . . .
There was a corroborating witness, and
she's downstairs ready to identify you,
right now. . . . You're getting pale, Kurt.
(Kurt laughs softly to himself) What are
you laughing at?

KURT. Nothing.

MCLEOD. That's right! That's just what
you've got to laugh about—nothing.
You're on the bottom of this joke.

KURT. Maybe I am. Maybe I'm not.
Maybe somebody else is.

MCLEOD. What's that mean?

KURT. I know why you're out to get
me.

MCLEOD. Why? . . . *(Kurt shakes his
head)* Why, Kurt? This is your last
chance. Do you want to talk?

KURT. My name is Kurt Schneider. I

live in Oakdale, New Jersey. That's all I'm obliged to say by law.

MCLEOD. You should have been a lawyer, Kurt. A Philadelphia lawyer. (*Crosses to the rail, shouts downstairs*) Line-up, Gus!

GUS (*off-stage, shouts up*). Coming. (*He can be heard approaching singing the melody of* The Rose of Tralee)

MCLEOD (*to Dakis*). Nick, put on your hat and coat for a line-up.

(*Brody crosses down to Arthur again. Arthur hands him the glass.*)

ARTHUR. Thanks.

(*A pause. As Brody looks at the boy, something of agony creeps into his face.*)

BRODY. My boy was in the Navy, too. The *Juneau*. Know her?

ARTHUR. She was a cruiser.

BRODY. Yeah.

ARTHUR. Didn't she go down with all hands? In the Pacific?

BRODY. There were ten survivors. He wasn't one of them.

ARTHUR. Too bad.

BRODY. Yeah! He was my only boy. It's something you never get over. You never believe it. You keep waiting for a bell to ring . . . phone . . . door. Sometimes I hear a voice on the street, or see a young fellow from the back, the set of his shoulders—like you—for a minute it's him. Your whole life becomes like a dream . . . a walking dream.

ARTHUR. Maybe he was one of the lucky ones.

BRODY. Don't say that!

ARTHUR. Why not?

BRODY. Because it wouldn't make sense then.

ARTHUR. Does it?

BRODY (*fiercely*). Yes, damn it! Yes.

MCLEOD. Say, Lou! Will you put on your hat and coat for a line-up?

(*Enter policemen in civilian clothes, and detectives putting on hats and coats, joking and laughing.*)

BRODY. Yeah.

MCLEOD. John, Nick, hat and coat!

(*The men line up.*)

DAKIS (*to Charley*). Sit over there, Charley. (*Indicates the bench*)

MCLEOD (*coming down to Kurt*). Kurt. Put on your hat and coat. Pick your spot. End, middle, any place. No alibis later. (*Kurt finds a place in the line and stands there stiffly. McLeod calls off*) Come in,

Miss Hatch. (*Enter Miss Hatch, a hard-looking young woman with hair bleached a lemon yellow. She wears an elaborate fur stole*) How do you do, Miss Hatch?

MISS HATCH. I'm fine, thank you. (*Crosses down to McLeod. McLeod scrutinizes her, frowns*) What's the matter?

MCLEOD (*indicating the fur piece*). Rushing the season, aren't you?

MISS HATCH (*laughs nervously*). Oh!

MCLEOD. New?

MISS HATCH. Yes.

MCLEOD. Mink?

MISS HATCH. Uh, uh! Dyed squirrel! Looks real though, doesn't it?

MCLEOD. Mmm. It was nice of you to come down and help us. We appreciate that.

MISS HATCH. Don't mention it. Let's just get it over with, huh? I got an engagement. What do I—(*She looks about for an ash tray in which to deposit her cigarette*)

MCLEOD. Throw it on the floor. (*She obeys. He steps on it*) You have your instructions?

MISS HATCH. Yeah. I look at them all, then touch the one on the shoulder. (*He nods. She walks slowly down the line, nervously scrutinizing the faces, a little too quickly to be convincing. She turns to McLeod*) He isn't here.

MCLEOD. You haven't looked.

MISS HATCH. I looked. Of course I did.

CALLAHAN. It's the new look.

MCLEOD. Just look, will you. Not at me. Over there.

MISS HATCH. I don't recognize anyone. I never saw any of them in my life before.

MCLEOD. You identified a picture of one of these men.

MISS HATCH. What are you trying to do . . . make me give you a wrong identification? Well, I ain't gonna do it.

MCLEOD (*rubs his thumb and forefinger together, suggestively*). Do you know what this means?

MISS HATCH (*sharply*). Yeah. That's your cut on the side.

MCLEOD. You're fresh! (*Phone rings, Brody answers it*)

BRODY. 2-1 Squad. Brody. (*Conversation sotto voce*)

MCLEOD. I've a good mind to prefer charges against you.

MISS HATCH (*screams at him*). That's

what I get for coming all the way downtown to help you. You cops are all the same. Give you a badge and you think you can push the world around.

MCLEOD. You identified one of these men. Now point him out or I'm going to throw you in the clink.

MISS HATCH. You'll do *what?*

BRODY *(hangs up the phone, calls him to one side)*. Jim!

MCLEOD. Yes?

BRODY *(in subdued tones)*. That was the D.A.'s office. The Harris girl died.

MCLEOD. When?

BRODY. A couple of hours ago.

MCLEOD. Why weren't we informed?

BRODY. I don't know.

MCLEOD. There goes the case.

BRODY. The D.A. says just go through the motions. He can't get an indictment now. Just book him and forget it, he says.

MCLEOD. Sure, forget it. Let him fill the morgues! *(Crosses over to Kurt)* Congratulations, Kurt! The girl died. Sit down over there, Kurt. All right, Miss Hatch. You've earned your fur piece. I hope you'll enjoy it.

MISS HATCH *(flaring)*. You can't talk to me that way. I'm no tramp that you can talk to me that way. Who the hell do you think you are anyway?

MCLEOD. Get out! Take a couple of drop-dead pills! Get lost!

MISS HATCH *(exit, murmuring)*. Big cheese! See my lawyer about him.

MCLEOD. All right, men, thank you. *(As they go, we hear snatches of the following conversation from the men.)*

GUS. I was waiting for her to put the finger on you, boy.

DAKIS. Me? Do I look like an ice-tong man?

O'BRIEN. Regular Sarah Heartburn.

CALLAHAN. One minute more we'd have gotten the witches' scene from *Macbeth.* *(Exit)*

(Willie, the janitor, has entered during the above.)

WILLIE *(sweeping vigorously, muttering all the while)*. Now look at this joint, will you? You filthy slobs. You live in a stable. *(To shoplifter)* Come on, get up. *(She rises. He sweeps right through her)* Wouldn't think I swept it out an hour ago. Boy, I'd like to see the homes you bums live in. Pig pens, I bet. *(Exit)*

MCLEOD *(crosses up to the duty chart, takes it off the wall, crosses down to the desk with it, murmuring for Joe's benefit).* Why am I wasting my life here? I could make more driving a hack. I like books, I like music, I've got a wonderful, wonderful wife—I could get a dozen jobs would give me more time to enjoy the good things of life. I should have my head examined. All this work, these hours! What for? It's a phony. *(He removes the letters spelling out Gallagher and Dakis, places them in the drawer, takes out other letters, inserts his name and Brody's)*

JOE *(comes down)*. Was she *reached,* you think?

MCLEOD. What do *you* think?

JOE. I don't know.

MCLEOD *(groans)*. Oh, Yussel.

JOE. I don't know.

MCLEOD. This is a phony. The thieves and murderers could have written the penal code themselves. Your democracy, Yussel, is a Rube Goldberg contraption. An elaborate machine a block long—you set it all in motion, 3,000 wheels turn, it goes *ping.* *(He crosses up again, replaces the chart on the wall)*

JOE. That's what's great about it. That's what I love. It's so confused, it's wonderful. *(Crosses to McLeod)* After all, Seamus, guilt and innocence!—The epistomological question! Just the knowing . . . the mere knowing . . . the ability to ken. Maybe he didn't do it. Maybe she can't identify him. How do you know? *(Brody enters, sits at desk.)*

MCLEOD. How do you know anything? You've got a nose, you can smell; you've got taste buds, you can taste; you've got nerve endings, you can feel; and, theoretically, you've got intelligence . . . you can judge.

JOE. Ah, ha! That's where it breaks down!

MCLEOD *(to Brody)*. Got an aspirin? *(Brody hands him a box of aspirin, McLeod takes the box and crosses over into the Lieutenant's office. Joe follows him.)*

JOE. I was talking to Judge Mendez today. He just got on the bench last year, Seamus. Twenty-nine years a successful lawyer. He thought this would be a cinch. He's lost forty pounds. He's nervous as a cat. His wife thinks he has a mistress. He has:—The Law. He said to me, "Joe! I've got to sentence a man to death tomorrow. How can I do it? Who am I to judge? It takes a God to know!—To really know!"

MCLEOD (*in Lieutenant's office, draws a glass of water, tosses the aspirin into his mouth*). Bunk!

JOE. I'm quoting Judge Mendez.

MCLEOD. Then he's a corrupt man, himself. All lawyers are, anyway. I say hang all the lawyers, and let justice triumph. (*Washes down the aspirin with a drink, sits, takes off his tie, rolls up his sleeve, then slowly, with mounting bitterness*) Evil has a stench of its own. A child can spot it. I know . . . I know, Yussel. My own father was one of them. No good he was . . . possessed. Every day and every night of my childhood I saw and heard him abuse and maliciously torment my mother. I saw that sadistic son-of-a-bitch of a father of mine with that criminal mind of his drive my mother straight into a lunatic asylum. She died in a lunatic asylum. (*He controls himself*) Yes, I know it when I smell it. I learned it early and deep. I was fourteen and alone in the world. I made war on it. Every time I look at one of these babies, I see my father's face!

(*Phone rings in the outer office. Brody answers.*)

BRODY. 2-1 Squad. Brody. (*Pause*) Lock the door. Don't let him out! I'll be right over. (*Hangs up, rushes into the inner office, grabs his hat and coat*) Say, Jim, there's a guy at O'Donovan's bar with a badge and gun, arresting a woman. Claims he's a cop. Might be, might be a shakedown. I'll be right back. Catch the phone for me! (*Takes his gun out of the drawer and runs off*)

JOE (*runs after him*). Could be some shooting. Wait for me, baby! (*Exit*)

(*McLeod comes out of Lieutenant's office, his face grim, black, the veins in his temple standing out.*)

MCLEOD (*to Kurt*). You're a lucky man, Kurt. Kissed in your cradle by a vulture. So the girl died, Kurt.

KURT. That's too bad.

MCLEOD. What have you got, Kurt, in place of a conscience? (*Kurt starts to speak*) Don't answer!—I know—a lawyer. I ought to fall on you like the sword of God.

KURT. That sword's got two edges. You could cut your own throat.

MCLEOD (*takes out a cigarette, turns away to light it, his face twitching neurotically*). *Look!* The gate's open! While I'm lighting my cigarette—why don't you run for it? One second, you'll be out in the street.

KURT. I'll go free anyway. Why should I run?

MCLEOD. Give me the little pleasure— (*Touching his gun*) of putting a hole in the back of your head.

KURT. You wouldn't do that. Talk!

MCLEOD. Is it?

KURT. You're an intelligent man. You're not foolish.

MCLEOD. Try me, Kurt. Why don't you? Go ahead, dance down that hall!

KURT (*smiles and shakes his head*). Soon as you book me, I'm out on bail. When I go to trial, they couldn't convict me in a million years. You know that. Even if I were guilty, which I'm not . . . The girl is dead. There are no witnesses. That's the law.

MCLEOD. You've been well briefed. You know your catechism.

KURT. I know more than my catechism!

MCLEOD. What, for example? (*Kurt smiles and nods*) What, Kurt? What goes on under that monkey-skull of yours, I wonder! (*Kurt is silent*) On your feet! (*Kurt looks up at McLeod's face, is frightened by its almost insane intensity. McLeod roars at him*) Get up!! (*Kurt rises*) Go in there! (*Points to the Lieutenant's office. Kurt goes into the Lieutenant's office. McLeod follows him, shuts the door*) Sit down, Kurt. (*Kurt sits*) I'm going to give you a piece of advice. When the courts and the juries and the judges let you free this time, get out of New York. Go to Georgia. They won't extradite criminals to us. So, you see, Kurt, take my advice, go to Georgia, or go to hell, but you butcher one more girl in this city, and law or no law, I'll find you and I'll put a bullet in the back of your head, and I'll drop your body in the East River, and I'll go home and I'll sleep sweetly.

KURT. You have to answer to the law the same as I. You don't frighten me. Now, I'll give you some advice. I've got plenty on you, too. I know why you're so vindictive. And you watch your step! Because I happen to have friends, too, downtown . . . with pull, lots of pull!

MCLEOD. Have you? What do you know? Aren't you the big shot! *Pull!* Have you got any friends with *push!* Like *that! (Kicks him; Kurt goes over, chair and all)*

KURT. Cut that out! You let me alone now. . . . *(McLeod grabs him by the lapels, pulls him to his feet)* You let me go! Let me go!

MCLEOD. No. Kurt! Everybody else is going to let you go. You got it all figured . . . exactly. The courts, the juries, the judges—*(He slaps him)* Everybody except me. *(He slaps him again. Kurt starts to resist, growls and tries to push McLeod away. McLeod hits him in the belly. Kurt crumples to the floor. McLeod's rage subsides. He sighs, disgusted with himself for losing his temper)* Why didn't you obey your lawyer and keep your mouth shut? All right! Get up, Kurt! Come on! Get up!

KURT *(moaning and writhing)*. I can't . . . I can't . . . Something inside . . . broke! *(He calls feebly)* Help! *(He screams)* Help!

MCLEOD. Get up! You're all right. Get up!

(Kurt's eyes roll up exposing the whites. Lieutenant Monoghan enters quickly, wiping shaving-lather off his face with a towel.)

LIEUTENANT. What's going on? *(He sees Kurt, goes to him, bends down)*

KURT. Inside! It broke. He hurt me . . . *(Dakis rushes in.)*

LIEUTENANT. Take it easy, son, you'll be all right.

KURT. I feel terrible.

LIEUTENANT. Nick! Quick! Get an ambulance.

DAKIS. Yes, sir. *(Goes to the phone, puts in a call)*

LIEUTENANT. Did he resist you? *(Gallagher enters on the double.)*

MCLEOD. No.

LIEUTENANT. No? You lunatic! Didn't I just get through warning you. *(To Kurt who is on the floor, moaning in agony)* What happened?

KURT *(gasping for breath)*. He tried to kill me!

LIEUTENANT. Why should he do that?

KURT. Tami Giacoppetti . . . Same thing! . . . She got him after me too. . . . Tami Giacoppetti . . . *(Kurt's mouth opens and closes with scarcely any further sound emerging)*

LIEUTENANT. What? Tami Giacoppetti? Who's he? What about him? *(Puts his*

ear to Kurt's mouth)* A little louder! Just try and talk a little louder, lad. *(Kurt's eyes close, his head falls back. To Gallagher)* Wet some towels! *(Gallagher rushes to the wash-room. Dakis loosens Kurt's collar, tries to restore him to consciousness. The Lieutenant rises, confronts McLeod, glaring at him)* Who's Tami Giacoppetti?

MCLEOD. I've no idea.

LIEUTENANT. What's the pitch here, McLeod?

MCLEOD. He needled me. He got fresh. He begged for it, and I let him have it. That's all.

(Gallagher returns with several wet towels. Dakis takes them from him, applies them to Kurt's head.)

LIEUTENANT. Don't con me! That ain't all. Come on! Let's have it! What about this Tami Giacoppetti?

MCLEOD. I never heard of him.

GALLAGHER. Giacoppetti? I know him. A black-market guy. Runs a creep joint in the village.

(Kurt groans.)

MCLEOD. He's putting on an act, Lieutenant. Can't you see . . .

(Kurt groans.)

LIEUTENANT. This could be a very hot potato. If this man's hurt, the big brass'll be down here throwin' questions at me. And I'm going to have the answers. What plays between you two guys? What's he got on you? What's the clout?

MCLEOD. Nothing.

LIEUTENANT. Then what was his mouthpiece yellin' and screamin' about?

MCLEOD. Red herring. Red, red herring!

LIEUTENANT. That I'm gonna god-damn well find out for myself. There's something kinky about this. McLeod, if you're concealing something from me, I'll have your head on a plate. *(To Gallagher)* This Giacoppetti! Find him and bring him in!

GALLAGHER. Yes, sir. *(Goes)*

LIEUTENANT *(calls after him)*. My car's downstairs. Use it.

GALLAGHER. Yes, sir. *(Goes)*.

(The Lieutenant bends down to Kurt. McLeod, grim-faced, lights another cigarette.)

CURTAIN

ACT TWO

SCENE: *The scene is the same, fifty-four minutes later by the clock on the wall.*

At rise, the lawyer, Endicott Sims, is closeted in the Lieutenant's office, scolding the Lieutenant and McLeod. In the squad-room the shoplifter is reading the comics. Arthur is seated quietly, his head bowed in thought. Dakis, the janitor and Gus are in a huddle, whispering, glancing over toward the Lieutenant's door. Brody is talking sotto voce to an excited man and woman, who are glaring at a tough-looking specimen. The setting sun is throwing long and ominous shadows into the darkening room.

———

SIMS *(fulminating at McLeod who pointedly ignores him by focusing attention on a hangnail).* How dare you take the law in your own hands? Who are you to constitute yourself a court of last appeal?

LIEUTENANT *(oil on the surging waters).* Nah, Counselor . . .

(The phone rings in the squad-room. Brody crosses to answer.)

BRODY. 21st Squad, Detective Brody . . . Yeah! . . . The hospital! Yeah. How is he? *(Jotting notation)*

SIMS. No, Lieutenant! This is a felony. *(Wheels back to McLeod)* I'm going to press a felonious assault here. So help me, I'm going to see you in jail!

MCLEOD *(calmly, biting the hangnail).* On which side of the bars, Counselor?

SIMS. Be careful. I'm an attorney and an officer of the court, and I don't like that talk.

MCLEOD. I'm an officer of the peace and I don't like collusion.

SIMS. What do you mean by that?

MCLEOD *(looks up, sharply).* By that I mean *collusion.* Subornation of witnesses, Counselor.

SIMS. What the devil are you talking about?

MCLEOD. I'm charging you with subornation.

SIMS. Your lips are blistering with lies.

MCLEOD *(sardonically).* Praise from an expert. I had a witness here today you bought off, Counselor.

SIMS. That's so absurd, I'm not even going to answer it.

MCLEOD. I'll prove it!

LIEUTENANT. All right! Cut it! Cut it out. Enough's enough.

SIMS *(to Lieutenant).* I intend to carry this to the Commissioner.

LIEUTENANT *(pushes the phone across the desk toward Sims).* Call him now. That's your privilege.

SIMS. And don't think *you're* entirely free of blame in this, Lieutenant.

LIEUTENANT. Me? What have I . . .

SIMS. I warned you personal motives are involved in this case. I was afraid this was going to happen. You should have taken the necessary steps to prevent it. Luckily, I came armed with photos and affidavits.

LIEUTENANT. Mystery! Mystery! *What* motives?

MCLEOD *(rises).* Yes. Why don't you tell us? Let's get it out in the open! What are these motives?

SIMS. It is not to my client's interests to reveal them at this moment.

MCLEOD. Legal bull.

LIEUTENANT. I'm beginning to think so, myself.

SIMS. Sure. One hand washes the other. *(Brody knocks at the door.)*

LIEUTENANT. Come in!

BRODY. Phone, Lieutenant.

LIEUTENANT *(picks up the phone).* 21st Squad, Lieutenant Monoghan . . . Yeah . . . Yeah . . .

(Brody returns to the squad-room, hangs up the phone.)

SIMS *(softly, to McLeod).* On what evidence do you make these serious charges?

MCLEOD *(taunting him).* The evidence of my intelligent observation.

SIMS. Insufficient, incompetent and irrelevant.

LIEUTENANT *(looks up, annoyed).* Sh! Sh! *(Turns back to the phone)*

SIMS. You're pretty cagey, McLeod, but your tactics don't fool me for a second. You're not going to duck out of this so easily. You're in a position of responsibility here and you have to answer for your actions. You can't use your badge for personal vengeance. That doesn't go. The public isn't your servant; you're theirs. You're going to be broken for this.

MCLEOD *(roaring back at him).* Go ahead! Break me! You're worse than the criminals you represent, Counselor. You're so damn respectable. Yet, look at you! The clothes you wear, your car downstairs, your house in Westchester, all bought with stolen money, tainted with blood.

LIEUTENANT. Shut up! I got the hospital.

SIMS. How is he? *(They listen attentively)*

LIEUTENANT *(on phone)*. Yes. Yes. I see. Keep in touch with me. Let me know right away. *(Hangs up)* See, Counselor, it always pays to await the event. There are no external lacerations on your client that would warrant a felony assault. They're now making X-rays and tests to see if there are any internal injuries. So far you haven't got a leg to stand on.

MCLEOD. Let him, let him! *(To Sims)* Bring your felony charge. It'll give me a chance to get your client on the stand and really tear his clothes off. And yours, too, Counselor.

LIEUTENANT. McLeod! Step outside! *(McLeod crosses out of the Lieutenant's office, shuts the door.)*

BRODY *(murmurs to McLeod)*. What's the score?

MCLEOD. Tempest in a teapot. *(Turns to his personal file)*

SIMS. What kind of an officer is that?

LIEUTENANT. Detectives are like fingerprints. No two alike. He has his quoiks.

SIMS. The understatement of the year.

LIEUTENANT. We've all got 'em. He has a value here. He's honest. He ain't on the take. I stand up for him on that. Got no tin boxes.

SIMS. I wasn't saying he had.

LIEUTENANT. I thought you was, maybe.

SIMS. No . . .

LIEUTENANT. Then what was you saying? I guess I fumbled it.

SIMS. I can't discuss it with you.

LIEUTENANT *(sarcastically)*. I'd live to discuss it with someone. Who do you suggest?

SIMS. McLeod.

LIEUTENANT. Nah, Counselor!

SIMS. Or his wife!

LIEUTENANT *(looks up sharply)*. His wife? What do you mean by that?

SIMS. Never mind! Skip it!

LIEUTENANT. You mentioned his wife. What do you mean by that? Look! I got to get a clear-up here. A little co-operation would go a long way.

SIMS. When it serves my client's interests . . . not before.

LIEUTENANT. Four years ago I threw my radio set the hell outa the window. You know why? Because, goddamn it, I hate mysteries.

SIMS *(smiles, shakes his head)*. Lieutenant, I'm not free to discuss this, yet. *(Looks at his watch)* Gouverneur Hospital?

LIEUTENANT. Yeah.

SIMS. I want to see my client. Will I be allowed in?

LIEUTENANT. Yeah, yeah.

SIMS. I'll be back. *(He leaves the Lieutenant's office. In the squad-room, he pauses to confront McLeod)* I'll be back. I'm not through with you.

MCLEOD. I can't wait.

(Exit Sims.)

BRODY *(to McLeod, indicating the tough, surly-looking character)*. This creep was impersonating an officer.

WOMAN. I didn't know. I thought he might be a policeman. His badge looked real.

BRODY. A shake-down. After he got you outside he'd a taken all your money and let you go. You see, Mrs. Feeney, that's how we get a bad reputation. Now you will appear in court in the morning, won't you?

MRS. FEENEY. Oh, yes.

MR. FEENEY. Tomorrow morning? Hey! . . . I've got a job.

MRS. FEENEY. You'll explain to your boss. You'll just take off, that's all.

MR. FEENEY. But, Isabel . . .

MRS. FEENEY. He'll be there. Don't you worry. Thank you. Thank you. *(They go off, arguing)*

BRODY *(to McLeod)*. I'm going down to book this crumb-bum.

CRUMB-BUM *(aggressively)*. What did you call me?

BRODY. A crumb-bum. Come on! *(Exit Brody and the glowering crumb-bum)*
(Inside, the Lieutenant squints at his cigar a moment, rises, bellows.)

LIEUTENANT. McLeod!

MCLEOD *(crosses to the Lieutenant's door, opens it)*. Yes, sir?

LIEUTENANT. What the hell is this about? What's he driving at? I want the truth.

MCLEOD. Lieutenant, I give you my solemn word of honor . . .

LIEUTENANT *(pauses, studies him, sighs, waves him out)*. Shut the door!
(McLeod shuts the door and crosses to the desk. A sad-looking man appears at the gate.)

MCLEOD. Yes, sir? What can I do for you?

MAN. I want to report someone picked my pocket.

MCLEOD (*sitting at the desk*). Come in!

MAN (*exposes his back-side, revealing a patch cut out of his trousers*). Look! They cut it right out.

MCLEOD. They work that way, with a razor blade. Sit down! Did you see the man?

MAN. No. First I knew I was in a restaurant. (*Sits down*) I ate a big meal, reached in my pocket to pay the check. Boy, I almost dropped dead. I'm lucky I'm not here under arrest myself.

MCLEOD (*smiles*). Yes. What's your name?

MAN. Gallantz. D. David.

MCLEOD. Address?

WILLY (*pail in one hand, broom in the other, taps Gallantz on the shoulder with the broom*). Git up!

GALLANTZ (*rises, staring at Willy*). 419 West 80th Street.

WILLY (*bends down to the basket under the desk, empties the contents into his pail, muttering under his breath, rises heavily, paying no attention to anyone as he crosses off*). Look at this room, will you? Wouldn't think I cleaned up an hour ago! Detectives! The brains of the department?! Ha! Couldn't find a Chinaman on Mott Street. (*Exit*)

MCLEOD. What did you lose?

GALLANTZ. My wallet.

MCLEOD. Can you describe it?

GALLANTZ. Black leather.

MCLEOD (*picks up the phone*). Lost property. McLeod.

SHOPLIFTER (*lays down the newspaper, addresses Dakis*). Have you got one of them two-way radio wrist-watches like Dick Tracy?

DAKIS. No.

SHOPLIFTER. Behind the times, ain't you?

DAKIS. Yeah, behind the behind.

SHOPLIFTER (*feels her pulse*). Gee, I think I'm getting a reaction. Emotions are bad for me. I got diabetes. I'm not supposed to get emotions.

DAKIS (*belches, then, indignantly*). I got ulcers—I'm not supposed to eat sandwiches. A hot meal was waiting for me at home. Do me a favor!—Next time get yourself arrested before four o'clock. Let a fellow eat a home-cooked meal.

SHOPLIFTER (*genuinely contrite*). I'm sorry.

DAKIS. Do you realize this is on my own time? (*With mounting anger*) Look at all these forms I had to type up. And when we get to court, what'll happen? The judge'll probably let you off. I won't even get a conviction. You cause me all this work for nothin'.

SHOPLIFTER. I'm sorry.

DAKIS. That's a big help.

(*In his office the Lieutenant fishes an address book out of his desk-drawer, thumbs through it for a number, reaches for the phone, dials.*)

MCLEOD (*hangs up. To Gallantz*). Sorry. Nothing yet. We'll follow it up. If we hear anything, we'll let you know.

GALLANTZ. Thanks! (*As he goes, he looks mournfully at his exposed derrière*) My best pants, too. (*Exit*)

LIEUTENANT (*on the phone*). Hello, Mrs. McLeod? This is Lieutenant Monoghan of the 21st. No, no! He's all right. Nothing like that!

(*The rest of his conversation is drowned out by the entrance of Callahan, Policeman Barnes, Brody and Charley, the burglar, all talking at once. Callahan and Barnes are carrying two suitcases and several pillowcases filled with "loot" from Charley's apartment. Brody completes the parade, carrying more loot. Callahan knocks at the Lieutenant's door.*)

LIEUTENANT. Come in!

CALLAHAN (*opens the Lieutenant's door, holds up the "loot"*). Look what we found, boss. And by a strange coincidence —in Charley's apartment.

(*The Lieutenant covers the phone, nods approval.*)

BARNES (*unlocks Charley's handcuffs*). Sit down! There! (*Charley sits in the designated chair*)

CALLAHAN. O'Brien is taking Lewis around to identify the houses.

LIEUTENANT. Good! (*Waves him out*) Shut the door!

(*Callahan slams the door with his knee; then aided by McLeod and Brody and Dakis, he begins unloading the stolen goods.*)

CALLAHAN (*holding up some "loot"*). Look at this! These jockeys sure get around! . . . (*The Lieutenant picks up his phone and continues his conversation, which is drowned out by the racket in the squad-room as the men proceed to lay out and examine the stolen goods. Callahan holds up an expensive clock, shakes it)* This worth anything?

MCLEOD *(examines it).* Very good piece —Tiffany. Where'd you get this, Charley?

CHARLEY. I bought it.

MCLEOD. Where?

CHARLEY. Outside the jewelry exchange. On the street.

MCLEOD. Who from?

CHARLEY. Some guy.

MCLEOD. What's his name?

CHARLEY. I don't know. I never saw him again.

MCLEOD. Or before?

CHARLEY *(nods).* Yeah.

MCLEOD. Or at all. The little man that wasn't there.

SHOPLIFTER *(feeling her pulse).* I am getting a reaction. Emotions are bad for me.

DAKIS *(checking a stolen article against a list).* Girls with diabetes shouldn't steal pink panties.

SHOPLIFTER. It wasn't pink pants.

DAKIS *(sighs).* I know.

SHOPLIFTER. It was a bag. . . .

DAKIS *(closes his eyes, sighs).* I know.

SHOPLIFTER. Alligator.

DAKIS. I know.

SHOPLIFTER. Imitation alligator.

DAKIS *(sorry he started it all).* I know.

BRODY *(holds up a piece of jewelry).* This any good?

MCLEOD *(examines it).* Junk! Wait! Here's something! Monogrammed: J. G. *(Checks with list)* Sure. This is some of the Gordon stuff. Where'd you get this, Charley?

CHARLEY *(hangs his head, disgusted).* I ain't talking.

BRODY. Where?

(Charley shakes his head.)

CALLAHAN. Where'd you get it, Charlay? *(Takes out a "billy")* Know what this is? A "persuader." *(Bangs it on the desk)*

CHARLEY. Go ahead! Beat me! Beat me unconscious. Go ahead!

(The janitor enters.)

CALLAHAN *(laughs, puts the "persuader" away).* You're too eager, Charley. Some-a them creeps like it, you know. Gives 'em a thrill. Look at that kisser! I'm a son-of-a-bitch, I'm right.

BRODY *(holding up a piece of silver).* Where'd you get this, Charley?

(Charley hangs his head.)

DAKIS *(annoyed, walks over him).* Why don't you be professional, Charley. He's talking to you. . . . What's the matter? What are you hanging your head for? What are you ashamed of? Nobody made you be a burglar. You wanted to be a burglar—you're a burglar. So be a good one! Be proud of your chosen profession! Hold your head up. *(Dakis lifts Charley's head up by the chin)* That's better. You're a good thief, Charley. You're no bum. They wear sweaters. Not you!—You got a hundred-dollar suit on you. You . . . Wait a minute! *(Opens Charley's coat, looks at label)* Take it off, you bum. Stolen! The name's still in it. Where'd you get it?

CHARLEY *(takes off the coat, talking fast).* You mean it's stolen? O.K. O.K. I'll tell you the whole story . . . may I drop dead on this spot.

CALLAHAN. On this one? Be careful, Charley.

CHARLEY *(faster and faster, the nervous hands weaving in the air).* Honest! The truth! But don't tell Lewis!—He'll kill me. He makes out like he's a dummy, don't he? He ain't. He's smart. Ooh, he's as smart as they come. Look . . . I just been in New York two weeks. I came here from Pittsburgh two weeks ago. So help me, I lose my valise in the station. I meet this guy, Lewis, in a poolroom. . . .

CALLAHAN. Where? What poolroom?

CHARLEY. 14th Street, corner of 7th Avenue . . . Look it up! Check it! I'm telling you the truth, so help me. I shoot a game of pool with him. He says to me, "You got a place to stay?" I says, "No." He says, "Share my flat." I say, "O.K." My suit's all dirty. He lends me this one. Says it belongs to his brother who's in Florida. *(Pause. He looks up at the unbelieving faces circling him, smiles feebly)* So help me.

CALLAHAN. Charley, my boy—I could tell you a story would bring tears to your eyes. Get in there and take off your pants! *(He pushes Charley into the wash-room)*

BRODY. Willy! Got an old pair of pants?

WILLY. Yeah, I got some downstairs! *(Exit)*

BRODY. Not even smart enough to take out the label. The name's still in it. Jerome Armstrong . . .

CALLAHAN *(examining his list).* Wait! I got that squeal right here. I think there was a rape connected with this one.

BRODY. I wouldn't be surprised. *(Leaves the door of the toilet for a second. Goes to the desk, picks up the lists)*

LIEUTENANT *(calls).* Dakis!

(Dakis hurries to the Lieutenant's door, opens it.)

DAKIS. Yes, sir?

LIEUTENANT *(beckons him in; then, softly).* Wait downstairs for Mrs. McLeod. When she gets here let me know foist.

DAKIS *(startled, murmurs).* Right, Chief.

LIEUTENANT. And . . . a . . . Nick . . . *(Touches his lips)* Button 'em up.

DAKIS. Yes, sir.

(As he crosses to the gate, he glances at McLeod, his forehead furrows. Exit. The Lieutenant studies his cigar, frowns, goes off. Through the little window we see Charley throw up the bathroom shade and tug at the iron grill-work. McLeod crosses to the wash-room door, calls in.)

MCLEOD. The only way you can get out of there, Charley, is to jump down the toilet and pull the chain.

(Joe Feinson comes in, tense and disturbed. He glances at McLeod curiously, comes over to Brody.)

JOE. Lots of loot. They do the Zaza robbery?

BRODY *(calls in to Charley).* You robbed that Zaza dame's flat, Charley?

CHARLEY *(calls out).* I don't know nuttin'!

BRODY. He don't know from nuttin'!

CALLAHAN. He's ignorant and he's proud of it.

JOE. Any good names?

BRODY. Don't know yet—

JOE. Any good addresses?

BRODY. They're taking the other bum around. He's identifying the houses. We'll crack it in an hour.

JOE *(saunters over to McLeod).* What's with Kurt Schneider?

MCLEOD. No story.

JOE. He left here twenty-five minutes ago in an ambulance. What happened? He trip?

MCLEOD. Yes.

JOE. Over his schnozzola?

MCLEOD. Could have. It's long enough.

JOE. No story?

MCLEOD. No.

JOE. His lawyer's sore as a boil. What happened?

MCLEOD. You tell me. You always have the story in your pocket.

JOE. Look, Seamus! There are angles here I don't feel happy about.

MCLEOD. What angles?

JOE. I don't know . . . yet. Come! Give! Off the record.

MCLEOD. You can print it if you want to. Kurt Schneider was a butcher who murdered two girls and got away with it. High time somebody put the fear of God in him. The law wouldn't, so I did. Print it, Yussel. Go ahead. You don't like cops. Here's your chance?

JOE. I don't like cops? For a smart guy, Seamus, you can be an awful schmoe. If I got fired tomorrow, you'd still find me here, hanging around, running errands for you guys, happy as a bird dog! I'm a buff from way back. I found a home. You know that.

MCLEOD. Sentimental slop, Yussel.

(A short, stout, timid man enters and looks about apprehensively.)

JOE. My sixth sense is still bothering me, Seamus.

MCLEOD. Have a doctor examine it. *(To the newcomer)* Yes, sir? *(The nervous man looks about, moistens his lips with his tongue, mops his brow, starts to speak. McLeod recognizes him)* Oh! Come in, Mr. Pritchett. We've been waiting for you.

MR. PRITCHETT. Did you get my money back?

MCLEOD. I'm afraid not.

MR. PRITCHETT. What'd he do with it?

MCLEOD. Women and plush saloons.

MR. PRITCHETT. Cabarets? I wouldn't have thought it. He seemed such an honest boy. I don't make many mistakes. I'm a pretty good student of human nature . . . usually.

MCLEOD. You'll be in court tomorrow morning?

MR. PRITCHETT. Oh, yes.

MCLEOD. We can count on you?

MR. PRITCHETT. When I make my mind up, I'm like iron.

MCLEOD. Fine! Thank you, Mr. Pritchett.

MR. PRITCHETT. Like iron.

MCLEOD. Arthur, on your feet! *(Arthur rises)* Is this the boy?

MR. PRITCHETT (*with a huge sigh*). I'm afraid it is.

MCLEOD. Arthur, over here. (*Arthur crosses to them. The phone rings. McLeod goes to the desk, picks up the receiver*) 21st Squad! McLeod!

BARNES (*at the wash-room door*). All right, Charley. (*He leads Charley back into the squad-room. Charley is now wearing an ill-fitting, torn and filthy pair of trousers at which the eloquent hands pantomime disgust*)

MR. PRITCHETT. Well, Arthur, is this your journey's end?

ARTHUR. I guess so.

MR. PRITCHETT. Did I treat you badly?

ARTHUR. No, Mr. Pritchett.

MR. PRITCHETT. Did I pay you a decent salary?

ARTHUR. Yes.

MR. PRITCHETT. Then why did you do this to me?

(*Susan appears at the gate.*)

SUSAN (*catches McLeod's eyes*). May I? (*He nods. She enters, fumbling in her purse*)

MR. PRITCHETT (*to Arthur*). You spent my money on fast women?

ARTHUR. Just a second . . .

MR. PRITCHETT. No! I didn't grow my money on trees. I built up my business from a hole in the wall where I sold neckties two for a quarter. Thirty years I built it. By the sweat of my brow. I worked darn hard for it. I want my money back.

SUSAN. And you'll get it. I promise you. (*She takes some money out of her purse*) The bank was closed. All I could scrape together, tonight, was $120. (*She hands the money to Mr. Pritchett*) I'll have the rest for you tomorrow.

ARTHUR. Susan! Take that back!

SUSAN. Let me alone! Don't interfere, Jiggs!

MR. PRITCHETT. Who is this? Who are you, Miss?

SUSAN. I'm an old friend of Mr. Kindred's family. And I'd like to straighten this out with you, Mister . . . What is your name?

MR. PRITCHETT. Pritchett, Albert J. Pritchett.

SUSAN. Mr. Pritchett. How do you do? I'm Susan Carmichael.

MR. PRITCHETT. How do you do? You say you're prepared to return the rest of my money, young lady?

SUSAN. Yes. I'll sign a promissory note, or whatever you suggest.

MCLEOD (*into the phone*). One second! (*To Susan*) Where'd you get that cash, Miss Carmichael?

SUSAN. I had some and I pawned some jewelry. Here are the tickets. Do you want to see them?

MCLEOD. If you don't mind. (*Takes them, examines them*) Anything of your sister's here?

SUSAN. Nothing. Not a bobby pin.

MR. PRITCHETT. Is this the young lady who . . .

ARTHUR. No. She doesn't know anything about it.

SUSAN. I know all there is to know. (*To Mr. Pritchett*) Mr. Pritchett, this whole mess you can blame on *my* sister.

ARTHUR. What's the matter with you, Suzy? What are you dragging Joy into this for? She's got nothing to do with it.

SUSAN. Hasn't she?

ARTHUR. No.

SUSAN. I've got news for you. I just spoke to her on the phone. (*Pause*)

ARTHUR. You didn't tell her?

SUSAN. Of course I did.

ARTHUR. What'd she say?

SUSAN. She was upset.

ARTHUR. Naturally, she would be. You shouldn't have . . .

SUSAN. Naturally! My blue-eyed sister was in a tizzy because she didn't want to get involved in your troubles. You know where I called her? At Walter Forbes' in Connecticut. She's afraid this might crimp her chances to be the next Mrs. Forbes. . . . Big deal!

ARTHUR. I know, Suzy. That's not news to me. I know.

SUSAN. Till ten minutes ago, I thought my sister was the cherub of the world. There wasn't anything I wouldn't have done for her. But if she can do this to you—to you, Jiggs—then I don't want any part of her. And I mean that. I'm through with her. I loathe her.

ARTHUR. Suzy! Take it easy.

SUSAN. All my life everything I wanted Joy got. All right! I didn't mind. I felt she was so special. She was entitled to be Queen. But now I'm through.

ARTHUR. Suzy, maybe you don't understand. Like everybody else, Joy is frightened. She wants to grab a little security.

Don't blame her for it. I don't.

SUSAN. Security? You've seen Walter Forbes. He's had four wives. He gets falling-down drunk every single night of his life. Some security!

ARTHUR. He's very rich. You can't have everything.

SUSAN. Jiggs! Don't! Don't you be disgusting too. *(To Mr. Pritchett)* Should I make out a note for the rest?

MCLEOD. Wait a minute. *(He hangs up the phone, crosses to Mr. Pritchett, takes the money from him and hands it back to Susan)* We don't run a collection agency here! This man is a thief. We're here to prosecute criminals, not collect money. *(Detective Dakis enters, crosses into the Lieutenant's office.)*

SUSAN. He's not a criminal.

MCLEOD. Miss Carmichael, you seem like a very nice young lady. I'm going to give you some advice. I've seen a thousand like him. *He's no good!* Take your money and run.

DAKIS *(to the Lieutenant)*. She's downstairs.

LIEUTENANT *(grunts, rises, goes to the door, calls)*. McLeod!

MCLEOD. Yes, sir?

LIEUTENANT. Get me the old files on that Cottsworth squeal!

MCLEOD *(thinks)*. 1938?

LIEUTENANT. Yeah.

MCLEOD. March 12th . . . *(Lieutenant nods)* That'll be buried under a pile inside, I'll have to dig them up.

LIEUTENANT. Dig 'em up! Do it now!

MCLEOD. Yes, sir. *(As he crosses off left, he throws his judgment at Arthur and Susan)* He spells one thing for you— misery the rest of your life. He's no good. Believe me, I know! *(Exit)*

SUSAN *(indignantly)*. That isn't true! *(To Mr. Pritchett)* That isn't true. I've known Arthur all my life. He never did anything before that was dishonorable. He was the most respected boy in Ann Arbor. *(The Lieutenant nods to Dakis, who goes off to bring up Mrs. McLeod. Brody crosses down, listening to Susan and Mr. Pritchett.)*

MR. PRITCHETT. Little lady, once I saw a picture, *Less Miserables.*—A dandy! That was before your time. This Gene Valjeane—his sister's nine children are starving. He steals a loaf of bread. He goes to jail for—I don't know—twenty years. I'm on Gene Valjeane's side there. Impressed me very much. I gave a little talk on it at my lodge. . . . But this? I don't go along with. He wasn't starving. He had a good job. He went cabareting . . . with my money. Heck, I don't go to them myself!

BRODY. Mr. Pritchett, maybe once a year we get someone in here steals because he's actually hungry. And we're all on his side. I'd do the same, wouldn't you?

MR. PRITCHETT. Absolutely. I always say self-preservation is the first law of nature.

BRODY. But that's one in a thousand cases.

MR. PRITCHETT. Exactly my point! And what did *he* do it for?

ARTHUR *(softly)*. I did it because I was hungry.

MR. PRITCHETT. What?

ARTHUR. Hungry. You can be hungry for other things besides bread. You've been decent to me, Mr. Pritchett. You trusted me, and I let you down. I'm sorry . . . It's hard to explain, even to myself. I'd been separated from my girl for five years—five long, bloody years! The one human being in the world I loved. She's very beautiful, Mr. Pritchett. Tall, a silvery blonde girl, warm, understanding.

SUSAN. Jiggs, don't!

ARTHUR. At least she was right. She was, Susan. We all change. When I came back from the war, I tried going back to school, but I couldn't get settled. I came to New York just to be near her. She'd moved on into a new world. She was out of my reach. I should have accepted that. I couldn't. To take her out to dinner and hold her hand cost a month's salary. I hung on anyway. Last Wednesday I had to face it. I was going to lose my girl. She told me she wanted to marry someone else. I made a final grandstand play for her. Late collections had come in. Your money was in my pocket. I blew the works on her. I didn't give a damn about anything except holding on to her. It was my last chance. I lost anyway. . . .

BRODY. You admit you did wrong?

ARTHUR. Yes, God, yes!

BRODY. You're willing to make restitution?

ARTHUR. If I get the chance.

SUSAN. Tomorrow morning. I promise you!

BRODY. That's in his favor. How do you feel, Mr. Pritchett?

MR. PRITCHETT. Well . . .

BRODY. This kid has a fine war record, too, remember.

MR. PRITCHETT. I know.

BRODY. He took a lot of chances for us. Maybe we ought to take one for him. You see, these kids today got problems nobody ever had. We don't even understand them. New blood. We're varicosed. If a new world is gonna be made outa this mess looks like they're the ones gotta do it.

MR. PRITCHETT. It's funny you should say that. I was talking to my brother-in-law only the other night about my nephew and I made exactly that point. I was saying to him . . .

BRODY. Mr. Pritchett, do you mind stepping over here a minute?

MR. PRITCHETT. Not at all! (Rises, follows him)

BRODY. You, too, Miss!

(Susan follows Brody off left.)

CHARLEY (stamps his foot). Give me another cigarette.

BARNES. What do you do? Eat these things?

CHARLEY. Give me a cigarette!

(Barnes gives him another cigarette. Dakis enters, leading Mrs. McLeod to the Lieutenant's office. Mary McLeod is a pretty young woman, with blonde hair, big gray, troubled eyes, a sweet mouth and delicate nose. She is inexpensively but attractively dressed. There is something immediately appealing about her. She is very feminine and very soft, and at the moment her evident terror augments these qualities.)

JOE (sees her, is startled, rises, stops her). How do you do, Mrs. McLeod! Remember me? I'm Joe Feinson, the reporter.

MARY (disturbed and overwrought, studies him for a split second, then recalls him). Oh, yes, of course. I met you with my husband. (Her mouth trembles. Joe smiles, nods) What's happened to Jim?

JOE (grins, reassuringly). Nothing. He's all right. He's in there.

MARY. Mr. Feinson, please tell me!

JOE. I am.

DAKIS. This way, please . . . (She fol-lows him into the Lieutenant's office)

LIEUTENANT. How do you do, Mrs. McLeod?

MARY. Lieutenant Monoghan?

LIEUTENANT. Yes, mam.

MARY. What is this about, Lieutenant?

LIEUTENANT. Have a seat?

MARY. Where's my husband?

LIEUTENANT. He'll be back in a few minutes.

MARY. He hasn't been *shot*?

LIEUTENANT (reassuringly). No!

MARY. I had a terrible feeling that he . . .

LIEUTENANT. Nothing like that. He's all right.

MARY. You're sure? You're not trying to break it easy?

LIEUTENANT. Nothing like that! I give you my word. You'll see him in a few minutes.

MARY. Then what is it? What's wrong?

LIEUTENANT. A certain situation has come up, and you might be able to help us out.

MARY. Me? . . . I'm all at sea, Lieutenant!

LIEUTENANT. Mrs. McLeod, your husband and I never got along too well, but I want you to know that right now I'm sticking my neck out a mile to save him. I'm not doing it because I like him—I don't. I'm doing it because he has a value here and I need him on the squad. So, like I say, I'm going to help him, if you help me.

MARY. What kind of trouble is Jim in?

LIEUTENANT. A prisoner here was assaulted, maybe injured, by your husband.

MARY. Jim wouldn't do that.

LIEUTENANT. He did. You'll have to take my word for it.

MARY. Then there must have been a reason. A very good reason.

LIEUTENANT. That's what I have to find out.

MARY. Jim is kind and gentle.

LIEUTENANT. That's one side of him.

MARY. It's the only side I know. I've never seen any other. (Pause)

LIEUTENANT. Please sit down!

MARY. Is this man badly hurt?

LIEUTENANT. I don't know yet. This could become serious, Mrs. McLeod. This might cost your husband his job. He could even wind up in jail.

MARY (*sinks into the chair*). How can I help?

LIEUTENANT. By answering some questions. By telling me the truth. Are you willing to go along?

MARY. Yes, of course.

LIEUTENANT. Did you ever run into a man named Kurt Schneider?

MARY (*hoarsely*). No. (*Coughs*)

LIEUTENANT. My cigar bothering you?

MARY. No. I love the smell of a cigar. My father always smoked them.

LIEUTENANT. Did you ever hear your husband mention that name?

MARY. What name?

LIEUTENANT. This prisoner's name. Kurt Schneider.

MARY (*shakes her head*). Jim made it a rule never to discuss his work with me.

LIEUTENANT. It's a good rule. We don't like to bring this sordid stuff into our homes.

MARY. I'm well trained now. I don't ask.

LIEUTENANT. How long you been married?

MARY. Three years.

LIEUTENANT. It took me ten years to train my wife. It's a tough life—being married to a cop.

MARY. I don't think so. I'm happy.

LIEUTENANT. You love your husband?

MARY. Very much.

LIEUTENANT. Where did you live before you were married?

(*The phone in the squad-room rings.*)

DAKIS (*picks up the receiver*). 21st Squad—Detective Dakis.

MARY. New York.

LIEUTENANT. You don't sound like a native. Where you from? Upstate?

MARY. Highland Falls. You've got a good ear.

LIEUTENANT. It's my business.

DAKIS (*knocks at the Lieutenant's door, opens it*). Captain on the phone, Lieutenant.

LIEUTENANT (*nods to Mrs. McLeod*). Excuse me! . . . (*He picks up the phone, turns away from her, and talks into the mouthpiece sotto voce. In the squad-room, the shoplifter rises and stretches*)

SHOPLIFTER (*coyly to Callahan, who is at the desk, typing*). You don't look like a detective.

CALLAHAN. No? What does a detective look like?

SHOPLIFTER. They wear derbies. (*She giggles archly*) You're a nice-looking fellow.

CALLAHAN. Thanks.

SHOPLIFTER. Are you married?

CALLAHAN. Yes.

SHOPLIFTER (*disgusted—this is the story of her life*). Ya-a-a! (*She slaps the paper on the chair, sits down again*)

LIEUTENANT. Thanks, Captain! (*Hangs up, turns to Mrs. McLeod, resumes his interrogation*) When'd you leave Highland Falls?

MARY. The spring of 1941. I got a job in a defense plant.

LIEUTENANT. Where?

MARY. In Newark.

LIEUTENANT. This doctor was practicing in Newark at about that time.

MARY. Doctor?

LIEUTENANT. Schneider.

MARY. Oh, he's a doctor?

LIEUTENANT. Yes. You never met him? Around Newark, maybe?

MARY. No. I don't know him.

LIEUTENANT. He knows you.

MARY. What makes you think that?

LIEUTENANT. He said so.

MARY (*avoids his probing stare*). I'm afraid he's mistaken.

LIEUTENANT. He was positive . . . Kurt Schneider! Ring any bells?

MARY. No. I'm afraid not.

LIEUTENANT. You averted my gaze then. Why?

MARY. Did I? I wasn't conscious of it.

LIEUTENANT. Are you sure a Dr. Schneider never treated you?

MARY (*indignantly*). Certainly not. I just told you, "No."

LIEUTENANT. Why are you so indignant? I didn't say what he treated you for.

MARY. Did this man tell my husband he treated me?

LIEUTENANT. If you'll tell the truth, Mrs. McLeod, you'll help your husband. You'll save me time and trouble. But that's all. In the end I'll get the correct answers. We got a hundred ways of finding out the truth.

MARY. I don't know what you're talking about, Lieutenant. I'm not lying.

(*Detective Gallagher enters with Tami Giacoppetti, handsome, swarthy, on the sharp, loud side, very sure of himself, very sure.*)

GIACOPPETTI. Can I use the phone, Champ?

GALLAGHER. Not yet, Tami. (*Knocks at the Lieutenant's door*)

GIACOPPETTI. O.K., Champ.

LIEUTENANT. Yeah! (*Gallagher enters and hands a note to the Lieutenant. The Lieutenant glances at it, pockets it and dismisses Gallagher with a gesture*) Mrs. McLeod, I'm going to ask you a very personal question. Now, don't get angry. I would never dream of asking any woman this type of question unless I had to. You must regard me as the impersonal voice of the law. Mrs. McLeod, did Dr. Schneider ever perform an abortion on you?

MARY. You've no right to ask me that.

LIEUTENANT. I have to do my job—and my job is to find out the truth. Let's not waste any more time! Please answer that question!

MARY. It seems to me I have some rights to privacy. My past life concerns nobody but me.

LIEUTENANT. You have the right to tell the truth. Did he?

MARY. No, Lieutenant Monoghan, he did not.

LIEUTENANT. Does this name mean anything to you: Tami Giacoppetti?

MARY. No.

(*The Lieutenant goes to the door, beckons. Gallagher nudges Tami, who walks inside, sees Mary, stops in his tracks. The smile on his face fades.*)

GIACOPPETTI (*very softly*). Hello, Mary. (*She withers, all evasion gone, her head droops as she avoids their glances.*)

LIEUTENANT (*to Mrs. McLeod, indicating the ante-room*). Would you mind stepping in here a minute! (*To Giacoppetti*) Be right with you. (*He leads her into the ante-room*)

(*Whistling a gay tune, Detective O'Brien enters the squad-room, followed by the burglar, Lewis, and a cop.*)

BARNES. Here's your boy friend, Charley!

DAKIS. How'd you do?

O'BRIEN. We got the addresses and most of the names.

DAKIS. How many?

O'BRIEN. Nine. (*To Lewis*) Sit down! Over here! Lewis has been very co-operative.

(*Callahan has taken off his coat and puts his gun in his holster again. As he bends down over the desk, Charley eyes the gun, tries to edge over, stands up.*)

CALLAHAN. Whither to, Charley?

CHARLEY. I got to go.

CALLAHAN. Again? This makes the sixth time.

CHARLEY. Well, I'm noivous.

BARNES. Sit down, Charley!

CALLAHAN. He's noivous, poor kid.

O'BRIEN. He needs a vacation.

DAKIS. He's gonna get one. A long one. At state expense.

CALLAHAN (*dialing a number*) Nuttin's too good for Charley. (*On Phone*) Hello, Mrs. Lundstrom? This is Detective Callahan of the Twenty-foist Precinct. We got that property was burglarized from your apartment. Will you please come down and identify it? Yeah! Yeah! We got 'em. Right. Yes, Ma'am. (*Hangs up, looks at the squeal card, dials another number*)

O'BRIEN (*on phone, simultaneously*). Hello, Mr. Donatello, please . . . Mr. Donatello? This is Detective O'Brien of the 21st Squad. Yes, sir. I think we've caught them. Yes. I have some articles here. Not all. Would you mind coming down to the station house and identifying them? Right. (*He hangs up*)

CALLAHAN (*on phone*). Hello! Mrs. Demetrios? This is Detective Callahan. Remember me? Twenty-foist Squad. Yeah. I'm still roarin'! How are you, Toots? (*Laughs*) Retoin match? Where's your husband tonight? Okay. (*McLeod enters with an ancient bundle of records wrapped in a sheet of dusty paper and tied with twine. He is blowing off clouds of dust*) I'll be off duty after midnight. (*Starts to hang up, suddenly remembers the purpose of the phone call*) Oh, by the way, we got that stuff was boiglarized from your apartment. Come down and identify it. O.K., yuh barracuda! (*Hangs up*) A man-eater.

O'BRIEN. You watch it!

CALLAHAN. What I don't do for the good of the soivice. I should be getting foist-grade money.

MCLEOD (*undoing the package*). You'll be getting a "foist"-grade knock on the head.

CALLAHAN (*disdainfully*). Brain trust. (*He walks away*)

BRODY (*approaches McLeod*). Say, Jim. I had a long talk with Mr. Pritchett and he's willing to drop the charges.

MCLEOD. He is? *(Turns to Mr. Pritchett)* What's this about, Mr. Pritchett?

MR. PRITCHETT. I decided not to bring charges against . . . *(Nods toward Arthur)*

MCLEOD. I thought you were going to go through with this.

MR. PRITCHETT. I'd like to give the boy another chance.

MCLEOD. To steal from someone else?

MR. PRITCHETT. I wouldn't want this on my conscience.

MCLEOD. Supposing he commits a worse crime. What about your conscience then, Mr. Pritchett?

MR. PRITCHETT. I'll gamble. I'm a gambler. I bet on horses—this once I'll bet on a human being.

MCLEOD. Stick to horses—the percentage is better.

BRODY. Wait a minute, Jim. I advised Mr. Pritchett to do this. I thought . . .

MCLEOD *(harshly)*. You had no right to do that, Lou. This is my case. You know better.

BRODY. I didn't think you'd mind.

MCLEOD. Well, I do.

BRODY *(angrily)*. Well, I'm sorry!!

SUSAN. But I'm going to return the money. And if he's satisfied, what difference does it make to you?

MCLEOD. It isn't as easy as that. This isn't a civil action: this is a *criminal* action.

GUS *(enters with sheet in his hand)*. Jim! Look at this sheet on Charley! *(McLeod takes it, studies it)* As long as your arm. *(To Barnes)* Keep your eye on that son-of-a-bitch!

MCLEOD *(studying the sheet grimly)* Hm! *(He crosses with Gus to the gate, exits into the hallway)*

MR. PRITCHETT *(to Brody)*. But you said . . .

BRODY. I'm sorry. I made a mistake. It's his case. The disposition of it is up to him.

SUSAN. But if everybody concerned is . . .

BRODY. I'm sorry, girlie. You gotta leave me outa this. I got no right to interfere. Take it up with him. *(Walks off left leaving Susan and Pritchett suspended in mid-air. Susan sinks into a chair awaiting McLeod's return, glancing off despairingly in his direction. Pritchett walks up to the gate, leans on it, looking off into the hallway. The Lieutenant returns to his office from the ante-room)*

GIACOPPETTI *(rises)*. What's this about, Champ?

LIEUTENANT. Sit down, Tami! *(Picks up Tami's hat from the desk, looks at the label in it)* Dobbs Beaver? *(Impressed)* A twenty-buck hat. You must be rolling. *(Hands Tami his hat)*

GIACOPPETTI *(taking it)*. Forty bucks. I'm comfortable. No complaints. What's on your mind, Champ?

LIEUTENANT. The woman you just said hello to.

GIACOPPETTI. Mary! What kind of trouble could she be in?

LIEUTENANT. I'd just like a little information.

GIACOPPETTI *(frowns)*. That girl's a hundred percent. I wouldn't say a word against her.

LIEUTENANT. You don't have to. She ain't in no trouble.

GIACOPPETTI. No. That's good. What do you want from me, Champ?

LIEUTENANT. Mr. Giacoppetti, all this is off the record.

GIACOPPETTI. When I talk, it's always for the record, Champ. I only say something when I got something to say, Champ.

LIEUTENANT. Look, Giacoppetti, I'm Lieutenant Monoghan. I'm in charge here. Keep your tongue in your mouth, and we'll get along.

GIACOPPETTI. Mind if I phone my lawyer?

LIEUTENANT. It ain't necessary.

GIACOPPETTI. My lawyer gets mad.

LIEUTENANT. Nothing you say here will be held against you, understand? I give you my woid.

GIACOPPETTI. I won't hurt that girl.

LIEUTENANT. I don't want you to. She's only a witness. It's someone else.

GIACOPPETTI. O.K. Shoot!

LIEUTENANT. Married?

GIACOPPETTI. Yeah.

LIEUTENANT. How long?

GIACOPPETTI. Fifteen years. What a racket that is!

LIEUTENANT. You're an expert, ain't you?

GIACOPPETTI. On what? Marriage?

LIEUTENANT. Rackets.

GIACOPPETTI. I'm a legitimate business

man. Take it up with my attorney.

LIEUTENANT. Look, Mr. Giacoppetti. We've got a sheet on you. We know you're in black market up to your neck. But we don't operate in the State of New Jersey. And what went on there ain't none of our business. Unless you make it so. Kapish?

GIACOPPETTI. Yeah, I kapish.

LIEUTENANT. Got any kids?

GIACOPPETTI. No.

LIEUTENANT. I got five. You don't know what you're missing, Tami.

GIACOPPETTI (rises, furious). Don't rub salt in! I know. I got a wife as big as the Sahara Desert—and twice as sterile. I got nine brothers, four sisters . . . all on my payroll. None of 'em worth anything. They got kids—like rabbits they got 'em —nephews, nieces, all over the lot. But a guy like me, I should become a nation, and I got no kids. Not one. So don't rub salt in, eh?

LIEUTENANT (laughs). O.K. I guess I know how you feel.

GIACOPPETTI (controls himself, smiles sheepishly). You're a sharpshooter, Champ. You hit me right on my spot.

LIEUTENANT. When did you know this girl?

GIACOPPETTI. Seven years ago.

LIEUTENANT. You like her?

GIACOPPETTI. I was crazy about her. She was my girl. I'd a married her, if I could a gotten a divorce.

LIEUTENANT. What broke it up?

GIACOPPETTI. I don't know.

LIEUTENANT. What do you think?

GIACOPPETTI. I think maybe I better call my lawyer.

LIEUTENANT. Come on, Giacoppetti. What the hell—You've gone this far. It's off the record.

GIACOPPETTI. Aah, she give me the air! She got "caught" . . . and that soured her on me. Dames! Who can understand them?

LIEUTENANT. Send her to a doctor?

GIACOPPETTI. To a doctor? Me? I wanted that kid. I told her: "Give me a son—anything goes." Anything she wants. The moon out of the sky . . . I'd get it for her. Dames! Who can understand them? She goes off. That's the last I see of her. Next thing I know I hear she went to some doctor. I went looking for her. If I'd a' found her, I'd a' broken her

neck. I found him though. I personally beat the hell out of him. Sent him to a hospital.

LIEUTENANT. What was his name?

GIACOPPETTI. A Dutchman. Schneider . . . something.

LIEUTENANT. Kurt Schneider.

GIACOPPETTI. That's it.

LIEUTENANT (rises). Thank you, Tami!

GIACOPPETTI. That all?

(Lieutenant opens the door of the ante-room, beckons to Mary.)

LIEUTENANT. Almost.

GIACOPPETTI. Now will you tell me what this is about?

LIEUTENANT. Just a minute. (Mary enters) Mrs. McLeod, Mr. Giacoppetti has told me everything.

MARY. He has?

GIACOPPETTI. In a case like this, they find out anyway. It's better to . . .

(Mary begins to weep.)

LIEUTENANT. Now, now! . . . (Pause) I'm sorry, Mrs. McLeod. Would you like a glass of water?

MARY (nods). Please! (He fetches her a glass of water)

LIEUTENANT. Mr. Giacoppetti! (Nods toward the anteroom. They both exit)

(Outside, night perceptibly lowers over the city. The squad-room grows ominously dark. McLeod enters, Charley's sheet in his hand.)

MCLEOD. So you didn't done it, Charley? (He switches on the lights)

CHARLEY (weeping and wringing his hands). No! No! On my mother's grave!

MCLEOD. And you never been in jail?

CHARLEY (wailing). May I drop dead on this spot! What do you guys want from me?

MCLEOD (to Mr. Pritchett). Heartbreaking, isn't it? (Crosses to Charley) These are your fingerprints, Charley. They never lie. (He reads the sheet) Burglary, eight arrests. Five assaults. Seven muggings. Three rapes. Two arrests for murder. Six extortions. Three jail sentences. One prison break! Nice little sheet, Charley? (To Barnes) He's a four-time loser. You have a club. If he makes one false move —you know what to do with it—hit him over the head.

BARNES. Don't worry, I will.

MCLEOD. Book him! (Nods in Lewis' direction) This bum, too.

(Lewis rises.)

CHARLEY (*abandons his weeping act abruptly, looks at McLeod, and begins to grin*). Got a cigarette?

MCLEOD (*furiously*). What do you want—room service?

CHARLEY (*laughing*). It's the green-light hotel, ain't it?

MCLEOD. Take him away!

BARNES. O.K., Charley. (*To Lewis*) Come on.

(*Exit Barnes, Lewis and Charley, the latter laughing raucously at McLeod.*)

MCLEOD (*turns to Pritchett*). Don't invest these criminals with your nervous system, Mr. Pritchett. Sure! They laugh, they cry; but don't think it's your laughter or your tears. It isn't. They're a different species, a different breed. Believe me, I know.

(*Joe Feinson enters.*)

SUSAN (*shrilly*). My God—didn't you ever make a mistake?

MCLEOD. Yes. When I was new on this job we brought in two boys who were caught stealing from a car. They looked like babies. They cried. I let them go. Two nights later—two nights later—one of them held up a butcher in Harlem. Shot him through the head and killed him. Yes, I made a mistake, and I'm not going to make it again.

SUSAN. But, Officer, you . . .

MCLEOD (*harshly*). Young lady, I don't want to discuss this with you. Now don't interrupt me!

ARTHUR (*rises*). Don't talk to her like that. She has a right to speak.

MCLEOD (*his face goes black with anger. He roars at Arthur*). Shut up! Sit down! (*Arthur sits. McLeod controls himself, lights a cigarette, his hand trembling*) When you're dealing with the criminal mind, softness is dangerous, Mr. Pritchett.

MR. PRITCHETT. But if it's a first offense.

MCLEOD. It's never a first offense: it's just the first time they get caught.

SUSAN. Why are you so vicious?

MCLEOD. I'm not vicious, young lady. I didn't steal this man's money. (*Extinguishes the match violently and hurls it in Arthur's direction*) He did. (*To Mr. Pritchett*) This is a war, Mr. Pritchett. We know it, they know it, but you don't. We're your army. We're here to protect you. But you've got to co-operate. I'm sick and tired of massaging the complainant into doing his simple duty! You civilians are too lazy or too selfish or too scared or just too indifferent to even want to appear in court and see the charges through that you, yourselves, bring. That makes us—street-cleaners. They have a stick, sweep out the streets, we have a stick, sweep out the human garbage; they pile it in wagons, dump it in the East River, we pile it in wagons, dump it in the Tombs. And what happens?—The next day . . . all back again.

MR. PRITCHETT. But if I get paid . . .

MCLEOD (*impatiently*). I don't care about that. This is a criminal action. Are you or aren't you going through with it? Because I'm not going to let him go.

MR. PRITCHETT. If I don't bring charges?

MCLEOD. Then I'm going to book him, anyway, and *subpoena you* into court.

MR. PRITCHETT. Well . . . I . . . I . . .

MCLEOD. It's my duty to protect you, in spite of yourself.

MR. PRITCHETT. I guess I've got to leave it up to you, Officer. Whatever you say.

MCLEOD. I say, "Prosecute!"

MR. PRITCHETT. All right! You know best. (*To Susan*) I'm sorry. But he had no right to rob me in the first place. That was a terrible thing to do.

MCLEOD (*takes him by the arm, leads him to the gate*). We won't take up any more of your time. I'll see you in court tomorrow morning at ten.

(*Mr. Pritchett goes.*)

SUSAN. Mister Pritchett . . . (*She rises and runs after him*)

MCLEOD (*witheringly*). There goes John Q. Public, "a man of iron."

JOE. Humble yourself, sweetheart, humble yourself!

MCLEOD. What?

JOE. Seamus, Seamus, why must you always make everything so black and white? Remember, we're all of us falling down all the time. Don't be so intolerant.

MCLEOD. You're out of line.

JOE. Listen to me, Seamus. Listen! I love you, and I'm trying to warn you.

MCLEOD. What about? What's on your mind?

JOE. You're digging your own grave. A bottomless pit, baby. It's right there in front of you. One more step and you're in.

Humble yourself, sweetheart, humble yourself!

MCLEOD. You're very Delphia today, Yussel. What's the oracle of CCNY trying to tell me?

(There's a long pause. Joe examines his face. All friendship is gone out of it. It's hard as granite, now, the jaw muscles bulging. Joe smiles sadly to himself, shakes his head.)

JOE. Nothing. Forget it. *(He goes)*

LIEUTENANT *(returns to his office, followed by Giacoppetti. Mary rises).* Feel better now?

MARY. Yes. Thank you.

LIEUTENANT. Are you ready to tell me the truth?

MARY. Yes.

LIEUTENANT. Your husband's been persecutin' Schneider for over a year because of this?

MARY. No.

LIEUTENANT. Schneider's attorney says so.

MARY. I don't care what he says. Jim never knew. He never knew. I'm sure of that.

LIEUTENANT. Careful now! Weigh your words. This is very important. Any minute that phone'll ring. If Schneider is critically hurt, it's out of my hands. The next second this case'll be with the homicide squad. The Commissioner'll be here, the District Attorney. If that happens I gotta have all the facts.

MARY. Jim didn't know.

LIEUTENANT. That's the question I gotta be sure of . . . now. *(Thinks a moment, goes to the door, calls)* McLeod!

MCLEOD. Yes, sir? *(The Lieutenant motions him in. McLeod enters, sees Mary, stops short)* Mary! What are you doing here? What's this, Lieutenant? What's my wife . . .

LIEUTENANT. I sent for her.

MCLEOD. Why?

LIEUTENANT. This is Mr. Giacoppetti.

GIACOPPETTI. Hi, Champ!

MCLEOD. What's this about, Lieutenant?

LIEUTENANT. Schneider! Why'd you lie to me?

MCLEOD. I didn't lie to you.

MARY. May I . . . may I . . . please.

LIEUTENANT. Yes. Go ahead. *(Watching McLeod)*

MARY. Jim, the Lieutenant won't be-

lieve me that you knew nothing about this . . .

MCLEOD. About what, Mary?

MARY. Dr. Schneider.

MCLEOD. What's he got to do with you?

MARY. This man you struck, this Dr. Schneider . . .

MCLEOD. Don't keep saying that, Mary. He's no doctor.

MARY. He isn't? I thought he was. I . . . had occasion to see him once. I went to him once when I needed help.

MCLEOD. You *what?* *(After a long pause, studies her, murmurs to himself)*

MARY. A long time ago, Jim. *(To the Lieutenant)* I told you he didn't . . .

MCLEOD. Wait a minute! *(Turns to Giacoppetti)* What's he got to do with this?

MARY. We were going together.

MCLEOD. I see.

MARY. I . . .

MCLEOD. O.K. Diagrams aren't necessary. I get the picture.

GIACOPPETTI. I beat the hell out of this Schneider myself. *(He touches McLeod on the arm. McLeod, with a growl, slaps his hand.)* Geeze! *(Holds his hand in agony)*

LIEUTENANT. Cut that out!

GIACOPPETTI. I don't have to take that from you, Champ!

MCLEOD. Touch me again and I'll tear your arm out of the socket.

LIEUTENANT *(to McLeod).* You cut that out! In one second I'm going to flatten you, myself. *(There is a long pause)*

MCLEOD. Do you mind if I talk to my wife . . . alone?

(The Lieutenant looks at Mary.)

MARY. Please!

LIEUTENANT. All right, Tami. You can go.

(Giacoppetti goes. The Lieutenant walks into his anteroom, slams the door.)

MARY. I'm terribly sorry, Jim. Please forgive me. *(She touches him; he moves away to avoid her touch)* Is this man badly hurt?

MCLEOD. No.

MARY. Then you're not in serious trouble, Jim?

MCLEOD. He's only acting. Nothing will come of it.

MARY. You're sure?

MCLEOD. Yes.

MARY. Thank God for that.

MCLEOD. My immaculate wife!

MARY. I never said I was.

MCLEOD. You never said you weren't! Why didn't you tell me?

MARY. I loved you and I was afraid of losing you.

MCLEOD. How long did you go with him?

MARY. A few months.

MCLEOD. How many?

MARY. About four.

MCLEOD. Four isn't a few.

MARY. No, I suppose not.

MCLEOD. Did he give you money?

MARY. No.

MCLEOD. But he did give you presents?

MARY. Yes. He gave me some presents, of course.

MCLEOD. Expensive ones?

MARY. I don't know.

MCLEOD. What do you mean you don't know?

MARY. I don't know. What difference does it make?

MCLEOD. This difference. I'd just as soon Schneider died. I'd sooner go to jail for twenty years—than find out this way that my wife was a whore.

MARY. Don't say that, Jim.

MCLEOD. That's the word, I didn't invent it. That's what they call it.

MARY. I don't care about "they." I only care about you, Jim, and it isn't true. You know it isn't true.

MCLEOD. Why didn't you tell me?

MARY. I wanted to, but I didn't dare. I would have lost you.

MCLEOD. I thought I knew you. I thought you were everything good and pure . . . And with a pig like that! Live dirt!

MARY. Jim, don't judge me. Try and understand. Right and wrong aren't always as simple as they seem to you. I was on my own for the first time in a large city. The war was on. Everything was feverish! I'd only been out with kids my own age until I met this man. He paid me a lot of attention. I was flattered. I'd never met anyone like him before in my whole life. I thought he was romantic and glamorous. I thought I was in love with him.

MCLEOD. Are you trying to justify yourself in those terms?

MARY. Not justify! Just explain. It was wrong. I know it. I discovered that for myself.

MCLEOD. When? Just now?

(The phone rings. Dakis answers it.)

MARY. I'm trying to make my life everything you want it to be. If I could make my past life over I'd do that, too, gladly. But I can't. No one can. I made a mistake. I admit it. I've paid for it . . . plenty. Isn't that enough?

DAKIS *(crosses to the Lieutenant's office, enters)*. Where's the Lieutenant?

MCLEOD. Inside.

DAKIS *(shouting off)*. Lieutenant!—Hospital's on the phone.

LIEUTENANT *(enters and picks up the phone)*. Yeah! . . . Put him on! . . . Yeah? You're sure? O.K., Doc. Thank you. *(He hangs up)* The devil takes care of his own! . . . It looks like Schneider's all right. They can't find anything wrong with him.

(There is a long pause.)

MARY. May I go now?

LIEUTENANT. Yes, Mrs. McLeod.

(Exit Lieutenant.)

MARY. Jim, I beg you. Please understand.

MCLEOD. What's there to understand? . . . You got undressed before him . . .

MARY. Jim!

MCLEOD. You went to bed with him.

MARY. Jim! I can't take much more of this.

MCLEOD. You carried his child awhile inside you . . . and then you killed it.

MARY. Yes. That's true.

MCLEOD. Everything I hate . . . even murder . . . What the hell's left to understand!

(Mary, completely stunned, looks at his face, swollen with anger, the face of a madman. She backs up to the door, suddenly opens it, turns, flees.)

CURTAIN

ACT THREE

SCENE: *The scene is the same, eight-thirty by the clock on the wall. Night has fallen. The black, looming masses and the million twinkling eyes of "the city that never sleeps," the flashing General Motors sign, the church spire and cross seem to enter into and become a part of this strange room.*

At rise, the Lieutenant's office is dark and empty. The squad-room, however, is crowded and humming like a dynamo. Half a dozen civilians under the guidance of Dakis and Callahan are identifying the stolen property piled high on the table. Brody is fingerprinting Lewis. Charley is sitting, pantomiming to himself, the colored officer watching him closely. McLeod is seated at the typewriter tapping off Arthur's "squeal"; Arthur is seated to the right of the typewriter desk, his eyes registering the nightmare. Susan, behind Arthur's chair, hovers over him, staring down at him like some impotent guardian angel. Near the same desk the shoplifter's big innocent calf eyes are busy watching, darting in all directions at once, enjoying the Roman holiday. A very chic lady and gentleman in formal evening attire, who are here to claim stolen property, are being photographed by a newspaper photographer. Joe weaves in and out of the throng gleaning his information and jotting it down in a notebook.

———

PHOTOGRAPHER *(to the chic lady in the evening gown, who is posing for him, holding a stolen silver soup tureen)*. Hold up the loot! Little higher, please! *(She holds it higher. Flash!)* Just one more, please!

MCLEOD *(at the desk, to Arthur)*. Hair?

ARTHUR. Brown.

MCLEOD. Eyes?

ARTHUR. Eyes? I don't know . . . greenish?

MCLEOD *(peering at Arthur)*. Look brown.

SUSAN. Hazel. Brown and green flecked with gold.

(Photographer flash!)

MCLEOD. Hazel. *(Types)*

PHOTOGRAPHER. Ankyou! *(Reloads his camera)*

DAKIS *(to the gentleman)*. Sign here. *(He signs)* That's all. We'll notify you when to come down to pick up the rest of your property.

GENTLEMAN *(plucks out some tickets from his wallet, hands them to Dakis)*. Excellent work, Officer, excellent! My compliments.

(Exit gentleman and lady.)

PHOTOGRAPHER *(to Joe)*. Did you get the name?

JOE *(writing story in notebook)*. I got it, I got it.

PHOTOGRAPHER. Park Avenue?

JOE. Spell it backwards.

PHOTOGRAPHER. K-R-A-P.

JOE. You got it.

(The photographer chortles.)

DAKIS *(examines the tickets with a slow, mounting burn. To Callahan)*. How do you like that jerk? Two tickets for the flower show yet! There are two kinds of people in this precinct—the crumbs and the eelite; and the eelite are crumbs.

(Callahan laughs through his nose. Dakis sits down and checks through his "squeals.")

MCLEOD *(typing)*. You might as well go home now, young lady; as soon as we finish this we're through.

SUSAN. A few minutes more . . . Please!

MCLEOD *(sighs. To Arthur)*. Weight?

ARTHUR. A hundred and fifty-two.

MCLEOD. Height?

ARTHUR. Five eleven.

MCLEOD. Identifying marks? Scars? Come here! *(Pulls Arthur's face around)* Scar on the left cheek. *(Types)* And a tattoo. Which arm was that on? *(Arthur raises his left hand)* Left? A heart and the name "Joy."

(The phone rings. Callahan answers it.)

CALLAHAN. 21st Squad Detectives, Callahan. Yeah? A jumper? Fifty-thoid Street? *(McLeod stops typing, listens)* Her name? Mc . . . what . . . ? Geeze!

MCLEOD *(calls across the room, sharply)*. What was that name?

CALLAHAN *(on the phone)*. Wait a minute . . . ! *(To McLeod)* What's 'at, Jim?

MCLEOD *(tense with sudden apprehension)*. You got a jumper?

CALLAHAN. Yeah.

MCLEOD. Woman?

CALLAHAN. Yeah.

MCLEOD. She killed?

CALLAHAN. Sixteenth floor.

MCLEOD. Who is it?

CALLAHAN. What's with you?

MCLEOD. Who is it?

CALLAHAN. Name is McFadden. Old lady. Her son just identified her. Why?

MCLEOD *(mops his brow with his hand kerchief, mumbles)*. Nothing. That's my street. 53rd.

(Callahan looks at McLeod with puzzlement, concludes his phone conversation sotto voce.)

SUSAN (*smiling sadly at Arthur*). A tattoo?

ARTHUR (*sheepishly*). The others all had them. It made me feel like a real sailor. I was *such* a kid. Seven years ago.

SUSAN. Seven? It was yesterday, Jiggs.

ARTHUR. Seven years. Another world.

BRODY (*finishes fingerprinting Lewis*). All done, Lewis! Go in there and wash your hands. Next . . .

(*Lewis, dumb bravo, walks to the washroom, slowly, nonchalantly, his head lolling from side to side as if it were attached to his spine by a rubber band.*)

MCLEOD. Arthur!

(*Arthur rises, walks slowly to Brody at the fingerprint board. They exchange glances.*)

BRODY (*softly*). This hand, son. Just relax it. Aaat's it. This finger. Roll it toward me.

DAKIS (*rises*). Well, three old squeals polished off. I'm clean! (*He crosses, replaces the cards in the file*)

CALLAHAN. There's one here I'm sure they did. . . . (*Propels himself in the swivel chair over to Charley*) Charley, did you burglarize this apartment? (*Charley sniffs a contemptuous silence!*) Why don't you give us a break? You do us a favor we might help you.

CHARLEY. How the hell you gonna help me? I'm a four-time loser. I'm gone to jail for life. How the hell you gonna help me?

CALLAHAN. You lived a louse, you wanta die a louse?

CHARLEY. Yaa!

CALLAHAN. You quif!

CHARLEY. Careful! De sign says courtesy.

CALLAHAN. Coitesy? For you? You want coitesy? Here! (*Tears off the sign, hits him on the head with it. Charley laughs. Lewis comes swaggering out of the washroom*)

BRODY (*finishes fingerprinting Arthur*). That's all, son. Go inside and wash your hands.

(*Arthur goes in to the wash-room. Susan holds on to herself tightly.*)

SHOPLIFTER (*rises—to Susan, comforting her*). It don't hurt. You roll it. (*Demonstrates*) Like that. It just gets your hands a little dirty. It washes right off. It's nothing. (*Susan crumples into a chair*) What's a matter? Did I say something? (*Susan shakes her head*) Are you married? (*Susan shakes her head*) Me neither. Everybody tells you why don't you get married. You should get married. My mother, my father, my sisters, my brother—"Get married!" As if I didn't *want* to get married. Where do you find a man? Get me a man, I'll marry him. *Anything!* As long as it's got pants. Big, little, fat, thin . . . I'll marry him. You think I'd be *here*? For a lousy crocodile bag? I'd be home, cooking him such a meal. Get married!! It's easy to talk! (*She sits again, wrapped up in the tragedy of her spinsterhood*)

MCLEOD (*at the main desk—to Lewis*). Sign your name here, Lewis! (*Lewis signs. The photographer signals Joe*)

JOE (*to Barnes*). O.K., Steve! Get 'em over here.

BARNES (*elbowing Lewis over, nudges Charley with his stick*). Rise and shine, Charley. (*They line up in front of the desk*)

PHOTOGRAPHER (*to Barnes*). Stand on the end! (*Patrolman Barnes obeys*)

BARNES. Stand here, Lewis.

LEWIS (*comes close to Charley, murmurs in his ear*). You louse! I ought to kill you.

CHARLEY (*mutters*). Me? The thanks I get.

JOE (*to photographer*). Wait a minute! I want to line up those bullets. I want 'em in the shot. (*He stands the bullets on end*) Can you get 'em in?

(*McLeod picks up Arthur's "sheet," and crosses to the desk.*)

PHOTOGRAPHER. Yeah! Ready?

LEWIS. Thirty grand.

CHARLEY. Thirty bull!

LEWIS. I saw the list.

PHOTOGRAPHER (*to Barnes, posing them for the shot*). Grab that one by the arm!

CHARLEY (*mutters*). Lists? It's a racket! People get big insurance on fake stuff. They collect on it.

BARNES (*smiling for the photo, mutters through his gleaming teeth*). Sh! You spoil the picture. (*Flash. The picture is taken. Barnes drops the smile*) Over there! (*He waves them to a seat with his club, turns to the photographer to make sure his name is spelled correctly*)

LEWIS. What about that fourteen hundred dollars?

CHARLEY (*indignantly*). I had it on me for your protection. If this flatfoot had any sense, he was supposed to take it and let us go. . . . Dumb cop! Can I help it?

LEWIS (*pushes his face into Charley's, threateningly*). I want my share.

CHARLEY. All right, Lewis. I'm not gonna argue with you. If it'll make you happy, I'll give you the whole fourteen hundred. Satisfied?

LEWIS (*thinks it over*). Ya.

CHARLEY. Good.

BARNES (*crosses over to them*). No talking—you!

MCLEOD (*to Arthur*). Your signature. Here! (*Arthur glances at the card, hesitates*)

SUSAN. Shouldn't he see a lawyer first?

MCLEOD. It's routine.

SUSAN. Anyway a lawyer should . . . (*McLeod presses his temples, annoyed.*)

ARTHUR. Susan! (*Shakes his head*)

SUSAN. Excuse me. (*She forces a wan smile, nods, puts her fingers to her lips. McLeod hands Arthur the pen. Arthur looks about seeking a depository for his cigarette butt*)

MCLEOD. On the floor. (*Arthur throws it on the floor*) Step on it! (*Arthur steps on butt*)

ARTHUR. Where do I sign?

MCLEOD. Here. (*Indicates the line on the card. Arthur signs. Susan rises*)

SUSAN. I believe in you, Arthur. I want you to know. Deep inside—deep down, no matter what happens—I have faith in you.

JOE (*to photographer*). Now, this one. (*To McLeod*) You want to be in this?

MCLEOD (*pressing his temples*). No! Got an aspirin, Yussel?

JOE (*curtly*). No. (*Walks away*)

PHOTOGRAPHER (*to Arthur*). You mind standing up?

(*The flash, as he snaps the picture, galvanizes Susan.*)

SUSAN (*hysterically*). No! No! They don't have to do that to him! They don't have to. . . . (*To Brody*) Officer Brody. They're not going to print that in the papers, are they?

ARTHUR (*goes to her*). It's all right, Suzy! Stop trembling. Please. I don't care. . . .

BRODY (*beckons Joe and photographer out through the gate*). Joe! Teeney! (*They follow him off*)

SUSAN. I'm not . . . really. . . . It was the sudden flash! (*She buries her head in her hands, turns away to control herself. Charley laughs softly*)

DAKIS (*putting on his hat and jacket, glances at the clock*). Well, quarter to nine. Night Court'll be open by the time we get there.

SHOPLIFTER (*rising, picking up her bag and scarf*). What do I do?

DAKIS. They'll tell you. Your brother-in-law's gonna be there, ain't he?

SHOPLIFTER. Yeah. All I can do is thank goodness my sister's sexy. Well . . . (*She looks about*) So long everybody! You been very nice to me. Really very nice. And I'm sorry I caused you all this trouble! Good-bye! (*She and Dakis go*)

MCLEOD (*to Susan*). You better go home now, young lady. It's all over.

SUSAN. May I talk to Arthur? For two minutes, alone? Then I'll go. I won't make any more trouble, I promise.

MCLEOD. All right. (*He handcuffs Arthur to the chair*) Two minutes. (*He goes into the Lieutenant's office, sits in the darkened room*)

SUSAN (*to Arthur, her lips trembling*). Jiggs . . .

ARTHUR (*quickly*). Don't!

SUSAN (*dragging a chair over to him*). I'm not going to cry. This is no time for emotionalism. I mean we must be calm and wise. We must be realists. (*She sits down, takes his hand*) The minute I walk out of here I'm going to call Father.

ARTHUR. No, Susan, don't do that!

SUSAN. But he likes you so much, Arthur. He'll be glad to help.

ARTHUR. I don't want him to know. I'm ashamed. I'm so ashamed of myself.

SUSAN. Jiggs, it's understandable.

ARTHUR. Is it? God Almighty, I don't understand it! I stole, Suzy. I stole money from a man who trusted me! Where am I? Am I still floating around in the middle of the Pacific, looking for concrete platforms that aren't there? How mixed up can you get?

SUSAN. But, Jiggs, everybody gets mixed up, some time or other.

ARTHUR. They don't steal. (*Pause*) Delirium, isn't it?

SUSAN. O.K. So it is delirium, Jiggs. So what? You're coming out of it fine.

ARTHUR (*shakes his head*). Look around, Susan. Look at this. (*Studies the handcuffs*) The dreams I had—the plans I made . . . to end like this.

SUSAN. This isn't the end of the world, Jiggs.

ARTHUR. It is for me. *(He rattles the handcuffs)* All I ever wanted was to live quietly in a small college town . . . to study and teach. No! *(Bitterly)* This isn't a time for study and teachers . . . this is a time for generals.

SUSAN *(passionately)*. I hate that kind of talk, Jiggs. Everywhere I hear it. . . . I don't believe it. Whatever happens to you, you can still pick up and go on. If ever there was a time for students and teachers, this is it. I know you can still make whatever you choose of your life. *(She pauses, aware of his black anguish)* Arthur! Do you want Joy? Would that help? Would you like to see her and talk to her?

ARTHUR. No.

SUSAN. I'll go to Connecticut and bring her back?

ARTHUR. I don't want her.

SUSAN. I'll get her here. Say the word. I'll bring her here, Arthur. She'll come. You know she will.

ARTHUR. I don't want her, Suzy. I don't want Joy.

SUSAN. You're sure?

ARTHUR. Yes. *(Pause)* For five years I've been in love with a girl that doesn't exist. I wouldn't know what to say to her now. *(The noises of the city outside rise and fall)* That's finished. Washed up.

SUSAN. Oh, Arthur! Why couldn't you have fallen in love with me?

ARTHUR *(looks at her, for a long time, then, tenderly)*. I've always loved you, Suzy. You were always . . . my baby.

SUSAN. I've news for you. I voted for the President in the last election. I'm years past the age of consent.

ARTHUR. Just an old bag?

SUSAN. Arthur, why didn't you fall in love with me? I'd have been so much better for you. I know I'm not as beautiful as Joy, but . . .

ARTHUR. But you are. Joy's prettier than you, Susan, but you're more beautiful.

SUSAN. Oh, Jiggs, you fracture me! Let us not . . . *(She almost cries)*

ARTHUR. Let us not be emotional. We were going to be "realists." Remember?

SUSAN. Yes.

ARTHUR. Suzy, when I go to jail . . . *(Her lip quivers again)* Now . . . "Realists"??

SUSAN. I'm not going to cry.

ARTHUR. Be my sensible Susan!

SUSAN. Jiggs, I can't be sensible about you. I love you.

ARTHUR. Suzy, darling . . .

SUSAN. Jiggs, whatever happens, when it's over—let's go back home again.

ARTHUR. That would be wonderful, Suzy. That would be everything I ever wanted.

CHARLEY *(pretends to play a violin, humming "Hearts and Flowers." Then he laughs raucously, nudging Lewis)*. Hear that, Lewis? He's facin' five to ten? Wait'll the boys go to work on him. *(Arthur and Susan look at him. To Susan)* What makes you think *he'll* want *you* then?

SUSAN. What?

CHARLEY. A kid like this in jail. They toss for him.

SUSAN. What do you mean?

CHARLEY. To see whose chicken he's gonna be!

SUSAN. What does that mean? What's he talking about?

ARTHUR. Don't listen to him. *(To Charley)* Shut up! Who asked you to . . .

CHARLEY. After a while you get to like it. Lots a guys come out, they got no use for dames after that.

ARTHUR. Shut up!

CHARLEY. Look at Lewis, there. He's more woman than man, ain't you, ain't you, Lewis? *(Lewis grins)*

ARTHUR *(rises in a white fury, goes for Charley, dragging the chair to which he's handcuffed)*. Shut up! I'll crack your goddam skull!

(Barnes runs over to Charley.)

SUSAN. Stop it! Stop! *(Brody enters quickly)* Officer Brody, make him stop! Make him stop!

BRODY *(to Arthur)*. Take it easy! Sit down! *(Kicks Charley in the shins)* Why don't you shut up?

SUSAN. Oh, Officer Brody, help us! Help us!

BRODY. Take it easy. He ain't convicted yet. The Judge might put him on probation. He might get off altogether. A lot of things might happen.

CHARLEY *(bending over, feeling his bruised shin)*. Yak! Yak!

BRODY. One more peep outa you! One! *(He slaps Charley, turns to Barnes, irritated)* Take them inside!

(Barnes waves Charley and Lewis into the next room. As they pass Arthur, Lewis

eyes Arthur up and down, grinning and nodding. Charley hums his mockery, "Hearts and Flowers." Barnes prods Charley with his night-stick, muttering, "We heard the voice before." They exit.)

BRODY *(to Susan).* If the complainant still wants to give him a break, that'll help. You got a good lawyer? *(She shakes her head)* I'll give you the name of a crackerjack! I'm not supposed to, but I'll call him myself. There are a lot of tricks to this business.

SUSAN. Don't let it happen!

BRODY. Here's your picture. *(Crumples up the photographic plate, tosses it into the waste-basket; goes to his locker, fishes out of his bottle of liquor. Susan begins to weep)*

ARTHUR. Susan! Susan! The rest of my life I'm going to find ways to make this up to you. I swear. Whatever happens . . . *(He puts his arms around her, pulls her down into the chair alongside him, holds her tight)*

SUSAN *(clinging to him).* Arthur, I . . .

ARTHUR. Sh! Don't say anything more, Suzy. We've a minute left. Let's just sit here like this . . . quietly. *(Susan starts to speak)* Sh! Quiet! *(She buries her head in his shoulder and they sit there in a gentle embrace. After a second's silence, she relaxes)* Better?

SUSAN *(nods).* Mm!

BRODY *(goes into the Lieutenant's office, looking for McLeod).* What are you sitting here in the dark for? *(He switches on the light)* Want a drink, Jim?

MCLEOD. No.

BRODY *(pours himself a stiff one).* Jim, I've been your partner for thirteen years. I ever ask you for a favor?

MCLEOD *(pressing his hand to his temples).* What is it, Lou?

BRODY. That kid outside. *(McLeod groans)* I want you to give him a break.

MCLEOD. You know better. I can't adjudicate this case.

BRODY. And what the hell do you think you're doing?

MCLEOD. What makes him so special?

BRODY. A lot. I think he's a good kid. He's got stuff on the ball. Given another chance . . . *(Pause)* Jim, he reminds me of my boy.

MCLEOD. Mike?—was a hero.

BRODY. Why? Because he was killed? If Mike'd be alive today, he'd have the same problems this kid has.

MCLEOD. Lou, Lou—how can you compare?

BRODY. Thousands like 'em, I guess. New generation, a screwed-up world. We don't even understand them, Jim. I didn't Mike, till he was killed. *(Pause)* Too late then. *(He swallows his drink)* How about it?

MCLEOD. Don't ask me, will you?

BRODY. But, I am.

MCLEOD. I can't. I can't do it, Lou. I can't drop the charges.

BRODY. Louder, please! I don't seem to hear so good outa this ear.

MCLEOD. This fellow and Mike—day and night— There's no comparison.

BRODY. Jim, this is me, Lou Brody. Remember me? What do you mean you can't drop it? You coulda let him go two hours ago. You still can. The complainant left it up to you. I heard him.

MCLEOD. Be logical, Lou.

BRODY. To hell with logic. I seen you logic the life out of a thing. Heart! Heart! The world's crying for a little heart. *(Pause)* What do you say?

MCLEOD. No, Lou. No dice!

BRODY. My partner! Arrest his own mother.

MCLEOD. I'm too old to start compromising now.

BRODY. There's a full moon out tonight. It shows in your puss.

MCLEOD. You shouldn't drink so much, Lou. It melts the lining of your brain.

BRODY *(pushes the bottle to him).* Here! You take it. Maybe that's what you need. Maybe it'll melt that rock you got in there for a heart.

MCLEOD *(a moan of anguish).* For Christ's sake, stop it, Lou, will you? My nerves are like banjo strings.

BRODY. Well, play something on them. Play "Love's Old Sweet Song."

MCLEOD. Shut up! Lay off! God damn it! I'm warning you. Lay off! *(Silence)*

BRODY *(studies him, then . . . softer).* What's the matter?

MCLEOD. I'm drowning, Lou. I'm drowning. That's all. I'm drowning in my own juices.

BRODY. I wish I could understand what makes you tick.

MCLEOD. I don't expect you to understand me, Lou. I know I'm different than the others. I think differently. I'm not a little boy who won't grow up, playing cops and robbers all his life, like Callahan; and I'm not an insurance salesman, like you, Lou. I'm here out of principle!! Principle, Lou. All my life I've lived according to principle! And, God damn it, I couldn't deviate even if I wanted to.

BRODY. Sometimes you gotta bend with the wind . . . or break. Be a little human, Jim! Don't be such a friggin' monument!

MCLEOD. How, how? How do you compromise? How do you compromise, Christ! —convictions that go back to the roots of your childhood? I hate softness. I don't believe in it. My mother was soft; it killed her. I'm no Christian. I don't believe in the other cheek. I hate mushiness. You ask me to compromise for this kid? Who the hell is he? Now, right now, Lou, I'm faced with a problem of my own that's ripping me up like a .22 bullet bouncing around inside, and I can't compromise on that. So what do I do? What do I do?

(A long pause. Joe has entered quietly and has been standing in the doorway, listening.)

JOE. Try picking up that phone and calling her.

MCLEOD. Who?

JOE. Mary. *(Tosses an aspirin box onto the desk)* Here's your aspirin.

MCLEOD. What are you talking about?

JOE. This ".22 bullet" of yours.

MCLEOD. You don't know anything about it.

JOE. It's one story I had in my pocket years before it happened.

MCLEOD. Listening at keyholes, Yussel?

JOE. No, I'm prescient. *(Pause)* I met Mary years before you did. The spring of '41—I was on the Newark *Star*. She didn't remember me. I never forgot her, though. It's one of those faces you don't forget. She's one in a million, your Mary. I know. She's a fine girl, Seamus. She could have had anything she wanted—materially— anything. She chose you instead. Why? What'd you have to offer her? Buttons!— These crazy hours, this crazy life? She loves you. You don't know how lucky you are. I know. I'm little and ugly—and because I'm a lover of beauty I'm going to live and die alone. But you? . . . The jewel was placed in your hands. Don't throw it away. You'll never get it back, again!

(Callahan re-enters the squad-room, crossing to the files. He pauses to light a cigarette.)

BRODY *(softly)*. You know what you were like before you met Mary? You remember?

MCLEOD. Yes.

BRODY. Like a stick!—Thin.

MCLEOD *(his voice hoarse with emotion)*. Yes.

BRODY. Dried up, lonely, cold.

MCLEOD. Yes.

BRODY. And you know what tenderness and warmth she brought to your life?

MCLEOD. I know. I know better than you.

BRODY. So what the hell you asking me what to do? Pick up the phone! Get on your knees. Crawl!

(Mary enters the squad-room, stands within the gate, pale, worn. Callahan clears his throat, approaches her, adjusting his tie, a little "makey.")

CALLAHAN. Yesss, Miss?

MARY. Is Detective McLeod here?

CALLAHAN. He's busy, Miss.

MARY *(wearily)*. It's Mrs., Mrs. McLeod.

CALLAHAN. Oh! Yes, Ma'am. I'll tell him you're here. *(Crosses. Pokes his head into the Lieutenant's office to McLeod)* Your wife is out here. *(McLeod rises at once, comes out to Mary. Joe and Brody follow him out, and discreetly vanish into the wash-room)*

MARY *(digs into her purse to avoid his eyes. Her voice is low and brittle)*. I'm leaving now, Jim. I thought I'd come up and tell you. Here are the keys.

MCLEOD *(softly)*. Come inside.

MARY. My taxi's waiting.

MCLEOD. Send it away.

MARY. No. My things are in it.

MCLEOD. What things?

MARY. My valises and my trunk.

MCLEOD. Oh, Mary, be sensible.

MARY. I intend to. Let's not drag it out, Jim! Please! I don't want any more arguments. I can't stand them. *(Her voice becomes shrill. Callahan passes by. She clamps the controls on, becoming almost inaudible)* It's only going to make things worse.

MCLEOD. Come inside! I can't talk to you here.

MARY. The meter's ticking.

MCLEOD *(firmly)*. Let it tick! Come! *(She obeys, follows him into the Lieuten-*

ant's office. He shuts the door, turns to her) Mary, this isn't the time or place to discuss our lives, past, present or future. I want you to take your things and go home. I'll be back at eight A.M. and we'll work this out then.

MARY. You think we can?

MCLEOD. We'll have to.

MARY. I don't. I don't think it's possible.

MCLEOD. Wait a minute! Wait one minute! I don't get this. What are *you* so bitter about? Who's to blame for tonight? You put me in a cement-mixer. And now you're acting as if I were the . . .

MARY. The whore?

MCLEOD. Don't say that!

MARY. I didn't invent the word, either, Jim.

MCLEOD. I wasn't myself.

MARY. You were never more yourself, Jim. *(Pause)*

MCLEOD. I'm sorry, Mary.

MARY. It's all right. I'm beyond feeling. I'm nice and numb.

MCLEOD. You're certainly in no condition to discuss this, tonight.

MARY. I've thought everything over and over and over again and I don't see any other way out. Our life is finished. We couldn't go on from here.

MCLEOD. You're married to me. You can't just walk out. Marriage is a sacrament, Mary. You don't dissolve it like that.

MARY. You once told me when you bring a married prostitute in here, if she's convicted, her marriage can be dissolved just like that! Well, I've been brought in and I've been convicted.

MCLEOD. I don't like that. Stop that talk, will you, Mary? I'm trying, I'm trying . . .

MARY. To what?

MCLEOD. To put all this behind me.

MARY. But you can't do it?

MCLEOD. If you'll let me.

MARY. Me? What have I got to say about it? I know the way your mind works. It never lets go. The rest of our days, we'll be living with this. If you won't be saying it you'll be thinking it. *(Pause)* It's no good. It won't work. I don't want to live a cat-and-dog existence. I couldn't take it. I'd dry up. I'd dry up and die.

MCLEOD. Why didn't you ever tell me? If you'd come to me once, just once . . .

MARY. How could I? What good would

it have done? Would you have understood? Would you have been able to forgive me?

MCLEOD. Wasn't I entitled to know?

MARY. Yes, yes!

MCLEOD. Why didn't you tell me?

MARY. Jim, I can't go over this again and again and again. I refuse to.

MCLEOD. If I didn't love you and need you so, it'd be simple, you understand?

MARY. I understand.

MCLEOD. Simple. You go home now and wait till morning.

MARY. That won't help us. Please, I'm so tired. Let me go now, Jim.

MCLEOD. To what? What'll you go to? You, who turn on every light in the house when I'm not there!

MARY. Let me go, Jim.

MCLEOD. You, who can't fall asleep unless my arms are around you! Where will you go?

MARY. Jim, I beg you . . .

MCLEOD. No, Mary, I'm not going to. *(He grasps her by the arm)*

MARY. You're hurting my arm. Jim!

MCLEOD. I'm sorry . . . I'm sorry. *(He lets her go)*

MARY. You ripped my sleeve.

MCLEOD. You'll sew it up.

MARY. The taxi's waiting. Please, Jim, let me go, without any more razor-slashing. I hate it.

MCLEOD. You'd go without a tear?

MARY. I wouldn't say that. One or two, perhaps. I haven't many left.

MCLEOD. Mary, I . . . *(Callahan enters the Lieutenant's office, leaves paper on his desk, and goes)* Mary, you just don't stop loving someone.

MARY. I wouldn't have thought so. I wouldn't have believed it could happen. But, there it is. I suppose in this life we all die many times before they finally bury us. This was one of those deaths. Sudden, unexpected, like being run over by a bus. It happens.

MCLEOD. Who do you think you're kidding?

MARY. No one! *(Begins to cry)* Least of all, myself.

MCLEOD *(takes her in his arms)*. Mary, I love you.

MARY *(clinging to him, sobbing)*. Then help me! I'm trying to be a human being. I'm trying to bundle myself together. It took every bit of strength to go this far. Help me, Jim!

MCLEOD (*caressing her*). It's no use, sweetheart, it's no use. I couldn't go home if you weren't waiting for me with the radio going and the smell of coffee on the stove. I'd blow out my brains. I would, Mary, if I went home to an empty flat—I wouldn't dare take my gun with me. (*He gives her his handkerchief. She dries her eyes*) Now powder your nose! Put on some lipstick. (*She kisses him. Sims appears at the gate, outside*)

CALLAHAN (*crosses to Sims*). Yes, Counselor?

SIMS. I want to see Detective McLeod.

CALLAHAN. All right, Counselor. Come in. (*Knocks on the door*)

MCLEOD. Come in!

CALLAHAN. Someone outside to see you.

MARY. I'll go home, now.

MCLEOD. No. Wait a minute.

MARY (*smiling now*). That taxi bill is going to break us.

MCLEOD (*grins back at her*). Let it break us. What do we care? (*He goes out, sees Sims, his face goes grim again. He crosses to Sims*) You see, Counselor? I told you your client was acting.

SIMS. He's still in shock.

MCLEOD. He'll be okay in the morning.

SIMS. No thanks to you. When he's brought back here tomorrow, though, he'd better remain okay. This is not to happen again! You're not to lay a finger on him. If you do . . .

MCLEOD. Then advise him again to keep his mouth shut. And see that he does.

SIMS. You're lucky you're not facing a murder charge yourself right now.

MCLEOD. I could always get you to defend me.

SIMS. And I probably would. That's my job, no matter how I feel personally.

MCLEOD. As long as you get your fee?

SIMS. I've defended many men at my own expense.

MCLEOD. That was very noble of you.

SIMS. Nobility doesn't enter into it. Every man has a right to counsel, no matter how guilty he might seem to you, or to me, for that matter. Every man has a right not to be arbitrarily judged, particularly by men in authority; not by you, not by the Congress, not even by the President of the United States. The theory being these human rights are derived from God himself.

MCLEOD. I know the theory, Counselor.

SIMS. But you don't go along with it? Well, you're not alone. There are others. You've a lot of friends all over the world. Read the headlines. But don't take it on yourself to settle it. Let history do that.

MCLEOD. Save it for the Fourth of July, Counselor.

SIMS. I'll save it for the Commissioner. I intend to see him about you. I'm not going to let you get away with this.

MCLEOD. As long as Schneider gets away with it, Counselor, all's well. Why do you take cases like this, if you're so high-minded? Schneider killed the Harris girl—he's guilty. You know it as well as I do.

SIMS. I don't know it. I don't even permit myself to speculate on his guilt or innocence. The moment I do that, I'm judging . . . and it is not my job to judge. My job is to defend my client, not to judge him. That remains with the courts. (*He turns to go*)

MCLEOD. And you've got that taken care of, Counselor. Between bought witnesses and perjured testimony . . . (*Sims stops in his tracks, suddenly white with fury*)

SIMS. If you're so set on hanging Schneider, why don't you ask Mrs. McLeod if she can supply a corroborating witness? (*McLeod is stopped in turn, as if he'd been hit by a meat-axe. Sims goes. Charley, Lewis and Barnes enter*)

BARNES. Charley, sit over there. Over there for you, Lewis.

(*McLeod looks a little sick. He lights a cigarette slowly. He returns to the Lieutenant's office, his face twitching. Mary is just finishing powdering her face and removing the traces of the tears.*)

MARY. What's the matter, dear?

MCLEOD. Nothing.

MARY. This has been our black day.

MCLEOD. Yes.

MARY (*puts her vanity case back into her bag*). I'm sorry, darling. And yet, in a way I'm glad it's out in the open. This has been hanging over my head so long. I've had such a terrible feeling of guilt all the time.

MCLEOD (*mutters*). All right! All right!

MARY (*ignores the storm warnings*). I needed help and there was no one. I couldn't even go to my parents.

MCLEOD. They didn't know?

MARY. No.

MCLEOD. You didn't tell them?

MARY. I didn't dare. I didn't want to hurt them. You know how sweet and simple they are.

MCLEOD. You didn't go home then? After?

MARY. No.

MCLEOD (*acidly*). Where'd you go?

MARY. That's when I came to New York.

MCLEOD. And how long was that before I met you, Mary?

MARY. Two years.

MCLEOD. Who'd you go with, then?

MARY. No one.

MCLEOD. How many others were there, Mary?

MARY. Others?

MCLEOD (*all control gone*). How many other *men*?

MARY. None. (*Alarmed now*) What's the matter with you, Jim?

MCLEOD. Wait a minute! Wait a minute! (*He turns away, trying to control the insane turbulence inside*)

MARY. No! What's the matter with you?

MCLEOD. At an autopsy yesterday I watched the medical examiner saw off the top of a man's skull, take out the brain, and hold it in his hand—(*He holds out his hand*) like that.

MARY (*horrified*). Why are you telling me this?

MCLEOD. Because I'd give everything I own to be able to take out my brain and hold it under the faucet and wash away the dirty pictures you put there tonight.

MARY. Dirty pictures?

MCLEOD. Yes!

MARY. Oh! I see. (*A long pause. The brakes of a truck outside the window suddenly screech like a horribly wounded living thing*) I see. (*To herself*) Yes. That would be fine, if we could. (*She straightens, turns to him, wearily*) But when you wash away what I may have put there, you'll find you've a rotten spot in your brain, Jim, and it's growing. I know, I've watched it. . . .

MCLEOD (*hoarsely*). Mary! That's enough.

MARY (*stronger than he, at last*). No, let's have the truth! I could never find it in my heart to acknowledge one tiny flaw in you because I loved you so—and God help me, I still do—but let's have the

truth, for once, wherever it leads. You think you're on the side of the angels? You're not! You haven't even a drop of ordinary human forgiveness in your whole nature. You're a cruel and vengeful man. You're everything you've always said you hated in your own father.

MCLEOD (*starts to throw on his jacket*). I'm not going to let you wander off in the streets this way. I'm going to take you home, myself.

MARY. What for? To kill me the way your father killed your mother!! (*His hands drop to his side. He stares at her dumbly, stricken. She puts the keys down on the desk, turns to go*)

MCLEOD. Where are you going? (*Pause. She looks at him sadly*)

MARY. Far away . . . you won't find me. I'm scorching my earth . . . burning my cities.

MCLEOD. When will I see you?

MARY. Never. . . . Good-bye. (*She goes. McLeod, dazed, walks slowly back to the squad-room. Brody sees him from the wash-room and enters with Joe*)

BRODY. How'd it go?

MCLEOD (*almost inaudibly*). Fine.

BRODY. I mean Mary.

MCLEOD. Fine. Dandy. (*To Susan*) All right, young lady, your two minutes are up.

(*The Lieutenant enters.*)

LIEUTENANT (*to McLeod*). What the hell's the matter with you?

MCLEOD. Nothing. . . .

LIEUTENANT. Don't you feel well?

MCLEOD. Yes, sir. Feel all right.

LIEUTENANT (*to Brody*). Am I crazy? Look at him.

BRODY. You've gone all green, Jim.

MCLEOD. I've got a headache. ·

LIEUTENANT. You better go home. Buzz your doctor.

MCLEOD. I've got a squeal to finish off, Lieutenant.

LIEUTENANT. Brody! You finish it off.

BRODY (*reluctantly*). Yes, sir.

MCLEOD. I'd rather do it, myself.

LIEUTENANT. You go home. That's an order.

MCLEOD. Yes, sir.

LIEUTENANT. Callahan! You catch for Jim tonight.

CALLAHAN. Yes, sir. (*He crosses up to the duty chart, takes it off the wall*)

BRODY (to McLeod). What happened, Jim? What's wrong?

MCLEOD (sits heavily). Mary left me. Walked out. We're finished.

BRODY. Too bad. She'll come back.

MCLEOD. No. This was for keeps.

(The Lieutenant crosses.)

LIEUTENANT. What are you sitting there for? Why don't you go home? (Exit Lieutenant)

MCLEOD. Because I haven't got any.

JOE (comes down to him). You drove her away, didn't you? Why? (McLeod doesn't answer) I tried to warn you, you damn fool. Why?

MCLEOD. I don't know. Why? Why do we do these things, Yussel? Who knows? . . . I built my whole life on hating my father—and all the time he was inside me, laughing—or maybe he was crying, the poor bastard, maybe he couldn't help himself, either.

(An excited woman enters, rattles the gate.)

CALLAHAN. Yes, Miss? (He is at the desk now, reaching into the bottom drawer for the celluloid letters to replace the name on the duty chart)

WOMAN. Someone snatched my purse. . . .

CALLAHAN. Come in, Miss. We'll take care of you. (He bends over to pick up a letter)

WOMAN. This happened to me once before . . . on 72nd Street. . . .

(Charley lunges for Callahan's exposed gun, grabs it, hits Callahan on the head with the butt, knocking him to the floor. Barnes raises his club.)

CHARLEY. Drop that club! (He aims at Barnes)

BRODY. Drop it! He's a four-time loser. He'll kill you. (Barnes drops his club)

CHARLEY. God damn right! Rot in jail the rest of my life? I take five or six a you bastards with me first. (Barnes makes a movement)

BRODY. Take it easy! He can't get by the desk.

CHARLEY. Shut up! One word! One move! Anybody! (McLeod, seated center, laughs softly)

MCLEOD. I was wondering when you'd get around to it, Charley.

CHARLEY. None of your guff, you!

MCLEOD (rises). Give me that gun!

CHARLEY. In the gut you'll get it. One step! I'm warnin' you. One!

BRODY. Easy, Jim. He can't get by the desk.

MCLEOD (lunges for the gun). You evil son-of-a-bitch!

(Charley fires point-blank at McLeod. One, two, three quick shots. McLeod is hurled back and whirled around by the impact. Barnes goes into action, knocks the gun out of Charley's hand and starts beating him over the head with his billy. Several of the others rush in and swarm all over Charley. He screams twice and is silent. McLeod staggers, clutching his stomach.)

BRODY (rushes to him, puts his arms around him, supporting him). Jim! Did he get you? Are you hurt?

MCLEOD. Slightly. . . . (He unbuttons his coat. His shirt is a bloody rag. The sight stuns and sickens him) God! (A little boy for one second) Oh, Mary, Mary, Mary . . . (He wraps the coat tightly about him as if to shut in the escaping stream of life. He looks up, smiles crookedly) Slightly killed, I should say. . . .

(The Lieutenant comes running in, a number of policemen crowd in through the gate.)

LIEUTENANT. What's happened?

BARNES. That son-of-a-bitch shot Jim!

LIEUTENANT. Take him inside! Get him into bed, quick.

BRODY (to McLeod). Easy, baby. Come, I'll carry you to bed. . . .

MCLEOD. Wait a minute.

BRODY. Now, Jim.

MCLEOD. No, don't! Don't pull at me. . . . (He sinks back into a chair)

JOE. You got to lie down, Seamus.

MCLEOD. No. Once I lie down I'm not going to get up again. No.

LIEUTENANT. Notify the Communication Bureau! Get an ambulance. Quick!

MCLEOD. Never mind the doctor. Get a priest.

BRODY. Feel that bad, Jim?

GALLAGHER (on the phone). Communication Bureau.

LIEUTENANT. Why don't you lie down, Jim?

MCLEOD. Get me a drink. (He gasps, unable to speak. Brody starts for the water-cooler)

LIEUTENANT (whispers to Brody). With a belly wound . . . ?

BRODY (whispers). What difference does it make . . . ? Look at him!

MCLEOD. Don't whisper, Lou. I can hear you.

(The Lieutenant goes for glass of water.)

BRODY. Sure you can. You're all right, baby. They can't hurt you. You're one of the indestructibles, you're immortal, baby.

MCLEOD. Almost, Lou, almost. Don't rush me. Give me your hand, Lou. Squeeze! Harder!

(Susan begins to sob.)

ARTHUR. Don't cry, Suzy. Don't cry!

MCLEOD *(glances up at Arthur, studies him, turns to Brody)*. Give me Buster's prints! I don't know. I hope you're right, Lou. Maybe he'll come in tomorrow with a murder rap. I don't know any more. Get me his prints. *(Brody goes for them. Charley is dragged off, half unconscious, moaning)*

JOE. How're you feeling, Seamus?

MCLEOD. Yussel! Find her! Ask her to forgive me. And help her. She needs help . . . will you?

JOE. Sure. Now take it easy.

(Brody hands Arthur's fingerprint sheet to McLeod.)

MCLEOD. Tear it up! *(Brody tears it)* Unchain him, Lou. The keys are in my pocket. We have no case here, Lieutenant. The complainant withdrew. *(He crosses himself)* In the name of the Father and of the Son and of the Holy Ghost. Oh, my God, I am heartily sorry for having offended Thee and I detest all my sins because I dread the loss of Heaven. . . . *(He falls. Brody catches him, eases him to the*

ground, feels for his pulse. Joe kneels to help him. After an interminable pause)*

BRODY. He's gone!

JOE. He's dead.

LIEUTENANT *(completes the Act of Contrition)*. I firmly resolve with the help of Thy Grace to confess my sins, to do penance and to amend my life. Amen. *(Crosses himself)*

BRODY *(murmurs)*. Amen. *(Barnes uncovers, crosses himself. Brody crosses himself, rises clumsily, goes to Arthur, unlocks his handcuffs)* All right, son. Go on home! Don't make a monkey outa me! If I see you . . . *(Brody is crying now)* up here again, I'll kick the guts outa you. Don't make a monkey outa me!

ARTHUR. Don't worry! I won't.

SUSAN. He won't.

BRODY. Now get the hell outa here! *(Susan takes Arthur's hand. They go. At the door Arthur pauses to look back. Brody has turned to watch him go. They exchange glances)*

GALLAGHER *(on the phone)*. St. Vincent's? Will you please send a priest over to the 21st Precinct Police Station to administer last rites?

LIEUTENANT *(on the phone)*. Communication Bureau? Notify the Commissioner, the D.A., the homicide squad . . . 21st Precinct . . . Detective shot . . . killed.

(Brody, his face twisted, glances down at McLeod. Joe rises, slowly, taking off his hat.)

CURTAIN

Billy Budd

BY LOUIS O. COXE and ROBERT CHAPMAN

First presented by Chandler Cowles and Anthony B. Farrell at the Biltmore Theatre in New York on February 10, 1951, with the following cast:

JENKINS, *Captain of the Maintop*......Jeff Morrow

THE DANSKER, *Mainmast Man*......George Fells

JACKSON, *Maintopman*...............Bertram Tanswell

JOHN CLAGGART, *Master-at-Arms*
Torin Thatcher

TALBOT, *Maintopman*..........................James Daly

BUTLER, *Maintopman*.....................Leonard Yorr

KINCAID, *Maintopman*...................Kenneth Paine

PAYNE, *Maintopman*.........................Judson Pratt

O'DANIEL, *Maintopman*....................Walter Burke

MESSBOY ....Charles Hudson

SQUEAK, *Master-at-Arms' Man*.....Bernard Kates

DUNCAN, *Mate of the Main Deck*
Robert McQueeney

SURGEON ....Winston Ross

GARDINER, *a Midshipman*..............Jack Manning

BILLY BUDD, *Foretopman*..............Charles Nolte

EDWARD FAIRFAX VERE, *Captain, Royal Navy*...Dennis King

HALLAM, *a Marine*............................Lee Marvin

REA, *a Midshipman*.......................Henry Garrard

PHILIP MICHAEL SEYMOUR, *First Officer*
Guy Spaull

JOHN RATCLIFFE, *First Lieutenant*
Preston Hanson

BORDMAN WYATT, *Sailing Master*
Norman Ettlinger

STOLL, *Helmsman*........................Charles Carshon

BYREN, *Relief Helmsman*................Martin Brandt

DRUMMER ....David Long

The entire action takes place aboard *H.M.S. Indomitable* at sea, August, 1798, the year following the Naval mutinies at Spithead and the Nore.

THE dramatization of Melville's novel of the sea, *Billy Budd,* is, in part, a tribute to the effective teaching of Professor Willard Thorp, the distinguished authority on American literature and Melville enthusiast, under whom the Messrs. Coxe and Chapman studied at Princeton. Both young men joined the navy during the Second World War, and a first-hand acquaintance with the sea may have also contributed a stimulus. Later, Louis O. Coxe joined the English department at the University of Minnesota, Robert Chapman the English department at Harvard. Their collaboration started in 1947.

The play, which narrowly missed winning the Drama Critics Award for the best play of the 1950-51 season, was tried out under the title of *Uniform of Flesh* by ANTA's Experimental Theatre on January 29, 1949, ran for seven performances, and impressed those who wandered uptown to the Lenox Hill Playhouse to see it. It was then a sparer work, written in stricter poetic form. *Billy Budd,* the retitled drama unfolded on Broadway, is a much revised and amplified version, in which the authors took significant liberties with the Melville text, justifying Brooks Atkinson's statement that "although *Billy Budd* is the dramatization of a novel, it is a fully wrought play in its own right." It is especially so in the insistent force of its central point that neither absolute good nor absolute evil is complete reality; that only a mixture of those elements is in accord with nature and has possibilities of survival. Mr. Atkinson found a suitable epigraph for the work when he quoted Melville's lines:

Yea and Nay—
Each hath his say;
But God, He keeps the middle way.

The cultivated and intelligent authors, who were anything if not conscious of their intentions, lend support to this philosophical view of their play, although it is possible that playgoers were more strongly affected by Billy's trial as a case of legal injustice contrasted with moral justice. In an appendix to the text published by Princeton University Press, they wrote: "Perhaps the 'Melville Revival' influenced us; it may have been the desire to find a theme and action that was inherently poetic and non-realistic. Above all, one idea or purpose seems clear; that we saw in *Billy Budd* a morality play." They add that they were impelled to shape it out of Melville's matter by a response to their own day as well as to Melville's artistry: "For us, as inchoate playwrights, in January of 1947, Melville's story of good, evil, and the way the world takes such absolutes was material enough for the veterans of a war, a depression, and the moving cold war." And they conclude, "This is a morality play and we do not apologize for its being such," even though aware of the fact that a dramatic morality is neither popular in our time nor easy to compose.

ACT ONE

SCENE ONE

SCENE: *Although outside it is a fine morning in early August, the between-decks compartment of the crew's quarters assigned to the maintopmen is dark and shadowy except for the light spilling down the companionway from above and, through the open gun-ports, the flicker of sunlight reflected on the water. The smoking-lamp burns feebly over a wooden mess table and two benches lowered for use.*

Jenkins sits at the table mending a piece of clothing. In the shadow the Dansker sits motionless on a low sea chest, smoking a pipe. Neither man speaks for a long minute.

Then Jackson appears on deck at the top of the companionway and lurches down into the compartment. He is doubled up in pain.

———

CLAGGART *(off)*. You there! Jackson!

JACKSON. Oh Christ, he's followed me!

JENKINS. Who?

JACKSON. Master-at-Arms. He'll send me aloft again sure, and I can't hang on . . .

JENKINS. What the devil's wrong with you, jack? Here, sit down.

CLAGGART *(entering down the companionway)*. Why have you come down off the mainmast, Jackson? Your watch over?

JACKSON. Sick, Mister Claggart, I'm bloody sick, so I'm shaking up there on the yard till I near fell off.

JENKINS. Grab an arm, mate, I'll take you along to sick-bay.

CLAGGART. Stand away from him, Jenkins. *(To Jackson)* Just where does this sickness strike you, in the guts, or limbs? Or in the head? Does it exist at all?

JENKINS. You can see he's sick as a puking cat, plain as your stick.

CLAGGART. The role of Good Samaritan hardly fits you, Jenkins. *(To Jackson)* Now up, man. Turn topside.

JACKSON. I can't, I can't, I'm deathly sick, God help me, sir!

CLAGGART. That's hard. But this ship needs all hands. We're undermanned. The aches and pains of landsmen have their cures, but ours have none. You'll have to get aloft. Now move!

JACKSON. I ain't bluffing, sir, swear I'm not! Please, Mister Claggart . . . I got Cooper's leave, he says all right, I can come down.

CLAGGART. You have not got my leave. Cooper is captain of the maintop and ought to know better. Four men to every spar, and no replacements. Now up. Back where you belong.

JACKSON *(starts up the ladder)*. God, sir, I can't, I can't stand it! It'll be my death, sure!

CLAGGART. No more talk, man! Up you get! Start! *(Jackson goes painfully up the ladder and out of sight on deck. Claggart starts out after him)*

JENKINS *(mutters)*. God damn your bloody heart!

CLAGGART. Did you say something, Jenkins? *(Jenkins does not answer. Claggart goes out, calling after Jackson)* Now Jackson, get along. Up! Up!

JENKINS. I'll stick him one day before long! I will, if I hang for it.

(Laughter and talk in the next compartment followed by entrance of Butler, Talbot and Kincaid.)

BUTLER. Messboy!

TALBOT. Haul in the slops!

KINCAID. Suppose we'll get the new man? The jack they 'pressed this morning off that merchantman? I see 'em come alongside just now.

TALBOT. I pity that poor bastard, so I do. I hear they get good pay on merchant ships. Eat good, too, and them treated like the God-damn Prince of Wales. *(Messboy enters with an iron pot of food and spits on the deck)* Spit in it, damn you. Can't taste no worse.

MESSBOY. Ain't nobody making you eat it, mate. You can wash your feet in it if you like. *(O'Daniel and Payne enter)*

TALBOT. What's eating you, Jenkins? Ain't you going to join the banquet?

JENKINS. By God, I seen a thing just now I won't stand for! I'm sitting here off watch, and I seen it all. That blacksnake Claggart kicked Jackson back aloft, and him sick as a pinkass baby in a cradle, as any fool could see.

PAYNE. He's the Master-at-Arms, ain't he?

JENKINS. Cooper sent him down. Who's captain of the starboard watch, him or Claggart? Cooper could have found him a relief. Plain murder, by God!

TALBOT. You think Claggart can get away with what he does without Captain Starry Vere knows what's going on? Him and that red snapper Seymour, and them other bloody officers!

JENKINS. Jackson'll fall. By God, no man can hang to a spar sick like that. He'll fall sure.

O'DANIEL. Tush, man, nobody falls in His Majesty's Navy. We lose our footing. 'Tis flying we do, to be sure.

TALBOT. I tell you it's Vere that's the cause of it! Our glorious fine Captain Vere, with a league of braid around his arm and a ramrod up his bum.

O'DANIEL. Vere, is it. As captains go, mate, let me tell you, he's an angel with a harp alongside of the skipper on the *Royal George*. Every day that one flogged a dozen men. Picked 'em by lottery, by God. Never took the gratings down till they was rusty with blood. Ho! This Vere's a saint in heaven after him.

JENKINS. Ram the *Royal George* and everybody in her! Claggart's the man we want, and the sooner the better, say I!

O'DANIEL. Ah, we'd had him puking his blood at Spithead, the devil rot his wick.

BUTLER. You was there, O'Daniel? At Spithead?

O'DANIEL. Aye. I was. Wherever you do find Englishmen doing a smart thing, you'll find an Irishman is at the bottom of it. Oho, fine it was, every day of it, with the officers quaking in their cabins, spitting green, and the whole English government wetting their breeches from the fear of us! Ah, lovely it was, lovely!

TALBOT. Belay your Irish noise, you fat-mouthed mackerel-snatcher. I'll tell you this, we need men on here is not afraid to use their knives if it come to that. And you can be bloody sure it will come to that, mind my word, Mickey Cork.

JENKINS. What did you ever use your knife for, Talbot, but to scratch your lice? Ah, you're a dancing daredevil, you are for sure.

TALBOT. I'll be happy to show you, if you like.

JENKINS. Trouble will be hunting you out, mate, if you're not careful.

TALBOT. Trouble! You whoreson cockney cullion! There's not a man aboard don't know you for a coward, you whining bitch-boy!

JENKINS. Get out.

TALBOT. Damn your seed, I'm not afraid of you, or your sniveling hangbys, either!

JENKINS. Move! Get out of it, or by God I'll run my knife into you!

TALBOT. You son of a whore! Pigsticker! (*They attack one another with drawn knives, Jenkins reaching suddenly across the table to seize Talbot. Silently they thrash around the compartment upsetting benches and food while the others look on unmoved.*)

O'DANIEL. Ah, I do love to see two Englishmen fighting each other. It's fonder they are of killing themselves than fighting their proper enemies. (*Laughs hoarsely*)

PAYNE. Tomorrow's rum on Jenkins. Any bets?

KINCAID. He's never lost one yet. (*Jenkins throws Talbot on the deck and holds the knife at his throat for a moment before letting him up, first taking his knife. He holds out his hand.*)

JENKINS. I'm leading seaman in this compartment, mind that. (*Talbot hits Jenkins' hand and goes off angrily*)

KINCAID. You're captain, that's all right by me.

O'DANIEL. Eyes in the boat, lads. Here comes *pfft*-face. (*Squeak, Billy and Gardiner appear on deck and start down the companionway.*)

GARDINER. Hang it, step lively, boy! Your ship is . . . Doff your hat to officers when they speak to you! By God, I'll teach you to touch your hat to a midshipman's coat, if it's only stuck on a broomstick to dry!

BILLY. Aye, sir. (*The men react to Gardiner with yawns and gestures behind his back*)

GARDINER. Very well. Your ship is *H.M.S. Indomitable* now, and we sail her tautly, and we tolerate no nonsense. Is that clear?

BILLY. Aye, sir.

GARDINER (*to Squeak*). See this new man is assigned to a watch, and get him squared away. (*To Billy*) You're green, of course, I can see that. But I expect we'll ripen you. (*He trips going up the ladder and Squeak tries to help him*) Carry on. (*Gardiner exits*)

SQUEAK. My name's Squeak. I'm the Master-at-Arms' man. Have you met the Master-at-Arms yet, Mister Claggart? (*Billy shakes his head*) Oh, you'll like him. He's a nice fellow. (*O'Daniel chokes on his pipe smoke and the other men re-act similarly)* Stow your gear along in there. This here's the larboard section of the maintop. Captain of the watch is Jenkins. Him, there. Report to him. *(He pats Billy on the chest and grins before starting up the ladder)*

JENKINS. What's a green hand dumped in here for?

SQUEAK. Complaining, Jenkins?

JENKINS. I'm asking. What's wrong with that?

SQUEAK. Mister Claggart wants him here, that's why. Maybe he wants for Billy Boy to set you pigs an example. Refer any more complaints to the Master-at-Arms! *(Exits. Billy grins at the men, who return his look)*

BILLY. My name is Budd. Billy, if you like.

KINCAID. I'm Kincaid. This is where you swing your hammock. That's O'Daniel, this here's Payne, and Butler. This is Jenkins, captain of the watch, and that old jack's called the Dansker. Don't know why, unless maybe he's Danish. You ever had a real name, Dansker?

DANSKER. Not for many years.

BUTLER. You'd be the new impressed man?

BILLY. Aye, so I am. I just came off the *Rights of Man* this morning.

DANSKER. Forget about the Rights of Man now, lad.

JENKINS. How long you been going to sea, baby?

BILLY. About ten years, but in the merchant service.

O'DANIEL. Merchant service! Whissht! *(Laughs hoarsely)*

BILLY. I know I'm new at Navy work, and probably there'll be some things I'll need help with.

JENKINS. No doubt, little boy.

BILLY. I'll learn fast, never fear. But she's a big old girl, this ship. I never was in a ship-of-the-line before. I'd have got lost trying to find the mess by myself. Maybe fallen in the magazine!

O'DANIEL. Ah, you get used to it. She's big, is this tub, but she's not so big you can get lost in her.

PAYNE. Sometimes I wish to God you could. Maybe we could lose O'Daniel. *(Billy laughs and the others join)*

BILLY. You're Irish, aren't you? I like the Irish. There was an Irishman on the *Rights of Man,* with big red whiskers . . . when I came away, he gave me a silver knife. This is it.

O'DANIEL. It's a beauty. Mind you keep an eye on it.

BUTLER. What's the matter, boy?

BILLY. I was just thinking, maybe I won't ever see my friends again.

O'DANIEL. If they was Irish, don't you worry at all. The Irish is liable to turn up almost anywheres, excepting England and the fires of hell, which is much the same.

PAYNE. Danny, if it wasn't for the harps, the devil wouldn't have nothing to do. What was potato-eaters doing on a merchant ship?

BILLY. Just sailors, like me. Most of us had no other home, even the skipper. He was a kind old bloke. Looked fierce, but he always had a kind word. Used to keep a bird in a cage in his cabin. The skipper let me feed the bird sometimes. Worms right out of the ship's biscuit. That was mostly all the meat we got.

O'DANIEL. The bargemen is in Navy biscuit would eat the bird.

KINCAID. Sit down here, Bill. Maggots or not, this is what we get. You hungry?

BILLY. I'm always hungry.

KINCAID. Try your first sample of His Majesty's bounty. We don't know what it is, but we been eating it for a long time.

BUTLER. Here, eat mine. Tastes like it's been eat before, anyhow.

JENKINS. Give him more lobscouse, Butler. We got to keep the roses in his cheeks, ain't we, boy?

BILLY *(laughing)*. I could eat anything right now. Even this.

O'DANIEL. Help you to forget about home and mother, lad.

JENKINS. Tell us about home and mother, Baby Budd.

BILLY. There's not much to tell. I've got no home, and never had a family to remember.

JENKINS. Ain't that too bad.

BILLY. Oh, I'd feel a lot worse if I'd been 'pressed with a wife and children.

KINCAID. That's the truth.

O'DANIEL. We're all patriotic volunteers.

KINCAID. Guano! Wait till my hitch is up, you won't see no more of me.

BUTLER. Three weeks drunk in Portsmouth, then back in the ruddy fleet.

DANSKER. Men like us got no other home.

o'DANIEL. No other home, is it? Ah 'tis so thick the sweet thoughts is in here, I can scarce breathe.

PAYNE. Then you can strangle or get out.

JENKINS. Aye, get along, you lousy harp, give us some fresh air.

o'DANIEL. If you begged me to stay itself, I'd be off to where there's smarter lads. Boy, let you pay no heed to these white mice, mind what I say. And be hanged, the lot of yous! *(He starts up the ladder)*

KINCAID. You'll catch it, Danny, if Captain holds an inspection.

o'DANIEL *(returning)*. Ah whissht, I was forgetting that. And I do think that me figure shows up better here below than it does in the broad daylight.

BILLY. Inspection today?

PAYNE. Ah, the Old Man crawls over the ship from arsehole to appetite any time he ain't got nothing else to do. You never know when till you see him.

KINCAID. What the devil he wants to inspect this hooker for, I can't figure. He's seen it before.

BUTLER. He ain't seen Billy.

BILLY. What's the Captain like? On the *Rights of Man,* the captain . . .

JENKINS. You going to jaw some more about that rocking horse? I suppose *you* was at Spithead, too?

BILLY. Spithead? Where is that?

JENKINS. A little party the Navy had a year ago. A mutiny, Baby, a mutiny. Know what that is?

BILLY. Why did they mutiny?

o'DANIEL. Arra, it's easy to see you're new to the Navy.

JENKINS. Jimmy-Legs is ten good goddam reasons for it, himself.

BILLY. Who's Jimmy-Legs?

KINCAID. Master-at-Arms. We call him Jimmy-Legs.

BUTLER. Watch out for that one, Billy.

PAYNE. He's the devil himself between decks.

o'DANIEL. What d'you expect, the saints of heaven? Not in an English tub.

BILLY. Why don't you like the Master-at-Arms?

JENKINS. You'll find out soon enough, Baby.

BUTLER. Watch him, boy. Jenkins can tell you. He's had a time or two with Claggart.

JENKINS. Aye, and I'll have another one day before too long.

BUTLER. Sure, Jenkins. You look after Bill.

JENKINS. How old are you, kid? Sixteen?

BILLY. I don't know, maybe . . . twenty.

JENKINS. He don't even know how old he is! My guess is, too young to know what his parts are for.

o'DANIEL. Is it anybody is that young?

KINCAID. Stow it, Jenkins. Come on, don't pay no attention to him. He's feeling ugly today.

JENKINS. Well now, ain't you getting holier than a bloody bishop. Let him talk up for himself, if he don't like it.

KINCAID. Stow it, I say. You got no reason to crawl over Bill. Let him be.

BILLY. That's all right, Tom. I don't mind a joke. Black's the white of me eye, mates! *(All laugh except Jenkins)*

JENKINS. Mama taught you pretty manners, huh? Oh! Ain't got no mama, you say? Well now, think what that makes you! *(Laughs)*

BILLY. Tell me what you mean, Mister Jenkins.

PAYNE. What's gnawing your arse, Jenkins? Can't you see the boy's trying to be friendly?

JENKINS. You forgetting who's leading seaman here? Come on, Baby, talk back, why don't you? Scared?

BILLY. N-no. Why do you think I'd be scared, M-M-Mister Jenkins?

JENKINS. He stammers! What do you know! The little bastard's so scared he's stammering.

BILLY. Don't call me that again.

JENKINS. Sounds good, ha? Sounds fine. I like the way it rolls out your mouth. Bastard Baby Budd . . .

(Billy strikes him. Jenkins staggers and falls, pulls a knife and gets up, lunging at Billy. Payne, Butler and Kincaid get up and stand close to Billy, silently protecting him.)

JENKINS. Get away, God damn you! He's got to find out who gives orders here.

KINCAID. Not this time, Jenkins. Lay off.

o'DANIEL. Belay it. You're wearing me out, the pair of yous.

BUTLER. Put away the knife. *(Jenkins sees their determination and relaxes a little, uncertain what to do)*

BILLY. Will you shake hands? Or would you rather fight?

JENKINS. You little bas . . . (*Lunges forward. Billy catches his arm and bends it, holding Jenkins cursing and powerless*)

BILLY. That's enough, mate. Pipe down and let us be.

O'DANIEL. Good lad! Save the great strength is in you, Jenkins, for fighting the devil is after your soul.

JENKINS. All right, all right. You can let me go now.

O'DANIEL. Leave him go, lad. I won't hurt him at all.

BILLY. You're like Red Whiskers on the *Rights,* he liked to fight too. (*Freeing him*) Will you shake hands, mate?

JENKINS (*momentarily uncertain what to do*). Shake hands, is it? . . . Well, you beat me fair. You got guts, which is more than I give you credit for. (*They shake hands*)

KINCAID. You're a hell of a peacemaker, Bill.

PAYNE. That's the only time I ever hear Jenkins eating his own words.

O'DANIEL. Ah, that's a terrible diet, would make any man puke.

JENKINS. Don't you be getting any wrong ideas. I'm still a match for you!

KINCAID. Better belay your mess gear, Bill.

JENKINS. Where you come from, Baby?

PAYNE. Stow it! Jimmy-Legs! (*Billy goes on talking as Claggart enters*)

BILLY. I don't know, I guess from Portsmouth. I never lived ashore, that I can remember. Where do you come from? (*Drops a pot on deck. Claggart stands over him*)

CLAGGART. Handsomely done, young fellow, handsomely done. And handsome is as handsome did it, too. You can wipe that up, Jenkins. (*To Billy*) What is your name?

BILLY. Budd, sir. William Budd, ship *Rights of Man.*

CLAGGART. Your ship is *H.M.S. Indomitable* now.

BILLY. Aye, sir.

CLAGGART. You look sturdy. What was your station aboard the merchantman?

BILLY. M-m-mizzentopman, sir.

CLAGGART. You like that station?

BILLY. Aye, sir, well enough.

CLAGGART. How long have you been at sea?

BILLY. Ten years, sir, near as I can tell.

CLAGGART. Education?

BILLY. None, sir.

CLAGGART. So. You come aboard with nothing but your face to recommend you. Well, while beauty is always welcome, that alone may not avail us much against the French. There are other requirements in the service.

BILLY. I'll learn quickly, sir.

CLAGGART. The sea's a taskmaster, young fellow. It salts the sweetness out of boyish faces. You cannot tell what motion lies asleep in that flat water. Down where the manta drifts, and the shark and ray, storms wait for a wind while all the surface dazzles.

BILLY. I am a seaman, sir. I love the sea. I've hardly lived ashore.

CLAGGART. Then let the wind and sea have license to plunder at their will. As of today, a new maintopman swings between sky and water. (*He turns toward the ladder and notices the mess on deck*) I thought I asked you to wipe that up, Jenkins.

JENKINS. That's the messboy's job.

CLAGGART. Clean up, Jenkins. (*Jenkins hesitates*) That is an order. Turn to.

BILLY. I'll give you a hand, Jenkins. Come on.

CLAGGART. Ah, there. See how helpful Billy is. Why can't you take a leaf from this innocent young David's book, Jenkins? (*Turns away. Jenkins accidentally brushes against him and receives a savage cut from Claggart's rattan across his face*) Watch what you're doing, man!

JENKINS. I swear . . . !

CLAGGART. Yes, what is it that you swear? Well, speak. Nothing at all to say? Then hear me: I have my methods with unruly tempers.

(*On deck there is a loud crescendo scream and a crash. Running footsteps, shouts, voice calling for the Surgeon. The men surge toward the ladder.*)

CLAGGART. Stand fast! (*Squeak enters down the hatchway, whispers to Claggart*) All right, I know. (*Squeak comes down into the compartment and runs off*)

JENKINS. It's Jackson! I knew it, by God, I told you so!

(*Men turn to stare at Claggart as several*

sailors enter down the companionway, bearing the body of Jackson, inert and shattered. They carry him through the compartment and off to sick-bay.)

SURGEON *(as he moves through the compartment).* Clear the way, you men. Take him into the sick-bay, through here. Carry him gently. Easy, now. Easy. *(Exit)*

JENKINS *(pointing to Claggart).* He sent him back aloft. Killed him, he did!

O'DANIEL. Might as well have knifed him.

CLAGGART. Stand fast. Stop where you are. Your man Jackson is looked after.

O'DANIEL *(in a low voice).* Then he's a dead man surely.

CLAGGART. Who spoke?

JENKINS. We'll have a showdown now! After him, mates! Cut into him!

(The men move toward Claggart in a rush, drawing knives and cursing him, as Captain Vere appears in the companion hatchway.)

VERE. Stand fast! Hold where you are. Master-at-Arms, what is the matter here? *(The men stop in their tracks and stare at Vere, who comes part way down the ladder)*

CLAGGART. These dogs are out of temper, sir.

VERE *(to men).* You will come to attention when I address you! Let me remind you that this ship is at war. This is a wartime cruise, and this vessel sails under the Articles of War. Volunteer or 'pressed man, veteran seaman or recruit, you are no longer citizens, but sailors: a crew that I shall work into a weapon. One lawless act, one spurt of rebel temper from any man in this ship, high or low, I will pay out in coin you know of. You have but two duties: to fight and to obey, and I will bend each contumacious spirit, each stiff-necked prideful soul of you, or crush the spirit in you if I must. Abide by the Articles of War and my commands, or they will cut you down. Now: choose. *(The men are silent)* Very well. Master-at-Arms, this accident on deck, the sailor fallen from the yardarm. Do you know how it occurred?

CLAGGART. I do not, sir.

VERE. You are his messmates. Does any man of you know how this occurred? *(To Butler)* You?

BUTLER. No, sir.

VERE. Jenkins, do you?

JENKINS *(hesitates a moment. Claggart moves slightly, tapping his hand with the rattan).* No, sir.

VERE *(notices the cut on Jenkins' face).* What's this, what's this? Speak up, man. I want no random bloodshed aboard this ship.

JENKINS. I . . . fell, Captain. Fell, and . . . and cut my cheek.

VERE. I see. You fell. Master-at-Arms, you will excuse this man from duty till the Surgeon tends him.

CLAGGART. Aye, aye, sir.

VERE. We must not wound ourselves, draining the blood from enterprise that takes a whole man. *(He turns to go up the ladder and sees Billy)* Well. This is a new face. Who are you, boy?

CLAGGART. Maintopman 'pressed from the *Rights of Man* this morning, sir. William Budd.

VERE. Let him speak for himself. *(Billy tries to speak but can only stammer incoherently)* That's all right, boy, take your time. No need to be nervous.

BILLY. I saw a man go aloft, sir, as I came on board just a while ago. He looked sick, sir, he did. This officer was there, too, he can tell you. *(To Claggart)* Don't you remember, sir?

VERE. Did you send a sick man aloft, Master-at-Arms?

CLAGGART. I did not, sir.

VERE. Very well. *(To Billy)* Well, Budd. I hope you take to Navy life and duty without too much regret. We go to fight the French and shall need wits and hearts about us equal to the task.

BILLY. I'll do my best, sir.

VERE. I'm sure you will. We are all here to do our several duties, and though they may seem petty from one aspect, still they must all be done. The Admiral himself looks small and idle to the man like you who can see him from the maintop, threading his pattern on the quarterdeck. The Navy's only life. *(Surgeon enters)*

SURGEON. Captain—Jackson, the man who fell just now—he's dead, sir.

VERE *(after a pause).* Carry on, Master-at-Arms. *(He goes out up the companionway. Surgeon exits)*

CLAGGART. You've made a good impression on the Captain, Billy Budd. You have a pleasant way with you. If you wish to make a good impression on me, you will need to curb your tongue. Jenkins, I thought you were ordered to sick-bay. Jump to it. And I suggest you change that shirt. See how fouled it is with a peculiar stain. Why can't you keep clean like Billy here? *(He strikes Jenkins viciously on the arm with his rattan, smiles at him, and exits up the ladder)*

JENKINS. God damn his flaming soul! I can't stand it no more!

BILLY. I don't see what you can do, mate. He didn't mean it when he hurt you then.

JENKINS. Listen, boy, I know Jimmy-Legs. He lives on hurting people. Stay away from him, and keep your mouth shut, if you don't want trouble.

O'DANIEL. Did you hear the lad speak up to the skipper?

PAYNE. Aye, you watch your tongue, Bill. Claggart will be after you for talking up like that.

KINCAID. He's a cool one, Billy is. None of us got the nerve.

BUTLER. It's nerve gets a man in trouble in this tub.

DANSKER. Jimmy-Legs is down on you already, Billy.

BILLY. Down on me? Why he's friendly to me.

JENKINS. Claggart don't make no friends.

O'DANIEL. You seen Jackson when they brought him below. That's how friendly he gets. *(Bosun's pipe off)*

DUNCAN *(off)*. Relieve the watch!

KINCAID. First watch on the *Indomitable*, Bill. Better lay up to the mainmast and report. *(Exit)*

BUTLER. Don't slip off the yardarm.

PAYNE. Watch your step.

BILLY. Not me. You watch for me. Got to find the mainmast, and I'm in a hurry.

O'DANIEL. You'll never find your way in this old tub. I'll come along and show you. If anybody comes calling for O'Daniel while I'm out, take the message.

PAYNE. O'Daniel couldn't find his breeches if they wasn't buttoned on. You come with me. *(Billy and Payne go off)*

JENKINS. Poor bastard. I pity him, I do.

BUTLER. He's dead, ain't he? Better off than us.

JENKINS. Not Jackson. I mean the baby here. Billy.

BUTLER. We could have fared worse for a messmate.

JENKINS. Aye. He can take care of himself. Heave up the table.

SCENE TWO

SCENE: *In the early evening of the same day, the off-duty sections of the crew are mustered aft on the maindeck for Jackson's funeral. Above them Captain Vere stands uncovered at the forward break of the quarterdeck, reading the Committal Prayer. The westward sky is bright yellow and red, but fades into darkness as the scene progresses.*

The men are uncovered and stand at attention.

———

VERE. Unto Almighty God we commend the soul of our brother departed and we commit his body to the deep, in sure and certain hope of the resurrection unto Eternal Life, through our Lord Jesus Christ, at whose coming in glorious majesty to judge the world, the sea shall give up her dead, and the corruptible bodies of those who sleep in Him shall be changed and made like unto His glorious body according to the mighty working whereby He is able to subdue all things unto Himself. Amen.

MEN. Amen.

(Short drum-roll followed by a muffled splash as Jackson's body slips over the side. Then the bosun's pipe. Officers cover and march off.)

CLAGGART. Ship's company: Cover! Petty officers, dismiss your divisions.

VOICE *(off)*. Carpenters and gunners: Dismiss!

VOICE *(off)*. Afterguardsmen: Dismiss!

VOICE *(off)*. Fore, main, and mizzentopmen: Dismiss! *(The men break formation and go off, excepting Butler, Jenkins, Payne, Kincaid and Billy, who gather near the ratlines, at the rail)*

BUTLER. I suppose in this clear water you could see him go down for quite a way.

BILLY. We're moving slow in this calm.

JENKINS. There'll be wind enough before dawn.

BUTLER. And that's the end of Enoch Jackson. Over the side he goes, and his mates forget him.

JENKINS. Whatever's happened to Jackson, he ain't worried none. He's got a hundred fathoms over him to keep him warm and cosy.

BILLY. I'd rather be buried at sea than on the beach, when I come to die. Will you stand by the plank, Tom, so I'll shake a friendly hand before I sink? Oh! But it's dead I'll be then, come to think! (All laugh)

PAYNE. Don't you worry none. By that time, you won't give a sailmaker's damn.

KINCAID. It's only living makes sense to me, anyhow.

BILLY. Aye, I like to live. Even when it seems bad, there's a lot that's good in it.

JENKINS. Maybe for you, Bill. You wouldn't know trouble if it come up and spit in your eye.

BILLY. Don't you try now, mate! You might miss, and I got a clean jumper on!

PAYNE. That's the way to be, if you ask me. There's always trouble, if you know where to look for it.

BUTLER. You don't have to see nothing if you close your eyes.

KINCAID. When I close my eyes I sleep sound as a drunk marine.

BILLY. Aye, after I roll in my hammock, it's one, two, three, and I'm deep down under.

JENKINS. Well it's down under for me right now. Let's lay below.

KINCAID. Aye, we'll be on watch before long. Coming, Bill?

BILLY. I think I'll stay and watch the water for a while. I like to watch the sea at night.

JENKINS. Aye. It's deep and silent, and it can drown a man before he knows it.

BILLY. Sleep sound, mates. (All but Jenkins go down the companion hatchway)

JENKINS. Billy: stay clear of Jimmy-Legs.

(Jenkins exits down the hatchway. Billy is left alone staring over the side until Claggart enters. He does not see Billy, but stops near the quarterdeck ladder and gazes fixedly seaward.)

BILLY. Good evening, sir.

CLAGGART (startled, then subtly sarcastic). Good evening.

BILLY. Will it be all right if I stay topside a bit to watch the water?

CLAGGART. I suppose the Handsome Sailor may do many things forbidden to his messmates.

BILLY. Yes, sir. The sea's calm tonight, isn't it? Calm and peaceful.

CLAGGART. The sea's deceitful, boy: calm above, and underneath, a world of gliding monsters preying on their fellows. Murderers, all of them. Only the sharpest teeth survive.

BILLY. I'd like to know about such things, as you do, sir.

CLAGGART. You're an ingenuous sailor, Billy Budd. Is there, behind that youthful face, the wisdom pretty virtue has need of? Even the gods must know their rivals, boy; and Christ had first to recognize the ills before he cured 'em.

BILLY. What, sir?

CLAGGART. Never mind. But tell me this: how have you stomach to stand here and talk to me? Are you so innocent and ignorant of what I am? You know my reputation. Jenkins and the rest are witnesses, and certainly you've heard them talking to me. Half of them would knife me in the back some night and do it gladly; Jenkins is thinking of it. Doubtless he'll try one day. How do you dare, then? Have you not intelligence enough to be afraid of me? To hate me as all the others do?

BILLY. Why should I be afraid of you, sir? You speak to me friendly when we meet. I know some of the men . . . are fearful of you, sir, but I can't believe they're right about it.

CLAGGART. You're a fool, fellow. In time, you'll learn to fear me like the rest. Young you are, and scarcely used to the fit of your man's flesh.

BILLY. I know they're wrong, sir. You aren't like they say. Nobody could be so.

CLAGGART. So . . . ? So what, boy? Vicious, did you mean to say, or brutal? But they aren't wrong, and you would see it, but for those blue eyes that light so kindly on your fellow men.

BILLY. Oh, I've got no education, I know that. There must be a lot of things a man misses when he's ignorant. But learning's hard. Must be sort of lonely, too.

CLAGGART. What are you prating of, half-man, half-child? Your messmates crowd around, admire your yellow hair and your blue eyes, do tricks and favors for you out of love, and you talk about loneliness!

BILLY. I just noticed the way you were

looking off to leeward as I came up, sir. Kind of sad, you were looking.

CLAGGART. Not sadness, boy. Another feeling, more like . . . pleasure. That's it. I can feel it now, looking at you. A certain . . . pleasure.

BILLY (*flattered*). Thank you, sir.

CLAGGART (*annoyed at Billy's incomprehension*). Pah.

BILLY. Just talking with you, sir, I can tell they're wrong about you. They're ignorant, like me.

CLAGGART. Compliment for compliment, eh, boy? Have you no heart for terror, fellow? You've seen this stick in use. Have you not got sense and spleen and liver to be scared, even to be cowardly?

BILLY. No, sir, I guess not. I like talking to you, sir. But please, sir, tell me something.

CLAGGART. I wonder if I can. Well, ask it.

BILLY. Why do you want us to believe you're cruel, and not really like everybody else?

CLAGGART. I think you are the only child alive who wouldn't understand if I explained; or else you'd not believe it.

BILLY. Oh, I'd believe you, sir. There's much I could learn from you: I never knew a man like you before.

CLAGGART (*slowly*). Do you—like me, Billy Budd?

BILLY. You've always been most pleasant with me, sir.

CLAGGART. Have I?

BILLY. Yes, sir. In the mess, the day I came aboard? And almost every day you have a pleasant word.

CLAGGART. And what I have said tonight, are these pleasant words?

BILLY. Yes, sir. I was wondering . . . could I talk to you between watches, when you've nothing else to do?

CLAGGART. You're a plausible boy, Billy. Aye, the nights are long, and talking serves to pass them.

BILLY. Thank you, sir. That would mean a lot to me.

CLAGGART. Perhaps to me as well (*Drops his rattan. Billy picks it up and hands it back to him. Claggart stares at it a moment, then at Billy*) No. No! Charm me, too, would you! Get away!

BILLY (*surprised and puzzled*). Aye, sir. (*He exits down the hatchway. After a pause in which Claggart recovers his self-control Squeak appears*)

CLAGGART (*without turning*). Come here. I thought I told you to put that new seaman Budd on report. Why was it not done?

SQUEAK. I tried, Mister Claggart, sir. I couldn't find nothing out of place. Gear all stowed perfect.

CLAGGART. Then disarrange it. You know the practice. I want him on report.

SQUEAK. Two of his messmates is ones nearly caught me at it before.

CLAGGART. Then be more careful. Now get along and see you make out something. (*Squeak scurries off belowdecks as Vere comes into sight on the quarterdeck*)

VERE. Master-at-Arms. What is that man doing above decks?

CLAGGART. Ship's corporal, sir. A routine report.

VERE. There is nothing in this ship of so routine a nature that I do not concern myself in it. Remember that.

CLAGGART. Aye, aye, sir. With your permission, sir. (*Exit. Vere walks along the deck and scans the sails as Seymour enters*)

SEYMOUR. Fine evening, sir.

VERE. Yes, a fine evening, Seymour. How is the glass?

SEYMOUR. Falling, I believe, sir. I think we'll toss a little before morning. Well, I suppose I should be in my cabin inspecting the deck logs.

VERE. Stay for a moment, Seymour. In the days and nights to come, you and I will not often have an opportunity to stand easy and talk.

SEYMOUR. Aye, sir. I expect the French will put us to our stations any hour now.

VERE. Are you impressed by omens, Seymour? This seaman we've just buried: I think of him as an omen of some sort, a melancholy prologue to this voyage.

SEYMOUR. Aye, sir. Hard on the sailor, certainly, but that's the service. But we've been lucky in other ways. An accident, now, that's unavoidable.

VERE. It was more than an accident, Seymour.

SEYMOUR. This maintop sailor? How do you mean, sir?

VERE. The man was sent aloft sick, by the Master-at-Arms, contrary to my standing order. Budd, the new seaman, implied as much, and the maintop watch confirmed it. The Master-at-Arms lied to me.

SEYMOUR. What are you going to do, sir? What action can you take? He's a valuable man, one we can hardly do without as things are now.

VERE. I shall do nothing at present, only wait and observe him. No court-martial could do more than strip him of his rank for such misconduct. I will let him have his head until some act puts him squarely counter to the law, then let the law consume him.

SEYMOUR. Why trouble the natural order to no purpose? Shouldn't we let it be?

VERE. Must a man always shrug, let things alone and drift? Would to God I could take this power of mine and break him now, smash all the laws to powder and be a man again.

SEYMOUR. We must serve the law, sir, or give up the right and privilege of service. It's how we live.

VERE. Live? Oh, you're right. Below this deck are men who at a call skip on the hurling spars against the wind, at Beat-to-quarters run as if they willed it. Yet each of us steps alone within this pattern, this formal movement centered on itself. Men live and die, taken by pattern, born to it, knowing nothing. No man can defy the code we live by and not be broken by it.

SEYMOUR. You are the Captain, sir. You maintain that code.

VERE. Keep an order we cannot understand. That's true. The world demands it: demands that at the back of every peacemaker there be the gun, the gallows and the gaol. I talk of justice, and would turn the law gentle for those who serve here; but a Claggart stands in my shadow, for I need him. So the world goes, wanting not justice, but order . . . to be let alone to hug its own iniquities. Let a man work to windward of that law and he'll be hove down. No hope for him, none. (Enter Wyatt)

WYATT. Eight o'clock report, sir. Ship inspected and all in order.

SEYMOUR. Very well, carry on. (Wyatt goes off) By your leave sir. Good night. (Exit. Vere remains, crosses to the hatch and looks down, then slowly upward at the set of the sails)

SCENE THREE

SCENE: *The maindeck several nights later.*

Four bells is struck offstage. A sailor climbs wearily down the ratlines, drops to the deck and goes below. Claggart stands by the larboard rail.

As Billy enters from below decks, he sees the Master-at-Arms.

BILLY. Hello, sir. (*Claggart looks at him without answering, then turns and goes off forward. The Dansker follows Billy up onto the deck*) Well, that's all there is to tell, Dansker. I always lash my hammock just so, and stow my gear same as all the others. They don't get in trouble.

DANSKER. Mister Claggart is down upon you, Billy.

BILLY. Jimmy-Legs? Why he calls me the sweet and pleasant fellow, they tell me.

DANSKER. Does he so, Baby lad? Aye, a sweet voice has Mister Claggart.

BILLY. For me he has. I seldom pass him but there comes a pleasant word.

DANSKER. And that's because he's down upon you.

BILLY. But he's my friend. I know he talks a little strange, but he's my friend.

DANSKER. Nobody's friend is Jimmy-Legs. Yours the least of all, maybe. Lay aloft, Baby. You'll be late to relieve your watch.

BILLY. Aye, Dansker. (*He climbs up the ratlines out of sight. The Dansker watches him go. Claggart appears, but the Dansker ignores him and goes off aft. As Jenkins comes into view climbing down the ratlines, Claggart gestures off and fades into a shadowy corner of the deck near the quarterdeck ladder. Squeak enters as Jenkins drops to the deck, and intercepts him as he starts down the companionway*)

SQUEAK. It's all right, mate, slack off and stay a bit.

JENKINS. What do you want? I pick my own company.

SQUEAK. So does I, mate, so does I. And if I may make so bold to say it, you'll be smarter to pick your company more careful.

JENKINS. If you got something to say to me, talk up, else I'll get below.

SQUEAK. Don't be hasty, now, mate, don't be in a sweat. It's haste gets good men into trouble. What d'you think of our new hand here, Billy Boy? Mister Claggart's taken with him, too. Fine young fellow, ha?

JENKINS. Talk plain. What d'you mean?

SQUEAK. I overheard him talking just this day. Would maybe surprise you some, what he had to say about yourself and a few other lads.

JENKINS. What?

SQUEAK. Aoh, bit of talk about his messmates. He don't fancy us! Not like his feather boys aboard the merchantman.

JENKINS. You lying cut-throat, try something else! Billy's in my mess; since he come on board he's rare been out of my sight. You're lying, you bloody mark! I know you too well. You'll need to try some other way to get Bill into trouble. Get away, and don't come lying to me no more.

SQUEAK. Aoh, so it's that friendly you are! Well, now, ain't that sweet! You're not smart, Jenkins. Remember, man: I tried to help you out. When you're feeling the cat between your shoulders . . .

JENKINS (seizing him). Damn your lies! Get back to Jimmy-Legs and kiss his butt. And stay out of my way! (Throws Squeak down and exits. Squeak watches him go. Claggart steps out of the shadows)

CLAGGART. I heard your little talk. You lack subtlety; but I'm the greater fool to use you in these matters. You're inept.

SQUEAK. Aoh! Why don't you do it yourself, if you don't need me!

CLAGGART. I need nobody, least of all a rum-soaked footpad from the Old Bailey. If you wish to have free rein with your distasteful habits, mind your cockney manners! I stand between you and the flogging whip. Improve your style, or you stand tomorrow forenoon at the gratings!

SQUEAK. I only meant as you could do it better, Mister Claggart, I wouldn't say nothing to . . .

CLAGGART (cuts him on the arm with his rattan). Don't touch me!—Keep Budd in petty troubles, that you can do. Unlash his hammock. Keep him on report. In time I'll let you know what plans I have for him. Get aft! (Squeak, eager to get away, scuttles aft as the Dansker enters) Well, old man. Moon's in and out tonight. There's weather somewhere. (The Dans-

ker turns down the night lamp over the cabin door and starts off) Stay and have a pipe.

DANSKER. I have the watch.

CLAGGART. You take your duties as seriously as ever.

DANSKER. Aye. They are all of life for an old seaman like me. (Turns to go)

CLAGGART. You move away from me as though I were some kind of stalking beast. You avoid me, too.

DANSKER. Your word, John, "too."

CLAGGART. You know what I mean. The hands detest me. You are a hand, older than most, and older in your hatred, I have no doubt. But why, man? You at least should see me as I am, a man who knows how the world's made: made as I am.

DANSKER. How can I know what goes on in your head?

CLAGGART. The enigmatic Dansker. Come, it's dark, we can drop disguises when night serves to hold the disclosing soul apart.

DANSKER. You know who you remind me of . . . maintopman: Billy Budd.

CLAGGART. More enigmas! That sunny, smiling infant with no spleen nor knowledge in his head?

DANSKER. I'll leave you now.

CLAGGART. No, stay a while. This is a night for secrets and disclosures.

DANSKER. You have half the truth and Billy Budd the other. He can't see there's evil in the world, and you won't see the good.

CLAGGART. So. And I take it you come in between.

DANSKER. I keep outside. I am too old to stand between sky and water.

CLAGGART. And yet you hate me, too.

DANSKER. I hate an incomplete man.

CLAGGART. Damn all this talk. Hate me and have done. Let it alone, I say. Whatever else it is, this thing is Man, still!

DANSKER. I'll be off.

CLAGGART. Don't go. The moon's gone under. Let us talk this out. You are a wise man in your senile way.

DANSKER. Then take this for all my wisdom. You recognize the hatred of your shipmates as an honor paid to a soul they cannot understand. Your fine contempt for human love is nothing but regret.

CLAGGART. Stop there. I know the rest by heart. Nothing you say to me but clatters in my belly, watch on watch. Aye: when this arm moves out in gesture of love, it mocks me with a blow. Who lifts this arm? What officer commands this hireling flesh? Somewhere below the farthest marks and deeps, God anchors hearts, and his sea rusts mine hollow. The flukes break in the bottom, and I slack and stand, go in and out forever at God's humor. Look at this sea: for all her easy swell, who knows what bones, ribs and decay are fathomed at her base and move in her motion, so that on the flattest water, the very stricture of the dead can kill that beauty with a dance of death?—Here is a man. He holds, past fathom curves, drowned fleets of human agonies that gesture when the long tide pulls.

DANSKER. Aye, John. But you must know that other men are moved so. Look up some evening at the quarterdeck for another poor thoughtful devil like you, like me, pacing all night between his doubts.

CLAGGART. What, Vere? That fine-drawn manner doesn't deceive me. There's a whited sepulchre, like all soft-spoken charmers of this world.

DANSKER. You don't believe in anything besides yourself, eh John?

CLAGGART. I've said what I have said. I know myself, and look to that. You should try it. Go to your post, old man, and your ever-lasting duties. (*Claggart turns away. Billy scrambles into view down the ratlines and calls out excitedly*)

BILLY. Quarterdeck ho!

RATCLIFFE (*coming forward to the forward break of the quarterdeck*). Sound off!

BILLY. Strange sail one mile off the larboard beam!

CLAGGART (*to Dansker*). A Frenchman! Get to your station.

RATCLIFFE (*on the quarterdeck ladder*). Mister Duncan! Sound Beat-to-quarters! Clear for action!

DUNCAN (*offstage*). Aye aye, sir!

RATCLIFFE. Gardiner! (*Enter Gardiner*)

GARDINER. Sir?

RATCLIFFE. Report to the Captain, strange sail on the larboard beam. Then send Payne to the wheel. (*Exit Gardiner*) Master-at-Arms, send a man to the mast to relay lookout's reports. Inspect battle stations and report to me when they are fully manned.

CLAGGART. Aye aye, sir. (*Exit*)

VOICE (*off*). She's a French frigate! Steering east by south! (*Enter Vere and Seymour*)

VERE. Prepare to make chase. Have your quartermaster steer small.

RATCLIFFE. Aye aye, sir.
(*Enter the Drummer and sound Beat-to-quarters. Men run on, to gun stations, rigging, crossing stage and off.*)

SEYMOUR. She's too fast for us, sir. We'll never come up with her.

VERE. We are bound to try, though we were sure to fail. And we may smell powder before this chase is over.

CLAGGART (*re-entering*). Battle stations fully manned, sir!

SEYMOUR. May we try a shot at her now?

VERE. She's drawing south. Yes, commence firing, Mr. Seymour.

SEYMOUR. Larboard battery, fire one!

DUNCAN. Fire! (*Fire one gun*)

VERE. Fire at will!

SEYMOUR. Fire at will!
(*Guns fire dissynchronously.*)

ACT TWO

SCENE ONE

SCENE: *The quarterdeck and part of the maindeck a few minutes before 0800. A high wind. On the quarterdeck are Lieutenant Wyatt, Midshipman Rea and the helmsman, Stoll.*

REA. I'm glad this watch is over. I'm tired.

WYATT. Make your entry in the log before your relief comes up. Bring it out here and I'll sign it.

REA. Aye, sir. What was our last position, do you remember?

WYATT. Thirteen ten west, forty-three forty north.

REA. And an easterly breeze.

WYATT. Aye, make it so. That'll make Ratcliffe happy. Last time he had an east wind, she blew his hat over the side. And put down "Running ground swell."

REA. Aye aye, sir. (*Exits*)

WYATT. Helmsman, keep her close-hauled.

STOLL. I can't, sir. Too much cloth in the wind.

WYATT. Well hold her close as you can, and let the next watch reef sail if they like.

STOLL. Aye aye, sir. *(Enter Ratcliffe)*

WYATT. Morning, Johnny! You're on time!

RATCLIFFE. What's the course?

WYATT. Steady south. Wind's easterly. Glass is dropping.

RATCLIFFE. East wind? Damn it. *(Enter Byren, the relief helmsman)* By the way, you forgot to sign the order book.

WYATT. All right. Thanks.

STOLL. I've been relieved, sir. Byren has the helm.

WYATT. Very well. *(Exit Stoll)* Who's mate of your watch?

RATCLIFFE. The Admiralty midshipman. That lobcock Gardiner, hang him. *(Eight bells)*

WYATT. Where the devil is he? It's eight. *(Enter Rea and Gardiner separately, meeting)*

RATCLIFFE. There he comes. He looks happy. That means trouble for some poor devil. *(Gardiner snatches the log out of Rea's hands and bounds up to the quarter-deck)*

REA. I've been relieved, sir. Horatio, Lord Gardiner has the watch.

WYATT. Ah, Midshipman Gardiner. The backbone of the British Navy.

RATCLIFFE. The backside, if you ask me.

WYATT. All right, Rea. You can turn in. *(Rea exits)*

RATCLIFFE. Pity we lost that Frenchman last night. A little action would season the monotony of these interminable watches.

WYATT. Did you ever hear of a ship-of-the-line running down a frigate, even with the wind? Ah, it's a magnificent morning! Thickening overcast, heavy ground swell, a fresh levanter breeze, and you, Johnny, are the Pride of the Morning!

RATCLIFFE. Mmmm. Has the skipper been on deck yet?

WYATT. Not since sunrise. He came up then and paced the deck and stared off east like a sleepwalker. Then went below again without a word.

RATCLIFFE. He thinks too much.

WYATT. Well if you ever make captain, your crew won't have that to complain of, anyway. Am I relieved?

RATCLIFFE. Yes, I relieve you. *(Tosses his cap to Wyatt)* Here. Take this below, will you?

WYATT. What? You'll be out of uniform, man. Mister Gardiner wouldn't approve of your standing watch without a hat, would you, Midshipman Gardiner?

GARDINER. Sir, the Articles state that officers on watch . . .

RATCLIFFE. Well hang it, I lost twelve shillings the last time my hat went over the rail, and this is the only other one I've got. To hell with the Articles.

WYATT. Mind your language! It's downright mutinous. Well, don't expect me to stand your watches if you catch your death of cold. Good morning. *(Exit)*

GARDINER. Midshipman Rea, sir, I don't like to say it, but his log entries are impossible.

RATCLIFFE. Then enter yourself, Mister Gardiner. So are you.

GARDINER. Yes sir. But I do think he ought to be told . . .

RATCLIFFE. Go find the Captain and report to him the wind's abeam. Respectfully suggest we ought to take in topsails.

GARDINER. Aye aye, sir. *(Goes down stairs)*

RATCLIFFE. And don't forget to tell him I haven't got a hat.

GARDINER. What's that, sir?

RATCLIFFE. Nothing, sir! You got my order. Dump your ballast and shove off.

GARDINER. I thought you spoke to me, sir.

RATCLIFFE. I avoid that whenever possible. Move!

GARDINER. Yes, sir.

RATCLIFFE. Ye gods, what a brat. Nothing off, helmsman. She's well enough thus.

BYREN. Nothing off, sir.

GARDINER *(nearly bumping into Vere as he emerges from cabin, followed by Seymour and Hallam)*. Atten-tion!

RATCLIFFE. Good morning, sir.

VERE. Morning, Mister Ratcliffe.

GARDINER *(starting after Vere, bumps into Hallam)*. Damn it, man, watch what you're doing!

VERE. Midshipman Gardiner.

GARDINER. Sir?

VERE. How long, pray, have you been in this ship, or any ship?

GARDINER. This is my first cruise, sir.

VERE. Your first cruise. A wartime cruise as well. And you are a midshipman. A midshipman, Mister Gardiner, let me tell you, is neither fish, flesh, nor fowl, and certainly no seaman. You're a salt-water hermaphrodite, Mister Gardiner. And unless you have a mind to be generally known as Spit-kit Gardiner, I recommend more tolerance toward the men. Now, is that clear?

GARDINER. Aye aye, sir!

VERE. Very well, you may carry on.

RATCLIFFE. We've a weather helm, sir, and bow seas.

VERE. Take in topsails, if you please, Mister Ratcliffe.

RATCLIFFE. Aye aye, sir. Mister Duncan!

DUNCAN *(enters)*. Aye, sir?

RATCLIFFE. Douse your topsails and topgallants. Haul in the weather braces.

DUNCAN. Aye aye, sir. *(Exit)* Away aloft! Hands by topgallant sheets and halyards!

GARDINER. Aloft there! Keep fast the weather sheets till the yards are down, da . . . if you please!

RATCLIFFE. Get aloft yourself, Mister Gardiner, see they do it right, since you're not satisfied.

GARDINER. Sir, the Articles state that . . .

RATCLIFFE. Did you hear me?

GARDINER. Aye aye, sir. *(Exits up ratlines)*

DUNCAN *(off)*. Haul tort!

VERE. You disapprove of Gardiner, Mister Ratcliffe?

RATCLIFFE. He seems to think he's the only midshipman aboard capable of doing anything properly. He's always looking at you as if your hat weren't squared.

VERE. That is an unfortunate simile under the present circumstances.

RATCLIFFE *(caught)*. Oh, I—er— Keep her close to the wind, helmsman. Don't fall away!

DUNCAN *(off)*. Let go topgallant bowlines!

VERE. I think Gardiner has had enough correction for one day. Call him down to our level, Mister Ratcliffe.

RATCLIFFE. Aye, sir. Mister Gardiner! You may come off your perch now! *(Billy descends rigging and starts offstage)* What do you think of our new man Budd, Captain?

SEYMOUR. That boy did a smart piece of work for us last night, sir. He's the nimblest man on the tops I've ever watched. Wyatt wants him for captain of the foretop.

VERE. Very well, let Budd take the post. He certainly deserves it for his actions last night during the chase. I'll speak to him myself.

SEYMOUR. He'll like hearing it from you, sir.

VERE. Hallam, go call Budd, the lad moving forward there. *(Exit Hallam. Gardiner appears, looking sick)* Well done, Gardiner. You may lay below and draw an extra tot of rum. You look . . . chilly.

GARDINER. Thank you, sir. *(Exit)*

SEYMOUR. By the way, sir, Budd has been on the Master-at-Arms' report once or twice for some petty misdemeanor. Nothing serious. *(Steps aside with Ratcliffe. Billy enters, followed by Hallam)*

BILLY. You sent for me, sir?

VERE. Yes, Budd. Your division officer recommends you for a post of more responsibility. He thinks you can perform duties of a higher station, and so do I, after last night. So I've agreed that you shall have Williams' place on the foretop.

BILLY. But—Williams is captain of the foretop, sir.

VERE. The station calls for a younger man. Lieutenant Wyatt asked for you, and the spirit you showed last night warrants it. That is a real honor for a man so new on board.

BILLY. The Navy's new to me, Captain, but I hardly know anything else but the sea and ships.

VERE. And how do you like us, now that the awesomeness has worn away a bit?

BILLY. The Navy's a bustling world, sir. Bigger than the *Rights of Man,* and I get lost sometimes. But my mates lend me a hand. Why even Jimmy-Legs—beg pardon, sir, the Master-at-Arms, I mean—he's good to me, too.

VERE. The sea and the Navy exact a discipline, but it need not be a harsh one. In some ways I envy the man who dances across the tops and seems to rule the ship and sea below. Up there is a pleach of ropes for you to make a world of. Though winds have their way with tackle of your world, you live at ease against your strength and the round bole of the mast in your back. You are a king up there, while the water curds and frolics at the forefoot. I envy you that stance.

BILLY. You can trust me, Captain.

VERE. I do, boy. Very well, that's all.

BILLY. Aye aye, sir. Thank you, sir, thank you! *(Runs off)*

VERE. Hallam, find the Master-at-Arms and bid him report to me.

HALLAM. Aye aye, sir. *(Exit. Seymour joins Vere)*

VERE. If I had a son, I'd hope for one like Budd.

SEYMOUR. Aye, sir. Fine boy. He's a force for order in this ship, certainly. I hope his charm's contagious.

VERE. One such is enough. Men cannot stand very much perfection. It's a disease that we stamp out at its first rash showing. *(Enter Claggart. Seymour withdraws)* Master-at-Arms, I want to make a change on the Watch, Quarter and Station Bill. I needn't have troubled you about it until later, but I am especially interested in this change.

CLAGGART. The time of day is indifferent to me, sir.

VERE. Williams, present captain of the foretop, is assigned to the afterguard. I am replacing him with Budd.

CLAGGART. William Budd, sir? You do not mean the so-called Handsome Sailor?

VERE. Aye, William Budd, the new seaman from the *Rights of Man.*

CLAGGART. I know him, sir.

VERE. Do you find anything unusual in this replacement?

CLAGGART. You must be aware, sir, that he is . . .

VERE. Well? That he is what? I know he's an able seaman.

CLAGGART. Nothing, sir. But I wondered if he were entirely trustworthy. He has been aboard such a brief time.

VERE. Long enough to prove himself to me, and to his shipmates.

CLAGGART. Very good, sir.

VERE. He is captain of the foretop. That is all.

CLAGGART. With your permission, sir. Will there not be some dissatisfaction among the foretopmen who have been aboard much longer than Budd?

VERE. Master-at-Arms: I concern myself with these matters. They are none of your function. Until such time as the senior topmen formally object to Budd for incapacity, he is captain of the foretop. Make it so on the Bill. *(Exit)*

RATCLIFFE. What are you waiting for, man? Light to dawn? Promotion? You got the order.

CLAGGART. With your permission, sir. *(As Claggart goes off, Ratcliffe spits over the rail.)*

SCENE TWO

SCENE: *Forward part of the deck. Night. Eight bells. A man descends the rigging and goes off. Claggart enters, stands by the hatch for a moment, then exits forward. Billy comes down off watch, drops to the deck and remains in shadow, leaning over the rail, looking seaward. Jenkins stealthily and silently comes up from below deck.*

———

BILLY. Jenkins! What you doing topside . . . *(Jenkins puts his hand over Billy's mouth)*

JENKINS *(in a whisper).* Stow the noise! *(Releases Billy)*

BILLY. You're after Mister Claggart, like you said you would!

JENKINS. Well? What about it? You try and stop me?

BILLY. He knows, Jenkins! I tell you, he knows! He's ready for you!

JENKINS. Then by God, I'll oblige him! I been waiting up here every night, waiting for him to come by when it's dark. Now get away and let me do it!

BILLY. No! I won't let you hang yourself!

JENKINS. I don't give a fiddler's damn what happens to me! Move out of my way, mate!

BILLY. No! Give me the knife.

JENKINS. The knife's for Claggart. You're a nice boy, Bill, but I ain't playing with you. You get away below, quick. This game ain't for boys.

BILLY. Damme, no, Jenkins! You'll hang yourself!

JENKINS. Take your hands off! The moon's under, I can do it now! Oh, sweet mother of God, leave me go!

BILLY. No!

JENKINS. Yes, by God! *(Jenkins strikes Billy; struggle, in which Billy wrests knife from Jenkins, and it falls on desk. Billy knocks Jenkins down.)*

CLAGGART *(offstage).* What's that noise? Stand where you are! *(Entering)* You again! Well? Explain this pageant.

BILLY. He . . . I had to hit him, sir. He struck at me.

CLAGGART. Mm. And drew that knife on you, too, no doubt.

BILLY. Yes, sir.

CLAGGART. I have been waiting, forward there, for Jenkins. You intercepted him, I take it.

BILLY. I didn't know you were looking for him, sir.

CLAGGART. You shouldn't meddle, my fine young friend, in matters that don't concern you! I was expecting him. *(Enter Dansker)* There, help the body up. I do not thank you, boy, for cheating me of the pleasure of his punishment.

WYATT *(offstage)*. What's the disturbance there? You, forward on the spardeck!

CLAGGART. Master-at-Arms reports all in order, sir!

WYATT *(offstage)*. Stand where you are.

CLAGGART. The sweet and pleasant fellow saved you, Jenkins. But I reserve you still for my own justice in due time. Say nothing to this officer. *(Enter Wyatt)*

WYATT. What's the matter, Master-at-Arms? It's an odd hour for star-gazing.

CLAGGART. A slight matter, sir. I found these two men together here on deck, contrary to the Captain's orders. I was sending them below when you called out.

WYATT. Oh, is that all. Carry on, then.

CLAGGART. Aye aye, sir. Now then, get below, both of you. *(Enter Vere followed by Hallam. The Dansker goes off)* Attention!

VERE. Wyatt, what's this mean?

WYATT. Two men on deck without permission, sir.

VERE. Is there no more to this? The story's lame, man. What occurred? *(Silence)* Very well, then. Go along, both of you.

BILLY. Aye aye, sir. Come along, mate. *(Exits with Jenkins)*

VERE. Your knife, Master-at-Arms?

CLAGGART. William Budd's, sir, I believe.

VERE. Return it to him. *(Exits with Hallam and Wyatt)*

(Claggart raps rail with rattan. Squeak approaches warily.)

CLAGGART. Listen carefully; you may make up for your late mistake if you do this smartly. Give Budd just time enough to get to sleep. At four bells wake him. Bring him to the lee forechains. You understand?

SQUEAK. Mister Claggart, sir . . we

done enough to him. He's a good lad, Mister Claggart. Couldn't it be somebody else? Jenkins, maybe?

CLAGGART. So. He's softened your heart too, eh? Do as you're ordered, man, or I'll see your back laid raw with a flogging whip! Remember: I will be watching you. Bring him to the lee forechains. And when you're there . . .

SQUEAK. Dansker. Moving forward.

CLAGGART. Step back, you fool. Wait for me.

(Exit Squeak. The Dansker enters.)

DANSKER. Baby saved you, eh? And you are angry.

CLAGGART. Saved me, you say? From what? I've tried to tempt Jenkins to this blow, so as to break his toplofty spirit with his neck; and I am "saved" by that guileless idiot! He'd turn the other cheek to me, in Christian kindness! Well, there's a second pleasure in striking that same face twice. I can destroy him, too, if I choose to do it!

DANSKER. Crazy, crazy!

CLAGGART. All right, old man, call it madness then. Whatever its name, it will plunder the sweetness from that face, or it will kill us both.

DANSKER. You are afraid of him.

CLAGGART. Afraid? Of Budd? What nonsense is that?

DANSKER. He usurps the crew; they turn from hating you to loving him, and leave you impotent.

CLAGGART. That bastard innocent frighten me! That witless kindness that spills from him has neither force nor aim. Stand out from between us, or you founder together, sink in five hundred fathoms with him, if I want it so!

DANSKER. Aye, then, if you take that tack, let it be both of us. You expect me to sit by and watch your deliberate arm seize him and force him under?

CLAGGART. Why not? You have always done that. I thought your practice was to stay outside. What breeds the saintly knight errant in you?

DANSKER. I am old, but I have some manhood left.

CLAGGART. What can you do? You've drifted with the tide too long, old one. You are as involved as I am now.

DANSKER. So you may say. In this ship a man lives as he can, and finds a way to make life tolerable for himself. I did so.

That was a fault. But no longer.

CLAGGART. Stand clear. You haven't courage to cross me.

DANSKER. Eh, I'm not afraid of you; I see your scheme.

CLAGGART. Damn your feeble, ineffectual eyes! *(Striking him; the Dansker falls)* You can see only what I let you see!

DANSKER. Say what you like. I see your scheme; so will Captain if need be.

CLAGGART *(pulling him to his feet).* Take a warning for yourself, old man. And keep away! You are on watch, eh? Well, go back to sleep again, or I'll report you. *(Dansker exits. Claggart watches him go, then violently breaks his rattan and throws the pieces over the side.)*

Scene Three

SCENE: *Forward part of the main deck. Four bells. Claggart stands with one hand on the rail, waiting. After a short pause, hearing a sound, he fades into shadow. Squeak enters, bending over and running.*

———

SQUEAK. Hsssssssssst! *(Billy, sleepy and rubbing his eyes, enters)*

BILLY. You brought me all the way up here, out of my hammock. Now what do you want?

SQUEAK. I heard you're captain of the foretop, Bill. That right?

BILLY. Aye. What's that to do with you?

SQUEAK. Ah, now you can be more use to your shipmates then ever you was before.

BILLY. What?

SQUEAK. You was impressed, now, weren't you? Well, so was I. We're not the only impressed ones, Billy. There's a gang of us. Could you help . . . at a pinch?

BILLY. What do you mean?

SQUEAK. See here . . . *(Holds up two coins)* Here's two gold guineas for you, Bill. Put in with us. Most of the men aboard are only waiting for a word, and they'll follow you. There's more for you where these come from. What d'you say? If you join us, Bill, there's not a man aboard won't come along! Are you with us? The ship'll be ours when we're ready to take it!

BILLY. Damme, I don't know what you're driving at, but you had better go

where you belong! *(Squeak, surprised, does not move. Billy springs up)* If you don't start, I'll toss you back over the rail! *(Squeak decamps. Billy watches him and starts off himself. Dansker, offstage, calls out)*

DANSKER. Hallo, what's the matter? *(Enters)* Ah, Beauty, is it you again? Something must have been the matter, for you stammered. *(Claggart appears and comes forward)*

CLAGGART. You seem to favor the maindeck, Billy Budd. What brings you topside at this hour, man, against my orders and the Captain's?

BILLY. I . . . found an afterguardsman in our part of the ship here, and I bid him be off where he belongs.

DANSKER. And is that all you did about it, boy?

BILLY. Aye, Dansker, nothing more.

CLAGGART. A strange sort of hour to police the deck. Name the afterguardsman.

BILLY. I . . . can't say, Mister Claggart. I couldn't see him clear enough.

DANSKER. Don't be a fool, speak up, accuse him.

CLAGGART. Well?

BILLY. I can't say, sir.

CLAGGART. You refuse? Then get below, and stay where you belong.

BILLY. Aye aye, sir. Good night, sir. Good night, Dansker. *(Exits)*

CLAGGART. I'm glad you saw this mutinous behavior.

DANSKER. Your crazy brain squeezes out false conclusions. He has done nothing except find you out, though he's too innocent to know it.

CLAGGART. I am not hoodwinked by his weak excuse. What else would he be doing at this hour, but fanning rebel tempers like his own?

DANSKER. I stood in the shadows forward when your pander Squeak slipped by me, running from this place. You set him on, on purpose to trap Billy.

CLAGGART. And I will do that, old man. But you will say nothing about it; see you don't. *(Enter Vere followed by Hallam)*

VERE. Well, Master-at-Arms? You stand long watches.

CLAGGART. Sir. May I take the liberty of reserving my explanation for your private ear. I believe your interest in this matter would incline you to prefer some privacy.

VERE *(to Dansker and Hallam).* Leave

us. Hallam, stand within hail. *(Dansker and Hallam go off)* Well? What is it you wish to say, Master-at-Arms?

CLAGGART. During my rounds this night, I have seen enough to convince me that one man aboard, at least, is dangerous; especially in a ship which musters some who took a guilty part in the late serious uprisings . . .

VERE. You may spare a reference to that.

CLAGGART. Your pardon, sir. Quite lately I have begun to notice signs of some sort of movement secretly afoot, and prompted by the man in question. I thought myself not warranted, so long as this suspicion was only indistinct, in reporting it. But recently . . .

VERE. Come to the point, man.

CLAGGART. Sir, I deeply feel the cruel responsibility of making a report involving such serious consequences to the sailor mainly concerned. But God forbid, sir, that this ship should suffer the experience of the Nore.

VERE. Never mind that! You say there is one dangerous man. Name him.

CLAGGART. William Budd, the . . . captain of the foretop.

VERE. William Budd?

CLAGGART. The same, sir. But for all his youth and appealing manners, a secret, vicious lad.

VERE. How, vicious?

CLAGGART. He insinuates himself into the good will of his mates so that they will at least say a word for him, perhaps even take action with him, should it come to that. With your pardon, sir; you note but his fair face; under that there lies a mantrap.

VERE *(after a pause)*. Master-at-Arms, I intend to test your accusation here and now. Hallam! *(Enter Hallam)*

HALLAM. Aye, sir.

VERE. Find Budd, the foretopman. Manage to tell him out of earshot that he is wanted here. Keep him in talk yourself. Go along.

HALLAM. Aye aye, sir. *(Exits)*

VERE *(angry and perturbed)*. Do you come to me with such a foggy tale, Master-at-Arms? As to William Budd, cite me an act, or spoken word of his, confirming what you here in general charge against him. Wait; weigh what you speak. Just now, and in this case, there is the yardarm end for false witness.

CLAGGART. I understand, sir. Tonight, when on my rounds, discovering Budd's hammock was unused, I combed the ship, and found him in conclave with several growlers; men, who, like himself, spread unrest and rebellion in the crew. They were collected here, near the lee forechains, and when I ordered them below, young Budd and others threatened me, and swore they'd drop me, and some officers they hate, overboard, some misty night. Should you, sir, desire substantial proof, it is not far.

(Enter Hallam, followed by Billy.)

VERE. Hallam, stand apart and see that we are not disturbed. *(Hallam exits)* And now, Master-at-Arms, tell this man to his face what you told me of him.

CLAGGART *(moving near to Billy, and looking directly at him)*. Certainly, sir. I said this man, this William Budd, acting so out of angry resentment against impressment and his officers, against this ship, this Service, and the King, breeds in the crew a spirit of rebellion against the officers, the mates, and me, urging some outrage like the late revolt. I myself have seen and heard him speak with manifest malingerers and men who growl of mistreatment, harshness, unfair pay and similar complaints. I say this man threatened his officers with murder, and was bent tonight on urging other men to act concertedly in mutiny. I have nothing further to say, sir.

(Billy tries to speak, but can make only incoherent sounds. He seems to be in pain from the contortions of his face and the gurgling which is all he can effect for speech.)

VERE. Speak, man, speak! Defend yourself! *(Remembering Billy's impediment, goes to him and puts a hand on his shoulder reassuringly)* There is no hurry, boy. Take your time, take your time.

(After agonized dumb gesturing and stammering, increased by Vere's kindness, Billy's arm hits out at Claggart. Claggart staggers, falls, lies still.)

VERE. Stand back, man! It was a lie, then! *(Billy, shaking, only stares at the body. Vere raises the body to a sitting position. Since Claggart remains inert, Vere lowers him again slowly, then rises. Billy tries again to speak, without success; he is crying and badly frightened)* No need to speak now, Billy. Hallam! *(Enter Hallam)*

Tell the Surgeon I wish to see him here at once. And bid Mister Seymour report to my cabin without delay. *(To Billy)* Retire to the stateroom aft. Remain there till I summon you. *(Billy exits. Vere waits, turning once to stare at Claggart's body. Enter the Surgeon)* Surgeon, tell me how it is with him. *(Surgeon bends over Claggart briefly, then looks up in surprise)* Come, we must dispatch. Go now. I shall presently call a drumhead court to try the man who out of God's own instinct dropped him there. Tell the lieutenants that a foretopman has, in an accidental fury, killed this man. Inform the Captain of Marines as well, and charge them to keep the matter to themselves. *(Surgeon exits)* The divine judgment of Ananias! Struck dead by the Angel of God . . . and I must judge the Angel. Can I save him? Have I that choice?

ACT THREE

Scene One

Scene: *Captain Vere's cabin, a quarter of an hour later. Vere and Seymour.*

——

seymour. Budd beat a man to death! What had he done?

vere. Lied again: lied to Budd's face, hoping to kill him by it. Oh, the boy was tempted to it past endurance.

seymour. False witness has its penalty, sir. Budd has set our justice right.

vere. Aye, too right. This natural, right act, done in an instinct's fever of recognition, was late and fatal.

seymour. What are you going to do, Captain? Isn't this last lie of the Master-at-Arms the very act you were waiting for, so as to let the law destroy him, as you said? He should have suffered at the yard-arm if Billy hadn't killed him.

vere. Yes. He should. But by fair process of authority. Budd has prevented that, and turned the law against himself.

seymour. You can't condemn the boy for answering with his arm for lack of words! The motive was clearly justified.

vere. Aye, but was the act? For God's sake try, try to convince me I am wrong!

seymour. This Master-at-Arms, you knew him for a liar, a vicious dog.

vere. A dog's obeyed in office. Claggart was authority.

seymour. Then authority's an evil!

vere. It often is. But it commands, and no man is its equal, not Billy, nor you, nor I. It will strike us down, and rightly, if we resist it.

seymour. Rightly! What power gives evil its authority? We should thank God the man's dead, and the world well rid of that particular devil.

vere. Our life has ways to hedge its evil in. No one must go above them; even innocents. Laws of one kind or other shape our course from birth to death. These are the laws pronouncing Billy's guilt; Admiralty codes are merely shadows of them.

seymour. That's tyranny, not law, forcing conformity to wrongs, giving the victory to the devil himself!

vere. I thought so once. But without this lawful tyranny, what should we have but worse tyranny of anarchy and chaos? So aboard this man-of-war. Oh, if I were a man alone, manhood would declare for Billy.

seymour. Then do it. Put your strength and your authority behind Budd, and let him go.

vere. When I think I could have watched him grow in comely wholesomeness of manhood . . . all lost now. What could have been, quenched in evil, swept out by that undertow.

seymour. It's more than anyone can have to answer for, Captain; to his peers, or to his God. Let him go free and try on mortal flesh! Will you urge a noose for him, marked like a common felon, and that devil still to have his wish, killing the boy at last?

vere. Can I do otherwise? I'd give my life to save his, if I could.

seymour. It's in your hands, Captain. Only you can help him now.

vere. Billy, Billy. What have we done to you? *(Knock)* Yes, come in. *(Enter Hallam)*

hallam. Lieutenants Ratcliffe and Wyatt, sir.

vere. Let them come in. *(Enter Ratcliffe and Wyatt)*

seymour. You both know why you've been summoned hither?

wyatt. Yes, sir.

ratcliffe. Aye, sir, in a general sort of way.

SEYMOUR. Then take your chairs. Ratcliffe. You here, Wyatt. You are appointed members of a court-martial convened under extraordinary circumstances by Captain Vere. I am Senior Member, and I declare this court open. (*Wyatt, Ratcliffe, and Seymour sit. Vere remains standing, apart*) Sentry, bring the prisoner in. (*Hallam salutes and exits*) As you know, the Master-at-Arms has been killed by the foretopman, Budd. Whether by accident or by design, and whether the act shall carry the penalty of death or no, you are to decide. There is only one witness, Captain Vere. I shall call upon him to give his deposition as soon as the sentry brings in the prisoner. (*An uneasy silence*)

WYATT. Budd wouldn't kill a minnow without good reason.

RATCLIFFE. What did the . . .

SEYMOUR. I had rather you did not express an opinion until after you have heard the evidence. (*Another awkward silence. Hallam finally enters with Billy*) Sentry, stand outside. (*Exit Hallam*) You may sit down.

BILLY. Th-th-thank you, sir.

SEYMOUR. Captain: will you be good enough to give us your account?

VERE (*turning toward them*). I speak not as your Captain, but as witness before this court. The Master-at-Arms early this morning detailed to me an account of mutinous sentiments expressed by Budd, and in particular, spoke of overhearing a specific conversation last night on the midwatch. He alleged that Budd offered him violence and threatened further violence against the officers.

WYATT. Budd a mutineer! That's absurd, he's the best-liked man . . .

RATCLIFFE. Did the Master-at-Arms specify who the other malcontents were, sir?

VERE. He did not. He said merely that he was in possession of substantial proof of his accusation.

SEYMOUR. With your permission, sir . . . Budd, did you speak with anyone in the Master-at-Arms' hearing last night?

BILLY. I . . . spoke a little . . . with the Dansker, sir.

WYATT. Who is the Dansker?

BILLY. He's just called the Dansker, sir. He's always called so.

RATCLIFFE. I know him. A mainmast sailor.

SEYMOUR. Sentry. (*Enter Hallam*)

HALLAM. Sir.

SEYMOUR. Do you know a mainmast sailor referred to as "the Dansker"?

HALLAM. Aye, sir.

SEYMOUR. Go on deck and find him. Let him know apart that he is wanted here, and arrange it so that none of the other people notice his withdrawing. See you do it tactfully. I want no curiosity aroused among the men.

HALLAM. Aye aye, sir. (*Exits*)

SEYMOUR. Please go on.

VERE. I sent at once for Budd. I ordered the Master-at-Arms to be present at this interview, to make his accusation to Budd's face.

RATCLIFFE. May I ask what was the prisoner's reaction on being confronted by the Master-at-Arms?

VERE. I perceived no sign of uneasiness in his demeanor. I believe he smiled.

RATCLIFFE. And for the Master-at-Arms?

VERE. When I directed him to repeat his accusation, he faced Budd and did so.

WYATT. Did Budd reply?

VERE. He tried to speak, but could not frame his words.

SEYMOUR. And then, sir?

VERE. He answered with blows, and his accuser fell. . . . It was apparent at once that the attack was fatal, but I summoned the Surgeon to verify the fact. (*Turns away*)

SEYMOUR (*to Billy*). You have heard Captain Vere's account. Is it, or is it not, as he says?

BILLY. Captain Vere tells the truth. It is just as Captain Vere says, but it is not as the Master-at-Arms said. I have eaten the King's bread, and I am true to the King.

VERE. I believe you, boy.

BILLY. God knows . . . I . . . thank you, sir.

SEYMOUR. Was there any malice between you and the Master-at-Arms?

BILLY. I bore ·no malice against the Master-at-Arms. I'm sorry he is dead. I did not mean to kill him. If I'd found my tongue, I would not have struck him. But he lied foully to my face, and I . . . had to say . . . something . . . and I could only say it . . . with a blow. God help me.

SEYMOUR. One question more—you tell us that what the Master-at-Arms said against you was a lie. Now, why should he have lied with such obvious malice, when you have declared that there was no malice between you? *(Billy looks appealingly at Vere)* Did you hear my question?

BILLY. I . . . I . . .

VERE. The question you put to him comes naturally enough. But can he rightly answer it? Or anyone else, unless, indeed, it be he who lies within there. *(Knock and enter immediately Hallam)*

HALLAM. The mainmast man, sir.

SEYMOUR. Send him in. *(Hallam nods off and the Dansker enters. Hallam withdraws, closing door)* State your name and station.

DANSKER. I have no name. I'm called the Dansker, that's all I know. Mainmast man.

SEYMOUR. You have been summoned in secrecy to appear as a witness before this court, of which I am Senior Member. I may not at this time disclose to you the nature of the offense being tried. However, the offender is William Budd, foretopman. *(Pause)* Do you consent to give this court your testimony, though ignorant of the case at trial, and further, to keep in strictest confidence all that passes here?

DANSKER. Aye.

SEYMOUR *(pushes forward a Bible)*. Do you so swear?

DANSKER *(touching the Bible)*. I do.

SEYMOUR. Then this is my question. In your opinion, is there malice between Budd and the Master-at-Arms?

DANSKER. Aye.

VERE *(wheeling around)*. How!

SEYMOUR. Explain your statement.

DANSKER. How should he not have hated him?

SEYMOUR. Be plain, man. We do not deal in riddles here.

DANSKER. Master-at-Arms bore malice towards a grace he could not have. There was no reason for it.

RATCLIFFE. In other words, this malice was one-sided?

DANSKER. Aye.

RATCLIFFE. And you cannot explain how it arose?

DANSKER. Master-at-Arms hated Billy . . .

SEYMOUR. One moment. I notice that you have been using the past tense in your testimony. Why?

DANSKER. I look around and sense finality here.

WYATT. You cannot explain further the cause of Claggart's hate for Budd?

DANSKER. Master-at-Arms made his world in his own image. Pride was his demon,

and he kept it strong by others' fear of him. Billy could not imagine such a nature, saw nothing but a lonely man, strange, but a man still, nothing to be feared. So Claggart, lest his world be proven false, planned Billy's death. The final reason is beyond my thinking.

VERE. Aye, that is thoughtfully put. There is a mystery in iniquity. But it seems to me, Seymour, that the point we seek here is hardly material.

SEYMOUR. Aye, sir. Very well, you may go.

DANSKER. One thing more. Since this Master-at-Arms first came on board from God knows where, I have seen his shadow lengthen along the deck, and being under it, I was afraid. Whatever happened here, I am in part to blame—more than this lad. *(To Billy)* I am an old man, Billy. You—try to—forgive me. *(Exits)*

SEYMOUR. Have you any further questions to put to the accused?

RATCLIFFE. No.

WYATT. None.

SEYMOUR. William Budd, if you have anything further to say for yourself, say it now.

BILLY *(after glance at Vere)*. I have said all, sir.

SEYMOUR. Sentry. *(Enter Hallam)* Remove the prisoner to the after compartment. *(Hallam and Billy exit. A long pause)* Have you anything to say, Ratcliffe?

RATCLIFFE. Yes, sir. Claggart was killed because Budd couldn't speak. In that sense, that he stammers, he's a cripple. You don't hang a man for that, for speaking the only way he could.

WYATT. If you condemn him, it's the same thing as condoning the apparent lie the Master-at-Arms clearly told. I'd have struck him, too. The boy is clearly innocent, struck him in self-defense.

RATCLIFFE. Aye. I'm ready to acquit him now.

SEYMOUR. Good. Then we can reach a verdict at once.

VERE. Hitherto I have been a witness at this trial, no more. And I hesitate to interfere, except that at this clear crisis you ignore one fact we cannot close our eyes to.

SEYMOUR. With your pardon, sir, as Senior Member of this court, I must ask if you speak now as our commanding officer or as a private man.

VERE. As convening authority, Seymour. I summoned this court, and I must review its findings and approve them before passing them on to the Admiralty.

SEYMOUR. Aye, sir, that is your right.

VERE. No right. Which of us here has rights? It is my duty, and I must perform it. Budd has killed a man—his superior officer.

SEYMOUR. We have found a verdict, sir.

VERE. I know that, Seymour. Your verdict sets him free, and so would I wish to do. But are we free to choose as we would do if we were private citizens? The Admiralty has its code. Do you suppose it cares who Budd is? Who you and I are?

SEYMOUR. We don't forget that, sir. But surely Claggart's tales were simply lies. We've established that.

VERE. Aye. But the Nore and Spithead were brute facts, and must not come again. The men were starved out before, but if they should think we are afraid . . .

RATCLIFFE. Captain, how could they? They certainly know Budd is no mutineer.

WYATT. Of course not. Since he came on board, he's done more to keep the crew in hand than any of us.

SEYMOUR. That's true. The men took naturally to him.

VERE. As officers we are concerned to keep this ship effective as a weapon. And the law says what we must do in such a case as this. Come now, you know the facts, and the Mutiny Act's provisions. At sea, in time of war, an impressed man strikes his superior officer, and the blow is fatal. The mere blow alone would hang him, at least according to the Act. Well then, the men on board know that as well as you and I. And we acquit him. They have sense, they know the proper penalty to follow, and yet it does not follow.

SEYMOUR. But they know Budd, sir, and Claggart too, I daresay. Would they not applaud the decision that frees Budd? They would thank us.

WYATT. String him to a yard, and they'll turn round and rescue him, and string us up instead!

RATCLIFFE. Aye, that's a point. It's twice as dangerous to hang the boy as it would be to let him go. If there's a mutinous temper in the crew, condemning Budd would surely set it off.

VERE. That is possible. Whatever step we take, the risk is great; but it is ours. That is what makes us officers. Yet if in fear of what our office demands we shirk our duty, we only play at war, at being men. If by our lawful rigor mutiny comes, there is no blame for us. But if in fear, miscalled a kind of mercy, we pardon Budd against specific order, and then the crew revolts, how culpable and weak our verdict would appear! The men on board know what our case is, how we are haunted by the Spithead risings. Have they forgotten how the panic spread through England? No. Your clemency would be accounted fear, and they would say we flinch from practising a lawful rigor lest new outbreaks be provoked. What a shame to us! And what a deadly blow to discipline!

RATCLIFFE. I concede that, sir. But this case is exceptional, and pity, if we are men, is bound to move us, Captain.

VERE. So am I moved. Yet we cannot have warm hearts betraying heads that should be cool. In such a case ashore, an upright judge does not allow the pleading tears of women to touch his nature. Here at sea, the heart, the female in a man, weeps like a woman. She must be ruled out, hard though it be. (Pause) Still silent? Very well, I see that something in all your downcast faces seems to urge that not alone the heart moves hesitancy. Conscience, perhaps. The private conscience moves you.

WYATT. Aye, that's it, sir. How can we condemn this man and live at peace again within ourselves? We have our standards; ethics, if you like.

VERE. Challenge your scruples! They move as in a dusk. Come, do they import something like this: if we are bound to judge, regardless of palliating circumstances, the death of Claggart as the prisoner's deed, then does that deed appear a capital crime whereof the penalty is mortal? But can we adjudge to summary and shameful death a fellow creature innocent before God, and whom we feel to be so? Does that state the case rightly?

SEYMOUR. That is my feeling, sir.

VERE. You all feel, I am sure, that the boy in effect is innocent; that what he did was from an unhappy stricture of speech that made him speak with blows. And I believe that, too; believe as you do, that he struck his man down, tempted beyond endurance. Acquit him, then, you say, as innocent?

RATCLIFFE. Exactly! Oh, I know the Articles prescribe death for what Budd has done, but that . . .

WYATT. Oh, stow the Articles! They don't account for such a case as this. You yourself say Budd is innocent.

VERE. In intent, Wyatt, in intent.

WYATT. Does that count for nothing? His whole attitude, his motive, count for nothing? If his intent . . .

VERE. The intent or non-intent of Budd is nothing to the purpose. In a court more merciful than martial it would extenuate, and shall, at the last Assizes, set him free. But here we have these alternatives only: condemn or let go.

SEYMOUR. But it seems to me we've got to consider the problem as a moral one, sir, despite the fact that we're not moralists. When Claggart told you his lie, the case immediately went beyond the scope of military justice.

VERE. I, too, feel that. But do these gold stripes across our arms attest that our allegiance is to Nature?

RATCLIFFE. To our country, sir.

VERE. Aye, Ratcliffe; to the King. And though the sea, which is inviolate Nature primeval, though it be the element whereon we move and have our being as sailors, is our official duty hence to Nature? No. So little is that true that we resign our freedom when we put this on. And when war is declared, are we, the fighters commissioned to destroy, consulted first?

WYATT. Does that deny us the right to act like men? We're not trying a murderer, a dockside cut-throat!

VERE. The gold we wear shows that we serve the King, the Law. What does it matter that our acts are fatal to our manhood, if we serve as we are forced to serve? What bitter salt leagues move between our code and God's own judgments! We are conscripts, every one, upright in this uniform of flesh. There is no truce to war born in the womb. We fight at command.

WYATT. All I know is that I can't sit by and see Budd hanged!

VERE. I say we fight by order, by command of our superiors. And if our judgments approve the war, it is only coincidence. And so it is with all our acts. So now, would it be so much we ourselves who speak as judges here, as it would be martial law operating through us? For that law, and for its rigor, we are not responsible. Our duty lies in this: that we are servants only.

RATCLIFFE. The Admiralty doesn't want service like that. What good would it do? Who'd profit by Budd's death?

WYATT. You want to make us murderers!

SEYMOUR. Wyatt! Control yourself!

VERE. What is this vessel that you serve in, Wyatt, an ark of peace? Go count her guns; then tell your conscience to lie quiet, if you can.

RATCLIFFE. But that is war. This would be downright killing!

SEYMOUR. It's all war, Ratcliffe; war to the death, for all of us.

VERE. You see that, Seymour? That this war began before our time?

SEYMOUR. And will end long after it.

VERE. Here we have the Mutiny Act for justice. No child can own a closer tie to parent than can that Act to what it stems from: War. This is a wartime cruise and in this ship are Englishmen who fight against their wills, perhaps against their conscience, 'pressed by war into the service of the King. Though we as fellow creatures understand their lot, what does it matter to the officer, or to the enemy? The French will cut down conscripts in the same swath with volunteers, and we will do as much for them. War has no business with anything but surfaces. War's child, the Mutiny Act, is featured like the father.

RATCLIFFE. Couldn't we mitigate the penalty if we convict him?

VERE. No, Ratcliffe. The penalty is prescribed.

RATCLIFFE. I'd like to think it over, Captain. I'm not sure.

VERE. I repeat, then, that while we ponder and you hesitate over anxieties I confess to sharing, the enemy comes nearer. We must act, and quickly. The French close in on us; the crew will find out shortly what has happened. Our consciences are private matters, Ratcliffe. But we are public men, controlling life and death within this world at sea. Tell me whether or not in our positions we dare let our consciences take precedence of the code that makes us officers and calls this case to trial.

RATCLIFFE (*after a pause; quietly*). No, sir.

WYATT. Can you stand Budd's murder on your conscience?

SEYMOUR. Wyatt! Hold your tongue!

WYATT *(jumping up)*. I say let him go!

SEYMOUR. Sit down, sir!

VERE. Let him speak.

WYATT. I won't bear a hand to hang a man I know is innocent! My blood's not cold enough. I can't give the kind of judgment you want to force on us! I ask to be excused from sitting upon this court.

SEYMOUR. Do you know what you're saying? Sit down and hold your tongue, man!

VERE. The kind of judgment I ask of you is only this, Wyatt: that you recognize your function in this ship. I believe you know it quite as well as we, yet you rebel. Can't you see that you must first strip off the uniform you wear, and after that your flesh, before you can escape the case at issue here? Decide you must, Wyatt. Oh, you may be excused and wash your hands of it, but someone must decide. We are the law; law orders us to act, and shows us how. Do you imagine Seymour, or Ratcliffe here, or I, would not save this boy if we could see a way consistent with our duties? Acquit Budd if you can. God knows I wish I could. If in your mind as well as in your heart, you can say freely that his life is not forfeit to the law we serve, reason with us! Show us how to save him without putting aside our function. Or if you can't do that, teach us to put by our responsibility and not betray ourselves. Can you do this? Speak, man, speak! Show us how! Save him, Wyatt, and you save us all. *(Wyatt slowly sits down)* You recognize the logic of the choice I force upon you. But do not think me pitiless in thus demanding sentence on a luckless boy. I feel as you do for him. But even more, I think there is a grace of soul within him that shall forgive the law we bind him with, and pity us, stretched on the cross of choice. *(Turns away)*

SEYMOUR. Well, gentlemen. Will you decide. *(Officers write their verdicts on paper before them, and hand them to Seymour, who rises, draws his dirk and places it on the table, pointing forward)* He is condemned, sir. Shall we appoint the dawn?

Scene Two

SCENE: *Captain Vere's cabin, 0400. Ship's bell strikes offstage. Vere sitting alone at his desk. Knock at the door.*

VERE. Come in. *(Enter Seymour)* Oh, it's Seymour.

SEYMOUR. It's eight bells, Captain.

VERE. What's the hour of sunrise?

SEYMOUR. Four fifty-two, sir.

VERE. Eight bells. And one bell at four-thirty. Odd and even numbers caught between two hands. Budd shall not live to head the odd made even or wrong made right.— Call all hands to quarters at four-thirty.

SEYMOUR. Aye aye, Captain. *(Turns irresolutely)*

VERE. The wind has slackened, I think. How is the glass?

SEYMOUR. It's risen slightly. Sea has flattened out.

VERE. Fair weather after foul . . . it's all nature, nature and law. How exigent are these Mediterranean climates of the heart, and temperate zones of mind!

SEYMOUR. Have you been here all night, sir?

VERE. All night, Seymour . . . all my life moving between dark and dark. It has been a long night, but day will be quick and deadly on the mainyard. D'you think, Seymour, a man can forgive a wrong done of the heart's own election?

SEYMOUR. Most people are decent enough. You can forgive them trespasses.

VERE. No, by God. There's wickedness alive. It's dead now in one man, but it's alive to feel and smell at night. . . Seymour, go below. Get Budd and bring him here.

SEYMOUR. But Captain . . .

VERE. Do as you're told. Get Budd and bring him here. *(Seymour exits. Vere sits motionless for a few moments, then rises and goes to the cabin door)* Sentry.

HALLAM. Yes, sir?

VERE. Who has the deck this watch?

HALLAM. Mister Ratcliffe, Captain.

VERE. Very well. *(Pause)* Sentry!

HALLAM. Sir?

VERE. When Mister Seymour has returned, admit him right away.

HALLAM. Aye aye, Captain.

VERE. The wind's still sharp. You must be cold there, Hallam. Go to the leeward side. I'll be responsible.

HALLAM. Thank you, sir. This is the coldest hour now, just before sunrise.

VERE *(closes door, returns slowly to his desk)*. The lamp holds steady when the vessel heels. Does the law hang straight in crooked lives? It burns, and shapes nothing but shadows here, plumb in the twisting cabin of the mind. *(Footsteps, voices. Vere turns to door. Enter Seymour, Billy, and Hallam)* Take off the manacles. *(Hallam frees Billy)*

SEYMOUR *(to Hallam)*. Outside, man. Bear a hand. *(Exits with Hallam)*

VERE. Sit down. No, it's better that I stand.

BILLY. I was thinking, locked up below there . . . the Captain knows the rights of this. He'll save me if it's right. Then you sent for me. Is there hope for me, Captain?

VERE. Billy, what hope is there?

BILLY. Tell me why. I only want to understand.

VERE. How young you still are, Billy! Oh, I can tell you this: nothing is lost of anything that happens. I have given you the judgment of the world . . . deadly constraint . . . a length of hemp and a yardarm. I have done this to you, no one else.

BILLY. I can't get the rights of all that's happened.

VERE. There's not much right, Billy. Only necessity. You and Claggart broke man's compromise with good and evil, and both of you must pay the penalty.

BILLY. Penalty? What for? Would anyone make laws just to be broken by fellows like me?

VERE. Aye, boy. You have learned this late. Most of us find out early and trim to a middle course.

BILLY. Do you mean . . . it's better to be like that?

VERE. Better as this world goes. When a man is born, he takes a guilt upon him, I can't say how or why. And life takes its revenge on those who hurt its pride with innocence.

BILLY. Do you think Claggart knew it would come to this?

VERE. He knew he would kill you, and he died to gain that end. But if you trust me, he'll not win entirely.

BILLY. How could he hate me like that?

VERE. The world we breathe is love and hatred both, but hatred must not win the victory.

BILLY. Claggart is dead. Now I'm to hang. Doesn't that show the law is wrong, when it can't choose between him and me?

VERE. Yes, it's all wrong, all wrong.

BILLY. I don't know, Captain. I never was a hand to wonder about things, but now I think that maybe there's a kind of cruelty in people that's just as much a part of them as kindness, say, or honesty, or m-m-m . . . I can't find words, I guess. Captain.

VERE. There are no words. We are all prisoners of deadly forms that are made to break us to their measure. Nothing has power to overcome them, except forgiveness . . . Can you forgive what I have done?

BILLY. I *can* trust you, can't I? *Can* you show me it's all right, my being . . .

VERE *(turns away; a long pause)*. It's nearly dawn, lad. In the Spanish villages they're lighting fires.

BILLY. I'm not afraid, sir. *(Steps toward Vere)* It's getting light.

VERE. There's no time for either of us left. Go, take the morning. God knows you have the right to it. And when you are on the mainyard, think of me, and pray for those who must make choices. Hallam. *(Enter Hallam in doorway)* Take Budd into your charge. *(Billy and Hallam go out)* Time has run out.

SCENE THREE

SCENE: *Main deck aft. Drum-to-formation. Crew forming up. Wyatt, Midshipmen Gardiner and Rea.*

WYATT. Bear a hand. Form the men up in ranks.

GARDINER. Aye, sir. All right, you! Close ranks! Move up, Stoll. That's better. Talbot, square your hat. Form up straight there, damn it! *(Drum. Men come to attention)*

WYATT. Division commanders report!

VOICE *(off)*. Carpenters and gunners, present or accounted for, sir!

VOICE *(off)*. Marine Detachment, present or accounted for, sir!

VOICE *(off)*. Afterguard, present or accounted for, sir!

GARDINER. Fore, main and mizzentopmen . . . one absentee!

WYATT. All hands will stand by to witness punishment! Stand easy.

VOICES *(off)*. Stand easy! *(Wyatt walks away from men. Murmur in ranks)*

KINCAID. Where the devil is Billy? He

wasn't in his hammock when they piped us up.

o'DANIEL. He'll be getting himself in trouble if he don't fall in.

KINCAID. Who the hell they punishing, and what for?

JENKINS. It's got to be flogging, or they wouldn't have us all up here.

KINCAID. Vere never flogs anybody. And there ain't no gratings up.

DANSKER. They flog men at noon. The early morning's for hanging.

KINCAID. Hanging! (*The word travels back*) Who? What for?

o'DANIEL. The skipper, he don't confide in me no more.

KINCAID. I thought they waited till they got ashore before they hanged a man.

DANSKER. Not in wartime.

JENKINS. He goes up them ratlines, out on the yard, they slips a noose around his neck, and then he jumps and hangs himself.

o'DANIEL. They'd have the devil's work getting O'Daniel to jump.

KINCAID. It's jump, or get pushed.

JENKINS. Where's Claggart? God, you don't suppose it's Claggart! Oh, Judas, let it be that fishblooded nark!

KINCAID. Not him. He's too smart, he is.

JENKINS. Where is he, then? He ain't here.

DANSKER. He is here.

KINCAID. Where? I don't see him.

DANSKER. He is here.

KINCAID. Ah . . . you're balmy, old man. (*Enter Vere, Seymour, Ratcliffe and the Surgeon. Drum sounds Attention.*)

WYATT (*to Seymour*). Ship's company present to witness execution, sir.

SEYMOUR. Very well. (*To Vere*) Ship's company present to witness execution, sir. (*Vere nods.*)

SEYMOUR (*to Wyatt*). Lieutenant Wyatt, have the prisoner brought forward.

WYATT. Aye, aye, sir. (*Marches to wing*) Sentries, bring forward the prisoner. (*Marches back to his post*) (*Enter Billy with two sentries. Astonished murmur through the crew, who momentarily break ranks.*)

WYATT. No talking in ranks! (*Continued restless movement and murmurings*) Form up!

GARDINER. You men are at attention!

WYATT (*over subdued muttering*). You hear me? Silence in ranks!

(*Silence. Sentries lead Billy to the foot of the ropes. Seymour looks at Vere, who nods. Seymour steps forward and reads.*)

SEYMOUR. Proceedings of the court-martial held aboard H.M.S. *Indomitable* on the eighth August, 1798. Convened under the authority of Edward Fairfax Vere, Senior Captain, Royal Navy, and composed of the First Officer, the Sailing Master, and the First Lieutenant of said vessel. In the case of William Budd, foretopman, Royal Navy. While attached and so serving in the aforesaid vessel, he did, on the 8th day of August, 1798, strike and kill his superior officer, one John Claggart, Master-at-Arms, Royal Navy.

(*Crew breaks out uneasily, astonished, talking excitedly.*)

JENKINS. Billy! Did you, boy? ⎤
VOICE. Good lad! | *All*
VOICE. Serves him proper!   ⎱ *together*
KINCAID. Hi, Billy! Hurrah! ⎦

WYATT. Quiet! Silence, you men! Form up!

GARDINER. Stand at attention, hang you! Silence in the ranks!

WYATT. Do you hear? (*Excited muttering, low voices*)

SEYMOUR. You will be silent and remain at strict attention until dismissed. (*Silence*) . . . Master-at-Arms, Royal Navy. Therefore, the court sentences the aforementioned William Budd, foretopman, Royal Navy, to die by hanging on the first watch of the day following these proceedings. By authority of his Gracious Majesty George Rex and Alan Napier, Viscount Kelsey, First Sea Lord. Signed, Philip Seymour, Senior Member.

(*During the last phrases of the reading, the crew, upon hearing the sentence, breaks out again, some stepping forward, shouting; they are in an ugly temper.*)

VOICES. No he don't!   ⎤
Not if I know it! |
Hang the jemmies instead, |
    I say! |
You ain't hanging Billy,   ⎱ *All*
Not Billy, you bloody   ⎰ *together*
    swineheads! |
Not him, by Christ! |
    damn your eyes! |
Let them dance on a rope's |
    end!   ⎦

WYATT. Stand back! Sentries, guard your prisoner, if you have to fire!

GARDINER. Stand back, you damned clods! Keep back!

SEYMOUR *(steps forward)*. Silence there! You will resume discipline instantly! Be warned. *(Waits a silent moment. Men stop in disordered formation)* Stand back into ranks.

GARDINER. Form up again, quick about it now! *(There is a surly movement into irregular lines)*

SEYMOUR *(warily resuming procedure)*. Prisoner, have you anything to say? *(Billy shakes his head)* If you have nothing to say, when the drum roll is sounded, you will proceed to carry out the sentence of this court. *(Signals to Wyatt)*

WYATT. Sound off!

(Drum roll. Billy turns and starts up the ropes.)

VOICES. Get him! Now! Bill! Stay where you are, boy, don't do it! Wait, Billy! Wait! Rush the deck, mates! Don't let them do it! We're here, Bill, don't you worry! } *All together*

BILLY *(stops, turns forward, looks at Vere, and shouts out loud and clear, without trace of stammer)*. God bless Captain Vere!

(A second's pause; Vere is profoundly shaken; Billy goes quickly up the ropes and out of sight. The crew moves back a step, is silent; officers and men in deep breathless quiet watch him out of sight and are staring overhead as the curtain falls.)

Medea

Freely Adapted from the "Medea" of Euripides

BY ROBINSON JEFFERS

First presented by Robert Whitehead and Oliver Rea at the National Theatre in New York on October 20, 1947, with the following cast:

THE NURSE....................................Florence Reed	JASON ....John Gielgud
THE TUTOR.................................Don McHenry	AEGEUS ....Hugh Franklin
THE CHILDREN.................Gene Lee, Peter Moss	JASON'S SLAVE...........................Richard Hylton
FIRST WOMAN OF CORINTH..........Grace Mills	ATTENDANTS TO MEDEA
SECOND WOMAN OF CORINTH..Kathryn Grill	Martha Downes, Marian Seldes
THIRD WOMAN OF CORINTH....Leone Wilson	SOLDIERS ....Ben Morse, Jon Dawson,
MEDEA ....Judith Anderson	Richard Boone, Dennis McCarthy
CREON ....Albert Hecht	

———————

The entire action of the play occurs before Medea's house in Corinth.

———————

OUR THEATRE is indebted to Judith Anderson not only for memorable performances, among which the one she gave in *Medea* is the most unforgettable, but for a large share in introducing Robinson Jeffers as a playwright. It was her West Coast performance as Clytemnestra in John Gassner's adaptation of *The Tower Beyond Tragedy* that first called Broadway's attention to the power of Jeffers' dramatic verse, although that power had been recognized in literary circles some fifteen years earlier. The John Gassner version had been made for the Theatre Guild in 1938 but had been shelved by the Guild's directorate in favor of a less distinguished but more topical play, Stefan Zweig's *Jeremiah* as adapted by Worthington Miner and John Gassner. The Guild's Lawrence Langner, however, made an attempt to put the play into production a year or so later and invited Miss Anderson to assume the leading role. Although Miss Anderson responded to the call, it was found difficult to cast the other parts of this exacting poetic drama, and the project was dropped. From then on, interest in the play cropped up in one quarter or another, but it finally yielded precedence to *Medea,* which Miss Anderson urged Mr. Jeffers to adapt for her from Euripides' play. *The Tower Beyond Tragedy,* in the meantime produced in various adaptations by community theatres, did finally reach New York in a stage version prepared by Jeffers himself, and was given an ANTA (American National Theatre and Academy) production in 1950. An attempt was also made to present his dramatic poem *Dear Judas* as a play. But it was *Medea,* produced on Broadway by Oliver Rea and Robert Whitehead, that made Jeffers known to a large body of playgoers who would not have otherwise made the acquaintance of this harrowing Euripidean drama and of Mr. Jeffers' dramatic poetry. *Medea* properly bears the following dedication: "To Judith Anderson for whom this was written."

Robinson Jeffers was born in Pittsburgh in 1887, but was taken to Europe by his parents on two occasions and educated there from the ages of thirteen to fifteen. At fifteen, he enrolled at Occidental College in Los Angeles and was graduated three years later. Subsequently he studied at the University of Southern California, the University of Zurich, and a medical school in Los Angeles. In 1914, however, he abandoned every intention to pursue a profession when a legacy of $10,000 enabled him to devote himself to the writing of poetry. He built himself a home in Carmel, California, and isolating himself from modern civilization, whose commercialism and tameness repelled him, he composed numerous poems expressive of his nihilistic philosophy and admiration for primitive nature. Especially notable were his long narratives dealing with the lusts, passions, and pride of men and women who despise a commonplace life or an easy felicity, succumb to dark inner promptings and violate taboos. For his violent subject matter, moreover, he developed a granitic style of poetry in the form of long, clause- and phrase-studded lines.

Jeffers had always been a dramatic, as well as epic, poet, but in *Medea* he wrote a completely dramatic work directly intended for the stage. It follows the outlines of Euripides' celebrated tragedy, but Jeffers' style and grim view of life are his own. The play departs considerably not only from Euripides' lyricism, but from the old master's liberal feminism and sympathy with victims of discrimination and oppression. If Jeffers' *Medea* is a dream of love frustrated and turned vengeful, this is not merely because the Greek Argonaut legend used by Euripides contains this often retold story, but because it accords with Jeffers' formidable, Nay-saying disposition and his fascination with destructive passion. This disposition and interest appeared early in the powerful poetry of *Tamar* (1924), *Roan Stallion* (1925), *Cawdor* (1928), and other volumes. *Medea* is the one distinguished high tragedy written by an American poet. Underlying this poetic drama is the same view, too extreme to be Greek or classic, that Jeffers expressed so plainly in the lines of his poem *Meditation on Saviors,* written in 1928:

> "But while he lives let each man make his health in his mind,
>   to love the coast opposite humanity
> And so be freed of love, laying it like bread on the waters; it is worst
>   turned inward, it is best shot farthest.
> Love, the mad wine of good and evil, the saint's and murderer's,
>   the mote in the eye that makes its object
> Shine the sun black . . ."

ACT ONE

The NURSE *comes from the door Left toward the front of the stage)*

THE NURSE.

I wish the long ship Argo had never passed that perilous channel between the Symplegades,
I wish the pines that made her mast and her oars still waved in the wind on Mount Pelion, and the gray fishhawk
Still nested in them, the great adventurers had never voyaged
Into the Asian sunrise to the shores of morning for the Golden Fleece
                    For then my mistress Medea
Would never have seen Jason, nor loved and saved him, nor cut herself off from home to come with him
Into this country of the smiling chattering Greeks and the roofs of Corinth: over which I see evil
Hang like a cloud. For she is not meek but fierce, and the daughter of a king.
                    Yet at first all went well.
The folk of Corinth were kind to her, they were proud of her beauty, and Jason loved her. Happy is the house
Where the man and the woman love and are faithful.
        Now all is changed; all is black hatred. For Jason has turned from her; he calls the old bond a barbarian mating, not a Greek marriage; he has cast her off
And wedded the yellow-haired child of Creon, the ruler here. He wants worldly advantage, fine friends,
And a high place in Corinth. For these he is willing to cast Medea like a harlot, and betray the children
That she has borne him. He is not wise, I think
                    But Medea
Lies in the house, broken with pain and rage; she will neither eat nor drink, except her own tears,
She turns her face toward the earth, remembering her father's house and her native land, which she abandoned
For the love of this man: who now despises her.
And if I try to speak comfort to her she only stares at me, great eyes like stones. She is like a stone on the shore
Or a wave of the sea, and I think she hates
Even her children.
She is learning what it is to be a foreigner, cast out, alone and despised.
She will never learn to be humble, she will never learn to drink insult
Like harmless water. O I'm in terror of her: whether she'll thread a knife through her own heart,
Or whether she'll hunt the bridegroom and his new bride, or what more dreadful evil stalks in the forest
Of her dark mind. I know that Jason would have been wiser to tempt a lioness, or naked-handed
Steal the whelps of a tiger.
    (From up Right she sees MEDEA'S BOYS *coming with their* TUTOR, ELDER BOY *first with seashell,* YOUNGER BOY *on* TUTOR'S *back.)*
                    Here comes the happy children. Little they know
Of their mother's grief.
(During this speech TUTOR *lets Boy off his back. Boys go up and sit up Right corner of house.* TUTOR *crosses down Center to Left of* NURSE.*)*

THE TUTOR.

            Old servant of my lady, why do you stand out here, keeping watch in solitude
With those grim eyes? Is it some trouble of your own that you are lamenting? I should think Medea
Would need your care.

THE NURSE.

It is all one to Medea, whether I am there or here. Yes, it is mine,
My trouble. My lady's grief is my grief. And it has hurt me .

So that I had to come out and speak it to the earth and sky.

THE TUTOR.

    Is she still in that deep despair?

THE NURSE.

                    You are lucky,
Old watchdog of Jason's boys. I envy you,
You do not see her. This evil is not declining, it is just at dawn. I dread the lion-eyed
Glare of its noon.

THE TUTOR.

            Is she so wrought? Yet neither you nor Medea
Knows the latest and worst.

THE NURSE. *(Rises from rock)*
                    What? What?

THE TUTOR. *(Crosses to Center)*

                    I shouldn't have spoken.

THE NURSE.

        Tell me the truth, old man. You and I are two slaves, we can trust each other,
We can keep secrets.

THE TUTOR

            I heard them saying—when we walked beside the holy fountain Peirene,
Where the old men sit in the sun on the stone benches —they were saying that Creon, the lord of this land,
Intends to drive out Medea and the children with her, these innocent boys, out of this house
And out of Corinth, and they must wander through the wild world
Homeless and helpless.

THE NURSE.

            I don't believe it. Ah, no! Jason may hate the mother, but he would hardly
Let his sons be cast out.

THE TUTOR.

            Well—he has made a new alliance.
He is not a friend of this house.

THE NURSE. *(She crosses below* TUTOR *to Left)*
If this were true!—

MEDEA. *(Within house. She is Asiatic and laments loudly)* Death.

THE NURSE.
Listen! I hear her voice

MEDEA. *(Within)*

Death. Death is my wish. For myself, my enemies, my children. Destruction.

THE NURSE.
Take the children away, keep them away from her.
Take them to the other door. Quickly.

    (During "Deaths" YOUNGER BOY *rises from rock.* TUTOR *crosses, picks him up and exits Left, followed by* ELDER BOY. *They go out, toward rear door of the house.* THE NURSE *looks after them, wringing her hands.)*

MEDEA.
That's the word. Grind, crush, burn. Destruction. Ai— Ai—

THE NURSE. *(Wringing her hands)*
            This is my terror:
To hear her always harking back to the children, like · a fierce hound at fault. O unhappy one,
They're not to blame.
    (Sits step Right of pillar down Left.)

·MEDEA. *(Within)*

            If any god hears me: let me die.
Ah, rotten, rotten, rotten: death is the only
Water to wash this dirt.

    *(*FIRST *and* SECOND WOMAN *are coming in*

up Right, but the NURSE *does not yet notice them. She is intent on* MEDEA'S *cries and her own thoughts.)*

THE NURSE.

Oh, it's a bad thing

To be born of high race, and brought up wilful and
  powerful in a great house, unruled.
And ruling many: for then if misfortune comes it is
  unendurable, it drives you mad. I say that poor
  people

Are happier: the little commoners and humble people,
  the poor in spirit: they can lie low
Under the wind and live:
          (Enter THIRD WOMAN; *joins* FIRST *and*
          SECOND *up Right Center.)*
                    while the tall oaks and cloud-
  raking mountain pines go mad in the storm,
Writhe, groan and crash.
          MEDEA.
Ai!
          THE NURSE.
This is the wild and terrible justice of God: it brings
  on great persons
The great disasters.
          MEDEA.
Ai!!!
          THE NURSE. *(Becomes aware of the* WOMEN *who
have come in, and is startled from her reverie.* FIRST
WOMAN *crosses down Center)*
          What do you want?
          FIRST WOMAN.
                    I hear her crying again: it
  is dreadful.
          SECOND WOMAN. *(Crosses down to Right of* FIRST
WOMAN)
                    Her lamentation.
She is beautiful and deep in grief: we couldn't help
  coming.
          THIRD WOMAN. *(Crosses down to Right of* SECOND
WOMAN)
We are friends of this house and its trouble hurts us.
          THE NURSE.
You are right, friends; it is not a home. It is broken.
A house of grief and of weeping.
          MEDEA. *(Within)*
                    Hear me, God, let me
  die. What I need: all dead, all dead, all dead
          (THIRD WOMAN *crosses down Right of rock.)*
Under the great cold stones. For a year and a thousand
    years and another thousand: cold as the stones,
    cold,
But noble again, proud, straight and silent, crimson-
    cloaked
In the blood of our wounds.

          (FIRST WOMAN crosses to 3rd step, Center.)

FIRST WOMAN.
                    O shining sky, divine earth,
Harken not to the song that this woman sings.
It is not her mind's music; her mind is not here.
She does not know what she prays for.
Pain and wrath are the singers.
          SECOND WOMAN. *(Crosses to second step, facing
door)*
                    Unhappy one,

Never pray for death, never pray for death,
He is here all too soon.
He strikes from the clear sky like a hawk,
He hides behind green leaves, or he waits
Around the corner of the wall.
O never pray for death, never pray for death—
Because that prayer will be answered.
          MEDEA. *(The rise and fall of her voice indicate that
she is prowling back and forth beyond the main door-
way, like a caged animal)*

I know poisons. I know the bright teeth of steel. I
  know fire. But I will not be mocked by my enemies,
          (THIRD WOMAN *crosses up Right of rock to
          Right Center.)*
And I will not endure pity. Pity and contempt are
  sister and brother, twin-born. I will not die tamely.
I will not allow blubber-eyed pity, nor contempt either,
  to snivel over the stones of my tomb.
I am not a Greek woman.
          THIRD WOMAN. *(Crosses to step Center)*
                    No, a barbarian woman from
  savage Colchis, at the bitter end
Of the Black Sea. Does she boast of that?
          SECOND WOMAN.
                              She doesn't
  know what she is saying.
          MEDEA. *(Within)*
Poisons. Death-magic. The sharp sword. The hemp
  rope. Death-magic.
Death—
          SECOND WOMAN. *(Crosses down Right of rock.*
THIRD WOMAN *joins her)*
                    I hate Jason, who made this sorrow.
          FIRST WOMAN. *(Crosses to* NURSE *in front of doors)*
Old and honored servant of a great house, do you think
  it is wise
To leave your lady alone in there, except perhaps a
  few slaves, building that terrible acropolis
Of deadly thoughts? We Greeks believe that solitude
  is very dangerous, great passions grow into
  monsters
In the dark of the mind; but if you share them with
  loving friends they remain human, they can be
  endured.
          MEDEA. *(Within)*
Ai!
          FIRST WOMAN.
I think you ought to persuade Medea to come from the
  dark dwelling, and speak with us, before her heart
  breaks,
Or she does harm to herself. She has lived among us,
  we've learned to love her, we'd gladly tell her so.
It might comfort her spirit.
          THE NURSE.
                    Do you think so? She
  wouldn't listen
          (Door BOLT is heard. NURSE *rises.* FIRST WOMAN
          crosses down Right, joining other two WOMEN,
          and sits on rock)
                    —Oh, oh, she is coming!
Speak carefully to her: make your words a soft music.

          *(MEDEA comes through the doorway, prop-
          ping herself against one of the pillars, and
          stands staring.)*

THE NURSE.
Oh, my dear, my poor child.
          (NURSE sits.)
          SECOND WOMAN. *(Whispering)*
They say she is dangerous. Look at her eyes.
          FIRST WOMAN.
She is a witch, but not evil. She can make old men
  young again: she did it for Jason's father.
          THIRD WOMAN.
All the people of her country are witches. They know
  about drugs and magic. They are savages, but they
  have a wild wisdom.
          SECOND WOMAN.
Poor soul, it hasn't helped this one much.
          MEDEA. *(She does not see the gaping and whispering*
WOMEN)
I will look at the light of the sun, this last time. I wish
  from that blue sky the white wolf of lightning
Would leap, and burst my skull and my brain, and like
  a burning babe cling to these breasts— Ai!—Ai!
          (She checks and looks fiercely at the WOMEN
          below)
Someone is here?
          (Her hostile eyes range back and forth; she

sees the WOMEN *clearly now, and assumes full self-control. Her voice is cautious and insincere)*

I did not know I had visitors.—Women of Corinth:
If anything has been spoken too loudly here, consider
That I believed I was alone; and I have some provocation. You've come—let me suppose
With love and sympathy—to peer at my sorrow. I understand well enough
That nothing is ever private in a Greek city; whoever withholds anything
Is thought sullen or proud—
(With irony).
                              undemocratic
I think you call it. This is not always just, but we know that justice, at least on earth,
Is a name, not a fact; and as for me, I wish to avoid any appearance
Of being—proud. Of what? Of affliction? I will show you my naked heart.
(The THREE WOMEN *rise; cross to Center.)*
                     You know that my lord Jason
Has left me and made a second marriage, with the bright-haired child
Of wealth and power. I too was a child of power, but not in this country; and I spent my power
For love of Jason. I poured it out before him like water, I made him drink it like wine. I gave him
Success and fame; I saved him his precious life; not once, many times. You may have heard what I did for him:
I betrayed my father for him, I killed my brother to save him; I made my own land to hate me forever;
And I fled west with Jason in the Greek ship, under the thunder of the sail, weeping and laughing,
That huge journey through the Black Sea and the Bosphorus, where the rocks clang together, through the Sea of Marmora,
And through Hellespont,
                              watched by the spearmen of
wealthy Troy, and home to Greek water: his home, my exile,
My endless exile.
(Crosses to pillar Left of house)
                     And here I have loved him and borne
him sons; and this—man—
Has left me and taken Creon's daughter, to enjoy her fortune, and put aside her soft yellow hair
And kiss her young mouth.
*(*MEDEA *stands rigid, struggling for self-control.)*

FIRST WOMAN.
She is terrible. Stone with stone eyes.
SECOND WOMAN.
Look: the foam-flake on her lip, that flickers with her breathing.
THIRD WOMAN.
She is pitiable: she is under great injuries.
MEDEA. *(Low-voiced)*
I do not know what other woman—I do not know how much a Greek woman
Will endure. The people of my race are somewhat rash and intemperate. As for me, I want simply to die.
(She sits at pillar Left)
But Jason is not to smile at his bride over my grave, nor that great man Creon
Hang wreaths and make a feast-day in Corinth. Or let the wreaths be bright blinding fire, and the songs a high wailing,
And the wine, blood.
FIRST WOMAN. *(Crosses to Center)*
                     Daughter of sorrow, beware.

It is dangerous to dream of wine: it is worse
To speak of wailing or blood:
For the images that the mind makes
Find a way out, they work into life.

MEDEA.
                              Let them work into life!
FIRST WOMAN.
There are evils that cannot be cured by evil.
Patience remains, and the gods watch all.
MEDEA. *(Dully, without hope)*
Let them watch my enemies go down in blood.

(First TRUMPET off up Right is heard. The THREE WOMEN *cross up Right.)*

SECOND WOMAN.
                              Medea, beware!
Some great person is coming.—
(Second TRUMPET is heard)
It is Creon himself.
(Third TRUMPET)
THIRD WOMAN.
Creon is coming.

(The THREE WOMEN *cross down stage of rock Right.)*

THE NURSE.
                     He is dark with anger. O my lady—
my child—bend in this wind,
And not be broken!

*(*MEDEA *rises.* CREON *comes in up Right with* MEN *attending him. The* WOMEN *move to one side. He speaks to* MEDEA, *with an angry gesture toward* WOMEN.)*

CREON. *(At Center)*
You have admirers, I see. Abate your pride: these people will not be with you where you are going.
(A pause. MEDEA *does not answer.* CREON *brings his wrath under control and crosses up to second step to Right of* MEDEA)*
Medea, woman of the stone forehead and hate-filled eyes: I have made my decision. I have decided
That you must leave this land at once and go into banishment
THREE WOMEN.
Oohh!
CREON.
          with your children.
THREE WOMEN.
Oohh.
CREON.
I intend to remove
A root of disturbance out of the soil of Corinth. I am here to see to it. I will not return home
Until it is done.

(The THREE WOMEN *sit.)*

MEDEA.
                     You mean—banishment?
CREON.
                              Exile: banishment:
go where you may, Medea, but here
You abide no more.
MEDEA.
                     —I with my children?
CREON.
                              I will not
take them away from you.
MEDEA.
                     The children, my lord—
(Her lips move angrily, but the voice is not heard.)
CREON.
What are you muttering?
MEDEA.
Nothing—I am praying to my gods for wisdom,
And you for mercy. My sons are still very young, tender and helpless. You know, my lord,
What exile means—to wander with fear and famine for guide and driver, through all the wild winter storms

And the rage of the sun; and beg a bread-crust and be
    derided; pelted with stones in the villages,
Held a little lower than the scavenger dogs, kicked,
    scorned and slaved—the children, my lord,
Are Jason's children. Your chosen friend, I believe,
    and now
Even closer bound. And as for me, your servant, O
    master of Corinth, what have I done? Why
Must I be cast?

CREON.
                    I will tell you frankly: because you
    nourish rancorous ill will toward persons
Whom I intend to protect: I send you out before you've
    time to do harm here. And you are notorious
For occult knowledge: sorcery, poisons, magic. Men
    say you can even sing down the moon from heaven,
And make the holy stars to falter and run backward,
    against the purpose
And current of nature. Ha? As to that I know not: I
    know you are dangerous. You threaten my daugh-
    ter: you have to go.

MEDEA.
But I wish her well, my lord! I wish her all happiness.
    I hope that Jason may be as kind to her
As—to me.

CREON.
                    That is your wish?

MEDEA.
                    I misspoke. I thought of
    old days—
    (She seems to weep.)

CREON.
                    I acknowledge, Medea,
That you have some cause for grief. I all the more
    must guard against your dark wisdom and bitter
    heart.

MEDEA.
You misjudge me cruelly. It is true that I have some
    knowledge of drugs and medicines: I can some-
    times cure sickness.
Is that a crime? These dark rumors, my lord,
Are only the noise of popular gratitude.
    (Crosses down to one step above him)
You must have observed
    it often: if any person
Knows a little more than the common man, the people
    suspect him. If he brings a new talent,
How promptly the hateful whispers begin. But you
    are not a common man, lord of Corinth; you
Will not fear knowledge.

CREON.
                    No. Nor change my decision.
    I am here to see you leave this house and the city:
And not much time. Move quickly, gather your things
    and go. I pity you, Medea,
But you must go.
    *(He crosses off steps, with back to her down
    Right Center.)*

MEDEA.
                    You pity me? You—pity me?
    (She comes close to him, wild with rage)
I will endure a dog's pity or a wart-grown toad's. May
    God who hears me— We shall see in the end
Who's to be pitied.

    *(NURSE rises, crosses in to steps. MEDEA
    crosses down Left, then up Right between
    pillar and edge of house, then back to NURSE in
    her arms.)*

CREON.
                    Yes, and I'll keep her safe of your
    female hatred: therefore I send you
Out of this land.

    *(NURSE resumes her sitting position down
    Left.)*

MEDEA.
                    It is not true, I am not jealous. I
    never hated her.

Jealous for the sake of Jason? I am far past wanting
    Jason, my lord. You took him and gave him to her,
And I will say you did well, perhaps wisely. Your
    daughter is loved by all: she is beautiful: if I were
    near her
I would soon love her.

CREON.
                    You can speak sweetly enough,
    you can make honey in your mouth like a brown
    bee
When it serves your turn.

MEDEA.
                    Not honey: the truth.

CREON.
                    Trust
    you or not, you are going out of this country,
    Medea.
What I decide is fixed;
    (MEDEA crosses away from him to Center.)
                    it is like the firm rocks of Acro-
    corinth, which neither earthquake can move
Nor a flood of tears melt. Make ready quickly: I have
    a guest in my house. I should return to him.

THE NURSE. *(Comes to Left of MEDEA and speaks
    to her)*
What guest? O my lady, ask him
Who is the guest? If powerful and friendly
He might be a refuge for us—

MEDEA. *(Pays no attention to her. Crosses; kneels;
    to CREON)*
I know that your will is granite. But even on the harsh
    face of a granite mountain some flowers of mercy
May grow in season. Have mercy on my little sons,
    Creon,
Though there is none for me.

    *(She reaches to embrace his knees. He steps
    backward from her.)*

CREON.
                    How long, woman? This
    is decided; done; finished.

    (NURSE crosses back Left and sits down.)

MEDEA. *(Rising from her knees, turns half away
    from him)*
                    I am not a beggar.
I will not trouble you. I shall not live long.
    *(Crosses two steps to Left; turns to him
    again)*
Sire: grant me a few hours yet, one day to prepare in,
    one little day
Before I go out of Corinth forever.

CREON.
                    What? No! I told
    you. The day is today. Medea, this day.
And the hour is now.

MEDEA.
                    There are no flowers on this
    mountain: not one violet, not one anemone.
Your face, my lord, is like flint.—If I could find the
    right words, if some god would lend me a touch of
    eloquence,
I'd show you my heart.

    (Crosses to CREON)
                    I'd lift it out of my breast and
    turn it over in my hands; you'd see how pure it is
Of any harm or malice toward you or your household.
    (She holds out her hands to him)
Look at it: not a speck: look, my lord. They call mercy
The jewel of kings. I am praying
To you as to one of the gods: destroy us not utterly.
    To go out with no refuge, nothing prepared,
Is plain death: I would rather kill myself quickly and
    here. If I had time but to ask the slaves
And strolling beggars where to go, how to live: and I
    must gather some means: one or two jewels
And small gold things I have.

(Crosses away from CREON *to Left)*
                    to trade them for bread
and goat's milk.
(Crosses up steps to Center of doorway)
        Wretched, wretched, wretched I am,
I and my boys.

(She kneels again)
        I beseech you, Creon,
By the soft yellow hair and cool smooth forehead and
    the white knees
Of that young girl who is now Jason's bride: lend me
    this inch of time: one day—half a day.
For this one is now half gone—and I will go my sad
    course and vanish in the morning quietly as dew
That drops on the stones at dawn and is dry at sunrise.
You will never again be troubled by any word
Or act of mine. And this I pray you for your dear
    child's sake. Oh Creon, what is half a day
In all the rich years of Corinth?
    CREON.
                    I will think of it. I am
    no tyrant.
I have been merciful to my own hurt, many times.
    Even to myself I seem to be foolish
If I grant you this thing— No, Medea,
I will not grant it.
    (THREE WOMEN rise, cross down Right of
    CREON, *imploringly)*
        Well— We shall watch you: as a
hawk does a viper. What harm could she do
In the tail of one day? A ruler ought to be ruthless,
    but I am not. I am a fool
In my own eyes, whatever the world may think. I
    can be gruff with warriors; a woman weeping
    (MEDEA weeps.)
Floods me off course.—Take it, then. Make your
    preparations.
But if tomorrow's sun shines on you here—Medea,
    you die—
    *(MEDEA and WOMEN make a gesture of
    thanks.)*
        Enough words. Thank me not. I want
my hands
Washed of this business.
    *(He departs quickly up Right, followed by
    his* MEN. *MEDEA rises from her knees.)*

MEDEA.
            I will thank you.
And the whole world will hear of it.
    *(MEDEA crosses around to Right of house
    on top step; makes a violent gesture after
    him, then sits at pillar Right.)*
FIRST WOMAN. *(Crosses up Center watching him
    out then turns to other* WOMEN)
I have seen this man's arrogance, I watched and heard
    him.
I am of Corinth, and I say that Corinth
Is not well ruled.
    SECOND WOMAN. *(Crosses up Center.* THREE
    WOMEN *join hands at Center on end of this speech)*
The city where even a woman, even a foreigner,
Suffers unjustly the rods of power
Is not well ruled.

    (THREE WOMEN take a step to MEDEA.)*

FIRST WOMAN.
Unhappy Medea, what haven, what sanctuary, where
    will you wander?
Which of the gods, Medea,
Drives you through waves of woe, the mooring broken,
    the hawsers and the anchor-head,
Hopeless from harbor?·
    MEDEA.
            —This man—this barking dog
    —this gulled fool—
    (MEDEA rises)
            gods of my father's country,
You saw me low on my knees before the great dog of

Corinth; humble, holding my heart in my hands
For a dog to bite—break this dog's teeth!

    (WOMEN cross down stage of rock Right.)
            Women: it is
a bitter thing to be a woman.
A woman is weak for warfare, she must use cunning.

    Men boast their battles: I tell you this, and we
    know it:
    (Starts down steps Center)
It is easier to stand in battle three times, in the front
    line, in the stabbing fury, than to bear one child.
And a woman, they say, can do no good but in child-
    birth. It may be so. She can do evil.
    (WOMEN make pleading gesture to her)
            she can do evil.
    (She snarls at them and they turn away)
I wept before that tall dog, I wept my tears before
    him, I degraded my knees to him, I gulled and
    flattered him.
O triple fool, he has given me
    (She crosses up Right Center. FIRST WOMAN
    sits on rock Right)*
            all that I needed: a little time, a
    space of time.
    (Crosses back to Left Center)
            Death is dearer to me
Than what I am now; and if today by sunset the world
    has not turned, and turned sharp too—let your
    dog Creon
Send two or three slaves to kill me and a cord to
    strangle me: I will stretch out
My throat to it. But I have a bitter hope, women. I
    begin to see light
Through the dark wood, between the monstrous trunks
    of the trees, at the end of the tangled forest an
    eyehole,
A pin-point of light:

            I shall not die perhaps
As a pigeon dies. Nor like an innocent lamb, that feels
    a hand on its head and looks up from the knife
To the man's face and dies.—No, like some yellow-
    eyed beast that has killed its hunters let me lie
    down
On the hounds' bodies and the broken spears.—Then
    how to strike them? What means to use? There
    are so many
Doors through which painful death may glide in and
    catch— Which one, which one?
    (She stands meditating down Left. The NURSE
    comes from behind her and speaks to the* FIRST
    WOMAN.)*
    THE NURSE.
                Tell me: do you
    know what guest
Is in Creon's house?
    FIRST WOMAN..
                What?—Oh. An Athenian ship
came from the north last night: it is Ægeus.
The lord of Athens.
    THE NURSE.
            Ægeus! My lady knows him: I
    believe he will help us. Some god has brought him
    here,
Some savior god.
    FIRST WOMAN.
            He is leaving, I think, today.
    THE NURSE. *(Hobbling back toward* MEDEA)*
                    My lady!
Lord Ægeus
Is here in Corinth, Creon's guest: Ægeus of Athens.
    *(MEDEA looks at her silently, without atten-
    tion.)*
If you will see him and speak him fairly,
We have a refuge.
    MEDEA.
            I have things in my hand to do. Be
    quiet.

THE NURSE.
        Oh, listen to me!
You are driven out of Corinth; you must find shelter.
Ægeus of Athens is here.

(MEDEA *turns from her. The* NURSE *catches at her clothing, servile but eager, slave and mother at the same time.*)

MEDEA. (*Angrily turning on her*)
What's that to me?
THE NURSE. (*Kneels at her feet*)
I lifted you in my arms when you were—this long. I
        gave you milk from these breasts, that are now
        dead leaves.
I saw the little beautiful body straighten and grow
        tall: Oh—child—almost my child—how can I
Not try to save you? Life is better than death—
MEDEA.
                                Not now.
THE NURSE.
        Time's running out!
MEDEA.
                        I have time. Oh, I have time.
It would be good to stand here a thousand years and
        think of nothing
But the deaths of three persons.
THE NURSE.
                        Ai! There's no hope then.
Ai, child, if you could do this red thing you dream of,
        all Corinth
Would pour against you.
MEDEA.
                        After my enemies are punished
and I have heard the last broken moan—Corinth?
What's that? I'll sleep. I'll sleep well. I am alone
        against all: and so weary
That it is pitiful.

(MEDEA *sits.* NURSE *rises, wringing her hands. On trumpet call the* THREE WOMEN *cross up Right.*)

FIRST WOMAN.
                Look: who is coming? I see the
sunlight glitter on lanceheads.

SECOND WOMAN.
Oh, it is Jason!
THIRD WOMAN.
Jason's Medea's worst enemy, who should have been
Her dearest protector.

(MEDEA *leans wearily against one of the pillars of the doorway, her back to the stage, unconscious of what they are saying.* JASON *enters in haste up Right, followed by armed* ATTENDANTS, *and speaks angrily.*)

JASON. (*Crossing to Center on 2nd step*)
                        What business have you here,
        you women
Clustered like buzzing bees at the hive-door?
Where is Medea?

(*They do not answer for a moment, but look involuntarily toward* MEDEA, *and* JASON *sees her. She jerks and stiffens at the sound of his voice, but does not turn.*)

FIRST WOMAN. (*Pointing*)
                        There: mourning for what you have
        done.

(NURSE *takes a step above* MEDEA, *disclosing her to* JASON.)

JASON.
        Ha? What she has done.

Not I. Not by my will she and my sons are exiled.
MEDEA. (*Slowly turns and faces him, her head high, rigid with inner violence*)
Is there another dog here?

(THREE WOMEN *sit on steps up Right Center.*)

JASON.
                        So, Medea,
You have once more affronted and insulted the head
        of Corinth. This is not the first time
I've seen what a fool anger is. You might have lived
        here happily, secure and honored—I hoped you
        would—
By being just a little decently respectful toward those
        in power. Instead you had to go mad with anger
And talk yourself into exile. To me it matters little
        what you say about me, but rulers are sensitive.
Time and again I've smoothed down Creon's indigna-
        tion, then you like a madwoman, like a possessed
        imbecile,
Wag your head and let the words flow again; you
        never cease
From speaking evil against him and his family. So
        now— Call yourself lucky, Medea,
Not to get worse than exile.
        (*Crosses a few steps to* MEDEA *on 2nd step*)
                        In spite of all this, I have
        your interest at heart and am here to help you.
Exile's a bitter business. I want to make some pro-
        vision for you. I wish you no harm,
Although you hate me.
        (*He waits for her to speak, but she is silent. He continues*)
                        And in particular the children,
        my sons; our sons.—You might have been decent
        enough
To have thought of our sons.
MEDEA. (*Slowly*)
                        Did you consider them
When you betrayed this house?
JASON.
                        Certainly I considered
        them. It was my hope that they would grow up
        here,
And I, having married power, could protect and favor
        them. And if perhaps, after many years, I become
Dynast of Corinth—for that is Creon's desire, to make
        me his heir—our sons
Would have been a king's sons— I hope to help them
        wherever they go: but now of course must look
        forward
To younger children.
        (*Steps down off steps and turns from her.*)
MEDEA. (*Trembling*)
                        Ah—it's enough. Something might
        happen. It is—likely that—something might happen
To the bride and the marriage.
JASON.
                        I'll guard against it. But
        evidently Creon is right to be rid of you.

(*He crosses as if to go off Right. She stops him when he is up Right Center. He gives helmet to* SLAVE; *crosses down Right.*)

MEDEA. (*Rises and crosses to Center*)
Have you finished now? I thought I would let you
        speak on and spread out your shamelessness
Before these women: the way a Tyrian trader unrolls
        his rare fabrics: "Do you like it, ladies?"

                                It is the
Dog's daughter's husband. It is a brave person: it has
        finally got up its courage—with a guard of
        spears—
To come and look me in the face.
        (JASON *turns away from her.* MEDEA *makes gestures as if to take him in her arms, then stops*)

O Jason: how have you pulled me down
To this hell of vile thoughts? I did not use to talk like
a common woman. I loved you once:
And I am ashamed of it:
(JASON sits rock Right. She crosses two steps Left)
           but there are some things
That ought to be remembered by you and me. That
blue day when we drove through the Hellespont
Into Greek sea, and the great-shouldered heroes were
singing at the oars, and those birds flying
Through the blown foam: that day was too fine I sup-
pose
For Creon's daughter's man to remember
(JASON rises as if to leave.)
          —but you might remember
Whether I cheated my father for you and tamed the
fire-breathing
Brazen-hoofed bulls; and whether I saved your life in
the field of the teeth; and you might remember
Whether I poisoned the great serpent and got you the
Golden Fleece; and fled with you, and killed my
brother
When he pursued us, making myself abominable
In my own home; and then in yours I got your enemy
Pelias hacked to death
By his own daughter's hands—whatever these fine
Corinthian friends of yours
May say against my rapid and tricky wisdom: you it
has served,
You it has served well:
(JASON starts to speak.)
           here are five times, if I counted
right—and all's not counted—
That your adventure would have been dusty death
If I'd not saved you—but now you think that your
adventures are over; you are safe and high placed
in Corinth,
And will need me no more.
           It is a bit of a dog, isn't it,
women? It is well qualified
To sleep with the dog's daughter.
(JASON makes a gesture of wrath.)
           But for me, Jason, me
driven by the hairy snouts from the quadruped
marriage-bed,

What refuge does your prudent kindness advise? Shall
I fly home to Colchis—
To put my neck in the coil of a knotted rope, for the
crimes
I served you with? Or shall I go and kneel to the
daughter of Pelias? They would indeed be happy
To lay their hands on my head: holding the very knives
and the cleavers
That carved their sire. The world is a little closed to me,
eh?
By the things I have done for you

(Crosses away from him to down Center.)
THE NURSE.
           I'll go to the palace
And seek Ægeus. There is no other hope.
(She hurries out door Left.)
JASON. *(Slowly crossing to Center to Right of MEDEA)*
           I see, Medea,
You have been a very careful merchant of benefits.
You forget none, you keep a strict reckoning.
But—
Some little things that I on my side have done for you
Ought to be in the books too: as, for example, that I
carried you
Out of the dirt and superstition of Asiatic Colchis into
the rational
Sunlight of Greece, and the marble music of the Greek
temples: is that no benefit? And I have brought
you
To meet the first minds of our time, and to speak as

an equal with the great heroes and the rulers of
cities:
Is that no benefit? And now—this grievous thing that
you hate me for:
That I have married Creon's young daughter, little
Creusa:
(MEDEA sits 2nd step.)
           do you think I did it like a boy or a woman.

Out of blind passion? I did it to achieve power here;
and I'd have used that power to protect
You and our sons, but your jealous madness has
muddled everything. And finally:
(NURSE appears behind house and exits up Right. JASON crosses above MEDEA to top step)
As to those acts of service you so loudly boast—whom
do I thank for them? I thank divine Venus, the
goddess
Who makes girls fall in love. You did them because
you had to do them; Venus compelled you; I
Enjoyed her favor.
(Crosses down two steps to her Left)
           A man dares things, you know; he
makes his adventure
In the cold eye of death; and if the gods care for him
They appoint an instrument to save him; if not, he dies.
You were that instrument.
MEDEA.
           Here it is: the lowest.
The obscene dregs; the slime and the loathing; the
muddy bottom of a mouthed cup: when a scoun-
drel begins
To invoke the gods
JASON.
Ha!
MEDEA.
You had better go, Jason. Vulgarity
Is a contagious disease; and in a moment what could I
do but spit at you like a peasant, or curse you
Like a drunken slave? You had better take yourself
back to
"Little Creusa."
JASON.
           I came to help you and save you if
possible.
(Reaches down and touches her arm.)
MEDEA.
           Your help
Is not wanted. Go. Go.
JASON. *(Crosses below her to Right Center, then stops)*
           If I could see my boys—
MEDEA.
           Go
quickly.
JASON.
           Yours the regret then.

(Exits up Right. Watching him go, MEDEA strokes her wrist and hand to the tips of the spread fingers, as if she were scraping off slime.)
MEDEA.
This is it. I did not surely know it: loathing is all. This
flesh
He has touched and fouled. These hands that wrought
for him, these knees
That ran his errands. This body that took his—what
they call love, and made children of it. If I could
peel off
The flesh, the children, the memory—
(Again she scarifies one hand with the other. She looks at her hand)
           Poor misused
hand; poor defiled arm; your bones
Are not unshapely. If I could tear off the flesh and be
bones; naked bones;
Salt-scoured bones on the shore
At home in Colchis.

FIRST WOMAN. (*Rises and crosses down Right*)
God keep me from fire and the hunger of the sword,
Save me from the hateful sea and the jagged lightning,
And the violence of love.
SECOND WOMAN. (*Joins* FIRST WOMAN)
A little love is a joy in the house,
A little fire is a jewel against frost and darkness.

(*During these two speeches* THIRD WOMAN
goes up Right Center, then returns to
WOMEN *down Right.*)

FIRST WOMAN.
A great love is a fire
That burns the beams of the roof.
(THIRD WOMAN *kneels.*)
A great love is a lion in the cattle-pen,
The herd goes mad, the heifers run bawling
And the claws are in their flanks.
Too much love is an armed robber in the treasury.
He has killed the guards and he walks in blood.
SECOND WOMAN.
And now I see the black end,
The end of great love, and God save me from it:
The unburied horror, the unbridled hatred,
The vultures tearing a corpse!
God keep me clean of those evil beaks.
THIRD WOMAN.
What is she doing, that woman,
Staring like stone, staring?
(MEDEA *looks up.*)
Oh, she has moved now.
MEDEA.
Annihilation. The word is pure music: annihilation. To
annihilate the past—
Is not possible: but its fruit in the present—
Can be nipped off. Am I to look in my sons' eyes
And see Jason's forever? How could I endure the end-
less defilement, those lives
That mix Jason and me? Better to be clean
Bones on the shore. Bones have no eyes at all, how
could they weep? White bones
On the Black Sea shore—
Oh, but that's far. Not yet.
Corinth must howl first.
FIRST WOMAN.
The holy fountains flow up from the earth,
The smoke of sacrifice flows up from the earth,

The eagle and the wild swan fly up from the earth,
Righteousness also
Has flown up from the earth to the feet of God.
It is not here, but up there; peace and pity are de-
parted;
Hatred is here; hatred is heavy, it clings to the earth.
Love blows away, hatred remains.
SECOND WOMAN.
Women hate war, but men will wage it again.
Women may hate their husbands, and sons their
fathers,
But women will never hate their own children.
FIRST WOMAN.
But as for me, I will do good to my husband,
I will love my sons and daughters, and adore the gods.
MEDEA.
If I should go into the house with a sharp knife
To the man and his bride—
(MEDEA *rises.* THIRD WOMAN *rises.*)
Or if I could fire the room they sleep in, and hear them
Wake in the white of the fire, and cry to each other,
and howl like dogs.
THREE WOMEN.
Oh!!!
(*Cringe together.*)
MEDEA.
And howl and die—
But I might fail; I might be cut down first;
The knife might turn in my hand, or the fire not burn,
and my enemies could laugh at me.

No: I have subtler means, and more deadly cruel; I
have my dark art
That fools call witchcraft. Not for nothing I have
worshipped the wild gray goddess that walks in
the dark, the wise one,
The terrible one, the sweet huntress, flower of night,
Hecate,
In my house at my hearth.
(*She crosses up to pillar Right and sits.*)
THE NURSE. (*Hurries in toward* MEDEA, *to her Right*)
My lady: he was leaving Creon's
door: he is coming.
(MEDEA *pays no attention.*)
Ægeus is coming?
The power of Athens.
MEDEA. (*Prays*)
Ancient Goddess to whom I and my people
Make the sacrifice of black lambs and black female
hounds,
Holy one, haunter of cross-roads, queen of night,
Hecate,
Help me now: to remember in my mind the use of the
venomous fire, the magic song
And the sharp gems.
(*She sits in deep thought.* ÆGEUS *comes in up
Right.*)
THE NURSE.
He is here, my lady,
Athens is here.

(MEDEA *pays no attention.* THREE WOMEN
*curtsy, then resume their original positions at
rock.* FIRST WOMAN *sits.*)

ÆGEUS. (*Crosses down Left and up steps to top
step, Left of* MEDEA)
Medea, rejoice! There is no fairer
greeting from friend to friend.
(*She ignores him. He speaks more loudly*)
Hail and rejoice! Medea.
MEDEA. (*Lifts her head and stares at him*)
"Rejoice?" It may be so. It
may be I shall—rejoice
Before the sun sets.
ÆGEUS.
What has happened to you?
Your
eyes are cavernous!
And your mouth twitches.

MEDEA.
Nothing: I am quite well:
fools trouble me.—Where are you travelling from,
Ægeus?
ÆGEUS.
From Delphi, where I went to consult
The ancient oracle of Apollo.
MEDEA. (*Abstractedly*)
Oh— Delphi—
Did you get a good answer?
ÆGEUS.
An obscure one.
Some god or other has made me unable to beget a child:
that is my sorrow: but the oracle
Never gives plain responses.
(*Crosses two steps nearer her*)
I tell you these things
because you are skilled in mysteries, and you might
help me
To the god's meaning.
MEDEA. (*Wearily*)
You want a child? What did
Apollo
Say to you?
ÆGEUS.
That I must not unloose the hanging foot
of the wine-skin until I return
To the hearth of my fathers.
MEDEA. (*Without interest, but understanding the
anatomical reference*)

You have never had a child?

ÆGEUS.
No.
And it is bitterness.
(Turns away from her and takes one step down.)

MEDEA.
But when misfortune comes it is bitter to have children, and watch their starlike Faces grow dim to endure it.

ÆGEUS.
When death comes, Medea, It is, for a childless man, utter despair, darkness, extinction. One's children Are the life after death.

MEDEA. *(Excited)*
Do you feel it so? Do you feel it so?
Then—if you had a dog-eyed enemy and needed absolute vengeance—you'd kill The man's children first. Unchild him, ha?
And then unlife him.

ÆGEUS.
I do not care to think of such horrors.
I have no enemy.
(MEDEA rises, making violent movement; sits again. He stares, and slightly recoils from her. Crosses back up to her) What is it? What is the matter, Medea? You are trembling; wild fever Flames in your eyes.

MEDEA.
I am well enough— Fools trouble me, and dogs; but not that— Oh—

ÆGEUS.
What has happened to you?

THE NURSE. *(Crouches by her, trying to comfort her)*
My dear—my love—

MEDEA. *(Pushes her gently aside; looks up at ÆGEUS)*
I would not hurt my children. Their father hurts them.

ÆGEUS.
What do you mean—Jason? What has Jason done?

MEDEA.
He has betrayed and denied Both me and them.

ÆGEUS.
Jason has done that? Why? Why?

MEDEA.
He has cast me off and married Creon's young daughter.
And Creon, this very day, is driving us Into black exile.

ÆGEUS.
Jason consents to that?

MEDEA.
He is glad of it.

ÆGEUS. *(Crossing down steps to WOMEN down Right)*
Why—it's atrocious, it's past belief.

THE NURSE. *(Says in MEDEA's ear)*
Ask him for refuge! Ask him to receive you in Athens!

MEDEA. *(Straight and rigid)*
Do you not think such men ought to be punished, Ægeus?

ÆGEUS.
I think it is villainous.
They told me nothing of this—

MEDEA.
Do you not think such men ought to be punished, Ægeus?
(Crossing down steps to 2d step Center.)

ÆGEUS.
Where will you go?

MEDEA. *(Solemnly)*
If there is any rightness on earth or in heaven, they will be punished.

ÆGEUS.
Where Will you go to, Medea?

MEDEA. *(Crossing Left, still on 2nd step)*
What? To death, of course.

THE NURSE. *(Crosses to ÆGEUS)*
Oh— She is all bewildered, sir, In the deep storm and ocean of grief, or she would ask of you
Refuge in Athens.

MEDEA. *(In bitter mockery, seeing ÆGEUS hesitate)*
Ah? So I should. That startled the man.—Ægeus:
Will *you* shelter me in *Athens?*

ÆGEUS.
Why—yes. Yes—I will not take you now from Corinth; it would not be right.
I want no quarrel with Creon, I am his guest here.
(Crossing below NURSE to Center)
If you by your own means come to Athens I will take care of you.

(THE NURSE sits on 1st step to Right of ÆGEUS.)

MEDEA.
I could repay you for it. I know the remedies—that would make a dry stick flame into fire and fruit.

ÆGEUS. *(Eagerly)*
You'd cure my sterility?

MEDEA.
I could do so.

ÆGEUS.
You are famous for profound knowledge Of drugs and charms.
(Eagerly)
You'll come to Athens?

MEDEA.
If I choose.
If the gods decide it so. But, Ægeus, Would you protect me if I came? I have certain enemies. If powerful enemies came, baying for my blood,
Would you protect me?

ÆGEUS.
Why—yes. What enemies?— Yes.
Athens protects.

MEDEA.
I should need peace and a free mind While I prepared the medicines to make you well.

ÆGEUS.
You'll have them, you'll have them, Medea. You've seen the huge stones
In the old sacred war-belt of Athens. Come the four ends of the world, they will not break in: you're safe there:
I am your pledge.
(Extends arm, which she later takes.)

MEDEA.
Will you swear it, Ægeus?

ÆGEUS.
Ah? Why?
I promised.

MEDEA. *(She takes his arm)*
I trust you: the oath is formal: your cure
Depends on it.
(She crosses below him to down Right and then turns to him, raising her hand)
You swear by the fruitful earth and high shining heaven that you will protect me in Athens

Against all men. Swear it.
ÆGEUS. (*Raises his hand*)
　　　　　　　　　I swear by the fruitful earth
and high shining heaven to protect you in Athens
Against all men.

　　　　　(BOTH *lower their arms.*)
MEDEA.
　　　　　　　And if you should break this oath?
ÆGEUS.
　I will not break it.
MEDEA.
　　　　　　If you should break it, the earth
Will give you no bread but death, and the sky no light
But darkness.
ÆGEUS. (*Visibly perturbed*)
　　　　　I will not break it.
MEDEA.
　　　　　　　　　You must repeat the
words, Ægeus.
ÆGEUS.
If I break it, the earth
Will give me no bread but death, and the sky no light
But darkness.
MEDEA.
　　　　　　You have sworn: the gods have heard
　you.
　　　　　(*Crosses below* ÆGEUS *to Center. Pause.*)
ÆGEUS. (*Uneasily*)
　When will you come to Athens?
　　　　　(*Turning to her.*)
MEDEA.
　　　　　　　　　　To Athens?
Oh,
To Athens. Why:—if I come, if I live—it will be soon.
The yoke's
On the necks of the horses.
　　　　　(*Crosses up to top step at door of house*)
　　　　　　　—I have some things to do
That men will talk of afterwards with hushed voices:
　while I and my children
Safe in Athens laugh. Is that it? Farewell, Ægeus.
　　　　　(*She turns abruptly from him; goes slowly,
　　　　　deep in thought, into the house. The doors
　　　　　close.*)
ÆGEUS. (*Staring after her*)
　May the gods comfort you, Medea.—to you also
　farewell,
Women of Corinth.

　　　　　(THREE WOMEN *rise.*)

FIRST WOMAN.
　　　　　　　Fair be the gale behind you, sir,
　and the way ahead.
　　　　　(*Exit* ÆGEUS *up Right. She turns to* NURSE)
What is she plotting in her deep mind?
She is juggling with death and life, as a juggler
With a black ball and a white ball.

　　　　　(NURSE *slowly goes up to 2nd step, looking at
　　　　　door of house.*)

SECOND WOMAN. (*Crosses to Left of the* FIRST
WOMAN)
No: she is like some distracted city
Sharpening its weapons. Embassies visit her:
The heads of state come to her door:
She receives them darkly.
THE NURSE.
　　　　　　I beseech you, women,
Not to speak words against my lady whom I love. You
　know that wicked injustice she has to suffer.
　　　　　(*She prays*)
O God, protector of exiles, lord of the holy sky, lead us
To the high rock that Athens loves, and the olive
Garland of Athens.
　　　　　(THE NURSE *crosses down Left and sits on
　　　　　steps.*)

FIRST WOMAN.
　　　　　　　　　Athens is beautiful
As a lamp on a rock.
The temples are marble-shafted; light shines and
　lingers there.
Honey-color among the carved stones

And silver-color on the leaves of the olives.
The maidens are crowned with violets: Athens and
　Corinth
Are the two crowns of time.
　SECOND WOMAN. (*Crosses to* FIRST WOMAN *and
they join hands*)
Mycenae for spears and armor; Sparta
For the stern men and the tall blonde women; and
　Thebes I remember,
Old Thebes and the seven gates in the gray walls—
But rather I praise Athena, the ivory, the golden,
The gray-eyed Virgin, her city.
And also I praise Corinth of the beautiful fountains,
On the fair plain between the two gulfs.
　FIRST WOMAN.
God-favored cities of the Greek world.
Fortunate those that dwell in them, happy that behold
　them.
　SECOND WOMAN.
How can one wish to die? How can that woman
Be drowned in sorrow and bewildered with hatred?

　　　　　(*The BOLT on door is heard opening.
　　　　　MEDEA enters and stands in doorway.*)
For only to be alive and to see the light
Is beautiful. Only to see the light;
To see a blade of young grass,
Or the gray face of a stone.
　FIRST WOMAN. (*Pointing toward* MEDEA)
Hush.
　MEDEA. (*Proudly and falsely*)
　　　　　As you say. What a marvelous privilege it is
Merely to be alive. And how foolish it would be
To spend the one day of life that remains to me—at
　least in Corinth—this tag end of one day
On tears and hatred! Rather I should rejoice, and
　sing, and offer gifts; and as to my enemies—
I will be reconciled with them.
　FIRST WOMAN. (*Amazed*)
　　　　　　　　　Reconciled with them!

　　　　　(THREE WOMEN *cross a few steps to* MEDEA.)
MEDEA.
　　　As you say. Reconciled. Why should they hate me?
Surely I can appease those people.
They say that gold will buy anything; even friendship,
　even love: at least in Greece,
Among you civilized people, you reasonable and civil-
　ized Hellenes.—In fact,
We've seen it happen. They bought Jason; Jason's
　love. Well—
I shall buy theirs.
I still have two or three of the treasures that I brought
　from home, things of pure precious gold, which
　a god
Gave to the kings of my ancestors.
　　　　　(*The LIGHT darkens, a cloud passing over
　　　　　the sun. HARP effect offstage. The* THREE
　　　　　WOMEN *huddle together.*)
　　　　　　　　　　Is it late? It seems
　to me
That the light darkens.
　　　　　(*To* THE NURSE)
　　　　　　　　Is it evening?
THE NURSE. (*Trembling*)
　　　　　　　　No— No— A cloud.
MEDEA.
　I hope for thunder: let the sky rage: my gifts
　　　　　(*Enter* TWO SLAVES *from door with gift.
　　　　　Kneel on top step.*)
Will shine the brighter.—Listen, old woman! I want
　you
　　　　　(THE NURSE *rises.*)
To go to Jason and tell him—tell him— Tell him that

I am sick of hating and weary of evil!
I wish for peace.
> (MEDEA *crosses and stands between* TWO
> SLAVES)

I wish to send precious gifts to that pale girl with the
yellow hair

Whom he has married: tell him to come and take them
——and to kiss his boys
Before we go into exile. Tell him to come speedily. Now
run, run, find him.
> (MEDEA *turns her head away.*)

THE NURSE. (*Crossing to* WOMEN *stage Center*)
Oh, I'll go. I'll run.
> (*Tremulously, to* WOMEN)
> Let me pass, please.
> (WOMEN *make way for* THE NURSE. MEDEA
> *stands looking after her.* THE NURSE *turns
> back at the limit of the scene, Right, and says,
> wringing her hands*)

But I am terrified. I do not know— I am terrified.

Pray to the gods, women, to keep
Evil birds from our hearts!
> (*She hurries away up Right.*)
MEDEA. (*Crossing down two steps*)
Run! Run! Find him!!!!
> (MEDEA *goes into the house.*)

CURTAIN

ACT TWO

MEDEA *is sitting on the upper doorstep. A cloak of
woven gold lies across her knee and down the stone
steps. Beside her are two open cases of dark
leather. From one she takes a coronet of gold vine
leaves, looks at it and replaces it.*

TWO SERVING WOMEN *stand in the doorway behind her. On the Right, at some distance, the
THREE WOMEN are huddled, like sheep in a storm.
The Scene is darker than it was, and the gold
cloth shines.*

MEDEA.
These are the gifts I am sending to the young bride;
this golden wreath
And this woven-gold veil. They are not without value;
there is nothing like them in the whole world, or
at least
The Western world; the God of the Sun gave them to
my father's father, and I have kept them

In the deep chest for some high occasion; which has
now come.
I have great joy in giving these jewels to Creon's
daughter, for the glory of life consists of being
generous

To one's friends, and—merciless to one's enemies—you
know what a friend she has been to me. All Corinth
knows.
The slaves talk of it. The old stones in the walls
Have watched and laughed.

(MEDEA *looks at the gold cloth, and strokes it cautiously with her hand. It seems to scorch her
fingers.* THIRD WOMAN *has come nearer to look;
now starts backward.*)

MEDEA.
See, it is almost alive. Gold is a living thing: such
pure gold.
> (NURSE *enters from up Right; crosses to foot of
> steps*)
But when her body has warmed it, how it will shine!
> (*To the* NURSE)
Why doesn't he come? What keeps him?
NURSE. (*Evidently terrified*)

Oh, my lady: presently.
I have but now returned from him. He was beyond
the gate, watching the races—where a monstrous
thing
Had happened: a young mare broke from the chariot
And tore with her teeth a stallion.
MEDEA. (*Stands up, shakes out the golden cloak,
which again smoulders. She folds it cautiously, lays it
in the leather case. The LIGHT has darkened again.
She looks anxiously at the clouded sun*)
He takes his time, eh? It
is intolerable
To sit and wait.
> (*To the* SERVING WOMEN)
> Take these into the house. Keep them at hand
For when I call.
> (*They take them in.* MEDEA *moves restlessly, un-
> der extreme nervous tension; speaks to the* NURSE.

> NURSE *crosses below steps to stage Left, then up
> two steps*)
You say that a mare attacked a stallion?
THE NURSE.
She tore
him cruelly.
I saw him being led away: a black racer: his blood
ran down
From the throat to the fetlocks.
MEDEA.
You're sure he's coming. You're
sure?
THE NURSE.
He said he would.
MEDEA.
Let him make haste, then!
SECOND WOMAN. (*She crosses to Left below* NURSE)
Frightening irrational things
Have happened lately; the face of nature is flawed
with omens.
FIRST WOMAN. (*Crosses to Left, joining* SECOND
WOMAN)
Yesterday evening a slave
Came up to the harbor-gate, carrying a basket
Of new-caught fish: one of the fish took fire
And burned in the wet basket with a high flame: the
thing was witnessed
By many persons.
THIRD WOMAN. (*Crosses Left of other* TWO WOMEN,
joining them)
And a black leopard was seen
Gliding through the market-place—
MEDEA. (*Abruptly, approaching the* WOMEN)
You haven't told
me yet: do you not think that Creon's daughter
Will be glad of those gifts?
FIRST WOMAN.
O Medea, too much wealth
Is sometimes dreadful.
MEDEA.
She'll be glad, however. She'll
take them and put them on, she'll wear them, she'll
strut in them,
She'll peacock in them.—I see him coming now.—the
(THREE WOMEN *retire to up Left corner.* NURSE
sits below Left pillar)
whole palace will admire her.—Stand away from
me, women,
While I make my sick peace.

(MEDEA *crosses way down Right as* JASON *enters up
Right to stage Center.* NURSE *points at* MEDEA.
who goes across the scene to meet JASON, but more
and more slowly, and stops. Her attitude indicates
her aversion.*)

JASON.
Well, I have come. I tell you plainly,
Not for your sake: the children's. Your woman says
that you have your wits again, and are willing
To look beyond your own woes.

(MEDEA *is silent.* JASON *observes her and says*)
                                   It appears doubtful.
(She turns from him)
—Where are the children? I have made inquiry: I can find fosterage for them
In Epidarurus; or any other of several cities
That are Creon's friends. I'll visit them from time to time, and watch
That they're well kept.
MEDEA. *(With suppressed violence)*
                         You mean—take them from me!
Be careful, Jason, I am not patient yet.
(More quietly)
                    I am the one who labored in pain to bear them, I cannot
Smile while I lose them. But I am learning: I am learning.—
No, Jason: I will not give up my little ones
To the cold care of strangers.
Hard faces, harsh hands. It will be far better for them to share
My wandering ocean of beggary and bleak exile:
I love them, Jason. Only if you would keep them and care for them here in Corinth,
I might consent.
JASON.
          Gladly—but they are exiled.
MEDEA.
                                    —In your own
house.
JASON.
      Gladly I'd do it—but you understand
They are exiled, as you are. I asked Creon and he refused it.
MEDEA.
       You asked Creon to take my children from me?
(She reaches her hands toward him)
Forgive me, Jason,
As I do you.
       (Crosses up steps to his Right)
              We have had too much wrath, and our acts
Are closing on us. On me, I mean. Retribution is from the gods, and it breaks our hearts: but you
Feel no guilt, you fear nothing, nothing can touch you.
It is wonderful to stand serene above fate
While earthlings wince. If it lasts. It does not always last.
—Do you love the children, Jason?
JASON.
          Ha? Certainly. The children? Certainly!
I am their father.
MEDEA.
         Oh, but that's not enough. If I am to give them up to you—be patient with me,
I must question you first. And very deeply; to the quick. If anything happens to them,
Would you be grieved?
JASON.
                   Nothing will happen to them,
Medea, if in my care. Rest your mind on it.
MEDEA. *(She crosses up to top step in back of* JASON*)*
You must pardon me: it is not possible to be certain of that.
If they were—killed and their blood
Ran on the floor of the house or down the deep earth—
Would you be grieved?
JASON.
                  You have a sick mind. What a weak thing a woman is, always dreaming of evil.
MEDEA.
Answer me!
JASON.
          Yes, after I'd cut their killer into red collops—I'd grieve.
MEDEA.
               That is true: vengeance
Makes grief bearable.—But—Creon's daughter, your wife—no doubt will breed

Many other boys.—But, if something should happen to—Creon's daughter—
JASON.
      Enough, Medea. Too much. Be silent!
MEDEA.
I am to conclude that you love—Creon's daughter—
More than your sons They'll have to take the sad journey with me.
              (To the NURSE*)*
Tell the boys to come out
And bid their father farewell.
              (The NURSE *goes into the house.)*
JASON. *(Coming to her and taking her arm)*
                              I could take them from you
By force, Medea.
MEDEA. *(Violently)*
            Try it, you!

(Controlling herself)
          No, Creon decided otherwise; he said
          *(*JASON *crosses down Right as if to go)*
they will share my exile.—Come, Jason,
Let's be friends at last!
    (The BOYS *come out with their* TUTOR, *followed by the* NURSE. JASON *makes to clasp her arm. She pulls away to Center)*
I am quite patient now; I have learned.—Come, boys, come,
         *(*BOYS *run straight to* MEDEA.*)*
Speak to your father.
         *(*NURSE *and* TUTOR *remain on top step at either side of door. They shrink back)*
         No, no, we're friends again. We're not angry any more.
JASON. *(Has gone eagerly to meet them on the steps. He drops to one knee to be more nearly level with them, but they are shy and reluctant)*
         Big boys. Tall fellows, ha?
You've grown up since I saw you.
MEDEA.
                     Smile for him, children.
Give him
         (She turns, and stands rigidly turned away, her face sharp with pain)
         your hands.
THE NURSE. *(To* JASON*)*
            I think he's afraid of you, sir.
JASON. *(To the* YOUNGER BOY*)*
                                  What?
What? You'll learn, my man,
         (During this speech ELDER BOY *crosses to him. He picks him up)*
Not to fear me. You'll make your enemies run away from you
When you grow up.
         (To the ELDER BOY*)*
                        And you, Captain,
How would you like a horn-tipped bow to hunt rabbits with?
Wolves, I mean.
         (Takes ELDER BOY *by the hand and crosses with him to rock Right. He sits* YOUNGER BOY *on his lap.* ELDER BOY *sits on floor. He plays with the* BOYS. *They are less shy of him now.)*
FIRST WOMAN. *(Coming close to* MEDEA*)*
            Don't give them to him,
Medea. If you do it will ache forever.
SECOND WOMAN.
                            You have refuge;
take them there.
Athens is beautiful—
MEDEA. *(Fiercely)*
             Be silent!
Look at him: he loves them—ah? Therefore his dear children
Are not going to that city but a darker city, where no games are played, no music is heard.—Do you think
I am a cow lowing after the calf? Or a bitch with pups, licking

The hand that struck her? Watch and see. Watch this man, women: he is going to weep. I think
He is going to weep blood, and quite soon, and much more
Than I have wept. Watch and keep silence.
(She goes toward the GROUP *on the steps)*
Jason,
Are the boys dear to you? I think I am satisfied that you love them,
These two young heroes.
*(*JASON *stands up and turns to her, one of the* BOYS *clinging to each of his hands. He has made friends with them.)*
MEDEA. *(She weeps)*
Oh—Oh—Oh!
JASON.
—God's hand, Medea, what is it?
What is the matter?
MEDEA. *(Makes with both hands a gesture of pushing down something, flings her head back proudly)*
Nothing. It is hard to let them go.
—This I have thought of:
You shall take them to—Creon's daughter, your wife—and make them kneel to her, and ask her
To ask her father to let them stay here in Corinth. He'll grant it, he is growing old, he denies her nothing.
Even that hard king loves his only child.
What she asks is done.—You will go with the boys, Jason, and speak for them,—they are not skillful yet
In supplication—and I'll send gifts. I'll put gifts in their hands. People say that gifts
Will persuade even the gods.—Is it well thought of? Will she listen to us?
JASON.
Why, if I ask it! She'd hardly refuse me anything. And I believe that you're right,
She can rule Creon.
MEDEA. *(To the* TUTOR)
Bring me those gold things.
*(*TUTOR *exits main door.)*
(She extends hands to BOYS. *Sits on step. They cross to her)*
Dear ones, brave little falcons—little pawns of my agony—
Go, ask that proud breastless girl of her bitter charity
Whether she will let you nest here until your wings fledge, while far your mother
Flies the dark storm—
(She weeps again.)
JASON.
I'm sorry for you. Parting is hard.
(He crosses down Right off steps.)
MEDEA.
I can
bear it.
And worse too.
(The TUTOR *and* SERVING WOMEN *bring the gifts)*
Oh, here: here are the things: take them, darlings,
Into your little hands.
(Giving them to the BOYS. *Crown goes to* YOUNGER BOY. *Cloak to* ELDER BOY. *Each show them to* TUTOR *and* NURSE, *then sit on the 3rd step.* SERVING WOMEN *exit as soon as gifts are taken from them)*
Hold carefully by the cases: don't touch the gold,
Or it might—tarnish.
JASON.
Why! These are king's treasures. You shouldn't, Medea: it's too much. Creon's house
Has gold enough of its own.
MEDEA.
Oh—if she'll wear them. What should I want with woven gold vanities —Black is my wear. The woman ought to be very happy

(Throws wedding ring in box with cloak)
With such jewels—and such a husband—ah? Her sun is rising,
*(*MEDEA *crosses Left)*
mine going down—I hope
To a red sunset.—The little gold wreath is pretty, isn't it?

*(*YOUNGER BOY *holds it up to* JASON.)*

JASON. *(Doubtfully)*
It looks like fire—
MEDEA.
Vine leaves: the flashing
Arrow-sharp leaves. They have weight, though.
*(*BOYS *put down boxes)*
Gold is too heavy a burden
for little hands. Carry them, you,
Until you come to the palace.
*(*NURSE *takes gold wreath; exits up Right, followed by* TUTOR *with cloak.* JASON *follows with* BOYS *by the hand)*
—Farewell, sweet boys: brave
little trudging pilgrims from the black wave
To the white desert: take the stuff in, be sure you lay
it in her own hands.
Come back and tell me what happens.
(Crosses up to front of pillar Right and waves goodbye to them as they leave. She turns abruptly away from them)
Tell me what happens.
(The BOYS *go out reluctantly,* JASON *holding their hands.)*
Rejoice, women,
The gifts are given; the bait is laid.
The gods roll their great eyes over Creon's house and quietly smile:
That robe of bright-flowing gold, that bride-veil, that fish-net
To catch a young slender salmon—not mute, she'll sing: her delicate body writhes in the meshes,
The golden wreath binds her bright head with light: she'll dance, she'll sing loudly:
Would I were there to hear it, that proud one howling.
(She crosses to Center between pillars)
—Look, the sun's out again, the clouds are gone,
All's gay and clear. Ai! I wish the deep earth would open and swallow us—
Before I do what comes next.
I wish all life would perish,
(Crosses down to 3rd step and sits)
and the holy gods in high heaven die,
before my little ones
Come home to my hands.
FIRST WOMAN. *(Going to* MEDEA)
It would be better for you, Medea, if the earth
Opened her jaws and took you down into darkness.
But one thing you will not do, for you cannot,
You will not hurt your own children, though wrath like plague-boils
Aches, your mind in a fire-haze
Bites the purple apples of pain—no blood-lapping
Beast of the field, she-bear nor lioness,
Nor the lean wolf-bitch,
Hurts her own tender whelps, nor the yellow-eyed,
Scythe-beaked and storm-shouldered
Eagle that tears the lambs has ever made prey
Of the fruit of her own tree—
MEDEA.
How could that girl's death slake me?
THIRD WOMAN. *(Coming forward from the* OTHERS)
I am sick with terror.
I'll run to the palace, I'll warn them.
MEDEA.
Will you?—Go. Go if you will.
God and my vengeful goddess are doing these things: you cannot prevent them, but you could easily fall
In the same fire.

THIRD WOMAN. *(Retreating)*
            I am afraid to go.
MEDEA.
                You are wise. Anyone
Running between me and my justice will reap
What no man wants.
FIRST WOMAN.
             Not justice; vengeance.
You have suffered evil, you wish to inflict evil.
MEDEA.
I do according to nature what I have to do.
FIRST WOMAN.
I have heard evil
Answering evil as thunder answers the lightning.
A great waste voice in the hollow sky,
And all that they say is death. I have heard vengeance
Like an echo under a hill answering vengeance,
Great hollow voices: all that they say is death.
SECOND WOMAN.
                The sword speaks
And the spear answers: the city is desolate.
The nations remember old wrongs and destroy each
    other.
And no man binds up their wounds.
FIRST WOMAN.
                But justice
Builds a firm house.
MEDEA.
         The doors of her house are vengeance.
SECOND WOMAN.
            I dreamed that someone
Gave good for evil, and the world was amazed.
MEDEA. *(Rises. Crosses up between pillar and col-*
umn Right)
Only a coward or a madman gives good for evil.—Did
    you hear a thin music
Like a girl screaming? Or did I perhaps imagine it?
    Hark, it is music.

THIRD WOMAN. *(Crossing towards Center below*
steps)
Let me go, Medea!
I'll be mute, I'll speak to no one. I cannot bear—
Let me go to my house!
MEDEA.
             You will stay here,
And watch the end.
         (The WOMEN are beginning to mill like
         scared cattle, huddled and circular)
            You will be quiet, you women. You
came to see

How the barbarian woman endures betrayal: watch
    and you'll know.
SECOND WOMAN. *(Kneels)*
My heart is a shaken cup
Of terror: the thin black wine
Spills over all my flesh down to my feet.

FIRST WOMAN.
She fled from her father's house in a storm of blood,
In a blood-storm she flew up from Thessaly,
Now here and dark over Corinth she widens
Wings to ride up the twisted whirlwind
And talons to hold with—
Let me flee this dark place and the pillared doorway.
SECOND WOMAN.
I hear the man-wolf on the snow hill
Howl to the soaring moon—
THIRD WOMAN.
The demon comes in through the locked door
And strangles the child—
SECOND WOMAN.
Blood is the seed of blood, hundredfold the harvest,
The gleaners that follow it, their feet are crimson—
FIRST WOMAN.
I see the whirlwind hanging from the black sky.
Like a twisted rope,
Like an erect serpent, its tail tears the earth,
It is braided of dust and lightning,

Who will fly in it? Let me hide myself
From these night-shoring pillars and the dark door.

MEDEA.
                Have patience,
    women. Be quiet.
I am quite sure something has happened; presently
    someone
Will bring us news.
THIRD WOMAN.
            Look! The children are coming.
SECOND WOMAN. *(Rises)*
They have bright things in their hands: their faces are
    clear and joyous; was all that fear
A dream, a dream?

         (MEDEA crosses to pillar Left. The TUTOR
         enters up Right with the BOYS. The ELDER
         BOY carries a decorated bow and arrows;
         the YOUNGER BOY has a doll, a brightly
         painted wooden warrior. MEDEA, gazing at
         the BOYS, retreats slowly backward from
         them.)

THE TUTOR. *(Crossing up to MEDEA on top step;*
BOYS *stand behind him on 2nd and 3rd steps)*
           Rejoice, Medea, I bring good news. The
    princess graciously
Received your presents and smiled: it is peace between
    you. She has welcomed the little boys, they are
    safe from exile.
They'll be kept here. Their father is joyful.
MEDEA. *(Coldly, her hands clenched in the effort of*
self control)
                     Yes?
THE TUTOR.
All Creon's house is well pleased. When we first went in
The serving-women came and fondled the children;
    it was rumored through all the household that
    you and Jason
Were at peace again: like word of a victory
Running through a wide city, when people gather in
    the streets to be glad together: and we brought
    the boys
Into the hall; we put those costly gifts in their hands;
    then Jason
Led them before the Princess. At first she looked
    angrily at them and turned away, but Jason said,
"Don't be angry at your friends. You ought to love
Those whom I love. Look what they've brought you,
    dear," and she looked and saw
In the dark boxes the brilliant gold: she smiled then,
And marveled at it.
         (He turns to them and YOUNGER BOY crosses
         up to him)
           Afterwards she caressed the children;
    she even said that this little one's
Hair was like fine-spun gold. Then Jason gave them
    these toys and we came away.
MEDEA.
                Yes.—If this
Were all. If this were all, old man—
I'd have your bony loins beaten to a blood-froth
For the good news you bring.
TUTOR.
                My lady—!
MEDEA.
                There's more, however
It will come soon.

         (The BOYS shyly approach her and show their
         toys. She, with violent self-constraint, looks
         at them; but folds her hands in her cloak, not
         to touch them.)

ELDER BOY. *(Crosses to her. Drawing the little bow)*
Look, Mother.
MEDEA. *(Suddenly weeping)*
                Take them away from me!
I cannot bear. I cannot bear.

THE TUTOR.

Children, come quickly.
(He shepherds them up the steps, and disappears in the house.)
FIRST WOMAN.
If there is any mercy or forbearance in heaven
Let it reach down and touch that dark mind
To save it from what it dreams—
THE SLAVE. *(A young SLAVE dashes in up Right, panting and distraught. He has run from CREON'S house)*

Where is Medea?
(SLAVE crosses to base of steps Right, throwing himself across them.)
SECOND WOMAN.

What has happened? What horror drives you?
Are spears hunting behind you?

THE SLAVE. *(He sees MEDEA on the steps)*

Flee for your life, Medea! I am
Jason's man, but you were good to me
While I was here in the house. Can you hear me?
Escape, Medea!
MEDEA.

I hear you.
Draw breath; say quietly
What you have seen. It must have been something
notable, the way your eyes
Bulge in the whites.
THE SLAVE.

If you have horses, Medea, drive! Or
a boat on the shore,
Sail!
(Rises and crosses down stage Right.)
MEDEA.

But first you must tell me about the beautiful
girl who was lately married:
SLAVE.
Ooh!
MEDEA.

your great man's daughter:
SLAVE.
Ooh!
MEDEA.
Are they all quite well?
SLAVE.

My ears ring with the crying,
my eyes are scalded. She put on the gold garments—
Did you do it, Medea?
MEDEA.

I did it.
SLAVE.
Ooooh!!!
MEDEA.
Speak quietly.
THE SLAVE.

You are avenged.
You are horribly avenged. It is too much.
The gods will hate you.
(Collapses on podium.)
MEDEA. *(Avid, but still sitting)*
That is my care. Did anyone die with her?
THE SLAVE.

Creon!
THREE WOMEN.
Oooh!!!!
MEDEA. *(Solemnly)*
Where is pride now?
Tell me all that you saw. Speak slowly.
THE SLAVE.

He tried to save her—

he died! Corinth is masterless.
All's in amazed confusion, and some are looting, but
they'll avenge him—
(He hears someone coming behind him)
I'm going on!
Someone is going to die.

(He runs Left to the far side of the scene, and exits while MEDEA speaks. Meanwhile the light has been changing, and soon the sun will set.)

MEDEA.

Here comes a more stable witness.
(The NURSE enters from up Right)
Old friend:
Catch your breath; take your time. I want the whole
tale, every gesture and cry. I have labored for this.
THE NURSE.
Death is turned loose! I've hobbled and run, and
fallen—
(Crosses to 4th step and sits.)
MEDEA.

Please
Nurse: I am very happy: go slowly.
(MEDEA sits and puts her head in NURSE's lap)
Tell me these things in order from the beginning.
As when you used to dress me, when I was little, in my
father's house: you used to say
"One thing at a time; one thing and then the next."
(The LIGHT has changed to a flare of sunset)

(THREE WOMEN have assembled themselves after NURSE's entrance in following fashion: FIRST sitting first step Center, SECOND standing to her Left, THIRD standing to Left of SECOND.)

THE NURSE.

My eyes are blistered,
My throat's like a dry straw— There was a long mirror
on the wall, and when her eyes saw it—
After the children had gone with Jason—she put her
hands in the case and took those gold things—and I
Watched, for I feared something might happen to her,
but I never thought
So horribly—she placed on her little head the bright
golden wreath, she gathered the flowing gold robe
Around her white shoulders,
And slender flanks,—
(MEDEA rises; crosses to below rock down Right)
And gazed at the girl in the metal mirror, going back
and forth
On tiptoe almost;
But suddenly horror began. I— Oh, oh—
MEDEA. *(Crosses up to Right of NURSE, shaking her by the shoulders)*
You are not suffering.
You saw it, you did not feel it. Speak plainly.
THE NURSE.

Her face went white;
She staggered a few steps, bending over, and fell

Into the great throne-chair; then a serving woman
Began to call for water thinking she had fainted, but
saw the foam
Start on her lips, and the eyes rolling, and screamed
instead. Then some of them
Ran after Jason, others ran to fetch Creon: and that
doomed girl
Frightfully crying started up from the chair; she ran,
she was like a torch, and the gold crown
(MEDEA races up to door of house writhing)
Like a comet streamed fire; she tore at it but it clung
to her head; the golden cloak
Was white-hot, flaying the flesh from the living bones:
blood mixed with fire ran down, she fell, she
burned
On the floor, writhing. Then Creon came and flung
himself on her, hoping to choke
That rage of flame, but it ran through him, his own
agony
Made him forget his daughter's. The fire stuck to the
flesh, it glued him to her; he tried to stand up,
He tore her body and his own. The burnt flesh broke

In lumps from the bones.
(She covers her eyes with her hands)
I have finished. They lie there.
Eyeless, disfaced, untouchable; middens of smoking
flesh—
(Nearly a scream)
No!
I have no more.
MEDEA. *(Crossing down to* NURSE; *takes her arms)*
I want all.
Had they died when you came away?
THE NURSE.
I am not able—have mercy—
No, the breath
Still whistled in the black mouths. No one could touch
them.
Jason stood in their smoke, and his hands tore
His unhelmeted hair.
MEDEA.
You have told good news well: I'll reward you.
As for those people, they will soon die. Their woes are
over too soon.
*(MEDEA crosses down, then paces up Right
and back down Right; sees* WOMEN *at end of
speech and crosses to them)*
Mine are not.
Jason's are not.
*(She turns abruptly from them, toward the
BOYS, who have been standing by the doorway,
fascinated, not comprehending but watching)*
My little falcons!—Listen to me! Laugh and
be glad: we have accomplished it.
Our enemies were great and powerful, they were full
of cold pride, they ruled all this country—they are
down in the ashes.
(Sitting on steps with BOYS)
Crying like dogs, cowering in the ashes, in their own
ashes. They went down with the sun, and the sun
will rise
And not see them again. He will think "Perhaps they
are sleeping, they feasted late.
At noon they will walk in the garden." Oh, no, oh, no!
They will not walk in the garden. No one has ever
injured me but suffered more
Than I had suffered.
(She turns from the BOYS)
Therefore this final sacrifice I
intended glares in my eyes
Like a lion on a ridge.
(Turning back to the BOYS)
We still hate, you know;—a person
nearer than these, more vile, more contemptible,
Whom I—I cannot. If he were my own hands I would
cut him off, or my eyes, I would gouge him out—
But not you: that was madness.
(She turns from them)
So Jason will be able to
say, "I have lost much,
But not all: I have children: My sons are well."
*(She stands staring, agonized, one hand pick-
ing at the other)*
No! I want him crushed, boneless, crawling—
I have no choice.
(Resolutely, to the THREE WOMEN. *She rises
and crosses down Left to* WOMEN)
You there! You thought me soft and
submissive like a common woman—who takes a
blow
And cries a little, and she wipes her face
And runs about the housework, loving her master? I
am not such a woman.
FIRST WOMAN.
Awake, Medea!
Awake from the evil dream. Catch up your children and
flee,
Farther than Athens, farther than Thrace or Spain,
flee to the world's end.
Fire and death have done your bidding,
Are you not fed full with evil?

Is it not enough?
MEDEA.
No, Loathing is endless.
Hate is a bottomless cup, I will pour and pour.
(She turns fiercely to the BOYS)
Children—
(Suddenly melting)
—O my
little ones!
What was I dreaming?—My babes, my own!
(She kneels to them, taking their hands)
Never, never, never, never
Shall my own babes be hurt. Not if every war-hound
and spear-slave in headless Corinth
Were on the track.
(Still kneeling; to WOMEN)
Look, their sweet lips are trembling:
look, women, the little mouths: I frightened them
With those wild words: they stood and faced me, they
never flinched.
Look at their proud young eyes! My eaglets, my golden
ones!
*(She kisses them, then holds them off and
gazes at them)*
O sweet small faces—like the pale wild-roses
That blossom where the cliff breaks toward the brilliant
sea: the delicate form and color, the dear, dear
fragrance
Of your sweet breath—
*(She continues gazing at them; her face
changes)*

THE NURSE. *(Sits up)*
My lady, make haste, haste!
Take them and flee. Flee away from here! Someone
will come soon.
(MEDEA still gazes at the BOYS)
Oh—listen to me.
Spears will come, death will come. All Corinth is in
confusion and headless anarchy, unkinged and
amazed
Around that horror you made: therefore they linger:
yet in a moment
Its avengers come!
(MEDEA looks up from staring at the BOYS.
*Her face has changed; the love has gone out
of it. She speaks in a colorless, tired voice)*
MEDEA.
I have a sword in the house.
I can defend you.
(She stands up stiffly and takes the BOYS *by
their shoulders; holds the* ELDER *in front of
her, toward* WOMEN: *speaks with cold in-
tensity)*
Would you say that this child
Has Jason's eyes?
(The WOMEN *are silent, in terror gazing at
her)*
—They are his cubs. They have his blood.
As long as they live I shall be mixed with him.
*(Crosses to pillar up Right. She looks down
at the* BOYS; *speaks tenderly but hopelessly.)*
Children:
It is evening. See, evening has come. Come, little ones.
Into the house.
(BOYS cross to her; arms about her waist)
Evening brings all things home. It brings
the bird to the bough and the lamb to the fold—
And the child to the mother.
(She pushes BOYS *gently into house)*
We must not think too much:
people go mad
If they think too much.
(In the doorway, behind BOYS, *she flings up
her hands as if to tear her hair out by the
roots; then quietly goes in. The great door
closes; the iron noise of the* BOLT *is driven
home.)*
THE NURSE.

No!
(She rushes toward the door, helpless, her hand reaching up and beating feebly against the foot of the door.)

FIRST WOMAN.
What is going to happen?

SECOND WOMAN.
That crown of horrors—
(They speak like somnambulists, and stand frozen. There is a moment of silence.)

CHILD'S VOICE. *(In the house, shrill, broken off)*
Mother Ai—!
(The WOMEN *press toward the door, crying more or less simultaneously)*

THE WOMEN.
Medea, no!
Prevent her! Save them!
Open the door—
(They listen for an answer.)

THIRD WOMAN.
A god is here, Medea, he calls to you, he forbids you—

*(*NURSE *has risen, and beats feebly on the door, stooping and bent over.* FIRST WOMAN *stands beside her, very erect, with her back against the door, covering her ears with her hands. They are silent.)*

ELDER BOY'S VOICE. *(Clear, but as if hypnotized)*
Mother— Mother—ai!

MEDEA. Aaahh!!!!

(Lamentation— keening —is heard in the house. It rises and falls, and continues to the end, but often nearly inaudible. It is now twilight.)

THE NURSE. *(Limps down the steps and says)*
There is no hope in heaven or earth. It is done.
It was destined when she was born, now it is done.
(Wailing.)
Oh, oh, oh.

THIRD WOMAN. *(With terror, looking into the shadows)*
Who is coming?
Someone is running at us!

FIRST WOMAN. *(Quietly)*
The accursed man.
Jason.

SECOND WOMAN.
He has a sword.

FIRST WOMAN.
I am more afraid of the clinging contagion of his misfortunes.
A man the gods are destroying.

JASON. *(Enters rapidly up Right, disheveled and shaking, a drawn sword in his hand. Crosses in to Right at foot of steps)*
Where is that murderess? Here in the house?
Or has she fled? She'll have to hide in the heavy metal darkness and caves of the earth—and there
I'll crawl and find her.
(No answer. The THREE WOMEN *draw away from him as he moves toward the door. He stops and turns on them, drawing his left hand across his face, as if his eyes were bewildered.)*

JASON.
Are you struck dumb? Are you shielding her?
Where is Medea?

FIRST WOMAN.
You caused these things. She was faithful to you and you broke faith.
Horror is here.

JASON.
Uncaused. There was no reason— Tell me at once—
Whether she took my boys with her? Creon's people

would kill them for what she has done: I'd rather save them
Than punish her. Help me in this.

THE NURSE. *(Wailing, sinks to ground down Left)*
Oh, oh, oh—

JASON. *(Looking sharply at* NURSE*)*
So she has killed herself.
Good. She never lacked courage— I'll take my sons away to the far end of the earth, and never
Speak of these things again.

THE NURSE. *(Wailing)*
Oh, oh, oh—

(Lamentation from the house answers.)

JASON. *(With a queer slyness, for he is trying to cheat himself out of believing what he dreads. He glances at the door, furtively, over his shoulder)*
Is she lying in there?
Honorable at least in her death.—I might have known it.
(They remain silent)
Well, answer!

FIRST WOMAN. *(Pointing toward* CREON'S *house)*
Death is there; death is here.
But you are both blind and deaf: how can I tell you?

JASON. *(Is silent, then says slowly)*
But—the— children are well?

FIRST WOMAN.
I do not know
Whether Medea lives or is dead.

JASON. *(Flings down the sword and sets his shoulder against the door; pushes in vain)*
Open! Open! Open!
(Returns halfway down the steps, and says pitiably)
Women, I am alone.
Help me.
Help me to break the bolt.
Go and find help—

*(*JASON *runs down Right as door opens. This stops him and he turns. It is now fairly dark; the interior of the house is lighted.* WOMEN *draw back in fear;* JASON *stands on the steps, bewildered.* MEDEA *comes into the doorway; her hand and clothing are blood-marked. The door closes.)*

MEDEA.
What feeble night-bird overcome by misfortune beats at my door?

*(*JASON *takes two steps up to her)*
Can this be that great adventurer,
The famous lord of the seas and delight of women, the heir of rich Corinth—this crying drunkard
On the dark doorstep?—Yet you've not had enough.
You have come to drink the last bitter drops.
I'll pour them for you.
(She displays her hand which is covered with blood.)

JASON.
What's that stain on your hands?

MEDEA.
The wine
I was pouring for you spilled on my hand—
Dear were the little grapes that were crushed to make it; dear were the vineyards.

JASON.
I came to kill you, Medea,
Like a caught beast, like a crawling viper. Give me my sons, that I may save them from Creon's men,
I'll go quietly away.

MEDEA.
Hush, they are sleeping. Perhaps
I will let you look at them: you cannot have them.
But the hour is late, you ought to go home to that highborn bride: the night has fallen, surely she longs for you.

Surely her flesh is not crusted black, nor her forehead
  burned bald, nor her mouth a horror.
        (JASON *kneels on the steps, painfully groping*
        for his sword)
                                        She
is very young. But surely she loves and desires
  you—
Surely she will be fruitful.—Your sword you want?
There it is. Not that step, the next lower. No, the next
  higher.
JASON. *(Stands erect. Goes up two steps to her)*
I'll kill you first and then find my sons.

MEDEA.
                        You must be careful, Jason.
  Do you see the two fire-snakes
That guard this door?
        (Indicating the two snakes)
        Here and here: one on each side: two
  serpents.
  Their throats are swollen with poison,
Their eyes are burning coals and their tongues are fire.
  They are coiled ready to strike: if you come near
  them,
They'll make you what Creon is. But stand there very
  quietly.
        I'll let you
Look at your sons.
        (MEDEA *crosses to pillar Left*)

Open the doors that he may see them.
        (The doors open revealing the Two Boys
        soaked in blood.)
JASON. *(Flinging his hands to his temples and cross-*
ing up to pillar Right)
        I knew it already.
I knew it before I saw it. No wild beast could have
  done it.
MEDEA.
                                I have
  done it: because I loathed you more
Than I loved them.
JASON.
        Did you feel nothing, no pity, are you pure evil? I
        should have killed you
The day I saw you.
MEDEA.
        I tore my own heart and laughed: I was tearing
        yours.
JASON. Will you laugh while I strangle you?
MEDEA.
I would still laugh.

        (JASON *lunges at her but is sent back by*
        snakes)
                —Beware my door holders, Jason! these
  eager serpents.—I'd still be joyful
To know that every bone of your life is broken: you
  are left helpless, friendless, mateless, childless,
Avoided by gods and men, unclean with awful excess
  of grief—childless

JASON.
        It is no matter now
Who lives, or who dies.
        (As next speech is said JASON *starts slowly*
        down steps to Right.)
MEDEA.
        You had love and betrayed it: now of all men
You are utterly the most miserable. As I of women.
        But I, as woman, despised, a foreigner, alone
Against you and the might of Corinth,
Have met you, throat for throat, evil for evil, vengeance
  for vengeance.
JASON. *(Turning to her on bottom step)*
        What does it matter now?
Only give me my boys: the little pitiful violated bodies:
  that I may bury them
In some kind place.
MEDEA.

To you?—You would betray even the little bodies:
  coin them for silver.
Sell them for power. No!
        JASON. *(Crawling up two more steps at her feet)*
        Let me touch their dear flesh, let me touch
        their hair!
MEDEA.
                No. They are mine.
                        (HARP EFFECT off Right)
They are going with me: the chariot is at the gate.

        (During this speech JASON *rises and goes*
        slowly down Right)

                Go down to your ship Argo and weep beside
        it, that rotting hulk on the harbor-beach
Drawn dry astrand, never to be launched again—even
        the weeds and barnacles on the warped keel
Are dead and stink:—that's your last companion—
And only hope: for some time one of the rotting tim-
        bers
Will fall on your head and kill you—meanwhile sit
        there and mourn, remembering the infinite evil,
        and the good
That you made evil.

        Now I go forth
Under the cold eyes of heaven—those weakness-despis-
        ing stars:—not me they scorn.

(MEDEA *goes into the house—*JASON *starts after her*
        but the door is bolted in his face. He collapses to
        the ground in front of doors. MEDEA *is seen com-*
        ing out Left door bearing the Two Boys. *Then as*
        final fanfare of MUSIC comes slow

                        CURTAIN

Mister Roberts

BY THOMAS HEGGEN and JOSHUA LOGAN

First presented by Leland Hayward at the Alvin Theatre in New York on February 18, 1948, with the following cast:

CHIEF JOHNSON	Rusty Lane	DOLAN	Casey Walters
LIEUTENANT (JG) ROBERTS	Henry Fonda	GERHART	Fred Barton
DOC	Robert Keith	PAYNE	James Sherwood
DOWDY	Joe Marr	LIEUTENANT ANN GIRARD	Jocelyn Brando
THE CAPTAIN	William Harrigan	SHORE PATROLMAN	John Jordan
INSIGNA	Harvey Lembeck	MILITARY POLICEMAN	Marshall Jamison
MANNION	Ralph Meeker	SHORE PATROL OFFICER	Murray Hamilton
LINDSTROM	Karl Lukas	SEAMEN, FIREMEN AND OTHERS:	
STEFANOWSKI	Steven Hill	Tiger Andrews, Joe Bernard, Ellis Eringer,	
WILEY	Robert Baines	Mikel Kane, Bob Keith, Jr., Walter Mullen,	
SCHLEMMER	Lee Krieger	John (Red) Kullers, Jack Pierce, Len Smith,	
REBER	John Campbell	Jr., Sanders (Sandy) Turner	
ENSIGN PULVER	David Wayne		

Scene: Aboard the U.S. Navy Cargo Ship, *AK 601*, operating in the back areas of the Pacific.

Time: A few weeks before V-E Day until a few weeks before V-J Day.

Mister Roberts was the most successful war play of the American theatre since *What Price Glory?* It was originally a novel written by Thomas O. (Orlo) Heggen out of his experience in the Navy, from which he was discharged in the fall of 1945. Mr. Heggen, who is of Norwegian descent and therefore qualifies for seafaring, was born on December 23, 1919, in Fort Dodge, Iowa. He attended the University of Minnesota, where he successfully discharged an apprenticeship in journalism by contributing a popular comic column to the college paper, the Minnesota *Daily,* and received his bachelor's degree in 1941. Joining the American Navy, he attained the rank of lieutenant, spent three years in the service, and saw action at Guam, Iwo Jima, and Okinawa. By the time he was ready for discharge, he had as much right as any man of letters to report on naval life. He found a position on the editorial staff of *Reader's Digest.* His *Mister Roberts* was published in 1946.

Its success attracted the Texas-born and Princeton-educated Joshua Logan, until then known only as a director and as an extremely talented one who had studied with Stanislavsky in Moscow on a fellowship and had subsequently staged, since 1938, such noteworthy productions as *On Borrowed Time, I Married an Angel, Knickerbocker Holiday,* and *Charley's Aunt*—the Broadway production that introduced another Princetonian, José Ferrer, as an actor to be reckoned with. Mr. Logan, whose own overseas experience had led to a captaincy in the Air Forces Combat Intelligence, found the play agent Leland Hayward favorably disposed toward turning producer and sponsoring a production of *Mister Roberts* if it were turned into a play. Mr. Logan collaborated on the dramatization with Mr. Heggen. For the leading part he recruited Henry Fonda, who had been a member of the University Players company Logan had founded on Cape Cod after leaving Princeton. A better choice could not have been made, and the results were gratifying to everyone involved in the extremely successful enterprise. The play, like the novel, was, in the words of John Mason Brown, "tough-fibered, muscular, and exuberant in its animalism," and "wonderfully unromantic and unorthodox" in its realization "that boredom is one of the chief conditions and horrors of war." At the same time, it was appealingly romantic as a tribute to the young officer-hero who was eager to see active service instead of navigating constantly on a supply ship "from Apathy to Tedium and back again." It would have been a miracle if the American public had been able to resist the Broadway production. Encouraged by the success of the play he had written as well as staged, Mr. Logan continued to try his hand at playwriting. He collaborated on the libretto of *South Pacific* with Oscar Hammerstein the Second, and he based *The Wisteria Trees* on *The Cherry Orchard* by Anton Chekhov the first and, alas, last.

ACT ONE

SCENE ONE

The curtain rises on the main set, which is the amidships section of a navy cargo ship. The section of the ship shown is the house, and the deck immediately forward of the house. Dominating center stage is a covered hatch. The house extends on an angle to the audience from downstage left to upstage right. At each side is a passageway leading to the after part of the ship. Over the passageways on each side are twenty-millimeter gun tubs; ladders lead up to each tub. In each passageway and hardly visible to the audience is a steep ladder leading up to a bridge. Downstage right is a double bitt. At the left end of the hatch cover is an opening. This is the entrance to the companionway which leads to the crew's compartment below. The lower parts of two kingposts are shown against the house. A life raft is also visible. A solid metal rail runs from stage right and disappears behind the house. Upstage center is the door to the Captain's cabin. The pilothouse with its many portholes is indicated on the bridge above. On the flying bridge are the usual nautical furnishings: a searchlight and two ventilators. Over the door is a loudspeaker. There is a porthole to the left of the door and two portholes to the right. These last two look into the Captain's cabin.

The only object which differentiates this ship from any other navy cargo ship is a small scrawny palm tree, potted in a five-gallon can, standing to the right of the Captain's cabin door. On the container, painted in large white letters, is the legend: "PROP.T OF CAPTAIN, KEEP AWAY."

At rise, the lighting indicates that it is shortly after dawn. The stage is empty and there is no indication of life other than the sound of snoring from below.

Chief Johnson, a bulging man about forty, enters through passageway upstage left. He wears dungaree shirt and pants and a chief petty officer's cap. He is obviously chewing tobacco, and he starts down the hatchway, notices the palm tree, crosses to the Captain's door cautiously, peering into the porthole to see that he is not being watched, then deliberately spits into the palm tree container. He wipes his mouth smugly and shuffles over to the hatch. There he stops, takes out his watch and looks at it, then disappears down the hatchway. A shrill whistle is heard.

——

JOHNSON (offstage—in a loud singsong voice which is obviously just carrying out a ritual). Reveille . . . Hit the deck . . . Greet the new day . . . (The whistle is heard again) Reveille . . .

INSIGNA (offstage). Okay, Chief, you done your duty—now get your big fat can out of here!

(Johnson reappears at the head of hatchway calling back.)

JOHNSON. Just thought you'd like to know about reveille. And you're going to miss chow again.

STEFANOWSKI (offstage). Thanks, Chief. Now go back to bed and stop bothering us.

(His duty done, Johnson, still chewing, shuffles across the stage and disappears. There is a brief moment of silence, then the snoring is resumed below.)

(After a moment, Roberts enters from the passageway at right. He wears khaki shirt and trousers and an officer's cap. On each side of his collar he wears the silver bar indicating the rank of Lieutenant [junior grade]. He carries a rumpled piece of writing paper in his left hand, on which there is a great deal of writing and large black marks indicating that much has been scratched out. He walks slowly to the bitt, concentrating, then stands a moment looking out right. He suddenly gets an idea and goes to hatch cover, sitting and writing on the paper. Doc enters from the left passageway. Doc is between thirty-five and forty and he wears khakis and an officer's fore-and-aft cap; he wears medical insignia and the bars of Lieutenant [senior grade] on his collar. A stethoscope sticks out of his hip pocket. He is wiping the sweat off his neck with his handkerchief as he crosses above hatch cover. He stops as he sees Roberts.)

DOC. That you, Doug?

ROBERTS (wearily, looking up). Hello, Doc. What are you doing up?

DOC. I heard you were working cargo today so I thought I'd get ready. On days when there's any work to be done I can always count on a big turnout at sick call.

ROBERTS (*smiles*). Oh, yeah.

DOC. I attract some very rare diseases on cargo days. That day they knew you were going to load five ships I was greeted by six more cases of beriberi—double beriberi this time. So help me, I'm going down to the ship's library and throw that old copy of *Moby Dick* overboard!
(*He sits on hatch cover.*)

ROBERTS. What are you giving them these days for double beriberi?

DOC. Aspirin—what else? (*He looks at Roberts*) Is there something wrong, Doug?

ROBERTS (*preoccupied*). No.

DOC (*lying back on the hatch*). We missed you when you went on watch last night. I gave young Ensign Pulver another drink of alcohol and orange juice and it inspired him to relate further sexual feats of his. Some of them bordered on the supernatural!

ROBERTS. I don't doubt it. Did he tell you how he conquered a forty-five-year-old virgin by the simple tactic of being the first man in her life to ask her a direct question?

DOC. No. Last night he was more concerned with quantity. It seems that on a certain cold and wintry night in November, 1939—a night when most of us mortal men would have settled for a cup of cocoa—he rendered pregnant three girls in Washington, D. C., caught the 11:45 train, and an hour later performed the same service for a young lady in Baltimore.

ROBERTS (*laughing*). Oh, my God!

DOC. I'm not sure what to do with young Pulver. I'm thinking of reporting his record to the American Medical Association.

ROBERTS. Why don't you just get him a job as a fountain in Radio City?

DOC. Don't be too hard on him, Doug. He thinks you are approximately God. . . . Say, there *is* something wrong, isn't there?

ROBERTS. I've been up all night, Doc.

DOC. What is it? What's the matter?

ROBERTS. I saw something last night when I was on watch that just about knocked me out.

DOC (*alarmed*). What happened?

ROBERTS (*with emotion*). I was up on the bridge. I was just standing there looking out to sea. I couldn't bear to look at that island any more. All of a sudden I

noticed something. Little black specks crawling over the horizon. I looked through the glasses and it was a formation of our ships that stretched for miles! Carriers and battleships and cans—a whole task force, Doc!

DOC. Why didn't you break me out? I've never seen a battleship!

ROBERTS. They came on and they passed within half a mile of that reef! Carriers so big they blacked out half the sky! And battlewagons sliding along—dead quiet! I could see the men on the bridges. And this is what knocked me out, Doc. Somehow—I thought I was on those bridges—I thought I was riding west across the Pacific. I watched them until they were out of sight, Doc—and I was right there on those bridges all the time.

DOC. I know how that must have hurt, Doug.

ROBERTS. And then I looked down from our bridge and saw our Captain's palm tree! (*Points at palm tree, then bitterly*) Our trophy for superior achievement! The Admiral John J. Finchley award for delivering more toothpaste and toilet paper than any other Navy cargo ship in the safe area of the Pacific. (*Taking letter from pocket and handing it to Doc*) Read this, Doc—see how it sounds.

DOC. What is it?

ROBERTS. My application for transfer. I've been rewriting it ever since I got off watch last night.

DOC. O God, not another one!

ROBERTS. This one's different—I'm trying something new, Doc—a stronger wording. Read it carefully.
(*Doc looks for a moment skeptically, then noticing the intensity in his face decides to read the letter.*)

DOC (*reading*).
"From: Lieutenant (jg) Douglas Roberts
To: Bureau of Naval Personnel
16 April 1945
Subject: Change of Duty, Request for ..."
(*He looks up.*)
Boy, this is sheer poetry.

ROBERTS (*rises nervously*). Go on, Doc.

DOC (*reads on*).
"For two years and four months I have served aboard this vessel as Cargo Officer. I feel that my continued service aboard can only reduce my own usefulness to the Navy and increase disharmony aboard this ship."

(He looks at Roberts and rises. Roberts looks back defiantly.)

ROBERTS. How about *that!*

DOC *(whistles softly, then continues).* "It is therefore urgently requested that I be ordered to combat duty, preferably aboard a destroyer."

ROBERTS *(tensely, going to Doc).* What do you say, Doc? I've got a chance, haven't I?

DOC. Listen, Doug, you've been sending in a letter every week for God knows how long . . .

ROBERTS. Not like this . . .

DOC. . . . and every week the Captain has screamed like a stuck pig, *dis*approved your letters and forwarded them that way. . . .

ROBERTS. That's just my point, Doc. He *does* forward them. They go through the chain of command all the way up to the Bureau . . . Just because the Captain doesn't . . .

DOC. Doug, the Captain of a Navy ship is the most absolute monarch left in this world!

ROBERTS. I know that.

DOC. If he endorsed your letter "approved" you'd get your orders in a minute . . .

ROBERTS. Naturally, but I . . . *(Turns away from Doc)*

DOC. . . . but "disapproved," you haven't got a prayer. You're stuck on this old bucket, Doug. Face it!

ROBERTS *(turns quickly back).* Well, grant me this much, Doc. That one day I'll find the perfect wording and one human guy way up on top will read those words and say, "Here's a poor son-of-a-bitch screaming for help. Let's put him on a fighting ship!"

DOC *(quietly).* Sure . . .

ROBERTS *(after a moment).* I'm not kidding myself, am I, Doc? I've got a chance, haven't I?

DOC. Yes, Doug, you've got a chance. It's about the same chance as putting your letter in a bottle and dropping it in the ocean . . .

ROBERTS *(snatching letter from Doc).* But it's still a chance, goddammit! It's still a chance!

(Roberts stands looking out to sea. Doc watches him for a moment then speaks gently.)

DOC. I wish you hadn't seen that task force, Doug. *(Pauses)* Well, I've got to go down to my hypochondriacs.

(He goes off slowly through passageway.)

(Roberts is still staring out as Dowdy enters from the hatchway. He is a hard-bitten man between thirty-five and forty and is wearing dungarees and no hat. He stands by hatchway with a cup of coffee in his hand.)

DOWDY. Morning, Mister Roberts.

ROBERTS. Good morning, Dowdy.

DOWDY. Jeez, it's even hotter up here than down in that messhall! *(He looks off)* Look at that cruddy island . . . smell it! It's so hot it *already* smells like a hog pen. Think we'll go out of here today, sir?

(Roberts takes Dowdy's cup as he speaks and drinks from it, then hands it back.)

ROBERTS. I don't know, Dowdy. There's one LCT coming alongside for supplies . . . *(Goes to hatchway, looks down)* Are they getting up yet?

DOWDY *(also looking down hatch).* Yeah, they're starting to stumble around down there—the poor punch-drunk bastards. Mister Roberts, when are you going to the Captain again and ask him to give this crew a liberty? These guys ain't been off the ship for over a year except on duty.

ROBERTS. Dowdy, the last time I asked him was last night.

DOWDY. What'd he say?

ROBERTS. He said "No."

DOWDY. We gotta get these guys ashore! They're going Asiatic! *(Pause)* Will you see him anyhow, Mister Roberts—just once more?

ROBERTS. You know I will, Dowdy. *(Hands Dowdy the letter)* In the meantime, have Dolan type that up for me. *(He starts off right)*

DOWDY *(descending hatchway).* Oh, your letter. Yes, sir!

ROBERTS *(calling over his shoulder).* Then will you bring a couple of men back aft? *(He exits through passageway)*

DOWDY. Okay, Mister Roberts. *(He disappears down hatchway. He is heard below)* All right, you guys in there. Finish your coffee and get up on deck. Stefanowski, Insigna, off your tails . . .

(After a moment the center door opens and the Captain appears wearing pajamas and bathrobe and his officer's cap. He is carrying water in an engine-room oil can.

He waters the palm tree carefully, looks at it for a moment tenderly and goes back into his cabin. After a moment, Dowdy's voice is heard from the companionway and he appears followed by members of the crew.)

DOWDY. All right, let's go! Bring me those glasses, Schlemmer. *(Schlemmer exits by ladder to the bridge. Other men appear from the hatchway. They are Insigna, Stefanowski, Mannion, Wiley, Reber and Lindstrom—all yawning, buttoning pants, tucking in shirts and, in general, being comatose. The men do not appear to like one another very much at this hour—least of all Insigna and Mannion)* All right, I got a little recreation for you guys. Stefanowski, you take these guys and get this little rust patch here. *(He hands Stefanowski an armful of scrapers and wire brushes, indicating a spot on the deck. Stefanowski looks at instruments dully, then distributes them to the men standing near him. Schlemmer returns from the bridge, carrying four pairs of binoculars and a spy glass. He drops them next to Insigna who is sitting on the hatch)* Insigna, I got a real special job for you. You stay right here and clean these glasses.

INSIGNA. Ah, let me work up forward, Dowdy. I don't want to be around this crud, Mannion.

MANNION. Yeah, Dowdy. Take Insigna with you!

DOWDY. Shut up, I'm tired of you two bellyaching! *(Nodding to others to follow him)* All right, let's go, Reber . . . Schlemmer.

(Dowdy, Reber and Schlemmer leave through passageway right. The others sit in sodden silence. Lindstrom wanders slowly over to Insigna. He picks up spy glass and examines it. He holds the large end toward him and looks into it.)

LINDSTROM. Hey, look! I can see myself!

STEFANOWSKI. Terrifying, ain't it?

(Insigna takes the spy glass from him and starts polishing it. Lindstrom removes his shoe and feels inside it, then puts it back on.)

MANNION *(after a pause)*. Hey, what time is it in San Francisco?

INSIGNA *(scornfully)*. When?

MANNION. Anybody ask you? *(Turns to Wiley)* What time would it be there?

WILEY. I don't know. I guess about midnight last night.

STEFANOWSKI *(studying scraper in his hand)*. I wonder if you could get sent back to the States if you cut off a finger. *(Nobody answers.)*

INSIGNA *(looking offstage)*. Hey, they got a new building on that island. Fancy—two stories . . . *(Nobody shows any curiosity.)*

MANNION. You know, I had a girl in San Francisco wore flowers in her hair—instead of hats. Never wore a hat . . . *(Another sodden pause.)*

INSIGNA *(holding spy glass)*. Hey, Stefanowski! Which end of this you look through?

STEFANOWSKI. It's optional, Sam. Depends on what size eyeball you've got. *(Insigna idly looks through spy glass at something out right. Another pause.)*

INSIGNA. Hey, the Japs must've took over this island—there's a red and white flag on that new building.

MANNION. Japs! We never been within five thousand miles of a Jap! Japs! You hear that, Wiley?

WILEY. Yeah, smart, ain't he?

MANNION. Japs! That's a hospital flag!

INSIGNA. Anybody ask you guys? *(Nudging Lindstrom and pointing to the other group)* The goldbrick twins! *(Looks through spy glass)* Hey, they got a fancy hospital . . . big windows and . . . *(Suddenly rises, gasping at what he sees)*

STEFANOWSKI. What's the matter, Sam?

INSIGNA. Oh, my God! She's bare-assed!

STEFANOWSKI. *She!*

INSIGNA. Taking a shower . . . in that bathroom . . . that nurse . . . upstairs window!

(Instantly the others rush to hatch cover, grab binoculars and stand looking out right.)

WILEY. She's a blonde—see!

LINDSTROM. I never seen such a beautiful girl!

MANNION. She's sure taking a long time in that shower!

WILEY. Yeah, honey, come on over here by the window!

INSIGNA. Don't you do it, honey! You take your time!

STEFANOWSKI. There's another one over by the washbasin—taking a shampoo.

INSIGNA *(indignantly)*. Yeah. But why the hell don't she take her bathrobe off!

That's a stupid goddamn way to take a shampoo!

(For a moment the men watch in silent vigilance.)

STEFANOWSKI. Ah-hah!

WILEY. She's coming out of the shower!

MANNION. She's coming over to the window! *(A pause)* Kee-ri-mi-ny!

(For a moment the men stand transfixed, their faces radiant. They emit rapturous sighs. That is all.)

LINDSTROM. Aw, she's turning around the other way!

MANNION. What's that red mark she's got . . . there?

INSIGNA *(authoritatively)*. That's a birthmark!

MANNION *(scornfully)*. Birthmark!

INSIGNA. What do you think it is, wise guy?

MANNION. Why, that's paint! She's sat in some red paint!

INSIGNA. Sat in some red paint! I'm tellin' you, that's a birthmark!

MANNION. Did you ever see a birthmark down there?

INSIGNA *(lowers his spy glass, turns to Mannion)*. Why, you stupid jerk! I had an uncle once had a birthmark right down . . .

WILEY. Aww!

(Insigna and Mannion return quickly to their glasses.)

STEFANOWSKI *(groaning)*. She's put her bathrobe on!

MANNION. Hey, she's got the same color bathrobe as that stupid bag taking the shampoo!

(The four men notice something and exclaim in unison.)

INSIGNA. Bag, hell! Look at her now with her head out of the water . . .

LINDSTROM. She's just as beautiful as the other one . . .

STEFANOWSKI. They look exactly alike with those bathrobes on. Maybe they're twins.

MANNION. That's my gal on the right—the one with the red birthmark.

INSIGNA. You stupid crud, the one with the birthmark's on the left!

MANNION. The hell she is . . .

(Mannion and Insigna again lower their glasses.)

INSIGNA. The hell she ain't . . .

WILEY. Awwww!

(Mannion and Insigna quickly drop their argument and look.)

STEFANOWSKI. They've both leaving the bathroom together. . . .

(The men are dejected again.)

LINDSTROM. Hey, there ain't no one in there now!

STEFANOWSKI *(lowering his glasses)*. Did you figure that out all by yourself? *(He looks through his glasses again)*

MANNION *(after a pause)*. Come on, girls, let's go!

WILEY. Yeah. Who's next to take a nice zippy shower?

INSIGNA *(after a pause)*. They must think we got nothing better to do than stand here!

LINDSTROM. These glasses are getting heavy!

STEFANOWSKI. Yeah. We're wasting manpower. Let's take turns, okay? *(The others agree)* All right, Mannion, you take it first.

(Mannion nods, crosses and sits on bitt, keeping watch with his binoculars. The others pick up their scrapers and wire brushes.)

INSIGNA *(watching Mannion)*. I don't trust that crud.

LINDSTROM. Gee, I wish we was allowed to get over to that island. We could get a closer look.

STEFANOWSKI. No, Lindstrom. They'd see us and pull the shades down.

LINDSTROM. No, they wouldn't. We could cover ourselves with leaves and make out like we was bushes—and sneak up on them—like them Japs we seen in that movie . . .

(He starts to sneak around front of hatch, holding his wire brush before his face. Stefanowski hears a noise from the Captain's cabin and quickly warns the others.)

STEFANOWSKI. Flash Red! *(The men immediately begin working in earnest as the Captain, now in khaki, enters. He stands for a moment, looking at them, and then wanders over to the group scraping the rust patch to inspect their work. Then, satisfied that they are actually working, he starts toward passageway. He sees Mannion, sitting on the bitt, looking through his glasses and smiling. The Captain goes over and stands beside him, looking off in the same direction. Stefanowski tries frantically to signal a warning to Mannion by beating out code with his scraper. Mannion suddenly sees the Captain and quickly lowers his glasses and pretends to clean them, alternately wiping the lenses and holding them up to his eyes to see that they are clean. The Captain watches him suspiciously for a moment, then he exits by the ladder to the bridge. Stefanowski rises and looks up ladder to make certain the Captain has gone)* Flash White! *(He turns and looks at Mannion)* Hey, Mannion. Anyone in there yet?

MANNION *(watching something happily through glasses).* No, not yet!

INSIGNA *(picks up spy glass and looks, and rises quickly).* Why, you dirty, miserable cheat!

(Instantly all the men are at the glasses.)

LINDSTROM. There's one in there again!

STEFANOWSKI. The hell with her—she's already got her clothes on!

INSIGNA. And there she goes! *(Slowly lowers his glass, turning to Mannion threateningly)* Why, you lousy, cheating crud!

MANNION *(idly swinging his glasses).* That ain't all. I seen three!

STEFANOWSKI. You lowdown Peeping Tom!

LINDSTROM *(hurt).* Mannion, that's a real dirty trick.

INSIGNA. What's the big idea?

MANNION. Who wants to know?

INSIGNA. *I* want to know! And you're damn well going to tell me!

MANNION. You loud-mouthed little bastard! Why don't you make me?

INSIGNA. You're damn right I will. Right now! *(He swings on Mannion as Lindstrom steps clumsily between them)*

LINDSTROM. Hey, fellows! Fellows!

INSIGNA. No wonder you ain't got a friend on this ship . . . except this crud, Wiley. *(He jerks his head in direction of Wiley who stands behind him on hatch cover. Wiley takes him by shoulder and whirls him around)*

WILEY. What'd you say?

STEFANOWSKI *(shoving Wiley).* You heard him!

(Mannion jumps on hatch cover to protect Wiley from Stefanowski. Insigna rushes at Mannion and for a moment they are all in a clinch. Lindstrom plows up on the hatch and breaks them apart. The men have suddenly formed into two camps—Mannion and Wiley on one side,

Insigna and Stefanowski facing them, Lindstrom is just an accessory, but stands prepared to intervene if necessary.)

MANNION *(to Wiley).* Look at them two! Everybody on the ship hates their guts! The two moochingest, no-good loudmouths on the ship!

(Stefanowski starts for Mannion but Insigna pulls him back and steps menacingly toward Mannion.)

INSIGNA. Why, you slimy, lying son-of-a-bitch!

(Suddenly Mannion hits Insigna, knocking him down. He jumps on Insigna who catches Mannion in the chest with his feet and hurls him back. Wiley and Stefanowski start fighting with Lindstrom, attempting to break them apart. Mannion rushes back at Insigna. Insigna sidesteps Mannion's lunge and knocks him to the deck. Insigna falls on him. They wrestle to their feet and stand slugging. At this point Roberts and Dowdy run on from passageway. Roberts flings Insigna and Mannion apart. Dowdy separates the others.)

ROBERTS. Break it up! Break it up, I tell you!

(Insigna and Mannion rush at each other. Roberts and Dowdy stop them.)

DOWDY. Goddamn you guys, break it up!

ROBERTS. All right! What's going on?

INSIGNA *(pointing at Mannion).* This son-of-a-bitch here . . .

ROBERTS. Did you hear me?

MANNION *(to Insigna).* Shut your mouth!

DOWDY. Shut up, both of you!

INSIGNA. Slimy son-of-a-bitch! *(Picks up scraper and lunges at Mannion again. Roberts throws him back)*

ROBERTS. I said to cut it out! Did you hear me? *(Wheels on Mannion)* That goes for you too! *(Includes entire group)* I'm going to give it to the first one who opens his mouth! *(The men stand subdued, breathing hard from the fight)* Now get to work! All of you! *(They begin to move sullenly off right)* Mannion, you and the rest get to work beside number two! And, Insigna, take those glasses way up to the bow and work on them! Stefanowski, keep those two apart.

STEFANOWSKI. Yes, sir.

(The men exit. Roberts and Dowdy look after them.)

DOWDY (tightly). You seen that, Mister Roberts. Well, last night down in the compartment I stopped three of them fights—worse than that. They've got to have a liberty, Mister Roberts.

ROBERTS. They sure do. Dowdy, call a boat for me, will you? I'm going ashore.

DOWDY. What are you going to do?

ROBERTS. I just got a new angle.

DOWDY. Are you going over the Captain's head?

ROBERTS. No, I'm going around his end —I hope. Get the lead out, Dowdy.

(He exits left as Dowdy goes off right and the lights fade out.)

During the darkness, voices can be heard over the squawk-box saying:

Now hear this . . . now hear this. Sweepers, man your brooms. Clean sweep-down fore and aft. Sweep-down all ladders and all passageways. Do *not* throw trash over the fantail.

Now, all men on report will see the master-at-arms for assignment to extra duty.

Now hear this . . . now hear this. Because in violation of the Captain's orders, a man has appeared on deck without a shirt on, there will be no movies again tonight—by order of the Captain.

SCENE TWO

The lights dim up revealing the stateroom of Pulver and Roberts. Two lockers are shown, one marked "Ensign F. T. Pulver," the other marked "Lt. (jg) D. A. Roberts." There is a double bunk along the bulkhead right. A desk with its end against the bulkhead left has a chair at either side. There is a porthole in the bulkhead above it. Up center, right of Pulver's locker is a washbasin over which is a shelf and a medicine chest. The door is up center.

An officer is discovered with his head inside Roberts' locker, throwing skivvy shirts over his shoulder as he searches for something. Dolan, a young, garrulous, brash yeoman, second class, enters. He is carrying a file folder.

DOLAN. Here's your letter, Mister Roberts. *(He goes to the desk, taking fountain pen from his pocket)* I typed it up. Just sign your old John Henry here and I'll take it in to the Captain . . . then hold your ears. *(No answer)* Mister Roberts! *(Pulver's head appears from the locker)* Oh, it's only you, Mister Pulver. What are you doing in Mister Roberts' locker?

PULVER (hoarsely). Dolan, look in here, will you? I know there's a shoe box in there, but I can't find it.

(Dolan looks in the locker.)

DOLAN. There ain't no shoe box in there, Mister Pulver.

PULVER. They've stolen it! There's nothing they'll stop at now. They've broken right into the sanctity of a man's own locker. *(He sits in chair at desk)*

DOLAN (disinterested). Ain't Mister Roberts back from the island yet?

PULVER. No.

DOLAN. Well, as soon as he gets back, will you ask him to sign this baby?

PULVER. What is it?

DOLAN. What is it! It's the best damn letter Mister Roberts writ yet. It's going to blow the Old Man right through the overhead. And them big shots at the Bureau are going to drop their drawers too. This letter is liable to get him transferred.

PULVER. Yeah, lemme see it.

DOLAN (handing letter to Pulver). Get a load of that last paragraph. Right here.

PULVER (reading with apprehension). ". . . increase disharmony aboard this ship . . ."

DOLAN (interrupting gleefully). Won't that frost the Old Man's knockers? I can't wait to jab this baby in the Old Man's face. Mister Pulver, you know how he gets sick to his stomach when he gets extra mad at Mister Roberts—well, when I deliver this letter I'm going to take along a wastebasket! Let me know when Mister Roberts gets back.

(Dolan exits. Pulver continues reading the letter with great dismay. He hears Roberts and Doc talking in the passageway, offstage, and quickly goes to his bunk and hides the letter under a blanket. He goes to the locker and is replacing skivvy shirts as Roberts and Doc enter.)

ROBERTS. . . . so after the fight I figured I had to do something and do it quick!

DOC. What did you do over on the island, Doug?

ROBERTS (sitting in chair and searching through desk drawer). Hey, Frank, has Dolan been in here yet with my letter?

PULVER (*innocently*). I don't know, Doug boy. I just came in here myself.

DOC. You don't know anybody on the island, do you, Doug?

ROBERTS. Yes. The Port Director—the guy who decides where to send this ship next. He confided to me that he used to drink a quart of whiskey every day of his life. So this morning when I broke up that fight it came to me that he might just possibly sell his soul for a quart of Scotch.

PULVER (*rises*). Doug, you didn't give that shoe box to the Post Director!

ROBERTS. I did. "Compliments of the Captain."

DOC. You've had a quart of Scotch in a shoe box?

ROBERTS. Johnny Walker! I was going to break it out the day I got off this ship —Resurrection Day!

PULVER. Oh, my God! It's really gone! (*He sinks to the bunk*)

DOC. Well, did the Port Director say he'd send us to a Liberty Port?

ROBERTS. Hell, no. He took the Scotch and said, "Don't bother me, Roberts. I'm busy." The rummy!

PULVER. How could you do it!

DOC. Well, where there's a rummy, there's hope. Maybe when he gets working on that Scotch he'll mellow a little.

PULVER. You gave that bottle to a goddamn *man!*

ROBERTS. Man! Will you name me another sex within a thousand miles . . . (*Pulver, dejected, goes up to porthole*) What the hell's eating you anyhow, Frank?

(*Doc crosses to bunk. He sees two fancy pillows on bottom bunk, picks up one and tosses it to Roberts. He picks up the other.*)

DOC. Well, look here. Somebody seems to be expecting company!

ROBERTS. Good Lord!

DOC (*reads lettering on pillowcase*). "Toujours l'amour . . . Souvenir of San Diego . . . Oh, you kid!"

ROBERTS (*reading from his pillowcase*). "Tonight or never . . . Compliments of Allis-Chalmers, Farm Equipment . . . We plow deep while others sleep." (*He looks at Doc, then rises*) Doc—that new hospital over there hasn't got nurses, has it?

DOC. Nurses! It didn't have yesterday!

PULVER (*turning from porthole*). It has today!

DOC. But how did you find out they were there?

PULVER (*trying to recall*). Now let me think . . . it just came to me all of a sudden. This morning it was so hot I was just lying on my bunk—thinking . . . There wasn't a breath of air. And then, all of a sudden, a funny thing happened. A little breeze came up and I took a big deep breath and said to myself, "Pulver boy, there's women on that island."

ROBERTS. Doc, a thing like this could make a bird dog self-conscious as hell.

PULVER (*warming up*). They just flew in last night. There's eighteen of them— all brunettes except for two beautiful blondes—twin sisters! I'm working on one of those. I asked her out to the ship for lunch and she said she was kind of tired. So then I got kind of desperate and turned on the old personality—and I said, "Ain't there anything in the world that'll make you come out to the ship with me?" And she said, "Yes, there is, one thing and one thing only—" (*Crosses to Roberts, looks at him accusingly*) "A good stiff drink of Scotch!" (*He sinks into the chair*)

ROBERTS (*after a pause*). I'm sorry, Frank. I'm really sorry. Your first assignment in a year. (*He pats Pulver on the shoulder*)

PULVER. I figured I'd bring her in here . . . I fixed it up real cozy . . . (*Fondling pillow on desk*) . . . and then I was going to throw a couple of fast slugs of Scotch into her and . . . but, hell, without the Scotch, she wouldn't . . . she just wouldn't, that's all.

ROBERTS (*after a pause*). Doc, let's make some Scotch!

DOC. Huh?

ROBERTS. As naval officers we're supposed to be resourceful. Frank here's got a great opportunity and I've let him down. Let's fix him up!

DOC. Right! (*He goes to desk. Roberts begins removing bottles from medicine chest*) Frank, where's the rest of that alcohol we were drinking last night?

PULVER (*pulling a large vinegar bottle half filled with colorless liquid from the wastebasket and handing it to Doc*). Hell, that ain't even the right color.

DOC (*taking the bottle*). Quiet! (*Thinks deeply*) Color . . . (*With sudden decision*) Coca-Cola! Have you got any?

ROBERTS. I haven't seen a Coke in four months—no, by God, it's five months!

PULVER. Oh, what the hell! (*He rises, crosses to bunk, reaches under mattress of top bunk and produces a bottle of Coca-Cola. The others watch him. Doc snatches the bottle. Pulver says apologetically*) I forgot I had it.

(*Doc opens the bottle and is about to pour the Coca-Cola into the vinegar bottle when he suddenly stops.*)

DOC. Oh—what shade would you like? Cutty Sark . . . Haig and Haig . . . Vat 69 . . .

PULVER (*interested*). I told her Johnny Walker.

DOC. Johnny Walker it is! (*He pours some of the Coca-Cola into the bottle*)

ROBERTS (*looking at color of the mixture*). Johnny Walker Red Label!

DOC. Red Label!

PULVER. It may look like it—but it won't taste like it!

ROBERTS. Doc, what does Scotch taste like?

DOC. Well, it's a little like . . . uh . . . it tastes like . . .

ROBERTS. Do you know what it's always tasted a little like to me? Iodine.

DOC (*shrugs as if to say "Of course" and rises. He takes dropper from small bottle of iodine and flicks a drop in the bottle*). One drop of iodine—for taste. (*Shakes the bottle and pours some in glass*)

PULVER. Lemme taste her, Doc!

DOC (*stops him with a gesture*). No. This calls for a medical opinion. (*Takes a ceremonial taste while the others wait for his verdict*)

PULVER. How about it?

DOC. We're on the right track! (*Sets glass down. Rubs hands professionally*) Now we need a little something extra—for age! What've you got there, Doug?

ROBERTS (*reading labels of bottles on desk*). Bromo-Seltzer . . . Wildroot Wave Set . . . Eno Fruit Salts . . . Kreml Hair Tonic . . .

DOC. Kreml! It has a coal-tar base! And it'll age the hell out of it! (*Pours a bit of Kreml into mixture. Shakes bottle solemnly*) One drop Kreml for age. (*Sets bottle on desk, looks at wrist watch for a fraction of a second*) That's it! (*Pours drink into glass. Pulver reaches for it. Roberts pushes his arm aside and tastes it*)

ROBERTS. By God, it does taste a little like Scotch!

(*Pulver again reaches for glass. Doc pushes his arm aside and takes a drink.*)

DOC. By God, it does!

(*Pulver finally gets glass and takes a quick sip.*)

PULVER. It's delicious. That dumb little blonde won't know the difference.

DOC (*hands the bottle to Pulver*). Here you are, Frank. Doug and I have made the Scotch. The *nurse* is your department. (*Pulver takes the bottle and hides it under the mattress, then replaces the pillows.*)

PULVER (*singing softly*). Won't know the difference . . . won't know the difference. (*Doc starts to drink from Coca-Cola bottle as Pulver comes over and snatches it from his hand*) Thanks, Doc. (*Puts cap on the bottle and hides it under the mattress. Turns and faces the others*) Thanks, Doug. Jeez, you guys are wonderful to me.

ROBERTS (*putting bottles back in medicine chest*). Don't mention it, Frank. I think you almost deserve it.

PULVER. You do—really? Or are you just giving me the old needle again? What do you really think of me, Doug—honestly?

ROBERTS (*turning slowly to face Pulver*). Frank, I like you. No one can get around the fact that you're a hell of a likable guy.

PULVER (*beaming*). Yeah—yeah . . .

ROBERTS. *But* . . .

PULVER. But what?

ROBERTS. But I also think you are the most hapless . . . lazy . . . disorganized . . . and, in general, the most lecherous person I've ever known in my life.

PULVER. I am not.

ROBERTS. Not what?

PULVER. I'm not disorganized—for one thing.

ROBERTS. Have you ever in your life finished anything you started out to do? You sleep sixteen hours a day. You pretend you want me to improve your mind and you've never even finished a book I've given you to read!

PULVER. I finished *God's Little Acre*, Doug boy!

ROBERTS. I didn't give you that! (*To Doc*) He's been reading *God's Little Acre* for over a year! (*Takes dog-eared book *from Pulver's bunk)* He's underlined every erotic passage, and added exclamation points—and after a certain pornographic climax, he's inserted the words "well written." *(To Pulver)* You're the Laundry and Morale Officer and I doubt if you've ever seen the laundry.

PULVER. I was down there only last week.

ROBERTS. And you're scared of the Captain.

PULVER. I'm not scared of the Captain.

ROBERTS. Then why do you hide in the passageway every time you see him coming? I doubt if he even knows you're on board. You're scared of him.

PULVER. I am not. I'm scared of myself —I'm scared of what I might do to him.

ROBERTS *(laughing)*. What you might do to him! Doc, he lies in his sack all day long and bores me silly with great moronic plots against the Captain and he's never carried out one.

PULVER. I haven't, huh.

ROBERTS. No, Frank, you haven't. What happened to your idea of plugging up the line of the Captain's sanitary system? "I'll make it overflow," you said. "I'll make a backwash that'll lift him off the throne and knock him clean across the room."

PULVER. I'm workin' on that. I thought about it for half an hour—yesterday.

ROBERTS. Half an hour! There's only one thing you've thought about for half an hour in your life! And what about those marbles that you were going to put in the Captain's overhead—so they'd roll around at night and keep him awake?

PULVER. Now you've gone too far. Now you've asked for it. *(Goes to bunk and produces small tin box from under mattress. Crosses to Roberts and shakes it in his face. Opens it)* What does that look like? Five marbles! I'm collecting marbles all the time. I've got one right here in my pocket! *(Takes marble from pocket, holds it close to Roberts' nose, then drops it in box. Closes box)* Six marbles! *(Puts box back under mattress, turns defiantly to Roberts)* I'm looking for marbles all day long!

ROBERTS. Frank, you asked me what I thought of you. Well, I'll tell you! The day you finish one thing you've started out to do, the day you actually put those marbles in the Captain's overhead, and then have the guts to knock on his door

and say, "Captain, I put those marbles there," that's the day I'll have some respect for you—that's the day I'll look up to you as a man. Okay?

PULVER *(belligerently)*. Okay!

(Roberts goes to the radio and turns it up. While he is listening, Doc and Pulver exchange worried looks.)

RADIO VOICE. . . . intersecting thirty miles north of Hanover. At the same time, General George S. Patton's Third Army continues to roll unchecked into Southern Germany. The abrupt German collapse brought forth the remark from a high London official that the end of the war in Europe is only weeks away—maybe days . . .

(Roberts turns off radio.)

ROBERTS. Where the hell's Dolan with that letter! *(Starts toward the door)* I'm going to find him.

PULVER. Hey, Doug, wait! Listen! *(Roberts pauses at the door)* I wouldn't send in that letter if I were you!

ROBERTS. What do you mean—*that* letter!

PULVER *(hastily)*. I mean any of those letters you been writin'. What are you so nervous about anyway?

ROBERTS. Nervous!

PULVER. I mean about getting off this ship. Hell, this ain't such a bad life. Look, Doug—we're a threesome, aren't we—you and Doc and me? Share and share alike! Now look, I'm not going to keep those nurses all to myself. Soon as I get my little nursie organized today, I'm going to start working on her twin sister—for you.

ROBERTS. All right, Frank.

PULVER. And then I'm going to scare up something for you too, Doc. And in the meantime you've got a lot of work to do, Doug boy—improvin' my mind and watching my grammar. And speaking of grammar, you better watch your grammar. You're going to get in trouble, saying things like "disharmony aboard this ship!" *(Roberts looks at Pulver quickly. Pulver catches himself)* I mean just in case you ever said anything like "disharmony aboard this ship" . . . or . . . uh . . . "harmony aboard this ship" or . . .

ROBERTS. Where's that letter?

PULVER. I don't know, Doug boy . . . *(As Roberts steps toward him, he quickly produces the letter from the blanket)* Here it is, Doug.

ROBERTS (*snatching the letter*). What's the big idea!

(*Roberts goes to desk, reading and preparing to sign the letter. Pulver follows him.*)

PULVER. I just wanted to talk to you before you signed it. You can't send it in that way—it's too strong! Don't sign that letter, Doug, please don't! They'll transfer you and you'll get your ass shot off. You're just running a race with death, isn't he, Doc? It's stupid to keep asking for it like that. The Doc says so too. Tell him what you said to me last night, Doc—about how stupid he is.

ROBERTS (*coldly, to Doc*). Yes, Doc, maybe you'd like to tell me to my face.

DOC (*belligerently*). Yes, I would. Last night I asked you why you wanted to fight this war. And you said: anyone who doesn't fight it is only half-alive. Well, I thought that over and I've decided that's just a crock, Doug—just a crock.

ROBERTS. I take it back, Doc. After seeing my task force last night I don't even feel half-alive.

DOC. You are stupid! And I can prove it! You quit medical school to get into this thing when you could be saving lives today. Why? Do you even know yourself?

ROBERTS. Has it ever occurred to you that the guys who fight this war might also be saving lives . . . yours and mine, for instance! Not just putting men together again, but *keeping* them together! Right now I'd rather practice that kind of medicine—Doctor!

DOC (*rising*). Well, right now, that's exactly what you're doing.

ROBERTS. What, for God's sake!

DOC. Whether you like it or not, this sorry old bucket does a necessary job. And you're the guy who keeps her lumbering along. You keep this crew working cargo, and more than that—you keep them *alive*. It might just be that right here, on this bucket, you're deeper and more truly in this war than you ever would be anywhere else.

ROBERTS. Oh, Jesus, Doc. In a minute, you'll start quoting Emerson.

DOC. *That* is a lousy thing to say!

ROBERTS. We've got nothing to do with the war. Maybe that's why we're on this ship—because we're not good enough to fight. (*Then quietly with emotion*) May-be there's some omniscient son-of-a-bitch who goes down the line of all the servicemen and picks out the ones to send into combat, the ones whose glands secrete enough adrenalin, or whose great-great-grandfathers weren't afraid of the dark or something. The rest of us are packed off to ships like this where we can't do any harm.

DOC. What is it you want to be—a hero or something?

ROBERTS (*shocked*). Hero! My God, Doc! You haven't heard a word I said! Look, Doc, the war's way out there! I'm here. I don't want to be here—I want to be out there. I'm sick and tired of being a lousy spectator. I just happen to believe in this thing. I've got to feel I'm *good* enough to be in it—to *participate!*

DOC. Good enough! Doug, you're good enough! You just don't have the opportunity. That's mostly what physical heroism is—opportunity. It's a reflex. I think seventy-five out of a hundred young males have that reflex. If you put any one of them—say, even Frank Thurlowe Pulver, here—in a B-29 over Japan, do you know what you'd have?

ROBERTS. No, by God, I don't.

DOC. You'd have Pulver, the Congressional Medal of Honor winner! You'd have Pulver, who, singlehanded, shot down twenty-three attacking Zeroes, then with his bare hands held together the severed wing struts of his plane, and with his bare feet successfully landed the mortally wounded plane on his home field. (*Pulver thinks this over*) Hell, it's a reflex. It's like the knee jerk. Strike the patella tendon of any human being and you produce the knee jerk. Look. (*He illustrates on Pulver. There is no knee jerk. He strikes again—still no reaction*)

PULVER. What's the matter, Doc?

DOC. Nothing. But stay out of B-29's, will you, Frank?

ROBERTS. You've made your point very vividly, Doc. But I still want to get into this thing. I've got to get into it! And I'm going to keep on sending in these letters until I do.

DOC. I know you are, Doug.

ROBERTS (*signs the letter. Then to Doc*). I haven't got much time. I found that out over on the island. That task force I saw last night is on its way to start our last big push in the Pacific. And it went by me, Doc. I've got to catch it. *(He exits)*

PULVER *(after a pause)*. Doc, what are you going to give Doug on his birthday?

DOC. I hadn't thought of giving him anything.

PULVER. You know what? I'm gonna show him he's got old Pulver figured out all wrong. *(Pulls small cardboard roll from under mattress)* Doc, what does that look like?

DOC. Just what it is—the cardboard center of a roll of toilet paper.

PULVER. I suppose it doesn't look like a firecracker.

DOC. Not a bit like a firecracker.

PULVER *(taking a piece of string from the bunk)*. I suppose that doesn't look like a fuse.

DOC *(rising and starting off)*. No, that looks like a piece of string. *(He walks slowly out of the room. Pulver goes on)*

PULVER. Well, you just wait till old Pulver gets through with it! I'm going to get me some of that black powder from the gunner's mate. No, by God, this isn't going to be any peanut firecracker—I'm going to pack this old thing full of that stuff they use to blow up bridges, that fulminate of mercury stuff. And then on the night of Doug's birthday, I'm going to throw it under the Old Man's bunk. Bam—bam—bam! *(Knocks on Roberts' locker, opens it)* Captain, it is I, Ensign Pulver. I just threw that firecracker under your goddamn bunk.

(He salutes as the lights fade out.)

(In the darkness we hear the sound of a winch and shouted orders.)

LCT OFFICER. On the AK—where do you want us?

AK VOICE. Starboard side, up for'd—alongside number two!

LCT OFFICER. Shall we use our fenders or yours?

AK VOICE. No, we'll use ours! Stand off till we finish with the barge!

SCENE THREE

The curtain rises and the lights dim up on the deck. Roberts stands on the hatch cover. Schlemmer, Gerhart and another seaman are sitting on the hatch cover. They are tired and hot. A cargo net, filled with crates, is disappearing off right. Off stage we hear the shouts of men working cargo. Two officers walk across the stage. Everyone's shirt is wet with perspiration.

———

ROBERTS *(calling through megaphone)*. Okay—take it away—that's all for the barge. On the LCT—I'll give you a bow line.

LCT OFFICER *(offstage)*. Okay, Lieutenant.

ROBERTS *(to crew)*. Get a line over!

DOWDY *(offstage)*. Yes, sir.

REBER *(off right)*. Heads up on the LCT!

ROBERTS. That's good. Make it fast. *(Payne, wearing the belt of a messenger, enters from companionway as Dowdy enters from right.)*

PAYNE. Mister Roberts, the Captain says not to give this LCT any fresh fruit. He says he's going to keep what's left for his own mess.

ROBERTS. Okay, okay . . .

PAYNE. Hold your hat, Mister Roberts. I just saw Dolan go in there with your letter. *(He grins and exits as Roberts smiles at Dowdy)*

DOWDY. Here's the list of what the LCT guy wants.

ROBERTS *(reading rapidly)*. One ton dry stores . . . quarter-ton frozen food . . . one gross dungarees . . . twenty cartons toothpaste . . . two gross skivvy shirts . . . Okay, we can give him all that.

DOWDY. Can these guys take their shirts off while we're working?

ROBERTS. Dowdy, you know the Captain has a standing order . . .

DOWDY. Mister Roberts, Corcoran just passed out from the heat.

ROBERTS *(looks at men, who wait for his decision)*. Hell, yes, take 'em off. *(Dowdy exits. Schlemmer, Reber and seaman remove shirts saying, "Thanks, Mister Roberts" and exit right. Roberts calls through megaphone)* LCT, want to swap movies? We've got a new one.

LCT *(offstage)*. What's that?

ROBERTS. *Charlie Chan at the Opera.*

LCT *(offstage)*. No, thanks, we've seen that three times!

ROBERTS. What you got?

LCT *(offstage)*. Hoot Gibson in *Riders of the Range.*

ROBERTS. Sorry I brought the subject up.

DOWDY (*entering from right*). All set, Mister Roberts.

LCT (*offstage*). Lieutenant, one thing I didn't put on my list because I wanted to ask you—you couldn't spare us any fresh fruit, could you?

ROBERTS. You all out?

LCT (*offstage*). We haven't seen any for two months.

ROBERTS (*to Dowdy*). Dowdy, give 'em a couple of crates of oranges.

DOWDY. Yes, sir.

ROBERTS. Compliments of the Captain.

DOWDY. Aye-aye, sir. (*He exits*)

ROBERTS (*to LCT*). Here comes your first sling-load! (*There is the grinding sound of a winch. With hand-signals Roberts directs placing of the sling-load. Then he shouts*) Watch that line!

DOWDY. Slack off, you dumb bastards! Slack off!

(*Payne enters. Roberts turns to him sharply.*)

ROBERTS. What!

PAYNE. The Captain wants to see you, Mister Roberts.

DOWDY (*offstage*). Goddammit, there it goes! You've parted the line!

ROBERTS. Get a fender over! Quick! (*To Payne*) You go tell the Captain I'm busy! (*Payne exits. Roberts calls offstage*) Get a line over—his bow's coming in!

REBER (*offstage*). Heads up!

GERHART (*offstage*). Where shall we secure?

DOWDY (*offstage*). Secure here!

ROBERTS. No. Take it around the bitt!

DOWDY (*offstage*). Around the bitt!

ROBERTS. That's too much! Give him some slack this time! (*Watches intently*) That's good. Okay, let's give him the rest of his cargo.

GERHART (*entering quickly and pointing toward companionway*). Flash Red! (*He exits. The Captain enters, followed by Payne and Dolan*)

CAPTAIN. All right, Mister! Let's have this out right here and now! What do you mean—telling me you're busy!

ROBERTS. We parted a line, Captain. You didn't want me to leave the deck with this ship coming in on us?

CAPTAIN. You're damn right I want you to leave the deck. When I tell you I want to see you, I mean *now*, Mister! I mean jump! Do you understand?

(*At this point a group of men, attracted by the noise, crowd in. They are naked to the waist. They pretend they are working, but actually they are listening to the Captain's fight with Roberts.*)

ROBERTS. Yes, Captain. I'll remember that next time.

CAPTAIN. You're damn right you'll remember it! Don't *ever* tell me you're too busy to see me! Ever! (*Roberts doesn't answer. The Captain points to the letter he is carrying*) By God, you think you're pretty cute with this letter, don't you? You're trying to get me in bad with the Admiral, ain't you? Ain't you?

ROBERTS. No, I'm not, Captain.

CAPTAIN. Then what do you mean by writing "disharmony aboard this ship"?

ROBERTS. Because it's true, Captain. (*The men grin at each other.*)

CAPTAIN. Any disharmony on this ship is my own doing!

ROBERTS. That's true too, Captain.

CAPTAIN. Damn right it's true. And it ain't gonna be in any letter that leaves this ship. Any criticism of this ship stays on this ship. I got a reputation with the Admiral and I ain't gonna lose it on account of a letter written by some smart-alec college officer. Now you retype that letter and leave out that disharmony crap and I'll send it in. But this is the last one, understand?

ROBERTS. Captain, every man in the Navy has the right to send in a request for transfer . . . and no one can change the wording. That's in Navy regs.

CAPTAIN (*after a pause*). How about that, Dolan?

DOLAN. That's what it says, sir.

CAPTAIN. This goddamn Navy! I never put up with crap like that in the merchant service. All right, I'll send this one in as it is—disapproved, like I always do. But there's one thing I don't have to do and that's send in a letter that ain't been written. And, Mister, I'm tellin' you here and now—you ain't gonna write any more. You bring one next week and you'll regret it the rest of your life. You got a job right here and, Mister, you ain't *never* going to leave this ship. Now get on with your work. (*He looks around and notices the men. He shouts*) Where are your shirts?

ROBERTS. Captain, I . . .

CAPTAIN. Shut up! *Answer me, where are your shirts?* (*They stare at him*) Get those shirts on in a goddamn quick hurry.

(The men pick up their shirts, then pause, looking at Roberts.)

ROBERTS. Captain, it was so hot working cargo, I . . .

CAPTAIN *(shouting louder)*. I told you to shut up! *(To the men)* I'm giving you an order: get those shirts on!

(The men do not move.)

ROBERTS *(quietly)*. I'm sorry. Put your shirts on.

(The men put on their shirts. There is a pause while the Captain stares at the men. Then he speaks quietly.)

CAPTAIN. Who's the Captain of this ship? By God, that's the rankest piece of insubordination I've seen. You've been getting pretty smart playing grab-ass with Roberts here . . . but now you've gone too far. I'm givin' you a little promise—I ain't never gonna forget this. And in the meantime, every one of you men who disobeyed my standing order and appeared on deck without a shirt—every one—is on report, do you hear? On report!

ROBERTS. Captain, you're not putting these men on report.

CAPTAIN. What do you mean—I'm not!

ROBERTS. I'm responsible. I gave them permission.

CAPTAIN. You disobeyed my order?

ROBERTS. Yes, sir. It was too hot working cargo in the sun. One man passed out.

CAPTAIN. I don't give a damn if fifty men passed out. I gave an order and you disobeyed it.

LCT *(offstage)*. Thanks a million for the oranges, Lieutenant.

CAPTAIN *(to Roberts)*. Did you give that LCT fresh fruit?

ROBERTS. Yes, sir. We've got plenty, Captain. They've been out for two months.

CAPTAIN. I've taken all the crap from you that I'm going to. You've just got yourself ten days in your room. Ten days, Mister! Ten days!

ROBERTS. Very well, Captain. Do you relieve me here?

CAPTAIN. You're damn right, I relieve you. You can go to your room for ten days! See how you like that!

LCT *(offstage)*. We're waiting on you, Lieutenant. We gotta shove off.

(Roberts gives the megaphone to the Captain and starts off. The Captain looks in direction of the LCT then calls to Roberts.)

CAPTAIN. Where do you think you're going?

ROBERTS *(pretending surprise)*. To my room, Captain!

CAPTAIN. Get back to that cargo! I'll let you know when you have ten days in your room and you'll damn well know it! You're going to stay right here and do your job! *(Roberts crosses to the crew. The Captain slams the megaphone into Roberts' stomach. Pulver enters around the corner of the house, sees the Captain and starts to go back. The Captain sees Pulver and shouts)* Who's that? Who's that officer there?

PULVER *(turning)*. Me, sir?

CAPTAIN. Yes, you. Come here, boy. *(Pulver approaches in great confusion and can think of nothing better to do than salute. This visibly startles the Captain)* Why, you're one of my officers!

PULVER. Yes, sir.

CAPTAIN. What's your name again?

PULVER. Ensign Pulver, sir.

(He salutes again. The Captain, amazed, returns the salute, then says for the benefit of Roberts and the crew:)

CAPTAIN. By God, I'm glad to see one on this ship knows how to salute. *(Then to Pulver)* Pulver . . . oh, yes . . . Pulver. How is it I never see you around?

PULVER *(terrified)*. I've wondered about that myself, sir.

CAPTAIN. What's your job?

PULVER *(trembling)*. Officer in charge of laundry and morale, sir.

CAPTAIN. How long you been aboard?

PULVER. Fourteen months, sir.

CAPTAIN. Fourteen months! You spend most of your time down in the laundry, eh?

PULVER. Most of the time, sir. Yes, sir. *(Roberts turns his face to hide his laughter.)*

CAPTAIN. Well, you do a good job, Pulver, and . . . you know I'd like to see more of you. Why don't you have lunch with me in my cabin today?

PULVER. Oh, I can't today.

CAPTAIN. Can't? Why not?

PULVER. I'm on my way over to the hospital on the island. I've got to go pick up a piece . . . of medical equipment.

ROBERTS *(calling over)*. Why, I'll take care of that, Frank.

CAPTAIN. That's right, Roberts. You finish here and you go over and fetch it.

ROBERTS. Yes, sir. (*He nods and turns away, grinning*)

CAPTAIN (*to Pulver*). Well, how about it?

PULVER. This is something I've got to take care of myself, sir. If you don't mind, sir.

CAPTAIN. Well, some other time then.

PULVER. Yes, sir. Thank you, sir.

CAPTAIN. Okay, Pulver.

(*The Captain baits another salute from Pulver, then exits. Pulver watches him go, then starts to sneak off.*)

ROBERTS (*grinning and mimicking the Captain*). Oh, boy! (*Pulver stops uneasily. Roberts salutes him*) I want to see more of you, Pulver!

PULVER (*furiously*). That son-of-a-bitch! Pretending he doesn't know me! (*He looks at watch and exits. Roberts turns laughing to the crew who are standing rather solemnly*)

DOWDY (*quietly*). Nice going, Mister Roberts.

SCHLEMMER. It was really beautiful the way you read the Old Man off!

GERHART. Are you going to send in that letter next week, Mister Roberts?

ROBERTS. Are we, Dolan?

DOLAN. You're damn right we are! And I'm the baby who's going to deliver it!

SCHLEMMER. He said he'd fix you good. What do you think he'll do?

REBER. You got a promotion coming up, haven't you?

SCHLEMMER. Yeah. Could he stop that or something?

DOLAN. Promotion! This is Mister Roberts. You think he gives a good hoot-in-hell about another lousy stripe?

ALL. Yeah.

GERHART. Hey, Mister Roberts, can I take the letter in next week?

DOLAN (*indignantly*). You can like hell. That's my job—isn't it, Mister Roberts?

GERHART. Can I, Mister Roberts?

ROBERTS. I'm afraid I've promised that job to Dolan.

DOLAN (*pushing Gerhart away*). You heard him. (*To Roberts*) We gotta write a really hot one next week.

ROBERTS. Got any asbestos paper?

(*He starts off, the men follow happily as the lights fade out.*)

SCENE FOUR

The lights come up immediately on the main set. Reber and Gerhart enter from right passageway. As they get around the corner of the house, they break into a run. Reber dashes off through left passageway.

GERHART (*excitedly, descending hatchway*). Hey, Schlemmer! Schlemmer! (*Miss Girard, a young, attractive, blonde Army nurse, and Pulver enter from right passageway.*)

PULVER. Well, here it is.

MISS GIRARD. This is a ship?

PULVER. Unh-hunh.

MISS GIRARD. My sister and I flew over some warships on our way out from the States and they looked so busy—men running around like mad.

PULVER. It's kinda busy sometimes up on deck.

MISS GIRARD. Oh, you mean you've seen a lot of action?

PULVER. Well, I sure as hell haven't had much in the last year . . . Oh, battle action! Yeah . . . Yeah . . .

MISS GIRARD. Then you must have a lot of B.F. on here.

PULVER. Hunh?

MISS GIRARD. You know—battle fatigue?

PULVER. Yeah, we have a lot of that.

MISS GIRARD. Isn't that too bad! But they brief us to expect a lot of that out here. (*Pause*) Say, you haven't felt any yourself, have you?

PULVER. I guess I had a little touch of it . . . just a scratch.

MISS GIRARD. You know what you should do then? You should sleep more.

PULVER. Yeah.

MISS GIRARD. What's your job on the ship?

PULVER. Me? I'm . . . Executive Officer . . .

MISS GIRARD. But I thought that Executive Officers had to be at least a . . .

PULVER. Say, you know what I was thinking? That we should have that little old drink of Scotcharoo right now—

MISS GIRARD. I think so too. You know, I just love Scotch. I've just learned to drink it since I've joined the Army. But I'm already an absolute connoisseur.

PULVER (*dismayed*). Oh, you are?

MISS GIRARD. My twin sister has a nickname for me that's partly because I like a particular brand of Scotch . . . *(Giggles)* and partly because of a little personal thing about me that you wouldn't understand. Do you know what she calls me? "Red Label!" *(They both laugh)* What are you laughing at? You don't know what I'm talking about—and what's more you never will.

PULVER. What I was laughing about is —that's the kind I've got.

MISS GIRARD. Red Label! Oh, you're God's gift to a thirsty nursie! But where can we drink it? This is a Navy ship . . . isn't it?

PULVER. Oh, yeah, yeah, we'll have to be careful . . . We mustn't be seen . . . Lemme see, where shall we go . . . *(Considers)* I have it! We'll go back to my cabin. Nobody'd bother us there.

MISS GIRARD. Oh, you're what our outfit calls an operator. But you look harmless to me.

PULVER. Oh, I don't know about that.

MISS GIRARD. What's your first name— Harmless?

PULVER. Frank.

MISS GIRARD. Hello, Frank. Mine's Ann.

PULVER. Hello, Ann.

MISS GIRARD. All right. We'll have a little sip in your room.

PULVER. Right this way. *(They start off toward left passageway. Insigna, Mannion, Stefanowski, Wiley and Lindstrom enter from right, carrying the spy glass and binoculars. Stefanowski trips on hatch cover. Miss Girard and Pulver turn)* Hello, Mannion . . . Insigna . . . Stefanowski . . .

MANNION *(hoarsely)*. Hello, Mister Pulver . . .

PULVER. This is—Lieutenant Girard. *(The men murmur a greeting.)*

MISS GIRARD. What're you all doing with those glasses?

INSIGNA. We're . . . cleaning them. *(Suddenly pulls out shirt tail and begins lamely polishing spy glass. The others follow his example. More men crowd onto the stage.)*

PULVER. Well, don't work too hard . . . *(They turn to leave, but find themselves hemmed in by the men)* It's getting a little stuffy up here, I guess we better . . . *(Roberts enters, very excited, carrying a piece of paper and a small book)*

ROBERTS *(entering)*. Hey, Insigna . . . Mannion . . . get a load of this . . . Hey, Frank . . . *(He stops short, seeing Miss Girard)*

PULVER. Hiya, Doug boy! This is Ann Girard—Doug Roberts.

ROBERTS. How do you do?

MISS GIRARD *(beaming)*. How do you do? You're Frank's roommate. He's told me all about you.

ROBERTS. Really?

MISS GIRARD. What are you doing on this ship?

ROBERTS. Now there you've got me.

MISS GIRARD. No, I mean what's your job? Like Frank here is Executive Officer.

ROBERTS. Oh, I'm just the Laundry and Morale Officer.

MISS GIRARD. Why, that's wonderful— I've just been made Laundry and Morale Officer in our outfit!

PULVER. Oh, for Christ's sake! *(Mannion and Insigna begin an argument in whispers.)*

MISS GIRARD. Maybe we can get together and compare notes.

ROBERTS. I'd enjoy that very much.

PULVER *(attempting to usher Miss Girard off)*. Look, Doug. Will you excuse us? We're going down to have a little drink.

MISS GIRARD. Frank, I don't think that's very nice. Aren't you going to ask Doug to join us?

PULVER. Hell, no—I mean—he doesn't like Scotch.

ROBERTS. That's right, Miss Girard. I stay true to alcohol and orange juice.

PULVER. Come on, Ann . . .

MISS GIRARD. Wait a minute! A lot of the girls at the hospital swear by alcohol and orange juice. We ought to all get together and have a party in our new dayroom.

INSIGNA *(to Mannion)*. I bet you fifty bucks . . . *(Stefanowski moves Insigna and Mannion away from Miss Girard.)*

MISS GIRARD. Seems to be an argument.

PULVER. Yeah.

MISS GIRARD. Well, anyhow, we're fixing up a new dayroom. *(She looks offstage)* Look, you can see it! The hospital! And there's our new dormitory! That first window . . . *(Pulver takes glasses from Wiley to look at island.)*

INSIGNA *(to Mannion, his voice rising)*. All right, I got a *hundred* bucks says that's the one with the birthmark on her ass. *(There is a terrible silence. Miss Girard, after a moment, takes the glasses from Pulver and looks at the island. After a moment she lowers the glasses and speaks to Pulver.)*

MISS GIRARD. Frank, I won't be able to have lunch with you after all. Would you call the boat, please? *(To Roberts)* Good-bye, Doug. It was nice knowing you. You see, I promised the girls I'd help them hang some curtains and I think we'd better get started right away. Good-bye, everybody. *(To Mannion)* Oh, what's your name again?

INSIGNA. Mine?

MISS GIRARD. No. Yours.

MANNION. Mine? *(Miss Girard nods)* Mannion.

MISS GIRARD. Well, Mannion. I wouldn't take that bet if I were you because you'd lose a hundred bucks. *(To Pulver)* Come on, Harmless. *(She exits, followed by a bewildered Pulver. The men watch her off. Stefanowski throws his cap on the ground in anger)*

MANNION *(to Insigna)*. You loud-mouthed little bastard! Now you've gone and done it!

ROBERTS. Shut up! Insigna, how did you . . .

INSIGNA. We seen her taking a bath.

LINDSTROM. Through these glasses, Mister Roberts! We could see everything!

STEFANOWSKI *(furious)*. You heard what she said—she's going to hang some curtains.

MANNION. Yeah . . .

LINDSTROM. Gee, them nurses was pretty to look at. *(He sighs. There is a little tragic moment)*

ROBERTS. She's got a ten-minute boat ride. You've still got ten minutes.

WILEY. It wouldn't be any fun when you know you're going to be rushed.

LINDSTROM. This was the first real good day this ship has ever had. But it's all over now.

ROBERTS. Well, maybe you've got time then to listen to a little piece of news . . . *(He reads from the paper in his hands)* "When in all respects ready for sea, on or about 1600 today, the *AK 601* will proceed at ten knots via points X-Ray, Yolk and Zebra to Elysium Island, arriving there in seven days and reporting to the Port Director for cargo assignment." *(Emphatically)* "During its stay in Elysium, the ship will

make maximum use of the recreational facilities of this port."
(The men look up in slow surprise and disbelief.)

STEFANOWSKI. But that means liberty!

LINDSTROM. That don't mean liberty, Mister Roberts?

ROBERTS. That's exactly what it means!

INSIGNA *(dazed)*. Somebody must've been drunk to send us to a Liberty Port! *(Roberts nods.)*

LINDSTROM. Has the Old Man seen them orders?

ROBERTS. He saw them before I did.
(Now the men are excited.)

WILEY. Elysium! Where's that?

MANNION. Yeah! Where's that, Mister Roberts?
(The men crowd around Roberts as he sits on the hatch.)

ROBERTS *(reading from guide-book)*. "Elysium is the largest of the Limbo Islands. It is often referred to as the 'Polynesian Paradise.' Vanilla, sugar, cocoa, coffee, copra, mother-of-pearl, phosphates and rum are the chief exports."

INSIGNA. Rum! Did you hear that? *(He gooses Lindstrom.)*

LINDSTROM. Cut that out!
(Dolan gooses Insigna.)

INSIGNA. Cut that out!

MANNION. Shut up!

ROBERTS. "Elysium City, its capital, is a beautiful metropolis of palm-lined boulevards, handsome public buildings and colorful stucco homes. Since 1900, its population has remained remarkably constant at approximately 30,000."

INSIGNA. I'll fix that!
(The men shout him down.)

ROBERTS. That's all there is here. If you want the real dope on Elysium, there's one man on this ship who's been there.

STEFANOWSKI. Who's that?

MANNION. Who?

ROBERTS. Dowdy!
(The men run off wildly in every direction, shouting for Dowdy. The call is taken up all over the ship. Roberts listens to them happily, then notices a pair of binoculars. He looks toward the island for a moment, shrugs and is lifting the binoculars to his eyes as the lights fade out.)

SCENE FIVE

During the darkness we can hear the

exciting strains of Polynesian music.

*The lights come up slowly through a porthole, casting a strong late-afternoon shaft of light onto motionless white figures. It is the enlisted men's compartment below decks. Except for a few not yet fully dressed, the men are all in white uniforms. The compartment is a crowded place with three-tiered bunks against the bulkheads. Most of the men are crowded around the porthole, downstage left. The men who cannot see are listening to the reports of Insigna, who is standing on a bench, looking out the porthole. The only man who is not galvanized with excitement is Dowdy, who sits calmly on a bench, downstage center, reading a magazine—*True Detective.

GERHART *(to Insigna).* What do you see now, Sam?

INSIGNA. There's a lot of little boats up forward—up around the bow.

PAYNE. What kind of boats?

INSIGNA. They're little sort of canoes and they're all filled up with flowers and stuff. And there's women in them boats, paddling them . . .

PAYNE. Are they coming down this way?

INSIGNA. Naw. They're sticking around the bow.

STEFANOWSKI. Sam, where's that music coming from?

INSIGNA. There's a great big canoe up there and it's all filled with fat bastards with flowers in their ears playing little old git-tars . . .

SCHLEMMER. Why the hell can't we go up on deck? That's what I'd like to know!

LINDSTROM. When are we going ashore! That's what I'd like to know!

(Insigna suddenly laughs.)

PAYNE. What is it, Sam?

INSIGNA. I wish you could see this . . .

(Chief Johnson enters, looking knowingly at the men, shakes his head and addresses Dowdy.)

JOHNSON. Same story in here, eh? Every porthole this side of the ship!

DOWDY. They're going to wear themselves down to a nub before they ever get over there . . .

LINDSTROM *(takes coin from pocket and thrusts it at Insigna).* Hey, Sam, here's another penny. Make them kids down below dive for it.

INSIGNA *(impatiently).* All right! *(Throws coin out the port)* Heads up, you little bastards!

(The men watch tensely.)

LINDSTROM. Did he get that one too?

INSIGNA. Yeah . . . *(The men relax somewhat)*

LINDSTROM. Them kids don't ever miss!

INSIGNA. Hey, Dowdy—where's that little park again? Where you said all the good-looking women hang out?

DOWDY. For the last time—you see that big hill over there to the right . . .

INSIGNA. Yeah.

DOWDY. You see a big church . . . with a street running off to the left of it.

INSIGNA. Yeah.

DOWDY. Well, you go up that street three blocks . . .

INSIGNA. Yeah, I'm there.

DOWDY. That's the park.

INSIGNA. Well, I'll be damned . . .

LINDSTROM. Hey, show me that park, Sam?

(The other men gather around Insigna, asking to see the park.)

INSIGNA *(the authority now).* All right, you bastards, line up. I'll show you where the women hang out.

(The men form a line and each steps up to the porthole where Insigna points out the park.)

JOHNSON *(to Dowdy).* Smell that shoe polish? These guys have gone nuts!

DOWDY. I went down the ship's store the other day to buy a bar of soap and, do you know, they had been sold out for a week! No soap, no Listerine, no lilac shaving lotion—hell, they even sold eighteen jars of Mum! Now these bastards are bootlegging it! They're gettin' ten bucks for a used jar of Mum!

(Reber, wearing the messenger's belt, enters. The men greet him excitedly.)

STEFANOWSKI. What's the word on liberty, Reber? Is the Old Man still asleep?

MANNION. Yeah, what's the word?

REBER. I just peeked in on him. He's snoring like a baby.

GERHART. Jeez, how any guy can sleep at a time like this!

INSIGNA. I'll get him up! I'm going up there and tap on his door! *(Picks up a heavy lead pipe)*

DOWDY *(grabbing Insigna).* Like hell you are! You're going to stay right here and pray. You're going to pray that he wakes up feeling good and decides he's kept you guys sweating long enough!

MANNION. That's telling the little crud! *(Insigna and Mannion threaten each other.)*

REBER. Hey, Lindstrom. I got good news for you. You can take them whites off.

LINDSTROM. I ain't got the duty *tonight?*

REBER. That's right. You and Mister Roberts got the duty tonight—the twelve to four watch. The Exec just posted the list . . . *(He is interrupted by the sound of static on the squawk box. Instantly all men turn toward it eagerly)*

DOLAN *(on squawk box)*. Now hear this! Now hear this!

WILEY. Here we go! Here we go!

STEFANOWSKI *(imitating the squawk box)*. Liberty . . . will com-mence . . . immediately!

GERHART. Quiet!

DOLAN *(on squawk box)*. Now hear this! The Captain's messenger will report to the Captain's cabin on the double!

REBER. My God! He's awake! *(He runs out)*

PAYNE. Won't be long now!

WILEY. Get going, Mannion! Get into those whites! We're going to be the first ones over the side!

MANNION. Hell, yes! Give me a hand! *(Now there is a general frenzy of preparation—the men put the last-minute touches to shoes, hair, uniforms.)*

GERHART *(singing to the tune of "California, Here I Come")*.
Ee-liss-*ee*-um, here I come! . . . Ta-ta-ta-ta-*ta*-da-tah . . .

SCHLEMMER *(to Gerhart)*. Watch where you're going! You stepped on my shine!

INSIGNA. Schlemmer . . . Stef . . . Gerhart . . . come here! *(These men gather around him. Lindstrom remains unhappily alone)* Now listen! Stefanowski and me are going to work alone for the first hour and a half! But if you pick up something first . . . *(Produces small map from his pocket)* We'll be working up and down this street here . . . *(They study the map. Now the squawk box is clicked on again. All the men stand rigid, listening.)*

DOLAN *(on squawk box)*. Now hear this! Now hear this! The Captain is now going to make a personal announcement. *(Sound of squawk-box switch.)*

CAPTAIN *(on squawk box)*. Goddammit, how does this thing work? *(Sound of squawk-box switch again)* This is the Captain speaking. I just woke up from a little nap and I got a surprise. I found out there were men on this ship who were expecting liberty. *(At this point, the lights start dimming until the entire scene is blacked out. The speech continues throughout the darkness. Under the Captain's speech the strains of Polynesian music can be heard)* Now I don't know how such a rumor got around, but I'd like to clear it up right now. You see, it's like this. Because of cargo requirements and security conditions which has just come to my personal attention there will be no liberty as long as we're in this here port. And one other thing—as long as we're here, no man will wear white uniforms. Now I would like to repeat for the benefit of complete understanding and clearness, NO LIBERTY. That is all.

SCENE SIX

The lights come up on the Captain's cabin. Against the left bulkhead is a settee. A chair is placed center. Up center is the only door. The Captain is seated behind his desk, holding a watch in one hand and the microphone in the other, in an attitude of waiting. Just over the desk and against the right bulkhead is a ship's intercommunication board. There is a wall-safe in the right bulkhead. After a moment there is a knock on the door.

———

CAPTAIN. Come in, Mister Roberts. *(As Roberts enters, the Captain puts the microphone on the desk)* Thirty-eight seconds. Pretty good time! You see, I been expectin' you ever since I made my little announcement.

ROBERTS. Well, as long as you're expecting me, what about it—when does this crew get liberty?

CAPTAIN. Well, in the first place, just kinda hold your tongue. And in the second place, sit down.

ROBERTS. There's no time to sit down. When are you going to let this crew go ashore?

CAPTAIN. I'm not. This wasn't my idea —coming to a Liberty Port. One of my officers arranged it with a certain Port Director—gave him a bottle of Scotch whiskey—compliments of the Captain. And the Port Director was kind enough to send me a little thank-you note along with our orders. Sit down, Mister Roberts. (Roberts sits) Don't worry about it. I'm not going to make trouble about that wasted bottle of Scotch. I'll admit I was a little pre-voked about not being consulted. Then I got to thinking maybe we oughta come to this port anyway so's you and me could have a little talk.

ROBERTS. You can make all the trouble you want, Captain, but let's quit wasting time. Don't you hear that music? Don't you know it's tearing those guys apart? They're breakable, Captain! I promise you!

CAPTAIN. That's enough! I've had enough of your fancy educated talk. (Rises, goes to Roberts) Now you listen to me. I got two things I want to show you. (He unlocks the wall-safe, opens it and takes out a commander's cap with gold braid "scrambled eggs" on the visor) You see that? That's the cap of a full commander. I'm gonna wear that cap some day and you're going to help me. (Replaces cap in safe, goes back to Roberts) I guess there's no harm in telling you that you helped me get that palm tree by working cargo. Now don't let this go to your head, but when Admiral Finchley gave me that award, he said, "You got a good Cargo Officer, Morton; keep him at it, you're going places." So I went out and bought that hat. There's nothing gonna stand between me and that hat—certainly not you. Now last week you wrote a letter that said "disharmony aboard this ship." I told you there wasn't going to be any more letters. But what do I find on my desk this morning . . . (Taking letter from desk) Another one. It says "friction between myself and the Commanding Officer." That ain't gonna go in, Mister.

ROBERTS. How are you going to ~top it, Captain?

CAPTAIN. I ain't, you are. (Goes to his chair and sits) Just how much do you want this crew to have a liberty anyhow? Enough to stop this "disharmony"? To stop this "friction"? (Leans forward) Enough to get out of the habit of writing letters ever? Because that's the only way this crew is ever gonna get ashore. (Leans back) Well, we've had our little talk. What do you say?

ROBERTS (after a moment). How did you

get in the Navy? How did you get on our side? You're what I joined to fight against. You ignorant, arrogant, ambitious . . . (Rises) jackass! Keeping a hundred and sixty-seven men in prison because you got a palm tree for the work they did. I don't know which I hate worse—you or that other malignant growth that stands outside your door!

CAPTAIN. Why, you goddamn . . .

ROBERTS. How did you ever get command of a ship? I realize that in wartime they have to scrape the bottom of the barrel, but where the hell did they ever scrape you up?

CAPTAIN (shouting). There's just one thing left for you, by God—a general court-martial.

ROBERTS. That suits me fine. Court-martial me!

CAPTAIN. By God, you've got it!

ROBERTS. I'm asking for it!

CAPTAIN. You don't have to ask for it, you've got it now!

ROBERTS. If I can't get transferred off here, I'll get court-martialed off! I'm fed up! But you'll need a witness. Send for your messenger. He's down below. I'll say it all again in front of him. (Pauses) Go on, call in Reber! (The Captain doesn't move) Go on, call him. (Still the Captain doesn't move) Do you want me to call him?

CAPTAIN. No. (He walks upstage, then turns to Roberts) I think you're a pretty smart boy. I may not talk very good, Mister, but I know how to take care of smart boys. Let me tell you something. Let me tell you a little secret. I hate your guts, you college son-of-a-bitch! You think you're better than I am! You think you're better because you've had everything handed to you! Let me tell you something, Mister—I've worked since I was ten years old, and all my life I've known you superior bastards. I knew you people when I was a kid in Boston and I worked in eating-places and you ordered me around. . . . "Oh, bus-boy! My friend here seems to have thrown up on the table. Clean it up, please." I started going to sea as a steward and I worked for you then . . . "Steward, take my magazine out to the deck chair!" . . . "Steward, I don't like your looks. Please keep out of my way as much as possible!" Well, I took that crap! I took that for years from pimple-faced bastards who weren't good enough to wipe my nose! And now I don't have to take it any more! There's a war on, by God, and I'm the Captain and you can wipe my nose! The worst thing I can do to you is to keep you on this ship! And that's where you're going to stay! Now get out of here! *(He goes to his chair and sits. Roberts moves slowly toward the door. He hears the music, goes to the porthole and listens. Then he turns to the Captain.)*

ROBERTS. Can't you hear that music, Captain?

CAPTAIN. Yeah, I hear it. *(Busies himself at desk, ignoring Roberts)*

ROBERTS. Don't you know those guys below can hear it too? Oh, my God.

CAPTAIN. Get out of here.

(After a moment, Roberts turns from the porthole and slumps against the Captain's locker. His face is strained.)

ROBERTS. What do you want for liberty, Captain?

CAPTAIN. I want plenty. You're through writin' letters—ever.

ROBERTS. Okay.

CAPTAIN. That's not all. You're through givin' me trouble. You're through talkin' back to me in front of the crew. You ain't ever gonna open your mouth—except in civil answer. *(Roberts doesn't answer)* Mister Roberts, you know that if you don't take my terms I'll let you go out that door and that's the end of any hope for liberty.

ROBERTS. Is that all, Captain?

CAPTAIN. No. Anyone know you're in here?

ROBERTS. No one.

CAPTAIN. Then you won't go blabbin' about this to anyone ever. It might not sound so good. And besides I don't want you to take credit for gettin' this crew ashore.

ROBERTS. Do you think I'm doing this for credit? Do you think I'd *let* anyone know about this?

CAPTAIN. I gotta be sure.

ROBERTS. You've got my word, that's all.

CAPTAIN *(after a pause)*. Your word. Yes, you college fellas make a big show about keeping your word.

ROBERTS. How about it, Captain. Is it a deal?

CAPTAIN. Yeah. *(Roberts picks up the microphone, turns on a switch and thrusts the microphone at the Captain)* Now hear

this. This is the Captain speaking. I've got some further word on security conditions in this port and so it gives me great pleasure to tell you that liberty, for the star board section . . .

ROBERTS *(covering the microphone with his hand)*. For the entire crew, goddammit.

CAPTAIN. Correction: Liberty for the entire crew will commence immediately. *(Roberts turns off the microphone. After a moment we hear the shouts of the crew. Roberts goes up to porthole. The Captain leans back on his chair. A song, "Roll Me Over," is started by someone and is soon taken up by the whole crew.)*

ROBERTS *(looking out of the porthole. He is excited and happy)*. Listen to those crazy bastards. Listen to them. *(The crew continues to sing with increasing volume. Now the words can be distinguished:*

Roll me over in the clover,
Roll me over, lay me down
And do it again.)

CURTAIN

ACT TWO

SCENE ONE

The curtain rises on the main set. It is now 3:45 A.M. The night is pitch-black, but we can see because of a light over the head of the gangway, where a temporary desk has been rigged; a large ship's logbook lies open on this desk. A small table on which are hospital supplies is at left of the door.

At rise, Roberts, Doc, Lindstrom, Johnson and four seamen are discovered onstage. Lindstrom, in web belt, is writing in the log. Roberts is standing with a pile of yellow slips in his hand; he wears the side-arms of the Officer of the Deck. Johnson and a seaman are standing near the hatchway, holding the inert body of another seaman, who has court plaster on his face. Two more seamen lie on the hatch cover where Doc is kneeling, bandaging one of them. As the curtain rises we hear the sound of a siren off right. Everyone turns and looks—that is, everyone who is conscious.

LINDSTROM. Here's another batch, Mister

Roberts—a whole paddy wagon full. And this one's an Army paddy wagon.

ROBERTS. We haven't filed away this batch yet. *(To Doc)* Hurry up, Doc.

JOHNSON *(to Doc, indicating body he is carrying)*. Where do we put number twenty-three here, Doc? Sick bay or what?

DOC. Just put him to bed. His condition's only critical.

JOHNSON *(carrying seaman off)*. They just roll out of their bunks, Doc. Now I'm stacking 'em on the deck down there—I'm on the third layer already.

VOICE *(offstage)*. Okay, Lieutenant! All set down here! You ready?

ROBERTS *(calling offstage—and giving hand signal)*. Okay! *(To Doc)* Here they come, Doc! Heads up!

SHORE PATROLMAN'S VOICE *(offstage)*. Lieutenant!

ROBERTS. Oh, not you again!

SHORE PATROLMAN'S VOICE *(offstage)*. I got a bunch of real beauties for you this time.

ROBERTS *(calling offstage)*. Can they walk?

SHORE PATROLMAN'S VOICE *(offstage)*. Just barely!

ROBERTS *(calling)*. Then send 'em up.

LINDSTROM. Man, oh, man, what a liberty! We got the record now, Mister Roberts! This makes the seventh batch since we went on watch!

(The sound of a cargo winch and a voice offstage singing the Army Air Corps song are heard. Roberts is looking offstage.)

ROBERTS *(signaling)*. Looks like a real haul this time. Schlemmer, look out!

LINDSTROM. Schlemmer, look out!

ROBERTS. Okay, Doc. *(Doc and Roberts lift the two bodies from the hatch cover and deposit them farther upstage. At this moment, the cargo net appears, loaded with bodies in once-white uniforms and leis. Riding on top of the net is Schlemmer, wearing a lei and singing "Off We Go into the Wild Blue Yonder")* Let her in easy . . .

LINDSTROM. Let her in easy . . .

(The net is lowered onto the hatch cover and Lindstrom detaches it from the hook. All start untangling bodies.)

ROBERTS. Well, they're peaceful anyhow. *(At this point a Shore Patrolman enters from the gangway.)*

SHORE PATROLMAN *(handing Roberts a sheaf of yellow slips)*. For your collection.

(Points down gangway) Take a look at them.

ROBERTS *(looks offstage)*. My God, what did they do?

SHORE PATROLMAN. They done all right, Lieutenant. Six of them busted into a formal dance and took on a hundred and twenty-eight Army bastards. *(Calls off)* All right, let's go!

(Stefanowski, Reber, Wiley, Payne and Mannion, with his arm around Insigna, straggle on—a frightening sight—followed by a Military Policeman. Insigna's uniform is torn to shreds. Mannion is clad in a little diaper of crepe paper. All have bloody faces and uniforms. A few bear souvenirs —a Japanese lantern, leis, Army caps, a Shore Patrol band, etc. They throw perfunctory salutes to the colors, then murmur a greeting to Roberts.)

MILITARY POLICEMAN. Duty Officer?

ROBERTS. That's right.

MILITARY POLICEMAN *(salutes)*. Colonel Middleton presents his compliments to the Captain and wishes him to know that these men made a shambles out of the Colonel's testimonial dinner-dance.

ROBERTS. Is this true, Insigna?

INSIGNA. That's right, Mister Roberts. A shambles. *(To Mannion)* Ain't that right, Killer?

MANNION. That's right, Mister Roberts.

ROBERTS. You men crashed a dance for Army personnel?

MANNION. Yes, sir! And they made us feel unwelcome! *(To Insigna)* Didn't they, Slugger?

ROBERTS. Oh, they started a fight, eh?

WILEY. No, sir! *We* started it!

STEFANOWSKI. We finished it too! *(To Military Policeman)* Tell Mister Roberts how many of you Army bastards are in the hospital.

MANNION. Go on.

MILITARY POLICEMAN. Thirty-eight soldiers of the United States Army have been hospitalized. And the Colonel himself has a very bad bruise on his left shin!

PAYNE. *I* did that, Mister Roberts.

MILITARY POLICEMAN. And that isn't all, Lieutenant. There were young ladies present—fifty of them. Colonel Middleton had been lining them up for a month, from the finest families of Elysium. And he had personally guaranteed their safety this evening. Well, sir . . .

ROBERTS. Well?

MILITARY POLICEMAN. Two of those young ladies got somewhat mauled, one actually got a black eye, six of them got their clothes torn off and then went screaming off into the night and they haven't been heard from since. What are you going to do about it, Lieutenant?

ROBERTS. Well, I'm due to get relieved here in fifteen minutes—I'll be glad to lead a search party.

MILITARY POLICEMAN. No, sir. The Army's taking care of that end. The Colonel will want to know what punishment you're going to give these men.

ROBERTS. Tell the Colonel that I'm sure our Captain will think of something.

MILITARY POLICEMAN. But . . .

ROBERTS. That's all, Sergeant.

MILITARY POLICEMAN (salutes). Thank you, sir. (He goes off)

SHORE PATROLMAN. Lieutenant, I been pretty sore at your guys up till now—we had to put on ten extra Shore Patrolmen on account of this ship. But if you knew Colonel "Chicken" Middleton—well, I'd be willing to do this every night. (To the men) So long, fellows!

((The men call "So long." Shore Patrolman exits, saluting Roberts and quarterdeck.)

ROBERTS. Well, what've you got to say for yourselves?

STEFANOWSKI (after a moment). Okay if we go ashore again, Mister Roberts?

ROBERTS (to Lindstrom) Is this the first time for these guys?

LINDSTROM (showing log). Yes, sir, they got a clean record—they only been brought back once.

ROBERTS (to Doc). What do you say, Doc?

(The men turn eagerly to Doc.)

DOC. Anybody got a fractured skull?

MEN. No.

DOC. Okay, you pass the physical.

ROBERTS. Go down and take a shower first and get into some clothes.

(The men rush to the hatchway.)

STEFANOWSKI. We still got time to get back to that dance!

(As they descend hatchway, Insigna pulls crepe paper from around Mannion as he is halfway down the hatchway.)

ROBERTS. How you feeling, Doc?

DOC. These alcohol fumes are giving me a cheap drunk—otherwise pretty routine. When do you get relieved, Doug? (Takes

box from table and gestures for men to remove table. They carry it off)

ROBERTS. Soon as Carney gets back from the island. Any minute now.

DOC. What are you grinning like a skunk for?

ROBERTS. Nothing. I always grin like a skunk. What have you got in the box?

DOC (descending hatchway—holding up small packet he has taken from the box). Little favors from the Doc. I'm going to put one in each man's hand and when he wakes up he'll find pinned to his shirt full instructions for its use. I think it'll save me a lot of work later on. (His head disappears)

LINDSTROM. I wish Gerhart would get back here and relieve me. I've got to get over to that island before it runs out of women.

(Dolan enters from gangway.)

DOLAN. Howdy, Mister Roberts! I'm drunk as a goat! (Pulls a goat aboard) Show him how drunk I am. Mister Roberts, when I first saw her she was eatin', and you know, she just eat her way into my heart. She was eatin' a little old palm tree and I thought to myself, our ship needs a mascot. (He points out palm tree to goat) There you are, kid. Chow!

(Roberts blocks his way.)

ROBERTS. Wait a minute . . . wait a minute. What's her name?

DOLAN. I don't know, sir.

ROBERTS. She's got a name plate.

DOLAN. Oh, so she has . . . her name is . . . (Reads from tag on goat's collar) . . . Property Of.

ROBERTS. What's her last name?

DOLAN. Her last name . . . (Reads again) Rear Admiral Wentworth.

(Approaching siren is heard offstage.)

ROBERTS. Okay, Dolan, hit the sack. I'll take care of her.

DOLAN. Okay, Mister Roberts. (Descends hatchway) See that she gets a good square meal. (He points to the Captain's palm tree and winks, then disappears. Gerhart enters from gangway)

LINDSTROM. Gerhart! (He frantically removes his web belt and shoves it at Gerhart)

GERHART. Okay, okay—you're relieved.

LINDSTROM (tosses a fast salute to Roberts and says in one breath). Requestpermissiontogoashore! (He hurries down gangway)

(Shore Patrolman enters from gangway.)

SHORE PATROLMAN. Lieutenant, has one of your men turned up with a . . . *(Sees goat and takes leash)* Oh, thanks. *(To goat)* Come on, come on, your papa over there is worried about you. *(Pulls goat down gangway)*

GERHART. Where's your relief, Mister Roberts?

ROBERTS *(sitting on hatch)*. He'll be along any minute. How was your liberty, Gerhart?

(Gerhart grins. So does Roberts. Doc enters from hatchway.)

DOC. What are you looking so cocky about anyway?

ROBERTS. Am I looking cocky? Maybe it's because for the first time since I've been on this ship, I'm seeing a crew.

DOC. What do you think you've been living with all this time?

ROBERTS. Just a hundred and sixty-seven separate guys. There's a big difference, Doc. Now these guys are bound together. You saw Insigna and Mannion. Doc, I think these guys are strong enough now to take all the miserable, endless days ahead of us. I only hope I'm strong enough.

DOC. Doug, tomorrow you and I are going over there and take advantage of the groundwork that's been laid tonight. You and I are going to have ourselves a liberty. *(Pulver enters slowly from the gangway and walks across the stage. Doc calls Roberts' attention to him.)*

ROBERTS. Hello, Frank. How was your liberty?

(Pulver half turns, shrugs and holds up seven fingers, then exits. A Shore Patrol Officer enters from the gangway and calls offstage. He speaks with a Southern accent.)

SHORE PATROL OFFICER. That's your post and that's your post. You know what to do. *(He salutes the quarter-deck, then Roberts)* Officer of the Deck? *(Roberts nods. The Shore Patrol Officer hesitates a moment)* I hope you don't mind but I've stationed two of my men at the foot of the gangway. I'm sorry but this ship is restricted for the rest of its stay in Elysium. Your Captain is to report to the Island Commander at seven o'clock this morning. I'd recommend that he's there on time. The Admiral's a pretty tough cookie

when he's mad, and he's madder now than I've ever seen him.

ROBERTS. What in particular did this?

SHORE PATROL LIEUTENANT. A little while ago six men from your ship broke into the home of the French Consul and started throwing things through the plate-glass living-room window. We found some of the things on the lawn: a large world globe, a small love seat, a lot of books and a bust of Balzac—the French writer. We also found an Army private first class who was unconscious at the time. He claims they threw him too.

ROBERTS. Through the window?

SHORE PATROL LIEUTENANT. That's right! It seems he took them there for a little joke. He didn't tell them it was the Consul's house; he said it was a—what we call in Alabama—a cat-house. *(Roberts and Doc nod)* Be sure that your Captain is there at seven o'clock sharp. If it makes you feel any better, Admiral Wentworth says this is the worst ship he's ever seen in his entire naval career. *(Laughs, then salutes)* Good night, Lieutenant.

ROBERTS *(returning salute)*. Good night. *(The Shore Patrol Lieutenant exits down gangway—saluting the quarter-deck.)*

GERHART. Well, there goes the liberty. That was sure a wham-bam-thank you, ma'am!

DOC. Good night. *(He exits through left passageway)*

GERHART. But, by God, it was worth it. That liberty was worth anything!

ROBERTS. I think you're right, Gerhart.

GERHART. Hunh?

ROBERTS. I think you're right.

GERHART. Yeah.

(He smiles. Roberts looks over the log. Gerhart whistles softly to himself "Roll Me Over" as the lights slowly fade out.)

During the darkness we hear Johnson shouting:

JOHNSON. All right, fall in for muster. Form two ranks. And pipe down.

SCENE TWO

The lights come up, revealing the deck. Morning sunlight. A group of men, right and left, in orderly formation. They are talking.

JOHNSON. 'Ten-shun!

(The command is relayed through the ship. The Captain enters from his cabin, followed by Roberts. The Captain steps up on the hatch cover. Roberts starts to fall in with the men.)

CAPTAIN *(calling to Roberts and pointing to a place beside himself on hatch cover)*. Over here, Roberts. *(Roberts takes his place left of Captain)* We're being kicked out of this port. I had a feeling this liberty was a bad idea. That's why we'll never have one again. We're going to erase this blot from my record if we have to work twenty-four hours a day. We're going to move even more cargo than we've moved before. And if there ain't enough cargo work, Mister Roberts here is gonna find some. Isn't that right, Mister Roberts? *(Roberts doesn't answer)* Isn't that right, Mister Roberts?

ROBERTS. Yes, sir.

CAPTAIN. I'm appointing Mister Roberts here and now to see that you men toe the line. And I can't think of a more honorable man for the job. He's a man who keeps his word no matter what. *(Turns to Roberts)* Now, Roberts, if you do a good job—and if the Admiral begins to smile on us again—there might be something in it for you. What would you say if that little silver bar on your collar got a twin brother some day? *(Roberts is startled. The Captain calls offstage)* Officer of the Deck!

OFFSTAGE VOICE. Yes, sir!

CAPTAIN *(to Roberts)*. You wasn't expectin' that, was you? *(Calling offstage)* Get ready to sail!

OFFSTAGE VOICE. Aye-aye, sir!

CAPTAIN. You men are dismissed!

JOHNSON. Fall out!

(The men fall out. Some exit. A little group forms downstage.)

CAPTAIN. Wait a minute! Wait a minute! Roberts, take these men here back aft to handle lines. And see that they work up a sweat. *(Roberts and men look at him)* Did you hear me, Roberts? I gave you an order!

ROBERTS *(carefully)*. Yes, Captain. I heard you.

CAPTAIN. How do you answer when I give an order?

ROBERTS *(after a pause)*. Aye-aye, sir.

CAPTAIN. That's more like it . . . that's more like it! *(He exits into his cabin)*

STEFANOWSKI. What'd he mean, Mister Roberts?

ROBERTS. I don't know. Just what he said, I guess.

GERHART. What'd you let him give you all that guff for?

DOLAN *(stepping up on hatch, carrying a file folder)*. Because he's tired, that's why. He had the mid-watch last night. Your tail'd be dragging too if you had to handle all them customers.

ROBERTS. Come on. Let's get going . . .

DOLAN. Wait a minute, Mister Roberts. Something come for you in the mail this morning—a little love letter from the Bureau. *(Pulls out paper from file folder)* Get a load of this! *(Reads)* "To All Ships and Stations: Heightened war offensive has created urgent need aboard combat ships for experienced officers. *(He clicks his teeth and winks at Roberts)* All commanding officers are hereby directed to forward with their endorsements all applications for transfer from officers with twenty-four months' sea duty." *(Roberts grabs the directive and reads it. Dolan looks at Roberts and smiles)* You got twenty-nine months—you're the only officer aboard that has. Mister Roberts, the Old Man is hanging on the ropes from the working-over the Admiral give him. All he needs to flatten him is one more little jab. And here it is. Your letter. I typed it up. *(He pulls out triplicate letter from file cover—then a fountain pen which he offers to Roberts)* Sign it and I'll take it in—

MANNION. Go on, sign it, Mister Roberts. He'll take off like a bird.

DOLAN. What're you waitin' for, Mister Roberts?

ROBERTS *(handing directive back to Dolan)*. I'll want to look it over first, Dolan. Come on, let's get going.

DOLAN. There's nothing to look over. This is the same letter we wrote yesterday —only quoting this new directive.

ROBERTS. Look, Dolan, I'm tired. And I told you I wanted—

DOLAN. You ain't too tired to sign your name!

ROBERTS *(sharply)*. Take it easy, Dolan. I'm not going to sign it. So take it easy! *(Turns to exit right, finds himself blocked by crew)* Did you hear me? Let's get going! *(Exits)*

STEFANOWSKI. What the hell's come over him?

(They look at one another.)

INSIGNA. Aye-aye, sir—for Christ's sake!

MANNION *(after a moment)*. Come on. Let's get going.

DOLAN *(bitterly)*. "Take it easy . . . take it easy!"

(The men start to move off slowly as the lights fade out.)

During the darkness we hear a radio. There is considerable static.

AMERICAN BROADCASTER. Still, of course, we have no official word from the Headquarters of the Supreme Allied Command in Europe. I repeat, there is no official announcement yet. The report that the war in Europe has ended has come from only one correspondent. It has not been confirmed by other correspondents or by SHAEF headquarters. But here is one highly intriguing fact—that report has not been denied either in Washington or in SHAEF headquarters in Europe. IT HAS NOT BEEN DENIED. Right now in those places the newsmen are crowded, waiting to flash to the world the announcement of V-E Day.

SCENE THREE

The lights come up on Roberts' and Pulver's cabin. Doc, at the desk, and Pulver, up in his bunk, are listening to the radio.

————

PULVER. Turn that damn thing off, Doc. Has Doug ever said anything to you about wanting a promotion?

DOC. Of course not. I doubt if he's even conscious of what rank he is.

PULVER. You can say that again!

DOC. I doubt if he's even conscious of what rank he is.

PULVER. That's what I said. He doesn't even think about a promotion. The only thing he thinks about is the war news—up in the radio shack two weeks now—all day long—listening with a headset, reading all the bulletins . . . Anyone who says he's bucking for another stripe is a dirty liar.

DOC. Who says he is, Frank?

PULVER. Insigna, Mannion and some of the other guys. I heard them talking out-side the porthole. They were talking loud on purpose so I could hear them—they must've guessed I was lying here on my bunk. What's happened to Doug anyway, Doc?

DOC. How would I know! He's spoken about ten words to me in as many days. But I'm damn well going to find out.

PULVER. He won't talk, Doc. This morning I followed him all around the room while he was shaving. I begged him to talk to me. I says, "You're a fellow who needs a friend and here I am." And I says, "What's all this trouble you're having with the crew? You tell me and I'll fix it up like that." And then I give him some real good advice—I says, "Keep your chin up," and things like that. And then do you know what he did? He walked out of the room just as though I wasn't here.

(There is a knock on the door.)

DOC. Come in.

(Dowdy enters.)

DOWDY. Doc, Mister Pulver—could we see you officers a minute?

DOC. Sure. *(Gerhart and Lindstrom enter, closing the door)* What is it?

DOWDY. Tell them what happened, Gerhart.

GERHART. Well, sir, I sure don't like to say this but . . . Mister Roberts just put Dolan on report.

LINDSTROM. Me and Gerhart seen him.

PULVER. On report!

GERHART. Yes, sir. Tomorrow morning Dolan has to go up before the Captain—on account of Mister Roberts.

LINDSTROM. On account of Mister Roberts.

GERHART. And we was wondering if you officers could get him to take Dolan off report before . . . well, before—

DOC. Before what, Gerhart?

GERHART. Well, you see, the guys are all down in the compartment, talking about it. And they're saying some pretty rough things about Mister Roberts. Nobody just ever expected to see him put a man on report and . . .

LINDSTROM. He ain't gonna turn out to be like an officer, is he, Doc?

DOWDY. Lindstrom . . .

LINDSTROM. Oh, I didn't mean you, Doc . . . or even you, Mister Pulver!

DOC. That's all right, Lindstrom. What was this trouble with Dolan?

DOWDY. This letter business again!

GERHART. Yes, sir. Dolan was just kiddin' him about not sending in any more letters. And all of a sudden Mister Roberts turned just white and yelled, "Shut up, Dolan. Shut your goddamn mouth. I've had enough." And Dolan naturally got snotty back at him and Mister Roberts put him right on report.

LINDSTROM. Right on report.

(Roberts enters.)

PULVER. Hello, Doug boy. Aren't you listening to the war news?

DOWDY. All right, Doctor. We'll get that medical store room cleaned out tomorrow. *(Dowdy, Gerhart and Lindstrom leave.)*

PULVER. We thought you were up in the radio shack.

ROBERTS *(to Pulver)*. Don't you want to go down to the wardroom and have a cup of coffee?

PULVER *(jumping down from bunk)*. Sure. I'll go with you.

ROBERTS. I don't want any. Why don't you go ahead?

PULVER. Nah. *(He sits back on bunk. There is another little pause)*

ROBERTS. Will you go on out anyway? I want to talk to Doc.

PULVER *(rising and crossing to door)*. All right, I will. I'm going for a cup of coffee. *(Stops, turns and gets cup from top of locker)* No! I'm going up to the radio shack. You aren't the only one interested in the war news. *(He exits)*

ROBERTS *(with emotion)*. Doc, transfer me, will you? *(Doc looks at him)* Transfer me to the hospital on this next island! You can do it. You don't need the Captain's approval! Just put me ashore for examination—say there's something wrong with my eyes or my feet or my head, for Christ's sake! You can trump up something!

DOC. What good would that do?

ROBERTS. Plenty! I could lie around that hospital for a couple of weeks. The ship would have sailed—I'd have missed it! I'd be off this ship. Will you do it, Doc?

DOC. Doug, why did you put Dolan on report just now?

ROBERTS *(angrily)*. I gave him an order and he didn't carry it out fast enough to suit me. *(Glares at Doc, who just studies him. Roberts rises and paces right)* No, that's not true. It was the war. I just heard the news. The war was ending and

I couldn't get to it and there was Dolan giving me guff about something—and all of a sudden I hated him. I hated all of them. I was sick of the sullen bastards staring at me as though I'd sold them down the river or something. If they think I'm bucking for a promotion—if they're stupid enough to think I'd walk ten feet across the room to get anything from that Captain, then I'm through with the whole damn ungrateful mob!

DOC. Does this crew owe you something?

ROBERTS. What the hell do you mean by that?

DOC. You talk as if they did.

(Roberts rises and crosses to bunk.)

ROBERTS *(quietly)*. That's exactly how I'm talking. I didn't realize it but that's exactly the way I've been feeling. Oh, Jesus, that shows you how far gone I am, Doc. I've been taking something out on them. I've been blaming them for something that . . .

DOC. What, Doug? Something what? You've made some sort of an agreement with the Captain, haven't you, Doug!

ROBERTS *(turns)*. Agreement? I don't know what you mean. Will you transfer me, Doc?

DOC. Not a chance, Doug. I could never get away with it—you know that.

ROBERTS. Oh, my God!

PULVER *(offstage)*. Doug! Doc! *(Entering)* Listen to the radio, you uninformed bastards! Turn it up!

(Roberts reaches over and turns up the radio. The excited voice of an announcer can be heard.)

ANNOUNCER. . . . this broadcast to bring you a special news flash! The war is over in Europe! THE WAR IS OVER IN EUROPE! *(Roberts grasps Doc's arm in excitement)* Germany has surrendered unconditionally to the Allied Armies. The surrender was signed in a schoolhouse in the city of Rheims . . .

(Roberts stands staring. Doc turns off the radio. For a moment there is silence, then:)

DOC. I would remind you that there's still a minor skirmish here in the Pacific.

ROBERTS. I'll miss that one too. But to hell with me. This is the greatest day in the world. We're going to celebrate. How about it, Frank?

PULVER. Yeah, Doug. We've got to celebrate!

DOC (*starting to pull alcohol from waste basket*). What'll it be—alcohol and orange juice or orange juice and alcohol?

ROBERTS. No, that's not good enough.

PULVER. Hell, no, Doc! (*He looks expectantly at Roberts*)

ROBERTS. We've got to think of something that'll lift this ship right out of the water and turn it around the other way. (*Pulver suddenly rises to his feet.*)

PULVER (*shouting*). Doug! Oh, my God, why didn't I think of this before. Doug! Doc! You're going to blow your tops when you hear the idea I got! Oh, Jesus, what a wonderful idea! It's the only thing to do. It's the only thing in the whole world to do! That's all! Doug, you said I never had any ideas. You said I never finished anything I started. Well, you're wrong—tonight you're wrong! I thought of something and I finished it. I was going to save it for your birthday, but I'm going to give it to you tonight, because we gotta celebrate . . .

ROBERTS (*waves his hands in Pulver's face for attention*). Wait a minute, Frank! What is it?

PULVER. A firecracker, by God. (*He reaches under his mattress and pulls out a large, wobbly firecracker which has been painted red*) We're gonna throw a firecracker under the Old Man's bunk. Bam-bam-bam! Wake up, you old son-of-a-bitch, IT'S V-E DAY!

ROBERTS (*rising*). Frank!

PULVER. Look at her, Doc. Ain't it a beauty? Ain't that the greatest hand-made, hand-painted, hand-packed firecracker you ever saw?

ROBERTS (*smiling and taking firecracker*). Yes, Frank. That's the most beautiful firecracker I ever saw in my life. But will it work?

PULVER. Sure it'll work. At least, I think so.

ROBERTS. Haven't you tested it? It's got to work, Frank, it's just got to work!

PULVER. I'll tell you what I'll do. I'll take it down to the laundry and test it—that's my laboratory, the laundry. I got all the fixings down there—powder, fuses, everything, all hid behind the soapflakes. And if this one works, I can make another one in two minutes.

ROBERTS. Okay, Frank. Take off. We'll wait for you here. (*Pulver starts off*) Be sure you got enough to make it loud. What'd you use for powder?

PULVER. Loud! This ain't a popgun. This is a firecracker. I used fulminate of mercury. I'll be right back. (*He runs out*)

ROBERTS. Fulminate of mercury! That stuff's murder! Do you think he means it?

DOC (*taking alcohol bottle from waste basket*). Of course not. Where could he get fulminate of mercury?

ROBERTS. I don't know. He's pretty resourceful. Where did he get the clap last year?

DOC. How about a drink, Doug? (*He pours alcohol and orange juice into two glasses*)

ROBERTS. Right! Doc, I been living with a genius. This makes it all worth while—the whole year and a half he spent in his bunk. How else could you celebrate V-E Day? A firecracker under the Old Man's bunk! The silly little son-of-a-bitch!

DOC (*handing Roberts a drink*). Here you are, Doug. (*Doc holds the drink up in a toast*) To better days!

ROBERTS. Okay. And to a great American, Frank Thurlowe Pulver . . . Soldier . . . Statesman . . . Scientist . . .

DOC. Friend of the Working Girl . . . (*Suddenly there is a tremendous explosion. Doc and Roberts clutch at the desk.*)

ROBERTS. Oh, my God!

DOC. He wasn't kidding! That's fulminate of mercury!

CAPTAIN (*offstage*). What was that? (*Roberts and Doc rush to porthole, listening.*)

JOHNSON (*offstage*). I don't know, Captain. I'll find out!

(*We hear the sounds of running feet.*)

ROBERTS. Doc, we've got to go down and get him.

DOC. This may be pretty bad, Doug. (*They turn to start for the door when suddenly a figure hurtles into the room and stops. For a moment it looks like a combination scarecrow and snowman but it is Pulver—his uniform tattered; his knees, arms and face blackened; he is covered with soapsuds and his eyes are shining with excitement. Roberts stares in amazement.*)

PULVER. Jeez, that stuff's terrific!

DOC. Are you all right?

PULVER. I'm great! Gee, you should've been there!

ROBERTS. You aren't burned—or anything?

PULVER. Hell, no. But the laundry's kinda beat up. The mangle's on the other side of the room now. And there's a new porthole on the starboard side where the electric iron went through. And I guess a steam-line must've busted or something—I was up to my ass in lather. And soap-flakes flyin' around—it was absolutely beautiful!

(During these last lines, Doc has been making a brisk, professional examination.)

DOC. It's a miracle. He isn't even scratched!

PULVER. Come on down and see it, Doug. It's a Winter Wonderland!

CAPTAIN *(offstage)*. Johnson!

ROBERTS. Quiet!

JOHNSON *(offstage)*. Yes, sir.

CAPTAIN *(offstage)*. What was it?

JOHNSON *(offstage)*. The laundry, Captain. A steam-line must've blew up.

PULVER *(explaining)*. Steam-line came right out of the bulkhead. *(He demonstrates)* Whish!

CAPTAIN *(offstage)*. How much damage?

JOHNSON *(offstage)*. We can't tell yet, Captain. We can't get in there—the passageway is solid soapsuds.

PULVER. Solid soapsuds. *(He pantomimes walking blindly through soapsuds)*

CAPTAIN *(offstage)*. Tell those men to be more careful.

ROBERTS *(excitedly)*. Frank, our celebration is just getting started. The night is young and our duty's clear.

PULVER. Yeah! What're we gonna do now, Doug?

ROBERTS. Get cleaned up and come with me.

PULVER. Where we goin' now, Doug?

ROBERTS. We're going down and get the rest of your stuff. You proved it'd work—you just hit the wrong target, that's all. We're going to make another firecracker, and put it where it really belongs.

PULVER *(who has slowly wilted during Roberts' speech)*. The rest of my stuff was—in the laundry, Doug. It all went up. There isn't any more. I'm sorry, Doug. I'm awful sorry.

ROBERTS *(sinks into chair)*. That's all right, Frank.

PULVER. Maybe I can scrounge some more tomorrow.

ROBERTS. Sure.

PULVER. You aren't sore at me, are you, Doug?

ROBERTS. What for?

PULVER. For spoilin' our celebration?

ROBERTS. Of course not.

PULVER. It was a good idea though, wasn't it, Doug?

ROBERTS. Frank, it was a great idea. I'm proud of you. It just didn't work, that's all. *(He starts for the door)*

DOC. Where are you going, Doug?

ROBERTS. Out on deck.

PULVER. Wait'll I get cleaned up and I'll come with you.

ROBERTS. No, I'm going to turn in after that. *(To Pulver)* It's okay, Frank. *(He exits)*

(Pulver turns pleadingly to Doc.)

PULVER. He was happy there for a minute though, wasn't he, Doc? Did you see him laughing? He was happy as hell. *(Pause)* We gotta do something for that guy, Doc. He's in bad shape. What's the matter with him anyhow, Doc. Did you find out?

DOC. No, he couldn't tell me. But I know one thing he's feeling tonight and that's panic. Tonight he feels his war is dying before he can get to it. *(He goes to radio and turns up volume)*

PULVER. I let him down. He wanted to celebrate and I let him down. *(He drops his head)*

(Announcer's Voice on radio comes up as the lights fade out.)

During the darkness and under the first part of Scene Four we hear the voice of a British broadcaster:

BRITISH BROADCASTER. . . . we hope that the King and the Queen will come out. The crowds are cheering—listen to them —and at any second now we hope to see Their Majesties. The color here is tremendous—everywhere rosettes, everywhere gay, red-white-and-blue hats. All the girls in their summer frocks on this lovely, mild, historic May evening. And although we celebrate with joyous heart the great victory, perhaps the greatest victory in the history of mankind, the underlying mood is a mood of thanksgiving. And

now, I believe, they're coming. They haven't appeared but the crowd in the center are cheering madly. Handkerchiefs, flags, hands waving—HERE THEY COME! First, Her Majesty, the Queen, has come into view. Then the King in the uniform of an Admiral of the Fleet. The two Princesses standing on the balcony— listen to the crowd—
(Sound of wild cheering.)
(This broadcast continues throughout the blackout and the next scene. Several times the station is changed, from a broadcast of the celebration in San Francisco to the speaker in New York and the band playing "The Stars and Stripes Forever" in Times Square.)

SCENE FOUR

The lights dim up on the main set. It is a few minutes later, and bright moonlight. The ship is under way—this is indicated by the apparent movement of the stars, slowly up and down. A group of men are sitting on the hatch cover in a late bull session. They are Insigna, Mannion, Dolan and Stefanowski. Gerhart stands over them; he has obviously just returned from some mission for the group.

——

GERHART. I'm telling you, that's all it was. A steam pipe busted in the laundry —they're cleaning it up now. It ain't worth going to see.
(The others make way for him and he sits down beside them. Insigna cocks his head toward the sound of the radio.)
INSIGNA. What the hell's all that jabbering on the radio now?
MANNION. I don't know. Something about the King and Queen . . .
(The men listen for a moment without curiosity; then, as the radio fades, they settle back in indolent positions.)
INSIGNA. Well, anyhow, like I was telling you, this big sergeant in Elysium was scared to fight me! Tell 'em how big he was, Killer.
MANNION. Six foot seven or eight . . .
STEFANOWSKI. That sergeant's grown eight inches since we left Elysium . . . Did you see me when I swiped that Shore Patrol band and went around arresting guys? That Shore Patrol Lieutenant said

I was the best man he had. I arrested forty-three guys . . .
MANNION *(smiles at Dolan who is looking depressed)*. Come on, Dolan, don't let him get you down.
INSIGNA. Yeah, come on, Dolan.
(Roberts enters. He looks at the men, who have their backs turned, hesitates, then goes slowly over to them.)
GERHART *(idly)*. What was them croquette things we had for chow tonight? *(Stefanowski looks up and notices Roberts. Instantly he sits upright.)*
STEFANOWSKI. Flash Red!
(The men sit up. There is an embarrassed silence.)
ROBERTS. Good evening. *(The men smile politely. Roberts is very embarrassed)* Did you hear the news? The war's over in Europe.
MANNION *(smiling)*. Yes, sir. We heard.
STEFANOWSKI *(helping out the conversation)*. Sure. Maybe somebody'll get on the ball out here now . . .
(Dolan rises, starts down hatchway.)
ROBERTS. Dolan, I guess I kind of blew my top tonight. I'm sorry. I'm taking you off report.
DOLAN. Whatever you want, sir . . . *(He looks ostentatiously at his watch and yawns)* Well, I guess I'll hit the old sack . . . *(He goes down hatchway)*
MANNION. Yeah, me too . . .
INSIGNA. Yeah . . .
GERHART. It's late as hell.
STEFANOWSKI. I didn't realize how late it was . . .
(All the men get up, then go down the hatchway. Roberts stands looking after them. Now the radio is heard again. Roberts goes to hatchway and sits listening.)
SPEAKER. . . . Our boys have won this victory today. But the rest is up to you. You and you alone must recognize our enemies: the forces of ambition, cruelty, arrogance and stupidity. You must recognize them, you must destroy them, you must tear them out as you would a malignant growth! And cast them from the surface of the earth!
(The end of the speech is followed by a band playing "The Stars and Stripes Forever." Roberts' face lights up and a new determination is in it. He repeats the words "malignant growth." The band music swells. He marches to the palm

tree, salutes it, rubs his hands together and, as the music reaches a climax, he jerks the palm tree, earth and all, from the container and throws it over the side. Then, as the music continues, loud and climactic, he brushes his hands together, shrugs, and walks casually off left singing the tune to himself.)

(For a moment the stage is empty. Then the lights go up in the Captain's cabin. The door to the Captain's cabin opens and the Captain appears. He is in pajamas and bathrobe, and in one hand he carries his watering can. He discovers the empty container. He looks at it, then plunges into his cabin. After a moment, the General Alarm is heard. It is a terrible clanging noise designed to rouse the dead. When the alarm stops, the Captain's voice is heard, almost hysterical, over the squawk box.)

CAPTAIN. General Quarters! General Quarters! Every man to his battle station on the double!

(Johnson, in helmet and life jacket, scurries from hatchway into the Captain's cabin. Wiley enters from right passageway and climbs into the right gun tub. Now men appear from all directions in various degrees of dress. The stage is filled with men frantically running everywhere, all wearing helmets and life preservers.)

INSIGNA *(appearing from hatchway).* What happened? *(He runs up the ladder and into the left gun tub. Payne enters from left and starts to climb up to left gun tub)* Get the hell out of here, Payne. This ain't your gun—your gun's over there!

DOLAN *(also trying to climb the ladder with Payne).* Over there . . . over there . . .

(Payne crosses to right gun tub.)

REBER *(entering from hatchway).* What the hell happened?

SCHLEMMER. Are *we* in an air raid?

PAYNE. Submarine . . . must be a submarine!

GERHART. Hey, Wiley, what happened?

DOWDY *(calling to someone on life raft).* Hey, get away from that life raft. He didn't say abandon ship!

(During the confusion, Stefanowski, bewildered, emerges from the hatchway and wanders over to right gun tub.)

STEFANOWSKI. Hey, Wiley, Wiley—you sure you're supposed to be up there?

WILEY. Yeah.

STEFANOWSKI *(crossing to left gun tub).* Hey, Sam. Are you supposed to be up there?

INSIGNA. Yeah, he was here last year!

STEFANOWSKI. Hey, Dowdy. Where the hell's my battle station?

DOWDY. I don't know where your battle station is! Look around!

(Stefanowski wanders aimlessly about. Wiley, in the gun tub right, is receiving reports of battle readiness from various parts of the ship:)

WILEY. Twenty millimeters manned and ready. *(Pause)* Engine room manned and ready. *(Pause)* All battle stations manned and ready.

STEFANOWSKI *(sitting on corner of hatch).* Yeah, all but mine . . .

JOHNSON'S VOICE *(in Captain's cabin).* All battle stations manned and ready, Captain.

CAPTAIN'S VOICE. Give me that thing.

JOHNSON'S VOICE *("on mike"—that is, speaking directly into squawk-box microphone. "Off mike" means speaking unintentionally into this live microphone).* Attention . . . Attention . . . The Captain wishes to . . .

CAPTAIN'S VOICE *(on mike).* Give me that thing! *(On mike)* All right, who did it? Who did it? You're going to stay here all night until someone confesses. You're going to stay at those battle stations until hell freezes over until I find out who did it. It's an insult to the honor of this ship, by God! The symbol of our cargo record has been destroyed and I'm going to find out who did it if it takes all night! *(Off mike)* Johnson, read me that muster list!

JOHNSON'S *voice (reading muster list off mike).* Abernathy . . .

MANNION. Symbol of our cargo record? What the hell's that?

(Stefanowski rises, sees empty container, kneels and ceremoniously bows to it.)

DOWDY. For God's sake, Stefanowski, find some battle station!

CAPTAIN'S VOICE. No, not Abernathy . . .

JOHNSON'S VOICE. Baker . . .

CAPTAIN'S VOICE. No . . .

JOHNSON'S VOICE. Bartholomew . . . Becker . . . Billings . . .

Carney . . .
Daniels . . .
(Stefanowski points Dexter . . .
to empty container. Ellison . . .
Dowdy sees it and Everman . . .
spreads the news to Jenkins . . .
the men on left. Kelly . . .
Schlemmer sees it Kevin . . .
and tells the other Martin . . .
men. Now from all Olsen . . .
parts of the ship O'Neill . . .
men enter and ju- CAPTAIN'S VOICE.
bilantly look at the No, not O'Neill . . .
e m p t y container. JOHNSON'S VOICE.
Bits of soil fly into Pulver . . .
the air as the men CAPTAIN'S VOICE.
group around the No, not Pulver. He
empty can.) hasn't the guts . . .
JOHNSON'S VOICE.
Roberts . . .

CAPTAIN'S VOICE *(roaring, off mike).* Roberts! He's the one! Get him up here!

JOHNSON'S VOICE *(on mike).* Mister Roberts will report to the Captain's cabin on the double!

(The men rush back to their battle stations.)

CAPTAIN'S VOICE. Get him up here, I tell you! Get him up here . . .

JOHNSON'S VOICE *(on mike).* Mister Roberts will report to the Captain's cabin on the . . .

CAPTAIN *(on mike).* Give me that thing. *(On mike)* Roberts, you get up here in a goddamn quick hurry. Get up here! Roberts, I'm giving you an order—get the lead out of your pants.

(Roberts appears from left passageway and, walking slowly, enters the Captain's cabin.)

(The men move onstage and Lindstrom gets to a position on the ladder where he can look through the porthole of the Captain's cabin.)

ROBERTS' VOICE. Did you want to see me, Captain?

CAPTAIN'S VOICE. You did it. You did it. Don't lie to me. Don't stand there and lie to me. Confess it!

ROBERTS' VOICE. Confess what, Captain? I don't know what you're talking about.

CAPTAIN'S VOICE. You know damn well what I'm talkin' about because you did it. You've doublecrossed me—you've gone back on your word!

ROBERTS' VOICE. No, I haven't, Captain.

CAPTAIN. Yes, by God, you have. I kept my part of the bargain! I gave this crew liberty—I gave this crew liberty, by God, but you've gone back on *your* word.

(Dowdy takes off his helmet and looks at the men.)

ROBERTS' VOICE. I don't see how you can say that, Captain. I haven't sent in any more letters.

(Dolan, on gun tub ladder, catches Insigna's eye.)

CAPTAIN'S VOICE. I'm not talking about your goddamn sons-a-bitchin' letters. I'm talkin' about what you did tonight.

ROBERTS' VOICE. Tonight? I don't understand you, Captain. What do you think I did?

CAPTAIN. Quit saying that, goddammit, quit saying that. You know damn well what you did. You stabbed me in the back. You stabbed me in the back . . . aaa . . . aa . . .

JOHNSON'S VOICE. Captain! Get over to the washbasin, Captain!

CAPTAIN'S VOICE. Aaaaaaa . . .

INSIGNA. What the hell happened?

DOLAN. Quiet!

JOHNSON *(on mike).* Will the Doctor please report to the Captain's cabin on the double?

(Doc appears from left, pushing his way through the crowd, followed by two Medical Corpsmen wearing Red Cross brassards and carrying first-aid kits and a stretcher. Doc walks slowly; he is idly attaching a brassard and smoking a cigarette. He wears his helmet sloppily.)

DOC. Gangway . . . gangway . . .

DOWDY. Hey, Doc, tell us what's going on.

DOC. Okay. Okay.

(He enters the Captain's cabin followed by the Corpsmen who leave stretcher leaning against the bulkhead. The door closes. There is a tense pause. The men gather around the cabin again. Lindstrom is at the porthole.)

REBER. Hey, Lindstrom, where's the Old Man?

LINDSTROM. He's sittin' in the chair—leaning way forward.

PAYNE. What's the Doc doin'?

LINDSTROM. He's holdin' the waste basket.

REBER. What waste basket?

LINDSTROM. The one the Old Man's got his head in. And he needs it too. *(Pause)*

They're helpin' him over to the couch. *(Pause)* He's lying down there and they're takin' off his shoes. *(Pause)* Look out, here they come. *(The men break quickly and rush back to their battle stations. The door opens and Roberts, Doc and the Corpsmen come out.)*

DOC *(to Corpsmen)*. We won't need that stretcher. Sorry. *(Calls)* Dowdy! Come here.

(Dowdy comes down to Doc. He avoids Roberts' eyes.)

ROBERTS. Dowdy, pass the word to the crew to secure from General Quarters.

DOC. And tell the men not to make any noise while they go to their bunks. The Captain's resting quietly now, and I think that's desirable.

ROBERTS. Pass the word, will you, Dowdy?

DOWDY. Yes, Mister Roberts. *(He passes the word to the crew who slowly start to leave their battle stations. They are obviously stalling)*

DOC *(to Roberts)*. Got a cigarette? *(Roberts reaches in his pocket and offers Doc a cigarette. Then he lights Doc's cigarette. Doc notices the men stalling)* Well, guess I'd better get back inside. I'll be down to see you after I get through.

(He enters cabin and stands there watching. The men move offstage, very slowly, saying "Good night, Mister Roberts," "Good night, sir." Suddenly Roberts notices that all the men are saying good night to him.)

DOLAN *(quietly)*. Good night, Mister Roberts. *(Roberts does not hear him)* Good night, Mister Roberts.

ROBERTS. Good night, Dolan.

(Dolan smiles and exits down hatch. Roberts steps toward hatch, removes helmet, looks puzzled as the lights fade out.)

During the darkness, over the squawk box the following announcements are heard:

FIRST VOICE. Now hear this . . . Now hear this . . . C, E and S Divisions and all Pharmacist's Mates will air bedding today —positively!

SECOND VOICE. There is now available at the ship's store a small supply of peanut brittle. Ship's store will be open from 1300 to 1315.

THIRD VOICE. Now, Dolan, Yeoman Second Class, report to the radio shack immediately.

SCENE FIVE

The lights come up on the stateroom of Roberts and Pulver. Pulver is lying in the lower bunk. Doc is sitting at the desk with a glass and a bottle of grain alcohol in front of him. Roberts is tying up a sea bag. A small suitcase stands beside it. His locker is open and empty. Wiley picks up the sea bag.

WILEY. Okay, Mister Roberts, I'll take these down to the gangway. The boat from the island should be out here any minute for you. I'll let you know.

ROBERTS. Thanks, Wiley.

WILEY *(grinning)*. That's okay, Mister Roberts. Never thought you'd be taking this ride, did you? *(He exits with the bags)*

ROBERTS. I'm going to be off this bucket before I even wake up.

DOC. They flying you all the way to the *Livingston?*

ROBERTS. I don't know. The radio dispatch just said I was transferred and travel by air if possible. I imagine it's all the way through. They're landing planes at Okinawa now and that's where my can is probably running around. *(Laughs a little)* Listen to me, Doc—my can!

PULVER *(studying map by Roberts' bunk)*. Okinawa! Jeez, you be might-y careful, Doug.

ROBERTS. Okay, Frank. This is *too* much to take, Doc. I even got a destroyer! The *Livingston!* That's one of the greatest cans out there.

PULVER. I know a guy on the *Livingston*.. He don't think it's so hot.

DOLAN *(entering. He has a file folder under his arm)*. Here you are, Mister Roberts. I typed up three copies of the radio dispatch. I've got to keep a copy and here's two for you. You're now officially detached from this here bucket. Let me be the first.

ROBERTS. Thanks, Dolan. *(They shake hands. Roberts takes papers, and looks at them)* Dolan, how about these orders? I haven't sent in a letter for a month!

DOLAN *(carefully)*. You know how the Navy works, Mister Roberts.

ROBERTS. Yeah, I know, but it doesn't seem . . .

DOLAN. Listen, Mister Roberts, I can tell you exactly what happened. Those guys at the Bureau need men for combat duty awful bad and they started looking through all the old letters and they just come across one of yours.

ROBERTS. Maybe—but still you'd think . . .

DOLAN. Listen, Mister Roberts. We can't stand here beating our gums! You better get cracking! You seen what it said there, "Proceed immediately." And the Old Man says if you ain't off of here in an hour, by God, he's going to throw you off!

ROBERTS. Is that all he said?

DOLAN. That's all he said.

ROBERTS (grinning at Doc). After fighting this for two years you'd think he'd say more than that . . .

CAPTAIN'S VOICE (offstage). Be careful of that one. Put it down easy.

DOC. What's that?

DOLAN. A new enlarged botanical garden. That's why he can't even be bothered about you today, Mister Roberts. Soon as we anchored this morning he sent Olsen over with a special detail—they dug up two palm trees . . . He's busy as a mother skunk now and you know what he's done—he's already set a twenty-four-hour watch on these new babies with orders to shoot to kill. (To Pulver) That reminds me, Mister Pulver. The Captain wants to see you right away.

PULVER. Yeah? What about?

DOLAN. I don't know, sir. (To Roberts) I'll be back to say good-bye, Mister Roberts. Come on, Mister Pulver. (He exits)

PULVER (following Dolan out). What the hell did I do with his laundry this week?

(Roberts smiles as he starts putting on his black tie.)

DOC. You're a happy son-of-a-bitch, aren't you?

ROBERTS. Yep. You're happy about it too, aren't you, Doc?

DOC. I think it's the only thing for you. (Casually) What do you think of the crew now, Doug?

ROBERTS. We're all right now. I think they're nice guys—all of them.

DOC. Uuh-hunh. And how do you think they feel about you?

ROBERTS. I think they like me all right . . . till the next guy comes along.

DOC. You don't think you're necessary to them?

ROBERTS (sitting on bunk). Hell, no. No officer's necessary to the crew, Doc.

DOC. Are you going to leave this ship believing that?

ROBERTS. That's nothing against them. A crew's too busy looking after themselves to care about anyone else.

DOC. Well, take a good, deep breath, Buster. (He drinks some alcohol) What do you think got you your orders? Prayer and fasting? Sending in enough Wheatie box tops?

ROBERTS. My orders? Why, what Dolan said—one of my old letters turned up . . .

DOC. Bat crap! This crew got you transferred. They were so busy looking out for themselves that they took a chance of landing in prison for five years—any one of them. Since you couldn't send in a letter for transfer, they sent one in for you. Since they knew the Captain wouldn't sign it approved, they didn't bother him—they signed it for him.

ROBERTS. What do you mean? They forged the Captain's name?

DOC. That's right.

ROBERTS (rising). Doc! Who did? Which one of them?

DOC. That would be hard to say. You see, they had a mass meeting down in the compartment. They put guards at every door. They called it the Captain's-Name-Signing contest. And every man in this crew—a hundred and sixty-seven of them—signed the Captain's name on a blank sheet of paper. And then there were judges who compared these signatures with the Captain's and selected the one to go in. At the time there was some criticism of the decision on the grounds that the judges were drunk, but apparently, from the results, they chose well.

ROBERTS. How'd you find out about this, Doc?

DOC. Well, it was a great honor. I am the only officer aboard who does know. I was a contestant. I was also a judge. This double honor was accorded me because of my character, charm, good looks and because the medical department contributed four gallons of grain alcohol to the contest. (Pauses) It was quite a thing to see, Doug. A hundred and sixty-seven guys with only one idea in their heads—to do something for Mister Roberts.

ROBERTS (*after a moment*). I wish you hadn't told me, Doc. It makes me look pretty silly after what I just said. But I didn't mean it, Doc. I was afraid to say what I really feel. I love those bastards, Doc. I think they're the greatest guys on this earth. All of a sudden I feel that there's something wrong—something terribly wrong—about leaving them. God, what can I say to them?

DOC. You won't say anything—you don't even know. When you're safely aboard your new ship I'm supposed to write and tell you about it. And at the bottom of the letter, I'm supposed to say, "Thanks for the liberty, Mister Roberts. Thanks for everything."

ROBERTS. Jesus!

(*Pulver enters, downcast.*)

PULVER. I'm the new Cargo Officer. And that's not all—I got to have dinner with him tonight. He *likes* me!

(*There is a polite rap on the door.*)

DOC. Come in. (*Enter Payne, Reber, Gerhart, Schlemmer, Dolan and Insigna, all carrying canteen cups except Insigna whose cup is in his belt. He carries a large, red fire extinguisher*) What's this?

INSIGNA. Fire and rescue squad. Heard you had a fire in here.

(*All are looking at Roberts.*)

ROBERTS. No, but—since you're here—I—

INSIGNA. Hell, we got a false alarm then. Happens all the time. (*Sets extinguisher on desk*) In that case, we might as well drink this stuff. Give me your glass, Mister Roberts, and I'll put a head on it—yours too, Doc. I got one for you, Mister Pulver. (*He fills their glasses from the fire extinguisher*)

ROBERTS. What's in that, a new batch of jungle juice?

INSIGNA. Yeah, in the handy, new, portable container. Everybody loaded?

(*All nod.*)

DOLAN. Go ahead, Sam.

INSIGNA (*to Roberts*). There's a story going around that you're leaving us. That right?

ROBERTS (*carefully*). That's right, Sam. And I . . .

INSIGNA. Well, we didn't want you to get away without having a little drink with us and we thought we ought to give you a little sort of going-away present. The fellows made it down in the machine shop. It ain't much but we hope you like it. (*Reber prompts him*) We all sincerely hope you like it. (*Calls offstage*) All right, you bastards, you can come in now.

(*Enter Lindstrom, Mannion, Dowdy and Stefanowski. Mannion is carrying a candy box. He walks over to Roberts shyly and hands him the box.*)

ROBERTS. What is it?

SCHLEMMER. Open it.

(*Roberts opens the box. There is a deep silence.*)

PULVER. What is it, Doug?

(*Roberts holds up the box. In it is a brass medal shaped like a palm tree attached to a piece of gaudy ribbon.*)

LINDSTROM. It's a palm tree, see.

DOLAN. It was Dowdy's idea.

DOWDY. Mannion here made it. He cut it out of sheet brass down in the machine shop.

INSIGNA. Mannion drilled the words on it too.

MANNION. Stefanowski thought up the words.

STEFANOWSKI (*shoving Lindstrom forward*). Lindstrom gets credit for the ribbon from a box of candy that his sister-in-law sent him. Read the words, Mister Roberts.

ROBERTS (*with difficulty*). "Order . . . order of . . ." (*He hands the medal to Doc*)

DOC (*rises and reads solemnly*). "Order of the palm. To Lieutenant (jg) Douglas Roberts for action against the enemy, above and beyond the call of duty on the night of eight May 1945." (*He passes the medal back to Roberts*)

ROBERTS (*after a moment—smiling*). It's very nice but I'm afraid you've got the wrong guy.

(*The men turn to Dowdy, grinning.*)

DOWDY. We know that, but we'd kinda like for you to have it anyway.

ROBERTS. All right, I'll keep it.

(*The men beam. There is an awkward pause.*)

GERHART. Stefanowski thought up the words.

ROBERTS. They're fine words.

(*Wiley enters.*)

WILEY. The boat's here, Mister Roberts. I put your gear in. They want to shove off right away.

ROBERTS (*rising*). Thanks. We haven't had our drink yet.

REBER. No, we ain't.

(*All get to their feet. Roberts picks up his glass, looks at the crew, and everyone drinks.*)

ROBERTS. Good-bye, Doc.

DOC. Good-bye, Doug.

ROBERTS. And thanks, Doc.

DOC. Okay.

ROBERTS. Good-bye, Frank.

PULVER. Good-bye, Doug.

ROBERTS. Remember, I'm counting on you.

(*Pulver nods. Roberts turns to the crew and looks at them for a moment. Then he takes the medal from the box, pins it on his shirt, shows it to them, then gives a little gestured salute and exits as the lights fade out.*)

During the darkness we hear voices making announcements over the squawk box:

FIRST VOICE. Now hear this . . . now hear this . . . Sweepers, man your brooms. Clean sweep-down fore and aft!

SECOND VOICE. Now hear this! All men put on report today will fall in on the quarter-deck—and form three ranks!

THIRD VOICE. Now hear this! All divisions will draw their mail at 1700—in the mess hall.

SCENE SIX

The lights come up showing the main set at sunset. Doc is sitting on the hatch, reading a letter. Mannion, wearing side-arms, is pacing up and down in front of the Captain's cabin. On each side of the door is a small palm tree in a five-gallon can—on one can is painted in large white letters, "Keep Away"; on the other, "This Means You." After a moment, Pulver enters from the left passageway, carrying a small packet of letters.

———

PULVER. Hello, Mannion. Got your mail yet?

MANNION. No. I've got the palm tree watch.

PULVER. Oh. (*To Doc*) What's your news, Doc?

DOC. My wife got some new wallpaper for the living room.

(*Pulver sits on hatch cover. Dowdy enters wearing work gloves.*)

DOWDY. Mister Pulver, we'll be finished with the cargo in a few minutes.

PULVER. How'd it go?

DOWDY. Not bad. I've got to admit you were right about Number Three hold. It worked easier out of there. Mister Pulver, I just found out what the Captain decided —he ain't going to show a movie again tonight.

PULVER. Why not?

DOWDY. He's still punishing us because he caught Reber without a shirt on two days ago. You've got to go in and see him.

PULVER. I did. I asked him to show a movie yesterday.

DOWDY. Mister Pulver, what the hell good does that do us today? You've got to keep needlin' that guy—I'm tellin' you.

PULVER. Don't worry. I'll take care of it in my own way.

DOWDY (*going off, but speaking loud enough to be heard*). Oh, God, no movie again tonight.

(*Dowdy exits. Pulver starts looking at his packet of mail.*)

PULVER (*looking at first letter*). This is from my mother. All she ever says is stay away from Japan. (*He drops it on the hatch cover*) This is from Alabama. (*Puts it in his pocket and pats it. Looks at third letter*) Doc! This is from Doug!

DOC. Yeah? (*Pulver rips open the envelope*) What does he say?

PULVER (*reading*). "This will be short and sweet, as we're shoving off in about two minutes . . ." (*Pauses and remarks*) This is dated three weeks ago.

DOC. Does he say where he is?

PULVER. Yeah. He says: "My guess about the location of this ship was just exactly right." (*Looks up*) That means he's around Okinawa all right! (*Reads on and chuckles*) He's met Fornell. That's that friend of mine . . . a guy named Fornell I went to college with. Listen to this: "Fornell says that you and he used to load up your car with liquor in Omaha and then sell it at an indecent profit to the fraternity boys at Iowa City. How about that?" We did too. (*Smiles happily*) "This part is for Doc." (*Doc gestures for him to read it*) "I've been aboard this destroyer for two weeks now and we've already been through four air attacks. I'm in the war at last, Doc. I've caught up with that task force that passed me by. I'm glad to be here. I had to be here, I guess. But I'm thinking now of you, Doc, and you, Frank, and Dolan and Dowdy and Insigna and everyone else on that bucket—all the guys everywhere who sail from Tedium to Apathy and back again—with an occasional side trip to Monotony. This is a tough crew on here, and they have a wonderful battle record. But I've discovered, Doc, that the most terrible enemy of this war is the boredom that eventually becomes a faith and, therefore, a sort of suicide—and I know now that the ones who refuse to surrender to it are the strongest of all.

"Right now, I'm looking at something that's hanging over my desk: a preposterous hunk of brass attached to the most bilious piece of ribbon I've ever seen. I'd rather have it than the Congressional Medal of Honor. It tells me what I'll always be proudest of—that at a time in the world when courage counted most, I lived among a hundred and sixty-seven brave men.

"So, Doc, and especially you, Frank, don't let those guys down. Of course, I know that by this time they must be very happy because the Captain's overhead is filled with marbles and . . ." *(He avoids Doc's eyes)* "Oh, hell, here comes the mail orderly. This has to go now. I'll finish it later. Meanwhile you bastards can write too, can't you?"

"Doug."

DOC. Can I see that, Frank?
(Pulver hands him the letter, looks at the front of his next letter and says quietly:)
PULVER. Well, for God's sake, this is from Fornell!
DOC *(reading Roberts' letter to himself).* ". . . I'd rather have it than the Congressional Medal of Honor." I'm glad he found that out. *(He looks at Pulver, sensing something wrong)* What's the matter? *(Pulver does not answer)* What's the matter, Frank?

(Pulver looks at him slowly as Dowdy enters.)
DOWDY. All done, Mister Pulver. We've secured the hatch cover. No word on the movie, I suppose.
DOC *(louder, with terror).* Frank, what is it?
PULVER. Mister Roberts is dead. *(Looks at letter)* This is from Fornell . . . They took a Jap suicide plane. It killed everyone in a twin-forty battery and then it went on through and killed Doug and another officer in the wardroom. *(Pause)* They were drinking coffee when it hit.
DOWDY *(quietly).* Mister Pulver, can I please give that letter to the crew?
DOC. No. *(Holding out Roberts' letter)* Give them this one. It's theirs. *(Dowdy removes gloves and takes the letter from Doc and goes off)* Coffee . . .
(Pulver gets up restlessly. Doc stares straight ahead. Pulver straightens. He seems to grow. He walks casually over to Mannion.)
PULVER *(in a friendly voice).* Go on down and get your mail. I'll stand by for you.
MANNION *(surprised).* You will? Okay, thanks, Mister Pulver.
(Mannion disappears down hatch. As soon as he exits Pulver very calmly jerks the rooted palms, one by one, from their containers and throws them over the side. Doc looks up to see Pulver pull second tree. Doc ducks as tree goes past him. Then Pulver knocks loudly on the Captain's door.)
CAPTAIN *(offstage. His voice is very truculent).* Yeah. Who is it?
PULVER. Captain, this is Ensign Pulver. I just threw your palm trees overboard. Now what's all this crap about no movie tonight?
(He throws the door open, banging it against the bulkhead, and is entering the Captain's cabin as the curtain falls.)

State of the Union

BY HOWARD LINDSAY and RUSSEL CROUSE

First presented by Leland Hayward at the Hudson Theatre in New York on November 14, 1945, with the following cast:

JAMES CONOVER............................Minor Watson	SAM PARRISH................................Herbert Heyes
SPIKE MacMANUS.................Myron McCormick	SWENSON ....Fred Ayres Cotton
KAY THORNDYKE............................Kay Johnson	JUDGE JEFFERSON DAVIS ALEXANDER
GRANT MATTHEWS....................Ralph Bellamy	G. Albert Smith
NORAH ....Helen Ray	MRS. ALEXANDER......................Maidel Turner
MARY MATTHEWS..........................Ruth Hussey	JENNY ....Madeline King
STEVENS ....John Rowe	MRS. DRAPER..........................Aline McDermott
BELLBOY ....Howard Graham	WILLIAM HARDY....................Victor Sutherland
WAITER ....Robert Toms	SENATOR LAUTERBACK.............George Lessey

---

ACT ONE

Scene One: The study in James Conover's home in Washington, D. C.
Scene Two: A bedroom in the Conover home. The following evening.

ACT TWO

The living room of a suite in the Book-Cadillac Hotel, Detroit. Several weeks later.

ACT THREE

Scene One: The living room of the Matthews' apartment in New York. Two weeks later.

Scene Two: The same, an hour later.

WITH *State of the Union,* which received the Pulitzer Prize in 1946, Lindsay and Crouse reached the peak of a joint artistic career already exalted by their *Life with Father.* The authors applied their well-tested talent for comedy to an immediate political issue—that of making fair and liberal politics prevail in the land of the free and the home of the brave. The liberal spirit was at its zenith then, the American eagle having acquitted itself triumphantly against the vultures of Nazism and Fascism. Now was the time for all good men to get together and expel native monstrosities of race hatred from the land and to clean up politics in general by denouncing whatever tendencies to play one ethnic group against another might exist or might arise in the political game. Some such idea buzzed in the busy factory of the two expert fun-makers, who are among the most reputable as well as successful of Broadway's showmen.

The story of their separate careers and partnership is by now authentic Broadway history, and there is no reason to revise the report written in the previous volume of our *Best Plays* series.

Mr. Lindsay, who was born in Waterford, New York, in 1889, became an elocutionist at the tender age of ten in Atlantic City, and his unprofessional success led him to cast an eye on the stage until the close of his freshman year at Harvard. Although he then entertained notions of preparing himself for the ministry (he would have filled a pulpit quite impressively), he soon found himself examining a catalogue of the American Academy of Dramatic Arts. He abandoned Harvard for the Academy and, after a year's preparation, started his stage career in 1909 by appearing in *Polly of the Circus.* He spent four years in road companies, worked as an extra in Hollywood, played in vaudeville, and joined Margaret Anglin's repertory as an actor and assistant stage manager. He regards his five years with Miss Anglin as his university education. The first World War found him in the infantry sporting a corporal's stripes. When he reappeared on Broadway, it was to play in Kaufman and Connelly's celebrated farce-comedy *Dulcy.* He also began to write plays, in collaboration with Bertrand Robinson: *Tommy, Your Uncle Dudley* (1929), and *Oh Promise Me* (1930). After another term in Hollywood, he directed *Gay Divorce,* starring Fred Astaire on Broadway, and both wrote and directed the successful college play *She Loves Me Not* (1933), which started the acting career of Burgess Meredith. The year 1935 saw a collaboration with Damon Runyon, *A Slight Case of Murder.* Lindsay and Crouse were introduced to each other in the summer of 1934 by Vinton Freedley, who was then trying to launch the musical comedy *Anything Goes,* for which he needed a new story. Mr. Lindsay was then recuperating from the "flu" and needed support from Mr. Crouse, who is a generous dispenser of sunshine, humor, and wit.

Mr. Crouse hailed from Findlay, Ohio, where he had been born in 1893 to an editor and owner of various Midwestern newspapers. Mathematics was the vulnerable part of Mr. Crouse's education, and it lost him an appointment to Annapolis. Journalism and the theatre gained thereby. Mr. Crouse did a two years' stint as reporter on the Cincinnati *Commercial-Tribune,* moved to the Kansas City *Star,* and after seeing service with the Navy during the first World War, worked on New York newspapers and graduated into the ranks of columnists on the *Post.* He published books (one of them was on Currier and Ives) and wrote two musical comedies; one of these was the successful Joe Cook show *Hold Your Horses.*

The first Lindsay-Crouse collaboration, *Anything Goes,* with music by Cole Porter, was a striking success. The next, somewhat less successful, collaborative effort was the musical *Red, Hot and Blue* (1936), which introduced Bob Hope to the public. Then the friends served Ed Wynn with the clever musical satire on "merchants of death" and international espionage, *Hooray for What.* This was in 1937, and in that year they began speculating on a dramatization of Clarence Day's books of reminiscence which eventuated in the memorable *Life with Father* in 1939. Next, Lindsay and Crouse branched out as the producers of *Arsenic and Old Lace* and *The Hasty Heart,* and put a portion of their fabulous earnings into the purchase of the Hudson Theatre. They did not lay down their pens, however. They tried to contribute to war-time morale with *Strip for*

Action, which fell short of success, and they retrieved their laurels with *State of the Union* in the season of 1945-46.

State of the Union, we must add, did not represent a commitment to political writing, as one could infer from the substantial presence of domestic comedy in the play. In the season of 1948-49, they produced their overdue sequel to *Life with Father*, the quite enchanting if rather tenuous comedy *Life with Mother*. They then made an even more strenuous return to unadulterated show-business by producing the musical *Call Me Madam*, and astutely cast Ethel Merman in the role of our first lady ambassador. And at this writing they are completely upsetting the public's equanimity with the farce-melodrama *Remains to Be Seen*, a fabrication of theirs to which they have added non-verbal percussion with an ampler set of drum-traps than any seen on the stage rather than under it. It is, however, conceivable that when the genial partners appear before the judgment seat, *State of the Union* will speak more loudly or at least more persuasively for them.

ACT ONE

SCENE ONE

The study in the home of James Conover in Washington, D. C. It is a wood-paneled library. There is a recessed window upstage, with the curtains drawn. The wall brackets and lamps are lighted. There is a large desk at the right of the room and several easy chairs. At the left of the room there is a table on which stands a tray containing bottles of liquor, soda, glasses and a container filled with ice cubes.

Four persons are seated in the room: James Conover, a quiet-spoken man of about 60, not quite the type the audience would expect as a politician. Mrs. Katherine Thorndyke, known hereafter as Kay, a handsome woman in her late thirties, the kind you would find talking to men more often than women. Spike MacManus, who has been for years a Washington political reporter, pudgy and genial and with a rough charm. Grant Matthews, a distinguished-looking man in his middle forties, a successful business man, but also much more than that.

James Conover is seated to the right of his desk engaged in a telephone conversation. His share of the conversation consists almost entirely of listening, with an occasional murmur of assent. The other three are obviously waiting for him to finish. Their attention wanders away from Conover to themselves. Kay consults her handbag mirror and passes her hand over her hair. Grant takes a fresh cigarette and lights it from the one he is about to discard. Spike takes a paper out of his pocket, glances at some notes on it and puts it back. Kay looks toward Grant and, when their eyes meet, she smiles and nods an indication that everything is going all right.

In reply Grant shrugs noncommittally. They both look at Spike, who makes a reassuring gesture with his hands, palms down.

Conover interrupts the flow of conversation coming from the other end of the telephone, speaking with quiet authority.

CONOVER *(into telephone)*. Dave, I'm sorry, but I have to give the Senator a free hand in this. *(Pause)* Has this occurred to you? The reason you and the Senator are fighting over this one appointment is because we lost the last election and the one before that and the one before that! We have to win the next one! The Senator feels that an appointment will strengthen the party in his district. So there's no argument. *(Short pause)* Certainly, any time. Good night, Dave. *(He hangs up and turns to the others)*

SPIKE. You're being pretty tough on Tisdale, Jim. If he can't swing that appointment, how's he going to stay out of jail?

CONOVER. Spike, you know too much.

SPIKE *(grinning)*. I've been blackmailing Tisdale for years. He's one of my best sources.

CONOVER. Spike's just trying to show off in front of his boss, Mrs. Thorndyke.

KAY. He doesn't have to. I'm not the only publisher who thinks Spike's the best newspaper man in Washington.

CONOVER. Well, I think Walter Lippmann writes a little better.

KAY. Oh, we wouldn't let Spike write a paragraph.

SPIKE. They even took away my typewriter—but they gave me six telephones.

KAY. Spike knows more about what's going on in Washington than you and Bob Hannegan put together. That's why I'm willing to lend him to you for the campaign—but I want him back!

CONOVER *(half kidding)*. Too bad you weren't running Dewey's campaign, Spike.

SPIKE. Well, if Dewey had listened to me when I saw him in Pawling he'd have had a much better chance. *(The others look at Spike with smiling disbelief)* I didn't say he'd have had a *chance*. I said he'd have had a much better chance.

KAY *(to Conover)*. Jim, do you think you're going to have trouble stopping Dewey?

CONOVER *(quietly)*. He's built up a strong organization. But I think it can be done. That's why we have to start early.

SPIKE. Republicans never have nominated a defeated candidate. That's on the record. The boys feel that way about Dewey, don't they, Jim?

CONOVER. I can't speak for the Republican Party . . .

SPIKE. Hell, who can these days? But, Jim, you're certainly strong enough to stop anyone on the horizon now. So why can't you name your own man?

CONOVER. If we get a strong candidate in '48 we've got better than a fighting chance. Jim, my newspapers are city papers, but small cities, with a rural circulation too. They make a pretty good sounding board. Here's what comes back to me. The party's best chance in '48 is to put up a candidate who's never been identified with politics.

SPIKE. Look what happened in '40. If the election had been held a month after Philadelphia, Willkie would have won.

KAY. Yes, and why? Because people had the idea Willkie was someone you politicians didn't want.

SPIKE (to Conover). You wouldn't mind if that impression got around about the candidate in '48, would you?

CONOVER. Not if the candidate was someone I did want.

SPIKE. That's what I mean.

CONOVER. It seems to me at this point we ought to hear from Mr. Matthews. (They all look at Grant.)

GRANT. Let me make this clear—I don't want to be President of the United States. (They smile at his vehemence.)

CONOVER. That decision may not be in your hands.

GRANT. Mr. Conover, I can understand Mrs. Thorndyke telling me I should be President. But you—you must be talking about somebody else.

CONOVER. You're a national figure—and you have been ever since the war started.

SPIKE. Is Henry Kaiser a national figure? For every ship he's built you've built a hundred planes.

KAY. Grant, everybody in the country knows you and everybody respects you.

GRANT. Oh, they know I make good airplanes and I've made a hell of a lot of them.

SPIKE. They know more than that. (He rises and goes to Grant) When you fought the aluminum combine! When you slugged it out with the War Production Board until they broke those bottlenecks! The time you talked back to that Senate Investigating Committee! Three times you crowded the war off the front page!

CONOVER. Mrs. Thorndyke and I aren't the only Republicans who've been thinking about you. Those speeches you've been making—especially that last one in Cleveland.

GRANT (putting his glass down on the table). When I made that speech in Cleveland I was trying to put both parties on the spot. I wasn't speaking as a Republican. I was speaking as a citizen. (He rises and moves toward Conover, as he warms to his subject) I'm worried about what's happening in this country. We're splitting apart. Business, labor, farmers, cattlemen, lumbermen—they're all trying to get the biggest bite of the apple. We talk about the war being over—well, we've got a war on here at home now—a civil war—an economic war. That's what I said in Cleveland. That's why I was surprised you asked me down here.

CONOVER. Why were you surprised?

GRANT. Because you politicians are trying to make capital out of this situation—you appeal to each one of these pressure groups just to get their votes. But let me tell you something. I don't think that's good politics. A lot of people wrote me after that speech in Cleveland. (With a grin) Of course I will admit that the business men liked best what I said about labor, and the unions said I was absolutely right about big business, and the farmers were pretty pleased with what I said about everybody but the farmers. (He becomes serious again) But they all knew what I was talking about. They know we've all got to work in harness, if we're going to take our place in this world. And if we don't there won't be any world. We may be kidding ourselves that our party is going to win in '48—that the people here will want a change the way they did in England—but if our party does win, whoever is President has to have guts enough to pull us together and keep us together. I'm for that man, Mr. Conover—I don't care who he is.

KAY. That man is you, Grant.

GRANT. You're prejudiced, Kay. (To Conover) The boys who are back from fighting the war deserve something better . . .

(There is a knock on the door.)

CONOVER. Go ahead, finish.

GRANT. No, that may be important.

CONOVER. Come in.

(Norah, a middle-aged maid, wearing glasses, enters. She has a slip of paper in her hand.)

NORAH. I'm sorry to interrupt you. It's a telephone call. *(She hands Conover the slip of paper. He looks at it)*

CONOVER. Thank you. You go to bed, Norah. I'll take the rest of the calls myself.

NORAH *(starting out)*. Thank you, Mr. Conover. *(Turns back at the door)* It's turned cool. I've put an extra blanket in your room, Mrs. Thorndyke. Yours, too, Mr. Matthews.

GRANT. Thank you, Norah. Good night.

KAY. Good night, Norah.

(Norah exits.)

CONOVER. Do you mind? I'll try to make this short. *(He picks up telephone and speaks into it)* Hello, there! How are you? *(Pause)* Oh—can you call me on that in the morning? *(Pause)* Well, hold on. I'll have to take this in another room. Spike MacManus is here.

(Conover rises, holding the telephone. Spike crosses to the desk, reaching for the telephone.)

SPIKE. I'll hang up as soon as you're on.

CONOVER *(giving him a look, then extending the telephone to Kay)*. Mrs. Thorndyke, do you mind? Spike has a little Drew Pearson blood. *(Conover exits)*

SPIKE *(to Kay)*. If he doesn't want me to hear that, it's something we ought to hear.

(There is a long pause, Kay holding the receiver to her ear.)

KAY *(watching Spike, but speaking into the telephone)*. Are you on? All right, I'll hang up. *(To amuse Spike she listens for a moment before putting the receiver down. Grant has been pacing the room nervously. Spike sits in Conover's chair and picks up a volume of* Who's Who *that is on Conover's desk and opens it)*

GRANT. I've never felt so uncomfortable in my life. When he comes back, I'm going to tell him to drop the whole subject.

KAY *(going to Grant)*. I didn't come all the way to Washington to tell Jim Conover not to talk about something we came down here to talk about.

GRANT *(taking Kay's hands in his)*. Now, Kay, we've had a lot of fun between ourselves dreaming about all this—but damn it, to ask a man like Conover to take it seriously . . .

KAY *(pushing Grant into his chair)*. Now behave yourself. Mr. Conover and I

are going to talk about you and you're going to sit right down and listen.

(Grant looks up and grins.)

GRANT. All right, I'll listen. But if Conover is serious about considering me, the Republican Party must be pretty desperate.

SPIKE *(looking up from the book)*. You're damn right they're desperate!

GRANT. But Conover—he's always played along with the reactionaries. Why should he be interested in me?

SPIKE. If Conover isn't the guy who picks the Republican candidate for '48, he might as well turn Democrat.

KAY. You know, Grant, the last thing he has to boast about is Warren Harding. *(Spike is studying the book in his lap.)*

SPIKE. And don't think he isn't serious about you! There was a bookmark in this *Who's Who* at your page. You know this even impresses me. *(He runs his finger down a page)* Twelve boards of directors! Say, there's a lot of swell angles about you! For instance, Honorary President of the Society for the Preservation of Wild Life. *(He puts the book back on the desk)* How can we use that in the campaign?

KAY. Spike, I don't think the wild-life vote is very important.

SPIKE. No, I mean from a publicity angle. Say, for instance, a picture in *Life*. *(He points to Grant)* You and a grateful duck.

(Conover enters.)

CONOVER. After that call I need a drink.

SPIKE *(pointing to the telephone)*. Oh, Senator Taft!

CONOVER *(laughs, then turns to mix a drink)*. Anyone else?

SPIKE. I'll tend bar. *(Spike mixes drinks and serves them during the following)*

CONOVER. Oh, thank you.

KAY *(to Conover)*. Jim, do you think Taft's serious about being a candidate himself?

CONOVER. You can always figure that Senator Taft is serious. *(He returns to his chair and sits)* He'll go into the convention with Ohio and some Southern delegations.

GRANT. Don't kid yourselves. Truman isn't going to be easy to beat. He's made some strong appointments.

KAY. He's also made some weak ones.

CONOVER. Those are the ones that interest me—the weak ones. Between now and the campaign the Administration can run into some ugly trouble.

SPIKE. Well, all we can do is hope. *(He places drinks in front of Kay and Conover)*

KAY. Jim, Labor's already asking Truman for more than he can give them. I think we've got a chance for the labor vote if we have the right candidate.

SPIKE. That rules out Sewell Avery!

KAY. But it doesn't rule out Grant. *(She rises)* No employer in the country's got a better labor record. And business is bound to go along with him. Jim, don't you see the strength we have in Mr. Matthews? Phil Murray and Sewell Avery would both vote for him.

GRANT. I'm not so sure—because I wouldn't promise either one of them anything.

SPIKE. You'd have to promise them something. *(He hands Grant a drink and pauses for thought)* Still, Dewey outpromised Roosevelt and it didn't get him anywhere.

GRANT. That's one of our most serious problems. There's not enough difference between the two parties.

SPIKE. Well, not to change the subject, I would like to pause at this moment and take a one-man Gallup poll. What do you think of Mr. Matthews' chances, Jim?

CONOVER. That's not an easy question to answer. I haven't got much to go on. After Mr. Matthews makes his speech here Monday night I'd know a little more about what the feeling is here in Washington. Is Mrs. Matthews coming down to hear you speak?

GRANT *(amiably)*. No, she takes bringing up the children more seriously than she does my speeches. And I think she's right. This has all been very flattering—but as I said to Mrs. Thorndyke while you were out of the room—let's drop the whole idea.

KAY *(quickly. To Conover)*. Jim, Tuesday Grant's starting a tour of his plants. Everywhere he's going he's been invited to speak.

SPIKE. Minneapolis, Seattle, San Francisco, Los Angeles, Denver, Wichita, Detroit—

KAY. If Grant made those speeches, at the end of the tour could you tell him whether he had a chance, or whether we should give up the whole idea?

CONOVER *(with a little thought)*. That covers a lot of territory. Yes, I think if Mr. Matthews made those speeches I could be pretty definite.

KAY *(going to Grant)*. Grant, you've got to go along with us that far! You've got to make those speeches.

GRANT *(looking up at Kay)*. Kay, I'm going to be pretty busy on this trip. I've got problems in every one of those plants. I've got to do my damnedest to keep those men working. Besides, I wish I knew how much you had to do with those invitations for me to speak.

KAY *(decisively)*. Spike, you're going to make the trip with him. You've been telling everyone for years how to run a political campaign. Now we'll find out whether you can run one. The bureau can get along without you for a couple of weeks. It will be a vacation for you.

CONOVER. It will be a vacation for everyone in Washington. *(Briskly)* Now that we've reached that decision, there's a lot for all of us to talk about. On this tour, Mr. Matthews . . . *(Telephone rings)* Damn! Pardon me! *(Conover answers the telephone)* Hello. *(With some interest)* Oh, yes, I've been waiting to hear from you. *(Looks around room unhappily)* Hold on. Wait a minute. *(He rises)* Spike, why don't you go home? *(He hands the telephone to Kay)* Do you mind, Mrs. Thorndyke?

KAY *(rises and takes the telephone)*. I'm glad you trust publishers.

CONOVER *(going to the door)*. Just Republican publishers.

SPIKE. I thought it was agreed we were all to trust each other.

CONOVER. Only when we're in the same room. *(He exits)*

SPIKE *(gleefully rubbing his hands)*. Mr. Conover has just leaped gracefully onto the front seat of the bandwagon.

GRANT. Take it easy, Spike. Conover hasn't brought up the payoff yet.

SPIKE. Well, there's one promise I want.

GRANT. What?

SPIKE. That I'm not to be the next Postmaster General.

GRANT. I'll settle for that, Spike—you're not the next Postmaster General. And that's the only commitment I'm going to make.

SPIKE. You settled awfully quick. I just threw that in for a laugh. *(He turns to*

Kay) Mrs. Thorndyke—tell Sir Galahad here . . .

KAY *(into the telephone).* Are you on? All right, I'll hang up. *(Again to amuse Spike, she keeps her ear to the receiver. Suddenly her expression changes sharply. She presses down the disconnector with her free hand, then releases it immediately and continues to listen in, giving the men a warning gesture. Grant rises indignantly and starts toward her)*

GRANT. Kay!

(Spike stops him with a gesture. Grant obviously disapproves and walks unhappily away, as if he will have none of it. Spike beams in admiration of Kay at first, but as she listens in and flashes a look toward Grant, Spike realizes it is a serious matter and his smile vanishes. Even Grant's attention is arrested. The two men stand watching Kay. She hangs up and goes immediately to Grant, speaking quickly and with deep concern.)

KAY. It's a report from New York. He's had someone looking you up. They've picked up some gossip about you and me.

SPIKE. Oh—oh!

KAY. And there's been talk about Mary, too—Mary and some Major.

SPIKE. Who's Mary?

KAY. Mrs. Matthews.

SPIKE. Oh—ho!

GRANT. What Major? What's his name?

KAY. I couldn't get his name.

GRANT. What'd the name sound like?

(Kay gestures him to be quiet.)

KAY. Sh-h. He'll be back in a minute. *(She raises her voice, making a pretense of normal conversation)* Of course, Spike, that's one way of looking at it, but you never can be sure.

GRANT *(sitting down).* A Major!

SPIKE *(to Grant as Conover enters).* On the other hand, if what you say is true, Mr. Matthews, that makes the migratory flamingo a very interesting bird.

CONOVER. What makes the flamingo an interesting bird, Spike?

SPIKE *(caught short, but not very).* Tell him what you just told us, Mr. Matthews.

GRANT *(at no loss whatever).* I don't think Mr. Conover's interested in the wild life of America.

CONOVER. Staying up this late is a little more wild life than I'm used to. I think we'd better call it a night.

(They are caught flatfooted by his tone of dismissal.)

SPIKE *(tentatively).* Nothing else you want to bring up, Jim?

CONOVER. Not now. *(Grant rises)* Spike, you may have a little trouble getting a taxi. Good night. *(Conover shakes hands with Spike)*

SPIKE. Good night, Jim. Good night, Boss. *(He turns to Grant)* Grant, if the lights are still on in the White House, I'll drop in and tell the Trumans to start packing.

KAY. Spike, you'd better get off some wires accepting those speaking dates for Grant.

CONOVER. I'd like to give some of those cities a little more thought. *(Spike gets his hat and crosses to the door)* Tomorrow's time enough for that, isn't it?

GRANT. Yes—I guess so. *(He goes to Conover)* Well, Mr. Conover, if I never get any closer to the White House than this, it's been a very pleasant evening. I'll say good night, too.

CONOVER. You and I might take time to finish our drinks.

KAY. I haven't finished mine— *(No one asks her to stay)* I'll finish it in my room. *(She starts to rise, picking up her bag and drink)*

CONOVER. I thought Mr. Matthews and I might chat for a few minutes longer.

KAY. I'll run along then. I can't tell you how grateful we are for your having us here. Good night. Good night, Grant.

GRANT. Good night, Kay.

KAY *(she starts to door, stops and turns back to Conover; Spike is holding door open for her).* Jim, I want you to know how completely we trust you. *(She goes directly to Grant)* Good night, darling. *(She puts her arms around him and they kiss. She starts out again)*

CONOVER. Mrs. Thorndyke! *(Kay stops and turns)* You might as well finish your drink here. That's what I was going to talk about. *(Kay raises her eyebrows, comes back and sits down. Spike closes the door, and drops his hat on a chair)* Naturally, Mr. Matthews, when your name first came up as a possible candidate, I made some inquiries. It seems there's been some talk about you and Mrs. Thorndyke.

GRANT. What kind of talk?

CONOVER *(easily).* I think you know what I mean when I say talk.

KAY. We wouldn't pretend to deny there's basis for it, but it can't be very widespread.

GRANT. Kay, let Mr. Conover tell us what he's heard.

CONOVER. That's about all. There's been some gossip. That's nothing unusual, and as long as it's about a man who makes airplanes, even though you're very well known, I don't think it would spread a great deal, but the minute you become a public figure . . .

KAY. You think it might be used against Mr. Matthews?

CONOVER. Not openly. What it would come down to would be a whispering campaign.

GRANT (firmly). Frankly, Mr. Conover, I don't give a damn for the kind of opinion that sort of thing would influence.

CONOVER. I haven't any respect for it, either; but I have to reckon with it. You see, Mr. Matthews, while Mrs. Thorndyke happens to be divorced, you're a married man.

GRANT. Well, if you think that's a major— (His mind sticks momentarily on the word) —a vital factor . . . Kay, that seems to settle it.

KAY. Wait a minute, Grant! Jim, there must be some way around this.

CONOVER. Yes, there's a very obvious one.

GRANT. So? What is it?

CONOVER. I'd like to see your wife with you when you speak here Monday night, and I'd like to see her make this trip with you.

GRANT (laughing). That's not the solution. If Mary knew that I even thought of myself as President of the United States . . .

KAY. Jim, we've got to think of something else. It's a little difficult for me to talk about Mrs. Matthews in this situation but—you've seen the kind of wife—the more important her husband becomes the more determined she is to make him feel unimportant.

GRANT. Now, wait a minute, Kay! Be fair to Mary. (To Conover) I don't want you to get the wrong impression of my wife, Mr. Conover. She's no shrew. She's a damn bright woman.

KAY. Grant, you know Mary's always cutting you down.

GRANT. I can't deny that. Still, I suppose her criticism of me has been valuable

sometimes. (To Conover) But a man doesn't reach a saturation point.

CONOVER. If you become a candidate you'll have to take a lot of criticism.

SPIKE. Yes, your wife might be good training for you. Toughen you up.

KAY. I think it's more important that Grant should have his self-confidence.

CONOVER (sitting on the edge of his desk). The most important thing of all is to kill this gossip. We haven't got a chance unless we do. The American people like to think of a married candidate as happily married. They want to see him and his wife together. They like to see them make the campaign together. It's an American tradition. You'd have to face that sooner or later. I think the sooner you face it the better.

GRANT. Yes, Mary may solve the whole situation for us. I'm not so sure she would campaign with me even if I asked her to.

CONOVER. Why don't you call her and find out?

(Kay and Grant exchange a look of mutual inquiry.)

GRANT (to Conover). Why not? (Conover picks up the telephone and dials)

SPIKE. There's been that gossip about every candidate except Herbert Hoover. They didn't pull it on Hoover because nobody would have believed it

CONOVER (into telephone). This is Dupont 4108. I want a New York call. I want to speak to Mrs. Grant Matthews at . . . (He looks inquiringly at Grant)

GRANT. Plaza 5-8249.

CONOVER (into phone). Plaza 5-8249. (He rises and hands the telephone to Grant) Invite her to stay here, of course.

GRANT (taking the telephone). There's no way of a man being elected President before his wife hears about it, is there? (He sits beside the desk) Hello. Well, put it through as soon as you can and call me. (He hangs up and there is an uneasy pause. They are not looking at each other. Finally Spike speaks up brightly)

SPIKE. Shall we dance?

(Jim Conover gives him a look that's an answer, but not to his question.)

GRANT. Mr. Conover, I'm glad there's a delay in that call because before it comes through there's something I'd like to ask you.

CONOVER. Yes?

GRANT. If it works out that we can go

ahead, you and I, what are you going to expect of me?

CONOVER. I'd expect you to be elected.

GRANT. Mr. Conover, I'm inexperienced in politics, but I am not—shall I say—completely naive. Let's put it this way—if I were elected, naturally I'd be very grateful to you. Is there any particular way in which you'd expect me to show my gratitude?

KAY. Grant, aren't you being a little premature? *(To Conover)* It's probably pre-natal influence. Grant was a premature baby.

SPIKE. You were? Say, drop that into an interview some time. There may be some votes in that. There are a lot of bastards who think they were seven-month babies.

CONOVER. In answer to your question, Mr. Matthews, if you mean have I a list of Federal appointments in my pocket?—No.

GRANT. I'd be very glad to see any list of names you wanted to show me. I just want it to be clear I'm not making any commitments.

CONOVER. I can't ask for more than an open mind. Mrs. Thorndyke said you two came down here for my advice. Well, politics is my business. If we do get into a campaign together I hope you'll be open-minded about any advice I might give you then.

GRANT. I'd welcome it—only I can't promise I'd always follow it.

KAY. Now, Grant, don't turn down advice before you get it.

GRANT *(to Conover, with a disarming laugh)*. All right. Give me some!

CONOVER *(amused, but still serious)*. Well, in that list of speaking dates, you mentioned Minneapolis. I wouldn't speak there. You might just stir up trouble. That's Stassen territory. The local boys would resent it and you might start a backfire.

GRANT. That's damn good advice. I'll take it. How do you feel about Stassen?

CONOVER. There's a good deal of opposition to him in the party. Oh, that prompts me to venture some more advice, if you don't mind?

GRANT. No—shoot!

CONOVER. If you make this preliminary tour, keep whatever you have to say pretty general. Don't be too specific.

GRANT. There I'm afraid I can't go all the way with you. The only reason I have for speaking at all is because there are some things I feel deeply about.

KAY. Grant, it's only that at this early stage . . .

GRANT. No, Kay! I'm not going to pull any punches! I want that understood!

KAY. Grant, if you keep on being belligerent about your honesty, we'll begin to suspect you.

CONOVER *(serenely)*. Mr. Matthews, most candidates have to spend a lot of time explaining things they wish they hadn't said. You're not carrying that weight because you haven't said very much yet. Your danger at this point might be in raising minor issues that would come back to plague you later.

KAY. Grant, this isn't the airplane business. You're used to dealing with tangible things. I know what Jim's talking about because I have to go out after circulation. You'll have to go out after votes.

GRANT. Oh, I know you have to appeal for votes. But I think what I believe in . . .

(The telephone rings. Spike picks it up.)

SPIKE *(into telephone)*. Hello. New York? Just a minute. *(He hands the telephone to Grant. Kay goes to a chair on the farther side of the room and sits)*

GRANT *(into telephone)*. Hello, Hello. What's that? *(With a little impatience)* Well, get them back. No, I'll hang on.

CONOVER. Have you your speech for Monday night prepared?

GRANT. Yes. Want to look at it tomorrow? I'll listen to anything you have to say.

KAY. And on the tour you listen to Spike. He can be very valuable.

GRANT *(grinning)*. If I know Spike, he's going to give me plenty of advice.

SPIKE. No, Mr. Matthews, my big job is to humanize you.

GRANT *(in amused surprise)*. Oh, is it?

SPIKE. I've got a lot of things dreamed up. Do you know what first sold Willkie to the country as a human being? His going on Information Please. He came over as a regular guy and he held his own, too.

GRANT. Just a minute! I'm no Wendell Willkie—I'm willing to take on Harry Truman, but not John Kieran.

SPIKE. We've got to do something to counteract those speeches.

GRANT. Counteract them! Well then, why am I making them?

SPIKE. Oh, no, you've got to make them. But sometimes your speeches get a little fancy. We don't want people to think you're stuffy.

GRANT. Do you know, Spike, you sound just like my wife. (*At this moment he hears his wife's voice on the telephone and speaks to her with some surprise*) Hello, Mary. (*Pause*) I'm in Washington. How's Joyce? (*Pause*) Doctor been there today? (*Pause*) That's fine . . . If she's that well, Sonny won't catch it now. (*Pause*) Mary, I'm making another speech down here Monday night. (*Pause—then somewhat indignantly*) No, they *asked* me to! I'd like to have you come down and listen to it, if it wouldn't bore you too much (*Pause*) As a matter of fact, I won't *be* home for a few weeks. I'm making a tour of the plants. How'd you like to make the trip with me?—I wish you would. We haven't made the circuit together in a long time. (*Pause*) But how about coming down here, anyway? We'll be house guests at Jim Conover's. (*Pause*) Conover—a friend of mine, but in spite of that you'll like him. (*Pause*) Get here tomorrow night—It doesn't matter how late. I'll send the plane back for you— Swell! (*Pause*) Bring enough clothes for the trip, anyway. We can talk it over when you get here. Mary, you'll need a dinner dress here Monday night. It's a banquet. (*Gaily*) You'll get my speech for dessert. (*Pause*) What? (*Not so gaily*) All right— Of course you'll look a little funny sitting there with earmuffs on. Good night. (*He hangs up*) I'm not sure the Presidency's worth it.

CONOVER. She's coming?

GRANT. Yes, Heaven help me.

KAY. Grant, you know what that means. If Mary's coming here I've got to go home tomorrow.

CONOVER. I confess that would ease the housing situation. The National Committee seems to think I run a hotel.

KAY (*starting for the door*). Well, for the next few weeks I'll be sitting alone in New York, while you tour the country with your wife.

SPIKE (*thoughtfully*). Politics makes strange bedfellows.

(*Kay looks at him sharply. Spike catches the look, picks up his hat and starts out of the room.*)

CURTAIN

SCENE TWO

The next night.

A bedroom in Jim Conover's house. There is a double bed with bed tables on each side of bed. There are two overstuffed chairs with a small table between them. The entrance to the bedroom is upstage to the left. There is a window downstage left. On the right there is a door leading to a dressing room and bathroom offstage. Below the door is a desk with a chair.

Grant, wearing horn-rimmed glasses, is discovered alone, seated at the desk, editing the loose pages of his typewritten speech. There is a knock at the door.

GRANT (*taking off his glasses*). Come in!

(*Conover enters.*)

CONOVER. How's the speech coming along?

GRANT. All right, I guess. What Spike said last night had me worried. I'm trying to unfancy it a little bit.

CONOVER. Don't let Spike worry you. I think it's very good. When you finish, drop back downstairs. I think it would be a good idea to have the boys see as much of you as possible. You made a very good impression at dinner.

GRANT. I was thrown a little by the way Senator Fosdick kept yessing me. He's an America Firster, isn't he?

CONOVER. He was—until he was defeated. (*He starts to leave*) I'll see you later then. (*Turns back*) Oh! I came up to tell you I've sent the car down to the airport.

GRANT (*looking at his watch*). He might have quite a wait. I don't think Mary will be in much before midnight. (*A little disturbed*) If she could have told me when she was getting in I could have met her myself.

(*Spike enters.*)

SPIKE. Jim, Governor Dunn just arrived.

CONOVER (*to Grant*). Oh, that's fine!

want you to meet him. He can be very valuable to you in the Northwest. I'm glad he dropped in.

SPIKE. Like hell you are! He brought his bags with him.

CONOVER. Oh, damn! Where am I going to put him? Well, I guess I'll have to take him into my room, and I was hoping for a good night's sleep. Spike, you're an expert in these matters. Why do all Governors snore?

SPIKE. It's an occupational disease.

GRANT. Where are you putting Mary? *(Conover is taken a little by surprise.)*

CONOVER. In here with you. If we're going to create the impression about you two that we want to, this would be a good start.

GRANT *(troubled)*. I don't think she'd welcome the idea. We rushed into this decision and it's been on my conscience ever since. Look, Jim, when Mary finds out what's up, she can still say no. But moving her in here with me tonight . . .

CONOVER *(thinking)*. Well, Senator Fosdick's room is about the only one. He's in there alone. But where can I put the Senator? There's nothing left but the billiard table.

SPIKE. Why not? The son-of-a-bitch didn't even carry his own state.

CONOVER. I'll put him on a cot somewhere. Come on down with me. I want you to meet the Governor.

SPIKE. He's got to finish that speech. I want to take it with me tonight.

GRANT. I'm almost through.

CONOVER *(turning at the door)*. Shall I send up a drink?

SPIKE. Send up a couple.
(Conover exits.)

GRANT. Why are you in such a hurry? There's plenty of time to get this copied before tomorrow night.

SPIKE. All the wire services will want it by noon, and even if they don't want it they're going to get it. If they don't have it in advance you may only get a couple of paragraphs. Are you out on a limb anywhere in here? *(He picks up first few pages of the manuscript and starts glancing through it)* Because we could play it the other way. Not give out any copies— then you could always claim you've been misquoted.

GRANT. I wish I was as sure as you seem to be that I'll be quoted at all.

SPIKE. This isn't as bad as I thought it was going to be.

GRANT. Those changes were all made for your benefit.

SPIKE *(placing one sheet in front of Grant)*. This spot in here sounds a little like a speech. *(He points)*

GRANT. Damn it!—It *is* a speech!

SPIKE. That's what I meant.
(There is a knock on the door.)

GRANT. Come in!
(Norah enters, loaded down with two bags and a hatbox.)

NORAH *(from doorway)*. These are Mrs. Matthews' bags.

GRANT *(rising)*. Oh, is my wife here?

NORAH. She just came. I'll put these in the dressing room.
(Grant stops her.)

GRANT. No, they don't go there. Mrs. Matthews is in another room.

NORAH *(bewildered)*. What other room?
(Conover enters.)

CONOVER. Grant, Mrs. Matthews is here!
(Mary follows Conover in. Mary is an attractive woman in her thirties, brisk and self-assured. She is dressed in a smart traveling suit and hat.)

GRANT. Hello, dear.

MARY. Hello, Grant. *(She goes to Grant and they kiss)*

GRANT. I didn't expect you to get here this early.

MARY. I think we broke the record— and both my ear drums.

GRANT. Spike, I want you to meet Mrs. Matthews. *(To Mary)* This is Mr. MacManus.

MARY. How do you do, Mr. MacManus?

SPIKE *(standing near window)*. Hello, Mrs. Matthews.

GRANT. You seem to have met Mr. Conover.

MARY. Oh, yes, downstairs. *(She smiles at Conover)* It's so nice of you to have us here. I'm really quite excited. I hope you'll notice, Grant, I've packed for the whole trip. *(She points to the bags, which Norah is still holding, then speaks to Norah)* Just put those down anywhere.

NORAH. I was told you were going to be in another room. *(Norah looks toward Conover)*

CONOVER. Leave the bags here for a minute, Norah. You're moving Senator Fosdick.

NORAH. Again?

CONOVER. Put him in the south bedroom with Mr. Godfrey.

NORAH. The Commissioner's in there with Mr. Godfrey.

CONOVER. We have another cot, haven't we?

NORAH. That army cot.

MARY. That's nonsense. Don't move Senator Fosdick. Grant and I can stay here. *(She looks around at the group)* We're really married. *(Conover hesitates)* Unless the rest of the Senate is in here with Grant.

GRANT. Mr. Conover just thought you'd be more comfortable with a room to yourself.

MARY *(to Norah)*. I'll stay here. *(Norah crosses to the dressing room with the bags. Grant holds the door open for her. Mary goes to the bed and throws hat and bag on it. She starts removing her gloves)* After all, Senator Fosdick's an isolationist. I think he ought to be isolated.

SPIKE *(grinning)*. I'm going to like you.

(Mary answers him with a smile.)

NORAH *(at dressing-room door)*. Shall I unpack for you, Ma'am?

MARY. Just the small bag. And you can take the shoes out of my hat box. *(Norah starts out)* Oh, there's a print dress in the suitcase I'd like to wear tomorrow. Could it be pressed for me?

NORAH. Surely. *(She exits into the dressing room with the bags)*

MARY *(pressing her ears)*. Those plane trips always leave me deaf.

GRANT. If that lasts through tomorrow you'll be spared hearing my speech.

MARY *(smiling at him)*. That's a little more than I could hope for.

(The others are politely amused. There is a knock on the door. Stevens, the butler, enters with two drinks on a tray. He's a little bewildered to find four people.)

STEVENS. Scotch and soda?

MARY. I'm not as deaf as I thought I was. What a perfect host! *(She takes one of the highballs)*

CONOVER. I'll take the other one, Stevens. *(To Grant)* You and Spike get your drinks downstairs. I want you to meet the Governor.

(Stevens exits.)

GRANT. Want to meet a Governor, Mary?

MARY. I'd like to get a little better acquainted with this highball.

CONOVER. That was my idea. You and I, let's finish our drinks quietly up here. *(To Grant)* We'll join you later.

SPIKE. How about the rest of this Gettysburg Address? Finished with it?

GRANT. Yes, I think the end's all right. Take it along. *(He hands Spike his speech)*

CONOVER. Spike, see that Grant and Governor Dunn get together.

SPIKE *(exiting)*. All right.

CONOVER. Grant, I'm sure the Governor will be very interested in meeting you.

GRANT *(with a touch of self-importance)*. I'll be glad to talk to him. *(Grant exits. Mary smiles at Conover and goes to one of the easy chairs and sits down)*

MARY. This is very pleasant.

CONOVER. It is for me.

MARY. Now I can boast that I've really been behind the scenes in Washington.

CONOVER. You certainly can! The Republican Party's been behind the scenes for fourteen years. However, that's about over. I think we're going to win next time.

MARY. If I needed an excuse to drink, that would be it. *(She lifts her glass to Conover. They drink)* But you'll have to offer the Democrats a good reason for voting Republican.

CONOVER. Your husband's been lecturing me along those lines.

MARY. Then I'd better change the subject. Grant can be very outspoken—but not by anybody I know.

CONOVER. Everything he said about politicians we had coming to us. I have a great admiration for your husband.

MARY. I'm many years ahead of you on that.

CONOVER. Of course, everyone admires him as a business man. What impresses me is that he doesn't limit his thinking to his own field. *(Conover sits in the other easy chair)* He has a very clear vision about the whole country—what it needs— what the world needs. Any man who sees our problems as clearly as he does—it imposes on him a certain responsibility.

MARY. Oh, I think you're sure of a big check from him.

(Conover smiles, then becomes serious.)

CONOVER. No, I mean a responsibility to the country. I've been trying to persuade your husband to take an active part in the Government.

MARY. Mr. Conover, Grant's talking politics is one thing—but he has a big enough job ahead of him—that is, if you know anything about his plans for post-war aviation.

CONOVER. I don't think his usefulness should be limited to that. I think the country will feel that way, too, after hearing what he says here tomorrow night, and the speeches he's going to make on this trip.

MARY. Is he going to make speeches on the trip?

CONOVER. Yes, in several places.

MARY (dismayed). Oh, dear. (Catching herself) Oh, I didn't mean that the way it sounded. Grant really can make a very good speech. But public appearances for me—I'm not good at that—I'm so uncomfortable. Would it be bad form if I just stayed quietly at the hotel and listened to him over the radio?

CONOVER. Yes, I'm afraid it would. It would defeat the whole purpose.

MARY. Purpose? What purpose?

CONOVER (avoiding a direct answer). Mrs. Matthews, you must know how concerned your husband is about this country's splitting apart—how deeply he feels that it must be held together.

MARY. Oh, yes. We've been talking about it for months. Grant's been trying to figure out what could be done.

CONOVER. I think you can help him do something about it.

MARY. Oh, not me. I just get angry! I can't read the newspapers any more! While the war was on we were a united country—we were fighting Germany and Japan. Now we're just fighting each other. No, I just get angry.

CONOVER. I'm glad you feel that strongly about it because it's important that wherever Grant goes now—wherever he makes these speeches—you're right there alongside of him.

(Mary senses for the first time that there is more than meets the ear in Conover's conversation.)

MARY. Why should that be important?

CONOVER (smoothly). Well, for a man who's going to be in the public-eye—people like to know his wife—like to see what she looks like—like to see the two of them together.

MARY (thoughtfully, putting her drink on the table). I was a little puzzled by Grant's invitation to make this trip with him.

CONOVER. Oh, Grant wants you to go along. These public appearances—they're my idea. It's just an old politician's habit of cashing in on an opportunity.

MARY (rising and walking away). It all fits in a little too neatly, Mr. Conover. I don't know whether you know—(She stops and looks at him sharply)—or perhaps you do—that Grant and I haven't been very close for the last year or so.

CONOVER. Wouldn't you prefer to create a contrary impression?

MARY. Oh, then you do know! Let's be open about this. These public appearances that Grant and I are to make together—are they designed to kill off any talk about my husband and Mrs. Thorndyke?

CONOVER. There's that kind of talk about every important man. But if there are any rumors about your husband, this would be a good chance to kill them. (Conover is watching Mary carefully) You see, Mrs. Matthews . . .

(Norah enters from the dressing room, carrying a print dress.)

NORAH. Is this the dress, Ma'am?

(Mary stares at the dress and then comes to the surface.)

MARY. Oh, yes. But don't bother to press it.

NORAH. It's no trouble at all, Ma'am. It won't take me long. I'll have it back tonight.

MARY. No! Please! (But Norah has gone. Mary to Conover) May I use your telephone?

CONOVER. Certainly.

MARY. I want to get back to New York tonight if I can. (She goes to the telephone, picks up the receiver and starts to dial)

CONOVER (rising). Mrs. Matthews, I think any man who has a chance to become President of the United States deserves that chance.

(Mary slowly puts down the telephone, turns and stares at Conover in astonishment.)

MARY. President of the United States?

CONOVER. Yes. (There is a short pause) Don't you think he'd make a good President?

MARY (after consideration). Yes, I do.

CONOVER. Then you understand this goes beyond personal considerations. Let's not think of this in terms of you—and Grant—

MARY. —and Mrs. Thorndyke.

CONOVER. And Mrs. Thorndyke. I'm sure you will go along with us. You're a good citizen.

MARY. Right now, Mr. Conover, I'm not feeling like a good citizen! I'm feeling like a woman!

CONOVER. All right, as a woman!

MARY. As a woman, no, I won't go along with you. I resent being used!

CONOVER. Mrs. Matthews, let's think of it in terms of the country. That's what I've had to do. I am prepared to make some sacrifices.

MARY (*turning to him*). What sacrifices?

CONOVER. Frankly, your husband isn't the kind of man a politician would prefer to deal with.

MARY. I've been wondering why any political party should choose Grant, knowing the things he stands for.

CONOVER. I want the people to make the choice.

MARY. That's damn white of you!

CONOVER. That's the purpose of this trip. I want the American people to get better acquainted with your husband. We don't know yet what's coming out of it, but I've told him that when this trip is over I can let him know whether to go ahead with the idea or forget the whole thing.

MARY. Oh, I don't think Grant could ever forget it. I'll bet he's running a pretty high fever right now. When he left the room I thought he walked as though he was trying to be two inches taller.

CONOVER. Mrs. Matthews, you see your husband at pretty close range. Take my word for it, he's a big man.

MARY. There's no argument about that, Mr. Conover. I know he's a big man and you know he's a big man. My bad days are when *he* knows he's a big man! (*She thinks for a moment*) You don't suppose there's any way of Grant being elected President and keeping it a secret from him, do you? (*Conover laughs. Mary sits on the side of the bed*) Is Grant speaking in Seattle?

CONOVER. Yes, why?

MARY. We were married in Seattle. When I think of Grant speaking there as a candidate for President—

CONOVER (*going to her quickly*). He's not speaking now as a candidate. That's a deep, dark secret. The whole idea of this trip is to create the demand.

MARY. That clears up something you just said—he's your choice first and then the people's choice.

CONOVER. I'm a citizen. I have a right to a choice. I think I've made a good one. And I want to help Grant all I can. He's new at this and needs advice.

MARY. What advice are you giving him?

CONOVER. Oh, so far it's chiefly along the lines of what not to say. Your husband is so afraid of not being completely honest.

MARY. You want him to be honest, don't you?

CONOVER. Oh, yes! (*There is a knock on the door*) Yes? Come in!
(*Stevens enters.*)

STEVENS. There's a long-distance call for you, sir. It's Wilkes-Barre.

CONOVER. Thank you, Stevens. (*He hesitates for a moment*) I'll take it here. (*He goes to the telephone. Stevens exits*)

MARY. Am I in the way?

CONOVER. Not at all. I won't be a minute. (*He picks up the receiver*) Hello. Put him on. (*Pause*) Yes, how are you? (*Pause*) Uh-huh. Yes, Joe, I want the campaign in your district strictly along those lines. If what happens down there is what I think will happen, it'll be a large part of the campaign in '48. How many Italians down there? (*Pause*) What's the size of your Polish vote? (*Pause*) That many? Well, tell them their hope lies in our party. Russia can't be trusted and we'll be tough with her—force her to correct those injustices. (*Mary turns and looks at Conover*) You don't have to tell 'em *how.* (*Mary rises, still watching Conover*) Go after it, hammer and tongs. You swing that district and we'll get you that veterans' hospital. (*Pause*) Not at all. Good luck. And thanks for calling. (*He hangs up*) Sorry for the interruption.

MARY. I'm glad it happened. It gave me a chance to change my mind. I'll go with Grant.

CONOVER (*heartily*). That's fine. That pleases me very much. (*He goes to the table and picks up his glass*) That's our first big campaign contribution. To you, my dear, the most attractive plank in your husband's platform.

MARY. That's a hell of a thing to call a woman.

CONOVER (laughing). Suppose we go downstairs? I'd like to have you meet the rest of my guests.

MARY. Would it be rude if I postponed that until tomorrow? I have to get a little used to this idea—and I have to get a little used to Grant.

CONOVER. Well, this trip—working along with Grant—by the time you come back you two may be much closer together.

MARY. Even if that could happen, I don't think you'd want it to. It might cost you the support of Mrs. Thorndyke's newspapers.

CONOVER (laughing). Don't worry about that. They're Republican newspapers in Republican territory. They couldn't afford to risk their circulation. A chain of newspapers is a very valuable property.

MARY. Mrs. Thorndyke must have thought so. In the divorce settlement Dick Thorndyke got the children and she got the newspapers. And if that sounds bitchy, I hoped it would. You may succeed in killing the rumors, but unfortunately you won't kill Mrs. Thorndyke.

CONOVER (knowingly). We may kill more than one rumor.

MARY. Oh, dear! Is there someone I don't know about?

CONOVER (with a smile). There have been some rumors about you.

MARY (enormously pleased, she walks over to Conover). There have?

CONOVER. Yes. About you and a certain Major.

MARY. That's wonderful! That's the best news I've had in weeks. Does Grant know about the Major?

CONOVER. Not so far as I know.

MARY. Well, you're going to tell him, aren't you? I deserve something out of this! I was hoping he'd told you.

CONOVER. No, Mrs. Matthews, I have a little intelligence service of my own.

MARY. Well, it can't be too intelligent. They're considerably behind the times. The Major's been in China for six months. But when you tell Grant about him, don't let him know the Major's out of the country.

CONOVER. As far as I'm concerned, the whole thing's a military secret.

MARY (gaily). You know, I think I'll go downstairs with you at that! I feel a lot better than I did! Can you wait until I put on a new face? (She picks up her bag. The door opens and Grant enters. To Grant) We were just starting down.

GRANT. You're a little late. The party's breaking up.

CONOVER. We forgot all about you. We've been having a very interesting talk.

GRANT. That puts you one up on me. I've been listening to Governor Dunn. He's just about talked himself to sleep.

CONOVER. I'd better get down there! He doesn't even know where his room is! I'm the night clerk around here. I'll make your excuses, Mrs. Matthews.

MARY. Thanks. Thanks for everything!

CONOVER. Good night. Good night, Grant. (He starts for the door)

GRANT. See you in the morning.

CONOVER (at the door). Grant, I couldn't wait. I told Mrs. Matthews all about it. (He gives Grant a reassuring smile and exits quickly. Grant turns and looks at Mary. He seems a little uncertain. There is a pause)

MARY. Grant, I'm very proud of you.

GRANT. Well, Mary, don't think I'm taking this too seriously.

MARY. I'm taking it seriously. (Grant gives her a quick look) I think it would be a wonderful thing for the country.

GRANT. That's about as nice a thing as you could say, Mary. It's a damn big job. I'm not so sure I've got what it takes.

MARY. Well, I am. It isn't only that you have the brains for it—the important thing to me is—you've always tried to be honest.

GRANT. Tried to be?

MARY. Oh, you've cut some corners in business to get where you wanted to. That's what frightens me a little. But I will say this—you always had the decency to be unhappy about it.

GRANT (wryly). With some help from you.

MARY. But when you weren't thinking of yourself—when it came to what was best for the airplane industry as a whole, I've seen you take some pretty big losses.

GRANT. Right now I'm thinking about the country as a whole. I'm scared, Mary. (He sits down on the side of the bed)

MARY. About being President?

GRANT. No, about what's happening to the country. It's breaking up again . . .

MARY. What do you think you can do about it?

GRANT. I think somebody can appeal to what's best in people instead of what's worst.

MARY. And still be in politics?

GRANT. That's my whole case, Mary. If I can make the people see the choice they've got to make—the choice between their own interests and the interests of the country as a whole—damn it, I think the American people are sound. I think they can be unselfish.

MARY. All of them?

GRANT. Hell, we both know there are plenty of bastards in this world who'll always be out for themselves. But that's where I differ from Conover. I think they're in the minority.

MARY. I do, too. *(Mary sits on the other side of the bed, facing him)* How much do you and Conover differ?

GRANT. He's a politician. Politicians think you have to bribe people to vote for you—one way or another.

MARY. You mean groups like the Poles and the Italians?

GRANT. Yes—and labor and the farmers and the rest of them. But I'm not going to play politics.

MARY. That will take a lot of courage.

GRANT. No, it won't. I have faith in the American people.

MARY. So have I. *(There is a pause)* The Presidency's a great temptation!

GRANT. I don't even want the job. Whether I become President or not is completely unimportant.

(They look at each other for a moment. Then Mary turns away.)

MARY. Grant, when I first learned the purpose of this trip, I wasn't very happy about making it with you.

GRANT. I can understand that.

MARY *(looking back at Grant)*. But I am now.

GRANT. Mary, there are some things I should say—*(There is a pause, and then he turns away)*—but I can't.

(The moment is almost too intense. Mary stares at Grant's back for a moment or two, then rises, taking up her hat, gloves and bag from bed.)

MARY. I think I'll get out of these clothes. *(She exits into the dressing room, leaving the door open. Grant rises and turns to watch the door for a moment. Then Mary's voice comes from the dressing room)* Grant!

GRANT. Yes?

MARY *(offstage)*. I wish you'd call up Joyce tomorrow.

GRANT *(sitting in one of the easy chairs)*. She'll be in school, won't she?

MARY *(offstage)*. No, the doctor thinks she shouldn't go back until Wednesday. Oh, she's better. She had no temperature at all today.

GRANT. I'll call around dinner time. Then I can talk to Sonny, too.

MARY *(offstage)*. They were both pretty disappointed they couldn't go along.

GRANT *(dreamily)*. We ought to be thinking about a good boarding school for those kids.

MARY *(offstage)*. For heaven's sake, why?

GRANT. Well, I'm not so sure the White House is a good place to raise children.

MARY *(offstage)*. Grant!

GRANT. Yes?

MARY *(offstage)*. When are you going to break the news?

GRANT. You mean that I'm a candidate?

MARY *(offstage)*. Oh, you're way beyond the nomination—you've elected yourself.

GRANT *(grinning)*. I walked into that one—*(Then, defensively)*—but I didn't mean it quite the way it sounded.

MARY *(offstage)*. Which one of the plants are we going to first?

GRANT. Minneapolis.

MARY *(offstage)*. What are you speaking about there?

GRANT. I'm not making a speech there. That's Stassen territory. Conover thought I might just stir up trouble.

MARY *(offstage)*. Uh-huh. I suppose that's good politics. Tell me some more about your differences with Conover.

GRANT *(irritated)*. Now wait a minute, Mary! *(He goes to dressing-room door)* That was my decision! I'm making all the decisions! I've told Conover where I stand and he knows I'm going to tell the American people where I stand. *(Starts walking around the room)* The American people are facing problems today that will affect the future of the entire world. There's only one way to face them—with complete honesty—with utter frankness—

MARY (offstage). Grant!

GRANT. What?

MARY (offstage). Take it easy. I'm going to vote for you.

GRANT. No, I want to straighten you out on this too! If I have anything to offer, it's to change the whole complexion of political campaigns. I'm not going before the American people telling them what I can do for them. (Mary enters in nightgown, negligee and mules) But what I can do for them is to show them that the strength of this country, within our own borders . . .

MARY. Grant! I'm through with the dressing room.

GRANT. I'm in no hurry. (Resuming his "broadcast") The power of this country, outside our own borders . . .

MARY. Wouldn't you feel more comfortable if you took off that stuffed shirt? (Grant throws himself down in the chair, sulkily.)

GRANT. Aw, hell—I don't want to be President.

MARY (going to him). Darling, when we were talking a little while ago, you said the same things and they sounded so right—I wish you could just talk to the people that way.

GRANT (not entirely mollified). That's the way I plan to talk to them.

MARY. That's all I meant. Got a cigarette? (Grant offers her one from his case and lights it for her) Bill and Amy know we're coming to Seattle? (She crosses to the bench at foot of bed and sits)

GRANT. Bill knows—he expects me at the plant. But they don't know you're coming.

MARY. I'll wire Amy. (She shakes her head) Amy—with eight children?

GRANT. Yep, Bill's got the best production record of anyone in the industry.

MARY. I hope Amy's done something about the way she dresses. She always looks as though somebody bet her she couldn't.

GRANT (laughing). Do you remember the way she looked as your bridesmaid?

MARY. No, I was in a complete daze until we got to Victoria.

GRANT. And even in Victoria! When we went into the dining room you shook hands with the headwaiter! (They both laugh. There is an embarrassed pause.

Grant straightens up in his chair, steals a look at Mary who is stealing a look at him at the same time. Grant rises) Well, I've got a tough day tomorrow. (He exits into the dressing room, unbuttoning his coat as he goes and leaving the door open. Mary goes back into her memories for a moment, then throws them off and starts for her drink on the table. There is a knock on the door and Mary goes to door and opens it. Norah enters with Mary's dress, pressed)

NORAH. I was afraid you might have gone to bed. I'll hang it up for you. (Norah starts for the dressing room)

MARY (running in front of Norah to dressing-room door). My husband's in there!

NORAH. Oh.

GRANT (offstage). Did you say something, darling?

MARY. No, dear. It's just the maid with my dress. (She closes the dressing-room door. Norah drapes the dress carefully over the back of a chair) What's your name?

NORAH. Norah, Ma'am. (She takes a blanket from the bed and puts it over the back of chair)

MARY. Thank you for pressing it, Norah. I'll hang it up later. (Norah starts preparing the bed, removing spread and turning back the covers.)

NORAH. I'm sorry I was so late with it. Just as the iron got hot we got another guest.

MARY. Gracious, where did you put him?

NORAH. He's on a cot in Mr. Conover's room.

MARY. Oh, dear, that makes me feel very guilty.

NORAH. Don't you worry, Mrs. Matthews. A cot's good enough for most of them. They just come down here to get something out of Mr. Conover. Not the people we put in this room. This room is for special guests. We even had a Democrat in this bed one night.

MARY. Oh, I wish you hadn't told me that.

NORAH. He wasn't a Roosevelt Democrat. (Norah has finished with the bed and turns on the bed light on table near the bed, then turns to the service-bell cord) When you wake up in the morning just press this button and I'll have breakfast right up for you.

MARY. Thank you, Norah. Good night.

NORAH. Good night, Ma'am. (*She starts out, then stops and turns*) Oh, I was going to ask your husband but maybe you can tell me. Do you know Mrs. Thorndyke's address?

MARY. Mrs. Thorndyke?

NORAH. She forgot her glasses when she left this morning. And I know what it is to be without glasses. I want to mail them back to her.

MARY. Are you sure they're Mrs. Thorndyke's?

NORAH (*getting the glasses from pocket and showing them*). Yes, they're them Chinese kind. What women won't do! Won't they?

MARY. Yes—won't they? (*Mary places her drink on the desk with considerable emphasis, goes to dressing-room door and opens it, calling in to Grant*) Grant, can you step out for a minute? Norah wants some information.

GRANT (*offstage*). Be right with you. (*Mary goes to the window and looks out, standing immovable. Grant appears, tying his dressing gown*) Hello, Norah, What can I do for you?

NORAH. Mrs. Thorndyke left her glasses. I wanted to know where to mail them back to her.

GRANT. Oh!— (*He glances toward Mary*) —1276 Park Avenue. Shall I write it down for you?

NORAH. No, I can remember it. 1276. 76 —that's the year of the revolution, and twelve for the Twelve Commandments. (*Norah exits. Grant glances toward Mary, who raises the window sharply, her back to him. Grant retreats into the dressing room, closing the door. Mary turns, looks after him, studies the bed for a moment and then her eyes go to the overstuffed chairs. She goes into action. She removes three cushions from the overstuffed chairs, placing them in a line on the floor. She then goes to the bed and removes the sheets and blankets. Folding one sheet and one blanket, she makes a bed for one person on one side of the double bed. Then with the other sheet and blanket, she makes a bed on the three cushions on the floor. As she is finishing this, Grant enters from the dressing room in pajamas and dressing gown. He takes in the situation.*)

GRANT. Mary, what do you think you're doing? Now stop that nonsense and make up that bed again. (*Mary finishes fixing the bed on the floor*) Damn it, I'm not going to let you do this! (*Grant goes to her. Mary, ignoring him, takes off her dressing gown, switches off the lights, leaving only the bed lamp burning*) You wouldn't get any sleep down there on the floor and I wouldn't get any sleep lying there worrying about you. (*He points to the double bed. Mary crosses quickly to the double bed*)

MARY. Good night, Mr. President! (*She pops into the double bed, turning off the bed lamp. Grant looks at the bed on the floor with dismay as the curtain falls*)

ACT TWO

The living room of a suite at the Book-Cadillac Hotel in Detroit. It is furnished the way a living room in the Book-Cadillac Hotel would be furnished—in fact the Book-Cadillac has furnished it for us—a desk, a telephone, a sofa, several easy chairs, and a highboy. The pictures on the wall are surprisingly enough not French prints but modern paintings.

The entrance from the hall is upstage, center. Down right and down left are the two doors leading into the bedroom of the suite.

At rise the stage is dark; then the door to the hall opens and a bellboy enters, puts down three bags he is carrying and switches on the lights.

Mary and Grant follow him, arm-in-arm. Grant is carrying a handful of telegrams, some of them already opened.

———

BELLBOY. Well, we made it.

GRANT. Thanks! That was slick. We'd have never got through that crowd in the lobby.

BELLBOY. Remember that if you get trapped again. The service elevators are right back of the passenger elevators.

MARY. It was exciting, wasn't it? At the station, too. What a mob!

GRANT. I thought Spike would meet us. I guess he didn't get my telegram.

MARY. Just the same I'm glad he came on ahead. This is more like it.

BELLBOY. Where shall I put the bags?

GRANT. Mary, pick a room for yourself,

will you? *(Grant throws his coat and hat on a chair, goes to the desk, puts down the telegrams, and picks up the telephone. Mary opens the door of the bedroom to the left and looks in)* Hello, what room is Mr. MacManus in?

MARY. That's a nice room. *(She crosses to the right bedroom)*

GRANT *(into the telephone)*. What? *(Pause)* E. J. MacManus. *(Pause)* Ring it, will you?

MARY *(looking into the right bedroom)*. One room's as good as another. *(She turns to the bellboy)* Where are Mr. Matthews' bags?

BELLBOY. I'll bring them right up.

MARY. Well, you can put those in here. *(She exits into the right bedroom followed by Bellboy with her bags)*

GRANT *(into the telephone)*. Hello, Spike. *(Pause)* Just this minute. We were grounded in Springfield. Come on up. We're in 2519. *(Pause)* Jim? The hell he is! Telephone the desk and tell them when he gets here to send him right up to the suite. *(Pause)* We're having a drink. What will you have, an old-fashioned? *(Pause)* Right. I'll order a drink for Jim too. Come on up. *(He clicks the receiver, staying on the phone)* Room service. *(Pause)* Room service? This is 2519. Will you send up two martinis— *(Mary enters from the right bedroom)* —one old-fashioned, and a Scotch and soda right away? Thanks.

MARY. Who are all the drinks for?

GRANT. Spike and Jim.

MARY. Is Conover here?

GRANT. He's on his way up from the station. That's a good sign, Mary. It looks as though Jim's afraid somebody might get his front seat on the bandwagon. *(Grant has started opening the telegrams)* Here! Let's get to work on these telegrams. *(He hands Mary some of the wires, then goes left to sofa and sits)*

MARY. I'm not so sure that's the reason Jim came out here.

GRANT *(absorbed in the telegrams)*. Yeah?

MARY *(going to him)*. Grant, don't talk to Jim about what you're going to say tonight.

GRANT *(excitedly)*. These wires are all about the Wichita speech. They're terrific. I've never had anything like this before.

MARY. That's what I mean. Spike tried to talk you out of making that speech. So remember what I just said.

GRANT *(looking up)*. What'd you just say?

MARY. Don't talk to Jim about your speech tonight.

GRANT. O.K. Mary, listen to this one. . . . *(The Bellboy enters from the right bedroom.)*

BELLBOY. I turned on the radiator and opened the windows. You've got plenty of towels. Is there anything else I can do?

MARY. Yes, you can get the other bags.

BELLBOY. Oh, yes. Coming right up. *(He exits)*

MARY *(glancing through the telegrams)*. Grant—these are simply wonderful! You see, you didn't have to be afraid of shooting the works. That's the way they want to hear you talk.

GRANT. Just look at these, Mary—it shows how hungry the American people are for leadership.

MARY. This one's nice, Grant. It mentions your modesty and humility.

GRANT. Well, here's one who didn't like it.

MARY. Who's that?

GRANT. I don't know. Executive Secretary, Local 801. . . . *(He crumples the telegram and throws it away)*

MARY. Look, darling—they want you to speak in Omaha next Monday.

GRANT. That's nothing. They want me in New Orleans on Thursday and Atlanta on Friday.

MARY. Let's go— *(She sits on the sofa beside him)* —let's go to all three of them!

GRANT. Mary, Omaha is way back there— *(He gestures)* —New Orleans and Atlanta are way down there— *(He gestures)* —New York is over there— *(Another gesture)* —and the work on my desk is up to here. *(He indicates his chin)*

MARY. I don't know why you bother with business when this is so much fun. *(They grin at each other.)*

GRANT. Do you know, this trip has done you a lot of good? You have no right to look that young at your age! On the field at Denver, just before we took off, I had the damnedest sensation. You were standing there in the moonlight with the wind from the propeller blowing your hair and your dress—I knew we were in Denver, but you were the girl standing on the deck of the boat on our way to Victoria.

MARY (*after a reminiscent pause*). Now I'll tell you something. Remember in Victoria when we stood on the balcony of the hotel and you were telling me what the world should be like? That same boy was standing on the platform last night in Wichita.

GRANT. I'm glad you said that, Mary. It was a wonderful satisfaction, that speech —just saying what I really believed.

MARY (*she holds up the telegrams*). You see what that speech did! (*She looks down at the top telegram*) Grant, who's Herbert Bayard Swope?

(*There is a knock on the door.*)

GRANT. Come in! (*Spike enters, carrying the Detroit newspapers. Mary and Grant rise and greet him*) Hello, Spike.

SPIKE. Hi-ya.

MARY. Hello, Spike, we finally got here.

SPIKE. You had me worried. You jammed up a lot of appointments when your plane was grounded.

MARY. Don't tell Grant I said so—but there's nothing like a train.

GRANT. Those the evening papers? (*He takes the papers from Spike and starts reading them*) Hmm! Front-page spread!

SPIKE. Did the newspaper boys get you at the station?

GRANT (*sitting in chair left*). Yeah—a flock of them. (*He is still reading paper*) Mary! (*In the play Grant reads a headline that would be in a Detroit newspaper the night of the performance. This headline is changed every night*) Jim's coming out here makes things look pretty hot.

MARY. Is he staying here?

SPIKE. Yes, damn it—and I have to split my bed with him. You know what kind of split a politician takes.

MARY. That's silly. We have two bedrooms here and we don't need both of them. Grant, you're moving in with me. We're putting Jim in the other bedroom. (*Grant is absorbed in the paper*) Grant! Yoo-hoo! Mr. Candidate! Mr. President!

GRANT (*looking up*). Huh?

MARY. That got him! (*To Grant*) I'm playing a little politics for you. I'm saving Jim from sleeping with Spike. We're putting him in our extra bedroom.

GRANT. Fine! Be with you in a minute, Spike. Let me finish this editorial.

(*There is a knock on the door.*)

SPIKE. I've got some people coming to see you but they're not due this early.

(*Spike goes to the door and opens it. Conover enters*) Hello, Jim!

CONOVER. Hello, Spike. (*He greets Mary*) Mary!

MARY. So nice seeing you, Jim. We didn't expect you. (*She offers him her cheek, which he kisses. Grant rises*)

CONOVER (*going to Grant and shaking hands*). Hello, Grant! Politics agrees with you—you're looking fine.

GRANT. I feel great. Look, headlines and a damn good editorial! It's about the Wichita speech—the responsibility of the labor unions. Says it's about time somebody brought it out into the open.

MARY. Jim, it was the best speech Grant ever made. It was the first time I felt sure he could be elected. You never heard such applause.

CONOVER. Mary, if applause elected Presidents, William Jennings Bryan would have had three terms.

GRANT. It's good to see you.

MARY. We're putting you in our other bedroom.

CONOVER. Fine! My bags are down in the lobby.

GRANT. What news have you brought us? I'm certainly glad you're here.

MARY. Yes, it will give you a chance to see Grant in front of an audience.

CONOVER. Oh, I'm not making any public appearances. I'm not supposed to be in Detroit. Don't let anyone know I'm in town. I thought I should come out and bring you up to date on things and go over the situation. What are you talking about here tonight?

GRANT. Well, it's the last speech of the tour, Jim. It's got a little bit of everything.

CONOVER. Anything controversial?

MARY. Not for anybody that agrees with him. I want you to see these telegrams. (*Mary goes to the desk*)

SPIKE. They got here three hours late. (*To Grant*) I was pretty sure you'd make the broadcast. You don't go on until after the banquet.

MARY. Is this another banquet?

SPIKE. Yeah.

MARY. Then we'd better have dinner before we go. (*Mary picks up the telephone and speaks into it*) Room service, please. What do you want to eat, Grant?

(*Spike takes the telegrams from Mary and hands them to Conover who glances at them casually.*)

GRANT. Anything that's ready—hamburger if they've got it.

SPIKE. I won't have time to eat with you. Better make it snappy. You're going to be busy.

MARY. Jim, what shall I order for you?

CONOVER. I'll have some chicken—and some coffee.

MARY. You can't have chicken and eat with us. I never want to see another chicken.

GRANT. Every time we sit down in a chair, somebody puts chicken in front of us. (*He pulls up a trouser-leg and points to his calf*) Look—pin-feathers!

CONOVER. All right. I'll have hamburger too—hamburger and onions.

MARY (*into the telephone*). Room service? (*Pause*) This is room— (*She looks inquiringly toward the men*)

SPIKE. 2519.

MARY. 2519. Have you any hamburger? (*Pause*) That's fine. Three hamburger steaks, one with onions—two without, damn it, and whatever goes with it—except spinach. (*To the men*) Anybody want dessert? Ice cream's always safe.

GRANT. Fine!

CONOVER. None for me.

MARY (*into the telephone*). One chocolate ice cream. And three coffees. Will you hurry it, please? (*She hangs up. There is a knock on the door*) Come in! (*The Bellboy enters with Grant's bags. He is followed by Waiter with a tray of drinks. To the Bellboy*) Put all the bags in there. (*She indicates the right bedroom. She takes a cocktail from the tray*) We ordered a highball for you, Jim.

CONOVER. Thanks.

(*The waiter serves the others their drinks.*)

SPIKE. Are you the floor waiter?

WAITER. Yes, sir.

SPIKE. There's a dinner order in. Hurry it up for us, will you? (*To Grant*) I've got a lot of people lined up for you to see.

GRANT. Can't I see them after the banquet?

SPIKE. You were supposed to see them this afternoon, but you didn't get in, so I bunched them all between seven and seven-thirty.

CONOVER. Well, I can't have dinner here if a lot of people are coming in.

SPIKE. No, it's O.K. I can keep this room clear. I'll juggle the visiting firemen

between the two bedrooms. Grant can duck in and say hello, and come back and eat. We'll clear them all up in a hurry.

(*The Bellboy enters from the right bedroom.*)

BELLBOY. I've turned off the radiator and closed the windows. Anything else I can do?

GRANT. No, thanks. (*Grant tips the Bellboy, who exits. The Waiter goes to Grant who takes the check and writes on it*)

CONOVER. Are you touching on labor again tonight?

GRANT. No!

MARY (*cutting in quickly*). Grant, we won't have time to dress after dinner. We ought to be changing now.

GRANT. Yes, we can be changed by the time dinner gets here.

(*The Waiter starts out and Mary stops him.*)

MARY. Waiter! Another drink, Jim?

CONOVER. No, thanks.

MARY. Spike?

SPIKE. Not now.

MARY. How about you, Grant? Another cocktail while you're dressing?

GRANT. I don't dare. I've got to make a speech.

MARY (*to the Waiter*). Bring another martini to the bedroom.

WAITER. Right away, Ma'am. (*He exits*)

MARY (*moving toward the right bedroom*). That's the difference between Grant and me—I'd rather be tight than be President. (*She exits*)

GRANT. Spike, we haven't opened all those telegrams. Look through them, will you? (*He starts to exit*)

CONOVER. Grant, while you're dressing, have you got a copy of your speech tonight that I could be glancing at?

GRANT (*at the bedroom door*). It's not a set speech, Jim. I'm talking from notes.

CONOVER. Could I be looking over the notes?

GRANT. They're just some memos I scribbled down—I'm sorry, Jim, they wouldn't mean a thing to you. (*Spike has picked up the telegrams*) I'll tell you what you can read. Spike, show him some more of my fan mail. (*Grant exits into the right bedroom. Spike turns to look at Conover*)

CONOVER (*angrily*). You're a hell of a campaign manager!

SPIKE (*on the defensive*). That's why I

wired for you, Jim. He's gotten away from me.

CONOVER. It's a damn shame! The boys in the Northwest and all along the Coast —they were swinging right in behind him. Then he had to stick out his chin in Wichita.

SPIKE. How much damage has he done?

CONOVER. We may have lost labor. I must have had thirty calls after that speech. How did you let it happen?

SPIKE. I talked him out of that labor stuff in Denver—that is, I gave him something to use instead—local stuff—Rocky Mountain stuff.

CONOVER. Didn't you get a look at the speech for Wichita?

SPIKE. No, and I'll tell you why. She— *(He points to the right bedroom)* —knew he was planning to talk about labor in Denver and when he didn't she spent the rest of the night tossing harpoons into him. But the next day on the plane to Wichita they were clubby as hell—and I couldn't get any advance copy of the speech. You just sent the wrong dame with him!

CONOVER. I even talked him into taking her along.

SPIKE. When we get back to New York, Kay can straighten him out. She put this Presidential bee in his bonnet. She never tears Grant down. She always builds him up. If you ask me, that's why he fell for her. But that doesn't help us tonight.

CONOVER. What are you afraid of tonight?

SPIKE. I don't know— *(The telephone rings)* —but she's too damn happy. *(Spike answers the telephone)* Hello. *(Pause)* Oh —give me the desk. *(To Conover)* That's why I sent for you. We can't take a chance on his making another mistake here tonight. *(Into the telephone)* Hello. This is MacManus. There are some people down there to see Mr. Matthews. And there are a lot more coming. Send them all up to the twenty-fifth floor, Parlor B, and tell them to wait for me there. *(He hangs up. Then speaks to Conover)* You've got to find out what he's talking about here. *(Spike picks up telegrams and joins Conover on the sofa)*

CONOVER. That's what I was trying to do —and you saw how far I got. *(Conover glances through some of the telegrams, then tosses them aside)*

SPIKE. Well, keep after him.

CONOVER. If you've got people coming to see him, what chance have I?

SPIKE. I wasn't sure you were going to get here. I figured I had to put some kind of pressure on him. I've got everybody— dairy farmers, automobile people, even the labor boys, mad as they are.

CONOVER. Maybe they ought to be talking to Mrs. Matthews.

SPIKE. Look, Jim, this guy's vulnerable. He's got the bug.

CONOVER. That's what I was counting on. How bad has he got it?

SPIKE. He wants to be President, all right. So what I keep throwing at him is votes—get those votes—don't lose those votes. *(Conover rises. Spike looks up from the telegrams he has been reading)* Say, maybe that Wichita speech didn't do as much harm as we thought it did.

CONOVER. Oh, those are just from people.

SPIKE. They don't count, eh?

CONOVER. You don't see any signed "State Chairman," do you?

SPIKE. Don't kid yourself, this guy does something to people. I've been on a lot of campaigns. They don't shake hands with Grant just to say they've shaken hands with him. They're up there with a light in their eyes—they practically mob him. If he gets away from us, you may be heading a "Stop Matthews" movement.

CONOVER. Stopping him wouldn't be any trouble. He hasn't any organization. I don't want to stop him. I think we can elect him, if we can keep him in line. *(Spike is studying another telegram.)*

SPIKE. Say, Jim, did you arrange this?

CONOVER. What?

SPIKE. He's speaking in New York—the 23rd—Foreign Policy Association.

CONOVER. The hell he is! Why doesn't he consult us?

SPIKE. He didn't even mention it to me. Just because I don't trust him doesn't mean he shouldn't trust me.

CONOVER. That forces us right out into the open. What's that date?

SPIKE. The twenty-third.

CONOVER. He can't speak there and pretend he's not a candidate. Besides that, he's got to go along with us on foreign policy. Our big chance to win is with the foreign vote. Well, I guess we've got to fence him in. Damn!

SPIKE. He wants that nomination. He wants to be President.

CONOVER. Then I'd better face him with some people who can deliver delegates—people he knows he has to have to win—I'd like to throw them at him all at once.

SPIKE. Better line up a big shot from labor.

CONOVER. Yes—Bill Hardy would do that for me. I could get Senator Lauterback to scare hell out of him on the farm vote.

SPIKE. You'd better have Kay there. I know damn well he listens to her.

CONOVER. Who would talk for business? Look around at the banquet tonight, Spike, and see if there's anybody who could be useful.

(There is a knock at the door.)

SPIKE. Damn it. I told them to send everybody to Parlor B. *(He goes to door and opens it. It is the Waiter)*

WAITER. I have the dinner—and the extra cocktail.

SPIKE. Wheel it in!

(The Waiter wheels in a table with service for three and Mary's second cocktail. Spike goes to the bedroom door and knocks.)

GRANT *(offstage)*. Yes?

SPIKE. Dinner's here.

GRANT *(offstage)*. We'll be right out.

SPIKE. Does Mary want her other cocktail in there?

MARY *(offstage)*. Cocktails don't have to come to me. I come to them. *(Mary enters in a dinner dress. The Waiter serves Mary the cocktail)*

WAITER. I have the dinner right outside. *(He exits and returns immediately with portable oven. During the following scene, he sets the table and puts three chairs in their proper places)*

SPIKE *(going to the bedroom door)*. Grant, is your room free?

GRANT *(offstage)*. All set. I'm just tying my tie.

SPIKE. When you're through, will you unlock the hall door to your room?

GRANT *(offstage)*. Okay.

MARY *(to the Waiter)*. Serve it as soon as you're ready.

SPIKE *(hurriedly going to the other bedroom)*. I'd better unlock the hall door to this one, too. *(Spike exits into left bedroom)*

CONOVER *(to Mary)*. My dear, that's a little unfair.

MARY. What?

CONOVER. I'm afraid that instead of listening to Grant they'll be just looking at you tonight.

MARY. Thank you, Jim. I'm so willing to believe that, I'm going to pretend you're not a politician.

(Spike returns from the left bedroom.)

SPIKE. All right. Here we go. I'll bring in the first batch of patriots. *(To Mary)* Remind Grant they've got votes.

MARY. Spike does take the nobility out of a crusade.

SPIKE *(at the hall doorway)*. Am I expected to be noble? On my salary! *(He exits into the hall)*

CONOVER. Why don't you just spend the evening here with me? You've probably read Grant's speech anyway, haven't you?

MARY. I'm sorry you won't be there.

CONOVER. I'll listen to it on the radio—if I can get a radio—and if I can't—what's he speaking about?

MARY. Oh, I think we can get you a radio. *(She goes to the telephone. Grant enters from the right bedroom)*

GRANT. I damn near left these notes in my other suit. *(He starts looking through some notes he has in his hand)*

MARY *(into the telephone)*. Could you have a radio sent up to 2519 right away? *(Pause)* It's very important. *(Pause)* Thank you! *(She hangs up)* It looks as though you'll have to listen, Jim. They think you can have one.

CONOVER *(to Grant)*. If you want to rehearse any of that, Grant, I'll be glad to have you try it out on me.

GRANT. I'll give you the start— *(He speaks as though he were addressing a large auditorium)* Ladies—and members of the Automotive Council of Detroit. I know that I am among friends here tonight—and it would be unfriendly of me not to talk to you with utter frankness and naked honesty. In the economic anarchy we are facing today—

(The Waiter has taken two plates of food out of the portable oven.)

WAITER. Who's with onions?

CONOVER *(sourly)*. I'm with onions.

(Mary goes to the center place at the table and sits. The two men go to either side and sit. The Waiter serves them.)

WAITER. Watch the plates—they're very hot.

GRANT. Looks good—I can hardly wait.

Waiter, you've got a starving man on your hands.

WAITER. Watch the plate. I'll bring the dessert in fifteen minutes. (*He exits, with the portable oven*)

GRANT. Ah—meat! And can I use it? (*He has his knife and fork poised when Spike enters from the right bedroom*)

SPIKE. Grant, your public is waiting.

GRANT. My hamburger's waiting.

SPIKE. Hamburgers don't vote. These are dairy farmers. (*He goes to Grant and hands him a slip of paper, pointing to a name at the top*) The fellow with the mustache is the one to play for.

GRANT. Just the Number Five handshake, Spike?

SPIKE. No, a little talk. You know— cows, butter, milk, cheese—since the war American cheese has become big industry.

GRANT. What do I know about American cheese?

SPIKE. Walk this way and meet three perfect specimens. (*Grant rises and starts out*) Remember— (*Grant turns*) They mean votes! (*Grant exits into the right bedroom*) Well—now I'll set 'em up in the other alley. (*He exits into the hall*)

MARY (*eagerly*). How do you think Grant's doing? What are your reports?

CONOVER. First let me tell you about my reports on you. You've done a great job, and I want to congratulate you.

MARY. Well, I'd like to admit something if I could be sure it wouldn't be used against me. I've enjoyed it—every minute of it.

CONOVER. Even the speeches?

MARY. That's been the best part of it. I don't mean just listening to Grant. I mean listening to the people—feeling the way they respond. Of course they laugh and yell when he talks about the troubles he's had getting things through in Washington . . .

CONOVER (*busily eating*). Yes, I've heard those laughs. He does it very cleverly. That's what they like to hear.

MARY. Jim, over the radio you only hear the audience when it's making noise. What you don't hear is the silence—when Grant has them so that they're not thinking of themselves—when he has them thinking of the country—that's when it takes your breath away.

CONOVER. I'm glad to hear Grant can do

that. I know how effective it can be in a speaker.

MARY. Jim, I'm not talking about Grant. When they rush up after the speeches—I wish you could see their faces. You know, I'd forgotten how good it was to be with people—I used to see a lot of them when Grant first started and had small plants— when we moved to New York I got too far away from them— They're so eager to do whatever is the best thing to do—and they're so quick—they're so intelligent. (*She laughs*) They've thrown a couple of questions at Grant that had him stopped cold. He just had to admit he didn't know enough to answer them. And they liked him for it.

CONOVER. That's smart. Shows he uses his head.

MARY (*sitting back in her chair and regarding Conover quizzically*). Jim, you fascinate me. You have such a complete lack of faith in sincerity—and you're so sincere about it. (*Conover gives her an understanding smile*) What puzzles me is that I dislike so thoroughly the way your mind works—and yet I'm so very fond of you.

CONOVER. It is puzzling, isn't it, because I feel the same way toward you. (*Mary pats his hand with fond reproof.*)

MARY. You're so cynical. (*Conover pats her hand in same manner.*)

CONOVER. You're so unrealistic. (*They grin at each other. Grant enters from the right bedroom.*)

MARY (*to Grant*). Well, how's the farmer's choice?

GRANT (*going to the table*). After the beautiful things I have just said about cows, I shouldn't touch this hamburger. It's like eating an old friend. But I'm going to. (*He sits down and gets ready to eat the hamburger. Spike enters from the left bedroom*)

SPIKE. Ah, back from the pastures. Wipe off your feet and come in and meet the A. F. of L.

GRANT. Look, Spike, give me a chance to eat . . .

SPIKE. Nope. This is a crisis. I have to know you're holding the A. F. of L. in there while I sneak the C.I.O. into the other bedroom.

GRANT. Put them both in the same room. I'll talk to them both at the same time.

SPIKE. Little Boy Blue, haven't you

heard? They ain't keeping steady company any more. Besides these aren't big shots—just small fry—officers in the locals.

GRANT. They're both labor groups. They both want the same thing. That's what I've been talking about all this time—getting people to work together—now let's put it into action.

SPIKE. Now, boss . . .

GRANT. I'm serious about this, Spike. Tell those men in there you're bringing in the C.I.O., and then I'll come in and talk to them!

(Spike shrugs and exits into the left bedroom. Mary preens herself, looking proudly from Grant to Conover.)

CONOVER. Grant, aren't you just asking for trouble?

GRANT. Jim, I've got both organizations working in my plants. I can walk into a recreation room where C.I.O. and A. F. of L. men are there together and talk to them—talk labor to them. Bill Green and Phil Murray will both sit down with each other. The big boys in labor are all right, except for Lewis. *(He points to the left bedroom)* This is the type of men we've got to get together.

CONOVER. I don't mind your having your head in the clouds—but I wish you'd keep your feet in the voting booth.

GRANT. Jim, if I can ever make people like these in the next room see something bigger than their job as head of their own locals and the little power they get from that . . .

MARY *(to Conover)*. There may be some votes in that, too.

CONOVER. One of the things I came down to talk to you about—I got a very bad reaction to your speech in Wichita.

GRANT. Did you read those telegrams?

CONOVER. You may have picked up a few votes there in the auditorium, but you've chilled off most of the labor leaders in the country. I know! I've talked to them!

GRANT. I said that business had to give labor a voice in management. That didn't chill them off, did it?

CONOVER. No, no, that was all right—for labor.

GRANT. I said that labor had to have a fairer share of the profits. Did they object to that?

CONOVER. No, damn it—it was the stand you took on strikes.

GRANT *(earnestly)*. No, Jim, not on strikes. I mentioned only one kind of strike. I asked labor to give the people of this country the answer to this question: "Is there any moral justification for the jurisdictional strike?" Can you answer that question? Can the labor leaders you talked to answer that question?

CONOVER. Of course they can't. That's what makes them so sore. Too bad you didn't talk about the other kind of strikes.

GRANT. All right, it's true—some unions are abusing their right to strike at this time. They're sacrificing the country for their own special interest. What do you propose to do? Take their right to strike away from them? Freedom of the press is being abused. Do you want to take that right away from publishers?

CONOVER *(grudgingly)*. Well—labor's pretty sore about what you said about opening their books, too.

GRANT. Not all of them are. Some of the biggest and best unions in the country have opened their books.

MARY. Jim, the audience was full of union men—I don't mean union leaders, I mean union members—and they cheered Grant. I had a feeling they'd like to get a look at those books themselves.

CONOVER. Some of that money goes into campaign contributions.

(Spike enters from the left bedroom.)

GRANT. Well?

SPIKE. No dice. They're even mad they're in the same hotel together.

GRANT. That makes me pretty mad, too.

SPIKE. Boss, you've got to speak to them.

GRANT *(he throws down napkin and rises)*. Of course I'll speak to them. How am I going to do what I want to do if I don't speak to them?

SPIKE. Here are the names. *(He hands Grant a slip of paper)* Watch out for the little guy they call Mac. *(Grant angrily grabs the paper, and exits into the left bedroom)* Now for some counter-espionage. *(Spike exits into the hall)*

MARY *(earnestly)*. Jim, Grant's got something. Don't take it away from him! When he's just cockeyed drunk with sincerity people can't resist him!

CONOVER. That statement sounds as though it includes you, too.

MARY. Let me straighten you out about Grant and me. Our personal relations are strictly political.

CONOVER. I thought I saw Grant throw

a look or two at you tonight that wasn't entirely impersonal.

MARY. Jim, you're a bachelor, aren't you?

CONOVER. Theoretically. Why?

MARY. It's just that if you'd been married, you'd understand?

CONOVER. Understand what?

MARY. When a man and woman have been married for a long time even their closest friends can't always tell whether they're still in love with each other. They themselves wonder about it sometimes.

CONOVER. Well, then the trip's accomplished something—if you're at the point of wondering.

MARY. No, there are things that happen that make you sure—little things that don't really mean anything except that you know how much they do mean. For instance, Grant found out once the girls at school used to call me Maizie. He knew I hated it. So sometimes he used to call me Maizie—just to tease me—but you don't tease people that way unless you love each other. Well, Maizie doesn't live here any more. And another thing—Grant always hated to hear me swear—whenever I let go with something—he used to smack me on the behind—hard. I've done a lot of swearing on this trip—

CONOVER. And no smacks?

MARY (wistfully). It's a small request—but I'd give anything for a good smack on the behind.

CONOVER. I wish there were something I could do about that.

(Spike enters from the right bedroom.)

SPIKE. Still in with them?

MARY. Yes, and all's quiet on the Western front.

SPIKE. Well, the Eastern front is ready. (Grant enters from the left bedroom, closing the door behind him.)

GRANT (to Spike). Are the C.I.O. boys in there?

SPIKE. Yes—and in what I would call an ugly mood.

GRANT. Keep your back turned, Jim. (Grant opens the left bedroom door) This way, gentlemen. (Three stony-faced labor leaders march in front the left bedroom, and Grant leads them toward the right bedroom. Mary springs up to greet them. As each one is introduced, they shake hands with Mary, then continue into the right bedroom) This is Mrs. Matthews! Mr. Vincent.

MARY. How do you do?

GRANT. Mr. Solly.

MARY. How do you do?

GRANT. Mr. Mack.

MARY. How do you do?

GRANT. Right in here, gentlemen. (He opens the right bedroom door and they file in. Grant turns and gives a broad wink to Mary and Conover and follows in after them, closing the door. Spike puts his fingers in his ears and stands shuddering as though he expects an explosion behind him, then relaxes with a grin)

SPIKE. You know, Grant might be able to unite the United Nations. (He starts out, sees Grant's food, walks to Grant's place, sits and picks up the knife and fork)

MARY. Spike, don't you dare touch that! (Spike rises.)

SPIKE. All right, I can starve. But that's the way you make Communists. (He exits into the hall)

MARY. Poor Grant. He's not getting a thing to eat. (She goes to the desk and gets a cigarette from her evening bag and lights it)

CONOVER. I was hoping we three could have a quiet dinner together and talk.

MARY. We'll see you after we get back here.

CONOVER. I'd like to go over with Grant what he's speaking about tonight. Tell me something about it.

MARY. Well, it's his last speech of the trip. It's sort of a summary.

CONOVER. Detroit's a dangerous city politically—almost anything you say here is controversial.

MARY. Isn't a Presidential campaign supposed to be controversial?

CONOVER. Yes, but they've had a lot of trouble here—strikes—race riots—and for some reason or other it seems to be the headquarters of the lunatic fringe.

MARY. You mean the subversive groups . . .

CONOVER. Mary, subversive is a very dangerous word— (Apprehensively) Grant's not using that word in his speech tonight, is he?

MARY. I think Grant's saving anything like that—and the international situation —for his speech in New York.

CONOVER. Oh, is he speaking in New York?

MARY. Yes! *(Grant enters from the right bedroom)* Still alive?

GRANT. Yes, and so are they. *(He goes to the table)* As a matter of fact, the Congress of Industrial Organization has just extended an invitation to the American Federation of Labor to have a glass of beer.

CONOVER *(with a bit of a grin)*. Under whose jurisdiction?

GRANT. The Arcade Bar and Grill! *(He starts to eat)*

CONOVER. Mary tells me you're making a speech in New York.

GRANT *(gratified)*. Yes. The twenty-third. Foreign Policy Association! That's moving into the big time!

CONOVER. You couldn't postpone that, could you? I don't see how you can open up on the international situation and still pretend you're not a candidate.

GRANT. I didn't think I could turn it down.

CONOVER. Well, it's too late, I guess. *(Disturbed)* I couldn't very well advise you about something I didn't know anything about.

(Spike enters from the left bedroom.)

SPIKE. Okay, Grant, if you're ready!

GRANT *(starting to eat again)*. Spike, they can't be more important than this hamburger.

SPIKE. Well, they're all your friends. It's the Detroit tycoon set.

GRANT *(rising with alacrity)*. Oh, somebody I really want to see? You're slipping, Spike. *(He exits into the left bedroom)*

SPIKE. I've got one more set. They're gate crashers. Even I don't know who they are. *(He exits into the hall)*

MARY *(putting out her cigarette)*. I wonder whether I have time to sneak a look in a mirror? *(She starts for the right bedroom, then stops. Conover rises)* Oh, I forgot to thank you for telling Grant the gossip about me.

CONOVER. I didn't tell him.

MARY. Well, somebody must have told him.

CONOVER. Has he said anything?

MARY. No, but he's very rude to all army Majors. *(Conover chuckles)* And it's so unfair to those poor Majors. My Major's been a Colonel for months.

CONOVER. I hadn't heard about that.

MARY. Jim, your secret service works backwards. They keep secrets from you! *(Grant enters from the left bedroom.)*

GRANT. Mary, Sam Parrish is in here. He'd like to say hello to you.

MARY. Good! I haven't seen Sam for ages.

CONOVER. Wait, Mary! Grant, I'd like to have a few words with Parrish myself. Could you have him step in here?

GRANT. Sure, I'll tell him.

CONOVER. Oh, Grant—don't let the others know I'm here.

(Grant exits into the left bedroom. Conover moves up out of range of door, pulling his chair with him.)

MARY. We've known Sam for years. We're very fond of him.

CONOVER. So am I. He's raised a lot of money for the party.

(Sam Parrish enters from the left bedroom. He is the successful American business man and looks it. He sees Mary and goes to her.)

SAM. Hello, Mary! You're a sight for sore eyes! *(He kisses her)*

MARY. Hello, Sam!

SAM. Mary, I'll be in New York for our annual dinner on the seventeenth. This time it's on me!

MARY. No, Sam, you're having dinner with us.

SAM. My, you're just as pretty as you ever were! I could eat you with a spoon. . . . *(He swings Mary around exuberantly and catches sight of Conover)* Why, Jim Conover, you old son-of-a-gun!

CONOVER. Hi-ya, Sam!

SAM. What are you doing here?

CONOVER. Take it easy, Sam. You're the only one in Detroit who knows I am here —and keep it to yourself!

SAM. What the hell's going on? Say— *(He looks from Conover to Mary and then the dawn breaks)* Damn it, I might have known! Jim, do you know you're psychic? I'm due in Washington on the eighteenth —I had it all planned to come and see you with the idea of selling you Grant Matthews for President, and damn it you beat me to it. Frankly, I was going to bribe you—with the biggest campaign contribution you ever saw.

CONOVER *(grabbing Sam's hand and shaking it)*. That's a date, Sam! Lunch in Washington on the eighteenth and bring cash!

SAM (*gleefully*). Mary, you go right home and start packing. You're moving into the White House. Give me another kiss! (*He kisses her again*) I've never been so happy about anything in my life. Wait until I tell Hilda!

CONOVER. Sam, you're not telling anybody, including Hilda.

MARY. How is Hilda? Is she coming to the banquet?

SAM. No, damn it, she's in bed with the flu. She's so mad she's going to miss Grant's speech she's not fit to live with. Look—why don't you call her up? Niagara 2956.

MARY. I'd better call her now because I'm not sure you and Hilda will be speaking to us after Grant's speech tonight. (*She goes to the telephone and picks up the receiver*)

CONOVER (*to Mary, sharply*). Why do you say that?

SAM (*to Conover*). The last time I was in New York, Grant and I had a hell of a knockdown drag-out fight about reconversion and full employment.

CONOVER (*to Mary*). Mary, is that what Grant's talking about tonight?

MARY (*into the telephone*). Just a minute. (*To Sam*) What's that number again, Sam?

SAM. Niagara 2956.

MARY (*into the telephone*). Niagara 2956.

SAM (*to Conover*). You know Grant—likes to talk like a radical, but, hell, anybody that's made as much money as Grant has is a sound American.

(*Grant enters from the left bedroom.*)

GRANT. The other boys thought they ought to hurry over there, Sam. Why don't you stick around a while and go over with us?

SAM. No, I've got to go with them. I'm chairman of the committe.

GRANT. You can catch them at the elevator. I'll let you out this way. (*He takes Sam to the hall door*)

SAM. I'll come back after the banquet. Got something to talk to you about, eh, Jim? (*He gives Conover a wink, then to Grant*) That was a hell of a good speech you made in Wichita. I could go along with two-thirds of it—especially that stuff about strikes. The other third—I suppose you've got to say those things—but look out people don't get the idea you're too

far to the left. Talk to you about it later.

MARY (*into the telephone*). Keep trying and call me when you get them. (*She hangs up*)

SAM. See you later, Mary.

MARY. Good-bye, Sam.

SAM (*shaking hands with Grant*). Damn it, Grant! I'll be telling people I knew you when.

GRANT. Don't tell them yet!

SAM (*outside the door*). Hey, wait! Going down! (*Grant closes the door after him*)

CONOVER (*accusingly*). You're talking about reconversion and full employment tonight.

GRANT. Touching on them, among other things. (*He lights a cigarette*)

CONOVER. What angle are you taking?

GRANT. We talked about it in Washington. You know how I stand.

CONOVER. In Washington you were pretty specific. You're not being that specific here tonight?

GRANT. You're damn right I am!

CONOVER. What are you going to say?

GRANT. I'm going to tell them they did a great job in war production—and they did! But I'm going to remind them there wasn't any risk in that— The Government paid them for it. They had their engineering brains, and plenty of manpower to do the work.

CONOVER. All right. Why don't you let it go at that?

GRANT. Oh, no! I've got to tell them that now they're up against the test. Now they're on their own. They talk about how they want to save the private-enterprise system. All right, now they've got a chance to do it!

CONOVER (*agreeably*). Yes?

GRANT. They're not going to save it by lowering production so they can raise prices. And they're not going to save it by closing down plants to cut down competition. They're not going to save it if they don't work with unions instead of against them. And those babies who are stirring up war veterans to fight labor— I'm going to take their hide off!

CONOVER. Grant, you can't do that!

GRANT. Jim, you know reconversion goes deeper than re-tooling our plants. We need a moral reconversion. Take full employment—I don't mean the Bill—I mean the principle of it. What's behind most of the opposition to full employment—behind opposing the whole idea of the Government supplying work. To give private enterprise the chance to supply the employment? Nuts! It's to keep prices up on everything but labor. Let labor starve for a while! Jim, there isn't going to be a free-enterprise system if it means that men are free to starve!

CONOVER. Grant, you can't say those things now, and you can't say them here! This town is one of my best sources for silent money!

GRANT. You'll have to take your chances on the silent money, Jim!

MARY. What is silent money?

CONOVER (ignoring her). I warn you, Grant, you can't get out on this limb before the nomination.

MARY. People ought to know where he stands before they nominate him.

CONOVER (angrily). The people have damn little to say about the nomination. You two have lived in this country all your lives. Haven't you got that through your heads yet? You're not nominated by the people—you're nominated by the politicians! Why? Because the voters are too damned lazy to vote in the primaries! Well, politicians are not lazy! Remember what happened to Willkie in Wisconsin!

GRANT. They've got to know what I think, Jim! I told you that from the start. I've got to be on record.

CONOVER. All right—but not here—not tonight! Later. When you're out in Nebraska or Oklahoma.

(Spike enters from the right bedroom.)

SPIKE. O.K., Grant. This is the last group. And are they fruity?

CONOVER. Stall them, Spike. We're discussing something.

GRANT. No, Jim, I'm seeing them. (Grant turns to Spike) Who are they?

SPIKE. I don't know. They call themselves the Americans Incorruptible.

GRANT. I never heard of them.

SPIKE. They're dressed for the McKinley campaign. I didn't take their names. The Head Incorruptible is the fat dame with the big cowcatcher.

GRANT. What's their angle? What are they for?

MARY. With a name like that they're not for anything. They're against something.

SPIKE. Yes. (He takes Grant's cigarette away from him) Let's take no chances! But remember—they've got votes!

(Grant opens the door to the right bedroom, looks in and then turns back to Spike.)

GRANT. They shouldn't have! (He exits into the right bedroom. Mary crosses to the sofa and picks up a newspaper and starts reading the editorial on Grant)

SPIKE. I think I'd better go and air out Parlor B. (He starts out. The telephone rings)

MARY. That's probably Hilda Parrish for me.

SPIKE (into the telephone). Hello . . . This is MacManus. (He shakes head negatively at Mary) It's for you, Jim. (Spike exits. Conover goes to the desk and picks up the receiver)

CONOVER (into the telephone, casually as though talking to an old political friend). Hello. Oh, hello. How are you? (Pause) Who told you I was here—Sam? (Pause) Where are you? (Pause) All right. I'll come up to your room. (He hangs up and turns to Mary) Mary, will you tell Grant— (The telephone rings again)

MARY (drops the paper and starts for the telephone). That must be Hilda.

CONOVER. Tell Grant I'll be right back. (He exits into the hall)

(The waiter enters with ice cream and coffee; he pours the coffee.)

MARY (into the telephone). Hello . . . Oh, hello, Hilda. (Pause) This is Mary . . . Mary Matthews! (Pause) Yes. I'm here with Grant. I'm so sorry you're sick. (Pause) Well, if it isn't too much for you we'd love to run out for a few minutes after the banquet. (Pause) Good. Oh, Grant's busy in the next room with some women. (She laughs) No, he's safe. There's a whole committee of them. (Pause) All right . . . see you later. Good-bye, dear. (Mary hangs up and turns to the Waiter) Have you the check?

WAITER. Yes, Ma'am. (Waiter hands Mary a pencil and offers the check. She starts writing on the check)

MARY. I'll write your tip on the check.

WAITER. Is your husband Grant Matthews?

MARY. Yes.

WAITER. He certainly don't pull any punches, does he?

MARY (smiling). You said that just in time. (She writes the tip on the check and *hands it to the Waiter. He looks at it and smiles broadly)*

WAITER. Oh, thank you! *(He hurries out)*

GRANT *(entering from the right bedroom, carrying his hat and coat, which he places on a table near the door).* Well, we've lost the Americans Incorruptible.

MARY *(taking a cup of coffee).* Who were they? What did they want?

GRANT *(sitting down to his ice cream and coffee).* They don't want America to be too harsh on poor little Germany and Japan. We shouldn't have gotten into it in the first place!

MARY. Oh, that crowd! Against war—but we may have to fight the Russians!

GRANT. Exactly! I wound up making a campaign speech for Stalin. *(He looks around)* Where's Jim?

MARY. He'll be back in a minute. He had a telephone call. Grant, what is silent money?

GRANT. Oh, it's a way they get around the Hatch Act.

MARY. What's the Hatch Act?

GRANT. It's a law they passed a few years ago about campaign funds. Only individuals can give money and nobody more than $5,000, and you have to account for how it's spent. It's a very pretty law—and we feel very moral that it's on the books —but it just doesn't work.

MARY. There must have been some reason for passing it.

GRANT. Yes, there was! It had gotten to be a bad situation. But you know how we do things in this country sometimes. When human nature gets to behaving like human nature, they pass a law repealing human nature. But the Hatch Act is too tough. So men who can afford it, walk in and put silent money down on the barrelhead—cash that can't be traced. It's been done by both parties before the law was passed and since. I've told you before, Mary, there's damn little difference between Democrats and Republicans.

MARY. But if silent money's illegal, I don't think you should take it!

GRANT. Oh, I wouldn't take it. That would be Jim's business.

MARY. But, Grant— *(She puts her coffee cup on the table)*

GRANT *(stopping her).* Now, Mary, we both drank during Prohibition, didn't we? Put it down to political education, the

way the PAC does. *(Seeing she is still troubled)* I can't be too righteous about taking silent money. I've given it.

MARY. If you take money, you have to pay it back some way.

GRANT *(indignantly).* Mary! You know damn well I'm not for sale!

MARY *(sharply).* You've arranged that very neatly in your mind, Grant. All they have to do is buy Conover! I warned you the Presidency was a great temptation!

GRANT *(after a tight-lipped pause).* You certainly have a gift for making it tough for me.

MARY *(distressed with herself).* I know. I hear myself saying those things. I suppose it's a gift I picked up in exchange for some illusions.

GRANT *(with sober reasoning).* Mary, people change. We've both changed. Life does that to you. We would have been happier if we could have stayed the two kids who went on a honeymoon to Victoria. I'm just as unhappy as you are that we didn't.

(There is a pause. Mary moves about the room restlessly, then turns the conversation to a less personal subject.)

MARY. I'm sorry Jim got a line on what you're going to say here.

GRANT. Yes, damn it! I was all keyed up for tonight's speech.

MARY *(disturbed).* Are you going to change it?

GRANT. Oh, no! Don't worry. I'm going to speak my mind about reconversion.

MARY. Grant, you have to! You told labor they had to take the responsibility that goes with their power! You certainly have to be just as frank with business!

GRANT. I'm going to! Jim's argument was just not to say it here in Detroit.

MARY. In Wichita you said what you really believed. *(She goes to Grant)* Remember the satisfaction it gave you? I hope you feel that way tonight.

GRANT. I'd like to feel that way all the time. But you know yourself, you get into spots where you just can't afford it. *(He turns away. Mary realizes Grant is torn between ambition and integrity. She speaks to him quietly and sincerely)*

MARY. Grant—you know you don't have to be President.

GRANT *(the big liar).* Oh—I don't even expect to be! *(Then with deep sincerity)*

But I know this much—I could do a lot of good.

MARY (*smoothing his hair*). Well, Grant, you may have to make up your mind whether you want that inner satisfaction or . . .

(*Conover enters from the outer hall.*)

GRANT (*rising and putting on his coat*). Hello, where's Spike? It's getting late. We ought to be going.

CONOVER. He may be getting the car around. Grant, before you go, I'd like to pick up where we left off about your speech tonight.

GRANT. Jim, we haven't got time for it. Let's talk about my speech after I've made it.

(*Spike enters from the left bedroom.*)

SPIKE. I hate to pull this on you, Grant, but there's one more delegation.

GRANT. To hell with them! Tell them I've left.

SPIKE (*handing a slip of paper to Grant*). You can't do that. They might see you on your way out.

GRANT (*taking the slip and glancing at it*). Okay. (*He starts for the left bedroom*)

MARY. Grant, we're the guests of honor. We can't be late.

GRANT. I'll make this short. Get your things, Mary. (*Grant exits into the left bedroom*)

SPIKE. Mary, you've got at least five minutes. I'll go down and check up on the police escort. (*He exits into the outer hall*)

MARY. It's a wonderful country! You take the police along with you so they can help you break the speed laws. (*She exits into the right bedroom, leaving the door open. Conover wanders down to the open door*)

CONOVER. Take your time, Mary. The way you look tonight I want everybody there before you make your entrance.

MARY (*offstage*). Don't be so flattering, Jim, or I'll think you want something from me!

CONOVER (*laughing*). As a matter of fact, I do. I was just going to ask you a favor.

MARY (*entering from the right bedroom wearing her evening wrap*). Fine! What can I do for you?

CONOVER. You're having Sam Parrish to dinner on the seventeenth. Do you mind inviting me, too?

MARY. Why, no. I'd love to have you.

CONOVER. Can I impose on you by inviting some other guests—say four or five?

MARY (*hesitating*). I hadn't planned that kind of a party on the seventeenth but . . .

CONOVER. If Grant's speaking on the twenty-third on International Policy, it may be important for him to see these people first.

(*Mary hesitates again, then comes to a decision.*)

MARY. All right, Jim. I think we can handle it! Do I know any of these people?

CONOVER. Well, you know Sam— And there's one other I'd like to talk to you about. You remember the reason I wanted you to make this trip in the first place?

MARY (*tightening*). Yes, I remember well enough.

CONOVER. Mary, I've been looking into how that talk got started. Mrs. Thorndyke used to be a frequent guest at your house. Then about a year ago she was crossed off your list, but Grant went on seeing her.

MARY. Yes.

CONOVER. Let's kill off those rumors once and for all. I want Mrs. Thorndyke there on the seventeenth.

MARY (*in cold anger*). No, Jim! Not in my house! And of all nights not on the seventeenth! It happens to be our wedding anniversary.

CONOVER (*with some heat*). Mary, I'm doing my damnedest to go along with Grant, even though he doesn't always go along with me. I need Mrs. Thorndyke there for more reasons than one. Let me win this one, will you?

MARY. Sorry, Jim, that's more than I can take. (*There is a knock on the door*) Come in! (*The Bellboy enters with a radio*)

BELLBOY. Here's your radio. I had to steal it from another room.

MARY. That's fine. Can you connect it for us?

CONOVER. Let's talk about this some more after the banquet.

(*The Bellboy puts the radio on the desk and plugs it in. Grant enters from the left bedroom.*)

MARY. Ready!

(*Grant takes a swig of coffee and Mary gets his hat. The Bellboy switches on the radio.*)

BELLBOY. Everybody wanted a radio tonight.

GRANT (*pleased*). So?

BELLBOY. Special broadcast from Holly-wood—Bob Hope and Jack Benny.

GRANT. Yes, I've got a break tonight, Jim —I'm following Hope and Benny.

MARY *(handing Grant his hat)*. After all that nonsense they'll be glad to hear Grant make some sense.

(The door opens and Spike sticks his head in.)

SPIKE. All set? I've got the elevator wait-ing for you.

MARY. Grant, fix your tie. Listen in, Jim. You'll find out what Grant's talking about!

GRANT. Good-bye, Jim. *(Grant and Mary exit into the hall)*

CONOVER. Good luck.

(We hear some music over the radio; then the Bellboy turns it off. Mary rushes back in excitement, looking desperately around the room.)

MARY. Where's my bag, my bag, my bag?

CONOVER. What's that in your hand? *(She looks down and sees her bag in her hand)*

MARY. That's my bag! *(She wheels and runs out)*

BELLBOY *(at the radio)*. Works all right. Do you want it on?

CONOVER. No. I can turn a radio on—and off. *(He tips the Bellboy, who thanks him and exits. Conover takes a chair from the table and places it at the right of the desk. Then he crosses to the left bedroom, opens the door, and speaks through it)* We may as well sit in here and be comfortable! *(Conover turns back into the room. Kay Thorndyke enters. She strolls across the room to the chair by the desk, places her furs and hat on the desk and sits down. Conover draws up a chair)* I have a radio. Do I dare listen?

KAY. I think so. Of course, I had less than five minutes with him.

CONOVER. Yes. And Mary's had five weeks! *(He lights a cigar)*

KAY *(confidently)*. I think he was glad to see me. I told you in Washington I could handle him.

CONOVER. Well, we'll find out. *(He sits down)*

KAY. I made it pretty strong. I said the Democrats would never take a chance like that. But that brought up a question that's on his mind, Jim, and you'd better have an answer ready for him.

CONOVER. An answer to what?

KAY. Is there any real difference between the Democratic Party and the Republican Party?

CONOVER. All the difference in the world. *(He turns on the radio)* They're in—and we're out!

CURTAIN

ACT THREE

SCENE ONE

The living room of the Matthews' apart-ment in New York. It is a fairly large room, the entrance from the hall being from an arch upstage, left of center; the door from the elevator is somewhere off-stage left. In this left arch we see stairs leading to an upper floor. Right of center there is a corresponding arch. Recessed be-hind this arch is an alcove bar with bottles of liquor and glasses, and it is through this arch that the guests proceed to the dining room, which is off right. Down-stage left there is a single door leading to a powder room and a place for the ladies' wraps.

There is a fireplace in the right wall. There is a small table and an ottoman be-low the fireplace. On a line with the fire-place and facing the audience is an up-holstered couch. On stage left there are two large comfortable upholstered chairs with a small table between them. Upstage between the two arches, there is a cabinet with single chairs at either end. On the cabinet is a vase of flowers, and above it on the wall hangs a painting of Mary and the two children.

Spike is sitting on the sofa, his hat be-side him. On the floor at his feet are an ashtray and a package which obviously contains a bottle of liquor. He has a piece of paper in his hand and a pencil.

Swenson, the butler, is standing facing Spike, with a piece of note-paper in his hand and a pencil.

———

SPIKE *(consulting the slip of paper he holds)*. Judge Alexander—bourbon—bour-bon and plain water—he may take a cock-tail, but I doubt it—he'll probably stick to straight bourbon.

SWENSON. Yes, sir. *(He makes a note)*

SPIKE. Now his wife—do you know how to mix a Sazarac?

SWENSON. No, sir, but I can look it up.

SPIKE. Well, I'll tell you. Take an old-fashioned glass and put a lump of sugar in it, soaked in Pernod.

SWENSON. I don't think we have any Pernod, sir.

SPIKE. I brought some. It's in there. *(He points to the package)* Then a jigger of bourbon, a twist of lemon peel on the top and give it a good stir. Don't sample that one, Swenson, it'll light up your vest buttons. *(Swenson makes a note)* That's all Mrs. Alexander drinks, but she drinks a lot of them. It's all right for her to get tight, if she wants to—but take it easy on the rest of them. We want to keep them sober. The Senator likes martinis before dinner, then he goes on a steady diet of Scotch and sodas.

SWENSON. Yes, sir.

SPIKE. Now, Mr. Parrish . . .

SWENSON. Manhattans for Mr. Parrish, and then rye.

SPIKE. And Mrs. Thorndyke—?

SWENSON. Mrs. Thorndyke likes a martini before dinner—very dry.

SPIKE. All right, give her one. Same for Mrs. Draper. Just have plenty of martinis and Manhattans—and Scotch and soda for Mr. Conover. And remember, Swenson, except for Mrs. Alexander nobody gets too much to drink—and that goes for Mr. and Mrs. Matthews too.

(Grant has entered through the left arch during the last sentence of Spike's speech. He is wearing a hat and a topcoat, and carries a small wrapped box. He drops the hat and the box on a chair.)

GRANT. What goes for Mr. and Mrs. Matthews?

SPIKE. I'm straightening Swenson out on the drinks—and nobody's to get too many. If there's one thing I don't want around here tonight, it's too much frankness—especially from you. I'm thinking of that time you got tight in San Francisco. We'd been in a hell of a fix if the newspaper men hadn't gotten drunker. Swenson wanted to know where to put the place cards. I've got a diagram here. *(He takes a piece of cardboard out of his pocket)*

GRANT. Wait till I get Mary. *(He hurries up the stairs)*

SWENSON. There's a Mr. Hardy on the list, sir.

SPIKE. Those labor boys are smart cookies. He doesn't drink anything.

(Swenson picks up the package at Spike's feet and goes through the right arch to the bar. He leaves the package behind the bar and exits right. We hear Grant before we see him.)

GRANT. Well, make it as soon as you can. I'm late. I should be changing. *(He comes downstairs, taking off his topcoat and holding it over his arm)* She'll be here in a minute. *(He goes to the fireplace)*

SPIKE. Nervous about tonight?

GRANT. Yes, a little. I feel as though I'm being quietly surrounded.

SPIKE. Take it easy. Let them do the talking.

GRANT. Oh, I'm not making any commitments here tonight. You and Jim and I are meeting over at Kay's after they've gone.

SPIKE. Look, they're going to throw the book at you tonight. That goes for Conover too. They don't expect you to take it all—it's just as Kay said last night—they'll be willing to compromise.

GRANT. Before I got into this, it all seemed so clear and simple. I suppose it does to almost everybody who doesn't have to make the decisions.

SPIKE. Yeah, Mary, for instance.

GRANT. I know now it isn't just black and white—but damn it, where do you draw the line? *(He thinks a moment)* I know damn well once I got to be President—*(A pause)* Well!

SPIKE. I'll drop back about midnight and pick you up and we can talk it out at Kay's.

GRANT. Spike, keep that to yourself—we're supposed to be meeting . . .

(Mary enters down the stairs. She is in evening dress. There is a lack of warmth between her and Grant.)

MARY *(crossing to arm of sofa and sitting)*. Hello, Spike. I'm sorry to get you up here, but I told Grant you had to help seat these people.

SPIKE. I've got a diagram here. *(He shows Mary the diagram)* You're here—and Grant's at the other end.

GRANT *(sitting on the sofa beside Spike)*. Well, if we're going to observe any protocol, Senator Lauterback ranks. I think he ought to be on Mary's right.

SPIKE. Okay, and I'll put Mrs. Draper on your right. We're short of women, some of the men will have to sit together.

MARY. Why don't you put Sam Parrish on Grant's left?

GRANT. Don't you want Sam up near you? It'll give you someone to talk to.

MARY. Well, I thought that after what you *didn't* say about reconversion in Detroit, you and Sam might want to hold hands under the table.

GRANT. Mary, we've been over that often enough. I *did* talk about reconversion in Detroit.

MARY. I wouldn't say about it, Grant. I'd say around it. You did come right out and mention the word once.

GRANT *(rising, and speaking with angry finality)*. Mary, I've heard all I want to hear about Detroit.

SPIKE *(to the rescue)*. Here's a good couple to pair off. Hardy and Mrs. Alexander. He never opens his mouth and she never closes hers. *(He writes their names down)* How about Mrs. Thorndyke up here? *(He points to one end of the diagram)*

MARY. How about Mrs. Thorndyke down there? *(She points to the other end of the diagram)*

SPIKE. Okay. Then the Judge here, and Jim here. *(He writes and then holds up the diagram)* That looks all right. *(He hands it to Mary)*

GRANT *(looking at his watch)*. Hell, I've got to get dressed. *(He starts for the stairs)*

MARY. Grant, you're looking in on Sonny and Joyce?

GRANT. I certainly am. *(He goes back to Mary)* Mary, I know this dinner isn't going to be much fun for you. It's damn nice of you to do it for me. I appreciate it.

MARY. Nonsense, Grant. I hope it's everything you want it to be. I'll do my best. Just to show you how serious I am about it, I'm not even going to have a cocktail.

GRANT. I'm going light myself. *(He starts off, then notices his hat and the box on the chair. He picks them up)* Oh, Mary, I almost forgot. This is for tonight. *(He hands her the box and hurries upstairs. Mary rises and watches Grant as he leaves)*

MARY. I didn't think he even remembered it.

SPIKE. Remembered what?

MARY. Today's our wedding anniversary. Excuse me, Spike! *(She takes off the wrapping eagerly, revealing a box of cigars)* My error! *(Jenny, a maid, enters from the right arch)* Jenny!

JENNY. Yes, Madam?

MARY. Here's the table diagram. Will you take care of the place cards? And these cigars?

JENNY *(taking both diagram and cigars)*. Very good, Madam. *(She exits left into the hall)*

SPIKE *(with forced gaiety)*. Those cigars are Llaranaguas, the only brand Conover smokes. Don't tell me Grant doesn't know how to play politics.

MARY. Oh, I know he plays politics! I've found that out! *(In unhappy puzzlement)* I *wish* I knew *why* he changed his speech in Detroit!

SPIKE *(casually)*. Jim talked to him, didn't he? Warned him not to say anything that would cost us any campaign contributions?

MARY. No, Spike, it wasn't for money. So if you do know, you won't tell me. You're not on my team. And I've often wondered why. You know, Spike, you've got a very wide streak of decency.

SPIKE. Yes, and if I don't watch it, it gets in my way. *(Seriously)* Mary, I'll pull every trick I know to get Grant in the White House, but once he's there and I'm back on the newspaper, I'll be on the same team with you; and if Grant isn't in there pitching for the people, I'll burn his pants off!

MARY. I'll light the matches for you.

SPIKE *(rising)*. But don't start any bonfires here tonight. *(Jenny crosses the hall, on her way to the outer door)* These educated apes that are coming here—Grant can't be nominated without their support, and in the election they can deliver a lot of votes.

MARY *(scornfully)*. How can you deliver the votes of a free people?

SPIKE. Mary, lazy people and ignorant people and prejudiced people are not free. *(We hear the voice of Judge Alexander offstage.)*

ALEXANDER *(offstage)*. Is Mrs. Matthews in?

JENNY *(offstage)*. This way, sir.

SPIKE *(picking up the ashtray and putting it on the table)*. Somebody's here.

I'd better run. I'll be back in time to help you sweep them out.

MARY. Wait until whoever this is comes in, will you, Spike? I don't know them all.

(*Judge Jefferson Davis Alexander and Mrs. Lulubelle Alexander enter. She is still wearing her wrap, which she hands to Jenny who exits with it to room down left. The Alexanders are from the deep South. He is tall and lean. She is short and plump.*)

SPIKE (*holding out his hand*). Hello, Judge. I'm Spike MacManus. Remember me?

ALEXANDER (*expansively, crossing to shake hands with Spike*). Indeed I do! It's a great pleasure to see you again, sir! This is Mrs. Alexander.

SPIKE. How do you do? Mrs. Matthews, this is Judge Alexander and Mrs. Alexander.

MARY (*holding out her hand*). How do you do, Judge Alexander?

ALEXANDER (*shaking hands*). It's an honor to be here, Mrs. Matthews.

MARY (*to Lulubelle*). I'm especially glad you could come, Mrs. Alexander. We women are going to be outnumbered here tonight.

LULUBELLE. That's nothing new to me, Mrs. Matthews. When I go to dinner with the Judge's Republican friends I'm always outnumbered. I make it a point to tell my hostess right off that while Jeff's a Republican, I'm a Democrat. But you can speak freely. You Republicans can't say anything about the Administration mean enough for us Democrats down South. (*She laughs; she is incurably good-natured*)

SPIKE (*amused*). I'll leave you my proxy, Mrs. Alexander. I've got to run along. Good night. Good night, Mary. Good night, Judge. (*He exits left.*)

ALEXANDER (*calling after him heartily*). It's been very pleasant seeing you again, sir! Good night! (*He turns to Mary*) Who is he?

MARY. A newspaperman. He's been helping my husband. Won't you sit down? (*Lulubelle goes to one of the easy chairs and sits. Jenny enters from the room down left and exits through the arch toward the outer door.*)

MARY. Mr. Matthews will be down in a minute.

ALEXANDER. Mrs. Alexander and I are certainly looking forward to meeting him. (*Swenson enters from the left arch and stands awaiting Mary's orders.*)

MARY. You must be looking forward to a cocktail, too.

LULUBELLE. Frankly, I'm looking forward to both.

SWENSON (*to Alexander*). Bourbon, sir?

ALEXANDER. You read my mind.

LULUBELLE. He can't read my mind.

SWENSON (*turning to Lulubelle*). A Sazarac, I believe?

ALEXANDER. Lulubelle, your reputation's getting too far north.

MARY. Swenson, can you make a Sazarac?

SWENSON. I think so, Ma'am.

LULUBELLE. If he just thinks so, Jeff, you'd better mix that Sazarac.

ALEXANDER. Yes, honey.

MARY (*indicating*). The bar's right over there.

SWENSON. This way, sir. (*He leads Alexander to the alcove bar, where the Judge goes to work mixing a Sazarac*)

MARY. Do you get up North often?

LULUBELLE. Being a Republican down South, the Judge only gets important every four years, around Convention time. Jim Conover getting him way up here this early must mean they're pretty serious about running your husband for President, which I hope they don't.

MARY. Really?

LULUBELLE. Yes, you seem like such a nice woman. Politics is too good an excuse for a man to neglect his wife.

MARY. Well, if you're neglected tonight —you and I will be neglected together. (*She hears voices in the hall and moves up to greet the new guests*)

(*Jenny ushers in Mrs. Grace Draper and Jim Conover. They are followed by Bill Hardy, and later Senator Lauterback. Mrs. Draper is a positive woman whose mind has been closed ever since Roosevelt's first term. Conover is dressed in a conservative business suit. Bill Hardy, the labor leader, obviously hasn't just come from the factory. He is dressed in dinner clothes and wishes he weren't. Senator Lauterback represents the farm bloc, but has been doing his farming in the Senate for a great many years. Jenny takes Mrs. Draper's wrap and exits with it into the room downstage left.*)

CONOVER. Hello, Mary. This is Mrs. Draper, Mrs. Matthews. Hello, Lulubelle. Where's the Judge?

LULUBELLE. Mixing me a drink.

CONOVER. Well, this is where I went out. *(He waves to the Judge)* Hello, Judge!

ALEXANDER *(from the bar)*. Hello, Jim!

MRS. DRAPER *(to Lulubelle)*. You're Judge Alexander's wife. I met you in Chicago.

LULUBELLE. Oh, yes, at the Convention. I was so glad to get back down South away from that heat.

(Mrs. Draper crosses to the sofa and sits down. Swenson has entered from the bar with a tray of drinks.)

MRS. DRAPER *(crossing to Mary and shaking hands)*. I've been so eager to meet you and your husband.

MARY. It's so nice that you could come. Do you know Mrs. Alexander?

(Mrs. Draper goes to Lulubelle.)

CONOVER. Mrs. Matthews, this is Bill Hardy.

(Hardy shakes hands with Mary.)

MARY. Hello, Mr. Hardy.

HARDY *(aggrieved)*. Nobody told me not to dress.

CONOVER. My fault, Bill. I slipped up on that.

MARY. I'm glad you did dress. Men are getting all too lazy about dressing.

CONOVER. Isn't that what you're after, Bill? Put labor in evening clothes and let the rest of us go without? Have a drink! *(He points to the bar)* Oh, Mary, this is Senator Lauterback.

SENATOR *(shaking hands with Mary)*. Wanted to meet you ever since you made that trip with your husband. You were just as big a hit as he was. He talks well, but you're prettier.

CONOVER. Mr. Matthews will be down in a minute, Senator, and the bar's over there.

(The Senator goes to the bar.)

MARY *(as Swenson comes up with the tray)*. You want a highball, don't you, Jim?

CONOVER. Well, we've just come from a little caucus in my room at the hotel. We did some drinking there. Oh, all right. *(He takes a highball. Swenson turns to offer a drink to Mary)*

MARY. No, thank you, Swenson. I'm not having anything to drink tonight. *(Swenson serves a drink to Mrs. Draper. Kay Thorndyke enters and stands in the left arch. Mary turns and sees her. There is a moment of tension)* Hello, Kay.

KAY. Hello, Mary. *(Kay walks forward with outstretched hand)* You're looking very pretty tonight.

MARY *(taking a martini from Swenson's tray and putting it in Kay's outstretched hand)*. You're just in time for a cocktail. Do you know everyone here?

KAY. I know Mrs. Draper.

(The Judge has entered from the bar with Lulubelle's Sazarac, which he takes to her. The Senator and Bill Hardy remain at the bar.)

MARY. Mrs. Alexander, this is Mrs. Thorndyke—and Judge Alexander.

KAY. How do you do?

LULUBELLE. Hello, Mrs. Thorndyke. *(She starts her drinking)*

ALEXANDER. Mrs. Thorndyke, I'm very pleased to meet you. I was raised in the old traditions of the South, where it was looked down on for a woman to go into anything like newspaper business. But no gentleman of the South could deny as attractive a woman as you your outstanding success. Which reminds me of a story! A number of years ago when I was a small boy . . .

LULUBELLE. Jeff, this is the best Sazarac I ever had in my life. Mix me another one right away!

ALEXANDER. Yes, honey.

MRS. DRAPER. Kay, after you left, Jim and I went into the situation in Chicago. Jim, tell her what you said.

KAY. Oh, Grace, let's take time out of politics for a little drinking. You're in for a bad evening, Mary.

(The Judge, having lost his audience, goes to the bar.)

MARY. Oh no! Politics is new to me, but I'm very interested.

CONOVER *(amiably, but sardonically)*.

You've got the "very" in the wrong place, Mary. Interested, but very new.

MARY *(to the others, smiling)*. Mr. Conover means I haven't lost my amateur standing.

CONOVER. You're learning—I hope!

MARY. That's a dangerous hope, Jim. You politicians have stayed professionals because the voters have remained amateurs.

(Sam Parrish appears in the left arch.)

SAM. Hello, everybody! Late as usual! Had a hell of a day! *(He goes to Mary)* How's my sweetheart?

MARY. Hello, Sam.

(Sam kisses her.)

SAM. That's for Hilda! *(He kisses her again)* That's for me! *(Hearing Sam, Hardy and the Senator drift into the room)* Jim, I won't get down to Washington until afternoon. How about dinner instead of lunch?

CONOVER. That suits me even better.

SENATOR. Hello, Sam.

SAM. *Senator!* You'll be glad to hear I'm starting a back-to-the-farm movement. Just closed down two plants. *(Hardy steps into view from behind the Senator)* Oh, hello, Bill! Shouldn't have said that in front of you! Mary, do I have to sit down with Labor again tonight? Where's Grant?

MARY. He'll be down any minute.

MRS. DRAPER. Hello, Sam!

SAM. Hello, Grace!

MARY. Do you know Mrs. Alexander? Mr. Parrish.

SAM. How are you, Mrs. Alexander?

MARY. And have you met Mrs. Thorndyke?

KAY. Oh, yes, we know each other. Nice seeing you, Mr. Parrish.

SAM *(to Kay)*. Where did you get to that night? I looked all over the banquet hall for you.

KAY *(after a second's pause)*. I didn't go to the banquet.

CONOVER *(to change the subject)*. Say, how's Hilda?

SAM. She's fine now. Mrs. Thorndyke, I thought that was why you were in Detroit—to hear Grant's speech.

MARY. Were you in Detroit when we were there, Kay?

SAM. Yes, you must have seen her, Mary. She was on her way to your suite. I'd just left you, remember?

MARY. I didn't see Mrs. Thorndyke in Detroit. *(Fitting the pieces together)* Oh, you must have dropped in to talk to Grant about reconversion.

SAM. What Grant said about reconversion in his speech that night was all right. You couldn't argue with it.

MARY. Well, I think you can thank Mrs. Thorndyke for that.

CONOVER *(interrupting and going center to Sam)*. Sam, did you get that finance report I sent you?

SAM. Yes, and it's a damn bad job. I've made you a whole new list. *(He searches through his pockets)*

KAY *(to Mrs. Draper)*. Grace, I'm having another cocktail.

MRS. DRAPER. I'll have one, too. *(They both go to the bar.)*

MARY *(turning to Conover)*. Well, Jim, you hoped I'd learn. I'm learning.

(The Judge enters from the bar with two Sazaracs and goes to Lulubelle.)

SAM. Left it in my overcoat. I'll get it. *(He starts out and sees the Judge)* Hello, Judge! You drinking with both hands now?

ALEXANDER. Hello, Sam! These aren't for me. *(Sam exits into the hall. The Judge places the drinks on the table beside Lulubelle)* Honey, I want to talk to some of these people, so I brought you two of them.

LULUBELLE. Thank you, Jeff. *(She takes a fresh drink)*

MARY. Judge, I'll have one of those. *(The Judge hands her a drink.)*

CONOVER *(concerned)*. Mary, those are pretty powerful. I thought you weren't drinking anything tonight.

MARY *(incisively)*. I've just been reconverted! *(She takes a healthy swallow)*

LULUBELLE. Jeff, make another one for me right away.

ALEXANDER. Yes, honey. *(He starts for the bar)*

MARY. Hm-m, I like these. Judge, would you make another one for me too?

(Mary sits in the comfortable chair next to Lulubelle. The Judge starts toward the bar. Grant Matthews comes down the stairs into the arch as Sam enters from the left with a sheaf of papers in his hand.)

GRANT. Hello, Sam!

SAM. Grant! All I've got to decide tonight is whether we're going to run you for a third term.

(They shake hands and come into the room together.)

CONOVER. How're you, Grant? You certainly took time to pretty yourself up.

GRANT. Was it successful? Sorry I'm late.

(The Judge has crossed down in front of sofa.)

ALEXANDER. Mr. Matthews, I'm Judge Alexander.

GRANT *(with a gesture)*. Not guilty!

(He crosses to the Judge and they shake hands. Sam takes Conover aside into conference)

ALEXANDER. Sir, I reject your plea. I'm sentencing you to four years in the White House!

GRANT *(laughing)*. You're taking Jim Conover more seriously than I am.

(Mary and Lulubelle are drinking steadily.)

ALEXANDER. Mr. Conover's a man to be taken seriously. Due to his efforts I almost had the honor of being the last man appointed to public office by Herbert Hoover. But the Federal Judge we expected to die held on a few days and the first thing we knew Mr. Roosevelt was in office. So I'm still on the State bench. However, my term expires in 1948. So ...

LULUBELLE. Jeff!

ALEXANDER. Yes, honey?

LULUBELLE. I'm going to be needing my other drink.

ALEXANDER. Yes, honey.

MARY. Grant, this is Mrs. Alexander.

(Grant turns to Lulubelle. Again without an audience, the Judge returns to the bar.)

GRANT. How do you do, Mrs. Alexander?

LULUBELLE *(to Mary)*. Handsome, isn't he? *He's* the first good reason I've ever seen for voting Republican. *(To Grant)* I warned your wife I was a Democrat.

GRANT. Some of my best friends are Democrats.

LULUBELLE. Well, you know us Southerners. We vote Democratic at home, but we've got an awfully good Republican record in Congress.

(Kay, Mrs. Draper, Hardy and the Senator come in from the bar. Swenson arrives at this moment at Grant's side with a tray of drinks. Grant takes a martini and turns to Mary.)

GRANT. Cocktail, Mary? Oh, you're not drinking anything, are you?

MARY *(holding glass aloft)*. Yes! Sazaracs!

GRANT *(surprised)*. Oh?

KAY. Hello, Grant!

(Grant turns and goes to her.)

GRANT. Oh, hello, Kay! Nice seeing you again.

(They shake hands.)

KAY. Do you know Bill Hardy?

GRANT. Glad you're here, Mr. Hardy.

HARDY. Nobody told me not to dress. *(He shakes hands with Grant, then turns to the fireplace to nurse his sense of social injustice)*

KAY. And this is Grace Draper.

GRANT. I've been looking forward to meeting you, Mrs. Draper. You're on the National Committee, I believe.

KAY. And they're going to run Mrs. Draper for Congress.

GRANT. Fine! I always say a woman's place is in the House.

SENATOR *(coming down to Grant)*. Just so they stay out of the Senate. How are you, Mr. Matthews? I'm Senator Lauterback.

(They shake hands.)

GRANT. Oh, of course.

(Conover comes down and joins the group.)

SENATOR. We met before, in a manner of speaking. Remember? You testified before my Committee. You made a very strong impression on us.

GRANT *(amused)*. Well, I would never have guessed it from the Committee's report.

CONOVER. The Senator was just telling me about that, Grant. He can give you the inside on it. I think you'll find it very interesting.

(Swenson approaches the group around Grant with a tray of drinks.)

GRANT. Senator, we'll have to go into that later. I'd like to hear about it. Another cocktail, Mrs. Draper?

MRS. DRAPER. Thank you. They're very good. *(She takes one)*

GRANT. How about you, Kay?

LULUBELLE *(to Mary)*. You see, that's what happens when your husband gets into politics. You just sit off in a corner.

MARY. We have each other for company tonight and it gives us time to attend to our drink-

KAY. No, two's my limit.

GRANT. How about you, Senator? Or would you rather have a highball?

SENATOR. No, I'll stick to these. *(He takes a cocktail)* And very good too!

GRANT *(to Hardy)*. Want that refreshed, Mr. Hardy?

HARDY. No, you can drink just so much Coca-Cola.

ing. *(She finishes her Sazarac just as the Judge arrives with two more. Both women take fresh drinks)*

LULUBELLE. Just in time, Jeff. Fix us some more right away.

ALEXANDER, Honey, there are a lot of things I want to talk to Mr. Matthews about.

LULUBELLE. Mix the drinks before you start talkin', Jeff; you know how I hate to interrupt you.

ALEXANDER. Yes, honey.

(Judge hurries back to bar, muttering.)

(Swenson returns to bar and then disappears into dining room.)

KAY. Grant, Mrs. Draper is very interested in what you plan to say at the Foreign Policy Association Thursday night.

GRANT *(to Mrs. Draper)*. Yes, Thursday's the night I settle world affairs.

KAY. Grace is the Party's expert on the foreign vote.

MRS. DRAPER. I think the election in '46 is going to turn on it, and in '48 too.

KAY. Take the Italians, for instance. Everybody knows we've made a mess of things in Italy.

MRS. DRAPER. The Italians over here are all unhappy about it, and they're going to be even unhappier when the final peace terms are drawn up.

KAY. Truman has to take responsibility for the peace terms. So it's not going to be hard to appeal to the Italian vote.

GRANT. I think we have to wait and find out what the peace terms are.

KAY. We don't have to wait. We just have to demand justice for Italy.

MARY *(who has been listening to this, speaks up, with Sazarac-inspired articulateness)*. If you favor Italy, won't that lose you the Abyssinian vote?

MRS. DRAPER *(turning to Mary)*. Mrs. Matthews, there isn't any Abyssinian vote.

MARY. Good! We don't have to worry

about justice for the Abyssinians. *(She goes back to her drinking)*

KAY *(to Grant)*. Grace thinks that in this election the Polish vote is the most important.

MRS. DRAPER. Indeed I do! Now in your speech Thursday night you should come out for the reopening of the whole Polish question—boundaries, government, reparations—

KAY. Any strong stand, Grant, would clinch the Polish vote.

MARY. I thought the Poles voted in Poland.

KAY *(to Mary, kindly)*. We're talking about Polish-Americans.

MARY. Oh, can you be both?

SAM *(looking up from his papers)*. Mary, you're a sweet girl and I love you, but this is practical politics, and you're way out over your head.

MARY. If they're Americans I should think you'd ask them to vote as Americans, not as Poles!

GRANT *(too heartily)*. Mary, I think we could all use some more hors d'œuvres.

(Mary rises and goes to bell in the left wall, which she presses.)

KAY. Take Pennsylvania for instance . . .

MARY. Is this what's called power politics?

SENATOR *(strolling toward Mary)*. Mrs. Matthews, power politics is what they play in Europe.

MARY *(crossing back to her chair)*. It seems to me we're beginning to play it right here. Let's disunite the United Nations and keep Pennsylvania safe for the Republicans. *(She sits. Judge Alexander comes out of the bar with a tray holding four Sazaracs. He crosses to Lulubelle)*

ALEXANDER. Doggone it, I miss everything. Who says we're not going to carry Pennsylvania? *(He places the tray on the table and addresses Lulubelle)* Honey, I made four this time. I'm missing out on everything. I'm starved for some good Republican talk.

(Jenny enters from left arch in answer to bell. Mary and Lulubelle each take a fresh Sazarac.)

LULUBELLE *(raising her glass to Mary)*. More power to you!

MARY. Thanks! They're full of it, aren't they? *(She starts on her third Sazarac.)*

GRANT *(to Jenny)*. Jenny, some hors d'œuvres, please.

(Jenny takes a tray of hors d'œuvres from a table at the foot of the stairs and passes them.)

ALEXANDER. Mr. Matthews, if I may say so, I think you're the hope of the new South.

SENATOR. Here we go again! The Judge is going to promise that we'll break the solid South.

ALEXANDER. Senator, you don't understand the conditions down there!

SENATOR. All I have to say is that when a state votes the same way for one hundred years, it a reflection on the intelligence of the electorate. *(Turns to Mary)* Don't you agree with me, Mrs. Matthews?

MARY. I'm from Vermont. *(She drinks)*

SENATOR. That's not the same thing. Vermont's always been a good sound Republican state *(To Grant)* Mr. Matthews, in your speech Thursday I know you have to tie up world peace with tariff reductions and we realize industry has to make some sacrifice along that line . . .

SAM. Oh, industry has to make the sacrifices!

SENATOR. But I think you'll have to reassure the American farmer that he won't be forced to compete with Russian wheat and Danish butter and Argentine beef.

GRANT. Senator, there's a direct connection between world trade and world peace.

KAY. Grant, the farmer has a special case.

SENATOR. And twenty million votes!

GRANT. Senator, I want you to talk to me very, very frankly and very fully, and give me all the information you can—but please don't expect me to make any decisions here tonight.

MARY. That's the way Grant works. He likes to listen to people before he makes any decish—*(Mary stops short, looks down at the drink, puts the drink on the table, then continues somewhat defiantly)* —before he decides anything.

SAM. I thought we were going to talk turkey tonight. If I'm going to raise this money, I've got to take word back to Detroit how Grant stands on certain issues.

CONOVER *(following Sam down to center)*. After you've gone, Grant and I are going to hold a caucus. We'll have word for all of you tomorrow.

SENATOR *(to Sam)*. Sam, Mr. Matthews' strength is with big business. Why should they be worried about him?

SAM. You know what we're worried about. Are we going to be in for a lot of government competition, or is this country going to be put back in the hands of private enterprise?

(Swenson enters from arch left and tries to catch Mary's eye.)

MARY *(rising)*. Oh, Grant believes in private enterprise. *(She stares across at Kay)* Doesn't he, Kay?

SWENSON. Dinner is served, Ma'am. *(Swenson exits.)*

GRANT. Dinner. Good! Take your cocktails with you if you haven't finished. *(He crosses to center)* Mary!

MARY *(leading the guests out)*. Just find your own place cards. I hope some of you men don't mind sitting together. There aren't enough women to go around.

(Mary exits through the right arch, followed by Mrs. Draper and Lulubelle, then Hardy, Alexander, Sam, Senator and Conover. Kay delays following the others so that when all are gone but Grant she can seize the opportunity to speak to him.)

KAY *(with cold anger)*. Grant, Mary's tight. Is there any way you can talk to her—do something with her?

GRANT *(worried)*. What happened?

KAY. It was Sam. The minute he walked into the room he . . .

(Mary enters from dining room, speaking back over her shoulder.)

MARY. Find your place cards, everyone. I forgot my—*(She turns and sees Grant and Kay)*—cocktail.

(Kay brushes past her to dining room. Mary stares after her.)

GRANT. Mary, I'm depending on you to help me tonight.

MARY *(crossing to the table)*. I'm afraid I interrupted you and Kay before she had a chance to tell you what you think. *(She picks up drink from table)*

GRANT. Leave that drink here, and get some food into you as soon as you can!

MARY *(challengingly)*. Well! Seems to me you're getting a little belligerel.

GRANT. Mary, I'm on a spot here tonight. We both are. We have to be ready to do some quick thinking.

MARY *(starting for the dining room)*. Don't worry about me. *(She stops and looks back at Grant)* I'm a very thick quinker.

(Mary continues toward the dining room,

walking with careful deliberation. Grant starts to follow.)

CURTAIN

SCENE TWO

The same, some time after dinner.
Mary and Lulubelle are seated in the comfortable chairs. Mary is drinking coffee with a certain desperation.
On the table between them is Lulubelle's demitasse, untouched. Lulubelle is at work on a bourbon and soda. Mary finishes her coffee, puts it down on the table and notices Lulubelle's full cup. She eyes it for a second and then speaks to Lulubelle.

MARY. You haven't touched your coffee.
LULUBELLE. Never use it. Keeps me awake nights.
MARY *(picking up the cup)*. Do you mind?
LULUBELLE. Help yourself, honey.
(Mary starts on Lulubelle's coffee. Lulubelle is sipping her highball as though her immediate memories gave her some amusement. Swenson appears with a coffee pot on a tray. He approaches the empty cup which Mary has put down.)
SWENSON *(to Lulubelle)*. More coffee, Ma'am?
MARY *(promptly)*. Yes, Swenson.
(He fills the empty cup, then turns to Mary.)
SWENSON. Coffee, Ma'am?
MARY. Yes, please. *(She quickly finishes coffee in her cup, then holds it out for Swenson to refill)* Be sure everyone in the dining room is taken care of. And did you remember Mr. Conover's cigars?
SWENSON. Yes, Ma'am.
(Swenson starts back to the dining room. Mrs. Draper enters. He allows her to pass and then exits. Mrs. Draper heads for the powder room, but stops center and points toward it.)
MRS. DRAPER. Am I right?
(Mary nods, giving her the best smile she can muster. Mrs. Draper hurries into the powder room.)
LULUBELLE *(to Mary, reassuringly)*. I thought she spoke to you real friendly.
MARY. Shouldn't she have? What did I say to *her?*

LULUBELLE. I can't quite remember, honey, but it was followed by one of the loudest silences I've ever heard.
(Mary suffers and gulps some coffee.)
MARY. I can't remember anything that happened before the salad.
LULUBELLE. You missed the best part. You certainly were whamming away at them. You picked them off one by one—like settin' birds. I haven't enjoyed myself so much since Huey Long died.
MARY *(after taking another gulp of coffee)*. Can you remember any of the things I said?
LULUBELLE *(thinking)*. Now let me see—what was it you said to the Senator? I kept wishing I had a pencil so I could write 'em down. It may come back to me later. That was the time Sam Parrish had the choking spell. You remember that, don't you?
MARY *(disconsolately)*. No.
LULUBELLE. Oh, he had to leave the table. Then when he came back you started on *him.*
MARY. Oh, dear! *(She puts her empty cup down and takes up Lulubelle's full one and starts drinking from it)*
LULUBELLE. It was something personal that I couldn't rightly follow. Your husband got it. That's when he knocked over his wine. My!—And that looked like an expensive dress Mrs. Thorndyke is wearing. *(Mary comes out of coffee cup with a broad smile and turns to Lulubelle)* I don't think she likes you, honey. She was the only one that tried to get back at you. But you took care of her!
MARY. What were they talking about?
LULUBELLE. It was kinda hard to keep track of it, because every time you said something they changed the subject. *(Mary suffers)* After we've gone, you'd better make up to your husband. I don't think he thought that talk about the thermometer was very funny.
MARY *(bewildered)*. Thermometer? What thermometer?
LULUBELLE. Oh, you just kept bedeviling him to take his temperature.
MARY. Why?
LULUBELLE. Well, you said he was getting another one of his attacks of gallopin' self-importance. *(Mary winces)* I remember that one! I'm saving that up to use on Jeff! *(She finishes her drink)*
MARY. I certainly picked a good day for

this. (*Turns to Lulubelle*) It's our wedding anniversary.

LULUBELLE (*thoughtfully*). Well, honey, this is one anniversary you'll both always remember. (*Jenny crosses back of arch toward the outer door. Swenson enters from the dining room with a tray holding a silver coffee pot and a bourbon and soda. Lulubelle helps herself to the highball*) Thank you!

SWENSON (*pouring coffee for Mary*). Shall I leave this here?

MARY. Yes, please. Thanks, Swenson. (*He puts the tray with the coffee pot on the table. Spike enters through the arch*)

SPIKE (*blithely*). Hello, there! How's everything going?

MARY. Just daisy. (*Swenson picks up Lulubelle's empty glass and starts to exit.*)

SPIKE (*to Swenson*). Will you tell Mr. Matthews I'm here? (*Swenson bows and exits.*)

MARY. They're still in the dining room, talking politics.

SPIKE. Did it get too much for you?

MARY. I got too much for them.

SPIKE (*concerned*). Oh-oh!

MARY. And don't ask for a copy of my speech. No matter what they tell you, I've been misquoted. (*Grant appears in the right arch.*)

GRANT. Hello, Spike, come on in! You know everybody.

SPIKE. How's it going?

GRANT. I don't know.

SPIKE. If it's a smoke-filled room, I can tell you—you're nominated. (*Spike exits into dining room. Grant looks at his watch. He speaks in Mary's general direction.*)

GRANT. I didn't know it was that late. Spike came to get Jim and me. We're going over to Jim's hotel afterwards for a post-mortem. Swenson taking care of you, Mrs. Alexander?

LULUBELLE. Yes, thank you. We're having a good time in here.

GRANT. We're having a good time in there—now. (*He exits into the dining room. Mary hastily drinks more coffee.*)

LULUBELLE. You blame it all on me, honey. You tell him I started you drinking those Sazaracs.

MARY (*painfully*). What's in those buzz bombs?

(*Mrs. Draper enters from the powder room.*)

LULUBELLE. Mrs. Draper, you've given me an idea. (*She rises and exits into the powder room*)

MARY (*to Mrs. Draper*). Won't you sit down and have a drink with us?

MRS. DRAPER. I have to catch a train. I'm just going back to say my good nights. (*Conover enters from the dining room.*)

CONOVER. Oh, Grace, I was afraid you'd gone. The talk has swung around to your territory. They need some information.

MRS. DRAPER. I can only stay a couple of minutes. (*She exits. Conover looks at Mary thoughtfully*)

CONOVER. Can I get you a drink?

MARY. Not until about 1952.

CONOVER. Oh, I forgot to tell you. There's been a shake-up in my secret service. I'll prove it to you. The Colonel, who used to be a Major, is now a General.

MARY (*disinterestedly*). Really?

CONOVER. He must be quite a guy.

MARY. He is.

CONOVER. Better keep in touch with him. Send him congratulations.

MARY. No, Jim. When he was a Major —I admit he was a major interest. But now, although he's a General, he's just a general interest. (*Conover studies Mary for a minute.*)

CONOVER. Mary, you once spoke of a spanking as an indication of deep affection. There were some moments tonight when I could have turned you over my knee, but there wouldn't have been any affection in it.

MARY. All right, Jim. I'll agree I've behaved badly as a hostess. I'm not proud of my bad manners. But I'll bet you I'd be proud of what I said—if I could remember what I said.

CONOVER (*amused in spite of himself*). You did let go some beauts.

MARY. Well, I think they're all stupid, selfish people.

CONOVER. I'd like to tell you how stupid I think you are. (*He goes to her*) Mary, I think it's time you were a little selfish, *and* a little intelligent. There's such a thing as enlightened self-interest you know. Why should you be stupid, just because Kay's being stupid?

MARY. Jim, that's one thing even I can't say about Kay—she's not stupid.

CONOVER. Isn't she? She's in there now

doing her damnedest to get Grant into the White House. And the White House is the one place where she can't be with him. She can't follow him there, Mary. Have you ever thought of that?

MARY (given pause). No, I hadn't.

CONOVER. Well, isn't it a little unintelligent of you to do anything to stop Grant from getting there? If he doesn't become President, I'm not so sure what's going to happen between you and him. But if he is elected—then you'll be the First Lady—in more ways than one.

MARY (painfully). That doesn't necessarily follow.

CONOVER. I think it does—and I'll tell you why. I know how you feel toward Grant. You've never bothered to conceal it from me.

MARY. Okay. So I love him.

CONOVER. Mary, when I saw you and Grant in Detroit—before he spoke that night—there were two people in love. Maybe Grant hadn't said so—maybe Grant hadn't shown it in those little ways you were looking for—but if you had had another month alone together, you know what would have happened.

MARY (not daring to believe it). I think you're wrong, Jim.

CONOVER. No, my dear, what he feels toward you goes pretty deep—and I'll tell you how he gives himself away. It's in his respect for your opinion—for what you think.

MARY. Don't kid me, Jim. We both know what happened to Grant's speech on reconversion.

CONOVER (sitting on the arm of her chair). Well, here's something you don't know—how unhappy Grant is about that. He's good and sore at himself and I know in my bones that some day what he thinks about reconversion—and Big Business—and what you think—is going to pop right out in the middle of a speech. I'm only praying that it doesn't happen before the nomination, and you'd better add a prayer, too.

MARY. But I want him to say it.

CONOVER. No, Mary! Not before the nomination! That's playing Kay's game. (Spike enters.)

SPIKE. Jim, can you come back in here? They're just breaking up.

CONOVER. I'll be there in a minute. (Spike exits) Mary, use your head. You can keep Grant from being President, but if you do, you're going to lose him. (He rises) Will you do something for me before I go tonight?

MARY. What?

CONOVER. I'd like to hear you say something to Grant that would let him know that if he does come our way just a little, you won't make life miserable for him. (Mary is silent) You're not the only one to be considered, Mary. Think of your children. That's a pretty good heritage—to be able to say, "My father was President of the United States."

MARY. Thanks, Jim. You're better than black coffee. You'd better get back in there.

CONOVER (strolling toward the dining room). Oh, I'll hear it all later.

MARY. Oh, yes, Grant and Spike are going over to your hotel with you. (Conover stops in the arch and looks back at Mary.)

CONOVER. No, Mary, we're going over to Mrs. Thorndyke's. (Conover stands for a minute watching Mary who slowly turns and stares at him; then he exits. Mary sits thinking for a moment; then rises with determination and starts for the dining room but hears voices offstage and stops.)

MRS. DRAPER (offstage). Good night, everybody! (She enters with Grant and Hardy) I'm sorry I have to run. I'm afraid I broke up the party.

GRANT. I'm sure you'll have time to get your train.

MRS. DRAPER. I have to stop at the hotel first. I'll get my wrap.

MARY. Can I help you?

MRS. DRAPER. No. I know right where it is. (She exits into the powder room. The Senator and Conover enter but stay in the bar alcove talking together confidentially)

HARDY (to Mary). I'll say good night, Mrs. Matthews.

MARY. Good night. It was very nice having you here.

HARDY (to Grant). I hope to hear from you on that.

GRANT. You'll be in touch with Jim.

HARDY. Just keep in mind what I said. Our funds are our secret weapon. If an employer knows how much we've got in the bank, he knows just how long we can stay out on strike. We can't afford to open our books.

GRANT *(smiling)*. As an employer I can understand that. Of course, I have to show my books.

HARDY. Well, good night. Good night, Mrs. Matthews. See you in Washington, Senator. *(He exits)*

SENATOR *(going to Mary)*. What you said about Sam Parrish—I can't wait to get back to Washington to tell it on him— *(Turns to Grant)* Good night, Mr. Matthews— *(He draws him downstage)* Look, will you promise me this? Before you speak in the Middle West again, will you have another talk with me—and I'd like to have Ed O'Neal and Earl Smith there. We can handle the farm problems in Congress, but we'd like to be sure we won't run into any vetoes.

GRANT *(laughing)*. Vetoes! Senator, you're moving a little too fast for me. I haven't even started to work on my inaugural address.

MARY *(trying to take part)*. Inaugural address! My, that makes me nervous—and excited!

CONOVER. I'll be there holding your hand, Mary.

SENATOR. Jim, I know everything's safe in your hands. *(We hear a laugh from dining room)* Good night, Mr. Matthews. *(He shakes hands with Grant)* Good night, Mrs. Matthews. *(Kay and Alexander enter)* Good night, everybody! *(He exits)*

KAY. I'll remember that, Judge, the next time I'm in New Orleans.

ALEXANDER. Where's Lulubelle?

MRS. DRAPER *(who has just entered with wrap)*. She's in the bedroom getting her things.

KAY *(crossing Mrs. Draper downstage to door at left)*. I'd better get mine. *(She exits)*

ALEXANDER. My coat is out there, isn't it? *(He indicates hall and exits into it)*

MRS. DRAPER *(going to Mary)*. It was so nice meeting you, Mrs. Matthews.

MARY. Thank you. I hope we see each other soon.

MRS. DRAPER. You don't mind my falling in love with your husband, do you?

MARY. I don't see how you could help it.

MRS. DRAPER *(to Grant)*. I hope you and Jim get together on everything.

GRANT. Whoever the candidate is, you're going to be very valuable to him. I realize that.

(Kay enters from the powder room with her wrap.)

MRS. DRAPER. Well, if there's one group I do know how to swing, it's the foreigners. I don't pretend to be an intellectual, but since our so-called great minds have gotten us into the United Nations, we can't overlook the political advantage it gives us. Remember, there are lots of voters who are afraid of Russia!—And you'd be surprised how many people hate the British!

GRANT. I don't think we can capitalize on that, Mrs. Draper. We can't build world peace on hate. We have a certain leadership in the United Nations. We have to be very jealous of it.

KAY. Yes, but, Grant, if the Party's to win, remember each nationality in America will be thinking of their home country. We can use that. Am I right, Jim?

CONOVER. In Jersey City, Mayor Hague promised the Italians we'd rebuild Italy.

KAY. Exactly!

MRS. DRAPER. We've got to promise them that, and more, too!

CONOVER. It's bound to be part of the campaign. I don't see how we can very well avoid it. *(He has been eyeing Mary)* Do you, Mary?

MARY *(taking time to swallow)*. Well, some of the Democrats are being pretty open about it.

MRS. DRAPER. I do have to run. Goodbye, Mr. Matthews. You'll find I'm right about all this! *(She shakes hands with Grant. To Mary)* Good night, Mrs. Matthews. It was a wonderful dinner—and such good talk! *(She crosses to the left arch and pauses to speak again to Mary who has followed her)* Of course my friends accuse me of thinking God is a Republican. But I'm fair-minded. I thank Him every night for Senator Bilbo. *(Mrs. Draper and Mary exit together. Kay crosses to sofa and sits. Lulubelle enters from the powder room, wearing her wrap. Judge Alexander enters from the left arch, with his topcoat on, carrying his hat.)*

ALEXANDER *(crossing to Grant)*. Mr. Matthews, I just happened to find in my overcoat pocket here a little pamphlet. It's a reprint of some of my most important decisions. I thought you might like to look it over. *(He hands pamphlet to Grant)*

GRANT. I'll be very glad to study it.

ALEXANDER. And I think I can safely

promise you the votes of five Southern States.

GRANT (*unbelieving*). In the election?

ALEXANDER. Hell, no!—In the convention! (*He crosses to the left arch*)

LULUBELLE. Mr. Matthews, I can't tell you how crazy I am about that wife of yours. And that reminds me— (*She offers her hand to shake*) Congratulations!

GRANT. Congratulations? I don't think the Democrats have conceded yet.

LULUBELLE. No, I mean on your anniversary—your weddin' anniversary!

(*Grant looks a bit blank, then it comes to him.*)

GRANT (*shaking her hand vigorously*). Oh, yes, of course! Well, thank you!

(*Sam and Spike enter from the dining room.*)

SAM. Spike, I hate to bother you with it . . .

ALEXANDER (*to Grant*). Remember, when you speak in New Orleans, you're going to be our house guest.

LULUBELLE. Good night, Mr. Matthews. But if you campaign through the South, you'd better change your name from Grant to Lee!

(*Lulubelle and Alexander exit through left arch.*)

SPIKE (*to Conover*). Jim, I'm going to try to switch Sam to your train tomorrow. You're on the Congressional, aren't you?

CONOVER. Yes.

SPIKE (*to Sam*). Better give me your space.

(*Sam hands Spike a railroad envelope. Spike sits down and makes notes on the envelope.*)

CONOVER. Yes, that's fine, Sam. I think on the way down we can have a pretty definite talk.

SPIKE. I'll get to work on it in the morning.

(*Mary enters from the left arch.*)

SAM. Well, I've got to catch up on my beauty sleep. Can I drop you, Mrs. Thorndyke?

GRANT. I'm going over to Jim's hotel with him. We can drop Mrs. Thorndyke. It's on the way.

SAM. Grant, the evening turned out fine. It was a great idea getting all these people together. Must have been something of an education for you. You see, Grant, you have to run your politics the same way you run your business. It's a question of taking practical measures.

(*Mary has come down to left of Sam. Conover is watching Mary.*)

GRANT. Sam, you'd better go home. You know you rule me. Pretty soon we'll be in an argument. (*He gives Sam a affectionate push*)

SAM. You're in a spot now where you can't indulge in any more of that radical talk. My God, look at the effect it's had on Mary!

GRANT. Sam, if you have nightmares, I'll bet they're all about Henry Wallace!

SAM (*remembering something*). Oh, say! —Hilda'd never forgive me if I forgot to show you this. (*He takes a leather picture case from his pocket*) Look! It's Bobby, taken in Japan. Made a hell of a record— sixteen Jap planes.

GRANT. You must be very proud of Bobby.

SAM. He'll be out soon. He wants to go right into the business when he gets back. No more college. And I'm going to let him. Want to train him. I haven't got too many more years left. I want to leave him the soundest business in these whole United States. (*To Mary with almost pathetic justification*) That isn't anything to be ashamed of, is it, Mary?

MARY (*distressed*). Give him my love when you write—and next time bring Hilda.

SAM. Good night, Mary. (*He kisses Mary and shakes hands with Grant*)

SPIKE. I'll leave your ticket at the hotel in the morning.

(*Jenny enters from the right arch with a tray.*)

SAM. See you on the train, Jim.

CONOVER. Good night, Sam.

(*Sam exits.*)

GRANT (*to Jenny*). Jenny, will you ask Swenson to bring down my coat? I left it upstairs.

(*Jenny exits and goes upstairs. Grant goes to the ottoman and sits.*)

KAY. Spike, why don't you get Jim's coat?

(*Spike rises and starts for the left arch. Swenson is seen going upstairs.*)

CONOVER. Well, Grant, you're still alive. I know you didn't look forward to this evening—but it wasn't so tough, was it?

GRANT. They certainly don't mind asking for heaven and earth, do they?

CONOVER. They don't expect to get heaven.

SPIKE. No, they'll settle for the earth. *(He exits into hall left. Mary sits on the arm of one of the chairs)*

KAY. I was pretty frank with them. I told them there were some things they just couldn't ask Mr. Matthews to do. They were pretty reasonable—on the whole. Of course, there's no question about it—we'll have to meet them half way. *(She sees Grant looking at her and smiles at him)* Part way, at least.

CONOVER. I'll get all these people alone. They know they can't get too tough with me. Of course there are some points we'll have to concede. We can't get through life without conceding some things, can we, Mary? *(He goes to Mary and puts his arm around her shoulder as if in reminder, but doesn't wait for an answer. Spike enters with Conover's coat)* I think all the Senator wanted to know was that Grant wouldn't fight the farm bloc. Hell, we all know we can't fight the farm bloc. They're too powerful.

(Spike helps Jim into his coat.)

GRANT. I'm afraid, Jim, that when it comes to concessions, the Senator and his crowd will have to make some. *(Swenson enters with Grant's coat and hat)* They want a floor under farm prices but no ceiling. They can't have it both ways.

CONOVER. Oh, there's always a margin of give and take. We won't have any trouble there.

GRANT *(getting into his coat)*. Don't wait up, Swenson. I'm going to be late. *(He hands Swenson the Judge's pamphlet)* And throw this away, will you? *(To the others)* Well, we'd better get going.

SPIKE. I don't think the Senator is going to be half as tough as Mrs. Draper. I started kidding her. I said it was too bad we couldn't dig up Hitler. There might be some votes in it. *(He chuckles)*. She didn't know whether I was on the level or not. And from her answer, I don't know whether she was on the level or not.

GRANT *(buttoning up his coat)*. If you ask me, I don't think she was kidding. I can't go whole hog with her, Jim.

CONOVER. Of course she goes a little overboard—but you can't dismiss the fact those issues are coming up, and we've got to find some way of making a play for the foreign vote.

KAY. We know that every nation is going to feel the peace terms have done them an injustice. We can make a perfectly honest appeal for justice, and if that gets us some votes—I don't think we should quibble.

GRANT. Which are you thinking of first, the votes or the justice?

CONOVER. Grant, we can't help ourselves! The Democrats are going to play that side of the street—they're doing it already! Mary agrees with us on that. *(He has been watching Mary. She, instead of making any comment, rises and starts for the stairway)* We can find some way to take a stand for justice and still appeal to the foreign vote—and with a clear conscience. Don't you think so, Mary?

MARY *(turns)*. No! I don't! I tried to get out of the room before I got sick, but you wouldn't let me! I've sat here listening to you making plans for Grant to trade away the peace of the world to get a few votes! Now that we're in the United Nations let's use it—use it to get Italian votes and Polish votes—let's use it to get the votes of those who hate the Russians and those who hate the British! How long is it going to be before you ask us to forgive Germany to get the German vote?

CONOVER *(warningly)*. Mary!

MARY. You heard Mrs. Draper and how much did it mean to you? "She's a little overboard"—"You can't quite go whole hog with her." And you heard Kay, too, cheering her on! None of you had the guts to tell them they are starting another war and to slap them down for it!

KAY. Now, Grant. Really!

CONOVER. Mary, do you know what you're doing?

MARY. Yes, Jim, I know what I'm doing! Look at Sam—he wants to leave a fortune to Bobby. What kind of a world is he going to leave to Bobby? The kind he wants isn't good enough for my children. Don't you know what's happened in the world? Are you willing to trust the people you brought here tonight with atomic power?

CONOVER *(harshly)*. We may not be as bright as you are, Mary, but the people here tonight were pretty representative.

MARY. Representative of what? Nobody represented the American people! They don't even represent the Republican Party. You represent what's dead in the Republican Party . . . and what's dead in the Democratic Party!

KAY. For Heaven's sake, Mary, have a little faith in Grant!

MARY. What have you got faith in? The people? You're afraid to let them know what Grant really thinks. Don't you believe in democracy?

KAY (sharply). Why do you suppose we were here tonight? What do you think we were doing? All we were planning was the next election.

MARY. Yes, I know. Everybody here tonight was thinking of the next election. Well, it's time somebody began thinking of the next generation! (She covers her face with her hands, sobbing, as she runs upstairs. There is a pause)

KAY. Well! . . . (She turns to look at Grant. Jim is also watching him. Grant is standing in thought, without moving. There is another pause) I think we could all use a drink. Let's go over to my house and go to work on some highballs. (There is another pause as they wait for Grant to break away from his thoughts)

CONOVER. Grace Draper will do what I tell her to do. But we have some things to settle. I want to be able to kid these people along.

GRANT. I'm not going to kid anybody along. I never have.

KAY (pleadingly). Grant, everybody here tonight was thinking of the future—which is how to get you elected. It's stupid right now to think in any other terms. (Grant unbuttons his coat and takes it off. Kay turns to Conover in alarm.)

CONOVER (going to Grant). Grant, I've got to talk to these people, and that means you've got to talk to me!

GRANT. I'm talking to a lot of people in my speech Thursday night. You'll be one of them. I promised myself when I went into this that I'd appeal to the best in the American people. The only advice I've ever had from any of you was to appeal to their worst. And that's what both parties are starting to do today. Let's end rationing! Who cares if Europe starves? Let's lift price ceilings—suppose it does bring inflation. Let's lower taxes and all get rich!

CONOVER. I see. You're the only honest man in politics.

GRANT. No, Jim! We have some damn good men! There are some wonderful men in the Senate and in the House, too—

Democrats and Republicans. But damn it, Jim, there aren't enough of them to shape party policies. So, to get votes, both parties are out to buy the American public. I can't do that, Jim. So I'm afraid I can't be of any use to you.

(There is a slight pause.)

KAY. Well, Grant, I won't accept that decision. Oh, Grant, we've always talked these things out together. All right, we won't discuss it any more tonight. You're upset. I'll be in touch with you tomorrow. Come on, Jim. (She starts to exit and turns back) Be sure to tell Mary it was a charming evening. (She exits)

CONOVER. I think Kay's right, Grant. You'd better sleep on it. I can stay over for another day.

GRANT. No, Jim. I've made up my mind.

CONOVER. Grant, you're wrong! In this country we play politics—and to play politics you have to play ball! (He starts out)

GRANT. I'm sorry, Jim. I've become very fond of you.

CONOVER. Oh, don't send any flowers. It's not my funeral. (He exits)

SPIKE (after a pause). Mr. Matthews, will you marry me?

GRANT (laughing). Be careful, Spike. I'm in the mood for it! I've never felt so relieved in my life. Thank God, that's settled. I hope they're all listening in Thursday night! I'm going to burn their ears off. Any candidate for any office who threatens world peace for the sake of a few votes—there's the international criminal for you, Spike! I'll take care of them Thursday night—and from now on!

SPIKE. You know, Jim may have to take you on your own terms.

GRANT. No, Spike, it's all over but the shouting—but, oh, boy, am I going to shout!

(Grant starts to take off his coat and roll up his shirt sleeves. Mary enters downstairs, is surprised to find Grant and Spike there. Grant pays no attention to her; he is busy with his thoughts.)

MARY. I thought you were gone. Where's Jim?

SPIKE. I think he's cabling General MacArthur.

GRANT (pacing). We've got to run business on a different basis . . .

MARY. What's happened?

SPIKE. Quiet, please, we're on the air.

GRANT. Sam and his type are dead! They

want to go back to something they've had before. We've got to move on to something we've never had before. And I'm going to tell off the Senator, too. . . . *(Goes to Mary)* It's time somebody spoke up for the farmers. The American farmer is not the unpatriotic, selfish, grasping bastard the farm bloc makes him out to be! Thank God, I can speak my mind now— *(He looks back at Spike)* I don't have to worry about being a candidate!

SPIKE. Now you're on the beam. Talk as though you're not a candidate and I think they'll have to make you one.

GRANT. Forget it, Spike. *(He goes to Spike and shakes his hand)* It's been great working with you. But it's all over. I'll be seeing you. This isn't good-bye.

SPIKE. You're damn right it isn't good-bye. I'll be around first thing Friday morning. *(He starts out)* See you later, Mary.

GRANT. No, Spike, it's cold. But I'm in a great spot for my speech Thursday night. I haven't any commitments.

SPIKE. You've got one.

GRANT. What?

SPIKE. You promised not to make me Postmaster General. But I'll tell you what I'm doing, Grant—I'm releasing you from that. I'll be Postmaster General. *(He exits)*

MARY. But, Grant, what happened?

GRANT. Mary, I'm not running for President. But that doesn't mean I'm out of politics. Nobody can afford to be out of politics. I'm going to be yelling from the sidelines; you've got to be yelling; everybody's got to be yelling! I'm going to be in there asking questions, and I'm going to see that the people get the answers!

MARY. There are a lot of questions to ask, Grant. You're going to be a busy man.

GRANT. You're damned right I'll be busy. Say, I didn't do a real job in any one of my plants. Let's make the trip all over again.

MARY. But, Grant, you need a rest first. We both do.

GRANT. All right. What do you say we go back to Victoria?

MARY. Victoria?

GRANT. Say—do you know something? *(He crosses to Mary, shaking finger at her)* You forgot this is our wedding anniversary!

MARY *(pretending surprise)*. I did? Oh, damn it all to hell!

(Grant gives Mary a resounding smack on the behind.)

GRANT. Cut that out, Maizie! *(The realization comes to Mary that he has smacked her and called her "Maizie." Her face slowly lights up. Grant continues pacing and talking to Mary and the world)* I've got to get back to work! We've all got to get back to work! There is a big job ahead for all of us! *(He stops and looks at Mary and then goes to her)* Darling, you're right about the future. We've got something great to work for! *(He reaches Mary and takes her in his arms)*

CURTAIN

Darkness at Noon

Based on the novel by Arthur Koestler

BY SIDNEY KINGSLEY

First presented by The Playwrights' Company at the Alvin Theatre in New York on January 13, 1951, with the following cast:

RUBASHOV	Claude Rains	IVANOFF	Alexander Scourby
GUARD	Robert Keith, Jr.	BOGROV	Norman Roland
402	Philip Coolidge	HRUTSCH	Robert Crozier
302	Richard Seff	ALBERT	Daniel Polis
202	Allan Rich	LUIGI	Will Kuluva
LUBA	Kim Hunter	PABLO	Henry Beckman
GLETKIN	Walter J. Palance	ANDRE	Geoffrey Barr
1st STORM TROOPER	Adams MacDonald	BARKEEPER	Tony Ancona
RICHARD	Herbert Ratner	SECRETARY	Lois Nettleton
YOUNG GIRL	Virginia Howard	PRESIDENT	Maurice Gosfield
2nd STORM TROOPER	Johnson Hayes	SOLDIERS, SAILORS, JUDGES AND JURORS	

ACT ONE—FIRST HEARING
A Prison—March, 1937

ACT TWO—SECOND HEARING
The Same—Five Weeks Later

ACT THREE—THIRD HEARING
The Same—One Week Later

The action of the play oscillates dialectically between the Material world of a Russian prison during the harsh days of March, 1937, and the Ideal realms of the spirit as manifested in Rubashov's memories and thoughts moving freely through time and space.

Darkness at Noon, Arthur Koestler's fascinating anti-Stalinist psychological novel, challenged the utmost skill of any playwright who would dramatize it for the stage. Sidney Kingsley proved himself a daring dramatist when he undertook the assignment. He also proved that he had the competence necessary for it when he made this taut and ingenious dramatization. Although Kingsley's forte has been realistic dramaturgy, he has not been unalterably wedded to it. That he is a flexible playwright, willing and able to employ a looser structure requiring multiple settings and short scenes, was already apparent in his anti-cartel tract *Ten Million Ghosts* (1936) and in his Jefferson-Hamilton drama *The Patriots.* In *Darkness at Noon,* the latest example of his skill, Kingsley managed to transfer the Koestler novel to the stage by means of forward and backward action without losing the advantages of unified drama, and without losing tension and excitement.

Any loss sustained in the dramatization concerns the psychological subtleties present in the Koestler novel. Kingsley, however, sacrificed these values partly as a necessity of the playwriting craft and partly as a consequence of his intention to launch an attack on Stalin's totalitarian system. Koestler's main objective had been to explain how a courageous revolutionist, a victim of the Moscow trial purges, could bring himself to the point of confessing crimes of which he was innocent, even though he knew that the confession would not save his life. For Kingsley, this was a matter of secondary interest. His main concern was with the evils of communist dictatorship. At the same time, however, he found a possibility of deepening his drama by situating this dictatorship in the more complex story of the old revolutionist Rubashov who had helped to inaugurate it, starting with noble intentions but discovering, as he reviews his life, how hazardous it is to follow the philosophy that the ends justify the means. Perhaps in writing this play, Kingsley also remembered a statement by his favorite hero, Thomas Jefferson: "Sometimes it is said that man cannot be trusted with the government of himself. Can he then be trusted with the government of others?" *Darkness at Noon* was not merely a technical feat; it was a humanized thesis drama.

Darkness at Noon did not receive unanimous endorsement from influential New York critics and won less public support than most of Kingsley's other plays. It was perhaps too grim for the taste of an entertainment-seeking clientèle. But Kingsley received the Drama Critics Award for the season of 1950-51, and a national tour was scheduled for the production, with Edward G. Robinson replacing Claude Rains in the role of Rubashov. It is difficult to imagine how a better play could have been made out of the novel without writing an Elizabethan chronicle. *Darkness at Noon,* however, was easily the most stirring of the period's small number of topical dramas.

ACT ONE

March, 1937

Granite and iron! The corridor of an ancient Russian prison buried deep underground. To the left, set into a soaring, Byzantine arch, is a thick, iron portcullis. Beyond it, visible through the bars, a steep flight of stone steps curves up out of sight. To the right a tier of cells forms an ominous column of sweating granite, towering up to vanish in the shadows above. A Guard with rifle and bayonet paces the corridor. He halts as the iron portcullis slides up to the clangor of chains, revealing an Officer and a Prisoner. The Prisoner, N. S. Rubashov, is a short, stocky, smooth-shaven, bespectacled man in his early fifties. His head is large beyond the proportions of his body, and characterized by an expanse of forehead. His eyes are set far apart and mongoloid in cast. He carries himself very erect and with fierce authority. The Guard opens the door of a cell, throws a switch in the corridor which turns on the light, and the Prisoner is pushed inside. The door clangs behind him. The heavy metallic sound of bolts being closed and a key turned. The Prisoner surveys his cell slowly: a solid, windowless cubicle with an iron bed and a straw mattress, nothing else. There is no day here, no night; it is a timeless dank grave for the living corpse. He reaches into his pocket automatically for cigarettes, then he remembers, turns to the judas-hole and observes the eye of the Guard staring at him.

———

RUBASHOV. Comrade guard! *(He turns his empty pockets inside out)* They've taken away my cigarettes, too! Can you get me a cigarette?

GUARD *(harshly)*. It's late, go to bed.

RUBASHOV. I've been dragged out of a sick-bed. I have a fever. I need some cigarettes.

GUARD *(mutters)*. Your mother! *(Turns out the light in the cell, leaving the Prisoner lit only by the light streaming through the judas-hole. The Guard goes off)*

RUBASHOV *(rubs his inflamed cheek, shakes his head, sighs, looks about, takes off his coat, slowly, painfully; throws it on the cot, murmurs to himself)*. So, it's come. You're to die, Rubashov. Well, the old guard is gone! *(He sits on the bed; rolls up his coat for a pillow, murmuring to himself)* For golden lads and girls all must as chimney sweepers come to dust. *(He takes off his spectacles, places them on the floor, and lies back, staring grimly at the ceiling)* Yes. The old guard is gone. *(He sighs again, repeats mechanically)* For golden lad and girls all must . . . *(A ticking sound is heard. Three ticks, then a pause, then three more ticks. He sits up, listening)* . . . as chimney sweepers . . . *(The ticking becomes louder. He picks up his spectacles, rises, glances at the judas-hole to make certain he is not being observed, places his ear to one wall, taps on it with his spectacles, listens, then tries another wall. Returning to the wall left, he listens, murmurs "Ah," taps three times. The answering taps become louder. He repeats the series, placing his ear to the wall; the taps now come in a different series, louder, rapid, more excited)* Easy! Slow . . . Slow. *(He taps slowly, deliberately. The answering taps slow down)* That's better . . . *(He counts the taps)* 5-3, W; 2-3, H; 3-5, O. "Who?" *(The Prisoner smiles and addresses himself softly to the wall)* Direct enough, aren't you, Comrade?

(The lights come up in the adjoining cell, the wall dissolves, the Prisoner in 402 appears. He is verminous, caked with filth, his hair matted, his old Tsarist uniform in rags, but he has somehow preserved his monocle and the tatters of an old illusion. He strokes his moustache and swaggers about as if he were still a perfumed dandy.)

402 *(As he taps on the wall, his lips unconsciously form the words and utter them. In their communications by tapping, all the prisoners unconsciously voice the messages as they tap them through)*. Who are you? *(Pause, as Rubashov shakes his head but doesn't answer. Taps again)* Is it day or night outside?

RUBASHOV *(glances again at the judas-hole, taps)*. 4:00 A.M.

402 *(taps)*. What day?

RUBASHOV *(taps)*. Tuesday.

402 *(taps)*. Month?

RUBASHOV *(taps)*. March . . .

402 *(taps)*. Year?

RUBASHOV *(taps)*. 1937.

402 *(taps)*. The weather?

RUBASHOV *(taps)*. Snowing.

402 *(to himself)*. Snow. *(Taps)* Who are you?

RUBASHOV *(to himself)*. Well, why not? *(He taps)* Nicolai Semonovitch Rubashov.

402 *(straightens up with a cry)*. Rubashov? *(He bursts into wild ugly laughter. He taps)* The wolves are devouring each other! *(Crosses over to the opposite wall. Taps three times, and listens, his ear to the wall. The cell above lights up and the occupant rises painfully from his cot. He is a young man, thin, with a white ghostlike face, bruises and burns on it, and a split lip. He crosses with effort to the wall, taps three times, then listens as 402 taps)* New prisoner. Rubashov.

302 *(taps)*. Nicolai Rubashov?

402 *(laughing hoarsely as he taps)*. N. S. Rubashov. Ex-Commissar of the People, ex-Member of the Central Committee, ex-General of the Red Army, Bearer of the Order of the Red Banner. Pass it along.

302 *(crouches, stunned, cries out suddenly)*. Oh! Father, Father, what have I done? . . . *(He crosses to the opposite wall, taps three times. An answering tap is heard. The cell above lights up; 202, a peasant with insane eyes, puts his head to the floor as 302 taps)*

302 *(taps)*. N. S. Rubashov arrested. Pass it along.

202. Rubashov? Well, well! *(Crosses to other wall, taps)* N. S. Rubashov arrested. Pass it along.

(The tiers of cells darken and vanish, leaving only Rubashov visible, leaning against the wall, staring into space. The taps echo and re-echo throughout the prison, to the whispering accompaniment: "N. S. Rubashov arrested! N. S. Rubashov arrested!" The whispers grow into the roar of a mighty throng calling out, "Rubashov! Rubashov!" Rubashov's voice is heard, young and triumphant, addressing the crowd.)

RUBASHOV'S VOICE. Comrades! *(The tumult subsides)* Proletarians, soldiers and sailors of the Revolution. The great, terrible and joyful day has arrived! *(The crowd roars. Rubashov, listening to the past, head bowed, paces his cell slowly)* Eight months ago the chariot of the bloodstained and mire-bespattered Romanov monarchy was tilted over at one blow. *(The oceanic roar of the crowd)* The gray, stuttering Provisional Government of bourgeois democracy was already dead and only waiting for the broom of History to sweep its putrid corpse into the sewer. In the name of the Revolutionary Committee I now declare the Provisional Government overthrown. *(The roar swells)* Power to the Soviets! Land to the peasants! Bread to the hungry! Peace to all the peoples! *(The victorious shouts of "Rubashov! Rubashov!" mount to a crescendo, fade away and die, leaving only the blanketed stillness of the cell and Rubashov listening to his memories. Three taps from 402's wall arouse him. He responds, ear to the wall. The wall dissolves, revealing 402.)*

402 *(taps, gloating)*. Serves you right.

RUBASHOV *(to himself)*. What is this? *(Taps)* Who are you?

402 *(taps)*. None of your damned business . . .

RUBASHOV *(taps)*. As you like.

402 *(taps)*. Long live His Majesty, the Tsar!

RUBASHOV. So that's it. *(Taps)* I thought you birds extinct.

402 *(beats out the rhythm with his shoe)*. Long live the Tsar!

RUBASHOV *(grins sardonically, taps)*. Amen! Amen!

402 *(taps)*. Swine!

RUBASHOV *(amused, taps out)*. Didn't quite understand.

402 *(in a frenzy, hammers out)*. Dirty swine . . .

RUBASHOV *(taps)*. Not interested in your family tree.

402 *(fury suddenly passes, taps out slowly)*. Why have you been locked up?

RUBASHOV *(taps)*. I don't know. *(Pause)*

402 *(taps)*. Anything happened? Big? Assassination? War?

RUBASHOG *(taps)*. No. Can you lend me tobacco?

402 *(taps)*. For you? I'd be castrated first.

RUBASHOV *(taps)*. Good idea.

(402 walks away, lies down on his cot. The lights fade out on him.)

RUBASHOV *(paces his cell, counting off the steps)*. 1-2-3-4-5- and a half . . . *(He wheels back)* 1-2-3-4 . . . *(Strange ghostly voices are dimly heard)* It starts. So soon. *(The vague outline of ghostly faces hover above him)* The waking, walking dreams. *(Other ghostly faces appear in space)* Yes, you sailors of Kronstadt—I shall pay . . . And you nameless ones. *(The face of a little hunchback appears, smoking a pipe and smiling)* And Comrade Luigi. *(Some plates appear dancing in space—then a big moon-face of a man, juggling them, grinning)* And Pablo. *(The luminous face of a young woman appears in space. A striking face; large, soft brown eyes; dark hair; white skin)* And Luba. *(The voices and faces fade away)* My debts will be paid—my debts will be paid.

(The young woman materializes. The cell becomes the office of the Commissar of the Iron Works. Huge graphs hang on the walls. Through the window, a vista of factory chimneys and the skeletons of incompleted buildings may be seen. The young woman is bent over her notebook, taking down dictation. Rubashov walks up and down, dictating. In the pauses, she raises her head, and her soft, round eyes follow his wanderings through the room. There is wonder and worship in the way she looks at him. She wears a white peasant blouse, embroidered with little flowers at the high neck. Her body is generously formed and voluptuous.)

RUBASHOV *(dictates)*. "To meet the Five-Year Plan we must step up our tempo. A twelve-hour day if necessary. Tempo! Tempo!" *(The girl tosses her head as she writes, and her dangling earrings attract his attention. He frowns. Her head buried in her notebook, she does not observe this)* ". . . The Unions will dismiss workers who come late and deprive all laggards of their food cards . . ." *(She quickly reaches down to scratch her ankle, and he notices she is wearing high-heeled slippers. He frowns again)* ". . . In the building of a new, hitherto undreamt-of Communist state, we must be guided by one rule, dash, the end justifies the means, period. Relentlessly, exclamation point." *(The girl bobs her head, the earrings sway. He suddenly growls)* Why do you wear those earrings? And those high heels? With a peasant blouse. Ridiculous! *(The girl looks up)* What's your name?

LUBA. Loshenko.

RUBASHOV. Loshenko?

LUBA. Yes, Comrade Commissar. Luba Loshenko. *(Her voice is low and hoarse, but gentle)*

RUBASHOV. And how long have you been working here?

LUBA. For you, Comrade Commissar?

RUBASHOV *(growls)*. Yes, for me. Of course, for me.

LUBA. Three weeks.

RUBASHOV. Three? Really? Well, Comrade Loshenko, don't dress up like a ceremonial elephant in the office!

LUBA. Yes, Comrade Commissar, I'm sorry.

RUBASHOV. You weren't wearing those earrings yesterday?

LUBA. No, Comrade Commissar, I wasn't.

RUBASHOV. Then what are you getting dressed up for now? What's the occasion? This is an office. We've work to do. Ridiculous . . . Where was I?

LUBA *(glances at her notebook)*. "The end justifies the means, period. Relentlessly, exclamation point."

RUBASHOV. Mm! *(He picks up some papers from the desk, glances at them)* "You liberals sitting on a cloud, dangling your feet in the air . . ." *(He turns and looks at her; she is watching him, but quickly turns back to her notebook)* You—you've really very pretty little ears. Why do you ruin them with those survivals of barbaric culture? *(She plucks off the earrings)* That's better. And don't look so frightened. I'm not going to eat you. What do you people in this office think I am? An ogre? I don't eat little children.

LUBA *(looks at him)*. I'm not frightened.

RUBASHOV. You're not?

LUBA. No.

RUBASHOV *(surprised)*. Humph! Good! Good! Where was I?

LUBA *(scans her notebook)*. "Sitting on a cloud, dangling your feet in the air."

RUBASHOV. Ah! *(She looks up at him and smiles. In spite of himself he returns her smile)* Yes . . . *(Then soberly again)* "You liberals are wrong." *(He begins to pace)* "And those who are wrong will pay . . . !" *(The image of the girl fades; the office vanishes, and he is back in his cell)* Yes, Luba, I will pay. I will pay my debt to you, above all. . . . *(Three taps are heard from 402's wall. He turns to the wall, fiercely)* But not you. I owe you nothing. How many of your people have I killed? No matter. You taught us to hate. *(Three taps from 402)* You stood over us with the knout and the hangman. *(Three taps from 402)* Your police made us fear this world, your priests the next, you poured melted lead down our throats, you massacred us in Moscow, you slit the bellies of our partisans in Siberia and stuffed them with grain. No! (*Crossing to the wall*) You? I owe no debt to you. (*Three taps from 402. Rubashov places his ear to the wall, taps curtly*) What do you want?

402 (*appears, tapping*). I'm sending you tobacco.

RUBASHOV (*after a long pause, taps*). Thanks. (*Sighs, murmurs to the wall*) Do I owe you a debt too? We at least acted in the name of humanity. Mm. But doesn't that double our debt? (*He shakes his head, cynically*) What is this, Rubashov? A breath of religious madness? (*A feverish chill shakes him. He puts on his coat*)

402 (*rattles his door, peers through the judas-hole, calls*). Guard! Guard! (*The Guard is heard shuffling across the corridor*)

GUARD (*through the bars of the judas-hole*). What do you want?

402. Could you take this tobacco to cell 400?

GUARD. No.

402. I'll give you a hundred rubles.

GUARD. I'll give you my butt in your face.

402 (*walks away*). For two rubles he'd cut his mother's throat.

GUARD (*returns to the judas-hole, menacingly*). What did you say?

402 (*cringes, whining*). Nothing! I said nothing. (*The Guard shuffles off. 402 crosses to wall, taps*) You're in for it.

RUBASHOV (*on sudden impulse goes to the iron door of his cell, bangs on it, shouting*). Guard! Guard! (*The Guard is heard approaching down the corridor*)

GUARD. Quiet! You're waking everyone. (*His shadow appears in the judas-hole*)

RUBASHOV (*peremptorily commands*). Tell the Commandant I must speak to him.

GUARD (*cackles*). Oh, sure.

RUBASHOV. At once!

GUARD. Who do you think you are?

RUBASHOV. Read your Party history.

GUARD. I know who you are.

RUBASHOV. Then don't ask idiotic questions.

GUARD. You're Number 400, in solitary, and you're probably going to be taken down in the cellar and shot. Now don't give me any more trouble or you'll get a butt in your face.

RUBASHOV. You try it and we'll see who'll be shot. (*The Guard hesitates. Rubashov again hammers on the door*)

GUARD. You're waking everyone. Stop that or I'll report you.

RUBASHOV. Do so! Report me! At once!

GUARD. I will. (*He goes*)

(*Rubashov continues to hammer on the cell door. The lights come up in the cell tier, bringing the other prisoners into vision. They have been listening to this exchange through the judas-hole. 302 turns from the door and seats himself on his cot. Slowly, painfully, he begins to tap the signal to 402.*)

(*402 stands on his cot, responds and listens.*)

302 (*taps*). Outside?

402 (*taps*). It's morning, 4:00 A.M., Tuesday. March. Snowing.

302 (*taps*). Send Rubashov my greetings.

402 (*taps*). Who shall I say?

302 (*taps*). Just say an old friend.

(*402 crosses to Rubashov, summons him with a tap. Rubashov rises and listens at the wall as 402 taps: 302 sends greetings.*)

RUBASHOV (*taps*). What's his name?

402 (*taps*). Won't say. Just old friend. He was tortured last week.

RUBASHOV (*taps*). Why?

402 (*taps*). Political divergencies.

RUBASHOV. Your kind?

402 (*taps*). No, your kind.

RUBASHOV (*taps*). How many prisoners here?

402 (*taps*). Thousands. Come and go.

RUBASHOV (*taps*). Your kind?

402 (*taps*). No. Yours. I'm extinct. Ha! Ha!

RUBASHOV (*taps*). Ha! Ha! (*Footsteps approaching ring out in the corridor. He taps quickly*) Someone's coming.

(*402 vanishes. Rubashov throw himself on the cot.*)

(*A huge, young man in an officer's uniform enters. His shaven head, his deep-set, expressionless eyes, and his jutting, Slavic cheek-bones give him the appearance of a death's head. His stiff uniform creaks, as do his boots. The officer who arrested Rubashov and the guard are visible in the doorway. The young man enters the cell which becomes smaller through his presence. His name is Gletkin.*)

GLETKIN (*fixes Rubashov with a cold stare*). Were you the one banging on the door? *(He looks about)* This cell needs cleaning. *(To Rubashov)* You know the regulations? *(He glances behind the door, turns to the guard)* He has no mop. Get him a mop! *(The Guard hurries off)*

RUBASHOV. Are you the Commandant here?

GLETKIN. No. Why were you banging on the door?

RUBASHOV. Why am I under arrest? Why have I been dragged out of a sick-bed? Why have I been brought here?

GLETKIN. If you wish to argue with me you'll have to stand up.

RUBASHOV. If you're not the Commandant, I haven't the slightest desire to argue with you . . . or even to speak to you for that matter.

GLETKIN. Then don't bang on the door again—or the usual disciplinary measures will have to be applied. *(Turns to the arresting officer)* When was the prisoner brought in?

ARRESTING OFFICER. Ten minutes ago.

GLETKIN *(glances at his watch, sternly)*. His arrest was ordered for three A.M. sharp. What happened?

ARRESTING OFFICER. The car broke down.

GLETKIN. That's inexcusable. It's the Commandant's new car, and it was in perfect condition. This looks very suspicious. *(He takes out a note-book and writes in it)* Send the driver up to my office at once!

RUBASHOV. It's not his fault. It wasn't sabotage.

GLETKIN *(writes, without glancing up)*. How do you know it wasn't?

RUBASHOV. Make allowances.

GLETKIN. For what?

RUBASHOV. Our roads.

GLETKIN *(puts away the note-book and measures Rubashov impersonally)*. What's the matter with our roads?

RUBASHOV. They're primitive cow paths.

GLETKIN. Very critical, aren't we? I suppose the roads in the bourgeois countries are better?

RUBASHOV *(looks at Gletkin, smiles cynically)*. Young man, have you ever been outside of our country?

GLETKIN. No. I don't have to . . . to know. And I don't want to hear any fairy tales.

RUBASHOV. Fairy tales? *(Sits up)* Have you read any of my books or articles?

GLETKIN. In the Komsomol Youth I read your political-education pamphlets. In their time I found them useful.

RUBASHOV. How flattering! And did you find any fairy tales in them?

GLETKIN. That was fifteen years ago. *(Pause)*. Don't think that gives you any privileges now! *(The Guard appears, flapping a dirty rag. Gletkin takes it, throws it at Rubashov's feet)* When the morning bugle blows, you will clean up your cell. You know the rules. You've been in prison before?

RUBASHOV. Yes. Many of them. But this is my first experience under my own people. *(He rubs his inflamed jaw)*

GLETKIN. Do you wish to go on sick call?

RUBASHOV. No, thanks. I know prison doctors.

GLETKIN. Then you're not really sick?

RUBASHOV. I have an abscess. It'll burst itself.

GLETKIN *(without irony)*. Have you any more requests?

RUBASHOV. Tell your superior officer I want to talk to him and stop wasting my time!

GLETKIN. Your time has run out, Rubashov! *(He starts to go, pulling the door behind him)*

RUBASHOV *(murmurs in French)*. Plus un singe monte . . .

GLETKIN *(re-enters quickly)*. Speak in your own tongue! Are you so gone you can't even think any longer except in a filthy, foreign language?

RUBASHOV *(sharply, with military authority)*. Young man, there's nothing wrong with the French language as such. Now, tell them I'm here and let's have a little Bolshevik discipline! *(Gletkin stiffens, studies Rubashov coldly, turns and goes, slamming the iron door. The jangle of the key in the lock; his footsteps as he marches off down the corridor. Suddenly Rubashov bounds to the door. He shouts through the judas-hole)* And get me some cigarettes! Damn you! *(Rubs his inflamed cheek, ruefully. To himself)* Now, why did you do that, Rubashov? What does this young man think of you? "Worn-out old intellectual! Self-appointed Messiah! Dares to question the party line! Ripe for liquidation . . ." There you go again, Rubashov—the old disease. *(Paces)* 4 . . . 5. Revolutionaries shouldn't see through

other people's eyes. Or should they? How can you change the world if you identify yourself with everybody? How else can you change it? *(Paces)* 3 . . . 4. *(He pauses, frowning, searching his memory)* What is it about this young man? Something? *(Paces)* 3 . . . 4. Why do I recall a religious painting? A Pietà, a dead Christ in Mary's arms? Of course—Germany. The Museum, Leipzig, 1933. *(Slowly the prison becomes a museum in Germany. A large painting of the Pietà materializes. An S.S. Officer in black uniform and swastika arm-band is staring at the Pietà. His face, though different from Gletkin's in features, has the same, cold, fanatical expression. Rubashov, catalogue in hand, walks slowly down, studying a row of invisible paintings front; then he crosses over, studies the Pietà. The S.S. Officer glances at him with hard searching eyes, then goes.)*
(A middle-aged man with a sensitive face, sunken cheeks, enters, looks alternately at the catalogue he is holding and the paintings in space. He halts next to Rubashov, squinting to make out the title.)
MAN *(softly, reading)*. "Christ Crowned With Thorns."
RUBASHOV *(turns, front, nods)*. Titian.
MAN *(to Rubashov)*. What page is it in your catalogue, please? *(Rubashov, without looking at him, hands over his catalogue. Man glances at it, looks about hurriedly, returns it, whispers hoarsely)* Be very careful. They're everywhere.
RUBASHOV. I know. You're late, Comrade Richard.
RICHARD. I went a round-about way.
RUBASHOV. Give me your report.
RICHARD. It's bad.
RUBASHOV. Give it to me.
RICHARD. Since the Reichstag fire, they've turned the tables on us. It's a massacre. All Germany is a shambles. Two weeks ago we had six hundred and twelve cells here—today there are fifty-two left. The Party is a thousand-headed mass of bleeding flesh. Two of my group jumped out of a window last night in order to avoid arrest! *(His lips start to tremble; his entire body is suddenly convulsed)*
RUBASHOV *(sharply)*. Control yourself! *(Glances about)* You're one of the leaders here. If you go on this way, what can we expect of the other comrades?

RICHARD *(controls himself with an effort)*. I'm sorry.
RUBASHOV. For a man who has written such heroic plays of the proletariat, this is surprising.
RICHARD. This is a bad moment for me. My wife, Comrade Truda, was arrested two days ago. The Storm Troopers took her and I haven't heard since.
RUBASHOV. Where were you at the time?
RICHARD. Across the street, on a roof. *(His voice becomes shrill as he begins to lose control again. A stutter creeps into his speech)* I w-w-watched them take her away.
RUBASHOV *(glances around to see if they are observed, motions Richard to the bench under the Pietà)*. Sit down. *(They both sit on the bench)* We have a big job here. We have to pull the Party together. We have to stiffen its backbone. This is only a temporary phase.
RICHARD. We carry on, Comrade. We work day and night. We distribute literature in the factories and house to house.
RUBASHOV. I've seen some of these pamphlets. Who wrote them?
RICHARD. I did.
RUBASHOV. You did?
RICHARD. Yes. Why?
RUBASHOV. They're not quite satisfactory, Comrade Richard.
RICHARD. In what respect?
RUBASHOV. A bit off the line. We sense a certain sympathy with the Liberals and the Social Democrats.
RICHARD. The Storm Troopers are . . . *(The stammer again creeps into his speech)* Sl . . . sl . . . slaughtering them, too, like animals in the street.
RUBASHOV. Let them! How does that affect us? In that respect the Nazis are clearing the way for us by wiping out this trash and saving us the trouble.
RICHARD. Trash?
RUBASHOV. The Liberals are our most treacherous enemies. Historically, they have always betrayed us.
RICHARD. But that's inhuman, man. You comrades back there act as if nothing had happened here. Try and understand! We're living in a j . . . j . . . jungle. All of us. We call ourselves "dead men on ho . . . holiday."
RUBASHOV. The party leadership here carries a great responsibility and those

who go soft now are betraying it. You're playing into the enemies' hands!

RICHARD. I . . . ?

RUBASHOV. Yes, Comrade Richard, you.

RICHARD. What is this? I suppose Truda betrayed the Party, too?

RUBASHOV. If you go on this way . . . *(Suddenly, urgently)* Speak quietly, and don't turn your head to the door! *(A tall young man in the uniform of a Storm Trooper has entered the room with a girl and they stand nearby, studying their catalogues and the pictures. The S.S. Officer whispers to the girl. She titters. Rubashov rises; in a low calm voice).* Go on talking.

RICHARD *(rises, glances at his catalogue, talking rapidly).* Roger van der Weyden, the elder, 1400 to 1464. He's probably Van Eyck's most famous pupil.

RUBASHOV. His figures are somewhat angular.

RICHARD. Yes, but look at the heads. There's real power there. And look at the depth of physiognomy. *(Again the stammer)* Compare h . . . h . . . him with the other masters; you'll see his coloring is softer . . . and I . . . I . . . lighter. *(His eyes stray to the S.S. Officer in panic and hatred)*

RUBASHOV. Did you stammer as a child? *(Sharply)* Don't look over there!

RICHARD *(looks away quickly).* S . . . sometimes.

RUBASHOV. Breathe slowly and deeply several times. *(Richard obeys. The girl with the Storm Trooper giggles shrilly, and the pair move slowly toward the exit. In passing, they both turn their heads toward Richard and Rubashov. The Storm Trooper says something to the girl. She replies in a low voice. They leave, the girl's giggling audible as their footsteps recede)*

RICHARD *(softly, to himself).* Truda used to laugh at my stutter. She had a funny little laugh.

RUBASHOV *(motioning Richard to reseat himself).* You must give me your promise to write only according to the lines laid down by the Comintern.

RICHARD *(sitting).* Understand one thing, Comrade: Some of my colleagues write easily. I don't. I write out of torment; I write what I believe and feel in here. I have no choice—I write what I must, because I must. Even if I'm wrong, I must write what I believe. That's how we arrive at the truth.

RUBASHOV. We have already arrived at the truth. Objective truth. And with us Art is its weapon. I'm amazed at you, Comrade Richard. You're seeking the truth for the sake of your own ego! What kind of delusion is this? The individual is nothing! The Party is everything! And its policy as laid down by the Comintern must be like a block of polished granite. One conflicting idea is dangerous. Not one crack in its surface is to be tolerated. Nothing! Not a mustard seed must be allowed to sprout in it and split our solidarity! The "me," the "I" is a grammatical fiction. *(He takes out his watch, glances at it)* My time is up. *(He puts his watch back in his pocket, rises)* You know what's expected of you. Keep on the line. We will send you further instructions.

RICHARD *(rises).* I don't think I can do it.

RUBASHOV. Why not?

RICHARD. I don't believe in their policy.

RUBASHOV. Against our enemies, we're implacable!

RICHARD. That means . . . ?

RUBASHOV. You know what it means.

RICHARD. You'd t . . . turn me over to the Nazis?

RUBASHOV. Those who are not with us are against us.

RICHARD. Then what's the difference between us and them? Our people here are going over to them by the tens of thousands. It's an easy step. Too easy. *(A pause. He speaks almost inaudibly)* Who can say what your Revolution once meant to me? The end of all injustice. Paradise! And my Truda now lies bleeding in some S.S. cellar. She may be dead even now Yes. In my heart—I know she's dead.

RUBASHOV *(buttons his coat).* We'll have to break this off now. We'd better go separately. You leave first, I'll follow.

RICHARD. What are my instructions?

RUBASHOV. There are none. There's nothing more to be said.

RICHARD. And that's all?

RUBASHOV. Yes, that's all! *(Walks off into the shadows)*

RICHARD *(groans).* Christ!

(Richard, the Pietà, and the Museum vanish, leaving Rubashov alone, pacing his cell. A tap from 402 brings him across

to 402's wall. Rubashov taps three times.)

402 *(becomes visible, tapping).* I've a very important question.

RUBASHOV *(taps).* What?

402 *(taps).* Promise answer?

RUBASHOV *(taps).* Your question?

402 *(taps).* When did you last sleep with a woman?

RUBASHOV *(groans; after a long pause, laughs sardonically).* Now what would you like? *(Taps)* Three weeks ago.

402 *(taps).* Tell me about it.

RUBASHOV. Ach! *(Turns away)*

402 *(taps).* Tell me! Tell me! What were her breasts like?

RUBASHOV *(to the wall).* I suppose I have to humor you. *(He taps)* Snowy, fitting into champagne glasses. *(Murmurs to the wall)* Is that your style?

402 *(taps).* Go on. Details. Her thighs.

RUBASHOV *(taps).* Thighs like wild mares. *(To the wall)* How's that?

402. Good fellow! *(Taps)* Go on! More!

RUBASHOV *(taps).* That's all. You idiot —I'm teasing you.

402 *(taps).* Go on, go on. Details, please.

(Suddenly the joke goes stale. Rubashov's face clouds as a haunting memory rises to torment him. Soft strains of distant music are heard. His hand brushes his face as if to wipe away the memory.)

RUBASHOV *(taps).* No more.

402 *(taps).* Go on, please. Please!

RUBASHOV *(to himself).* No more. No more. *(He lies down on his cot, throws his coat over him, brooding. The music rises)*

402 *(taps)* Please! *(On his knees, pleading)* Please! *(Moans and taps)* Please! *(He buries his head in his cot, pleading inaudibly as the lights fade out on him) (The lights in Rubashov's cell dim. The music swells to the strains of a piano recording of Beethoven's "Appassionata." As the lights come up, the cell dissolves and becomes Luba Loshenko's bedroom. Rubashov's cot becomes part of a large double bed. At the edge of the bed Luba, clad only in her chemise, sits smoking, dreamily staring into space, listening to the music which is coming from a small gramophone on the table nearby.)*

LUBA. So tomorrow I'll have a new boss.

RUBASHOV. Yes.

LUBA. I'll hate him.

RUBASHOV. No. He'll be all right. *(They listen in silence. He smiles, musing)* This music is dangerous.

LUBA. You'll be gone long?

RUBASHOV. I don't know.

LUBA. I'll miss you terribly *(She hums the melody of the music)*

RUBASHOV *(taking out a cigarette).* Get me a match, will you, Luba?

LUBA *(smiles, rises, walks to the table, picks up some matches, crosses to him, swaying to the music).* I love this. It always makes me feel like crying. *(She lights his cigarette)*

RUBASHOV *(smiling).* Do you enjoy that?

LUBA. Crying? *(She blows out the match, laughs)* Sometimes.

RUBASHOV. Our racial weakness.

LUBA. What?

RUBASHOV. Tears and mysticism.

LUBA. You mean the Slavic soul?

RUBASHOV *(smiling cynically).* The soul? Soul?

LUBA. I believe in it.

RUBASHOV. I know you do.

LUBA. Petty bourgeois?

RUBASHOV. Yes, Luba, you are. *(He looks at her fondly, leans over, pulls her to him, kisses her throat. The music rises)* This music is dangerous. *(They listen in silence a while. She goes to the gramophone and winds it. She leans against the wall near Rubashov)*

LUBA. When I was a little girl in the Pioneer Youth I would start crying at the most unexpected moments.

RUBASHOV. You? In the Pioneer Youth? You, Luba?

LUBA. You're surprised? I wasn't in very long. I wasn't good material. *(Rubashov smiles)* I would cry suddenly for no reason at all.

RUBASHOV. But there was a reason?

LUBA. I don't know. *(She smokes for a moment)* Yes, I do. Our primer books made little Pavelik such a hero. All of us children wanted to turn our mothers and fathers over to the G.P.U. to be shot.

RUBASHOV. Was there anything to turn them in for?

LUBA *(laughs gently).* No. Nothing. But I would picture myself doing it anyway and becoming a great national hero like Pavelik. Then I would burst out crying. I loved my parents very much. Of course no one knew why I was crying. So I was expelled, and my political career ended at the age of nine! (*Rubashov smiles. Luba hums the melody*) My father loved this. He and mother used to play it over and over and over.

RUBASHOV. Where are they now?

LUBA. They died in the famine after the Revolution. My father was a doctor.

RUBASHOV. Have you any family left?

LUBA. One brother. He's a doctor too. He's married. My sister-in-law is very nice. She's a Polish woman . . . an artist. (*Luba picks up a small painting, crosses to Rubashov, kneels at his side*) She painted this picture. It's their baby. A little boy. Two years old. Isn't he fat?

RUBASHOV (*studies it*). Yes, he is fat. (*He puts it aside, looks at Luba*) Why don't you get married, Luba, and have some fat babies of your own? Isn't there a young man at the office . . . ?

LUBA. Yes.

RUBASHOV. I thought so. And he wants to marry you?

LUBA (*rests her cheek on his knee, lovingly caresses his hand*). Yes, he does.

RUBASHOV. Well . . . ?

LUBA. No!

RUBASHOV. Why not?

LUBA. I don't love him.

RUBASHOV. Mm, I see, I see. (*A pause*)

LUBA (*suddenly*). You can do anything you wish with me.

RUBASHOV (*studies her*). Why did you say that? (*Luba shrugs her shoulders*) You don't reproach me?

LUBA. Oh, no, no, no! Why should I? (*The music swells and fills the room*)

RUBASHOV. This music is dangerous. When you listen to this and you realize human beings can create such beauty, you want to pat them on the head. That's bad. They'll only bite your hand off.

LUBA (*takes his hand, and kisses it*). Like this?

RUBASHOV (*gently*). Luba, you know, with us, there can never be anything more.

LUBA. I don't expect anything more. Did I give you the impression I expected anything more?

RUBASHOV. No. You've been very kind, Luba, and sweet. (*Pause*) I may be gone a long time. I may never see you again.

LUBA. Where are you going?

RUBASHOV (*hands her the painting*). Wherever the Party sends me.

LUBA (*rises*). I understand. I'm not asking anything. Only, wherever you go, I'll be thinking of you. I'll be with you in my mind always!

RUBASHOV (*snuffs out cigarette*). But this is exactly what I don't want.

LUBA (*turns toward him*). You don't?

RUBASHOV. No Luba, no!

LUBA (*quietly*). Oh! (*She crosses slowly to the gramophone*)

(*Suddenly the phantasmagoria of Luba and the bedroom vanish as the lights are switched on in the cell. The jangle of the key in the lock. The door flies open. A young Guard enters.*)

GUARD. All right! Get up. Come with me.

RUBASHOV. Are you taking me to your Commandant?

GUARD. Don't ask questions! Do as you're told.

RUBASHOV. Very well. (*Rises*) All the posters show our young people smiling. (*He puts on his overcoat*) Have you ever smiled?

GUARD (*humorlessly*). Yes.

RUBASHOV. Wonderful! When? On what occasion short of an execution?

(*The Guard grimly motions him out. They go. The light is switched off in his cell, as the lights come up on the prison tier.*)

402 (*crosses to 302's wall and taps*). They've taken him up.

302 (*taps*). So soon?

402 (*taps*). Pass it on.

302 (*taps*). They've taken Rubashov up. Pass it on.

202 (*taps*). I hope they give him a bad time.

302 (*taps*). Oh, no! He was a friend of the people.

202 (*taps*). Yes. (*His eyes bulge wildly as he addresses an imaginary group about him*) They're all friends of the people. Didn't they free us? Look at us. Free as birds! Everything's all right, Comrades. The land belongs to us! But, the bread belongs to them. The rivers are ours! But the fish are theirs. The forests are ours, but not the wood! That's for them. Everything's for them. (*He crosses taps*) They've taken Rubashov up! Pass it on!

(*The taps echo and re-echo throughout the prison: "Rubashov taken up," "Rubashov taken up." The lights dim and the prisoners in the honeycomb of cells vanish behind the scrim, leaving only a huge pillar of granite and iron shrouded in shadows. The lights come up on an office in the prison. A barred window reveals dawn, and snow falling, outside. The bayonet of a guard cuts back and forth across the window like a metronome. On the wall, over the desk, is a portrait of The Leader seen vaguely in shadow. The rest of the wall is empty except for faded patches where other pictures have been hung and removed. Seated at the desk, smoking a long Kremlin cigarette, is a middle-aged man in officer's uniform. He is rough, heavy-set, jowly, graying at the temples, a face once handsome, now dissipated and cynical. He is grimly examining some papers, carelessly dribbling cigarette ashes over his jacket. There is a knock at the door. The officer, Ivanoff, calls out, "Come in." The Guard enters with Rubashov.)*

IVANOFF *(gruffly, to the Guard).* Shut the door. *(Exit the Guard. Ivanoff rises, shakes his head at Rubashov, laughs; then familiarly).* Kolya!

RUBASHOV. Well . . . !

IVANOFF. Surprised?

RUBASHOV. Nothing surprises me any more. *(Ivanoff laughs, opens a drawer, takes out a box of cigarettes, limps across the room to him)* Are you the Commandant here?

IVANOFF *(shaking his head).* I'm your investigator.

RUBASHOV. That makes it difficult.

IVANOFF. Not at all. Not if we're intelligent . . . which we are. *(Offers him the box of cigarettes)* Cigarette? *(Rubashov pauses)*

RUBASHOV. Have hostilities begun yet?

IVANOFF. Why?

RUBASHOV. You know the etiquette.

IVANOFF. Take one! *(Forces the box into his hand)* Put them in your pocket, keep them.

RUBASHOV. All right. *(He takes a cigarette, and puts the box in his pocket)* We'll call this an unofficial prelude.

IVANOFF. Why so aggressive?

RUBASHOV. Did I arrest you? Or did you people arrest me?

IVANOFF. You people? *(Shakes his head, lights his own cigarette)* What's happened to you, Kolya? What a falling off is here! *(Sighs)* Ekh! Ekh!

RUBASHOV. Why have I been arrested?

IVANOFF *(gives Rubashov a match, geni-*

ally*).* Later. Sit down. Light your cigarette. Relax. *(He limps to the door, closes the judas-hole, and locks it. Rubashov sits down)* I saw you last three years ago.

RUBASHOV *(smoking his cigarette with relish).* Where?

IVANOFF. Moscow. *(As he talks he crosses up to the window and pulls the chain, letting down the iron shutters)* You were speaking. You'd just escaped from the German prison. They gave you a bad time, didn't they? They didn't dull your edge, though. *(Crosses back to Rubashov)* Good speech, plenty of bite. I was proud of my old General.

RUBASHOV. Why didn't you come back stage?

IVANOFF. You were surrounded by all the big wigs.

RUBASHOV *(dryly).* Mm, a fine assortment of opportunists, bureaucrats, and variegated pimps. *(Ivanoff grins, shakes his head, hobbles to his desk. Rubashov points to his leg)* Your leg's very good. I hadn't even noticed.

IVANOFF *(nods, smiles, sits on the desk, tapping his legs).* Automatic joints, rustless chromium plating. I can swim, ride, drive a car, dance, make love. You see how right you were? And how stupid I was.

RUBASHOV. You were young and emotional, that's all. Tell me, Sascha, does the amputated foot still itch?

IVANOFF *(laughs).* The big toe. In rainy weather.

RUBASHOV *(smoking).* Curious.

IVANOFF *(lowers his lids, squints at Rubashov, blows a smoke ring).* Not at all. Doesn't your recent amputation itch?

RUBASHOV. Mine?

IVANOFF *(calmly, blowing smoke rings).* When did you cut yourself off from the Party? How long have you been a member of the organized opposition?

RUBASHOV *(throws his cigarette away, grinds it out under his foot).* The unofficial part is over.

IVANOFF *(rises, stands over him).* Don't be so aggressive, Nicolai!

RUBASHOV *(takes off his glasses, rubs his eyes).* I'm tired, and I'm sick and I don't care to play any games with you. Why have I been arrested?

IVANOFF *(cynically, crossing back to his desk-chair).* Supposing you tell me why.

RUBASHOV *(bounds to his feet, furious).*

Stop this nonsense now! Who do you think you're dealing with? What are the charges against me?

IVANOFF *(shrugs his shoulders, leans back in his chair)*. What difference does that make?

RUBASHOV. I demand that you either read the charges—or dismiss me at once!

IVANOFF *(blows a smoke ring)*. Let's be sensible, shall we? Legal subtleties are all right for others, but for the likes of you and myself? *(He taps his cigarette ash off into the tray)* Why put on an act? When did you ever trouble about formal charges? At Kronstadt? *(He rises, confronts Rubashov)* After all—remember—I served under you. I know you.

RUBASHOV. No man fights a war without guilt. You don't win battles with rose water and silk gloves.

IVANOFF. Not our kind of battles, no!

RUBASHOV *(heatedly)*. A bloodless revolution is a contradiction in terms. Illegality and violence are like dynamite in the hands of a true revolutionary—weapons of the class struggle.

IVANOFF. Agreed.

RUBASHOV. But, you people have used the weapons of the Revolution to strangulate the Revolution! You've turned the Terror *against* the people. You've begun the blood bath of the Thermidor. *(He controls himself, speaks quietly)* And that's something quite different, my one-time friend and comrade. *(Sits)*

IVANOFF. Damn it, Kolya. I'd hate to see you shot.

RUBASHOV *(polishing his glasses, smiles sarcastically)*. Very touching of you. And exactly why do you people wish to shoot me?

IVANOFF *(flares up)*. "You people!" Again. What the hell's happened to you? It used to be "we."

RUBASHOV *(on his feet again)*. Yes, it used to be. But who is the "we" today? *(He points to the picture on the wall)* The Boss? The Iron Man and his machine? Who is the "we"? Tell me.

IVANOFF. The people, the masses . . .

RUBASHOV. Leave the masses out. You don't understand them any more. Probably I don't either. Once we worked with them. We knew them. We made history with them. We were part of them. For one little minute we started them on what promised to be a new run of dignity for man. But that's gone! Dead! And buried. There they are. *(He indicates the faded patches of wallpaper)* Faded patches on the wall. The old guard. Our old comrades. Where are they? Slaughtered! Your pock-marked leader has picked us off one by one till no one's left except a few broken-down men like myself, and a few careerist prostitutes like you!

IVANOFF. And when did you arrive at this morbid conclusion?

RUBASHOV. I didn't arrive at it. It was thrust on me.

IVANOFF. When? On what occasion would you say?

RUBASHOV. On the occasion when I came back from the Nazi slaughter house, when I looked about for my old friends, when all I could find of them were those *(Again he waves his spectacles at the tell-tale patches)* faded patches on every wall in every house in the land.

IVANOFF *(nods his head, murmurs reasonably)*. Mm, hm! I see. That's logical. And that, of course, was when you . . . *(The telephone rings. Ivanoff picks up the receiver, barks)* I'm busy . . . *(And hangs up)* When you joined the organized opposition . . .

RUBASHOV *(slowly, deliberately)*. You know as well as I do, I never joined the organized opposition.

IVANOFF. Kolya! Please! We both grew up in the tradition.

RUBASHOV *(sharply)*. I never joined the opposition.

IVANOFF. Why not? You mean you sat by with your arms folded? You thought we were leading the Revolution to destruction and you did nothing? *(Shakes his head)*

RUBASHOV. Perhaps I was too old and used up.

IVANOFF *(sits back again, clucks with good-natured disbelief)*. Ekh, ekh, ekh!

RUBASHOV *(shrugging his shoulders)*. Believe what you will.

IVANOFF. In any event, we have all the proofs.

RUBASHOV. Proofs of what? Sabotage?

IVANOFF. That, of course.

RUBASHOV. Of course.

IVANOFF. If that were all.

RUBASHOV. There's more?

IVANOFF *(nods)*. And worse. *(Rises)* Attempted murder.

RUBASHOV. Ah! And who am I supposed to have attempted to murder?

IVANOFF. Not personally. You instigated the act. Naturally.

RUBASHOV. Naturally.

IVANOFF. I told you we have proofs. *(Picks up a sheaf of typewritten pages and waves them under his nose)*

RUBASHOV. For instance?

IVANOFF. Confessions.

RUBASHOF. Whose?

IVANOFF. For one, the man who was to do the killing.

RUBASHOV. Congratulations. And who was it I instigated to murder whom?

IVANOFF. Indiscreet question.

RUBASHOV. May I read the confession? *(Rubashov reaches out for the papers. Ivanoff smiles, draws them out of his reach)* May I be confronted with the man? *(Ivanoff smiles again, shakes his head)* Who the hell would I want to murder?

IVANOFF. You've been sitting there for ten minutes telling me. *(He opens a drawer, drops in the sheaf of papers)* The man you tried to murder is the Leader. *(He slams the drawer shut)* Our Leader.

RUBASHOV *(takes off his glasses, leans forward, speaks deliberately, between his teeth)*. Do you really believe this nonsense? *(He studies Ivanoff)* Or are you only pretending to be an idiot? *(He suddenly laughs knowingly)* You don't believe it.

IVANOFF *(sits slowly, adjusting his prosthetic leg)*. Put yourself in my place. Our positions could very easily be reversed. Ask yourself that question—and you have the answer. *(Ivanoff rubs his thigh at the amputation line, stares moodily at the false leg)* I was always so proud of my body. Then to wake, to find a stump in a wire cage. I can smell that hospital room. I can see it as if it were happening now: you sitting there by my bed, soothing, reasoning, scolding, and I crying because they had just amputated my leg. *(He turns to Rubashov)* Remember how I begged you to lend me your pistol? Remember how you argued with me for three hours, till you persuaded me that suicide was petty bourgeois romanticism? *(He rises, his voice suddenly harsh)* Today the positions are reversed. Now it's you who want to throw yourself into the

abyss. Well, I'm not going to let you. Then we'll be quits.

RUBASHOV *(putting on his glasses, studies Ivanoff for a second, with an ironic smile)*. You want to save me? You've a damned curious way of doing it. I am unimpressed by your bogus sentimentality. You've already tricked me into talking my head off my shoulders. Let it go at that!

IVANOFF *(beams)*. I had to make you explode now, or you'd have exploded at the wrong time. Haven't you even noticed? *(Gestures about the room)* No stenographer! *(He crosses back to his desk, opens a drawer)* You're behaving like an infant. A romantic infant. Now you know what we're going to do? *(Extracts a dossier out of the drawer)*

RUBASHOV *(grimly)*. No, what are we going to do?

IVANOFF. We are going to concoct a nice little confession.

RUBASHOV. Ah!

IVANOFF. For the public trial.

RUBASHOV *(nods his head in amused comprehension)*. So that's it? There's to be a public trial? And I'm to make a nice little confession?

IVANOFF. Let me finish . . .

RUBASHOV *(biting out each word)*. That is to say, I'm to transform myself into a grinning chimpanzee in a zoo? I'm to beat my breast and spit at myself in a mirror, so the People can laugh and say, "The Old Guard—how ridiculous!" I'm to pick at my own excrement and put it in my own mouth, so the People can say, "The Old Guard—how disgusting!" No, Sascha, no! You've got the wrong man.

IVANOFF *(drawling with exaggerated patience)*. Let me finish. *(The patience vanishes. He shouts at Rubashov)* Which are we to save? Your dignity or your head? *(He controls his impatience, begins to talk rapidly, thinking out the plan in his own mind, as he paces to and fro)* You make this confession now. You admit developing a deviation. You joined such and such an opposition bloc. You give us their names. (They've all been shot by now, anyway, so nothing's lost.) However, when you learned of their terroristic plans, you were shocked. You broke off with them. You see?

RUBASHOV. Yes, I see.

IVANOFF. Your case then goes to public

trial. We refute the murder charge completely. Even so, you'll get twenty years. But in two, perhaps three years, a reprieve. In five years you'll be back in the ring again. And that is all that matters. *(He stops and nods cheerfully at Rubashov)*

RUBASHOV. No, I'm sorry.

IVANOFF *(his smile fades, he lights a fresh cigarette, speaks slowly, dryly).* Then your case will be taken out of my hands. You'll be tried in secret session administratively. You know what that means?

RUBASHOV. Yes. The rubber ball in my mouth, the bullet in the back of the neck.

IVANOFF *(shakes out the match, blows a perfect smoke ring, and smiles).* The methods follow logically. You just disappear into thin air. As far as your followers are concerned, no demonstrations. How can they? Perhaps you're off on a mission? Perhaps you've run away? Hidden somewhere? Suspicious, of course. But what does that matter? N. S. Rubashov has vanished. Pf! Quietly! Forever! That's your alternative. *(The phone rings. Ivanoff picks up the receiver)* Look here, I'm . . . What? Oh! Yes? Yes. I see. I'll investigate at once. *(He hangs up, turns to Rubashov, chuckles, and nods his head)* You fox! Oh, you old fox! *(He picks up the phone, presses a button. An answering voice responds)* Gletkin? Ivanoff. Come to my office at once! The Rubashov arrest. You bungled it, that's what. Yes. At once! *(He hangs up. Turns again to Rubashov)* Very adroit.

RUBASHOV. Really? What have I done now?

IVANOFF. You've no idea?

RUBASHOV. I have a small notion. Nuisance tactics! Of no real importance. You overestimate them.

(Gletkin enters; crosses above the desk, salutes stiffly. Ivanoff returns the salute.)

IVANOFF. I have just received a phone call from the prosecutor's office. Your men were instructed to arrest Citizen Rubashov as quietly as possible. What the hell went wrong?

GLETKIN. I'm interrogating the arresting officers now. The prisoner refused them entrance and barricaded his door against them.

IVANOFF. So they shot off the lock?

RUBASHOV *(with mock indignation).* Woke up the whole neighborhood.

GLETKIN *(not glancing at him).* There was no alternative.

RUBASHOV *(over his shoulder to Gletkin).* There were five alternatives. You need some lessons in elementary tactics. *(Stung, Gletkin turns toward Rubashov.)*

IVANOFF *(quickly, commanding).* Go on!

GLETKIN. Then he refused to accompany them on his feet. They were forced to pick him up and carry him out bodily, screaming like a woman.

RUBASHOV. Wrong! Roaring like a bear. A wounded bear. And they tore my pants. *(Gletkin stands there, straight as a ramrod, his eyes expressionless, in perfect control now.)*

IVANOFF. Your instructions were to treat him with care. You will see that the prisoner gets cigarettes and medical attention.

RUBASHOV. Not unless you furnish an outside physician. I know these prison doctors.

GLETKIN. That is against regulations.

IVANOFF *(to Rubashov).* We'll see what can be done. *(To Gletkin)* Wait outside. *(Exit Gletkin)* You'll be given every consideration. Pencil and paper, if you wish . . .

RUBASHOV. Many thanks, but it won't work. I've had my bellyful of this farce. *(He rises)* Kindly have me taken to my cell.

IVANOFF. As you like. *(He picks up the phone, presses a button, and barks)* Guard! *(He hangs up)* I didn't expect you to confess at once. Take your time. You have plenty of time. Think it over. When you are ready to confess, send me a note. *(The men stare at each other. Ivanoff smiles)* You will. I'm sure you will.

RUBASHOV. Never, Sascha. That's final! *(The door is opened. The Guard enters.)*

IVANOFF. The next decade will decide the fate of the world in our era. Don't you want to be here to see it? *(Rubashov glances at Ivanoff, then turns and goes off with the Guard)*

(As soon as Rubashov leaves, Ivanoff drops his monumental calm, rises and calls out irritably, "Gletkin!" As Gletkin enters, Ivanoff speaks quickly and harshly, hobbling up and down nervously.)

IVANOFF. By now all Moscow knows. Make a full report. Send the arresting officers over to Headquarters. *(Indicates the chair)* Sit down. *(Gletkin sits)* Now, look here! I want it clearly understood. This is no ordinary prisoner. We can't afford any more bungling. When you handle this man you dance on eggs! The political and historical importance of these trials is enormous. And N. S. Rubashov is the key figure. We must have his confession. Those are our orders. From the top.

GLETKIN. Then why not turn him over to me? I'll bring you his confession in three days.

IVANOFF. Thanks! And you'll carry N. S. Rubashov to the witness stand in pieces? Wonderful. No, your harsh methods won't work here. Not with this man. (Lights a fresh cigarette, calms down) He'll confess. There's enough of the old Bolshevik left in him. He'll confess. You're to leave him in peace. I don't want him disturbed. He's to have paper, pencils, cigarettes, extra rations . . .

GLETKIN. Why?

IVANOFF. To accelerate the processes of thought. He has to work this out alone. (Taps his head) In here.

GLETKIN. This approach, in my opinion, is all wrong.

IVANOFF (looks at Gletkin with veiled amusement). You don't like him? You had a little trouble with him a few minutes ago, didn't you?

GLETKIN. That has nothing to do with it.

IVANOFF. Old Rubashov can still spit a sword! What'd he do? Cut you up the middle?

GLETKIN (coldly). His personality has nothing to do with it. I hope I'm a better Party member than that. I never allow likes or dislikes to interfere with my judgment.

IVANOFF. Very commendable.

GLETKIN. Only, since this confession is so important to the Party, I consider your method wrong. This won't get you results. I know how to handle these old-timers. They're all rotten at the core. They're all infected with the Western leprosy. If you want a confession, turn him over to me.

IVANOFF. You young people amuse me. You know everything, don't you? The Nazis captured this man, broke his leg, smashed his jaw, killed him and brought him to life again—I don't know how many times—but they couldn't extract one admission out of him. And finally, he escaped. And you're going to break him for me in three days? (Musing) No! If he confesses it won't be out of cowardice. (To Gletkin) Your methods won't work with him. He's made out of a material, the more you hammer it, the tougher it gets.

GLETKIN. I don't agree. My experience with these old counter-revolutionaries proves otherwise. The human nervous system at best can only stand so much—and when they have these bourgeois flaws in them, a little pressure—in the right places—and they split like rotten logs.

IVANOFF (laughs softly, shakes his head). I'd hate to fall into your hands.

GLETKIN. It's my experience that every human nervous system has a breaking point under pain. It's only necessary to find the lever, the special pain . . .

IVANOFF (abruptly and harshly). That'll do!

GLETKIN (rises stiffly). You asked me.

IVANOFF (pause). Comrade Gletkin, in the early days . . . (He goes to his desk, opens a drawer, takes out a bottle and several glasses. He fills the glasses, pushes one over to Gletkin) . . . before you were born, we started the Revolution with the illusion that some day we were going to abolish prisons and substitute flower gardens. Ekh, ekh! Maybe, some day. (He tosses off his drink)

GLETKIN. Why are you all so cynical?

IVANOFF. Cynical? (Turns and surveys him) Please explain that remark!

GLETKIN. I'd rather not, if you don't mind.

IVANOFF. I do mind. Explain it.

GLETKIN (picks up the glass, drains it). I notice you older men always talk as if only the past were glorious . . . or some distant future. But we're already far ahead of any other country, here and now! As for the past, we have to crush it. The quicker, the better.

IVANOFF. I see. (He sits, shaking his head, amused) In your eyes, then, I am the cynic?

GLETKIN. Yes, I think so. (He crosses to the table, sets down the glass, abruptly)

IVANOFF. Well, that may be. As for Rubashov, my instructions remain. He's to be left alone, and he will become his own torturer.

GLETKIN. I don't agree.

IVANOFF. He'll confess. (He catches the expression in Gletkin's face, then sharply)

You're to leave him alone! That's an order.

GLETKIN. As you command. *(Clicks his heels, jerks to attention, wheels about and marches out as if on parade. Ivanoff curls his lip in disgust, pours himself a stiff drink, sighs heavily, and drinks . . . as the scene fades out)*

(The lights come up on all the cells. Rubashov is seated on his cot, smoking, wrapped in thought. The other prisoners are passing communications down the grapevine.)

202 *(taps)*. All the prisoners ask Rubashov not to confess. Die in silence.

302 *(taps)*. Prisoners ask Rubashov not to confess. Die in silence.

(402 crosses to Rubashov's wall and signals. Rubashov raises his head, pauses, slowly rises, glances at the judas-hole, then crosses to the wall, responds to the signal.)

402 *(taps)*. Prisoners ask you not to give in. Don't let them make you go on trial.

RUBASHOV *(pause, then taps)*. How was 302 tortured?

402 *(taps)*. Steam.

(Rubashov, grimly, puffs at his lit cigarette, till it glows, blows off the ashes, presses the live coal into the back of his hand, and holds it there without flinching, staring stoically at the blue wisps of smoke that curl up from his burning flesh. Finally, he grinds out the cigarette, tosses it away.)

402 *(taps again)*. You'll die in silence? You'll die in silence?

RUBASHOV *(taps wearily)*. I will. Tell them. I will.

402 *(taps)*. My respects. You're a man! *(He crosses, taps on 302's wall)* Rubashov will die in silence. Pass it on.

302 *(taps)*. Rubashov will die in silence. Pass it on.

(The news is tapped through the prison and a murmur like a wind rises and falls: "Rubashov will die in silence . . . Rubashov will die in silence . . ." The lights fade, and the prisoners in the tier vanish.)

(Rubashov, staring at the scorched hand, crosses to his cot, sits, nods his head, and murmurs: As chimney sweepers come to dust . . . to dust . . . to dust . . . The lights fade on him.)

CURTAIN

ACT TWO

SCENE: *Rubashov's cell, five weeks later.*

AT RISE: *Darkness. Bars of light from the judas-hole illuminate Rubashov's feverish face. His eyes are closed; he is dreaming evil dreams. He breathes heavily, moaning and tossing about fitfully on his cot. Ghostly images hover over and around him; ghostly voices whisper hollowly: "Rubashov! Rubashov!" Echoes of the past—Richard's voice calling: "Christ crowned with thorns!", Luba's voice, rich and low, "You can do anything you want with me." The nameless ones appear and disappear, whispering, "Rubashov, Rubashov."*

Rubashov, dreaming, raises his head, his eyes shut, and cries out: Death is no mystery to us. There's nothing exalted about it. It's the logical solution to political divergencies. *His head falls back again, turning from side to side, moaning.*

The lights come up in the corridor. A sound of heels on a stone floor. Gletkin enters from a door right, coming up from the execution cellar; he is followed by a young fellow officer. They move toward Rubashov's cell, talking inaudibly. Ivanoff enters through the gate, glimpses them, stops short, then calls out sharply: "Gletkin!" Gletkin halts, turns to face Ivanoff.

IVANOFF *(hobbles down to Gletkin, scrutinizing him suspiciously)*. What are you up to?

GLETKIN *(very correct)*. I don't understand you, Comrade.

IVANOFF. No. I'm sure you don't. Have you been at my prisoner?

GLETKIN. Been at him?

IVANOFF *(irritably)*. Laid your hands on him. You understand that, don't you?

GLETKIN. I haven't seen Citizen Rubashov for five weeks. However, I am informed, in the line of duty, his fever is worse. I suggest it would be advisable I bring him to the prison doctor.

IVANOFF *(blows a smoke ring, then slowly, measuring his words)*. Keep away from him. And keep that prison doctor away from him. *(Sharply)* My orders still stand.

GLETKIN. Very well, Comrade. They'll be obeyed.

(Ivanoff snorts, blows smoke into his face

*then turns and limps off. They watch him
go. The Young Officer turns to Gletkin
who has taken out his note-book and is
writing in it.)*

YOUNG OFFICER. Comrade Ivanoff's
nerves are wearing thin.

GLETKIN. I'm afraid this prisoner is
proving stubborn. I told them when they
brought him in that I could break him.

YOUNG OFFICER. Easily.

GLETKIN. Comrade Ivanoff wants to use
psychological methods only.

YOUNG OFFICER *(scornfully)*. These old
bookworms of the Revolution!

GLETKIN. Tonight I'm using psychological methods. *(Closes his note-book,
puts it away)* I'll break this prisoner.

YOUNG OFFICER. Against orders?

GLETKIN. No. I won't so much as go
near his cell. But *(Glances at his watch)*
inside an hour he'll be ready to confess.

YOUNG OFFICER. How?

GLETKIN *(enigmatically)*. It'll be very
interesting.

*(Rubashov wakes, sits up with a sudden
start, listening. The lights in the tier of
cells come up.)*

*(402 sits up abruptly, wakening suddenly,
also listens, frozen. 302 and 202 also
awaken—suddenly and listen to the
ominous stillness. The lights fade on Gletkin and the Young Officer.)*

*(The prisoners rise, one by one, and be-
gin to pace nervously to and fro like
caged animals. Once in a while one of
them will pause, listen, and then continue
to pace. Rubashov rises, wipes the perspiration from his face with the sleeve of
his coat, listens, then crosses to 402's wall,
taps, waits, and 402 responds.)*

RUBASHOV *(taps)*. Did I wake you?

402 *(taps)*. No.

RUBASHOV *(taps)*. Something's happening . . .

402 *(taps)*. You feel it too?

RUBASHOV *(taps)*. What?

402 *(taps)*. Don't know. Something.
How's your fever?

RUBASHOV *(taps)*. Not good.

402 *(taps)*. Try to sleep. *(Overhead
302 taps signal)* Wait! *(Crosses over to
302's segment of wall, and answers the
signal)*

302 *(taps)*. Who is Bogrov?

402 *(taps)*. Don't know. *(Returns, taps)*
Who is Bogrov?

RUBASHOV *(taps)*. Mischa Bogrov?

402 *(taps)*. No first name.

RUBASHOV *(taps)*. I know a Mischa Bogrov. Why?

402 *(taps)*. Name tapped through.

RUBASHOV *(taps)*. He arrested?

402 *(taps)*. Don't know. Name Bogrov.
That is all.

RUBASHOV *(taps)*. What connection?

402 *(taps)*. Don't know.

RUBASHOV *(to himself)*. Curious.

*(The lights fade on the other prisoners as
they start to pace nervously. Rubashov,
alone, thinking, smiles, murmurs: Mischa.
He sits on his cot, shaking his head.
Mischa!)*

*(A chorus of men singing is faintly heard.
It grows louder. The bronze of a flickering campfire. Russian soldiers and marines
of the Revolution, in conglomerate uniforms, half-military, half-civilian, laden
with assorted weapons, dangling stick
grenades and daggers, are gathered around
the fire, smoking, warming their hands,
singing. General Rubashov, his face shining with reflected firelight, shakes his
head and beats out the tune as a big, snub-
nosed, sandy-haired marine with thick
shoulders and an enchanting smile, sings
out in a mellow, ringing voice:*

"In the dawn's light, faintly gleaming
Stand the ancient Kremlin walls;
And the land, no longer dreaming,
Now awakes as morning calls.
Though the winds are coldly blowing,
Streets begin to hum with noise;
And the sun with splendor glowing
Greets the land with all its joys.
We'll shout aloud for we are proud;
Our power is invincible.
We'll ne'er disband, we'll always stand
Together for dear Moscow's land."

*The marine punctuates the finish by toss-
ing his hat in the air. The others applaud
and shout: "Bravo Mischa! Bravo Mischa
Bogrov!")*

MISCHA *(laughs, crosses to Rubashov, un-
hooks from his belt a curved, elaborately
chased, silver-handled dagger)*. Kolya . . .

RUBASHOV. Yes, Mischa?

BOGROV *(presenting the dagger to him)*.
Here, I want you to have this. To remember me.

RUBASHOV *(laughs)*. You may need it,
yourself.

BOGROV *(shakes his head, grins. There is
something of the good-natured, ingenuous
child in this big man)*. No. The Civil

War is over. No more killing. Now we go home. We build a new life. (*He extends the gift again*) Please, take it.

RUBASHOV (*accepts it*). All right, Mischa. Thank you. Now, I have something for you. Can you guess?

BOGROV (*thinks hard, frowning, then his eyes open wide*). Kolya, is it . . . Am I . . . They're . . . ?

RUBASHOV (*beaming, nods*). Tomorrow you'll be a member of the Party.

BOGROV (*overcome with joy*). Me? Me? Mischa Bogrov a member of the Party!

RUBASHOV. You've earned it. You fought well for the Revolution.

BOGROV. I'm ignorant, Kolya; I'm just a stupid peasant and I don't know enough yet—but I'd die for the Revolution.

RUBASHOV. We know that. Now you must learn the meaning of it. You must go to school. You must study, Mischa.

BOGROV. I will, I will. You'll see, you'll be very proud of me. Wherever I am, every year on this day, I'll send you a letter and I'll sign it. "Your Comrade, Faithful to the Grave." (*The soldiers call for more song. "Come on, Mischa. More!"*) For you, I sing this just for you, Kolya.

BOGROV (*sings in a rich voice the chorus of "Red Moscow"*).
"We'll shout aloud for we are proud,
Our power is invincible.
We'll ne'er disband, we'll always stand
Together for dear Moscow's land."

(*Gradually Bogrov and the campfire and the men singing with him fade away as do their voices, leaving Rubashov alone in his dank, silent, gray cell, nodding and humming the tune quietly to himself. Lights come up on 402 who is tapping on Rubashov's wall. Rubashov crosses to the wall, responds.*)

402 (*taps*). What day?

RUBASHOV (*taps*). Lost track.

402 (*taps*). What you doing?

RUBASHOV (*taps*). Dreaming.

402 (*taps*). Sleeping?

RUBASHOV (*taps*). Waking.

402 (*taps*). Bad. What dreams?

RUBASHOV (*taps*). My life.

402 (*taps*). You won't confess?

RUBASHOV (*taps*). I told you no.

402 (*taps*). Die in silence is best. (*Pause*)

RUBASHOV (*to himself, sardonically*). Yes. Die in silence! Fade into darkness!

Easily said. Die in silence! Vanish without a word! Easily said.

402 (*taps*). Walking?

RUBASHOV (*taps*). Yes.

402 (*taps*). Careful of blisters. Walking dreams bad for feet. I walked twelve hours in cell once. Wore out shoes. (*He laughs hoarsely*) Didn't mind. (*He licks his lips, rolls his eyes, and moans voluptuously*) Mm! I was dreaming women. Ah-h-h! Question: When is woman best? Answer: After hot bath, well soaped all over, slippery. Ha! Ha! (*His laughter is tinctured with agony and madness*) Ha! Ha! (*He stops, listens. The want of a response from Rubashov makes him suddenly angry*) What's matter? You didn't laugh. Joke!

RUBASHOV (*shrugs his shoulders, taps*). Ha! Ha!

402 (*bursts into laughter again, taps*) Ha! Ha! Funny, ha!

RUBASHOV (*taps*). Funny.

402 (*taps*). How many women you love? (*Pause*) How many?

RUBASHOV (*taps*). None.

402 (*taps*). Why not?

RUBASHOV (*taps*). My work. No time.

402 (*taps*). You and Revolution. Some love affair! Don't you fellows have sex?

RUBASHOV (*taps*). Oh, yes.

402 (*taps*). What you use it for? Write in snow? Ha! Ha! (*He doubles up with laughter, plucking at the lean flesh on his arms and thighs*) Good joke?

RUBASHOV (*taps*). Not good.

402 (*soured, taps*). No sense humor No wonder. Your women are half men. Your women have moustaches. You killed the beauty of our women. Son of bitch, son of bitch, son of bitch!

RUBASHOV (*dryly, taps*). Repeating yourself.

402 (*taps*). Confess. Never in love? Once?

RUBASHOV (*taps*) No. Never. (*He sighs heavily, frowns, thinking. 402 vanishes*)

(*A gray-haired man, Hrutsch, materializes, sighing heavily and clutching his breast over the heart.*)

HRUTSCH (*laughs timidly*). It's nothing. My heart skips about a bit.

(*The cell fades away. Hrutsch is standing at the desk in the office of the Commissariat of the Iron Works. The vista outside the window reveals the new-com-*

pleted factory buildings. Hrutsch is obvi-ously frightened and nervous.)

HRUTSCH *(squeezes his speech out in short spasmodic gasps).* Yes, the files are ready for you, and of course you'll want to see the charts. *(He turns to the dark-ness. Luba Loshenko materializes, stand-ing there with the charts in her hand, staring at Rubashov with large luminous eyes and parted lips. She hands the charts to Hrutsch, but her eyes never leave Ru-bashov)* Ah, here we are. Now, anything you want explained, our secretary here knows them backwards. *(He observes them staring at each other)* You remem-ber Comrade Loshenko? *(Hands the charts to Rubashov)*

RUBASHOV *(leaning heavily on a cane, steps forward. He walks with a slight limp).* Yes. How have you been, Com-rade Loshenko?

LUBA. Very well, thank you, Comrade Rubashov. Welcome back home.

HRUTSCH. Many changes since you've been gone. The factories are completed.

RUBASHOV *(depositing the charts on the desk).* You haven't filled your quota. Iron is off 23 per cent, steel 38 per cent.

HRUTSCH. Yes, yes, the sabotage is a problem. *(He sighs, clutches his heart. He laughs apologetically, indicating his heart)* Every once in a while it just starts ham-mering . . . I should complain—look at him. The stories you could tell, Comrade Rubashov? Those Nazis! What they did to you! And he escapes, comes home, and right to work. Wonderful spirit. Wonder-ful. What an example to us! *(He laughs feebly, pants, holding his heart)* Of course, as for us filling the new quota, mechani-cally it can't be. It's physically . . .

RUBASHOV *(coldly, impersonal).* Those are the orders.

HRUTSCH *(again the fear rises; he essays a feeble smile).* Well, if those are the or-ders, it will just have to be done, won't it?

RUBASHOV. Yes. I'll send for you. *(He dismisses him. Hrutsch goes quickly. Ru-bashov turns. He looks at Luba in silence, smiles)*

LUBA. I wondered if I'd ever see you again.

RUBASHOV. It was a question whether anyone would.

LUBA. I know. My prayers were an-swered. I prayed for you.

RUBASHOV. To which god?

LUBA. I did. I prayed.

RUBASHOV. The same little bourgeoise, Luba. Are you married yet?

LUBA. No.

RUBASHOV. Why not? *(Luba shrugs her shoulders)* Any babies?

LUBA. No. *(Luba laughs)* You've no idea of the excitement here when we read that you were alive and home. We saw a picture of you when you arrived at Mos-cow, and our Leader had his arm around you. I was so proud. *(There is an em-barrassed pause)*

RUBASHOV *(glances at the charts).* Hrutsch is in trouble.

LUBA. Poor man, it's not his fault.

RUBASHOV. Whose fault is it?

LUBA. No one's. The men are over-worked, and . . . *(She stops herself abruptly)*

RUBASHOV. Go on.

LUBA *(shakes her head).* That's all. Who am I to tell you?

RUBASHOV. Go on! Go on!

LUBA *(a sudden outpouring).* They're frightened. Last week more than forty workers were taken away by the G.P.U.

RUBASHOV. Well, we have to have dis-cipline. Socialism isn't going to drop down on us from your nice neat heaven.

LUBA. Yes, but the machines don't know that. The machines break down, too.

RUBASHOV. Why?

LUBA. The same reason. They're over-worked.

RUBASHOV *(sighs).* Problems. *(He puts the charts away, turns to her)* Tell me about yourself. Any lovers?

LUBA *(seriously).* No.

RUBASHOV *(teasing her).* No? Why not? Put on those old earrings and find your-self a lover.

LUBA. I thought you were dead and I didn't want to go on living. I found that out. I wouldn't want to live in a world without knowing you were somewhere in it.

RUBASHOV. Come here. *(Luba goes to him. He puts his arms around her and kisses her)*

LUBA *(begins to tremble and cry).* I thought you were dead. I thought the Nazis had killed you.

RUBASHOV *(burying his face in her hair).* I'm hard to kill.

LUBA. But they hurt you so. Your poor legs—they broke them?

RUBASHOV. The pieces grow together.

LUBA. Was it awful?

RUBASHOV. I forget. (*Holds her at arm's length, studies her face*) It's good to see you again, Luba.

LUBA. Do you mean that?

RUBASHOV (*impersonally*). Yes. (*He turns from her, picks up the charts*) I have some dictation. Get your pad and pencil. And call in Hrutsch. I'm afraid we're going to have to get rid of that milksop. (*Crossing away from her into the shadows*)

LUBA (*very quietly*). Yes, Comrade Commissar.

(*The memory scene fades. Rubashov, alone, leaning against the stone wall, sighs heavily. Three taps are heard. He responds.*)

402 (*appears, taps*). Sad!

RUBASHOV (*taps*). What?

402 (*taps*). You! Never in love. To die without ever being in love. Sad!

(*A chill seizes Rubashov; he groans, puts his hand to his swollen cheek, and shivers.*)

RUBASHOV (*taps*). Good night.

402 (*taps*). What's wrong?

RUBASHOV (*taps*). My fever's back.

402 (*taps*). Again? Maybe you should try the prison doctor?

RUBASHOV (*taps*). No, thanks.

402 (*taps*). Don't blame you. A butcher!

(*They both turn from the wall, pace a few steps, and simultaneously freeze, listening, listening as if the silence itself contained some unheard and unholy sound.*)

RUBASHOV (*crosses to 402, taps*). What's that?

402 (*taps*). You felt it again?

RUBASHOV (*taps*). In the air . . .

402 (*taps*). Yes . . . (*The lights fade on 402*)

(*Rubashov wipes his feverish brow with the back of his sleeve and slowly paces to and fro; to himself:* What if the Leader is right? In spite of everything. In spite of the dirt and blood and lies. Suppose the Leader is right? *A chill shakes him. He puts on his coat, continues to pace.* Suppose the true foundations of the future are being built here? History has always been an inhumane and unscrupulous builder, mixing its mortar of lies and blood and filth. *He shivers again, pulls his coat tighter.* Well, what of it, Rubashov? Be logical. Haven't you always lived under the compulsion of working things out to their final conclusions? *He accelerates his pacing, counting the steps:* 1 . . . 2 . . . 3 . . . 4 . . . 5 . . . and a half; 1 . . . 2 . . . 3 . . . 4 . . . 5 and a half. *He stops abruptly as a thought strikes him:* Yes. Yes.)

(*A sound of distant laughter. Slowly the figures of some dockworkers materialize, sitting at a small iron table in a pub on the waterfront of the Marseilles docks. They are eating bread and cheese and drinking wine, talking loudly and laughing good-naturedly. A big stocky man wearing a sailor's sweater and stocking cap is seated next to a little hunchback who wears a sailor's cap and a seaman's pea-jacket. Next to the little hunchback sits a third dockworker. The big man is juggling some apples and the others are watching and roaring with laughter. On the wall over the table is a militant poster demanding sanctions against Mussolini for his rape of Ethiopia. Benito's caricature dominates the scene: the jutting jaw, the pop-eyes, the little fez on the shaved dome.*)

(*Rubashov, accompanied by Albert, a sharp-featured, young French intellectual, with long expressive hands which are forever gesturing, and a mincing, epicene manner, approaches the table. The little hunchback sees them and rises.*)

ALBERT (*waving to him*). Comrade Luigi, head of the Dockworkers' Union. This is the comrade from Moscow.

LUIGI (*smiles and extends his hand*). We're honored. We're honored. (*He shakes Rubashov's hand vigorously*) Please sit down. (*He motions to the big dockworker*) Comrade Pablo, business manager of the union.

PABLO (*shakes hands*). How do you like the job we're doing here?

RUBASHOV. You've the strongest dockworkers' union in Europe.

PABLO. Nothing'll get by us. We'll strangle Il Duce.

LUIGI (*introduces the third dockworker*). Comrade André, our secretary.

ANDRE. Comrade. (*They shake hands. Rubashov and Albert sit*)

PABLO. Those Italian ships out there will rot before we call off this strike.

LUIGI. Drink?

RUBASHOV. Coffee, black.

ALBERT. A double fine.

PABLO *(calls off)*. One coffee, black. One double fine.

VOICE *(off)*. Coming.

PABLO *(pointing off, shouts a warning to Luigi)*. Luigi, look—Here comes that cat again.

ANDRE. Meow! Meow!

LUIGI *(jumping to his feet in panic, growls at the unseen cat)*. Get out! Fft—out! *(He throws a spoon across the floor. The cat obviously flees. André and Pablo collapse in their chairs, holding their sides, filling the café with booming laughter. Luigi looks at them, shakes his head, laughs sheepishly)*

PABLO *(to Rubashov)*. Luigi don't like cats.

ANDRE. But they love him. They come to him like a bowl of cream.

LUIGI. They got no reason to. *(The three laugh. Luigi's laughter becomes a racking cough. The Waiter enters and sets the drinks on the table. They are silent until he leaves)*

ANDRE. When Luigi escaped from Italy he lived by killing cats.

PABLO. And selling their skins.

LUIGI. I had no papers. I couldn't get a job.

RUBASHOV. You're Italian?

LUIGI. I'm a man without a country. *(He spits at Benito's caricature)* Three years ago I escaped. Benito was after me. I got here in France. No passport. The French police arrest me. Take me at night to the Belgian border. "We catch you here again, God help you!" In Belgium the Belgian police arrest me . . . "No passport?" Take me to the French border. Kick me back here into France. Six times back and forth. Luigi, the human football. *(He grimaces. His two comrades laugh appreciatively)* A man without a country. *(They laugh louder and slap him on the back. He laughs)* Well, I can laugh now, too, thanks to Pablo. I meet him in jail. He gets me passport. Finds me this job with the union. I'm alive again, I belong.

PABLO *(leans across the table confidentially to Rubashov)*. If you need any passports, I have a man will make you anything. A real artist.

RUBASHOV *(nods)*. Thanks. I'll remember that.

ALBERT *(half rises, significantly)*. The comrade from Moscow has a message for us.

LUIGI. For us? *(They all lean forward, intent)*

RUBASHOV. In connection with this strike.

PABLO. Ah! The strike? Don't worry. Nothing'll get by us.

LUIGI. Sh, Pablo! *(To Rubashov)* Your message?

RUBASHOV. As you know, our strength in the Soviet Union is the strength of the revolutionary movement all over the world.

PABLO *(hits the table with his fist)*. You can count on us!

LUIGI. Sh, Pablo! *(To Rubashov)* The strike?

RUBASHOV. The Italian shipyards are completing two destroyers and a cruiser for us.

ALBERT. For the Motherland of the Revolution!

RUBASHOV. The Italian Government has informed Moscow if we want these ships this strike must be called off at once.

PABLO. What?

ANDRE. You want us to call off this strike?

(The dockworkers look at each other, stunned, bewildered.)

LUIGI. But Moscow called on the world for sanctions!

ALBERT. The comrade from over there has explained this is in the interest of the defense of the Motherland of the Revolution.

PABLO *(angrily)*. But the Fascists are taking on supplies to make war.

ANDRE. To kill Ethiopian workers!

LUIGI. To make slaves of them.

ALBERT. Comrades, sentimentality gets us nowhere.

LUIGI *(gesticulates with his dirty handkerchief)*. But this isn't right; we can't do this! It isn't fair, it isn't just, it isn't . . .

RUBASHOV *(quickly, sharply)*. It isn't according to the rules laid down by the Marquis of Queensberry? No, it isn't. But revolutions aren't won by "fair play" morality. That's fine in the lulls of history, but in the crises, there is only one rule: The end justifies the means.

LUIGI. No, there are principles; the whole world looks to you back there for an example. . . . *(He coughs violently into the handkerchief)*

ANDRE *(pointing at the scarlet stains on Luigi's handkerchief)*. You see? Blood. He spits blood. Benito gave him that. And took two brothers in exchange. If you knew . . .

LUIGI. That doesn't matter.

PABLO. This is just scabbing.

ANDRE. I vote to continue the strike.

PABLO. Strike.

LUIGI. Strike. The meeting is closed. *(He stands up)*

RUBASHOV *(rises quickly, decisively)*. No, it isn't! I'm in authority now. We have a job to be done here and it will be done.

ALBERT. In spite of agents provocateurs. *(Pablo reaches over, grabs Albert by the lapels of his coat, and shakes him)*

LUIGI *(rises)*. No, Pablo, stop that! Stop! *(Pablo releases Albert. Luigi addresses Albert)* Provocateurs? For who, in God's name?

ALBERT *(furious, his voice shrill)*. For the Fascists.

PABLO. Because we won't load their ships? You hear, Comrades. That's a joke —a rotten joke, isn't it?

LUIGI *(softly)*. No, it's not a joke, Pablo; it's rotten, but it's not a joke. *(He looks up at the caricature of Mussolini)* The joke is Benito brought me into socialism, me and my two brothers. We lived in Forli, 1911. Italy was starting a war with Tripoli. There was a big anti-war meeting, banners, posters. Benito took the platform. Benito, the humble socialist, in a dirty black suit and a bow tie. *(He imitates the crowd)* "Bravo, Benito!" *(He mimics the gestures and facial expressions of Mussolini)* "Fellow workers, militarism is our enemy! We hate war!" *(He becomes the crowd)* "Bravo, Benito!" *(Again he is Mussolini)* "We don't want iron discipline, we don't want colonial adventures! We want bread and schools and freedom." "Bravo, Benito!" *(He angrily admonishes the invisible crowd)* "Don't applaud me! Don't follow me. I hate fetichism. Follow my words!" *(Softly, nodding to himself)* Benito. *(He leans on the table; to Rubashov)* We followed his words; my two brothers and I. Ten years later he gives my brothers the castor-oil treatment. To some that sounds like a joke, too. You know what happens when a quart of castor oil is poured down your throat? It tears your intestines to pieces, like you put them in a butcher's grinder, to little pieces. Two brothers I had. Not like me. Well-formed, beautiful, like Michelangelo carved them out of Carrara marble—one a David and one a Moses. I, the ugly one, I escaped. *(Softly, tenderly)* Two brothers I had . . . and now, *(fiercely)* Mother of God, I'm a Fascist! *(He coughs convulsively into his handkerchief)* Back where I started with Benito. *(He spits at the caricature of Mussolini)*

PABLO *(fervently)*. I swear to God it's all true.

ANDRE. Luigi's not a Fascist!

ALBERT *(rises, gesticulating with the long slender hands)*. Now, Comrades, you're thinking mechanistically. Dialectically, the fact is that, whoever does not serve the long-distance aims of the Party is an enemy of the Party and therefore, even though he may think himself subjectively an anti-Fascist, he is in fact objectively a Fascist . . .

PABLO *(ironically seizes some dishes, tosses them into the air, juggles them, catches them, then proffers them to Albert with an ironic bow)*. Here! You do it better than I.

RUBASHOV *(rising)*. The ships are to be unloaded tomorrow.

LUIGI. Over my dead body.

PABLO. And mine.

ANDRE. And mine.

RUBASHOV. You can tear up your cards! *(Silence)* The meeting is adjourned. *(Indicating the phone)* Albert. *(Albert nods, crosses to the phone, picks it up)*

LUIGI *(to the others)*. Come. *(The three men leave, Luigi coughing as he does)*

ALBERT *(at phone)* André, Pablo, Luigi. Yes. Publish their pictures in tomorrow's press. Front page. Agents provocateurs. Any Party member who even talks to them will be dismissed at once.

RUBASHOV. Their passports!

ALBERT. Ah, of course. *(On phone)* Also notify the French police their papers here are forged. Arrange for their immediate arrest and deportation. *(He hangs up, grins smugly)* That'll do it! Now little Luigi is really a man without a country!

RUBASHOV *(stonily)*. Yes. *(Albert laughs. Rubashov turns a withering look of re-*

vulsion on him, and then, unable to endure it, shouts at him) What the hell are you laughing at? What's so funny? *(Albert's laughter dies in his throat. He looks pained and puzzled. With an exclamation of disgust Rubashov walks away)*
(The scene fades. Rubashov is back in his cell, pacing nervously.)

RUBASHOV. Yes . . . We lived under the compulsion of working things out to their final conclusions. I thought and acted as I had to; I destroyed people I was fond of; I gave power to others I disliked . . . Well—History put you in that position, Rubashov. What else could you do? . . . But, I've exhausted the credit she gave me. Was I right? Was I wrong? I don't know. . . . The fact is, Rubashov, you no longer believe in your infallibility. That's why you're lost.
(A tapping. Rubashov crosses to the wall and replies. The lights come up on 402.)

402 *(taps)*. Knew something was happening.

RUBASHOV *(taps)*. Explain.

402 *(taps)*. Executions.

RUBASHOV *(to himself)*. Executions? *(Taps)* Who?

402 *(taps)*. Don't know.

RUBASHOV *(taps)*. What time?

402 *(taps)*. Soon. Pass it on.

RUBASHOV *(goes to another wall of his cell, taps, receives an answering click, then he taps out the message)*. Executions soon. Pass it on. *(To himself, pacing)* Perhaps this time it is you, Rubashov. Well, so long as they do it quickly. *(He stops, rubs his swollen cheek thoughtfully)* But is that right? You can still save yourself. One word—"Confess." *(Fiercely)* What does it matter what you say or what you sign? Isn't the important thing to go on? Isn't that all that matters?—To go on? *(An agonized look appears on his face, as an unbidden memory rises)*
(Faint strains of music. Luba's voice humming the melody of the "Appassionata." The prison vanishes. We are in Luba's room. It is a bright Sunday afternoon. The sun is pouring through the window, flooding the room with golden warmth. Luba, kneeling, is snipping sprays of apple blossoms from a large bough spread out on a cloth laid on the floor. She is pruning the twigs preparatory to arranging them in a vase on the table. She hums

happily. Rubashov enters, stands, watching her. She turns.)

LUBA. Oh! I didn't hear you come in. *(She rises, goes to him, holding out the flowers as an offering)*

RUBASHOV *(touches them)*. Beautiful! Where did you get them?

LUBA. I took a long walk this morning in the country. They were lying on the ground. The branch had broken off an old apple tree. *(Luba notices that Rubashov's face is strained and lined with fatigue)* You look tired.

RUBASHOV. I am. I've been walking too.

LUBA. Not in the country?

RUBASHOV. No.

LUBA *(crosses to the table, arranges the flowers in the vase)*. If you want to walk you should go out to the country. *(Disposing of the flowers, she opens a drawer, takes out a bar of chocolate and hands it to him)* Yesterday was my lucky day.

RUBASHOV. Chocolate?

LUBA *(triumphantly)*. Two bars. I ate one. They were the last in the store. I stood in line three hours. I had to battle for them, but I won.

RUBASHOV *(softly, under the strain of some deep emotion)*. Thank you.

LUBA *(kneels, cutting more sprays off the branch, reminiscing)*. We had some apple trees at home. On Sundays we'd help Father prune them. There was one huge old tree so gnarled and full of bumps. We had a special affection for that tree. Tch, the pains Father took to save it. We called it his "patient." *(Rises with the blooms)* One spring morning he took us out to look at the "patient." It was blossom time. The other apple trees didn't have many blossoms that year—but the "patient" . . . You've never seen so many blossoms on one tree. It took our breath away. The tree was all covered with blossoms like snow. Then Father said, "I'm going to lose my patient."

RUBASHOV. Why'd he say that?

LUBA. An apple tree puts out its most beautiful bloom just before it dies.

RUBASHOV. I didn't know that.

LUBA. It's true. The next year the "patient" was gone.

RUBASHOV. Oh!

LUBA. When I'm working at the factory, everything seems matter-of-fact; but whenever I go out to the country, the world suddenly becomes full of mystery.

(Luba looks at Rubashov. He sits slowly, a strained expression on his face) What is it? What's wrong?

RUBASHOV *(shakes his head)*. Troubles.

LUBA. At the factory?

RUBASHOV *(tastes the chocolate)*. There too. All over. Upheavals. *(He glances at the chocolate evasively)* This chocolate is made of soya beans. Tastes almost like real chocolate. *(He sighs, pauses)* Luba . . .

LUBA. Yes?

RUBASHOV *(carefully places the chocolate on the table, speaks softly, deliberately)*. Orders came in late yesterday, after you left. You'll have to report back to Moscow. *(Luba's hand, lifting a spray of blossoms to the vase, freezes in mid-air)* You're to leave tonight.

LUBA. Tonight?

RUBASHOV *(evading her glance)*. Those are the orders. There's a train at ten o'clock.

LUBA *(trying desperately to control her mounting terror)*. Why am I being sent back there?

RUBASHOV. They're investigating the files and production records.

LUBA. How long will I be gone?

RUBASHOV. I don't know that, Luba.

LUBA. Why didn't you tell me last night?

RUBASHOV. I wanted to find out what it is about.

LUBA. But I've so much work at the office to clean up. So many . . .

RUBASHOV *(rises)*. It's hurried, I know. But that's the way the Bureau does things.

LUBA. What have I done wrong?

RUBASHOV. Nothing.

LUBA. Has my work been unsatisfactory?

RUBASHOV. It's been excellent.

LUBA *(the terror in her voice now)*. Then why am I being sent back?

RUBASHOV *(patiently, soothingly)*. I told you, they're examining the books.

LUBA *(dully wiping her wet hands on a cloth)*. Someone else will take on my job here?

RUBASHOV. Only while you're gone.

LUBA *(turns to Rubashov, childishly)*. I don't want to go.

RUBASHOV. You have to, Luba.

LUBA *(crossing to Rubashov, pleading)*. Can't you help me?

RUBASHOV. You understand, I have ene-

mies. It would look bad for you, if I interceded.

LUBA. For me?

RUBASHOV. For both of us. As if I wanted to conceal something.

LUBA *(her love and her fear for him taking precedent, she studies him)*. You're not in any trouble?

RUBASHOV. No.

LUBA. You're sure?

RUBASHOV. Yes. *(There is a long pause)*

LUBA *(very simply and directly)*. They're not going to arrest me?

RUBASHOV. Of course not.

LUBA. I'm frightened. *(She sits, looks about helplessly, a trapped animal)*

RUBASHOV *(goes to her, places his hands soothingly on her shoulders)*. There's no need to be. If they should interrogate you, tell them the truth. You have nothing to fear. Just tell them the truth.

LUBA *(whispers)*. I'm frightened *(Suddenly the waves of panic explode, and she cries out)* I'm not going to Moscow. I just won't go.

RUBASHOV *(quickly, trying to control the panic)*. Then it would look as if you had done something wrong, wouldn't it?

LUBA *(turns to Rubashov, hysterically)*. But I haven't, I haven't.

RUBASHOV. I know that, Luba.

LUBA *(her hysteria mounting, her body trembling, her voice becoming shrill)*. Oh God! I want to run away. I want to hide! I want to run away.

RUBASHOV *(grips her arms tightly)*. Nothing's going to happen to you. Understand? There are no charges against you. Nothing's going to happen. Nothing, nothing! *(He holds her tight and kisses her. She clings to him with all her strength, wildly, passionately returning his embrace. Then she goes limp, withdraws, looks at him, smiles sadly, shakes her head)*

LUBA. I'm sorry. I'm stupid. *(She turns to gather up the flowers from the floor)* I'll be all right. *(Kneeling)* Ten o'clock?

RUBASHOV. Ten o'clock.

LUBA. The tickets? And my travel warrant? *(Rubashov plucks them out of his pocket and hands them to her. She takes them quietly. She rises, and, tonelessly)* I'll have to pack now.

RUBASHOV. Yes. I'll go.

LUBA. Not yet.

RUBASHOV. It would be best . . . for both of us, at this time.

LUBA. Yes, I suppose so. *(She looks at the bouquet of blossoms in her hands)* Wouldn't it be wonderful if we could just say "No" to them? If we could come and go as we wished, all of us?

RUBASHOV. But we can't, Luba. That would be anarchy. We haven't the right. *(He crosses into the shadows)*

LUBA *(almost inaudibly)*. No. of course not. We haven't the right.

(Luba, flowers, room and sunlight, all fade away, leaving Rubashov alone in his dank cell, talking to himself.)

RUBASHOV. And have *I* the right to say "No"? Even now? Have I the right to leave—to walk out, to die out of mere tiredness, personal disgust and vanity? Have I this right?

(The lights come up in the other cells. The prisoners, ears to the wall, are listening for the news. 202 has just received a message. He crosses to 302's wall.)

202 *(taps)*. They're reading death sentence to him now. Pass it on. *(He shuttles back to the other post to listen)*

302 *(crosses, taps on 402's wall)*. They're reading death sentence to him now. Pass it on. *(Shuttles back to listen)*

402 *(taps)*. They're reading death sentence now. Pass it on.

RUBASHOV *(taps)*. Who is he? *(But 402 has crossed back to listen to the next message. Rubashov crosses to the rear wall, taps)* They're reading death sentence to him now. Pass it on. *(Rubashov crosses back to 402's wall to listen)*

202 *(crosses to wall, taps to 302)*. They are bringing him, screaming and hitting out. Pass it on. *(202 returns to his other post, listening)*

302 *(crosses, taps to 402)*. They are bringing him, screaming and hitting out. Pass it on. *(302 returns to his other post)*

402 *(taps to Rubashov)*. They are bringing him, screaming and hitting out. Pass it on.

RUBASHOV *(taps, urgently)*. Who is he? *(But 402 has gone back to the opposite wall to listen for more news. Rubashov shuffles over to the rear wall and taps)* They are bringing him screaming and hitting out. Pass it on. *(Then he moves back to 402's wall and taps insistently)* Who is he? *(402 crosses to Rubashov's wall, lis-*

tening. *Rubashov, very clearly)* What's his name?

402 *(taps)*. Mischa Bogrov.

RUBASHOV *(suddenly becomes faint; wipes the sweat from his forehead and for a moment braces himself against the wall; walks slowly to the rear wall and leans heavily against it as he taps through to 402)* Mischa Bogrov, former sailor on Battleship Potemkin, Commander of the Baltic Fleet, bearer of Order of Red Banner, led to execution! Pass it on.

202 *(taps)*. Now! *(He crosses to the door and starts drumming on the iron surface)*

302 *(taps)*. Now! *(He crosses to the door and starts drumming on the iron surface)*

402 *(taps)*. Now! *(He crosses to the door and starts drumming on the iron surface)*

RUBASHOV *(taps)*. Now! *(Drags himself across the cell and starts drumming on the door's iron surface)*

(The prison becomes vibrant with the low beat of subdued drumming. The men in the cells who form the acoustic chain stand behind their doors like a guard of honor in the dark, create a deceptive resemblance to the muffled solemn sound of the roll of drums, carried by the wind from the distance. At the far end of the corridor, the grinding of iron doors becomes louder. A bunch of keys jangle. The iron door is shut again. The drumming rises to a steady, muffled crescendo. Sliding and squealing sounds approach quickly, a moaning and whimpering like the whimpering of a child is heard. Shadowy figures enter the field of vision. Two dimly lit figures, both in uniform, drag between them a third whom they hold under their arms. The middle figure hangs slack and yet with doll-like stiffness in their grasp, stretched out its full length, face turned to the ground, belly arched downwards, the legs trailing after, the shoes scraping on the toes. Whitish strands of hair hang over the face, the mouth is open. As they turn the corner of the corridor and open the trap-door to the cellar, we see that this tortured, mangled face is Bogrov's. Gletkin now appears, whispers in his ear. Bogrov straightens up, looks about, flings off his captors for a moment and moans out some vowels.)

BOGROV. Oo . . . a . . . ah; Oo . . . a

... ah! (*Then with a mighty effort, he articulates the word and bellows out*) Rubashov; Rubashov!

RUBASHOV (*pounds on his door like a madman, screaming*). Mischa! Mischa! (*The other prisoners accelerate their drumming. Bogrov is dragged through the cellar-door; it clangs shut, and we can hear his voice as he is being dragged down to the execution cellar, growing fainter and fainter, calling "Rubashov! Rubashov!" Gradually the drumming dies down, the other prisoners vanish, a deep terrible silence settles on the prison. Rubashov stands in the middle of his cell, clutching his stomach to prevent himself from vomiting. He staggers to his cot, collapses on it, and is enveloped by complete darkness.*)

(*There is a long silence. From somewhere above a prisoner cries out, "Arise, ye wretched of the earth!"*)

(*The electric light in Rubashov's cell is suddenly turned on. Ivanoff is standing next to his bed with a bottle of brandy and a glass. Rubashov, his eyes glazed, is staring, unseeing, into space.*)

IVANOFF. You feel all right?

RUBASHOV. It's hot! Open the window! (*He looks up at Ivanoff*) Who are you?

IVANOFF. Would you like some brandy? (*Rubashov's eyes follow him, dull, uncomprehending. Ivanoff pours a drink, extends it to Rubashov. Sits next to him*) Drink this. (*Ivanoff holds the glass, feeding the drink to Rubashov*)

RUBASHOV (*finishes the drink, looks at him*). You been arrested too?

IVANOFF. No. I only came to visit you. (*He places the bottle and the glass on the floor*) I think you're ill. Are you in pain?

RUBASHOV. No.

IVANOFF. Your cheek is swollen. I think you've a fever.

RUBASHOV. Give me a cigarette. (*Ivanoff gives him a cigarette, lights it for him. Rubashov inhales the smoke deeply, hungrily. After a few moments of this, his eyes come into focus, his breathing becomes a little more regular, and he looks at Ivanoff who is patiently blowing smoke rings*) What time is it?

IVANOFF. Two thirty A.M.

RUBASHOV. How long have I been here?

IVANOFF. Five weeks tomorrow.

RUBASHOV (*examines Ivanoff. He is beginning to think quite clearly now*). What are you doing here?

IVANOFF. I want to talk to you. Some more brandy? (*Picks up the bottle*)

RUBASHOV (*the iron creeping into his voice*). No, thank you.

IVANOFF. Lie down. Rest!

RUBASHOV (*sits up, spits out*). You pimp! Get out of here. You're a pimp like all the rest of them! You disgust me—you and your filthy tricks.

IVANOFF. Tricks? (*Pours a drink*)

RUBASHOV (*raging*). You drag him by my cell—Bogrov—or what you've left of him, and when my bowels are split open, a savior appears with a bottle of brandy. You think I can be taken in by a cheap trick like that? You think you can wheedle a confession out of me with a bottle of brandy?

IVANOFF (*smiles and shows his gold teeth*). You really believe that I have such a primitive mind?

RUBASHOV. Take your whorish mind the hell out of here! It stinks! It's choking me.

IVANOFF (*drinks*). Very well. I'll go if you want me to.

RUBASHOV. You cannot begin to understand how you disgust me. All of you.

IVANOFF. But first, you must listen to me for one second.

RUBASHOV. I don't want to hear any more ...

IVANOFF (*outshouts him*). I'm afraid you'll have to! (*Pause, gently*) Now listen —logically and calmly, if you can. First, to remove any doubts, Bogrov has already been shot!

(*There is a long silence as Rubashov absorbs this news, then:*)

RUBASHOV (*low, strangulated*). Good!

IVANOFF. He was also tortured for several days.

RUBASHOV. That was obvious.

IVANOFF. It was meant to be. But not by me. (*Sits next to Rubashov, placing the bottle on the floor*) I'm going to put my life in your hands, Kolya. (*Rubashov looks at him*) If you mention what I tell you, to anyone, I am done for. This filthy trick, as you call it, was arranged by my young colleague, Gletkin, against my instructions. I would never make this mistake, not out of concern for you, but because it's bad psychology. You've recently been suffering humanitarian scruples? A scene with Bogrov could only intensify them. Obvious? Only a fool like Gletkin makes such mistakes. He's been urging me to use his methods on you too!

RUBASHOV. You can torture me; it will get you no results.

IVANOFF. Won't it? *(He smiles cynically, reaches for the bottle)* You don't know Gletkin. *(He fills the glass, studies it)* He's something new in the world—the Neanderthal Man! He came after the flood. He had no umbilical cord to the past. He was born without a navel. He doesn't approve of us old apes in general, and of *you* in particular. *(He shakes his head at Rubashov)* It seems the other day you showed him your behind. He didn't like that. *(Ominously)* He wants to lay his big hands on you.

RUBASHOV. I'm quite prepared to die.

IVANOFF. But I'm not prepared to let you die. Your martyrdom, Kolya, will consist of not being allowed to become a martyr. That's not why you're here. We need you, and we need you logical, because when you've thought the whole thing out clearly, then, but only then, will you make your confession. Am I right?

RUBASHOV. Go away, it's no use.

IVANOFF. Do you believe that I'm telling you the truth? *(Pause)* Do you?

RUBASHOV. Yes . . . I suppose so.

IVANOFF. Then why do you want me to go? *(He bends forward, pushing his face into Rubashov's, mockingly)* Because you are afraid of me, because my way of reasoning is your way and you're afraid of the echoes in your own head.

RUBASHOV *(impatiently)*. I've had enough of this reasoning. We've been running amok with it for thirty years. Enough.

IVANOFF. Get thee behind me, Satan. *(Rises, goes to the door, peers out the judas-hole, turns back)* In the old days temptation was carnal. It took the form of little naked women running around shaking their things in your face. Today it's cerebral. It takes the form of naked reason pushing facts in your face. Values change. *(He drinks)*

RUBASHOV. Why was Bogrov tortured?

IVANOFF. He was stubborn like you.

RUBASHOV. Did you hear him whimpering?

IVANOFF. No, I didn't hear it. But I've heard and seen others. *(He wheels on Rubashov, stabbing an accusing finger at him)* And so have you! And so have you,

my General! *(He hobbles to Rubashov, face thrust forward, accusingly)* What of it? A conscience is as unsuited to a revolutionary as a double chin. Since when did N. S. Rubashov develop this bourgeois conscience? Hm? When? *(Pause)* Shall I tell you? The day, the hour, the minute? Nine months, two weeks ago—at 3:10 A.M.—when your little secretary, Luba Loshenko, was shot! *(He sits next to Rubashov)* You were sleeping with her, weren't you? Now she's dead. So you're making the world a metaphysical brothel for your emotions. What have the shape of Luba Loshenko's breasts or Bogrov's whimperings to do with the new world we're creating?

RUBASHOV. Bogrov's dead, she's dead. You can afford a little pity.

IVANOFF. I have many vices:—I drink; for a time, as you know, I took drugs; but so far I've avoided the vice of pity. One drop of that and a revolutionary's lost. *(He fills his glass)* The great temptation! To renounce violence, to make peace with ourselves . . . Hm? *(He drinks)* I prefer my synthetic ecstasy in a glass. You get over it in the morning.

RUBASHOV *(after a long silence, shakes his head, murmurs sadly.)* Our golden dream! *(Then savagely)* What a stinking mess we've made of it.

IVANOFF *(setting down the glass, articulates carefully).* Have we? *(He lights a fresh cigarette)* We've taken the land from the landlords. *(He blows a smoke ring)* We've freed them from industrial exploitation. *(He blows another)* For the first time in history a revolution is functional.

RUBASHOV. Functional? *(He jumps to his feet, furious)* So functional in taking the land, in one year, we let five million farmers and their families die of starvation! Deliberately. So functional *(He begins to pace up and down)* in freeing the people from industrial exploitation we sent ten million of them to forced labor under worse conditions than galley slaves. *(He plucks off his spectacles nervously and waves them at Ivanoff)* So functional, to settle a difference of opinion, the omnipotent Leader knows only one argument—Death!—whether it's a matter of submarines, manure, or the party-line in Indo-China. Death! *(He replaces his spectacles and glares at Ivanoff)*

IVANOFF *(rises, belligerently).* That

woman has really given you softening of the brain! What of the millions who die of starvation in China and India, of tuberculosis in rice fields, cotton plantations . . . ?

RUBASHOV. In negatives we agree. Where has it led us?

IVANOFF. Well, where?

RUBASHOV. Our standard of living is lower than the most backward country in Europe. Labor conditions are harder; discipline's more inhuman. Our country is run by the police. (*Again he plucks off the glasses for emphasis*) We've torn the living skin off our people and left them standing with bare tissues, muscles and nerves quivering.

IVANOFF. Well, and what of it? (*With warmth and conviction*) Don't you find that wonderful? Has anything more wonderful ever happened in history? We're tearing the old skin off mankind and giving it a new one! That's not an occupation for people with weak nerves, but there was a time it filled you with enthusiasm.

RUBASHOV. I know.

IVANOFF. Look at the pamphlets put out by the antivivisectionists. When you read how some poor cur, who has just had his liver cut out, whines and licks his tormentor's hand, it breaks your heart. But if we listened to these sentimentalists we'd have no cures for typhus, cholera, diphtheria . . .

RUBASHOV. I know, I know. (*He turns away, sits, moodily*)

IVANOFF (*following him, persistently*). Of course you do. Better than I. And you still insist on being a martyr? (*He waits for an answer. Finally he throws up his hands and growls in disgust*) All right. Have it your way. (*He picks up the bottle and glass*) If you must throw yourself into the dust-bin of history, I can't stop you. Go. Let Gletkin have you. You're his. (*He turns to the door, pauses, turns back. His voice becomes soft*) Only tell me, why? Why are you so in love with death? It stinks! Why do you want to die?

RUBASHOV (*hoarsely*). I don't want to die. No one does.

IVANOFF. You act as if you do.

RUBASHOV. It's a fake. (*He clutches his throat*) From here up, I'm resigned. From here down, I'm frightened.

IVANOFF. Yet I offer you your life.

RUBASHOV. On what terms?

IVANOFF. The only terms that matter. To go on being useful. (*He places the bottle on the floor and fumbles in his pocket*)

RUBASHOV. To act the fool in public trial? No, thanks. The terms are too high.

IVANOFF (*taking out an official communication, pushes it under Rubashov's nose*). Here's a confidential report I received today. (*Rubashov takes it, glances at it*) Read between the lines.

RUBASHOV (*dryly*). I need no instructions, thank you. (*Studies the document*)

IVANOFF. What do you see?

RUBASHOV. War! It's coming.

IVANOFF. How soon?

RUBASHOV. Depends on how we play our cards. Perhaps years, perhaps months.

IVANOFF. The last war gave us Russia, Kolya; the next gives us the world. Or does it?

RUBASHOV. It could, if . . .

IVANOFF. If . . . ? Good! (*He sits next to him*) There's a breach in the Party, in the whole country; the people are restless, dissatisfied; our economy is in pieces. The breach must be mended first; and you, and those who think like you, must mend it!

RUBASHOV. Hence the trials! (*Hands him back the document, contemptuously*) They're better than the opera or the theater.

IVANOFF. The goal, Kolya. It's coming. Nearer. Listen. You can hear it on the wind. And when that day comes . . .

RUBASHOV. The Gletkins take over.

IVANOFF. They're brutes. They don't count.

RUBASHOV (*plucking off his spectacles and glaring at Ivanoff*). Who made them brutes? We did! Their Byzantine leader worship is frightening. Their cultivated ignorance is disgusting.

IVANOFF. Would they have been any use to us any other way?

RUBASHOV. You'd trust our revolution to them?

IVANOFF. Why do you think I'm risking my neck to save you? It's your brain I want to save. When the day comes, your brain will be needed. We'll get rid of them. You'll be needed more than ever!

RUBASHOV (*studies him, replaces his spectacles, shakes his head*). If I thought that . . .

IVANOFF (*strongly*). Think it! Think it! (*He watches Rubashov wrestle with the thought, then leans forward, and softly*)

What other choice have you? To become a Christian martyr? For the Western democracies?

RUBASHOV *(rises, angrily)*. What are you talking about, "the Western democracies"? What have I to do with those decadent humanists—those phantoms of religion and superstition?

IVANOFF *(pressing his point, sharpening his irony)*. Do you want their liberal press, that hated your guts while you were alive, to sanctify you after your death?

RUBASHOV. The liberal press? Those puking jackals of holy property? What have I to do with them? I'd rather be two feet of manure in a Russian field. *(He nervously polishes the glasses with his shirt)*

IVANOFF. Nevertheless they'll put you in a stained-glass window. Saint Rubashov—the martyr for the Western world! Is that what you want?

(Rubashov looks at him, looks away, ponders, replaces the spectacles, sighs. For a long time he stands there, head bowed, wrapped in thought. Ivanoff watches him patiently.)

RUBASHOV *(finally, wearily)*. I'll think it over.

IVANOFF *(triumphantly picks up his bottle, rises, and going to the judas-hole, calls)*. Guard! *(He turns back to Rubashov, beaming)* You old war-horse. You've had an attack of nerves. *(The Guard opens door)* But that's over now. Go to bed. Get some sleep. You'll need a clear head tomorrow when we make up your statement.

RUBASHOV *(frowning)*. I said I'll think it over.

IVANOFF *(nods, laughs)*. Good night, Kolya.

RUBASHOV. Good night, Sascha.

(Ivanoff goes. Rubashov stands, thinking, thinking. In the corridor Ivanoff sees Gletkin, leaning against the wall, watching Rubashov's cell.)

IVANOFF *(crosses to Gletkin, with supreme contempt)*. What genius inspired you tonight? *(Pause. He blows a smoke ring)* It's all right. He'll confess. But I had to sweat blood to repair the damage you did. You are all still suffering from personal feelings. In his place you'd be even more stubborn.

GLETKIN. I have some backbone, which he hasn't.

IVANOFF. But you're an idiot! For that answer alone, you ought to be shot before he is! *(He blows a cloud of cigarette smoke directly into Gletkin's face, shows his gold teeth in a grin of utter disdain, and hobbles off down the corridor)*

(Gletkin stands there as if he were made of stone, the face completely without expression, then he raises his hand and waves aside the fumes of smoke with a sudden, quick gesture.)

DIM-OUT AND CURTAIN

ACT THREE

SCENE: *Rubashov's cell; several days later.*

AT RISE: *Rubashov seated on the cot, his shoes off, his coat thrown over his shoulders, a pad of blank paper on his knee, is writing intently, completely absorbed. He pauses, chews his pencil, studies the page, writes rapidly. Alongside him is a stack of completed pages. The tensions and the fever appear to have abated. As he writes, three taps are heard from 402's wall. He ignores them. Three more taps. Then three more. He glances up, annoyed, but continues to work. The taps now flow rapidly and insistently in a staccato stream. With an exclamation of annoyance, Rubashov tears off the page he has just completed, lays it carefully on the pile next to him, rises and, crossing to the wall, taps. The lights come up on 402.*

402 *(taps)*. I tried to talk to you all day. Why didn't you answer?

RUBASHOV *(taps)*. I've been busy.

402 *(taps)*. How?

RUBASHOV *(taps)*. Writing.

402 *(taps)*. What?

RUBASHOV *(taps)*. A new theory.

402 *(taps)*. What about?

RUBASHOV *(smiling ironically, taps)*. The immaturity of the masses. The historical necessity for dictatorship.

402 *(taps)*. Repeat!

RUBASHOV *(taps)*. Never mind.

402 *(taps)*. What's happened?

RUBASHOV *(taps)*. I'm waiting for word. Upstairs.

402 *(taps)*. Why?

RUBASHOV *(taps)*. I am confessing.

402 *(pauses, stunned by this volte-face, then angrily, taps)*. I'd rather hang.

RUBASHOV (*cynically, taps*). Each in his own way.

402 (*taps slowly*). I thought you an exception. Have you no honor?

RUBASHOV (*taps*). Our ideas of honor differ.

402 (*taps*). Honor is to live and die for your beliefs.

RUBASHOV (*taps*). I am living for mine.

402 (*taps louder and more sharply*). Honor is decency.

RUBASHOV (*taps slowly, calmly*). What is decency?

402 (*very excited, taps*). Something your kind will never understand.

RUBASHOV (*taps*). We have replaced decency by reason.

402 (*taps*). What reason?

RUBASHOV (*taps*). Pure Reason.

402 (*taps*). You're pure son of bitch.

RUBASHOV (*amused, chuckles and taps*). Flattery does not impress me.

402 (*taps*). I'll never talk to you again. (*The scene is interrupted by a jangling sound. The door of Rubashov's cell is thrown open. A Young Officer enters.*)

OFFICE. Put on your shoes!

RUBASHOV. Well! It's about time! (*Crosses to the cot, sits and proceeds to put on his shoes, leisurely*) I've been waiting on Commissar Ivanoff for several days.

OFFICE. Put on your shoes, and come with me.

RUBASHOV. You might have timed it a little more considerately. But, I suppose you Neanderthal men only come out after midnight.

OFFICE. Don't talk so much. Just put on your shoes and hurry up.

RUBASHOV (*looks at the Officer, smiles, shakes his head as he ties the laces*). Brutes! (*He rises, the Officer motions him out with a jerk of the head. Rubashov goes, remarking over his shoulder*) But then you wouldn't be any use to us if you weren't, would you? (*Exit. The Officer frowns, follows him out. The lights in the cell dim out*)

402 (*watching at the judas-hole*). Son of a bitch! (*He crosses up to 302's wall, taps*)

(*The lights come up in the tier above. 302 is pacing. He stops at the sound of tapping, crosses, and listens.*)

402 (*taps*). Rubashov is a filthy coward.

302 (*taps*). You're wrong. He's brave. My father told me.

402 (*taps*). Your father is mistaken . . .

302 (*taps*). What's he done?

402 (*taps*). He's saving his skin. He's confessing. They've taken him up now.

302 (*taps*). Oh, my God! Pray for me.

402 (*taps*). For you?

302 (*taps*). Yes, for me. (*He crosses, taps on 202's wall. The lights come up on 202, who responds and listens. 302 taps*) Rubashov confessing. Pass it on.

202 (*groans, crosses to opposite wall, taps*). Rubashov confessing. Pass it on . . . (*The tappings multiply and the murmur "Rubashov confessing, Rubashov confessing," echoes back and forth through the prison. The cells dim out slowly as the lights come up on Ivanoff's office. Seated at the desk, his chair wheeled around, his back to us is a man in uniform, apparently Ivanoff. Rubashov enters, accompanied by the Guard. There is a faint ironic smile on Rubashov's lips as he enters. The man seated at the desk swings his chair round to face Rubashov. It's not Ivanoff, it's Gletkin! He looks at Rubashov, stony-faced. The smile on Rubashov's lips vanishes, he pauses in his stride, looks about quickly. Near Gletkin a grim-lipped young woman, obviously a secretary, sits, sharpening her pencils.*)

GLETKIN (*rises, waves the Guard out*). Shut the door! (*The Guard goes, shutting the door behind him. Gletkin turns to a heavy floor lamp nearby and switches it on. There is a humming sound, and a fierce, white light strikes Rubashov full in the eyes. He jerks his face away as if he'd been struck, then turns back to face Gletkin, squinting and shielding his eyes with his hand. Gletkin sits, picks up some official documents*) We will proceed with your examination. You wish to make a full confession?

RUBASHOV (*takes off his glasses and wipes his eyes*). Yes. To Commissar Ivanoff. Not to you.

GLETKIN. You will make your confession to me, here and now, or this investigation is closed, and you will be sentenced at once. Those are my orders from above. (*Rubashov puts on his spectacles and tries to meet Gletkin's gaze, but the harsh light blinds him. He removes his glasses again*) You have your choice. Which is it?

RUBASHOV (*avoiding the light*). I am ready to make a statement.

GLETKIN. Sit there.

RUBASHOV. On one condition. (*He turns to Gletkin firmly, even though he has to almost shut his eyes*) Turn off that dazzle-light! Save these devices for gangsters.

GLETKIN (*calmly*). You're in no position to make conditions. The fact is you are charged with being the worst kind of "gangster."

RUBASHOV (*controls his anger*). Exactly what are these charges? Please read them to me. Up till now this hasn't been done.

GLETKIN. Very well. Sit here! (*Rubashov sits in the chair upon which the dazzle-light has been trained. Gletkin reads the official statement in a rapid monotone*) "Enemy of the people, Nicolai Semono-vitch Rubashov, you are charged with be-ing a counter-revolutionary in the pay of hostile, foreign governments; of having, at the instigation of their agents, committed such acts of treason and wreckage as to cause vital shortages—undermining the military power of the U.S.S.R. You are also charged with having incited an accom-plice to attempt the assassination of the Leader of the Party. I.e., you are charged with crimes covered by Articles 58-1A; 58-2; 58-7; 58-9 and 58-11 of the Criminal Code." (*He drops the official papers and looks up*) You've heard the charges? You plead guilty?

RUBASHOV (*turns to face him, shielding his eyes with his hand*). I plead guilty to having fallen out of step with historical necessity. I plead guilty to bourgeois senti-mentality. I plead guilty to having wanted an immediate alleviation of the Terror, and extension of freedom to the masses. (*The secretary who is writing this in shorthand smiles contemptuously. Ruba-shov glances at her*) Don't be cynical, young woman. (*To Gletkin*) I now realize fully that the regime is right and I am wrong. The times demand a tightening of the dictatorship; any sentimental aberra-tions at the present moment in history could become suicide. In this sense can you call me a counter-revolutionary, but in this sense only. With the insane charges made in the accusation I have nothing to do. I deny them categorically.

GLETKIN. Have you finished?

RUBASHOV. I deny that I, Rubashov, ever plotted against my country. I deny that I am in the pay of a foreign government. I deny any act of sabotage. I deny ever having taken the least part in any act of terror against the Leader of the Party. (*To the stenographer, quietly*) Have you all that, young woman?

GLETKIN. Have you finished?

RUBASHOV. I have finished.

GLETKIN. Wipe your lips then. They're slimy with lies. Lies! Lies! Vomit! (*He snatches a thick dossier off the desk, and cracks Rubashov across the face with it*) The statement you have just made is vomit. Enough nobility! Enough postur-ing! Enough strutting! What we demand of you is not high talk, but a full confes-sion of your real crimes!

RUBASHOV (*his hand to his face, breath-ing hard, biting back the indignation, fighting for control*). I cannot confess to crimes I have not committed.

GLETKIN (*pressing a button the desk*). Oh, no, that you cannot. (*The Guard en-ters, bringing in 302, whose eyes at once fix on Gletkin, and who moves and talks like a sleepwalker. There is something in his manner of the helpless child, desper-ately eager to be "good" and to please. Gletkin dismisses the Guard with a nod, then points to a spot on the floor*) Step over here. (*Immediately 302 nods and shuffles over to stand correctly as desig-nated. Gletkin crosses above the desk. To Rubashov*) Do you know this person? (*Pause. Harshly*) You will please pay at-tention! Do you know this person?

RUBASHOV. The light's in my eyes.

GLETKIN (*softly*). Stand up! (*Rubashov hesitates. Gletkin roars*) Stand up! (*Ruba-shov rises*) Step over there! (*He points to 302. Rubashov walks up closer*) Do you recognize him now?

RUBASHOV (*shielding his eyes from the blinding light, scrutinizes 302, then shakes his head*). No.

GLETKIN. You've never met him before?

RUBASHOV (*hesitates*). Mm . . . No.

GLETKIN. You hesitated. Why?

RUBASHOV (*studies 302's face*). I don't place him.

GLETKIN. Your memory was once pro-verbial in the Party. (*A long pause*) You refuse to answer?

RUBASHOV. I do not refuse to answer. I simply do not place him.

GLETKIN. Good. Sit down. (*Rubashov sits. Gletkin turns to 302*) Help Citizen Rubashov's memory. Where did you last meet him?

302. Citizen Rubashov instigated me to

murder the Leader of the Party by poison . . .

GLETKIN (*irritably*). I didn't ask you
that. I asked you where you last met him.

RUBASHOV (*smiles grimly, and mutters*).
Wrong lever.

GLETKIN (*turns on him, snaps*). What?

RUBASHOV. The automatic barrel organ
played the wrong tune.

GLETKIN (*ominously*). I warn you. Remember where you are. We want none of
your so-called wit. (*Nods to 302*)

302. I met Citizen Rubashov in Brussels.

GLETKIN. Can you remember the date?

302. Distinctly. It was on the 17th anniversary of the Revolution. At his apartment!

RUBASHOV (*studying 302, suddenly puts
his hands to his forehead*). Yes, of course.
The date is correct. I didn't recognize
Joseph Kieffer. (*To Gletkin*) Congratulations!

GLETKIN. You admit you knew him
then? You met him on the day and occasion aforementioned?

RUBASHOV (*his eyes glued to the terrible
spectacle of 302's mangled, ghost-like
mask*). I've just told you that. If you'd
informed me at once that he was the son
of my unfortunate friend, Professor Kieffer, I'd have identified him sooner.

GLETKIN (*turns to 302*). How did this
meeting come about?

302. After the reception at the Legation
my father took me up to Citizen Rubashov's apartment.

GLETKIN (*nods*). Go on.

302. He and my father hadn't seen each
other for years. They talked about the
early days of the Revolution.

GLETKIN. They were drinking?

302. Yes. They drank and talked. (*A
far-away look and a gentle smile illumine
his face at the memory*) In the last few
years I've never seen my father in such a
good mood.

GLETKIN (*quietly*). That was three
months before the discovery of your father's counter-revolutionary crimes and his
execution!

(*302 darts a glance at him, licks his lips,
and stands there dumb. Rubashov turns to
Gletkin on a sudden impulse, but, blinded
by the light, he shuts his eyes and turns
slowly away, taking off his spectacles and
wiping them on his sleeve. The secretary's*

*pencil scratches on the paper and stops.
After a long pause 302 regains himself.*)

302. Yes.

GLETKIN. Proceed! Repeat their conversation. Only essentials.

302. He said . . .

GLETKIN. Rubashov?

302. Yes. Rubashov said, since the Boss
sat on the Party with his broad posterior,
the air underneath was no longer breath-
able. He said they must hold tight and
wait the hour.

GLETKIN. What did he mean by that?
"Wait the hour"?

302. The hour in which the Leader
would be eliminated. (*Rubashov smiles*)

GLETKIN. These reminiscences seem to
amuse you.

RUBASHOV. Two old friends get a little
drunk, talk carelessly, and you make a
conspiracy.

GLETKIN. So Rubashov spoke of the hour
in which the Leader of the Party would
be eliminated? How eliminated?

302. My father said some day the Party
would force him to resign.

GLETKIN. And Rubashov?

302. Laughed. He said the Boss had
made the Party bureaucracy his puppets.
He said the Boss could only be removed
by force.

RUBASHOV. By this I meant political action.

GLETKIN. As opposed to what?

RUBASHOV. Individual terrorism.

GLETKIN. In other words, you preferred
civil war?

RUBASHOV. No, mass action.

GLETKIN. Which leads to civil war. Is
that the distinction on which you place so
much value?

RUBASHOV (*loses patience, shouting*). I
cannot think straight with that damned
light in my eyes.

GLETKIN (*outshouts him*). I can't change
the lighting in this room to suit you. (*To
302, quietly*) So Rubashov said they had
to use violence? (*302 nods*) And his wild
talk, plus the alcohol he'd fed you, inflamed you?

302 (*after a pause*). I didn't drink, but
he—yes, he made a deep impression on
me.

GLETKIN. And later that evening he out-
lined his plan for you to murder the
Leader? (*302 is silent. He blinks into the
light. Rubashov raises his head. A pause,*

during which one hears only the lamp humming) Would you like your memory refreshed?

302 *(quivers as though struck by a whip).* It didn't happen that evening, but next morning.

RUBASHOV *(to Gletkin).* I believe the defendant has the right to ask questions.

GLETKIN *(fiercely).* You have no rights here! *(He leans forward to make some notations, and after a brief pause, without looking up)* Go ahead; ask your questions.

RUBASHOV *(rises, steps toward 302, very gently).* Now, Joseph, if I remember correctly, your father received the Order of Lenin the day after the celebration of the 17th anniversary of the Revolution.

302 *(whispers).* Yes.

RUBASHOV *(gently).* So that is correct. If I again remember rightly, Joseph, you were with him at the time he received it. *(302 nods)* And as I recall it, the Order was presented at Moscow. Right, Joseph? *(302 nods. Rubashov pauses, turns to Gletkin)* Professor Kieffer took a midnight plane and young Kieffer went with him. This alleged instigation to murder never took place because at the alleged moment young Kieffer was hundreds of miles away, high in the clouds.

(The secretary's pencil comes to a sudden standstill. She turns to Gletkin. 302, his face twisting with bewilderment and fear, also looks to Gletkin.)

GLETKIN *(calmly).* Have you any more questions?

RUBASHOV. That is all for the present. *(Sits)*

GLETKIN. Now, Joseph— *(Rises, assumes Rubashov's gentleness, even exaggerates it, crosses to 302)* —did you leave with your father? Or did you, in fact, join him later after your rendezvous with Rubashov?

302 *(almost a sob of relief).* After! I joined my father later.

GLETKIN. In time to be with him for the presentation?

302. Yes. Yes.

GLETKIN *(nods, turns to Rubashov).* Have you any more questions?

RUBASHOV. No.

GLETKIN *(turns to 302).* You may go.

302. Thank you . . .

GLETKIN *(calls).* Guard!

(A uniformed Guard enters and leads 302 out. At the door 302 turns his head once

more to Rubashov. Rubashov meets 302's imploring glance for a second, then turns away. Exit 302.)*

RUBASHOV *(angrily).* Poor devil! What have you done to him?

GLETKIN *(who has walked away, the full diameter of the room, turns, bellowing).* What can be done to you. *(And with incredible speed for such a huge man he hurls himself across the room, grabs Rubashov by the throat and pulls him to his feet)* We have many ways of making a man tell the truth.

RUBASHOV *(quickly).* Very well, what do you want me to sign? *(Gletkin relaxes his grip)* If you torture me I will sign anything you place before me. I will say anything you wish me to say at once. But tomorrow I will recant. At the public trial I'll stand up in open court and I'll cry out for all the world to hear, "They are drowning the Revolution in blood. Tyranny is afoot. She strides over our dead bodies." You've become quite pale. It would end your career, wouldn't it? You hold me by the throat, young man, but I hold you by the throat too. Remember that!

GLETKIN *(slowly releasing Rubashov).* Why do you make this so personal?

RUBASHOV. Death, even in an impersonal cause, is a personal matter. Death and promotions. *(Sits)*

GLETKIN. I am here only to serve the Party. I am nothing. *(He sits at the desk, gathering up his papers)* The personal element in this case has been removed along with your friend Ivanoff.

RUBASHOV *(his face clouding, apprehensively).* Removed?

GLETKIN. There'll be no partial confessions; there'll be no bargains. We promise you nothing.

RUBASHOV. What's happened to Ivanoff?

GLETKIN. Enemy of the people Ivanoff was executed early this morning.

RUBASHOV *(after a long pause, nods to himself, murmurs).* I see. *(Looks up at Gletkin)* Why? Was it because of me?

GLETKIN. Perhaps.

RUBASHOV. Perhaps he thought I was innocent.

GLETKIN. Then he shouldn't have conducted your investigation.

RUBASHOV *(sighs heavily, murmurs).* Go, Sascha. Go, in peace!

GLETKIN. He was corrupt, like so many

ot your old guard, and his counter-revolutionary action in your examination . . .

RUBASHOV (*jumps to his feet, all his pent-up feelings exploding*). Counter-revolutionary? You ignorant young ass! What the hell do you know about the Revolution or the old guard? When you were peeing in your diapers we were working and fighting and studying and writing one thing: Revolution! Revolution! Half our lives we lived like moles—underground; we rotted away in every prison in Europe; we knew poverty, we knew persecution, we knew starvation, but every living second we dreamed and built the Revolution with our blood and our bones! And now you have the gall to sit there and (*He waves his hand to the faded patches on the wall*) spit at these, the heroes of your boyhood? Are you insane? Do you really believe that we have all suddenly become venal and corrupt?

GLETKIN (*leans forward, rising slowly, his face apoplectic*). Quiet! You washed-out, disgusting, rotten old man! You didn't make the Revolution—the Revolution made you. You adventurers rode along, scum on the flood of the people's uprising. But don't make any mistake! You never fooled our Leader! He used you, because he had to use whatever was at hand, but he knew you were defective. That's why our Leader has taken such pains with us. We have learned to recognize your defectiveness by the smell of you. You were needed for a while like the white-collared intelligentsia after the Revolution. But a new generation is at the helm now and your day is over. Understand! There'll be no bargains! You, we offer nothing! You are going to die! The only question is whether you'll die uselessly, or whether you will confess and perform a last service for the Party. But, die you will, you understand?

RUBASHOV (*stares at him. Something dies; something of the will, and the battle, and the spirit go out of Rubashov forever. He suddenly becomes a very tired, sick old man. He nods, whispers hoarsely*) I understand.

GLETKIN (*harshly, triumphant*). Then let's have no more arrogance. (*He pushes a button, picks up the phone*) Next witness! (*The lights flicker, and as Rubashov slowly sits the scene vanishes*)

(*The lights come up on the tier of cells.*

We see 402 and the wraith-like 302. They are eating their meager supper of black bread and cabbage soup.)

302 (*taps to 402*). Is Rubashov back yet?

402 (*taps*). No.

302 (*taps*). How long?

402 (*taps*). They've had him upstairs—it must be ten hours now.

302 (*taps*). I wonder are they torturing him now.

402 (*taps*). Why should they? He's confessed.

302 (*taps*). They want more than that from him.

402 (*taps*). What more is there?

302 (*taps*). There's more. I hope he understood. I think he did. I looked into his eyes before I left. He seemed to understand. My father used to talk so well of him. (*Suddenly overcome, to himself*) Oh, my father, my father!

402 (*taps*). Eat your supper.

(*The lights fade and the prisoners vanish. The lights come up again, revealing the office. A new Interrogator and Secretary have replaced Gletkin and the Young Woman. As the scene appears the Interrogator, red-eyed, perspiration-soaked, purple-faced, is standing over Rubashov, hammering away at him. On the verge of fainting from fatigue, white-faced as the ghosts that haunt him, Rubashov exerts every ounce of will power to resist the fanatical onslaught. The Secretary is also washed out with fatigue, his hair in disarray, his tie loosened.*)

INTERROGATOR (*bellowing*). Is this true? Answer yes or no!

RUBASHOV. I can't . . .

INTERROGATOR. Yes or no!

RUBASHOV. Partially . . .

INTERROGATOR (*harshly*). Yes or no! Yes or no!

RUBASHOV (*wearily*). Yes . . . Yes.

INTERROGATOR (*grunts*). Yes. Good. (*Returns to the chair at the desk, seats himself*) And now we return to the Kieffer episode. (*Picks up the documents*) You admit this conversation with Professor Kieffer? (*Pause. He glances up; Rubashov's eyes have closed, his head, fallen, rests on his chest. The Interrogator shouts*) You will pay attention!

RUBASHOV (*opens his eyes, raises his head*). What?

INTERROGATOR. Don't you feel well?

RUBASHOV. I'm all right.

INTERROGATOR (with quiet threat). Would you like me to call in the doctor?

RUBASHOV (quickly, alert again). No.

INTERROGATOR. Stand up! (Rubashov pulls himself to his feet) Straight! Head up! Hands at your sides! At attention! (Rubashov obeys) Perhaps that will keep you awake. You admit this conversation? (Pause) Yes or no!

RUBASHOV. There were conversations.

INTERROGATOR. I didn't ask you about conversations, I ask you about this one.

RUBASHOV. In Hegel's philosophy, every yes has a no and every no has a yes.

INTERROGATOR. You're not here as a philosopher, you're here as a criminal. You'd better not talk about Hegel's philosophy. It'd be better first of all for Hegel. Do you admit this conversation? Yes or no.

RUBASHOV. Yes.

(The door opens, Gletkin and his Secretary enter briskly. They are fresh and rested. She has changed her dress. Gletkin carries an armful of books, with slips inserted.)

INTERROGATOR. Yes. Good.

RUBASHOV. But I deny your conclusions.

GLETKIN (interrupting). That is to say you admit everything except the logical consequence of your admissions? (He nods to the seated Secretary, who folds his notebook and rises. Gletkin's Secretary occupies the chair and proceeds to make notes)

INTERROGATOR. Stop this crude lying!

RUBASHOV. I'm not lying, young man.

GLETKIN (crosses to the desk). You've been here for ten hours poisoning the air with your Jesuit tactics. What do you expect to gain by this?

RUBASHOV. Gain? Nothing?

GLETKIN (touches the Interrogator who nods, rises). Then admit your crimes and get it over with!

RUBASHOV. Admit to crimes I didn't commit? Even Danton in the French Revolution was allowed to defend himself.

INTERROGATOR (now up out of the chair). And what happened to the French Revolution?

GLETKIN (sliding into the seat, leaning across the desk, without interrupting the interrogation. The effect is of a well-oiled machine) Powdered pigtails declaiming about personal honor! All that mattered to Danton and Company was to go with a swan song. Is that what you want? (The Interrogator and the male Secretary exit, stretching, yawning wearily)

RUBASHOV. I certainly don't want to go howling like a wolf in the night.

GLETKIN. Whether it does good or harm to the Cause, that doesn't matter?

RUBASHOV. My whole life has been a single purpose: to serve the Cause.

GLETKIN. There's only one way you can serve it now. A full confession in open court. A voluntary confession of all these crimes.

RUBASHOV (sways, leans on the desk to support himself). I've pleaded guilty to a false and harmful policy. Isn't that enough?

GLETKIN. Our country today is the bastion of the new era. Everything depends on our keeping the bastion intact, keeping the country solidly united.

RUBASHOV. How does it unite the country? How does it serve the Party that her members have to grovel in the dust? The name N. S. Rubashov is a piece of Party history. By dragging me in the mud you besmirch the Revolution. I—

GLETKIN. I, I, me, me, I! (He picks up one of the books, opening it to a marked page) Do you recognize this book?

RUBASHOV (puts on his glasses. His hands are trembling. It takes him some time to focus his vision as he peers at the book). Yes.

GLETKIN. Who wrote it?

RUBASHOV. I did.

GLETKIN (reads from the page). "With us the objective result is everything. With us objective good faith is of no interest. Those who prove wrong will pay!" You said that?

RUBASHOV (his body sags again). Yes.

GLETKIN. Well, you are wrong.

(The ghost-like image of Richard appears, pointing a finger at Rubashov.)

RUBASHOV (staring into space, nods). Yes.

GLETKIN. And you will pay.

(The phantom of Richard vanishes.)

RUBASHOV. I am paying.

GLETKIN. With your life!

RUBASHOV. My life has been the Party. My life would be worthless unless I could go on working for it. (His knees buckle, he sways, about to collapse)

GLETKIN. Sit down! (Rubashov sinks to the chair) There's only one way you can serve the Party now. As an example to the masses. *(He opens another book, reading from it)* "For the masses, what is right must be gilded, what is wrong must be black as pitch." You wrote that?

RUBASHOV. Yes.

GLETKIN. Even if we let you go on living—as you say—what would you have to live for?

RUBASHOV *(to himself)*. Nothing. A man without a country. *(The ghostly image of Luigi appears, smiling, gesticulating)* Like little Luigi.

GLETKIN. Who?

(Luigi's phantom vanishes.)

RUBASHOV *(shakes his head)*. Never mind.

GLETKIN. You admit your guilt?

RUBASHOV. In thought.

GLETKIN. In thought? *(Holds up a book)* And this?

RUBASHOV. Yes. Mine too.

GLETKIN *(reads)*. "The consequences of our thinking will be felt unto the seventh generation. Hence a wrong thought from us is more criminal than a wrong deed from others." You wrote that?

RUBASHOV. Yes. I wrote it.

GLETKIN. Then, when you say you are not guilty, aren't you thinking mechanistically, Citizen Rubashov? *(Albert's image appears. He is waving his hands with the ridiculously exaggerated gestures. Pablo's image appears, juggling plates)* *(Rubashov laughs softly.)*

GLETKIN. What are you laughing at?

(The phantoms of Pablo and Albert vanish.)

RUBASHOV *(startled, looks up)*. Was I laughing?

GLETKIN. Yes.

RUBASHOV *(passes his hand over his forehead)*. I wasn't conscious of it.

GLETKIN. Do you usually do things you're not conscious of?

RUBASHOV. No. Not often.

GLETKIN. These acts of sabotage, for example.

RUBASHOV. I deny them.

GLETKIN. Perhaps you committed them unconsciously.

RUBASHOV. I didn't commit them at all.

GLETKIN. These factories had great losses.

RUBASHOV. Yes.

GLETKIN. Sabotage is a weapon of the class struggle.

RUBASHOV. Yes. But I didn't employ it.

GLETKIN. You've advocated its use again and again?

RUBASHOV. Yes. But I didn't employ it here.

GLETKIN. Didn't you? *(Pause. He looks through the papers)* The case of the woman Luba Loshenko. She was your secretary? Correct?

RUBASHOV. Yes.

GLETKIN. And you were sleeping with her. *(Rubashov straightens up)*. Correct? *(Silence)* Shall I give you the place, dates, conversations? *(He waves the dossier)* They're all here.

RUBASHOV *(almost inaudible)*. Yes, I was sleeping with her.

GLETKIN. Speak up!

RUBASHOV *(loudly)*. Yes. I admit the relationship.

GLETKIN. You admit it?

RUBASHOV. I said yes.

GLETKIN. She was tried and shot for sabotage, correct?

RUBASHOV *(wildly)*. She was innocent.

GLETKIN. Innocent? *(He rises)*

RUBASHOV. Yes.

GLETKIN. She had no political motives? Is that when you mean?

RUBASHOV. Precisely.

GLETKIN. Precisely. She was an ordinary young woman, infatuated—blindly, stupidly, the slave and tool of one man who, however, did have considerable political motives—you!

RUBASHOV. What motives?

GLETKIN. You hated the Revolution, and you taught her to hate us.

RUBASHOV *(desperately)*. That's not true. She was innocent.

GLETKIN. Why didn't you say so at the time?

RUBASHOV. You know as well as I there wasn't anything I could do to save her.

GLETKIN. So you did nothing?

RUBASHOV. Nothing.

GLETKIN. You were silent.

RUBASHOV. I was silent.

GLETKIN. To save your own neck!

RUBASHOV. To go on working.

GLETKIN. Without a neck one cannot work; hence, to save your own neck. And this silence of yours was finally responsible for her execution. Correct?

RUBASHOV. So I was informed.

GLETKIN. For your further information, I was one of her interrogators.

RUBASHOV *(raises his head)*. You?

GLETKIN *(thumbs through the transcript).* I have here a transcript of her interrogation. I think it might interest you. Ninth day. Tenth day. Yes, here we have it. This Loshenko woman was surprising. These thin delicate ones sometimes really stand up. Listen! *(He reads)* Interrogator: "Under whose orders?" Loshenko: "No one's . . ."

(Luba's image appears in space, bowed, drenched with pain. She shakes her head slowly, moving her lips silently at first, then her trembling voice becomes barely audible, grows stronger, finally topping and supplanting Gletkin's voice. Gletkin continues to read from the transcript.)

LUBA. No one's. I've told you a hundred times there were no orders.

GLETKIN. Stop lying.

LUBA. No matter what I say you don't believe me. Oh, God! I'm so tired.

GLETKIN. I want the truth.

LUBA. I've told you the truth, over and over and over and over. I'm so tired, I can't . . .

GLETKIN. Who gave you these instructions?

LUBA. No one.

GLETKIN. You sabotaged without instructions?

LUBA. No, no, no. You're twisting my words.

GLETKIN. That's what you said.

LUBA. I didn't say that! I said I didn't do these things and no one asked me to.

GLETKIN. We've all the proofs.

LUBA. What are you trying to make me say?

GLETKIN. Stop shielding Rubashov!

LUBA. I'm not shielding anyone.

GLETKIN. You're shielding Rubashov.

LUBA. A man like that doesn't need shielding. A man like that . . .

GLETKIN. You were sleeping with him, weren't you?

LUBA. I loved him.

GLETKIN. You loved him?

LUBA. Yes.

GLETKIN. You'd do anything he asked you?

LUBA. He wouldn't ask me to commit crimes.

GLETKIN. Idiot! This man has used you.

LUBA. No!

GLETKIN. He's made a fool of you.

LUBA. No!

GLETKIN. And now when you need him, where is he? Where is he?

LUBA. Oh, God, God, make them leave me alone!

GLETKIN. God is dead, Luba Loshenko! God is dead.

LUBA. What do you want of me?

GLETKIN. Rubashov's making you responsible for his guilt.

LUBA. He's not.

GLETKIN. Use your head! He's refused to testify for you.

LUBA. I don't believe that.

GLETKIN. Here are the proofs! Look, look!

LUBA. I don't want to look.

GLETKIN. He was asked to testify and he's refused.

LUBA. I don't believe that. I don't believe you . . . I don't believe you . . .

RUBASHOV *(staring into space, murmurs).* I had no choice, Luba. Don't you see? I had no choice. I couldn't have saved you. It was only a trap to destroy my usefulness. *(The Secretary rises, leans forward to catch Rubashov's words and writes them down)* I tried! I went everywhere—to my friends in high places. They said no, nothing will help.

GLETKIN *(reads on).* Save yourself! This is your last chance, Luba Loshenko! You admit these acts of sabotage.

LUBA. I can't admit them because there weren't any. There was no sabotage. There were only tired men and sick men and frightened men.

GLETKINS *(slaps his hand as he reads).* You stupid bitch! *(Luba's image recoils as if she'd been struck)* All right! Then you'll be shot in the back of your neck!

LUBA. What are you doing to us? What are you doing to us? We're not stones, we're not machines! We're human beings. We feel, we think, we see, we dream, we're a part of God. Why have you done this to us? You say God is dead, but you've made your own god out of darkness, out of misery and lies and pain! Why? Why are you doing this to us?

RUBASHOV *(stands up unsteadily, staring into space, calls out).* This was not the way it was to be.

(Gletkin glances quickly at Rubashov who is no longer aware of his surroundings, nods to the Secretary. She rises and leans closer to Rubashov, taking down his words.)

LUBA. You've made a prison . . . out of our wonderful country—a prison.

RUBASHOV. We wanted to build a new and better world.

LUBA. You've put chains on our people. Chains. In their hearts, inside their skulls. Why? Why?

RUBASHOV. I don't understand why myself. Our principles were right.

LUBA. Our people are more miserable than before the Revolution.

RUBASHOV. We diagnosed the disease, but wherever we applied the healing knife . . .

LUBA. Our people are covered with sores.

RUBASHOV. Our will was pure. We should have been loved by the people . . .

LUBA. They hate you.

RUBASHOV. Why? Why are we so hated? We brought truth.

LUBA. In your mouths everything becomes a lie.

RUBASHOV. We brought living life . . .

LUBA. The trees in the forest wither.

RUBASHOV. I sang of hope.

LUBA. Your tongues stammer and bark.

RUBASHOV. Yes, yes, and every premise of unimpeachable truth has led me to this final weird and ghostly game. Why? Why?

LUBA. Kolya! Kolya, darling! Wherever you are . . . (*She vanishes and only her voice is heard crying "Kolya! Kolya!"*)

RUBASHOV. Luba! Luba! What have I done? What have I done? (*He whispers*) Guilty, guilty, guilty! (*Then, very simply*) I'm going to faint. (*He slides gently and quietly out of the chair and falls to the floor*)

GLETKIN (*rings for his colleague, snaps his fingers at his Secretary*). The ammonia! (*The Secretary rushes across to the table, opens a drawer, takes out a bottle of ammonia and hands it to him. Gletkin, on one knee, slaps Rubashov's face and administers the restorative. The door is thrown open and the other Interrogator enters*)

GLETKIN (*nods, indicating Rubashov's crumpled body*). We've got him. We've got the lever. (*The sharp fumes of the ammonia begin to revive Rubashov*) Stand him up! (*The other Interrogator lifts Rubashov to his feet and holds him there, limp as a rag-doll. Gletkin waves the ammonia bottle under his nose until he responds, then, putting one huge hand gently on his shoulder, speaks softly, caressingly*) You haven't eaten your food today, Comrade Rubashov. Would you like some hot soup?

RUBASHOV (*murmurs*). Sleep. I must sleep.

GLETKIN. You understand, Comrade Rubashov, what the Party expects of you.

RUBASHOV. Yes.

GLETKIN. This is the last service you can perform for the Party.

RUBASHOV. I must sleep. Sleep.

GLETKIN. Very well. (*To Guard*) Take him back to his cell. (*To Rubashov, gently*) I'll see that you are not disturbed.

RUBASHOV (*like a child, eagerly*). Thank you, Comrade Gletkin. (*The Guard takes Rubashov out*)

GLETKIN (*to the Interrogator*). In exactly twenty minutes wake him up and bring him back here. I'll interrogate him till midnight, you take him till five A.M., and I'll take him again at five. (*Blinks his eyes, avoids the dazzle-light*) This Loshenko thing—that's the lever. Work it around in his belly. Keep returning to it. It's simply a question of time now. (*The Interrogator nods, feels his aching back, and goes, yawning. Gletkin snaps off the dazzle-light*)

SECRETARY. Congratulations, Comrade Gletkin.

GLETKIN (*sits down to his desk, stretches his legs, pleased*). It's just a matter of constitution.

(*The scene fades out. The lights come up. The Supreme Court of the U.S.S.R. This scene is another memory in the mind of the brooding Rubashov after the event has occurred. The President, bathed in a hot white light, is seated at a long covered table, three judges to his left, three to his right. The rest are shadowy figures.*)

PRESIDENT. Comrade Judges, you have heard the evidence against Citizen Rubashov. Comrade Procurateur of the U.S.S.R. has summed up for the prosecution. Accused Rubashov step forward. (*Rubashov appears in the white light before the judge's bench. The Guard brings on a microphone and sets it in front of Rubashov*) Accused Rubashov may make his last plea.

RUBASHOV (*bending a little, speaking into the microphone, in a dead voice*). Citizen Judges. Covered with shame, trampled in the dust, about to die—let me serve my final purpose. Let my horrible story demonstrate how the slightest deflection from the Party line must inevitably drag one down into counter-revolutionary banditry. If I ask myself today: "For what am I dying?" I am confronted by absolute nothingness. Therefore, on the threshold of my final hour, I bend my knees to my country and to my people. The political masquerade is over. We were dead long before the Public Prosecutor demanded our heads. With this my task is ended. I have paid my debts. To ask for mercy would be derision. You must hate me, and you must kill me! I have nothing more to say. (*He stands with lowered head. The Guard removes the microphone*)

PRESIDENT. I will announce the sentence of the Military Collegium of the Supreme Court. (*He reads*) "The Sentence. The Military Collegium of the Supreme Court of the U.S.S.R. sentences N. S. Rubashov to the supreme penalty—to be shot, with the confiscation of all his personal property . . ."

(*His voice trails off. The lights fade. The court vanishes. Only Rubashov remains, sitting in his cell, wrapped in meditation, his head between his hands, his brow furrowed, his face old and gray as if all the blood had been drained out of him. An insistent tapping. 402 comes into view, tapping three times, waiting, and gently repeating the code.*)

RUBASHOV (*coming out of his reverie, rises feebly, crosses unsteadily to the wall, taps*). Yes?

402 (*taps*). I thought 302 behaved quite well. He went like a brave man.

RUBASHOV (*taps*). Yes.

402 (*taps*). You still have about ten minutes. What are you doing?

RUBASHOV (*taps*). I'm thinking.

402 (*taps*). Thinking's bad. You won't show the white feather! We know you're a man. A man. (*Pause*) Do you still remember "Breasts fit champagne glasses!" Ha! Ha! What a man you are! (*Rubashov listens for a sound from the corridor. 402 senses his thoughts*) Don't listen. I'll tell you in time when they are coming. (*Pause*) What would you do if you were pardoned?

RUBASHOV (*thinks, taps*). I'd study astronomy.

402 (*taps*). Ha! Ha! Me too, perhaps.

But they say other stars are perhaps also inhabited. That would spoil it. (*Pause*) May I give you some advice?

RUBASHOV (*taps*). Yes.

402 (*taps*). But don't take it wrong. Technical suggestion of an old soldier. Empty your bladder. Is always better in such case. The spirit is willing but the flesh is weak. Ha! Ha!

RUBASHOV (*smiles, taps*). Thanks. (*Pause*)

402 (*taps*). Why astronomy?

RUBASHOV (*taps*). As a boy I loved to watch the stars. I wanted to solve the riddle of the universe.

402 (*taps*). Why? Talk to me.

RUBASHOV (*to himself*). Recently I read they have discovered the Universe is finite. Forty years pass and I read that. If the Public Prosecutor had asked, "Defendant Rubashov, what about the Infinite?," I would not have been able to answer. Perhaps there is my real guilt.

402 (*taps*). It's too late to worry about guilt.

RUBASHOV (*taps*). How can I die till I find out what I'm dying for? (*Pause, taps*) Sorry! Tell me, what are your prospects?

402 (*taps slowly*). Eighteen years more. Not quite. Only six thousand five hundred thirty days. (*Pause*) Think of it. Another six thousand five hundred thirty days without a woman. I envy you really. My brain is turning to water. I have returned to the habits of my childhood. I loathe myself!

RUBASHOV (*to the wall*). Oh, you poor, poor devil! (*To the entire prison, to all Russia*) All of you! My hundred and eighty million fellow prisoners, what have I done to you? What have I created? If History is all calculation, Rubashov, give me the sum of a hundred and eighty million nightmares. Quickly calculate me the pressure of a hundred and eighty million cravings. Where in your mathematics, Rubashov, is the human soul? At the very beginning you forgot what you were searching for?

(*Footsteps ring out in the corridor.*)

402 (*taps*). They're coming. (*The footsteps grow louder*) What a shame. We were having such a pleasant talk.

RUBASHOV (*taps*). You've helped me a lot. Thanks.

402 *(taps)*. Farewell. I envy you, I envy you.

(The door of Rubashov's cell is thrown open with a clang. Gletkin enters.)

GLETKIN. Enemy of the People Nicolai Semonovitch Rubashov, before you are executed, have you any last wish? *(A long pause)*

RUBASHOV. One. *(He tries to catch Gletkin's eyes)* If I could only make you understand where in the very beginning we failed.

GLETKIN. These are your last words. Don't waste them.

RUBASHOV *(passionately)*. You don't build a Paradise out of concrete. My son . . .

GLETKIN *(quickly, distastefully)*. I am not your son.

RUBASHOV *(after a long pause, sadly)*. Yes, you are. That's the horror. *(He shakes his head, bitterly)* The means have become the end; and darkness has come over the land.

GLETKIN. Have you any last wish?

RUBASHOV. To die.

(Gletkin motions him to walk. Rubashov moves slowly out of the cell; Gletkin takes out his pistol, cocks it and follows. The Guard opens the gate to the cellar, a shaft of light coming up catches them. 402 begins to drum on the door. From all over the prison comes the hollow muffled drumming, which mounts higher and higher as Rubashov and Gletkin descend, and the iron gate clangs behind them. The drumming reaches a climax as the curtain falls slowly.)

Anne of the Thousand Days

BY MAXWELL ANDERSON

First presented by The Playwrights' Company at the Shubert Theatre in New York on December 8, 1948, with the following cast:

ANNE BOLEYN.................................Joyce Redman	MADGE SHELTON...................Margaret Garland
HENRY ....Rex Harrison	JANE SEYMOUR..............................Monica Lang
CARDINAL WOLSEY.....................Percy Waram	SIR THOMAS MORE.......................Russell Gaige
THOMAS BOLEYN......................Charles Francis	THOMAS CROMWELL.........Wendell K. Phillips
SERVANT ....Ludlow Maury	BISHOP FISHER................................Harry Irvine
HENRY NORRIS.........................Allan Stevenson	PRIOR HOUGHTON......................George Collier
MARK SMEATON...........................John Merivale	A MESSENGER...................................Harry Selby
DUKE OF NORFOLK.....................John Williams	BAILIFF ....Fred Ayres Cotton
PERCY, EARL OF NORTHUMBERLAND	BAILIFF ....Harold McGee
Robert Duke	CLERK ....Terence Anderson
ELIZABETH BOLEYN.........................Viola Keats	SINGERS:
SERVING WOMAN.....................Kathleen Bolton	Richard Leone, Frank Myers, Donald Conrad
SERVANT ....Cecil Clovelly	MUSICIANS:
MARY BOLEYN...............................Louise Platt	Harold McGee, Malcolm Wells, Charles Ellis

An historical drama in two acts dealing with Anne Boleyn's courtship and marriage to Henry VIII, and finally her execution. The action of the play takes place in England between the years 1526 and 1536.

In Maxwell Anderson the American theatre has had one of its most skillful as well as literate practitioners. In him it has also had a playwright who has always had large designs upon the stage, and these have been far less disputed than the actual results of Mr. Anderson's ambition. His highest intentions have been most manifest in the series of verse plays he has given us with considerable regularity since the writing of *Elizabeth the Queen*, produced by the Theatre Guild in 1930. Although Anderson's boldest effort was *Winterset*, in 1935, and his most lyrical *High Tor*, in 1937, his safest ventures into formal poetic drama have been his Elizabethan dramas *Elizabeth the Queen, Mary of Scotland*, and *Anne of the Thousand Days*. Although the derivativeness of these plays subjected them to charges of academicism, they never failed to exert a strong theatrical effect; and least open to criticism is *Anne of the Thousand Days*, except in its soliloquies. Comparatively muscular and downright robust in its humor, and also written less loquaciously than his other pieces, this reworking of the story of Anne Boleyn and Henry VIII is the most forceful historical drama Mr. Anderson has written to date. His characters, too, have less than his usual measure of romanticized reality.

Anderson belongs to the playwriting generation of the nineteen-twenties. Born in 1888, well educated, a college teacher of English, and a journalist whose last position was on Pulitzer's *New York World*, Anderson first made an impression in 1924 with the war play *What Price Glory?*, a collaboration with Laurence Stallings. Previously, he had published a volume of verse and presented an unsuccessful verse play, *White Desert*, in 1923. During the nineteen-twenties, he had another success with a tidy comedy of marriage, *Saturday's Children*, in 1927. In the strenuous nineteen-thirties, he wrote a stinging satire on Congressional log-rolling, *Both Your Houses*, and earned a Pulitzer Prize for playwriting. But he devoted most of his time to verse drama, composing, in addition to his first two Elizabethan plays and *Winterset*, the romantic protest against materialism *High Tor*, the George Washington drama *Valley Forge*, the Hapsburg tragedy *The Masque of Kings*, the New England Medea piece *The Winged Victory*, and a play about social responsibility set in Spain during the Civil War and Florida under gangster rule, *Key Largo*. In the early forties, Mr. Anderson's efforts were less effective, although the patriotic drama *The Eve of St. Mark* won strong public support. In the latter part of that decade, he also won favor with his ingenious Joan of Arc play *Joan of Lorraine*, with his music-drama *Lost in the Stars*, based on Alan Paton's novel *Cry, the Beloved Country*, and with *Anne of the Thousand Days*. For an American playwright to retain the respect of a large public for nearly three decades was no small accomplishment. Mr. Anderson remained a considerable figure in the Broadway theatre.

ACT ONE

PROLOGUE

The curtain rises in darkness. Then a single spotlight comes up to show, sitting at stage right, a young woman dressed in a gray fur-trimmed costume of a fashion usual at the time of Henry VIII. There are dark hangings behind her, broken only by a small, barred window which the lights project on one panel of the curtains. The young woman is Anne Boleyn, and the time is the evening of May 18, 1536.

———

ANNE. If I were to die now—
but I must not die yet,
not yet.
It's been too brief. A few weeks and days.
How many days, I wonder, since the first
   time
I gave myself, to that last day when he—
when he left me at the lists and I saw
   him no more?
Well, I can reckon it.
I have time enough. Those who sit in the
   Tower
don't lack for time.
(She takes out a little wax tablet, with a stylus)
He could never cipher.
He was shrewd and heavy—
and cunning with his tongue, and wary in
   intrigue,
but when it came to adding up an account
he filled it with errors and bit his tongue—
and swore—
till I slapped his hands like a child and
   took the pen
and made it straight.
"A king," I said, "a king, and cannot
   reckon."
I was his clever girl then, his Nan;
he'd kiss me then, and maul me, and take
   me down.
On the rushes. Anywhere.
Why do I think of it now? Would he kill
   me? Kill me?
(She laughs)
Henry? The fool? That great fool kill
   me?
God knows I deserve it. God knows I
   tried to kill,
and it may be I succeeded.
I did succeed. I know too well I succeeded,
and I'm guilty, for I brought men to death
   unjustly,

as this death of mine will be un[
   comes—
only I taught them the way. A[
   die
in the way I contrived. . . . It may be. .. . .
No, but Henry. He could not. Could
   not . . .
Could I kill him, I wonder?
I feel it in my hands perhaps I could.
So—perhaps he could kill me.
Perhaps he could kill me.
If it came tomorrow, how many days
would it have been,
(She makes a mark on the tablet)
beginning with our first day?
(The lights dim down and go out except on Anne's face. She remains visible in reverie during the first few moments of the first scene.)

SCENE ONE

The lights come up on a circle at stage left. A great window, partly of stained glass, is projected on the curtain background, and Mary Boleyn (she is the wife of William Carey, but that hardly counts, for she has been the mistress of King Henry for four years, and she is only twenty-three) stands, peering through one of the panes. We are in the castle at Hever, owned by Thomas Boleyn, the king's treasurer, and the year is 1526. It is early spring. Thomas Boleyn enters from stage right.

———

BOLEYN. Mary?
MARY. Yes, father.
BOLEYN. You watch for someone?
MARY. I thought I saw the king on the road below.
BOLEYN. We were to talk over the enclosure of a hunting park near Hever.
MARY. He's here to see you, then?
BOLEYN. I think so, child.
MARY. Not me?
BOLEYN. Not this time.
MARY. But I may speak to him in passing, surely?
BOLEYN. Perhaps—but—*(He pauses in embarrassment)* I wonder if you could do this? Could you go to your room while he's here—and not see him—and send no message?
MARY. Why?
BOLEYN. Could you do this?

MARY. Go to my room! But for what reason? I have some rights in this house I should think—as your daughter, if not as the wife of my husband. And in the kingdom as the king's mistress, which, God help me, I am, and which you have encouraged me to be!

BOLEYN. Did you need encouraging, Mary? Think back on the fever you were in those days. Did you need encouragement?

MARY. If I am sent out of the way I shall ask the king why.

BOLEYN. Very well.

MARY. And now. I shall ask him now!

BOLEYN. The truth is, the king sent ahead to make sure we two could speak alone. He and I.

MARY. He asked—not to see me?

BOLEYN. Not in so many words—but—

MARY. That could mean—I was not to see him again.

BOLEYN. One never gets used to these things—there's always a hell to go through. But when a girl gives herself so completely—

MARY. You knew when I gave myself! And where. It has helped you! Yes, you live by it! Steward of Tunbridge and Penshurst, sheriff of Bradsted, viscount, king's treasurer—and all these revenues have come to you since I opened my bedroom door to him!

BOLEYN. Mary, girl, I've always loved you. I wouldn't want to hurt you in any way. And all these things are true. The king has been generous to me because you were generous to him—and I know that and I've known it all the time. But could I have refused what he gave? I've been grateful to you, Mary—and ashamed of having to be grateful—yet I couldn't refuse what was offered. And now—if you've lost the king, I don't know how to help with that. I shall help any other way I can. . . . You still have your husband.

MARY. Who wants my husband?

BOLEYN. I'm caught here, Mary—we're all caught. . . .

MARY. It's true, though. The moment I became all his, and held nothing back, I had lost the king, and I knew it. Yes, I've lost him—

(Mary turns away. As she does so an elegantly robed prelate enters from stage right. The girl goes out past the ecclesiastic without trusting herself to speak. The newcomer is Cardinal Wolsey.)

WOLSEY. You've told her?

BOLEYN. Yes.

WOLSEY. And Anne?

BOLEYN. The earl is with her.

WOLSEY. The king rode close behind me, Thomas.

BOLEYN. My dear Cardinal, I have encouraged Anne with the young noble. He'll have the greatest estates in the north of England. It was something off my mind that Anne should like him and want him, for she's not easy to please. It never entered my head that the king had noticed her. What can I say to her now?

WOLSEY. To send the earl away.

BOLEYN. I think they have a sort of engagement between them.

WOLSEY. Well—the king's here.

BOLEYN. I think it would need more time.

WOLSEY. Suppose you take the king to look at your hounds. Tell him that Anne had ordered a new dress and there's some trouble with it—her hands tremble over the fastenings, and other rubbish of that sort. I'll speak to Anne and to the earl.

BOLEYN. Well—if you'll manage it.

(A servant enters.)

SERVANT. My lord—

(Henry VIII enters behind the servant. A rough, shrewd, merry, brutal man in the thirties, accustomed to making himself at home in this house and with all his subjects when he thinks the effect might be good. Norris and Smeaton enter after him.)

HENRY (to Norris and Smeaton). Wait for me, gentlemen. Only your king, Thomas. No ceremony. Only your Henry. (Nevertheless he gives his hand to be kissed and Boleyn kisses it. Norris and Smeaton go out) And how's the vicar of hell this chilly spring morning?

(The Servant goes out.)

WOLSEY. I keep warm, Majesty.

HENRY. I'm sure you do. With your feet on the devil's fender. Meanwhile toasting your paddocks at God's altar.

WOLSEY. And running the king's errands. It's a busy life.

HENRY. Has he done my errand?

BOLEYN. Yes, he has.

HENRY. May I smell this pretty posy of yours?

BOLEYN. My lord, if you mean Anne, she's still at her mirror, and—if you could give her a half hour.

HENRY. We've this whole day.

BOLEYN. There was a clump of red deer grazing within view when I last looked out. In velvet, but they give promise of sport later.

HENRY. We'll see them. We'll see your red deer, and afterward we'll appraise what was seen in that same looking glass. *(He turns.)*

WOLSEY. Good hunting, Majesty.

HENRY. You won't be with us?

WOLSEY. It happens there is a poor soul in the house who seeks the ministrations of a religious. I must go where I am called.

HENRY. You will go wherever it's most profitable for the Cardinal of York to be at any given time. So go there, and no more of these holy thin excuses.

WOLSEY. Yes, Majesty.

(He goes out.)

HENRY. There's no hurry about the deer. I want three words with you.

BOLEYN. Yes?

HENRY. There's always a temptation, when a man's in my position, that he'll think of the nation as his own trough, and get all four feet in it and eat from one end to the other. I don't want to look like that to anybody.

BOLEYN. You don't, my sovereign.

HENRY. I'm a religious man, Boleyn. I want to do what's right in the eyes of God and the church. And myself—and my people—and you.

BOLEYN. That's a swath of folk to satisfy —if you include God.

HENRY. I include both God and the women—among them your daughters. What will your daughters say of me—the two of them together—talking at night?

BOLEYN. What two women say together— talking at night of one man who has wanted them both—and taken both. No man will ever know that. But I think—if you don't mind—

HENRY. I've asked you.

BOLEYN. I think you go a little rapid with Annie. You'll need to be gentle.

HENRY. But she'll have me—in the end?

BOLEYN. She's no fool, my lord.

HENRY *(after a pause)*. What I do is God's will.

BOLEYN. Now, if a man or a monarch could be sure of that!

HENRY. I've worked it out, in my mind— I pray to God.

(He hesitates)

I tell you this first, Boleyn.

God answers prayer. That's known. Every morning I go on my knees

and pray that what I do may be God's will.

I pray him to direct me—that whatever thought

comes to my mind—whatever motion

floods in my heart—shall be God's will— and I

only His instrument. Wherever I turn,

whatever I do—whether to reach for food,

or thread my way among the crossed paths of the law,

or interpret the holy word,

or judge men innocent—or guilty—

every morning I pray Him on my knees

nothing shall rise in my brain or heart but He

has wished it first.

And since He answers prayer,

and since He's given me such heavy power to act,

power for good and evil,

He must answer this. He does answer.

I find such peace

in this, that not one morning my whole life long

shall I fail these devotions.

BOLEYN. This is a noble thought, of course,

but Your Majesty realizes that it might be used as an excuse for—

HENRY. For what?

BOLEYN. For doing as you please.

HENRY. I'm quite serious, Boleyn. I want no trifling.

BOLEYN. It was not my intention to trifle.

HENRY. But you do! I tell you I pray and God answers!

BOLEYN. Yes, my lord.

HENRY. I am younger than you. I am younger than Wolsey.

I am younger than many dukes and earls and peers.

But I am the king of England. When I pray God answers.

I will not have this questioned.

BOLEYN. Yes, my lord.

(Norris and Smeaton enter.)

NORRIS. We're sent as a delegation, my lord.

HENRY. Come in, come in. Pour it on, whatever it is. Your king is your natural receptacle for whatever you can't hold any longer.

NORRIS. The fact is we are sent to keep you amused while Sir Thomas Boleyn confers with his lady wife. There is a sort of kitchen rebellion afoot and his voice is needed.

HENRY. Go, Boleyn, mollify your women.

BOLEYN. If you'll excuse me.

(He goes.)

HENRY. Come in, lads. I want a word with you, anyway—man to man, kingship aside. You buzz the girls you two— you've thrust your hands in amongst a flutter of larks often enough and pulled out the one you wanted. Tell me, what's the best cast of all for a maiden?

SMEATON. A maid, Your Majesty?

HENRY. I wouldn't swear to that. Not medically. But a young one—a bit wild— uncaught.

NORRIS. I couldn't say of my own knowledge, sir, but Tom Wyatt has an unfailing way. He writes them poems.

SMEATON. But you can't catch a ticklish hoyden with madrigals. That's for matrons.

HENRY. Then your lure, Smeaton? Your favorite?

SMEATON. My king, my acquaintance doesn't run among the grade of females you seek. I'm more successful with waiting women and ladies' maids.

HENRY. Don't be modest, lad. I've followed your spoor so close there was scarce time to close the window you left by—or change perfumes to put me off the scent—

SMEATON. Truly, truly—

HENRY. I've breathed your same air in some close quarters, singer. So speak on. Your lure. Your most seductive.

SMEATON. Why, being a singer, I sing to them a good deal—but, in addition to that—you will not be offended?

HENRY. I'll be offended if you keep back, musician. Be ashamed of nothing. We live in a new age, a new time. I was born within a year of the discovery of the new world. We revise all the old laws to suit ourselves. And the mysteries and manners.

SMEATON. Why, then, if you truly want her, make her believe you're potent only with her, Majesty, and that will do the business. Make out that you've tried with numbers of others, gone to bed and kissed hotly, and hung embarrassed and unable. But with her you rouse up. You're a man again. They can't resist that. They open like—

HENRY. Never mind the simile. There's nothing like it. But, lad, this is new, this device.

SMEATON. I think it's my own.

HENRY. And ingenious. *(Norfolk enters)* We're speaking of the best way to woo a green maid, Norfolk. You're a man of expedients. You know these things—if you haven't forgotten them.

NORFOLK. Why, my advice is, if you want a woman, take her.

HENRY. There are certain preliminaries. There's consent, anyway. You must have consent.

NORFOLK. Nonsense. Take her and make her like it. Why should a woman have anything to say about it?

HENRY. It may have been so in the good old days. Today we woo—and wait.

NORRIS. Do you wish her to be in love with you, my lord?

HENRY. That I do.

NORRIS. Do you wish to be in love with her?

HENRY. In love with her? I? Personally? Now, I'll tell you the truth, so far my experience of being in love is like this: love is a kind of wanting, a panting and sighing and longing. What does a man desire of a lass, anyway? To be assuaged. He wants his pain assuaged. Well, that done, what more's to be done?

SMEATON. Is it *lèse-majesté*, or may I ask—

HENRY. Nothing is *lèse-majesté* in this conversation.

SMEATON. Have you ever been refused by a maid?

HENRY. Refused? I? No, I think not. When I've wanted them I've had them. And once I've had a wench, I'm cured. That's general, isn't it? Broad and narrow?

NORRIS. My king, with me it's the opposite. Once I've mixed flesh and lips with her I'm in danger of a golden wedding— should we both live.

HENRY. It can happen so?

SMEATON. The poor gudgeon's hooked now. He'll never swim free again.

NORRIS. And she won't look at me.

HENRY. Keep me from that, good God!

NORFOLK. Can you youngsters leave talking of virgins long enough to look at the venison?

HENRY. Yes—come. Next to the haunch of a virgin there's nothing like a haunch of venison.

(The lights go out on the scene.)

SCENE TWO

The lights go up on a circle at stage left, where Anne Boleyn and Percy, Earl of Northumberland, sit on a bench, their arms about each other. Anne is younger than in the Prologue, and dressed in a simple morning dress of the period. Percy is a young, headstrong, handsome fellow, not without brains and spirit. A half-open casement takes shape on the curtains at the rear.

———

ANNE. I'm angry with myself about one thing.

PERCY. Yes, dear.

ANNE. I spent two years at the court of Queen Claude. I met there the silkened flower of the aristocracy. Such manners, such grace, such horsemanship and dancing! They spoke Greek, they spoke Latin, they spoke Italian—and they spoke their own French with a wit and a fencer's point that gave me a new glimpse of what a language could be!

PERCY. But what disappointed you?

ANNE. Among them there were—well, truly gallant men. Captivating men. Charmers. With an ease of carriage—and a way with women that . . . and I fell in love with none of them. I came home and promptly fell in love with a—a thistle. A countryman from the north. With no graces at all. Can't dance. Can't sing. Can hardly speak English.

PERCY. Can put his arm around you.

ANNE. Doesn't do that well. Not as well as I've known it done. But it's the one arm I want—for some God-knows-what reason. You do everything badly—everything awkwardly—and I love it the way you do it.

PERCY. I'm glad I wasn't educated in France.

ANNE. Why?

PERCY. You wouldn't have loved me.

ANNE. I wonder. It may be true.

PERCY. Silks are for holiday. Honest homespun wears through the years.

ANNE. One thing though. If we love enough to marry we must love enough to keep nothing back. I shall keep nothing from you.

PERCY. Nor I from you, sweet.

ANNE. But you have. You don't know what I mean.

PERCY. Are we to lie together? Before?

ANNE. If you like. But that's not it.

PERCY. My bonny, what more can there be than that?

ANNE. Kiss me hard.

(He kisses her.)

PERCY. I wish I had you in my house.

ANNE *(musing)*. That's part of it, too. To be Lady Anne, and live with you in your house, and sleep with you at night, and in the morning—well, the servants will bring in breakfast to the earl—to Percy, the Earl of Northumberland, and his wife.

PERCY. Will you like that?

ANNE. Yes. It's far from the court. It's buried in the north hills, a long way off. But it's power, and I love you, and I'll like it. Tell me, are you a virgin?

PERCY. I?

ANNE. Yes, Earl of Northumberland—you.

PERCY. I'm a man.

ANNE. I know. But are you a virgin? When we bed together shall I be your first?

PERCY. I—

ANNE. Don't be confused, dear. Folk are such barbarians here in England! Say it out as it was. For me, I'll say it all frankly, the way they do in France. In England we make muddy mysteries of such things. As if they were crimes—but they've happened to all of us. We don't come out of a rainbow at seventeen and there's no use pretending we did. You may ask me whatever you like.

(A pause.)

PERCY. Are you a virgin?

ANNE. No.

(They look away from each other.)

PERCY. Was this something that happened in France?

ANNE. Yes. But long before France, too. When I was little I was playing with a boy in the woods near Hever, not far from here. We quarreled about something, and he threw me down and—

(She rises)

God help me, I'm blushing. All over. I thought I'd finished with that. But no— it began at my heels—I could feel it—and rushed up in a wave till now it burns at the roots of my hair. And I've told this before—

PERCY. Without blushing?

ANNE *(defiantly)*. Yes! But there's something in the foggy, torpid air of this islaɒ ' that makes people want to hide things. Like savages.

PERCY. There might be another reason.

ANNE. What?

PERCY. Look at me.

(She does so)

Were you ever in love before?

ANNE. I think—no. No.

PERCY. Now I'm no spring of wisdom in these matters, Anne, but it may be you're not a woman till you're in love. It may be you've nothing to hide till then.

ANNE (slowly). Yes. It may be. It may be that you're wiser than you think.

PERCY. I hope so. A man has to be wiser than he thinks or he won't go far.

ANNE. It's strange. I stand here still trying to say it to you—and it's a perfectly natural thing—and my tongue won't say it.

PERCY. Never mind. I don't want to hear it.

ANNE. You are a Boeotian, aren't you, darling? You're horribly embarrassed. But you shouldn't be, and I shouldn't. I won't take up with these shamefaced country manners—

PERCY. I don't want to hear it. I'm afraid I don't like this game you learned in Paris.

ANNE. Were you an angel, darling?

PERCY. No. I was not.

ANNE. Tell me about the girls. How many and when.

PERCY. One thing you'd best learn now, my sweet. I'll be the man of the house when we have a house, and if any game's to be played I'll lead in that game and not follow. I don't want to sear my tongue or redden my forehead with this kind of thing. The game I like now is to put my arms about you and say nothing.

ANNE. You know, I think I like that better, too. Come, then.

(Percy takes Anne in his arms again. At the same moment a shadow moves toward them from the center of the stage, and Anne puts up a hand to hold Percy's lips from hers)

I think the Cardinal is here.

(She rises. Percy keeps his seat and holds her hand. Wolsey steps toward them into the light. Percy rises.)

WOLSEY. I'm glad I find you together, for I have to speak to you both. I'm sorry to find you so intimate, for it's about that I have to speak to you. My lord, your father and the king have given some thought to where you shall marry, and an alliance with the Talbots, through one of the daughters of the Earl of Shrewsbury, is thought best.

PERCY. An—alliance with—! Not by me, my lord Cardinal.

WOLSEY. Anne, my dear, your father has a claim on the Ormond estates in Ireland. He and the king have agreed that you will marry the Earl of Ormond to reinforce that claim.

ANNE. I—marry into Ireland?

WOLSEY. It's so decided.

ANNE. But how can you—? It's not so decided! Not one word of this has been said to me! Of Ormond or Ireland—!

WOLSEY. Your father will deal with you. As for Lord Percy, remember, if you will, that I brought you to court and that you are still a member of my household. A half-grown steer and a leggy girl will not be allowed to overturn the policies of England, fixed in council.

PERCY. But, my lord, I am of full age, and I have pledged myself to this girl before many witnesses—among them her own father! It's a good match for both of us, and nothing's been said against it till this moment! More than that, we've pledged ourselves to each other, and our hearts go with that pledge!

WOLSEY. No doubt. And this is the reward I get for my kindness to you.

(He turns away.)

ANNE (softly). My lord Cardinal, that we two are in love, and have been these two months, every servant in the house knows, for we've made no secret of it before them or anyone. That we are in love, that we mean to marry, has been no secret from the whole world all that time. Why you've come here now to tell us suddenly that we're to match elsewhere, we don't know. There must be some reason behind it. Tell us what it is.

WOLSEY. I have told you.

ANNE. Then you talk nonsense, and I won't listen!

PERCY. Nor I!

WOLSEY. I stand here as the king's minister, and you're aware of that. I knew a great lord to die for less than you have just said. His name was Buckingham.

PERCY (more humbly). You know I have no wish to anger the king. But tell us what this means and why you say it to us.

WOLSEY (thundering). Do you think the

king and I come lightly to such decisions as this? Do you think we have not weighed every reason for and against before we issue a command? One thing I can tell you, you will obey or your estates are forfeit! If you continue disloyal it's doubtful how long you will live! Go now, for I wish to speak to Anne alone.

PERCY. Anne—

ANNE. Yes, you must go.

PERCY. Kiss me then.

WOLSEY. Do not touch her.

PERCY. All this talk of sudden death makes it very easy for you, my lord. But I shall kiss her if I like.

(And he does so.)

ANNE. Only take care of yourself. I shall see you.

PERCY. Yes.

(He turns and goes stage right, into darkness. Anne stands silent and defiant, looking at Wolsey.)

WOLSEY. Look your knives through and through me, mistress. At my age it will do me no hurt—and at yours, though you hurt easily, you will cure quickly. Are you serious about this thorn apple from the north?

ANNE. My lord—he's mine—and I'm his.

WOLSEY. But if there were another and worthier, well, you could change?

ANNE. No.

WOLSEY. But I think when you see him you will.

ANNE. The Lord of Ormond? Hardly.

WOLSEY. That was only a name plucked out of the air. I had another in mind.

ANNE. I want no other. And if you do him harm—this my chosen husband—I am only a girl, but you will know you have an enemy!

WOLSEY. Look down at your necklace, Anne. Do you see a writing on it?

ANNE. There's no writing on it.

WOLSEY. There is, though, and I can see it, though it may not be visible to you as yet. The writing is a quotation from a poem. It says: "Noli me tangere, for Caesar's I am." You have studied Latin?

ANNE. Yes.

WOLSEY. "Touch me not," the translation might go, "I belong to the king."

ANNE. What king?

WOLSEY. We have only one king in England.

ANNE. I want no king. I want only the person of my choice.

WOLSEY. When Harry of England turns his eyes on a girl she can hardly look away.

ANNE *(after a pause)*. Forgive me if I seem slow to understand what you say. Do you mean that King Henry has looked at me?

WOLSEY. Yes.

ANNE. And sent you to me?

WOLSEY. It is sometimes my pleasure to anticipate his desires.

(Two figures come toward them out of shadow from stage right.)

ANNE. Perhaps you would be wise to anticipate the answer he will receive from me if he comes. We have had him in the bosom of our family for some years. My sister is probably with child by him at the moment. And of no further use to him. I shall not go the way of my sister, thank you—

(Thomas Boleyn and his wife, Elizabeth, come forward out of the shadow.)

BOLEYN. Anne!

ANNE. Do you also offer me up to this royal bull—you, my father? And you, my mother?

BOLEYN. Hush, daughter! Manage your voice. He's in the house.

(There is a silence.)

ANNE. Why is he here?

BOLEYN. To see you.

ANNE. Well—you've let him come—I haven't. Find some way out of it.

BOLEYN. It's not my doing. It's his. He came quite openly demanding you. And since that is what every girl in England prays for, how was I to know it would displease you?

ANNE. Do you know what it is to be in love? Either of you? Do you remember? Remember what it's like to have your whole life follow one person out at the door—and not to live again, and not want to live, till he returns?

BOLEYN. You have been in France—and at the court.

ANNE. I've been many places, and done more things than you know—yet there's only one man I want now! And I'll have no one else! No one! Mother!

ELIZABETH *(softly)*. Yes—I said these things once—all of them—and I would help you now if I could. But I know now that we're not free to have or take or choose. You are here—and you live—and we all of us live—because we took advantage when it came our way, because we stood at the door and waited, because we smiled where a smile would help, and kissed when a kiss would help—

BOLEYN. And struck down where a death would help! And we're not safe now! If you think we're safe, or that you are, or that we'll ever be safe, or that you will, you're more of a fool than any daughter of mine has a right to be!

ELIZABETH. Do you know what it means when a king asks for you? Do you know what goes with it?

ANNE. Yes—I know that. I know, all too exactly.

WOLSEY. If he feels a coldness in you he'll not want you, I can assure you of that. Indicate only a slight doubt—and the king will be gone. He is not accustomed to hesitations.

ELIZABETH. And do you know what it means when a king asks for you and you turn him away? We can say farewell to all we've worked for and all we have if we lose the king's favor.

ANNE. Then say good-by to all that—all of you—this whole family and house—for I won't have the king! I don't want him and I won't have him!

BOLEYN. As for this boy you've set your heart on—this Northumberland—don't count on him beyond the castle gate. Would he dare touch a girl the king had bid for?

WOLSEY. Would he dare marry into a family which had displeased his sovereign?

ANNE. He would dare anything!

WOLSEY. He will not dare either of these.

ANNE. My lord Cardinal, we are only one family among many at court—and in this family only two sisters, Mary and I. Surely one of two sisters should be enough. Surely he could look elsewhere now.

WOLSEY. There are only two things to blame—the king's will, and your own self, your form and face and words. The king has seen you and heard your voice and liked you. I can't change you and I can't change him.

ELIZABETH. He is our king, Anne. He is a great king. He is young and handsome. He knows poetry and music; he speaks and dances better than any other in the court. Surely it's not hard to think well of him.

ANNE. Yes, mother. I've been well trained. I'm trying now. . . . Young? Well, it's true

he married at eighteen, but he's been married nearly seventeen years, and if all his children had lived, legitimate and illegitimate, there would have been at least a dozen. He can be only fairly faithful to a mistress. I think my sister Mary kept him longest. That lasted four years—and now that's over. And what becomes of Mary? No, I won't ask that. He's a great king, you say. It's true that his father, who was unscrupulous and a miser, left him a mountain of money. It's true therefore that he has great power, but as for his being a great king, I rather doubt it, for he's neither wise nor just nor merciful. You say he knows poetry and music. He's much praised for his poetry and music at the court, where, as you have noticed, if you don't praise him you're likely to be unlucky. You say he speaks and dances better than any about him—and wouldn't it be a silly courtier who outdanced the proud Henry? When it comes to warfare his wife Katharine is a better soldier than he. She won the great battle of Flodden Field while he was abroad subjugating two minor French towns with an army sufficient to conquer all Europe.

(A shadow moves into the darkness at stage center and Henry's voice is heard.)

HENRY (still unseen). You there! Kindly inquire if the king may enter! Right! Right! I speak to you! A sovereign has so little privacy that he knows how to respect the privacy of others. So ask! Inquire!

SERVANT (appearing at the edge of the ring of light). May the king come in?

HENRY. That says it. That puts it bluntly. A good honest half-witted servingman you have here, if ever I saw one. Aren't you, fellow?

(He claps the servant on the back.)

SERVANT. If Your Majesty please, yes, Sire.

BOLEYN. Your Majesty knows that you are always welcome in this house.

HENRY. As you in mine, Sir Thomas. And now my manners. I have greeted all here, I think, save only the Lady Anne. Sweet Nan, will you give me a kiss?

ANNE. Yes, Your Majesty.

(He comes forward with his arms jovially outstretched. Anne bows, then takes one of his hands and kisses it coolly.)

HENRY. It was not such a kiss I meant, my dear.

ANNE. I have been drinking foul medicines

for a cold, my lord. You would never forgive my breath.

HENRY. Have you tried hippocras, a strong glassful every hour, steaming hot?

ANNE. No, I haven't.

HENRY. You shall have some of my own brewing. I'll send it today. For your health is very dear to me, sweet Nan, and you must keep well. We live all too brief a time—and what little we have should not be wasted in sickness.

(He stops suddenly and kisses her)

There is neither fever nor medicine on your lips, sweetheart, but such a honey scent as bashful maidens breathe. . . . Shall I send away this chaperonage that rings us round?

ANNE. No.

HENRY. I will, though, by your leave; no, without your leave. Mothers, fathers, churchmen, all these may depart.

(Wolsey and the Boleyns, Thomas and Elizabeth, bow out backward toward stage right)

You would never credit how fast my heart beats, nor how hard it is to draw breath. A king is not fortunate in these matters, Nan. I come to you as frightened as a 'prentice who takes his first nosegay to a wench—but whether you like me or not— whether any woman likes me or not—I shall never know. I shall never be sure I have the truth—because I am the king, and love is paid to me like taxes. . . . Do me this favor, Nan. Look on me not as a monarch who commands and may demand, but as the doubting, hoping, tremulous man I am—wishing to be loved for myself.

ANNE. If you were a common man, doubtful of yourself, and tremulous, would you have sent an ambassador to warn me and make sure of me?

HENRY. Did I send an ambassador?

ANNE. Wolsey speaks for you, I believe.

HENRY. Has he spoken clumsily?

ANNE. No, very deftly. He made it plain that what the king wanted he would have.

HENRY. Then he was clumsy. I swear to you, Nan, only this very cruel thing has happened to me: I have fallen in love. I tried to argue myself out of it, but seeing you day by day here, and trying not to see you, not to think about you, I have tangled myself deeper day by day, till now I can't keep it to myself. I must tell you.

And ask your pity. . . . The truth is I dared not speak to you first myself. I was afraid.

ANNE. You were afraid?

HENRY. Yes.

ANNE. Of what?

HENRY. That you wouldn't care for me.

ANNE. Then perhaps you will understand the very cruel thing that has happened to me: I have fallen in love. And not with you.

HENRY. By God!

ANNE. You were complaining a moment ago that such remarks were not made to kings.

HENRY. By God, I got it full in the face that time! Who is it? Northumberland?

ANNE. Would I be wise to tell you?

HENRY. Never mind. I know. I've been told but I didn't believe it. How far has it gone?

ANNE. We mean to be married.

HENRY. Yes?

ANNE. But not as my sister's married. He would not be a complaisant husband— and I would not be an accessible wife.

HENRY. All wives are accessible—any husband can be placated!

ANNE. Not all.

HENRY. Yes, all! But I don't want you that way! Damn my soul, and yours—I want you to myself!

ANNE. What can I do?

HENRY. Give up this young wattle and daub—

give him up, I tell you,

and this kingdom shall turn round you, bishops and peers—

and whatever you've wanted, for anyone, a knighthood,

an estate, a great income rolling in forever, titles and places, you shall dispose of them just as you please!

ANNE. And be thrown out in the end like a dirty rag. I haven't seen Mary disposing

of revenues.

HENRY. She asked for nothing. Look, Anne,

I stand here desperate. I can't bargain with you.

Ask for what you want.

ANNE. To be free. To be free to marry where I love.

(Henry pauses.)

HENRY. No.

ANNE. I've seen you too close

and known you too long. I've heard what
your courtiers say
and then I've seen what you are. You're
spoiled and vengeful,
and malicious and bloody. The poetry they
praise
so much is sour, and the music you write's
worse.
You dance like a hobbledehoy; you make
love
as you eat—with a good deal of noise and
no subtlety.
It was my doubtful pleasure once to sleep
in Mary's room—
or to lie awake when you thought me
asleep—and observe
the royal porpoise at play—

HENRY. This is not safe.

ANNE. Yes, I've been told it's not safe for
any of us
to say no to our Squire Harry. This put-
on, kindly
hail-fellow-well-met of yours. My father's
house
will be pulled down—and Northumberland's, too, they tell me
Well, pull them down. You are what I
said.

HENRY. I had no wish to come here. I
came
because I must, and couldn't help myself.
Well—I'm well out of it. Let it end here
this morning.
I thank you for your anger,
and for raising anger in me. There's no
better way
to make an end.
Say farewell to all here.
I'll go back to my ancient wife and my
cold statecraft,
card houses and card empires . . .
and card ruins.
(He turns.)

ANNE. You will not—touch—Northumberland?

HENRY. I'll try not.
Bloody as I am, I'll try not.
(He calls)
Wolsey!
(He turns and goes into darkness)
Where's the fat saddlebags? Where's this
vicar of hell?
(The lights go out.)

SCENE THREE

The lights come up on Anne as we saw
her in the Prologue, wearing the fur-
trimmed dress. The same little barred win-
dow of the Tower cell comes slowly into
focus.

————

ANNE. Then I could only wait,
and pace my room,
and write to Northumberland in secret,
saying, "I've sent him away. Take care of
yourself.
But for God's sake come if you can—
for I'm alone."
And I waited alone. In my little room.
It was my father's pleasure
to keep me prisoner in my little room.
And over and over the one dream, the one
dream
whenever I'd fall asleep—
Northumberland standing
with his arms stretched out to me
(At stage right a figure is glimpsed in
darkness)
and his eyes torn out and bleeding—
(We see Percy with bloody eyes, reaching
out his hands)
as I see him now.
I tried not to sleep, for when I slept,
day or night, I saw him there.
Till the news came.
(The figure of Percy vanishes)
They wouldn't tell me at first.
The messenger came to the kitchen.
(A half-light comes up at stage left. In it
a courier can be seen with a woman
servant.)

COURIER. I've ridden thirty-five hours and
I'm dead for sleep.
This is for the Lady Anne. Nobody's to
know.
(He hands over a letter.)

SERVANT. Where are you from?

COURIER. From Northumberland. Let me
lie down here—anywhere.
I'm dead.
(He throws himself on the floor and sleeps
instantly.)

SERVANT (fingering the letter). Is it good
or bad? He's under already Man!
(She shakes him)
Man! Is it good or bad?
(There's no response from the courier)
It can't be good or it 'ud 'a' traveled
slower. I'd
best keep it in my pocket.
(She pockets the letter. The lights go out
on stage left.)

ANNE. But when she brought it at last
it cut through my years
like a dull knife through screaming flesh.
 I feel it yet.
"I'm a prisoner, too,
and I'm to be married," it said.
"To the Shrewsbury hag. She hates me
and I hate her.
One of us will murder the other. I'm
 afraid God's on her side,
and she'll kill me first.
Anne, my bonny, forgive me."
Well, she did kill him. Anyway, there was
 no love between them,
and within two years he was dead.
And the king came back to Mary,
and she took him, took him again,
and began to have a child by him—
and again he left her.
And still I sat in my room.
And again the king came to see us.
*(Mary Boleyn appears near stage center
and speaks to Anne, who seems to sit at
the window of her bedroom at the right.)*
MARY. Father says
you're to make yourself ready in the best
 you have.
The king will be here tonight.
(Anne is silent)
Make yourself pretty, dear.
I know you're weary of your room. It's
 you he wants to see.
Make yourself charming.
And don't think of me.
Oh, I'm to appear.
(She comes over to Anne and kisses her)
But you know, dear, the human liver or
 lights—
or heart—or whatever one loves with—
these are tough, perdurable organs. I can
 look at him
and it won't matter. I've . . . I can look
 at him.
(Anne is still silent)
Yes, as you do.
I don't even dislike him.
I begin to be in love with someone else.
ANNE. Oh?
MARY. Yes—so—I mean it—
wear the best you have.
(She moves toward stage right)
I'd stay and help you—only—
I'm dressing up—for somebody else.
It's still, but I am.
(The lights go out on Mary.)
ANNE *(again in the Tower cell)*. He had

been hunting, they said, and threw down
his bow and said, "I must see her."
*(At stage right the lights come up on King
Henry sitting in a hunting pavilion,
stringing a bow. Wolsey holds spare staves
and arrows near-by.)*
WOLSEY. The first buck you struck died in
 the midst of a leap.
The arrow pierced him through and
 brought out heart's blood on the other
 side.
HENRY. Is there any other sovereign in
Europe who could plant an arrow behind
the shoulder of a stag in motion?
WOLSEY. There is not one who could kill
a deer in any decent fashion. I have heard
that the Emperor Charles hunts the boar
with powder and ball.
HENRY. Let us not believe evil of any man
or prince till proved.
WOLSEY. True. It was only a rumor.
HENRY. Give me the longbow. *(Quoting)*
"Who list to hunt, I know where is an
hind—."
*(An Attendant in shadow hands him a
bow.)*
WOLSEY. As for the longbow, there is no
other man in all Europe, commoner, noble,
or sovereign, who could flex this stave of
yours a full yard.
HENRY *(fitting a cord to the bow)*. A
man's not as good at thirty-five as at
twenty though.
(He throws down the bow and arrow)
Damn the hunting—and damn all entertainment! And damn all women! Why
must it be this one girl I want—who
doesn't want me? We'll give over here.
"Since in a net I seek to hold the wind."
I'll see her.
*(The lights go out on Henry and Wolsey,
then, after the next scene begins, on
Anne.)*

SCENE FOUR

*The lights go up at stage left on a Woman
Servant carrying a little table on which
there is a silver basket full of cakes. A
Man Servant follows behind with a carved
chair.*

———

WOMAN. Set it here and I'll put the basket
of cakes beside it. When I make seed-
cakes like these he eats the basket empty,
down to the last. I've made plenty this
time.

MAN. That's right, feed him up and fat him. He's got himself trained down till he can jump in the air in the middle of a dance and crack his hocks together three times. You'll ruin that with your cakes.

WOMAN. Would you have every man thin but you, you great hunk?

MAN. I'd keep my king thin because he'll live longer.

WOMAN. He was born to be oversize. Has a king no right to be heavy?

MAN. Not my king hasn't. . . . Where do I put the chairs for the musicians?

WOMAN. Here, near His Majesty. Come in, masters.

(Three Musicians, with violins of the period, come in through the curtains from stage right)

We'll put the chairs for you here, and the king himself will bring you the music. He writes a round, clear hand, music and words, and you'll read it easily.

(The Servants place chairs for the musicians, who sit to tune their instruments. One of them plays a little mournful sprig of a tune.)

MAN. When you've finished with that sad kind of stuff there's sweet sack in the buttery.

1ST MUSICIAN. We'll have it afterward, if you'll save it. Here they come.

(The whole stage begins to light up. The curtains at the rear now look like a wall tapestry showing the return of the Prodigal Son. The musicians' stools and the king's chair and table are seen at stage right. Elizabeth and Mary enter, dressed for a formal occasion. Anne follows them.)

MARY. There was more than a little talk about you and the king—when you were young.

ELIZABETH. Well, be sure it all came to nothing, and none of you children are his—though I'm not sure I could have held him off if he'd tried hard for me. We were about of an age, and we danced together a good deal, and he had the face of an angel in those days. And danced like an angel. But he was naïve and gentle —and I think he'd have been afraid to ask me. There was something innocent and pure about him then. He wanted to be a good king. He wanted to be a great king—almost a Messiah.

MARY. He's changed indeed.

ELIZABETH. Yes. He reads Machiavelli now.

(Elizabeth and Mary take their places.)

MARY. But when he came to me first, he was still naïve. He was afraid of women who might be difficult. He wanted someone to whom he could say, "Open sesame," and she'd open. I'm afraid that's what attracted him to me. He said, "Open, sesame," and there I was. His—his mule. It's his own word.

ELIZABETH. You may yet be the mother of a king of England.

(Anne sits beside her mother.)

MARY. Small chance of that. And small reward in it.

ELIZABETH. It's more than I've ever had— of anything. And it won't happen so easily again. He's grown infinitely more complex—and brutal. He wants a woman who will resist—a woman hardly won, a Roman conquest.

ANNE. I've hated him from the beginning. I hate him now.

ELIZABETH. That's what he wants.

ANNE. I hate him and I hate Wolsey. What they did was like a murder. . . . It killed him. I think it will kill me too.

ELIZABETH. If women died as easily as men there would be no women in this world.

MARY. If you ever go to him, lock up your heart, never surrender yourself, keep a cold reserve of hate and anger and laughter and unfaith—

ANNE. Thank you—I shall not go to him.

MARY. For the moment you are won and conquered and a worshiper he will give you back to yourself and walk away. He'll want no more of you.

ANNE. I shan't go to him, nor let him come to me. I'm not sure I shall live. Tell me why I should wish to live.

(Thomas Boleyn enters from stage left.)

BOLEYN. Are we ready?

ELIZABETH. Quite ready, Thomas.

BOLEYN. I think the king is waiting and anxious.

ELIZABETH. We are waiting.

(Boleyn crosses the stage and looks within the curtains at stage left, then returns to stand behind his wife. Three Boy Singers enter and take places near the musicians. King Henry comes from stage left, his hands full of manuscripts. The women rise and bow. Wolsey follows Henry in and waits.)

HENRY. I am not here tonight as your king. Something was said at one time—I forget by whom—about my bad poetry and bad music. It rankled deep—but then I saw that there was only one answer: to write great poetry and great music. And since I have a cause for anguish in my life, and songs come out of anguish, I have heard these strains in the night when I woke out of sleep, and I have risen and written them down. Many songs came to me. This is only one. It may be it is not a great song, but when I hear it I know it sings what is in my heart—the pain and the loss and the parting that's like death. Here are your parts, masters. Play it and sing it as it is written, and sing it gravely, for it carries the awkward burden of a grief.

(The King sits in his chair after giving out the music. The Musicians look over the parts briefly, then the leader raps for attention and they begin. Wolsey stands behind the king.)

SINGERS. Alas, alas,
What shall I do
For love, for love,
Alas what shall I do—
Since now so kind I do you find—
To keep you me unto?
To keep you me unto?

Oh my heart,
Oh my heart,
My heart it is so sore,
Since I must needs from my love depart,
And know no cause therefore—
And know no cause therefore!

(The Singers go out stage right. Henry crosses to Anne.)

HENRY. The music will now play a saraband of my writing. Will you dance it with me, Nan?

(Anne looks down at the floor for a moment, rises silently and puts out her hands for the dance. The music begins and they take the first steps of the saraband. Then the lights dim down and close in till we see nothing but the faces of Henry and Anne. The music hushes to pianissimo, so that we can hear their voices. They cease dancing, and now we see only their two faces motionless in a medallion of light.)

ANNE. Northumberland is dead.

HENRY. Not by my order.

ANNE. You sent him to marry elsewhere— and it killed him.

HENRY. I couldn't let him marry you. I tried—but I couldn't.

ANNE. When I look in your face I see his murderer.

HENRY. I have learned something that makes me very humble, Nan. One cannot choose where he will love. Even a king cannot choose. I tried again and again to love elsewhere. I didn't want to come here, this year or last. But here I am. Bringing you the best I have—my music and my poetry and my love for you.

ANNE. Even if I loved you, you offer me nothing. You're not free.

HENRY. Not free?

ANNE. You are married to Katharine.

HENRY. Does that matter to a king? A king makes his own rules.

ANNE. Does he? A king or no king, if he's married he's not free.

HENRY. If you loved me you'd find me free.

ANNE. From your marriage?

HENRY. Here is my marriage, Nan. My older brother Arthur was heir to the kingdom. To make an alliance with Spain he married Katharine of Aragon. Then Arthur died—and I was heir to the throne of England. To continue the alliance with Spain I was advised to marry Arthur's widow, six years my senior. And I did. At seventeen I married her. I never loved her. I should never have married my brother's widow. There's a curse on the marriage. We cannot have sons. Our sons are all born dead. There is no heir male to the English crown because of this accursed union. The kingdom faces anarchy when I die, and I face anarchy in my own life, because I have no male heir—yet because of the church and our friendship with Spain, I remain Katharine's husband. More than anything in this world I want a son, and she can't give me one—yet I must not publicly put her aside. Do you understand now? This marriage is a form—important only in statecraft and churchcraft, not to you or me.

ANNE. Important or not, you can't break it. It's stronger than you are—and so you offer me nothing.

HENRY. It's not nothing. Nan. It's my whole life. I know because I tried to erase you and fill my life with other things. It won't work. I can think of nothing but you.

(She has been looking straight into his eyes. She drops her head)

It's not only this pain, this stitch in the

side, this poetry I can't keep from writing,
this music that I hear when I think of
you and must write down. . . . I'm a man,
too, Nan. I want you—and only you. I
find myself—when I'm talking to an ambassador, perhaps—I find myself thinking
of you. And what am I thinking of? Of
you and me playing at dog and bitch. Of
you and me playing at horse and mare.
Of you and me every way there is. I
want to fill you up—night after night. I
want to fill you with sons.

ANNE. Bastards? For they would be bastards, you know.

*(There is a long pause. The music stops.
The lights come up on the whole scene,
revealing Henry and Anne in the middle
of the stage, the others watching.)*

HENRY. If you say one more word I shall
strike you. One word more.

ANNE *(in his teeth)*. But it's quite obvious
that if you and I had children they would
be bastards.

*(There is another long pause, then Henry
strikes Anne heavily across the face. She
goes down to one knee. Wolsey and Boleyn step forward, but do not interfere.)*

WOLSEY *(low)*. Your Majesty.

*(Anne gets slowly to her feet, a little
dazed, then faces the king.)*

ANNE. You have not yet understood what
I mean, I think. What I am trying to tell
you is that you not only offer me nothing
—you offer yourself nothing. You say you
want a son, an heir to the throne. You
need such an heir, and the kingdom needs
him. But an heir must be legitimate—
not baseborn—and while you are married
to Katharine you can have only bastards.
Fill me with as many sons as you like,
you would still have no heir, and I would
have—nothing. As for your music and
your poetry and your love for me—you
know I don't love you. You've given me
good reason not to love you.

HENRY. Would you marry me if I were
free of Katharine?

ANNE. You can't get free of Katharine.
You know that. And I know it.

HENRY. But if I were free of her, and free
to marry you, and would make you queen
of England, would you marry me?

(There is a long pause.)

ANNE. None of these things could be. Yes.
If you'll make me queen of England I
will marry you.

HENRY. Wolsey!

WOLSEY. We can do many things, as you
know, my sovereign. We can shake the
thrones of the Emperor and of the King
of France. We can sometimes get our way
to Rome. But this we could not do. Try
to divorce Katharine and you'll have the
whole world against you. You'll be at war
with all Europe.

ANNE. Very well.

HENRY. You knew you'd get this answer.

ANNE. Yes. I knew it.

WOLSEY. The king asks very little of you,
Anne. Any other woman would give it
readily.

ANNE. Out of fear.

WOLSEY. No.

ANNE. Out of gratitude, then. But I'm not
flattered, and I'm not afraid. If he will
marry me and make me queen of England
I will give him boys in plenty. But I will
take nothing less.

HENRY. It's true that I go through life
dragging a sick woman—cold and sick—
blotched and middle-aged—and fanatic—
who can give neither pleasure nor a living
son.
I have worked at that long enough, I
think. I know
what can come from that bed.
There never was much need for the hair
shirt
she wears next her skin. And none now.

WOLSEY. Any son of the king could be
made legitimate—
could be made the heir.

HENRY. Yes. It's true.

ANNE. Your Majesty
already has a natural son. Have you made
him the heir?
Is he legitimate?

WOLSEY. He's made Duke of Richmond.

ANNE. Could the Duke of Richmond inherit the throne?

WOLSEY. He may. It could be. The lad's
not well.
Not like to live.

ANNE. But he would come first, shall we
say? And then Mary's child.
It happens that any baseborn son I might
have
would be younger than Mary's. Her child
would come before mine.
My entry would be third.
Now we
are affectionate sisters, Mary and I.
We forgive each other
the little things that sisters must forgive.

Yet she would rather her son sat on the
  throne
than mine.
I'd rather mine than hers.
I'd rather have no son than a son baseborn.
HENRY. I shall rid myself of Katharine.
I shall make this girl queen.
I shall settle the question of the succession
  once for all!
WOLSEY. Oh, my lord, I beg you,
as your faithful servant, I beg you,
don't promise this now.
It may mean your death—or the loss of
  your kingdom—
Or her death.
You are not yourself. This is not a small
  error.
It—
HENRY. I shall make this girl queen.
WOLSEY. She's never said she loved you!
HENRY. I shall make her queen.
If it breaks the earth in two like an apple
and flings the halves into the void,
I shall make her queen.
(The lights go out.)

EPILOGUE

*A center of light comes up on Anne at
stage right, in the furred gown of the Prologue, the barred window behind her.*

ANNE. He knew very well I'd love him
when once he'd make me his. And so it
  was.
This is the night on which he made me
  his—
the night I write here.
After that night I loved him more and
  more
and hated him less and less—
and I was lost.
(The lights dim down.)

CURTAIN

ACT TWO

PROLOGUE

*The curtain rises in darkness, then the
lights come up on Henry, alone, seated
stage left at a table with a paper before
him and a quill pen, ready to sign. On
the curtains at the rear a window sharpens
into focus gradually, showing in its colored panes the royal arms of the king of
England.*

HENRY. This is hard to do—
when you come to put pen on paper.
You say to yourself:
She must die. And she must—
if things are to go as planned.
Yes, if they are to go at all. If I am to rule
and keep my sanity and hold my England
  off the rocks.
It's a lee shore—and a low tide—and the
  wind's a gale—
and the Spanish rocks are bare and sharp.
Go back to it, Henry, go back to it.
Keep your mind
on this parchment you must sign.
Dip the pen in the ink; write your name.
*(He dips the pen, draws the paper toward
him, then lays down the pen)*
You've condemned men, nobles and
  peasants.
She's struck down a few herself—
or driven you to do it.
It's only that a woman you've held in your
  arms
and longed for when she was away,
and suffered with her
and waited
for the outcome of her childbed—
No, but she promised me an heir.
Write it down.
Write Henry Rex and it's done.
And then the headsman
will cry out suddenly, "Look, look there!"
(He points suddenly off stage)
and point to the first flash of sunrise,
and she'll look,
not knowing what he means, and his
  sword will flash
in the flick of sun, through the little bones
  of her neck
as she looks away,
and it will be done.
What will it seem to men
I was like when I did this?
It will be written and studied.
The histories of kings are not secure.
The letters they have hidden, the secret
  ciphers
are unraveled and chuckled over.
"He loved her and he had her and he
  killed her,"
the books will say. The letters will be
  printed,

the stolen love letters where I played the
fool
like a country boy to his milkmaid.
There's a heart drawn
at the bottom of one, and in the heart
"A. B."
laboriously printed. "Henry Rex seeks
A. B., no other."
(He prints the A. B. on the air with his
finger)
So the legend reads,
and will read so forever.
When she first refused me
I made off in a lash of anger and blood
and spume—
a bull whale with the ocean at his prow—
"There's a whole world of women with
eyes and pursestring mouths
and legs and pockets! Let her keep
empty!"
But the harpoon had sunk deep, and it
tugged me in,
and I came again—and took her—
and must have her.
And now I seek her death.
But she betrayed me. She has earned
death.
Take the pen and write the name.
Let us pretend it's not your name at all,
but the name of a just judge.
You prayed this morning. You were long
on your knees.
God will not allow you to condemn
unjustly.
If you write your name here it is just.
But then, this hesitation to write my name,
is that, too, from God?
If I question that I question my whole
life and all I've done.
Well, I do question it. At times.
(He takes up the pen)
Could she have betrayed me?
I think, as I loved her less she loved me
more.
Even in anger could she have betrayed
me?
(The lights dim down on Henry, coming
up on stage right and center, though we
still see the king as he watches the first
scene.)

SCENE ONE

Four players sit about a card table at stage
right. They are Anne Boleyn; Mark
Smeaton, a good-looking young gallant;
Jane Seymour, a girl of Anne's own age—
lady in waiting to Anne; and Henry Norris, a gentleman about the court. About
them are grouped, some sitting, some
standing, Elizabeth and Thomas Boleyn;
the old Duke of Norfolk, Anne's uncle;
Madge Shelton, another of Anne's waiting
women; and Sir Thomas More, who
stands watching in half-shadow. The players are placed so that Norris sits facing
the audience. Anne faces toward stage left.
Jane faces stage right, and Smeaton faces
stage rear. An elaborate tapestry is gradually etched on the rear curtain.

NORRIS. This is a new game they play in
Paris now.
ANNE. Does it have a name?
NORRIS. They call it King's Ransom. First
we all ante a noble
(They ante)
and then I deal four cards to each player,
including myself. Face up, thus.
(He deals)
Then, when all have four cards showing,
the eldest hand—that's you, darling—bets
that she can beat the next card in the deck
with one of her own. You can bet any
part of the money on the table—or all of
it—or nothing.
JANE. I must beat it in the same suit?
NORRIS. You must.
JANE. But I have only one suit here, all
clubs, and no court cards.
NORRIS. Oh—your chances are very bad.
You shouldn't bet at all.
JANE. I thought so. I retire.
(She picks up her cards.)
SMEATON. I'm afraid this is not a game for
wise men.
ANNE. But you can play, my dear.
SMEATON. Touché. I'll risk one noble.
(Norris turns up a card.)
NORRIS. Seven of diamonds. You win. You
have the nine there.
SMEATON. So I do.
NORRIS. Here's your noble.
ANNE. I'll bet what's on the table.
NORRIS. Ah, you have four kings. You
couldn't possibly lose.
(He turns up a card)
And you don't.
ANNE. Is there no way I could bet more?
NORRIS. None, alas. It's the chances of war.
Like Alexander, you can't win more than
there is at stake.
BOLEYN. Do you need money, Jane?

JANE. No, I'm even so far.

(Norris pushes the money toward Anne.)

NORRIS. Another gold noble, please. All round.

(They ante.)

BOLEYN. I ask because the king's treasury stands behind you tonight.

JANE. Why does it, sir?

BOLEYN. Because you are sitting in the king's chair. Whoever plays in the king's place may draw on the resources of the king. I have known an earl to lose a thousand pounds in that seat, and walk away paying nothing because the king's treasury paid.

JANE. But if he had won?

BOLEYN. Oh, what you win you keep.

NORRIS. Now, that's the way to live.

SMEATON. Aye. That's the arrangement I'd like to have with my bankers.

MORE. How men love injustice.

NORRIS. Don't they? They know what would happen to them if they got what they earned.

ANNE. Do you love justice, Sir Thomas?

MORE. Now where would I have seen it?

(Henry is seen standing at the entrance, listening)

Still, men do seem to get what they deserve—in a rough way—over a long period.

ANNE. You think so, truly?

MORE. Well, it's my guess. There's no proving it. Nobody's ever made up the accounts. Think of the accounting system they'd have to have in heaven to reckon our follies and sins and good deeds, and decide what we should get. Think of the decisions they'd have to make—and revise. And reverse. Think of the good deeds that turned out badly—and of the murders that turned out to be a good thing. Yet—on the whole—it's my guess that what should come to a man does come to him.

ANNE. Or to a woman.

MORE. They're not exempt.

NORRIS. I wonder who makes these intricate calculations. For example, I slapped my wife last Thursday. Now I thought it was good for her. I think she thought it was bad for her. Anyway, she gave me a black mark for it. But suppose it definitely improved her character? What mark would heaven give me for it?

ANNE. Think what it did to your character.

NORRIS. That's another complication. It may have been bad for my moral structure to slap my wife. But suppose it was good for her? Am I then a martyr, having sacrificed myself, and acquired a black mark, in order to make her a better woman?

ANNE. There must be a machine up above that computes these things, and filters them automatically—and keeps the score.

MORE. But who built it? And suppose it gets out of order?

NORFOLK. It's out of order all the time. I know. I've been watching it these many years.

ELIZABETH. There may have been an error in it from the beginning.

MORE. But somehow we came here. Somehow we are as we are.

NORRIS. We're not as you made us in *Utopia*.

NORFOLK. I hope God's happy in heaven. And got what he wanted.

SMEATON. It's your play, Norris.

NORRIS. I'll stay out of it. I've nothing here. Turn in your hands and Jane will shuffle and deal.

(They throw in their cards. Sir Thomas Wyatt comes in from stage right.)

MADGE. Ah—now we have another Sir Thomas—and the evening grows more and more literary!

SMEATON. Take my chair, Wyatt. I don't half like this game.

ANNE. Let's break it up. Tommy promised to bring a poem if it was finished—and might even read it for us. Won't you?

WYATT. It's the usual thing. After you've written a poem, you read it. And then, if you're a man of sense, you run for your life. Any other poets present?

MORE. Only a plodding prose writer, friend.

WYATT. They're the worst, of course. They hold all prose superior to all verse.

MORE. True. And make no distinctions. Read your bad verses, man.

WYATT. My bad verses?

MORE. All verse is bad. Its intention is to mislead.

ANNE. Is this a quarrel?

MORE. Oh, an ancient one, my dear. A quarrel to the death, but unimportant. Only writers involved.

ANNE *(rising)*. I feel very foolish saying this to wise and learned men, but one thing we must not forget here in the court. It's the things we say and do here that set the pace for what is said and done in England. If Sir Thomas More is honored at court for his *Utopia,* then he is honored through England. If Sir Thomas Wyatt's verses are read at court, then through England men will want to read them—and it will be, well, honorable to write verses. And we should be aware of this—

MORE. But not too much aware—

WYATT. Lest the verses should not be good.

ANNE. Do I speak too much like a queen? I am not queen yet, as you know, and yet if I am not queen there is no queen in England—for Katharine says nothing, is never sure—and the things a queen should do are not done.

MORE. If you are hoping for a renaissance of letters—and of the spirit—in our England, my dear Nan, I fear you're ahead of your time. Men are always hoping for that kind of thing—and how often does it happen? Well—it happened once, in Greece, as everybody knows, and a sort of substitute renaissance happened in Rome later on. But that's all. The rest is darkness through all Europe, through all later time. I hardly think we shall roll it back with our few books and sonnets.

ANNE. But you write your books.

MORE. I write them. I hope for no great upswing—till all men are free—and changed.

MADGE. Still, I'd like to hear the poem.

ANNE. Yes, Tommy.

WYATT. Only if it's unanimous.

NORFOLK. It's unanimous, lad. I know nothing about poetry, but I'll sit quiet and make the proper faces.

ANNE. No excuse—no haw, no hem—no hanging back. Sit in the light here and read.

WYATT. Here I sit, and here I read:

They flee from me that sometime did me
  seek,
With naked foot stalking within my
  chamber:
Once I have seen them gentle, tame, and
  meek,
That now are wild, and do not once
  remember
That sometime they have put themselves
  in danger
To take bread at my hand; and now they
  range,

Busily seeking in continual change.

SMEATON. Is this about birds or women?

ANNE. Hush!

NORFOLK. It's about his women, son. Nobody has that much bellyache over birds.

WYATT. The advantage of poetry is that nobody knows what it means.

Thanked be fortune, it hath been other-
  wise,
Twenty times better; but once especial,
In thin array, after a pleasant guise,
When her loose gown did from her
  shoulders fall,
And she me caught in her arms long and
  small,
And therewithal so sweetly did me kiss,
And softly said, "Dear heart, how like
  you this?"

NORFOLK. Yes, he's had his troubles with human females.

WYATT. In the interests of the renaissance I continue.

It was no dream; for I lay broad awaking:
But all is turned now, through my gentle-
  ness,
Into a bitter fashion of forsaking;
And I have leave to go of her goodness;
And she also to use new-fangleness.
But since that I unkindly am so served,
"How like you this?"—What hath she
  now deserved?

MORE. We were talking about that before you came in—about what people deserve, and whether they get it. Anyways, never, or sometimes.

HENRY *(speaking out of half-darkness).* All three, I think. Some get it always, some get it never, some get it sometimes. *(The court rises and bows)* Sit, sit, bend no more, either at the half or the quarter or the three-quarters. Relax necks, knees, and middles, and, if you'll be more comfortable, unbutton. I'm unbuttoning my own doublet right now. That last portion—well, probably what I feel now is my just desert. . . . Did nobody understand that?

ANNE. We were being very quiet and respectful, my good lord.

HENRY. You were indeed. What's in the air tonight?

ANNE. Henry Norris has taught us a new card game from Paris and Sir Thomas Wyatt has read us a poem about women.

NORFOLK. His women.

ANNE. I gathered they're not his women any more.

HENRY (sitting). You'll forgive me for this, I know—I listened for a few moments before I entered. I said to myself, "Let me hear what my court's like when I'm not there." I listened to you all. And I believe we have now in England what no king of this island has ever had before, a beginning of those things that take a nation upstream to greatness. Quick minds, critical, witty, and yet willing to say, "Yes, this is good," when something good flashes out. A philosopher who has some fun in him, and a poet who can write lines that catch at the heart. We have not had this before. We have had a dull court. Religious and dutiful and dull. And the change has come with this my Nan, who stands embarrassed before you, and wants to quiet me. Come and quiet me with a kiss on the mouth, Nan, for you've brought me a nest of singing birds here, and for the first time I begin to believe I may go down as a great king, after a great reign, and over a great nation. Since you don't come to kiss me I go to kiss you.

(He does so)

This is what I've always wanted, you know, to feel a stirring of minds about me, to feel that my age will not go back into death without leaving a little something for men to recollect. . . . I wish I could spend my time here, and not with legates and ambassadors and politicians, good and bad. I've been with such a set all day, and all year, and the years before—and as if that were not enough here comes another set of them, and I must send away these larks my lover has gathered and go back to the quarrel among rats and hogs.

(Wolsey and Cromwell appear in the half-light)

Come in, gentlemen. Come in, my good Cardinal, you who labor while I sleep. The May flies are about to depart and we must go to work.

(A general exodus begins, to make way for the business session)

Wyatt, it's good poetry. It will need more than one reading.

WYATT. Then I'm afraid it needs another writing.

(He goes.)

HENRY. Maybe, maybe. Try it, try it.

More, it's more than four years since we sat on the palace roof together and considered the motions of the stars.

MORE. They haven't changed much, Your Majesty.

(He follows Wyatt.)

HENRY. That's the saddest subject I know, astronomy. But very good for kings. It teaches them that kings and subjects are no different.

NORFOLK. It's a lie, Majesty. The kings can coin money and the subjects can't.

HENRY. Under heaven that means nothing, Norfolk.

NORFOLK. Over hell it means a good deal. And I'm old enough to feel pretty close to hell. And I resent the king coining money when I can't! Especially when he cuts down the silver by half, and doubles the number of shillings in a pound!

(He goes.)

HENRY. You know, he has hold of something there. It was not quite honest, but I needed the money and I had to do it.

BOLEYN. Good night, my lord.

HENRY. Good night, my treasurer. Here's one man who knows how desperately I had to do it. Good night, good night.

(The last of the courtiers go, leaving only Henry, Anne, Wolsey and Cromwell.)

ANNE. I'll leave you two to conspire.

HENRY. Stay, my dear, stay. Help me with whatever it is.

WOLSEY. What I have to say is for Your Majesty's private ear.

HENRY. I have no private ear—not from Nan.

WOLSEY (shifting quickly). To be frank, it could go till tomorrow. I'm sorry I interrupted. Shall we call the court back?

HENRY. Come, come, what barrel of herrings is this you don't want to broach before Nan?

WOLSEY. My king, let us have the poets again—

HENRY. On pain of my displeasure—what did you come here to say?

WOLSEY (after a moment's hesitation). For the preservation of your good fortune—and that of England—I must endure your displeasure.

HENRY (angry). It has been your habit lately to slight my wife and overlook her presence and counsel! Speak now—and before her!

WOLSEY. Why, if I must, I shall. Our messenger returned from Rome today. We have the last word from that quarter.

HENRY. Oh?

WOLSEY. And not one we can welcome.

HENRY. What is it?

WOLSEY. The Pope will not annul your marriage to Katharine.

HENRY. But he must.

WOLSEY. He will not. He makes it quite definite and final.

HENRY. But what reason can he give?

WOLSEY. The reason he gives is unimportant. The true reason is that he is a prisoner, and cannot grant it.

HENRY. What kind of prisoner?

WOLSEY. An actual one. He was just about to annul your marriage to Katharine. He had quite sufficient ground for it—she was your brother's widow, and that's enough. But now the Emperor Charles has invaded Italy and captured the Vatican. He can give orders there and does. And the Emperor Charles is Katharine's nephew, and he doesn't want his aunt divorced from you. Pope Clement has been forbidden to favor us in the matter.

HENRY. How do you know this?

WOLSEY. From my agents in Rome. . . . Times will change, of course. There will be another pope; there will be another emperor. But there can be no divorce this year.

HENRY. There must be a divorce this year. Nan is with child—and her child must be heir to the throne.

WOLSEY. I warned you when you first contemplated this marriage—

ANNE. It was you who came first to me, demanding me for King Henry!

WOLSEY. There was. no thought of marriage at that time.

ANNE. You are a man of the church! You speak for the church!

WOLSEY. I am King Henry's minister. I speak for what can be done. I speak against what cannot.

HENRY. You will somehow get this divorce for me.

WOLSEY. My king, you and I have worked together on this. We've tried everything we could lay hands or wits on. *(To Anne)* For two years, Lady Anne, step by step, with patience and cunning and the best skill there is about us, we have tried to bring about the divorce from Katharine. Henry went to her and asked directly for it. He told her, which is true, that from the beginning he and she had been living in mortal sin. She refused him. As for me, I have marshaled cardinals and bishops like storm troops to assail the Pope's position. I have tried from every angle, from every direction, with money, influence, and temporal power. I have run my head against this wall like a bull in a stone barn—till there's blood dripping in my eyes and I'm worn out. And when we were about to win—when the wall was crumbling and going down before us— the Emperor broke into Italy and made the church his vassal. In that situation I'm powerless. And so is Henry.

ANNE. What are we to do?

WOLSEY. Live as you were. Live as you are. Wait.

ANNE. Children don't wait for these changes among the dynasties. They come at their own time, convenient or inconvenient. They don't wait.

WOLSEY. I know no other answer. Am I dismissed, my lord?

HENRY. Yes.

(Wolsey and Cromwell bow and go out stage right)

I hoped to win suddenly and have good news for you some morning, but it hasn't come. This comes instead. . . . Am I forgiven, Nan?

(He puts his hand over hers.)

ANNE. Is anything ever forgiven?

HENRY. Is that your answer?

ANNE. How do I know what you've agreed with Wolsey? In all your pacts with kings and princes of the whole earth, I've never known you to tell the truth—never!

HENRY. But I've told it to you!

ANNE. I thought you had. I've tried to take the place you wanted me to take— and do what must be done—because I had promised, and you had promised. But what I feared has come about—

(Henry leaps to his feet.)

HENRY. God in Heaven damn this spotted bitch! To be called a liar by my own bitch! Damn you!

ANNE. I've heard you lie to too many. You've never yet told truth when a lie would serve! And we had a bargain, remember. I said, "If you will make me queen I will marry you!" But our marriage was at night and in secret; the church does not hold it valid; I am not the queen, and my child will not inherit the throne! Was this planned? It's like many plans I've known you to make!

HENRY. I'll strangle you yet! I'll make an end of you!

ANNE. No doubt.

HENRY. You've lied at times! And to me! What's all this sudden passion about lying?

ANNE. I could have said, "I love you, I love you, I love you!" I didn't say it. Because I don't. And whether you love me I don't know. You've been unfaithful to me often enough—and I've known where and with whom!

HENRY. If I have you've spoiled it for me, with your damned mocking face watching me through the walls! You spoil everything for me! Faithful—what kind of faith do you want of me? To be impotent in every bed but yours? Well, that's happened, too! They've laughed at me in their beds—more than one. Laughed at their king—and he impotent—with all but you! It's as if you were a disease in me—so that I'm in a fever when you're with me and a fever when you're absent—and it grows worse with the years that should burn it out! What more can I give, in faith or anything I have?

ANNE. What you promised? What you gave your pledged word to do?

HENRY (gently). Anne—I have tried. Not always the right way, perhaps, but my best.

ANNE. You see—if I have a child before this divorce is granted—well, you are still as you are, untouched, but I'm not.

HENRY. I know, Anne. And it's unfair. But it's not what I meant. I meant it all quite honestly—quite as I said. I like what you've done with the court. I want you for my queen. I've lied to all the others, but not to you. . . . Why must she anger me? Why am I tied to this alabaster face and this pinched-up mouth and these slanted eyes?

(A shadow moves at stage right and Cromwell's voice is heard.)

CROMWELL. May I come in, Your Majesty?

HENRY (angry). Who is it? Who disturbs me here?

CROMWELL. I am the lord Cardinal's secretary, Your Majesty. My name is Cromwell.

HENRY. Stay out! No—come in.

(Cromwell approaches)

You were just here.

CROMWELL. Yes, Majesty.

(He bows.)

HENRY. Well, what do you want? Has the Cardinal forgotten something?

CROMWELL. He forgets nothing, my liege, except his duty to his king.

HENRY. I'm in no mood for riddles.

CROMWELL. I mean that Your Majesty may have your divorce, and the Lady Anne be crowned queen, and the child to come made heir apparent very simply. It needs only the will to do it.

HENRY. Whose will?

CROMWELL. The Cardinal's. He has something else in mind. He's playing his hand to get himself made pope in Rome. He's not thinking of you or your divorce.

HENRY. You have been dismissed once— now once again!

ANNE. What makes you say this?

CROMWELL. I know it.

HENRY. I've worked with Wolsey. This man is mad or fanatic—

ANNE. If the Pope will not grant the divorce—and can't grant it—how can any of these things you say be done?

CROMWELL. Forgive me, Your Majesty. I am not a fanatic, not a madman. All my life I have been an earnest student at the inns of court. I have read the laws of England, something which few seem to have bothered to do. There is a law of this land that makes it treason to acknowledge any higher authority than the will of the king. The church in England must grant the king a divorce if he wishes it. To maintain that the Pope may govern the king in such a matter—or in any matter—is traitorous and punishable by death. Say this to Cardinal Wolsey. He will turn white to the roots of his beard. For he too knows of this law. . . . To bring about all these things you wish, the king has only to appoint a new primate who will legalize his divorce and a new marriage.

HENRY. That would mean excommunication and a complete break with Rome. If there is such a law.

CROMWELL. Yes, Majesty. But there is such a law. Of that you may be sure. It is called the law of praemunire.

HENRY. I have always been a defender of the faith. And of the church. That is my greatest strength with my people. I can't change there.

CROMWELL. Allow me to say a word on that subject, Your Grace. As matters stand you are but half a king. We are only half-subject to you. If you were truly king in England could a foreign prelate call you to account? England is only half-free. You are only half-free. What the king of England wants he should have, without hindrance from abroad.

HENRY *(dryly)*. I fear such independence might be purchased very dearly.

CROMWELL. Dearly? You have sometimes found yourself in need of money, Your Majesty.

HENRY. Well?

CROMWELL. At one stroke you could obtain your divorce and make yourself the wealthiest monarch in Europe. The monasteries of England are richer than the gold mines of the new world. Quarrel with Rome, set yourself at the head of the English church, and these riches are yours.

HENRY. You are a man without scruple, Master Cromwell.

CROMWELL. Entirely without scruple, Your Majesty. I have learned my trade, as you know, under Cardinal Wolsey. For your information I have brought with me a list of the church properties which the Cardinal has already condemned for his own use. And an itemized history of how and where he obtained the furnishings for his palace at York—as well as the titles to the estate. Cardinal Wolsey is a richer man than you, Your Majesty.

HENRY. For the third time, you are dismissed, Master Cromwell. . . . But I shall be able to find you if I need you?

CROMWELL. Yes, Your Majesty.

ANNE. I should like to see those papers.

CROMWELL *(smiling grimly)*. Yes, Your Majesty.

(He hands the papers to Anne and goes.)

ANNE *(after a pause)*. Do you think he tells the truth?

HENRY. There would be little point in his coming to us unless he told the truth.

ANNE. Is there such a law?

HENRY. I've never heard of it, but he convinces me there is.

ANNE *(who has the papers before her)*. The Cardinal seems to have stolen an immense amount of money.

HENRY. Doubtless.

(He rises, pondering)

Doubtless he stole more than I knew. Though I'm not exactly innocent in the matter. We sometimes went halves.

ANNE. Are you also a pupil of the Cardinal's?

HENRY. I am the son of Henry the Seventh. I studied under a real master—my father. Whatever crookedness was lacking in the world when my father was born he invented before he left it. No other king of our island ever stole so widely, so successfully, so secretly—or died so rich. And the central principle he taught me was this: always keep the church on your side.

ANNE. Then he didn't steal from the church?

HENRY. Oh, yes. He stole from everybody. But not enough to turn it against him. I've stolen from the church too. But not enough to turn it against me. So far.

ANNE. If this law exists—you could have the divorce, we could be married legally—and you could be richer than your father.

HENRY. I'm thinking of just that.

(He takes a turn or two up and down as he speaks)

And of my father's advice. And they pull me two ways. . . . I'm your prisoner, Nan. Little as I like it, I'm your prisoner, and I mean to make you my queen. You've never told me you loved me. But if you were my queen—it would happen. You would say it and it would be true. . . . And now a hatch opens. As if in the floor. It may be I could make you my queen at once. And make myself wealthy beyond hope—but I'd have to make the church my enemy.

ANNE. And you love me—not quite enough.

HENRY. Suppose I set out to make myself head of the church. I shall be opposed by many who are now my friends. They will be guilty of treason and I shall have to kill them. Those whom I like best—those who have some integrity of mind—will speak first against me. They must die. Parliament and the nation can then be bludgeoned into silence—but a lot of blood will run before they're quiet. Most of my people will hate me—and even more will hate you. Yes, I can make my Nan queen—but we must consider the price. In how much we dare be hated. Are we willing to pay it?

ANNE. I am.

HENRY. You are new at this work, of course. You don't know quite what it means. To see blood run. If you knew, I wonder if you'd still wish it.

ANNE. I am with child.

(Henry comes back to his chair.)

HENRY. The altar at St. Paul's will stand ankle-deep in blood. The shopkeepers will mop blood from their floors. . . . But it must be done if we're to marry. Well, so be it.

ANNE. Must so many die?

HENRY. Many must die. And it will look as if I had done this for money. Like my father.

ANNE. He killed for money?

HENRY. It was his main source of income —to attaint a well-lined noble for treason, do away with him, and take what he had. It brought in millions. I've been trying not to think of that.

ANNE. Don't think of it.

HENRY. It will bring in the money anyway. And—the money would be useful. If only you could love me a little—no, not a little—with your whole heart . . . then —it wouldn't matter what happened—or what's thought of me.

ANNE *(putting out her hand)*. Sometimes —no. If you were ever honest—if you were ever true. . . .

HENRY *(taking her hand)*. Yes?

ANNE. But you never are.

(The lights go out.)

SCENE TWO

A great sunburst window brightens first, then we see York Palace.

Norfolk and Cromwell enter to the window and listen to the sounds of cheering without. A few voices cry:

VOICES. Long live the new queen! Long live Queen Anne!

A VOICE. Long live Queen Katharine! Long live—

VOICES. Down with him! He took foreign money! Long live Queen Anne!

NORFOLK. It seems to me the shouting for Queen Anne was somewhat sparse along the streets—not what you'd expect for a royal wedding and a coronation. You should have paid them a bit and we'd have heard something really spontaneous.

CROMWELL. They were paid.

NORFOLK. How many of them?

CROMWELL. A thousand apprentices.

NORFOLK. How much were they paid?

CROMWELL. One groat each.

NORFOLK. A groat? Man, that won't buy a whole drink of good liquor! They should have had a silver penny apiece and they'd have shaken the foundations! They'd have rung the bells! They'd have jumped out of windows! Anyway, they'd have thrown their caps in the air! The rabble I saw must have had the mange. Their headgear was stuck tight on their skulls and when they yelled it was more like a growl.

CROMWELL. For a half-crown each, or a whole one, they wouldn't cheer Queen Anne—not as they'd like to be cheering Queen Katharine.

NORFOLK. Why man, have you lost faith in money? And in King Henry? They'll go along with Henry in time. Give him a few years and he'll make them love this queen as much as the first.

CROMWELL. Those that were yelling loudest were calling her a whore.

NORFOLK. Those were paid, too, Cromwell. Those were paid, too—and probably more. By the Spanish ambassador. Or by our friend Wolsey. I'm pretty sure they were paid more than you paid, because what they shouted came straight from the heart.

(The cheering begins again.)

VOICES. God save Queen Anne!

(Henry and Anne enter from the right and pause to listen to the cheering.)

ANNE. Wasn't it rather flimsy applause?

NORFOLK. Nonsense, Your Majesty. It was what you always get in London when the folk are truly moved. It goes too deep for noise. They just stand there and weep.

ANNE. Uncle, uncle, you're an unprincipled old sinner. There were no tears. They didn't even bother to uncover.

HENRY. Let's be thankful for the friends we have, my dear. Will you be happy here?

ANNE. I've never known there was anything so perfect in England.

HENRY. There isn't, anywhere else. This must have been his library.

CROMWELL. Yes, it was. He worked in this room.

HENRY. And so, will you be happy?

ANNE. Who else will live here?

HENRY. Only you.

ANNE. There's room for so many.

HENRY. There'll be no apartment here for anyone save you. Not even for me unless you ask me.

ANNE. I've never had a place that was mine.

CROMWELL. There's someone here.

(The lights come up a little at stage right, and we see an old man bowed over papers at a table. He looks up. It is Cardinal Wolsey, much changed.)

WOLSEY. Ah, forgive me. Go on with whatever you have in hand, you young people. I'm only finishing an inventory for the new owner.

CROMWELL. His Majesty waits for you to rise, Cardinal Wolsey.

WOLSEY. You must forgive me. I can rise only with assistance. My legs are not for dancing, any more. But the inventory's ready, and now I write my name.

(He writes.)

ANNE. I'm afraid we disturb you here.

WOLSEY. It's better that you should. The palace is much too beautiful for an old man. It needs youth in it. Here's the paper. I'm sorry that I can't rise and bring it to you—or kneel before you. I can only reach it out.

ANNE *(going to him)*. I've been your enemy—but I can't take it from you.

WOLSEY. Take it. Take it. My life is broke square in two. I have no use for it now, and you have. So take it.

(She doesn't put out her hand)

Or I'll leave it here.

(He lays the paper down)

It's yours.

HENRY. We thought you had left for Esher.

WOLSEY. It was my intention to be gone when you came, my lord, but some friends of mine were here, and they wished to see you, and they persuaded me to stay.

HENR. Some friends of yours?

WOLSEY. And of yours. Sir Thomas More, Bishop Fisher, and John Houghton, Prior to the Charter House in London.

HENRY. They are here?

WOLSEY. Yes. Will you see them?

HENRY. We thought to escape conferences this one day, but

(He looks at Anne)

kings and queens are never excused. Let them come in.

(Wolsey claps his hands and Three Men enter from stage right. Henry welcomes them as they come in)

Welcome, Sir Thomas More! Welcome, Bishop of Rochester! Welcome, Prior John Houghton! I know what you come to say, but welcome!

MORE. It's good of you to see us, Your Majesty.

HENRY. Make it plural, More. Our Majesties are both seeing you. We have come from the coronation.

MORE. It's about that we wish to speak, my lord. But Bishop Fisher is the eldest and most learned among us. I ask him to speak first.

FISHER. I have known you from a child, King Henry. I was present when you took your first three steps. You know I would not willingly say any word unpleasing to you. I have not opposed your divorce. I have not opposed your new marriage or the coronation of Queen Anne. Such things are sometimes necessary in the conduct of a state. But you also ask that every religious in England swear fealty to you as spiritual head of the church. And I cannot accept your guidance in spiritual matters.

HENRY. But if I were not head of your church there could be no divorce and no marriage to Anne. Anne could not be crowned. Her child could not succeed me.

FISHER. I know that. And still I cannot accept you as my spiritual guide.

HENRY. Do you accept the church of Rome?

FISHER. Yes.

HENRY. Is the Pope moved by spiritual considerations?

FISHER. Your Majesty, I accept the spiritual authority of the church. I cannot accept your usurpation of that authority.

HENRY. Then—though I'm very sorry to lose my friend—I'm afraid you are guilty of treason and will die for it.

FISHER. If it were only I, my king, it wouldn't matter. But there are thousands of my order and of similar orders who cannot take this oath. Must they all die?

HENRY. If they wish to die, they may. If they insist, they will.

And I'll tell you why!

You have no right to question me, but I'll answer!

I had no mind to cut adrift from Rome when this thing started. But I was driven to it—by Rome—

and now the cable's cut, and we're adrift unless we anchor to something! Church and all,

we're adrift! And I see no anchor but the king,
and it happens I'm the king!
John Houghton, why are you here?

HOUGHTON. I could sign everything that's asked, Your Majesty,
except the act that constitutes the king head of the church I serve.

HENRY. You will sign it or die.

HOUGHTON. Then all my Charter House dies with me.

HENRY. Have you not seen I have no alternative?
Rome denies my divorce. If I go and take it
I deny Rome's authority, and set up an authority of my own! It's Rome or the king!
I had to choose—and now you must! Sir Thomas?

MORE. I have watched you govern for many years, King Henry. It's a tyranny—and not a tyranny.

HENRY. I thank you.

MORE. You keep no standing army. You use your power
unjustly, illegally often, but your way is never to go beyond what the people's will
supports—or will support. You're very shrewd
in judging what you dare do. It's as if you had
an extra sense—the king's finger—and you kept it
on the pulse of your subjects—on your whole kingdom—
and knew—before they knew—where they were going—
and how far in the year. Only this time I don't follow you at all. How can you hope
your people will go with you when you rob
their mother church, devour her children, slip
your cuckoo eggs into the nest, and ask that we sit and say nothing's happened?

HENRY. You're a great man,
Sir Thomas More, but it may be there's some truth
in that about the king's finger. They'll go with me.
The people will.

MORE. Tell me why.

HENRY. It's—they don't like Rome.

They want to be free of Rome. They'll take me rather
than some foreigner overseas. This wasn't true
ten years ago. It's beginning to be true only now. This year.

MORE. It may be true. I don't know.
I've known these things to happen before with you.
Not quite like this. Not on this scale.

HENRY. It will happen. Must you still refuse to sign?

MORE. I must follow my own conscience.
I have no king's finger. I can't sign.

FISHER. And I can't.

HOUGHTON. Nor I, my lord.

HENRY. I'm very sorry.

MORE. We may go?

HENRY. Yes, gentlemen. You move away from this world of your own will.

MORE. Your Majesty, it will go on without us.

HENRY. No doubt of that. Farewell, then. Go with them, Norfolk.

NORFOLK. Yes, Majesty.

(More, Houghton, and Fisher bow and go out stage right, accompanied by Norfolk.)

WOLSEY. Tom, will you help me up?

CROMWELL. Yes, sir.

(He helps Wolsey to his feet.)

WOLSEY. Some men die for their principles, I observe; others because it's the next thing to do. Good-by, Your Majesties.

HENRY. Good-by, Wolsey.

ANNE *(low)*. Good-by.

(Cromwell helps Wolsey out stage right.)

HENRY. And that answers the last of them that dare speak. The rest will die silent.

(He turns to her)

Anne?

ANNE. Yes.

HENRY. Now I've done all you asked of me,
all you asked
when we first danced together.
And more.
For you said nothing about a place of your own
back there at our beginning.

ANNE. Yes. You've done more.

HENRY. I think there's never been
in all this world
a king who gave so much to find his way to the heart of her he loved.
Over many years,

winter and summer, I have fought and
  chopped
and hacked and stabbed my path through
  the jungle of laws
and events and churchly rules—
and the flesh of friends—
to come to this day.
To come to this day when I can say it's
  done,
and I have earned her love.
For all these days,
Sweet, we have lain together, and kissed
  and drawn
apart from the world into a world of our
  own,
but not once, not once have you said,
"I love you."
Surely now—surely
my Nan will say it now?
ANNE *(after a pause).* Yes, I do love you.
HENRY. So.
Then that's not it. Not what I wanted.
ANNE. What did you want, my lord?
HENRY. Why—I don't know.
Only—I still don't have you. You're not
  mine.
ANNE. Is it something I could say?
HENRY. Why, yes, I think it is, if you
  wished to say it.
But you don't. Perhaps it's better.
Let it go. Let us look at the palace.
ANNE. Yes, let us look at York Palace—
and find your rooms for you.
HENRY. You'll want me here?
ANNE. Yes.
HENRY. You're sure?
ANNE. Yes.
HENRY. Nan?
ANNE. My lord?
HENRY. Did someone say to you—some-
  time—
"Never be all his,
never melt to him—never forget to hate
  him
at least a little—for that way you'll lose
  him"?
ANNE. I've said it to myself.
HENRY. Do you say it now?
ANNE. Yes.
HENRY. I see. That's what I feel. That
you're never mine.
ANNE. Isn't it better so?
HENRY. Because you might lose me?
No—don't answer that. Let's look at the
rooms.
ANNE. Yes.
HENRY. And yet . . .

I think I'm not as I was.
I think I've earned your heart—all your
  heart—
over these years.
Yet keep it if you wish.
Only—Nan, Nan,
last night while I lay thinking of you,
and couldn't sleep, and cursed myself for
  not sleeping,
I found myself writing the words of a
  lyric,
a little poem,
and trying the music for it in my mind.
It was a poem that grew from three words
  I heard
once, from this same Sir Thomas More
  who must die,
three words, "Always, never, sometimes."
I rose and wrote the poem down, and the
  music,
and as I wrote I said to myself:
"Do I mean what is said by this music,
or by these words?"
And now I ask myself, "Do I mean them
  now?"
Here I stand, a king, with the woman I
  love,
planning murder for her sake,
planning to rob, lost in a copse of lies,
sweating, falling over boulders,
without a star. It's a king's life. A king
  lives so.
Yet the music I wrote and remember says
  something simple and sweet
and the words are undressed truth.
Something within me drove me to write
  them
out of the undergrowth of sweat and lies.
looking for a star. It's that way always.
I haven't meant to do ill.
I've meant to do well.
I have known that good was better than
  evil,
when I've known which was evil, which
  was good,
but what test is there—what star, what
  beacon of fire?
Is it the church, held in thrall?
Is it the Christ?
Withdraw your guards,
make no wars,
strike no man down who strikes you,
and how long will you be there, you or
  your nation?
I found it better to let all that go and
  write a lyric with music,

writing to one I loved, a bitch who does
  not love me,
but writing truly, thus, out of myself:
Waking at night, I go to my window,
  Scanning the stars in a portion of sky,
Fixing on one that hangs yonder—and
  over
  The street of the house where you lie.
If you sleep, do you dream,
If you dream, is it of me?
The clock strikes; I hear your voice in the
  chimes,
     Repeating your words
     When I ask if you love me:
     "Always, never, sometimes."
ANNE. I didn't say it.
HENRY. No, Sir Thomas More said it. But
  you might have.
Writing's like that. You never write down
  what happened.
But what you write comes closer to what's
  true
than what did happen, or was said.
ANNE. I love you.
HENRY. Nan!
ANNE. I love you. Now I know. I love you.
HENRY. I think you mean this.
ANNE. I've said it, and it's true.
These men who were to die, Henry—
Sir Thomas More
and all the others—they must live.
HENRY. That was all done for you, sweet.
ANNE. Yes, but we must let them live.
HENRY. Our marriage may not be valid,
nor my divorce from Katharine,
nor the succession to your issue,
if they refuse to swear, and live—
ANNE. It doesn't matter.
It doesn't matter about the divorce—or the
  marriage—
or having this palace. Let them swear or
  not swear
as they like. Let Katharine keep her
  throne, and Mary
inherit. You love me, and I love you,
and I can say it.
HENRY. Why can you say it?
ANNE. Because of the poem—
and the things you put in it—
and the things you are—
when we speak, and are close together.
I've been afraid to say it, afraid to be it,
but now—
Let it come, whatever it brings. I'm deep
  in love.
With one I hated.

Who took me anyway. Took me from my
  first love.
With you.
HENRY. I thought you'd never say it.
Oh, if it's true, and you'll lie in my arms
  and love me,
then I can be the king you've wished me
  to be,
the king I've wished to be,
just, generous, magnanimous to enemies,
royal enough to treat all men royally,
only I'll need you to help me.
ANNE. If I can.
HENRY. It's not because of the palace?
Never a fair woman but loved silks
and oriel windows and coronets.
ANNE. No, dear, it's you,
and hearing your thoughts,
and being close to you,
and thinking of the men that must not
  die.
HENRY. Then it's a new age. Gold
or some choicer metal—or no metal at all,
but exaltation, darling. Wildfire in the air,
wildfire in the blood!
Have you room in your heart for much
  loving?
ANNE. All you have.
HENRY. For now you'll have no rest.
ANNE. I want none. Here.
*(She opens her arms. He kisses her and
they stand embraced.)*
HENRY. I was a pirate till I met you, Nan.
No girl could call me hers,
her minion.
But I'm yours.
Is it some trick of the way you turn your
  eyes
suddenly, and smile?
Sometimes I think it's that.
Is it the triangle of eyes and mouth,
and the way they go together
like no others?
Is it your lips?
Let me see.
(He kisses her)
Now I think it's your lips.
Or is it that little trill of speech you
  brought
from France—
hesitating over a word,
and bewitching it with a laugh?
Is it your brows?
(He kisses her brows)
Is it the delicacy of all you are,
the flower face,

and the minuscule breasts that I cup in
my hands,
and the tiny dancing feet
like a figurine's
but tireless to dance with?
ANNE. Never mind my size—
I've been teased about it.
HENRY. There's one way to decide—
I'll kiss you all, feet to crown—
and it won't take long,
it's not far to go!
ANNE. Not now.
No, it's because I was hard to get, King
Henry.
But for whatever it was, I'm happy—
to have it as it pleases you.
And, as for you,
I know what it is about you.
HENRY. What about me?
ANNE. There's everything in you.
Good and bad.
There's so much in you, you hardly know
who you are.
You're a world. With one
you're a man about courts, a fantastic,
with another
you're an authority on religion,
monastic, grim, savage, learned,
then again
a pedant, running with ink, ink on your
fingers,
ink in your hair—if you cut yourself you
bleed ink.
With another a sportsman,
talking shafts, or deer, or pheasants,
or the habits of eels.
Then you're a lover of old manuscripts
and libraries, an illuminator of Chaucer.
Or a despot, or a king, a magnifico. Sometimes.
Or a host, or a poet—
or a merry guest, or a dancer, or a devil.
God what a devil you can be!
You hardly know who you are.
HENRY. I know with you.
ANNE. But for all of these—
I kiss you. For the devil, too.
HENRY. Kiss me for all of them,
for each one separately,
and then again, twice as many, for my-
self.
*(She kisses him, lips, eyes, and brow.
Cromwell returns, stage right.)*
CROMWELL. Forgive me, Your Majesty.
HENRY. We're reversing a policy, Crom-
well.

The oath to the Act of Succession is not
required.
Let them swear or not swear, as they
please.
CROMWELL. But, Your Majesty—there are
men sentenced—many
HENRY. Lift the sentences. Go now, and
leave us alone.
CROMWELL. Yes, Majesties.
(He goes, stage right.)
HENRY. And now— it's your palace.
I have no place here till I'm asked.
ANNE. Then I ask it.
You won't need an apartment here.
My place is yours.
Whatever I am is yours. Or what I have.
Put your arms round me.
HENRY. Yes, sweet.
(He puts his arms round her.)
ANNE. I want to be yours only.
HENRY. I have been yours only—thesↄ
many years. And now, for the first time—·
(He kisses her. The lights go out)
you are mine, too.

SCENE THREE

*A bedroom in York Palace. Anne Boleyn
lies in bed with an infant beside her.
Elizabeth Boleyn, Madge Shelton, and
Norfolk are in the room. Madge and Elizabeth bend over the child.*

———

ELIZABETH. What beautiful little hands!
What a beautiful face!
ANNE. I think I shall call her after you,
mother.
ELIZABETH. Hush!
ANNE. Well, he must know sooner or later.
It may as well be soon.
NORFOLK. The king's at the door now, in
case you wish to know.
ELIZABETH. He must come in, of course.
ANNE. Not yet—not yet! Make some ex-
cuse. Not quite yet.
ELIZABETH. My dear, it's her father—the
king.
ANNE. She is beautiful.
ELIZABETH. Yes, she is.
NORFOLK *(at the door)*. It seems all's
ready, Your Majesty.
*(Henry enters and stands at the door,
looking at the bed.)*
HENRY. Nan, sweet—
ANNE. Yes, Henry?
HENRY. Do I come too soon? Will it tire

you to speak?

ANNE. No, Henry. I'm glad to see you.

(Henry comes into the room, staring at the child.)

HENRY. I won't say much. Nor stay long. I just want to look at you two—the most precious freight ever a bed carried. My queen—and my prince—my son.

ANNE. My lord—

HENRY. Hush. Rest, my dear, and get strong. I shall call him Edward. It's been a lucky name for English kings. A lucky name and a great name. Oh, little lad, little lad, may you better them all for fortune and fair renown!

ANNE. My lord, we—

HENRY. All my life as a king I have asked only one thing of heaven—that it grant me a son to carry on what I leave. And now heaven has given me more than I asked, for this is a handsome, bold boy's face, and already there's wit behind those eyes—

ANNE. Her name's to be Elizabeth.

HENRY. Whose—name?

ANNE. We have a little daughter . . . and her name's Elizabeth.

HENRY. A daughter! Why did no one tell me?

NORFOLK. They're all afraid of you, my lord. I offered to go. What can he do to an old man, I said, beyond the usual disemboweling? But they said no, wait.

HENRY. They were wrong. Whatever happens we must look our hap in the face. Why, girl, don't look so down. If we can have a healthy girl together we can have a healthy boy together. We shall get one yet.

ANNE. I'm sorry, Henry. As if it were my fault.

HENRY. It's no fault of anyone. There must be girls as well as boys. She has a sonsie sweet face. . . . I like her no less than I did—not a groat less. Get better, lass; eat well and get on your legs quickly. We'll have a good life, we'll let this beauty grow a foot or two, and then we'll have our son—and so nothing's lost. Norfolk, I'm off for the hunting. Come with me.

NORFOLK. I, my lord?

HENRY. Aye—come with me and talk treason! It amuses me! Nan, sweet, nurse the moppet and—remember me.

ANNE. Yes, my lord.

HENRY. Give me a kiss—

(He kisses her)

I'm off.

ANNE. Will you kiss our little one, Henry?

HENRY. When she's a shade older, my dear —when she's in petticoats, and can run. Why, I'll kiss her now!

(He does so)

Come, Duke—and be thinking of a jest for the road.

God keep all here—

(The lights go out.)

SCENE FOUR

Shows Henry sitting as in the Prologue to the act, pen in hand.

———

HENRY. There is a load every man lugs behind him,
heavy, invisible, sealed, concealed, perfumed,
a package of dead things he drags along, never opened
save to put in some horror of the mind—
some horror of his own doing—to seal up
and rot in secret. He pretends
there's no such thing. He tries to walk
as if he had no burden. The stench is covered
with purchased scents and flowers.
The deeds in this bag,
man and king, he utterly cancels, denies, forgets,
for they would prove him an idiot, criminal,
subhuman.
Yet they are his.
He did them, and put them there.
And they are mine.
I did them, and put them there.
All men have done the same—
or done the like. And will.
Have you done so much better,
you out there in the future,
you whom I see with the thousand eyes, looking back
on my secret ways?
If you have, then you're young and unlucky—
it's still to come.
Or else you're old and unlucky—
it never was.
With kings as with men
there is the mask and tongue among your friends
with a steady smile and word,
and there is the hog behind the eyes, the rat

behind the tongue, the dog that runs
    before
and brings you after—
or lags, and holds you back.
And you obey them,
the hog, the rat, the dog.
Man, woman, and child, you have obeyed
    them always,
and I have. The carrion and the beast
decide where we shall love, and when
    leave off
to love another;
not our high purpose, our resolve, our
    brain,
but the vermin underneath,
the unacknowledged boar, the hidden
    wallow,
the invisible decay.
Whatever she did, I had done first.
For when I knew for the first time she
    was all mine,
then, having loved her many years,
suddenly I loved her only a little,
and could look at others.
And then I loved her not at all—
And her lips were an over-eaten plate,
and my body would not answer hers,
and when I felt my child move beneath
    her skin
I had no liking for it, and turned away.
Was this her blame or mine?
Or was there blame?

SCENE FIVE

*A room in York Palace. The lights come
up stage right to show Jane Seymour
crocheting at a window. A Servant enters,
bringing her a letter and a leather purse.*

JANE. Yes?
SERVANT. It's from the king, if it please
you. Both these.
JANE. From—?
SERVANT. I'm to wait for an answer.
JANE. Is this a purse of gold?
SERVANT. I think it is, mistress.
JANE. I would not have the king think
me ungrateful, but I have no need of gold,
and no wish for it. And I think it would
be better if I were not to know what is
written here.
(She gives back letter and purse.)
SERVANT. Am I to tell him this?
JANE. If you will.
(The lights go out on the scene.)

SCENE SIX

*The king's hunting pavilion. A Servant is
tying a bracer on Henry's arm. Norfolk is
reading to him out of a huge volume.*

——

HENRY. What does he say about the
bracer?
NORFOLK. "In a bracer a man must take
heed of three things: that it have no nails
in it, that it have no buckles, that it be
laced without aiglettes."
HENRY. These three every fool knows.
What else?
NORFOLK. Nothing.
HENRY. Throw the book away!
*(Norfolk starts to hand the book to a
servant)*
Throw it, I said! Am I a king, or not a
king?
NORFOLK. How far am I to throw it, Your
Grace? My arm is not what it was.
HENRY. Keep it. Here's a glum bird that
portends no good.
(Cromwell enters from stage left)
Portend, blackbird, portend.
CROMWELL. I come to tell Your Majesty
that you have perhaps left me in charge
too long. The Commons and the Church
are both out of hand. Nobody swears to
the Act of Succession. It's a matter of open
debate whether Katharine or Anne is your
queen, and whether Mary or Elizabeth
shall succeed you.
HENRY. I intend to reign another forty
years. And to have sons. And not by
Katharine or Anne. Not by Katharine or
Anne! You hear! Let them fight it out.
CROMWELL. Queen Anne has sent Jane
Seymour away from court.
HENRY. Where?
CROMWELL. It's not known where.
HENRY. Has she harmed her?
CROMWELL. That I don't know. But Jane
was sent away, guarded.
HENRY. I must go.
*(He starts to walk away with the bracer
still on his arm, carrying a bow.)*
SERVANT. Your Majesty—shall I take this
off?
HENRY. Aye—tear it off—cut it off!
(He pauses, impatient)
No, leave it! I must go.
*(He starts out, tossing the bow away,
Cromwell hurrying after him. The lights
go out.)*

SCENE SEVEN

The lights come up on full stage, show-
ing the nursery of the child Elizabeth at
York Palace. There is a cradle and a chair
or two. The rest is suggested by projec-
tions on the rear curtain. Elizabeth Boleyn
and Henry Norris are at the cradle, watch-
ing the child. Mark Smeaton is singing a
lullaby, and playing on a stringed instru-
ment. Anne and Madge Shelton are listen-
ing.

———

SMEATON *(singing)*.
I had a little nut tree,
Nothing would it bear,
But a silver nutmeg,
And a golden pear.

NORRIS *(going to Anne)*. Shall we dance
to it?

ANNE. Surely.

(During the next stanza they take a few
steps together.)

ELIZABETH. Hush! Don't wake her.

SMEATON *(singing)*.
The king of Spain's daughter
Came to visit me,
And all for the sake
Of my little nut tree.

ELIZABETH. She's asleep.

NORRIS. Whether to escape the singing or
for delight in it, no man knows.

ANNE. It was well sung. But you could
keep the king of Spain's daughter out of
it, after this. I've had enough trouble with
the king of Spain's daughter.

SMEATON. Next time I will.

(Norfolk appears at stage right.)

NORFOLK. The king's here, my chicks.

ANNE. The king of Spain?

HENRY *(entering behind Norfolk, with*
Cromwell). No, lassie, the king of England.

ANNE. I thought the king of Spain more
likely.

HENRY. Yes. We stayed long at our hunting.

ANNE. The princess has grown. Would
you care to look at her?

HENRY. Indeed I would.

(Norris and Smeaton have bowed and re-
treated. Henry looks into the cradle)
She looks like you.

ANNE. And you.

HENRY. And me. She'll never be hung for
her beauty.

ANNE. I think she's beautiful.

HENRY. She gathers a court, I notice.
(He looks about)
We must see you for a moment, Cromwell
and I.

ANNE. Mother, will you take Elizabeth
back to her room? Mark and Norris will
carry the cradle.

ELIZABETH. Yes, dear.

(Smeaton and Norris carry the cradle off
to stage right. Elizabeth and Madge fol-
low)
Softly now.

SMEATON. I sang her to sleep. I'll take
care not to wake her.

ANNE *(speaks after they are gone. Henry,*
Anne, Cromwell, and Norfolk are on
stage). Yes, King Henry, there was some
question you wished to discuss with your
queen?

HENRY. Two gentlemen of my court,
Edward and Thomas Seymour, came to
me
an hour or two ago, demanding of me
where they could find their sister.

ANNE. Does this frighten you?

HENRY. They are my friends.
I have especial cause
at this moment not to offend them.

ANNE. Yes, I think so.

HENRY. Where is Jane Seymour?

ANNE. In Northumberland. And a very
good place for her.

HENRY. Her brothers have made it plain
that they resent the slur you cast on her
in sending her from court.

ANNE. I don't care for her.
She has the face of a sheep. And the
manners.
But not the morals.
I don't want her near me.

HENRY. You will bring her back.

ANNE. No, I think not.
If you want her near you, why, find a
suite for her
in your own palace. This York place is
mine.
You gave it to me for my own. And while
it's mine, Jane Seymour must lie elsewhere.

HENRY. Lassie—well—
Speak to her, Norfolk.

NORFOLK. The truth is, girl, you're on
slippery ground.
More and more the common folk cry
down your name.
There used to be a penalty for speaking
against you.

There's none now.
And the people take advantage of it,
in the church, in the government,
 wherever they meet.
You have no defenders.
ANNE. Am I at the mercy of the people?
NORFOLK. We're all at the mercy of the
 people.
Sooner or later, what they want they'll
 have,
unless you're willing and able.
to do unlimited murder on them.
ANNE. I gave my voice for mercy.
NORFOLK. It happens you stand for some-
 thing they don't want.
They're for having the old queen back.
HENRY. Speak to her, Cromwell.
CROMWELL. If things go as they're going
the Commons will revolt, Your Majesty.
The divorce will be invalidated,
and your marriage also.
We've slackened our hold, and the dogs
 are at our throats,
yours and mine! Not the king's.
ANNE. Why yours?
CROMWELL. I've worked hard at sup-
 pressing monasteries
and squeezing money out of them.
You—and the king's love for you—
have sliced off England from the mother
 church.
We shall never be forgiven, you or I.
Nor your child.
She will not rule. Not as things go now.
HENRY. And so, my dear,
be a little less absolute in what you'll have
and not have.
ANNE. Jane Seymour will not couch here.
HENRY. She will live here, among your
 women,
and you'll accept her.
I've sent for her to come.
ANNE. There are ways of making
a woman so unwelcome . . .
(She pauses)
No, she may come—
and we'll make her welcome.
But More and Fisher and Houghton must
 not live,
and all who refuse to sign the Act of
 Succession
must die with them.
Elizabeth must succeed you. See to that
and Jane will be accepted here. We made
this bargain before. And some of it you've
 kept.
Now keep the rest.

HENRY. This part I can't keep.
These men are my friends.
ANNE. By the year when I loved elsewhere,
but must have you because you were the
 king—
by the years when I loved no one
but bore your weight because the earth
 was empty—
by the year when I must carry your child
without loving you, because you were
 royal—
my child must be royal, too!
HENRY. Let me off from this, Nan. I can't
 kill these men.
ANNE. You've killed before!
HENRY. One learns a little. Never since
 Buckingham
have I touched a man in high place,
one I respected,
or whose death might become a symbol.
If you love me, Nan,
forget the succession.
ANNE. I love you now.
I shall go to my grave loving you, no
 doubt,
and hating you.
But if you remember how it all came
 about,
and how your word's dishonored,
how can you look in my eyes and say our
 daughter
will not succeed?
HENRY. Because I cannot look on these
 deaths.
In all honesty!
Other deaths, but not these!
Could you sign these death warrants?
ANNE. Oh, King of England, King of
 England,
you blind king!
I'd sign ten thousand to die
rather than warm that white-faced serpent
 you love
and disinherit my blood!
(Henry stands silent before her, then
speaks slowly.)
HENRY. It would need unlimited murder,
 as Norfolk said.
Unlimited, pitiless murder. It would mean
 tearing
the world apart!
Look at me, Nan—you know me—
as I know myself.
Is it fitting I should be head of a church?
It's laughable—it can't be serious,
and yet it is. If I impose myself there
I'm king and they dare not answer,

and there I am—king and pope in one.
To legalize a divorce,
and a child, and a marriage!
ANNE. Our dead marriage.
But you will demand it, Henry, and take
it!
Make yourself head of the church, stand
by me as
my husband, and father Elizabeth, the
heir!
And if it costs heads and blood and fires
at Smithfield
let the blood run and the fires burn!
It's that, or else it's my blood, and Cromwell's—
and Elizabeth's.
Cromwell knows that, your butcher-cleaver
man knows that!
Send him out to implement these deaths
and let it be done quickly,
let there be no mistaking,
no leniency, no mercy!
High or low, they will sign—or depart
without entrails!
And you will keep your word to me, un-
loved
though I may be!
I wish I were loved, but I'm not,
and so I shall be queen of this island, and
Elizabeth shall be queen!
(A pause.)
HENRY. No.
But you're beautiful when you're angry.
Now if we had a son . . .
(He steps toward her)
Help me to prove that I can father kings—
ANNE. What do you mean?
HENRY. For Elizabeth, no.
For her I will not commit these murders.
But if we had a male heir . . .
(He steps closer to her)
Your son and mine—
ANNE. I can be angrier than you've seen
me yet,
and not beautiful!
I know where your heart is! It's not with
me!
HENRY. What has the heart to do
with the getting of kings?
I am not young—I am not true—
I'm bitter and expert and aging and
venomous—
not to be trusted.
It's your misfortune that you love me
now that I no longer love you.
Yet at this moment I want you—because
of your anger

and the flash of blood in your face—
and, if you give me a prince, things may
change—
even I may change!
(He comes still closer.)
ANNE. No. Not unless you kill them—
More and Houghton and Fisher
and all who will not sign—
not unless Elizabeth is your heir.
HENRY (to Cromwell). Put them to death,
then. Go out and do it.
(Cromwell and Norfolk go out)
See, now. I rob and murder at your order.
And commit sacrilege.
ANNE. You do what you wish to do
and call it my deed.
(He puts his arms round her)
I hate you. I hate your desire.
And mine.
(She pulls away from him.)
HENRY. Things could change.
Even I. I loved you once.
I saw that fire in your face.
Give me a son.
(He takes her in his arms again. The
lights go out. After a moment three vio-
lins are heard playing the air of a song
somewhere in the darkness.)

SCENE EIGHT

King Henry is sitting in his closet at window, writing and humming the song to
himself as he writes it down. Cromwell
enters.

———

HENRY. You're late, sir—and we have
much to do.
CROMWELL. I have ill news.
HENRY. What news?
CROMWELL. The queen is brought to bed
of a son, and it's born dead.
HENRY (not comprehending). A son. Born
dead.
CROMWELL. Yes.
HENRY. I don't trust you in this.
CROMWELL. I didn't trust anyone else. I
went to see it. And it's a son. And dead.
HENRY. Leave me. I won't work today.
CROMWELL. Yes, master.
(He goes.)
HENRY. A son. Born dead. Like the sons
of Katharine.
Born—and a son—but cursed with the
curse of God

se I've had her sister—
cause . . .
for whatever reason,
as dead.
, my God, help me! What do you want
of me?
Was this girl not to your mind? Not ever?
Or am I
not to your mind?
But I am the king, God's chosen,
potent and virile. I am a man. The
  woman's failed me.
I must look elsewhere.
*(The lights fade. The music of the song
plays again.)*

SCENE NINE

*The lights come up on Henry, sitting at
the table, stage left. The three singers
stand before him.*

HENRY. Sing the song tenderly—
no, you're young, you wouldn't know
  about tenderness.
Sing it lightly, softly, to the lady who sits
  reading.
*(The lights come up on Jane Seymour,
who sits with a book in hand. The singers
go toward her.)*
JANE. Yes?
HENRY. They are about to sing to you,
Jane.
JANE. I thank Your Majesty.
SINGERS. Waking at night, I go to my
  window,
  Scanning the stars in a portion of sky,
Fixing on one that hangs yonder—and
  over
  The street of the house where you lie.
*(Anne Boleyn enters, unseen by the others,
and listens)*
  If you sleep, do you dream,
  If you dream, is it of me?
The clock strikes; I hear your voice in
  the chimes,
    Repeating your words
    When I ask if you love me:
    "Always, never, sometimes."
*(As the song ends Henry catches sight of
Anne in the shadow. She drops him a
little mocking curtsy.)*
HENRY. Come near me, Anne.
(She does so)
You think me happy, Anne, but I'm not
happy.

ANNE. Play out your play.
(She goes out.)
HENRY. Sing the song again.
(As the song begins the lights go out.)

CURTAIN

ACT THREE

PROLOGUE

*Anne Boleyn is seen sitting in her cell in
the fur-trimmed gown, as at the beginning
of the play. She has her tablet and stylus
and begins to write.*

ANNE. From the day he first made me his,
to the last day I made him mine,
yes,
let me set it down in numbers,
I who can count and reckon, and have
  the time.
Of all the days I was his and did not love
  him—
this; and this; and this many.
Of all the days I was his—
and he had ceased to love me—
this many; and this. In days.
(She writes)
It comes to a thousand days—
out of the years.
Strangely, just a thousand.
And of that thousand—
one—   •
when we were both in love. Only one
when our loves met, and overlapped and
  were both mine and his.
When I no longer hated him—
he began to hate me,
except for that day. And the son we had—
the one son—born of our hate and lust—
died in my womb. When Henry was hurt
  at the jousting.
Then Henry looked in my face and said,
"This marriage is cursed like the other.
I've known it all along.
There's a curse on it."
And he turned and left me.
Have you no hate in your heart, Anne?
You had hate enough when you were
  young!
Hate him now, and curse him, and it
  won't matter
what he does—or has done! I can't hate
  him.
It's as he said long ago:

You love where you love.
You can't change it. And this great fool
  and bully,
I'd take him now
if he came and put out his hand
and said one word.
*(The lights dim, remaining on Anne's
face, then coming up on stage left)*
Even when they came . . .

SCENE ONE

*The little, barred window has disap-
peared and instead we are in the castle at
York. At stage left Norris, Smeaton, and
Madge Shelton are seated at a card table.
Anne is at the cradle, stage right, bending
over it to sing a lullaby.*

———

ANNE. Sleep, little coddling,
  Sleep, sleep warm,
Your mother's in a taking,
  There will be a storm.
Sleep, little hatchling,
  Sleep, little squirrel,
Your father's losing money,
  There will be a quarrel.
MADGE. Can you pick up your cards, Nan?
ANNE. Play for me, will you, Madge?
Never mind, I can leave her.
*(She rises and goes to the card table. Nor-
folk comes in from stage left, followed
by Cromwell)*
We have visitors. We are honored, gentle-
men, but why were you not announced?
NORFOLK *(to Cromwell)*. Norris and
Smeaton.
CROMWELL. Yes, I know the names.
NORFOLK. I have a warrant for your ar-
rest, niece. I could have let others bring
it, but I thought I could do it more gently
than some.
ANNE. What . . . am I to be arrested for?
NORFOLK. Also any gentlemen found in
your chamber are to be taken with you.
ANNE. But—why? What for? I am the
queen.
NORFOLK *(embarrassed, looking at a
paper)*. For—it says for adultery. With
these—and three others.
ANNE. But—this is—
NORFOLK. Niece, it's pure nonsense. But
here it is.
CROMWELL. You will take a few things and
come.
ANNE. But the child?

CROMWELL. You will leave her with your
women.
ANNE. Then—what women may I take
with me?
CROMWELL. You will be furnished with at-
tendants at the Tower.
SMEATON. We go to the Tower, too?
CROMWELL. You go to the Tower.
*(The lights flick out and come up on
Henry, sitting at his table as in Act Two.)*

SCENE TWO

Cromwell comes in and bows to Henry.

———

HENRY. What have you done?
CROMWELL. She's safe in a room without
windows.
HENRY. We can't keep her there. We have
no evidence. There's no precedent for the
trial of a queen.
CROMWELL. No evidence? Smeaton admits
adultery with her.
HENRY. What?
(He leaps to his feet)
Smeaton!
CROMWELL. And there will be others.
HENRY. Where is Smeaton?
CROMWELL. In the Tower.
HENRY. He's been tortured?
CROMWELL. Would that impugn his evi-
dence?
HENRY. I've sometimes wondered.
CROMWELL. There will be others.
HENRY. I want to be just. I must be just
in this. Smeaton! Tell me. Is this true?
CROMWELL. The truth is what the judges
will find, what the king will decide.
HENRY. You'll go too far with this verbal
juggling some day! What I want to know
is, did this happen?
CROMWELL. He confesses it.
HENRY. Under what torture?
CROMWELL. Only a rope around his brows.
No more.
HENRY. God knows she could. Any woman
could. And I've given her cause. But you
have reasons for wishing her guilty, you
know! You're not an impartial judge. You
need a scapegoat to blame for the robbery
of the church!
CROMWELL. My lord—
HENRY. And I need a scapegoat! I'm no
impartial judge! I'd want to find her
guilty, and you know that, you play on
that!

CROMWELL. My lord, if you wish to accuse me—

HENRY. I accuse both of us! I want to marry elsewhere! There was a time when getting rid of Anne wouldn't have helped. I'd have had Katharine round my neck again. But now Katharine's dead. And if Anne were dead I'd be free! And you saw this and so you put the temptation before me! Liar, butcher, sewer rat! And yet she may truly be guilty.

CROMWELL. So Smeaton says.

HENRY (after a pause). Let her be tried. Let Norfolk sit over her as judge. Let her own uncle be the judge. Let her be tried by a group of peers. And if she speaks in her defense I wish it to be where I may hear her speak—without being seen.

CROMWELL. Yes, my lord.

(The lights go out on Henry and Cromwell, come up on . . .)

SCENE THREE

Anne at her cell window. After a moment we see that there are three men standing before her: Norfolk, Cromwell, and Kingston, the keeper of the Tower.

NORFOLK. I'd have preferred to see you alone, Anne, that's true, but there are reasons why I couldn't.

ANNE. You may send the others out, I think.

NORFOLK. The point is, they won't go. Kingston won't go because he has orders that nobody's to see you alone. Cromwell won't go because he doesn't want anything said to you—or by you—that he doesn't hear. And I don't dare to be alone with you here, because I'm your judge, and it would be thought I was in collusion with you.

ANNE. I'm glad to see you even on these terms, Uncle Norfolk. I've had little company. I'd ask you to sit, but my cell's poorly furnished.

NORFOLK. Thank you, we do nicely.

ANNE. I could have some chairs, perhaps?

KINGSTON. I'm sorry, Your Majesty.

ANNE. No?

(She smiles)

Well, it's you who stand, not I.

NORFOLK. What I came to ask is whether I can help you in any way.

ANNE. Would you?

NORFOLK. If I can.

ANNE. There are three things I've wanted very much. One is to walk out and look at the sky—a few minutes every day. I get such a longing to see the sky. And . . .

NORFOLK. Yes?

ANNE. I'd like to see one or two friends—only one or two—if they could come here. Somebody could be with us—but I'd like to see them.

NORFOLK. Yes.

ANNE. And my Elizabeth. Couldn't she visit me—or even stay here? She'd be company for me—she's three now—and the days are so horribly long.

NORFOLK. Kingston?

KINGSTON. These things have all been thought of, my lord.

ANNE. Oh?

KINGSTON. And all forbidden.

ANNE. By whom?

KINGSTON. By him who thinks of everything.

ANNE. By Henry?

(Kingston doesn't answer)

By the king?

NORFOLK (after a pause). He is not allowed to answer, my dear.

ANNE. Yes. By Henry. I understand. But why it's all taken so seriously and black-browed, that I don't understand at all. Nobody can actually believe that I'm guilty. Or actually find me guilty.

NORFOLK. My dear, do you think you could bring yourself to live quietly somewhere—out of the kingdom—such a place as Antwerp—and not claim your rights here further?

ANNE. I could be quiet. I'd be glad to be quiet. You're offering me something. If I resign my queenship—and the succession?

NORFOLK. Suppose you made it easy—to annul your marriage? Could you do that?

ANNE. What would it mean for Elizabeth?

NORFOLK. She'd go to Antwerp with you.

ANNE. And it would go back to what Henry wanted in the first place. I'd be a mistress—a discarded mistress with an unfathered child. No. I'd have to refuse that.

NORFOLK. But—if you do—won't the peers have to find you guilty, Anne?

ANNE. Even though I'm not?

(He is silent)

And you?

NORFOLK. I'd have no choice. I must impose a sentence commensurate with the guilt they find.

ANNE. I'd have to die then?

(He is silent)

By the headsman?

(He is still silent)

I can't believe it.

NORFOLK. It's not certain, of course. I'm not sure. Speak well at your trial, girl. You can do it, none better. None as well. Make them listen. That way there may be hope.

(The lights dim.)

ANNE. At my trial?

NORFOLK. Yes. Make it difficult for him. Speak—as if he were there.

(The lights go out. The little barred window appears, then Anne. She is alone in her cell.)

SCENE FOUR

The lights come up on Norfolk seated as a judge at stage left, a clerk below him writing the proceedings of the trial. He writes in a large book that lies on his knees, using an inkhorn that sits on the floor. Henry Norris is in the witness chair. Cromwell, standing, acts as prosecutor. A group of peers are faintly seen above and behind Norfolk.

CROMWELL. I ask you this question for the last time, Henry Norris, and I warn you that there is mercy in this court only for those who tell truth. What were your relations with the queen?

NORRIS. Speaking truly, Master Cromwell, I can say only what I have said before— that I have always honored Her Majesty, Queen Anne, for her wit and presence and her conduct of the court, and also for her known and unquestioned virtue. Whoever has slandered her enough to say that there was ever a breath of wrong between her and me—he lies, no matter who he is, or where.

(As Norris speaks we see Anne seated listening as the defendant in the trial. Then, on the opposite side of the stage, we see that a curtain, or arras, is hung along the wall, and that King Henry sits concealed behind it, hearing the trial.)

CROMWELL. Your guilt is open and known, sir. You will find it useless to deny it.

NORRIS. You have brought no witnesses against me. I am unjustly accused in this star chamber and quite guiltless—and I believe the queen to be quite as guiltless as I am.

CROMWELL. Remove Henry Norris and bring Mark Smeaton in again.

(A bailiff comes forward to lead Norris out.)

NORRIS. Lord Norfolk, this is no just procedure! Do you continue to lend it your countenance?

NORFOLK. Every man to his own conscience, lad.

NORRIS. God keep me from yours!

NORFOLK. That he will do.

NORRIS. The one witness the prosecution has found is a loose-mouthed woman of sinister reputation! The queen has denied her guilt! The five men accused with her deny their guilt and hers—in spite of torture, bribes, and promises of acquittal!

(Henry rises in his place, uneasy.)

NORFOLK. Let us proceed with the case The next witness.

(Norris is led out. Smeaton is brought in He is pale and broken. The mark of a rope appears on his forehead. He sits and looks down.)

CROMWELL. Swear him.

(A bailiff takes a Bible to Smeaton, lays his hand on it. Henry sits.)

BAILIFF. Do you swear to tell the truth at this trial?

SMEATON. Yes.

(The bailiff takes the Bible away.)

CROMWELL. Again I warn you, Mark Smeaton, that there will be mercy only for those who tell truth. What were your relations with the woman who sits here, the former Queen Anne?

SMEATON. My lord, I have told only the truth. So far as I know she is innocent. I am innocent.

CROMWELL. Do you wish to spend another half hour with the executioner?

SMEATON. No.

CROMWELL. Then truthfully. Did you have carnal relations with Queen Anne?

SMEATON. My lord, you don't want the truth—

CROMWELL. Did you have carnal relations with Queen Anne? And this time have a care of yourself. I shan't ask you again!

(A silence)

Answer!

SMEATON *(looking desperately round the court, then again at the floor)*. Yes.

CROMWELL. Did you answer yes?

SMEATON *(low)*. Yes.

CROMWELL. He confesses it. *(To the clerk)* Be sure this is written. *(To Smeaton)* You had relations with the queen at sundry times and places?

SMEATON. Yes.

CROMWELL. Why, now you begin to talk like a man. Now we begin to think well of you, and you shall be treated like a man. Take him to his cell and let him rest. Let us have Norris again!

ANNE *(to Norfolk)*. My lord! My lord of Norfolk!

NORFOLK. Yes, Lady Anne.

ANNE. May I question this man—Mark Smeaton?

NORFOLK. Why do you wish to question him?

ANNE. You know this is not a trial, Uncle Norfolk! It's like an evil dream, with no witnesses, no defense for the accused, no sifting of evidence, no waft of air from outside, and yet I'm being tried here for my life—and five men are being tried! Since no man speaks for me or examines for me, let me speak and examine for myself!

CROMWELL. Take him to his cell.

NORFOLK. Lord Cromwell examines for you.

ANNE. He! He brought me here! He is my accuser!

NORFOLK. Why, let her question Mark Smeaton.

(Smeaton is brought back.)

ANNE. Thank you, my lord. Mark, look at me.

(He looks at her, then away)

I know well you've been tortured, but you know it's not true—what you've said about you and me. Why do you say it?

SMEATON *(low)*. It is true.

CROMWELL *(to the clerk)*. Write that. He says it is true.

ANNE. Mark, you poor lad, I've been at the other end of the process, and I know the wiles they use on the rats and rabbits they catch in their trap. I know why you've changed your mind and say now that I'm guilty. They've promised you your life if you'll say it. But they won't keep their word, Mark. After you've testified they'll find you guilty and worthy of death.

(Smeaton is silent.)

CROMWELL. He's said it three times now. We have our evidence.

ANNE. Isn't it better, if we're to die, that we die with the truth on our lips? You can't save me or save yourself, but you will save something if you refuse to utter a falsehood with the last breath you have. It's a pernicious falsehood, and its influence will go on forever. It's the word you will be remembered for.

SMEATON *(desperate)*. It's not a falsehood! It's true! I'm guilty! I was guilty with the queen! Let me go! Let me go! I was guilty! The queen was guilty! Let me go free!

CROMWELL. Take him to his cell.

ANNE. Who do you say it for, Mark? For Cromwell, here, this hollow-ground death's man? He's promised life to uncounted monks and men—and seen them hastily buried. It's his trade. He's done it for me—to my shame!

SMEATON. She came to my bed! I swear it!

ANNE. Mark, Mark!

CROMWELL. Take him out!

(The bailiff leads Mark Smeaton toward the exit, but before they can go Henry has risen in his chair suddenly, tipping it over backward, and making enough noise to startle the court. He strides into the scene, his eyes on Smeaton.)

ANNE. Ah! He who sees everything, who knows everything! The king!

(At his entrance, though he takes no note of them, the peers all rise and bow. Cromwell bows.)

HENRY *(to Smeaton)*. Give your testimony again! You say the queen came to your bed. When? How many times?

SMEATON *(not looking up)*. Many times.

HENRY. When was this?

SMEATON. I don't remember.

HENRY. You will remember! Call it to mind, man, or you'll speak with those who can jog your memory? When did this happen? Where?

SMEATON. At York place.

HENRY. You lie. It could never have happened at York place—for you slept in a room with two others!

SMEATON. No, no, it was at Windsor!

HENRY. Fool! She went to Windsor only with me. Can you find no better lie!

SMEATON. It was many places! She came to my bed! It was wherever you like, whenever you like! Oh, God help me, let me go! Let me go free! I'll say whatever you like!

HENRY. Did Cromwell promise you your

life if you said this?

CROMWELL. My lord!

HENRY (*knocking pen and book from the clerk's hand*). Cease this pen-scratching! Answer me! Did he say you would live?

SMEATON. Yes.

HENRY. He lied to you. You're to die, musician. Say what you like, you're to die! Speak now without lying, for it gains you nothing!

SMEATON. Why am I to die?

HENRY. You're to die in any case, whatever's said from here on. And now that you know that, what happened between you and the queen?

SMEATON (*coming to himself*). Between the queen and me? Nothing. She was kind and pleasant and just. I wouldn't hurt her. But they've broken me with ropes and irons—and wooden wedges.

HENRY. Take him out.

(*A bailiff leads Smeaton out*)

And yet it could be true. (*To Anne*) You were no virgin when I met you first. You told me as much. You knew what it was to have men.

ANNE. Have you stepped into your own trap, my lord? Any evidence you have against me you yourself bought and paid for. Do you now begin to believe it?

HENRY (*looks at her steadily for a moment, then turns*). I was a fool to come here!

ANNE. Why did you come?

HENRY. Because I wanted to know!

(*He faces her again*)

Because I wanted to know! And still I don't know!

And no man ever knows!

ANNE. Whether I was unfaithful to you?

HENRY. Yes! Just that! Whether you were unfaithful to me while I loved you! But I'll never know! Whether you say aye or no I won't be sure either way! Fool that I am! That all men are!

ANNE. There are fools and fools, King Henry. Do you have a moment to hear my side of it?

HENRY. No.

ANNE. Go then.

But when you speak of fools—you've shut me up here

to be tried for adultery and treason toward you.

I'm tried as if in a coffin—and those with me—

in a coffin—the lid closed—no evidence—

no voice—no air to breathe—no cell mates for us but torture—

or lies—or false promises.

You've done this because you love elsewhere—

you want to forget me utterly, go on, have sons—

and it's easy with me—it's only a death—

not like that dreadful years-long tug of worlds

you had to go through with Katharine.

So you do this—and I know it—

but now you come here

to make sure whether there were truly adultery,

because that would touch your manhood—or your pride!

And you sit and listen, a cat in a corner,

watching the pet mouse run before it dies.

And then you come out—to make sure!

And, oh fool of fools,

even so, my heart and my eyes

are glad of you!

Fool of all women that I am,

I'm glad of you here!

Go, then. Keep your pride of manhood.

You know about me now.

HENRY. Nan—

ANNE. Mind, I ask no pity of you—

for I'm as proud as you—though my heart has played me this trick—

and puts me here and you there—

but I would like to ask you, what kind of court is this

where the peers sit along the wall like painted figures,

saying nothing, and the judge fears the prosecutor,

and the truth isn't wanted?

Are you so afraid of me? Am I such a danger?

HENRY. This court was set up for a purpose.

You know that.

You've seen such courts.

ANNE. Yes.

HENRY. You were given a choice.

ANNE. When?

HENRY. A man you know

came offering you a choice.

I think you recall it.

ANNE. There was some suggestion

the marriage could be nullified.

I said no to that.

The suggestion came from you?

HENRY. It came from me.

ANNE. I'd have to say no again.

HENRY. But think still once more
about it, Nan. I have no wish to harm
you.
I am much moved by what you said. I'd
rather
a year cut out of my life than do you
wrong.
After those words of yours.
Did you say—
Did you say truly, you were glad of me
here?
ANNE. I won't say it again.
But I did say it.
And it was true.
HENRY. Then,
let's do this all gently, Nan,
for old times' sake.
I have to prove that I can father a king
to follow me.
That was why I left Katharine—
why I turned to you.
It's why I must leave you now and turn
to someone else,
but it can be done all simply and gently,
without this court or the headsman.
ANNE. How?
HENRY. If I'm to marry again
you must somehow free me. Divorce won't
do,
because that would leave Elizabeth the
heir.
Nullification of our marriage—that—
if you would agree to it, and sign away
all rights, and live at some distance—
that would do it.
ANNE. Why must you leave a king to
follow you, Henry?
Why not a queen?
HENRY. This country's never been ruled
by a queen.
I doubt that it could be.
You and I,
we'll not have a son now.
God has spoken there.
I must have my king's sons elsewhere.
And it grows late.
I'm not young as I was.
ANNE. And what do you want of me?
HENRY. Go quietly. Sign the nullification.
Live abroad with Elizabeth. You'll be
cared for.
Leave me free.
ANNE. No.
Once we danced together, and I told you
any children we had
would be bastards. You promised me

to change that—now you dance out of
your promise
and reduce to bastards again. Well, I
won't do it.
We were king and queen, man and wife
together. I keep that.
Take it from me as best you can.
HENRY. You do leave no choice.
ANNE. Would you let this grind on
the way it's going?
HENRY. You would, if it served your pur-
pose.
ANNE. I?
HENRY. I remember
your saying, "Let them die," upon a time.
You've forgotten it, no doubt.
ANNE. No, I did say it.
These things look different from the other
end.
If I'd known then what I feel now—
I couldn't have done it.
HENRY. No.
ANNE. I've been your wife.
Could you do it to me?
HENRY. Yes. If you stood in my way.
Defiantly. As you do.
ANNE. You're not old. You've been long a
king.
But you're still young and could change.
You said—on that one day when we loved
each other—
you remember—that one day when I
loved you
and you loved me—that you would change
—would seek justice—
would be such a king as men had hoped
you'd be
when you came to the throne?
It's not too late for that.
Only if you harden in your mind toward
me,
and say, it's nothing, like the other rats
and rabbits
let her be cut and torn and buried—
then I think
it will be indeed too late.
The king—the great king
you might have been, will have died in
you.
HENRY. Now I'll tell you truly.
I do want to begin again.
And I can't with you.
You brought me into blood—that bloody
business
of the death of More and all the pitiful
folk
who were like him and wouldn't sign.

Your hand was to that. It's bloodstained.

ANNE. And yours? Not yours?
Will you give back what you stole from the monasteries,
and the men executed?
Will you resume with Rome?
When you do that I'll take your word again.
But you won't do it.
And what you truly want—
you may not know it—
is a fresh, frail, innocent maid who'll make you feel
fresh and innocent again,
and young again.
Jane Seymour is the name. It could be anyone.
Only virginal and sweet. And when you've had her
you'll want someone else.

HENRY. It's not true.

ANNE. Meanwhile, to get her,
You'll murder if you must.

HENRY *(angry)*. Why, then you've decided. And so have I.
Norfolk!
(He starts away.)

ANNE *(flashing out)*. Before you go, perhaps
You should hear one thing—
I lied to you.
I loved you, but I lied to you! I was untrue!
Untrue with many!

HENRY. This is a lie.

ANNE. Is it? Take it to your grave! Believe it!
I was untrue!

HENRY. Why, then, it's settled.
You asked for it. You shall have it.

ANNE. Quite correct.
Only what I take to my grave you take to yours!
With many! Not with one! Many!

HENRY *(to Norfolk)*. She's guilty! She dies!
Proceed with this mummery.
(He turns.)

NORFOLK. May we have your signature, my lord?

HENRY. Lend me your pen.
(He takes the clerk's pen from his hand, pulls a paper from his pocket, and sits to write. The lights dim on all those present save Henry and Anne)
She lies, she lies. She was not unfaithful to me.

And yet—if she were—
She could—any woman could—
and yet she lies!
If she lies, let her die for lying!
Let her die.
(He writes)
Oh God, oh God,
sometimes I seem to sit in a motionless dream,
and watch while I do a horrible thing
and know that I do it,
and all the clocks in all the world stand still—waiting.
What is she thinking in this halted interval
while no mote falls through the shaft of sunlight
and no man takes a breath?

ANNE *(to herself, as the lights dim on Henry)*. I've never thought what it was like to die.
To become meat that rots. Then food for shrubs,
and the long roots of vines.
The grape could reach me.
I may make him drunk before many years.
Someone told me the story
of the homely daughter of Sir Thomas More
climbing at night up the trestles of London Bridge
where they'd stuck her father's head on a spike—
and climbing down with it, and taking it home.
To bury in the garden perhaps.
Even so, it was death. And I ordered it.
And Bishop Fisher, the old frail man.
And Houghton.
And the thousands.
They lie there now. And the roots find them.
—That was my dream! I remember—
poor homely Margaret
climbing into the darkness above the bridge
and hunting among the stinking and bloody heads
of criminals, till she found her father's head,
and pulling it from the spike,
holding on with one hand, crying, almost falling,
his beard matted and hard with blood.
Then she must clasp the horrible thing against her breast,

and climb down in the dark, holding by
  one hand,
slipping, near falling, unable to see for
  tears.
"Where is your father's head?" they asked
  her.
"In earth," she said proudly. "How far
  do you pursue a great man after his
  death?"
And they haven't found it, still. . . .
Would they fix my head up on London
  Bridge?
No. Even Henry would object to that.
I've been his queen. He's kissed my lips.
He wouldn't want it. I'll lie in lead—or
  brass. Meat. Dead meat.
But if my head were on the bridge he
  wouldn't climb to take it down.
Nobody'd climb for me. I could stay and
  face up the river,
and my long hair blow out and tangle
  round
the spikes—and my small neck.
Till the sea birds took me,
and there was nothing but a wisp of hair
and a cup of bone.
Sir Thomas More made a jest before he
  died.
He spoke to the headsman at the foot of
  the scaffold—
"Friend," he said, "if you'll help me to
  get up,
I'll see to the coming down."
I must think of something to say when
  the time comes.
If I could say it—with the ax edge toward
  me.
Could I do it? Could I lay my head
  down—
and smile, and speak? Till the blow
  comes?
They say it's subtle. It doesn't hurt.
  There's no time.
No time. That's the end of time.
I wonder what will come of my little girl
when she must go on alone.
HENRY (*rising, the paper in his hands*).
  Shall I tear this?
ANNE. No.
Go your way, and I'll go mine.
You to your death, and I to my expiation.
For there is such a thing as expiation.
It involves dying to live.
HENRY. Death is a thing the coroner can
  see.
I'll stick by that.

ANNE. A coroner wouldn't know you died
  young, Henry.
And yet you did.
HENRY (*turning away*). Burn these records!
(*He kicks the clerk's book, which lies on
the floor, and goes out. The lights go out
on the scene.*)

SCENE FIVE

*The lights come up on Henry, who sits
writing in his accustomed place. There
are papers before him, and a number of
pens, also an inkhorn. A penknife lies
with the pens.*

———

HENRY. I've worked all night.
There's light in the window.
They say you need less sleep as you grow
  older.
Or more.
One or the other. This night I've had
  none.
(*He puts out a hand*)
Yet my hand's steady as a tree.
And the writing's firm as a boy's.
This is the morning she's to die. I'd al-
  most forgotten.
That would have shaken me, ten years
  ago.
Not now.
(*He lays the quill down*)
I need a new pen.
(*He takes up the penknife and begins to
cut a new quill with practiced hand. The
boom of a single cannon is heard*)
Nan is dead. Well, so much for Nan.
  That's over.
(*He pares tranquilly at the quill. Sudden-
ly there's blood on the paper and on his
hands. He rises, throws down the knife
and quill, stanching the blood with a
handkerchief*)
And so your hands are steady, are they?
(*He needs and finds another kerchief*)
Open the bag you lug behind you, Henry.
Put in Nan's head.
Nan's head,
and her eyes, and the lips you kissed.
Wherever you go they'll follow after you
  now.
Her perfume will linger
in every room you enter, and the stench
of her death will drive it out. . . .
Get on with your work.

(He sits, wraps a kerchief about his hand, dips the new pen, and writes)
These are not empty things you do.
(As he bends over his table Anne is seen standing opposite him. Her hair is piled on top of her head, and the fur collar turned down. There is a ring of blood about her neck. Henry looks up)
It's Nan.
No doubt I'll sometimes see you when I'm alone.
It's not over yet between us, is it?
Strangely enough
it will never be over between us, or in our world,
Nan girl. More than that—what we did, thinking we did it for ourselves—our hate and our passion—
these were somehow arranged for us by our masters—
by the people of this kingdom—
or made use of by them.
You thought you did what you wished.
I thought, no, I was the cleverer—all went as I wished.
But truly it all went as the people wished.

We were the puppets and they dangled us to a tune they were playing.
(She smiles)
Why do you smile?
That's not quite true, is it? That's my sophistry again.
I can hear you saying that the blame is ours, that for what we do we pay, that nothing's ever forgiven.
Perhaps.
But one thing we do know—it will never be ended,
never be put back the way it was.
Nothing can ever be put back the way it was.
The limb that was cut from Rome won't graft to that trunk again.
What we were will be permanent in England,
however it came about,
whether your will,
or mine,
or theirs.

CURTAIN

Bell, Book and Candle

BY JOHN VAN DRUTEN

First presented by Irene Mayer Selznick at the Ethel Barrymore Theatre in New York on November 14, 1950, with the following cast:

GILLIAN HOLROYD	Lilli Palmer	NICKY HOLROYD	Scott McKay
SHEPHERD HENDERSON	Rex Harrison	SIDNEY REDLITCH	Larry Gates
MISS HOLROYD	Jean Adair		

ACT ONE

Scene One: Christmas Eve.
Scene Two: About three hours later.

ACT TWO

Two weeks later.

ACT THREE

Scene One: Four hours later.
Scene Two: Two months later.

The action passes throughout in Gillian Holroyd's apartment in the Murray Hill district of New York City.

Bell, Book and Candle is not the weightiest of John van Druten's contributions to either the British or the American stage, but the expertness with which this fantastic comedy is maneuvered on the stage is derived from long experience in the theatre. Many less seasoned playwrights might have come a cropper in writing comedy and many more in managing fantasy; season after season is strewn with their wreckage.

John van Druten, who was born in London in 1901 of an English mother and a Dutch father, served a novitiate as a schoolmaster, which is not uncustomary for British authors. Familiarity with academic backgrounds was, indeed, usefully present in one of his latest and most serious plays, *The Druid Circle*, produced in 1947. Van Druten became a lecturer in English law and legal history at University College in Wales after receiving a Bachelor of Laws degree from London University. During the three years of his lectureship, however, he wrote steadily, turning out poems, articles, stories—and plays. His second attempt at playwriting was the celebrated drama of school life and adolescence, *Young Woodley*. It did not immediately settle him in the theatre because the play was not approved by the Lord Chancellor, by whom all professional stage productions must be licensed in England. Van Druten therefore turned his material into a novel. *Young Woodley* was first presented in New York City—in 1925; London first saw the piece in 1928. After that date, however, Mr. van Druten became a prolific playwright. His forte proved to be comedy of manners, such as *Old Acquaintance* and the vastly popular war-time romance *The Voice of the Turtle*, which started a long Broadway run in December, 1943. He diversified his work the next year with the affecting dramatization *I Remember Mama*, which was made especially memorable by the performance of the recently deceased sweet lady of the theatre Mady Christians. And Mr. van Druten, having acquired an enviable mastery of directing for the stage by watching many productions, also kept his hand in the theatre by staging his own plays.

While still a British subject, Mr. van Druten visited us in 1926 and 1927, and toured our lecture circuits as a successful author. We approved him as a lecturer and we liked him as a playwright. The affection proved reciprocal and Mr. van Druten, taking up residence here, became a naturalized American in 1944. Neither the playwright nor the nation has had reason to regret the association, which continued to be mutually profitable during the season of 1951-52, to which he contributed the successful *I Am a Camera*, winner of the Drama Critics Award for the best American play of the year.

ACT ONE

SCENE ONE

The scene throughout is Gillian Holroyd's apartment in New York. It is a first-floor apartment of a converted brown-stone house in the Murray Hill district—the East thirties.

The living room is interesting and comfortable. There is nothing of the interior decorator about it. It is a little on the dark side—paneled walls, maybe; a number of drawings and books; a large and comfortable couch. The furniture is good, but neither modern nor antique: family-looking stuff, mainly, from Gillian's childhood. Some colored glass, and a witchball or two.

There is a swing door to the kitchen, and another door to the bedroom—probably on the same side of the stage. An open fireplace with a fire burning. An alcove with windows, looking on to the street. The front door to the apartment is at the back, and opens straight into the room.

It is Christmas Eve, about six in the evening. The curtains are open. There is a Christmas tree, trimmed and lighted.

When the curtain rises, Gillian is alone on the stage. She is twenty-seven, small, alert, direct, very attractive. She wears a simple and perhaps slightly arty dinner dress. She is seated with a cat in her arms, stroking and talking to it. She is in the half-dark, lighted only by the fire and the street lamps through the window.

GILLIAN *(talking to the cat).* Oh, Pye—Pye—Pyewacket—what's the matter with me? Why do I feel this way? It's all such a *rut.* And you can't get away from it. It was just the same in Mexico. You know it was. Were the Mexican cats any different from the ones you know in New York? *(She starts to wander, still carrying the cat)* Why don't you give me something for Christmas? What would I like? I'd like to meet someone *different.* Yes, all right. Like the man upstairs, then. *(She looks out of the window, then draws back a step, so as not to be seen)* There he is, coming in now. Did *you* do that? No, you couldn't have. But he *is* attractive, don't you think? Why don't I ever meet people like that? . . . What's the matter? Want to go out? *(She opens the swing door to the kitchen)* All right, then, Pyewacket. There you are. *(She sets the cat down, outside, and returns. There is a knock on the door)* Who's there? *(She switches on the lights and opens the door. Shep Henderson is standing outside. He is a man of anywhere from thirty-five up, masculine and attractive. He wears day clothes, a topcoat and carries his hat. He also carries a couple of Christmas-wrapped packages)* Oh . . .

SHEP. Miss Holroyd?

GILLIAN. Yes.

SHEP. My name's Shepherd Henderson. I live on the floor above. Are you my landlady?

GILLIAN. Yes. How do you do?

SHEP. Are you busy, or could I see you for a minute?

GILLIAN. Certainly. Come in, won't you?

SHEP. Thanks. *(He does so, shutting the door behind him)*

GILLIAN. Take off your coat.

SHEP *(doing so).* Thanks. I won't keep you, long. I imagine you're going out. I am, too. *(Showing the packages)* I've just been getting some last-minute presents I forgot. Well, now . . .

GILLIAN *(interrupting).* Would you like a drink?

SHEP. I don't think I ought to take time for that. And . . . I don't know that this is an altogether friendly call. . . .

GILLIAN. Oh?

SHEP. You've been away ever since I moved in. . . .

GILLIAN. Is anything wrong? You should have called the agents.

SHEP. I did. But—well, I'm afraid it doesn't seem to have done much good.

GILLIAN. What's the trouble?

SHEP. The lady on the floor above me. I think she's your aunt.

GILLIAN. Yes?

SHEP. Did you ever give her a key to my apartment?

GILLIAN *(astonished).* No, of course not. Why?

SHEP. Well, she's been in it a couple of times. I found her there. And I'm afraid I don't awfully like it.

GILLIAN. No. Naturally. But how did she get in?

SHEP. She said she found the door open. That *may* have been true the first time, though I don't think so. I know it wasn't true, the second. And—even if it were ...

GILLIAN (*shutting up somewhat; something almost guilty about her, as though she knows more than she is saying*). Oh, I'm sorry.

SHEP. Yes, well, I thought I'd better tell you, now that you're back.

GILLIAN (*worried*). Yes, of course. Is that all?

SHEP. Isn't it enough?

GILLIAN (*laughing, but uncomfortably*). I didn't mean that.

SHEP. As a matter of fact, it's *not* really all. I—er—think your aunt is rather a peculiar lady.

GILLIAN (*still worried, and not giving at all*). Oh?

SHEP. Is she by any chance studying dramatics?

GILLIAN. Dramatics?

SHEP. Well, I can hear her at night through the ceiling, and it sounds as if she were *reciting*—or something.

GILLIAN (*with obviously embarrassed knowledge*). Oh.

SHEP. Oh, you know about that? What *is* it that she's doing—or shouldn't I ask?

GILLIAN. Well, it is a *kind* of dramatics. You can't hear what she says?

SHEP. No. And I'm sorry, but there's another thing. Her cooking. At least, again I guess that's what it is. Unless she's an amateur chemist. It doesn't smell like anything I'd be willing to eat.

GILLIAN. It's not cooking. She—she *makes* things. Perfumes and—lotions, and things.

SHEP. It's not *my* idea of perfume.

GILLIAN (*smiles, but still uneasily*). And that *is* all?

SHEP (*half-amused*). You sound as if you were expecting something worse.

GILLIAN (*unconvincingly*). No. No.

SHEP. Well, I'm sorry, but there *is* something else. Though I can't be sure it's she who does it.

GILLIAN. What's that?

SHEP. Well, ever since I caught her in my place—and talked to the agents about it—rather firmly, I'm afraid—I imagine they spoke to *her*—my telephone's started ringing at eight o'clock every morning—and around midnight, too—and when I answer it, there's no one there. I've talked to the telephone company, but they can't trace anything.

GILLIAN. And you think it's Aunt Queenie?

SHEP. I've no *proof* that that is. But—well ...

GILLIAN (*with decision, frankly*). Mr. Henderson, I'm most awfully sorry. I'll talk to Aunt Queenie. She *is* a little—eccentric, but I promise you none of this will happen again.

SHEP. *Can* you promise?

GILLIAN. Yes. I can. I really can.

SHEP. Well, thanks, then. I don't mean to be unpleasant. ...

GILLIAN. I'm only sorry I've not been here before.

SHEP (*rising*). You've been traveling about, I understand.

GILLIAN. Yes, I've been in Haiti, and Mexico.

SHEP. Whereabouts in Mexico?

GILLIAN. I had a house in Taxco.

SHEP. You didn't, by any chance, run into Redlitch down there, did you? The man who wrote that book on magic. *Magic in Mexico.*

GILLIAN. No, he'd left by the time I got there. (*Rather searchingly*) Why—are you interested in that sort of thing?

SHEP. Not personally—but professionally. I'm a publisher.

GILLIAN. Did you publish his book?

SHEP. No, but I wish I had. It sold like the Kinsey Report.

GILLIAN. I can't think why.

SHEP (*shrugging*). It was sensational.

GILLIAN. And completely phony. They fed him a whole lot of fake tourist stuff, and he swallowed it whole.

SHEP. Maybe they did that to Kinsey, too. But I hear that Redlitch is ready to change publishers, and I'd kind of like his next one. I've written to him several times, but I got no answer.

GILLIAN (*eagerly*). If you'd like to meet him ...

SHEP. Oh, do you know him?

GILLIAN. No, but I know people who do. I can arrange it.

SHEP. I'd appreciate that, very much. Well, I'll get along.

GILLIAN. You won't have that drink now? There are some Martinis in the kitchen.

SHEP. I mustn't. I'm late. But—if I may have a raincheck ...

GILLIAN. Yes, of course. And I'll have Redlitch here to meet you.

SHEP. That would be fine. I hear he's a drunk and a nut, but . . . (*Looking at a drawing on the wall*) Say, that's kind of interesting. Who did that?

GILLIAN. My brother.

SHEP. He's good. Ought I to know his stuff?

GILLIAN. I don't think so. Nicky's very lazy.

SHEP (*looking at the drawing again*). It's a strange face. Who is it, do you know?

GILLIAN (*after a half beat's pause*). It's a Brazilian girl who used to dance in a night club here. A place called the Zodiac.

SHEP. I don't know it.

GILLIAN. I don't imagine you would.

SHEP. Why not?

GILLIAN. Oh, because—well, it's a sort of—*dive*.

SHEP (*smiling*). But *you* know it?

GILLIAN. I've *been* there. . . .

SHEP. Well . . . (*A knock on the door*) You've got visitors. I must be getting along.

(*Gillian goes to the door. Miss Holroyd is outside. She is an odd-looking woman, vague, fluttery and eccentric. She is dressed in a wispy evening gown, bitty and endy, with a trailing scarf, bangles and a long necklace. When she talks it is in a high, feathery voice, and a trilling little laugh. She carries her cloak, and three gift-wrapped packages.*)

GILLIAN. Oh, Aunt Queenie . . .

MISS HOLROYD. Hello, darling, Merry . . . (*She stops on seeing Shep*) Oh, I didn't know you had company.

GILLIAN. It's all right. this is . . . (*Then, with some meaning*) Oh, yes . . . you know each other.

SHEP (*amused, friendly*). Hello, Miss Holroyd.

MISS HOLROYD (*formally*). How do you do?

SHEP (*starting to leave*). Well . . .

MISS HOLROYD. Don't let me drive you away.

SHEP. I have to go. (*Holding out his hand to Gillian*) Well, good night, and—Merry Christmas.

GILLIAN (*taking his hand*). And to you.

SHEP. Thank you. (*Bowing to Miss Holroyd*) Good night.

(*Miss Holroyd bows, without replying, and he goes. Miss Holroyd walks away with exaggerated nonchalance, aware of the scolding that is coming to her, and trying only to postpone it. Gillian stands watching her, like a cat waiting to pounce.*)

MISS HOLROYD. So you've met him, after all. Do you still think he's attractive?

GILLIAN (*quietly*). Yes, I do. Very.

MISS HOLROYD. Did you—bring him here?

GILLIAN. No. He came here to talk to me. (*Pause. Then, springing it*) About *you.*

MISS HOLROYD (*naïvely*). Me?

GILLIAN. Yes, and it's no good acting innocent. I'm angry. *Really* angry.

MISS HOLROYD. Why, what have I done?

GILLIAN. You know. Broken into his apartment—played tricks with his telephone . . .

MISS HOLROYD. That was because he reported me to the agents. That was just to pay him out.

GILLIAN. I don't care *what* it was. You *promised* when I let you move in here . . .

MISS HOLROYD. I promised to be careful.

GILLIAN. And do you call that being careful? Getting caught in his apartment? Twice!

MISS HOLROYD. What harm did I do? I didn't *take* anything. Yes, I read his letters, but it's not as if I were going to make *use* of them. Though I'm tempted to now —now that he's told on me—to you.

GILLIAN (*menacingly, and quite frighteningly*). Auntie, if you do—well, you'll be sorry. And you know I can *make* you sorry, too.

MISS HOLROYD (*defensively*). He'd never suspect, darling. Not in a million years. No matter *what* I did. Honestly, it's amazing the way people don't. Why, they don't believe there *are* such things. I sit in the subway sometimes, or in busses, and look at the people next to me, and I think: What would you say if I told you I was a witch? And I know they'd never believe it. They just wouldn't believe it. And I giggle and giggle to myself.

GILLIAN. Well, you've got to stop giggling here. You've got to swear, swear on the Manual . . .

MISS HOLROYD (*retreating a step*). Swear what?

GILLIAN. That you'll stop practicing— in this house—ever.

MISS HOLROYD. *You* practice here.

GILLIAN. I can be discreet about it. You can't.

MISS HOLROYD (*very hurt*). I shall move to a hotel.

GILLIAN. Very well. But if you get into trouble there, don't look to *me* to get you out.

MISS HOLROYD (*huffily*). I've other people I can turn to.

GILLIAN (*scornfully*). Mrs. de Pass, I suppose.

MISS HOLROYD. Yes, she's done a lot for me.

GILLIAN. Well, I wouldn't count on Mrs. de Pass, if *I* turn against you. I'm a lot better than *that* old phony. Now . . . (*She gets a large white-bound book from a closet*)

MISS HOLROYD (*really scared*). Oh, please —not on the Manual.

GILLIAN (*relentlessly*). On the Manual. (*She brings it*) Now, put your hand on it. (*Miss Holroyd does so, terrified*) Now, then, I swear that I will not practice witchcraft ever in this house again. So help me Tagla, Salamandrae, Brazo and Vesturiel. Say, "I swear."

MISS HOLROYD (*after a moment*). I swear.

GILLIAN. Good. (*She replaces the book*)

MISS HOLROYD. I think you're very cruel.

GILLIAN (*returning, somewhat softened*). Oh, Auntie, if you'd only have a little sense!

MISS HOLROYD (*continuing*). And hypocritical. Sometimes I think you're *ashamed* of being what you are.

GILLIAN. Ashamed? I'm not in the least ashamed. No, it's not a question of that, but . . . (*Suddenly*) Auntie, don't you ever wish you *weren't*?

MISS HOLROYD (*amazed*). No.

GILLIAN. That you were like those people you sit next to in the busses?

MISS HOLROYD. Ordinary and humdrum? No, I *was*. For years. Before I came into it.

GILLIAN. Well, you came in late. And, anyway, I don't *mean* humdrum. I just mean unenlightened. And I don't hanker for it all the time. Just sometimes.

MISS HOLROYD. Darling, you're depressed. . . .

GILLIAN. I know. I expect it's Christmas. It's always upset me.

MISS HOLROYD. You wait till you get to Zoe's party, and see all your old friends again.

GILLIAN. I don't *want* to see all my old friends again. I want something different.

MISS HOLROYD. Well, come with me to Mrs. de Pass's, then. She's got some very interesting people. Some French people. From the Paris chapter.

GILLIAN (*laughing*). I didn't mean *that*, when I said I wanted something different. I think maybe I'd like to spend the evening with some everyday people for a change, instead of *us*.

MISS HOLROYD (*archly*). With Mr. Henderson?

GILLIAN. I wouldn't mind.

MISS HOLROYD. It's too bad he's getting married. Still, I suppose . . .

GILLIAN. He's getting married?

MISS HOLROYD. Yes, quite soon. They're announcing it New Year's Eve.

GILLIAN. How do you know that? Oh, the telephone, I suppose.

MISS HOLROYD. Yes, dear.

GILLIAN. Who's he getting married to? Do you know?

MISS HOLROYD. I don't know her last name. Her first name's Merle.

GILLIAN. Merle? The only Merle I ever knew was a girl I was in college with. Merle Kittredge. She used to write poison-pen letters. I caught her writing one about me, once. That's why we had all those thunderstorms that spring. She was terrified of them. (*Smiling at the recollection*) We had one every day for a month. It was most extraordinary.

MISS HOLROYD. You mean that that was *you*? (*Delighted*) Oh, Gillian, you were naughty!

GILLIAN. She was a nervous wreck by the end of the term.

MISS HOLROYD. And you think this might be the same girl? What was she like?

GILLIAN. Southern, and blonde, and helpless . . .

MISS HOLROYD. This one's blonde. He's got her picture on his bureau.

GILLIAN (*continuing her catalogue*). And appealing. And underneath, a liar and a sneak and a beau-snatcher.

MISS HOLROYD. Did you ever hear what happened to her?

GILLIAN. I think she became a decorator.

MISS HOLROYD. This one's a decorator.

GILLIAN (*after a moment's pause*). Well,

there's probably more than one decorator in New York called Merle. And, if he's engaged, that rules him out.

MISS HOLROYD. I don't see why.

GILLIAN. I'm not a Southern belle. I don't take other women's men. Though I would, if it *were* Merle Kittredge.

MISS HOLROYD. I could find out for you.

GILLIAN. But — New Year's. That wouldn't leave me much time.

MISS HOLROYD. You wouldn't *need* time. Just a quick little potion. Or—four words to Pyewacket, you once told me.

GILLIAN. Yes, but I wouldn't want him that way. That would take the challenge out of it. Especially with her. Other girls can make men like them in a week, without that. Why can't I?

MISS HOLROYD. Did he seem to like you this afternoon?

GILLIAN (*with rueful humor*). Not very much. No.

MISS HOLROYD (*with sudden alarm*). Gillian, you—you haven't fallen in love with him, and lost your powers, have you? That isn't what this is all about?

GILLIAN (*laughing*). No, of course not.

MISS HOLROYD. Oh, thank goodness!

GILLIAN. You don't *believe* that old wives' tale?

MISS HOLROYD. Of course I do! It's true. They say it's true.

GILLIAN. It's the other way around. We can't fall in love. (*Pause*) Merle Kittredge. I haven't thought of her in years. (*Pause again*) Do you think—if it were she—I could do it in a week—without tricks?

MISS HOLROYD. Darling, it's no good asking me. I never could do it at all. But if it is, why don't you pull a quick one, and have done with it?

GILLIAN. No. I don't say I wouldn't be tempted, but if I've got a week—I'd like to see how good I am, the other way. (*The buzzer sounds. She answers it, unhooking the mouthpiece*) Hello?

NICKY'S VOICE (*in the mouthpiece*). It's me. Nicky.

GILLIAN. Good. (*She buzzes and hangs up*) I'll get the drinks.

(*She goes into the kitchen. Miss Holroyd looks after her—goes to the telephone and stands for a moment with her hand on the receiver, as though to make a call. Then she thinks better of it. The front door opens and Nicky comes in. He is Gillian's brother, a little younger, and has*

an engaging, impish and somewhat impertinent personality. He wears a dinner jacket, topcoat, and carries some small Christmas-wrapped packages.)

MISS HOLROYD. Nicky, dear!

NICKY. Hello, Auntie. Merry Christmas. (*He kisses her*) Where's Gill?

MISS HOLROYD. In the kitchen. (*Looking over her shoulder, and speaking low*) Nicky, will you do something for me?

NICKY (*taking off his coat*). Sure. What??

MISS HOLROYD. Have you got a pencil and paper? (*Sees the block by the telephone*) Oh, this will do. (*She writes on it, tears off the sheet*) Nicky, this number. I want you to fix it for me.

NICKY. Fix it?

MISS HOLROYD. *You* know.

NICKY. Why, who is it?

MISS HOLROYD. Someone I want to—pay back for something.

NICKY. But you can pull that one for yourself. I taught you.

MISS HOLROYD. Yes, but I just had to promise Gillian that I wouldn't in this house any more. So will you do it for me?

NICKY. Anything to oblige. (*He lifts the receiver, holds down the bar and begins to mutter*) Actatus, Catipta, Itapan, Marnutus. (*Gillian returns with a pitcher of Martinis*) Murray Hill 6-4476. (*He hangs up*) Hello, darling.

GILLIAN. What are you two up to? (*Warningly*) Auntie . . .

MISS HOLROYD. I haven't done a thing.

GILLIAN. Whose number was that you were fixing?

NICKY (*putting the paper in his pocket*). No one you know, dear.

GILLIAN. Just a little Christmas present for a friend? No telephone for a week? Oh, Nicky, when will you grow up? How are you?

NICKY. Fine. (*They kiss*) Merry Christmas, darling.

GILLIAN. Pour the drinks, will you, and then we'll have presents.

NICKY (*going to do so*). I'm afraid mine's pretty mingy, dear—but I've never been more broke. You know, I used to wonder when I was a kid why all the witches in history were always poor and miserable old men and women, living in hovels, when you'd have thought they could have anything they wanted. But

I've learned why, since. *(He passes drinks)*

MISS HOLROYD. It's only because they weren't *good enough at it*. Any more than *we* are.

NICKY. Or else they got scared, like Gill here. *(Giving Gillian her glass)* She admitted to me once that she could hex the whole Stock Market if she wanted.

MISS HOLROYD. Oh, Gillian, could you? Really, dear? Why don't you do it?

NICKY. She said she was afraid of the repercussions.

GILLIAN. I didn't say that, at all. Nicky, you still don't know what this kind of thing can do to you—if you go too far. *(Then, breaking off)* But that's nothing to talk about tonight. *(Raising her glass)* Merry Christmas.

MISS HOLROYD AND NICKY. Merry Christman. *(They all drink)*

GILLIAN. Now. *(Getting presents from the tree)* Nicky. Aunt Queenie.

MISS HOLROYD *(bringing her two packages)*. For you, darling. And for Nicky.

NICKY *(doing likewise)*. Gillian. Auntie. *(They start to open their packages.)*

MISS HOLROYD. You two are the hardest people to find presents for. I gave you both the same thing.

GILLIAN *(opening hers)*. A book.

NICKY *(looking at his)*. *Magic in Mexico,* by Sidney Redlitch.

MISS HOLROYD. They're autographed.

GILLIAN. Why—do you know him?

MISS HOLROYD. No, but Mrs. de Pass does. She got them for me.

NICKY. Well, thank you very much. I've heard a lot about it.

MISS HOLROYD. I hope you haven't read it.

GILLIAN. I have. But I'm very glad to have it. Thank you, Auntie. *(To Nicky, who is unwrapping his present)* Careful with those, Nicky. Those are records.

NICKY. Oh, fine. Only . . . *(Ruefully)* I don't have a phonograph any more.

GILLIAN *(smiling)*. I think you'll find you have, when you get home.

NICKY. Oh, darling—no! You shouldn't.

GILLIAN. Why not?

NICKY. It's so extravagant. Or did you . . . *(With a gesture)* "get" it for me? Was it witched, or paid for?

GILLIAN *(smiling)*. None of your business.

NICKY. I know. But tell me.

GILLIAN *(as before, teasingly)*. I will not.

MISS HOLROYD *(severely)*. You shouldn't ask that, Nicky. It's like asking what it cost!

NICKY. Thanks all the same, darling— either way. *(Inspecting the records)* What *are* these?

GILLIAN. A man at a party in Mexico. We took some recordings of the incantations.

NICKY. Oh, wonderful. What are they for?

GILLIAN *(smiling)*. Try them and see. You'll be surprised. Like to have music come out of your ears?

NICKY. No???

GILLIAN. That's the least of them.

NICKY. I'll take them to Natalie's party with me. Think they'll help me make any headway with her?

GILLIAN *(amused)*. Well, this man had quite a way with him. He had a mink as his familiar.

MISS HOLROYD *(unwrapping an elaborate lace mantilla)*. Oh, this is lovely, darling. Simply lovely. *(She puts it on)* What does it *do*?

GILLIAN. It makes you look fascinating.

MISS HOLROYD *(hopefully)*. You mean . . . ?

GILLIAN *(smiling)*. No, Auntie, I'm afraid it has no powers. I just thought it was pretty.

MISS HOLROYD *(very disappointed)*. Oh, it is. Very pretty. I love it.

NICKY *(to Gillian)*. Why didn't you say it had powers, and that you wouldn't tell her what they were? Then she'd have had such fun wearing it, and trying to find out.

MISS HOLROYD *(severely, as before)*. Gillian doesn't tell lies—*ever*.

NICKY. No, but she manages to hold out plenty! *(He hands her a small bottle)* Here's something that has got powers for you, Auntie. It's an unguent. You feel colors. Quite a sensation. *(Teasing her)* Kind of sexy, too. *(She giggles. Then, to Gillian, as she unwraps a small phial)* I got that in a new little shop I've found. It's a sort of paint. For summoning. You just paint it on an image—or a drawing or a photograph, they said—of anyone you want, and then set light to it. And they have to come. I hope it works for you. *I* couldn't even make it light. Try it. Now.

GILLIAN. Whom do we want here?

MISS HOLROYD (*archly*). Him! (*She points to the ceiling*)

GILLIAN. No, *I* know.

NICKY. Who?

GILLIAN (*holding up Redlitch's book*). This man.

NICKY. Redlitch? What on earth for?

GILLIAN. I want to meet him. I've promised to introduce him to somebody. I thought I'd find someone who knew him, but this will save a lot of time. It's got his picture on the back. Auntie, you don't mind if I cut it off?

MISS HOLROYD. Not if I can stay and watch.

GILLIAN (*getting scissors from desk drawer*). How soon is it supposed to work?

NICKY. Depends on how far they've got to come. But within twenty-four hours, nowadays, anyway, I should think. You don't have to stay home, if that's what you're worried about. They'll find you, wherever you are. He'll probably turn up at your party tonight.

GILLIAN (*who has cut out the picture*). Put out the lights, will you? (*Nicky puts out the lights. Again the room is lighted by the fire and the street-lamp*) Auntie, the big ash tray.

NICKY (*bringing a giant square glass ash tray*). There's a little brush in the cork.

GILLIAN. I've found it. (*She smears paint on the picture*) Any words?

NICKY. They said not.

GILLIAN. All right, then. Got a match? (*Nicky produces one.*)

NICKY. Go.

(*Gillian touches a match to the picture, which she has placed in the ash tray. It goes up in blue flame. Miss Holroyd squeals.*)

NICKY. You're a marvel. (*There is a knock on the door*) Not *already*? Gill, that's genius!

GILLIAN (*laughing*). No, of course it isn't. Go and see who it is.

(*Nicky opens the door. Shep is standing outside. He has changed into a dinner jacket, wears a dark topcoat, and carries a carton filled with presents.*)

NICKY. Yes?

SHEP. Is Miss Holroyd in?

GILLIAN. Oh . . . Mr. Henderson—come in. (*She rises, switching on a lamp*)

SHEP. I'm sorry if I'm disturbing you. Are you having indoor fireworks?

GILLIAN. Oh—no—no, it's just some nonsense that my brother gave me. This is my brother. Mr. Henderson.

SHEP AND NICKY (*together*). How do you do?

SHEP. Please go on with what you were doing.

GILLIAN. It's all right. We'd finished. Really. (*She blows out the flame in the ash tray*) Is there something I can do for you?

SHEP. I just wondered if I might use your telephone? Mine's really turned into a problem child. It's gone right out of order.

GILLIAN (*with a quick look at Miss Holroyd and Nicky, who evade her eyes*). Of course. Come in and help yourself.

SHEP. Well, thank you. (*He sets down the carton, and goes to the phone, talking while he does so and while he dials*) I used mine right after I left here, and it was doing fine. Then, for the last fifteen minutes, I've been getting nothing but a lot of hiccups in my ear.

(*Gillian turns accusingly to Miss Holroyd, who hurries to her cloak.*)

MISS HOLROYD. I really must be going!

SHEP (*hanging up*). Busy. May I wait just a minute?

GILLIAN. Of course. Maybe you'd like to report your line?

SHEP. Oh, thanks. (*He sits again, and dials O*)

GILLIAN. Nicky, that piece of paper you put in your pocket? I'd like to see it for a minute. (*She holds out her hand for it*)

SHEP (*into phone*). Hello, Operator? I want to report a line out of order. Murray Hill 6-4476. (*Gillian receives the paper from Nicky and compares the numbers, simultaneously with this*) I don't know. I can't get a dialing tone. If you would. Thanks. (*He hangs up*)

MISS HOLROYD (*seeing Gillian's face*). It was Nicky.

GILLIAN. I know.

MISS HOLROYD (*smiling, archly*). But I think it's worked out wonderfully. Well, good-bye. And . . . (*With a playful glance at Shep's back*) Good luck.

NICKY. Well, good-bye, Mr. Henderson. I'm glad to have met you.

SHEP. Me, too.

(*They shake hands.*)

NICKY *(to Gillian)*. Can I leave these records here? I'm going to a cocktail party first, and I don't want them to get broken. You know, under all the coats on the bed. I'll pick them up on my way to Natalie's.

GILLIAN. I won't be here.

NICKY. *I* can get in.

GILLIAN *(dubiously)*. Oh—well, all right, then.

MISS HOLROYD *(indignantly)*. Well, really, if Nicky can, I . . .

GILLIAN *(amused)*. I know, Auntie. It's not fair. It's not a bit fair. Take her away, Nicky.

MISS HOLROYD *(put out)*. Good-bye, Mr. Henderson. I hope your telephone gets well, soon.

(Nicky and Miss Holroyd leave.)

SHEP *(going back to the phone)*. I'll try just once more, and then I'll go, too.

GILLIAN. There's no hurry.

SHEP *(dialing)*. You're going out, aren't you?

GILLIAN. Later. But it's not important . . .

SHEP *(getting his number)*. Ah—luck! *(Gillian starts for the kitchen)* You don't have to go.

GILLIAN. I'll be back.

SHEP *(into phone)*. Hello . . . Is Miss Kittredge there? *(Gillian hears this, registers it and then goes into kitchen)* Merle? It's me. I got delayed. I tried to get you, but the phone's gone off again. Darling, they're fed up with my complaints by now. I'm getting a taxi in two shakes, but . . . What? Oh, darling, won't you mind? Really? Well, that's wonderful, bless you. I'll meet you there, then. What is it? *(Gillian returns with the shaker refilled with Martinis)* What's your idea? Tonight? Announce it tonight? Well, wonderful. I thought you were so keen on New Year's Eve. Well, that's fine. Let's tell them all. *(Gillian, having registered this, too, returns to the kitchen)* Yes, I've got everything. All the presents. Yours, theirs, everybody's. Yes, darling, I've got that, too, though why you want it, I can't think. Sure. O.K. *(Gillian returns again, carrying the cat)* Fifteen minutes. I can't wait. Good-bye, darling. Darling! *(He hangs up. Turns and sees Gillian, who moves to a chair, where she sits nursing the cat)* Oh . . . I didn't hear you come back. Is that your cat? I've seen him on the stairs here lately, watch-ing me come in and out. What's his name?

GILLIAN. Pyewacket.

SHEP. How's that?

GILLIAN. Pyewacket.

SHEP *(trying to shake hands with the cat)*. How do you do? Ouch!

GILLIAN. Did he scratch you?

SHEP *(finger in mouth)*. No, he didn't make it.

GILLIAN *(slaps the cat lightly and play-fully)*. Bad cat.

SHEP *(moving as though to say good-bye)*. Well, I've bothered you enough.

GILLIAN. Won't you have that drink now?

SHEP. Thanks, but I'm terribly sorry. I know it must sound as if I were trying to duck it. I'm not—really—but I am late and—tonight's kind of an important night. So if you don't mind . . .

GILLIAN. No, of course not.

SHEP. Thanks all the same. Well . . . *(He puts on his overcoat and hat, and lifts the carton, with his back to her. She goes on stroking the cat)*

GILLIAN. Pye—Pye—Pyewacket—this is Mr. Henderson. Mr. Shepherd Henderson. *(She goes on stroking, and mutters quietly, rhythmically)* Reterrem, Salibat, Cratares, Hisaster.

SHEP *(turning)*. What was that?

GILLIAN. I was talking to Pyewacket. I think he wants to go out.

(She rises, avoiding his eye, and goes into the kitchen. Shep stands for a moment still holding the carton, staring after her. She comes back, without the cat. She holds his eye. She takes a few steps into the room, then stops. Shep takes two steps forward, then sets down the carton, throws his hat aside and moves toward her. She takes a step toward him—then they are in each other's arms.)

CURTAIN

SCENE TWO

The same. About three hours later.

When the curtain rises, Gillian and Shep are stretched on the couch. The room is darker than it was—the curtains are drawn—only one lamp is on, lighting the couch. Shep's hat, coat and muffler are thrown aside. The carton is where it last was. The door to the bedroom is partly open.

———

SHEP *(after a long moment).* Say something.

GILLIAN. What?

SHEP. Anything. It doesn't matter. I just want to hear your voice again.

GILLIAN. Do you like my voice?

SHEP. No. *(She looks up, surprised)* I don't like anything about you. I'm just—*insane* over you. All of you. You should know that, by now. Don't you?

GILLIAN. Well . . .

SHEP. Don't you?

GILLIAN *(with a satisfied smile).* Well, you made it charmingly apparent.

(A long silence of sheer contentment falls on them.)

SHEP. You know, there's a wonderful, suspended, *timeless* feeling to this moment, and the two of us like this. I feel—spellbound.

GILLIAN *(quietly).* Stay that way.

SHEP. I don't ever want to move. *(Another pause)* What are you thinking?

GILLIAN. Nothing. Not a thing. And you?

SHEP. Nothing, either. I can't think. Certainly not this close to you. I've got to start soon, though. Very soon. *(He rises. She remains curled on the couch)*

GILLIAN. What about?

SHEP *(grimly).* A lot of things. *(He goes to the drink table)* I think I'd better fix myself a drink. Can I fix you one?

GILLIAN. No, thanks.

(Shep mixes himself a highball. She watches him, stilly, rather like a cat. Then he looks, amazed, at his watch.)

SHEP. Do you happen to know what time it is?

GILLIAN. No.

SHEP. It's ten o'clock. A good three hours since I came in here. Since I went to that door to leave.

GILLIAN. Well?

SHEP. Doesn't that seem strange to you?

GILLIAN. Not strange . . . It—happened . . .

SHEP. Nothing like this has ever happened to *me*, before.

GILLIAN. Do you mind?

SHEP. I *ought* to mind. . . .

GILLIAN. Why?

SHEP. In the first place, I was on my way to a party.

GILLIAN. And you found something you'd rather do.

SHEP. That, my girl, is an understatement. I found something I couldn't resist doing.

GILLIAN *(smiling).* You don't have to explain to me.

SHEP. It's fantastic. *(He comes back to the couch, sets down his drink, sits beside her, taking her hands)* Gillian—tell me—just what has it meant to you?

GILLIAN. Meant?

SHEP. These three hours.

GILLIAN. They've been—enchantment.

SHEP. And that's all?

GILLIAN. What more?

SHEP. I don't know. I know it doesn't make sense, but somewhere, I've got an idea—that I must be in love with you. . . . Are you—at all in love with me?

GILLIAN. I like you more than I can say.

SHEP. That wasn't what I asked you.

GILLIAN. Do we have to talk about it?

SHEP. Yes, I've got to know.

GILLIAN. Why?

SHEP. Because I've got to face a few decisions.

GILLIAN. Now?

SHEP. I should think so. There are people waiting for me—wondering where the hell I am. There's a whole future that's either got completely shot to hell, or else—well, I've got to do some fast talking. Some *very* fast talking. And I'd like to know where I stand. Where *we* stand.

GILLIAN. What do you want to do?

SHEP *(slowly).* Right at the moment, I want never to stop seeing you. *(He stares into her eyes, and then kisses her deeply, tenderly, hungrily)* Is it possible—that I can—never stop seeing you?

GILLIAN. You can see me all you want.

SHEP. It hasn't hit you as it has me.

GILLIAN. I want you just as much as you want me.

SHEP. You do?

GILLIAN. And I'm happy. Very happy.

SHEP. Look, I haven't asked you, but—I guess you're free and unattached.

GILLIAN. Yes.

SHEP. Well, that makes a difference—for you. You don't have to ask yourself questions. I do. I'm not free. The thing I've got to decide is—am I going to cut free?

GILLIAN. Do you want to?

SHEP. I've told you I want to. But—what future is there in it?

GILLIAN. It can go on like this.

SHEP. For always?

GILLIAN. Does anything go on for always?

SHEP. One likes to think that some things can. I don't know whether this is one of those things that burn themselves out—but if it is, well, it's a hell of a fire. Maybe that's the kind that burns out quickest. I don't know. I know it's crazy to talk about love—yet—but I just wish I could be sure.

GILLIAN. Of what?

SHEP. Whether this is it. If it's not, it's a pretty good facsimile.

GILLIAN. I think—that for me, too.

SHEP. And that will do for the answer. And now I think I'll have to use your telephone.

GILLIAN. Go right ahead.

SHEP. And this time—do you mind?— I'd like to be left alone.

GILLIAN. Of course. *(She rises, and starts for the bedroom. He stops her)*

SHEP. You're amazing, do you know it? *(He kisses her passionately, and holds her)* More than amazing!

GILLIAN *(in his arms)*. Shep—it has hit me—quite hard.

(They stay together a long moment, then she leaves and goes into the bedroom, closing the door. Shep stands where he is for a moment, then he finishes his drink in one big swallow to nerve himself—goes to the telephone, and then dials.)

SHEP *(into phone)*. Is that Miss Carlson's apartment? I'd like to speak to Miss Kittredge, please. And—is there some place where she can sit down for a minute? I mean, where she can talk without being disturbed Yes, I wish you would. *(He holds on, carrying the phone to the coffee table, where he nervously and absent-mindedly lights two cigarettes, one after the other. Then he answers, again, in a high, nervous voice)* Merle? This is me. I'm—out some place. I know. That's what I'm calling about. I can't get there. I can't get there! No, not at all. Never. I've suddenly realized—it's no good. It's no use. Us. I mean—us! Yes, I'm afraid that is—just what I mean. I can't explain. I don't understand it, myself. Yes—yes— okay, let's have it. *(He listens, wretchedly)* Yes . . . yes . . . Ouch! No, it's all right. I'm still here. Go on, I deserve it. Say it all. Yes, I am. Yes, I'm that. Yes, I guess

I'm that, too! No, wait a minute, I'm *not* that! *(She has hung up. He clicks the receiver hook, then slowly hangs up, himself)* I guess I am. *(He replaces the phone. Then calls, off)* You can come back now. *(Gillian returns.)*

GILLIAN. Well?

SHEP. It's done. Do you want to know about it?

GILLIAN. Do you want to tell me?

SHEP. I'd rather not.

GILLIAN. Then you needn't.

SHEP *(sincerely)*. Thank you.

GILLIAN. Are you unhappy about it?

SHEP. No. I ought to be—I guess. But I'm not. At all. *(Then, dismissing it all)* Do you know something?

GILLIAN. What?

SHEP. We haven't eaten.

GILLIAN. No.

SHEP. Let's go out and have caviar and champagne. How does that sound?

GILLIAN. It sounds just right!

(They kiss, lightly.)

SHEP. It's so ridiculous that I know nothing about you. Nothing at all.

GILLIAN. What do you want to know?

SHEP. At the moment, nothing, except about us. Tell me, when did you first know—that you liked me?

GILLIAN. The moment I saw you. Coming down the stairs, three days ago. I thought: "That's for me."

SHEP. Oh, you did, did you? And did nothing about it?

GILLIAN *(smiling)*. What can a nice girl do?

SHEP. You could have asked me down for a cocktail.

GILLIAN. I offered you a cocktail earlier this evening. Three times, actually. You wouldn't have it.

SHEP. Isn't that extraordinary? I really didn't notice you. That sounds awful.

GILLIAN *(amused)*. I'm not hurt.

SHEP. Was that why you offered to arrange for me to meet Redlitch? As a come-on?

GILLIAN. I guess—in a way.

SHEP. Well, now you don't need to. Though I'd still like to meet him.

GILLIAN. You'll meet him.

SHEP. Oh, you've done something about it already?

GILLIAN. I've—set things in motion.

SHEP. When are you meeting him?

GILLIAN. Soon.

(Buzzer sounds.)

SHEP. Damn. Don't answer that.

GILLIAN *(oddly)*. Do you mind if I do?

SHEP. No, I don't mind, but why?

GILLIAN. Oh—just an idea. We're going out, anyway. *(She answers the buzzer. Into buzzer mouthpiece)* Hello?

REDLITCH'S VOICE *(off)*. Miss Holroyd?

GILLIAN *(as before)*. Yes, who is it?

REDLITCH'S VOICE *(as before)*. This is Sidney Redlitch. You don't know me, but . . .

GILLIAN *(assuming astonishment)*. Mr. Redlitch? Yes, of course—come in. *(She hangs up and buzzes)*

SHEP *(astonished)*. Well, that's the damnedest thing. You weren't expecting him, were you?

GILLIAN. Not—quite like that. *(She opens the door. Redlitch comes in. He is a man in the fifties—shambling, messy and slightly drunk)* How do you do, Mr. Redlitch?

REDLITCH. Do you know me?

GILLIAN. I've seen your picture on your book. Come in, won't you? This is Mr. Henderson. Mr. Shepherd Henderson.

REDLITCH. Oh—you've been writing to me.

SHEP *(smiling)*. And you've not been answering. How do you do?

REDLITCH. I've been out of town for a couple of weeks. Only got in on the train an hour ago. *(To Gillian)* Look, I know Christmas Eve is hardly the right time for a call, but I was sitting in a bar right around the corner just now, going through my wallet, and I came across your address.

GILLIAN. Who gave you my address?

REDLITCH. Some people in Mexico. I wrote down there about a mask I'd seen, and they wrote back that you'd bought it. A kind of long black mask, with gold eyes. I wondered if you'd let me photograph it for an article I'm doing.

GILLIAN. It's coming in the trunk I sent by rail.

REDLITCH. You don't happen to know what that mask is, do you?

GILLIAN *(playing innocent)*. No, what?

REDLITCH *(heavily)*. Just one of the most potent witch-masks that I ran across down there.

GILLIAN. Oh, they told me that, but . . .

REDLITCH. But you didn't believe it? No, nobody does. Say, you wouldn't feel like offering a poor author a glass of Christmas cheer, would you?

SHEP. Yes, of course. Scotch or Bourbon?

REDLITCH. It doesn't make a bit of difference.

SHEP. Water or soda?

REDLITCH. Either one. As a matter of fact, straight. With a water chaser.

SHEP. Oh! I see. . . . Gillian?

GILLIAN. No, thank you.

(The door opens, and Nicky enters.)

NICKY. Oh . . . Excuse me . . . I didn't know. . . . *(He sees Shep)* Oh, you're still here.

SHEP *(with some concealed embarrassment)*. Er . . . Yes.

GILLIAN. Nicky, this is Mr. Redlitch. Mr. Sidney Redlitch. My brother.

(The men shake hands. Then Nicky crosses to Gillian.)

NICKY. Well, what do you know?

GILLIAN. Pretty good, eh?

NICKY. I'll say.

REDLITCH *(taking his drink from Shep)*. Thanks. Well, Merry Christmas.

GILLIAN AND SHEP. Merry Christmas!

SHEP. Are you writing anything more about witchcraft, Mr. Redlitch?

REDLITCH. Just getting ready to.

SHEP. Oh, that interests me. Very much.

REDLITCH. Oh? I just got my room in Brooklyn back.

GILLIAN. Brooklyn?

REDLITCH. That's where I write best. And boy, is this one going to knock them over. *(He flicks his ashes in his trouser cuff)*

GILLIAN. More witchcraft? Where this time?

REDLITCH. Right here.

GILLIAN. Here?

REDLITCH. In New York. *Witchcraft Around Us.* What do you think of that for a title?

SHEP. It sounds provocative. What does it mean—exactly?

REDLITCH. It means exactly what it says. Witchcraft around us. All around us.

NICKY *(fascinated and amused)*. Is it?

REDLITCH. It sure is, boy. You probably thought that sort of thing was confined to the tropics and the jungles—if you thought of it at all. So did I, until now.

GILLIAN. Oh?

REDLITCH. You won't believe this, but right here—all around you—there's a whole community devoted to just that.

SHEP. That's a novel idea.

REDLITCH. Hell, it's not an idea. It's true.

GILLIAN. How do you know?

NICKY. Tell us.

(From here on, he and Gillian play to each other. He, perching on the arm of the couch, mischievously amused; she slightly so, but also very much on the alert and watchful.)

REDLITCH. Well, I've met a couple. Met them through my book. They let me in on a few things. Then, from there—well, I've made it my business to find out. You've no idea. They have their regular hangouts—cafés, bars, restaurants. Ever hear of a night club called the Zodiac?

NICKY. Yes.

SHEP *(to Gillian)*. Say, isn't that the place you were talking about? That drawing . . . *(He points to it)*

REDLITCH. What drawing? *(He crosses to it)* Sure. She used to dance there. Who did that?

SHEP. He did. *(Points to Nicky)*

REDLITCH. And I suppose it never occurred to you that she was one?

NICKY *(acting incredulity)*. No!

REDLITCH. Sure. Ever look at the proprietor there?

NICKY. Don't tell me he's a witch, too!

REDLITCH. Well, when it's a man, they're called warlocks. *(He gives Shep a sudden, odd, suspicious look and then turns away)* Say, I'd like to have this for an illustration, too.

NICKY. I daresay Gill would loan it to you. Go on. This is fascinating.

REDLITCH. Maybe you don't take it seriously . . .

GILLIAN AND NICKY. Oh, but we do!

NICKY. Tell us more about them, and their—doings.

REDLITCH. Well, then there are the places where they hold their meetings. You think of witches meeting on a blasted heath, don't you?

SHEP *(dryly)*. I don't think I think of their meeting at all.

GILLIAN. Where do they meet? Do you know?

REDLITCH. Sure, I know. One of their main places is up in Harlem. It's an old vaudeville house. There's another down in the Village. And sometimes they have them in a suite of offices on the top of the Woolworth Building. *(He finishes his drink, and hands the glass to Nicky to replenish)* You'd be amazed what's going on under your nose that you'd never suspect. Talk about spy-rings and organized vice—they're nothing compared to it.

SHEP. What do they look like? The witches, I mean?

REDLITCH. Like anyone else. Like you—or you—or you. *(He points to each in turn)* You couldn't tell them, but I could.

GILLIAN. You can—recognize them?

REDLITCH. Like a shot.

GILLIAN. How?

REDLITCH. Well, that's hard to say. It's a something. A look. A feeling. I don't know. But if one were to walk in here right now, I'd know. *(He looks at Shep's hand, on the back of the couch. Shep, nervously, removes it and rises, very uncomfortably)*

NICKY. Gill, I wonder if we know any.

GILLIAN. I wonder.

REDLITCH. I'll bet you do. I bet that I could tell you names that . . .

NICKY. Oh, do!

REDLITCH. Uh-huh. Can't do that. I'm careful. That's why there can't be any names in my book. Though I've got protection, up to a point.

SHEP. Protection?

REDLITCH. There's a woman—pretty high up in the movement. She's considered about the best there is. Well, I've got her on my side.

GILLIAN *(with a touch of professional jealousy)*. Who's that?

REDLITCH. A Mrs. de . . . Well, I shouldn't give her name, though she's pretty open about it. Kind of flaunts it. Some of them do, you know. Go about dressed up so that people will recognize them. You may have seen this woman. She goes to opening nights in robes with Cabalistic what-d'-you-call-them all over them.

GILLIAN. A Mrs. de Pass.

REDLITCH. That's the one. Matter of fact, I'm going up to her house a bit later.

GILLIAN *(alarmed)*. Tonight?

REDLITCH. Yes. She's got a party. I'll tell you another couple of things about them. Witches can't cry. Shed tears, I mean. Or blush.

SHEP. Oh, really?

REDLITCH. And if you throw them in the water, they float.

SHEP. Anyone tried that lately?

REDLITCH. And they almost all have pets.

They're called "familiars." You know—familiar spirits who have to carry out their masters' bidding.

GILLIAN (*rising suddenly*). Shep, we ought to go.

REDLITCH. Oh, everyone is bored, all of a sudden.

GILLIAN. No, no, I'm not. I'm sure there is a lot of it around.

SHEP (*involuntarily*). Like influenza.

REDLITCH. Okay. Okay. Make fun of it. I'm used to that.

SHEP. No, I'm sorry, I didn't mean to. I really am interested. In fact, I'd like to hear more about it. I understand your contract with Seldens is just about up.

REDLITCH. It is.

SHEP. Well, I wish you'd lunch with me and my partner one day.

REDLITCH. Sure. Glad to. (*To Gillian*) And if you'll let me know when that mask turns up . . . I'll give you my address. (*He gets out pencil and paper*)

SHEP. Give it to me, too, will you? (*He stands over Redlitch. Gillian moves to Nicky, worriedly, talking in an undertone*)

GILLIAN. Nicky, you know where Aunt Queenie was going tonight . . .

NICKY. No. Where? Oh, yes . . .

GILLIAN (*with an inclination of her head toward Redlitch and Shep*). I don't think *that's* a good idea.

NICKY (*with an understanding glance and nod*). What do you want me to do?

GILLIAN. Stop it. Can you?

NICKY. Sure!

REDLITCH. Here you are, Miss Holroyd.

GILLIAN. Thank you very much. I'm sorry to have to turn you out, but . . .

SHEP. We do have to go out. Well, I'll call you.

NICKY (*to Redlitch*). You know, I'd like to hear some more about this book. I'll walk along with you.

REDLITCH. We'll stop in for a drink some place.

NICKY. Fine.

REDLITCH (*to the room*). Well, good-bye then.

SHEP. I'll be in touch with you.

REDLITCH. Okay! (*As he and Nicky go out*) There's a place on Third Avenue called "The Cloven Hoof" I'd like to show you.

(*They are gone.*)

SHEP. This has been the most extraordi-nary evening! He seemed to think that *I* was one of them! (*He comes to Gillian*) And now, if we're going to have our first meal together . . .

GILLIAN. I'll get my wrap. (*She goes into the bedroom. Shep puts on his coat and his muffler. Then he sees the carton full of presents. He picks up a couple and stands turning them over in his hands. Gillian returns, wearing an evening cloak*) What are you going to do with all those?

SHEP. Have them sent around, in the morning, I guess. With apologies. *Most* of them. (*He replaces the packages*) All these presents—and none for you.

GILLIAN. Give me one.

SHEP. Which?

GILLIAN. Any one. Shut your eyes, and —dip. Go on.

(*Shep closes his eyes and rootles in the carton. Finally brings out a small package. He opens his eyes and looks at it.*)

SHEP. How extraordinary!

GILLIAN. Why—what is it? (*He hands it to her, without a word*) What is it?

SHEP. Open it. It's a locket. Rather a revolting locket, really. I was giving it to some—it has some significance, or other.

GILLIAN (*stopping her unwrapping*). Do you still want to give it to them?

SHEP. No. (*She unwraps the package. Inside is a small jeweler's box. She opens it and takes out an old-fashioned locket*)

GILLIAN. It's beautiful. (*She holds it up*)

SHEP. You think so, too? It belonged to my—damn it, why can't one say "my mother" without sounding sentimental? (*As she starts to open it*) You can guess what's inside.

GILLIAN. You?

SHEP (*nodding*). Aged . . . (*He holds his hand at eight-year-old height*)

GILLIAN (*looking at it*). I should have met you earlier.

SHEP (*half amused*). You think so?

GILLIAN. Yes, I do.

SHEP. Shall I put it on for you?

GILLIAN. If you're really sure?

SHEP. I am.

(*She turns and he fastens it around her neck.*)

GILLIAN (*with a little satisfied smile*). Well, then—thank you. *Very* much.

SHEP (*taking her in his arms*). Merry Christmas, my darling.

GILLIAN. Merry Christmas to you. (*They kiss*) Shall we go?

SHEP. Sure.

(He goes to the door and opens it. Gillian turns out the lights in the room. The only light now comes from the hall outside, and from the glow of the fire, silhouetting them as they stand in the doorway. Shep stands, looking back at the room. Gillian joins him.)

GILLIAN. What are you looking at?

SHEP. This place. The place you happened to me in. This room.

GILLIAN. It's just an ordinary room.

SHEP. Not by a long shot. It may *look* like one, but . . . *(He shakes his head)*

GILLIAN. Well, you'll see it again.

SHEP *(forcibly)*. You bet I will.

(Gillian goes out ahead of him. He stands a moment longer, staring at the room. Then he shakes his head and shrugs his shoulders in complete bewilderment and disbelief, and follows her out.)

CURTAIN

ACT TWO

The same. Two weeks later. Afternoon. The stage is empty when the curtain rises. The light outside the windows is fading to darkness. The Christmas tree has gone. The Mexican mask is hanging prominently on the back wall.

The door opens and Gillian and Shep come in. Gillian switches on the hall light. Shep takes the latchkey from the door and puts it in his pocket. Gillian carries a large box of candy and some letters. She comes to the sofa table, switches on the lamp, and puts the candy box down. Shep takes off his coat and hat and puts them on the hall bench. Gillian crosses, looking at the letters.

SHEP *(standing near coffee table)*. Darling, come here.

GILLIAN *(she comes to him)*. Yes?

(He takes her in his arms and kisses her.)

SHEP. I've been aching to do that for the last three hours. Since before lunch.

GILLIAN. Is that why you wouldn't take me to tea?

SHEP. My, but your nose stays cold a long time.

GILLIAN. I'm cold-blooded.

SHEP *(holds her away from him)*. I'd hardly say that. You know something?

You get better all the time. To be with. To do things with. Everything. I've never known what to do with Saturday afternoons in New York before, except wait for them to become Saturday night. This one's been wonderful.

GILLIAN. Lunching at the Plaza—going to an art exhibit—walking down Park Avenue? The most ordinary things!

SHEP. And what a bit of magic can do to them!

GILLIAN. Magic?

SHEP. Well, isn't it? Two weeks ago tonight we met. And they've been magic weeks.

GILLIAN *(starts to take off coat)*. I know. They have. They've been exactly that. Enchanted! *(Shep starts toward her. She holds out her hand to stop him)* No, Shep! We're going to have tea.

SHEP *(agreeing)*. First . . . Right. *(He starts to the kitchen, stops to pick up something)*

GILLIAN. Oh, Shep, not another pin! You, who won't even pick up a newspaper!

SHEP. I've always picked up pins. Okay. I know. Sheer superstition. Doesn't mean a thing. *(Puts the pin in the lapel of his jacket)*

GILLIAN. How many have you got in there already? *(She looks at his lapel)* Four!

SHEP. I have not! *(He takes them out)* I'll throw them in the fire.

GILLIAN *(quickly and unguardedly)*. No!

SHEP. Why not?

GILLIAN. It's bad luck. Yes, I'm superstitious, too. I'll take them. Give them to me. *(She takes the pins from him)*

SHEP. What are you going to do with them?

GILLIAN. Keep them. *(Vaguely)* They come in handy!

SHEP. What for?

GILLIAN *(as before)*. Different things. *(She goes into the bedroom, carrying her hat and coat. Shep starts for the kitchen again then stops below the door and looks at the mask. Gillian returns)*

SHEP *(teasingly)*. Consistent, aren't you? Superstitious—yet you'll have this thing in the place, after what Redlitch said about it?

GILLIAN *(smiling)*. I think it's kind of friendly.

SHEP *(looking at its ugliness, dubiously)*.

Well, not toward *me*, I don't think! *(He looks at it, then says to it, sharply and suddenly)* Boo! *(He goes into the kitchen. The telephone rings. Gillian answers it)*

GILLIAN. Hello? Oh, Nicky. Well, *I've* been busy, too. Quite busy. No, not the way *you* think. Just busy. What can I do for you? Shep? You mean Shepherd Henderson? Yes, I see him—now and then. What do you want with him? Well, call him. Why ask me? Well, certainly not today. I just don't want you to. Maybe I can arrange for you to meet him next week. *(Shep returns with the tea-tray, minus the teapot. He puts it on the coffee table, and sits, listening puzzledly)* I can't talk now. No, I can't do that now, either. All right, then, say it over to me, and I'll correct you. Yes. Yes. No, the other way around. That's it, and count ten between the last two. Okay? What? Oh, Natalie's party? No, I'd love to, but I can't, tonight.

SHEP. Look, if this is something . . .

GILLIAN *(quieting him)*. Ssh! *(Back into phone)* No, nothing's going on. No, no, don't come over.

(Nicky has hung up. She bangs the hook a couple of times, then hangs up.)

SHEP. What was that all about?

GILLIAN. Oh, just someone I've known for ages—and ages.

SHEP. Were they asking you to coach them in a part or something?

GILLIAN. Yes—or something. But it's not important.

SHEP. Look, sweet, we've spent all our time together, all our meals and everything. It's just occurred to me, there must be lots of people you're neglecting.

GILLIAN. No one I care about.

SHEP. I've been neglecting *everything.* There's a whole stack of manuscripts piled up by my bed—only I never seem to get there any more! You go to your party tonight. Maybe I'll join you there later.

GILLIAN *(too quickly)*. Oh, no!

SHEP. Why not?

GILLIAN *(evasively)*. You'd hate it.

SHEP. Do you know I haven't met a single friend of yours?

GILLIAN. And you're not going to. They're awful.

SHEP *(he laughs)*. What are they like?

GILLIAN *(surprised)*. Like? They're— *(Reflecting)* irresponsible—and malicious —and unprincipled—and *fun!*

SHEP. Well, that's something.

GILLIAN. I'm not sure that's not the worst part.

SHEP. Hey, what's eating you all of a sudden?

GILLIAN *(disturbed and restless)*. I don't know. I just don't like myself very much, that's all.

SHEP. I'm crazy about you. Gillian, when are we going to get married? *(She stares at him in astonishment)* What's the matter?

GILLIAN. I must have missed a chapter somewhere.

SHEP. Darling, after the last two weeks, you can't say, "This is so sudden."

GILLIAN. No, but I hadn't thought of marriage.

SHEP *(lightly)*. Darling, that's the *man's* remark—usually.

GILLIAN *(smiling, but half-serious)*. You mean you've been thinking of it—all along?

SHEP. Well, not *all* along, but—now it's getting pretty bad. I never knew a man could feel this way. I'm going crazy. I've let everything slide. My business has got shot to hell. My secretary glares at me, and my partner isn't speaking to me. I can't stay in the office for wanting to get to this place, and to you. When I get here, I can't wait to get close to you. And then I never can get close enough.

GILLIAN *(keeping up the banter)*. And how do you think marriage would cure that?

SHEP. I don't know. I don't care. But we can't go on like this.

GILLIAN. Darling—that's the *woman's* remark—usually!

SHEP. You know I'm in love with you. Marriage is the logical next step. Doesn't it seem that way to you? *(She does not answer)* Gill, why are you ducking this? Tell me, be serious.

GILLIAN *(moving away)*. I don't think I'm cut out for marriage, that's all.

SHEP. In what way?

GILLIAN. The way I've lived . . .

SHEP. How have you lived?

GILLIAN. Selfishly—restlessly—one thing after another. *(Quickly)* I don't mean *affairs.*

SHEP *(amused and relieved)*. I'm glad to hear that. What do you mean?

GILLIAN *(vaguely)*. Just—one thing after another.

SHEP *(crossing to her, turns her to him;).*

Well, anyhow, there's a time to stop. There's a moment when we get the chance to go one of two ways forever. But you've got to recognize the moment when it comes. This is it—for *me*. I thought for *you*, too. (*Pause*) No?

GILLIAN (*slowly, very torn by an inner conflict*). I don't know. It would mean—giving up a whole way of living—and thinking. I've wondered sometimes if I could. And wished I could.

SHEP. Settle down, you mean?

GILLIAN. You can call it that. But that's not what's worrying me.

SHEP. What is?

GILLIAN. I told you. Me.

SHEP. So long as it's not me.

GILLIAN. It's not.

SHEP. Then let me do the worrying. (*He puts his arms around her. She does not answer*) Well?

GILLIAN (*slowly*). You're tempting me.

SHEP (*still holding her*). That's better.

GILLIAN (*stalling*). That kettle must be boiling by now.

SHEP (*with double meaning*). They don't boil if you watch them—eh? (*He goes into the kitchen. Gillian stands alone*)

GILLIAN (*to herself*). I wonder. I wonder if I could. Suppose he found out, afterward. That would be bad. (*With a little giggle*) And what would all the others say? (*She seems to hear a chuckle from the mask, and turns to it*) Don't look at me like that. I will, if I want to. (*Shep returns, carrying the teapot. He crosses with it to the coffee table. Gillian keeps her eyes on him, as though measuring her whole future with him. Then she comes to the sofa and pours the tea. The silence between them is long and tense. She hands him his tea. He takes the cup, and they both sip in unison. Then, with her cup still in her hand, she speaks at last*) Shep, I will.

SHEP. I'd like to hear that again.

GILLIAN. I will. I want to.

SHEP (*moving to embrace her*). I think you will have to put that cup down. (*He takes it from her*) Oh, darling . . . darling . . . (*He embraces her*) Darling! (*Then, with an intake of the breath*) What do we say now? (*They lean back*) Where shall we live? Shall I buy this place from you? Then we can throw the other tenants out and unconvert it.

GILLIAN. I've only got a lease on this house. And anyway, I'd like to start some-where afresh.

SHEP. What—again? You know, I wish you'd make a list of your past activities. A primitive art gallery on Twelfth Street. Book shop—herb shop. I can't keep up with them.

GILLIAN (*disturbed*). Shep—don't ask me questions about my past.

SHEP (*a shade worried, but trying to laugh it off*). You do make it sound lurid.

GILLIAN. I don't mean it that way. Though there have been—episodes. Do you want to know about them?

SHEP (*humorously uncomfortable*). Er—no. I don't think I do.

GILLIAN. Well, that's the way I feel about it all. My life's been sort of—raffish—at least, seen through your eyes. And I don't want to talk about it.

SHEP. Yes, but your childhood, every-thing that makes you what you are—I'm jealous of these things. Oh, I know you don't feel that way. You're not jealous, in the remotest degree, about anything. You knew there was another woman—right up to the moment we met—yet you've never asked me one thing about her. Who she was, or anything. That seems incredible to me.

GILLIAN (*rises*). Yes, but that—whatever it was—is over. I know it is.

SHEP. Even so, a little twinge of jealousy would be flattering.

GILLIAN (*with a change*). Oh, don't think I can't be jealous. I can—in my own way. It's my worst thing. Almost. That, and trying to get something for nothing. Eating my cake, and having it, too. But I'll be different from now on. I promise you. I swear!

SHEP. I don't want you different.

GILLIAN. But I want to be different. Quite different.

SHEP. I won't stand for it! (*He kisses her*) I wonder if two people have ever had a romance like this before.

GILLIAN. Very few! Very few!

SHEP. Damn few.

GILLIAN. Yes. Damn few.

(*The buzzer sounds.*)

SHEP. Hell! There's life breaking in.

GILLIAN. Tell it to go away.

SHEP. We've got to start meeting it again, sometime. And now we've got the rest of our lives together. . . .

GILLIAN. All right. I'll be polite to it.

(She rises to go to buzzer)

SHEP. Maybe it's Aunt Queenie. Does she know about us, by the way?

GILLIAN. Certainly. She's been tickled to death about it.

SHEP. Oh, not only eccentric, but immoral, too!

GILLIAN. No. Just romantic. *(She answers the buzzer)* Hello?

NICKY'S VOICE. Gill? It's Nicky.

GILLIAN. Oh, Nicky—please!

NICKY'S VOICE. I want to come up.

(Gillian buzzes for him. Then she turns to Shep.)

GILLIAN. There you are. Interruptions.

SHEP. We won't let him stay long. We'll get rid of him.

(Nicky enters, and sees Shep.)

NICKY *(eagerly shaking hands)*. Hello! Well, how very nice. *(He turns)* Thanks, Gill. *(He sees the mask)* Say, that's new, isn't it? Is that the one Redlitch was talking about? It looks just like that German governess we used to have.

SHEP. You're quite a stranger.

NICKY. That's right. Not since Christmas Eve.

SHEP. Where have you been?

NICKY. Believe it or not, in Brooklyn!

GILLIAN. What for?

NICKY. I've got a hotel room there. It's handier for work.

GILLIAN. Work? *You?*

NICKY. Yes, dear. And it's not nearly as tough as standing in line for unemployment insurance.

GILLIAN. What are you up to?

NICKY. I've got a surprise for you. *(To Shep)* For you, too. *(Holding up the envelope)* Sid's new book. Sid Redlitch.

SHEP. What, already?

NICKY. Oh, not all of it. This is just an outline, and the first two chapters. But it will give you an idea.

SHEP. Well, that's pretty quick.

NICKY. Oh, we've been at it, night and day.

GILLIAN. Did you say "we"?

NICKY *(smugly)*. Yes, dear. *(He taps the envelope)* Witchcraft Around Us, by Sidney Redlitch and Nicholas Holroyd. With illustrations by N. Holroyd.

GILLIAN. You mean—you're writing it with him? *(He nods, beaming. She giggles)* Oh—oh, what fun!

SHEP. But—what do you know about that sort of thing?

NICKY. I know as much as he does. *(Airily)* You—pick things up.

SHEP. Well, this is a surprise. Isn't it, Gill?

GILLIAN *(with twinkling eyes)*. It certainly is.

SHEP. We've got a surprise for you, too. *(Putting his arm around Gillian)* Think you could stand me as a brother-in-law?

NICKY. Do you mean it?

SHEP. Well, I do. Don't you? *(He turns to Gillian. She nods)*

NICKY *(lightly, almost casually)*. Well, for goodness' sake. Well, bless your hearts. *(He kisses Gillian)* Congratulations, darling. *(Shakes hands with Shep)* Both of you.

SHEP. Thanks.

NICKY. That was pretty quick, too, wasn't it?

SHEP. No, not at all!

NICKY *(with sudden realization)*. Say, you've been here all along.

SHEP. Well, not *all* along.

GILLIAN *(quickly)*. Shep, I'd like to talk to Nicky. Do you mind?

SHEP. To exchange some sentimental tears?

GILLIAN. Well, maybe.

SHEP. I'll go up to my apartment for a bit.

NICKY *(going to the door with him)*. Why don't you look that book over now?

SHEP. Now?

NICKY. Sure. It won't take you long. It's good.

SHEP. Well, I might glance at it.

NICKY. Fine!

SHEP. Bless you, Gill dearest. *(He exits. Gillian and Nicky smile at each other)*

NICKY. Well, well, well! Marriage, no less.

GILLIAN. Uh-huh.

NICKY. What fun!

GILLIAN. It is—very.

NICKY. Between the two of us, he's going to have quite a time.

GILLIAN. The two of us?

NICKY. Me and my book. I'm going to need your help. You know I've never kept up with all the manifestoes.

GILLIAN *(lightly)*. Oh, invent anything you like. What's it matter?

NICKY. Oh, I can't. Sid's a stickler for accuracy.

GILLIAN. What? Nicky, you're not giving him the truth?

NICKY. Sure, I am.

GILLIAN. But I thought this book was a joke. You don't mean he knows about *you?*

NICKY. Of course. You've no idea the things I've shown him and told him.

GILLIAN *(alarmed)*. You didn't tell him about *me?*

NICKY. No, darling. I told him it was *I* who summoned him. But if you want to take credit . . .

GILLIAN *(interrupting, angrily)*. I do not want to take credit. Oh, Nicky, why —why did you do this? Don't you know by now it never pays to tell outsiders?

NICKY *(blandly)*. It's going to pay beautifully. I gather Shep has made Sid a very generous offer.

GILLIAN. You mean that's what Shep is reading upstairs now? *(He nods)* You can't publish that book. I won't let you.

NICKY. What harm can it do to you? There are no names in it.

GILLIAN. But your name is going to be on it, and it's too close to home to be safe. Nicky, Shep doesn't know about me. And he's not going to.

NICKY *(ribbing her)*. Oh, I suppose you're going to tell me you're renouncing, too.

GILLIAN. I *have* renounced.

NICKY *(as before)*. Since when?

GILLIAN. Well, actually, since half an hour ago.

NICKY *(growing serious)*. You don't mean this marriage is on the level?

GILLIAN. Certainly.

NICKY. That's crazy. You can't be in love with him. What are you marrying him for, anyway?

GILLIAN. Because I want to. *(Urgently)* That's why you've got to stop that book.

NICKY *(firmly)*. I'm sorry, dear, but no. It's important to me.

GILLIAN *(equally firmly)*. It's more important to me!

NICKY *(quietly)*. No, dear, I'm sorry. But quite firmly—*no!*

GILLIAN *(after a moment)*. Very well, then. I'll have to do something about it.

NICKY. You don't mean "pull one"? I thought you'd retired.

GILLIAN *(again, after a second)*. Yes, I have. But I'll make a farewell appearance, to stop this!

NICKY. We've got people on our side, remember.

GILLIAN. Mrs. de Pass? Well, I'm better than that old battle-axe.

NICKY. Yes, but she can take it up higher. To the big boys. She'll get the whole organization back of it!

GILLIAN. That bunch of phony fuddy-duddies! There isn't one of them that gives anyone a flat tire, without having to go to bed for a week! *(She moves to him)* Now, will you bring me every copy in existence, or am I going to have to go to work? You know I can, don't you? *(She picks up the tea-tray)* Think it over while I take these out.

(She goes out with it. Nicky stands baffled and angry. He goes to the telephone, dials a number and gets the busy signal.)

NICK. Damn! *(Then he gets an idea, lifting the receiver again)* Actatus, Catip-ta, Marnutus . . .

(Gillian returns, carrying the cat.)

GILLIAN *(silkily)*. Nicky, I wouldn't do that, whatever it is. If I were you. Well, what's it to be? Yes or no?

NICKY. Not on your life.

GILLIAN. Very well, then. *(She sits, nursing the cat and stroking it)* Pye—Pye—Pyewacket. Eloas, Bejulet, Phidibus. I don't want that book to be published. Do you hear? Not by anyone.

NICKY *(warningly)*. Gill, watch out.

GILLIAN. And that'll teach you to threaten me with the organization.

NICKY. Okay, you asked for it. I'm going to see that your little romance goes on the rocks, my girl. Shep's going to know all about you. And before the day is out, too.

(Shep re-enters.)

SHEP. Oh, you're still here, Nicky. Good. Hello, there's Pyewacket again. I haven't seen him in a long time.

NICKY. What are you going to do with Pye, now?

GILLIAN. I'm going to put him out. *(She takes the cat into the kitchen)*

NICKY. I meant, now that you two are getting married.

SHEP. Oh, did she tell you that he doesn't like me? Can't bear me to touch him, for some reason?

(Gillian returns.)

NICKY. Did you read it? How did you like it?

SHEP. Do you want me to talk in front of Gillian?

NICKY. Sure. Why not?

SHEP. Gill, I'm afraid Nicky, here, has been a bad boy. I don't think Aunt Queenie's the only member of your family who goes in for practical jokes.

NICKY. You think this book's a joke?

SHEP. It's crazy. You should call it *What Every Young Witch Ought to Know.* How you imagined for one instant that I'd fall for it! *(To Gillian)* I've just been talking to Redlitch on the phone and he said that Nicky had convinced him that he was one of them. I think that was going a little far.

NICKY. Did he tell you how he got here, in the first place?

SHEP. Yes, I had all that. Luminous paint, or something. And all your references, including a Mrs. de Pass, who seems to be a sort of Head Witch or something. But now the joke's over. So you'd better tell Redlitch the whole thing was a gag, or that book will have to find another publisher.

NICKY *(after a pause)*. No, I don't guess any other publisher would be any good, either. *Now.* Do you, Gill?

GILLIAN *(faintly alarmed)*. Nicky, what are you up to?

NICKY *(gaily)*. Not a thing, darling. Okay, Shep. I guess it was silly of me to think you'd believe it—like that. Well, good-bye—and—no hard feelings?

SHEP. You're an ass, Nicky.

NICKY *(at the door, smiling)*. So long, Gill. You'll be hearing from me. Later in the day. *(He exits)*

SHEP. Is anything the matter?

GILLIAN. No.

SHEP. You look peculiar. Nothing wrong between you and Nicky?

GILLIAN. No.

SHEP *(crossing to the fireplace)*. The young scamp. I don't think he's going to have an easy time with Redlitch. *(He stoops to mend the fire. There is a long pause. Gillian raises her head, with terrific determination)*

GILLIAN. Shep, I've got to tell you something.

SHEP *(back to her)*. What?

GILLIAN *(she makes two desperate, determined efforts, and nothing comes out. Then, at last, her voice strangling so that it comes out almost in a squeak)*. Shep—I'm one.

SHEP. What did you say?

GILLIAN. I said—I'm one. I was one.

SHEP. One what?

GILLIAN. One of the people that that book's about. Nicky's one, too!

SHEP *(with a roar of laughter)*. Oh, that's what it is. *(Puts poker back)* He's persuaded you to come in on it. I suppose that's to carry on the joke? Sorry, dear, but it won't work.

GILLIAN. No, no, no! You've got it all wrong! You've got to listen. I've got to try and explain something to you.

SHEP. Not if it's to prove to me that Nicky is a witch. No.

GILLIAN *(irritated)*. The word is warlock.

SHEP. Well, we don't have to get technical about it!

GILLIAN. You don't believe there are such things—at all?

SHEP. No, dear, and it's no good trying to make me.

GILLIAN. No matter who told you?

SHEP. No matter who told me.

GILLIAN. I wish I could trust that!

SHEP *(sensing her real distress)*. Look nobody's threatening you with anything are they? Nicky isn't?

GILLIAN. I guess—in a way—he is.

SHEP. Well, he can go to hell. What is it? Threatening to tell something about you, to me?

GILLIAN. Yes.

SHEP. Well, that's easily dealt with.

GILLIAN. How?

SHEP. Tell me yourself.

GILLIAN *(loudly and angrily)*. That's what I'm trying to do!

SHEP. What is it? Something in your past that you didn't want questions asked about? What have you been up to? Have you been engaging in un-American activities?

GILLIAN. No. I'd say very American. *Early* American! Shep—look—you say you don't believe in anything supernatural. How about superstitions? Picking up pins?

SHEP. There's nothing in that. That's just habit.

GILLIAN. Yes, but what's the habit based on? Isn't it just in case there were something governing those things?

SHEP. No. Not at all.

GILLIAN. Shep, there *is* something *(With a breath)* There are the laws of gravity....

SHEP *(amused)*. So I've always heard.

GILLIAN. I don't mean you can set those aside—exactly . . .

SHEP. That's a relief.

GILLIAN. But there are ways of—well—altering things . . .

SHEP (as before). Are there now?

GILLIAN. Manipulating things for yourself. . . .

SHEP. How interesting!

GILLIAN. Short cuts to getting your own way.

SHEP. No, now I've lost you.

GILLIAN. Shep, the people who live by those short cuts are the people who—I've got to say it—live by *magic*.

SHEP (totally disbelieving). Magic?

GILLIAN. Shep, there is such a thing as magic. I know, I can do it.

SHEP (as before). You can?

GILLIAN. Yes.

SHEP. Well, do it, then. Show me some.

GILLIAN (after a tempted pause). No!

SHEP. Oh, come on.

GILLIAN. No, I mustn't. It would go on and on. It always does. I've broken down once this afternoon, already.

SHEP (immensely tickled). You have? What did you do?

GILLIAN. I stopped that book being published.

SHEP. Oh, no, you didn't. That's my province. Sorry to spoil your story, but I decided I wasn't going to publish it after I'd read two pages.

GILLIAN (angrily). I didn't say I stopped *you* publishing it. I stopped *anyone* publishing it!

SHEP (still amused). Oh, can you do that?

GILLIAN. Yes!

SHEP. How very useful. What did you do?

GILLIAN (after a second). I can't tell you. It would sound too silly.

SHEP. No. Come on. What *did* you do?

GILLIAN. I put on a spell.

SHEP. And how does one "put on a spell"?

GILLIAN. I used Pyewacket.

SHEP (still kidding her). You mean—you spoke to him about it? And what's he supposed to do? Go out and call on all the publishers? And talk them out of it? Is Pyewacket a witch too?

GILLIAN. He's a—familiar!

SHEP (beginning to get angry). And what's that? Oh, yes, a pet who's supposed to do his master's bidding. I remember. Gill, what the hell are you getting at?

GILLIAN (turning to him). I'll tell you other things. The luminous paint—that was true. Only, it wasn't Nicky. It was I. You saw me doing it, even. You thought that it was indoor fireworks. And your coming here. You remember how that happened? Your telephone went out of order.

SHEP. That was Providence.

GILLIAN. No, that was Nicky! He put it out of order.

SHEP. Well, I've heard of *repair* men! Why would Nicky do that?

GILLIAN. As a prank. That's what he uses it all for, mainly. Playing tricks. Turning all the lights on Fifty-seventh Street green at the same moment. That, and for his sex life.

SHEP. Look, Gil, you're going crazy. I don't know about Nicky's sex life, but Redlitch coming here—my phone going out of order—even the lights on Fifty-seventh Street—damn it, those things are coincidences.

GILLIAN (urgently). They look like coincidences. They have to. You can't do it any other way. I can't bring Niagara Falls down to Grand Central Station, or turn this house into the Taj Mahal. It doesn't work that way. There's always a rational explanation—if you want it.

SHEP. Then I'll take the rational explanation.

GILLIAN (turning away). Just as you took the rational explanation of *us*!

SHEP. What's that?

GILLIAN (sitting, desperately). There—now, I've said it.

SHEP. You mean—*that* was . . . ?

GILLIAN. Yes. That *was*!

SHEP. Now, wait a minute. . . .

GILLIAN. Why? You thought it strange enough yourself when it happened. You called the whole thing magic, only this afternoon.

SHEP. I didn't mean it literally.

GILLIAN. Well, was it rational, what happened to you here on Christmas Eve?

SHEP. It happened . . .

GILLIAN. How? Think back. What did happen? You came in here to use the telephone. It was busy. Then you got your number. Can you remember what happened next?

SHEP. I can remember every single thing. You went into the kitchen. I made my call. . . . You came back with the cat. . . .

GILLIAN. Go on.

SHEP. I went to the door—turned back—and suddenly I seemed to see you for the first time . . . And you were in my arms. . . .

GILLIAN. You've left out something. What did I do before that?

SHEP. You didn't do anything. You sat down and you talked to the cat. . . . *(He stops and stares at her)* Goddamn it! No, I won't believe it!

GILLIAN. What made you suddenly take me in your arms?

SHEP. Because I wanted to. More than I've ever wanted to do anything in my whole life. And you think you made me do it? Why? What for?

GILLIAN. Because I wanted you to. So I did that.

SHEP. You mean *I* had nothing to do with it, at all?

GILLIAN. I'm sorry, Shep. It's true. These powers do exist. All kinds of powers. All you've got to do is use them.

SHEP. You mean, everyone's got them? I could do things?

GILLIAN. I guess you might do—some things. If someone showed you how. Don't ever let them.

SHEP. Don't worry about that!

GILLIAN. It's bad. The whole thing's bad.

SHEP. Why is it bad?

GILLIAN *(urgently)*. It's habit-forming! You don't know. I do. I've lived among it. And I know what it can do to you. It's like pulling rank, or abusing influence. And it can destroy you as a person. Well, now I've told you. And I don't have to worry about anyone else telling you now.

SHEP *(embraces her)*. You don't have to worry about anything.

GILLIAN. You don't believe a word of it, do you?

SHEP. I certainly do!

GILLIAN *(hopefully)*. You do?

SHEP. I believe you cast an absolutely wonderful spell on me, and I'm crazy about it. *(He kisses her. There is a knock on the door)* Oh, damn . . . Don't answer it.

GILLIAN *(pulling reluctantly away)*. Darling, now that we've got the rest of our lives together . . . ? *(She goes to door opens it. Miss Holroyd is there)* Oh . . . Aunt Queenie!

MISS HOLROYD. Hello, darling. Oh, hello, Shep, too! *(Gillian gestures to her to sit down)* No, darling, I'm not staying. But something wonderful happened to me this afternoon, and I've simply got to tell you.

GILLIAN. Well, tell us, then.

MISS HOLROYD. Well, Gill, you know how utterly lost I've been here—without my kitchen—or anything. Well, this afternoon, I met a lady at the Roxy—in the Ladies' Room. My pocketbook fell open, and some things dropped out—some pamphlets—and—well, we got to talking and we found we had a lot in common. . . . You know what I mean?

GILLIAN *(amused)*. I think I do.

SHEP *(briefly)*. I don't.

MISS HOLROYD. Well, we had a soda together, she and I, and she told me about the club she lives in—a place where I can do anything I want. She said there was a vacancy right now, so I thought I'd let her introduce me, and then I could pay my entrance fee right away. I'm dining with Mrs. de Pass tonight, and it's right around the corner. *(At the mention of Mrs. de Pass, Shep rises, does a prodigious take)* Why, what's the matter, Shep?

SHEP. Did you say Mrs. de Pass?

MISS HOLROYD. Why—do you know her?

SHEP. Gill—you don't mean that she . . . *(He indicates Miss Holroyd. Gillian nods)* Oh, no!!

MISS HOLROYD. What's this all about?

GILLIAN. Auntie, I'd better tell you. Shep—knows. I've told him.

MISS HOLROYD. Oh, how wonderful. And is he—*(Hopefully)* sympathetic?

SHEP. Now, wait a minute. Let's get this straight. You mean that *she* thinks *she's* one, too?

MISS HOLROYD *(proudly)*. Yes, Shep. How else do you think I got into your apartment, when the door was locked?

SHEP. You mean you can get through locked doors?

MISS HOLROYD. Usually.

SHEP. Could you get through that one if I locked it?

MISS HOLROYD. I think so.

SHEP *(steps up to door)*. Good!

MISS HOLROYD *(follows him. She stops,*

looks at Gillian, who waves a forbidding finger). No, I mustn't. I can't.

SHEP *(closing the door again).* No. I suspected that.

MISS HOLROYD *(to Gillian).* Well, *you* do it then.

GILLIAN. No, Auntie. I've stopped. Shep and I are getting married.

MISS HOLROYD. Oh, how lovely! How exciting! But, if he knows . . .

GILLIAN. That makes no difference. I've stopped.

MISS HOLROYD *(very disappointed).* Oh, well. I'm sorry, Shep, about the door.

SHEP. I'm sorry, too.

MISS HOLROYD. It would have been such fun!

SHEP. Yes, I'd have liked to see it.

MISS HOLROYD *(to Gillian).* Well, darling, now you're getting married, you won't think I'm deserting you? *(The cries of a cat are heard)* Why, what's that?

GILLIAN. That's Pyewacket. It must be his dinner time. *(She looks at her watch)* Goodness, it's long past. I forgot all about him. Pardon me. *(She goes into the kitchen)*

SHEP. We shall miss you here.

MISS HOLROYD. Oh, how nice of you. I don't know why I had to come and tell you. But I just felt an impulse. An irresistible impulse.

SHEP. What's this place you're moving into? A sort of Witch's Hostel?

MISS HOLROYD. Yes, they have a communal kitchen we can all use for our brewing!

SHEP. Oh, for God's sake!

MISS HOLROYD. I know how hard it is to take in, at first, Shep. I don't know how much Gillian has told you about it all. About that spell she put on you?

SHEP. Yes, I had all that.

MISS HOLROYD. Maybe I should lend you some books, to explain things to you. They helped me a lot.

SHEP. Did they?

MISS HOLROYD. Yes. Of course, I always knew that I had something, but I thought it was artistic temperament. I don't think I would ever have become a witch, if my parents had let me go on the stage.

SHEP. You might have combined your talents. Gone into vaudeville and done card tricks.

MISS HOLROYD. Oh, I've never had any real talent, in either direction. Just itty-bitty ones. Gillian's the one who's really gifted.

SHEP. Miss Holroyd, you don't really believe that Gillian has any powers?

MISS HOLROYD. I know she has.

SHEP. Name me one thing she has ever done.

MISS HOLROYD. She's done wonderful things. Those thunderstorms. While she was in college on account of *(Intimately)* you-know-who!

SHEP *(irritable).* I have no idea who.

MISS HOLROYD. Your friend. Merle Kittredge.

SHEP. Oh, nonsense! Gillian has never heard of Merle Kittredge.

MISS HOLROYD. But, of course she has! I told her myself that you were getting married. That's why she went after you with Pyewacket.

SHEP *(stopping and staring at her).* I beg your pardon?

MISS HOLROYD. Oh, but I promise you she wouldn't have used magic, if she'd had time for the usual feminine methods. No matter how great enemies she and Miss Kittredge were.

SHEP. You mean—she went after me because of Merle?

MISS HOLROYD. Well—she thought you very attractive, already. You've no idea how much she likes you. Or, perhaps you have. . . .

SHEP. Miss Holroyd, what are you trying to say?

MISS HOLROYD. Well, Shep—with us, it's like the Saints.

SHEP. Saints?

MISS HOLROYD. Yes, only the other way around! At least, that's what the books say. Saints love everyone. Just everyone. With no thought of themselves. But with us, it's just the contrary.

SHEP. Look, maybe I'd better read some of those books of yours, after all.

MISS HOLROYD. Yes, Shep, then you'll see how impractical—well, how impossible, really—*love* is. Not sex. Sex is allowed. In fact, it's almost encouraged! But, of course, you must know that.

SHEP *(turning, angrily).* Miss Holroyd . . .

MISS HOLROYD. Oh, no, Shep, can't I be Auntie now?

SHEP. Miss Holroyd, I don't think we had better go on with this.

MISS HOLROYD. Oh, dear, I haven't been too bold, have I?

(*Gillian returns from the kitchen.*)

GILLIAN. Pyewacket is acting very strangely. I had to coax and coax him.

MISS HOLROYD. I must go, darling. I was late, even when I came. But I couldn't resist it. I just couldn't resist the urge.

GILLIAN (*with a sudden suspicion*). Auntie, Nicky didn't send you, did he?

MISS HOLROYD (*vaguely and innocently*). Nicky? No. I just passed Nicky on the street. He waved to me—rather a funny kind of wave, but . . . Darling, I must trot. Good-bye. Good-bye, Shep—*dear!* (*She goes out*)

SHEP (*after a moment*). Gillian, there are some things I want to ask you. Have you told me the truth—about yourself?

GILLIAN. Yes.

SHEP. And about us?

GILLIAN. Yes, why?

SHEP. You didn't tell me that you know Merle Kittredge. You did know her, didn't you? You were at college together. You knew about her and me, too, didn't you? You knew from the beginning? And that was why you went after me, deliberately, to spite her.

GILLIAN. No, not to spite her.

SHEP. Why, then?

GILLIAN. Because I wanted you.

SHEP. Because you were in love with me?

GILLIAN. How could I be in love with you? I didn't know you.

SHEP. Are you in love with me now? (*Silence*) Well?

GILLIAN (*after a moment, evasively*). I'm more in love with you than I've ever been with anyone. . . .

SHEP. Can you be in love, at all? Can you?

GILLIAN. I don't know. I never have, but then . . . I've never felt about anyone as I do about you, either. (*Turns to him*) How does one *tell* if one's in love?

SHEP. One knows.

GILLIAN. But how?

SHEP (*slowly*). Could you go on without me? I think that's the best test. If I wasn't there? Could you?

GILLIAN. I'd—have to, wouldn't I?

SHEP. And there's the answer. (*He turns away*)

GILLIAN (*follows him*). But wouldn't I?

SHEP. Maybe. But you shouldn't feel that you could. Why do you think it's hitting me the way it is? To find out the whole thing was a frame-up—of whatever kind—to find that you just haven't been there, the whole time?

GILLIAN (*turning away, deeply unhappy*). I don't think I knew. (*Sits on ottoman*)

SHEP. Knew what?

GILLIAN. What I was doing. That it would be like this. I'm sorry. (*She puts her hand to her head*)

SHEP (*angrily*). That's great. And you needn't pretend to cry. Because you can't do that, either, if I remember rightly.

GILLIAN (*angrily*). I'm not crying. (*Then, with realization*) Oh, so you believe it, now.

SHEP. No, I don't believe a word of it. Not a Goddamned word. (*A pause*) Can you take off spells that you put on? Because I think you'd better.

GILLIAN (*urgently*). No, no, I wouldn't do that. No, I won't! I won't!

SHEP (*again, after a pause*). Okay! (*He goes to the door, picking up his coat*)

GILLIAN. Where are you going?

SHEP. I don't know, but I'm getting the hell out of here. For good and all!

GILLIAN. No, no, you can't.

SHEP. Oh, yes, I can! I don't know how one deals with witches, but don't think, because you put a spell on me, that I'm coming back. Because I'm not. Ever. (*He goes out, slamming the door*)

GILLIAN (*urgently, moving forward*). Shep! (*Then she stops*) The spell! He'll have to come back. (*The front door is heard to slam*) Won't he?

(*She starts to the window. Then, suddenly, the door bursts open, and Shep breaks in again. He looks wild and utterly bewildered. He takes one step forward, and then freezes, staring at Gillian.*)

SHEP (*after a second—and as though struggling*). NO! No! Good God, No! (*He retreats slowly, as though fighting conflicting forces, and as though his feet were in glue*) No! No!! No!!! (*He manages to exit and to slam the door again*)

CURTAIN

ACT THREE

SCENE ONE

The scene is the same, later on tha

night. The mask, which was on the wall, is now broken into two pieces, lying on the chair and on the floor.

Gillian sits in the window-seat, staring out into the street, lighted only by the street-lamp.

After a moment, Nicky enters, silently. He sees the broken fragments of the mask, and registers them. Then he steps forward.

NICKY *(gaily)*. Ah, a dull moment around here!

GILLIAN *(rising and turning)*. Nicky, how did you get in?

NICKY. Don't ask silly questions. Through the door. Where's Shep?

GILLIAN. Out some place.

NICKY. You two haven't had a quarrel, or anything, have you?

GILLIAN *(coldly)*. No, not a quarrel. Just a visitor. Thank you, Nicky.

NICKY *(picking up the pieces of the mask)*. Say, what's this? Goodness, someone's been careless.

GILLIAN. No one has been careless.

NICKY. What a pity it got broken! It would come in so handy right now. Don't tell me Shep broke this.

GILLIAN. You know perfectly well who did it.

NICKY. Yes, you. But was it in reform or anger? Not just because Shep walked out on you?

GILLIAN. Nicky, you've seen him. Where?

NICKY. At Sid's place. He came straight there from you. *(Gillian is already half-way to the telephone)* Oh, it's no good your calling him. He isn't there now.

GILLIAN. Where is he?

NICKY. Well, that, I'm afraid I can't tell you.

GILLIAN. He's not with Merle? He's not thinking of Merle, is he?

NICKY. No, but I think he thinks he ought to be. After all, maybe he's still in love with her, underneath.

GILLIAN. Don't think I haven't thought of that. I've been sitting here battling with the temptation to take the spell off. That's when I broke the mask. Oh, but if I leave things as they are, he'll still love me, and loathe me for it.

NICKY. Yes, I don't think it was very smart of you to tell him all about the spell. Don't you know what it always says

on love potions? "Shake well, and don't tell."

GILLIAN *(not listening)*. This is what happens to you. You think you're getting away with something, and you forfeit almost everything. You end up in a little world of separateness from everyone. That's what I've found out. *(There is a knock on the door)* Who's that? It can't be Shep. Shep's got his key. *(The knock is repeated. Nicky opens the door. Shep is outside)* Shep!

SHEP *(in doorway)*. Nicky, I want to talk to Gillian. Alone. Will you clear out? It won't take more than a couple of minutes.

NICKY. Sure. Sure. I'll go and get a pack of cigarettes around the corner. *(He takes his coat over his arm and goes)*

GILLIAN *(urgently, as soon as the door is closed)*. Shep, won't you please . . . ?

SHEP *(interrupting firmly)*. Listen to me. I've got something to say, and I want to say it fast. I don't want to be here. And I wouldn't be, only I was told I had to, so here I am. *(Pause)* For your information, I've been to see Mrs. de Pass.

GILLIAN *(appalled)*. Oh, no! Why? What for?

SHEP. For a hair of the dog that bit me! After listening to Redlitch and to Nicky, they convinced me that there might be just a shred of truth in all this stuff of yours, so I thought I'd take a fling at the full treatment. I'd heard quite a lot about this de Pass dame from all of you, so I got Redlitch to take me up there.

GILLIAN *(aghast)*. Not to get her to take my spell off? Oh, no!

SHEP *(roughly)*. What the hell else?

GILLIAN. And—did she? Shep, did she?

SHEP. Sure, she did. For whatever it was worth.

GILLIAN. How?

SHEP. With a whole lot of hocus-pocus and a very dirty old parrot. From what I've seen, it's a lot more complicated to take a spell off than to put one on.

GILLIAN *(bitterly)*. It would be. For her. *(Pause)* And how do you feel now?

SHEP. I don't feel anything, except God-damned mad.

GILLIAN. At me?

SHEP. At the whole business. And at myself for getting into it. Going up, hat in hand, to a crummy joint like that . . . making me learn a little poem . . . having to say, "Yes, ma'am" and "No, ma'am" to that old bag. . . . It's stomach-turning, and humiliating!

GILLIAN *(ashamed)*. I know. Don't tell me.

SHEP *(ignoring her)*. To say nothing of being out a hell of a lot of dough, into the bargain.

GILLIAN. Why, what did she charge you?

SHEP. Plenty.

GILLIAN. How much?

SHEP. I don't want to go into it. Any of it. The only reason that I came was that she said the thing wouldn't be complete until I'd seen you and told you.

GILLIAN *(bitterly)*. That was nice of her. To make that a condition.

SHEP. Well, now I have, and I can get out of here. *(He starts to go, then stops)* And, by the way, she's fixed it so you can't undo this one.

GILLIAN *(incensed)*. And how did she do that?

SHEP. How would I know? She pretended it was something she put into that disgusting mess she made me drink.

GILLIAN. I never heard such rubbish in all my life. For her to think that she could stop me like that. Oh, it's all right. I'll let you go. . . .

SHEP. You're damned right you will.

GILLIAN. But don't think that decision is due to anything *she* did.

SHEP. We won't go into it—any of it. I've said what I had to say.

GILLIAN *(with an effort)*. What about—Merle?

SHEP. What about her?

GILLIAN. Are you going back to her—if she'll have you?

SHEP. Right now the only thing I'm going to do is to get a couple of stiff drinks under my belt, and knock myself out. Forget the whole business—if I can . . . I'll say good night.

GILLIAN *(faintly)*. You mean—good-bye?

SHEP. Yes, I mean good-bye.

GILLIAN *(staring at him)*. I'll never see you again.

SHEP. I wouldn't know what for. *(He turns and goes. Offstage, Nicky's voice can be heard)*

NICKY *(off)*. All through? *(Shep does not answer. Nicky comes in. Sunnily)* Well? What cooks?

GILLIAN. You knew that's where he was.

NICKY. Yes, dear.

GILLIAN. That was *your* bright idea.

NICKY. No, darling, it was his. All his. He got Sid to call her up.

GILLIAN *(with sudden revulsion)*. Oh, it's revolting! *His* getting mixed up with it. Going to see *her*. He's too good for that sort of thing.

NICKY *(protesting)*. Now, wait a minute . . .

GILLIAN. He is. It's cheapening to him. Scrabbling about in the gutters of the supernatural with Mrs. de Pass.

NICKY *(insinuatingly)*. Are you going to let her get away with it? Come on back to us, where you belong. Come to Natalie's party with me.

(There is a tap on the door. He opens it. Miss Holroyd enters.)

MISS HOLROYD. Gillian, I've got Mr. Redlitch outside.

GILLIAN. Since when do you know Redlitch?

MISS HOLROYD. We met tonight at Mrs. de Pass'. And then we left together when Shep—went in. Will you see him? Just for a minute. It's important.

GILLIAN. I can't see anyone now.

MISS HOLROYD. Yes, but you see, it's about Shep and Mrs. de Pass. Mr. Redlitch is afraid you may be holding it against him.

GILLIAN *(turning slowly, letting her distress take itself out in anger)*. Oh, yes—he took Shep up there, didn't he? All right. I'll see him.

MISS HOLROYD. I don't think you should be cross with him, darling.

GILLIAN *(coldly)*. Don't you? Bring him in.

(Miss Holroyd goes out.)

NICKY. Boy, will he need a drink! *(He goes into the kitchen. Miss Holroyd comes back, followed by Redlitch)*

REDLITCH *(very conciliatory)*. Good evening, Miss Holroyd. It's very nice of you to see me like this.

GILLIAN. It's you I have to thank for taking Shep up to Mrs. de Pass', isn't it, Mr. Redlitch? Taking him to be cured of me.

REDLITCH. Oh, it wasn't that, Miss Holroyd.

GILLIAN. What was it, then?

REDLITCH. Well, it was—to put him back to where he was when he first met you. You know, like in Shakespeare . . . "Be as thou wast wont to be—See as thou wast wont to see." *Midsummer Night's Dream*, when they take off the power of the flower and . . .

GILLIAN (*finishing for him*). And Titania falls out of love with the ass. Thank you for the comparison.

REDLITCH. Oh . . . Yes, I guess that was putting my foot in it. (*Nicky returns from the kitchen, with a straight bourbon which he silently hands Redlitch, who downs it hastily*) But—but what I want to explain is—*I* couldn't help myself. I figured at the time that you mightn't altogether like it . . .

GILLIAN. Oh, you did? Well, that was smart of you.

REDLITCH. And then when your aunt here told me you'd always had a hate on old Bianca . . .

GILLIAN. Bianca?

REDLITCH. Mrs. de Pass. Well, when I heard that—that you'd always been rivals, so to speak . . .

GILLIAN (*furious*). We've never been rivals. That third-rate, vulgar, self-advertising, *mail-order* sorceress . . .

NICKY. Hey, take it easy, darling. She's about the best in the business. . . .

GILLIAN (*interrupting*). It's people like her who make me wish we had the Inquisition back again. Do you know what she made him do? She made him come down here and tell me. Tell me what she'd done. Told him it was part of it.

MISS HOLROYD. Well, maybe it is, dear.

GILLIAN. Not for anyone who knows their business. She can't be as bad at it as that. No, that was just to crow over me.

REDLITCH. Look, Miss Holroyd, I don't know anything about that side of it. But I know you're no slouch yourself when it comes to revenge and that sort of thing. I don't want you to take it out on me. It was Shep's idea, the whole thing. All I did was take him there.

GILLIAN. And now you're afraid of the consequences.

REDLITCH. Well, only from you. I mean . . .

GILLIAN. Why don't you ask Mrs. de Pass to protect you, if you think so highly of her? I'm sure she wouldn't consider a little thing like rendering me impotent beyond her powers. Or you might go to the local minister and get me exorcised—with Bell, Book and Candle.

REDLITCH. Now, listen, don't get mad. I haven't done anything, except what I was asked to do!

GILLIAN. Suppose you'd been asked to commit a murder. Or introduce someone to a murderer, who'd do the job for the sum of . . . Yes, what does she charge for a little chore like this?

MISS HOLROYD. Well, she varies her prices, dear. According to people's means. She asked me about Shep . . .

GILLIAN. And what did you tell her?

MISS HOLROYD. I told her I thought he was quite well off. You see, I'd seen his bank book, and letters from his broker . . .

NICKY. What did that set him back?

MISS HOLROYD. She said she was going to ask five thousand dollars.

GILLIAN. *What?*

MISS HOLROYD. Well, I thought it was a little high, but she did point out that—supposing you and he had been married, it would cost him a lot more than that to get divorced. . . .

GILLIAN. Another pretty comparison.

REDLITCH. Look, Miss Holroyd, I don't want to intrude on you in your—hour of grief, but—put yourself in my place.

GILLIAN. I'd rather not, Mr. Redlitch. But don't worry, I won't do anything to *you*.

REDLITCH. Gee, that's swell of you, Miss Holroyd. Thank you, thank you. And—just one thing more. About the book. Nicky said you'd sort of—put a stopper on it. . . .

GILLIAN. Yes, I did.

REDLITCH. Well, don't you think—I mean, now that Shep's not—don't you think you might—I mean—well, sort of release it? (*Hastily*) Oh, I don't mean right now—naturally. But some time when you've nothing else on your mind. . . . If you could just flip that off . . .

GILLIAN (*breaking in*). Mr. Redlitch, don't you think from now on that you'd better stay clear of this kind of thing? I don't think you've got the temperament for it. Or the nerve, apparently.

REDLITCH. Maybe you're right. I only meant . . .

GILLIAN. Mr. Redlitch—*go away!*

REDLITCH. Oh, sure, sure. And thanks a lot, anyway. Good-bye. Good-bye, Miss Holroyd.

MISS HOLROYD. Good-bye. It was so nice meeting you. And . . . (*Intimately*) I'll try and talk Gillian around about the book.

REDLITCH. Yeah, but—don't upset her. It's not worth it. Good-bye. *(He goes hurriedly)*

NICKY. Well, darling, how do you feel now?

GILLIAN *(inarticulate with rage)*. Feel? Feel?

NICKY. Feel like coming to Natalie's party with me?

GILLIAN. Maybe. But I've got a little job to do here first.

NICKY. Old Bianca?

(Gillian nods grimly.)

MISS HOLROYD. You know, you're wrong about her, Gillian. She was very nice about you tonight. She really was.

GILLIAN. Yes, I'm sure she was. "Dear Gillian, I'm so fond of her. Just an amateur, of course, but really quite gifted in her way." Wasn't that it?

MISS HOLROYD. Well, sort of—yes, But . . .

GILLIAN. Amateur. I'll show her.

NICKY. That's my little sister.

GILLIAN. She and her five thousand dollars. With her potions and her . . . I wondered why he said it tasted bad. I suppose she thought if it didn't, he wouldn't feel that he was getting his money's worth. It must have tasted revolting for that.

NICKY. Maybe she gave him a candy, after.

GILLIAN. It'll cost her a lot more than five thousand to get out of what I'll do to her. She's got a lot of valuable Chinese rugs, you once told me. And that mink coat! Well, we'll start with some *moths!*

MISS HOLROYD. Gillian, you mustn't!

GILLIAN. Come to that, there's Merle, too. *(Furiously)* "Be as thou wast wont to be." And how was that? In love with Merle Kittredge. No. She's not going to get him back. Not if I have anything to do with it. Where's Pyewacket? *(She opens the kitchen door and calls)* Pye— Pye—Pyewacket? Pye, where are you? *(She goes into the kitchen)*

MISS HOLROYD. I've never seen her like this before.

NICKY *(happily)*. Yes, but don't stop her.

GILLIAN *(returning)*. He's not there.

MISS HOLROYD. Well, then, darling, why don't you wait and think it over till the morning?

GILLIAN. I can do without him. *(She goes to a closet; takes a key from behind some books, and opens it)* Let's see what I've got. *(She starts taking out bottles and looking at them)*

MISS HOLROYD. Darling, you can't have the moths in. Think of the other people in the building.

NICKY. Think of the moths!

GILLIAN *(muttering over labels)*. Where's that stuff I got in Haiti?

MISS HOLROYD. And Merle . . What are you going to do to her? Why don't you transport her somewhere?

GILLIAN *(still hunting)*. And have Shep go after her?

MISS HOLROYD. Then make her fall in love with someone else. Someone very unsuitable. *(Giggling)* The garbage man, maybe.

GILLIAN. Here. Here we are. I've been waiting for an opportunity to try this.

NICKY. What is it?

GILLIAN *(closing the closet)*. Something really fancy. For revenges. Now, what have we got of theirs? *(To Miss Holroyd)* Do you have anything belonging to her?

MISS HOLROYD. Mrs. de Pass? I've got her picture upstairs. But I don't think I should let you use that.

GILLIAN. I can write her name, and use that. That'll do. It'll also do for Miss Poison-Pen, too!

NICKY. This is a double-header. Quite a comeback you're staging.

MISS HOLROYD. Gillian, please, darling . . .

GILLIAN. Auntie, if you don't like it, you don't have to stay.

NICKY. Ah, let her see.

GILLIAN. Well, then, she must keep quiet. *(Writing)* Bianca—eh? Has she any middle name?

MISS HOLROYD. I think it's Flo.

GILLIAN *(writing)*. Bianca Flo. de Pass. Good. *(She gets another sheet)* Merle Emily Kittredge. Funny I should remember that it's Emily.

NICKY. Things do come back when they're needed.

GILLIAN. There. Put out the lights, Nicky. *(He puts out all lights. The scene is now a repeat of the summoning of Redlitch in Act One)* Auntie, the big ash tray.

MISS HOLROYD *(timidly proffering it)*. Here.

GILLIAN. Good. *(She settles. Crumples the two papers into the ash tray. Takes a pinch of herbs from the bottle and sprinkles them into the ash tray with the paper. She mutters)* Zaitux, Zorami, Elastot. . . . Got a match? *(Nicky produces some. She strikes a match, applies it to the contents of the ash tray. It sputters and goes out)* Damn. Give me another. *(She strikes another match. Same result)* It won't light.

NICKY. The stuff must be old, or something.

GILLIAN *(scared)*. The paper won't light.

MISS HOLROYD. Maybe the ash tray is damp.

GILLIAN. That wouldn't make any difference. I'll use the whole book this time. *(She strikes another match, then throws the book of matches into the tray and applies the lighted match. Again it splutters and goes out)* That's strange. . . . *(She rises, with a sudden knowledge)* Oh . . . ! *(She switches on the light)*

NICKY. What is it?

GILLIAN. We're not going on with this.

NICKY. Why not?

GILLIAN. I've changed my mind.

NICKY. But, Gill . . .

GILLIAN *(more firmly)*. I've changed my mind.

NICKY *(suspicious)*. There's nothing wrong, is there?

GILLIAN. No, no, of course not. You'd better go to your party, Nicky, I'll join you later. Nothing further is going to happen here tonight.

NICKY. Say, something really is wrong. You haven't been—defrosted, have you?

GILLIAN. No, of course not.

NICKY. Show me. Prove that.

GILLIAN *(moving away)*. I'll do no such thing. I'm tired.

NICKY *(after a pause)*. So, it is true, after all? The old wives' tales are true. Well, well, well! Let me hear from you some time, Gill. When you're feeling better, maybe? Good night. *(He goes out)*

MISS HOLROYD *(rises)*. Gill, what is it?

GILLIAN *(returning)*. Auntie—it *is* true.

MISS HOLROYD. You mean—you have lost your powers? You've fallen in love?

GILLIAN. I guess so. I guess it's happened to me.

MISS HOLROYD. With Shep, you mean?

GILLIAN *(angrily)*. Who else?

MISS HOLROYD. Oh, but, darling—now—now . . .

GILLIAN. Yes, it's a fine time, isn't it? I've been coming down with it all evening.

Only, I just didn't know what it was. Well, that's that. I guess I'm through. Through as a witch, anyway.

MISS HOLROYD. Gillian, what is love like? You know, I've never had it. Is it—wonderful?

GILLIAN. No—it's awful! *(She bursts into tears)*

MISS HOLROYD. Oh, darling! Tears. Real tears.

GILLIAN *(weeping)*. Yes, and to think I've always envied people who *could* cry! It feels horrible! *(The tears turn into floods)* Oh, Auntie, I don't *want* to be human—*now!*

(She sobs in Miss Holroyd's arms.)

CURTAIN

SCENE TWO

Two months later.

Afternoon. All the objects savoring of witchcraft have been removed.

When the curtain rises, Nicky is discovered, trying to pour himself a drink at the liquor console. He finds the whiskey bottle almost empty. He pours the last dregs from it, then tries the door of the console. It is locked. He snaps his fingers at it four times, tries it again, and it opens. He takes out a fresh bottle of Scotch and pours himself a drink. The buzzer sounds, and he answers it.

———

NICKY. Hello?

MISS HOLROYD'S VOICE. Is that Nicky? It's Aunt Queenie.

NICKY. Come on in.

(He buzzes her in, takes swallow of drink, and then opens the door. Miss Holroyd comes in, in a breathless fluster.)

MISS HOLROYD. Nicky, dear—how nice. *(She kisses him)* It's been such ages. Oh, I'm exhausted. Really, the traffic. You must teach me how to handle that.

NICKY. Yes, it's made you so late, I can't stay.

MISS HOLROYD *(urgently)*. You must stay till Gillian gets here. That's why I got you here. You two can't go on this way. Especially when she's so unhappy.

NICKY. Is she still in love with Shep?

MISS HOLROYD. Yes, and he hasn't set foot in this building since that night.

NICKY. What does Gill do with herself these days, anyway?

MISS HOLROYD. Well, she has a job.

NICKY. A job?

MISS HOLROYD. She goes to the movies. At first, she just went because they were a good place to cry in. And she said, too, that if she was going to start having human emotions, she'd better learn something about them.

NICKY. From the movies?

MISS HOLROYD. And then one day she met a lady whose job was seeing movies, and she asked Gillian if she'd like to do it, too. Gill sees two double features a day, and then reports on them. Writes them up in the evening.

NICKY. Wouldn't she rather be dead?

MISS HOLROYD. Nicky, you mustn't say things like that. You must be kind.

NICKY. Auntie, how can you, a self-respecting witch, say that?

MISS HOLROYD. Nicky, I don't want to scold you today, not about anything, but ever since your book died you've been very discourteous to Sidney.

NICKY. Sidney?

MISS HOLROYD *(coyly)*. You know—Mr. Redlitch.

NICKY *(amused)*. Hey, since when?

MISS HOLROYD *(as before)*. Oh, quite a little while. We have dinner every Wednesday.

NICKY. I didn't mean to be discourteous, but things have been pretty slim for me.

(Gillian enters. She wears hat and coat.)

GILLIAN. Auntie! Nicky! Oh, how nice. I haven't seen you since—well, not since. What brought you here?

NICKY. I just thought I'd come around, and say hello. Or, rather, Aunt Queenie thought so.

GILLIAN. Oh, well, lovely. Come and sit down.

NICKY. Look, I can't, today.

GILLIAN. Oh, just for a little. Won't you? Please, Nicky, please stay.

NICKY. I'm late as it is. I've got a date with Natalie. I'll come back some other time. I really will. How's Pyewacket?

GILLIAN. He ran away.

NICKY. Because of . . . ?

GILLIAN. I guess so.

NICKY. Nothing for him to do around here any more? *(He looks at her)* You know, Gill, you *look* different. I don't know *how*, exactly, but . . .

GILLIAN. Better or worse?

NICKY. That depends upon your taste, I guess. Good-bye, Gill. Good-bye, Auntie. *(He goes)*

MISS HOLROYD. What did you see this afternoon, dear?

GILLIAN. I didn't stay. They were two comedies. *(She starts to pace)*

MISS HOLROYD. You're very nervous.

GILLIAN *(with a sudden intensity)*. Auntie . . . Shep's upstairs!

MISS HOLROYD. Oh, darling, how do you know?

GILLIAN. I saw him at his window. Just a flash of him.

MISS HOLROYD. Did he see you?

GILLIAN. I don't know. I'm afraid he may have.

MISS HOLROYD. Not afraid!

GILLIAN. I've been so thankful that he's not been in the place—that I've not bumped into him. And now, the feeling that he's just up there is more than I can stand. Let's not have dinner here. *(Panicky)* Let's go out! Let's go out right now!

MISS HOLROYD *(firmly)*. I wish I could summon him. Then we could tell him what's happened to you. About your—accident. And what caused it.

GILLIAN. Tell him? I'd go to any lengths to stop his finding out.

MISS HOLROYD. But, darling, why?

GILLIAN. Something called pride, I guess. Or shame. They're new emotions to me. Or else they're very old ones, in reverse. The other side of the coin.

(There is a knock on the door. She retreats a step, startled.)

MISS HOLROYD. Oh, it's him! *(Correcting herself)* It's he!

GILLIAN *(distracted)*. It can't be! Help me. Open the door, but don't leave me. Promise.

(The knock is repeated. Miss Holroyd goes to the door. She opens it. Shep is standing outside. He carries a suitcase.)

SHEP. Hello.

MISS HOLROYD. Hello, Shep.

SHEP *(to Gillian)*. Are you busy, or could I see you for a moment?

GILLIAN. I have Aunt Queenie here.

MISS HOLROYD *(to Gillian)*. Darling, I'm going to run along. I have a dinner engagement.

GILLIAN. But I thought we . . .

MISS HOLROYD. No, darling. I forgot to

tell you. But I'll call you. Later. See? Good-bye, Shep. It's so lovely you dropped in! *(She goes)*

SHEP. I'm afraid Miss Holroyd has the wrong idea of what I came here for. This isn't a friendly visit.

GILLIAN. I didn't imagine that it was.

SHEP. I'm leaving for Europe and I came down here to get some things I needed. *(Indignantly)* I've only just discovered that I still have an apartment here. I told my secretary right after—that night—to move me the hell out of here and never mention the place to me again. *(Belatedly)* I don't mean to be offensive.

GILLIAN. I understand.

SHEP. Today I found my stuff is not in storage at all. I'm stuck with this place. No sublet. You can't expect me to believe nowadays there are suddenly no tenants to be had. I see your hand in this, and I don't intend to put up with it.

GILLIAN. What have I done?

SHEP. You know damn well what you've done. Fixed it that way.

GILLIAN. What did the agents tell your secretary?

SHEP. I don't know what they told her. I didn't let her get that far. I intend to deal with this, myself.

GILLIAN. You mean—deal with *me?* I can't do anything about it.

SHEP. You mean, you won't.

GILLIAN. If it will end this interview, I will accept that.

SHEP. But I won't accept it. This is sheer vindictiveness. Trying to hold me here.

GILLIAN *(bursting out)*. And I won't accept *that*. The whole thing is in your lease, as you could have found out if you'd been willing to look or listen, instead of jumping to insane conclusions. The owner here won't let me give a sublet clause. And if you think I fixed that, in some way or other, I'll dispel that illusion, too. I don't want you in this house. I'd far rather you were out of it. And I'll make that clear by canceling your lease, if that will suit you.

SHEP. You will?

GILLIAN. Gladly.

SHEP. Done.

GILLIAN. Good.

SHEP. Fine!

GILLIAN. Finished!

SHEP *(glancing at his watch)*. Oh . . .

GILLIAN. What is it?

SHEP. I was wondering if my secretary would still be in the office.

GILLIAN. Do you want to call and see?

SHEP *(eyeing the telephone, half-humorously)*. On this phone?

GILLIAN. Well, if you prefer not to . . .

SHEP. It's not my favorite telephone. But I'll take a chance. *(He goes to it, and dials)* I'm sorry I got sore.

GILLIAN. I did, too.

SHEP *(forcing friendliness)*. How have you been?

GILLIAN *(doing likewise)*. Fine. And you?

SHEP. Fine. How's Pyewacket?

GILLIAN. He . . . *(She checks herself)* He's fine.

SHEP. Keeping busy?

GILLIAN. Him or me?

SHEP. Both of you. *(He answers the phone)* Hello . . . Miss Bishop? I'm sorry I flew off the handle. I'm at Miss Holroyd's apartment. I've arranged to cancel the lease. Will you look after it? I won't be in the office in the morning, so why don't I leave the key here? With Miss Holroyd. Then you can get it from her. *(To Gillian)* Is that all right?

GILLIAN. Certainly.

SHEP *(into phone)*. Okay, then. What? What rent? Well, haven't you been . . . ? Well, why not? All right. All right. I'll deal with it. Good-bye. *(He hangs up)* I gather I owe you some rent. Three months, to be exact.

GILLIAN. No. No, you don't.

SHEP. Why not?

GILLIAN. I owe you far more than that.

SHEP. What do you owe me?

GILLIAN. Well—well, five thousand dollars, anyway.

SHEP. Huh?

GILLIAN. That Mrs. de Pass charged you. That was outrageous.

SHEP. I thought it was a bit excessive, myself. But I'd nothing to compare it with.

GILLIAN. I wish that I could pay it. I ought to, I know. But I can't.

SHEP. I don't see that it's your responsibility. But thanks for thinking of it. Do you mind if I leave a note for my secretary? She's terribly dumb.

GILLIAN *(very tentatively)*. How is it—going? I mean—how's Merle?

SHEP *(after a tiny pause)*. She's fine—I guess.

GILLIAN. You—guess? Didn't you—go back to her? Or was that spoiled?

SHEP (*unwillingly*). No, I went back to her.

GILLIAN. Then what did happen? I'm sorry to be inquisitive, but it has been rather like—not knowing the end of a movie.

SHEP. Yes, I can see that. Well, I went back, but—it didn't work.

GILLIAN. Because of me? What did you tell her about me?

SHEP. Nothing.

GILLIAN. Didn't she want to know? How you had come to leave her?

SHEP. Yes, but I wouldn't go into it. Beyond the fact that I'd been—well, "bewitched" was the word I used. I didn't say I meant it literally. And then—something happened. Something she had done. I can't tell you what, but—it finished things.

GILLIAN. It wasn't—a letter? An anonymous letter, was it?

SHEP (*surprised*). What makes you ask that? Was that a habit of hers?

GILLIAN. I'm afraid it was.

SHEP. Actually, it was a letter she had written to my partner while I was—with you.

GILLIAN. Oh, yes, you said he had been acting strangely.

SHEP. That was why.

GILLIAN (*genuinely*). I'm sorry. Very sorry.

SHEP. You know, this is odd—for you.

GILLIAN. What is?

SHEP. All this—interest. This curiosity . . . You look different, too.

GILLIAN (*scared*). How—different?

SHEP. I don't know. But something about you. There's something different about this place, too.

GILLIAN (*hastily*). I've changed some things in the apartment. That's all the difference is. (*Eager to end the interview*) And—look, please, you don't have to stay and be polite.

SHEP. Yes, I have got a great deal to do. . . . (*He makes a move, then stops, remembering something*) Oh—my key. (*He takes a single key from his pocket*) Will you give it to my secretary? (*He hands it to her*)

GILLIAN (*taking it*). Of course.

SHEP (*awkwardly*). And that reminds me. There's something else. I've been wondering how I could go about returning it. (*Pause*) It's the key to—this apartment. (*He takes out his key-ring*)

GILLIAN (*turning away*). Will you excuse me for a moment?

(*She goes swiftly into the bedroom. Shep looks after her, surprised by the suddenness of her exit. Then he takes the key off the ring. Gillian returns, carrying something in her hand.*)

SHEP (*holding out the key to her*). Here.

GILLIAN (*unwilling to touch it*). Put it down, will you? (*He does so. There is a tiny pause. Then, with equal embarrassment*) I've been wondering how I could go about returning this to *you*.

SHEP. What is it?

GILLIAN. Your locket.

SHEP. I gave you that.

GILLIAN. Under false pretenses. I've felt worse about having that, than over anything. Like a thief, almost. Please take it.

SHEP. It doesn't mean that much.

GILLIAN. It does to me. Please.

SHEP. Very well, then. (*He takes it. Looks at it, then slips it into his pocket*)

GILLIAN. I feel better. And now, I think I'd like you to go.

SHEP (*slowly*). Yes . . . Yes . . . (*He stands, looking at her*)

GILLIAN. Don't stare at me. Please go.

SHEP (*continuing to stare*). It's strange to look at you like this. The way I see you now is like a kind of—double image. Someone who's completely new and strange—and someone I've known intimately. (*With implication*) Very intimately. It would be hard to forget that. Here, especially. (*She turns away*)

GILLIAN (*with her back to him*). Do you mind going?

SHEP (*goes to her, turns her around to him; she averts her face*). Gill—you're not blushing?

GILLIAN. No, of course I'm not. (*She struggles to keep her head turned away*)

SHEP. You're crying, too.

GILLIAN (*angrily*). All right, then I'm crying!

SHEP. But I thought . . .

GILLIAN. You thought we couldn't—didn't you? Well, you were wrong!

SHEP (*slowly*). Are you quite sure of that?

GILLIAN. Quite sure.

SHEP. Well, I'm not! You're different. You're completely different. Why?

GILLIAN. What does it matter?

SHEP. It matters to me. One hell of a lot! Tell me—are you—not one, any more? Is that it? Is it? I've got to know.

GILLIAN *(turning, violently)*. All right, then. I have lost my powers. Now you do know. I guess you're entitled to that much satisfaction. And now will you please leave me alone?

SHEP *(after a beat, quietly)*. How did you lose them?

GILLIAN. They just—went.

SHEP. Is that apt to happen?

GILLIAN *(shortly)*. Under certain circumstances.

SHEP. What circumstances?

GILLIAN. There are all kinds.

SHEP *(forcibly)*. No, there's only one way. It was in that book of Redlitch's.

GILLIAN. Redlitch doesn't know anything about it.

SHEP. But Nicky does. And he helped write it.

GILLIAN *(desperately)*. Shep, if you've ever had any regard for me, please go now. What's the point in going on at me like this?

SHEP *(slowly)*. Because something has been happening since I came into this room. I want to be sure that it's the real thing—this time. *(She looks up at him, getting his meaning. Her face begins to shine with an incredulous rapture. Shep smiles, then moves)* I *will* go now. *(He picks up his hat and suitcase. She stands staring at him, bewildered, dazed. He comes back into the room)* And maybe I won't go to Europe—just yet. I'd like to give those images a chance to blend. *(Smiling, teasingly)* I suppose you have got some idea of what I'm talking about?

GILLIAN *(slowly)*. I—think so. It's been happening to me, too—for—such a long time.

SHEP *(gently, smiling)*. It has?

GILLIAN *(in a small voice)*. I'm only human!

(He sets down the suitcase. They are in the same spot as at the end of the first scene of Act One. Slowly, as before, they move toward each other, ending in each other's arms.)

CURTAIN

The Moon Is Blue

BY F. HUGH HERBERT

First presented by Aldrich & Myers, with Julius Fleischmann, at Henry Miller's Theatre in New York on March 8, 1951, with the following cast:

PATTY O'NEILL......................Barbara Bel Geddes	DAVID SLATER...................... ......Donald Cook
DONALD GRESHAM......................Barry Nelson	MICHAEL O'NEILL..........................Ralph Dunn

---

ACT ONE

Scene One: The Observation Tower of the Empire State Building. Early evening.
Scene Two: An apartment on East 49th Street. An hour later.

ACT TWO

The same. Two hours later.

ACT THREE

Scene One: The same. Several hours later.
Scene Two: The Observation Tower of the Empire State Building. The following
　　　　　afternoon.

The entire action of the play takes place in New York City within 24 hours. Spring, 1951.

The English-born F. Hugh Herbert gravitated into show business after service in the advertising department of London's famous department store, Selfridge's. After spending a well-earned vacation in the United States in 1920, Mr. Herbert decided to transplant himself permanently and became a resident and, finally, a citizen. A versatile gentleman, he published a number of popular novels, contributed successfully to magazines, worked in motion pictures (starting in Paramount's old Long Island studio), and gave radio one of its most successful serials, *Meet Corliss Archer,* originally a magazine serial by him. Having found a seemingly inexhaustible subject in the complications of girlhood, Mr. Herbert placed it at the disposal of the Broadway stage by writing the immensely liked war-time comedy *Kiss and Tell,* produced by George Abbott on March 17, 1943, with the attractive young actress Joan Caulfield playing Corliss Archer and Richard Widmark playing her brother. A second piece of entertainment by the author, *For Love or Money,* presented on November 4, 1947, was less rapturously received in town. (It is not to be assumed, of course, that Mr. Herbert had been laboring at it all these years. He continued to exercise his versatility frequently and profitably in Hollywood.) But *The Moon Is Blue,* a more sparkling comedy, won immediate acclaim and restored amity for its author even among drama critics.

In *The Moon Is Blue,* Mr. Herbert turned out a gay comedy by marrying innocence and sophistication, wholesome young love and slightly decadent but decidedly entertaining middle-aged cynicism. The cynicism was especially welcome when conveyed with brilliant aplomb by the reliable Donald Cook, previously seen on Broadway in the season of 1948-49, as Tallulah Bankhead's sparring partner in Noel Coward's *Private Lives. The Moon Is Blue* made the best of the two worlds of low-comedy and high-comedy, pleasing both low-brow and high-brow, or at least middle-brow playgoers.

Astutely effecting a compromise, Herbert made wit profitable on Broadway. Ben Hecht, who wrote a foreword to the published play, called it "the perfect example of successful mental comedy" in spite of the fact that the "plot, characters, and problems are almost as naïve as those in a musical show." The virtues of this comedy do not depend so much on the triumph of virtue and love, a foregone conclusion in the author's contrivance, as on its pyrotechnics of discussion, in which the candor and perverse reasoning on the subject of seduction are droll and hilarious. This could not, of course, be effected without whimsical and neat dialogue. Ben Hecht summarized the nature of the author's success by declaring that "F. Hugh Herbert is one of the few witty writers for the American stage who has managed to land an audience rather than himself in the aisles."

ACT ONE

Scene One

The Observation Tower of the Empire State Building. The stage is empty for a few moments. Then a young girl strolls out. She is about twenty-one. Her name is Patty O'Neill. She wears a light spring coat over a little street dress. She is hatless but wears gloves. She comes downstage, glancing over her shoulder toward the tower as if she were expecting someone. There is a rather amused, excited smile on her face. There is an eager, fresh quality about Patty that is very engaging.

She stands at the balustrade, gazing out, but out of the corner of her eye she is still watching the tower.

A few moments later a young man enters from the tower. His name is Don Gresham. Over his arm he carries a light, spring overcoat, and he wears no hat. He carries a small package.

Patty is well aware of the fact that he is there, but affects to pay no attention. Don comes down to the balustrade. He is whistling with an air of nonchalance. She affects to be absorbed in the slot-machine binoculars nearby.

———

DON (*finally*). Why were you in such a tearing hurry?

PATTY. What?

DON. I was just putting away my wallet and I spoke to the woman selling tickets—and, *bingo*—you'd vanished into thin air.

PATTY. I'm sorry. . . . I didn't know for sure whether . . . Why didn't you *say* something?

DON. I *did*. I yelled "Hey!"—but you were already off in a cloud of dust.

PATTY. No, I don't mean then. Why didn't you say something before in the drug store when we—when we first sort of noticed each other? (*Points to his little package*) Why were you buying pumice stone?

DON. Because I get ink on my hands and pumice stone takes it off.

PATTY. Oh. And all those rubber bands —what do you need them for?

DON (*amused*). I need those in my business. I didn't know you were watching me that closely.

PATTY. I was just across the counter from you and I couldn't help hearing, and, besides, I'm always *fascinated* by what other people buy in drug stores. You got razor blades, too.

DON. I shave. You didn't buy anything, I noticed.

PATTY. I was flirting with a divine new shade of lipstick, but it was a dollar-fifty and I decided to be sensible. It's so beautiful too—it's called . . .

(*Don instantly produces a little package from his pocket and puts it on the balustrade in front of her.*)

DON. "Dusty Dawn"—and a damn silly name, if you ask me.

(*Patty takes a lipstick out of the package and looks at him wonderingly.*)

PATTY. For me?

DON. I rarely use lipstick.

PATTY. How perfectly sweet of you! You must've been watching me in the drug store.

DON. When a man's waiting for pumice stone and rubber bands, he has to watch something.

PATTY. Why didn't you speak to me then?

DON. I was just rehearsing a suitable gambit—when you mooched off.

PATTY. I did not mooch off.

DON. You never looked back once.

PATTY. Well, I should hope not. (*Giggles*) I tried to create the impression that I'd suddenly remembered an urgent appointment.

DON. You almost fooled me (*They look at each other, smiling*) Why didn't you smile at me like that in the drug store?

PATTY. I don't smile at men in drug stores.

DON. Well, a few minutes later then— when I obviously followed you into the lobby where they sell tickets for up here. It wouldn't have hurt you to smile then.

PATTY. Did I look very aloof?

DON. Aloof and forbidding—and rather scared. You scowled.

PATTY. Nonsense, I was trying to look sultry and provocative.

DON. You beat me to the elevator, too.

PATTY (*slightly fussed*). I know . . . I got in before I realized . . . I wondered what happened to you. (*She yawns vigorously*) Are your ears still popping? Mine are.

DON. That's just your imagination.

PATTY. Don't be silly. Of course they're

popping. It's the pressure or something. Haven't you ever been up in an airplane? *(Another yawn)* It's okay now. They unpopped. Now I feel fine. *(Gazes out)* Gosh! Isn't this wonderful?

DON. Not particularly. Fog's coming in. Can't see much today.

PATTY. You can see Staten Island.

DON *(amiably)*. You're crazy. You can hardly see a thing.

PATTY. I can.

DON *(points)*. You can't even see the Chrysler Building.

PATTY. I can.

DON. You're nuts.

PATTY. Well, I can imagine it, anyway.

DON. Couldn't you imagine it just as well from the street? They told you it was crazy downstairs. Remember the sign: Visibility Poor. Look—There's not a soul up here.

PATTY. I'm glad I came. I love it up here. Just think—we're over a thousand feet up. The tallest building in the world. I think it's wonderful. I mean—just look —doesn't it take your breath away. *(An ecstatic sigh)* It's a wicked extravagance, but I don't care. It's worth every penny of it.

(Don takes out a dollar bill and two dimes and puts them in front of her on the balustrade.)

DON. By the way, here's your dollar-twenty.

PATTY. What? What do you mean?

DON. Despite your sultry scowl, I paid for two tickets—and when the woman said you'd paid for yours, I told her we'd had a little spat—so she gave me the money back.

PATTY. You mean you're treating me to this? How perfectly sweet of you. Thanks a lot. *(Puts the money in her purse)* Now I can really enjoy it. One always gets a bigger kick out of things for free. And you don't even know my name, even. I think that's perfectly charming of you. *(Looks him over)* What's your name? Mine's Patty—Patty O'Neill.

DON. Don Gresham.

PATTY. Don. Yes. That suits you. You look like a Don.

DON. Patty, let me ask you a question. I don't usually do things like this, and I have a . . .

(Patty pretends to be absorbed in the slot-machine binoculars. She wants to duck questions.)

PATTY. I wonder how this gadget works?

DON *(gives her a dime)*. For a dime you can find out.

PATTY. Thanks. You *are* nice. Before—when you came out, I was pretending.

DON. I gathered that.

(She drops in the dime and swivels the gadget around. She is enchanted.)

PATTY. Oh, this is terrific. Now you can really see. . . . Wouldn't you like a look?

DON. I've been up here before. My office is in this building. Patty, listen to me a minute. I'd like to tell you . . .

PATTY *(adjusts binoculars)*. Oh, stop jabbering. I want to enjoy this, and I can't while you keep on talking. . . . Are you drumming like that because you're bored or nervous—or do you want to hold my hand? You can if you want to. . . .

(She takes off her glove and slips her hand into his. He fondles it gently. She gazes into space—with the binoculars and then without. Her face is troubled.)

DON. You are a screwball—and no fooling. And you have very sweet hands. *(Looks into her face)* What are you thinking about?

PATTY. I want to cry.

DON. What for?

PATTY *(points)*. All those people . . .

DON. What people?

PATTY. In Brooklyn.

DON *(points over his shoulder)*. Brooklyn's over there.

PATTY. I don't care. It doesn't matter. I still want to cry.

DON. Why?

PATTY. Because it's so sad.

DON. What? Living in Brooklyn?

PATTY. Please don't be funny. I was born in Brooklyn.

DON. I'm not trying to be funny. I swear I don't know what you're talking about.

PATTY *(in a reverie)*. The poor, drab, little people, sweating their lives out in a . . .

DON *(shivering)*. Nobody's sweating on a day like this. Don't worry.

PATTY. Don't be so darn practical.

DON. Then quit talking like a play by Saroyan.

PATTY. I adore him, don't you?

DON. Huh? Who?

PATTY. Saroyan.

DON. I can take him or leave him.

PATTY. I think he's wonderful. *(Into the void)* Hello out there!

DON. Huh?

PATTY. *Hello Out There.* It's a play of his. Saroyan's. *Hello Out There,* by William Saroyan. It's about a man who was in jail. *(Gently)* He loves little, drab, gentle people. Saroyan—not the man who was in jail.

DON *(baffled)*. Look, Patty—let's go down, shall we? It's getting all fogged in.

PATTY. No, I like it up here.

DON. Aren't you cold?

PATTY. Only my hands. They always get cold when I get excited.

DON. What are you excited about?

PATTY. Coming up here. I've wanted to for years.

DON. Then why didn't you?

PATTY. Frankly, because I couldn't afford it. You can get a lovely pair of nylons for a dollar-twenty. I don't know why I decided to splurge tonight.

DON *(chuckles gently)*. You're terribly sweet. . . .

PATTY. Look, I swear I had no idea you'd . . . I *was* splurging . . . Fancy charging a dollar-twenty just to ride to the top of a building. It's enough to make you a Communist.

DON. You think Stalin doesn't charge admission to go to the top of the Kremlin?

PATTY *(seriously)*. You know, I never thought of that.

DON. Are you hungry?

PATTY. Starving.

DON. Let's go down and get some dinner.

PATTY *(shakes her head)*. No.

DON. Why not?

PATTY. You've spent enough on me already.

DON. Don't be silly.

PATTY. You have, too. A ticket to the tower and a lovely lipstick . . .

DON *(ribbing)*. Don't forget the dime for the gadget.

PATTY *(gravely)*. That's right.

DON. Now, don't be a little dope. We're going someplace to eat. I don't want any arguments out of you.

PATTY. Where would we go?

DON. You name it.

PATTY. Are you very flush?

DON. Just name it.

PATTY. Would you take me to the Stork Club?

DON. Sure.

PATTY. It's awfully expensive.

DON. Oh, well. Mr. Billingsley has to live.

PATTY. Do you like the Stork Club?

DON. I've only been there a few times. It's mostly for people in show business, and I don't know many of those. Do you like it?

PATTY. Gosh, yes, I've only been there once—an agent took me—but I'd just adore to go again. None of the boys I know can afford it. We usually go Dutch to a spaghetti joint. I love spaghetti, don't you?

DON. Frankly, I prefer a good steak. Come on, let's go.

PATTY *(hesitates, stalling)*. It's early. I'm not that hungry.

DON. Fine. We'll go to my place first and have a drink. How about it?

PATTY *(looks him over for a long time)*. Would you try to seduce me?

DON *(amused)*. I don't know. Probably. Why?

PATTY. Why? A girl wants to know.

DON. A girl is supposed to be intuitive about those things. You don't go around bluntly asking people such questions.

PATTY. I do. I always do.

DON. And what happens if they say yes, they're going to try and seduce you?

PATTY. I generally believe them, and then I'm out one dinner.

DON. And if they say their intentions are honorable?

PATTY. I generally believe *them*—but you get fooled sometimes. I hate men like that. After all, there are lots of girls who don't mind being seduced. Why pick on those who do?

DON. Okay. I won't make a single pass at you. Do you believe me?

PATTY *(a long look)*. Yes, I do. You're nice. I like you.

DON. I could be lying.

PATTY. That's true. Are you?

DON. Frankly, I don't know. I've never run up against anybody like you.

PATTY *(delighted)*. How nice!

DON. I won't take an oath that I'm not going to kiss you.

PATTY. Oh, that's all right. Kissing's *fun.* I've *no* objection to that.

DON. I'll be damned if I know whether

you're just incredibly naïve or whether you're ribbing the pants off me.

PATTY (*bluntly*). Look, it's very simple. Let's face it—going to a man's apartment almost always ends in one of two ways: Either the girl's willing to lose her virtue —or she fights for it. I don't want to lose mine—and I think it's vulgar to fight for it. So I always put my cards on the table. Don't you think that's sensible?

DON (*smiling*). Okay. Sold. Affection, but no passion. My word of honor.

PATTY (*happily*). "Affection, but no passion." That's *lovely*. You could run for president on that.

(*Laughing, he pulls her to him, tilts up her face, and they kiss.*)

DON. You're terribly sweet—even if you are a little bit nuts. (*Kisses her. After kiss*) Patty O'Neill. You must be very Irish.

PATTY. Both of my parents were born in Brooklyn, but Pop's Irish from way back. When he gets good and mad, he can even talk with a thick brogue.

DON. What does he do?

PATTY. He's a cop.

DON. Oh. Then you probably have lots of brothers and sisters.

PATTY. No. Why?

DON. I always thought Irish cops had at least ten kids.

PATTY. No. I was the only one. My mother died when I was twelve. She was swell.

DON. You live at home?

PATTY (*shakes her head emphatically*). Uh uh. Irish cops are too strict and old-fashioned, and Pop's a holy terror. All my beaux were scared to death of him. I've been on my own since I was eighteen. (*Looks him over*) Are you married?

DON. No.

PATTY. That's good. You shouldn't get married for ages. You're too young. What do you do?

DON. Architect.

PATTY. Oh, that explains the ink and the pumice stone! Are you a draftsman?

DON. Believe it or not—I'm a full-fledged architect. I can build you anything from a cathedral to a bomb shelter.

PATTY. This'll be a lesson to you. You shouldn't pick up girls in the Empire State Building. Then you get hooked for tickets to the tower, and a dinner at the Stork Club—and no prospects before or after. There's not much percentage in it for you, is there?

DON. It's not every day that I can pick up a charming little lunatic like you.

PATTY. Do you really think I'm nuts?

DON. No, not really. But I'm an architect, and I have a rather orderly mind and lead quite an orderly life.

PATTY (*thoughtfully*). I'm too young to tidy up my life yet. You see, at my age, when you're just learning a lot of new things, you haven't the remotest idea what to keep, or what to discard, or even what to get. You just go on collecting them— and hope for the best.

DON. As for instance?

PATTY. A career, if possible. Failing that —marriage. I'm just dying to get married —but I'm very choosy, so it's not going to be easy. The kind of men I want don't grow on trees.

DON. Do they prowl the lobby of the Empire State Building picking up girls?

PATTY. You didn't pick me up. I made you. My gosh, I did everything but actually drop my handkerchief. (*Amused. Looks in his face, laughing*) But don't worry—you're not the type I'm looking for at all.

DON. No?

PATTY. Nope. You looked sort of forlorn and I wanted to talk to you, but you're much too young. When I get married, I want a nice, middle-aged man with gobs of dough. Preferably one who's been married before and had a simply lousy time. He can have five kids, for all I care.

DON. Doesn't sound very romantic.

PATTY. Oh, pooh! Romance is for bobby-sockers. I'd much rather have a man appreciate me than *drool* over me.

DON. Do you think I have a tendency to drool?

PATTY (*thoughtfully*). Yes, I think you're quite demonstrative. I think that's swell. I'm very affectionate myself.

DON. How old are you?

PATTY. I'll be twenty-one in a few weeks. Old enough to vote. (*Gazes into space—points vaguely*) Just think—every day thousands of people my age become old enough to vote—and none of us really know what to vote for. I always want to cry—the poor, little, ignorant people....

DON. No! No! Don't go Saroyan on me again. I'm getting hungry. Aren't you?

PATTY. Yes—let's go.

DON. And you'll let me take you to my place for a drink first?

PATTY (*gravely*). Yes.

DON. Without any qualms?

PATTY. Without a qualm in the world. (*Hastily*) And I'm not reflecting on your virility either.

DON. Let's leave my virility out of it.

PATTY. Well, I just didn't want to hurt your feelings. (*Philosophically*) Boys are so funny. They're not a bit flattered to be trusted.

DON. You met me ten minutes ago. Why do you trust me so implicitly?

PATTY (*simply*). It sounds awfully corny —but I think you're a man of honor. A girl can tell.

DON (*touched*). You're really terribly sweet. (*He raises her chin and kisses her gently on the lips*)

PATTY Thank you. (*Contented sigh*) I'm so glad you don't mind.

DON. Mind what?

PATTY (*brightly—taking his arm*). Oh, men are usually so bored with virgins. I'm so glad you're not.

(*As they walk toward exit.*)

CURTAIN

SCENE TWO

The living room of Don's apartment in the East Forties. It is on the fifth floor of a large apartment building, well lit by table and floor lamps. It is a large, very masculine room. Windows look out onto the street. Under these windows there is a narrow window seat of leather. On the left is a door leading to the two bedrooms and on the right is a door to the kitchen. There is a fireplace at right, and, nearby, a comfortable chair with an ottoman. Behind this there is a small, well-stocked portable bar. The lamps are all lit. It's about an hour later. Outside, it's raining, a steady, hissing downpour. The drapes are not yet drawn. There is a backing which shows the dimly lit windows of houses across the street. Patty is curled up comfortably on a large couch. She is studying a blueprint—a building designed by Don. She has removed her coat, which hangs over the back of a straight chair. There is a coffee table in front of the

couch. Patty has also removed her shoes, which stand neatly under the coffee table, on which she has placed her purse and gloves. Patty's feet are curled up under her, modestly covered by her skirt. Behind the couch, there is a library table with a handsome, massive table lamp. On the table, there is a large silver-framed photograph of a pretty girl. It is a studio portrait of the glamor type. There is no sign of Don. After a few moments, the phone rings. The telephone, on a long cord, is on the library table behind the couch.

———

PATTY (*yelling toward kitchen*). Hey! Telephone! (*Silence*) Do you want me to answer it?

(*Don enters from kitchen. He is preparing to fix drinks and carries an ice-bucket in one hand. He sets the ice-bucket down on the bar and then crosses to answer the phone.*)

DON. No, I'll get it. (*Into phone*) Hello? (*Very cordial*) Oh, hello, Mike—sorry, pal, not tonight. Just going out. Sure, later this week. Love to. So long. (*He hangs up and crosses to bar, where he mixes drinks*)

PATTY. Who's Mike?

DON. Friend of mine.

PATTY. Are you mad at him?

DON. No, of course not. Why?

PATTY. Why did you hang up so quickly?

DON (*amused*). Because there wasn't anything more to say. He wanted me to dine with him, and I told him I couldn't.

PATTY. Yes—but you could have talked to him. I always talk by the hour to my friends.

DON. I'll bet you do. (*Glancing around*) Where did I put that bottle of Vermouth?

PATTY (*pointing*). Over there. (*Unrolling blueprint further*) This is fascinating. What's it going to be? Oh . . . I see. . . . (*Reads from blueprint*) Ground plan— Freeport Civic Center—Donald Gresham, architect. . . . Oh, boy, that's something. Are you famous?

DON. No. Not in the least. I'm just a good, practical, modern run-of-the-mill architect. (*Hands her another rolled-up blueprint*) You can get a better idea from this. It's an elevation.

(*She removes rubber band from rolled-up plan, spreads it out. He mixes cocktail thoughtfully.*)

PATTY. Now I know why you needed rubber bands. *(Looks at plan)* That's swell. Is it built already?

DON. Building now.

PATTY. Have you planned many buildings?

DON. Quite a few. Used to be with a big firm. Went on my own a couple of years ago.

PATTY. Don't you get an awful kick out of looking at a building—and knowing that it all started in your head?

DON. Sure. I'll let you in on a secret. First job I did off my own bat was a large, hideous warehouse. I sometimes drove out late at night when there wasn't a soul around and I sat in my car and gloated over it.

PATTY. All alone?

DON. Uh huh. Large, boxlike brick warehouses don't appeal to many people.

PATTY. I think it's more fun to have someone to gloat *with*.

DON. Might be. Are you sure you won't have a martini?

PATTY. Quite sure. I only want a lemonade, that's all. Or a Coke, or something.

DON. I'm sorry, but I'm fresh out of lemons and/or Cokes.

PATTY. Never mind. I'll settle for an olive. I really don't want a thing.

DON. Don't you like martinis?

PATTY. I used to like them, but I gave up drinking.

DON. Why?

PATTY. I think it's sort of high school to drink and smoke when you don't actually crave it. *(Looking around)* I love your apartment. Do you live here alone?

DON *(fixing martinis)*. All alone.

PATTY. But you showed me two bedrooms.

DON. One's for guests—if, as and when I have guests.

PATTY. Oh. *(Slight pause)* Do you have a mistress?

DON. Mistress? Isn't that a rather old-fashioned term?

PATTY. Well, it may be old-fashioned but at least it's specific. Do you have one?

DON. You ask the damnedest questions.

PATTY. Why? You're a bachelor, and you're obviously quite well off. It's a natural question.

DON. It isn't a bit natural. You don't go around asking people bluntly if they have a mistress.

PATTY. I do. It saves so much time. I mean, one always finds out sooner or later. Do you? Have one, I mean?

DON. No, as a matter of fact, I don't.

PATTY. That's good. I'm glad. *(A pause)* Why *don't* you have one? *(Hastily)* You needn't tell me unless you want to.

DON. Well, maybe I think it's sort of high school to have a mistress unless you actually crave one.

PATTY *(promptly)*. You know, that's really very true. *(Points to picture)* Who's that?

DON. Her name is Cynthia.

PATTY. She's quite cute. *(A closer look)* Very cute. *(A questioning look)* Are you in love with her?

DON *(vaguely)*. No. Not now. I used to be. Sort of, I think. I don't know. Not any more, anyway.

PATTY. Oh. Why do you have her picture?

DON. Because she gave it to me.

PATTY. Is she in love with you?

DON. How can a man tell?

PATTY. When a girl gives a man her picture, that's usually a sign.

DON. I dunno. Could be. Probably thought she was. She's only eighteen.

PATTY. Were you engaged?

DON *(gloomily)*. More or less, I suppose.

PATTY *(compassionately)*. Oh. How sad for you! *(Looks at picture again)* She's so pretty. Was she . . . ?

DON *(grimly)*. She was *not* my mistress.

PATTY. I never said she was.

DON. You were just going to!

PATTY. Don't be disagreeable. *(Brightly)* You're not engaged to her now? I mean, not even *sort* of?

DON. Nope. All off.

PATTY. When did you split up?

DON. Last night. Or maybe this morning. Sometime in between.

PATTY. Oh. How sad! Were you crushed? I'm always simply devastated when I break up with people. I was engaged to a boy once, and when I sent him back the ring, I absolutely wept buckets.

DON. Never gave Cynthia a ring, and the only time she ever weeps is into the fifth daiquiri.

PATTY. What an *awful* thing to say. I don't believe you even liked her.

DON. I'm beginning to wonder about that myself.

PATTY. Then why are you so unhappy about it?

DON. I'm not a bit unhappy.

PATTY. You're keeping her picture. And when I asked if you were still in love with her, you shilly-shallied.

DON (cheerfully). Okay, she's left an aching void in my heart.

PATTY. Is that why you picked me up—sort of on the rebound?

DON. Could be.

PATTY. Why did you split up?

DON. You ask too many questions.

PATTY. I know. I'm sorry. (Looks at picture again) She has a very pretty chin.

DON. She's very pretty all over.

PATTY (significantly). Oh. How sad! Then she *was* your mistress?

DON. She was nothing of the sort.

PATTY. You said she was pretty all over. I naturally thought . . .

DON. Why are you so preoccupied with sex?

PATTY (indignant). Who? Me?

DON. Yes—you.

PATTY. Do you really think I am?

DON. Well, you're always asking people if they plan seduction, or whether they're bored with virgins, or if they have a mistress. If that isn't being preoccupied with sex, I'd like to know what is.

PATTY. You may be right. (Brightly) But don't you think it's better for a girl to be preoccupied with sex than occupied?

DON (strolls to window). You win. Much better. (Peers through drapes) Raining like hell.

PATTY (rises, points to the TV set). Say, listen, is your TV working?

DON. Sure, why?

PATTY. What's the time?

DON. About seven-twenty.

PATTY. Oh, well, there's lots of time yet. Can you watch TV from the Stork Club?

DON. I don't know.

PATTY. Remind me to turn it on at ten, will you? They're doing a show on CBS that I'd have been absolutely perfect for, but they gave it to another girl and I want to see if she stinks. It was a nice little part too.

DON. What kind of parts do you play?

PATTY. Well, I've only done three dra-matic shows so far—the competition is simply brutal—but each time I've done a sort of—well, I suppose you'd call it a sort of tart. I'm good, too. I got a call from Studio One. Friday I'm going to read for another tart.

DON. You don't look very much like a tart.

PATTY. I do on TV. I look all haggard and dissipated and simply crawling with vice.

DON. Doesn't that apply to everyone on TV?

PATTY. Don't you be snotty above TV. Maybe some of the shows are rather crummy yet, but it's bread and butter to hundreds of girls like me.

DON. Talking of bread and butter—I'm hungry. Let's go and eat.

PATTY. Okay.

DON. You're going to get drenched without a raincoat.

PATTY. Let's not go out! Let's fix dinner up here. I'm a sensational cook.

DON. Unfortunately, I haven't any sensational food.

PATTY. Don't you have anything?

DON. Afraid not.

PATTY. No leftovers? What I can do with leftovers is nobody's business. Do you like kedgeree?

DON. Beg pardon?

PATTY. Kedgeree—it's made with finnan haddie. Do you have any finnan haddie?

DON. God, no.

PATTY. Don't say "God, no" like that. You've never tasted it. It's delicious.

DON. Look, Patty—all I have in the kitchen is a box of crackers that are very stale, and a small crock of cheese that was sent to me last Christmas.

PATTY. Blue cheese?

DON. It's going blue. That's all. No eggs even, no milk—nothing.

PATTY. Don't you ever eat meals here?

DON. No.

PATTY. No wonder you're unhappy and maladjusted.

DON. I'm not a bit unhappy, and my adjustment is just dandy.

PATTY. You broke up with Cynthia.

DON. It was not for lack of home cooking, believe me.

PATTY. How do you know? I think that's awful. That darling kitchen going to waste. And that lovely ice box and stove. I want to cry. Honestly.

DON. You're the strangest girl I've ever known.

PATTY. You don't know me. You picked me up.

DON. You don't have to rub it in.

PATTY. Yes, I do. I think both of us ought to bear it in mind all the time.

DON. Why?

PATTY. Because— (A sigh) I just think we should, that's all.

DON. Why?

PATTY. Just in case we start feeling romantic about each other.

DON. Is that bad?

PATTY. Yes. You picked me up, and no matter what happened, you'd always wonder.

DON. What about?

PATTY. About all the other men who might have picked me up before you did —in just the same way.

DON. I have been wondering about that. Do you do it often?

PATTY. Once is enough to leave doubts.

DON. Mine are completely dispelled.

PATTY. For the time being. They'd come creeping back, though.

DON (earnestly). Never. You see, you're rather . . .

PATTY. Oh, shut up. I don't want to talk about it any more.

DON. Okay. Would you like to fix dinner for us here?

PATTY. Even I can't do much with stale crackers and moldy old cheese.

DON. There's a market down the block. I have a raincoat. I could get whatever you need.

PATTY (she's obviously enchanted). Would you like to?

DON. Sure. Would you?

PATTY. I'd love it. I adore cooking, and I rarely get a chance to cook for a man. My roommate's a girl.

DON (amused). I'm relieved to hear it.

PATTY (smiling at him). Now who's preoccupied with sex?

DON. Okay, okay. What'll I buy?

PATTY. Let's splurge. Let's have steak and mushrooms and a salad and cake and coffee. And strawberries. You'll have to buy a sponge cake. I won't have time to bake one. Be sure to get whipping cream, and we'll have a strawberry shortcake.

DON. Okay. Sold. Make out a list.

PATTY. Oh, you don't need a list. Tell them at the store that you haven't any-thing—tell 'em what we're going to have and they'll tell you what you need. Tell 'em you're just setting up housekeeping.

DON. All right. (The phone rings. She glances at it then at him. He picks up receiver) Hello? Oh, hello, Shirley. How are you, baby? No, not tonight, I'm afraid. Nope—dining with an important client. Give me a raincheck, will you? Okay, Shirley. Be seeing you. 'Bye. (He hangs up)

PATTY. Who's Shirley?

DON. Girl I know. Blonde, blue eyes. Hundred and ten pounds. Very beautiful. All over. Any more questions?

PATTY. What did she want?

DON. She asked me to dinner. She lives with her parents. They're out tonight.

PATTY. Oh. Personally, I don't think it's right for girls to call men up.

DON (ribbing). It is rather disgusting, isn't it?

PATTY. I know what you're thinking. I picked you up—and that's worse than calling up.

DON. Will you stop harping on that— you sweet little dope? (He moves toward her. She backs away. He takes her by the shoulders)

PATTY. Run along and do your marketing.

DON (gently). Patty—I . . .

PATTY (deliberately matter-of-fact). And don't forget the staples—the flour, and salt and sugar and coffee and stuff . . . (She wriggles herself free of his hands on her shoulders. He stands looking at her very intently) Well, go on—what are you waiting for?

DON. I've decided not to run for president—at least not on that platform you drafted for me.

PATTY. What?

DON. "Affection, but no passion." I think . . .

PATTY. You're not passionate now— you're just hungry. And so am I. Go out and get the groceries.

DON. Okay. (Gets his raincoat) I'll be back in a flash. Hold the fort.

PATTY. Hey, wait! What'll I do if the phone rings while you're gone?

DON. Answer it.

PATTY. Aren't you afraid of being compromised?

DON. Not particularly. Of course, if my mother called at four A.M. and a girl answered, she might raise an eyebrow, but it's only seven P.M. and my mother's in Europe.

(*Patty has walked to the door with him. Suddenly she points to a framed picture.*)

PATTY. Did you build this house?

DON. Not yet. Some day I plan to. It's just a sketch. It's a sort of hideaway cabin.

PATTY. I like it. Of course you'll never find lovely old trees like that.

DON (*takes picture off hook*). The trees are already there. I plan to build this shack to fit into the trees.

PATTY. How do you mean?

DON. It's a piece of property I own.

PATTY. Gosh? Do you own property?

DON. Don't be too impressed. It's just five acres of land up in Maine. Cost me all of a thousand dollars. (*He laughs*) Bought it four years ago—and went in hock to pay for it. Clear now.

PATTY. Oh. Is that where you'd have lived if you'd married Cynthia?

DON. She didn't like it.

PATTY. You're kidding. She didn't like this darling cabin?

DON. She said she didn't want to live in a neck of the woods up in Maine.

PATTY. Why not? She's crazy.

DON. No, she isn't. You'd be surprised at the number of people who don't want to live in Maine.

(*Patty stands gazing at picture. He looks over her shoulder.*)

PATTY. What's this long, flat business?

DON. Influence of Frank Lloyd Wright. Car port under it—sun deck on top. Modern as hell.

PATTY. Is this the bedroom?

DON. Yep. Windows on three sides. Fireplace here. Huge fireplace. Roast an ox on it, if you felt like it.

PATTY. It might be fun to roast an ox in a bedroom.

DON. Limb of that oak tree just misses the sun deck by two feet. That's quite a tree.

PATTY (*she stares at him*). It must be wonderful to own a tree.

DON. Huh?

PATTY. I have a window box with geraniums—but it must be simply terrific to actually own an enormous tree.

DON (*indulgently*). I own a stream, too. (*Points to picture*) It's way back there. It's barely a trickle, but it does flow. It

could be dammed up to make a swimming hole.

PATTY. How wonderful! Do you ever drive out to gloat over it?

DON. My child, it's a good sixteen-hour drive. Haven't seen it for a couple of years. Only remember that I own it when I pay the taxes.

PATTY. If I owned an oak tree, I'd live in it.

DON. Want to drive out with me some week end and look at it?

PATTY (*after a long pause*). No.

DON. Why not?

PATTY (*unhappily*). Because I hinted—and I didn't mean to.

DON. I'd have asked you even if you hadn't hinted. I have rather an affinity for trees myself.

PATTY. When I was a kid . . . (*Stops short—a new thought*) Do you like children?

DON (*poker-faced*). Can't stand the sight of them.

PATTY. Why not?

DON (*amused*). Oh. They're all right, I guess. I've never been exposed to them very much.

PATTY. Isn't that funny? You're quite proud of loving trees, but you're a little ashamed to admit you like kids. I'd like to have at least five.

DON. I know. You plan to acquire them ready-made with a rich middle-aged husband.

PATTY. Oh, yes, but I'd like five of my own too. I suppose you think it isn't fair to bring kids into this—this mess of a world?

DON. Ever hear of a mess being cleaned up by unborn kids?

PATTY (*soberly*). I never thought of it that way.

DON. Think about it while I get all this food you've ordered.

PATTY. Okay. I will. (*Pause*) How old are you?

DON. Twenty-eight. Why?

PATTY. Twenty-eight. Let's see—half of that is fourteen—plus seven . . . (*Smiles happily*) Twenty-one. Isn't that amazing? It just works out.

DON. What does?

PATTY. Haven't you ever heard that the girl is supposed to be half the man's age, plus seven?

DON. What girl? What man?

PATTY. Never mind. Beat it.

DON *(walks to door, pensively).* Say, I think I'll get some ham and eggs, too.

(After his exit Patty goes to table and gets plate of olives, carries it to couch, settles herself comfortably with phone from sofa table and dials.)

PATTY *(into phone).* Hello, Vicki? Hello, sweetie. Were you getting worried about me? Well, don't. I'm okay, but I won't be home for dinner. No, you can eat up all the spaghetti, you lucky girl. *(Munches on olives)* What? I am not chewing gum. I'm eating olives—and you'll never guess where. I'm in a man's apartment. Now, please stop worrying. No, you don't know him, but he's just divine. What? No, he wouldn't harm a fly, honestly. His name's Gresham—Donald Gresham—and he's an architect and he has a perfectly darling apartment on East 49th Street—and he's a bachelor—and he has a crew haircut—and he owns a perfectly gorgeous old oak tree —oak tree, that's right. . . . Never mind, I'll explain it later. What? I don't know, sweetie—I only met the man a couple of hours ago— No, no, don't worry. . . . He's practically a child, and very sweet. . . . Don't worry. Does he know what? *(She laughs)* Sure. Sure. I told him—and he doesn't mind a bit. Isn't that refreshing? Okay then, stop worrying. Any messages? Oh, how very dull. *(Door buzzer sounds)* Look, I'll call you back later, maybe. There's someone at the door. G'bye.

(She hangs up, primps and goes to the front door. Enter David Slater. David is around forty and is endowed with entirely too much charm for his own good. Despite the fact that he's tanned and healthy, there's a vague aura of dissipation about him. He speaks with a marked Southern drawl. David also has too much money for his own good. It is doubtful if he ever did a day's work in his life. He wears obviously expensive but very informal-looking clothes. At the moment, he has on a raincoat (dry) over a rather hearty tweed suit. He wears a brown felt hat at a rather rakish angle. When Patty opens the door to him, he is obviously very much surprised. He remains in the doorway, gaping at her.)

DAVID. Well, I'll be damned!

PATTY *(smiling).* Why will you be damned?

DAVID. I'm sorry. You caught me off base. I didn't expect to find—a girl here.

PATTY. Why not? It's a very respectable hour.

DAVID *(fussed).* Yes—yes, of course. I didn't mean—you see, is—er—is Mr. Gresham in?

PATTY. No, but he'll be back in a little while. He went to the market at the corner. Won't you come in?

DAVID *(hesitating).* Well, I was just going out—and I thought maybe Don was free—and—you see, I live a couple of floors above—so I guess I'd better just . . .

PATTY. Don't be silly. Come in. Would you like a drink?

DAVID *(gravely).* I would like a drink very much indeed. *(Disarmingly)* Frankly, I'm still slightly hung over from—er— from last night, and a drink . . .

PATTY *(soothingly).* I know. A hair of the dog. You'll be all right. I've cured more hangovers than you could shake a stick at.

DAVID *(shuddering).* Never shake a stick at a hangover. It brings on the screaming willies. *(He comes in, removes his hat and coat, throws them on window seat, while Patty pours him a drink)* My name's David Slater. What's yours?

PATTY. Patty. Patty O'Neill.

DAVID. Known Don for long?

PATTY *(glibly).* Oh, yes. Of course, it isn't really long—but it just seems like ages. He's a darling. I'm crazy about him. *(Brings him his drink)*

DAVID *(sipping his cocktail).* That's very interesting. Is he crazy about you?

PATTY. Oh, it's purely platonic on both sides.

(David glances significantly at her stockinged feet.)

DAVID *(very skeptical).* Of course.

PATTY *(amused).* I took off my shoes because my feet hurt.

DAVID. You should never say that your feet hurt.

PATTY. Why not? They do.

DAVID. My foot singular hurts is an intriguing statement. My feet plural hurt is a rather sordid admission.

PATTY *(laughs, puts on her shoes).* Well, anyway, these were on sale at less than half price, and they're divine, but they're too tight. They were killing me. *(She sees that he's finished his cocktail and pours him another)* Here, there's lots left.

DAVID. Aren't you having one?

PATTY. No, thanks. I don't drink. Have you known Don long?

DAVID. Oh, about a year. Little less. Since he moved in here.

PATTY (*points to picture*). Do you know Cynthia?

DAVID. Yes, indeed.

PATTY. She was sort of Don's fiancée, you know. I mean—so to speak.

DAVID. What do you mean—so to speak?

PATTY. Well, it seems to have been a sort of loose arrangement.

DAVID. Loose? Did he say it was loose?

PATTY. Oh, no. But anyway it's all off now.

DAVID. Yes. I know.

PATTY. Was she a pill?

DAVID. That's a rather difficult question.

PATTY. Why? Either she was or she wasn't.

DAVID. It's not quite as simple as that.

PATTY. Why isn't it?

DAVID. Well, since you must know, Cynthia happens to be my daughter.

PATTY. Oh. Oh, I see. I see what you mean.

DAVID. That's good.

PATTY. I'm terribly sorry. If I'd had any *idea* you were her father, I wouldn't have dreamed of asking you if she was a pill.

DAVID (*sadly*). You couldn't have come to a better source. She is.

PATTY (*mulling this over*). Uh huh. I see. . . . (*Handsomely*) Well anyway, she's awfully pretty. (*Brightly*) Don went out to buy steaks. I'm going to fix dinner up here. I'm a terrific cook. Do you like steak?

DAVID. Mad about it.

PATTY. Why don't you stay and have dinner with us?

DAVID. I think not, thanks very much all the same.

PATTY. Oh, you mean because of Cynthia?

DAVID. There's a connection.

PATTY. Did they split up because of you? I mean, did you disapprove or something?

DAVID. On the contrary. I was prepared to love him like a son. More than a son. I've been practically fawning on him—ready to give my blessing any moment. Damn.

PATTY. Oh. Is Cynthia all broken up about it?

DAVID. No. She doesn't break up so eas-ily. But I am. I was counting on that boy. (*Sighs*) Damnation.

PATTY. Then you're sore because they split up. (*Disarmingly*) You see, I don't know anything about what happened except that he told me it was off.

DAVID (*growling*). Uh huh.

PATTY. You seem to be sore at Don. Are you? I mean, did he do something he shouldn't have done?

DAVID. That's what I'd like to find out. That's why I'm here. (*Grimly*) The theory prevails that Mr. Donald Gresham should be horsewhipped. By me.

PATTY. Why?

DAVID. That's what Cynthia said this morning. (*A pause*) I think.

PATTY. Don't you know?

DAVID. I was not in good shape this morning. She said a lot of things.

PATTY. Like what?

DAVID. Well, it appears that he—I think the phrase is "played fast and loose" with my daughter's affections.

PATTY. That doesn't sound like Don.

DAVID. It isn't Don whom I'm quoting.

PATTY. Oh. Mrs. Slater?

DAVID. Nope. She divorced me years ago. "Fast and loose" was Cynthia's rather dull cliché. (*Sadly*) There's that word "loose" again. Unfortunate.

PATTY. Did she send you down just now to horsewhip poor Don?

DAVID. No. She's out somewhere. She's always out. I never know where she is. (*Sighs*) I was not cut out to raise a daughter.

PATTY. She needs a good influence. She probably needs a mother.

DAVID. Either that—or a good swift kick in the pants.

PATTY. Well, couldn't you provide one or the other? You look awfully young. Why don't you marry again?

DAVID. Unfortunately, all the women to whom I am attracted are not a desirable influence.

PATTY. Then why don't you kick her in the pants?

DAVID. It's an attractive thought. (*Starts to rise*) Well, I've enjoyed our chat, I think I'll . . .

PATTY. Don't dash off. You don't want to eat alone. Stay here. Don't be silly. Come on, do stay.

DAVID. No. I don't think so. I . . .

PATTY. Look, just because they seem to

have had a fight is no reason why you . . .
(She breaks off—muses) Why did they
break it off, anyway?
*(David considers for a moment, frowning.
He can't quite make this girl out. He set-
tles down again.)*

DAVID. Look, since you seem to know
him pretty well, tell me something. Do
you consider our friend a man of high
principles?

PATTY. I certainly do. He's charming.

DAVID *(ruefully)*. I have been told that I
am not without charm, but I have no principles whatsoever. Answer my question: is
he a man who . . . ?

PATTY. I don't know what you're driving at.

DAVID *(unhappily)*. You would if you
were a father.

PATTY. Oh. Are you worried about Cynthia?

DAVID. Extremely worried.

PATTY. Is she pregnant?

DAVID *(startled)*. Good God, no! *(Suddenly)* What made you ask that question?

PATTY. Well, isn't that what fathers are
usually so worried about?

DAVID. I guess it is.

PATTY. My father used to worry himself
sick about it. If a boy so much as looked
at me, he'd go on and on about hell fire
and damnation.

DAVID. Do you believe in that?

PATTY *(dubiously)*. No. But it makes
you stop and think.

DAVID. I must make a note of that: speak
to Cynthia about hell fire and damnation.

PATTY. Yes, but don't go on and on.
That's one reason I left home. Pop never
drew the line. When boys took me out on
a first date they used to get a load of brim-
stone right off the bat. It scared them off.

DAVID. I wonder if Cynthia . . .

PATTY *(cheerfully)*. Look, you needn't
worry. I don't know anything about Cynthia, but Don would never do a thing like
that. He doesn't believe in it. Just forget
it. *(Brightly)* Is that why you came down?
Because you thought she was pregnant?

DAVID. No! I suspected that maybe they
. . . *(Suddenly)* Let's talk about something
else, shall we?

PATTY. Then you will stay for dinner,
won't you?

DAVID. Frankly, I'm tempted. But hadn't
we better check with Don first?

PATTY. Why? I'm sure it'll be okay with

him. You said you always got along fine.
Cynthia doesn't have to know.

DAVID. I wasn't thinking of Cynthia at
the moment.

PATTY. What were you thinking about?

DAVID. Well, if I had inveigled a pretty
girl to fix dinner for me in my apartment
on a rainy night, and somebody tried to
crash the party, I'd be sore as hell.

PATTY. Did you say "invaygled"?

DAVID *(hastily apologetic)*. Yes, but I assure you I . . .

PATTY. Is that how it's pronounced? I
always say "inveigled." Is "invaygled"
right?

DAVID. I think so. *(Tries them both)*
Inveigled—invaygled—inveigled. Now I
don't know. Silly word, isn't it?

PATTY. Well, whichever it is, Don didn't
have much to do of it. It was my idea. You
see, I didn't bring a raincoat, and he
wanted to take me out, and then it started
pouring—so I said I'd fix steaks. I make a
divine steak sauce. Oh, gosh, I hope he
brings mustard.

DAVID. Nevertheless, the fact remains . . .

PATTY. What fact?

DAVID. You and he will doubtless wish
to be alone.

PATTY. Why?

DAVID. He may have plans for after dinner.

PATTY *(cheerfully)*. Oh, no, that's all
understood. He promised he wouldn't even
try to make passes. Not one pass, he said,
and not one pass has he made. This is
purely a social visit—by mutual agreement.

DAVID. Has it occurred to you that after
a steak dinner he might become more affectionate?

PATTY. Oh, I hope he will. I like being
kissed. *(Musing)* D'you know that he's
never even kissed me since the Empire
State Building.

DAVID. You mean since it was built?

PATTY. Don't be silly. That's where we
met—in a lovely fog. *(Musing)* Gosh, I
hope he brings pepper and salt and stuff.
Men always like their food well seasoned,
but they never *think* of buying it. Do you
like kedgeree?

DAVID. Never met her.

PATTY. Kedgeree's a dish.

DAVID. I'll bet she is.

PATTY. It's a dish made of flaked finnan
haddie and rice and eggs.

DAVID. I've lost all interest.

(Telephone rings.)

PATTY. Excuse me. *(Picks up phone)* Hello—yes—just a sec—I'll look—yes, this is Plaza 9-8416—no—I'm afraid he's not here right now. But he'll be back in a few minutes. What? Oh, not more than another ten minutes, I'd say. He just went out to buy some steaks and groceries—that can't take him so very long. Oh, yes, I'm sure he'll be here—I'm fixing dinner for us and it's such lousy weather that I'm sure we'll stay home afterwards. Shall I tell him who called? Hello? Hello? H'um —hung up on me. *(Hangs up—dubiously)* I can't help it. He told me to answer the phone.

DAVID. Male or female?

PATTY. Female. Very female. She has such a pretty voice. A thick Southern accent that you could cut with a knife.

DAVID *(gulping)*. Oh—oh.

PATTY. You know her?

DAVID. Yes, indeed. That must've been Cynthia.

PATTY. Of course—you have a Southern accent, too. I might've guessed. I'm sorry. If I'd had any idea I'd have told her you were here and you could've . . .

DAVID. Thank God you didn't.

PATTY. Why? Didn't you tell me she asked you to come down and horsewhip poor Don?

DAVID *(significantly)*. Yes, but—well, never mind. You see—we—never mind.

PATTY *(amiably)*. Okay. It's none of my business, anyway. *(Hospitably)* Go on, fix yourself another drink.

DAVID *(crosses to bar)*. Don't mind if I do.

PATTY. Would you like me to turn on the TV?

DAVID. Is it in color?

PATTY. You're crazy. It won't be in color for years.

DAVID. Let's wait till then!

(Patty goes over to the windows, pulls aside the drapes, presses her nose to the pane, looking out.)

PATTY. Gosh, it's raining cats and dogs. *(Suddenly)* What kind of a car do you drive?

DAVID. Lincoln. Why?

PATTY. Have you seen the new Cadillac?

DAVID. Yes.

PATTY. They have a fascinating new gadget. Whenever it starts to rain, you press a little button and it squirts water onto your windshield so that the wiper won't get it all smeared. I think of it the moment it starts to rain.

DAVID *(sizing her up)*. You drive a Cadillac?

PATTY. Heavens, no! Don't be silly. But the boy Vicki goes with has one, and he lets me work it. Not drive it. Work the gadget. Vicki says . . .

DAVID. Who's Vicki?

PATTY. My roommate. You'd like her. She's wonderful. She's only a year older than I am, but she clucks over me like an old hen. She's a Conover model. This boy with the Cadillac is mad about her, and it's so sad, because he's married and has two kids and he won't do anything to distress his wife. He's a Princeton man.

DAVID. Is that what you are—a model?

PATTY *(modestly)*. Well, yes—sort of. I've modeled bras and girdles. Lots of girls don't like to. I don't either, for that matter. But I'm built right for it, and it pays awfully well. And a girl has to eat.

DAVID. What else do you do?

PATTY. Oh, any old thing that comes along. Salesgirl, receptionist, temporary jobs. Just to keep the pot boiling.

DAVID. What's it boiling for? What do you want to do?

PATTY. Act. I'm an actress. Or rather, I want to be an actress.

DAVID *(this seems to explain everything)*. Oh.

PATTY. I know. The woods are full of 'em. Dime a dozen. I know.

DAVID. Are you any good?

PATTY. I think I'm pretty good!

DAVID. Have you been in many plays?

PATTY. I've been in three TV shows.

DAVID. Does that count?

PATTY. Don't you ever watch TV?

DAVID. They have it in one of my favorite saloons, but I can't say I actually watch it. Last night they had a Roller Derby God, those poor girls! *(Slight pause)* Don't you find it awfully exhausting?

PATTY. I don't roller skate. I act.

DAVID. I know, I know.

PATTY *(pensively)*. Does Cynthia do anything—I mean like acting or modeling or something?

DAVID. No.

PATTY. Doesn't she do anything?

DAVID. No. At least nothing that fills me with paternal pride.

PATTY. Oh. *(Pause)* Do you do anything

to make her proud of you? *(He chews on this a second, rises, puts drink down, crosses to sofa and lies down. Patty rises)* What's the matter?

DAVID. You just connected with a vicious left hook below the belt.

(Patty sits down on the couch next to him.)

PATTY. I meant to. I always get burned up with parents who gripe about their kids. It's the parents' fault—that's what I always say.

DAVID. Don't say it again.

PATTY. Why?

DAVID. Because it's a dull thing to say—trite, banal and painfully true.

PATTY. It's never too late to mend.

DAVID. I'll bet you always say that, too.

PATTY. Well, it's true. You've probably got the makings of a very good father. *(She leans close, looking him over)* I like the way your eyes sort of crinkle. You're really very cute. *(He gets up suddenly and walks over to the window. She remains on the couch, looking at him)* Why did you get up?

DAVID. It seemed like a good idea.

PATTY. Why? We were just . . .

DAVID. Frankly, my child, I felt a sudden, powerful, very ignoble desire to kiss the hell out of you.

PATTY *(pleased)*. You did? How lovely! This *is* one of my good days. *(This is said rather smugly)*

DAVID. And, rather than yield to this ignoble desire . . .

PATTY. What's so ignoble about it? I think it's wonderful to be desired. As a rule, I don't attract men, physically, I mean. Not right off the bat, anyway. Vicki says I scare 'em off because I look too wholesome. Who wants to look wholesome? Gosh, I'd love to be so pretty that I could drive men absolutely crazy.

DAVID. You attract me.

PATTY *(pleased)*. Well, good! Now I'm really glad I asked you to stay for dinner.

DAVID. Er—look—aren't you—er—already spoken for by Don?

PATTY. No, of course not. *(She giggles)* Matter of fact, I only met him this afternoon. We met on top of the Empire State Building.

DAVID *(grinning)*. Oh. I see.

PATTY *(instantly)*. Oh, no, you don't. We may not have been formally intro-duced—as I'm sure Cynthia was—but I assure you it's every bit as respectable.

DAVID *(thoughtfully)*. That is not a reassuring statement.

(Loud rapping on the door.)

DON *(offstage)*. Hey! It's me! Open the door.

PATTY. Okay—coming!

(Patty runs to open the door. Enter Don. He is staggering under a huge carton of groceries. His coat and hat are drenched. He starts straight for the kitchen, without noticing David at first.)

DON. Boy—this weighs a ton! I bought enough food for a month's siege.

PATTY. Good for you. Look, Don—we've got a visitor.

DAVID *(vaguely)*. Hi, pal!

DON *(stares at him)*. What the hell are you doing here? *(He staggers into the kitchen without waiting for a reply)*

DAVID *(sotto voce)*. Hardly a cordial greeting, you'll have noted. I think I'll fade away.

PATTY. You stay here. *(Calling)* Don! Come here!

(Re-enter Don from kitchen. He looks at David truculently.)

DON *(very disagreeable)*. What the hell are you doing here?

PATTY *(suavely)*. I invited Mr. Slater to have dinner with us. Don't be so rude. I think you're terrible.

(The men both stare at her.)

DON *(finally)*. Did he accept?

PATTY. Of course he did.

DON *(stiffly)*. Then perhaps I should inform you that Mr. Slater . . .

PATTY *(interrupting)*. I know all about it. He's Cynthia's father. But don't worry. He's not a bit sore—and he's not going to horsewhip you.

DON *(blankly)*. He's not going to *what!*

DAVID *(to Patty, reproachfully)*. You talk too much. *(To Don)* The—er—horsewhipping is a—er—feature you haven't heard about yet.

DON *(dryly)*. No, but *do* tell. *(He looks at David challengingly)*

DAVID. Well, you see . . . *(He breaks off and stares at Patty. So does Don. There is a moment's silence. David smiles at Patty)* Man talk, honey. Will you excuse us?

PATTY. Okay, I'm going to start dinner, anyway, and you two can gab to your hearts' content. *(To Don)* How do you like your steak?

DON. Very rare.

PATTY. Swell, so do I. *(To David)* How about you? *(David looks to Don for a cue)*

DON. Look, Patty . . .

PATTY *(amiably, as to a naughty child)*. Oh, shut up—I'm not talking to you. I invited him, and he's going to stay. You like yours rare too, Mr. Slater?

DAVID. Sure do. Blood rare.

PATTY. Okay. That's all settled. *(Starts for kitchen. Over her shoulder to Don)* If you got your feet wet, go change your socks. They look wet.

DON. Listen, Patty—that stove is quite temperamental. Would you like me to . . . ?

PATTY. You leave it to me. I know all about stoves.

(Exit Patty into kitchen. The two men look at each other for quite a while.)

DAVID. That's a remarkable girl.

DON. Yes, she is. Sweet kid. *(Tentatively))* Known her for years. Nice family. *(Removes raincoat and hat)*

DAVID *(poker-faced)*. Lots of nice families live in the Empire State Building.

DON *(grins ruefully)*. Oh, my God. I might have guessed. You been here long?

DAVID. Ten—fifteen minutes. She never stopped talking.

DON. I can imagine. *(Shrugging)* Okay —so I picked her up. She's still an awfully sweet kid.

DAVID. Very.

DON. What's the horsewhipping routine?

DAVID *(sternly)*. My daughter got in at ten A.M. this morning.

DON. That's right.

DAVID. She was with you all night.

DON. She spent the night in this apartment. That's correct.

DAVID. She claims that . . .

DON. She lies. I never touched her. Moreover, I don't believe you. She'd never say . . .

DAVID. She told me, definitely, that you . . .

DON. She lies.

DAVID. Quit yapping "she lies" in that dramatic fashion before I can even finish a sentence. Let me try to recall exactly what she *did* say.

DON. Go ahead.

DAVID. Well, this morning I was fixing my breakfast—or, to be more accurate, a Bromo Seltzer, when Cynthia came traipsing in wearing a black, strapless formal.

You could have knocked me over with a feather. I mean—she's come in late before, two—three o'clock in the morning, but never at ten A.M.

DON. Go on.

DAVID. I asked her where in hell she'd been all night, and she told me she slept down here. No evasion. Just like that.

DON. Yes?

DAVID. So I said to her, "Good God, you shouldn't have done that!" Words to that effect, anyway. I always feel uncomfortable on a high moral plane.

DON. And what did she say?

DAVID. She said, "You're quite right. It was a grave mistake." Then she stomped off to her room, slammed the door and took a shower.

DON. While you searched for a horse-whip?

DAVID. No, that suggestion came later. I stuck around—asked her what she thought I ought to do about it.

DON. And what did she seem to think?

DAVID. She was in a very strange mood. Cynical as all get out. Bitter. Sore as hell. Said she never wants to lay eyes on you again. In effect, that she had trusted you and that you had done her wrong. Her very words.

DON. Even if it were true, I doubt that Cynthia would use such a corny phrase.

DAVID. My theory is that she would use it only if it were true. And she said it several times, "He done me wrong."

DON. Is that all she said? Wasn't she more specific?

DAVID. That's all she said!

DON *(slowly, with complete conviction)*. She's lying. I never touched her. Never. Believe it or not. I never touched her. *(David quite clearly believes him.)*

DAVID *(musing)*. You know, it just occurs to me—*that* might very well be the "wrong" you done her. In Cynthia's book. She said—anyway, she was sore as hell. Got me worked up.

DON *(coldly)*. Better start working yourself down.

DAVID *(burning)*. I can see her point, you know. Don't blame her. Hell hath no fury, and so forth and so forth. I think she's got something. Probably should beat you up anyway.

DON *(pacing, frowning)*. Let me get this straight: I'm to be horsewhipped for *not* seducing your daughter?

DAVID (grinning). It's quite a new twist, isn't it? However, don't worry. Just an idle figure of speech. Never even whipped a horse in my life.

DON. You're a hell of a father. It's none of my damned business. She's your kid and your responsibility. But does it ever occur to you that your cockeyed philosophy of life may not be what she . . .

(Enter Patty.)

PATTY. Quit picking on him.

DAVID. You see, she thinks I could still be salvaged.

PATTY (to Don). You did very well, but you forgot the whipping cream.

DON. No, I didn't. Got it here. (Goes to get it out of pocket of his raincoat)

PATTY (to David). Why was he bawling you out? I mean—shouldn't you be bawling him out?

DAVID. Well, it started off that way—but we got sidetracked. (Picks up empty martini shaker) Could you use your girlish charms to promote me another drink? All the martinis seem to have ebbed away.

(Don gives Patty a container of cream.)

DON. Here's the cream.

PATTY. Oh, thanks. (Gives shaker to Don) He wants another drink.

DON (puts shaker down). Want to switch to brandy?

DAVID. I'm not fussy—if you're too lazy.

PATTY (on her way out). Now don't get him tight, and don't start quarreling again. I like him, he's cute.

(Exit Patty.)

DAVID. You know, that's an exceptionally charming girl.

DON (curtly). Yes, she is.

DAVID. Directly after dinner, I'll make myself scarce.

DON. I didn't invite her here to spend the night.

DAVID. It could happen, though. Cynthia spent the night here yesterday.

DON. Do I have to tell you again? She slept in the guest room. I slept in mine. That's how she spent the night.

DAVID. I see. But why?

DON. I'll tell you why. We'd been to dinner and to a show. I brought her home about midnight. Cynthia wanted to come in here for a nightcap, but I said no. We went straight up in the elevator to your apartment. I said good night to her at the front door. Then I came down here. Five minutes later she came back here. She said she'd found you up there, extremely tight, and with—with a young lady.

DAVID (flippantly). She was young.

DON. You know, it's really very tragic. Cynthia thought it was rather funny, too.

DAVID (soberly). Go on.

DON. You're not going to like this.

DAVID. You think I've liked it so far?

DON. Well, we sat around for a while and had some drinks. She didn't want to go back to your apartment.

DAVID (ironically). Too degrading?

DON. No. She said she didn't want "to cramp your style." Said she'd known since she was about eleven that you were helling around with assorted women. . . . Finally she . . . (He hesitates) She—well, she . . .

DAVID. Offered to spend the night with you—not in the guest room?

DON (quickly, chivalrously). Yes, but she was all upset and mixed up. She didn't really mean it.

DAVID (burning up). Are you suggesting that she's a moron? She's not a fifteen-year-old high-school kid. A girl doesn't— Of course she meant it.

DON (stiffly). I chose to believe otherwise.

DAVID (savage mimicry). He chose to believe otherwise. My God, the girl's crazy about you, isn't she?

DON. I don't know—and I don't think she knows. Anyway, now you know what the score is.

DAVID. Let me ask you one question—as man to man.

DON (grins). When a man puts it that way, it's always bitchy.

DAVID. Okay, but perhaps we'll get nearer the truth. As man to man let me ask you this—and let's forget for a moment that I'm related to Cynthia, shall we?

DON. Shouldn't be hard for you—you're always forgetting.

DAVID. Let me ask you this: when a pretty girl offers herself to a man—under conditions such as you've described—what would stop him?

DON. Apart from moral barriers—which we needn't go into—nothing if the man's in love. Then he doesn't mind being committed.

DAVID. Correct me if I'm mistaken, but weren't you sort of engaged to her?

DON. There is an important distinction between an engagement and a commitment.

DAVID. Aha.

DON (*needling*). As man to man—I was unwilling to lose the initiative—I've given it a lot of thought.

DAVID (*growling*). Intellectual bastard, aren't you?

DON. When you're carrying the ball you don't like to lose it—on a fumble—in a casual bed . . .

DAVID. I'm not a football fan—but is it customary for the ball carrier to function also as the referee? Who blew the whistle? (*Enter Patty from kitchen, carrying tablecloth. She overhears the last line.*)

PATTY. What are you fighting about now? Football?

DAVID. Why, yes. We were just discussing an incompleted pass.

CURTAIN

ACT TWO

Time—couple of hours later. David is sprawled on the couch sipping brandy from a snifter. Patty is not in the room. She's out in the kitchen washing up. Patty's dress, looking somewhat limp and damp, is hanging over the back of the chair by the fireplace. Don's mood is surly and disagreeable. David is smug and complacent.

DAVID. Still raining. Yep. Makes for a nice, cozy evening indoors. Put another log on the fire.

DON. 'Smatter? You paralyzed?

DAVID. I'm a guest.

DON. And not a very welcome guest, may I add?

DAVID. You made that very clear throughout the meal. I was quite embarrassed. Such a good meal, too. You hardly spoke a word.

DON. Several words occurred to me, but there was a lady present.

DAVID. I did my best to keep the conversation rolling, but I must admit that I detected a slight feeling of strain.

DON. Yes, I thought that some of your jokes were rather strained. However, we'll give you an E for effort.

DAVID. Are you annoyed about something?

DON (*grimly*). Okay, Slater. You crashed the party. You've had your fun. Now why don't you blow?

DAVID. Do you think Patty would like that? I'm here at her invitation—repeated several times—even in your presence. She really twisted my arm.

DON. I feel sure she'll excuse you now.

DAVID. What makes you so sure? I got the impression that she really craved my presence here. She may have had some reason above and beyond the call of hospitality, to urge me to stay.

DON. Your irresistible charm, no doubt.

DAVID. No, I'd say it was a combination of natural curiosity—about me and Cynthia—and feminine fear of spending an evening alone with you.

DON. Don't worry. There was no fear. Before we even came up here I promised . . .

DAVID. My God! You promised . . . ? Then she *was* afraid—afraid of being bored to death. But why should we speculate? Let's ask her why she invited me. I'd be really interested. (*He rises*)

DON (*accepts the challenge*). Okay. Ask her.

DAVID. On second thought . . . (*David sits down.*)

DON. Lost interest?

DAVID. Women are never honest when they're put on a spot. (*Don laughs and strolls toward the kitchen. David sits back.*)

DON. I'm going to help her. Doesn't seem right to let the poor kid do all the work alone.

DAVID. Don't be sentimental. Women love to work. In her case I think it's rather a transparent device.

DON (*turning to him*). What are you talking about?

DAVID. Reached your heart via the stomach . . . The dinner was excellent. Now having established a beach-head in your heart, she's landing in full force on your whole bosom with this dish-washing, see-what-a-superb-housekeeper-I-am routine.

DON. You always look for an ulterior motive, don't you?

DAVID. Yes, and I nearly always find one. (*Don gives him a dirty look. He shoves open the swinging door into the kitchen.*)

DON. Sure you don't need any help?

PATTY (*offstage*). No, thanks. I'll be through in a few minutes.

DON. Just stack all the stuff. I get daily maid service. You don't have . . .

PATTY (offstage). Uh huh. I know. Daily maids are lazy slobs. You just leave me alone and don't stand there kibitzing. Go and read a book or something. . . . What's Mr. Slater doing?

DAVID (calling to Patty). I'm still here.

PATTY (offstage). That's good.

(David gives Don a triumphant look as he settles back on sofa, and Don goes to get a drink.)

DAVID (sprawling on the couch). Want to play some gin? I took you for a bundle, the other night, as I recall. Want to get it back?

DON. Are you planning to settle down for the rest of the evening?

DAVID (raised eyebrows). You feel that I'm offering you unfair competition?

DON (savagely). I just wish you'd call it a day and get the hell out of here.

DAVID (rising). My dear boy, forgive me. . . . Perhaps I'm a little confused.

DON. By what?

DAVID. Well, mainly by you. By your repeated—and quite unnecessary protestations throughout the evening that this was not to be construed as a rendezvous. (Confidentially) Now, if you'd been honest and would have come right out and told me . . .

DON. I'd hate to have a mind like yours. Haven't you ever wanted to spend the evening alone with a girl without trying to make her? (David suddenly sits down) What's the matter with you?

DAVID. I'm trying to think. . . . I take it you're referring to a young, pretty girl?

DON. You're overplaying it, Slater. You know that's a nice kid. There's a cleaned, scrubbed quality about her that even you could see.

DAVID. The greatest courtesans of history were all cleaned and scrubbed in appearance, as far as I know. Mandatory to the profession, you might almost say.

DON. You know very well what I mean.

DAVID. Okay, but keep the soap commercials out of it.

(The telephone rings. Don goes to answer it. David watches him. The kitchen door swings open and Patty enters with plate and dish towel. She wears a man's silk robe over her slip.)

DON (into phone). Hello—no, no—no . . . Yes. (He hangs up. Patty stares across at David who grins)

PATTY. What do you make of that, Watson?

DAVID. Three "no's" and one "yes." Department of utter confusion.

PATTY. I got the impression that he was deliberately noncommittal.

DAVID. Yes, he has a lot of experience in non-committing himself.

(Patty giggles.)

DON (prowls around, chewing his lip). I have to go some place.

(Don shrugs himself into his raincoat. David watches him.)

DAVID (tongue in cheek). Would you like me to keep her company until you return? I'll be delighted to stay.

(Don is debating what to do.)

PATTY. Where are you going?

DON. I have to go out for a few minutes.

PATTY. What for?

DON. It's—er . . .

DAVID. Don't be indiscreet, Patty. When your host walks out on you, never inquire into the reasons. (Strolls to get his hat and raincoat) Just finish the dishes, like a good girl.

PATTY. Are you leaving, too?

DAVID. Our young friend has made it clear to me that my presence is undesirable.

PATTY. You mean to me?

DAVID. To him. I think.

PATTY. Well! I certainly don't intend to stay here alone. (She rolls down her sleeves, unfastens her improvised apron)

DON. Look, Patty.

DAVID. Why don't you take her along with you, Don? Or would that be embarrassing?

DON. I won't be gone more than ten or fifteen minutes.

DAVID. He fears that during that time, I will attempt to alienate your affections.

PATTY (amused). Gosh! Sounds exciting. (To Don) Don't worry. He's really quite harmless.

DAVID. No comment.

DON (reluctantly). Well, okay. But just remember that she hates middle-aged men who make passes.

DAVID. And who can blame her?

DON (crossing to door). And you're old enough to be her father.

DAVID (flops into a chair). You're treading on dangerous ground. I'm a hell of a father. Remember?

DON *(at door)*. Just leave her alone.

(Exit Don. Patty folds her dish towel neatly, walks to kitchen, tosses it onto a shelf.)

PATTY *(pensively)*. Poor Don. Why do you needle him all the time?

DAVID. Now don't start feeling sorry for him.

(Patty, at the door, glances around kitchen, then closes door.)

PATTY. Well, anyway, I really did a job in there. Everything's washed up and cleaned up and put away neat as a pin.

DAVID. Don't be so smug about it. Tidiness is not a virtue.

PATTY. It is. They always say that cleanliness is next to godliness.

DAVID. Okay. But godliness does not appeal to me.

(Patty sits down comfortably in a chair and props her feet up on a table, in a relaxed, unladylike position, displaying generous portions of nylon slip and nylon hose.)

PATTY. What does appeal to you?

DAVIDS. Steaks—liquor—and sex—in that order.

(Patty lowers her legs promptly and gets up. She crosses to the fireplace and casually inspects her dress.)

PATTY. Oh, you're not nearly as depraved as you'd like people to think.

DAVID. Is it dry yet?

PATTY. I think it's getting dry, sort of. *(She holds the dress up for inspection)* Of course, this stain will never come out completely. There ought to be a law.

DAVID. What about?

PATTY *(mock indignation)*. About you. About people who haven't got more sense than to help themselves to ketchup like this.

(She demonstrates by holding an imaginary ketchup bottle and smacking the bottom of it sharply with a fist.)

DAVID *(grinning)*. Didn't I apologize in the most handsome and servile fashion?

PATTY. You weren't even aiming it at the plate.

DAVID. Oh, stop fussing. You look very charming in that robe of Don's. . . . And you probably know it.

PATTY. That must've been a girl on the phone.

DAVID. No question about it.

PATTY. Do you suppose it was Cynthia?

DAVID. I hope so.

PATTY. I suppose you'd like them to kiss and make up?

DAVID. Sure, I'm all for it.

PATTY. Do you realize we've practically driven him out of his own apartment?

DAVID *(piously)*. Let us console ourselves by the hope that we have driven them into each other's arms.

PATTY. What were you fighting about just before dinner?

DAVID. Weren't you listening at the door?

PATTY. No! You can't hear a thing from the kitchen, anyway. What were you . . . ?

DAVID. I was deploring his morality.

PATTY. And you *still* want him to marry your daughter?

DAVID. I deplored his morality, not his immorality.

PATTY *(relieved)*. Oh. *(Pause)* Wasn't that a good dinner I whipped up?

DAVID. How many times during the meal did I congratulate you?

PATTY. Quite often.

DAVID. You want to get married some day and stay married?

PATTY. Sure.

DAVID. My wife was a Southern girl. Cute little thing. She made popovers, superb popovers. I never ate less than three. I always said "swell popovers" or "wonderful popovers," or frequently, "some popovers." Then, maybe an hour later, while I was still digesting them, she always said, "Weren't those popovers good?" You want to know what happened?

PATTY. You divorced her.

DAVID. No. She divorced me. Extreme cruelty. I hit her with a skillet.

PATTY. You didn't!

DAVID. A stainless-steel skillet. Still warm from popovers. Right across her behind. Raised a welt that lasted for weeks, according to her lawyer. I was never privileged to see it.

PATTY. I don't believe you.

DAVID. Why not? It's the truth.

PATTY. You struck a woman?

DAVID. Certainly. Matter of fact, I rarely strike anyone but a woman. I'm not the belligerent type. I'm also a coward. Oh, once in a while, I'll strike a small, defenseless man.

PATTY. You're making it up.

DAVID. It's a fact.

PATTY. But—but you're a Southerner. They all . . .

DAVID. My child, geography has nothing to do with it. Hookworm, yes; chivalry, no.

PATTY. I think you're simply awful. I'm not surprised your wife divorced you. I'm only surprised that anyone ever married you in the first place.

DAVID. Now don't be silly. A predisposition to knock women about is not a characteristic that a man advertises while he's courting. I *can* be rather ingratiating.

PATTY. Yes, you can. That's your whole trouble. Too much charm. Entirely too much.

DAVID. Would you like to marry me?

PATTY. And be knocked about with skillets? Don't be silly.

DAVID. Yes, it was a mistake to tell you about that at this stage. Grave error. However, you're a strong, healthy, athletic-type girl. Much stronger than my ex. You'd hit back. I'd be more careful. How about it?

PATTY. How about what?

DAVID *(soberly)*. Would you like to marry me?

PATTY. Wouldn't you feel foolish if I said yes?

DAVID. No. I would like you to say yes. That's really why I asked you.

PATTY. Do you go around asking strangers to marry you?

DAVID. No. I've asked a few chance acquaintances if they'd like to live in sin with me.

PATTY. Why didn't you ask me?

DAVID. You know, there's a popular theory that nice little girls are always led astray or seduced by nasty old men. It isn't so. For every nice girl seduced by a nasty old man, there are *fifty* betrayed by inexperienced *nice* young men. *Only* nasty old men have an instinctive respect for innocence.

PATTY. You're rather sweet.

DAVID. I might add that since my divorce, I have never proposed marriage to anyone but you.

PATTY. You must be drunk.

DAVID. No. I'm comparatively sober.

PATTY. Well, in that case, you must be crazy.

DAVID. Why? You're on record as wanting to marry a well-heeled man of mature years. I'm forty-one.

PATTY. One wouldn't know it. You act like an adolescent.

DAVID. Should be an irresistible combination. You could mother me.

PATTY. No, thanks.

DAVID. You could mother Cynthia, then.

PATTY. Oh, sure. She'd just love that. I'm all of three years older.

DAVID. She's always urging me to get married to some nice young girl. Well, if Cynthia and Don get together you could be his mother-in-law. Does *that* appeal to you?

PATTY. You shouldn't joke about it. Marriage is much too serious. *(A long pause)* You must be absolutely crazy.

DAVID. For proposing marriage?

PATTY. Yes. What do you know about me?

DAVID. Enough. You're intelligent, you're efficient. You have an adventurous spirit. You're infectiously young and gay. You're an excellent cook. You have a charming face and figure, and you have admirable legs.

PATTY *(fascinated)*. Go on.

DAVID. That should be enough for you. It's enough for me.

PATTY. You haven't said a word about love.

DAVID. There are altogether too many words said about love.

PATTY. Nevertheless, a girl likes to hear them.

DAVID. Knowing that nine-tenths of them are empty, pretty lies?

PATTY. They don't have to be, always.

DAVID. I allowed a margin of ten per cent for romantic sentimentalists.

PATTY. I'll wait for somebody in that bracket.

DAVID. Someone like Don, maybe.

PATTY. Maybe.

DAVID. It was my impression that you were looking for a secure, stable, sanctified relationship with a man who would appreciate you.

PATTY. Yes. But a girl wants to be happy, too.

DAVID. I have an immense capacity for making people happy.

PATTY. With skillets?

DAVID. Ended the union with one clean blow. She married a rich Brazilian almost immediately. Happy as a clam, now. Got a handsome settlement, too. Any more questions?

PATTY. I wouldn't marry you if you were the last man on earth.

DAVID. That's an emotional and ill-considered figure of speech.

PATTY. I mean it.

DAVID. My child, if I were the last man on earth—and if there were a million women left, you'd be fighting tooth and claw with all of them for the privilege of being my mate. You'd be panting to re-populate the world.

PATTY. Don't kid yourself.

DAVID. Your loyalty to the human race would overcome your prejudice against me.

PATTY. You're completely wrong. I don't think the human race is so hot. And I'm not prejudiced against you. I think you're perfectly charming. And crazy.

(The telephone rings.)

DAVID. Let it ring.

PATTY. You mean not answer it at all?

DAVID. You couldn't bear that, could you?

(Phone rings again and again.)

PATTY. It could be an emergency.

DAVID. Somebody wants a house built right this minute.

PATTY. Emergencies can happen to any-one.

DAVID. All right. Don't torture yourself. *(Patty picks up phone eagerly. The line is obviously dead. She hangs up.)*

PATTY. Now they've gone. Why didn't you let me answer it in the first place? *(Looks at watch)* What time is it in Europe?

DAVID *(baffled)*. Pardon?

PATTY. I was just wondering if it could be his mother. She's in Europe—he told me. *(David gets up, takes the telephone off the hook, and sits down again. It remains off the hook, unnoticed, for the balance of Act Two)* You shouldn't do that.

DAVID. Why not?

PATTY. Because this is *his* apartment.

DAVID. And we are his guests. He never should have left. No manners.

PATTY. I hope he comes back and kicks you out.

DAVID. It isn't necessary. I'll leave at once if you'd like me to. Is that what you want?

PATTY. Yes.

DAVID *(starts to get up)*. All right.

PATTY *(smiling)*. But suppose he doesn't come back?

DAVID *(settling down again)*. In that case, you'd probably be bored stiff waiting for him. Or, of course, you could always go home.

PATTY. Oh, no, not before I see him. I couldn't. I mean—well, it's been such a crazy sort of evening. I'd have to wait for him.

DAVID. And if he stayed out all night?

PATTY. Where would he stay?

DAVID. There are places.

PATTY. He's not that kind.

DAVID. How do you know?

PATTY. Well, don't you? He *was* going to marry your daughter, you may recall.

DAVID. I asked for no certificate of chastity. Nor, I am sure, did Cynthia.

PATTY. Maybe she phoned from the corner drug store.

DAVID. People often do.

PATTY. Or even from the lobby.

DAVID. Could be.

PATTY. Look, will you promise to leave the instant he comes back?

DAVID. I will promise no such thing.

PATTY. You're a difficult man.

DAVID. However, I'll repeat my offer to leave now, if you'd rather.

PATTY. Where would you go?

DAVID. Upstairs, to my apartment.

PATTY. What would you do?

DAVID. Probably telephone to a dame I know and ask her to come over.

PATTY. Don't say "dame." It's vulgar. At least say "girl."

DAVID. This girl is quite vulgar in the sense that she's earthy and rather uninhibited. By common definition, she is essentially a "dame" rather than a "girl."

PATTY. Isn't that awfully sordid?

DAVID. It isn't spiritual, but it isn't sordid. This—er—character is a lot of fun.

PATTY *(ironically)*. Good clean fun?

DAVID. Don't be so contemptuous of healthy carnality.

PATTY *(puzzled)*. What's carnality?

DAVID. The sinful lusts of the flesh.

PATTY. Oh! That's from the Bible, isn't it?

DAVID. They've been doing it for a long time.

PATTY. Do you have anything else in common with her?

DAVID *(soberly)*. Yes.

PATTY. What?

DAVID. Companionship. Laughter. Friendship—believe it or not. She thinks I'm a very nice guy. I'm extremely fond of her.

PATTY. Why don't you ask her to marry you?

DAVID. Because she's highly intelligent, and would lose all respect for me if I made such an idiotic and obviously unworkable suggestion.

PATTY *(long pause)*. Why did you ask me to marry you just now?

DAVID. A: you want to get married. B: it might be a very good thing for me to get married again. C: it seemed to me that you'd make an excellent and stimulating wife. Are you reconsidering? My offer's still open.

PATTY. You know, it's very strange. You're really horrible, and cynical and shallow and selfish and immoral and completely worthless—and I *like you*. I like you very much.

DAVID. Enough to marry me?

PATTY. No, but I could probably do a lot worse. A lot worse.

DAVID. Think it over.

PATTY. Are you rich?

DAVID. Yes. Fairly rich. No, let's face it. I'm rich, period. I've never done a day's work, and if I never do, I'll always have a very large income, even after taxes. Why?

PATTY. I've never even thought of being even fairly rich, but security is a terrific temptation. *(Long pause, and then, suddenly reaching for her purse)* Do you have any idea how much money I've got in my purse?

DAVID *(blandly)*. Yes. You have seven dollars and forty-three cents. And a bank book that shows no balance whatsoever. *(She looks at him in amazement)* I'm not psychic. I looked while you were doing the dishes.

PATTY *(smiling)*. That wasn't very ethical.

DAVID. I've never claimed to be ethical. Don thought it was rather shabby of me, too.

PATTY *(counting her money)*. Next Tuesday, I'm doing a television show—maybe—and I'll get about $62.50. Then I'll have over seventy dollars. Once I had over two hundred dollars. For over a week, I had it. That's one thing you miss, being rich.

DAVID. What?

PATTY *(rises, walks around the room)*. The terrific thrill of knowing that you've got over two hundred dollars. It's won-derful. You just feel like going out and spit in somebody's eye.

DAVID *(thoughtfully)*. I won six hundred dollars in a gin game the other night.

PATTY. How wonderful! Weren't you thrilled to death?

DAVID. No.

PATTY. Oh, don't be so blasé! You can't be as rich as all that.

DAVID. No, I like to win, naturally. What I meant was this: I was just six hundred bucks ahead—and now I'm asking myself ahead of what? *(He takes out his wallet)* I have it here. Six crisp, new, one-hundred-dollar bills.

PATTY. You're a dope to carry so much money around. I lost a purse once with over twenty dollars in it. I was sick for weeks.

DAVID *(gently)*. Patty, I would like very much to give you the six hundred dollars.

PATTY. You must be crazy!

DAVID. Will you accept it?

PATTY. No. Of course not.

DAVID. There are no strings to it.

PATTY. Why should you give me six hundred dollars?

DAVID. Maybe I'm not as depraved as I think I am—if I may borrow your phrase.

PATTY. No. Seriously. Why?

DAVID. I told you I got no great kick out of winning it. Give me the kick I missed, by accepting it?

PATTY *(weakening)*. But look. I can't take money from . . .

DAVID. I said there were no strings to it.

PATTY. How much is forty into six hundred?

DAVID *(pause for mental arithmetic)*. Fifteen. Why?

PATTY. That's what I average. Forty a week. Gosh—fifteen weeks!

DAVID *(folds bills, holds them out to her)*. Sold?

PATTY. I don't know what to do. I've never taken money from a man.

DAVID. I won it from a very unpleasant, ruthless capitalist, who grinds the faces of the poor. *(Still proffering money)* Sold?

PATTY. It's an awful temptation. Would you think me a dope if I said no?

DAVID *(thoughtfully)*. Yes, but dopes who said no have added quite a bit to human dignity, such as it is.

PATTY. What would your little friend—*(A glance upward)*—the one we were talking about. What would she do? If you offered the money to her?

DAVID. I don't know. I've given her presents now and then. I've never offered to give her any money. I suspect that she'd say, "Thanks, kid, you're a peach," and that she would have the bills tucked in her stocking in two seconds flat. She's a creature of instinct. *(Shrugging)* On the other hand, she might be very indignant. I don't know. There's a vast difference, anyway.

PATTY. You mean because she's your mistress?

DAVID *(laughs)*. She's not my mistress, you sweet little idiot.

PATTY. But you said that . . .

DAVID. Having a mistress implies a beautiful, romantic, sentimental, passionate relationship of long standing. This girl would laugh at you if you suggested to her that she was my mistress or anybody else's mistress. In her set, a girl goes with a fella. At the moment, she's going with me. I wouldn't swear to it, but I fancy that she's going *exclusively* with me. Not that it matters. When she elects to go with somebody else, or maybe to remarry—she's divorced—there will be no hard feelings on either side, no scenes, no explanations, no recriminations, no broken vows.

PATTY. You make it sound very attractive.

DAVID. Make what sound attractive?

PATTY. Promiscuity.

DAVID. You don't know what promiscuity means.

PATTY. All right, then—sleeping around.

DAVID. Okay—I'll buy that—and don't let anyone ever tell you *that* isn't attractive—in its very limited way. *(Again proffering bills)* Well, are you going to accept it?

PATTY *(moves closer)*. I suppose it would be crazy not to—I mean, it's a fortune. *(Reaches out a hand, and then pulls it back)* Are you a writer, by any chance?

DAVID. Good God, no! Why?

PATTY. I used to know a writer. Last winter, when I had a foul cold, he asked me to go with him to Miami for a week. I was just dying to go, because I needed some sun, but I knew this writer was sort of a wolf. He was in Hollywood once, and he used to date people like Shelley Winters. He said he'd buy me airplane luggage and sport clothes and everything.

We had a terrific scene at Lord & Taylor's, because I finally said no. I never saw him again. He wanted to buy me the most adorable lizard-skin purse and shoes.

DAVID *(puzzled)*. I don't quite get the point.

PATTY. I'm just coming to the point. Months later, I read a short story of his. It was in the *New Yorker*. It was called "The Jaws of the Alligator." I was furious.

DAVID. Why?

PATTY. Because it was the whole story of our bust-up, that's why. The whole story, word for word. He just changed the names and he made it an alligator purse at Bergdorf-Goodman's instead of lizard skin at Lord & Taylor's. Because of the title, see? He was just using me for copy. I think that was pretty chintzy.

DAVID *(poker-faced)*. I vow never to use this incident for copy. In fact, I'll never tell it to a soul.

PATTY. Okay, then. I—I'll take it. *(She takes the money gingerly. Then, suddenly, she is overcome by shyness. She doesn't know what to say or do.)*

DAVID *(kindly)*. Good for you.

PATTY. Gosh, that's the first time I've even *seen* one! *(Unhappily)* I don't know what to say. I'm completely at a loss for words.

DAVID *(smiling)*. Oh, dear. That's bad. It must be unprecedented for you.

PATTY *(gravely)*. I know—I do talk a lot. But this . . . *(Shrugging)* Just to say "I thank you" seems so—well, I mean it sounds just silly.

DAVID. Sounded okay to me, the way you said it.

PATTY. It isn't enough, just "thank you." *(Looks at the money)* Fifteen weeks of security, for free. I just don't know what to say.

DAVID. Don't make a production of it, Patty. Skip it. I'm well repaid, already.

PATTY. By what?

DAVID. Your look of wholesome rapture.

PATTY *(long pause)*. You know—there are strings—on my side.

DAVID. What sort of strings?

PATTY. Gratitude—affection—a terrific desire to repay you some day—somehow . . .

DAVID. It was a gift—not a loan.

PATTY. That's what I mean by strings. You wipe out a loan when you pay it back. For a gift, you're always beholden. *(She puts the money away in her purse)* Oh, boy, when I show this to Vicki and tell her what happened, she'll fall over in a dead faint!

DAVID. You don't think she'll misunderstand?

PATTY. Six hundred dollars! *Nobody* could misunderstand *that* much. Besides, she knows I don't go in for that sort of thing, and she's a good girl, too. That's why we room together.

DAVID. How about the Princeton man, with the Cadillac?

PATTY. Nothing. It's all very hopeless and sad. They just go to very mushy movies once in a while and hold hands. His wife has very low blood pressure. Or maybe it's very high. Anyway, she's not very healthy.

DAVID. He doesn't sound too robust himself.

PATTY. Oh, you. Unless people are sleeping together, you think there's something wrong with them. *(She looks at him for several moments. Then she leans over and kisses him on the cheek)* There!

DAVID. I didn't like the way you said that.

PATTY. Why?

DAVID. It was patronizing, indulgent and maternal.

PATTY. Well, you offered to let me mother you. Didn't you want me to kiss you?

DAVID. Very much—but without the "there"!

PATTY *(amused)*. Oh, you're too fussy.

DAVID. Not at all. The whole point really is—did *you* want to kiss *me?*

PATTY. Of course.

DAVID. You'd have felt pretty silly if I'd said "there"!

PATTY *(thoughtfully)*. Maybe you're right. *(Grinning)* Okay, let's try it again. *(She gets up, and after a moment's mental debate kisses him again on the cheek. He is impassive)* That better?

DAVID. Not appreciably.

PATTY. It wasn't patronizing—or maternal.

DAVID. No, but it seemed to be on the daughterly side.

PATTY. Wasn't giving me all that money on the fatherly side?

DAVID. You're too logical. It's unbecoming in the young.

PATTY. Well, anyway, you're sweet. *(She sits on his knee. Again she kisses his cheek, sweetly and affectionately. He pats her shoulder reassuringly, rather clumsily. Manifestly, this is the first time he ever had a girl sitting on his lap and kissing him without making passes at her. The front door is suddenly opened by Don, who comes in very wet, and, when he sees what they are doing, very angry. Patty jumps up off David's lap, startled.)*

DON. Well, I'll be damned! What the . . . ? I'll be damned!

PATTY *(fussed)*. Gosh, you did get wet! What were you doing—standing in the rain?

DON *(furious)*. Get out of here—both of you.

DAVID *(soothingly)*. Now, now, let's not be hasty. *(Philosophical)* Things are not always what they seem to be.

DON. I've got eyes in my head. It was pretty obvious.

DAVID. The obvious is frequently misleading. Now, take little Patty here. She . . .

DON. You take her. You're welcome. *(To Patty)* You'll have lots of company. He has a whole raft of little playmates. *(Strides to door)* I'd appreciate it very much if you'd both get the hell out of my apartment.

PATTY *(with spirit)*. Oh, stop being so stuffy and so horrible. Okay, so you found me sitting on his knee and kissing him. Is that so awful? My gosh, I swear I'm never going to kiss a man again as long as I live.

DON. That might be an excellent resolve for you.

PATTY. It never fails. It always messes things up.

DON. And how! *(He opens the bedroom door. Patty goes to him)*

PATTY. Don, would you like to know exactly what happened? Why you found me . . .

DON. Does it make any difference, why or how?

PATTY. I think it might. *(Gravely)* You see, Mr. Slater had asked me to marry him.

DON *(amazed)*. Marry? He asked you to marry him?

PATTY. Yes. *(To David, anxiously)* I hope you don't mind my telling him that?

DAVID. It's none of his damned business.

DON (*to David, still incredulous*). You asked her to marry you? You only met her a few hours ago.

DAVID. That's correct. One of her dinners and I was putty in her hands.

DON (*to Patty*). What did you put in that steak sauce—marijuana? (*Stepping into bedroom*) I hope you'll be very happy.

DAVID. Wait a minute. She had the good sense to turn me down flat.

DON (*skeptically*). Uh huh. That must have been the close-up I saw when I came in. (*He goes into bedroom, sticks his head out again for a moment*) Again may I say that I'd appreciate it if you'd get the hell out of here.

(*Exit Don, slamming the door.*)

DAVID (*yelling*). Which one of us do you mean?

PATTY. Oh, dear, poor Don. What must he think?

DAVID. It's hard to know with such a clean-minded young man. They can think of the vilest things.

(*Patty crosses to the bedroom door and listens.*)

PATTY. I wonder what he's doing?

DAVID. Maybe he's changing his socks. He looked very damp all over.

PATTY. Look, you'd better go, I think.

DAVID. You mean now—like this—without an honest-to-God scene of some sort?

PATTY. You want him to throw you out?

DAVID. Don't be so melodramatic.

PATTY. He could. He's not a coward. He could easily.

DAVID (*considering*). Yes, but it'd make him feel awfully silly, now. He missed the right moment. Violence should never come as an afterthought.

PATTY. He told us both to get out.

DAVID. Yes, but rather ambiguously. He obviously wants me to blow—but he hopes you'll stick around. He hasn't finished with you, yet.

PATTY (*distressed*). Oh, gosh. (*Staring at bedroom door*) Now he probably doesn't believe a word I've told him. Now he probably thinks I'm just a little tramp.

DAVID. Don't worry about it.

PATTY. But I do. After all, I mean— well, what else could he think? He still doesn't know why I was sitting on your knee and kissing you.

DAVID. And if you have any sense, you won't tell him.

PATTY. He's a very nice boy and I don't want him to think I'm that sort of a girl. (*David rises, takes his hat, and puts his coat over his arm.*)

DAVID. Are you seriously interested in our young friend?

PATTY. How do you mean?

DAVID. Romantically?

PATTY. How would I know? I've spent practically the whole evening over a hot stove—or talking to you.

DAVID. Physically?

PATTY. Don't be coarse.

DAVID. Matrimonially?

PATTY. I only met him a few hours ago. I'll probably never see him again.

DAVID. But you'd like to?

PATTY. I just don't want him to think I'm a—(*Groping for an appropriate word*) —a pushover.

DAVID. You think he believes that now?

PATTY (*glances toward bedroom*). I wouldn't blame him. He has reason to have suspicions.

(*David puts on his hat at a rakish angle and opens the front door.*)

DAVID. Then take my advice, let them lurk.

PATTY (*puzzled*). What?

DAVID. Suspicions, my child, suspicions. The lurking doubt—is she, or isn't she? Does she—or doesn't she? Will she—or won't she? Suspicion—the most powerful aphrodisiac in the world. (*He goes out, closing the door behind him. Patty starts toward the bedroom. Almost immediately, David opens the front door again, watching her*) Now, don't go knocking on the door! Let him lead off.

PATTY (*startled, wheeling around*). You scared me. I thought you'd gone.

DAVID. On second thought, I decided to slam the door. He'll figure one of us is left. Should bring him out panting with curiosity. If things get too unpleasant you know where I live.

(*He waves to her, and then exits slamming the door as advertised. Patty, very pensive, crosses to inspect her dress, still draped in front of the fireplace. She is disappointed to note that the slam produced no immediate effect. A moment later, enter Don whistling from bedroom. He wears a bathrobe, around which he is just tying the belt. His feet are in bedroom slippers. He notes with obvious satisfaction that Patty is alone. Patty looks at him rather nervously. Don sits down on the couch and lights a cigarette. There is a long, pregnant silence.)*

DON. Where did Slater go?

PATTY. I don't know. How should I know?

DON. I assumed that by now you would know all about his movements.

PATTY. Well, I don't. And, what's more, I don't care.

DON *(very polite)*. Please excuse this robe. I got rather wet.

PATTY. Well, it's a very nice robe. *(Amiably)* Of course it does need mending— where the loop . . .

DON. I have a very gorgeous robe that doesn't need mending. You happen to be wearing it.

PATTY *(miffed)*. You shall have it back the moment my dress is dry enough for me to put on. I'd have gone before, but I just wanted to . . .

DON. That's all right. No hurry. *(He sneezes)*

PATTY. Gezundheit.

DON *(stiffly)*. Thank you. *(He sneezes again and gropes in the pocket of his robe for a handkerchief. There isn't one)* Nuts. *(Patty goes to her purse, takes out a folded wad of Kleenex and hands it to him.)*

PATTY. Kleenex.

DON. Thank you. *(He blows his nose)*

PATTY. Was that Cynthia on the phone?

DON. Yes.

PATTY. We figured it was.

DON. It was.

PATTY. Have you been standing talking to her in the rain?

DON. Yes. She phoned from Luigi's— that's a cocktail bar at the corner—but I didn't want to go in. *(He sneezes again)* We stood in the rain and talked.

PATTY. What about?

DON. About you, mostly.

PATTY. Me?

DON. Yes. I told her just how we met, and how you came up here to fix dinner— and what a nice kid you seemed to be.

PATTY. She didn't believe that, did she?

DON. She said, "I think I know the type. She sounds like a professional virgin."

PATTY. What an awful thing to say!

DON. Yes. I thought so, too. We had quite a fight about it.

PATTY *(gently, musing)*. In the rain.

DON. In the rain. Seemed very appropriate.

PATTY *(promptly)*. And? Go on.

DON *(slight hesitation)*. That's about all there was to it.

PATTY. Sounds like a very unsatisfactory conversation.

DON. I guess it was. *(Shrugging)* What is there to say to a girl when you—when everything is obviously . . . *(Another shrug, and a smile)* It was raining like hell.

PATTY *(gravely)*. I know.

DON. All I wanted was to come back— here—but I didn't expect to find you . . .

PATTY *(quickly)*. Necking with Mr. Slater?

DON. Nobody said anything about necking. You were getting along pretty well with him, weren't you?

PATTY *(savagely)*. Yes, he's adorable. Too bad you had to barge in just at that tender moment.

(Don looks at her for a long time. Then he pours himself a drink of brandy and sips it.)

DON *(suddenly)*. I wish the hell Al Smith had stuck to politics.

PATTY. Who?

DON. Al Smith.

PATTY. Who's he?

DON. He built the Empire State Building.

PATTY. Oh. Oh, I see. *(Musing)* Of course, it isn't really his fault. We might have met anywhere.

DON. Do you go around kissing every Tom, Dick and Harry?

PATTY *(furious)*. Yes. Yes. Always.

DON. You were kissing him.

PATTY. Yes. Yes. I was.

DON. A perfect stranger.

PATTY. Rubbish. He had dinner with us. I've known him almost as long as I've known you.

DON. I suppose he made love to you?

PATTY *(viciously)*. Of course. Violent love. How can you doubt it?

DON. I don't.

PATTY *(needling)*. In your apartment, too, to your pickup, wearing your robe and digesting your dinner.

DON. He never had any scruples. I might have warned you.

(They are working themselves up to a real fight. Suddenly, Patty deflates. She looks at him very earnestly.)

PATTY. Look, Don. Let's be sensible. Would you like me to tell you exactly what happened after you left?

DON (*surly*). No. What's the difference? (*Unhappily*) It just seems a pity—that's all.

PATTY. What's a pity?

DON. I really thought you were a nice girl. I really did. I told Cynthia you were worth fifty of her. I really thought you were a nice kid.

PATTY. And now you don't.

DON. And now I don't.

PATTY. Mr. Slater does. Still. (*Brief pause*) I think that's why he asked me to marry him. (*Don looks at her contemptuously*) Don't you believe me?

DON. I don't believe he ever asked you to marry him. I didn't believe it when you first told me—or when you asked him to confirm it—or now.

PATTY. Why not?

DON. Because I know David Slater—and he's not the type. That's why.

PATTY. Well, it's true.

DON. Oh, be your age. Slater's a playboy—an avowed rake and a libertine. He's a thoroughly deplorable character.

PATTY. I like him very much.

DON. That's pretty obvious. I gathered that when I came back with the groceries and found that you'd asked him to dinner. If I'd had any sense I'd have kicked you both out then.

PATTY. Why didn't you?

DON. Because I was a sucker. I was willing to give you the benefit of the doubt.

PATTY. Oh, thanks a lot!

DON. You're not even playing it smart. Now if you told me Slater asked you to sleep with him, I could have believed that.

PATTY. We discussed that.

DON. I'll bet you did.

PATTY. I didn't mean . . . Don't you believe anything I told you on the Empire State Building?

DON. No. Nothing. Did you give Slater the same line?

PATTY. It *wasn't* a line.

DON. He'd have laughed in your face.

PATTY. No, he wouldn't. He's much kinder than you.

DON. Kinder?

PATTY. Yes. He found me up here tonight—he knew how we met—and he had every reason to think the worst of me. He

didn't. You were gone—how long?—fifteen minutes—and you come back and look at me and talk to me as if I were just a little floozie. I offered to explain what happened. It's really very innocent. You wouldn't listen. Why? Did you think I'd lie to you?

DON. I don't care, that's all. I'm not interested.

PATTY. Mr. Slater believes . . .

DON (*pause*). I believed it too, this afternoon. It's a pretty good act.

PATTY (*she's almost crying*). I think you're horrible.

DON (*brutally*). Don't bother to cry. Cynthia tipped me off to that gag. She said that professional virgins . . .

(*Patty goes to fireplace and grabs her dress.*)

PATTY. I'm going.

DON. Okay. Going up to Slater's?

PATTY (*defiantly*). Yes. Yes—I am. (*She marches toward bedroom door, Don follows her*)

DON. Unfinished business?

PATTY. Yes. (*She opens the door. Looks back at Don. He strolls away*)

DON. If you run into Cynthia up there—tell her she won her bet.

(*Exit Patty, slamming the door. Don paces up and down savagely. Doorbell rings. Don opens the door. Enter Detective-Sergeant Michael O'Neill. He is a very large man and also a suspicious and angry man. He is in plain clothes. His coat and hat are drenched. He looks Don over quickly, noting the bathrobe.*)

O'NEILL. Your name Donald Gresham?

DON. That's right. (*O'Neill strides in, looks around, and heads for kitchen without saying a word. Don is at his heels*) Who are you? What do you want? (*O'Neill looks into kitchen, shoves Don aside and heads for bedroom. Still completely at sea, Don follows. He grabs O'Neill by the arms*) Where the hell do you think you are? (*O'Neill shoves him aside. Opens door to bedroom, peers in*)

PATTY (*offstage, alarmed*). Wait! I'm not buttoned up yet.

DON. What *is* this?

(*O'Neill turns on Don and hits him in the eye. He falls down, out cold. The door buzzer sounds. O'Neill opens the door and there stands David.*)

DAVID (*startled*). Evening. Mr. Gresham in?

o'neill. No, sir. Mr. Gresham is out. . . . *(Glances to prostrate Don)* Out like a light. . . .
(O'Neill kneels by Don's side, takes his pulse. David strolls over, fascinated.)

david *(casually).* Did you break his neck?
(Don starts to stir.)

o'neill. He's coming to. Thirty-five years on the force have taught me just how hard to hit a man.
(Patty enters, buttoning her dress.)

patty. Pop! *(Sees the fallen Don)* Oh, Pop, what have you done?
(She kneels by Don, chafing his hands, etc. He's stirring.)

o'neill. Leave him be. Are *you* all right?

patty. Of course I'm all right. How on earth did you know I was here? *(Sees David)* Did you . . . ?

david. Me? Heaven forbid.

o'neill. 'Tis by the grace of God I telephoned your apartment. Your roommate told me where I could find you.

patty. Oh, why can't she keep her big mouth shut?

david. Did he find you in each other's arms?

patty. I wasn't even in the room. We had a terrific fight—and my father seems to have come barging in and . . .

o'neill. Leave him be. You little fool—don't you know better than to come to a man's apartment and . . .

patty. Oh, Pop. You don't understand. He wasn't trying to—I know it looks bad, but he—can't you realize that he—he—he's an *architect* . . . *(As if that explained everything)*

o'neill. I'll hear your story later. Come.

patty *(protesting to her father).* Oh, Pop . . .

o'neill. Quiet. *(Patty goes to bar to get a glass of water for Don. To David)* Let me ask you something, sir. Wouldn't you have done what I did if you had found *your* daughter in a man's apartment?

david. That's a good question, Mr. O'Neill. A very good question.

o'neill. Thank you. Good night, sir. *(To Patty)* Didn't I tell you about hell fire and damnation? How many times . . . ?

patty. Pop, please!

o'neill. Come on!

patty *(as she's following her father out).* Oh, Mr. Slater, do something!
(Patty and her father exit. The door is closed. David looks at the prostrate Don, gets the brandy bottle and glass from coffee table, pours a drink without haste, puts down the bottle and, with glass in hand, steps over the prostrate Don near the end of sofa. Looks down at him, slowly drinks, then casually sits on sofa, gazing down thoughtfully at the prostrate Don.)

CURTAIN

ACT THREE

SCENE ONE

Stage is in darkness. Moonlight streams from windows. The door buzzer sounds several times. After a moment Don enters from bedroom wearing a robe over pajamas. He snaps on the lights and goes to front door, disclosing Patty. She wears the same suit as in the previous scene. Don stands at the door and does not admit her immediately. He is in a very disagreeable state and Patty promptly matches his mood.

———

don. Are you here again? D'you realize it's after two A.M.?

patty. Well, I'm very sorry but I couldn't get back before. I came as soon as I could. *(She tries to step into the room but Don is not yet willing to admit her)*

don. What do you want?

patty *(annoyed).* What do you *think* I want? I want to talk to you.

don. What about?

patty. Well, I certainly can't tell you in two seconds flat—and I can't do it standing out here in the hall.

don. Why not?

patty. All right. I just came back to ask you what Cynthia meant when she said that I was a professional virgin.

don *(he finally admits her. He closes the door and then follows her into the room).* This is no time to be calling on people.

patty. I know. It's taken me nearly three hours to get away from my father! That's why I'm so late. He took me to my apartment and we had the most awful row. He was livid. You should have seen him.

DON. I did. I caught the first show.

PATTY. Well, anyway, he knows now that it was all quite innocent and he said for me to tell you . . .

DON. I'd rather not hear. I've read about police brutality but it never hit me in the eye before.

PATTY. I tried to phone you . . . *(She sees the telephone still off the hook)* Oh, that man. No wonder they said the line was busy. I'd forgotten he did that. *(She puts the receiver back on its cradle and then goes to him. For the first time she gets a real good look at his shiner)* Gosh, that's quite an eye. Does it hurt?

DON. Yes. Very much.

PATTY *(judicially)*. My father shouldn't have done that.

DON *(grimly)*. Isn't that putting it rather mildly?

PATTY *(quite evenly)*. Look, I'm sorry my father slugged you. I said he shouldn't have. He should have asked a few questions first. But he's my father and—well—he's an old-fashioned man. He sees his duty and he does it. *(Another look at his eye)* That does look ghastly. Would you like me to fix it up for you?

DON *(very surly)*. No. It's just an old-fashioned shiner—from an old-fashioned father and I'll cherish it as such for several days.

PATTY. It's a horrible-looking eye—but you said a lot of horrible things to me—awful things—so in a sense I think you deserve it richly.

DON *(stares at her, amazed)*. Well, I'm filled with remorse!

PATTY. A shiner doesn't last more than a few days. Some of the things you said to me I'll never forget—never. *(She paces nervously)* You should have put some raw steak on it.

DON *(irate again)*. If you hadn't invited Slater for dinner there might have been some steak left for me to put on it.

PATTY. Now don't start that again.

DON *(with indignant yelp)*. Start, my God! Whose fault is all this? Who caused all the trouble? If you hadn't invited Slater . . .

PATTY *(very cold and dignified)*. I haven't come back to discuss Mr. Slater. *(A pause, and then, with feminine incon-*

sistency) Didn't he offer to do anything for your eye?

DON *(he's off again)*. When I came to, I found your friend Mr. Slater sitting over there like Rodin's *Thinker*—with a snootful—and instead of showing decent sympathy for me, all he did was tell me what a great guy your father was; and when he wasn't ranting about the great moral lesson your father had taught him, he looked at my eye and laughed.

PATTY. Oh, no.

DON. Oh, yes. Finally I got fed up and kicked him out. *(A long look at Patty, still very irate)* Look, it's getting late. What's on your mind?

PATTY. If you'll stop yelling at me, I'll try to tell you. *(Don stares at her fixedly)* And don't glare at me like that. I can't even think when you . . . *(Looks at his eye; quite friendly)* You know, an ice pack would take down that swelling.

DON *(grimly)*. And let's not discuss my eye.

PATTY *(gravely)*. All right. That seems reasonable enough. Let's discuss . . .

DON. It's late. I'm willing to forego *any* discussion. In fact, I'm willing to write the whole thing off as a hideous nightmare.

PATTY *(with a long look at him)*. The *whole* thing?

DON. From beginning to end. *(The telephone rings. He goes to answer it)* Hello. Oh, my God, what do you want? Yes, I'm all right. Look, do you realize it's about two A.M.? Oh, no, I left it off the hook. No, Cynthia, no. Let's just forget it. I don't want to talk about it. The fact remains . . .

(He hangs up slowly, looking at the instrument. As usual, Patty has listened to the conversation avidly.)

PATTY. What did *she* want?

DON. She's also overcome with concern about my eye.

PATTY. At *this* hour?

DON. May I remind you that you came in person—also at this hour?

PATTY. There's a slight difference. Whose father biffed you in the eye? *(Faintly malicious)* What did she do, hang up on you?

DON. No. Slater just picked up the extension and was bawling her out. He's had a rush of paternal solicitude to the head.

(He stands looking out of the window. Patty watches him thoughtfully.)

PATTY. You're tired, aren't you?

DON. I had a hard day.

PATTY. If Cynthia came down now— and cried over you a little—and fussed over your eye—I wonder . . .

DON *(turning on her acidly)*. Let's add Cynthia to the list of topics we won't discuss, shall we?

PATTY *(very feminine)*. No. She called me a professional virgin. That's what gripes me. That's what I came back to talk about. Not Cynthia—don't worry— only what she said. *(Friendly, but firm)*

DON *(uneasily)*. It was just a rather— unfortunate phrase—and I flung it in your teeth because we were having a fight.

PATTY. Yes, and they were fighting words the way you said them. May I ask you why does Cynthia object to virgins?

DON. Look, nobody in their right mind would seriously object to being called a virgin, even if they weren't one. . . .

PATTY. Okay, but it's this "professional" makes me mad. I'd like to have that explained.

DON. It's not necessary to advertise it. That's really all the phrase means.

PATTY. What's wrong with advertising?

DON. People who advertise are anxious to sell something.

(This stops Patty cold.)

PATTY. Oh, oh, I see what you mean. Maybe I yap about it too much. I hadn't met you for ten minutes before I started yapping about how virtuous I was. Then when Mr. Slater came I yapped about it some more, then . . .

DON. Then *quit* yapping!

PATTY. Maybe you're right. One shouldn't put one's cards on the table. That's a silly way to play cards.

DON *(uncomfortably)*. I find the topic rather uncomfortable.

PATTY. Why? It's *my* chastity we're discussing—not yours. *(Pokerface)* We could discuss *yours* if you'd rather. . . .

DON. No, thanks.

PATTY. All right. *(Suddenly)* Do you believe in fate?

DON. What kind of fate?

PATTY. Oh, I was just wondering what would have happened if it hadn't rained like crazy and you'd just taken me out to dinner as we'd planned.

DON. I think we'd have had a more conventional date.

PATTY. Yes. We just started off on the wrong foot, I guess. Anyway, I don't think we'd be sitting here now . . . *(The doorbell sounds)* Oh, my goodness!

(Both are startled. The doorbell sounds again and there is a rapping on the door.)

DON. Shshsh! *(Don dashes to the bedroom door, beckons to Patty and shoves her in. He closes the bedroom door and starts dubiously to the front door. Suddenly he notices Patty's purse and jacket and hastily puts them in the bedroom. Finally he goes to open the front door. Enter David. He wears a robe over his pajamas. David comes in uninvited. As previously, he is not entirely sober, yet not entirely drunk)* What are you prowling around for, dressed like that?

DAVID. Never mind my wardrobe. If it shocks the elevator boys, it's just too bad. *(Peering at Don's eye)* That's a grisly-looking eye.

DON. So I've observed—with the good eye. *(David promptly goes to the bar and pours himself a drink. Don follows him, irritated)* What do you want? Do you realize it's well after two A.M.?

DAVID. Exactly. That's why I'm here. This is no time for you and Cynthia to be chewing the rag over the telephone. Thought I'd come down right away and tell you.

DON *(indignantly)*. I never . . . *She* telephoned *me!* Why the hell don't you talk to *her?*

DAVID. My dear boy—I did. I am hoarse from talking to that girl. Can't get to first base with her. Moreover, I am running out of material. *(Stares at Don's eye)* That's the most unpleasant sight I've ever seen.

DON. Get out of here, will you?

(David pours himself another drink.)

DAVID. I'm sorry if it's painful, of course —but let's be fair about it. O'Neill had the right idea. Had it coming to you in spades.

DON. Are you still defending the actions of that imbecile flatfoot . . . ?

DAVID. He may be an imbecile, and he may be a flatfoot—but he's a father. He'd have been quite justified in killing you. So would I, for that matter. There is no closed season for seducers. The unwritten law protects us fathers.

DON (*contemptuously*). Unwritten law . . .

DAVID. Look, I'll grant that if somebody would want to write it down, more people would know just where they stand—but the principle's sound. Man has the right to protect his daughter. Duty to protect her. Now, getting back to Cynthia.

DON. Why don't you *get* back to Cynthia?

DAVID. All right—all right—don't rush me. She's safe at the moment. (*Displays key*) Locked her in her bedroom. Difficult girl, Cynthia. You know something? Spoke to that girl for an hour about hell fire and damnation—Patty's advice, too—never batted an eyelash. Laughed at me. (*Grinning*) Of course I found it hard to keep a straight face. Guess you have to believe in it yourself if you want to put the fear of God in anybody else. Bawled the hell out of that girl.

DON. Isn't that rather belated—this making a noise like a father?

DAVID. You know—that's exactly what Cynthia said. Stopped me cold. Good point. That's why I locked her in her bedroom. Anyway, for your information I have forbidden her to see you or to communicate with you under any and all circumstances. I think.

DON. So I gathered when you cut in on our telephone conversation.

DAVID. Yes, I knew she'd try to call you, but I heard her dialing. Made me quite sore. I'd expressly forbidden her to do that. (*Musing*) Got to do something drastic to save that girl. Flesh of my flesh, after all.

DON. Go to bed. You're breaking my heart.

DAVID. Don't be cynical. (*Goes to bar, pours himself a final drink. Quotes:*) "There is more joy in heaven over one sinner that repenteth."

DON. Okay. Repenteth in your own apartment, will you? I'd like to go to bed. Go away.

DAVID. That's what I plan to do—go away. Go far away. Yes, sir, I've decided to take Cynthia down to Brazil.

DON (*hopefully*). Good idea.

DAVID. Now why couldn't I have had a son? Nobody cares if they lose their virtue. People are all for it. There's no justice.

DON. Go away. Go to bed.

DAVID. Yes, sir, my ex-wife is in Brazil

and it's high time she took charge of Cynthia. What the hell do I know about raising daughters? Do Cynthia good to learn Portuguese. Keep her out of mischief. I'll make reservations right now. (*Politely*) Mind if I use your phone?

DON. You've got a phone in your place.

DAVID. I had a phone, but when you called Cynthia up just now—(*He sees that Don is about to protest and beats him to it*)—okay, when she called you—I ripped the damn thing right out of the wall. The only way I could figure to keep her incommunicado. (*Well pleased with himself*) Yes, sir, if more fathers ripped more phones out of more walls, more girls wouldn't get into trouble. (*Crosses to phone*) It's only a local call.

DON. All right. Make it snappy.

DAVID. You wouldn't by any chance know the number of Pan American, would you? I had lunch with Howard Hughes once, but didn't get the number.

DON. Howard Hughes is not with Pan American.

DAVID. Don't change the subject. Never mind, I'll get the number from information. (*He puts the receiver to his ear for a moment and is about to dial when he looks at Don in a puzzled way*) You got a party line?

DON. No.

(*Don glances around sharply, realizes that David must have heard Patty on the extension in the bedroom. David listens again for a few moments and hangs up. Don comes to him.*)

DAVID (*grinning amiably*). You low-down, no-good, lying, hypocritical son of a . . . I'll be damned. You've got that girl in there now. I recognized her voice. (*He goes to bedroom door. Don tries to head him off, but David beats him to it*)

DON. You don't know what you're talking about. She . . .

DAVID (*yelling*). Patty!

PATTY (*offstage*). Just a sec, I'm on the phone.

(*David looks triumphantly at Don, who sits down in a weary, resigned manner.*)

DON. Okay. And wipe that grin off your face. I told her to hide in there. She was just leaving. I didn't know who was at the door. I didn't want her to be embarrassed by . . .

DAVID (*holds up a hand to stop the flood of alibis. He is rather ruefully amused*).

You pillar of virtue! Did I tell you how much I hate nobility? I hate hypocrisy more. My God, you really fooled me. I must be slipping. *(Feigning great concern, confidentially)* Of course it's none of my business—since you're not going to be my son-in-law—but doesn't that homicidal father of hers dampen your ardor at all? He'd scare the hell out of me, I can tell you. *(He strolls toward the vestibule, then turns back)*

DON. Slater, you're completely wrong. Patty just stopped by for a moment to ...

DAVID *(gently, almost sadly)*. Look, why don't we try to stop kidding each other? It's no skin off my nose what you do— *(A glance toward bedroom)* or even what she does. I'm a little disappointed—maybe even a little disillusioned. But what the hell, she's not my daughter.

DON. Will you listen to me?

DAVID. Don't bother dreaming up alibis. I'm not sitting in moral judgment—either on her or on you. Okay, so she fooled me too. Pity. Seems like such a nice kid. *(Shakes his head)* Fooled me completely. Great pity. *(He walks toward the vestibule. Don looks back in a troubled way toward the bedroom door)*

DON. Wait a minute, Slater. She'll tell you. *(Calls)* Patty!

DAVID *(interrupting)*. No, I'd rather not hear. *(Don turns back to face him. The door of the bedroom opens silently and Patty stands there. Neither of them is aware of her presence)* Just tell her for me that—that I rather hoped she'd wait at least fifteen weeks.

DON *(puzzled)*. What?

DAVID. She'll understand.

(Patty, who has overheard this, now strides into the room, burning up.)

PATTY. She certainly will. *(Both men are startled to realize that she has overheard. Patty crosses to David)* How dare you say a thing like that?

DAVID. Well, it wasn't intended for your ears, but I thought it was rather well put.

PATTY. You're just as bad as Don. I think you're horrible.

DAVID. You do?

PATTY. Yes. I didn't think *you'd* have any doubts. What happened to your respect for innocence?

DAVID. You know in spite of all appearances I feel it coming on again.

DON. Look, Slater, why don't you go up to your apartment?

PATTY. You leave him to me. I haven't started telling him what I think of him yet. *(She opens her purse and starts groping in it. David watches her)*

DAVID. Now calm down. Don't say or do anything that you might regret. *(Handsomely)* I'm beginning to think I may have—jumped to the wrong conclusion.

PATTY *(indignantly)*. Just because you happened to find me in a man's bedroom is no reason ...

DAVID. It's considered good circumstantial evidence.

PATTY. That's a horrible thing to say.

DAVID. In my condition it's almost impossible to say—but I made it.

PATTY. You also said there were no strings—and I thought you meant it.

DAVID. I did.

PATTY. No—you didn't. *(Wisely)* I don't believe it would have entered your mind that there might be anything wrong—if I hadn't taken all that money.

DON *(puzzled)*. What? *What* money?

PATTY *(to David, ignoring Don. She is still groping in her purse and now produces the money)*. I never should have taken it—and now I want you to take it back.

DON. Will you kindly tell me what the hell you're talking about?

PATTY. I'm not talking to you. I'm talking to Mr. Slater—about the money he gave me.

DON. What on earth did he give you money for?

PATTY. I don't know. Ask him. I don't know.

DON. You gave her money?

(David pours himself a drink and looks at Patty reproachfully.)

DAVID. You have a genius for doing the wrong thing at the wrong time. You should be in the State Department.

PATTY *(to Don)*. That's why I was kissing him. I was thanking him for a gift. A gift of six hundred dollars. He said he won it playing gin with a bloated capitalist who grinds the faces of the poor.

(Don sits down with an amused grin on his face.)

DON. Well, I'll be damned. I'll be damned. *(He looks at David and they both laugh)*

PATTY. What's so funny?

DON. He won that from *me*. Only last week he took it from me. I'm still bleeding. That was *my* six hundred bucks.
(Both men are highly amused. Patty is furious.)

PATTY *(to Don)*. Okay. Then you take it. *(She marches over and hands him the folded bills. He pushes her away)*

DON. Oh, for God's sake. It's his dough.
(Patty marches over to David and extends the bills to him. They look at each other for a long time. He makes no move.)

PATTY. I'd like you to take it back, Mr. Slater. Please.
(He looks at her for another moment and then calmly takes the bills and folds them carefully, still looking straight at Patty.)

DAVID. Boy Scouts are supposed to be doing a good deed *every* day. They must have a hell of a time! *(Patty isn't quite sure whether he's making fun of her or not. She walks away irritably. For a moment they are all constrained. David is still folding the bills)* I wonder why it is that young men are always cautioned against bad girls. Anyone can handle a bad girl. It's the good girls men should be warned against.

PATTY. You're so right. *(Suddenly)* I'd like a drink.

DAVID *(promptly)*. Good idea.

DON. I thought you considered it high school to drink unless you actually craved it.

PATTY *(defiantly)*. Well, I crave it now.
(David goes to the bar and starts to pour a drink.)

DAVID. Soda or plain water?

PATTY. I'll take it straight.

DAVID *(as he pours)*. Say when . . .

PATTY *(the glass is almost full)*. When.

DON *(dubiously)*. Isn't that a pretty stiff drink?

PATTY *(taking the drink)*. No.

DAVID *(to Don)*. Haven't we confused this poor little girl enough for one day? Don't *you* start getting fatherly all of a sudden. *(He watches Patty who is sipping her drink very gingerly)* Bottoms up, baby. *(Patty takes a couple of good swallows. David watches her with quiet amusement)* Cigarette?

PATTY. Thanks. I think I will.
(She lights the cigarette and puffs on it. She doesn't choke but you get the feeling that she might at any moment.)

DON. You're really going high school with a vengeance, aren't you?

PATTY. Yes. Across the board.

DON *(annoyed, sternly)*. Why don't you quit trying to show off?
(For answer, Patty merely takes another swallow of her drink.)

DAVID. Now there's a man who's hard to please. Gripes when you're trying to be pure—and gripes when you're trying to be wanton.

DON *(gritting his teeth)*. Look, Slater, will you, for God's sake, go up to your own apartment?

DAVID. All right. *(To Patty)* Want to come with me? I mean if you're seriously planning to embark on a life of sin—I wouldn't attempt to dissuade you.
(Don shows his irritation and Patty is aware of it and is playing largely for his benefit. She smiles at David.)

PATTY. You wouldn't?
(Don goes toward the door of the bedroom.)

DAVID. We'd be very discreet, of course. Wouldn't want your father to suspect, but I know a very nice little apartment. . . .

PATTY. Gosh, could I have a maid?

DAVID. Sure. And a Cadillac with a gadget.

PATTY. And charge accounts?

DON *(contemptuously)*. It's a very bad routine, Patty. I bet you can't act, even on TV. Good night.
(Exit Don, slamming the door.)

DAVID. There's always roller skating.

PATTY. It wasn't a routine—except the last part. He goes out of his way to hurt me.

DAVID. Young men in love are always cruel.

PATTY. We've done nothing but fight.

DAVID. He suffers too.

PATTY. I'm fed up with being . . .

DAVID. The status to which I presume you're referring needn't be permanent. *(She lets that sink in)* There comes a time, my child, when you should follow your feminine instincts—when understanding is more precious than virtue.

PATTY. I know—but we've only known each other for such a little time. Wouldn't he lose all respect for me if . . .

DAVID. For a gift one is always beholden. Good night, Patty. You're a nice kid.
(He exits quietly as Patty sits thoughtfully. She is obviously debating whether

to take his advice or not. After a few moments she puts down her drink and cigarette and goes slowly to the bedroom door. She knocks. There is no answer. She is about to knock again when she gets cold feet. She picks up her purse and gloves and runs away, glancing back, fearfully, to the door. For a few seconds, after her exit, the stage is empty.)

CURTAIN

SCENE TWO

The Observation Tower again.
It's about 4:30 P.M. on the following day. The sun is beginning to sink but it's still broad daylight. Don is prowling around minus hat and coat. His hands are plunged in his pockets. His shiner is still quite conspicuous. He goes to the balustrade and stares moodily at the gadget. Almost sheepishly he fishes in his pocket for a dime and drops it in the machine. He looks through the binoculars. His mood is obviously reminiscent. After a brief glance he drapes himself across the gadget and peers out rather mournfully. We should get the impression that for two pins he would call out "Hello out there."
A moment later Patty comes out onto the platform. She wears a different suit, carries a different bag and gloves, but is hatless, as previously. Slowly she crosses to Don and leans across the balustrade. They look at each other for a long time.

DON (*finally*). Why were you in such a tearing hurry?
PATTY. What?
DON. Last night. You knocked on my door.
PATTY. I know. I—I wasn't sure if you'd heard.
DON. I heard. I was shaving.
PATTY. At three o'clock in the morning?
DON. That's right. By the time I wiped off the lather and opened the door—you'd vanished in a cloud of dust.
PATTY. I know.
DON (*gently*). Why did you knock?
(*Patty considers this for a moment and then comes back with another question by way of answering him.*)
PATTY. Why were you shaving?
(*They glance at each other for a moment*

and then look away. Don starts pacing again.)
DON. How did you know I was up here?
PATTY. I didn't—for sure. I went to your office. Your secretary said you'd mooched off—without saying a word.
DON. Yes—I couldn't work.
PATTY. She said you were in a filthy temper. (*Amiably*) Why did you tell her you ran into a door?
DON (*amused*). Because I didn't think she'd be interested in the details of my love life.
PATTY. You're crazy. She was fascinated. I told her the whole story.
DON (*wonderingly*). My God, I believe you did.
PATTY. Of course I did. She seems like a very nice girl. Did you know that her husband was a Thirty-Second Degree Mason? I think that's very nice. She . . .
(*Don interrupts her by suddenly grabbing her elbows.*)
DON. Did you get any sleep at all last night?
PATTY. No—not a whole lot. There wasn't much night left anyway.
DON. I didn't sleep a wink and I've eaten nothing all day.
PATTY. You're a dope. Why?
DON. You know damn well why. Because of you. Worrying about you. Wondering what insane . . . (*He holds her at arm's length, still gripping her elbows, and there should be some doubt as to whether he's going to shake her or kiss her*) I nearly went out of my mind when you dashed off—I didn't even know your telephone number.
PATTY. Don't worry—I knew yours.
DON (*grinning*). You don't think it's right for girls to call up men.
PATTY. Well, yes, but—well, I guessed you'd be worrying about me, and I *did* worry about your eye.
DON. Worry is right. What you need is a governess—or a keeper—or a guardian or a . . .
PATTY. Keep going!
DON. Accepting gifts of money from . . .
PATTY (*interrupting*). Say, listen, about that six hundred dollars—can you afford to lose that much? (*She is now thoroughly wifely*) I think that's terrible—gambling for stakes like that. I bet that's a month's salary—or do architects get salaries? Anyway, I'm quite sure you could find far bet-

ter things to do with your money than ...

DON. Will you kindly shut up? We're not married yet.

PATTY. Yes, but . . . *(With a sudden smile)* What did you say?

DON. I said, we're not married yet.

PATTY. That's just what it sounded like. *(He pulls her toward him and gives her a long hard kiss. She responds in a thoroughly satisfactory manner. They come out of it smiling at each other. She opens her purse and produces some Kleenex, wiping off his lips.)*

DON. Dusty Dawn?

PATTY. Uh huh. They claim it's kissproof but they're crazy.

(She crumples up the sheet of Kleenex and is about to throw it off the building but he takes it from her and throws it into the receptacle.)

DON. Want to know what I thought when you smiled at me in the drug store yesterday?

PATTY. I didn't smile till we got up here.

DON. Well, anyway I was thinking of the sun deck on that cabin I'm going to build. I thought to myself that smile would look pretty damn good up there.

PATTY. Did you?

DON. Yes. And then when you lolled on the couch looking at the blueprints—I thought to myself that it would be rather nice to have you along any time I felt like gloating over a building.

PATTY. You mean a lovely boxlike brick warehouse?

DON. And when you were fixing dinner —and even during dinner when you were flirting with Slater—I thought to myself ...

PATTY. Are you proposing to me?

DON. Well, if I haven't been proposing for the last five minutes, what do you suppose I've been doing? What else can I say?

PATTY. You could say "I love you" in so many words without all this shillyshallying.

DON. Haven't I said that yet?

PATTY. No, and I want to hear it. I want the real thing—with all the trimmings— an old-fashioned proposal. *(Suddenly)* Do you know how my father proposed to my mother?

DON. Popped her in the eye.

PATTY *(laughing)*. Now of course I can't tell you. You wouldn't believe it now. Anyway he wasn't ashamed to come right out and say "I love you." I'll give you that much of a hint.

DON. Okay. Now don't prompt me. *(Taking her face between his hands)* I love you, Patty—I love you very much— even if you are a screwball and even if you are a little bit nuts.

PATTY. Do they let children up here at half price?

DON. I don't know. Why?

PATTY. Well, I thought it would be rather nice to come up here for our anniversaries—but with five kids, that's going to be expensive.

DON. We can always leave them downstairs.

PATTY. No, I want them to see it. I'm so glad Mr. Smith put up that building. *(Patty stands on tiptoes and very gently kisses his damaged eye)* There. *(A pause)* Did you mind it when I said "there"?

DON. What?

PATTY. Oh, nothing, never mind.

DON. You're terribly sweet.

PATTY *(happily)*. Just think—we only met yesterday.

DON. It happens—once in a blue moon.

PATTY. Once in a blue moon. Imagine charging a dollar-twenty just to ride to the top of an old building. . . .

DON *(quickly gives her $1.20)*. Shshsh.

CURTAIN

Summer and Smoke

BY TENNESSEE WILLIAMS

First presented by Margo Jones at her theatre in Dallas, Texas; presented at the Music Box Theatre in New York on October 6, 1948, with the following cast:

ALMA, AS A CHILD....................Arlene McQuade	ALMA WINEMILLER...............Margaret Phillips
JOHN, AS A CHILD...................Donald Hastings	ROSA GONZALES...........................Monica Boyar
REV. WINEMILLER............Raymond Van Sickle	NELLIE EWELL...............................Anne Jackson
MRS. WINEMILLER...........Marga Ann Deighton	ROGER DOREMUS....................Earl Montgomery
JOHN BUCHANAN, JR..................Tod Andrews	MRS. BASSETT......................Betty Greene Little
A GIRL...Hildy Parks	VERNON ....Spencer James
DUSTY ....William Layton	ROSEMARY ....Ellen James
DR. BUCHANAN........................Ralph Theadore	PAPA GONZALES ....Sid Cassel
MR. KRAMER......................................Ray Walston	

PART ONE—A SUMMER

Prologue: The Fountain.
Scene One: The Same.
Scene Two: The Rectory Interior and Doctor's Office.
Scene Three: The Rectory Interior.
Scene Four: The Doctor's Office.
Scene Five: The Rectory Interior.
Scene Six: The Arbor.

PART TWO—A WINTER

Scene Seven: The Rectory and Doctor's Office.
Scene Eight: The Doctor's Office.
Scene Nine: The Rectory and Doctor's Office.
Scene Ten: The Fountain.
Scene Eleven: The Doctor's Office.
Scene Twelve: The Fountain.

The entire action of the play takes place in Glorious Hill, Mississippi. The time is the turn of the century through 1916.

As the concept of a design grows out of reading a play I will not do more than indicate what I think are the most essential points.

First of all—*The Sky*.

There must be a great expanse of sky so that the entire action of the play takes place against it. This is true of interior as well as exterior scenes. But in fact there are no really interior scenes, for the walls are omitted or just barely suggested by certain necessary fragments such as might be needed to hang a picture or to contain a door-frame.

During the day scenes the sky should be a pure and intense blue (like the sky of Italy as it is so faithfully represented in the religious paintings of the Renaissance) and costumes should be selected to form dramatic color contrasts to this intense blue which the figures stand against. (Color harmonies and other visual effects are tremendously important.)

In the night scenes, the more familiar constellations, such as Orion and the Great Bear and the Pleiades, are clearly projected on the night sky, and above them, splashed across the top of the cyclorama, is the nebulous radiance of the Milky Way. Fleecy cloud forms may also be projected on this cyclorama and made to drift across it.

So much for *The Sky*.

Now we descend to the so-called interior sets of the play. There are two of these "interior" sets, one being the parlor of an Episcopal Rectory and the other the home of a doctor next door to the Rectory. The architecture of these houses is barely suggested but is of an American Gothic design of the Victorian era. There are no actual doors or windows or walls. Doors and windows are represented by delicate frameworks of Gothic design. These frames have strings of ivy clinging to them, the leaves of emerald and amber. Sections of wall are used only where they are functionally required. There should be a fragment of wall in back of the Rectory sofa, supporting a romantic landscape in a gilt frame. In the doctor's house there should be a section of wall to support the chart of anatomy. Chirico has used fragmentary walls and interiors in a very evocative way in his painting called "Conversation among the Ruins." We will deal more specifically with these interiors as we come to them in the course of the play.

Now we come to the main exterior set which is a promontory in a park or public square in the town of Glorious Hill. Situated on this promontory is a fountain in the form of a stone angel, in a gracefully crouching position with wings lifted and her hands held together to form a cup from which water flows, a public drinking fountain. The stone angel of the fountain should probably be elevated so that it appears in the background of the interior scenes as a symbolic figure (Eternity) brooding over the course of the play. *This entire exterior set may be on an upper level, above that of the two fragmentary interiors.* I would like all three units to form an harmonious whole like one complete picture rather than three separate ones. An imaginative designer may solve these plastic problems in a variety of ways and should not feel bound by any of my specific suggestions.

There is one more set, a very small exterior representing an arbor, which we will describe when we reach it.

Everything possible should be done to give an unbroken fluid quality to the sequence of scenes.

There should be no curtain except for the intermission. The other divisions of the play should be accomplished by changes of lighting.

Finally, the matter of music. One basic theme should recur and the points of recurrence have been indicated here and there in the stage directions.

Rome, March, 1948.

Although *Summer and Smoke* was a tremendous success when first produced by Margo Jones in her Dallas arena theatre, her restaged Broadway production proved unsuccessful. Nevertheless, it managed to have a tour after the Broadway closing, and it won the esteem of the prominent critics Joseph Wood Krutch and Brooks Atkinson. The latter even preferred it to *A Streetcar Named Desire,* and it is plain that Tennessee Williams achieved his effects without resorting to the sensationalism that sustained the earlier play. It is also probable that readers will find considerably more force and distinction in the play than Broadway playgoers did. Broadway was rather impatient with *Summer and Smoke* because it suspected the author of being fixated forever on the subject of frustrated Southern womanhood. Williams proceeded to disprove that allegation when he presented his Sicilian folk-comedy *The Rose Tattoo* in the season of 1950-51.

The fact is that *Summer and Smoke* revealed Mr. Williams as a restive experimenter in dramatic style and form. *The Glass Menagerie* had been a memory-play, a drama of retrospective vignettes framed by a narration. *A Streetcar Named Desire* had been more conventionally constructed and possessed many of the attributes of a naturalistic melodrama in spite of the heroine's elevated, often poetic, language. *Summer and Smoke* represented a return to unconventional dramaturgy. Here Williams once more departed from the rules of tight realistic structure. His ruefully ironic chronicle of two lives crossing each other's orbit frequently yet somehow never actually touching, of two people never being ready for each other at the same time, is, in part, tone poem and, in part, novel. For the published edition, Williams chose an epigraph from Rilke's famous *Duino Elegies:* "Who, if I were to cry out, would hear me among the angelic orders?" Nobody hears the play's Alma Winemiller of Glorious Hill, Mississippi, although she stands often enough at the foot of the stone angel of the public fountain, the symbol of Eternity "brooding over the course of the play," which is the most prominent feature of the stage set.

That a novelistic play need not always fail has been noted more than once. In our theatre, O'Neill's *Strange Interlude* and Miller's *Death of a Salesman* also possessed a novel's extended picture of a multifarious life. But there is this difference: O'Neill's "novel" had the sharp outlines of a psychoanalytical schematization of personalities and relationships; Miller's "novel" not only had an explicit argument but a naturalistic density of texture—that is, the environment and the characters, all but the dream-brother Ben, were "solid." By contrast, Williams' "novel" is impressionistic; his writing is more elusive, flickering, and phosphorescent.

There is sufficient reason to doubt that Williams mastered the dramatic problems of his play. But his "impressionism" was neither whim nor literary preciosity. It was dictated by the nature of his subject, for his heroine's view of life is, by definition, indistinct. Her aims and desires are unclear to herself as well as to the young man with whom she is involved. The latter, too, arrives at self-understanding only slowly. *Summer and Smoke* is a drama of vague longings for love and ineffective attempts at self-realization, and of ironies of fate ruefully noted. Of necessity, the "Summer" brightness in Williams' world is fugitive, and the "Smoke" heavy and persistent.

For George Jean Nathan, Williams' method of composition was "a scrim treatment of character . . . hiding real delineation behind pseudo-poetical gauze which blurs his audience's vision." An indulgent view would extol this very quality as a poetic component of playwriting and as a relief from the Broadway theatre's surface realism. The truth, as often happens, lies somewhere between these extremes of unqualified depreciation and approval. *Summer and Smoke* is an incompletely realized but sensitive and affecting drama.

PART ONE—A SUMMER

PROLOGUE

In the park near the angel of the fountain. At dusk of an evening in May, in the first few years of this Century.

Alma, as a child of ten, comes into the scene. She wears a middy blouse and has ribboned braids. She already has the dignity of an adult; there is a quality of extraordinary delicacy and tenderness or spirituality in her, which must set her distinctly apart from other children. She has a habit of holding her hands, one cupped under the other in a way similar to that of receiving the wafer at Holy Communion. This is a habit that will remain with her as an adult. She stands like that in front of the stone angel for a few moments; then bends to drink at the fountain.

While she is bent at the fountain, John, as a child, enters. He shoots a pea-shooter at Alma's bent-over back. She utters a startled cry and whirls about. He laughs.

JOHN. Hi, Preacher's daughter. *(He advances toward her)* I been looking for you.

ALMA *(hopefully)*. You have?

JOHN. Was it you that put them handkerchiefs on my desk? *(Alma smiles uncertainly)* Answer up!

ALMA. I put a box of handkerchiefs on your desk.

JOHN. I figured it was you. What was the idea, Miss Priss?

ALMA. You needed them.

JOHN. Trying to make a fool of me?

ALMA. Oh, no!

JOHN. Then what was the idea?

ALMA. You have a bad cold and your nose has been running all week. It spoils your appearance.

JOHN. You don't have to look at me if you don't like my appearance.

ALMA. I like your appearance.

JOHN *(coming closer)*. Is that why you look at me all the time?

ALMA. I—don't!

JOHN. Oh, yeh, you do. You been keeping your eyes on me all the time. Every time I look around I see them cat eyes of yours looking at me. That was the trouble today when Miss Blanchard asked you where the river Amazon was. She asked you twice and you still didn't answer because you w' lookin' at me. What's the

idea? What've'y' got on y' mind anyhow?

ALMA. I was only thinking how handsome you'd be if your face wasn't dirty. You know why your face is dirty? Because you don't use a handkerchief and you wipe your nose on the sleeve of that dirty old sweater.

JOHN *(indignantly)*. Hah!

ALMA. That's why I put the handkerchiefs on your desk and I wrapped them up so nobody would know what they were. It isn't my fault that you opened the box in front of everybody!

JOHN. What did you think I'd do with a strange box on my desk? Just leave it there till it exploded or something? Sure I opened it up. I didn't expect to find no—*handkerchiefs!*—in it . . .

ALMA *(in a shy trembling voice)*. I'm sorry that you were embarrassed. I honestly am awfully sorry that you were embarrassed. Because I wouldn't embarrass you for the world!

JOHN. Don't flatter yourself that I was embarrassed. I don't embarrass that easy.

ALMA. It was stupid and cruel of those girls to laugh.

JOHN. Hah!

ALMA. They should all realize that you don't have a mother to take care of such things for you. It was a pleasure to me to be able to do something for you, only I didn't want you to know it was me who did it.

JOHN. Hee-haw! Ho-hum! Take 'em back! *(He snatches out the box and thrusts it toward her)*

ALMA. *Please* keep them.

JOHN. What do I want with them?
(She stares at him helplessly. He tosses the box to the ground and goes up to the fountain and drinks. Something in her face mollifies him and he sits down at the base of the fountain with a manner that does not preclude a more friendly relation. The dusk gathers deeper.)

ALMA. Do you know the name of the angel?

JOHN. Does she have a name?

ALMA. Yes, I found out she does. It's carved in the base, but it's all worn away so you can't make it out with your eyes.

JOHN. Then how do you know it?

ALMA. You have to read it with your fingers. I did and it gave me cold shivers! *You* read it and see if it doesn't give *you* cold shivers! Go on! Read it with your fingers!

JOHN. Why don't you tell me and save me the trouble?

ALMA. I'm not going to tell you.

(John grins indulgently and turns to the pediment, crouching before it and running his fingers along the worn inscription.)

JOHN. E?

ALMA. Yes, E is the first letter!

JOHN. T?

ALMA. Yes!

JOHN. E?

ALMA. E!

JOHN. K?

ALMA. No, no, not K!—R! *(He slowly straightens up)*

JOHN. Eternity?

ALMA. *Eternity!*—Didn't it give you the cold shivers?

JOHN. Nahh.

ALMA. Well, it did me!

JOHN. Because you're a preacher's daughter. Eternity. What is eternity?

ALMA *(in a hushed wondering voice).* It's something that goes on and on when life and death and time and everything else is all through with.

JOHN. There's no such thing.

ALMA. There is. It's what people's souls live in when they have left their bodies. My name is Alma and Alma is Spanish for soul. Did you know that?

JOHN. Hee-haw! Ho-hum! Have you ever seen a dead person?

ALMA. No.

JOHN. I have. They made me go in the room when my mother was dying and she caught hold of my hand and wouldn't let me go—and so I screamed and hit her.

ALMA. Oh, you didn't do that.

JOHN *(somberly).* Uh-huh. She didn't look like my mother. Her face was all ugly and yellow and—terrible—bad-smelling! And so I hit her to make her let go of my hand. They told me that I was a devil!

ALMA. You didn't know what you were doing.

JOHN. My dad is a doctor.

ALMA. I know.

JOHN. He wants to send me to college to study to be a doctor but I wouldn't be a doctor for the world. And have to go in a room and watch people dying! . . . Jesus!

ALMA. You'll change your mind about that.

JOHN. Oh, no, I won't. I'd rather *be* a

devil, like they called me and go to South America on a boat! . . . Give me one of them handkerchiefs. *(She brings them eagerly and humbly to the fountain. He takes one out and wets it at the fountain and scrubs his face with it)* Is my face clean enough to suit you now?

ALMA. Yes!—Beautiful!

JOHN. *What!*

ALMA. I said "Beautiful"!

JOHN. Well—let's—kiss each other.

(Alma turns away.)

JOHN. Come on, let's just try it!

(He seizes her shoulders and gives her a quick rough kiss. She stands amazed with one hand cupping the other.

(The voice of a child in the distance calls "Johnny! Johnny!"

(He suddenly snatches at her hair-ribbon, jerks it loose and then runs off with a mocking laugh.

(Hurt and bewildered, Alma turns back to the stone angel, for comfort. She crouches at the pediment and touches the inscription with her fingers. The scene dims out with music.)

SCENE ONE

Before the curtain rises a band is heard playing a patriotic anthem, punctuated with the crackle of fireworks.

The scene is the same as for the Prologue. It is the evening of July 4th in a year shortly before the first World War. There is a band concert and a display of fireworks in the park. During the scene the light changes from faded sunlight to dusk. Sections of roof, steeples, weathervanes, should have a metallic surface that catches the mellow light on the backdrop; when dusk has fallen the stars should be visible.

As the curtain rises, the Rev. and Mrs. Winemiller come in and sit on the bench near the fountain. Mrs. Winemiller was a spoiled and selfish girl who evaded the responsibilities of later life by slipping into a state of perverse childishness. She is known as Mr. Winemiller's "Cross."

MR. WINEMILLER *(suddenly rising).* There is Alma, getting on the bandstand! *(Mrs. Winemiller is dreamily munching popcorn.)*

AN ANNOUNCER'S VOICE *(at a distance).*

The Glorious Hill Orchestra brings you Miss Alma Winemiller, The Nightingale of the Delta, singing . . . "La Golondrina."

MR. WINEMILLER *(sitting back down again)*. This is going to provoke a lot of criticism.

(The song commences. The voice is not particularly strong, but it has great purity and emotion. John Buchanan comes along. He is now a Promethean figure, brilliantly and restlessly alive in a stagnant society. The excess of his power has not yet found a channel. If it remains without one, it will burn him up. At present he is unmarked by the dissipations in which he relieves his demoniac unrest; he has the fresh and shining look of an epic hero. He walks leisurely before the Winemillers' bench, negligently touching the crown of his hat but not glancing at them; climbs the steps to the base of the fountain, then turns and looks in the direction of the singer. A look of interest touched with irony appears on his face. A couple, strolling in the park, pass behind the fountain.)

THE GIRL. Look who's by the fountain!

THE MAN. Bright as a new silver dollar!

JOHN. Hi, Dusty! Hi, Pearl!

THE MAN. How'd you make out in that floating crap game?

JOHN. I floated with it as far as Vicksburg, then sank.

THE GIRL. Everybody's been calling: 'Johnny, Johnny—where's Johnny?'"

(John's father, Dr. Buchanan, comes on from the right, as Rev. and Mrs. Winemiller move off the scene to the left, toward the band music. Dr. Buchanan is an elderly man whose age shows in his slow and stiff movements. He walks with a cane. John sees him coming, but pretends not to and starts to walk off.)

DR. BUCHANAN. John!

JOHN *(slowly turning around, as the couple move off)*. Oh! Hi, Dad. . . . *(They exchange a long look)* I—uh—meant to wire you but I must've forgot. I got tied up in Vicksburg Friday night and just now got back to town. Haven't been to the house yet. Is everything . . . going okay? *(He takes a drink of water at the fountain)*

DR. BUCHANAN *(slowly, in a voice hoarse with emotion)*. There isn't any room in the medical profession for wasters, drunkards and lechers. And there isn't any room in my house for wasters—drunkards

—lechers! *(A child is heard calling "I sp-yyyyyy!" in the distance)* I married late in life. I brought over five hundred children into this world before I had one of my own. And by God it looks like I've given myself the rottenest one of the lot. . . . *(John laughs uncertainly)* You will find your things at the Alhambra Hotel.

JOHN. Okay. If that's how you want it. *(There is a pause. The singing comes through on the music. John tips his hat diffidently and starts away from the fountain. He goes a few feet and his father suddenly calls after him.)*

DR. BUCHANAN. John! *(John pauses and looks back)* Come here.

JOHN. Yes, Sir? *(He walks back to his father and stands before him)*

DR. BUCHANAN *(hoarsely)*. Go to the Alhambra Hotel and pick up your things and—bring them back to the house.

JOHN *(gently)*. Yes, Sir. If that's how you want it. *(He diffidently extends a hand to touch his father's shoulder)*

DR. BUCHANAN *(brushing the hand roughly off)*. You! . . . You infernal *whelp,* you!"

(Dr. Buchanan turns and goes hurriedly away. John looks after him with a faint, affectionate smile, then sits down on the steps with an air of relief, handkerchief to forehead, and a whistle of relief. Just then the singing at the bandstand ends and there is the sound of applause. Mrs. Winemiller comes in from the left, followed by her husband.)

MRS. WINEMILLER. Where is the ice cream man?

MR. WINEMILLER. Mother, hush! *(He sees his daughter approaching)* Here we are, Alma!

(The song ends. There is applause. Then the band strikes up the Santiago Waltz.

(Alma Winemiller enters. Alma had an adult quality as a child and now, in her middle twenties, there is something prematurely spinsterish about her. An excessive propriety and self-consciousness is apparent in her nervous laughter; her voice and gestures belong to years of church entertainment, to the position of hostess in a rectory. People her own age regard her as rather quaintly and humorously affected. She has grown up mostly in the company of her elders. Her true nature is still hidden even from herself. She is dressed in

pale yellow and carries a yellow silk parasol.
(As Alma passes in front of the fountain, John slaps his hands resoundingly together a few times. She catches her breath in a slight laughing sound, makes as if to retreat, with a startled "Oh!", but then goes quickly to her parents. The applause from the crowd continues.)

MR. WINEMILLER. They seem to want to hear you sing again, Alma.

(She turns nervously about, touching her throat and her chest. John grins, applauding by the fountain. When the applause dies out, Alma sinks faintly on the bench.)

ALMA. Open my bag, Father. My fingers have frozen stiff! *(She draws a deep labored breath)* I don't know what came over me—absolute panic! Never, never again, it isn't worth it—the tortures that I go through!

MR. WINEMILLER *(anxiously)*. You're having one of your nervous attacks?

ALMA. My heart's beating so! It seemed to be in my *throat* the whole time I was singing! *(John laughs audibly from the fountain)* Was it noticeable, Father?

MR. WINEMILLER. You sang extremely well, Alma. But you know how I feel about this, it was contrary to my wishes and I cannot imagine why you wanted to do it, especially since it seemed to upset you so.

ALMA. I don't see how anyone could object to my singing at a patriotic occasion. If I had just sung well! But I barely got through it. At one point I thought that I wouldn't. The words flew out of my mind. Did you notice the pause? Blind panic! They really never came back, but I went on singing—I think I must have been improvising the lyric! Whew! Is there a handkerchief in it?

MRS. WINEMILLER *(suddenly)*. Where is the ice cream man?

ALMA *(rubbing her fingers together)*. Circulation is slowly coming back . . .

MR. WINEMILLER. Sit back quietly and take a deep breath, Alma.

ALMA. Yes, my handkerchief—now . . .

MRS. WINEMILLER. Where is the ice cream man?

MR. WINEMILLER. Mother, there isn't any ice cream man.

ALMA. No, there isn't any ice cream man, Mother. But on the way home Mr. Dore-

mus and I will stop by the drug store and pick up a pint of ice cream.

MR. WINEMILLER. Are you intending to stay here?

ALMA. Until the concert is over. I promised Roger I'd wait for him.

MR. WINEMILLER. I suppose you have noticed who is by the fountain?

ALMA. Shhh!

MR. WINEMILLER. Hadn't you better wait on a different bench?

ALMA. This is where Roger will meet me.

MR. WINEMILLER. Well, Mother, we'll run along now. *(Mrs. Winemiller has started vaguely toward the fountain, Mr. Winemiller firmly restraining her)* This way, this way, Mother! *(He takes her arm and leads her off)*

MRS. WINEMILLER *(calling back, in a high, childish voice)*. Strawberry, Alma. Chocolate, chocolate and strawberry mixed! Not vanilla!

ALMA *(faintly)*. Yes, yes, Mother—vanilla . . .

MRS. WINEMILLER *(furiously)*. I said *not* vanilla. *(Shouting)* Strawberry!

MR. WINEMILLER *(fiercely)*. Mother! We're attracting attention. *(He propels her forcibly away)*

(John laughs by the fountain. Alma moves her parasol so that it shields her face from him. She leans back closing her eyes. John notices a firecracker by the fountain. He leans over negligently to pick it up. He grins and lights it and tosses it toward Alma's bench. When it goes off she springs up with a shocked cry, letting the parasol drop.)

JOHN *(jumping up as if outraged)*. Hey! Hey, you! *(He looks off to the right. Alma sinks back weakly on the bench. John solicitously advances)* Are you all right?

ALMA. I can't seem to—catch my breath! Who threw it?

JOHN. Some little rascal.

ALMA. Where?

JOHN. He ran away quick when I hollered!

ALMA. There ought to be an ordinance passed in this town forbidding firecrackers.

JOHN. Dad and I treated fifteen kids for burns the last couple of days. I think you need a little restorative, don't you? *(He takes out a flask)* Here!

ALMA. What is it?

JOHN. Applejack brandy.

ALMA. No thank you.

JOHN. Liquid dynamite.

ALMA. I'm sure.

(John laughs and returns it to his pocket. He remains looking down at her with one foot on the end of her bench. His steady, smiling look into her face is disconcerting her.

(In Alma's voice and manner there is a delicacy and elegance, a kind of "airiness," which is really natural to her as it is, in a less marked degree, to many Southern girls. Her gestures and mannerisms are a bit exaggerated but in a graceful way. It is understandable that she might be accused of "putting on airs" and of being "affected" by the other young people of the town. She seems to belong to a more elegant age, such as the Eighteenth Century in France. Out of nervousness and self-consciousness she has a habit of prefacing and concluding her remarks with a little breathless laugh. This will be indicated at points, but should be used more freely than indicated; however, the characterization must never be stressed to the point of making her at all ludicrous in a less than sympathetic way.)

ALMA. You're—home for the summer? *(John gives an affirmative grunt)* Summer is not the pleasantest time of year to renew an acquaintance with Glorious Hill—is it? *(John gives an indefinite grunt. Alma laughs airily)* The Gulf wind has failed us this year, disappointed us dreadfully this summer. We used to be able to rely on the Gulf wind to cool the nights off for us, but this summer has been an exceptional season. *(He continues to grin disconcertingly down at her; she shows her discomfiture in flurried gestures)*

JOHN *(slowly)*. Are you—disturbed about something?

ALMA. That firecracker was a shock.

JOHN. You should be over that shock by now.

ALMA. I don't get over shocks quickly.

JOHN. I see you don't.

ALMA. You're planning to stay here and take over some of your father's medical practice?

JOHN. I haven't made up my mind about anything yet.

ALMA. I hope so, we all hope so. Your father was telling me that you have succeeded in isolating the germ of that fever epidemic that's broken out at Lyon.

JOHN. Finding something to kill it is more of a trick.

ALMA. You'll do that! He's so positive that you will. He says that you made a special study of bacter—bacter . . .

JOHN. Bacteriology!

ALMA. Yes! At Johns Hopkins! That's in Boston, isn't it?

JOHN. No. Baltimore.

ALMA. Oh, Baltimore. Baltimore, Maryland. Such a beautiful combination of names. And bacteriology—isn't that something you do with a microscope?

JOHN. Well—partly. . . .

ALMA. I've looked through a telescope, but never a microscope. What . . . what do you—see?

JOHN. A—universe, Miss Alma.

ALMA. What kind of a universe?

JOHN. Pretty much the same kind that you saw through the lens of a telescope—a mysterious one. . . .

ALMA. Oh, yes. . . .

JOHN. Part anarchy—and part order!

ALMA. The footprints of God!

JOHN. But not God.

ALMA *(ecstatically)*. To be a doctor! And deal with these mysteries under the microscope lens . . . I think it is more religious than being a priest! There is so much suffering in the world it actually makes one sick to think about it, and most of us are so helpless to relieve it. . . . But a physician! Oh, my! With his magnificent gifts and training what a joy it must be to know that he is equipped and appointed to bring relief to all of this fearful suffering—and fear! And it's an expanding profession, it's a profession that is continually widening its horizons. So many diseases have already come under scientific control but the commencement is just—beginning! I mean there is so much more that is yet to be done, such as mental afflictions to be brought under control. . . . And with your father's example to inspire you! Oh, my!

JOHN. I didn't know you had so many ideas about the medical profession.

ALMA. Well, I am a great admirer of your father, as well as a patient. It's such a comfort knowing that he's right next door, within arm's reach as it were!

JOHN. Why? Do you have fits? . . .

ALMA. Fits? *(She throws back her head with a peal of gay laughter)* Why no, but I do have attacks!—of nervous heart trouble. Which can be so alarming that I run straight to your father!

JOHN. At two or three in the morning?

ALMA. Yes, as late as that, even . . . occasionally. He's very patient with me.

JOHN. But does you no good?

ALMA. He always reassures me.

JOHN. Temporarily?

ALMA. Yes . . .

JOHN. Don't you want more than that?

ALMA. What?

JOHN. It's none of my business.

ALMA. What were you going to say?

JOHN. You're Dad's patient. But I have an idea . . .

ALMA. Please go on! *(John laughs a little)* Now you have to go on! You can't leave me up in the air! What were you going to tell me?

JOHN. Only that I suspect you need something more than a little temporary reassurance.

ALMA. *Why?* Why? You think it's more serious than . . . ?

JOHN. You're swallowing air.

ALMA. I'm what?

JOHN. You're swallowing air, Miss Alma.

ALMA. I'm swallowing air?

JOHN. Yes, you swallow air when you laugh or talk. It's a little trick that hysterical women get into.

ALMA *(uncertainly)*. Ha-ha . . . !

JOHN. You swallow air and it presses on your heart and gives you palpitations. That isn't serious in itself but it's a symptom of something that is. Shall I tell you frankly?

ALMA. Yes!

JOHN. Well, what I think you have is a *doppelganger!* You have a *doppelganger* and the *doppelganger* is badly irritated.

ALMA. Oh, my goodness! I have an irritated *doppelganger!* *(She tries to laugh, but is definitely uneasy)* How awful that sounds! What exactly *is* it?

JOHN. It's none of *my* business. You are not *my* patient.

ALMA. But that's downright wicked of you! To tell me I have something awful-sounding as that, and then refuse to let me know what it is! *(She tries to laugh again, unsuccessfully)*

JOHN. I shouldn't have said anything! I'm not your doctor. . . .

ALMA. Just how did you arrive at this—diagnosis of my case? *(She laughs)* But of course you're teasing me. Aren't you? . . . There, the Gulf wind is stirring! He's

actually moving the leaves of the palmetto! And listen to them complaining. . . .

(As if brought in by this courier from the tropics, Rosa Gonzales enters and crosses to the fountain. Her indolent walk produces a sound and an atmosphere like the Gulf wind on the palmettos, a whispering of silk and a slight rattle of metallic ornaments. She is dressed in an almost outrageous finery, with lustrous feathers on her hat, greenish blue, a cascade of them, also diamond and emerald earrings.)

JOHN *(sharply)*. Who is that?

ALMA. I'm surprised that you don't know.

JOHN. I've been away quite a while.

ALMA. That's the Gonzales girl. . . . Her father's the owner of the gambling casino on Moon Lake. *(Rosa drinks at the fountain and wanders leisurely off)* She smiled at you, didn't she?

JOHN. I thought she did.

ALMA. I hope that you have a strong character. *(He places a foot on the end of the bench)*

JOHN. Solid rock.

ALMA *(nervously)*. The pyrotechnical display is going to be brilliant.

JOHN. The what?

ALMA. The fireworks.

JOHN. Aw!

ALMA. I suppose you've lost touch with most of your *old* friends here.

JOHN *(laconically)*. Yeah.

ALMA. You must make some *new* ones! I belong to a little group that meets every ten days. I think you'd enjoy them, too. They're young people with—intellectual and artistic interests. . . .

JOHN *(sadly)*. Aw, I see . . . intellectual. . . .

ALMA. You must come!—sometime—I'm going to remind you of it. . . .

JOHN. Thanks. Do you mind if I sit down?

ALMA. Why, certainly not, there's room enough for two! Neither of us are—terribly large in diameter! *(She laughs shrilly.)*

(A girl's voice is heard calling: "Goodbye, Nellie!" and another answers: "Goodbye!" Nellie Ewell enters—a girl of sixteen with a radiantly fresh healthy quality.)

ALMA. Here comes someone much nicer! One of my adorable little vocal pupils, the youngest and prettiest one with the least gift for music.

JOHN. I know that one.

ALMA. Hello, there, Nellie dear!

NELLIE. Oh, Miss Alma, your singing was so beautiful it made me cry.

ALMA. It's sweet of you to fib so. I sang terribly.

NELLIE. You're just being modest, Miss Alma. Hello, Dr. John! Dr. John?

JOHN. Yeah?

NELLIE. That book you gave me is too full of long words.

JOHN. Look 'em up in the dictionary, Nellie.

NELLIE. I did, but you know how dictionaries are. You look up one long word and it gives you another and you look up that one and it gives you the long word you looked up in the first place. *(John laughs)* I'm coming over tomorrow for you to explain it all to me. *(She laughs and goes off)*

ALMA. What book is she talking about?

JOHN. A book I gave her about the facts of nature. She came over to the office and told me her mother wouldn't tell her anything and she had to know because she'd fallen in love.

ALMA. Why the precocious little—imp! *(She laughs.)*

JOHN. What sort of a mother has she?

ALMA. Mrs. Ewell's the merry widow of Glorious Hill. They say that she goes to the depot to meet every train in order to make the acquaintance of traveling salesmen. Of course she is ostracized by all but a few of her own type of women in town, which is terribly hard for Nellie. It isn't fair to the child. Father didn't want me to take her as a pupil because of her mother's reputation, but I feel that one has a duty to perform toward children in such—circumstances. . . . And I always say that life is such a mysteriously complicated thing that no one should really presume to judge and condemn the bahavior of anyone else!

(There is a faraway "puff" and a burst of golden light over their heads. Both look up. There is a long-drawn "Ahhh . . ." from the invisible crowd. This is an effect that will be repeated at intervals during the scene.)

There goes the first sky-rocket! Oh, look at it burst into a million stars!

(John leans way back to look up and al-lows his knees to spread wide apart so that one of them is in contact with Alma's. The effect upon her is curiously disturbing.)

JOHN *(after a moment)*. Do you have a chill?

ALMA. Why, no!—no. Why?

JOHN. You're shaking.

ALMA. Am I?

JOHN. Don't you feel it?

ALMA. I have a touch of malaria linger-ing on.

JOHN. You have malaria?

ALMA. Never severely, never really severely. I just have touches of it that come and go. *(She laughs airily)*

JOHN *(with a gentle grin)*. Why do you laugh that way?

ALMA. What way?

(John imitates her laugh. Alma laughs again in embarrassment.)

JOHN. Yeah. That way.

ALMA. I do declare, you haven't changed in the slightest. It used to delight you to embarrass me and it still does!

JOHN. I guess I shouldn't tell you this, but I heard an imitation of you at a party.

ALMA. Imitation? Of what?

JOHN. You.

ALMA. I?—I? Why, *what* did they imi-tate?

JOHN. You singing at a wedding.

ALMA. My voice?

JOHN. Your gestures and facial expres-sion!

ALMA. How mystifying!

JOHN. No, I shouldn't have told you. You're upset about it.

ALMA. I'm not in the least upset, I am just mystified.

JOHN. Don't you know that you have a reputation for putting on airs a little—for gilding the lily a bit?

ALMA. I have no idea what you are talk-ing about.

JOHN. Well, some people seem to have gotten the idea that you are just a little bit—affected!

ALMA. Well, well, well, well. *(She tries to conceal her hurt)* That may be so, it may seem so to some people. But since I am innocent of any attempt at affectation, I really don't know what I can do about it.

JOHN. You have a rather fancy way of talking.

ALMA. Have I?

JOHN. Pyrotechnical display instead of fireworks, and that sort of thing.

ALMA. So?

JOHN. And how about that accent?

ALMA. Accent? This leaves me quite speechless! I have sometimes been accused of having a put-on accent by people who disapprove of good diction. My father was a Rhodes scholar at Oxford, and while over there he fell into the natural habit of using the long A where it is correct to use it. I suppose I must have picked it up from him, but it's entirely unconscious. Who gave this imitation at this party you spoke of?

JOHN *(grinning)*. I don't think she'd want that told.

ALMA. Oh, it was a *she* then?

JOHN. You don't think a man could do it?

ALMA. No, and I don't think a lady would do it either!

JOHN. I didn't think it would have made you so mad, or I wouldn't have brought it up.

ALMA. Oh, I'm not mad. I'm just mystified and amazed as I always am by unprovoked malice in people. I don't understand it when it's directed at me and I don't understand it when it is directed at anybody else. I just don't understand it, and perhaps it is better not to understand it. These people who call me affected and give these unkind imitations of me—I wonder if they stop to think that I have had certain difficulties and disadvantages to cope with—which may be partly the cause of these peculiarities of mine—which they find so offensive!

JOHN. Now, Miss Alma, you're making a mountain out of a molehill!

ALMA. I wonder if they stop to think that my circumstances are somewhat different from theirs? My father and I have a certain—cross—to bear!

JOHN. What cross?

ALMA. Living next door to us, you should know what cross.

JOHN. Mrs. Winemiller?

ALMA. She had her breakdown while I was still in high school. And from that time on I have had to manage the Rectory and take over the social and household duties that would ordinarily belong to a minister's wife, not his daughter. And that may have made me seem strange to some of my more critical contemporaries.

In a way it may have—deprived me of— my youth. . . .

(Another rocket goes up. Another "Ahhh . . ." from the crowd.)

JOHN. You ought to go out with young people.

ALMA. I am not a recluse. I don't fly around here and there giving imitations of other people at parties. But I am not a recluse by any manner of means. Being a minister's daughter I have to be more selective than most girls about the—society I keep. But I do go out now and then. . . .

JOHN. I have seen you in the public library and the park, but only two or three times have I seen you out with a boy and it was always someone like this Roger Doremus.

ALMA. I'm afraid that you and I move in different circles. If I wished to be as outspoken as you are, which is sometimes just an excuse for being rude—I might say that I've yet to see you in the company of a—well, a—reputable young woman. You've heard unfavorable talk about me in your circle of acquaintances and I've heard equally unpleasant things about you in mine. And the pity of it is that you are preparing to be a doctor. You're intending to practice your father's profession here in Glorious Hill. *(She catches her breath in a sob)* Most of us have no choice but to lead useless lives! But you have a gift for scientific research! You have a chance to serve humanity. Not just to go on enduring for the sake of endurance, but to serve a noble, humanitarian cause, to relieve human suffering. And what do you do about it? Everything that you can to alienate the confidence of nice people who love and respect your father. While he is devoting himself to the fever at Lyon you drive your automobile at a reckless pace from one disorderly roadhouse to another! You say you have seen two things through the microscope, anarchy and order? Well, obviously *order* is not the thing that impressed you . . . conducting yourself like some overgrown schoolboy who wants to be known as the wildest fellow in town! And you—a gifted young doctor—*Magna cum Laude! (She turns aside, touching her eyelids with a handkerchief)* You know what I call it? I call it a *desecration! (She sobs uncontrollably. Then she springs up from the bench. John catches her hand)*

JOHN. You're not going to run off, are you?

ALMA. Singing in public always—always upsets me!—Let go of my hand. *(He holds on to it, grinning up at her in the deepening dusk. The stars are coming out in the cyclorama with its leisurely floating cloud-forms. In the distance the band is playing "La Golondrina")* Please let go of my hand.

JOHN. Don't run off mad.

ALMA. Let's not make a spectacle of ourselves.

JOHN. Then sit back down.

(A skyrocket goes up. The crowd "Ahhh . . .s.")

ALMA. You threw that firecracker and started a conversation just in order to tease me as you did as a child. You came to this bench in order to embarrass me and to hurt my feelings with the report of that vicious—imitation! No, let go of my hand so I can leave, now. You've succeeded in your purpose. I *was* hurt, I *did* make a fool of myself as you intended! So let me go now!

JOHN. You're attracting attention! Don't you know that I really *like* you, Miss Alma?

ALMA. No, you don't.

(Another skyrocket.)

JOHN. Sure I do. A lot. Sometimes when I come home late at night I look over at the Rectory. I see something white at the window. Could that be you, Miss Alma? Or, is it your *doppelganger,* looking out of the window that faces my way?

ALMA. Enough about *doppelganger*—whatever that is!

JOHN. There goes a nice one, Roman candle they call it!

(This time the explosion is in back of them. A Roman candle shoots up puffs of rainbow-colored light in back of the stone angel of the fountain. They turn in profile to watch it.)

JOHN *(counting the puffs of light).* Four—five—six—that's all? No—seven! *(There is a pause. Alma sits down slowly)*

ALMA *(vaguely).* Dear me . . . *(She fans herself)*

JOHN. How about going riding?

ALMA *(too eagerly).* When . . . now?

(Rosa Gonzales has wandered up to the fountain again. John's attention drifts steadily toward her and away from Alma.)

JOHN *(too carelessly).* Oh . . . some afternoon.

ALMA. Would you observe the speed limit?

JOHN. Strictly with you, Miss Alma.

ALMA. Why then, I'd be glad to—John. *(John has risen from the bench and crosses to the fountain.)*

JOHN. And wear a hat with a plume!

ALMA. I don't have a hat with a plume!

JOHN. Get one!

(Another skyrocket goes up, and there is another long "Ahhh . . ." from the crowd. John saunters up to the fountain. Rosa has lingered beside it. As he passes her he whispers something. She laughs and moves leisurely off. John takes a quick drink at the fountain, then follows Rosa, calling back "Good night" to Alma. There is a sound of laughter in the distance. Alma sits motionless for a moment, then touches a small white handkerchief to her lips and nostrils. Mr. Doremus comes in, carrying a French horn case. He is a small man, somewhat like a sparrow.)

ROGER. *Whew!* Golly! Moses!—Well, how did it go, Miss Alma?

ALMA. How did—what—go?

ROGER *(annoyed).* My solo on the French horn.

ALMA *(slowly, without thinking).* I paid no attention to it. *(She rises slowly and takes his arm)* I'll have to hang on your arm—I'm feeling so dizzy!

(The scene dims out. There is a final skyrocket and a last "Ahhh . . ." from the crowd in the distance. Music is heard, and there is light on the angel.)

SCENE TWO

Inside the Rectory, which is lighted. Mrs. Winemiller comes in and makes her way stealthily to the love seat, where she seats herself. Opening her parasol, she takes out a fancy white-plumed hat which she had concealed there. Rising, she turns to the mirror on the wall over the love seat and tries on the hat. She draws a long, ecstatic breath as she places it squarely on her head. At that moment the telephone rings. Startled, she snatches off the hat, hides it behind the center table and quickly resumes her seat. The telephone goes ov ringing. Alma comes in to answer it.

———

ALMA. Hello. . . . Yes, Mr. Gillam. . . . She did? . . . Are you sure? . . . How shocking! . . . *(Mrs. Winemiller now retrieves the hat, seats herself in front of Alma and puts the hat on)* Thank you, Mr. Gillam . . . the hat is here.
(Mr. Winemiller comes in. He is distracted.)

MR. WINEMILLER. Alma! Alma, your mother . . . !

ALMA *(coming in)* I know, Father, Mr. Gillam just phoned. He told me she picked up a white plumed hat and he pretended not to notice in order to save you the embarrassment, so I—told him to just charge it to us.

MR. WINEMILLER. That hat looks much too expensive.

ALMA. It's fourteen dollars. You pay six of it, Father, and I'll pay eight. *(She gives him the parasol)*

MR. WINEMILLER. What an insufferable cross we have to bear. *(He retires despairingly from the room)*
(Alma goes over to her mother and seats her in a chair at the table.)

ALMA. I have a thousand and one things to do before my club meeting tonight, so you work quietly on your picture puzzle or I shall take the hat back, plume and all.

MRS. WINEMILLER *(throwing a piece of the puzzle on the floor)*. The pieces don't fit! *(Alma picks up the piece and puts it on the table)* The pieces don't fit!
(Alma stands for a moment in indecision. She reaches for the phone, then puts it down. Then she takes it up again, and gives a number. The telephone across the way in the doctor's office rings and that part of the scene lights up. John comes in.)

JOHN *(answering the phone)*. Hello?

ALMA. John! *(She fans herself rapidly with a palm leaf clutched in her free hand and puts on a brilliant, strained smile as if she were actually in his presence)*

JOHN. Miss Alma?

ALMA. You recognized my voice?

JOHN. I recognized your laugh.

ALMA. Ha-ha! How are you, you stranger you?

JOHN. I'm pretty well, Miss Alma. How're you doing?

ALMA. Surviving, just surviving! Isn't it fearful?

JOHN. Uh-huh.

ALMA. You seem unusually laconic. Or perhaps I should say more than usually laconic.

JOHN. I had a big night and I'm just recovering from it.

ALMA. Well, sir, I have a bone to pick with you!

JOHN. What's that, Miss Alma? *(He drains a glass of bromo)*

ALMA. The time of our last conversation on the Fourth of July, you said you were going to take me riding in your automobile.

JOHN. Aw. Did I say that?

ALMA. Yes indeed you did, sir! And all these hot afternoons I've been breathlessly waiting and hoping that you would remember that promise. But now I know how insincere you are. Ha-ha! Time and again the four-wheeled phenomenon flashes by the Rectory and I have yet to put my—my quaking foot in it!
(Mrs. Winemiller begins to mock Alma's speech and laughter.)

JOHN. What was that, Miss Alma? I didn't understand you.

ALMA. I was just reprimanding you, sir! Castigating you verbally! Ha-ha!

MRS. WINEMILLER *(grimacing)*. Ha-ha.

JOHN. What about, Miss Alma? *(He leans back and puts his feet on table)*

ALMA. Never mind. I know how busy you are! *(She whispers)* Mother, hush!

JOHN. I'm afraid we have a bad connection.

ALMA. I hate telephones. I don't know why but they always make me laugh as if someone were poking me in the ribs! I swear to goodness they do!

JOHN. Why don't you just go to your window and I'll go to mine and we can holler across?

ALMA. The yard's so wide I'm afraid it would crack my voice! And I've got to sing at somebody's wedding tomorrow.

JOHN. You're going to sing at a wedding?

ALMA. Yes. "The Voice That Breathed O'er Eden!" And I'm as hoarse as a frog!
(Another gale of laughter almost shakes her off her feet)

JOHN. Better come over and let me give you a gargle.

ALMA. Nasty gargles—I hate them!

MRS. WINEMILLER *(mockingly)*. Nasty gargles—I hate them!

ALMA. Mother, shhh!—please! As you no doubt have gathered, there is some interference at this end of the line! What I wanted to say is—you remember my mentioning that little club I belong to?

JOHN. Aw! Aw, yes! Those intellectual meetings!

ALMA. Oh, now, don't call it that. It's just a little informal gathering every Wednesday and we talk about the new books and read things out loud to each other!

JOHN. Serve any refreshments?

ALMA. Yes, we serve refreshments!

JOHN. Any liquid refreshments?

ALMA. Both liquid and solid refreshments.

JOHN. Is this an invitation?

ALMA. Didn't I promise I'd ask you? It's going to be tonight!—at eight at my house, at the Rectory, so all you'll have to do is cross the yard!

JOHN. I'll try to make it, Miss Alma.

ALMA. Don't say try as if it required some Herculean effort! All you have to do is . . .

JOHN. Cross the yard! Uh-huh—reserve me a seat by the punch bowl.

ALMA. That gives me an idea! We *will* have punch, fruit punch, with claret in it. Do you like claret?

JOHN. I just dote on claret.

ALMA. Now you're being sarcastic! Ha-ha-ha!

JOHN. Excuse me, Miss Alma, but Dad's got to use this phone.

ALMA. I won't hang up till you've said you'll come without fail!

JOHN. I'll be there, Miss Alma. You can count on it.

ALMA. Au revoir, then! Until eight.

JOHN. G'bye, Miss Alma.

(*John hangs up with an incredulous grin. Alma remains holding the phone with a dazed smile until the office interior has dimmed slowly out.*)

MRS. WINEMILLER. Alma's in love—in love. (*She waltzes mockingly*)

ALMA (*sharply*). Mother, you are wearing out my patience! Now I am expecting another music pupil and I have to make preparations for the club meeting so I suggest that you . . . (*Nellie rings the bell*) Will you go up to your room? (*Then she calls sweetly*) Yes, Nellie, coming, Nellie. All right, stay down here then. But keep your attention on your picture puzzle or there will be no ice cream for you after supper!

(*She admits Nellie, who is wildly excited over something. This scene should be played lightly and quickly.*)

NELLIE. Oh, Miss Alma!

(*She rushes past Alma in a distracted manner, throws herself on the sofa and hugs herself with excited glee.*)

ALMA. What is it, Nellie? Has something happened at home? (*Nellie continues her exhilaration*) Oh, now, Nellie, stop that! Whatever it is, it can't be *that* important!

NELLIE (*blurting out suddenly*). Miss Alma, haven't you ever had—*crushes?*

ALMA. What?

NELLIE. Crushes?

ALMA. Yes—I suppose I have. (*She sits down*)

NELLIE. Did you know that I used to have a crush on *you,* Miss Alma?

ALMA. No, Nellie.

NELLIE. Why do you think that I took singing lessons?

ALMA. I supposed it was because you wished to develop your voice.

NELLIE (*cutting in*). Oh, you know, and I know, I never had any voice. I had a crush on you though. Those were the days when I had crushes on girls. Those days are all over, and now I have crushes on boys. Oh, Miss Alma, you know about Mother, how I was brought up so nobody nice except you would have anything to do with us—Mother meeting the trains to pick up the traveling salesmen and bringing them home to drink and play poker—all of them acting like pigs, pigs, pigs!

MRS. WINEMILLER (*mimicking*). Pigs, pigs, pigs!

NELLIE. Well, I thought I'd always hate men. Loathe and despise them. But last night— Oh!

ALMA. Hadn't we better run over some scales until you are feeling calmer?

NELLIE (*cutting in*). I'd heard them downstairs for hours but didn't know who it was—I'd fallen asleep—when all of a sudden my door banged open. He'd thought it was the bathroom!

ALMA (*nervously*). Nellie, I'm not sure I want to hear any more of this story.

NELLIE (*interrupting*). Guess who it was?

ALMA. I couldn't possibly guess.

NELLIE. Someone you know. Someone I've seen you with.

ALMA. Who?

NELLIE. The wonderfullest person in all

the big wide world! When he saw it was me he came and sat down on the bed and held my hand and we talked and talked until Mother came up to see what had happened to him. You should have heard him bawl her out. Oh, he laid the law down! He said she ought to send me off to a girl's school because she wasn't fit to bring up a daughter! Then she started to bawl him out. You're a fine one to talk, she said, you're not fit to call yourself a doctor. *(Alma rises abruptly)*

ALMA. John Buchanan?

NELLIE. Yes, of course, Dr. Johnny.

ALMA. Was—with—your—mother?

NELLIE. Oh, he wasn't her beau! He had a girl with him, and Mother had somebody else!

ALMA. Who—did—he—have?

NELLIE. Oh, some loud tacky thing with a Z in her name!

ALMA. Gonzales? Rosa Gonzales?

NELLIE. Yes, that was it! *(Alma sits slowly back down)* But him! Oh, Miss Alma! He's the *wonderfullest* person that I . . .

ALMA *(interrupting)*. Your mother was right! He isn't fit to call himself a doctor! I hate to disillusion you, but this wonderfullest person is pitiably weak.

(Someone calls "Johnny" outside.)

NELLIE *(in hushed excitement)*. Someone is calling him now!

ALMA. Yes, these people who shout his name in front of his house are of such a character that the old doctor cannot permit them to come inside the door. And when they have brought him home at night, left him sprawling on the front steps, sometimes at daybreak—it takes two people, his father and the old cook, one pushing and one pulling, to get him upstairs. *(She sits down)* All the gifts of the gods were showered on him. . . . *(The call of "Johnny" is repeated)* But all he cares about is indulging his senses! *(Another call of "Johnny")*

NELLIE. Here he comes down the steps! *(Alma crosses toward the window)* Look at him jump!

ALMA. Oh.

NELLIE. Over the banisters. Ha-ha!

ALMA. Nellie, don't lean out the window and have us caught spying.

MRS. WINEMILLER *(suddenly)*. Show Nellie how *you* spy on him! Oh, she's a good one at spying. She stands behind

the curtain and *peeks* around it, and . . .

ALMA *(frantically)*. Mother!

MRS. WINEMILLER. She spies on him. Whenever he comes in at night she rushes downstairs to watch him out of this window!

ALMA *(interrupting her)*. Be still!

MRS. WINEMILLER *(going right on)*. She called him just now and had a fit on the telephone! *(The old lady cackles derisively. Alma snatches her cigarette from her and crushes it under her foot)* Alma's in love! Alma's in love!

ALMA *(interrupting)*. Nellie, Nellie, please go.

NELLIE *(with a startled giggle)*. All right, Miss Alma, I'm going. *(She crosses quickly to the door, looking back once with a grin)* Good night, Mrs. Winemiller!

(Nellie goes out gaily, leaving the door slightly open. Alma rushes to it and slams it shut. She returns swiftly to Mrs. Winemiller, her hands clenched with anger.)

ALMA. If ever I hear you say such a thing again, if ever you dare to repeat such a thing in my presence or anybody else's—then it will be the last straw! You understand me? Yes, you understand me! You act like a child, but you have the devil in you. And God will punish you—yes! I'll punish you too. I'll take your cigarettes from you and give you no more. I'll give you no ice cream either. Because I'm tired of your malice. Yes, I'm tired of your malice and your self-indulgence. People wonder why I'm tied down here! They pity me—think of me as an old maid already! In spite of I'm young. Still young! It's you—it's you, you've taken my youth away from me! I wouldn't say that —I'd try not even to think it—if you were just kind, just simple! But I could spread my life out like a rug for you to step on and you'd step on it, and not even say "Thank you, Alma!" Which is what you've done always—and now you dare to tell a disgusting lie about me—in front of that girl!

MRS. WINEMILLER. Don't you think I hear you go to the window at night to watch him come in and . . .

ALMA. Give me that plumed hat, Mother! It goes back now, it goes back!

MRS. WINEMILLER. *Fight! Fight!*

(Alma snatches at the plumed hat. Mrs. Winemiller snatches too. The hat is torn

between them. Mrs. Winemiller retains the hat. The plume comes loose in Alma's hand. She stares at it a moment with a shocked expression.)

ALMA *(sincerely)*. Heaven have mercy upon us!

SCENE THREE

Inside the Rectory.

The meeting is in progress, having just opened with the reading of the minutes by Alma. She stands before the green plush sofa and the others. This group includes Mr. Doremus, Vernon, a willowy younger man with an open collar and Byronic locks, the widow Bassett, and a wistful older girl with a long neck and thick-lensed glasses.

ALMA *(reading)*. Our last meeting which fell on July fourteenth . . .

MRS. BASSETT. Bastille Day!

ALMA. Pardon me?

MRS. BASSETT. It fell on Bastille Day! But, honey, that was the meeting before last.

ALMA. You're perfectly right. I seem to be on the wrong page. . . . *(She drops the papers)*

MRS. BASSETT. Butterfingers!

ALMA. Here we are! July twenty-fifth! Correct?

MRS. BASSETT. Correct! *(A little ripple of laughter goes about the circle)*

ALMA *(continuing)*. It was debated whether or not we ought to suspend operations for the remainder of the summer as the departure of several members engaged in the teaching profession for their summer vacations . . .

MRS. BASSETT. Lucky people!

ALMA. . . . had substantially contracted our little circle.

MRS. BASSETT. Decimated our ranks! *(There is another ripple of laughter)*

(John appears outside the door-frame and rings the bell.)

ALMA *(with agitation)*. Is that—is that—the doorbell?

MRS. BASSETT. It sure did sound like it to me.

ALMA. Excuse me a moment. I think it may be . . .

(She crosses to the door-frame and makes the gesture of opening the door. John steps

in, *immaculately groomed and shining, his white linen coat over his arm and a white Panama hat in his hand. He is a startling contrast to the other male company, who seem to be outcasts of a state in which he is a prominent citizen.)*

ALMA *(shrilly)*. Yes, it is—our guest of honor! Everybody, this is Dr. John Buchanan, Jr.

JOHN *(easily glancing about the assemblage)*. Hello, everybody.

MRS. BASSETT. I never thought he'd show up. Congratulations, Miss Alma.

JOHN. Did I miss much?

ALMA. Not a thing! Just the minutes— I'll put you on the sofa. Next to me. *(She laughs breathlessly and makes an uncertain gesture. He settles gingerly on the sofa. They all stare at him with a curious sort of greediness)* Well, now! we are completely assembled!

MRS. BASSETT *(eagerly)*. Vernon has his verse play with him tonight!

ALMA *(uneasily)*. Is that right, Vernon? *(Obviously, it is. Vernon has a pile of papers eight inches thick on his knees. He raises them timidly with downcast eyes)*

ROGER *(quickly)*. We decided to put that off till cooler weather. Miss Rosemary is supposed to read us a paper tonight on William Blake.

MRS. BASSETT. Those dead poets can keep!

(John laughs.)

ALMA *(excitedly jumping up)*. Mrs. Bassett, everybody! This is the way I feel about the verse play. It's too important a thing to read under any but ideal circumstances. Not only atmospheric—on some cool evening with music planned to go with it!—but everyone present so that nobody will miss it! Why don't we . . .

ROGER. Why don't we take a standing vote on the matter?

ALMA. Good, good, perfect!

ROGER. All in favor of putting the verse play off till cooler weather, stand up!

(Everybody rises but Rosemary and Mrs. Bassett. Rosemary starts vaguely to rise, but Mrs. Bassett jerks her arm.)

ROSEMARY. Was this a vote?

ROGER. Now, Mrs. Bassett, no rough tactics, please!

ALMA. Has everybody got fans? John, you haven't got one!

(She looks about for a fan for him. Not seeing one, she takes Roger's out of his

hand and gives it to John. Roger is non-plussed. Rosemary gets up with her paper.)

ROSEMARY. The poet—William Blake.

MRS. BASSETT. Insane, insane, that man was a mad fanatic! *(She squints her eyes tight shut and thrusts her thumbs into her ears. The reactions range from indignant to conciliatory)*

ROGER. Now, Mrs. Bassett!

MRS. BASSETT. This is a free country. I can speak my opinion. And I have *read up* on him. Go on, Rosemary. I wasn't criticizing your paper. *(But Rosemary sits down, hurt)*

ALMA. Mrs. Bassett is only joking, Rosemary.

ROSEMARY. No, I don't want to read it if she feels that strongly about it.

MRS. BASSETT. Not a bit, don't be silly! I just don't see why we should encourage the writings of people like that who have already gone into a drunkard's grave!

VARIOUS VOICES *(exclaiming)*. Did he? I never heard that about him. Is that true?

ALMA. Mrs. Bassett is mistaken about that. Mrs. Bassett, you have confused Blake with someone else.

MRS. BASSETT *(positively)*. Oh, no, don't tell me. I've read up on him and know what I'm talking about. He traveled around with that Frenchman who took a shot at him and landed them both in jail! Brussels, Brussels!

ROGER *(gaily)*. Brussels sprouts!

MRS. BASSETT. That's where it happened, fired a gun at him in a drunken stupor, and later one of them died of T.B. in the gutter! All right. I'm finished. I won't say anything more. Go on with your paper, Rosemary. There's nothing like contact with culture!

(Alma gets up.)

ALMA. Before Rosemary reads her paper on Blake, I think it would be a good idea, since some of us aren't acquainted with his work, to preface the critical and biographical comments with a reading of one of his loveliest lyric poems.

ROSEMARY. I'm not going to read anything at all! Not I!

ALMA. Then let me read it then. *(She takes a paper from Rosemary)* . . . This is called "Love's Secret."

(She clears her throat and waits for a hush to settle. Rosemary looks stonily at the

carpet. Mrs. Bassett looks at the ceiling. John coughs.)

Never seek to tell thy love,
Love that never told can be,
For the gentle wind doth move
Silently, invisibly.
I told my love, I told my love,
I told him all my heart.
Trembling, cold in ghastly fear
Did my love depart.

No sooner had he gone from me
Than a stranger passing by,
Silently, invisibly,
Took him with a sigh!

(There are various effusions and enthusiastic applause.)

MRS. BASSETT. Honey, you're right. That isn't the man I meant. I was thinking about the one who wrote about "the bought red lips." Who was it that wrote about the "bought red lips"?

(John has risen abruptly. He signals to Alma and points to his watch. He starts to leave.)

ALMA *(springing up)*. John!

JOHN *(calling back)*. I have to call on a patient!

ALMA. Oh, John!

(She calls after him so sharply that the group is startled into silence.)

ROSEMARY *(interpreting this as a cue to read her paper)*. "The poet, William Blake, was born in 1757 . . ."

(Alma suddenly rushes to the door and goes out after John.)

ROGER. Of poor but honest parents.

MRS. BASSETT. No supercilious comments out of you, sir. Go on, Rosemary. *(She speaks loudly)* She has such a beautiful voice!

(Alma returns inside, looking stunned.)

ALMA. Please excuse the interruption, Rosemary. Dr. Buchanan had to call on a patient.

MRS. BASSETT *(archly)*. I bet I know who the patient was. Ha-ha! That Gonzales girl whose father owns Moon Lake Casino and goes everywhere with two pistols strapped on his belt. Johnny Buchanan will get himself shot in that crowd!

ALMA. Why, Mrs. Bassett, what gave you such an idea? I don't think that John even knows that Gonzales girl!

MRS. BASSETT. He knows her, all right.

In the Biblical sense of the word, if you'll
excuse me!

ALMA. No, I will not excuse you! A
thing like that is inexcusable!

MRS. BASSETT. Have you fallen for him,
Miss Alma? Miss Alma has fallen for
the young doctor! They tell me he has lots
of new lady patients!

ALMA. Stop it! *(She stamps her foot furiously and crushes the palm leaf fan between her clenched hands)* I won't have
malicious talk here! You drove him away
from the meeting after I'd bragged so
much about how bright and interesting
you all were! You put your worst foot
forward and simpered and chattered and
carried on like idiots, idiots! What am I
saying? I—I—please excuse me!
(She rushes out the inner door.)

ROGER. I move that the meeting adjourn.

MRS. BASSETT. I second the motion.

ROSEMARY. I don't understand. What
happened?

MRS. BASSETT. Poor Miss Alma!

ROGER. She hasn't been herself lately....
*(They all go out. After a moment Alma
reenters with a tray of refreshments, looks
about the deserted interior and bursts into
hysterical laughter. The light dims out.)*

SCENE FOUR

In the doctor's office.
*John has a wound on his arm which he
is bandaging with Rosa's assistance.*

———

JOHN. Hold that end. Wrap it around.
Pull it tight. *(There is a knock at the
door. They look up silently. The knock is
repeated)* I better answer before they wake
up the old man. *(He goes out. A few
moments later he returns followed by
Alma. He is rolling down his sleeve to
conceal the bandage. Alma stops short at
the sight of Rosa)* Wait outside, Rosa. In
the hall. But be quiet! *(Rosa gives Alma
a challenging look as she withdraws from
the lighted area. John explains about Rosa)*
A little emergency case.

ALMA. The patient you had to call on.
(John grins) I want to see your father.

JOHN. He's asleep. Anything I can do?

ALMA. No, I think not. I have to see
your father.

JOHN. It's two A.M., Miss Alma.

ALMA. I know, I'm afraid I'll have to
see him.

JOHN. What's the trouble?
*(The voice of John's father is heard, call-
ing from above.)*

DR. BUCHANAN. John! What's going on
down there?

JOHN *(at the door)*. Nothing much,
Dad. Somebody got cut in a fight.

DR. BUCHANAN. I'm coming down.

JOHN. No. Don't! Stay in bed! *(He rolls
up his sleeve to show Alma the bandaged
wound. She gasps and touches her lips)*
I've patched him up, Dad. You sleep!
*(John executes the gesture of closing a
door quietly on the hall.)*

ALMA. You've been in a brawl with that
—woman! *(John nods and rolls the sleeve
back down. Alma sinks faintly into a
chair)*

JOHN. Is your *doppelganger* cutting up
again?

ALMA. It's your father I want to talk to.

JOHN. Be reasonable, Miss Alma. You're
not that sick.

ALMA. Do you suppose I would come
here at two o'clock in the morning if I
were not seriously ill?

JOHN. It's no telling what you would
do in a state of hysteria. *(He puts some
powders in a glass of water)* Toss that
down, Miss Alma.

ALMA. What is it?

JOHN. A couple of little white tablets
dissolved in water.

ALMA. What kind of tablets?

JOHN. You don't trust me?

ALMA. You are not in any condition to
inspire much confidence. *(John laughs
softly. She looks at him helplessly for a
moment, then bursts into tears. He draws
up a chair beside hers and puts his arm
gently about her shoulders)* I seem to be
all to pieces.

JOHN. The intellectual meeting wore
you out.

ALMA. You made a quick escape from
it.

JOHN. I don't like meetings. The only
meetings I like are between two people.

ALMA. Such as between yourself and the
lady outside?

JOHN. Or between you and me.

ALMA *(nervously)*. Where is the . . . ?

JOHN. Oh. You've decided to take it?

ALMA. Yes, if you . . .
(She sips and chokes. He gives her his

handkerchief. She touches her lips with it.)

JOHN. Bitter?

ALMA. Awfully bitter.

JOHN. It'll make you sleepy.

ALMA. I do hope so. I wasn't able to sleep.

JOHN. And you felt panicky?

ALMA. Yes. I felt walled in.

JOHN. You started hearing your heart?

ALMA. Yes, like a drum!

JOHN. It scared you?

ALMA. It always does.

JOHN. Sure. I know.

ALMA. I don't think I will be able to get through the summer.

JOHN. You'll get through it, Miss Alma.

ALMA. How?

JOHN. One day will come after another and one night will come after another till sooner or later the summer will be all through with and then it will be fall, and you will be saying, I don't see how I'm going to get through the fall.

ALMA. Oh . . .

JOHN. That's right. Draw a deep breath!

ALMA. Ah . . .

JOHN. Good. Now draw another!

ALMA. Ah . . .

JOHN. Better? Better?

ALMA. A little.

JOHN. Soon you'll be much better. *(He takes out a big silver watch and holds her wrist)* Did y' know that time is one side of the four-dimensional continuum we're caught in?

ALMA. What?

JOHN. Did you know space is curved, that it turns back onto itself like a soap-bubble, adrift in something that's even less than space. *(He laughs a little as he replaces the watch)*

ROSA *(faintly from outside)*. Johnny!

JOHN *(looking up as if the cry came from there)*. Did you know that the Magellanic clouds are a hundred thousand light years away from the earth? No? *(Alma shakes her head slightly)* That's something to think about when you worry over your heart, that little red fist that's got to keep knocking, knocking against the big black door.

ROSA *(more distinctly)*. Johnny!
(She opens the door a crack.)

JOHN. Calla de la boca! *(The door closes and he speaks to Alma)* There's nothing wrong with your heart but a little func-tional disturbance, like I told you before. You want me to check it? *(Alma nods mutely. John picks up his stethoscope)*

ALMA. The lady outside, I hate to keep her waiting.

JOHN. Rosa doesn't mind waiting. Unbutton your blouse.

ALMA. Unbutton . . . ?

JOHN. The blouse.

ALMA. Hadn't I better—better come back in the morning, when your father will be able to . . . ?

JOHN. Just as you please, Miss Alma. *(She hesitates. Then begins to unbutton her blouse. Her fingers fumble)* Fingers won't work?

ALMA *(breathlessly)*. They are just as if frozen!

JOHN *(smiling)*. Let me. *(He leans over her)* Little pearl buttons . . .

ALMA. If your father discovered that woman in the house . . .

JOHN. He won't discover it.

ALMA. It would distress him terribly.

JOHN. Are you going to tell him?

ALMA. Certainly not! *(He laughs and applies the stethoscope to her chest)*

JOHN. Breathe! . . . Out! . . . Breathe! . . . Out!

ALMA. Ah . . .

JOHN. Um-hmmm . . .

ALMA. What do you hear?

JOHN. Just a little voice saying—"Miss Alma is lonesome!" *(She rises and turns her back to him)*

ALMA. If your idea of helping a patient is to ridicule and insult . . .

JOHN. My idea of helping you is to tell you the truth. *(Alma looks up at him. He lifts her hand from the chair arm)* What is this stone?

ALMA. A topaz.

JOHN. Beautiful stone. . . . Fingers still frozen?

ALMA. A little. *(He lifts her hand to his mouth and blows his breath on her fingers)*

JOHN. I'm a poor excuse for a doctor, I'm much too selfish. But let's try to think about you.

ALMA. Why should you bother about me? *(She sits down)*

JOHN. You know I like you and I think you're worth a lot of consideration.

ALMA. Why?

JOHN. Because you have a lot of feeling in your heart, and that's a rare thing. It makes you too easily hurt. Did I hurt you tonight?

ALMA. You hurt me when you sprang up from the sofa and rushed from the Rectory in such—in such mad haste that you left your coat behind you!

JOHN. I'll pick up the coat sometime.

ALMA. The time of our last conversation you said you would take me riding in your automobile sometime, but you forgot to.

JOHN. I didn't forget. Many's the time I've looked across at the Rectory and wondered if it would be worth trying, you and me. . . .

ALMA. You decided it wasn't?

JOHN. I went there tonight, but it wasn't you and me. . . . Fingers warm now?

ALMA. Those tablets work quickly. I'm already feeling drowsy. (She leans back with her eyes nearly shut) I'm beginning to feel almost like a water lily. A water lily on a Chinese lagoon.

(A heavy iron bell strikes three.)

ROSA. Johnny?

(Alma starts to rise.)

ALMA. I must go.

JOHN. I will call for you Saturday night at eight o'clock.

ALMA. What?

JOHN. I'll give you this box of tablets but watch how you take them. Never more than one or two at a time.

ALMA. Didn't you say something else a moment ago?

JOHN. I said I would call for you at the Rectory Saturday night.

ALMA. Oh . . .

JOHN. Is that all right?

(Alma nods speechlessly. She remains with the box resting in the palm of her hand as if not knowing it was there. John gently closes her fingers on the box.)

ALMA. Oh! (She laughs faintly)

ROSA (outside). Johnny!

JOHN. Do you think you can find your way home, Miss Alma?

(Rosa steps back into the office with a challenging look. Alma catches her breath sharply and goes out the side door.

(John reaches above him and turns out the light. He crosses to Rosa by the anatomy chart and takes her roughly in his arms. The light lingers on the chart as the interior dims out.)

SCENE FIVE

In the Rectory.

Before the light comes up a soprano voice is heard singing "From the Land of the Sky Blue Waters."

As the curtain rises, Alma gets up from the piano. Mr. and Mrs. Winemiller, also, are in the lighted room.

———

ALMA. What time is it, Father? (He goes on writing. She raises her voice) What time is it, Father?

MR. WINEMILLER. Five of eight. I'm working on my sermon.

ALMA. Why don't you work in the study?

MR. WINEMILLER. The study is suffocating. So don't disturb me.

ALMA. Would there be any chance of getting Mother upstairs if someone should call?

MR. WINEMILLER. Are you expecting a caller?

ALMA. Not expecting. There is just a chance of it.

MR. WINEMILLER. Whom are you expecting?

ALMA. I said I wasn't expecting anyone, that there was just a possibility . . .

MR. WINEMILLER. Mr. Doremus? I thought that this was his evening with his mother?

ALMA. Yes, it is his evening with his mother.

MR. WINEMILLER. Then who is coming here, Alma?

ALMA. Probably no one. Probably no one at all.

MR. WINEMILLER. This is all very mysterious.

MRS. WINEMILLER. That tall boy next door is coming to see her, that's who's coming to see her.

ALMA. If you will go upstairs, Mother, I'll call the drug store and ask them to deliver a pint of fresh peach ice cream.

MRS. WINEMILLER. I'll go upstairs when I'm ready—good and ready, and you can put that in your pipe and smoke it, Miss Winemiller!

(She lights a cigarette. Mr. Winemiller turns slowly away with a profound sigh.)

ALMA. I may as well tell you who might call, so that if he calls there will not be any unpleasantness about it. Young Dr. John Buchanan said he might call.

MRS. WINEMILLER. See!

MR. WINEMILLER. You can't be serious.

MRS. WINEMILLER. Didn't I tell you?

ALMA. Well, I am.

MR. WINEMILLER. That young man might come here?

ALMA. He asked me if he might and I said, yes, if he wished to. But it is now after eight so it doesn't look like he's coming.

MR. WINEMILLER. If he does come you will go upstairs to your room and I will receive him.

ALMA. If he does come I'll do no such thing, Father.

MR. WINEMILLER. You must be out of your mind.

ALMA. I'll receive him myself. You may retire to your study and Mother upstairs. But if he does come I'll receive him. I don't judge people by the tongues of gossips. I happen to know that he has been grossly misjudged and misrepresented by old busybodies who're envious of his youth and brilliance and charm.

MR. WINEMILLER. If you're not out of your senses, then I'm out of mine.

ALMA. I daresay we're all a bit peculiar, Father. . . .

MR. WINEMILLER. Well, I have had one almost insufferable cross to bear and perhaps I can bear another. But if you think I'm retiring into my study when this young man comes, probably with a whiskey bottle in one hand and a pair of dice in the other, you have another think coming. I'll sit right here and look at him until he leaves. (He turns back to his sermon)

(A whistle is heard outside the open door.)

ALMA (speaking quickly). As a matter of fact I think I'll walk down to the drug store and call for the ice cream myself. (She crosses to the door, snatching up her hat, gloves and veil)

MRS. WINEMILLER. There she goes to him! Ha-ha! (Alma rushes out)

MR. WINEMILLER (looking up). Alma! Alma!

MRS. WINEMILLER. Ha-ha-haaaaa!

MR. WINEMILLER. Where is Alma?— Alma! (He rushes through the door) Alma!

MRS. WINEMILLER. Ha-ha! Who got fooled? Who got fooled! Ha-haaaa! Insuf-

ferable cross yourself, you old—windbag. . . .

(The curtain comes down.)

SCENE SIX

A delicately suggested arbor, enclosing a table and two chairs. Over the table is suspended a torn paper lantern. This tiny set may be placed way downstage in front of the two interiors, which should be darkened out, as in the fountain scenes. In the background, as it is throughout the play, the angel of the fountain is dimly visible.

Music from the nearby pavilion of the Casino can be used when suitable for background.

John's voice is audible before he and Alma enter.

———

JOHN (from the darkness). I don't understand why we can't go in the casino.

ALMA. You do understand. You're just pretending not to.

JOHN. Give me one reason.

ALMA (coming into the arbor). I am a minister's daughter.

JOHN. That's no reason. (He follows her in. He wears a white linen suit, carrying the coat over his arm)

ALMA. You're a doctor. That's a better reason. You can't any more afford to be seen in such places than I can—less!

JOHN (bellowing). Dusty!

DUSTY (from the darkness). Coming!

JOHN. What are you fishing in that pocketbook for?

ALMA. Nothing.

JOHN. What have you got there?

ALMA. Let go!

JOHN. Those sleeping tablets I gave you?

ALMA. Yes.

JOHN. What for?

ALMA. I need one.

JOHN. Now?

ALMA. Yes.

JOHN. Why?

ALMA. Why? Because I nearly died of heart failure in your automobile. What possessed you to drive like that? A demon?

(Dusty enters.)

JOHN. A bottle of vino rosso.

DUSTY. Sure. (He withdraws)

JOHN. Hey! Tell Shorty I want to hear the "Yellow Dog Blues."

ALMA. Please give me back my tablets.

JOHN. You want to turn into a dope-fiend taking this stuff? I said take one when you need one.

ALMA. I need one now.

JOHN. Sit down and stop swallowing air. *(Dusty returns with a tall wine bottle and two thin-stemmed glasses)* When does the cock-fight start?

DUSTY. 'Bout ten o'clock, Dr. Johnny.

ALMA. When does *what* start?

JOHN. They have a cock-fight here every Saturday night. Ever seen one?

ALMA. Perhaps in some earlier incarnation of my mine.

JOHN. When you wore a brass ring in your nose?

ALMA. Then maybe I went to exhibitions like that.

JOHN. You're going to see one tonight.

ALMA. Oh, no, I'm not.

JOHN. That's what we came here for.

ALMA. I didn't think such exhibitions were legal.

JOHN. This is Moon Lake Casino where anything goes.

ALMA. And you're a frequent patron?

JOHN. I'd say constant.

ALMA. Then I'm afraid you must be serious about giving up your medical career.

JOHN. You bet I am! A doctor's life is walled in by sickness and misery and death.

ALMA. May I be so presumptuous as to inquire what you'll do when you quit?

JOHN. You may be so presumptuous as to inquire.

ALMA. But you won't tell me?

JOHN. I haven't made up my mind, but I've been thinking of South America lately.

ALMA *(sadly)*. Oh . . .

JOHN. I've heard that cantinas are lots more fun than saloons, and senoritas are caviar among females.

ALMA. Dorothy Sykes' brother went to South America and was never heard of again. It takes a strong character to survive in the tropics. Otherwise it's a quagmire.

JOHN. You think my character's weak?

ALMA. I think you're confused, just awfully, awfully confused, as confused as I am—but in a different way. . . .

JOHN *(stretching out his legs)*. Hee-haw, ho-hum.

ALMA. You used to say that as a child—to signify your disgust!

JOHN *(grinning)*. Did I?

ALMA *(sharply)*. Don't sit like that!

JOHN. Why not?

ALMA. You look so indolent and worthless.

JOHN. Maybe I am.

ALMA. If you must go somewhere, why don't you choose a place with a bracing climate?

JOHN. Parts of South America are as cool as a cucumber.

ALMA. I never knew that.

JOHN. Well, now you do.

ALMA. Those Latins all dream in the sun—and indulge their senses.

JOHN. Well, it's yet to be proven that anyone on this earth is crowned with so much glory as the one that uses his senses to get all he can in the way of—satisfaction.

ALMA. Self-satisfaction?

JOHN. What other kind is there?

ALMA. I will answer that question by asking you one. Have you ever seen, or looked at, a picture of a Gothic cathedral?

JOHN. Gothic cathedrals? What about them?

ALMA. How everything reaches up, how everything seems to be straining for something out of the reach of stone—or human—fingers? . . . The immense stained windows, the great arched doors that are five or six times the height of the tallest man—the vaulted ceiling and all the delicate spires—all reaching up to something beyond attainment! To me—well, that is the secret, the principle back of existence—the everlasting struggle and aspiration for more than our human limits have placed in our reach. . . . Who was that said that—oh, so beautiful thing!—"All of us are in the gutter, but some of us are looking at the stars!"

JOHN. Mr. Oscar Wilde.

ALMA *(somewhat taken aback)*. Well, regardless of who said it, it's still true. Some of us are looking at the stars! *(She looks up raptly and places her hand over his)*

JOHN. It's no fun holding hands with gloves on, Miss Alma.

ALMA. That's easily remedied. I'll just take the gloves off. *(Music is heard)*

JOHN. Christ! *(He rises abruptly and*

lights a cigarette) Rosa Gonzales is dancing in the Casino.

ALMA. You *are* unhappy. You hate me for depriving you of the company inside. Well, you'll escape by and by. You'll drive me home and come back out by yourself. . . . I've only gone out with three young men at all seriously, and with each one there was a desert between us.

JOHN. What do you mean by a desert?

ALMA. Oh—wide, wide stretches of uninhabitable ground.

JOHN. Maybe you made it that way by being stand-offish.

ALMA. I made quite an effort with one or two of them.

JOHN. What kind of an effort?

ALMA. Oh, I—tried to entertain them the first few times. I would play and sing for them in the Rectory parlor.

JOHN. With your father in the next room and the door half open.

ALMA. I don't think that was the trouble.

JOHN. What was the trouble?

ALMA. I—I didn't have my heart in it. *(She laughs uncertainly)* A silence would fall between us. You know, a silence?

JOHN. Yes, I know a silence.

ALMA. I'd try to talk and he'd try to talk and neither would make a go of it.

JOHN. Then silence would fall?

ALMA. Yes, the enormous silence.

JOHN. Then you'd go back to the piano?

ALMA. I'd twist my ring. Sometimes I twisted it so hard that the band cut my finger! He'd glance at his watch and we'd both know that the useless undertaking had come to a close. . . .

JOHN. You'd call it quits?

ALMA. Quits is—what we'd call it. . . . One or two times I was rather sorry about it.

JOHN. But you didn't have your heart in it?

ALMA. None of them really engaged my serious feelings.

JOHN. You do have serious feelings—of that kind?

ALMA. Doesn't everyone—sometimes?

JOHN. Some women are cold. Some women are what is called frigid.

ALMA. Do I give that impression?

JOHN. Under the surface you have a lot of excitement, a great deal more than any other woman I have met. So much that you have to carry these sleeping pills with you. The question is why? *(He leans over and lifts her veil)*

ALMA. What are you doing that for?

JOHN. So that I won't get your veil in my mouth when I kiss you.

ALMA *(faintly)*. Do you want to do that?

JOHN *(gently)*. Miss Alma. *(He takes her arms and draws her to her feet)* Oh, Miss Alma, Miss Alma! *(He kisses her)*

ALMA *(in a low, shaken voice)*. Not "Miss" any more. Just Alma.

JOHN *(grinning gently)*. "Miss" suits you better, Miss Alma. *(He kisses her again. She hesitantly touches his shoulders, but not quite to push him away. John speaks softly to her)* Is it so hard to forget you're a preacher's daughter?

ALMA. There is no reason for me to forget that I am a minister's daughter. A minister's daughter's no different from any other young lady who tries to remember that she *is* a lady.

JOHN. This lady stuff, is that so important?

ALMA. Not to the sort of girls that you may be used to bringing to Moon Lake Casino. But suppose that some day . . . *(She crosses out of the arbor and faces away from him)* suppose that some day you—married. . . . The woman that you selected to be your wife, and not only your wife but—the mother of your children! *(She catches her breath at the thought)* Wouldn't you want that woman to be a lady? Wouldn't you want her to be somebody that you, as her husband, and they as her precious children—could look up to with very deep respect? *(There is a pause)*

JOHN. There's other things between a man and a woman besides respect. Did you know that, Miss Alma?

ALMA. Yes. . . .

JOHN. There's such a thing as intimate relations.

ALMA. Thank you for telling me that. So plainly.

JOHN. It may strike you as unpleasant. But it does have a good deal to do with—connubial felicity, as you'd call it. There are some women that just give in to a man as a sort of obligation imposed on them by the—cruelty of nature! *(He finishes his glass and pours another)* And there you are.

ALMA. There *I* am?

JOHN. I'm speaking generally.

ALMA. Oh.

(*Hoarse shouts go up from the Casino.*)

JOHN. The cock-fight has started!

ALMA. Since you have spoken so plainly, I'll speak plainly, too. There are some women who turn a possibly beautiful thing into something no better than the coupling of beasts!—but love is what you bring to it.

JOHN. You're right about that.

ALMA. Some people bring just their bodies. But there are some people, there are some women, John—who can bring their hearts to it, also—who can bring their souls to it!

JOHN (*derisively*). Souls again, huh?— those Gothic cathedrals you dream of! (*There is another hoarse prolonged shout from the Casino*) Your name is Alma and Alma is Spanish for soul. Some time I'd like to show you a chart of the human anatomy that I have in the office. It shows what our insides are like, and maybe you can show me where the beautiful soul is located on the chart. (*He drains the wine bottle*) Let's go watch the cock-fight.

ALMA. No! (*There is a pause*)

JOHN. I know something else we could do. There are rooms above the Casino....

ALMA (*her back stiffening*). I'd heard that you made suggestions like that to girls that you go out with, but I refused to believe such stories were true. What made you think I might be amenable to such a suggestion?

JOHN. I counted your pulse in the office the night you ran out because you weren't able to sleep.

ALMA. The night I was ill and went to your father for help.

JOHN. It was me you went to.

ALMA. It was your father, and you wouldn't call your father.

JOHN. Fingers frozen stiff when I . . .

ALMA (*rising*). Oh! I want to go home. But I won't go with you. I will go in a taxi! (*She wheels about hysterically*) Boy! Boy! Call a taxi!

JOHN. I'll call one for you, Miss Alma. —Taxi! (*He goes out of the arbor*)

ALMA (*wildly*). You're not a gentleman!

JOHN (*from the darkness*). Taxi!

ALMA. You're not a gentleman!

(*As he disappears she makes a sound in her throat like a hurt animal. The light fades out of the arbor and comes up more distinctly on the stone angel of the fountain.*)

PART TWO—A WINTER

SCENE SEVEN

The sky and the southern constellations, almost imperceptibly moving with the earth's motion, appear on the great cyclorama.

The Rectory interior is lighted first, disclosing Alma and Roger Doremus seated on the green plush sofa under the romantic landscape in its heavy gilt frame. On a tiny table beside them is a cut glass pitcher of lemonade with cherries and orange slices in it, like a little aquarium of tropical fish. Roger is entertaining Alma with a collection of photographs and postcards, mementoes of his mother's trip to the Orient. He is enthusiastic about them and describes them in phrases his mother must have assimilated from a sedulous study of literature provided by Cook's Tours. Alma is less enthusiastic; she is preoccupied with the sounds of a wild party going on next door at the doctor's home. At present there is Mexican music with shouts and stamping.

Only the immediate area of the sofa is clearly lighted; the fountain is faintly etched in light and the night sky walls the interior.

ROGER. And this is Ceylon, The Pearl of the Orient!

ALMA. And who is this fat young lady?

ROGER. That is Mother in a hunting costume.

ALMA. The hunting costume makes her figure seem bulky. What was your mother hunting?

ROGER (*gaily*). Heaven knows what she was hunting! But she found Papa.

ALMA. Oh, she met your father on this Oriental tour?

ROGER. Ha-ha!—yes. . . . He was returning from India with dysentery and they met on the boat.

ALMA (*distastefully*). Oh . . .

ROGER. And here she is on top of a ruined temple!

ALMA. How did she get up there?

ROGER. Climbed up, I suppose.

ALMA. What an active woman.

ROGER. Oh, yes, active—is no word for it! Here she is on an elephant's back in Burma.

ALMA. Ah!

ROGER. You're looking at it upside down, Miss Alma!

ALMA. Deliberately—to tease you. *(The doorbell rings)* Perhaps that's your mother coming to fetch you home.

ROGER. It's only ten-fifteen. I never leave till ten-thirty.

(Mrs. Bassett comes in.)

ALMA. Mrs. Bassett!

MRS. BASSETT. I was just wondering who I could turn to when I saw the Rectory light and I thought to myself, Grace Bassett, you trot yourself right over there and talk to Mr. Winemiller!

ALMA. Father has retired.

MRS. BASSETT. Oh, what a pity. *(She sees Roger)* Hello, Roger! . . . I saw that fall your mother took this morning. I saw her come skipping out of the Delta Planters' Bank and I thought to myself, now isn't that remarkable, a woman of her age and weight so light on her feet? And just at that very moment—*down she went!* I swear to goodness I thought she had broken her hip! Was she bruised much?

ROGER. Just shaken up, Mrs. Bassett.

MRS. BASSETT. Oh, how lucky! She certainly must be made out of India rubber! *(She turns to Alma)* Alma—Alma, if it is not too late for human intervention, your father's the one right person to call up old Dr. Buchanan at the fever clinic at Lyon and let him know!

ALMA. About—what?

MRS. BASSETT. You must be stone-deaf if you haven't noticed what's been going on next door since the old doctor left to fight the epidemic. One continual orgy! Well, not five minutes ago a friend of mine who works at the County Courthouse called to inform me that young Dr. John and Rosa Gonzales have taken a license out and are going to be married tomorrow!

ALMA. Are you—quite certain?

MRS. BASSETT. Certain? I'm always certain before I speak!

ALMA. Why would he—do such a thing?

MRS. BASSETT. August madness! They say it has something to do with the falling stars. Of course it might also have something to do with the fact that he lost two or three thousand dollars at the Casino which he can't pay except by giving himself to Gonzales' daughter. *(She turns to Alma)* Alma, what are you doing with that picture puzzle?

ALMA *(with a faint, hysterical laugh)*. The pieces don't fit!

MRS. BASSETT *(to Roger)*. I shouldn't have opened my mouth.

ALMA. Will both of you please go!

(Roger goes out.)

MRS. BASSETT. I knew this was going to upset you. Good night, Alma. *(She leaves. Alma suddenly springs up and seizes the telephone)*

ALMA. Long distance. . . . Please get me the fever clinic at Lyon. . . . I want to speak to Dr. Buchanan.

(The light in the Rectory dims out and light comes on in the doctor's office. Rosa's voice is heard calling.)

ROSA. Johnny!

(The offstage calling of John's name is used throughout the play as a cue for theme music.

(John enters the office interior. He is dressed, as always, in a white linen suit. His face has a look of satiety and confusion. He throws himself down in a swivel chair at the desk.

(Rosa Gonzales comes in. She is dressed in a Flamenco costume and has been dancing. She crosses and stands before the anatomy chart and clicks her castanets to catch his attention, but he remains looking up at the roofless dark. She approaches him.)

ROSA. You have blood on your face!

JOHN. You bit my ear.

ROSA. Ohhh . . . *(She approaches him with exaggerated concern)*

JOHN. You never make love without scratching or biting or something. Whenever I leave you I have a little blood on me. Why is that?

ROSA. Because I know I can't hold you.

JOHN. I think you're doing a pretty good job of it. Better than anyone else. Tomorrow we leave here together and Father or somebody else can tell old Mrs. Arbuckle her eighty-five years are enough and she's got to go now on the wings of carcinoma. Dance, Rosa! *(Accordion music is heard. She performs a slow and joyless dance around his chair. John continues while she dances)* Tomorrow we leave here together. We sail out of Galveston. don't we?

ROSA. You say it but I don't believe it.

JOHN. I have the tickets.

ROSA. Two pieces of paper that you can tear in two.

JOHN. We'll go all right, and live on fat remittances from your Papa! Ha-ha!

ROSA. Ha-ha-ha!

JOHN. Not long ago the idea would have disgusted me, but not now. (*He catches her by the wrist*) Rosa! Rosa Gonzales! Did anyone ever slide downhill as fast as I have this summer? Ha-ha! Like a greased pig. And yet every evening I put on a clean white suit. I have a dozen. Six in the closet and six in the wash. And there isn't a sign of depravity in my face. And yet all summer I've sat around here like *this,* remembering last night, anticipating the next one! The trouble with me is, I should have been *castrated!* (*He flings his wine glass at the anatomy chart. She stops dancing*) Dance, Rosa! Why don't you dance? (*Rosa shakes her head dumbly*) What is the matter, Rosa? Why don't you go on dancing? (*The accordion continues; he thrusts her arm savagely over her head in the Flamenco position*)

ROSA (*suddenly weeping*). I can't dance any more! (*She shrows herself to the floor, pressing her weeping face to his knees. The voice of her father is heard, bellowing, in the next room*)

GONZALES. The sky is the limit!

(*John is sobered.*)

JOHN. Why does your father want me for a son-in-law?

ROSA (*sobbing*). I want you—I, I want you!

JOHN (*raising her from the floor*). Why do you?

ROSA (*clinging to him*). Maybe because —I was born in Piedras Negras, and grew up in a one room house with a dirt floor, and all of us had to sleep in that one room, five Mexicans and three geese and a little game-cock named Pepe! Ha-ha! (*She laughs hysterically*) Pepe was a good fighter! That's how Papa began to make money, winning bets on Pepe! Ha-ha! We all slept in the one room. And in the night, I would hear the love-making. Papa would grunt like a pig to show his passion. I thought to myself, how dirty it was, love-making, and how dirty it was to be Mexicans and all have to sleep in one room with a dirt floor and not smell good because there was not any bathtub! (*The accordion continues*)

JOHN. What has that got to do with ... ?

ROSA. Me wanting you? You're tall! You smell good! And, oh, I'm so glad that you never grunt like a pig to show your passion! (*She embraces him convulsively*) Ah, but *quien sabe!* Something might happen tonight, and I'll wind up with some dark little friend of Papa's.

GONZALES (*imperiously*). Rosa! Rosa!

ROSA. Si, si, Papa, aqui estoy!

GONZALES (*entering unsteadily*). The gold beads ... (*He fingers a necklace of gold beads that Rosa is wearing*) Johnny ... (*He staggers up to John and catches him in a drunken embrace*) Listen! When my girl Rosa was little she see a string a gold bead and she want those gold bead so bad that she cry all night for it. I don' have money to buy a string of gold bead so next day I go for a ride up to Eagle Pass and I walk in a dry good store and I say to the man: "Please give me a string a gold bead." He say: "Show me the money!" And I reach down to my belt and I pull out—not the money—but this! (*He pulls out a revolver*) Now—now I have money, but I still have this! (*Laughing*) She got the gold bead. Anything that she want I get for her with this (*He pulls out a roll of bills*) or this! (*He waves the revolver*)

JOHN (*pushing Gonzales away*). Keep your stinking breath out of my face, Gonzales!

ROSA. Dejalo, dejalo, Papa!

GONZALES (*moving unsteadily to the couch, with Rosa supporting him*). Le doy la tierra y si la tierra no basta—le doy el cielo! (*He collapses onto the couch*) The sky is the limit!

ROSA (*to John*). Let him stay there. Come on back to the party.

(*Rosa leaves the room. John goes over to the window facing the Rectory and looks across. The light comes up in the Rectory living room as Alma enters, dressed in a robe. She goes to the window and looks across at the doctor's house. As Alma and John stand at the windows looking toward each other through the darkness music is heard. Slowly, as if drawn by the music, John walks out of his house and crosses over to the Rectory. Alma remains motionless at the window until John enters the room, behind her. The music dies away and there is a murmur of wind. She slowly turns to face John.*)

JOHN. I took the open door for an invitation. The Gulf wind is blowing tonight . . . cools things off a little. But my head's on fire. . . . *(Alma says nothing. John moves a few steps toward her)* The silence? *(Alma sinks onto the love seat, closing her eyes)* Yes, the enormous silence. *(He goes over to her)* I will go in a minute, but first I want you to put your hands on my face. . . . *(He crouches beside her)* Eternity and Miss Alma have such cool hands. *(He buries his face in her lap. The attitude suggests a stone* Pieta. *Alma's eyes remain closed)*

(On the other side of the stage Dr. Buchanan enters his house and the light builds a little as he looks around in the door of his office. The love theme music fades out and the Mexican music comes up strongly, with a definitely ominous quality, as Rosa enters the office from the other side.)

ROSA. Johnny! *(She catches sight of Dr. Buchanan and checks herself in surprise)* Oh! I thought you were Johnny! . . . But you are Johnny's father. . . . I'm Rosa Gonzales!

DR. BUCHANAN. I know who you are. What's going on in my house?

ROSA *(nervously)*. John's giving a party because we're leaving tomorrow. *(Defiantly)* Yes! Together! I hope you like the idea, but if you don't, it doesn't matter, because *we* like the idea and my father likes the idea.

GONZALES *(drunkenly, sitting up on the couch)*. The sky is the limit!

(Dr. Buchanan slowly raises his silver-headed cane in a threatening gesture.)

DR. BUCHANAN. Get your—swine out of —my house! *(He strikes Gonzales with his cane)*

GONZALES *(staggering up from the couch in pain and surprise)*. Aieeee!

ROSA *(breathlessly, backing against the chart of anatomy)*. No! No, Papa!

DR. BUCHANAN *(striking at the chest of the bull-like man with his cane)*. Get your swine out, I said! Get them out of my house!

(He repeats the blow. The drunken Mexican roars with pain and surprise. He backs up and reaches under his coat.)

ROSA *(wildly and despairingly)*. No, no, no, no, no, no!

(She covers her face against the chart of anatomy. A revolver is fired. There is a burst of light. The cane drops. The music stops short. Everything dims out but a spot of light on Rosa standing against the chart of anatomy with closed eyes and her face twisted like that of a tragic mask.)

ROSA *(senselessly)*. Aaaaaahhhhhh . . . Aaaaaahhhhhh . . .

(The theme music is started faintly and light disappears from everything but the wings of the stone angel.)

SCENE EIGHT

The doctor's office.
The stone angel is dimly visible above.
John is seated in a hunched position at the table. Alma enters with a coffee tray. The sounds of a prayer come through the inner door.

———

JOHN. What is that mumbo-jumbo your father is spouting in there?

ALMA. A prayer.

JOHN. Tell him to quit. We don't want that wornout magic.

ALMA. You may not want it, but it's not a question of what you want any more. I've made you some coffee.

JOHN. I don't want any.

ALMA. Lean back and let me wash your face off, John. *(She presses a towel to the red marks on his face)* It's such a fine face, a fine and sensitive face, a face that has power in it that shouldn't be wasted.

JOHN. Never mind that. *(He pushes her hand away)*

ALMA. You have to go in to see him.

JOHN. I couldn't. He wouldn't want me.

ALMA. This happened because of his devotion to you.

JOHN. It happened because some meddlesome Mattie called him back here tonight. Who was it did that?

ALMA. I did.

JOHN. It *was* you then!

ALMA. I phoned him at the fever clinic in Lyon as soon as I learned what you were planning to do. I wired him to come here and stop it.

JOHN. You brought him here to be shot.

ALMA. You can't put the blame on anything but your weakness.

JOHN. *You* call me weak?

ALMA. Sometimes it takes a tragedy like this to make a weak person strong.

JOHN. You—white-blooded spinster! You

so right people, pious pompous mumblers, preachers and preacher's daughter, all muffled up in a lot of wornout magic! And I was supposed to minister to your neurosis, give you tablets for sleeping and tonics to give you the strength to go on mumbling your wornout mumbo-jumbo!

ALMA. Call me whatever you want, but don't let your father hear your drunken shouting. *(She tries to break away from him)*

JOHN. Stay here! I want you to look at something. *(He turns her about)* This chart of anatomy, look!

ALMA. I've seen it before. *(She turns away)*

JOHN. You've never dared to look at it.

ALMA. Why should I?

JOHN. You're scared to.

ALMA. You must be out of your senses.

JOHN. You talk about weakness but can't even look at a picture of human insides.

ALMA. They're not important.

JOHN. That's your mistake. You think you're stuffed with rose-leaves. Turn around and look at it, it may do you good!

ALMA. How can you behave like this with your father dying and you so . . .

JOHN. Hold still!

ALMA. . . . so much to blame for it!

JOHN. No more than you are!

ALMA. At least for this little while . . .

JOHN. Look here!

ALMA. . . . you could feel some shame!

JOHN *(with crazy, grinning intensity)*. Now listen here to the anatomy lecture! This upper story's the brain which is hungry for something called truth and doesn't get much but keeps on feeling hungry! This middle's the belly which is hungry for food. This part down here is the sex which is hungry for love because it is sometimes lonesome. I've fed all three, as much of all three as I could or as much as I wanted— You've fed none—nothing. Well—maybe your belly a little—watery subsistence— But love or truth, nothing but—nothing but hand-me-down notions!—attitudes!—poses. *(He releases her)* Now you can go. The anatomy lecture is over.

ALMA. So that is your high conception of human desires. What you have here is not the anatomy of a beast, but a man. And I —I reject your opinion of where love is, and the kind of truth you believe the brain to be seeking!—There is something not shown on the chart.

JOHN. You mean the part that Alma is Spanish for, do you?

ALMA. Yes, that's not shown on the anatomy chart! But it's there, just the same, yes, there! Somewhere, not seen, but there. And it's *that* that I loved you with—that! Not what you mention!—Yes, did love you with, John, did nearly *die* of when you hurt me! *(He turns slowly to her and speaks gently)*

JOHN. I wouldn't have made love to you.

ALMA *(uncomprehendingly)*. What?

JOHN. The night at the Casino—I wouldn't have made love to you. Even if you had consented to go upstairs I couldn't have made love to you. *(She stares at him as if anticipating some unbearable hurt)* Yes, yes! Isn't that funny? I'm more afraid of your soul than you're afraid of my body. You'd have been as safe as the angel of the fountain—because I wouldn't feel *decent* enough to touch you. . . .

(Mr. Winemiller comes in.)

MR. WINEMILLER. He's resting more easily now.

ALMA. Oh . . . *(She nods her head. John reaches for his coffee cup)* It's cold. I'll heat it.

JOHN. It's all right.

MR. WINEMILLER. Alma, Dr. John wants you.

ALMA. I . . .

MR. WINEMILLER. He asked if you would sing for him.

ALMA. I—couldn't—now!

JOHN. Go in and sing to him, Miss Alma!

(Mr. Winemiller withdraws through the outer door. Alma looks back at John hunched over the coffee cup. He doesn't return her look. She passes into the blurred orange space beyond the inner door, leaving it slightly open. After a few minutes her voice rises softly within, singing. John suddenly rises. He crosses to the door, shoves it slowly open and enters.)

JOHN *(softly and with deep tenderness)*. Father?

(The light dims out in the house, but lingers on the stone angel.)

SCENE NINE

The cyclorama is the faint blue of a late

afternoon in autumn. There is band-music
—a Sousa march, in the distance. As it
grows somewhat louder, Alma enters the
Rectory interior in a dressing gown and
with her hair hanging loose. She looks as
if she had been through a long illness, the
intensity drained, her pale face listless. She
crosses to the window frame but the pa-
rade is not in sight so she returns weakly
to the sofa and sits down closing her eyes
with exhaustion.

The Rev. and Mrs. Winemiller enter the
outer door frame of the Rectory, a gro-
tesque-looking couple. Mrs. Winemiller
has on her plumed hat, at a rakish angle,
and a brilliant scarf about her throat. Her
face wears a roguish smile that suggests a
musical comedy pirate. One hand holds the
minister's arm and with the other she is
holding an ice cream cone.

———

MR. WINEMILLER. Now you may let go
of my arm, if you please! She was on her
worst behavior. Stopped in front of the
White Star Pharmacy on Front Street and
stood there like a mule; wouldn't budge
till I bought her an ice cream cone. I had
it wrapped in tissue paper because she had
promised me that she wouldn't eat it till
we got home. The moment I gave it to
her she tore off the paper and walked
home licking it every step of the way!—
just—just to humiliate me! *(Mrs. Wine-*
miller offers him the half-eaten cone, say-
ing "Lick?") No, thank you!

ALMA. Now, now, children.

(Mr. Winemiller's irritation shifts to
Alma.)

MR. WINEMILLER. Alma! Why don't you
get dressed? It hurts me to see you sitting
around like this, day in, day out, like an
invalid when there is nothing particularly
wrong with you. I can't read your mind.
You may have had some kind of disappointment, but you must not make it an
excuse for acting as if the world had come
to an end.

ALMA. I have made the beds and washed
the breakfast dishes and phoned the market and sent the laundry out and peeled
the potatoes and shelled the peas and set
the table for lunch. What more do you
want?

MR. WINEMILLER *(sharply)*. I want you
to either get dressed or stay in your room.
(Alma rises indifferently, then her father
speaks suddenly) At night you get dressed.

Don't you? Yes, I heard you slipping out
of the house at two in the morning. And
that was not the first time.

ALMA. I don't sleep well. Sometimes I
have to get up and walk for a while before I am able to sleep.

MR. WINEMILLER. What am I going to
tell people who ask about you?

ALMA. Tell them I've changed and you're
waiting to see in what way.

(The band music becomes a little louder.)

MR. WINEMILLER. Are you going to stay
like this indefinitely?

ALMA. Not indefinitely, but you may
wish that I had.

MR. WINEMILLER. Stop twisting that
ring! Whenever I look at you you're twisting that ring. Give me that ring! I'm going to take that ring off your finger! *(He*
catches her wrist. She breaks roughly away
from him)

MRS. WINEMILLER *(joyfully)*. Fight!
Fight!

MR. WINEMILLER. Oh, I give up!

ALMA. That's better. *(She suddenly*
crosses to the window as the band music
gets louder) Is there a parade in town?

MRS. WINEMILLER. Ha-ha—yes! They met
him at the station with a great big silver
loving-cup!

ALMA. Who? Who did they . . . ?

MRS. WINEMILLER. That boy next door,
the one you watched all the time!

ALMA. Is that true, Father?

MR. WINEMILLER *(unfolding his news-*
paper). Haven't you looked at the papers?

ALMA. No, not lately.

MR. WINEMILLER *(wiping his eyeglasses)*.
These people are grasshoppers, just as
likely to jump one way as another. He's
finished 'the work his father started,
stamped out the fever and gotten all of
the glory. Well, that's how it is in this
world. Years of devotion and sacrifice are
overlooked an' forgotten while someone
young an' lucky walks off with the honors!
(Alma has crossed slowly to the window.
The sun brightens and falls in a shaft
through the frame.)

ALMA *(suddenly crying out)*. There he
is! *(She staggers away from the window.*
There is a roll of drums and then silence.
Alma now speaks faintly) What . . . happened? Something . . . struck me! *(Mr.*
Winemiller catches her arm to support
her)

MR. WINEMILLER. Alma . . . I'll call a doctor.

ALMA. No, no, don't. Don't call anybody to help me. I want to die! *(She collapses on the sofa)*

(The band strikes up again and recedes down the street. The Rectory interior dims out. Then the light is brought up in the doctor's office. John enters, with his loving-cup. He is sprucely dressed and his whole manner suggests a new-found responsibility. While he is setting the award on the table, removing his coat and starched collar, Nellie Ewell appears in the door behind him. She stands by the anatomy chart and watches him until he discovers her presence. Nellie has abruptly grown up, and wears very adult clothes, but has lost none of her childish impudence and brightness. John gives a startled whistle as he sees her. Nellie giggles.)

JOHN. High heels, feathers . . . and paint!

NELLIE. Not paint!

JOHN. Natural color?

NELLIE. Excitement.

JOHN. Over what?

NELLIE. Everything! You! You here! Didn't you see me at the depot? I shouted and waved my arm off! I'm home for Thanksgiving.

JOHN. From where?

NELLIE. Sophie Newcombe's. *(He remains staring at her, unbelieving. At last she draws a book from under her arm)* Here is that nasty book you gave me last summer when I was pretending such ignorance of things!

JOHN. Only pretending?

NELLIE. Yes. *(He ignores the book. She tosses it on the table)* . . . Well? *(John laughs uneasily and sits on the table)* Shall I go now, or will you look at my tongue? *(She crosses to him, sticking out her tongue)*

JOHN. Red as a berry!

NELLIE. Peppermint drops! Will you have one? *(She holds out a sack)*

JOHN. Thanks. *(Nellie giggles as he takes one)* What's the joke, Nellie?

NELLIE. They make your mouth so sweet!

JOHN. So?

NELLIE. I always take one when I hope to be kissed.

JOHN *(after a pause)*. Suppose I took you up on that?

NELLIE. I'm not scared. Are you?

(He gives her a quick kiss. She clings to him, raising her hand to press his head against her own. He breaks free after a moment and turns the light back on.)

JOHN *(considerably impressed)*. Where did you learn such tricks?

NELLIE. I've been away to school. But they didn't teach me to love.

JOHN. Who are you to be using that long word?

NELLIE. That isn't a long word!

JOHN. No? *(He turns away from her)* Run along Nellie before we get into trouble.

NELLIE. Who's afraid of trouble, you or me?

JOHN. I am. Run along! Hear me?

NELLIE. Oh, I'll go. But I'll be back for Christmas!

(She laughs and runs out. He whistles and wipes his forehead with a handkerchief.)

SCENE TEN

An afternoon in December. At the fountain in the park. It is very windy.

Alma enters. She seems to move with an effort against the wind. She sinks down on the bench.

A widow with a flowing black veil passes across the stage and pauses by Alma's bench. It is Mrs. Bassett.

———

MRS. BASSETT. Hello, Alma.

ALMA. Good afternoon, Mrs. Bassett.

MRS. BASSETT. Such wind, such wind!

ALMA. Yes, it nearly swept me off my feet. I had to sit down to catch my breath for a moment.

MRS. BASSETT. I wouldn't sit too long if I were you.

ALMA. No, not long.

MRS. BASSETT. It's good to see you out again after your illness.

ALMA. Thank you.

MRS. BASSETT. Our poor little group broke up after you dropped out.

ALMA *(insincerely)*. What a pity.

MRS. BASSETT. You should have come to the last meeting.

ALMA. Why, what happened?

MRS. BASSETT. Vernon read his verse play!

ALMA. Ah, how was it received?

MRS. BASSETT. Maliciously, spitefully and

vindictively torn to pieces, the way children tear the wings of butterflies. I think next spring we might reorganize. *(She throws up her black-gloved hands in a deploring gesture)*
(Nellie Ewell appears. She is dressed very fashionably and carrying a fancy basket of Christmas packages.)

NELLIE. Miss Alma!

MRS. BASSETT *(rushing off)*. Goodbye!

NELLIE. Oh, there you are!

ALMA. Why Nellie . . . Nellie Ewell!

NELLIE. I was by the Rectory. Just popped in for a second; the holidays are so short that every minute is precious. They told me you'd gone to the park.

ALMA. This is the first walk I've taken in quite a while.

NELLIE. You've been ill!

ALMA. Not ill, just not very well. How you've grown up, Nellie.

NELLIE. It's just my clothes. Since I went off to Sophie Newcombe I've picked out my own clothes, Miss Alma. When Mother had jurisdiction over my wardrobe, she tried to keep me looking like a child!

ALMA. Your voice is grown-up, too.

NELLIE. They're teaching me diction, Miss Alma. I'm learning to talk like you, long A's and everything, such as "cahn't" and "bahth" and "lahf" instead of "laugh." Yesterday I slipped. I said I "lahfed and lahfed till I nearly died laughing." Johnny was so amused at me!

ALMA. Johnny?

NELLIE. Your nextdoor neighbor!

ALMA. Oh! I'm sure it must be a very fashionable school.

NELLIE. Oh yes, they're preparing us to be young ladies in society. What a pity there's no society here to be a young lady in . . . at least not for me, with Mother's reputation!

ALMA. You'll find other fields to conquer.

NELLIE. What's this I hear about *you?*

ALMA. I have no idea, Nellie.

NELLIE. That you've quit teaching singing and gone into retirement.

ALMA. Naturally I had to stop teaching while I was ill and as for retiring from the world . . . it's more a case of the world retiring from me.

NELLIE. I know somebody whose feelings you've hurt badly.

ALMA. Why, who could that be, Nellie?

NELLIE. Somebody who regards you as an angel!

ALMA. I can't think who might hold me in such esteem.

NELLIE. Somebody who says that you refused to see him.

ALMA. I saw nobody. For several months. The long summer wore me out so.

NELLIE. Well, anyhow, I'm going to give you your present. *(She hands her a small package from the basket)*

ALMA. Nellie, you shouldn't have given me anything.

NELLIE. I'd like to know why not!

ALMA. I didn't expect it.

NELLIE. After the trouble you took with my horrible voice?

ALMA. It's very sweet of you, Nellie.

NELLIE. Open it!

ALMA. Now?

NELLIE. Why, sure.

ALMA. It's so prettily wrapped I hate to undo it.

NELLIE. I love to wrap presents and since it was for you, I did a specially dainty job of it.

ALMA *(winding the ribbon about her fingers)*. I'm going to save this ribbon. I'm going to keep this lovely paper too, with the silver stars on it. And the sprig of holly . . .

NELLIE. Let me pin it on your jacket, Alma.

ALMA. Yes, do. I hardly realized that Christmas was coming. . . . *(She unfolds the paper, revealing a lace handkerchief and a card)* What an exquisite handkerchief.

NELLIE. I hate to give people handkerchiefs, it's so unimaginative.

ALMA. I love to get them.

NELLIE. It comes from Maison Blanche!

ALMA. Oh, does it really?

NELLIE. Smell it!

ALMA. Sachet *Roses!* Well, I'm just more touched and pleased than I can possibly tell you!

NELLIE. The card!

ALMA. Card?

NELLIE. You dropped it. *(She snatches up the card and hands it to Alma)*

ALMA. Oh, how clumsy of me! Thank you, Nellie. "Joyeux Noel . . . to Alma . . . from Nellie and . . . *(She looks up slowly)* John?"

NELLIE. He helped me wrap presents

last night and when we came to yours we started talking about you. Your ears must have burned!

(*The wind blows loudly. Alma bends stiffly forward.*)

ALMA. You mean you—spoke well of me?

NELLIE. "Well of"! We raved, simply raved! Oh, he told me the influence you'd had on him!

ALMA. Influence?

NELLIE. He told me about the wonderful talks he'd had with you last summer when he was so mixed up and how you inspired him and you more than anyone else was responsible for his pulling himself together, after his father was killed, and he told me about . . . (*Alma rises stiffly from the bench*) Where are you going, Miss Alma?

ALMA. To drink at the fountain.

NELLIE. He told me about how you came in the house that night like an angel of mercy!

ALMA (*laughing harshly by the fountain*). This is the only angel in Glorious Hill. (*She bends to drink*) Her body is stone and her blood is mineral water. (*The wind is louder.*)

NELLIE. How penetrating the wind is!

ALMA. I'm going home, Nellie. You run along and deliver your presents now. . . . (*She starts away*)

NELLIE. But wait till I've told you the wonderfullest thing I . . .

ALMA. I'm going home now. Goodbye.

NELLIE. Oh— Goodbye, Miss Alma.

(*She snatches up her festive basket and rushes in the other direction with a shrill giggle as the wind pulls at her skirts. The lights dim out.*)

SCENE ELEVEN

An hour later. In John's office.

The interior is framed by the traceries of Victorian architecture and there is one irregular section of wall supporting the anatomy chart. Otherwise the stage is open to the cyclorama.

In the background mellow golden light touches the vane of a steeple (a gilded weathercock). Also the wings of the stone angel. A singing wind rises and falls throughout scene.

John is seated at a white enameled table examining a slide through a microscope.

(*A bell tolls the hour of five as Alma comes hesitantly in. She wears a russet suit and a matching hat with a plume. The light changes, the sun disappearing behind a cloud, fading from the steeple and the stone angel till the bell stops tolling. Then it brightens again.*)

ALMA. No greetings? No greetings at all?

JOHN. Hello, Miss Alma.

ALMA (*speaking with animation to control her panic*). How white it is here, such glacial brilliance! (*She covers her eyes, laughing*)

JOHN. New equipment.

ALMA. Everything new but the chart.

JOHN. The human anatomy's always the same old thing.

ALMA. And such a tiresome one! I've been plagued with sore throats.

JOHN. Everyone has here lately. These Southern homes are all improperly heated. Open grates aren't enough.

ALMA. They burn the front of you while your back is freezing!

JOHN. Then you go into another room and get chilled off.

ALMA. Yes, yes, chilled to the bone.

JOHN. But it never gets quite cold enough to convince the damn fools that a furnace is necessary so they go on building without them.

(*There is the sound of wind.*)

ALMA. Such a strange afternoon.

JOHN. Is it? I haven't been out.

ALMA. The Gulf wind is blowing big, white—what do they call them? cumulus? —clouds over! Ha-ha! It seemed determined to take the plume off my hat, like that fox terrier we had once, named Jacob, snatched the plume off a hat and dashed around and around the back yard with it like a trophy!

JOHN. I remember Jacob. What happened to him?

ALMA. Oh, Jacob. Jacob was such a mischievous thief. We had to send him out to some friends in the country. Yes, he ended his days as—a country squire! The tales of his exploits . . .

JOHN. Sit down, Miss Alma.

ALMA. If I'm disturbing you . . . ?

JOHN. No—I called the Rectory when I heard you were sick. Your father told me you wouldn't see a doctor.

ALMA. I needed a rest, that was all. . . . You were out of town mostly. . . .

JOHN. I was mostly in Lyon, finishing up Dad's work in the fever clinic.

ALMA. Covering yourself with sudden glory!

JOHN. Redeeming myself with good works.

ALMA. It's rather late to tell you how happy I am, and also how proud. I almost feel as your father might have felt—if . . . And—are you—happy now, John?

JOHN (*uncomfortably, not looking at her*). I've settled with life on fairly acceptable terms. Isn't that all a reasonable person can ask for?

ALMA. He can ask for much more than that. He can ask for the coming true of his most improbable dreams.

JOHN. It's best not to ask for too much.

ALMA. I disagree with you. I say, ask for all, but be prepared to get nothing! (*She springs up and crosses to the window. She continues*) No, I haven't been well. I've thought many times of something you told me last summer, that I have a *doppelganger*. I looked that up and I found that it means another person inside me, another self, and I don't know whether to thank you or not for making me conscious of it!—I haven't been well. . . . For a while I thought I was dying, that that was the change that was coming.

JOHN. When did you have that feeling?

ALMA. August. September. But now the Gulf wind has blown that feeling away like a cloud of smoke, and I know now I'm not dying, that it isn't going to turn out to be that simple. . . .

JOHN. Have you been anxious about your heart again? (*He retreats to a professional manner and takes out a silver watch, putting his fingers on her wrist*)

ALMA. And now the stethoscope? (*He removes the stethoscope from the table and starts to loosen her jacket. She looks down at his bent head. Slowly, involuntarily, her gloved hands lift and descend on the crown of his head. He gets up awkwardly. She suddenly leans toward him and presses her mouth to his*) Why don't you say something? Has the cat got your tongue?

JOHN. Miss Alma, what can I say?

ALMA. You've gone back to calling me "Miss Alma" again.

JOHN. We never really got past that point with each other.

ALMA. Oh, yes we did. We were so close that we almost breathed together!

JOHN (*with embarrassment*). I didn't know that.

ALMA. No? Well, I did, I knew it. (*Her hand touches his face tenderly*) You shave more carefully now? You don't have those little razor cuts on your chin that you dusted with gardenia talcum. . . .

JOHN. I shave more carefully now.

ALMA. So that explains it! (*Her fingers remain on his face, moving gently up and down it like a blind person reading Braille. He is intensely embarrassed and gently removes her hands from him*) Is it—impossible now?

JOHN. I don't think I know what you mean.

ALMA. You know what I mean, all right! So be honest with me. One time I said "no" to something. You may remember the time, and all that demented howling from the cock-fight? But now I have changed my mind, or the girl who said "no," she doesn't exist any more, she died last summer—suffocated in smoke from something on fire inside her. No, she doesn't live now, but she left me her ring — You see? This one you admired, the topaz ring set in pearls. . . . And she said to me when she slipped this ring on my finger—"Remember I died empty-handed, and so make sure that your hands have *something in them!*" (*She drops her gloves. She clasps his head again in her hands*) I said, "But what about pride?"—She said, "Forget about pride whenever it stands between you and what you must have!" (*He takes hold of her wrists*) And then I said, "But what if he doesn't want me?" I don't know what she said then. I'm not sure whether she said anything or not—her lips stopped moving—yes, I think she stopped breathing! (*He gently removes her craving hands from his face*) No? (*He shakes his head in dumb suffering*) Then the answer is "no"!

JOHN (*forcing himself to speak*). I have a respect for the truth, and I have a respect for you—so I'd better speak honestly if you want me to speak. (*Alma nods slightly*) You've won the argument that we had between us.

ALMA. What—argument?

JOHN. The one about the chart.

ALMA. Oh—the chart!

(*She turns from him and wanders across to the chart. She gazes up at it with closed eyes, and her hands clasped in front of her.*)

JOHN. It shows that we're not a package of rose leaves, that every interior inch of us is taken up with something ugly and functional and no room seems to be left for anything else in there.

ALMA. No . . .

JOHN. But I've come around to your way of thinking, that something else is in there, an immaterial something—as thin as smoke—which all of those ugly machines combine to produce and that's their whole reason for being. It can't be seen so it can't be shown on the chart. But it's there, just the same, and knowing it's there—why, then the whole thing—this— this unfathomable experience of ours— takes on a new value, like some—some wildly romantic work in a laboratory! Don't you see?

(*The wind comes up very loud, almost like a choir of voices. Both of them turn slightly, Alma raising a hand to her plumed head as if she were outdoors.*)

ALMA. Yes, I see! Now that you no longer want it to be otherwise you're willing to believe that a spiritual bond can exist between us two!

JOHN. Can't you believe that I am sincere about it?

ALMA. Maybe you are. But I don't want to be talked to like some incurably sick patient you have to comfort. (*A harsh and strong note comes into her voice*) Oh, I suppose I am sick, one of those weak and divided people who slip like shadows among you solid strong ones. But sometimes, out of necessity, we shadowy people take on a strength of our own. I have that now. You needn't try to deceive me.

JOHN. I wasn't.

ALMA. You needn't try to comfort me. I haven't come here on any but equal terms. You said, let's talk truthfully. Well, let's do! Unsparingly, truthfully, even shamelessly, then! It's no longer a secret that I love you. It never was. I loved you as long ago as the time I asked you to read the stone angel's name with your fingers. Yes, I remember the long afternoons of our childhood, when I had to stay indoors to practice my music—and heard your playmates calling you, "Johnny, Johnny!" How

it went through me, just to hear your name called! And how I—rushed to the window to watch you jump the porch railing! I stood at a distance, halfway down the block, only to keep in sight of your torn red sweater, racing about the vacant lot you played in. Yes, it had begun that early, this affliction of love, and has never let go of me since, but kept on growing. I've lived next door to you all the days of my life, a weak and divided person who stood in adoring awe of your singleness, of your strength. And that is my story! Now I wish *you* would tell *me* —why didn't it happen between us? Why did I fail? Why did you come almost close enough—and no closer?

JOHN. Whenever we've gotten together, the three or four times that we have . . .

ALMA. As few as that?

JOHN. It's only been three or four times that we've come face to face. And each of those times—we seemed to be trying to find something in each other without knowing what it was that we wanted to find. It wasn't a body hunger although— I acted as if I thought it might be the night I wasn't a gentleman—at the Casino —it wasn't the physical you that I really wanted!

ALMA. I know, you've already . . .

JOHN. You didn't have that to give me.

ALMA. Not at that time.

JOHN. You had something else to give.

ALMA. What did I have?

(*John strikes a match. Unconsciously he holds his curved palm over the flame of the match to warm it. It is a long kitchen match and it makes a good flame. They both stare at it with a sorrowful understanding that is still perplexed. It is about to burn his fingers. She leans forward and blows it out, then she puts on her gloves.*)

JOHN. You couldn't name it and I couldn't recognize it. I thought it was just a Puritanical ice that glittered like flame. But now I believe it *was* flame, mistaken for ice. I still don't understand it, but I know it was there, just as I know that your eyes and your voice are the two most beautiful things I've ever known—and also the warmest, although they don't seem to be set in your body at all. . . .

ALMA. You talk as if my body had ceased to exist for you, John, in spite of the fact that you've just counted my pulse.

Yes, that's it! You tried to avoid it, but you've told me plainly. The tables have turned, yes, the tables have turned with a vengeance! You've come around to my old way of thinking and I to yours like two people exchanging a call on each other at the same time, and each one finding the other one gone out, the door locked against him and no one to answer the bell! *(She laughs)* I came here to tell you that being a gentleman doesn't seem so important to me any more, but you're telling me I've got to remain a lady. *(She laughs rather violently)* The tables have turned with a vengeance!—The air in here smells of ether—It's making me dizzy . . .

JOHN. I'll open a window.

ALMA. Please.

JOHN. There now.

ALMA. Thank you, that's better. Do you remember those little white tablets you gave me? I've used them all up and I'd like to have some more.

JOHN. I'll write the prescription for you. *(He bends to write)*

(Nellie is in the waiting room. They hear her voice.)

ALMA. Someone is waiting in the waiting room, John. One of my vocal pupils. The youngest and prettiest one with the least gift for music. The one that you helped wrap up this handkerchief for me. *(She takes it out and touches her eyes with it)*

(The door opens, first a crack. Nellie peers in and giggles. Then she throws the door wide open with a peal of merry laughter. She has holly pinned on her jacket. She rushes up to John and hugs him with childish squeals.)

NELLIE. I've been all over town just shouting, shouting!

JOHN. Shouting what?

NELLIE. Glad tidings!

(John looks at Alma over Nellie's shoulder.)

JOHN. I thought we weren't going to tell anyone for a while.

NELLIE. I couldn't stop myself. *(She wheels about)* Oh, Alma, has he told *you?*

ALMA *(quietly)*. He didn't need to, Nellie. I guessed . . . from the Christmas card with your two names written on it!

(Nellie rushes over to Alma and hugs her. Over Nellie's shoulder Alma looks at John. He makes a thwarted gesture as if he wanted to speak. She smiles desperately

and shakes her head. She closes her eyes and bites her lips for a moment. Then she releases Nellie with a laugh of exaggerated gaiety.)*

NELLIE. So, Alma, you were really the first to know!

ALMA. I'm proud of that, Nellie.

NELLIE. See on my finger! This was the present I couldn't tell you about!

ALMA. Oh, what a lovely, lovely solitaire! But solitaire is such a wrong name for it. Solitaire means single and this means *two!* It's blinding, Nellie! Why it . . . hurts my eyes!

(John catches Nellie's arm and pulls her to him. Almost violently Alma lifts her face; it is bathed in tears. She nods gratefully to John for releasing her from Nellie's attention. She picks up her gloves and purse.)

JOHN. Excuse her, Miss Alma. Nellie's still such a child.

ALMA *(with a breathless laugh)*. I've got to run along now.

JOHN. Don't leave your prescription.

ALMA. Oh, yes, where's my prescription?

JOHN. On the table.

ALMA. I'll take it to the drug store right away!

(Nellie struggles to free herself from John's embrace which keeps her from turning to Alma.)

NELLIE. Alma, don't go! Johnny, let go of me, Johnny! You're hugging me so tight I can't breathe!

ALMA. Goodbye.

NELLIE. Alma! Alma, you know you're going to sing at the wedding! The very first Sunday in spring!—which will be Palm Sunday! "The Voice That Breathed O'er Eden."

(Alma has closed the door. John shuts his eyes tight with a look of torment. He rains kisses on Nellie's forehead and throat and lips. The scene dims out with music.)

SCENE TWELVE

In the park near the angel of the fountain. About dusk.

Alma enters the lighted area and goes slowly up to the fountain and bends to drink. Then she removes a small white package from her pocketbook and starts to unwrap it. While she is doing this, a

Young Man comes along. He is dressed in a checked suit and a derby. He pauses by the bench. They glance at each other.

A train whistles in the distance. The Young Man clears his throat. The train whistle is repeated. The Young Man crosses toward the fountain, his eyes on Alma. She hesitates, with the unwrapped package in her hand. Then she crosses toward the bench and stands hesitantly in front of it. He stuffs his hands in his pockets and whistles. He glances with an effect of unconcern back over his shoulder.

Alma pushes her veil back with an uncertain gesture. His whistle dies out. He sways back and forth on his heels as the train whistles again. He suddenly turns to the fountain and bends to drink. Alma slips the package back into her purse. As the young man straightens up, she speaks in a barely audible voice.

——

ALMA. The water—is—cool.

THE YOUNG MAN *(eagerly)*. Did you say something?

ALMA. I said, the water is cool.

THE YOUNG MAN. Yes, it sure is, it's nice and cool!

ALMA. It's always cool.

THE YOUNG MAN. Is it?

ALMA. Yes. Yes, even in summer. It comes from deep underground.

THE YOUNG MAN. That's what keeps it cool.

ALMA. Glorious Hill is famous for its artesian springs.

THE YOUNG MAN. I didn't know that.

(The Young Man jerkily removes his hands from his pockets. She gathers confidence before the awkwardness of his youth.)

ALMA. Are you a stranger in town?

THE YOUNG MAN. I'm a traveling salesman.

ALMA. Ah, you're a salesman who travels! *(She laughs gently)* But you're younger than most of them are, and not so fat!

THE YOUNG MAN. I'm just starting out. I travel for Red Goose shoes.

ALMA. Ah! The Delt's your territory?

THE YOUNG MAN. From the Peabody Lobby to Cat-Fish Row in Vicksburg.

(Alma leans back and looks at him under half-closed lids, perhaps a little suggestively.)

ALMA. The life of a traveling salesman is interesting . . . but lonely.

THE YOUNG MAN. You're right about that. Hotel bedrooms are lonely.

(There is a pause. Far away the train whistles again.)

ALMA. All rooms are lonely where there is only one person. *(Her eyes fall shut)*

THE YOUNG MAN *(gently)*. You're tired, aren't you?

ALMA. I? Tired? *(She starts to deny it; then laughs faintly and confesses the truth)* Yes . . . a little. . . . But I shall rest now. I've just now taken one of my sleeping tablets.

THE YOUNG MAN. So early?

ALMA. Oh, it won't put me to sleep. It will just quiet my nerves.

THE YOUNG MAN. What are you nervous about?

ALMA. I won an argument this afternoon.

THE YOUNG MAN. That's nothing to be nervous over. You ought to be nervous if you *lost* one.

ALMA. It wasn't the argument that I wanted to win. . . .

THE YOUNG MAN. Well, I'm nervous too.

ALMA. What over?

THE YOUNG MAN. It's my first job and I'm scared of not making good.

(The mysteriously sudden intimacy that sometimes occurs between strangers more completely than old friends or lovers moves them both. Alma hands the package of tablets to him.)

ALMA. Then you must take one of my tablets.

THE YOUNG MAN. Shall I?

ALMA. Please take one!

THE YOUNG MAN. Yes, I shall.

ALMA. You'll be surprised how infinitely merciful they are. The prescription number is 96814. I think of it as the telephone number of God! *(They both laugh. He places one of the tablets on his tongue and crosses to the fountain to wash it down)*

THE YOUNG MAN *(to the stone figure)*. Thanks, angel. *(He gives her a little salute, and crosses back to Alma)*

ALMA. Life is full of little mercies like that, not *big* mercies but comfortable *little* mercies. And so we are able to keep on going. . . . *(She has leaned back with half-closed eyes)*

THE YOUNG MAN *(returning)*. You're falling asleep.

ALMA. Oh no, I'm not. I'm just closing my eyes. You know what I feel like now? I feel like a water-lily.

THE YOUNG MAN. A water-lily?

ALMA. Yes, I feel like a water-lily on a Chinese lagoon. Won't you sit down? *(The Young Man does)* My name is Alma. Spanish for soul! What's yours?

THE YOUNG MAN. Ha-ha! Mine's Archie Kramer. Mucho gusto, as they say in Spain.

ALMA. Usted habla Espanol, senor?

THE YOUNG MAN. Un poquito! Usted habla Espanol, senorita?

ALMA. Me tambien. Un poquito!

THE YOUNG MAN *(delightedly)*. Ha . . . ha . . . ha! Sometimes un poquito is plenty! *(Alma laughs . . . in a different way than she has ever laughed before, a little wearily, but quite naturally. The Young Man leans toward her confidentially)* What's there to do in this town after dark?

ALMA. There's not much to do in this town after dark, but there are resorts on the lake that offer all kinds of after-dark entertainment. There's one called Moon Lake Casino. It's under new management, now, but I don't suppose its character has changed.

THE YOUNG MAN. What was its character?

ALMA. Gay, very gay, Mr. Kramer. . . .

THE YOUNG MAN. Then what in hell are we sitting here for? Vamonos!

ALMA. Como no, senor!

THE YOUNG MAN. Ha-ha-ha! *(He jumps up)* I'll call a taxi. *(He goes off shouting "Taxi")*

(Alma rises from the bench. As she crosses to the fountain the grave mood of the play is reinstated with a phrase of music. She faces the stone angel and raises her gloved hand in a sort of valedictory salute. Then she turns slowly about toward the audience with her hand still raised in a gesture of wonder and finality as . . . the curtain falls.)

ANDERSON, MAXWELL: *Joan of Lorraine*. November 18, 1946. An ingenious Joan of Arc drama written in the "play within a play" form, showing an actress, who struggles with her role as Joan, arriving at an understanding of the nature and significance of the character. The play was a successful vehicle for Ingrid Bergman.

ARCHIBALD, WILLIAM: *The Innocents*. February 1, 1950. A dramatization of *The Turn of the Screw* by Henry James.

BARRY, PHILIP, with revisions by ROBERT SHERWOOD: *Second Threshold*. January 2, 1951. (Left nearly completed by Barry, who died on December 3, 1949.) A psychological comedy about the frustrations and death-wishes of a retired statesman and his conflict with his daughter, who restores his will to live when she contracts a wholesome marriage with a young American instead of marrying a British contemporary of her father's.

BERG, GERTRUDE: *Me and Molly*. February 26, 1948. A folk comedy about a poor Jewish family's struggles for material and cultural improvement.

GARDNER, DOROTHY: *Eastward in Eden*. November 18, 1947. A sensitive portrait of the New England poetess Emily Dickinson and a treatment of one of the frustrated romances attributed to her.

GIBBS, WOLCOTT: *Season in the Sun*. September 28, 1950. A sprightly comedy about summer resort life on Fire Island and of a magazine writer's bizarre attempt to abandon a sophisticated life for the dubious blessings of a commonplace existence.

GOETZ, RUTH and AUGUSTUS: *The Heiress*. September 29, 1947. A dramatization of Henry James's *Washington Square*.

GORDON, RUTH: *Years Ago*. December 3, 1946. A nostalgic reminiscence of the youth of an actress in an eccentric but affectionate household.

HAINES, WILLIAM WISTER: *Command Decision*. October 1, 1947. A Second World War drama revolving around the anguish and protests of an air force general obliged to send his flyers on suicidal bombing assignments over Germany.

HARRITY, RICHARD: *Hope Is a Thing with Feathers*. ANTA experimental "Six O'Clock Theatre" production, April 11-18, 1948; Broadway production, May 11-15, 1948. A wry one-act comedy about derelicts in a park.

HART, MOSS: *Light Up the Sky*. November 18, 1948. A comedy of the theatre describing the tensions of a Boston try-out and displays of egotism customary in the course of staging a play.

HELLMAN, LILLIAN: *Another Part of the Forest*. November 20, 1946. The author's sequel to *The Little Foxes* (1939). An account of the early career of her predatory "Little Foxes" Hubbards and the making of the family fortune by the unpatriotic contraband operations of the elder Hubbard during the Confederacy.

HEYWARD, DOROTHY: *Set My People Free*. November 3, 1948. An historical drama about an attempted uprising of slaves in Charleston in 1822 under the leadership of an historical figure, Denmark Vesey. Most interesting as the study of a house slave's effort to save his benevolent white master and his divided loyalties.

JEFFERS, ROBINSON: *The Tower Beyond Tragedy*. November 26, 1950. Playing version of Jeffers' dramatic poem, based on Aeschylus' *Oresteian trilogy* and the *Electra* plays of Sophocles and Euripides.

KANIN, FAY: *Goodbye, My Fancy*. November 17, 1948. A comedy of life in a woman's college revolving around the return of a celebrated alumna and Congresswoman and her efforts to liberalize the college president with whom she was once in love.

* Unless otherwise stated, the date refers to the Broadway opening.

KELLY, GEORGE: *The Fatal Weakness.* November 19, 1946. A character comedy revolving around a romantically disposed wife's inability to resist attending weddings and sympathizing with romantic attachments; this, even at her own expense when she loses her husband to a refugee woman.

KRASNA, NORMAN: *John Loves Mary.* February 4, 1947. A farcical comedy of misunderstandings caused by a young ex-soldier's inability to reveal the fact that he is unmarried after having come to the assistance of a fellow-soldier in France.

LINDSAY, HOWARD and CROUSE, RUSSEL: *Life with Mother.* October 20, 1948. A sequel to the same authors' *Life with Father,* revolving around the Day mother's efforts to get an engagement ring from Father Day after twenty-two years of married life with him.

LOGAN, JOSHUA: *The Wisteria Trees.* March 29, 1950. A free adaptation of Chekhov's *The Cherry Orchard* as a family story with a Southern background.

LOOS, ANITA: *Happy Birthday.* October 31, 1946. The successful Helen Hayes vehicle, in which a spinster, a New Jersey librarian, takes a vacation from her inhibitions in a Newark bar.

MABLEY, EDWARD and MINS, LEONARD: *Temper the Wind.* December 27, 1946. A drama of denazification efforts in Germany by an idealistic American officer.

McENROE, ROBERT E.: *The Silver Whistle.* November 24, 1948. A comedy of life in an old people's home enlivened by a philosophical tramp.

NASH, N. RICHARD: *The Young and the Fair.* November 22, 1948. An unsuccessful but intense study of life in a junior college for girls, to be remembered as the play in which Julie Harris made a successful Broadway debut.

ODETS, CLIFFORD: *The Country Girl.* November 10, 1950. A powerful drama of a woman's patient loyalty to a talented but weak alcoholic actor.

O'NEILL, EUGENE: *A Moon for the Misbegotten.* Opened in Columbus, Ohio, February 20, 1947; closed in St. Louis, March 29, 1947, and withdrawn. A drama about the life of an oversized Irish farm girl and a dissipated and disenchanted man who fall in love but fatefully separate.

RAPHAELSON, SAMSON: *Hilda Crane.* November 1, 1950. The "well-made" drama of a maladjusted and restive twice-divorced woman who settles for security rather than love but finds her marriage unendurable.

STAVIS, BARRIE: *Lamp at Midnight.* December 21, 1947. A dramatic account of Galileo's struggle for freedom of scientific inquiry.

STEINBECK, JOHN: *Burning Bright.* October 18, 1950. The chronicle of a sterile man's desire to beget a child and final realization that the continuity that really matters is not that of family lineage but that of the human race.

TAYLOR, SAMUEL: *The Happy Time.* January 24, 1950. A comedy about congenial French-Canadian family life and the growth of a boy under its raffish but benign influence. Based on the novel *The Happy Time* by Robert Fontaine.

VAN DRUTEN, JOHN: *The Druid Circle.* October 22, 1947. A psychological portrait of a frustrated professor at a small British university town and his attempt to wreck the lives of two young people.

VERNEUIL, LOUIS: *Affairs of State.* September 25, 1950. A sophisticated comedy of love and political intrigue in Washington.

WARREN, ROBERT PENN: *All the King's Men.* January 14, 1948. The play was originally written before Mr. Warren's Pulitzer Prize novel and was produced in New York by Erwin Piscator in a revised version. This treatment of the "Huey Long" story was constructed in the style of European "epic realism" and was an interesting experiment in play structure.

WILLIAMS, TENNESSEE. *The Rose Tattoo*. February 3, 1951. A Sicilian folk-comedy set along the Gulf Coast, revolving about a widow's attachment to memories of her husband and her frantically held belief in his fidelity until disillusionment frees her from her obsession and enables her to take a second husband.

WILSON, EDMUND: *The Little Blue Light*. April 29, 1951. A philosophical melodrama concerning a magazine editor's effort to oppose a reactionary, neo-fascistic pressure movement and his destruction by a lethal wonder-weapon as a result of the corrupt nature of his wife and associate. An ANTA production.

WOUK, HERMAN: *The Traitor*. March 31, 1949. An intelligent spy melodrama concerning the intellectual problems of an idealistic, anti-war young professor and his former teacher, an elderly liberal philosopher.

AMERICAN MUSICAL PLAYS OF THE PERIOD

in which the "book" was more or less important*

ANDERSON, MAXWELL and WEILL, KURT: *Lost in the Stars*. October 30, 1949. (A dramatization of Alan Paton's South African novel, *Cry, the Beloved Country*.)

BLITZSTEIN, MARC: *Regina*. October 31, 1949. (A musical version of Lillian Hellman's *The Little Foxes*.)

HARBURG, E. Y. and SAIDY, FRED; music by BURTON LANE: *Finian's Rainbow*. January 10, 1947.

LATOUCHE, JOHN and MOROSS, JEROME: *Ballet Ballads*. ANTA production, May 9, 1948; Broadway production, May 18, 1948.

LERNER, ALAN JAY and LOEWE, FREDERICK: *Brigadoon*. May 2, 1950.

LERNER, ALAN JAY and WEILL, KURT: *Love Life*. October 7, 1948.

MENOTTI, GIAN-CARLO: *The Medium*. Originally presented by the Ballet Society, February 18, 1947. Opened on Broadway, March 1, 1947. *The Consul*. March 15, 1950.

RICE, ELMER; music by KURT WEILL; lyrics by LANGSTON HUGHES: *Street Scene*. January 9, 1947. (Based on Elmer Rice's play, first produced on January 10, 1929.)

RODGERS, RICHARD, HAMMERSTEIN, OSCAR II and LOGAN, JOSHUA: *South Pacific*. April 7, 1949. (Adapted from James A. Michener's *Tales of the South Pacific*.)

RODGERS, RICHARD and HAMMERSTEIN, OSCAR II: *The King and I*. March 29, 1951. (Based on *Anna and the King of Siam* by Margaret Landon.)

SMITH, BETTY and ABBOTT, GEORGE; music by ARTHUR SCHWARTZ; lyrics by DOROTHY FIELDS: *A Tree Grows in Brooklyn*. April 19, 1951. (Based on Betty Smith's novel, *A Tree Grows in Brooklyn*.)

SPEWACK, BELLA and SAMUEL and PORTER, COLE: *Kiss Me Kate*. December 30, 1948. (Based on Shakespeare's *The Taming of the Shrew*.)

SWERLING, JO and BURROWS, ABE; music by FRANK LOESSER: *Guys and Dolls*. November 24, 1950. (Based on a story and characters by Damon Runyon.)

* Unless otherwise stated, the date refers to the Broadway opening.

ATKINSON, BROOKS: *Broadway Scrapbook*. New York: *Theatre Arts,* 1947. A selection of essays and criticism, mainly on plays, from *The Petrified Forest* to *Born Yesterday.*

BENTLEY, ERIC: *The Playwright as Thinker.* New York: Reynal and Hitchcock, 1946. This vigorously critical book presents a sharp minority report on O'Neill and other American playwrights. Its chapters on European drama supply an interesting frame of reference for American drama.

BLUM, DANIEL: *A Pictorial History of the American Theatre, 1900-1950.* New York: Greenberg, 1950. Also: *Theatre World.* A theatrical record published annually. See volumes beginning with *Theatre World: Season 1946-47.* Published first by Theatre World, and, after 1948, by Greenberg, Publisher.

BROOKS, CLEANTH and HEILMAN, ROBERT D.: *Understanding Drama.* New York: Henry Holt & Co., 1945, 1948. A useful critical introduction to drama, including twelve complete plays for study.

BROWN, JOHN MASON: *Seeing More Things.* New York: Whittlesey House, McGraw-Hill Book Company, 1948. Another collection of delightfully written essays by Mr. Brown reprinted from the *Saturday Review of Literature.*

CHAPMAN, JOHN: *The Burns Mantle Best Plays of 1947-48,* and subsequently published volumes covering the 1948-49 to 1950-51 seasons, and maintaining the late Burns Mantle's high editorial standards. New York: Dodd, Mead & Co.

COLE, TOBY and CHINOY, HELEN KRICH: *Actors on Acting.* New York: Crown Publishers, 1949. A compilation of essays on the theory and practice of acting. The last section, pp. 459-550, deals with acting on the American stage.

CLARK, BARRETT H. and FREEDLEY, GEORGE: *A History of Modern Drama.* New York: D. Appleton-Century Company, 1947. This most comprehensive book on the subject, with chapters contributed by experts on the various national theatres of the Western World, contains a long chapter on the American drama.

CLARK, BARRETT H.: *European Theories of the Drama. With a Supplement on the American Drama.* New York: Crown Publishers, 1947. Mr. Clark has added to this revised edition new material by American writers, including George Pierce Baker, George Jean Nathan, Ludwig Lewisohn, Joseph Wood Krutch, Eugene O'Neill, Maxwell Anderson, John Gassner and John Mason Brown.
Intimate Portraits. New York: Dramatists Play Service, 1951. Recollections of Edward Sheldon and Sidney Howard, as well as of Gorki, George Moore and Galsworthy.
Eugene O'Neill: The Man and His Plays. New York: Dover Publications, 1947. A revised edition of Mr. Clark's book, originally published in 1926 and now brought up to date, covering *The Iceman Cometh* and other new plays by O'Neill.

DOWNER, ALAN S.: *Fifty Years of American Drama: 1900-1950.* Chicago: Henry Regnery Company, 1951. A well-written and useful short history in the series "Twentieth-Century Literature in America."

EGRI, LAJOS: *The Art of Dramatic Writing.* New York: Simon and Schuster, 1946. A revised edition of a vigorously analytical approach to drama.

ELIOT, T. S.: *Poetry and Drama.* Boston: The Atlantic Monthly Co., 1951. Eliot's account of his problems in creating poetic drama.

FINCH, ROBERT: *How to Write a Play.* New York: Greenberg, 1948.

GAGEY, EDMOND M.: *Revolution in American Drama.* New York: Columbia University Press, 1947. A study of changing drama in America since 1912.

GALLAWAY, MARIAN: *Constructing a Play.* New York: Prentice-Hall, 1950. A thorough study of play construction drawing upon recent, as well as other examples of playwriting. Foreword by Tennessee Williams.

GASSNER, JOHN: *Best Plays of the Modern American Theatre: Second Series.* New York: Crown Publishers, 1947. Covers the war period from 1939 to 1945.
Twenty-five Best Plays of the Modern American Theatre: Early Series. New York: Crown Publishers, 1949. This volume covers the theatre from 1916 to 1929, the period of the formation of our modern theatre.
20 Best Plays of the Modern American Theatre. New York: Crown Publishers, 1939. Covers the theatre from 1929 to 1939.
A Treasury of the Theatre. 3 volumes (2 volume-college edition). New York: Simon and Schuster, 1951. (The third volume of the trade edition and the second volume of the college edition provide an anthology and history of the American theatre.)

GAVER, JACK: *Curtain Calls.* New York: Dodd, Mead & Co., 1949.

HEFFNER, HERBERT C., SELDEN, SAMUEL, and SELLMAN, HUNTON D.: *Modern Theatre Practice.* New York: F. S. Crofts, 1947. Third revised edition of an invaluable practical book on all phases of stage production in America.

HUGHES, GLENN: *A History of the American Theatre: 1700-1950.* New York: Samuel French, 1951. An economically written account, giving facts and dates; a useful one-volume record.

LANGNER, LAWRENCE: *The Magic Curtain.* New York: E. P. Dutton & Company, 1951. This autobiography chronicles the history of the Greenwich Village Players, the Theatre Guild, and the Westport Country Playhouse, and provides valuable material on American as well as foreign playwrights, especially O'Neill. An indispensable source-book.

LAWSON, JOHN HOWARD: *Theory and Technique of Playwriting.* New York: G. P. Putnam's Sons, 1949. A revised edition, to which has been added a useful section on screenwriting.

LEES, C. LOWELL: *Play Production and Direction.* New York: Prentice-Hall, 1948. A lucid review of the practice of American stage production.

MacGOWAN, KENNETH: *A Primer of Playwriting.* A compact and sensible treatment of the subject by a critic, producer, and teacher of wide experience.

MANTLE, BURNS: *Best Plays of 1946-47.* New York: Dodd, Mead & Co., 1947. This annual record of the theatre, which includes synoptic versions of ten American and foreign plays considered the best of the season, was continued by Mantle's associate, the critic John Chapman, after Mr. Mantle's death on February 9, 1948.

MOREHOUSE, WARD: *Matinee Tomorrow: Fifty Years of Our Theatres.* New York: Whittlesey House, McGraw-Hill Book Company, 1949. A lively informal history, well illustrated.

NATHAN, GEORGE JEAN: *The Theatre Book of the Year.* See the annual volumes from 1946-47 to 1950-51. Each volume contains lively and acute criticisms of each season's offerings, play by play. New York: Alfred A. Knopf, 1947, etc.

ODELL, GEORGE C. D.: *Annals of the New York Stage.* 15 volumes published. New York: Columbia University Press, 1949. (The last volume completed by Professor Odell brings this history up to 1894.)

RAPHAELSON, SAMSON: *The Human Nature of Playwriting.* New York: Macmillan Co., 1949. An original "organic" approach to the writing of plays, presented as a series of laboratory investigations.

SPER, FELIX: *From Native Roots: A Panorama of Our Regional Drama.* Caldwell, Idaho: The Caxton Printers, 1948. A comprehensive history of folk theatre in America.

THOMPSON, ALAN REYNOLDS: *The Anatomy of Drama.* Berkeley: University of California Press, 1946. A penetrating discussion of the forms and types of drama.

YOUNG, STARK: *Immortal Shadows: A Book of Dramatic Criticism.* New York: Charles Scribner's Sons, 1948. A collection of *New Republic* articles by Stark Young Some of the best dramatic criticism ever written in America.